# SPOUSAL SUPPORT IN CANADA

## Third Edition

AUTHORS

Ann C. Wilton, B.A., M.A. (Oxon), LL.B., of the Ontario Bar
Noel Semple, B.A., J.D., LL.M., of the Ontario Bar

**CARSWELL**®

**A cataloguing record for this publication is available from Library and Archives Canada.**

**ISBN 978-0-7798-6624-3**

Printed in Canada by Thomson Reuters

## TELL US HOW WE'RE DOING

Scan the QR code to the right with your smartphone to send your comments regarding our products and services.
Free QR Code Readers are available from your mobile device app store.
You can also email us at carswell.feedback@thomsonreuters.com

**THOMSON REUTERS**

CARSWELL, A DIVISION OF THOMSON REUTERS CANADA LIMITED

| | |
|---|---|
| One Corporate Plaza | **Customer Relations** |
| 2075 Kennedy Road | Toronto 1-416-609-3800 |
| Toronto, Ontario | Elsewhere in Canada/U.S. 1-800-387-5164 |
| M1T 3V4 | Fax 1-416-298-5082 |
| | www.carswell.com |
| | E-mail www.carswell.com/email |

# ACKNOWLEDGEMENT

The authors gratefully acknowledge Professor Carol Rogerson of the University of Toronto Faculty of Law, Professor Rollie Thompson of the Schulich School of Law and Wendy Bryans of the Federal Department of Justice for their guidance in the preparation of the material on spousal support. The authors gratefully acknowledge the help and support of MacDonald and Partners. They also appreciate the practical assistance they received with this edition from Andre Popadynec, Jennifer Weinberger and Kevin Phillips, all of Carswell, A Thomson Reuters business.

The authors in addition would like to acknowledge their appreciation of James C. MacDonald Q.C. for his contribution to *Canadian Divorce Law and Practice* which has increased their understanding of spousal support.

# TABLE OF CONTENTS

## Part I
### Divorce Act

# Part II
## Spousal Support Advisory Guidelines

# TABLE OF CASES

# PART I

# *Divorce Act*

## OVERVIEW

Spousal support is one of the three primary financial remedies in Canadian family law; the others being child support and matrimonial property division. Like child support, spousal support generally involves an obligation for periodic payments from one spouse to another. However, like matrimonial property remedies, it does not depend on the presence of children and it is at least partially intended to address the post-marital consequences of financial decisions made by spouses during marriage.

Spousal support evolved from alimony, a common law remedy, which, under certain circumstances, required husbands to support their wives after divorce or separation. Unlike alimony, spousal support is today available to husbands and to members of same-sex marriages in addition to wives. Also, unlike alimony, spousal support is a purely statutory remedy. The focus of this edition is spousal support under the *Divorce Act*, 1985, c. 3 (2nd Supp.), but the remedy is also available under provincial and territorial family law legislation. The general principles of the law are the same under both types of statutory authority, with certain exceptions. The most important difference is that provincial legislation allows spousal support claims between parties who have never been married or who have never been divorced.

Spousal support serves two purposes in Canadian family law. Firstly, it seeks to *compensate* the lower-earning spouse for sacrifices in earning power which he or she made during the relationship. This is the "compensatory" purpose of spousal support, and the focus of s. 6.2 of this edition. Secondly, if the lower-earning spouse is in financial *need*, and if the other spouse has the ability to pay, spousal support seeks to address the need. This is sometimes referred to as the "non-compensatory" purpose of spousal support, and is explained in s. 6.4. While in many cases a single order of spousal support will be intended to both compensate and relieve need, the two purposes are conceptually distinct. Either one, in the absence of the other, can be sufficient basis for a spousal support award. If neither is present in a given fact pattern, there is unlikely to be any entitlement to spousal support found.

However, entitlement to spousal support is found in the majority of cases in which there is a significant disparity between the parties' incomes after separation. An income disparity will often demonstrate a basis for compensation. Even if it does not, an income disparity is likely to establish the support applicant's *need* for support. This is because (i) if the party from whom support is sought is earning significantly more than the party seeking support, then it is likely that the standard of living of the party seeking support is lower than the marital standard; and (ii) need is usually established by reference to the marital standard of living.

Nonetheless, in certain cases, there will be no entitlement to spousal support despite an income disparity. This is usually because the lower-earning spouse has substantial assets or because the income disparity cannot be traced to anything which happened during the relationship. Entitlement to spousal support must always be established as a threshold issue, before quantum and duration are considered.

Spousal support is less frequently ordered and less frequently paid than child support. A number of individuals are considered by the law to have sufficient means to pay child support, but insufficient means to pay spousal support. One indication of this is the fact that the *Federal Child Support Guidelines* provide that a non-custodial parent should pay child support if he or she has an income in excess of $11,000 per year. By contrast, the Spousal Support Advisory Guidelines have a "floor" of $20,000 per year. If the higher-earning spouse earns less than this amount, it is not likely that a court will order spousal support.

The infrequency of spousal support awards by comparison to child support awards reflects the priority which the *Divorce Act* gives to the latter. Section 15.3(1) states. "Where a court is considering an application for a child support order and an application for a spousal support order, the court shall give priority to child support in determining the applications." The duty to support a child is considered by our law to be more pressing and more absolute than the duty to support a former spouse, who as an adult is presumed to have at least some capacity to support him or herself. However, the relative infrequency of spousal support awards was also a function of the pervasive uncertainty which characterized this area of the law for many years. Because potential spousal support claimants found it very difficult to predict the result of a spousal support application, they often chose to avoid incurring the costs of putting one forward.

The unlegislated Spousal Support Advisory Guidelines ("SSAG") were created, in part, as a response to this unpredictability. They were commissioned by the federal Department of Justice, and written by Professor Carol Rogerson of the University of Toronto Faculty of Law and Professor Rollie Thompson of Dalhousie Law School with the collaboration of a large group of lawyers and judges. The SSAG were released in draft form in January 2005, and in final form in July 2008. The SSAG utilize certain factual inputs to produce quantum and duration ranges. For example, suppose a 40 year-old wife seeks spousal support from her husband after a 10-year relationship without children. Suppose further that at the time of separation she is earning $25,000 per year while he is earning $65,000. On the basis of these facts, the SSAG would suggest spousal support of between $500 and $667 per month, lasting for between 5 and 10 years. The SSAG have found generally wide judicial approval, but they do not replace the individualized analysis called for by the *Divorce Act*.

Part I of this edition is about spousal support under the *Divorce Act*. Chapter 1 provides the introduction and is concerned with the application of the statutes. Chapters 2 and 3 deal with preliminary issues – the jurisdiction of various courts over spousal support issues and the parties to a spousal support application. Chapter 4 identifies the various types of spousal support litigation, which include interim, variation, and review proceedings. Chapter 5 focuses on the factors relevant to a spousal support determination, drawing on s. 15.2(4) of the *Divorce Act* – means, needs, length of relationship, functions performed during the relationship, and prior agreements between the parties. Chapter 6 is about the *objectives* of a spousal support order, according to s. 15.2(6). This chapter includes extended annotations of the two leading Supreme Court of Canada spousal support cases, as well as a number of cases in which no entitlement to spousal support was found. Chapter 7 is about the terms and conditions which can be part of a spousal support order, and Chapter 8 deals briefly with the determination of the parties' income for the purposes of spousal support. Because income determination in Canadian family law is primarily done according to the *Federal Child Support Guidelines,* readers should turn to MacDonald and Wilton, *Child Support Guidelines Law and Practice*, 2nd ed., for a detailed treatment of this topic. Finally, Chapter 9 addresses a series of miscellaneous issues which may be relevant to spousal support issues in certain cases and Chapter 10 addresses variation and review of spousal support orders.

Part II of this edition is about the Spousal Support Advisory Guidelines ("SSAG"). It takes the form of extracts from the text of the final SSAG, interspersed with case law annotations. Chapter 19 of the Part II contains a review of appellate decisions dealing with the Spousal Support Advisory Guidelines, as well as a quantitative analysis which seeks to analyze judicial reception of the SSAG. Chapter 19A deals with retroactive support and the SSAG. For convenience of reference, the *Spousal Support Advisory Guidelines* and relevant provisions of the *Divorce Act* have been reproduced as appendices.

# CHAPTER 1

# INTRODUCTION AND APPLICATION OF THE STATUTES

The portions of s. 15 of the *Divorce Act* that deal with Spousal Support are as follows:

## *Divorce Act*

### COROLLARY RELIEF

**INTERPRETATION**

**Definition of "spouse"**

15. In sections 15.1 to 16, "spouse" has the meaning assigned by subsection 2(1), and includes a former spouse.

R.S., 1985, c. 3 (2nd Supp.), s. 15; 1997, c. 1, s. 2.

**SPOUSAL SUPPORT ORDERS**

**Spousal support order**

15.2 (1) A court of competent jurisdiction may, on application by either or both spouses, make an order requiring a spouse to secure or pay, or to secure and pay, such lump sum or periodic sums, or such lump sum and periodic sums, as the court thinks reasonable for the support of the other spouse.

**Interim order**

(2) Where an application is made under subsection (1), the court may, on application by either or both spouses, make an interim order requiring a spouse to secure or pay, or to secure and pay, such lump sum or periodic sums, or such lump sum and periodic sums, as the court thinks reasonable for the support of the other spouse, pending the determination of the application under subsection (1).

**Terms and conditions**

(3) The court may make an order under subsection (1) or an interim order under subsection (2) for a definite or indefinite period or until a specified event occurs, and may impose terms, conditions or restrictions in connection with the order as it thinks fit and just.

## Factors

**(4)** In making an order under subsection (1) or an interim order under subsection (2), the court shall take into consideration the condition, means, needs and other circumstances of each spouse, including

(a) the length of time the spouses cohabited;

(b) the functions performed by each spouse during cohabitation; and

(c) any order, agreement or arrangement relating to support of either spouse.

## Spousal misconduct

**(5)** In making an order under subsection (1) or an interim order under subsection (2), the court shall not take into consideration any misconduct of a spouse in relation to the marriage.

## Objectives of spousal support order

**(6)** An order made under subsection (1) or an interim order under subsection (2) that provides for the support of a spouse should

(a) recognize any economic advantages or disadvantages to the spouses arising from the marriage or its breakdown;

(b) apportion between the spouses any financial consequences arising from the care of any child of the marriage over and above any obligation for the support of any child of the marriage;

(c) relieve any economic hardship of the spouses arising from the breakdown of the marriage; and

(d) in so far as practicable, promote the economic self-sufficiency of each spouse within a reasonable period of time.

1997, c. 1, s. 2.

## PRIORITY

### Priority to child support

**15.3 (1)** Where a court is considering an application for a child support order and an application for a spousal support order, the court shall give priority to child support in determining the applications.

### Reasons

**(2)** Where, as a result of giving priority to child support, the court is unable to make a spousal support order or the court makes a spousal support order in an amount that is less than it otherwise would have been, the court shall record its reasons for having done so.

### Consequences of reduction or termination of child support order

**(3)** Where, as a result of giving priority to child support, a spousal support order was not made, or the amount of a spousal support order is less than it otherwise would have been, any subsequent reduction or termination of that child support constitutes a change of circumstances for the purposes of applying for a spousal support order, or a variation order in respect of the spousal support order, as the case may be.

1997, c. 1, s. 2.

**15. History.** The corollary relief provisions were formerly section 15 of the *Divorce Act*, R.S.C. 1985, c. 3, s. 15 which read as follows:

**"Spouse" — Order for support — Interim order for support — Terms and conditions — Factors — Spousal misconduct — Objectives of order for support of spouse — Objectives of order for support of child — Assignment of order.**

**15.** (1) In this section and section 16, "spouse" has the meaning assigned by subsection 2(1) and includes a former spouse.

(2) A court of competent jurisdiction may, on application by either or both spouses, make an order requiring one spouse to secure or pay, or to secure and pay, such lump sum or periodic sums, or such lump sum and periodic sums, as the court thinks reasonable for the support of

(*a*) the other spouse;

(*b*) any or all children of the marriage; or

(*c*) the other spouse and any or all children of the marriage.

(3) Where an application is made under subsection (2), the court may, on application by either or both spouses, make an interim order requiring one spouse to secure or pay, or to secure and pay, such lump sum or periodic sums, or such lump sum and periodic sums, as the court thinks reasonable for the support of

(*a*) the other spouse

(*b*) any of all children of the marriage, or

(*c*) the other spouse and any or all children of the marriage,

pending determination of the application under subsection (2).

(4) The court may make an order under this section for a definite or indefinite period or until the happening of a specified event and may impose such other terms, conditions or restrictions in connection therewith as it thinks fit and just.

(5) In making an order under this section, the court shall take into consideration the condition, means, needs and other circumstances of each spouse and of any child of the marriage for whom support is sought, including

(*a*) the length of time the spouses cohabited;

(*b*) the functions performed by the spouse during cohabitation; and

(*c*) any order, agreement or arrangement relating to support of the spouse or child.

(6) In making an order under this section, the court shall not take into consideration any misconduct of a spouse in relation to the marriage.

(7) An order made under this section that provides for the support of a spouse should

(*a*) recognize any economic advantages or disadvantages to the spouses arising from the marriage or its breakdown;

(*b*) apportion between the spouses any financial consequences arising from the care of any child of the marriage over and above the obligation apportioned between the spouses pursuant to subsection (8);

(*c*) relieve any economic hardship of the spouses arising from the breakdown of the marriage; and

(*d*) in so far as practicable, promote the economic self-sufficiency of each spouse within a reasonable period of time.

(8) An order made under this section that provides for the support of a child of the marriage should

(*a*) recognize that the spouses have a joint financial obligation to maintain the child; and

(*b*) apportion that obligation between the spouses according to their relative abilities to contribute to the performance of the obligation.

**(9) An order made under this section may be assigned to**

(*a*) any minister of the Crown for Canada designated by the Governor in Council;

(*b*) any minister of the Crown for a province designated by the Lieutenant Governor in Council for the province;

(*c*) any member of the Council of the Yukon Territory designated by the Commissioner of the Yukon Territory; or

(*d*) any member of the Council of the Northwest Territories designated by the Commissioner of the Northwest Territories.

The corollary relief provisions were formerly sections 10, 11 and 12 of the *Divorce Act*, R.S.C. 1970, c. D-8 and are reproduced below.

### Interim orders

**10.** Where a petition for divorce has been presented, the court having jurisdiction to grant relief in respect thereof may make such interim orders as it thinks fit and just

(*a*) for the payment of alimony or an alimentary pension by either spouse for the maintenance of the other pending the hearing and determination of the petition, accordingly as the court thinks reasonable having regard to the means and needs of each of them;

(*b*) for the maintenance of and the custody, care and upbringing of the children of the marriage pending the hearing and determination of the petition; or

(*c*) for relieving either spouse of any subsisting obligation to cohabit with the other.

## Orders granting corollary relief — variation, *etc.* of order granting corollary relief

**11.** (1) Upon granting a decree *nisi* of divorce, the court may, if it thinks it fit and just to do so having regard to the conduct of the parties and the condition, means and other circumstances of each of them, make one or more of the following orders, namely:

(*a*) an order requiring the husband to secure or to pay such lump sum or periodic sums as the court thinks reasonable for the maintenance of

> (i) the wife,
>
> (ii) the children of the marriage, or
>
> (iii) the wife and the children of the marriage;

(*b*) an order requiring the wife to secure or to pay such lump sum or periodic sums as the court thinks reasonable for the maintenance of

> (i) the husband,
>
> (ii) the children of the marriage, or
>
> (iii) the husband and the children of the marriage; and

(*c*) an order providing for the custody, care and upbringing of the children of the marriage.

(2) An order made pursuant to this section may be varied from time to time or rescinded by the court that made the order if it thinks it fit and just to do so having regard to the conduct of the parties since the making of the order or any change in the condition, means or other circumstances of either of them.

### Payment and conditions

**12.** Where a court makes an order pursuant to section 10 or 11, it may

(*a*) direct that any alimony, alimentary pension or maintenance be paid either to the husband or wife, as the case may be, or to a trustee or administrator approved by the court; and

(*b*) impose such terms, conditions or restrictions as the court thinks fit and just.

---

This chapter is divided into the following subsections:

## 1.1 Introduction

Corollary relief consists of child support (s. 15.1), spousal support (s. 15.2), and custody of, and access to children (s. 16). See also the definition of "corollary relief proceeding" in s. 2(1). Orders made for corollary relief are never final and may be varied at a later date to accommodate changed circumstances: s. 17. This volume of *Canadian Divorce Law and Practice* will only consider spousal support under the *Divorce Act*, the *Spousal Support Advisory Guidelines* and the cases which consider the spousal support sections of the Act and/or the *Spousal Support Advisory Guidelines*. Entitlement issues are decided under the *Divorce Act*. The *Spousal Support Advisory Guidelines* have been established to assist courts and the parties in determining the quantum and duration of spousal support. They have not been legislated and are merely advisory.

The Act contemplates the possibility of a joint application by both spouses as well as the ordinary case of one spouse proceeding against the other: see ss. 15.1(1), 15.2(1) and 16(1).

The right to corollary relief comes into existence at the time of divorce, but a claim for that relief need not be joined with a claim for divorce, and need not be heard at the time of the divorce. It may be made in a proceeding independent of the divorce and may be commenced some time after the date on which the divorce is obtained. To accommodate these two options, the Act provides that the claim may be brought by a spouse or a former spouse: ss. 15 and 15.1 to 16.

Since, pursuant to s. 4, the court has jurisdiction to grant corollary relief only to "former" spouses — that is, only to parties who have been divorced — practitioners should, in the petition for divorce, join with the claim for support as corollary relief an alternative claim for support that stands alone under provincial legislation. Then, if the claim for a divorce is dismissed and the court is without corollary relief jurisdiction, it may proceed to exercise its jurisdiction under the provincial legislation on the alternative claim.

There is no time specified in the Act within which a corollary relief claim must be brought. Whether the court will hear a claim commenced long after the divorce has been granted is not a matter of jurisdiction — the jurisdiction continues indefinitely — but a question of whether defences based on that delay and other circumstances are available.

Severing the claim for corollary relief from its dependence on a claim for divorce, and giving it an existence of its own, creates the possibility of three distinct proceedings under the *Divorce Act*:

1. a divorce proceeding,
2. a corollary relief proceeding, and
3. a variation proceeding.

The usual reason for severing the divorce and corollary relief claims is that one of the parties is anxious to remarry and wishes to avoid the delay caused by the much slower pace needed to resolve disputed corollary relief issues. There is no dispute over the divorce because, in these situations, it is based on the ground of marriage breakdown by reason of separation and there is no issue about the required year having matured. The divorce, if cut loose from the claims for corollary relief, can be tried immediately as an uncontested proceeding, unhampered by the other disputed claims. They are off on their own with all the time needed to work through the various stages of litigation to settlement or trial. The severance, however, is not advantageous in all cases. Sometimes, the marriage should be kept in place to preserve, for example, rights to exclusive possession of the matrimonial home, or to property rollovers available only to spouses. This means that unless there is a need to rush the divorce, it should await the resolution of the corollary issues just in case marriage rights are needed in the settlement.

Settlements, not trials, are the preferred legislative objectives. In the document that commences a divorce proceeding, the lawyer with carriage of the proceeding must certify that he or she has discussed with the client the advisability of negotiating a settlement of the matters that may be the subject of a support order or a custody order, and must inform the client of the mediation facilities known to him or her that might assist the spouses in negotiating a settlement of those matters: s. 9(2).

## 1.2 Application of Statutes

See: *Divorce Act*, s. 15.

Spousal support is entirely a creature of statute. It is only because there is authority in the statute for support that support exists.

Spousal support orders may be made under s. 15.2 of the *Divorce Act* by a "court of competent jurisdiction." The "court" is defined by name in s. 2(1) for each province and territory and, generally speaking, is the highest division or court in the province or territory in which trials are conducted. This court is competent to try an issue of spousal support after a divorce has been granted where the claim is made in a corollary relief proceeding. A corollary relief proceeding is "a proceeding in a court in which either or both former spouses seek a child support order, a spousal support order or a custody order": s. 2(1). This proceeding is within the jurisdiction of the court if

(a) either former spouse is ordinarily resident in the province at the commencement of the proceeding; or

(b) both former spouses accept the jurisdiction of the court: *Divorce Act*, s. 4(1)(a) and (b).

The requirement of a divorce first being granted applies to permanent spousal support orders only. An interim order may be made before divorce, while the parties are still spouses. See ss. 15.1(2), 15.2(2) and 16(2).

The requirement that the granting of a divorce is a condition precedent to the support order is implicit in the description of the parties found in both the definition of a corollary relief proceeding and the provision setting out the basis of the court's jurisdiction in these proceedings, above. They are described, not as "spouses", but as "former" spouses; that is, spouses who have obtained a divorce.

The divorce may have been granted in the immediate past as where the claim for support is joined with a claim for divorce in the same proceeding and the divorce is granted first, with the order for support made an instant later, or the divorce may have been granted in the more distant past where the support claim is made in an independent corollary relief proceeding commenced on a date after the date of the granting of the divorce.

Support claimed in an independent corollary relief proceeding need not be ordered by the same court that granted the divorce. The divorce may have been granted on an earlier date in another province or territory. The new court may assume jurisdiction if either of the elements in s. 4(1)(a) or (b) are present. See JURISDICTION IN COROLLARY RELIEF PROCEEDINGS, 4§§1 and 2 in Volume 1.

Where two corollary relief proceedings are commenced on different days, the court in which the first proceeding was commenced has exclusive jurisdiction to hear and determine the matter: *Divorce Act*, s. 4(2).

Where two proceedings are commenced on the same day, the Federal Court – Trial Division has exclusive jurisdiction over the matter: *Divorce Act*, s. 4(3).

## 1.3 Grounds for Entitlement to Spousal Support

*Bracklow v. Bracklow*, 1999 CarswellBC 532, 1999 CarswellBC 533, 44 R.F.L. (4th) 1, [1999] 1 S.C.R. 420, 63 B.C.L.R. (3d) 77, 169 D.L.R. (4th) 577, [1999] 8 W.W.R. 740, [1999] R.D.F. 203, 236 N.R. 79, 120 B.C.A.C. 211, 196 W.A.C. 211, [1999] S.C.J. No. 14 (S.C.C.) identifies three "conceptual grounds for entitlement to spousal support: (1) compensatory; (2)

contractual; and (3) non-compensatory" grounds. See discussion of these grounds in **Chapter 6, section 6.1 Objectives — General**.

# CHAPTER 2

# JURISDICTION

See *Divorce Act*, s. 3 (Jurisdiction in divorce proceedings).
See *Divorce Act*, s. 4 (Jurisdiction in corollary relief proceeding).
See *Divorce Act*, s. 5 (Jurisdiction in variation proceedings).
See *Divorce Act*, s. 15.2(2).
See *Divorce Act*, s. 15.2(1).
See *Divorce Act*, s. 2.2 (Recognition of Foreign Divorce)

This chapter is divided into the following subsections:

## 2.1 Jurisdiction in Corollary Relief Proceedings

Section 4(1) of the Act provides that a corollary relief proceeding may be brought in any province in which either former spouse is ordinarily resident at the time of the commencement of the proceedings or in a province whose jurisdiction is acceptable to both former spouses.

If a divorce or corollary relief proceeding contains a claim for an order under s. 16 (custody or access) which is contested, and the child is most substantially connected with another province, the court may on application of a spouse or former spouse, or on its own motion, transfer the proceeding to that other province (s. 6(1) and (2)). That province then has exclusive jurisdiction to hear and determine the proceeding: s. 6(4).

Where corollary relief proceedings are pending in two courts, the first court approached will have exclusive jurisdiction: s. 4(2). If both proceedings were commenced on the same day, both will be transferred to the Federal Court — Trial Division for hearing: s. 4(3).

Section 4 mirrors the language of s. 5 of the *Divorce Act*.

For cases discussing ordinarily resident, see *Canadian Divorce Law and Practice*, Volume 1, s. 3§1 Ordinarily resident.

For case law, see *Canadian Divorce Law and Practice*, Volume 1, s. 4§1 Jurisdiction to grant corollary relief.

In divorce proceedings, corollary relief issues may be separated from the divorce and from each other and treated as separate claims: see *Canadian Divorce Law and Practice*, Volume 1, s. 4§2 Severance of corollary relief.

## 2.2 Jurisdiction in Variation Proceedings

See *Divorce Act*, s. 5.

Section 5(1) of the Act provides that a variation proceeding may be brought in any province in which either former spouse is ordinarily resident at the time of the commencement of the proceeding or in a province in which both spouses accept the jurisdiction of the court.

Where variation proceedings are pending in two courts, the court in which a proceeding was commenced first will have exclusive jurisdiction: s. 5(2). If the proceedings were commenced on the same day, they will be transferred to the Federal Court — Trial Division which will exercise exclusive jurisdiction: s. 5(3).

Section 6(3) provides that if a variation proceeding in respect to a custody order is opposed and the child involved is most substantially connected with another province, the court having original jurisdiction may, on application by a former spouse or on its own motion, transfer the proceeding to a court in that other province. Pursuant to s. 6(4) the court to which the variation proceeding is transferred will then have exclusive jurisdiction.

For cases discussing "ordinarily resident", see Volume 1, 3I1 Ordinarily resident.

## 2.3 Jurisdiction to Make Support Orders — Case Law

*Canadian courts have no jurisdiction under the* Divorce Act *to vary the provisions of corollary relief pursuant to a foreign divorce judgement — Leonard v. Booker*, 2007 CarswellNB 495, 2007 CarswellNB 496, 2007 NBCA 71, 44 R.F.L. (6th) 237, 286 D.L.R. (4th) 451, 321 N.B.R. (2d) 340, 827 A.P.R. 340 (N.B.C.A.). A foreign support order must be registered under the *Interjurisdictional Support Orders Act* before it can be varied. In New Brunswick, a foreign custody order can be recognized under the *Family Services Act* and then it can be varied under that Act where "there has been a material change in circumstances that affects or is likely to affect the best interests of the child" (s. 130.3(1)). The parties were married in Fredericton and then moved to Bermuda, where they subsequently divorced and a consent order dealing with custody and support was granted. The parties returned to New Brunswick, and the consent order was varied by the Court of Queen's Bench three times. The Court of Appeal determined that *Rothgiesser* (see below) applies to situations of child support as well as spousal support, and that the lower courts erred in varying the original consent order as they had no jurisdiction to do so.

*Custody and support matters outside of the context of a Canadian divorce can only be dealt with through provincial legislation — Leonard v. Booker*, 2007 CarswellNB 495, 2007 CarswellNB 496, 2007 NBCA 71, 44 R.F.L. (6th) 237, 286 D.L.R. (4th) 451, 321 N.B.R. (2d) 340, 827 A.P.R. 340 (N.B.C.A.).

*The Ontario court does not have jurisdiction to hear and determine corollary relief following a valid divorce in a foreign jurisdiction — Okmyansky v. Okmyansky*, 2007 CarswellOnt 3702, 2007 ONCA 427, 38 R.F.L. (6th) 291, 86 O.R. (3d) 587, 225 O.A.C. 60, 284 D.L.R. (4th) 152, [2007] O.J. No. 2298 (Ont. C.A.). The parties were married in Russia. While they were living in Ontario, the husband returned to Russia and was granted a divorce. At trial, the court determined that the Russian divorce decree was valid. On the grounds that Ontario was their last common habitual residence, the trial judge refused to stay the wife's application for support that was brought pursuant to the *Divorce Act* and the *Family Law Act* and her application for division of property brought under the *Family Law Act*. The husband's appeal was allowed in part. Although the court had no jurisdiction to hear the applications for corollary relief, it had jurisdiction to hear the equalization claim. Considering the language of s. 4 of the *Divorce Act*, the Ontario court does not have jurisdiction to hear and determine corollary relief following a valid divorce in a foreign jurisdiction. Corollary relief proceedings may only be heard if the court has granted a divorce to the parties in question.

*A court in province other than one in which the parties were divorced has jurisdiction to vary a corollary support order* — *Arsenault v. Arsenault*, 2006 CarswellNS 116, 2006 NSCA 38, 265 D.L.R. (4th) 1, 242 N.S.R. (2d) 340, 770 A.P.R. 340, [2006] N.S.J. No. 114 (N.S.C.A.). The parties were divorced in Manitoba. Prior to the divorce decree they had executed a full and final separation agreement, but failed to ask that it be incorporated into a corollary relief judgement. The trial court dismissed the wife's application for a corollary relief judgement to incorporate the separation agreement on the grounds that the court did not have jurisdiction. The appellate court determined that it had jurisdiction to incorporate the separation agreement. Following the 1993 amendment to s. 4(1) of the *Divorce Act*, a court no longer needs to have granted the parties a divorce in order to make a corollary relief judgement.

*No power to terminate contractual support* — *Zimmerman v. Shannon*, 2006 CarswellBC 2715, 2006 BCCA 499, 34 R.F.L. (6th) 32, [2007] 4 W.W.R. 35, 62 B.C.L.R. (4th) 255, 276 D.L.R. (4th) 659, 385 W.A.C. 122, 232 B.C.A.C. 122 (B.C.C.A.). It is an error in principle to interpret s. 15.2 of the *Divorce Act* to include the power to terminate a contractual support obligation.

*Canadian courts will only have jurisdiction to hear and determine a corollary relief judgement when the parties are divorced in Canada* — *V. (L.R.) v. V. (A.A.)*, 2006 CarswellBC 299, 2006 BCCA 63, 43 R.F.L. (6th) 59, 264 D.L.R. (4th) 524, 52 B.C.L.R. (4th) 112, 222 B.C.A.C. 178, 368 W.A.C. 178, [2006] B.C.J. No. 264 (B.C.C.A.). The parties divorced in the United States, and the husband was ordered to pay child support. The mother applied to vary the U.S. order, but it was found that the B.C. courts did not have jurisdiction to do so. The father was resident in the U.S. and had never resided in Canada. The court stated:

> [59] If one analyzes closely the sections of the Acts of 1968, 1986 and 1993, bearing on the jurisdiction to make support orders, the progression is this:
>
> 1. By the Act of 1968, only the court which pronounced the decree of divorce could grant corollary relief or subsequently vary the orders thus made.
>
> 2. By the Act of 1986 (s. 5(1)), the jurisdiction to "vary" an order for corollary relief could be exercised by any court if either spouse was ordinarily resident in the jurisdiction of that court at the time of the commencement of the proceeding.
>
> 3. By the Act of 1993, the jurisdiction to grant corollary relief in the first instance was extended to any court if either spouse was ordinarily resident in the jurisdiction of the court at the time of the commencement of the proceeding. The point of the 1993 amendment was to expand the jurisdiction granted by the Act of 1986. There is nothing at all in the change in the statute to lead to the conclusion that Parliament, even if it has the constitutional jurisdiction to do so, intended to give jurisdiction to a Canadian court to grant "corollary" relief founded upon a foreign divorce.

*Quebec courts have competence to determine and hear a corollary relief judgement even when the divorce took place outside of Canada* — *M. (G.) c. F. (M.A.)*, 2003 CarswellQue 1969, REJB 2003-46894, [2003] R.J.Q. 2516, [2003] R.D.F. 794, [2003] J.Q. No. 11325 (C.A. Que.). The parties, both Canadians, were divorced in Louisiana. Prior to the parties' divorce, however, an action for divorce was filed and dismissed in Montreal. The Court of Appeal determined that Quebec courts did have jurisdiction based on the fact that one of the parties was a habitual resident of Quebec.

"*A court will have jurisdiction to hear and determine a corollary relief proceeding, and can therefore make a support order, provided it is the court that has also granted either or both parties their divorce. Clearly, the 'court' can only be a Canadian court and would include the Ontario Court where it was the court that granted the parties their divorce*" — Rothgiesser v. Rothgiesser, 2000 CarswellOnt 50, 2 R.F.L. (5th) 266, 46 O.R. (3d) 577, 183 D.L.R. (4th) 310, 128 O.A.C. 302, [2000] O.J. No. 33 (Ont. C.A.), at para. 28. See also *Gyuzeleva v. Angelov*, 2012 CarswellOnt 14936, 2012 ONSC 6628 (Ont. S.C.J.), additional reasons at 2012 CarswellOnt 16101, 2012 ONSC 7193 (Ont. S.C.J.).

*Canadian courts do not have jurisdiction under the* Divorce Act *to vary a support order in a divorce judgement of another country* — Rothgiesser v. Rothgiesser, supra. Variations of foreign support orders can be addressed by Canadian courts only under the provincial legislation respecting reciprocal enforcement of support orders. The parties were divorced by the Supreme Court of South Africa. The final order of divorce incorporated terms of settlement including a provision for spousal support. After the divorce, the wife made her home in California and the husband in Ontario. The husband applied in the Ontario courts to terminate the spousal support contending that the wife had consented to the court having jurisdiction. In allowing an appeal from an order terminating the support, the Court of Appeal held that the Ontario courts do not have jurisdiction to vary a foreign support order and that the parties cannot confer such jurisdiction on them.

*Lack of jurisdiction — retroactive support prior to commencement of divorce proceedings* — Young v. Young, 2000 CarswellNB 85, 7 R.F.L. (5th) 228, 225 N.B.R. (2d) 272, 578 A.P.R. 272, [2000] N.B.J. No. 93 (N.B.C.A.). There is no jurisdiction under the *Divorce Act* to make a support order retroactive to a date prior to the commencement of divorce proceedings.

*Refusal to exercise jurisdiction regarding support* — Hughes v. Hughes, 1976 CarswellBC 25, 30 R.F.L. 199, [1997] 1 W.W.R. 579, 1 B.C.L.R. 234, 72 D.L.R. (3d) 577, [1976] B.C.J. No. 1400 (B.C.C.A.), at 201 [R.F.L.]. A court can refuse to exercise its jurisdiction to grant or refuse maintenance and may make no maintenance order at all. "There are many circumstances in which the matters of custody or maintenance are better left to the parties or to the provincial legislation".

*Judge seized of corollary relief application until application signed* — Cromwell v. Cromwell, 1995 CarswellNS 63, 14 R.F.L. (4th) 47, 140 N.S.R. (2d) 397, 399 A.P.R. 397 (N.S.C.A.). A judge remains seized of an application for corollary relief until the final order is signed. Accordingly where the judge was dissatisfied with the draft including the introduction of new evidence, he had jurisdiction to issue an order inconsistent with the first draft.

*No corollary relief where divorce not obtained* — Kalsi v. Kalsi, 1992 CarswellAlta 318, 41 R.F.L. (3d) 201, 131 A.R. 102, 25 W.A.C. 102 (Alta. C.A.). Section 4 of the *Divorce Act* prevents a chambers judge from ordering corollary relief where the parties are not yet divorced.

*Order for support may be granted after divorce* — Delaney v. Delaney, 1995 CarswellBC 24, 11 R.F.L. (4th) 155, 2 B.C.L.R. (3d) 227, 122 D.L.R. (4th) 439, [1995] 4 W.W.R. 599, 55 B.C.A.C. 258, 90 W.A.C. 258, [1995] B.C.J. No. 307 (B.C.C.A.). An order for support may be granted after the date on which a divorce judgement has been made and entered.

*Court ordering support cannot bar variation within specified time-frame* — Lidstone v. Lidstone, 1993 CarswellNS 44, 46 R.F.L. (3d) 203, 121 N.S.R. (2d) 213, 335 A.P.R. 213, [1993] N.S.J. No. 165 (N.S.C.A.). In making a support order, the court lacks jurisdiction to bar the payor from seeking a variation of the order within a specified timeframe. Section 17 of the Act specifies a statutory right of review for a former spouse, and the husband could not be precluded from exercising that right in the event of a material change in circumstances.

*A court will have jurisdiction to make a support order under the* Divorce Act *when a default judgment has been silent as to corollary relief* — Bull v. Bull, 2013 CarswellAlta 1094, 2013

ABQB 366 (Alta. Q.B.). The husband applied for, and was granted, an undefended desk divorce which did not provide for spousal support. The wife subsequently sought to set aside the divorce or alternately claim spousal support under the *Divorce Act*. The judge found there was no time limit on his jurisdiction to grant support under the *Divorce Act*, but rather that relief may not be available based on defences of delay or prejudice. The judge read into the original divorce judgment that corollary relief had been severed and considered the application for support.

*Where each party is ordinarily resident in Ontario when an application for interim spousal support was issued, the court will have jurisdiction over support* — Cantave v. Cantave, 2013 CarswellOnt 8644, 2013 ONSC 4082 (Ont. S.C.J.). The judge found that he had jurisdiction to determine interim spousal support as the parties were "ordinarily resident" at the time of application and Ontario was the forum conveniens, despite various relocations to France.

*Where part of the corollary relief judgment had already been made in one jurisdiction, a transfer will not be granted* — Godin v. Godin, 2013 CarswellNS 1060, 2013 NSSC 401, 340 N.S.R. (2d) 52, 1077 A.P.R. 52 (N.S.S.C.). The wife sought to transfer custody, access and support corollary relief proceedings from Nova Scotia to British Columbia. The Divorce Order had been granted, and the judge considered whether a transfer was appropriate under s. 6(2) of the *Divorce Act*. Spousal support had already been determined as a corollary order in Nova Scotia. The judge noted the objective of the legislation of not having "competing jurisdictions dealing with different aspects of corollary relief or even the divorce proceeding". He found that the fact that he had already ruled on the spousal support issue indicated continuing with a determination of other corollary relief in the same jurisdiction and not transferring the proceedings in the middle of a trial.

*Section 4 addresses which province has jurisdiction when claims for corollary relief are advanced in the Superior Courts of two different province* — Houle v. Trottier, 2012 CarswellOnt 17367, 2012 ONSC 6661, 34 R.F.L. (7th) 76, 313 O.A.C. 81 (Ont. Div. Ct.).

*Section 4 specifies that it operates in respect to "corollary relief proceedings" of "former spouses"* — D. (C.R.) v. D. (N.D.), 2009 CarswellAlta 586, 2009 ABQB 242 (Alta. Q.B.).

*Service in Ontario of a non-resident does not meet the criteria for jurisdiction set out in ss. 5(1) and 18(2) of the* Divorce Act — McCaffrey v. Dalla-Longa, 2007 CarswellOnt 7748 (Ont. S.C.J.). If one party has previously sought the aid of the Ontario court in an unrelated matter, it does not determine whether or not the party has accepted the jurisdiction of the court for the proceedings at hand.

*A second variation application is deemed discontinued where the original application is stayed* — Ridout v. Ridout, 2006 CarswellOnt 5788 (Ont. S.C.J.). The husband's application, brought in Ontario, to vary the divorce was stayed. The Alberta court had no jurisdiction to hear and determine a subsequent, nearly identical, application brought by the husband. The second application, which involved the same former spouses and the same subject-matter, was deemed discontinued by s. 5(2) of the *Divorce Act*.

*If s. 5(1) of the* Divorce Act *is read as mandatory, it would be in conflict with Articles 3, 12 and 13 of the* Hague Convention — Braatelien v. Horning, 2001 CarswellOnt 3402, [2001] O.J. No. 3799 (Ont. S.C.J.).

*Section 5(2) of the* Divorce Act *is mandatory, and there is nothing in the wording of that provision which gives a court discretion to order a result other than the one specified therein* — Wolch v. Wolch, 1995 CarswellOnt 1093, 17 R.F.L. (4th) 413 (Ont. Gen. Div.).

*Order for support may be granted after divorce* — Huazarik v. Fairfield, 2004 CarswellOnt 840, 48 R.F.L. (5th) 275, [2004] O.T.C. 209, [2004] O.J. No. 798 (Ont. S.C.J.). Under the *Divorce Act*, it is possible to make an order for spousal support following the parties' divorce. Section 15 of the *Divorce Act* includes a divorced spouse in the definition of "spouse" for the purposes of corollary relief.

*Order for support may be granted which would alter support arrangements in separation agreement — Huszarik v. Fairfield*, 2004 CarswellOnt 3962, 9 R.F.L. (6th) 130, [2004] O.T.C. 843, [2004] O.J. No. 798 (Ont. S.C.J.). Where the husband applied for a determination of spousal support which would have the effect of altering the support arrangements under the parties' separation agreement, he was not required to establish the "material change" required by s. 17 of the *Divorce Act*. The application was not a variation application but an originating application. Accordingly, the variation clause in the agreement itself was properly considered.

*Divorce granted by foreign court — Canadian court cannot grant corollary relief or vary foreign order — Jahangiri-Navaneh v. Taheri-Zengekani*, 2003 CarswellOnt 2934, 39 R.F.L. (5th) 103, 66 O.R. (3d) 272, [2003] O.T.C. 705, [2003] O.J. No. 3018 (Ont. S.C.J.). There is no authority to grant corollary relief under the *Divorce Act* where a divorce was granted in a foreign country. Nor is there any jurisdiction to vary that foreign order.

*Divorce granted by foreign court — Canadian court cannot grant corollary relief — Wlodarczyk v. Spriggs*, 2000 CarswellSask 700, 2000 SKQB 468, 12 R.F.L. (5th) 241, 200 Sask. R. 129 (Sask. Q.B.). Corollary relief under the *Divorce Act* is not available where the parties' divorce was granted by a foreign court.

*Summary application for support — inappropriate to grant orders dispensing with spousal support or order directing that neither party shall apply for spousal support at later date — Page v. Page*, 2003 CarswellAlta 1492, 2003 ABQB 847, 49 R.F.L. (5th) 157, 25 Alta. L.R. (4th) 321, [2003] A.J. No. 1300 (Alta. Q.B. [In Chambers]). Orders dispensing with spousal support are rare and orders directing that neither party shall apply for spousal support at a later date definitely require trial and hearing of surrounding issues and should not be granted in the context of a summary application for divorce.

*Original divorce judgement silent on issue of support — Hamonic v. Hamonic*, 1992 CarswellSask 484, 103 Sask. R. 29 (Sask. Q.B.) (a case involving child support, but the same principle applies to spousal support). Where the original divorce decree is silent on the issue of support, the proper procedure for obtaining support is by way of an original application and not a request for variation of the decree.

*Judicial separation — does not limit court's power to award support at later time — Ruel c. Thomas*, 1982 CarswellQue 480, [1982] C.A. 357 (C.A. Que.). A judicial separation granted under provincial legislation does not limit the court's power to award maintenance in a later divorce action.

*Role of registrar concerning support — Larson v. Larson*, 1993 CarswellBC 154, 80 B.C.L.R. (2d) 303, [1993] B.C.J. No. 661 (B.C.S.C.). On a reference to the Registrar on support issues, the Registrar lacks jurisdiction to adjudicate the support issues, but he or she does have the jurisdiction to make findings of fact on the issues of need and the ability to pay.

*Consent corollary relief order not intended to be final order may be re-opened — Russell v. Russell*, 1995 CarswellAlta 291, 16 R.F.L. (4th) 229, 33 Alta. L.R. (3d) 170, 175 A.R. 225 (Alta. Q.B.). Where neither the party nor the judge intended that a consent corollary relief order made during the course of proceedings was to be final, the wife was entitled to have the order re-opened by virtue of R. 390(1) of the *Alberta Rules of Court*.

*Support order — no jurisdiction in master to order spouse to continue mortgage payments — Fisher v. Fisher*, 1990 CarswellOnt 289, 28 R.F.L. (3d) 324, [1990] O.J. No. 1454 (Ont. H.C.). In the context of a support order, a Master has no jurisdiction under the *Divorce Act* to order a spouse to continue to make mortgage payments.

*Court has jurisdiction to award support where claimant has abandoned claim — Standing v. Standing*, 1991 CarswellSask 80, 37 R.F.L. (3d) 90, 96 Sask. R. 13, 85 D.L.R. (4th) 309 (Sask. Q.B.). The court has jurisdiction to award spousal support after divorce even where the claimant had abandoned the support claim prior to the granting of the divorce.

*Settlement agreement incorporated into consent order but not incorporated into divorce judgement. no change of circumstances needs to be proven* — *Fraticelli v. Fraticelli*, 2000 CarswellNB 19, 4 R.F.L. (5th) 222, [2000] N.B.J. No. 22 (N.B.C.A.). Where the parties' settlement agreement had been incorporated into a consent order under provincial legislation but had not been incorporated in the divorce judgement, the wife was not required to prove a change of circumstances in her subsequent application for support under the *Divorce Act*.

*No jurisdiction to grant application for support in different jurisdiction from that in which divorce judgement granted* — *Droit de la famille - 770*, 1989 CarswellQue 1223, EYB 1989-76539, [1990] R.J.Q. 581, [1990] R.D.F. 142 (C.S. Que.).The Quebec court dismissed the wife's application for alimony where she had not sought such an award in the original New Brunswick divorce proceedings. Only the court in New Brunswick had jurisdiction to make the order requested.

*Effect of divorce order on order of support under provincial legislation* — *Carson v. Carson*, 1979 CarswellPEI 22, 9 R.F.L. (2d) 209 (P.E.I.S.C.). An order for maintenance made under provincial legislation does not survive a decree absolute. Consequently, a provisional order made after the decree purporting to vary a provincial order made before the decree is made without jurisdiction and cannot be confirmed. This is so even though the divorce decree makes no provision for maintenance.

## 2.4 Constitutional Issues

*Federal power to grant maintenance under the* Divorce Act — *Zacks v. Zacks*, 1973 CarswellBC 134, 1973 CarswellBC 266, 10 R.F.L. 53, [1973] S.C.R. 891, 35 D.L.R. (3d) 420, [1973] 5 W.W.R. 289 (S.C.C.); *Jackson v. Jackson*, 1972 CarswellBC 217, 1972 CarswellBC 318, 8 R.F.L. 172, [1973] S.C.R. 205, 29 D.L.R. (3d) 641, [1972] 6 W.W.R. 419 (S.C.C.). See also *Vadeboncoeur c. Landry*, 1976 CarswellQue 27, [1977] 2 S.C.R. 179, 68 D.L.R. (3d) 165, 23 R.F.L. 360, 10 N.R. 469 (S.C.C.); *Whyte v. Whyte*, 1969 CarswellMan 54, 69 W.W.R. 536, 7 D.L.R. (3d) 7 (Man. C.A.); *Niccolls v. Niccolls*, 1969 CarswellBC 51, 68 W.W.R. 307, 4 D.L.R. (3d) 209 (B.C.S.C.); *Todd v. Todd*, 1969 CarswellBC 52, 2 R.F.L. 303, 68 W.W.R. 315, 5 D.L.R. (3d) 92 (B.C.S.C.); *Heikel v. Heikel*, 1970 CarswellAlta 76, 1 R.F.L. 326, 73 W.W.R. 84, 12 D.L.R. (3d) 311 (Alta. C.A.). The power to grant an order of maintenance pursuant to s. 11 [now ss. 15.1 and 15.2] of the *Divorce Act* is necessarily ancillary to jurisdiction in divorce and in that regard the Parliament of Canada was acting within its legislative competency conferred upon it by s. 91(26) of the *Constitution Act, 1867* (U.K.), c. 3. This principle applies equally to matters of custody, care and upbringing of children of the marriage under s. 11(1)(c) [now s. 16] and to the provisions dealing with interim orders.

*No reduction of property under the guise of spousal support* — *Shepley v. Shepley*, 2006 CarswellOnt 382, 24 R.F.L. (6th) 422, [2006] O.J. No. 293 (Ont. S.C.J.). It is beyond the jurisdiction of the federal divorce legislation to require a redistribution of property under the guise of spousal support. The husband could not be ordered to provide support from capital excluded from equalization. While in appropriate circumstances a court may consider the income from capital assets as available for the purpose of determining whether spousal support is payable, and the court may deem particular assets to be income-producing, the Ontario *Family Law Act* considers inherited property to be exempt from sharing upon the breakdown of a marriage.

*Charter of Rights* — *Divorce Act* — *grounds and corollary relief* — *not contrary to Charter* — *Qually v. Qually*, 1987 CarswellSask 312, 5 R.F.L. (3d) 365, [1987] 2 W.W.R. 553, 56 Sask. R. 165, [1987] S.J. No. 18 (Sask. Q.B.), affirmed 1988 CarswellSask 338, 18 R.F.L. (3d) 69, [1989] 2 W.W.R. 268, [1988] S.J. No. 736 (Sask. C.A.). The provisions under the *Divorce Act, 1985* relating to grounds and corollary relief are not contrary to the *Canadian Charter of Rights and Freedoms*.

*Judicial separation under provincial legislation — court can grant support in divorce action — Ruel c. Thomas*, 1982 CarswellQue 480, [1982] C.A. 357 (C.A. Que.). A judicial separation granted under provincial legislation does not limit the court's power to award maintenance in a later divorce action.

## Support under provincial statutes

### Paramountcy of federal legislation

*Paramountcy of federal legislation — Fancy v. Shephard*, 1997 CarswellNS 503, 35 R.F.L. (4th) 430, 155 D.L.R. (4th) 680, 51 C.R.R. (2d) 45, 164 N.S.R. (2d) 274, 491 A.P.R. 274, [1997] N.S.J. No. 517 (N.S.S.C.). Section 6(3) of the Nova Scotia *Family Maintenance Act*, R.S.N.S. 1989, c. 160, which calls for the termination of support upon the remarriage of the payee spouse, is unconstitutional. Federal legislation in the area of divorce prevails if there is apparent conflict with provincial legislation. As the *Divorce Act* does not specifically provide for variation of spousal support on the grounds of remarriage, there is serious incompatibility between the two statutes.

*Paramountcy of federal legislation — used to resolve conflicts — White v. White*, 1994 CarswellSask 216, 3 R.F.L. (4th) 201, [1994] 7 W.W.R. 249, 113 D.L.R. (4th) 582, 118 Sask. R. 293 (Sask. Q.B.), relying on the statement of Peter W. Hogg in *Constitutional Law of Canada*, 2nd edition (1985). Federal paramountcy is a doctrine of constitutional law used to resolve conflicts between orders made under federal, and orders made under provincial laws. Conflicts in the area of support became a possibility in 1968 when corollary relief provisions were introduced in the *Divorce Act— federal legislation. By this time, provincial support legislation of undoubted validity had already enjoyed a long history.*

*Paramountcy of federal legislation — marriage and divorce — support ancillary to divorce — Jackson v. Jackson*, 1972 CarswellBC 217, 1972 CarswellBC 318, 8 R.F.L. 172, [1973] S.C.R. 205, [1972] 6 W.W.R. 419, 29 D.L.R. (3d) 641 (S.C.C.), per Ritchie J. The powers of the federal Parliament to enact legislation to provide for support arises under s. 91(26) of the *Constitution Act, 1867*, which gives it the right to make laws in relation to "marriage and divorce". The provision for support "is necessarily ancillary to jurisdiction in divorce and . . . the Parliament of Canada was therefore acting within the legislative competency conferred upon it by the B.N.A. Act [now the *Constitution Act*], s. 91(26), in legislating to this end." The provincial legislatures find their jurisdiction in the powers allocated to them under s. 92(13) to make laws in relation to "property and civil rights in the province". (See *White v. White*, above.)

*Paramountcy of federal legislation — both federal and provincial legislatures — power to enact laws concerning support and custody — Radke v. Radke*, 1971 CarswellAlta 64, 4 R.F.L. 318, [1971] 5 W.W.R. 113, 20 D.L.R. (3d) 679, [1971] A.J. No. 131 (Alta. C.A.), at 338 [R.F.L.]. Both parliament and provincial legislatures have jurisdiction to enact provisions for support. "There can be little doubt that Parliament has power to enact provisions for maintenance and custody when these questions arise as a result of dissolution of the marriage in proceedings under the *Divorce Act*, and it also seems clear enough that the existence of such 'ancillary' jurisdiction does not oust the jurisdiction of the provincial legislatures to enact provisions conferring similar jurisdiction on the courts in other matrimonial proceedings", per Cairns J.A.

*Paramountcy of federal legislation — federal and provincial legislation — no distinction concerning spousal support — Bracklow v. Bracklow*, 1999 CarswellBC 532, 1999 CarswellBC 533, 44 R.F.L. (4th) 1, [1999] 1 S.C.R. 420, 63 B.C.L.R. (3d) 77, 169 D.L.R. (4th) 577, [1999] 8

W.W.R. 740, [1999] R.D.F. 203, 236 N.R. 79, 120 B.C.A.C. 211, 196 W.A.C. 211, [1999] S.C.J. No. 14 (S.C.C.). No distinction is made between spousal support under federal (*Divorce Act*) and provincial legislation. For a detailed discussion of the case, see Chapter 6.

*Paramountcy of federal legislation — support ancillary to divorce — federal — otherwise provincial — Yearley v. Yearley*, 1978 CarswellSask 18, 5 R.F.L. (2d) 301 (Sask. Dist. Ct.). The *Divorce Act* deals with support as a matter ancillary to divorce proceedings. When it is dealt with in divorce proceedings it comes within federal jurisdiction. Otherwise, it would fall within provincial jurisdiction as dealing with property and civil rights.

Where parliament and the legislatures under their respective heads of legislative jurisdiction enact the same, or substantially the same provisions with respect to support, the parliamentary enactments are considered to be paramount. This means that in a conflict they prevail over and make inoperative the provincial or territorial enactments.

*Paramountcy of federal legislation — no real conflict between federal and provincial legislation — Goldstein v. Goldstein*, 1975 CarswellAlta 4, 17 R.F.L. 346 (Alta. T.D.), at 348 [R.F.L.], reversed 1976 CarswellAlta 102, 23 R.F.L. 206, [1976] 4 W.W.R. 646, 67 D.L.R. (3d) 624 (Alta. C.A.). See also *Gillespie v. Gillespie*, 1973 CarswellNB 13, 13 R.F.L. 344, 6 N.B.R. (2d) 239, 36 D.L.R. (3d) 421, [1973] N.B.J. No. 33 (N.B.C.A.). "The apparent conflict between the provincial legislation and federal legislation in the area of corollary relief has been considered by a number of courts which, as far as I can ascertain, are in agreement that the federal legislation must prevail and is paramount over the provincial legislation", per Bowen J.

*Paramountcy of federal legislation — no conflict between support order under federal legislation and order for exclusive possession under provincial legislation — Lamb v. Lamb*, 1985 CarswellOnt 266, 1985 CarswellOnt 941, 46 R.F.L. (2d) 1, [1985] 1 S.C.R. 851, 20 D.L.R. (4th) 1, 59 N.R. 166, 9 O.A.C. 256, [1985] S.C.J. No. 43 (S.C.C.). The conflict must be direct. Thus there is no conflict between an order for support under the *Divorce Act*, and an order for exclusive possession of the matrimonial home under provincial legislation. Although the order for possession is relevant to the question of support, it is not in itself a support order. Since it is not a support order, there is no conflict and no reason to resort to the doctrine of paramountcy.

The test to determine whether there is a conflict between the two sets of laws, and hence the circumstances in which the doctrine of paramountcy should be invoked, has evolved from an application of the "occupied field theory" to a more narrow or specific test embraced by the "operational conflict theory".

### Paramountcy — occupied field theory

*Where provincial legislation deals with same subject-matter as federal legislation — provincial legislation not effective — Richards v. Richards*, 1972 CarswellOnt 126, 7 R.F.L. 101, [1972] 2 O.R. 596, 26 D.L.R. (3d) 264 (Ont. C.A.), at 102 [R.F.L.]. Chief Justice Gale of the Ontario Court of Appeal described what came to be known as the occupied field theory. "[When] the federal government entered the field of divorce and corollary relief by the passage of the *Divorce Act*, 1967-68 (Can.), c. 24, insofar as any provincial legislation in that field dealt with the same subject-matter as the federal legislation, it ceased to be effective. Although the provisions of the federal and provincial legislation are not exactly co-extensive, it is our opinion that any of the provincial legislation which appears to extend beyond the boundaries of the federal legislation is not effective because the federal legislation occupies the field", per Gale C.J.O.

## Paramountcy — operational conflict theory

Where no order made under Divorce Act, order made under provincial legislation — not deemed inconsistent — Keller v. Keller, 1987 CarswellAlta 339, 10 R.F.L. (3d) 268, 45 D.L.R. (4th) 74, 83 A.R. 313, [1987] A.J. No. 655 (Alta. Q.B.). Justice Dickinson (as he then was) in Multiple Access Ltd. v. McCutcheon, 1982 CarswellOnt 128, 1982 CarswellOnt 738, [1982] 2 S.C.R. 161, 18 B.L.R. 138, 138 D.L.R. (3d) 1, 44 N.R. 181, [1982] S.C.J. No. 66 (S.C.C.), is often credited with laying the foundation for the operational conflict theory, or the express contradiction theory. "In principle, there would seem to be no good reason to speak of paramountcy and preclusion except where there is actual conflict in operation as where one enactment says 'yes' and the other says 'no'; 'the same citizens are being told to do inconsistent things'; compliance with one is defiance of the other." On the basis of this theory, so long as no order has in fact been made under the Divorce Act, an order made under the provincial law would not be deemed inconsistent (operationally in conflict) with the Divorce Act and would, therefore, be legally effective. The operational conflict theory has ousted or overruled the occupied field concept. Keller, above.

Support order under provincial legislation not in conflict with federal legislation unless and until federal legislation is invoked — Lefebvre v. Lefebvre, 1982 CarswellOnt 325, 30 R.F.L. (2d) 184, 38 O.R. (2d) 683 (Ont. Co. Ct.). Accepting that the proper test for paramountcy is an express contradiction between the two legislative enactments, "a support order made pursuant to provincial legislation does not automatically lapse on the granting of a decree nisi [divorce judgement] where the judge has made no corollary relief order. While it is certainly within his prerogative to invoke federal divorce jurisdiction to make a support order, in the absence of his exercising such jurisdiction to make a support order, in the absence of his exercising such jurisdiction, it cannot be said that there can be a 'conflict' between federal and provincial legislation. Unless and until the federal legislation is invoked there can be no 'express conflict' or operating incompatibility. There can be no conflict until an actual order is made".

## Support under provincial statutes

Where there is a possibility of conflict with the exercise of jurisdiction under the Divorce Act, provincial legislatures may describe in their enabling statutes the circumstances in which a support order may be granted. These provisions can be seen as codifying the law in the areas in which the provincial legislation operates. For instance, the Family Law Act (Ontario) provides:

36. (1) When a divorce proceeding is commenced under the Divorce Act (Canada), an application for support under this Part [Family Law Act, Part III — Support Obligations] that has not been adjudicated is stayed, unless the court orders otherwise.

(2) The court that deals with a divorce proceeding under the Divorce Act (Canada) may determine the amount of arrears owing under an order for support made under this Part and make an order respecting that amount at the same time as it makes an order under the Divorce Act (Canada).

(3) If a marriage is terminated by a divorce or judgement of nullity and the question of support is not adjudicated in the divorce or nullity proceedings, an order for support made under this Part continues in force according to its terms.

The arrangement of the principles recorded in this section of the Ontario Act will be followed in the organization of the next part of this commentary.

## (1) Stay of Claim for Support in Proceedings under Provincial Legislation

*Commencement of proceedings under the Divorce Act stays proceedings under provincial legislation* — *Pope v. Pope*, 1995 CarswellNfld 7, 12 R.F.L. (4th) 391, [1995] N.J. No. 77 (Nfld. U.F.C.). Interpreting a similar provision to that found in the Ontario act. The first subsection of the Ontario provision sets out the principle of paramountcy developed in the common law that where a *Family Law Act* (Ontario) proceeding in which support is claimed has been started, and no order for support has been made in this proceeding, the mere commencement of a divorce proceeding stays the claim for support in the *Family Law Act* proceeding unless the court orders otherwise. See *Family Law Act* (Ontario), s. 36(1), In the *Pope* decision, the court stated, "There is no jurisdiction under the *Family Law Act* [Newfoundland] to consider a claim for support once a divorce proceeding is started. Once a divorce proceeding is commenced, subs. 43(1) of the *Family Law Act* [Newfoundland] makes it clear that application for support under that Act is stayed, except by leave of the Court."

The stay is automatic. The court that is empowered to lift the stay, or in the words of the *Ontario Act* to order "otherwise," is the court entertaining the *Family Law Act* proceeding; that is, the provincial court. But the court has no power to order a stay where the *Family Law Act* proceeding has resulted in an order for support. The power to order a stay is operative only from the commencement of the proceeding to the time if and when a support order is granted. Once granted, the support order continues in force according to its terms and may be enforced until varied or discharged by the court that made it, notwithstanding the commencement of divorce proceedings subsequent to the order in the provincial court, or until it is superseded by an order granted by the court in the divorce proceeding.

*"Upon the commencement of a divorce proceeding, an application for support brought under the* Family Law Reform Act *or under the* Family Law Act *may only be stayed if it has not been determined or adjudicated by way of an interim-interim or interim or a final order and then only by the court in which the application is pending"* — *Mongrain v. Mongrain*, 1986 CarswellOnt 255, 1 R.F.L. (3d) 33, [1986] O.J. No. 2511 (Ont. H.C.).

## (2) In Divorce Proceeding Court may Enforce Payment of Arrears Accumulated under Provincial Court Order

The second provision in the codifying provision of the *Family Law Act* (Ontario) clarifies the right of the court in a proceeding under the *Divorce Act* to make an order for the payment of arrears owing under *Family Law Act* order: *Family Law Act* (Ontario), s. 36(2).

*A court under* Divorce Act *cannot deal with support arrears under provincial legislation* — *Tweel v. Tweel*, 1994 CarswellPEI 16, 7 R.F.L. (4th) 204, 124 Nfld. & P.E.I.R. 40, 384 A.P.R. 40 (P.E.I.T.D.), additional reasons at 1995 CarswellPEI 54, 18 R.F.L. (4th) 222, 136 Nfld. & P.E.I.R. 148, 423 A.P.R. 148 (P.E.I. T.D.) The court, under the *Divorce Act*, lacks jurisdiction to deal with support arrears accumulating under an order made under a provincial statute. But see *Family Law Act* (Ontario), s. 36(2).

## (3) Order under *Divorce Act* Supersedes Provincial Court Order — *Divorce Judgement Silent Permits Provincial Court Order to Continue*

Lastly, the Ontario section touches on two further characteristics of the law of parmountcy in family law; first the right of the court in a proceeding under the *Divorce Act* to make an order superseding an order that has been made in a *Family Law Act* proceeding, and secondly, the fact that if this right is not exercised, and the question of support is not adjudicated in these proceedings, the *Family Law Act* support order continues in force: *Family Law Act* (Ontario), s. 36(3).

*Existing support order made under provincial legislation does not make support res judicata under* Divorce Act — *Callison v. Callison*, 1989 CarswellBC 171, 22 R.F.L. (3d) 123, 39 B.C.L.R. (2d) 379, [1989] B.C.J. No. 1731 (B.C.C.A.). The fact that a support order has been made under a provincial family law statute does not render the issue *res judicata* in subsequent divorce proceedings.

*Existing final order made under provincial legislation does not affect payor's right to seek or court's right to award a different order in divorce proceedings* — *Goodfellow v. Goodfellow*, 1982 CarswellOnt 433, 38 O.R. (2d) 54, 28 C.P.C. 212 (Ont. Master); *Lefebvre v. Lefebvre*, 1982 CarswellOnt 325, 30 R.F.L. (2d) 184, 38 O.R. (2d) 683 (Ont. Co. Ct.), affirming 1982 CarswellOnt 1432, 38 O.R. (2d) 121 (Ont. Prov. Ct.); *Ferraz v. Ferraz*, 1981 CarswellAlta 74, 24 R.F.L. (2d) 386, 16 Alta. L.R. (2d) 286 (Alta. Prov. Ct.). An existing order for support under the *Family Law Reform Act* does not give rise to *res judicata* in a subsequent application for interim maintenance under the *Divorce Act*.

*Existing final order made under provincial legislation does not affect payor's right to seek or court's right to make a different order in divorce proceedings* — *Delaney v. Delaney*, 1995 CarswellBC 24, 11 R.F.L. (4th) 155, 2 B.C.L.R. (3d) 227, 122 D.L.R. (4th) 439, [1995] 4 W.W.R. 599, 55 B.C.A.C. 258, 90 W.A.C. 258, [1995] B.C.J. No. 307 (B.C.C.A.). A "final order" of support made under a provincial statute does not affect the payor's right to seek nor the court's right to grant a different order in divorce proceedings.

*Child support based solely on previous support award under provincial legislation — inappropriate — Williams v. Williams*, 1999 CarswellNfld 243, 50 R.F.L. (4th) 446, 179 Nfld. & P.E.I.R. 283, 546 A.P.R. 283, [1999] N.J. No. 254 (Nfld. C.A.). It is inappropriate to base a child support award solely on a previous support award made under provincial legislation. A support order made under the *Divorce Act* is grounded in constitutionally separate federal legislation and does not "continue" an order made under provincial legislation. A support order made under the *Divorce Act* must have its own evidentiary base.

*Settlement agreement — not required to prove change in circumstances in application under* Divorce Act — *Fraticelli v. Fraticelli*, 2000 CarswellNB 19, 4 R.F.L. (5th) 222, 2000 N.B.J. No. 22 (N.B.C.A.). Where the parties' settlement agreement had been incorporated into a consent order under provincial legislation but had not been incorporated in the divorce judgement, the wife was not required to prove a change of circumstances in her subsequent application for support under the *Divorce Act*.

*Existing support order under provincial legislation — Strickland v. Strickland*, 1991 CarswellNS 53, 32 R.F.L. (3d) 179, 107 N.S.R. (2d) 111, 290 A.P.R. 111 (N.S.C.A.). In the case of an existing support order under provincial legislation, it is not necessary that a claimant prove a change in circumstances to bring a support claim under s. 15 of the *Divorce Act*.

*Interim maintenance order under* Divorce Act *supersedes final order under provincial legislation — Strong v. Strong*, 1987 CarswellOnt 280, 5 R.F.L. (3d) 209 (Ont. H.C.). The court has jurisdiction to make an interim maintenance award under the *Divorce Act* which supersedes a final support order made under provincial legislation.

*Support order under provincial legislation survives divorce judgement which is silent as to support — Keller v. Keller*, 1987 CarswellAlta 339, 10 R.F.L. (3d) 268, 45 D.L.R. (4th) 74, 83 A.R. 313, [1987] A.J. No. 655 (Alta. Q.B.). An order for support made under provincial legislation survives a decree of divorce where there is no mention of support in the decree. There is no operational incompatibility in continuing an order for support under provincial legislation where a divorce decree is silent as to support. The doctrine of paramountcy only renders the provincial order inoperative where it collides with or is repugnant to the federal legislation. Absent such conflict, the provincial support order remains in full force and effect.

*Court may make support order under provincial legislation where no order under federal legislation — White v. White*, 1994 CarswellSask 216, 3 R.F.L. (4th) 201, [1994] 7 W.W.R. 249, 113 D.L.R. (4th) 582, 118 Sask. R. 293 (Sask. Q.B.). The "divorce court" does not have exclusive jurisdiction over the issue of support. A "provisional court" under its enabling legislation may make an order for support, if the divorce court has not done so.

*No claim for corollary relief under* Divorce Act *— continue variation proceeding under provincial legislation — Gow v. Gow*, 1989 CarswellOnt 211, 18 R.F.L. (3d) 14, 67 O.R. (2d) 443 (Ont. H.C.). In the absence of a claim for corollary relief in a divorce petition, leave to continue an earlier support variation proceeding under provincial legislation should be granted as a matter of course.

*Where divorce decree silent as to child support — separation agreement concerning child support continues in force — Coutts v. Coutts*, 1995 CarswellSask 236, 14 R.F.L. (4th) 234, 132 Sask. R. 288 (Sask. Q.B.). Where the divorce decree was silent on the issue of child support, a separation agreement dealing with child support issues which had been filed with the Unified Family Court was found to continue in force. Under provincial legislation, the agreement was deemed to be an order of the court upon the filing and accordingly, the variation principles to be followed were those specified under the provincial legislation.

*Spousal support order under provincial legislation is suspended, no conflict with proceedings under the* Divorce Act *unless the order under provincial legislation is superseded by doctrine of paramountcy — Gaughan v. Gaughan*, 1998 CarswellOnt 5102, 45 R.F.L. (4th) 147 (Ont. Gen. Div.). Where a provision for spousal support in an order under provincial legislation is suspended until a change in circumstances occurs, there is no operational conflict with proceedings under the *Divorce Act* unless the order is superseded in those proceedings through the doctrine of paramountcy. In the absence of a paramount order, the Provincial Court Family Division may vary its order pursuant to the provincial legislation.

*Divorce judgement silent on issue of support does not affect support obligation in earlier separation agreement — Droit de la famille - 457*, 1988 CarswellQue 1179, [1988] R.J.Q. 769, [1988] R.D.F. 73 (C.S. Que.). A divorce judgement which is silent on the issue of support does not affect the support obligation engrossed in an earlier separation order.

## Support — discretion to proceed under the *Divorce Act* or under provincial legislation

*Support awarded on judicial separation cannot be reviewed in divorce proceedings — Droit de la famille - 1117*, [1987] R.D.F. 360 (C.S. Que.). It is not possible to review maintenance awarded on judicial separation in the context of divorce proceedings.

*Proceedings in Supreme Court for divorce and in Family Court where support is an issue in both courts — Family Court judge may hear application unless probable jurisdictional conflict exists — Tuz, Re*, 1976 CarswellOnt 135, 25 R.F.L. 87, 11 O.R. (2d) 617, 67 D.L.R. (3d) 41, [1976] O.J. No. 2075 (Ont. C.A.). In Ontario, where there are proceedings in the Supreme Court for divorce, in which maintenance is in issue, and there is an application for maintenance in Family Court under a provincial statute, the judge of the Family Court may proceed with the application unless he or she determines after considering the circumstances of the case before him or her that actual or probable conflict of jurisdiction exists.

Divorce Act *— not to retry support issues dealt with under provincial statute — Langner v. Langner*, 1987 CarswellBC 544, 11 R.F.L. (3d) 29 (B.C.S.C.). The *Divorce Act* is not to be used as providing a forum to retry support issues which already have been dealt with under a provincial statute.

*Support order under* Divorce Act — *should not vary existing support order under provincial legislation* — *Rehn v. Rehn*, 1988 CarswellOnt 236, 13 R.F.L. (3d) 440, [1988] O.J. No. 522 (Ont. U.F.C.). The court should not make an order for support under the *Divorce Act*, which has the effect of varying an existing support order made under provincial legislation. The federal Act was not intended as a vehicle to frustrate the variation requirements set out by provincial legislation.

*No final order under provincial legislation* — *prospective payee who is divorced and seeking support must pursue remedies under* Divorce Act — *B.(R.) v. B.(M.)*, 1989 CarswellOnt 221, 19 R.F.L. (3d) 92, 68 O.R. (2d) 32 (Ont. H.C.). Where there has been no final support order made under provincial legislation and where the prospective payee spouse intends to pursue a remedy for support, then if there is a divorce in being, the payee spouse is obligated to pursue the remedies under the *Divorce Act* if the other spouse demands it.

*Spouse paying support under provincial legislation may seek support determination under* Divorce Act — *Clayton v. Clayton*, 1989 CarswellOnt 232, 19 R.F.L. (3d) 430 (Ont. Div. Ct.). A spouse who is paying support under an order made under provincial legislation is entitled to request a support determination under the *Divorce Act*.

# CHAPTER 3
## PARTIES

### 3.1 Spouses or Former Spouses

The *Divorce Act* provides that a claim for spousal support can be brought by either a spouse or former spouse.

"Spouse" is defined in s. 2(1) in the *Divorce Act* as "either of two persons who are married to each other."

"Spouse" is defined in s. 15 of the *Divorce Act* as follows:

> In section 15.1 to 16, "spouse" has the meaning assigned by subsection 2(1), and includes a former spouse.

The Act contemplates the possibility of a joint application by both spouses as well as the ordinary case of one spouse proceeding against the other: see s. 15.2(1).

The parties in a variation application are the former spouses: see s. 17(1)(a). There is again a possibility of an application by one spouse or a joint application by both spouses. Section 17(1)(a) provides:

> A court of competent jurisdiction may make an order varying, rescinding or suspending, prospectively or retroactively,
>
> (a) a support order or any provision thereof on application by either or both former spouses;

Since the 1997 amendments, spousal support orders may be assigned to a federal or provincial ministry or agency. See *Divorce Act*, s. 20.1.

*Where the form of marriage undergone in a foreign country is not prohibited in Canada, the parties complied with the formal requirements of that country, and they held themselves out as married in Canada, they will be considered spouses* — Nafie v. Badawy, 2014 CarswellAlta 731, 2014 ABQB 262 (Alta. Q.B.). The parties underwent a religious marriage ceremony in Egypt. The husband claimed this was not a legal marriage. The wife claimed it complied with the laws of Egypt and the parties were spouses as set out in s. 2(1) of the *Divorce Act*. The judge found that the parties' marriage was recognized in Canada and the form of the Egyptian marriage, which was registered in the civil courts of Egypt, was not prohibited in Canada. The parties had three children and held themselves out as married in Canada.

*The court has no jurisdiction to vary spousal support provisions after the death of the payor spouse, as a claim for support or variation must be made against a living spouse* — Brubacher v. Brubacher Estate, 1997 CarswellOnt 2374, 30 R.F.L. (4th) 276, 18 E.T.R. (2d) 296, 33 O.T.C. 241, [1997] O.J. No. 2466 (Ont. Gen. Div.).

# CHAPTER 4

# INTERIM AND INDEFINITE SUPPORT

This chapter is divided into the following subsections:

## 4.1 General

This chapter will consider permanent and interim support. Varation applications and review proceedings will be considered under Chapter 10 Variation and Review.

The *Divorce Act* s. 15.2(1) and (2) provides:

> (1) A court of competent jurisdiction may, on application by either or both spouses, make an order requiring a spouse to secure or pay, or to secure and pay, such lump sum or periodic sums, or such lump sum and periodic sums, as the court thinks reasonable for the support of the other spouse.

> (2) Where an application is made under subsection (1), the court may, on application by either or both spouses, make an interim order requiring a spouse to secure or pay, or to secure and pay, such lump sum or periodic sums, or such lump sum and periodic sums, as the court thinks reasonable for the support of the other spouse, pending the determination of the application under subsection (1).

Pursuant to these subsections, a court is empowered to make either an order for interim or for permanent support.

## 4.2 Interim Support

On an application for spousal support the court may "make an interim order requiring a spouse to secure or pay, or to secure and pay, such lump sum or periodic sums, or such lump sum and periodic sums, as the court thinks reasonable for the support of the other spouse, pending the determination of the application": *Divorce Act*, s. 15.2(2). The order may be made "for a definite or indefinite period or until a specified event occurs," and the court "may impose terms, conditions or restrictions in connection with the order as it thinks fit and just": *Divorce Act*,

s. 15.2(3). In making the order "the court shall take into consideration the condition, means, needs and other circumstances of each spouse, including

(a)  the length of time the spouses cohabited;
(b)  the functions performed by each spouse during cohabitation; and
(c)  any order, agreement or arrangement relating to support of either spouse": *Divorce Act*, s. 15.2(4).

The spousal support order should

(a)  recognize any economic advantages or disadvantages to the spouses arising from the marriage or its breakdown;
(b)  apportion between the spouses any financial consequences arising from the care of any child of the marriage over and above any obligation for the support of any child of the marriage;
(c)  relieve any economic hardship of the spouses arising from the breakdown of the marriage; and
(d)  in so far as practicable, promote the economic self-sufficiency of each spouse within a reasonable period of time": *Divorce Act*, s. 15.2(6).

Where the court is considering both an application for child support and an application for spousal support, "the court shall give priority to child support in determining the applications": *Divorce Act*, s. 15.3(1).

## 4.2.1 Jurisdiction to Grant Interim Relief

*Interim support — not on application to vary — Y. (H.). v. Y. (D.)*, 1998 CarswellPEI 104, 42 R.F.L. (4th) 418, 170 Nfld. & P.E.I.R. 44, 522 A.P.R. 44, [1998] P.E.I.J. No. 97 (P.E.I.C.A.). Section 17 of the *Divorce Act* cannot be used as authority for granting interim spousal support in the context of an application to vary and extend limited term spousal support. The provision does not expressly authorize interim support on variation applications.

*No jurisdiction where divorce petition filed prematurely — Zemliak v. Zemliak*, 1992 CarswellMan 41, 40 R.F.L. (3d) 181, 78 Man. R. (2d) 104, 16 W.A.C. 104 (C.A.). The court is without jurisdiction to order interim support where the petition for divorce has been filed prematurely. An order made in such circumstances is properly stayed.

*Jurisdiction where claim referred to registrar — Vedovato v. Vedovato*, 1981 CarswellBC 335, 25 R.F.L. (2d) 297, 32 B.C.L.R. 360, 130 D.L.R. (3d) 283, [1982] 1 W.W.R. 752, [1981] B.C.J. No. 1509 (B.C.C.A.). Where the wife's claim for permanent maintenance is referred to the registrar contemporaneously with the granting of the decree *nisi*, the pronouncement of the decree does not deprive the trial judge of jurisdiction to make an interim order for maintenance under the *Divorce Act* pending the registrar's report.

*Master has jurisdiction to grant interim relief in a divorce action despite the existence of a final support order made under a provincial statute — Pantry v. Pantry*, 1986 CarswellOnt 333 50 R.F.L. (2d) 240, 53 O.R. (2d) 667, 25 D.L.R. (4th) 636,, 13 O.A.C. 48, [1986] O.J. No. 2347 (Ont. C.A.).

*Procedure — where no final order under provincial legislation — B. (R.) v. B. (M.)*, 1989 CarswellOnt 221, 19 R.F.L. (3d) 92, 68 O.R. (2d) 32 (H.C.). Where there is no final order for support under provincial legislation and the payee or prospective payee spouse intends to pursue a remedy for support or custody, if a divorce proceeding is initiated, support must be sought under the *Divorce Act*, if the other spouse demands it. The issue of spousal and child support should be determined as an interim motion under the *Divorce Act*, rather than as a variation of an interim order under the *Family Law Act*. The wife would not be disadvantaged by having the matter dealt with as an interim application under the *Divorce Act* either. The advantages of consolidation in one action take precedence.

*Procedure — Burton v. Burton*, 1982 CarswellBC 85, 27 R.F.L. (2d) 170, 36 B.C.L.R. 169, [1982] B.C.J. No. 3 (B.C.C.A.) — *Where maintenance has been granted in a previous order, it is incorrect for a court, at a later date, to make an order of interim maintenance, pending a recommendation from the registrar. The proper course is to order a variation of the original maintenance order until such time as the reference to the registrar is made an order of the court.*

*Procedure — Simpson v. Simpson*, 1982 CarswellOnt 263, 27 R.F.L. (2d) 130, 134 D.L.R. (3d) 209 (Ont. H.C.). There is no jurisdiction granted by the *Divorce Act* or other legislation to make interim maintenance orders pending cross-examination in an application to vary a maintenance order engrossed in a decree nisi.

*Divorce judgement silent on spousal support — Vipond v. Vipond*, 1990 CarswellOnt 226, 72 O.R. (2d) 82, 25 R.F.L. (3d) 128, [1990] O.J. No. 3292 (Ont. H.C.), at 133 [R.F.L.]. "If the divorce judgment is silent on spousal or child support, the application to provide for support by the judgment may be brought under s. 15(2), *i.e.*, as in the action for divorce, and the court may then make an interim order under s. 15(3) and there is no need to invoke the *parens patriae* powers of the court in respect of child support."

*Procedure — where variation hearing pending — McKillop v. McKillop*, 1985 CarswellOnt 238, 44 R.F.L. (2d) 221, [1985] O.J. No. 1544 (Ont. H.C.). In an application for increased maintenance, the court is without jurisdiction to make an interim order pending the variation hearing. In such an instance, however, the court can make a final order which itself can be subsequently varied.

*Interim or interim interim order of spousal support for a former spouse — Southgate v. Southgate*, 1984 CarswellOnt 276, 41 R.F.L. (2d) 246, [1984] O.J. No. 2562 (Ont. H.C.), at 250 [R.F.L.]. "[T]here are exceptional or compelling circumstances where it is within the jurisdiction of the court to make an interim or interim interim order for maintenance for a former spouse ...and where the court should exercise its discretion to grant that relief pending the hearing of the motion to vary a decree nisi . . . There is a heavy onus on the applicant to cause the court to exercise its discretion in this way".

*Order under provincial statute and application under* Divorce Act — *Bombier v. Bombier*, 1984 CarswellOnt 290, 42 R.F.L. (2d) 93 (Ont. Master). Where the wife had already obtained an interim interim support order under the *Family Law Reform Act*, her subsequent application for interim maintenance under the *Divorce Act* was struck. As both parties considered the first order to continue in effect and as the two applications were essentially identical as far as the relief sought, it was held that the wife's application had been effectively dealt with in the earlier proceeding.

*Procedure — MacNeil v. MacNeil*, 1982 CarswellOnt 1365, 134 D.L.R. (3d) 115 (Ont. H.C.). There is no statutory power authorizing the court to grant any interim relief once a decree *nisi* has been granted. Therefore, in an application to vary the maintenance provisions of a decree *nisi*, the court is without jurisdiction to grant interim maintenance pending the hearing of the variation application.

*Jurisdiction — Bickerton v. Bickerton*, 1983 CarswellNB 31, 31 R.F.L. (2d) 323, 45 N.B.R. (2d) 112, 118 A.P.R. 112 (N.B.Q.B.). A court making an interim order for corollary relief must also have jurisdiction to grant the actual divorce. Therefore, where a court on an application for interim relief adjourns a challenge to its jurisdiction until the trial of the divorce, such court lacks jurisdiction to make an interim order.

*Interim support prior to delivery of answer or counter-petition — Collis v. Collis*, 1983 CarswellOnt 294, 35 R.F.L. (2d) 8, [1983] O.J. No. 2382 (Ont. H.C.); *Mudrinic v. Mudrinic*, 1978 CarswellOnt 301, 6 R.F.L. (2d) 326, [1978] O.J. No. 2660 (Ont. H.C.); *Cisecki v. Cisecki*,

1972 CarswellBC 33, 8 R.F.L. 232 (B.C.S.C.). Where the wife, in response to her husband's petition for divorce, applied for interim maintenance prior to delivering an answer or counter-petition, her application was adjourned pending her delivery of pleadings. The court was without jurisdiction at that stage of the proceedings to grant the relief requested.

*Provisions for mortgage and utility payments on marital home deleted* — *Glass v. Glass*, 1997 CarswellMan 632, 34 R.F.L. (4th) 411, 123 Man. R. (2d) 239, 159 W.A.C. 239 (Man. C.A.). The court allowed the husband's appeal in part from an interim spousal support order. The provision in the motions judge's order that the husband make mortgage and utility payments on the marital home was deleted, as was the court's provision for an arbitrary amount of maintenance of $2,200 per month if the wife left the marital home, without having evidence to determine the wife's needs in other accommodation.

*Jurisdiction to make interim order final* — *Gidora v. Gidora* , 1997 CarswellBC 273, 27 R.F.L. (4th) 292, 85 B.C.A.C. 311, 138 W.A.C. 311 (B.C.C.A.). A judge has jurisdiction to make an interim support order finite in time even where counsel had agreed that the order should be open ended.

## 4.2.2 General — Case Law

*The failure to accept a settlement offer, whether or not it is reasonable, is not a reason to deny interim spousal support* — *Richards v. Richards*, 2012 CarswellNS 87, 2012 NSCA 7, 18 R.F.L. (7th) 287, 346 D.L.R. (4th) 653, 312 N.S.R. (2d) 282, 987 A.P.R. 282 (N.S.C.A.). The wife was in need, as she had no income or access to capital, and no immediate access to capital assets of or income from the parties' companies. The court imputed income of $157,000 to the husband and would order spousal support of $72,000 per year or $6,000 per month, but deferred making an order for two weeks to allow the parties to consider whether it would be preferable to have funds paid as dividend income, which as directors they could jointly authorize, and which could be embodied in the court's order.

*Interim support awarded despite court's failure to set out specific reasons, as it was clear the motions judge assessed the means and needs of the parties, as well as considered the* Spousal Support Advisory Guidelines *to determine the quantum of interim spousal support* — *Thomson v. Thomson*, 2011 CarswellMan 93, 2011 MBCA 28 (Man. C.A.). The appellant husband, who had proposed at first instance that the SSAG be applied, was more concerned with quantum than methodology. The quantum ordered in this case was not clearly wrong.

*A party should not have to deplete his or her capital to meet daily needs* — *interim spousal support ordered* — *Elgner v. Elgner*, 2009 CarswellOnt 7702, 85 R.F.L. (6th) 51, [2009] O.J. No. 5269 (Ont. S.C.J.). Leave to appeal refused 2010 CarswellOnt 1640, 2010 ONSC 1578, 85 R.F.L. (6th) 62, 99 O.R. (3d) 687, 267 O.A.C. 1, [2010] O.J. No. 1139 (Ont. Div. Ct.), additional reasons at 2010 CarswellOnt 3918, 2010 ONSC 2399, 85 R.F.L. (6th) 71 (Ont. Div. Ct.), affirmed 2010 CarswellOnt 6860, 2010 ONSC 3512, 92 R.F.L. (6th) 106, 103 O.R. (3d) 588, 324 D.L.R. (4th) 277, 268 O.A.C. 267, [2010] O.J. No. 3828 (Ont. Div. Ct.), affirmed 2011 CarswellOnt 5673, 2011 ONCA 483, 5 R.F.L. (7th) 1, 105 O.R. (3d) 721, 336 D.L.R. (4th) 159, 282 O.A.C. 28, [2011] O.J. No. 3040 (Ont. C.A.). Leave to appeal refused 2011 CarswellOnt 12421, 2011 CarswellOnt 12422, 429 N.R. 398 (note), 294 O.A.C. 396 (note) (S.C.C.). The husband earned $2,800,000 to $3,900,000 in the previous 3 years. The wife had no income.

*Interim spousal support can be awarded to maintain the status quo* — *Loesch v. Walji*, 2007 CarswellBC 3007, 2007 BCSC 1807, 48 R.F.L. (6th) 128, [2007] B.C.J. No. 2663 (B.C.S.C.), affirmed 2008 CarswellBC 982, 2008 BCCA 214, 81 B.C.L.R. (4th) 271, 52 R.F.L. (6th) 33, [2008] 10 W.W.R. 625, 255 B.C.A.C. 264, 430 W.A.C. 264, [2008] B.C.J. No. 897 (B.C.C.A.).

The court awarded spousal support of $50,000 a month. The husband had recently had an income of $7,000,000 a year.

*Neither party should have to use assets to provide interim support — Loesch v. Walji*, 2007 CarswellBC 3007, 2007 BCSC 1807, 48 R.F.L. (6th) 128, [2007] B.C.J. No. 2663 (B.C.S.C.), affirmed 2008 CarswellBC 982, 2008 BCCA 214, 81 B.C.L.R. (4th) 271, 52 R.F.L. (6th) 33, [2008] 10 W.W.R. 625, 255 B.C.A.C. 264, 430 W.A.C. 264, [2008] B.C.J. No. 897 (B.C.C.A.). If it were decided at trial that no support is payable, the court can take the payment of interim support into account at that time.

*Needs of the recipient may be determined by an examination of the parties' lifestyle — Loesch v. Walji*, 2007 CarswellBC 3007, 2007 BCSC 1807, 48 R.F.L. (6th) 128, [2007] B.C.J. No. 2663 (B.C.S.C.), affirmed 2008 CarswellBC 982, 2008 BCCA 214, 81 B.C.L.R. (4th) 271, 52 R.F.L. (6th) 33, [2008] 10 W.W.R. 625, 255 B.C.A.C. 264, 430 W.A.C. 264, [2008] B.C.J. No. 897 (B.C.C.A.). The parties had a 21-year relationship, including 17 years of marriage, and had four children. The husband earned in excess of $1 million annually. The judge awarded $50,000 in interim monthly spousal support, which was above the SSAG. The husband appealed the decision, but the Court of Appeal affirmed the trial decision, finding that the pure discretion approach to the SSAG ceiling was appropriate in this case. The needs of the recipient wife were determined based on the extravagant lifestyle the parties had always enjoyed prior to separation.

*An interim spousal support order attracts a high level of deference on appeal and will only be interfered with if it is clearly wrong — Gale v. Gale*, 2007 CarswellMan 503, 2007 MBCA 162, 220 Man. R. (2d) 306 (Man. C.A.). The husband appealed an order of spousal support. The Court of Appeal emphasized the high degree of deference to be given to interim orders in family cases, noting they were essentially discretionary and their purpose was to provide a "reasonably acceptable" solution pending trial. The Court of Appeal found the chambers judge correctly stated the applicable legal principles (means and needs) for interim support and applied her discretion reasonably.

*A judge should not attempt to resolve the conflicts on the record at a hearing for interim spousal support — Peterson v. Ardiel*, 2007 CarswellAlta 841, 2007 ABCA 218, 39 R.F.L. (6th) 41, [2007] A.J. No. 687 (Alta. C.A.). The parties had a 15-year relationship and no children. The Court of Appeal overturned the decision of a chambers judge who attempted to resolve conflicting evidence on the record and whose decision was akin to a final support order decision. The case was sent back to the lower courts for a determination of interim support.

*Interim support will be awarded pending a determination by a lower court when a decision is sent back to the trial judge — Lawson v. Lawson*, 2006 CarswellOnt 4789, 29 R.F.L. (6th) 8, 81 O.R. (3d) 321, 214 O.A.C. 94, [2006] O.J. No. 3179 (Ont. C.A.). Here, the Court of Appeal made an award of interim support pending a retrial of amount and duration of spousal support, as entitlement was not in issue. The parties had a 12-year marriage and three children.

*Entitlement to interim spousal support must be made out in an analysis under s. 15(2), not merely by determining the means and needs of the parties — Noonan v. Noonan*, 2006 CarswellPEI 48, 2006 PESCTD 41, 262 Nfld. & P.E.I.R. 78, 794 A.P.R. 78 (P.E.I.T.D.), reversed 2007 CarswellPEI 17, 2007 PESCAD 5, 281 D.L.R. (4th) 725, 264 Nfld. & P.E.I.R. 330, 801 A.P.R. 330 (P.E.I.C.A.). The Court of Appeal reversed the order of a motions judge which granted interim spousal support, on the grounds that the trial judge had not discussed entitlement other than means and needs under s. 15(2). Although the evidence was clear that the wife had need and the husband had the means to pay, these factors alone were not sufficient to make out entitlement.

*An interim spousal support order is based on judicial discretion — Peterson v. Horan*, 2005 CarswellSask 420, 2005 SKCA 82, 29 R.F.L. (6th) 241 (Sask. C.A.), additional reasons at 2006 CarswellSask 404, 2006 SKCA 61, 29 R.F.L. (6th) 241, 270 D.L.R. (4th) 450, [2006] 11 W.W.R.

396, 279 Sask. R. 94, 372 W.A.C. 94, [2006] S.C.J. No. 333 (Sask. C.A.). The Court of Appeal upheld the decision of a chambers judge on interim spousal support, finding that interim support awards are generally an exercise in judicial discretion.

*Interim orders — temporary — Miller c. Cameau,* 1991 CarswellQue 2158 (C.A. Que.). Interim support orders are temporary by nature and their purpose is to ensure the welfare of the parties, and any children, until the case can be heard on its merits. Such orders are not binding on the judge who rules on the merits.

*Difference in evidence for interim and permanent support — MacMinn v. MacMinn,* 1995 CarswellAlta 813, 174 A.R. 261, 17 R.F.L. (4th) 88, 102 W.A.C. 261, [1995] A.J. No. 893 (Alta. C.A.). Typically, an interim support award is made without benefit of discoveries, production of documents, evidence and the general safeguards which are found in a trial. It is intended to be made quickly to meet the immediate needs of the claimant based on the best evidence before the court. However, at trial, where full evidence has been adduced it is proper for the trial judge to make adjustments to the interim order based on that evidence.

*Spousal support in the guise of child support — Chutter v. Chutter,* 1989 CarswellBC 430, 23 R.F.L. (3d) 22 (B.C.S.C.), affirmed 1990 CarswellBC 467, 26 R.F.L. (3d) 463 (B.C.C.A.). Where there was sufficient concern as to whether the mother was seeking spousal support under the guise of child support and thereby abrogating her responsibility to contribute to the children's needs, her application for interim child support was dismissed.

*Proper considerations on interim applications for support — Lila v. Lila,* 1986 CarswellOnt 294, 3 R.F.L. (3d) 226, [1986] O.J. No. 2533 (Ont. C.A.). The effect granting interim relief to a spouse would have at the subsequent trial is not a proper consideration in determining that spouse's right to interim support.

*Income may be imputed on an interim application for spousal support — Whatley v. Whatley,* 2014 CarswellBC 842, 2014 BCSC 536 (B.C.S.C.). The parties were married for 23 years and had three children, one of whom remained a child of the marriage. The wife sought spousal support, *inter alia.* She had no income and had been out of the workforce for approximately 30 years. The judge found that many issues, including the marital standard of living, debts and gifts, were hotly disputed and could only be resolved at trial. The judge imputed income to the husband based on funds held in trust for him in his mother's estate. It was clear that he had the ability to access those funds.

*The purpose of an interim support award is to allow a dependant to maintain a reasonable lifestyle pending trial, not merely to "staunch the bleeding" — Newcombe v. Newcombe,* 2014 CarswellOnt 3524, 2014 ONSC 1094 (Ont. S.C.J.). The parties had an 8-year relationship. The wife sought interim support. The judge found that although the wife was not destitute, her income was one-fifth that of the husband. The judge found that the drop in her standard of living constituted economic hardship and entitled her to interim spousal support. Mid-range support was ordered.

*Interim support at the low end of the SSAG range will be ordered when there is a large disparity in income between the parties, even in situations where the recipient's expenses are low — Pelley v. Pelley,* 2014 CarswellBC 749, 2014 BCSC 473 (B.C.S.C.). The payor husband's income was significantly higher than that of the wife. The judge found that this indicated an award of interim support despite the fact that the wife and child were living with the wife's parents, which reduced their costs. Spousal support was ordered at the low end of the SSAG range.

*Interim spousal support may be ordered based on need and the statements made by the applicant are to be taken at face value in determining the quantum of interim spousal support — Devincenzo v. Devincenzo,* 2012 CarswellOnt 4422, 2012 ONSC 2326 (Ont. S.C.J.). This decision stemmed from an interim motion for child and spousal support (among other forms of relief). Spousal support was ordered at slightly above the midrange of the SSAG. The parties had been married for 21 years. The judge noted: "At the interim stage, the statements made by the applicant should be taken at face value. The matter of the applicant's physical and emotional health will ultimately have to be addressed by medical information on the ultimate disposition of this matter, but given the history and the situation existing at the time of separation, it is not appropriate, in my view, to impute income to the applicant at the interim stage".

*A spouse in a long-term marriage, where the parties have sufficient funds to live in a fashion similar to that enjoyed during the marriage, should not have to use up the capital the wife has in her name to support the expenses of her continuing to live in the matrimonial home — interim spousal support should be awarded retroactive to the date of separation — McCain v. McCain,* 2012 CarswellOnt 16853, 2012 ONSC 7344, 34 R.F.L. (7th) 82 (Ont. S.C.J.). The husband had a net worth of $500,000,000 at separation. Allegedly the wife had $15,000,000 to $17,000,000. She was awarded interim spousal support of $175,000 a month.

*On an interim application for spousal support, the court must provide a factual framework so that it is possible to determine whether the court properly apprehended the evidence — where the reasons do not provide this framework, the order for interim spousal support may be set aside — Fiorentino v. Fiorentino,* 2011 CarswellBC 1007, 2011 BCSC 527, 1 R.F.L. (7th) 428 (B.C.S.C.). It will be necessary to make findings as to the incomes of the parties in order to know how the decision as to quantum relates to the financial need of the party requiring support and the financial capacity of the other party to pay it. In this case, the inadequacy of the Master's reasons respecting spousal support constitutes an error in law requiring the court to reverse the reasons.

*"Interim orders are not, by their nature, intended to be a final or comprehensive solution to issues raised in matrimonial proceedings. They are typically imperfect solutions made to resolve pressing issues based on incomplete and usually untested evidence" — Lawless v. Lawless,* 2008 CarswellOnt 4632 (Ont. S.C.J.). The court dismissed the father's motion for declaration of income and reduction in child and spousal support, when the information had been available at a previous hearing, the father had failed to make proper disclosure. The father would not be permitted to relitigate an issue that had been litigated 3 months previously.

*Where the payor is the primary parent, the goal of interim spousal support will be to provide a comparable standard of living for the children rather than equalize net disposable income — André v. Van Gentevoort,* 2008 CarswellOnt 4329 (Ont. S.C.J.). The wife earned significantly more than the husband. The judge found that the husband was entitled to interim spousal support but, as the wife had been the primary parent and had been paying the expenses associated with the matrimonial home, it was not appropriate to equalize the parties' net disposable income. Rather, it was appropriate to base interim support on providing the father with the ability to provide a comparable standard of living for the children.

*Debts incurred since separation will provide information as to means and needs of the parties for the purpose of determining interim support — D'Vaz v. D'Vaz,* 2008 CarswellOnt 1492 (Ont. S.C.J.). The parties had a 23-year, traditional marriage, and the wife did not work outside the home. The wife had incurred debts since separation and lived in a modest rental property, whereas the husband was living in the mortgage-free matrimonial home. Interim spousal support was ordered at the mid-range of the SSAG.

*Means and need will form the basis of an interim support analysis — Carnegie v. Carnegie,* 2008 CarswellMan 494, 2008 MBQB 249, 60 R.F.L. (6th) 192, 234 Man. R. (2d) 22 (Man. Q.B.). The judge ordered interim support after finding that the wife suffered economic hardship as a result of the breakdown of the marriage and the husband had the means to support her. The wife was in the midst of retraining.

*Where need is established, interim support will be ordered even when the means of the payor are unclear — Fellinger v. Fellinger,* 2007 CarswellSask 462, 2007 SKQB 317 (Sask. Q.B.). The judge found that the wife was unable to make ends meet pending final adjudication of the issues and ordered interim support. A support order was made despite ongoing questions about the means of the payor husband.

*Principles in dealing with temporary spousal support motions* — *Kowalski v. Grant*, 2007 CarswellMan 422, 2007 MBQB 235, 43 R.F.L. (6th) 344, 219 Man. R. (2d) 260, [2007] M.J. No. 386 (Man. Q.B.), quoted with approval in *Jones v Hugo*, 2012 CarswellOnt 4722, 2012 ONCJ 211, [2012] O.J. No. 1735 (Ont. C.J.). The court in *Kowalski* set out the following

1. Interim support is to provide income for dependent spouses from the time the proceedings are instituted until trial.
2. The court need not conduct a complete inquiry into all aspects and details to determine what extent either party suffered economic advantage or disadvantage as a result of the relationship. That is to be left to the trial judge.
3. Interim support is a *holding order* to maintain the accustomed lifestyle if possible pending final disposition as long as the claimant is able to present a triable case for economic disadvantage.
4. Interim support is to be based on the parties' means and needs assuming that a triable case exists. The merits of the case in its entirety must await a final hearing.

*Where need is shown, interim support will be ordered even when the payor's income is not clear* — *Gonzalez v. Ross*, 2007 CarswellOnt 753, 36 R.F.L. (6th) 126, [2007] O.J. No. 529 (Ont. S.C.J.). The wife demonstrated that she had at least some need and the husband had the ability to pay. The matter was to proceed to trial shortly.

*Interim spousal support will be ordered even when the parties disagree on the date of separation and that issue must be determined at trial* — *Kemble v. Roy*, 2006 CarswellOnt 4274, [2006] O.J. No. 2853 (Ont. S.C.J.). There was a dispute about the date of separation as well as a potential limitations issue. The judge ordered interim support on the basis that the wife had need and the husband had the ability to pay.

*Interim support will be ordered when the provisions of a domestic agreement as to support are ambiguous* — *Bater v. Bater*, 2006 CarswellOnt 4107, [2006] O.J. No. 2740 (Ont. S.C.J.). The provisions of a cohabitation agreement were ambiguous as to support. The judge ordered interim support, finding that an interim motion was not the appropriate time to determine the validity of an agreement. The judge found a trial judge was required to weigh viva voce evidence and determine credibility.

*Purpose, for spouse to maintain reasonable lifestyle* — *Bennett v. Bennett*, 2005 CarswellAlta 1994, 2005 ABQB 984, 22 R.F.L. (6th) 399, 57 Alta. L.R. (4th) 380, [2006] 9 W.W.R. 62, [2005] A.J. No. 1824 (Alta. Q.B.). An order for interim spousal support should reflect the amount of income required by one spouse in order to allow that spouse to maintain a reasonable standard of living, having regard to the means of both parties. It should cover only those needs that will arise from the time of application until litigation is complete.

*Prima facie case for entitlement on application for interim support* — *Charbonneau v. Charbonneau*, 2004 CarswellOnt 5211, 9 R.F.L. (6th) 67, [2004] O.J. No. 5059 (Ont. S.C.J.). Although in-depth analysis of entitlement is not required on an application for interim spousal support, it is necessary that the claimant *establish a prima facie case of entitlement.*

*No interim support where payee spouse had capital fund to draw on* — *Camp v. Camp*, 2004 CarswellBC 1900, 2004 BCSC 1096, 9 R.F.L. (6th) 54, [2004] B.C.J. No. 1713 (B.C.S.C. [In Chambers]). Under the parties' separation agreement, the wife continued to have a capital fund to draw upon. Furthermore, there was no evidence indicating an economic disadvantage to the wife and it was uncertain whether her support claim would be successful at trial.

*Inappropriate considerations on application for interim support — defence of assault charge — Sharf v. Sharf*, 2004 CarswellOnt 4858, 10 R.F.L. (6th) 167, [2004] O.J. No. 3282 (Ont. S.C.J.). In a claim for interim interim spousal support, the fact that the husband had the expense of defending charges for an alleged assault of the wife was irrelevant. The wife should not have to fund the defence by a reduction in her support entitlement.

*Application dismissed, wife had significant assets — Tout v. Bennett*, 2003 CarswellOnt 1625, 38 R.F.L. (5th) 223, [2003] O.J. No. 1674 (Ont. S.C.J.). Where the wife had significant assets upon which she could draw to support herself until trial, her application for interim support was dismissed. The fact that the equalization payment owing to her was outstanding did not automatically entitle her to support.

*Application dismissed, brought after limited term support order expired — Cherneski v. Cherneski*, 2003 CarswellOnt 4896, 49 R.F.L. (5th) 299, [2003] O.J. No. 5036 (Ont. S.C.J.). The court refused the wife's claim for interim spousal support brought after the expiration of the limited term support provided for in the parties' separation agreement. The wife's allegations that she had been pressured to sign the agreement were not determinative of the issue and she was not financially desperate. Also the possibility existed that permanent support could be awarded at trial and enforced retroactively.

*Inappropriate claims on applications for interim support — Titchener v. Titchener*, 2003 CarswellBC 1771, 2003 BCSC 1120, 42 R.F.L. (5th) 461, [2003] B.C.J. No. 1683 (B.C.S.C. [In Chambers]). Expenses such as RRSP contributions, RESP contributions and charitable donations are inappropriate claims on an application for interim support.

*When ability to pay not issue — similar lifestyle determinative — Lakhani v. Lakhani*, 2003 CarswellOnt 3928, 43 R.F.L. (5th) 125, [2003] O.J. No. 4041 (Ont. S.C.J.), additional reasons at 2003 CarswellOnt 3927, [2003] O.J. No. 4039 (Ont. S.C.J.). The traditional approach to interim support based on established need and the ability to pay is not always an approach that is fair and just in the circumstances. Where the ability to pay is not an issue, the parties should have the financial ability to enjoy a similar lifestyle, regardless of whether they did in fact choose to enjoy such a lifestyle.

*Interim support — when paid out of capital — Plaxton v. Plaxton*, 2002 CarswellOnt 1343, 27 R.F.L. (5th) 135, [2002] O.J. No. 1226 (Ont. S.C.J.). An order for interim support to be paid out of capital should only be made where the recipient requires the funds to maintain a minimal standard of living.

*Objectives — periodic and lump sum payments — Volken v. Volken*, 2001 CarswellBC 1401, 2001 BCSC 970, 19 R.F.L. (5th) 205, [2001] B.C.T.C. 970, [2001] B.C.J. No. 1344 (B.C.S.C. [In Chambers]). The husband's annual income was found to be $2,000,000. The wife was not employed outside the home and had no income of her own. After the separation the husband made voluntary payments of $5,000 a month which reflected the relatively frugal lifestyle of the family before the separation. The wife's expenses after the separation exceeded these payments. She supplemented them by taking out a mortgage on her equity in the family home. She applied for interim child support for three children and spousal support for herself. The Guideline Table Amount of $25,723 per month in child support was awarded retroactive to the 1st of January, the month in which her application for interim support was made. For herself, the wife sought interim spousal support of $18,000 per month plus a lump sum of $10,000 to pay for repairs to the home and an automobile, $50,000 for payment of the services of a business valuator and $100,000 for a legal retainer. The husband's monthly expenses were about $9,000. The court found that after taking into account the child support obligation, the husband's after tax earnings would meet the needs of the wife and still leave him with more than enough for his own expenses. Exercising its discretion on the basis of the condition, means, needs, and other circumstances of each spouse in light of the objectives of spousal support orders described in s. 15.2 of the *Divorce*

*Act*, the court ordered interim monthly spousal support of $15,000 plus a lump sum payment of $10,000. The court refused to make the spousal support payments retroactive. The husband could not be faulted for his delay in making financial disclosure because of the complexities of his holdings. Any deficiencies in child support were made up by the retroactivity of that order, and the high amount compared to the "relatively frugal" lifestyle before separation. Also, any shortfall experienced by the wife was met by her borrowing against the equity in the family home. Any order that might be made as to retroactivity would have the undesirable effect of redistributing capital, or awarding additional spousal support, under the guise of child support.

*Purpose, similar standard of living* — *Harrison v. Harrison*, 2001 CarswellOnt 420, 14 R.F.L. (5th) 321, [2001] O.T.C. 107, [2001] O.J. No. 470 (Ont. S.C.J.). The trend in law is to ensure that each party's household enjoys a similar standard of living. The financial circumstances of each parent should not be so divergent that a child is tempted to make the more affluent household the primary residence. The *Divorce Act* requires a fair and equitable distribution of resources to alleviate the consequences of marriage breakdown. This principle is as applicable to interim situations as it is to final situations. Taking into account the fact that the applicant earned $20,000 a year and the respondent earned $99,000 a year, that the respondent would be paying child support and, possibly, a payment for extraordinary expenses, the court ordered interim spousal support of $2,400 a month.

*Commencement date* — *Radcliff v. Radcliff*, 2001 CarswellOnt 1928, 17 R.F.L. (5th) 417 (Ont. S.C.J.). The effective date for the commencement of interim support should be the date of the issue of the petition, when there are no special circumstances to favour an earlier date and where the divorce action is commenced a month after the separation began.

*Objective, similar after-tax income* — *Haroun v. Haroun*, 2001 CarswellOnt 2253, 20 R.F.L. (5th) 64, [2001] O.J. No. 2575 (Ont. S.C.J.), additional reasons at 2001 CarswellOnt 2450 (Ont. S.C.J.). In determining quantum of support, after a long-term traditional marriage, it is reasonable for the parties to have a similar after-tax income available to them.

*Objective, for quantum for lavish marital lifestyle* — *Bennett v. Bennett*, 12001 CarswellOnt 168, 3 R.F.L. (5th) 325, [2001] O.J. No. 224 (Ont. S.C.J.). Where a lavish and opulent lifestyle has been enjoyed by the spouse over several decades, the traditional "living modestly in retirement" approach to interim spousal support is inadequate and inappropriate.

*Limited-term interim spousal support, then wife to support herself* — *Fritze v. Day*, 2001 CarswellAlta 282, 2001 ABQB 172, 15 R.F.L. (5th) 60 (Alta. Q.B.). The court ordered interim spousal support for a limited term of 3 months where the wife, an intelligent, capable and university-educated woman without children had done nothing to obtain a job for 14 months. She was found to be capable of supporting herself.

*No economic disadvantage* — *Burmi v. Dhiman*, 2001 CarswellOnt 1812, 18 R.F.L. (5th) 9, [2001] O.J. No. 2010 (Ont. S.C.J.), additional reasons at 2001 CarswellOnt 2195 (Ont. S.C.J.). The court refused the wife's application for interim spousal support. The parties' marriage had been an arranged one in India, but the husband had left and returned to Canada after only 7 weeks of cohabitation. The wife could work and support herself in India and had not suffered any economic loss as a result of the marriage or its end.

*Payor of child support not necessarily precluded from receipt of spousal support* — *Richter v. Vahamaki*, 2000 CarswellOnt 2440, 8 R.F.L. (5th) 194 (Ont. S.C.J.). A lower income parent who is required to make child support payments under the Guidelines to the higher income custodial parent is not automatically precluded from receiving spousal support. The father was ordered to pay the mother $1000 per month in interim spousal support.

*No intermingling of child and spousal support* — *Y. (H.) v. Y. (D.)*, 1999 CarswellPEI 43, 49 R.F.L. (4th) 450, 175 Nfld. & P.E.I.R. 85, 537 A.P.R. 85 (P.E.I.T.D. [In Chambers]). The husband was not allowed to set off his monthly child support obligation against an interim spousal support overpayment owed by the wife. Child support and spousal support obligations should not be intermingled. It is unfair to the child and contrary to the spirit of the legislation to excuse a parent from paying child support on the basis of dealings between the spouses.

*Self-sufficiency not appropriate consideration* — Ridgeway-Firman v. Firman, 1999 CarswellOnt 1201, [1999] O.J. No. 1477 (Ont. Gen. Div.). In an application for interim spousal support, the parties must generally take each other as they find them. Accordingly, a husband's allegations that his unemployed wife was able to work and support herself may be appropriate in an application for long-term support, but it should not be adjudicated upon in an interim interim application.

*Comprehensive material not required on interim spousal support application* — Gearin v. Gearin, 1999 CarswellNfld 87, 45 R.F.L. (4th) 333, 176 Nfld. & P.E.I.R. 76, 540 A.P.R. 76, [1999] N.J. No. 97 (Nfld. U.F.C.). A detailed examination of an unequal property division in the wife's favour and her failure to seek retraining were found not to be appropriate in the case of an interim spousal support application in which the wife had established a prima facie case for support.

*Objective of interim support* — maintain status quo — Moschuk v. Moschuk, 1999 CarswellOnt 3193 (Ont. S.C.J.). The court was of the opinion that, "The purpose of an interim motion in family breakdown situations is to maintain, as far as it is possible, the status quo until such time as the matters at issue can be fully explored at trial."

*Primary responsibility for support with husband* — Cluett v. Cluett, 1998 CarswellNWT 38 (N.W.T.S.C.). Even though any amounts received as interim spousal support will reduce payments from social assistance, where the wife is at an economic disadvantage caused by the birth of the parties' child, the primary financial responsibility for her support should be with the husband, rather than the state.

*Dissatisfaction with interim order* — Jessome v. Jessome, 1998 CarswellOnt 5161, 43 R.F.L. (4th) 196, 87 O.T.C. 143, [1998] O.J. No. 5565 (Ont. Gen. Div.). If a party is dissatisfied with an interim interim support order the proper procedure is to arrange for cross-examination as quickly as possible and return a motion for a hearing on the interim application. Appealing from the order is not the appropriate approach.

*Prima facie case for interim support* — Gordon v. Gordon, 1998 CarswellOnt 966, 36 R.F.L. (4th) 443 (Ont. Gen. Div.). The wife who was unemployed and heavily indebted was able to make out a prima facie case for interim support, even though the husband also had serious debt obligations. The court took into account only the most basic needs of the parties. It assessed the wife's basic needs, deducted the amount the wife would receive in unemployment benefits and the remainder was the amount of the wife's interim support.

*No interim spousal support where no clear need* — Byerley v. Byerley, 1998 CarswellOnt 3649, 41 R.F.L. (4th) 50, 75 O.T.C. 73, [1998] O.J. No. 3781 (Ont. Gen. Div.). A court should deny interim spousal support where the dependant spouse fails to demonstrate, with cogent and compelling evidence, a current need for interim spousal support from the husband. In this case, the wife who was living in a common-law union did not provide the court with her common-law spouse's income and expenses. The wife had been self-supporting for a year and then her common-law husband had supported her for almost a year before she sought support. At the time of the hearing the wife and her common-law husband were expecting a child.

*Interim support not based solely on payor's income* — Warford v. Warford, 1998 CarswellOnt 781, [1998] O.J. No. 896 (Ont. Gen. Div.). An award of interim spousal support requires need on the part of the claimant and the ability to pay on the part of the payor and is not to be based solely on the income of the payor.

*Terms and conditions* — review order — Chambers v. Chambers, 1998 CarswellNWT 100, 40 R.F.L. (4th) 351, [1998] N.W.T.R. 252, [1998] N.W.T.J. No. 54 (N.W.T.S.C.). An interim spousal order, which is subject to review after a set period of time, is not truly a "time limited" award. Accordingly, such an award is properly open to review under s. 15.2 of the *Divorce Act*, even after it has expired.

*Means and needs* — *Gordon v. Gordon*, 1998 CarswellOnt 966, 36 R.F.L. (4th) 443 (Ont. Gen. Div.). Where both the husband and the wife had monthly incomes in deficit positions, the wife's need for interim spousal support purposes was properly determined by taking into account only her most basic requirements for sustenance.

*Capital can be used for interim support* — *Jackson v. Jackson*, 1997 CarswellOnt 4717, 35 R.F.L. (4th) 194, 46 O.T.C. 66, [1997] O.J. No. 4790 (Ont. Gen. Div.). Where there has been a fairly lengthy marriage and substantial history of the use of capital to support a joint lifestyle, a spouse should not be required to have a lifestyle based on income alone, rather than the other means available to the spouse, at least on an interim basis.

*Where options for support, consider more moderate claim* — *Webster v. Webster*, 1997 CarswellOnt 815, 37 R.F.L. (4th) 347, 32 O.R. (3d) 679, 28 O.T.C. 81 (Ont. Gen. Div.). Where there are two options for calculating interim child and spousal support, it is appropriate to modify the claimed needs of the petitioner and, consequently, the court ordered support of $45,000 per month and not the $60,000 per month claimed.

*Parties must choose option for calculating support* — *Thompson v. Thompson*, 1997 CarswellPEI 23, 30 R.F.L. (4th) 376, 150 Nfld. & P.E.I.R. 86, 470 A.P.R. 86 (P.E.I.T.D.). Where there were two options for calculating interim child and spousal support depending on whether the husband's pension plan benefits were included as part of the wife's income, the parties were ordered to choose an option.

*Interim support is to provide a reasonably acceptable standard of living until trial* — *Peel v. Griffin*, 1996 CarswellOnt 292, 19 R.F.L. (4th) 94 (Ont. Gen. Div.). The matters which are to be considered on interim or interim interim support orders are the means and needs of the parties. Such orders are to provide a reasonably acceptable solution to problems until trial. Although the parties were married for only 2 years, the wife relied on the relationship to her detriment and the court awarded the wife $2,000 per month in interim interim support. A different result might be obtained at trial.

*On an application for interim support, needs and means are the considerations which provide greater certainty* — *Short v. Short*, 1996 CarswellBC 893, 21 R.F.L. (4th) 429, [1996] B.C.J. No. 910 (B.C.S.C.). While the needs and means of the parties should not take a predominant position in the deliberations, they are considerations which provide greater certainty when all the information is not available and before the court has determined whether there is economic advantage or disadvantage or economic hardship arising from the marriage or its breakdown. It would seem that the court decided to grant the petitioner $700 per month in interim spousal support primarily on the basis of consideration of the needs and means and needs of the parties.

*On an application for interim interim support, means and needs are the most important considerations* — *Robertson v. Hotte*, 1996 CarswellOnt 1506, 21 R.F.L. (4th) 452, 2 O.T.C. 1, [1996] O.J. No. 1433 (Ont. Gen. Div.). The court was of the opinion that on an interim or interim interim application for support, the cases support a four-step analysis that concentrates on the parties' needs and means:

(1) Does the Applicant have standing to claim support?
(2) Is the Applicant entitled to the support?
(3) What are the dependant's needs?
(4) Does the payor have the ability to pay?

*On an interim application, if the applicant has made an arguable case for standing and entitlement, the court will decide support on basis of needs and means* — Robertson v. Hotte, 1996 CarswellOnt 1506, 21 R.F.L. (4th) 452, 2 O.T.C. 1, [1996] O.J. No. 1433 (Ont. Gen. Div.). Because of the nature of the proceedings, the court will not conduct an in-depth analysis of the first two issues, standing and entitlement. If the applicant is able to make out an arguable case for standing and entitlement the court will assess support on the basis of the parties' needs and means. The parties had lived together off and on for over 20 years. They had entered into a domestic contract that contained a provision releasing support, and the respondent contended that the applicant did not qualify as a spouse. The motions judge awarded interim support finding that the domestic contract was ambiguous and that it would be unconscionable if it provided for no support. The applicant was unemployed. The respondent's appeal to the General Division was dismissed. There was a triable issue with respect to the domestic contract, and the fact that the parties had three children provided a good argument that the applicant was a spouse within the meaning of the *Family Law Act*.

*Need for interim support based on relationship with respondent* — Thorvaldson v. Vanin, 1996 CarswellSask 617, 25 R.F.L. (4th) 273, 149 Sask. R. 231 (Sask. Q.B.). The applicant was granted interim spousal support where her current difficulty in obtaining employment was largely attributable to her eight-year relationship with the respondent who encouraged her to remain on the farm and not seek work elsewhere.

*Effect of child support on interim spousal support* — Lane v. Lane, 1996 CarswellOnt 506, 19 R.F.L. (4th) 168 (Ont. Gen. Div.). Where the husband, who was awarded custody of the parties' daughter, could no longer work overtime because of his child care responsibilities, the decrease in his income was considered in determining the quantum of interim spousal support to be paid by him.

*Purpose of interim support* — Eder v. Eder, 1995 CarswellNWT 37, 18 R.F.L. (4th) 454, [1995] N.W.T.J. No. 81 (N.W.T.S.C.). The purpose of interim support is to permit the recipient spouse to maintain an acceptable standard of living until trial. Absent evidence of need, the award should not be made.

*Presumptive equal standard of living* — Carr v. Carr, 1993 CarswellBC 260, 46 R.F.L. (3d) 326, 83 B.C.L.R. (2d) 363, 28 C.P.C. (3d) 274, [1994] 1 W.W.R. 213, [1993] B.C.J. No. 720 (B.C.S.C.). In an application for interim support, it is not sufficient merely to consider the factors of need and ability to pay. The presumptive claim to an equal standard of living, subject to the equitable sharing of the consequences of the marriage breakdown, should also be considered.

*Economic disadvantage as a result of marriage — matter for trial judge* — Cafik v. Cafik, 1993 CarswellOnt 321, 46 R.F.L. (3d) 321, [1993] O.J. No. 684 (Ont. Gen. Div.). The determination of whether either party suffered an economic disadvantage as a result of the marriage or its breakdown is not a proper issue on an application for interim support. Such a determination is best left for the judge at trial.

*Courts should be cautious changing interim awards* — Murray v. Murray, 1991 CarswellAlta 152, 35 R.F.L. (3d) 449, 82 Alta. L.R. (2d) 260, [1992] 1 W.W.R. 183, 123 A.R. 68 (Alta. Q.B.). In awarding interim support, the court should give as much care as when awarding final support, as the interim amount frequently becomes the final amount. Accordingly, courts should be cautious in changing interim awards prior to trial.

*Interim application — denial of support possible* — Polgari v. Polgari, 1991 CarswellBC 563, 36 R.F.L. (3d) 369 (B.C. Master). On an interim support application, the court is entitled to consider the prospect of denial of a permanent support order.

*Interim order — not final order* — De Grandis v. De Grandis, 1990 CarswellBC 168, 28 R.F.L. (3d) 45, 48 B.C.L.R. (2d) 53, [1990] B.C.J. No. 1479 (B.C.S.C.). By its very nature, an interim support order is not a final order. It does not in any way limit the trial judge's discretion in determining any issue as to final support.

*Interim order — prima facie case for entitlement —* Theriault v. Theriault, 1994 CarswellAlta 371, 2 R.F.L. (4th) 157, 113 D.L.R. (4th) 57, 149 A.R. 210, 63 W.A.C. 210, [1994] A.J. No. 187 (Alta. C.A.). On an application for interim support, a full inquiry concerning support issues is not necessary. The applicant must, however, establish a prima facie case for entitlement.

*Interim application — payable from both income and capital —* Manning v. Manning, 1990 CarswellBC 457, 26 R.F.L. (3d) 151, [1990] B.C.J. No. 1013 (B.C. Master). On an interim support application the court was of the opinion that support money to a wife need not be payable solely from income, as the word in the statute is "means", which would include both income and capital. The court also ruled that entertainment is not an allowable expense in the consideration of interim matters.

*Caution on interim support applications, repayment unlikely —* Segal v. Segal, 1988 CarswellMan 53, 14 R.F.L. (3d) 453, 54 Man. R. (2d) 142 (Man. Q.B.). The court must be cautious on interim applications for support because, if it transpires at trial that the evidence fails to support a finding of entitlement, it is not usually practical to order that the money be paid back.

*Interim support should only be awarded in case where support is likely to be awarded at trial —* Potschka v. Potschka, 1987 CarswellMan 91, 5 R.F.L. (3d) 225, 49 Man. R. (2d) 50 (Man. Q.B.).

*Economic disadvantage arising from the marriage —* Cuzzocrea v. Swain, 1995 CarswellOnt 485, 15 R.F.L. (4th) 300, [1995] O.J. No. 2824 (Ont. Gen. Div.), additional reasons at 1995 CarswellOnt 1085, 17 R.F.L. (4th) 245, [1995] O.J. No. 3298 (Ont. Gen. Div.). A husband sought support ,on the basis that he was economically disadvantaged as a result of assuming the role of a "househusband" during part of the marriage, and moved for interim support. He contended that in this role he helped the wife advance her career to the detriment of his own career opportunities. In dismissing his motion for interim support, the court held, in the circumstances, that the mere fact of marriage did not entitle the husband to support and the evidence did not show that his efforts at home advanced his wife's career or were the cause of his unemployment.

*On an application for interim support, the court is to take into account any benefit to the parties from use of family property as well as the cost of paying family debts —* Bettles v. Bettles, 1994 CarswellPEI 15, 7 R.F.L. (4th) 153, 122 Nfld. & P.E.I.R. 341, 379 A.P.R. 341, [1994] 2 P.E.I.R. 394 (P.E.I.T.D.). The court, through the award, should attempt an equitable distribution of the parties' resources although a fair reorganization of wealth is not automatically achieved through the equalizing of incomes.

*Interim support should be determined by assessing the parties' resources —* Forbes v. Forbes, 1994 CarswellSask 36, 2 R.F.L. (4th) 121, 117 Sask. R. 299 (Sask. Q.B.). Where the spouses had used all of their resources to meet their living expenses, interim support should be determined by considering all available resources and not the parties' estimated expenses. After the children's reasonable needs have been met, the remaining resources should be distributed equitably between the parties.

*Examination of objectives is superficial at interim hearings —* Labelle v. Labelle, 1993 CarswellMan 48, 46 R.F.L. (3d) 341, 87 Man. R. (2d) 207, [1993] M.J. No. 152 (Man. Q.B.). Interim orders are, by their nature, "holding orders" and whereas the support objectives outlined in the *Divorce Act* are, strictly speaking, applicable on an interim hearing, common sense dictates that the depth of the inquiry at that stage of the proceedings is quite different from that expected at trial.

*Interim support award likely to be greater than final support award where payee unemployed —* Offet v. Offet, 1993 CarswellAlta 435, 1 R.F.L. (4th) 203, 150 A.R. 11, [1993] A.J.

No. 1029 (Alta. Q.B.). Where the wife is unemployed, the quantum of interim spousal support is likely to exceed that finally awarded at trial to ease the transition between her nonworking status and her return to the workforce. The issue of her ability to achieve self sufficiency is a matter for determination by the trial judge.

*The fact that the wife left the husband for another man was found not to disentitle her from interim spousal support* — *Kendell v. Kendell*, 1993 CarswellNfld 25, 48 R.F.L. (3d) 146, 110 Nfld. & P.E.I.R. 213, 346 A.P.R. 213 (Nfld. T.D.). Her conduct was not relevant to her claim.

*The prevalent view of interim support is that the dependent spouse should be allowed to maintain his or her existing lifestyle pending resolution* — *Weil v. Weil*, 1993 CarswellNB 281, 143 N.B.R. (2d) 108, 366 A.P.R. 108, [1993] N.B.J. No. 560 (N.B.Q.B.).

*Relationship between spousal and child support — interim application — Lopez v. Lopez*, 1993 CarswellOnt 350, 48 R.F.L. (3d) 298 (Ont. Gen. Div.). Where the wife claimed both interim spousal and child support, and the child support claim was dismissed, it was held that the wife's spousal support claim was not limited to the amount specified in her application. The wife had anticipated that the child support order would also help to defray her costs. As that claim had been dismissed, it was not proper to hold her to the quantum of spousal support outlined in her pleading.

*The fact that a spouse might be found entitled to support at trial does not justify an interim support award where that spouse could not establish any immediate pressing need* — *Viswalingam v. Viswalingam*, 1992 CarswellNWT 6, 41 R.F.L. (3d) 155 (N.W.T.S.C.).

*The requirement that a spouse seek self sufficiency should not be scrutinized as closely on an interim application as it might be on a final hearing* — *Titchener v. Titchener*, 1991 CarswellBC 509, 31 R.F.L. (3d) 173 (B.C. Master).

*Interim support refused where wife had amount remaining from interim distribution of matrimonial property* — *Kujawa v. Kujawa*, 1990 CarswellSask 71, 28 R.F.L. (3d) 386, 87 Sask. R. 101, [1990] S.J. No. 469 (Sask. Q.B.). Where the wife had $20,000 remaining from an interim distribution of matrimonial property, her application for interim support was refused. Given her resources, she did not require the husband's assistance to live comfortably until trial.

*An application for interim spousal support should be refused where the claimant's earning capacity has not been altered or impaired during the course of the marriage* — *Home v. Home*, 1989 CarswellBC 390, 19 R.F.L. (3d) 399, [1989] B.C.J. No. 280 (B.C.S.C.).

*An award of interim support or interim interim support should not be made if there is no possibility of the claimant's success at trial* — *Smith v. Smith*, 1987 CarswellOnt 268, 11 R.F.L. (3d) 214, 63 O.R. (2d) 146, [1987] O.J. No. 1172 (Ont. H.C.). The onus is on the claimant to plead the facts necessary to support the case, the entitlement principles being the same for an interim disposition as for a final disposition.

*No interim support where wife able to maintain a reasonable standard of living pending trial* — *Koulack v. Saifer*, 1986 CarswellMan 269, 43 Man. R. (2d) 70, (Man. Q.B.). Where the wife had an annual salary of $41,200 her application for interim maintenance was dismissed. Although she would probably be entitled to maintenance at trial, she would be able to maintain a reasonable standard of living pending trial using her own resources.

## Interim spousal support granted — examples

*Where the parties in a domestic contract have waived spousal support, a court, in granting an interim award of spousal support, where the recipient has made out a prima facie case for support, will be limited to providing for basic needs and will order support below the SSAG range* — *Burden v. Burden*, 2013 CarswellNS 526, 2013 NSCA 30, 34 R.F.L. (7th) 255, 328 N.S.R.

(2d) 104, 1039 A.P.R. 104 (N.S.C.A.). The parties were married for 11 years, within a 14-year relationship, and had one child, who resided with the wife. The parties had concluded a cohabitation agreement which waived spousal support. The husband's income had increased from $100,000 to $250,000, and the wife's had diminished. She had returned to school and had no income. The husband appealed a motion judge's decision to award interim spousal support to the wife. The amount ordered by the motion judge was $3,000 monthly, which was approximately half of the amount at the low range for the with child formula. The motion judge limited spousal support in order to provide for the wife's basic needs, while recognizing that the parties had negotiated a comprehensive agreement, with assistance of counsel, that waived support. The motion judge found the wife had made out a reasonable prospect of success in setting aside the agreement. The Court of Appeal upheld this decision.

*An interim support award granted to the wife to permit her to perform urgent repairs on the family home was upheld on appeal* — Novak c. Bingle (11 décembre 1991), no C.A. Montréal 500-09-000988-907 (C.A. Que.).

*The purpose of interim spousal support is to address need, rather than compensatory entitlement — an award below the SSAG range was appropriate* — Betts v. Betts, 2014 CarswellNB 63, 2014 NBQB 47, 416 N.B.R. (2d) 355, 1079 A.P.R. 355 (N.B.Q.B.). The parties were married for 38 years and had five adult children. There was an unenforceable agreement between the parties, and the wife also claimed there were collateral agreements. The judge found the existence of collateral agreements required findings of credibility and a full hearing. The wife had no high school diploma and had never worked. The judge found she needed support and that interim support was intended to address need, rather than compensatory issues to be determined at trial, which indicated an award at the low end of the SSAG range. The judge considered other factors, such as the wife living rent-free in the marital home, the husband's income of over $350,000, and the property had not yet been equalized. In the circumstances, an award below the low end of the range was appropriate.

*A recipient's ability to work or efforts to work will not be considered on an interim motion* — Pasta v. Pasta, 2013 CarswellMan 744, 2013 MBQB 311, 300 Man. R. (2d) 290 (Man. Q.B.). The parties had three children who resided with the husband. The wife sought, *inter alia,* interim spousal support. The wife had not worked outside the home for 19 years. The judge found it was not appropriate to consider "the wife's ability to work and her lack of effort to find it" on an interim motion. Means and needs of the parties were considered, and spousal support at the mid-range of the SSAG was ordered.

*Where a recipient has suffered a heart attack which affects his or her ability to work, interim spousal support will be ordered at the higher end of the range* — Wallace v. Wallace, 2013 CarswellOnt 11098, 2013 ONSC 4324 (Ont. S.C.J.), additional reasons at 2013 CarswellOnt 18604, 2013 ONSC 8007 (Ont. S.C.J.).

*Where the parties have very divergent financial resources and the payor will continue to pay the carrying costs of the matrimonial home in which the recipient resides, interim support will be set at the mid-SSAG range* — Cardoso v. Cardoso, 2013 CarswellOnt 11144, 2013 ONSC 5092 (Ont. S.C.J.). The parties cohabited for 14 years, including 7 years of marriage. Since separation, the husband had voluntarily paid $1,200 monthly in support. Interim support was set at the mid-range to reflect that the payor husband was carrying the costs of the matrimonial home and that his financial resources were vastly superior to those of the wife.

*Even though the parties have a brief marriage (2 years in this case), a party will be ordered to pay interim spousal support where he has sponsored his spouse and brought her to Canada as a permanent resident, promised to help her become a Canadian citizen, and undertaken to support her for 3 years from the date that she becomes a permanent resident* — Kkabbazy v. Esfahani, 2012 CarswellOnt 11411, 2012 ONSC 4591 (Ont. S.C.J.). The wife, who was from Iran, did not have a bank account in Canada and did not have the ability to work in Canada in her profession as an optometrist. She was developing her English language skills, but was not proficient. If the wife were to return to Iran, her right to return to Canada might be revoked. One issue was whether the parties' Iranian marriage contract, a Meher Agreement, under which, at the time of their marriage, the husband had agreed to pay her the equivalent of approximately Cdn$540,000, among other things, in the event of separation, was enforceable in Canada. The husband was from a wealthy Iranian family. The court estimated that his income was at least $200,000 a year. Under the *Spousal Support Advisory Guidelines*, a payment of spousal support of $933 per month would be justified. In the circumstances, however, the court ordered the husband to provide the wife with a gross monthly amount that would leave her with a net monthly disposable income of $3,250.

*Where the recipient spouse has suffered economic disadvantage as a result of the marriage and the breakdown of the marriage, interim support will be awarded — Guignard v. Guignard,* 2009 CarswellOnt 3127, [2009] O.J. No. 2267 (Ont. S.C.J.). Income was imputed to the husband and spousal support was awarded because of the disparity in the parties' incomes and the wife's economic disadvantage as a result of the marriage.

*Lengthy marriage and childcare responsibilities — Bekkers v. Bekkers,* 2008 CarswellOnt 173, 49 R.F.L. (6th) 119, [2008] O.J. No. 140 (Ont. S.C.J.). The wife was awarded interim spousal support upon separation after 17 years of marriage. Even though she was employed, the wife was entitled to support based upon the lengthy marriage and the fact that she had previously stayed home for years to care for the parties' children.

*Where the recipient spouse supported the payor spouse during the relationship, a case for interim support will be made out — Desrochers v. Tait,* 2008 CarswellOnt 8179, 70 R.F.L. (6th) 165, [2008] O.J. No. 5419 (Ont. S.C.J.), additional reasons at 2009 CarswellOnt 4075, 70 R.F.L. (6th) 178 (Ont. S.C.J.). The parties had a 5-year relationship, including 1 year of marriage, and had a child. The husband had become very wealthy after the parties separated. The wife was found to be entitled to temporary, compensatory spousal support for her role in supporting the husband during the relationship. The husband's income was very high.

*Spousal support may be increased on an interim interim motion where the wife suffers a stroke which increases her monthly costs — Colville-Reeves v. Colville-Reeves,* 2007 CarswellOnt 7569 (Ont. S.C.J.).

*It is an error to refuse to order interim spousal support where a lower court has put too much reliance on the "means and needs of the parties" rather than the other factors enumerated in s. 15.2 of the* Divorce Act *— Christensen v. Christensen,* 2006 CarswellBC 3767, 2006 BCSC 2095 (B.C.S.C. [In Chambers]) .

*Interim spousal support will be awarded when a prima facie case for relief is made out — Brown v. Brown,* 2004 CarswellBC 231, 2004 BCSC 174, [2004] B.C.J. No. 218 (B.C.S.C.).

*Loss of career, parties' standard of living — Vandale v. Vandale,* 2003 CarswellAlta 724, 2003 ABQB 407, 39 R.F.L. (5th) 445, [2003] A.J. No. 672 (Alta. Q.B.). Where the wife had given up her nursing career to raise the parties' children and had enjoyed a high standard of living throughout the marriage, her application for interim support was allowed. The parties' high standard of living was relevant in establishing the wife's needs.

*Interim spousal support will be granted, even though access visits to children will be less frequent, since to receive support is in the children's best interests — Hahn v. Hahn,* 2001 CarswellAlta 559, 2001 ABQB 357, 17 R.F.L. (5th) 330 (Alta. Q.B.), additional reasons at 2001 CarswellAlta 1119, 2001 ABQB 722 (Alta. Q.B.).

*Interim support to assist in wife's support and to relieve economic hardship — Marshall v. Marshall,* 2001 CarswellNfld 111, 16 R.F.L. (5th) 347, 200 Nfld. & P.E.I.R. 120, 603 A.P.R. 120 (Nfld. U.F.C.). Where both parties worked during most of the marriage and the wife only became dependant after she left her employment, perhaps unreasonably, she should be entitled to some interim support to help her to contribute to her own support and to relieve her current economic hardship. The interim support was primarily needs based on noncompensatory grounds.

*Interim spousal support, payee not incapable of work* — Andrews v. Andrews, 2000 CarswellAlta 564, 2000 ABQB 384, 8 R.F.L. (5th) 1, [2000] A.J. No. 676 (Alta. Q.B.). Interim spousal support for 6 months was granted to the husband where he suffered a disability. However, the court did not accept that the husband was incapable of doing any work and he might receive increased disability payments from the government.

*Economic disadvantage related to the marriage* — *illnesses resulting from husband's treatment prevented wife from being self-supporting* — Kennedy v. Kennedy, 2000 CarswellOnt 3622, 11 R.F.L. (5th) 150, [2000] O.J. No. 3742 (Ont. S.C.J.). The court accepted the wife's evidence that her stress-related illnesses which prevented her from working were the result of emotional and psychological abuse imposed by the husband. Accordingly, the wife had established an economic disadvantage related to the marriage and she was awarded interim spousal support.

*Means and needs* — Dunn v. Menear, 2000 CarswellOnt 4778, 14 R.F.L. (5th) 293 (Ont. S.C.J.). The husband, a lawyer, had left a good position with a firm to start a practice on his own. At the time of the separation his billings were only $1,500 a month. His wife was earning $90,000 a year. On a motion by the husband for interim support, the court held that the test on the issue of spousal support at this stage is the need of the spouse seeking support and the ability to pay of the other spouse. While the husband had suffered an economic loss as a result of the separation, the low monthly billings prior to separation meant that the amount of that loss was not a great one. In addition, his proven ability to earn significant income had not been adversely affected by the separation on a permanent basis. Therefore, support should be provided to compensate directly for loss of income for the 6 months that he was prevented, for one reason or another, from carrying on his old practice and, at the same time, to provide some assistance in financing the start up costs of a new practice. To achieve these objectives, the wife was ordered to pay the husband compensatory interim support by way of a lump sum of $7,500. This was calculated using the average billings of the husband's practice prior to the separation for a period of 6 months (which was $1,500 times six or $9,000) less a reduction of $1,500 to allow for the fact that the lump sum payment would not be deductible to the wife and would not be taxable in the hands of the husband.

*Interim support granted to recognize economic disadvantage of marriage* — Bell v. Bell, 1998 CarswellNfld 246, 42 R.F.L. (4th) 301 (Nfld. U.F.C.). Where the wife stayed at home to raise the parties' four children and was definitely economically disadvantaged and currently has health problems, she should be granted interim spousal support to help her attain the objectives set out in s. 15(7).

*Relationship with third party does not affect entitlement to interim spousal support* — Bell v. Bell, 1998 CarswellNfld 246, 42 R.F.L. (4th) 301 (Nfld. U.F.C.). Where a spouse has formed a relationship with a third party but the relationship is transient only with no contemplation of a long term commitment, the applicant's entitlement to interim spousal support should not be eliminated nor reduced.

*Interim spousal support granted where wife's income considerably less than husabnd's and wife not so self sufficient as to preclude spousal support* — Nataros v. Nataros, 1998 CarswellBC 944, 40 R.F.L. (4th) 308, [1998] B.C.J. No. 1417 (B.C. Master). The husband's income was $158,000 a year and the wife earned $39,000 a year. Their son was in the wife's custody. On an application by the wife for interim child and spousal support, the court held the husband should pay child support including s. 7 expenses of $ 1,888 each month and interim spousal support of $750 each month on the ground that the wife's income was considerably less than the income enjoyed by the husband, and it could not be said that she had achieved a level of self sufficiency that would preclude spousal support. The amount awarded would enable each of the parties to enjoy comparable lifestyles and permit their son to continue to enjoy a lifestyle similar to that to which they have made him accustomed.

*Interim support granted despite fact payor's liabilities exceeded assets — Modry v. Modry*, 1998 CarswellAlta 949, 1998 ABQB 86842 R.F.L. (4th) 387, 231 A.R. 110, [1998] A.J. No. 1162, (Alta. Q.B.). The wife was granted $15,000 monthly interim support despite the fact that the husband's accountant gave evidence that the husband's liabilities exceeded his assets. The husband showed no evidence indicating any demand for loan repayments nor had he reduced his own lifestyle. The husband could liquidate assets to reduce his debt load, which had ballooned since separation, while paying support and maintaining his own lifestyle.

*Nominal interim support — wife economically advantged by marriage — Davidson v. Davidson*, 1998 CarswellAlta 879, 42 R.F.L. (4th) 154, 230 A.R. 151, [1998] A.J. No. 1040 (Alta. Q.B.). The wife was granted only nominal interim support. The wife had substantial assets, considerable rental income and had obtained two university degrees during the marriage. The parties had amassed a sizable fortune and the wife had actually been economically advantaged by the marriage by her entitlement to a share in these assets.

*Where the applicant has demonstrated a need for spousal support and the respondent has the means, interim support will be granted — Cote v. Cote*, 1995 CarswellOnt 91, 12 R.F.L. (4th) 194, [1995] O.J. No. 807 (Ont. Gen. Div.).

*Economic disadvantage arising from the marriage — Stefanyk v. Stefanyk*, 1994 CarswellNS 38, 1 R.F.L. (4th) 432, 128 N.S.R. (2d) 335, 259 A.P.R. 335, [1994] N.S.J. No. 67 (N.S.S.C.). The wife was ordered to pay interim support to the husband. The husband had given up his job to allow the family to move to Nova Scotia so that the wife could pursue a career opportunity. As a result, the husband had proven an economic disadvantage arising from the marriage.

*Economic disadvantage arising from the marriage — Mitchell v. Mitchell*, 1993 CarswellNS 620, 129 N.S.R. (2d) 351, 362 A.P.R. 351, [1993] N.S.J. No. 504 (N.S.S.C.). The court granted the 62-year-old husband's claim for interim support against the 67-year-old wife. The wife's income greatly exceeded that of the husband and in the later years of the parties' 12-year marriage, the husband had depended upon the wife's superior income. In the interim period, there was a need for a more equitable distribution of the parties' income.

*Objectives relevant on interim support application — Kendell v. Kendell*, 1993 CarswellNfld 25, 48 R.F.L. (3d) 146, 110 Nfld. & P.E.I.R. 213, 346 A.P.R. 213 (Nfld. T.D.). The support objectives set out in s. 15(7) [now s. 15.2(6)] of the *Divorce Act* are relevant to a claim for interim spousal support. Where the limited evidence presented by a wife on an interim support application indicated her need for funds to complete her education and to assist her in becoming self sufficient, she was found entitled to interim support. If at the final hearing the wife was found to be disentitled to support, an order requiring the repayment of the interim funds could be made.

*Upgrading of career reasonable before trial — Davison v. Davison*, 1992 CarswellNS 76, 42 R.F.L. (3d) 341 (N.S.T.D.). Where the wife planned to quit her part time career shortly after separation to pursue upgrading for long term career plans, she was found entitled to interim support. Given her age (46) and her position, she was under no obligation to defer her career plans until trial, particularly as the husband had not established that her plan was unreasonable.

*Interim support granted where wife had contributed at home during long-term marriage — Fabian v. Fabian*, 1987 CarswellSask 593, 65 Sask. R. 271 (Sask. Q.B.). The wife was awarded $780 monthly as interim support in recognition of her contribution at home during the parties' 25-year marriage. The wife had been employed as a medical technician but since losing her job had attempted to sell real estate with little success. The court rejected the husband's assertion that the wife's claim should be denied because of her refusal to attempt to find alternative employment as a medical technician.

## Interim spousal support not granted — examples

*Where no entitlement is found on the evidence, interim spousal support will not be awarded* — Gerlitz v. Gerlitz, 2005 CarswellAlta 1841, 2005 ABCA 424, [2005] A.J. No. 1708 (Alta. C.A.). The parties had a long-term, traditional marriage. The Alberta Court of Appeal upheld the decision of a lower court judge not to award interim spousal support. The judge had found the issues were best determined at trial and that entitlement to spousal support had not been made on the evidence she had available. The lower court decision not to award interim support was discretionary, and there was no error made by the trial judge.

*Provisions for mortgage and utility payments on marital home deleted* — Glass v. Glass, 1997 CarswellMan 632, 34 R.F.L. (4th) 411, 123 Man. R. (2d) 239, 159 W.A.C. 239 (Man. C.A.).The court allowed the husband's appeal in part from an interim spousal support order. The provision in the motions judge's order that the husband make mortgage and utility payments on the marital home was deleted, as was the court's provision for an arbitrary amount of maintenance of $2,200 per month if the wife left the marital home, without having evidence to determine the wife's needs in other accommodation.

*Where the parties essentially had no relationship despite being married, and the wife came to Canada against the wishes of her husband, entitlement to spousal support will not be found* — Mazloumisadat v. Zarandi, 2010 CarswellOnt 287, 2010 ONSC 524, 81 R.F.L. (6th) 82 (Ont. S.C.J.). The wife was not entitled to interim support because, although the husband had sponsored her for immigration purposes, she came to Canada against the husband's wishes. The marriage was never consummated. The fact of marriage alone did not create entitlement to support.

*Interim support will not be awarded when the current needs of the wife are met and a full compensatory analysis must be performed* — Geange v. Geange, 2009 CarswellNfld 121, 2009 NLTD 75, 286 Nfld. & P.E.I.R. 261, 883 A.P.R. 261 (N.L.T.D.). The wife's income had been higher than the husband's for the past 8 years. Although the wife had moved around in order to accommodate her husband's career, the judge found there was no entitlement to interim support. The evidence was extremely conflicting, and the judge found a full hearing was required.

*Increases in the husband's income since separation were considered, but were not applied to an interim award* — Boju v. Corr, 2009 CarswellOnt 563 (Ont. S.C.J.). The parties were married in the United States in 2001. The husband moved to Canada in 2005, and the wife remained in the United States. She was currently living in Arizona. The husband petitioned for divorce in 2008. The husband, who earned $52,000 per year and had received increases in salary since moving to Canada, opposed payment of spousal support. The wife's interim application for spousal support was granted. The wife, who was the primary caregiver of the parties' young child, was entitled to support on an interim basis. The wife's claim for support in the amount of $500 per month was reasonable. The amount claimed by the wife was less than half of the lowest amount payable under the *Spousal Support Advisory Guidelines*. The amount awarded took into account that the wife lived with her parents and was not currently paying rent, and that the cost of living was lower in Arizona than Toronto.

*When interim spousal support is ordered based on need, and the need is no longer present, a spousal support order will be rescinded from the date the need disappeared* — Hayward v. Hayward, 2003 CarswellOnt 5475, 50 R.F.L. (5th) 360, [2003] O.J. No. 5504 (Ont. S.C.J.). The original interim order was made based on a temporary need of the wife for support after losing her job. The judge ordered the wife to repay spousal support she received after she had found a new, well-paying job. Interim spousal support in this case was not ordered on a compensatory basis, but merely needs-based.

*Interim spousal support will be refused where the marriage or its breakdown have not caused any diminution in a spouse's ability to earn income as a result of the roles adopted in the marriage* — Burmi v. Dhiman, 2001 CarswellOnt 1812, 18 R.F.L. (5th) 9, [2001] O.J. No. 2010 (Ont. S.C.J.), additional reasons at 2001 CarswellOnt 2195 (Ont. S.C.J.). In this case, the parties had married in India in an arranged marriage and had cohabited for 7 weeks. The wife claimed that her husband's repudiation of the marriage had led to her ostracism and ridicule within her religious community and her inability to remarry well. The court was of the opinion that the wife had not suffered any economic loss as contemplated by the *Divorce Act.*

*No interim support, no explanation for failure to work* — Harris v. Harris, 1999 CarswellAlta 558, 1999 ABQB 325, 48 R.F.L. (4th) 341, 242 A.R. 382 (Alta. Q.B.). A claim for interim spousal support will be rejected where the wife had been recently employed at occupations which met her modest needs and there was no explanation for her decision not to return to work when it appeared that workers' compensation authorities had deemed her fit to work. Moreover, the wife had not shown that her move outside the jurisdiction was made with some reasonable assessment of employment opportunities available or with the welfare of the children in mind. The husband ought not to be required to subsidize the wife's personal choice. Lastly, the husband's assumption of all matrimonial debt should be taken into account as this action provided the wife with some financial benefit.

*No interim support where party married to third party during cohabitation* — Mahoney v. King, 1998 CarswellOnt 2348, 39 R.F.L. (4th) 361, [1998] O.T.C. 235, [1998] O.J. No. 2296 (Ont. Gen. Div.). An application for interim spousal support was refused where the parties had cohabitated in a 5- or 6-year relationship while one of the parties had been married to another person. The court ruled that if support were ordered at trial, the award would be retroactive to at least the date of the application.

*No interim support where husband paying expenses for matrimonial home* — Haddad-Hashem v. Hashem, 1997 CarswellPEI 32, 28 R.F.L. (4th) 225 (P.E.I.T.D. [In Chambers]). The husband, since separation, had been paying all expenses for the matrimonial home, including taxes, oil, electricity and upkeep and had permitted the wife to live in the house. Title to the home was in the name of the husband and his father. The court, in refusing the wife's application for interim spousal support, held that the husband was providing sufficient spousal support by paying the expenses and the arrangement should continue. If the wife had sought support at the time of separation, she probably would have received a support order in a specific amount. The wife claimed that the parties had separated in 1988. The husband claimed that the date was 1976.

## 4.2.3 Evidence and Disclosure

*Where a judge is clear that he is making an interim order with very little reliable evidence and that further evidence is required that can only be adduced at trial for a determination of the issues, an interim order will not be varied* — Blatherwick v. Blatherwick, 2014 CarswellOnt 2644, 2014 ONSC 1433, 44 R.F.L. (7th) 379 (Ont. S.C.J.).

*Where there is insufficient evidence of income, an interim interim order of support will be made at less than the low end of the SSAG range* — Strutzenberger v. Strutzenberger, 2013 CarswellOnt 11889, 2013 ONSC 5224 (Ont. S.C.J.). The parties were married for 34 years, and the wife sought interim spousal support. The judge found that there was insufficient evidence to determine the husband's income and made an interim interim order for 4 months at slightly less than the low end of the SSAG range.

*Where income is in flux and fuller evidence is required for an accurate calculation of support but income seems commensurate with the previous order, interim support will not be varied* — *W. (T.A.) v. W. (S.R.)*, 2013 CarswellBC 1523, 2013 BCSC 907 (B.C.S.C.). The parties were married for 4 years and had one child. The wife sought, *inter alia*, variation of spousal support. The parties sought to vary the Consent Order for interim support from the previous year. The judge found that the difference in the husband's income from that time was only $2,000 and the husband's income was very much in flux. Consequently, it was more prudent to wait for a full determination of financial issues at trial in order to calculate support accurately.

*Expert evidence as to income will be rejected on an interim support application when it does not have an air of reality* — *Ramlochan v. Ramlochan*, 2010 CarswellOnt 5726, 2010 ONSC 4323 (Ont. S.C.J.). The parties had a 10-year relationship. The court rejected the husband's expert report on his income as incredible and based income on the retained income of the husband's companies.

*Where there is insufficient evidence, interim spousal support will not be ordered* — *James v. James*, 2010 CarswellOnt 4671, 2010 ONSC 3445 (Ont. S.C.J.). There was no evidence as to the parties' incomes, and as such the judge was unable to make an order for interim support, noting that means and needs of the parties were very significant on an interim application.

*Where inadequate evidence is led concerning entitlement and need, interim support may not be ordered* — *Prikker v. Vaine*, 2010 CarswellOnt 7125, 2010 ONSC 2208 (Ont. S.C.J.), additional reasons at 2010 CarswellOnt 7126, 2010 ONSC 2914 (Ont. S.C.J.). The parties had a relatively short cohabitation and marriage (less than 5 years). The court found it was unable to find entitlement to interim support for the wife. The wife had received a settlement from a motor vehicle accident but did not provide evidence about the loss of income component of the settlement to the court or the husband. In the absence of knowing how much the third party tortfeasor would be compensating the wife for her loss of income, the court found it was unable to determine an appropriate spousal support quantum.

*Interim spousal support will be ordered even when a motion is adjourned in order to allow better evidence as to the means and needs of the parties to be collected* — *Poirier v. Poirier*, 2010 CarswellOnt 744, 2010 ONSC 920, 81 R.F.L. (6th) 161, [2010] O.J. No. 536 (Ont. S.C.J.), additional reasons at 2010 CarswellOnt 4889, 2010 ONSC 2291, 89 R.F.L. (6th) 459 (Ont. S.C.J.). The parties had a long-term, traditional marriage. Income was imputed to the husband, and he was ordered to pay interim support, while the motion was adjourned to allow for better evidence to be collected.

*An interim order for support will be made even when the parties' incomes are uncertain* — *Atkins v. Burgess*, 2010 CarswellOnt 339, 2010 ONSC 557, [2010] O.J. No. 275 (Ont. S.C.J.). The husband did not make financial disclosure, and the judge was required to estimate the wife's income. The judge ordered support at the low end of the SSAG because of the husband's imputed income and the uncertainty surrounding the wife's income.

*Where no financial disclosure is made by the payor, interim support may be ordered based on the SSAG for an imputed income* — *Hernandez v. Hernandez-Trueba*, 2008 CarswellOnt 1879, 53 R.F.L. (6th) 61, [2008] O.J. No. 1287 (Ont. S.C.J.). Here, the court imputed an income to the husband, who did not appear or submit financial information.

*Where a party's assertion of income clearly lacks credibility but income cannot be imputed, interim support will be ordered at a level that reflects the needs of the recipient* — *Stergiou v. Stergiou*, 2007 CarswellOnt 3167, 38 R.F.L. (6th) 160 (Ont. S.C.J.). The parties had a 4-year marriage and two children. The judge found that the husband's income was not credible and the husband had been mortgaging joint assets since separation. It was not possible to impute income to him, but a global amount was ordered for spousal and child support which took into account the needs of the children and wife based on their budget.

*Where adequate disclosure is not made, income may be imputed at the interim stage when the evidence supports it* — *Verwey v. Verwey*, 2006 CarswellMan 232, 2006 MBQB 149, 207 Man. R. (2d) 41, [2006] M.J. No. 326 (Man. Q.B.), affirmed 2007 CarswellMan 338, 2007 MBCA 102, 41 R.F.L. (6th) 29, 220 Man. R. (2d) 52, [2007] M.J. No. 309 (Man. C.A.). The parties were married for 24 years and had two children. The judge found that, even on an interim motion, each party was entitled to proper disclosure from the other and that the husband had not provided adequate disclosure and was deliberately evading his disclosure obligations. Income was imputed to him.

*A court may make an interim or temporary order on a final application where there is insufficient evidence to make a temporary order* — *Harris v. Harris*, 2004 CarswellOnt 1336, [2004] O.J. No. 1429 (Ont. S.C.J.).

## 4.2.4 Relationship of Interim Support to Permanent Support

*Quantum* — *Mosher v. Mosher*, 1995 CarswellNS 11, 13 R.F.L. (4th) 385, 140 N.S.R. (2d) 40, 399 A.P.R. 40, [1995] N.S.J. No. 133 (N.S.C.A.), reversing in part 1993 CarswellNS 391, 126 N.S.R. (2d) 367, 352 A.P.R. 367 (N.S.S.C.). In determining the quantum of permanent spousal support, significance should not be attached in all cases to the size of an interim support award.

*Interim award granted, husband's responsibility of rehabilitation of wife left until trial* — *Sencza v. Donohue*, 1995 CarswellOnt 1278, 18 R.F.L. (4th) 115, [1995] O.J. No. 3850 (Ont. Gen. Div.). Where the wife had developed alcoholism during the period of cohabitation which impaired her ability to work, her application for interim support was granted. It was reasonable to award support on an interim basis although the larger issue of whether the husband should be ordered to assist in the rehabilitation of the wife would require determination at trial.

*Matters inappropriate for interim spousal support application* — *Gearin v. Gearin*, 1999 CarswellNfld 87, 45 R.F.L. (4th) 333, 176 Nfld. & P.E.I.R. 76, 540 A.P.R. 76, [1999] N.J. No. 97 (Nfld. U.F.C.). A detailed examination of an unequal property division in the wife's favour and her failure to seek retraining were found not to be appropriate in the case of an interim spousal support application in which the wife had established a prima facie case for support.

## 4.2.5 Defences — Delay in Application for Interim Support

*There is no time limitation under the Divorce Act for a former spouse obtaining spousal support* — *a provincial legislature cannot abrogate a claim for spousal support under the Limitations Act of a spousal support claim under the federal Divorce Act* — *K. (H.J.) v. B. (J.E.)*, 1997 CarswellBC 2558, 33 R.F.L. (4th) 409, 44 B.C.L.R. (3d) 77, 100 B.C.A.C. 1, 163 W.A.C. 1 (B.C.C.A.). Since Parliament has enacted a complete scheme concerning the parties' support obligations, the equitable doctrine of *laches* does not apply. Furthermore, in this case, delay is not relevant. The former wife made every effort to be self-supporting but was eventually unable to work, as she looked after the parties' disabled child. The husband's appeal of a decision to award the wife interim spousal support was dismissed.

*An award of interim spousal support following a long delay will be linked to likely success at trial* — *Belcourt v. Chartrand*, 2006 CarswellOnt 2272, 28 R.F.L. (6th) 157, [2006] O.J. No. 1500 (Ont. S.C.J.). The judge found that interim support should not be ordered in this case as the financial difficulties of the wife likely stemmed from her break-up with her common-law spouse rather than the separation from the husband, which had occurred some 12 years previously. As such, a trial judge was unlikely to award spousal support.

*Delay of 4 years, not unreasonable.* — *Radcliff v. Radcliff,* 2001 CarswellOnt 1141, 15 R.F.L. (5th) 423, [2001] O.J. No. 1195 (Ont. S.C.J.), additional reasons at 2001 CarswellOnt 1928, 17 R.F.L. (5th) 417 (Ont. S.C.J.). At the time of the marriage breakdown, the wife held a well paying job and was economically self sufficient. She lost this job and found work at a lower salary that did not meet her needs. Her claim for support in a *Family Law Act* proceeding was dismissed on the ground that her need for support did not result from an economic disadvantage caused by the marriage. In subsequent divorce proceedings taken 4 years after the marriage breakdown, she claimed support again and moved for interim support. In allowing her motion, and granting interim support of $800 a month, the court held that the fact that she had achieved economic self sufficiency at the time of the marriage breakdown did not extinguish the support obligation founded on the marriage relationship. This obligation remained dormant for 4 years — which was not an unreasonable period considering that cohabitation under the marriage lasted 27 years — until the need for support arose. The loss of the job that gave rise to the need was not too remote. Her claim for support was neither tenuous nor uncertain, and there was no reason for not making an interim support order.

*The Divorce Act does not prescribe a time limit within which to bring a claim for interim spousal support* — *Interim support was however denied on the basis of delay* — *Byerley v. Byerley,* 1998 CarswellOnt 3649, 41 R.F.L. (4th) 50, 75 O.T.C. 73, [1998] O.J. No. 3781 (Ont. Gen. Div.), and *Bouchard v. Quesnel,* 1989 CarswellNB 368, 97 N.B.R. (2d) 273, 245 A.P.R. 273 (Q.B.). In the *Byerley* case, the parties lived together in a common law relationship for 3 years and were married for 8 years. The parties separated in 1996. A year after the parties' separation, the wife began to live in a common law relationship with another man. She quit her job and became pregnant. In the fall of 1998, almost 2 years from the date of separation, the wife sought interim spousal support. The court, in dismissing the motion, held that the wife was self supporting from the time of separation to the time of the hearing, first from her own earnings and latterly because of the support of her common law partner. The court was of the opinion that at the preliminary stage of awarding interim relief, the function of the court was to determine if the applicant had current needs during the period of the order, decide if the applicant required interim relief and whether the responding party had the means to provide interim support. In this case, the wife did not provide the court with material as to her common law spouse's income and expenses and the details of their joint expenses. The wife, according to the court, at page 52, "failed to demonstrate, with cogent and compelling evidence, a current need for interim spousal support from the husband."

*Delay because of payment of child support* — *Gearin v. Gearin,* 1999 CarswellNfld 87, 45 R.F.L. (4th) 333, 176 Nfld. & P.E.I.R. 76, 540 A.P.R. 76, [1999] N.J. No. 97 (Nfld. U.F.C.). The wife was awarded interim spousal support 7 years after a consent order that provided maintenance for the children only. The court was of the opinion that the wife had an honest belief that she obtained some benefits from the reasonably generous child support payments, benefits which, at the time of the hearing had ceased as child support was no longer payable. Further, the court considered that at the time of the consent order, it would have been unlikely that the husband would have been ordered to pay spousal support above the amount he was already paying for child support.

*Delay reasonable as wife had been living on capital* — *Williams v. Williams,* 1984 CarswellBC 640, 42 R.F.L. (2d) 110 (B.C.C.A.). Where the wife first brought an application for interim maintenance three and a half years after the parties' separation, it was held that the delay was not fatal to the application. As the wife had been living on the capital realized upon the sale of the matrimonial home, the delay in seeking maintenance could not be interpreted as a lack of financial need on her part.

## Interim support and domestic contracts

*Where a motion judge denies a wife's claim for interim spousal support on the basis that it was precluded by the terms of the existing marriage contract. an appellate court will affirm the decision where the motion judge correctly applied the* Miglin *test and did not make any error in law* — H. (C.M.) v. H. (J.R.), 2012 CarswellNB 525, 2012 CarswellNB 526, 2012 NBCA 71, 393 N.B.R. (2d) 154, 354 D.L.R. (4th) 31, 1017 A.P.R. 154, [2012] N.B.J. No. 314 (N.B.C.A.). The parties, who had cohabited since March 1999 and had a child, executed a marriage contract March 15, 2002, with both parties receiving independent legal advice, and were married April 16, 2002. Under the marriage contract, changes in the parties' "respective financial circumstances, whether by reason of health, employment, cost of living change or otherwise" would not entitle either party to spousal support. Each party contracted to "own assets in his or her own name free from any claim of the other." In 2007, the wife developed fibromyalgia and allegedly was unable to work. The wife received a disability pension. The motions judge had found that the changes were not sufficient to overturn the marriage contract. [See Epstein's This Week in Fam. Law 2012-45, where the author commenting on H. (C.M.) v. H. (J.R.) states: "I think there is fair argument to be made that the wife was entitled to at least interim support based on the first stage test of *Miglin* and the second stage test."]

*Agreements less important for interim support* — Ziniuk v. Ziniuk, 1986 CarswellBC 524, 2 R.F.L. (3d) 398 (B.C.C.A.). Although the court pays great heed to agreements made between parties regarding maintenance, less weight is to be accorded such agreements in the case of interim matters.

*Although the parties had signed a marriage contract, the court nullified the waiver of spousal support and granted interim spousal support of $175,000 a month to the wife, retroactive to the date of separation, where the wife was subject to duress at the time of signing the contract* — McCain v. McCain, 2012 CarswellOnt 16853, 2012 ONSC 7344, 34 R.F.L. (7th) 82 (Ont. S.C.J.). The husband was an extremely wealthy man, having an approximate net worth of $500,000,000 at the time of separation. At the insistence of the husband's father, who maintained that he would disinherit the husband if the husband and his wife did not sign a marriage contract, the parties executed an agreement 16 years into a 30-year marriage. According to the contract, the wife waived all her property rights on marriage breakdown, keeping only assets registered in her name, and waived all rights to spousal support. She would receive a lump sum amount of $7,000,000 after separation, as well as the matrimonial home and properties in her name. The court made its calculations assuming an income of $120,000 for the wife and $9,700,000 for the husband. The wife had stated that her expenses were $118,803.05. Madam Justice Greer applied a *Miglin* analysis in her consideration of the spousal support waiver in the contract. She was of the opinion that she could use a *Miglin* analysis as there was voluminous financial and affidavit evidence in the record, sufficient for her to come to a determination on the issue of interim/temporary spousal support. The court found that at the time of signing the contract, the wife was subject to duress and over time the provisions of the marriage contract led to a result that was unconscionable. The wife had significant assets, but little liquidity to earn income and provide support for herself. All parts of the marriage contract were severable from all other parts. Therefore, the issue of spousal support could be severed from the rest of the contract on an interim/temporary motion. The circumstances regarding the contract's execution, the improvident result for the wife and the extent of the husband's current wealth were sufficient to have the spousal support provisions of the contract set aside. Spousal support was ordered on an interim basis at $175,000 monthly.

*Agreement a bar to interim support* — *Rodrigues v. Rodrigues*, 2004 CarswellBC 1503, 2004 BCSC 855, 6 R.F.L. (6th) 365, [2004] B.C.J. No. 1353 (B.C.S.C.), the court refused the wife's application for interim support pending her challenge to the waiver of spousal support contained in the parties' separation agreement. Although it was not certain that the wife's action would be unsuccessful, the status quo established by the agreement should govern until the final disposition.

*Agreement not a bar to interim support* — *Salzmann v. Salzmann*, 2004 CarswellOnt 169, 50 R.F.L. (5th) 181, [2004] O.J. No. 166 (Ont. S.C.J.). The wife was awarded interim spousal support despite the existence of a cohabitation agreement in which she had waived her right to support. The wife had raised arguable issues on each element of the test for determining if the terms of the agreement were unconscionable. If she was unsuccessful in challenging the agreement at trial, payments made by the husband could be addressed through an unequal diversion of property.

*Agreement a bar to interim support* — *Palmer v. Palmer*, 2003 CarswellSask 690, 2003 SKQB 438, 45 R.F.L. (5th) 447, 240 Sask. R. 25, [2003] S.J. No. 671 (Sask. Q.B.). Where the wife had signed a separation agreement waiving her right to support after a specified date, her subsequent application for interim spousal support was refused. Although the wife challenged the validity of the agreement, the trial judge would be in the best position to assess that issue.

*Agreement did not bar right to interim support* — *Walmsley v. Moore*, 2002 CarswellOnt 584, 25 R.F.L. (5th) 462, [2002] O.J. No. 611 (Ont. S.C.J.), additional reasons at 2002 CarswellOnt 1865, [2002] O.J. No. 2116 (Ont. S.C.J.), the wife executed a separation agreement releasing her support rights in exchange for continuing employment with the husband's company. When her employment was terminated 1 year later, her application for interim spousal support was granted. In the circumstances, the release clause was not a bar to her claim for interim support pending determination of the issue of entitlement at trial.

*Interim support refused where agreement did not contemplate self-sufficiency* — *Borrelli-Steffes v. Steffes*, 2002 CarswellOnt 2152, 27 R.F.L. (5th) 265 (Ont. Master). The court dismissed the wife's application for interim support launched over 6 years after the expiration of her limited term support agreed to in the parties' separation agreement. Although the wife had failed to become self-sufficient, there was no evidence that her self-sufficiency had even been contemplated when the agreement was executed. Furthermore, the wife could offer no reasonable explanation for her delay in seeking an initial award of support.

*Interim order for support not required where support provided for in agreement* — *Woode v. Woode*, 2002 CarswellSask 49, 2002 SKQB 33, 26 R.F.L. (5th) 232, 216 Sask. R. 1 (Sask. Q.B.). The court refused the wife's application for interim nominal support. The wife already had such support pursuant to the parties' separation agreement and a formal order was not required.

*A separation agreement is a defence to a claim to interim support, but not necessarily to a claim for permanent support* — *Bedard v. Huard*, 2000 CarswellOnt 1129, 5 R.F.L. (5th) 282, [2000] O.J. No. 969 (Ont. S.C.J), additional reasons at 2000 CarswellOnt 1226 (Ont. S.C.J.).

*Agreement not a bar to interim spousal support* — *Kennedy v. Kennedy*, 2000 CarswellOnt 3622, 11 R.F.L. (5th) 150, [2000] O.J. No. 3742 (Ont. S.C.J.). An agreement signed by the wife in which she purportedly waived her right to spousal support was found to have been improperly executed and was entered into without independent legal advice or financial disclosure. Accordingly, the agreement was not a bar to the wife's application for interim spousal support.

*Agreement incorporated in interim support order* — *Sobey v. Sobey*, 2000 CarswellNS 279, 11 R.F.L. (5th) 401 (N.S.S.C.). The court allowed the wife's application to incorporate the spousal and child support provisions of the parties' maintenance agreement into an interim support order.

Both parties had been represented by experienced counsel and the agreement had actually been drafted by the husband's counsel. No change of circumstances had occurred since the signing of the agreement and it should not be ignored.

*Interim spousal support despite separation agreement provisions* — *Bailey v. Plaxton*, 2000 CarswellOnt 1194, 6 R.F.L. (5th) 29, 47 O.R. (3d) 593, [2000] O.T.C. 243, [2000] O.J. No. 1187 (Ont. S.C.J.). The court held that the former wife was entitled to interim spousal support pursuant to s. 15.2 of the *Divorce Act* despite a separation agreement which provided for spousal support for 3 years ending 10 years before the judgement. The court considered all factors required pursuant to s. 15.2, including the separation agreement, and concluded that in the circumstances it was warranted and reasonable to make an interim support order in the amount of $5,000 per month pending the determination of the application under s. 15.2(1).

*Court must consider other factors as well as contract on support application* — *Bailey v. Plaxton, supra.* While a contract is an important factor to consider in determining whether spousal support should be granted, there are other factors which a court must take into account. If the terms of the contract do not promote or cease to promote the objectives of the *Divorce Act*, a court should intervene to protect those objectives and policies. In that decision, the court held that the former wife was entitled to interim spousal support pursuant to s. 15.2 of the *Divorce Act*, despite a separation agreement which provided for spousal support for 3 years ending 10 years before the judgement.

*Waiver of support in separation agreement* — *Allen v. Allen*, 1999 CarswellAlta 1210, 2 R.F.L. (5th) 1, [2000] 3 W.W.W. 271, 75 Alta. L.R. (3d) 305, 256 A.R. 121 (Alta. Q.B.). Where the separation agreement contains a waiver of spousal support, the onus is on the applicant to satisfy the trial judge that he or she should invoke the inherent jurisdiction of the court to override the agreement.

*Agreement not a bar to interim spousal support* — *Scheel v. Henkelman*, 1999 CarswellOnt 1156, 45 R.F.L. (4th) 419, [1999] O.J. No. 1372 (Ont. Gen. Div.). The husband was not allowed to rely upon a mutual support waiver contained in the parties' cohabitation agreement as a defence to the wife's claim for interim spousal support. There were triable issues relating to the validity of the agreement arising out of issues of unconscionability and the husband's alleged breaches of the agreement.

*Effect of separation agreement on interim spousal support, agreement to be examined, no urgency* — *Lees v. Lees*, 1998 CarswellOnt 1329, [1998] O.J. No. 1397 (Ont. Gen. Div.), the wife had signed a separation agreement dealing with spousal support among other matters, against the advice of independent legal counsel. When the wife learned that the husband was cohabiting with his lawyer, she attempted suicide and injured herself so that she was now in a wheel chair. The wife moved for interim relief including spousal support. She sought to set aside the agreement on the grounds that it was improvident and unconscionable. The husband moved for an adjournment of the wife's motion. The court granted an adjournment since it considered that there was no urgency to the matter; the final separation agreement was in place and needed to be carefully examined. Further, the husband was looking after the children well.

*No change in amount of support from that specified in agreement* — *Beeching v. Beeching*, 1998 CarswellSask 432, 40 R.F.L. (4th) 15, 169 Sask. R. 18, [1998] S.J. No. 355 (Sask. Q.B.). Where an agreement provides for a combined monthly amount of spousal and child support, and the husband had been paying the amount until recently, the court will not interfere with the agreement on an interim basis other than to specify the amounts for spousal and child support separately.

*Agreement not a bar to interim spousal support* — *Burton v. Burton*, 1998 CarswellOnt 5186, 42 R.F.L. (4th) 310 (Ont. Gen. Div.). Where a party is receiving social assistance, and the other party has the means to pay support, interim spousal support will be granted despite the provisions of marriage contract in which support rights were given up. The validity of the agreement was an issue for trial but for the purposes of the interim spousal support application, the contract was considered valid.

*Effect of subsequent agreement dealing with property* — *Johnston v. Johnston*, 1997 CarswellBC 2403, 35 R.F.L. (4th) 37, [1997] B.C.J. No. 2597 (B.C. Master). Where there is an agreement which provides for interim spousal support and a subsequent agreement that deals only with property, the obligation to pay interim spousal support is not terminated by the second agreement. The second agreement specifically stated that it did not settle spousal support.

*Agreement not a bar to interim support* — *Lodjn v. Lodjn*, 1997 CarswellBC 2716, 34 R.F.L. (4th) 147, 43 B.C.L.R. (3d) 271, [1997] B.C.J. No. 2834 (B.C. Master). The wife was awarded interim spousal support despite the fact that she had executed a prenuptial agreement waiving her right to claim support. The agreement was entered into 2 years prior to the marriage and indicated the parties' intention not to have children. As they did in fact have a child which required the wife to be primary caregiver and had created an economic dependency, it was possible that the trial judge could find a radical change in circumstances justifying that the agreement be set aside.

*Where there is a separation agreement dealing with support, and an applicant is able to sustain herself before trial, the agreement should prevail until trial* — *Hay v. Hay*, 1997 CarswellOnt 2123 (Ont. Gen. Div.). The parties had signed a separation agreement and the wife had paid the husband $2,000 in full and final settlement of all support obligations as a result of the marriage relationship. The husband and wife worked for the same company and after separation the wife resigned from her position, alleging a history of her husband's violent conduct. The wife attempted to establish a business of her own, but to date had little success. The court was of the opinion that where there was a separation agreement in place, the party seeking interim spousal support could sustain himself or herself and where there was a serious issue of credibility, the terms of the separation agreement should prevail on an interim basis until the trial judge made a determination.

*Agreement not a bar to spouse in need* — *Munn v. Munn*, 1996 CarswellOnt 1240, 23 R.F.L. (4th) 115, [1996] O.J. No. 1188 (Ont. Gen. Div.). Where the wife released any claim for spousal support in the separation agreement if she obtained 2 years of full-time employment and her full-time employment was reduced to half time, the court could award interim spousal support because she was in need.

*Interim support granted where validity of separation agreement in dispute* — *Carlsen v. Carlsen*, 1990 CarswellOnt 243, 25 R.F.L. (3d) 461, [1990] O.J. No. 3091 (Ont. H.C.). Where the husband's obligation, under the parties' separation agreement, to pay spousal support had expired, but the wife had an arguable case on the validity of the agreement, she was granted interim support pending the hearing of the issue in the parties' divorce action. The quantum of interim support, however, recognized the fact that if the agreement were upheld, the funds would not be repaid.

*Agreement not a bar to interim support* — *Desimone v. Desimone*, 1993 CarswellBC 620, 48 R.F.L. (3d) 161, [1993] B.C.J. No. 1480 (B.C.S.C.). Where the wife was attempting to set aside some of the provisions of the parties' separation agreement at trial, it was held that the agreement, which limited her support rights, did not act to bar her claim for interim support.

*Agreement not a bar to interim support* — *Pineault v. Pineault*, 1993 CarswellOnt 358, 49 R.F.L. (3d) 411 (Ont. Gen. Div.). The court considered whether the wife was entitled to interim support, even though she had signed a marriage contract after the wedding and before the reception whereby she waived any right to spousal support. The court exercised its discretion and awarded interim support.

*Agreement a bar to interim support* — *Legg v. Legg*, 1991 CarswellBC 574, 38 R.F.L. (3d) 23 (B.C.S.C.). The wife's claim for interim support was dismissed on the basis of a variation to the parties' separation agreement whereby the wife had agreed to forgo spousal support. Although agreed to without legal advice, the variation was intended by the parties to result in a final agreement and could only be varied by proof of a radical change in circumstances. The wife could not establish any change and the final determination of the validity of the agreement was best left to the trial judge.

*Agreement a bar to interim support* — *Droit de la famille - 1222* (1988), [1989] R.D.F. 168 (C.S. Que.). The court refused the wife's application for interim support where the application would have required the court to override a provision in the parties' separation agreement whereby the wife waived all claims against the husband. Although the wife had spent all of the money she received under the agreement, the court could not override the agreement absent proof of a radical change in circumstances that resulted from the marriage.

*Oral agreement not binding* — *Hunkin v. Hunkin*, 1988 CarswellMan 48, 14 R.F.L. (3d) 157, 54 Man. R. (2d) 44 (Man. Q.B.). A settlement agreement which is orally varied by the parties is not a "final" settlement and in no way restricts the court's jurisdiction to award interim support which is inconsistent with a consent support award based upon the agreement.

*Separation agreement is only evidence to establish quantum of support* — *Conley v. Conley*, 1987 CarswellSask 86, 7 R.F.L. (3d) 372, 54 Sask. R. 17 (Sask. C.A.), affirming 1986 CarswellSask 570, 54 Sask. R. 21(Sask. Q.B.). In an application for interim maintenance, a separation agreement may only be considered as evidence to establish the appropriate alimony and maintenance which should be paid.

## 4.2.6 Interim support — Miscellaneous

### Interim support — securing payment

*Spousal support may be secured on an interim order through a charge on the proceeds of an estate* — *Whatley v. Whatley*, 2014 CarswellBC 842, 2014 BCSC 536 (B.C.S.C.). The parties were married for 23 years and had three children, one of whom remained a "child of the marriage". The wife sought spousal support, *inter alia*. She had no income and had been out of the workforce for 30 years. The judge found that many issues, including marital standard of living, debts and gifts, were hotly disputed and could only be resolved at trial. The judge imputed income to the husband based on funds held in trust for him from his mother's estate, which he had demonstrated he had the ability to access. The judge also placed a charge on the estate proceeds to secure spousal support, which the judge held he was empowered to do on an interim order by s. 15.2(2) of the *Divorce Act.*

*Securing support where payor not a Canadian citizen* — *Droit de la famille - 1231*, [1989] R.D.F. 189 (C.S. Que.). Where, in response to the wife's claim for interim spousal and child support, the husband, who was not a Canadian citizen, threatened to leave the country, the court required him to guarantee 1 year's interim support by way of a bank note or suretyship in the amount of $10,000.

### Interim support — duration of interim support order

*Time-limited support awards are not appropriate in interim proceedings* — *D. (L.) c. D. (J.)* (9 juin 1993), no C.A. Québec 200-09-000044-930 (C.A. Que.).

*Order subject to 6-month review* — *Watson v. Watson*, 1992 CarswellSask 443, 107 Sask. R. 127 (Sask. Q.B.). Where the parties disputed the amount of the husband's earnings on the wife's interim support application, the award was made subject to a review in 6 months' time.

*Interim support until wife employed* — *Nord v. Nord*, 1986 CarswellMan 244, 42 Man. R. (2d) 50 (Man. Q.B.). The wife's award of interim maintenance was stated to continue only until such time as she obtained employment.

## Retroactive payment of interim support

*Where interim support has been awarded and there is no evidence that it did not meet the payee spouse's reasonable needs, it is improper to award retroactive lump sum support for the pre-trial period* — *Elliot v. Elliot*, 1993 CarswellOnt 348, 48 R.F.L. (3d) 237, 15 O.R. (3d) 265, 106 D.L.R. (4th) 609, 65 O.A.C. 241, [1993] O.J. No. 2308 (Ont. C.A.). Leave to appeal refused 1994 CarswellOnt 5818, 1994 CarswellOnt 5819, 3 R.F.L. (4th) 290 (note), 18 O.R. (3d) xvi (note), 112 D.L.R. (4th) vii (note), 175 N.R. 324 (note), 74 O.A.C. 159 (note), [1993] S.C.C.A. No. 522 (S.C.C.).

*Interpretation* — *Yaholnitsky v. Yaholnitsky*, 1992 CarswellSask 464, 105 Sask. R. 255, 32 W.A.C. 255 (Sask. C.A.). An interim support award made on July 3, 1992 granting support from July 1, 1992 was found not to constitute an improper retroactive award. The award was merely intended as payment for the month of July and all subsequent months.

*Retroactive support may be ordered on an interim basis* — *McCain v. McCain*, 2012 CarswellOnt 16853, 2012 ONSC 7344, 34 R.F.L. (7th) 82 (Ont. S.C.J.). The court relied on *Desrochers v. Tait*, 2008 CarswellOnt 8179, 70 R.F.L. (6th) 165, [2008] O.J. No. 5419 (Ont. S.C.J.), at para. 31; and *Turk v. Turk*, 2008 CarswellOnt 512, 50 R.F.L. (6th) 211, [2008] O.J. No. 397 (Ont. S.C.J.), at para. 65.

*Needs and means, retroactive interim support awarded* — *Lakhani v. Lakhani*, 2003 CarswellOnt 3928, 43 R.F.L. (5th) 125, [2003] O.J. No. 4041 (Ont. S.C.J.), additional reasons at 2003 CarswellOnt 3927, [2003] O.J. No. 4039 (Ont. S.C.J.). Where in the 3 years since the parties' separation, the husband had managed to increase his asset base substantially while the wife had been forced to liquidate investments to support herself and the children, retroactive interim spousal and child support was awarded.

*Where there is no compelling reason to do so, retroactive support will not be ordered on an interim motion* — *M. (T.I.) v. M. (T.L.)*, 2003 CarswellBC 3168, 2003 BCSC 1918, 1 R.F.L. (6th) 266, [2003] B.C.J. No. 2902 (B.C.S.C.).

*Claim for retroactive spousal support payments denied as husband's delay in making financial disclosure reasonable as finances complex — any shortfall by wife made up for by wife borrowng against equity in the family home* — *Volken v. Volken*, 2001 CarswellBC 1401, 2001 BCSC 970, 19 R.F.L. (5th) 205, [2001] B.C.T.C. 970, [2001] B.C.J. No. 1344 (B.C.S.C. [In Chambers]). The husband's annual income was found to be $2,000,000. The wife was not employed outside the home and had no income of her own. After the separation the husband made voluntary payments of $5,000 a month which reflected the relatively frugal lifestyle of the family before the separation. The wife's expenses after the separation exceeded these payments. She supplemented them by taking out a mortgage on her equity in the family home. The court found that after taking into account the child support obligation of $25,723 per month, the husband's after tax earnings would meet the needs of the wife and still leave him with more than enough for his own expenses. Exercising its discretion on the basis of the condition, means, needs, and other circumstances of each spouse in light of the objectives of spousal support orders described in s. 15.2 of the *Divorce Act*, the court ordered interim monthly spousal support of

$15,000 plus a lump sum payment of $10,000. The court refused to make the spousal support payments retroactive. Any order that might be made as to retroactivity would have the undesirable effect of redistributing capital, or awarding additional spousal support, under the guise of child support.

No retroactive interim support to take account of increase in the cost of living — Zander v. Zander, 1994 CarswellOnt 452, 8 R.F.L. (4th) 35, [1994] O.J. No. 4003 (Ont. Gen. Div.). The court refused the wife's request for retroactive interim support to reimburse her for the fact that her interim support award had not been indexed to the cost of living. As she had not previously appealed or sought a variation of the award, an adjustment at the trial stage would be gratuitous.

## Interim support pending appeal

An order for interim support pending an appeal to the Supreme Court of Canada on a support issue will only be made in exceptional circumstances — B. (G.) c. G. (L.), 1994 CarswellQue 130, , [1995] 3 S.C.R. 367, 165 N.R. 237, 61 Q.A.C. 179, [1994] S.C.J. No. 114 (S.C.C.).

An application by the wife for a stay of an order which varied an interim support order pending appeal of the order was refused as the court was of the opinion that any damage which might result from the variation order was not irreparable — Armstrong v. Armstrong, 1998 CarswellBC 2172, 112 B.C.A.C. 186, 182 W.A.C. 186, [1998] B.C.J. No. 2309 (B.C.C.A. [In Chambers]).

The Ontario Court of Appeal held that the interlocutory order allowing the motion for interim support to proceed should be stayed pending the determination of a constitutional issue under appeal, since if the applicant were successful in her appeal, there would be no basis in law for proceeding with the interim support hearing — M. v. H., 1996 CarswellOnt 595, 20 R.F.L. (4th) 278 (Ont. C.A. [In Chambers]). It would be wasteful to proceed if the process was unnecessary and it is not certain that the applicant would be able to recover the costs if she were successful on appeal. The potential prejudice to the applicant outweighs any potential benefit to the respondent if the interim support hearing proceeded.

## Interim support pending re-hearing

Interim support pending re-hearing — Sadler v. Sadler, 1999 CarswellBC 1069, 1999 BCCA 335, 1999 BCCA 304, 46 R.F.L. (4th) 368 (B.C.C.A.). Where the appellate court determined that the issues at trial on an application to vary spousal support had not been satisfactorily adjudicated, a new hearing was ordered pending which the husband was required to pay $1,000 monthly as interim spousal support.

## Other

Interim orders are reviewable at trial, even when they were not appealed — S. (A.K.) v. L. (K.J.), 2014 CarswellAlta 514, 2014 ABQB 188 (Alta. Q.B.). The trial judge found that the interim spousal support orders were based on incomplete income information and that, despite the fact that the recipient wife did not appeal the orders, the general rule was that the "trial judge will revisit and adjust the amount of support provided for in interim orders, recognizing that such orders are often made on incomplete information and prior to full disclosure" (para. 77).

**Practice Tip — Spousal Support on an Interim Motion:** At the interim stage, a motions judge will place strong emphasis on the respective "needs and means" of the parties, within the context of the provisions of s. 15.2 of the *Divorce Act* and the factors set out at s. 15.2(6). The analysis of these factors at the interim stage on the basis of affidavit evidence cannot be fully carried out, at least in the absence of uncontested affidavit evidence. At this preliminary stage, the function of a motions court judge is to consider the current needs of the moving party during the period of the order and then to determine whether the moving party requires interim relief and whether the responding party has the means to provide that interim relief. Family law counsel should work with his or her client to prepare a properly sworn Financial Statement including a detailed current monthly budget showing expenses and deficits that can be fully supported, as well as a proposed budget. Questioning of the parties should be completed and undertakings answered before the support motion is adjudicated. When representing a self-employed payor, obtaining at least a draft report prepared by a qualified business valuator of his or her income for support purposes will be critical. A motions judge will place significant weight on the draft report, as well as on both parties' sworn financial statements. When representing a support recipient, counsel should be able to explain why the recipient is not working (if that is the case) and provide documentary proof of his or her efforts to retrain or find employment, such as job applications, a current curriculum vitae, etc. This will be less important in cases involving a long-term marriage. The *Spousal Support Advisory Guidelines* are particularly useful at the interim stage, which is now dominated by a needs-and-means analysis. A motions court judge with a lengthy court docket will want a quick, easily calculated support amount, knowing that more precise adjustments can be made at trial. It is important that counsel provide the court with properly completed SSAG calculations and be able to explain whether or not the ranges of support under SSAG are appropriate based on the needs and means of the parties within the context of the factors set out in the *Divorce Act.*

Gary S. Joseph,, Partner, & Michael J. Stangarone, Partner, MacDonald & Partners LLP

## 4.3 Indefinite Support

Meaning of "permanent". *Jakob v. Jakob*, 2010 CarswellBC 599, 2010 BCCA 136, 80 R.F.L. (6th) 264, 6 B.C.L.R. (5th) 212 (B.C.C.A.), additional reasons at 2010 CarswellBC 1530, 2010 BCCA 309, 82 R.F.L. (6th) 95, 289 B.C.A.C. 50, 489 W.A.C. 50 (B.C.C.A.). The court considered the effect of a support order that was "permanent". The Court stated, at para. 35:

> Before the introduction of the *Spousal Support Advisory Guidelines* ("*SSAG*") in 2005, the use of the term "permanent" for a spousal support order typically referred to a final order. "Permanent" in that context meant the opposite of an interim order. A permanent support order was a final order without duration. This was in contrast to a final support order for a fixed or time-limited duration. With the introduction of the SSAG, the use of the word "permanent" was replaced by the term "indefinite" for a final order where the duration is not specified.

The court was of the opinion that whether a final spousal support order is described as "permanent" or "indefinite", the order is subject to variation upon establishing a material change of circumstances.

Where the SSAG suggest an "indefinite" order, a date for review or termination will not be fixed — *Fielding v. Fielding*, 2014 CarswellOnt 4752, 2014 ONSC 2272 (Ont. S.C.J.). The parties were married for 17 years and had three children. The wife was disabled and was entitled to compensatory and non-compensatory spousal support. The judge noted that based on the length of the marriage, the SSAG suggested an indefinite order. Consequently, the judge declined to set a date for termination or review of the order, although he remarked that the order was open to change based on a material change in circumstances.

# CHAPTER 5

# FACTORS

This chapter is divided into the following subsections:

## 5.1 General

Section 15.2(4) describes the factors which a court must consider before making an original spousal support order. The first clause requires consideration of the "condition, means, needs and other circumstances" of the parties. The three subsections of s. 15.2(4) identify three factors which are are among the relevant circumstances:

(a) the length of time the spouses cohabited;

(b) the functions performed by each spouse during cohabitation; and

(c) any order, agreement or arrangement relating to support of either spouse.

The "factors" are closely intertwined with the "objectives" identified by s. 15.2(6). Both *Moge* and *Bracklow* held that the factors must be considered "against the background" of the objectives, and that the relative weights given to the various factors depends on the case. The factors that a court must consider on a variation of a spousal support order are different from those on an original order. Section 17 (4.1) of the *Divorce Act* provides that a court, before making a variation of a spousal support order, "shall satisfy itself that a change in the condition, means, needs or other circumstances of either former spouse has occurred since the making of the spousal support order or the last variation order made in respect of that order, and, in making the variation order, the court shall take that change into consideration."

*Conditions, means, needs, and other circumstances may require compensation through spousal support — Bracklow v. Bracklow,* 1999 CarswellBC 532, 1999 CarswellBC 533, 44 R.F.L. (4th) 1, [1999] 1 S.C.R. 420, [1999] 8 W.W.R. 740, 63 B.C.L.R. (3d) 77, 169 D.L.R. (4th) 577, 236 N.R. 79, 120 B.C.A.C. 211, 196 W.A.C. 211, [1999] S.C.J. No. 14 (S.C.C.). The requirement to consider the "condition, means, needs and other circumstances" of the spouses is one of the provisions in the *Divorce Act* that gives rise to the compensatory basis for support. This may encompass lack of ability to support oneself due to foregoing career opportunities during the marriage.

*1985* Divorce Act *requires broader spectrum of considerations than predecessor statutes —* Moge v. Moge, 1992 CarswellMan 143, 1992 CarswellMan 222, REJB 1992-67141, 43 R.F.L. (3d) 345, [1992] 3 S.C.R. 813, [1993] 1 W.W.R. 481, 99 D.L.R. (4th) 456, 145 N.R. 1, 81 Man. R. (2d) 161, 30 W.A.C. 161, [1993] R.D.F. 168, [1992] S.C.J. No. 107 (S.C.C.). The principles embodied in the current *Divorce Act* engage the courts in a different type of analysis than that which was required under the 1970 *Divorce Act* when considering the question of support. The most significant change is a shift away from "means and needs" as the exclusive test to a set of objectives which require the courts to accommodate a much wider spectrum of considerations. This change recognizes that the economic variables of marriage breakdown do not lend themselves to the application of only one objective. "All four of the objectives defined in the Act must be taken into account when spousal support is claimed or an order for spousal support is sought to be varied. No single objective is paramount."

*"While the objectives of the variation order are virtually identical to those in s. 15.2 dealing with an initial support order, the factors to be considered in ss. 17(4.1) and 15.2(4) are significantly different — s. 17(4.1) sets out 'a change in the . . . circumstances' of the parties as the sole factor" —* Droit de la famille - 091889, 2011 CarswellQue 13698, 2011 CarswellQue 13699, 2011 SCC 64, 6 R.F.L. (7th) 1, [2011] 3 S.C.R. 775, 339 D.L.R. (4th) 624, 424 N.R. 341, [2011] S.C.J. No. 64, [2011] A.C.S. No. 64 (S.C.C.), reversing 2010 CarswellQue 3636, 2010 CarswellQue 15612, 2010 QCCA 793, EYB 2010-172837, [2010] R.D.F. 235 (C.A. Que.), varied 2009 CarswellQue 7646, 2009 QCCS 3389, EYB 2009-162093 (C.S. Que.). In an initial application for spousal support under s. 15.2(4)(c), the court is directed to consider among other factors "any order, agreement or arrangement relating to support of either spouse". Subsection 17(4.1) makes no reference to agreements and instead just requires a court to be satisfied "that a change in the condition, means, needs or other circumstances of either former spouse has occurred" since the making of the prior order or the last variation of that order. See **Chapter 10, section 10.3 Variation — Change in Circumstances — Meaning**, for a detailed discussion of the case.

*Relevant factors can only be put in front of a judge when they have occurred, which was after the retirement of the payor in this case —* Vaughan v. Vaughan, 2014 CarswellNB 41, 2014 CarswellNB 42, 2014 NBCA 6, 44 R.F.L. (7th) 20, 372 D.L.R. (4th) 579, 415 N.B.R. (2d) 286, 1076 A.P.R. 286, [2014] N.B.J. No. 35 (N.B.C.A.). The parties separated in 2010 after 38 years of marriage. The husband wished to retire and sought an advance ruling on what spousal support after his retirement would be. The trial judge varied support but found that some post-retirement income should be imputed to the husband. The Court of Appeal held that the trial judge improperly made an order prior to the husband's actual retirement. Although the husband had the intention to retire, until he retired important information concerning the factors to be considered could not be truly known. The date of retirement was unknown at the time of the trial, and there was no evidence regarding post-retirement earning capacity. The decision was overturned, and the pre-retirement spousal support amount was reinstated until such time as the husband retired.

*A review must fully consider factors in s. 15.2, such as the parties' respective contributions to the relationship, means and needs —* Morck v. Morck, 2013 CarswellBC 1032, 2013 BCCA 186, 28 R.F.L. (7th) 279, 44 B.C.L.R. (5th) 235, 337 B.C.A.C. 125, 576 W.A.C. 125, [2013] B.C.J. No. 803 (B.C.C.A.). The parties separated in 2005 after almost 25 years of marriage. The wife had mental health issues that were well known to the husband. In 2006, the court awarded the wife support, reviewable after 2 years. The wife applied for a review, and the husband appealed the decision. The Court of Appeal found that the trial judge had treated the wife's application for review as an application for variation and noted that the review must be based on the parties' present circumstances rather than those of the original order. The trial judge had not adequately considered the parties' present circumstances, and the Court of Appeal sent the case back down to trial.

*On a variation application, it is an error for the judge to consider the factors under s. 15.2(4) as they are static as of the initial order for support and the court hearing the variation application should treat the first order as correct at the time it was made and confine its role to examining whether subsequent changes justify variation under s. 17 of the* Divorce Act — *Aspe v. Aspe,* 2010 CarswellBC 3077, 2010 BCCA 508, 89 R.F.L. (6th) 245, 11 B.C.L.R. (5th) 309, 327 D.L.R. (4th) 231, 294 B.C.A.C. 290, 498 W.A.C. 290 (B.C.C.A.).

*Although there is no legal obligation to support a sibling, if the parties supported the sibling during the marriage, this expense can form part of the recipient spouse's needs — Elgner v. Elgner,* 2009 CarswellOnt 7702, 85 R.F.L. (6th) 51, [2009] O.J. No. 5269 (Ont. S.C.J.), leave to appeal refused 2010 CarswellOnt 1640, 2010 ONSC 1578, 85 R.F.L. (6th) 62, 99 O.R. (3d) 687, 267 O.A.C. 1, [2010] O.J. No. 1139 (Ont. Div. Ct.), additional reasons at 2010 CarswellOnt 3918, 2010 ONSC 2399, 85 R.F.L. (6th) 71 (Ont. Div. Ct.), affirmed 2010 CarswellOnt 6860, 2010 ONSC 3512, 92 R.F.L. (6th) 106, 103 O.R. (3d) 588, 324 D.L.R. (4th) 277, 268 O.A.C. 267 (Ont. Div. Ct.), affirmed 2011 CarswellOnt 5673, 2011 ONCA 483, 5 R.F.L. (7th) 1, 105 O.R. (3d) 721, 336 D.L.R. (4th) 159, 282 O.A.C. 28 (Ont. C.A.), leave to appeal refused 2011 CarswellOnt 12421, 2011 CarswellOnt 12421 (S.C.C.). After the parties' separation, the wife used her capital to purchase a condominium for her ailing sister and continued to pay for her sister's medical expenses in the amount of $6,444 per month and her father's expenses. In ordering that this was a legitimate expense, the court noted that, "While one could say that the wife has no legal obligation to support her sister or assist her father financially, while the parties were married, the husband paid for the support of the sister, as the wife did not work. Secondly, the wife has a moral obligation to now continue that support rather than leave the sister in abject poverty."

*Evidence relating to financial circumstances at the time of the original order is required for a variation hearing — H. (L.A.) v. H. (A.M.),* 2014 CarswellBC 378, 2014 BCSC 241 (B.C.S.C.). The parties were married for approximately 6 years prior to separation and had three children. The husband sought to terminate spousal support, which had been set in 2009 pursuant to a consent order. The judge held that insufficient evidence regarding financial status at the time of the original order, as well as currently, prevented him from determining whether there had been a material change in circumstances.

*Factors considered in a s. 15.2 order and a s. 17.4 order varying support are different, and a variation order makes no specific reference to consideration of previous agreements or orders — Kordyban v. Kordyban,* 2013 CarswellAlta 1656, 2013 ABQB 500 (Alta. Q.B.).

*Section 15.2(4) factors are applicable in an application to vary interim spousal support — Clark-Smith v. Smith,* 2013 CarswellNB 104, 2013 CarswellNB 105, 2013 NBQB 74, 401 N.B.R. (2d) 206, 1041 A.P.R. 206 (N.B.Q.B.). The wife sought to vary interim spousal support. The judge held that factors under s. 15.2(4) were applicable in an application to vary interim spousal support, but that the husband had not met the onus of showing a material change of circumstances as required by s. 17.

*Factors considered when the original order was made were still relevant at a variation proceeding — MacNeil v. MacNeil,* 2013 CarswellNS 23, 2013 NSSC 23 (N.S.S.C.). The parties cohabited for 28 years and separated in 2007. The wife sought a variation of spousal support. The divorce decision allowed the husband not to pay spousal support for 2.5 years because of the unequal division of the matrimonial debt, on the condition he maintain the wife on his health insurance. The husband's income had also increased. The parties had a traditional marriage, and the wife had significant health problems which required additional insurance. Spousal support was awarded at the top end of the SSAG range after an examination of the roles played during the marriage, means and needs of the parties, ability to work, economic consequences of the marriage and its breakdown, which were considered when the original order was made.

*A judge will consider the relevant factors in determining support irrespective of whether the original order was based on compensatory or needs-based support* — Morigeau v. Moorey, 2013 CarswellBC 3177, 2013 BCSC 1923, 40 R.F.L. (7th) 223 (B.C.S.C.). The husband sought to terminate support. The parties were married for 18 years, cohabited for 20 years in total and had two adult children. Since separation, the wife had begun cohabiting with a new partner, who did not pay rent. The judge found that, irrespective of the spousal support model on which the original order was based (compensatory, needs-based or a combination), the variation analysis will be "a matter of applying the relevant factors and striking the balance that best achieves justice in the particular case".

*Conditions, means and needs to be evaluated at time of order* — Epp v. Epp, 1998 CarswellBC 1346, 40 R.F.L. (4th) 137 (B.C.S.C. [In Chambers]). "In cases where need is demonstrated as a result of the marriage breakdown, the condition, needs, means and other circumstances of the parties at the time of the maintenance order must be given emphasis."

*Needs and means analysis* — Ormerod v. Ormerod, 1990 CarswellOnt 270, 27 R.F.L. (3d) 225, [1990] O.J. No. 1035 (Ont. U.F.C.). In practice, the quantum of support has generally been determined by looking at both spouses' present needs and means.

## 5.2 Means and Needs of Party from Whom Support is Sought

The first clause of s. 15.2(4) states that the "means" and "needs" of both spouses must be taken into account. While always relevant, these considerations are more important to the needs-based purpose of spousal support than they are to its compensatory purpose. The central logic of compensatory support does not depend on the support applicant being in need or on the respondent having a surplus. By contrast, an award of needs-based support will not be made unless it is demonstrated that the applicant is in need and the respondent has the means to pay.

The income of a party is the most important, but not the only, component of his or her "means." Assets and debts are also relevant. For case law regarding the impact of the division of pensions or other assets on spousal support, please see s. 9.5 of this volume. An individual's income can vary substantially depending on the choices made in calculating it. For example, the word "income" could mean gross or net of tax, could include or exclude imputed income, and could include or exclude non-monetary benefits received from an employer. Section 15.2 of the *Divorce Act* does not set out for the court a matter of calculating income for the purpose of spousal support. However, for the purpose of child support, s. 15.1(3) does incorporate, by reference, the *Federal Child Support Guidelines*, P.C. 1997-469 ("FCSG"), which provide a complete code for calculating income. The calculation of income under the FCSG is dealt with comprehensively in MacDonald and Wilton, *Child Support Guidelines Law and Practice, 2nd Ed.*

Canadian judges usually rely on the FCSG to calculate income for the purpose of spousal support as well. The key difference is that, in most cases, only the income of the child support payor must be calculated under the FCSG. In spousal support law, by contrast, the incomes of both spouses are relevant and must therefore be calculated. The *Spousal Support Advisory Guidelines* also rely on the FCSG method for calculating income, although there are a few minor differences (see Part II, s. 1.3 of this volume).

An individual's income and assets may not accurately reflect his or her "means." If the individual has new family obligations (especially to children who are not the children of the other party), he or she may have more modest means than his or her financial position suggests.

However, cohabiting with an income-earning individual can also augment a party's means. If a party has the potential to improve his or her financial position, then his or her means may be more substantial than his or her financial position indicates. A party who is voluntarily under-employed or unemployed may have income imputed for the purpose of determining spousal support, even if there is no evidence that he deliberately reduced earnings in order to strengthen his spousal support case. The same is true of any decision taken by a party which results in his or her income being lower than it might otherwise be. A payor's decision to retire may be scrutinized and if it is found to be premature the amount of support may be relatively high for his actual post-retirement income.

An important issue is whether a spouse can share in post-separation increases in the other spouse's income. Factors that seem to be significant include whether there is a great discrepancy in the parties' incomes shortly after separation, whether the payee spouse contributed to the payor spouse's acquisition of employment skills or credentials during cohabitation, and whether the parties jointly made decisions during cohabitation which benefited the payor spouse's financial interests. Sharing of post-separation income is also more likely in a long-term marriage. See subsection below under 5.2.

*Pension already included in the division of property* — *Boston v. Boston*, 2001 CarswellOnt 2432, 2001 CarswellOnt 2433, 2001 SCC 43, REJB 2001-25002, 17 R.F.L. (5th) 4, [2001] 2 S.C.R. 413, 28 C.C.P.B. 17, 201 D.L.R. (4th) 1, 271 N.R. 248, 149 O.A.C. 50, 2001 C.E.B. & P.G.R. 8385 (headnote only), [2001] S.C.J. No. 45 (S.C.C.). Where the capitalized value of the payor's pension has been included in the division of property between the parties, it would be inequitable to continue support out of the payor's pension income. To do so would allow the payee to reap benefits from the payor's pension twice, or permit "double recovery". To avoid this result, the focus should be on the portion of the pension-holding spouse's income and assets that were not part of the equalization or division process.

*Where a payor earns less income because of personal preferences rather than factors beyond his control, no change in circumstances will be found* — *Hepburn v. Hepburn*, 2013 CarswellBC 2592, 2013 BCCA 383, 48 B.C.L.R. (5th) 251, 34 R.F.L. (7th) 267, 344 B.C.A.C. 6, 587 W.A.C. 6 (B.C.C.A.). A husband sought to vary a consent order for spousal support on the basis that his income had decreased. His income had decreased because of more time being spent on media opportunities, which were not lucrative, rather than on his primary occupation as a physician. He had changed clinics at the request of his employer, which led to reduced hours. The chambers judge found that, while the husband was free to pursue these non-remunerative opportunities, he was not able to use this as a basis for a reduction in spousal support. It was open to him to attempt to work more hours as a physician; and the reduction in income was as a result of his preferences, rather than circumstances. The chambers judge also found the relocation was voluntary. The original order was indefinite, and the wife was reliant on the support as there was no reasonable expectation she would return to the workforce and attain even partial self-sufficiency. The Court of Appeal found that there was evidence to support the chambers judge finding that the husband had reduced his hours as a physician to accommodate his unpaid media initiatives and upheld the finding that there was no material change in circumstances. However, the judge found the husband did lose some income through factors beyond his control, and this was found to be a material change sufficient to recalculate support.

*On appeal by the wife, spousal support awarded to the wife as trial judge had failed to fully address the impact of the allocation of family assets and debts on parties' means and needs since the wife's failed business was a family debt and the husband's business was a family asset* — *in addition, husband's non-disclosure of his means should not provide a way to avoid support obligation* — *Gonabady-Namadon v. Mohammadzadeh*, 2009 CarswellBC 2767, 2009 BCCA 448, 74 R.F.L. (6th) 1, 98 B.C.L.R. (4th) 23, 277 B.C.A.C. 48, 469 W.A.C. 48 (B.C.C.A.). The parties married in 1993 in Iran and had 2 children. They moved to Canada in 2001 and separated in 2006. The husband had a successful business and the wife had become a doctor in Iran. She requalified in Canada, but the medical clinic she established in Canada failed. The husband returned to Iran and the children remained with the wife. At trial, the husband, who did not make full disclosure, was imputed to have an income of $250,000 and the claim of the wife, who had an income of $156,000, was dismissed. On appeal, the income imputed to the husband was $350,000 and the wife was awarded spousal support of $2,300 a month for 6 years.

*Effect of second spouse's unemployment on support for first family* — Fisher v. Fisher, 2008 CarswellOnt 43, 2008 ONCA 11, 47 R.F.L. (6th) 235, 288 D.L.R. (4th) 513, 88 O.R. (3d) 241, 232 O.A.C. 213, [2008] O.J. No. 38 (Ont. C.A.). Where there is no evidence that a payor spouse's obligations to his first family would impoverish his second family, his endorsement of his second wife's preference not to work outside the home cannot be relied upon to reduce his support obligations to his first family.

*Undeclared income to be included in income for spousal support purposes* — Sipos v. Sipos, 2007 CarswellOnt 1084, 2007 ONCA 126, 277 D.L.R. (4th) 193, 222 O.A.C. 78, [2007] O.J. No. 711 (Ont. C.A.), additional reasons at 2007 CarswellOnt 2317, 2007 ONCA 293 (Ont. C.A.). Where the payor spouse received undeclared income that did not reduce his disability benefits, the undeclared moneys should be included in his income.

*Income from damage settlement, inheritance, CPP and private disability insurance is income for purposes of support* — Redman v. Korchinski, 2006 CarswellMan 436, 2006 MBCA 149, 33 R.F.L. (6th) 36, 277 D.L.R. (4th) 427, [2007] 2 W.W.R. 611, 212 Man. R. (2d) 90, 389 W.A.C. 90 (Man. C.A.). The husband who had suffered a permanent brain injury and was unable to work was still required to pay spousal support. He had an annual income of $77,000 resulting from a settlement, a bequest from his father's estate, CPP and private disability insurance, and accordingly had the ability to pay.

*Payor unemployed but employable, responsible to provide support* — Wyman v. Wyman, 1999 CarswellNS 49, 1999 NSCA 32, 49 R.F.L. (4th) 447, [1999] N.S.J. No. 38 (N.S.C.A.). When the 60-year-old husband's position had been eliminated he applied for and received a substantial reduction in the spousal support payable by him. The wife, whose only means of income after the dissolution of the parties' 30-year marriage was spousal support, successfully appealed. The husband, despite his age, still had marketable skills which could deliver a significant income. He had also remarried and his new wife, who was employed, could contribute to household expenses. The trial judge had erred in placing too much responsibility on the wife to obtain employment and not enough responsibility on the husband.

*Impact of subsequent family on ability to pay* — Wyman v. Wyman, supra. When the 60-year-old husband's position had been eliminated he applied for and received a substantial reduction in the spousal support payable by him. The wife, whose only means of income after the dissolution of the parties' 30-year marriage was spousal support, successfully appealed. The husband, despite his age, still had marketable skills which could deliver a significant income. He had also remarried and his new wife, who was employed, could contribute to household expenses. The trial judge had erred in placing too much responsibility on the wife to obtain employment and not enough responsibility on the husband.

*A party's health issues must be considered if a court assumes future income for that party* — Butler v. Butler, 1998 CarswellNB 131, 37 R.F.L. (4th) 226, 195 N.B.R. (2d) 156, 499 A.P.R. 156, [1998] N.B.J. No. 75 (N.B.C.A.). The wife appealed a spousal support order of $800 per month for 8 months and $400 per month thereafter. The lower court was of the opinion that when she received her share of the matrimonial home, she ought to be able to increase her earnings from virtually nothing to $15,000 a year. The appellate court held that the evidence disclosed that the wife had physical disabilities, mild depression and suffered from alcohol abuse, problems which made it difficult to project that her earnings would increase to $15,000 a year.

*Payor cohabits with new partner and stays home with children — ability to pay support to be based on income payor would earn if she returned to the work force, not on a portion of cohabitant's income — Lauderdale v. Lauderdale*, 1996 CarswellAlta 43, 21 R.F.L. (4th) 17, 180 A.R. 81, [1996] A.J. No. 53 (Alta. Q.B.), reversed on other grounds 1997 CarswellAlta 448, 29 R.F.L. (4th) 34 , 200 A.R. 198, 146 W.A.C. 198, [1997] A.J. No. 499 (Alta. C.A.). Where the wife had entered into a common-law relationship which permitted her financially to remain at home with the children rather than seek employment, the court found it inappropriate to attribute to her a portion of her common-law spouse's income in determining her ability to pay child support. In the circumstances, it was more appropriate to attribute to her the income she would likely earn were she to re-enter the workforce.

*Payor does not avoid support obligations by voluntarily leaving employment — Cross v. Cross*, 1994 CarswellSask 40, 3 R.F.L. (4th) 276, 119 Sask. R. 241 (Sask. Q.B.), additional reasons at 1994 CarswellSask 43, 4 R.F.L. (4th) 162, 119 Sask. R. 241 at 244 (Sask. Q.B.), affirmed 1995 CarswellSask 475, 16 R.F.L. (4th) 277, 134 Sask. R. 74, 101 W.A.C. 74 (Sask. C.A.). The husband could not rely upon the fact that he had voluntarily left his employment as a means of avoiding spousal support obligations.

*Definition of "means" — Marchak v. Fleury*, 1995 CarswellMan 226, 15 R.F.L. (4th) 458, 102 Man. R. (2d) 121, 93 W.A.C. 121, [1995] M.J. No. 263 (Man. C.A.). "Means" includes not only actual income earned but also the ability to earn it.

*Definition of "means" — Muirhead v. Muirhead*, 1995 CarswellBC 260, 14 R.F.L. (4th) 276, 6 B.C.L.R. (3d) 229, 59 B.C.A.C. 144, 98 W.A.C. 144, [1995] B.C.J. No. 1088 (B.C.C.A.). The term "means" as it is used in s. 15(5) of the *Divorce Act* includes not only what the parties are earning but also what they can "reasonably" expect to earn. The determination of what is "reasonable" is based upon the age, health and the employment prospects of the parties in the area in which they live.

*Compensation for career interruption limited by other spouse's ability to pay — Elliot v. Elliot*, 1993 CarswellOnt 348, 48 R.F.L. (3d) 237, 106 D.L.R. (4th) 609, 15 O.R. (3d) 265, 65 O.A.C. 241, [1993] O.J. No. 2308 (Ont. C.A.). Leave to appeal refused 1994 CarswellOnt 5818, 1994 CarswellOnt 5819, 18 O.R. (3d) xvi (note), 112 D.L.R. (4th) vii (note), 3 R.F.L. (4th) 290 (note), 175 N.R. 324 (note), 74 O.A.C. 159 (note), [1993] S.C.C.A. No. 522 (S.C.C.). Section 15(7)(a) [now s. 15.2(6)(a)] of the *Divorce Act* does not provide a right to full compensation through spousal support for the economic disadvantage that arises from a marriage or its breakdown, and any recovery is limited by the payor's ability to pay.

*Absence from workforce — retraining — payor's bankruptcy — entitled to spousal support — Mears v. Mears*, 1992 CarswellMan 406, 82 Man. R. (2d) 156 (Man. Q.B.), affirmed 1992 CarswellMan 191, 83 Man. R. (2d) 129, 36 W.A.C. 129 (Man. C.A.). The husband, despite his bankruptcy, was ordered to pay spousal support to the wife. Through the first half of the parties' 13-year marriage, the wife had remained in the home and cared for the children, allowing the husband to qualify as a teacher. Since separation the wife had made reasonable efforts to find employment but was hampered by her limited skills and the unfavourable economic climate. Her plans to return to school were reasonable in the circumstances.

*Payor's potential income from investments to be considered in assessing support — Robinson v. Robinson*, 1985 CarswellOnt 333, 49 R.F.L. (2d) 43 [1985] O.J. No. 192, (Ont. C.A.). The fact that the husband had a substantial investment portfolio was taken into account in determining the quantum of maintenance he was required to pay, despite the fact that the portfolio produced little income. The husband had an obligation to arrange his affairs so that the portfolio did produce income for his family.

*Definition of "means"* — *Osborne v. Osborne*, 1973 CarswellSask 31, 14 R.F.L. 61, [1973] S.J. No. 236 (Sask. Q.B.), at 68 [R.F.L.], varied 1973 CarswellSask 38, 23 R.F.L. 358 (Sask. C.A.). See also *Raffin v. Raffin*, 1971 CarswellOnt 114, 5 R.F.L. 274, [1972] 1 O.R. 173, 22 D.L.R. (2d) 497 (Ont. C.A). "The word 'means' includes all of a person's pecuniary resources, his capital assets, his income from his employment or his earning capacity, and any other sources from which he receives gains or benefits," per Disbery J.

*Tax-free disability income should be included in a consideration of the circumstances, means and needs of each spouse* — *Vaughan v. Vaughan*, 2014 CarswellNB 41, 2014 CarswellNB 42, 2014 NBCA 6, 44 R.F.L. (7th) 20, 372 D.L.R. (4th) 579, 415 N.B.R. (2d) 286, 1076 A.P.R. 286, [2014] N.B.J. No. 35 (N.B.C.A.). The parties separated in 2010 after 38 years of marriage. The husband wished to retire and sought an advance ruling on what spousal support after his retirement would be. The husband appealed the trial judge's decision to include his veteran's disability payments in his income. The Court of Appeal held that, after considering the broad policy objectives of the *Divorce Act*, tax-free disability payments should be considered when determining the "condition, means, needs and other circumstances of each spouse" for the purposes of determining spousal support.

*The husband had an income that was approximately $80,000 higher than that of the wife, and despite her superior capital position spousal support was ordered to continue* — *Holman v. Holman*, 2013 CarswellOnt 16472, 2013 ONSC 6988 (Ont. S.C.J.). The parties were married for 19 years prior to separation in 2002. They had two adult daughters. The wife had been a stay-at-home mother during the marriage. She had received $300,000 from an inheritance after separation, which the judge found must be considered as part of her assets and means under the *Family Law Act*. The judge also found that her means were equal or superior to those she enjoyed during the marriage. She had attained self-sufficiency. Spousal support was not terminated because it had been paid for 10 years and the husband had the means to pay.

*Means and needs that differ considerably from those anticipated by a previous order will be considered in a variation application* — *Peever v. Peever*, 2013 CarswellBC 486, 2013 BCSC 299 (B.C.S.C.). The husband sought to vary spousal support and extinguish support arrears because he was previously ordered responsible for the matrimonial debt, which was far higher than anticipated by the previous order. The wife did not oppose variation and recognized the husband's limited means in oral argument. Spousal support and arrears were terminated.

*Spousal support was to continue until the recipient wife had obtained self-sufficiency anticipated 4 years after a 20-year marriage when there was no evidence the husband could not afford to pay. This was consistent with the parties' previous agreement* — *C. (M.S.) v. C. (T.L.)*, 2013 CarswellNS 885, 2013 NSSC 378, 337 N.S.R. (2d) 177, 1067 A.P.R. 177 (N.S.S.C.). The parties had concluded a separation agreement, which provided for spousal support at below the Guidelines range and review at any time without showing a material change in circumstances. The parties were married for 20 years. The judge found that the wife was entitled to compensatory support, which was consistent with the original agreement for spousal support. The wife projected she would be self-sufficient within 4 years of separation, and spousal support was ordered to continue until that time. There was no evidence that the husband did not have the means to pay support.

*The principle against double recovery regarding pension income does not apply where the wife has pressing need and only a small portion of the pension was equalized* — *McKay v. Adams*, 2013 CarswellMan 555, 2013 MBQB 236, 298 Man. R. (2d) 97 (Man. Q.B.). The parties were married for 19 years. In 2010, the husband earned $70,500 (or $5,875 per month), and the wife earned no income apart from disability benefits. The husband had transferred a part of his pension to the wife as a result of equalization. In 2010, the court awarded the wife $1,000 per month in spousal support for eight years, which was below the low end of the SSAG ($1,233 to

$1,644 for nine to ten years) in terms of both amount and duration. In 2013, the husband retired at the age of 59, and his sole source of income became his pension, which was $2,377 per month. The husband brought a motion to reduce his spousal support obligation to $200 a month. The wife argued that the husband had no reason to retire early, that he knew she was counting on his support due to her disability, and that she was entitled to that support in view of their 19-year marriage. The wife sought support for an additional five years when she would be able to access her investment capital. Because of the transfer of a portion of the husband's pension, there was potentially an issue with "double recovery" (where the recipient spouse benefits from a pension as both an asset and income), which is generally not permitted. The wife had a clear need for support, she had invested the pension but could not yet access the principal, and only 21% of the husband's pension had been equalized. The court awarded the wife continued support.

*Support was terminated when the payor had reasonably retired without intention to thwart spousal support. The payor did not have means to pay large arrears* — Yerex v. Yerex, 2012 CarswellBC 2356, 2012 BCSC 1181 (B.C.S.C. [In Chambers]). The husband sought to terminate spousal support retroactively. The parties were married for 26 years prior to separation and had no children. In 2002, they entered into a consent order which was neither enforced nor abided by the payor. The wife registered the separation agreement with the enforcement agency in 2011, by which time some $49,000 of arrears had accumulated. The judge found that the accrual of arrears constituted a material change of circumstances and that the husband had made the decision to retire without knowledge of the wife's intention to enforce the consent order. The husband had limited income and no accumulated assets, and the judge found he did not have the means to pay the arrears or ongoing support. Arrears were reduced to $6,000 and were payable periodically in a step-down arrangement.

*Where no significant economic reliance had been created by a short-term marriage and the payor has no earning capacity, spousal support will terminate* — G. (C.A.) v. G. (S.), 2012 CarswellAlta 1619, 2012 ABQB 529, 24 R.F.L. (7th) 461, 70 Alta. L.R. (5th) 388, [2013] 2 W.W.R. 773, 548 A.R. 226 (Alta. Q.B.). The husband sought, *inter alia*, to terminate or reduce spousal support and spousal support arrears. The parties separated in 2001. The husband had been involved in a motor vehicle accident which was found to have reduced his ability to earn income. The judge considered the factors in s. 15.2(4) in determining that ongoing spousal support should be reduced to zero. The parties had a very short marriage of less than 2 years. The wife did not become economically dependent on the husband during cohabitation because the husband was unwilling or unable to work at that time and the wife was responsible for supporting the family. However, the judge found that the wife was entitled to compensatory support on the basis that she did not receive adequate compensation for her economic efforts given that she was also responsible for childcare. However, since the husband had no capacity to earn income and his income was under the $20,000 floor of the SSAG, support for her was terminated.

*Time until retirement was considered when determining means and needs of the parties* — M. (P.R.) v. M. (B.J.), 2012 CarswellBC 3748, 2012 BCSC 1795 (B.C.S.C.). The parties were married for 23 years and had four children. The wife sought spousal support. The wife had received significant assets of over $4 million through the division of property. The parties were found to have had a traditional marriage in which the wife devoted herself to child and home responsibilities during years critical to her professional prospects and the husband built a business. The wife was found to be entitled to compensatory support to reflect the affluent lifestyle the parties enjoyed. The husband had 10 years until retirement, and the judge found his income would likely increase, whereas the wife's income was unlikely to increase based on the role she had played in the marriage.

*Where a payor's income is reduced after involuntary retirement, the prudence of the payor's investments will not be considered in a means analysis under s. 17 but rather economic implications will be determined* — Star v. Bolster, 2012 CarswellOnt 15990, 2012 ONSC 4744 (Ont. S.C.J.). The husband sought to change the spousal support provisions of a 1999 order. The parties were married for 39 years prior to separation. Post-separation, they concluded Minutes of Settlement which were incorporated into a consent order. The husband's income subsequently increased exponentially and then plummeted as a result of his forced retirement in 2007. On the motion to change, the judge, in determining that a material change in circumstances had occurred, considered the economic implications of the decisions made after termination and the decrease in income, rather than second-guessing the payor's investment choices in the absence of expert evidence.

*Voluntary assistance by other family members will not relieve a payor spouse of responsibility or reduce the SSAG amounts that would otherwise be considered appropriate* — Gibson v. Gibson, 2009 CarswellOnt 6082, [2009] O.J. No. 4172 (Ont. S.C.J.). The parties were married for 12 years and had two children. The husband earned $90,000 annually and the wife's income was $15,000. After separation, the wife relied on her mother to support her and the children, who resided with their grandmother. The judge ordered interim spousal support and did consider the fact that the wife was assisted by her mother in determining quantum, stating "Mr. Gibson cannot rely on the fact that Ms. Gibson is presently being assisted by her mother to reduce his support obligation. Ms. Gibson has suffered both an economic disadvantage and economic hardship resulting from the breakdown of the marriage." He ordered support to be paid in the lower range of the SSAG.

*From a practical point of view, the amount of spousal support should be a reflection of a recipient's reasonable needs and not exceed the payor's means* — Phillips-Curwin v. Curwin, 2008 CarswellNS 328, 2008 NSSC 198, [2008] N.S.J. No. 267 (N.S.S.C.). The wife, age 34, had primary care of the parties' two children while the husband, age 42, was employed as a sales representative with an income of $156,000. The court ordered that the husband pay the wife spousal support in the amount of $2,000 per month in addition to child support.

*Income may be imputed where denial of income not credible* — Colquhoun v. Colquhoun, 2007 CarswellOnt 18, [2007] O.J. No. 9 (Ont. S.C.J.). The husband, on a corollary relief claim for support in a divorce proceeding, took the position that he was unemployed, had no income, and, therefore, could not pay support. The court found that he had deliberately avoided seeking employment, and that he had done so either to avoid paying spousal support or because he was in fact self-employed and earning income, or a combination of both. He was probably earning rental income from properties he owned, and receiving significant income (directly or indirectly) from a house cleaning franchise in the name of his common law partner in which he denied having any interest. He could be earning at least $50,000 a year from these two sources, without undertaking any other employment. With the help and support of his new partner, he could probably work, also, at a job outside the entrepreneurial ventures. In the circumstances, the court imputed an annual income of $50,000 to him and ordered that he pay $1,000 (indexed) a month in spousal support to his wife for whom the court imputed an income of $20,800 a year.

*Reasonable for husband to reinvest most of after-tax income into his business* — Williams v. Williams, 2007 CarswellAlta 1371, 2007 ABQB 620, 43 R.F.L. (6th) 333, [2007] A.J. No. 1137 (Alta. Q.B.). Where the husband's company's after-tax income was largely reinvested in the company, such income was not considered in calculating the husband's ability to pay spousal support. Since the husband had passed the reigns of the company to his son, who was now president, his actions to ensure the long-term success of the business were reasonable.

*Capital gains not certain to recur, therefore not considered part of income* — Williams v. Williams, 2007 CarswellAlta 1371, 2007 ABQB 620, 43 R.F.L. (6th) 333, [2007] A.J. No. 1137

(Alta. Q.B.). In calculating the wife's income for the purposes of determining her spousal support, capital gains earned by her as a result of some astute real estate investments were not included. This type of income could not be counted upon in the future.

*Payee entitled to support where payor making discretionary purchases and person living with him is making minimal financial contribution* — O. (D.P.) v. O. (P.E.), 2006 CarswellNS 208, 2006 NSSC 159, [2006] N.S.J. No. 205 (N.S.S.C.). While the husband did not dispute the wife's entitlement to support based on a non-compensatory dependency, the court did not accept that the husband was unable to pay. The court noted that the husband had made a number of discretionary purchases and that the female friend who lived with him made only a very minimal contribution to expenses. The court ordered spousal support of $900 per month, subject to review.

*Cost of husband's travel to exercise access has priority over spousal support* — Morgan v. Morgan, 2006 CarswellNfld 9, 2006 NLTD 6, 22 R.F.L. (6th) 419, [2006] N.J. No. 9 (N.L.T.D.). The wife was denied spousal support even though entitlement was established. The husband had to spend a considerable sum of money for travel to exercise access, and accordingly lacked the ability to pay.

*Impact of subsequent family on ability to pay* — O. (D.P.) v. O. (P.E.), 2006 CarswellNS 208, 2006 NSSC 159, [2006] N.S.J. No. 205 (N.S.S.C.).

*Northern Travel Grant related to medical treatment not part of husband's income* — Fraser v. Fraser, 2004 CarswellOnt 3343, 8 R.F.L. (6th) 125, [2004] O.T.C. 729, [2004] O.J. No. 3408 (Ont. S.C.J.). A Northern Travel Grant provided to the husband to assist with his travel expenses to obtain medical treatment should not be characterized as "income" in determining his claim for spousal support.

*Child Support Guidelines — provisions applicable in spousal support income calculations* — Murray v. Murray, 2003 CarswellOnt 3258, 40 R.F.L. (5th) 244, 66 O.R. (3d) 540, [2003] O.T.C. 780, [2003] O.J. No. 3350 (Ont. S.C.J.), additional reasons at 2003 CarswellOnt 3862 (Ont. S.C.J.), reversed on other grounds 2005 CarswellOnt 3900, 17 R.F.L. (6th) 248, 76 O.R. (3d) 548, 257 D.L.R. (4th) 320, 201 O.A.C. 254, [2005] O.J. No. 3563 (Ont. C.A.), additional reasons at 2005 CarswellOnt 7278, 79 O.R. (3d) 147, 205 O.A.C. 107, [2005] O.J. No. 5379 (Ont. C.A.). Leave to appeal refused 2006 CarswellOnt 1033, 2006 CarswellOnt 1034, 221 O.A.C. 399 (note), 352 N.R. 198 (note) (S.C.C.). The income calculation provisions found in ss. 15 through 19 of the *Federal Child Support Guidelines* apply to the calculation of the payor spouse's income for purposes of determining spousal support as well as for determining child support.

*In determining the payor's ability to pay, the court should consider the financial burden resulting from the payor's new marriage* — Petrin v. Hahn, 2003 CarswellOnt 4108, 47 R.F.L. (5th) 372, [2003] O.J. No. 4206 (Ont. S.C.J.). Where the wife had been receiving interim spousal support of $650 monthly for the 6 years since the parties' separation and was incapacitated by a brain injury occurring before the marriage, final spousal support in the reduced amount of $500 monthly was awarded. While the wife had suffered economically because of the breakdown of the marriage, the award also had to recognize the financial burdens on the husband resulting from his new marriage and two new children.

*Income differential offset by claimant's greater security and child support obligation — no support* — Leet v. Leet, 2002 CarswellNB 98, 2002 NBQB 87, 25 R.F.L. (5th) 302 (N.B.Q.B.). The court refused the wife's application for spousal support upon the dissolution of the parties' 15-year marriage. The wife's career had not been prejudiced by the marriage. She continued to work throughout the relationship and had enjoyed advancement to a responsible management position. Although the husband's income was larger than the wife's, her employment was more secure and the husband would be paying a significant amount in child support.

*Motion to strike accountant's affidavit speculating about husband's income — motion denied — Picard v. Picard*, 2001 CarswellOnt 2111, 18 R.F.L. (5th) 352, [2001] O.J. No. 2299 (Ont. S.C.J.). The court dismissed the husband's application to strike an affidavit prepared by the wife's accountant estimating the husband's income for the purposes of a temporary spousal and child support application. The accountant had carefully set out in detail his assumptions and the factual background he relied upon as well as the source of information. Accordingly, the court could determine the appropriate weight to be given to this piece of evidence without abdicating its responsibility to make findings of fact. The accountant's opinion amounted to evidence, it decided nothing and ultimately the court could accept or reject it, in whole or in part.

*Former income attributed to payor who voluntarily reduces employment income — Hildahl-Trauter v. Trauter*, 1996 CarswellSask 35, 140 Sask. R. 46 (Sask. Q.B.). Where the husband had willfully taken a leave of absence from his job which reduced his monthly income from $4,200 to $1,000, the quantum of spousal support payable by him was set by reference to his former income. The wife after their traditional marriage of 11 years could not be expected to fill the void left by the husband's failure to maintain his income at a reasonable level.

*Support based on potential income where payor voluntarily leaves employment — Martens v. Martens*, 1996 CarswellMan 221, 22 R.F.L. (4th) 411, 109 Man. R. (2d) 189 (Man. Q.B.). Where a spouse who has the potential to earn income and has an obligation to support his or her spouse and children decides to stop working and sets out on another course, the courts will determine what the person's potential to earn is and require support payments commensurate with that potential.

*Gross farming income to be established on what it would be if party were employed as wage earner — Moon v. Bechard*, 1996 CarswellSask 113, 21 R.F.L. (4th) 101, 140 Sask. R. 197 (Sask. Q.B.). Gross farming income cannot form the sole basis for the determination of means to pay maintenance, nor is it proper to use only net income as reported for income tax purposes. For such individuals, the court must do a calculation to determine, as near as possible, the gross income were the party employed for wages.

*Support awarded where payee's income mostly from investments and husband had substantial income and investments — Droit de la famille - 2129* (1994), [1995] R.D.F. 102 (C.S. Que.). Where the wife's main source of income was derived from her investments, she was awarded spousal support on the breakdown of the parties' 30-year marriage. The husband had a healthy income from which to draw, in addition to substantial investments, and was in a position to pay support.

*Payor working abroad in country which restricts amount of money which can be sent to Canada — Stebbins v. Stebbins*, 1995 CarswellNS 67, 14 R.F.L. (4th) 226 (N.S.S.C.). Currency restrictions should be considered in determining the husband's ability to pay support where he works in a country which limits the amount of money he can send out of the country to his wife.

*Temporary increase in income — McIntyre v. McIntyre*, 1995 CarswellNB 84, 160 N.B.R. (2d) 81, 412 A.P.R. 81, [1995] N.B.J. No. 140 (N.B.Q.B.). Where the husband's income had been inflated as a result of his working overseas on a limited term contract, spousal support was ordered on the basis of that income. However, when the husband returned to Canada and resumed normal employment, the parties would have to seek a review of the order which could ultimately result in a variation or the imposition of a time limitation.

*Possession of real estate and attempt to hide it indicates means to pay spousal support — Droit de la famille - 2140* (1994), [1995] R.D.F. 126 (C.S. Que.). Where only upon threats of contempt proceedings the husband revealed the existence of real estate assets in Florida, the wife's claim for spousal support was allowed. Although the husband claimed monthly income of only $475, the fact that he held American real estate indicated that he had sufficient resources to support his wife.

*In determining the payor's ability to pay, a common law spouse's contribution to expenses should be considered* — Underwood v. Underwood, 1994 CarswellOnt 394, 3 R.F.L. (4th) 457, 113 D.L.R. (4th) 571 (Ont. Gen. Div.), varied 1995 CarswellOnt 88, 11 R.F.L. (4th) 361, [1995] O.J. No. 4335 (Ont. Div. Ct.). The husband's ability to pay spousal support was based on the premise that half of the husband's household expenses were being borne by his common-law wife.

*In determining the payor's ability to pay, a new partner's salary should be considered* — MacLean v. MacLean, 1991 CarswellPEI 70, 94 Nfld. & P.E.I.R. 265, 298 A.P.R. 265, [1991] P.E.I.J. No. 89 (P.E.I.T.D.). The court held that it was appropriate to consider the salary of the husband's new partner in determining his ability to pay. While the court did not treat this amount as part of the husband's income, it held that it must be considered when the husband's standard of living or lifestyle is examined and in an assessment of his expenses in his new situation.

*Means to be calculated on the basis of real or actual income regardless of source* — McGuigan v. McGuigan, 1991 CarswellNS 57, 33 R.F.L. (3d) 183, 105 N.S.R. (2d) 170, 284 A.P.R. 170 (N.S.T.D.). Where the payor spouse's draws from his dental practice are derived indirectly from bank loans, periodic support should be calculated on the basis of the payor's real or actual income without reference to its source. The payee's property entitlement had been adversely affected by the payor's bank loans for his dental practice and the payee should not be forced to suffer doubly by having her income affected adversely as well.

*Unreasonable expenditures on hobbies added back to payor's income* — Glazier v. Glazier, 1991 CarswellOnt 325, 36 R.F.L. (3d) 84, 5 O.R. (3d) 183, [1991] O.J. No. 1552 (Ont. Gen. Div.). The husband was found to have given precedence to his hobbies over pursuit of his career. Accordingly, when assessing the quantum of spousal support which should be paid by him, the court found that the amount expended on hobbies was unreasonable and assessed his ability to pay after reducing his hobby expenditures to a reasonable amount.

*No income to be attributed to payor who retires at appropriate age* — Metcalf v. Metcalf, 1990 CarswellOnt 254, 26 R.F.L. (3d) 381 (Ont. H.C.). Where the husband had retired at age 67, it was not appropriate to attribute income to him for the purpose of the wife's support claim. He had reached the stage in life where he should not be forced to work and accordingly periodic support was not ordered.

*Support based on employment prospects where payor retired to reduce obligation* — Bellemare v. Bellemare, 1990 CarswellNS 50, 28 R.F.L. (3d) 165, 98 N.S.R. (2d) 140, 263 A.P.R. 140 (N.S.T.D.). A husband, who had retired after the parties' separation in an attempt to reduce his support obligation, was nevertheless ordered to pay support in an amount commensurate with the good employment prospects that he still possessed.

*Income attributed to payor who voluntarily left employment* — Titterton v. Titterton, 1990 CarswellMan 327, 66 Man. R. (2d) 259, [1990] M.J. No. 364 (Man. Q.B.). Where the husband quit his job to defeat his wife's support order, it was continued on the basis of income attributed to him.

*Severance pay not to be considered income for support purposes* — Melanson v. Melanson, 1989 CarswellNB 338, 104 N.B.R. (2d) 76, 261 A.P.R. 76 (N.B.C.A.), reversing 1989 CarswellNB 206, 98 N.B.R. (2d) 357, 248 A.P.R. 357 (N.B.Q.B.). For the purposes of determining support, severance pay in the hands of the payor spouse should not be considered as income.

*Appropriate for payor to reduce income to pay debt* — Northcut v. Ruppel, 1989 CarswellMan 48, 21 R.F.L. (3d) 195, 59 Man. R. (2d) 113, [1989] M.J. No. 371 (Man. Q.B.). Where the husband's decision to maintain his income at a reduced level was taken for the sound business reason of reducing business debts, the wife's application for support was dismissed as the parties' incomes were almost equal.

*Payor's fluctuating earnings should be calculated over a significant period — Boult v. Boult,* 1989 CarswellMan 307, 62 Man. R. (2d) 161 (Man. Q.B.). Where the payor spouse's income is based upon earnings from self-employment, the quantum of support payable should be based upon such earnings calculated over a significant period due to fluctuations in the business world.

*Not proper to make order where ability to pay in doubt — Day v. Day,* 1988 CarswellNB 35, 13 R.F.L. (3d) 313, 89 N.B.R. (2d) 207, 226 A.P.R. 207 (N.B.Q.B.). A court should not make an order for support if there is doubt as to the payor's ability to pay, even if the payor is willing to consent to such an order.

*Payor's income more relevant to ability to pay support than employment status — Sagoo v. Sagoo,* 1987 CarswellMan 94, 6 R.F.L. (3d) 128 (Man. Q.B.). A spouse's income rather than his or her state of employment is determinative of whether support should be payable.

*Husband lacks ability to pay and wife chooses to remain with child — no support — Storey v. Storey,* 1987 CarswellMan 328, 49 Man. R. (2d) 235 (Man. Q.B.). Where the husband had no means to pay spousal support and the wife chose to delay her re-entry into the work force at a high-income position to remain at home with the parties' young child, her application for support was refused.

*In determining the payor's ability to pay, the demands of a new relationship should be considered — McNeilly v. McNeilly,* 1987 CarswellOnt 318, 7 R.F.L. (3d) 385 (Ont. H.C.). Support under the *Divorce Act* is based on a needs and means test. In assessing needs and means, a court should take into account a potential payor's settled, new relationship and the demands which that places upon his or her resources.

*Income attributed to payor who voluntarily left employment — Mitchell v. Mitchell,* 1986 CarswellNS 285, 74 N.S.R. (2d) 435, 180 A.P.R. 435 (N.S.T.D.). Where the husband had voluntarily quit his job, the maintenance ordered payable to his incapacitated wife was calculated as if he continued to be employed.

*"Means" includes potential income — Hastings v. Hastings,* 1984 CarswellSask 51, 38 R.F.L. (2d) 462 (Sask. Q.B.). When determining the quantum of maintenance to be paid by a husband, the court in considering his "means" is entitled to have regard to his potential earning capacity. The husband was an undischarged bankrupt, but since his earning capacity was expected to improve, he was ordered to pay maintenance on a gradually increasing basis.

*Definition of "means" — capital position must be considered — Campbell v. Campbell,* 1981 CarswellOnt 280, 24 R.F.L. (2d) 59, [1981] O.J. No. 809 (Ont. H.C.), at 69 [R.F.L.]. "In order to determine the 'means' of the parties, the court must consider not only actual income generated by the assets owned by each party, but the income that would be generated if the assets owned were reasonably and intelligently managed, which latter potential income must be attributed to each party. Thus the term 'means' basically includes the capital assets of both parties, their savings, earnings and benefits from employment and otherwise, and money which would be generated if the assets are properly and intelligently managed", per DuPont J.

*In determining the payor's ability to pay, the contribution of common law spouse in an unstable relationship should not be considered — Gosney v. Gosney,* 1980 CarswellNfld 12, 17 R.F.L. (2d) 28, 26 Nfld. & P.E.I.R. 92, 72 A.P.R. 92 (Nfld. T.D.). The failure of the woman with whom the husband was living to pay a larger contribution toward their common household expenses was not a factor, given the unstable nature of their relationship.

*See also re payor cohabiting — Rathwell v. Rathwell,* 1974 CarswellSask 26, 16 R.F.L. 387 (Sask. Q.B.), at 392 [R.F.L.].

*Court may consider earning capacity as well as actual earnings in making a support order — Jaworski v. Jaworski,* 1973 CarswellOnt 99, 10 R.F.L. 190, 34 D.L.R. (3d) 44, [1973] 2 O.R. 420 (Ont. H.C.). The court held that a physician who had reduced his income by resigning from a medical clinic to devote himself entirely to research work should be deemed to have a higher income. The court was entitled to take into consideration not only his actual earnings, but his earning capacity in considering the reasonable amount of maintenance which he should provide for his wife.

## 5.2.1 Post-separation Increases in the Payor Spouse's Income — General

Whether a spouse can share in post-separation increases in the other spouse's income is an important issue. Whether there is a great discrepancy in the parties' incomes shortly after separation (*Francis v. Baker; Giguere; Emery*; below), whether the payee spouse contributed to the payor spouse's acquisition of employment skills or credentials during cohabitation (*Moge; Dextraze; Pendleton; Sawchuk*; below), whether the parties jointly made decisions during cohabitation which benefited the payor spouse's financial interests (*Hartshorne; Fitzpatrick*; below), whether the change in circumstances is temporary or permanent (*Kerman*, below), whether the change was contemplated at the time of the original order or agreement (*Fargey*, below) are all important factors in determining whether a payee spouse should share in a payor spouse's post-separation increases in income.

Many cases suggest that a direct contribution to future income earning potential by way of contributing to credentials or skills is a necessary precondition to sharing post-separation success. If the payor obtains skills or credentials during the marriage, the recipient is more likely to be entitled to share future increases in income. If the payor's post-separation success flows from a job different than that held during the marriage, the court is more likely to reject a claim for the sharing of post-separation success. In contrast, where the payor's job that generated the increased income is the same or similar to the payor's job during the marriage, the court is more likely to allow the other spouse to share in the increased income. As well, where there was a long-term marriage with a complete integration of the parties' personal and economic lives, there is more likely to be an entitlement to share in a post-separation increase in income.

Where a payor spouse's income increases post-separation, there is no automatic increase in spousal support: *Judd, Hariram; Rozen; Dextraze; Sarophim*; below.

Post-separation income is relevant to compensatory-based spousal support; postseparation income is usually not relevant to needs-based support because support on that basis is "generally restricted in quantum to the lifestyle enjoyed during the marriage": *Ludmer; M. (A.A.) v. K. (R.P.); Korkola*; below.

As far as the *Spousal Support Advisory Guidelines* are concerned, Carol Rogerson and Rollie Thompson, the authors of the SSAG, suggest that whether or not an increase in the other spouse's income should be shared is a matter of judicial discretion. They consider that circumstances "such as post-separation increases in the payor's income, re-partnering, remarriage and second families" are best left to a discretionary, case-by-case determination (*Spousal Support Advisory Guidelines*, July 2008, c. 8, s. 14). Rogerson and Thompson write in the Guidelines at "The Payor's Post-Separation Income Increase 14.3":

> There are two possible formulaic extremes here. At one extreme, one could decide that any post-separation income increase of the payor spouse should not affect the amount of spousal support. After all, some would suggest, the recipient is entitled to a sharing of the marital standard of living, but no more. Certainly, this bright-line method would be predictable and administratively simple. At the other extreme, one could argue that the formulas should just continue to be applied to any income increase for the payor. This again would offer a predictable result, but one which the basic principles of spousal support would not justify in all cases. This approach is most compelling after a long traditional marriage.

Under the current law, it is impossible to maintain either of these approaches to the exclusion of the other. Some rough notion of causation is applied to post-separation income increases for the payor, in determining both whether the income increase should be reflected in increased spousal support and, if it should, by how much. It all depends on the length of the marriage, the roles adopted during the marriage, the time elapsed between the date of separation and the subsequent income increase, and the reason for the income increase (e.g. new job vs. promotion within same employer, or career continuation vs. new venture). The extent of sharing of these post-separation increases involves a complex, fact-based decision.

We can propose one formulaic limit in these cases: the upper limit upon any increased spousal support ought to be the numbers generated by the formulas.

In contrast to the *Spousal Support Advisory Guidelines*, the *Federal Child Support Guidelines* specifically state that an objective of the Guidelines is "to establish a fair standard of support for children that ensures that they continue to benefit from the financial means of both spouses *after separation*: FCSG, s. 1(a) [emphasis added]. See also *R. v. R.*; *Logan*, below.

In addition to granting a spouse increased support where the payor spouse's income has increased post separation, there are cases where support is time limited but, because of the increase in the payor spouse's income, the termination date is extended (*Graca v. Graca*, below).

*Where there is a great discrepancy in incomes shortly after separation, the payee spouse would be entitled to an increase in support* – Francis v. Baker, 1997 CarswellOnt 1774, 28 R.F.L. (4th) 437, 150 D.L.R. (4th) 547, 30 O.T.C. 369, [1997] O.J. No. 2196 (Ont. Gen. Div.), additional reasons at 1997 CarswellOnt 3187 (Ont. Gen. Div.), affirmed 1998 CarswellOnt 931, 34 R.F.L. (4th) 317, 157 D.L.R. (4th) 1, 38 O.R. (3d) 481 (Eng.), 38 O.R. (3d) 509 (Fr.), 107 O.A.C. 161, 52 O.T.C. 80, [1998] O.J. No. 924 (Ont. C.A.), affirmed 1999 CarswellOnt 2734, 1999 CarswellOnt 2948, 50 R.F.L. (4th) 228, [1999] 3 S.C.R. 250, 177 D.L.R. (4th) 1, 125 O.A.C. 201, 246 N.R. 45, 44 O.R. (3d) 736 (headnote only), [1999] S.C.J. No. 52 (S.C.C.). The wife, 1 year after a separation agreement had been signed, commenced an action to have it set aside and to claim spousal support, among other things. The case did not reach trial until 9 years later (12 years after the separation). Although the evidence failed to establish that the agreement should be set aside, the court held that with the clear discrepancy existing between the incomes of the spouses very shortly after the separation, the wife would have been entitled to "top up" support. The separation agreement made provision for support for "herself and the children" and the court found that far from releasing spousal support, the agreement contemplated ongoing support "for herself. In any event, the agreement was only one of many factors that must be considered in determining the right to, and the amount and duration of spousal support. All four of the objectives of spousal support orders under subsection 15(7) of the *Divorce Act* must be considered. There was no evidence that the agreement sought to address these objectives. The wife had not received adequate support during the 12 years she had been separated. At the time of trial, she earned $63,000 a year as a teacher. The husband had a net worth of about 78 million dollars and an annual income of nearly $1,000,000. In the circumstances, the wife was awarded lump sum support. Her child-raising responsibilities clearly affected her careerearning potential and her career path would have been entirely different and more lucrative but for the children. Lump sum support was advisable as there would be no prejudice to the husband given his net worth; it would reduce the financial connection between the parties, recognize the economic disadvantages to the wife arising from her marriage and its breakdown relieve her economic hardship and promote her self-sufficiency. Recognizing that a lump sum would not be taxable to the wife, the spousal support claims were assessed at $500,000 payable as a lump sum to satisfy her entitlement to past support and future support. (The main thrust of the case, especially on appeal, was whether the Table Amount of child support was "inappropriate". Spousal support was only a secondary consideration. For child support, the current income of the payor — that is, his post-separation income — is the relevant income. However, the court made no distinction between post-separation income and income at the time of the separation in awarding the lump sum to the wife. The husband's circumstances at time of trial were the determining circumstances for both child and spousal support.)

*In order for the wife to share in the husband's post-separation increased income, she must show that she contributed to his skills or to the credentials he acquired that led to his ability to earn his increased income* (Moge v. Moge *(S.C.C.))* — *Dextraze* v. *Dextraze*, 2004 CarswellBC 287, 2004 BCSC 215, [2004] B.C.J. No. 266 (B.C.S.C.).

*No automatic annual increase in spousal support when the payor's income increases* — *Hariram* v. *Hariram*, 2001 CarswellOnt 732, 14 R.F.L. (5th) 88, 197 D.L.R. (4th) 377, 53 O.R. (3d) 131, 7 C.P.C. (5th) 115, 142 O.A.C. 381 (Ont. Div. Ct.). The portion of the judgement providing for the automatic increase was set aside.

*In deciding whether a spouse should share in the other spouse's post separation increase in income, the spouse's contribution during the marriage is determinative* — *Judd* v. *Judd*, 2010 CarswellBC 246, 2010 BCSC 153, 83 R.F.L. (6th) 314, [2010] B.C.J. No. 177 (B.C.S.C.). The resolution of the issue of post-separation increases in income is fact based. If the increase in salary is founded in expertise and seniority established during the marriage and no intervening event or events are the cause of the increase, then the increase is to be included unless the recipient's role during marriage necessitates a different determination. If an event after separation is the reason for the increase, in whole or in part, then the increase may be excluded from consideration, also in whole or in part.

*On an application to vary the fact that the husband's ability to pay may have increased since the settlement does not, in itself, constitute a basis for an increase in spousal support* — *Dextraze* v. *Dextraze*, 2004 CarswellBC 287, 2004 BCSC 215, [2004] B.C.J. No. 266 (B.C.S.C.).

## 5.2.2 Post-separation Increases in the Payor Spouse's Income — Increase in Support Granted or Time-limited Support Extended

*Husband's post-separation dramatic increase in income should benefit wife* — *O'Grady* v. *O'Grady*, 2010 CarswellAlta 752, 2010 ABCA 109, 82 R.F.L. (6th) 59, 319 D.L.R. (4th) 301, 477 A.R. 216, 483 W.A.C. 216 (Alta. C.A.). This was an appeal from the lower court that ordered the husband to pay $12,000 per month in spousal support, an amount the husband had previously agreed to pay. This amount was based on the fact that the husband's income had dramatically increased post-separation because he was a workaholic and rarely took holidays. The Court of Appeal found that although the trial judge failed to impute an income to the wife, there was no appealable error and upheld the award.

*The court should give full consideration to the payor's post-separation income* — *Hartshorne* v. *Hartshorne*, 2009 CarswellBC 1398, 2009 BCSC 698, 70 R.F.L. (6th) 106, [2009] B.C.J. No. 1050 (B.C.S.C.), reversed in part 2010 CarswellBC 1618, 2010 BCCA 327, 82 R.F.L. (6th) 1, 320 D.L.R. (4th) 398, 289 B.C.A.C. 244, 489 W.A.C. 244, [2010] B.C.J. No. 1271 (B.C.C.A.). Both parties were lawyers. The wife left her profession to remain with the parties' children for a lengthy period and then returned to work. The husband's post-separation income should be considered because first, the parties continued to function as a unit until at least the end of November 1999, after the court had underestimated the husband's income for the year. The court held that there was a clear temporal link between their marriage and this increase with no intervening change in the husband's career, or any other event, that could explain the increase.

Second, after separation, the wife continued to be the custodial parent of the parties' children, taking on the greater part of child-rearing responsibilities, including the additional burden created by their son's special needs. Her continued assumption of these responsibilities restricted her income-earning potential and allowed the husband to expend his energies to improving his business and increasing his income. Third, the court was satisfied that the years the parties lived together, from the time that the husband was 38 years old until he was 51 years old, were crucial years in the professional development of most lawyers. The wife's contributions during those years helped the husband establish his practice and contributed to his improved income in the 2000 to 2007 period. The court ordered a lump sum award of $350,000 to the wife.

*Increase in payor's income — spousal support increased, given the parties long-term marriage and the wife's dependency* — Beninger v. Beninger, 2009 CarswellBC 2963, 2009 BCCA 458, 77 R.F.L. (6th) 56, 277 B.C.A.C. 36, 469 W.A.C. 36, [2009] B.C.J. No. 2197 (B.C.C.A.). The increase in the payor's income constituted a material change. The grounds for awarding an increase were reasonable given the parties' long-term marriage and the wife's inability to become self-sufficient because of her economic sacrifices undertaken for the benefit of the marriage.

*Payee spouse entitled to increased support where payor spouse's income increased after separation* — Horner v. Horner, 2004 CarswellOnt 4246, 6 R.F.L. (6th) 140, 245 D.L.R. (4th) 410, 72 O.R. (3d) 561, 191 O.A.C. 28, [2004] O.J. No. 4268 (Ont. C.A.). The the wife brought a corollary relief application under the *Divorce Act* for spousal support for an indefinite period of time. As part of her application she sought to set aside the time-limited support provision in her separation agreement and claimed support in a higher amount. Based on the husband's increased post-separation income, the applications judge awarded spousal support for more than the amount set out in the separation agreement, made the increase retroactive to 1 month after she had requested it, but did not extend the duration of payment beyond the limited period. The Court of Appeal awarded a further increase in spousal support finding that the applications judge had used too low an amount for the husband's income, did not reflect in his award the contribution the wife had made to her husband's career advancement during the marriage, although he noted the fact of this contribution, and notwithstanding that the wife's budget was reasonable and not criticized, he did not award the amount requested to maintain this budget. The Court of Appeal also found that the amount awarded was below the median of awards made in cases involving similar circumstances. After the separation, the husband obtained an engineering degree and "advanced rapidly in his career to become Vice-President of Engineering" in his company. His income increased accordingly. The applications judge connected the husband's advance in his career to the marriage.

*Court assumed that wife would share in husband's post-separation increase in income* — Marinangeli v. Marinangeli, 2003 CarswellOnt 2691, 38 R.F.L. (5th) 307, 66 O.R. (3d) 40, 228 D.L.R. (4th) 376, 174 O.A.C. 76, [2003] O.J. No. 2819 (Ont. C.A.). The Court of Appeal dealt with the wife's application to vary her support on the assumption, which was not articulated, that she was entitled to share in the husband's post-separation increase in income.

*Wife entitled to share in husband's post-separation increase in income* — Mosher v. Mosher, 1995 CarswellNS 11, 13 R.F.L. (4th) 385, 140 N.S.R. (2d) 40, 399 A.P.R. 40 (N.S.C.A.), the court viewed the wife's claim for support "to a significant degree" in light of the husband's post-separation income. It came to this conclusion because of her contribution to the marriage and the upbringing of the children, her willingness to share in a compromise of the family's standard of living in order to purchase rental properties and to invest in the stock market. The court found that it would be inequitable if her claim was affected as a consequence of the reduction of her husband's income for the 2 years after he left his previous position, and not by the spectacular increases thereafter.

*Post-separation income is relevant to compensatory based spousal support but not relevant to need-based support because support on that basis is "generally restricted in quantum to the lifestyle enjoyed during the marriage" — parties returning to a lifestyle they had previously, for many years, enjoyed during marriage — payor's skills and credentials as a lawyer used to earn the post-separation income were acquired during the marriage, income flowing to him was from a law career and not from an entirely new venture — taking payor's post-separation income into account in determining spousal support is justified* — Ludmer v. Ludmer, 2013 CarswellOnt 1625, 2013 ONSC 784, 33 R.F.L. (7th) 331, [2013] O.J. No. 699 (Ont. S.C.J.). The court, taking into account the husband's post-separation income, ordered the husband to pay the wife $432,000 in lump sum spousal support on account, and in complete satisfaction, of her spousal support claims.

*Where the payor's financial circumstances have improved since signing of minutes of settlement, spousal support will not be terminated* — Graca v. Graca, 2012 CarswellOnt 8535, 2012 ONSC 3934 (Ont. S.C.J.). The husband sought to terminate spousal support on the basis that he had retired for medical reasons at age 58. The parties had concluded minutes of settlement at separation that provided for spousal support until either party died and the spousal support was terminated by a court order. The support was secured by a life insurance policy. The judge considered the means and needs of the parties and found that the husband was better off than he had been at the time of the signing of the minutes of settlement. The wife continued to be in need of support. Retirement was not set out as a material change in circumstances by the minutes of settlement.

*Where the payee had contributed to her partner's retraining during their union, she was entitled to share in his increased income post-separation; however, the payor's income may be discounted to take into consideration each party's contribution to post-separation increases in income* — Pendleton v. Pendleton, 2010 CarswellBC 2179, 2010 BCSC 1167, 90 R.F.L. (6th) 166, [2010] B.C.J. No. 1629 (B.C.S.C. [In Chambers]). The parties lived as common-law spouses for five years and were married for five years before separating. During the relationship, the parties relocated twice for the husband's employment. The wife left employment for each move. The wife's application for spousal support was granted. In 2006, when the parties separated, the husband earned $55,000 per year. The husband changed employment again and earned $82,000 at the time of the hearing. The wife's income was approximately $46,400. The wife had, at least indirectly, contributed to the husband's retraining during the marriage. A sufficient connection existed between the wife's contribution to the marriage and the husband's post-separation increases in income. Some of the husband's post-separation increase in income was solely attributable to his initiative. The husband's income was discounted to $72,500 to reflect the above factors. The husband was ordered to pay $350 per month in spousal support for three years.

*Post-separation increase in payor's income taken into account as it is an important element of a compensatory claim, as payee had contributed to the success of the payor husband's career* — M. (A.A.) v. K. (R.P.), 2010 CarswellOnt 1139, 2010 ONSC 930, 81 R.F.L. (6th) 370, [2010] O.J. No. 807 (Ont. S.C.J.). Both parties had trained to be veterinarians. The wife was found to be entitled to support on both compensatory and non-compensatory grounds. The court held that the compensatory component related not only to economic disadvantages that the wife experienced which delayed and undermined her veterinary career and income, but also that the husband had a concomitant economic advantage in that the wife's assumption of significant child-related responsibilities at least somewhat enhanced the husband's ability to devote time and attention to developing his very profitable business. While incomes for both parties increased since separation, the gap between them continued to be significant. Part of the wife's compensatory claim related to the fact that as a veterinarian her income still lagged behind the husband's and might always do so because of his head start when his career was given primacy during the early years of the parties' marriage. The court held at para. 207 that "To simply ignore continuing income gains by the payor, while factoring in changes in the recipient's earnings, would almost inevitably preclude consideration of an important component of a compensatory claim." The court ordered the husband to pay the wife $44,000.00 as lump sum spousal support, inclusive of pre-judgement interest.

*Spouse entitled to compensatory support should share in payor's post-separation increase in income — Korkola v. Korkola*, 2009 CarswellOnt 395, [2009] O.J. No. 343 (Ont. S.C.J.), The parties marriage was of a medium length. The wife already had educational qualifications and the ability to increase her earning ability with further education. Consequently, an appropriate award would include a consideration of the post-separation increases in the husband's income. This had already been accounted for in the award of retroactive support which recognized the differences in the husband's income year to year from 2004 to 2007. In addition, the court awarded the wife $12,000 which was a lump sum equivalent to 50% of the cost of the wife's education for the course of her 4-year nursing degree. The court also awarded the wife periodic support of $9,210 per month commencing January 1, 2009. Periodic spousal support is based on equalization of the parties' NDI and a projected income for the husband of $540,000 for 2008 with a projected RRSP contribution of $19,000.

*New payor income after retirement justifies continuation of support — Hurst v. Hurst*, 2008 CarswellOnt 5707, 58 R.F.L. (6th) 377, [2008] O.J. No. 3800 (Ont. S.C.J.). While the separation agreement provided that no support would be assessed on the basis of the husband's pension income, he had developed other sources of income after his retirement. Two years previously, the recipient's mother had come to live with her, and the recipient spent most of her time caring for her. The court found that while the recipient was not deliberately underemployed, she could probably increase her employment income slightly, to $5,000 per year. The husband was ordered to pay retroactive support plus $1,200 per month going forward.

*Payor's income increased substantially since support agreement signed — payee attempted to become self-sufficient — increased support ordered although 10 years after separation agreement — increase justified by special circumstances — Wagg v. Wagg*, 2008 CarswellNS 604, 2008 NSSC 315 (N.S.S.C.). The parties married in 1981, had two children, separated in 1998 and divorced in 2004. They agreed in minutes of settlement signed in 2004 that the husband, who at the time earned approximately $160,000, would pay spousal support of $1,070 per month to the wife. The minutes contained a review clause providing that the amount was not to be reviewed earlier than two years from the date of the agreement. Since the parties' separation in 1998, the wife began part-time employment in 2003 earning $25,000 per year; and she obtained higher paying employment in October 2007, but lost her job less than a year later due to factors outside her control. The husband, whose income had increased significantly since settlement, and whose total income in 2007 was $316,788 (US), applied for an order terminating spousal support. The support was increased to $1,070 per month through the remainder of 2008, $1,500 per month in 2009, and $1,200 per month for the next two years. The court found that the wife, who had been the full-time caregiver of the couple's two children until the date of separation and whom the husband had discouraged from obtaining employment until the date of separation, had diligently attempted to be employed and to move towards self-sufficiency after the separation. Her re-entry into the workforce after 17 years of being out of the workforce was a significant barrier to her self-sufficiency. The husband also impeded the wife's self-sufficiency by failing to live up to the terms of disclosure and by participating in the son's unexpected departure from the mother's home without consultation or notice. Full self-sufficiency must be sufficient to sustain existence and not necessarily a minimal existence. The wife planned to begin taking courses to attain her CGA status. In order to do so and to address the wife's current income instability, spousal support was ordered for three years at which time her financial situation should be reviewed and the onus would be on the wife to prove ongoing need. While it was unusual to order an increase in support payments after 10 years, the court held that the combination of special circumstances justified such an increase.

*Increase in payor's income combined with the termination of child support allowed for an increase in spousal support* — Farrah v. Farrah, 2008 CarswellNB 434, 2008 NBQB 176, 58 R.F.L. (6th) 162, 339 N.B.R. (2d) 11, 870 A.P.R. 11 (N.B.Q.B.). The court granted the wife's motion to vary the spousal support order which had initially been made with a child support order. The child support order had since terminated, as one child was no longer a dependant and the other child was now living with the husband. Where the husband experienced a significant change in his financial circumstances since the date of the initial spousal support order, given that his employment income had increased and the fact that he no longer had to pay child support, the amount of support payable to the wife was ordered increased from $500 to $1,300 per month.

*Payor's post-separation increase in income should be considered for interim support* — Meliambro v. Meliambro, 2007 CarswellOnt 7699, [2007] O.J. No. 4638 (Ont. S.C.J.). The husband was a broker and his income fluctuated. The court did not accept as accurate the amount that he had stated as his income at the time of the original temporary order where the husband had averaged his income over the past 3 years when his income had in fact increased each year. He had claimed to be earning $96,000 a year. The initial order awarded the wife $400 per month. At the subsequent interim hearing, the wife demonstrated need in relation to standard of living and the payor's ability to pay. The court took into account, among various factors, that the wife's household included the parties' two children and that weight should be given to the husband's post-separation increase in income. Support until trial was to be based on the husband's annual income of $57,500. The court set support at $1,500 per month until trial.

*A spouse is generally not entitled to share in the other spouse's post-separation increase in income, but can be entitled where non-compensatory obligations are greater than the need for finality* — Logan v. Logan, 2007 CarswellBC 1435, 2007 BCSC 904 (B.C.S.C. [In Chambers]). The court held that post-separation increases in income should only be taken into account where "there are circumstances as in *Bracklow*, where non-compensatory obligations arising from the marriage will outweigh the parties' needs for closure. Usually these extreme cases have come about because the hopes and aspirations of the separating parties have not materialized usually for circumstances beyond their control". [However the husband's income was $100,000 at the time of the consent order. The court, at the review hearing, based the amount of the spousal support on the husband's current income of $110,000. Consequently, the court did seem to take post-separation income into account. For a detailed discussion of the case, see 5.2.3 Post-separation Increases in the Payor Spouse's Income — Increase in Support Not Granted.]

*The payor spouse's increase in income after separation could be taken into account where the parties had made decisions which had helped his financial interests* — Fitzpatrick v. Fitzpatrick, 2004 CarswellOnt 2606, 3 R.F.L. (6th) 325, [2004] O.J. No. 2695 (Ont. S.C.J.). The husband's income increased significantly after the separation. In considering the question of spousal support the court observed that the husband's income had "taken off and that the process began at least a year before the parties separated. The husband's interests in the business from which his income was derived "were directly related to the roles of the spouses within the marriage, their joint decision to sacrifice salary for equity 8 years earlier when he joined [the company], and their mutual plan to adopt a modest lifestyle, emphasizing financial security for their retirement. When the parties separated . . . [the company] seemed poised for takeoff. Mrs. Fitzpatrick was on that plane until it left the ground." The award for her support was assessed against the husband's greatly increased post-separation income.

*A payee spouse is entitled to share in the post-separation income of the payor spouse where the payee had clearly suffered a disadvantage as a result of the separation, the payor's income had increased dramatically shortly after separation, the marriage was lengthy (26 years); however, the incomes should not be equalized* — *Giguere v. Giguere*, 2003 CarswellOnt 5006, 46 R.F.L. (5th) 184, [2003] O.J. No. 5102 (Ont. S.C.J.), additional reasons at 2004 CarswellOnt 273, [2004] O.J. No. 444 (Ont. S.C.J.). The husband's raise in income was attributable to the tremendous effort the husband had put into his work from the outset, when the parties were still residing together. They had been together for 26 years. Cases decided more than 10 years earlier may be read as holding that the standard of living of the wife ought to be that enjoyed during the marriage. These should be distinguished from recent cases. More recent cases have entitled a wife in a long-term marriage to increased support flowing from the husband's post-separation increased income. The wife was entitled to compensatory and needs-based support.

*Wife entitled to some benefit from husband's post-separation income increase* — *Giguere v. Giguere*, 2003 CarswellOnt 5006, 46 R.F.L. (5th) 184 (Ont. S.C.J.), additional reasons at at 2004 CarswellOnt 273, [2004] O.J. No. 444 (Ont. S.C.J.). Where, subsequent to separation, the husband's income had increased substantially, it was found that the wife, through spousal support, was entitled to enjoy a higher standard of living than that experienced by the parties throughout their long marriage. It was not, however, appropriate that the parties' income be equalized, given the substantial effort that the husband had made to earn his income.

*The wife could share in husband's post-serparation increase in income in part so that she could save for her own retirement* — *Rothenburg v. Rothenburg*, 2003 CarswellOnt 1380, 40 R.F.L. (5th) 363, [2003] O.T.C. 327, [2003] O.J. No. 1551 (Ont. S.C.J.). In assessing spousal support for the wife, the court considered the husband's post-separation increase in income finding that "her involvement in the husband's education and his consulting business, as well as the time devoted to child care and care of his parents, require the wife share in some of the financial gain received by the husband." She was not entitled to an equalization of incomes, but her relationship with her husband in a 28-year marriage entitled her to "more than just her actual need". And given their ages and the likelihood of a support variation on the husband's retirement, she should be allowed an amount from which she could save for her own retirement.

*Payor voluntarily increases mortgage payments after income increases* — *support varied upwards* — *Jang v. Jang*, 2001 CarswellAlta 555, 2001 ABQB 351, 17 R.F.L. (5th) 370, 300 A.R. 387, [2001] A.J. No. 563 (Alta. Q.B.). The wife was granted an upward variation of spousal support. The husband had arbitrarily renegotiated the mortgage on the matrimonial home by reducing the amortization period and thus increasing the monthly payments. The wife had actually requested that the husband extend the amortization, thus freeing up more money on a monthly basis. Given the negative impact of the husband's actions on the wife's cash flow and the fact that the husband's income had increased, the upward variation of spousal support was justified.

*Where there was a long-term relationship of 17 years; the payor was appointed to his present position in 1987 after the parties had been living together for 10 years and married for 3 of those years; the payor's post-separation increase in income came directly from that same position held since 1987; parties' personal and economic lives were fully integrated; the applicant payee is entitled to share in the post-separation increase in income* — *Farnum v. Farnum*, 2010 CarswellOnt 6732, 2010 ONCJ 378, 91 R.F.L. (6th) 457, [2010] O.J. No. 3795 (Ont. C.J.).The quantum of the support should be at the low end because the applicant payee did not confer "a career enhancing benefit" on the payor that led to his increase in income.

*Support granted, but would be increased when husabnd's income increased post-separation* — *Keast v. Keast*, 1986 CarswellOnt 257, 1 R.F.L. (3d) 401, [1986] O.J. No. 2537 (Ont. Dist. Ct.), the court determined the quantum of support in two amounts, $600 monthly in permanent support for the wife's lifetime and a quasi-restitutionary or compensatory support sum would be paid to her for her contributions to the husband's career potential, fixed at $1,000 monthly but commencing in 1990, when he was expected to have established his practice and be earning the average amount for a physician and continuing for 10 years thereafter.

### 5.2.3 Post-separation Increases in the Payor Spouse's Income — Increase in Support Not Granted

*Payor's post-separation income not considered* — Fisher v. Fisher, 2008 CarswellOnt 43, 2008 ONCA 11, 47 R.F.L. (6th) 235, 288 D.L.R. (4th) 513, 232 O.A.C. 213, [2008] O.J. No. 38, 88 O.R. (3d) 241 (Ont. C.A.). The court made it clear that a spousal support award will be based on the parties' respective incomes as of the date of separation. In that case, the Court of Appeal averaged the payor's increased income in the last 3 years before separation, as well as his increased income in the year of separation, to determine his income for support purposes. The payor's post-separation income was not considered.

In an annotation to *Fisher v. Fisher*, Philip Epstein writes,

> It is suggested that of the three types of spousal support described in *Bracklow v. Bracklow*, 1999 CarswellBC 532/533, 44 R.F.L. (4th) 1 (S.C.C.), only compensatory support allows a spouse to share in post-separation increases in income. Contractual spousal support is proscribed by the terms of the contract and needbased support is generally restricted in quantum to the lifestyle enjoyed during the marriage. Compensatory support considerations, on the other hand, might sometimes take into account post-separation increases in income, for example, where the claimant has conferred a substantial career enhancement benefit on the other spouse. See *Keast v. Keast*, 1986 CarswellOnt 257, 1 R.F.L. (3d) 401 (Ont. Dist. Ct.) and *Ferguson v. Ferguson*, 2008 CarswellOnt 1676 (Ont. S.C.J.)...

*Where there is insufficient connection between the husband's increased post-separation income and the marriage, there should not be any significant sharing of that increase* — Chalifoux v. Chalifoux, 2006 CarswellAlta 907, 2006 ABQB 535, [2006] A.J. No. 883 (Alta. Q.B.), additional reasons at 2007 CarswellAlta 230, 2007 ABQB 111 (Alta. Q.B.), reversed on other grounds 2008 CarswellAlta 211, 2008 ABCA 70, 425 A.R. 361, 418 W.A.C. 361, [2008] A.J. No. 174 (Alta. C.A.).

*No sharing of post-separation increase in income* — Robinson v. Robinson, 1993 CarswellOnt 349, 48 R.F.L. (3d) 265, 15 O.R. (3d) 485, 107 D.L.R. (4th) 78, 66 O.A.C. 381, [1993] O.J. No. 2172 (Ont. C.A.). The Ontario Court of Appeal refused the wife's application to share in the husband's post-separation income increase. The parties were married for 13 years. The wife was acknowledged to be a good mother and homemaker who attended social functions with the husband and entertained in their home. The court observed that the evidence did not show that she had assisted in any other important way to advance the husband's career.

*An anomalous increase in income in one year did not result in retroactively adjusted spousal support when the means of the payor were otherwise as projected in the original support order* — Kerman v. Kerman, 2014 CarswellBC 679, 2014 BCSC 428 (B.C.S.C.). The wife sought a retroactive increase in support. The parties were married for 17 years and had separated some 17 years prior to this application. An order for support was made in 2008 which anticipated the income each party would earn. The husband earned significantly more in 2008, but the motion judge found that this was an anomaly and the husband's subsequent income was in line with the projections of the original order.

*Payor's income increased after separation, but this change was contemplated at the time of the original order and no material change was found* — Fargey v. Fargey, 2013 CarswellBC 510,

2013 BCSC 331, 28 R.F.L. (7th) 115 (B.C.S.C.). The wife applied to reinstate spousal support based on the husband's increase in income. Support had been paid under the terms of a separation agreement, which provided for support to expire in 2012. The judge found that, based on the evidence available at the time of the signing of the separation agreement, the success of the husband's company was reasonably foreseeable and there were no grounds to set aside the agreement.

Where larger-than-normal bonuses had little impact on the husband's income, there was no material change in circumstances that warranted variation of spousal support — Menegaldo v. Menegaldo, 2012 CarswellOnt 6030, 2012 ONSC 2915, [2012] O.J. No. 2186 (Ont. S.C.J.), additional reasons at 2012 CarswellOnt 6189, 2012 ONSC 2940 (Ont. S.C.J.). The parties separated in 2004 following a 26-year, traditional marriage. The parties resolved the issues arising from their marital breakdown by way of minutes of settlement, which they executed in 2007. A final order, on consent of both parties, pursuant to the Minutes of Settlement was granted later in 2007. The husband failed to show a material change in circumstances regarding his income from 2007 to 2012. Although he had received larger-than-normal bonuses in 2009 and 2011, the husband's estimated 2012 income was not significantly different from his 2011 income. The failure of the wife to increase her income did not constitute a material change of circumstances that warranted variation of spousal support.

An increase in the payor's post-separation income does not necessitate an increase in spousal support — Sarophim v. Sarophim, 2010 CarswellBC 370, 2010 BCSC 216, 82 R.F.L. (6th) 318 (B.C.S.C. [In Chambers]). In addressing the issue of post-separation income, the court noted that simply because the husband was receiving extra income from employment above and beyond his full-time employment, does not mean that the wife is entitled to additional spousal support. The wife should not receive increased spousal support because the husband has decided to work harder and longer hours at his second job.

Spouse not entitled to share in other spouse's increased income earned after separation, where she had not provided sufficient evidence to show that she had contributed to the skills or credentials which specifically led to his ability to earn an increased income — Sawchuk v. Sawchuk, 2010 CarswellAlta 32, 2010 ABQB 5, 79 R.F.L. (6th) 135, 22 Alta. L.R. (5th) 383, 485 A.R. 183, [2010] A.J. No. 18 (Alta. Q.B.). There was no temporal link between the marriage and the post-separation salary increase. The husband, an electrician, had received a great increase in his income since separation. The increase was due to his overtime work. The wife was entitled to support as she was entitled to an equitable distribution of the benefits of the parties' marriage and because of her contributions, both monetary and non-monetary, to their collective union. As the parties had a long-term marriage of 24 years, and their lives had evolved together, there was a presumption on separation that their standards of living would be equalized. She was entitled to an equalization of their standards of living based upon the parties' at-separation standard of living. She was not, however, entitled to share in his post-separation increase in income.

There is no direct, automatic link between increased income and entitlement to increased support for the recipient spouse — Judd v. Judd, 2010 CarswellBC 246, 2010 BCSC 153, 83 R.F.L. (6th) 314, [2010] B.C.J. No. 177 (B.C S.C.). On a de novo application for support, the judge found that a one-time increase in the spouse's income because of responsibilities related to the Olympics should not be included in his income under the SSAG. The judge found that this increase was not related to the role played by the wife during the marriage and declined to include it.

Increases in the husband's income since separation were considered, but were not applied to the interim award — Boju v. Corr, 2009 CarswellOnt 563 (Ont. S.C.J.). The parties were married in the United States in 2001. The husband moved to Canada in 2005, and the wife remained in the United States. She was currently living in Arizona. The husband petitioned for divorce in 2008. The husband, who earned $52,000 per year and had received increases in salary since moving to Canada, opposed payment of spousal support. The wife's interim application for spousal support was granted. The wife, who was the primary caregiver of the parties' young child, was entitled to support on an interim basis. The wife's claim for support in the amount of $500 per month was reasonable. The amount claimed by the wife was less than half of the lowest amount payable under the *Spousal Support Advisory Guidelines*. The amount awarded took into account that the wife lived with her parents and was not currently paying rent, and that the cost of living was lower in Arizona than Toronto.

*No entitlement to spouse's post-separation increase in income* — *Bryant v. Gordon*, 2007 CarswellBC 1613, 2007 BCSC 946, 45 R.F.L. (6th) 99, [2007] B.C.J. No. 1460 (B.C.S.C. [In Chambers]). The parties had been married for over 20 years. At the time of the hearing, the wife's childcare duties were minimal. The court used the husband's income at separation, as otherwise the wife would have a higher standard of living than she had experienced during the marriage. The court emphasized the need for the wife to attain self-sufficiency. She was employed, but the court was of the opinion that she could be earning more, if she did not limit her work hours. The court imputed an income of $38,000 to the wife. Using the SSAG, she would receive in the range of between $1,145 and $1,820 per annum. The court granted the wife support of $1,800 monthly.

*A spouse is generally not entitled to share in the other spouse's post-separation increase in income* — *Logan v. Logan*, 2007 CarswellBC 1435, 2007 BCSC 904 (B.C.S.C. [In Chambers]). After their separation, the husband and wife settled all issues arising from the marriage and its breakdown pursuant to the terms of a consent order which specified the parties' respective Guideline incomes at $100,000 for the husband and $4,000 for the wife. The husband was to pay spousal support to the wife in the sum of $2,400 per month, an amount which would be reduced by her investment income and her gross monthly employment income in excess of $333.33 per month. The only change in circumstances since the time of the parties' consent order, when the husband earned $100,000 a year, was his increase in income. The husband's income was $118,989 in 2004, $117,472 in 2005, and $108,000 in 2006. As this proceeding was a review hearing, the court essentially looked at the circumstances of the parties and could again consider the three models of spousal support discussed in *Bracklow v. Bracklow*, 1999 CarswellBC 533, 1999 CarswellBC 532, 44 R.F.L. (4th) 1, [1999] 1 S.C.R. 420, 63 B.C.L.R. (3d) 77, [1999] 8 W.W.R. 740, 169 D.L.R. (4th) 577, 120 B.C.A.C. 211, 196 W.A.C. 211, 236 N.R. 79, [1999] S.C.J. No. 14 (S.C.C.), keeping in mind the factors and objectives of spousal support set out in s. 15.2(4) and (6) of the *Divorce Act*. The court held, at para. 40, that post-separation increases in income should only be taken into account where there are "circumstances as in *Bracklow*, where non-compensatory obligations arising from the marriage will outweigh the parties' needs for closure. Usually these extreme cases have come about because the hopes and aspirations of the separating parties have not materialized usually for circumstances beyond their control." The consent order contemplated that the wife would obtain employment. In fact, she only received income from disability pensions. The court considered that as the SSAG did not apply to a review, it was necessary to consider her property and financial statements to determine whether she was, with her income, in need of support. The court found that the wife was entitled to support on compensatory and non-compensatory grounds. The overriding principle was the equitable distribution to both parties of economic consequences of the marriage breakdown. The husband agreed that the wife was entitled to continued spousal support. He intended to retire on April 30, 2008. The husband's income was $110,000 annually and the wife's income was $10,000 annually. The court roughly calculated what the *Spousal Support Advisory Guidelines* would yield, and noted that the low range of spousal support would be $2,394, while the middle would be $2,688 and the highest level would be $2,981. The court ordered spousal support of $2,400 per month. [However the husband's income was $100,000 at the time of the consent order. The court, at the review hearing, based the amount of the spousal support on the husband's current income of $110,000. Consequently, the court did seem to take post-separation income into account.]

*When the conceptual basis for on-going support is need, then spousal support should be towards an amount based on the 'marital standard of living' rather than based on a standard taking into account post-separation increases in the payor's income* (obiter) — *Kelly v. Kelly*, 2007 CarswellBC 342, 2007 BCSC 227, [2007] B.C.J. No. 324 (B.C.S.C.). In 2001, the wife obtained divorce and spousal support orders. The husband was ordered to pay the wife $2,000 per month for the first 2 years, $1,500 for the third year, and $1,000 thereafter. The wife remarried. The husband brought an application for variation or termination of support. The wife brought an application for increased support. The husband's application was granted. The wife's application was dismissed. On the applications, the court looked at the husband's postseparation income in considering quantum. The court observed that the SSAG do not require that support be increased, if the payor spouse's income increases. The matter should proceed on a case by case basis to be determined at the judge's discretion. The husband was ordered to pay monthly support of $750 from January 2006 to November 2007 and $500 until November 2008, when it would end.

*An increase in the payor's income by itself may not justify an increase in spousal support* — *Emery v. Emery*, 2007 CarswellBC 2889, 2007 BCSC 1747, 47 R.F.L. (6th) 72 (B.C.S.C.). A great disparity in post separation standards of living could indicate an economic disadvantage following from the dissolution of the marriage or the roles assumed by the parties in the marriage. The concept of need should have to take into account the relative standards of living of the spouses after the marriage breakdown. The parties had been married for 23 years. Although the court found that the wife was capable of earning more income than she was earning, there was still a significant discrepancy between their incomes. The re-apportionment of the property assisted the wife, but she was not self-sufficient or independent. She continued to be in need of spousal support. The court reduced spousal support for the wife from $1,750 to $1,300 per month.

*No sharing of post-separation increase in income* — *C. (D.B.) v. W. (R.M.)*, 2006 CarswellAlta 1723, 2006 ABQB 905, 69 Alta. L.R. (4th) 170, [2006] A.J. No. 1629 (Alta. Q.B.). The wife was a supportive spouse and a good mother, but "there was no credible evidence to show that [the husband]'s post-separation success was in any way attributable to the wife's contributions". As a result, the court refused to allow the wife to share in the increased income.

*The portion of the husband's increased income attributable to his relationship with his employer was not linked to the wife and was consequently unavailable for sharing with her through support* — *Fletcher v. Fletcher*, 2003 CarswellAlta 1534, 2003 ABQB 890, [2003] A.J. No. 1333 (Alta. Q.B.).

*Payee spouse was not entitled to increased spousal support where the additional income was not related to the breakdown of the marriage or any sacrifice made by the wife during the marriage, but rather to a business reorganization and the husband's additional work* — *Rozen v. Rozen*, 2003 CarswellBC 1564, 2003 BCSC 973, 37 R.F.L. (5th) 205, [2003] B.C.J. No. 1486 (B.C.S.C.). The additional income was not, in the judge's view, related to the breakdown of the marriage or the sacrifice made by the wife during marriage. [See also Annotation by James G. MacLeod in *Rozen v. Rozen*, supra, at 209 [R.F.L.], where the author wrote: "Automatically sharing post-separation increases in income is akin to treating a job as if it were a family asset, shareable in specie. Rather than doing so as a matter of course, courts should investigate whether there is sufficient relationship between the increased income and the payee's efforts during marriage to justify allowing him or her to share in the increase."

## 5.3  Means and Needs of Party Seeking Support

A spousal support order, by contrast to a child support order, must always consider the means and needs of the party seeking support as well as those of the party from whom it is sought. Just like the means and needs of the party from whom support is sought, those of the party seeking support are to be considered in light of all relevant information and not merely income.

One common issue is whether it is significant that the party seeking support has started cohabiting with someone else. A support applicant who cohabits with an individual earning an income is likely to be less needy than he or she would otherwise be. However, cohabitation is by no means a bar to support, especially when there is a compensatory basis for it.

*Need may be a sufficient factual basis for support – Bracklow v. Bracklow*, 1999 CarswellBC 532, 1999 CarswellBC 533, 44 R.F.L. (4th) 1, 169 D.L.R. (4th) 577, [1999] 1 S.C.R. 420, [1999] 8 W.W.R. 740, 63 B.C.L.R. (3d) 77, 2120 B.C.A.C. 211, 196 W.A.C. 211, 36 N.R. 79, [1999] S.C.J. No. 14 (S.C.C.). While the 1985 *Divorce Act* represents a shift away from "means and needs" to some degree "it retains the older idea that spouses may have an obligation to meet or contribute to the need of their former partners where they have the capacity to pay, even in the absence of a contractual or compensatory foundation for the obligation – need alone may be enough."

*Need was de-emphasized and compensation emphasized as a basis of support by the 1985 Divorce Act – Moge v. Moge*, 1992 CarswellMan 143, 1992 CarswellMan 222, EYB 1992-67141, 43 R.F.L. (3d) 345, [1992] 3 S.C.R. 813, [1993] R.D.F. 168, [1993] 1 W.W.R. 481, 99 D.L.R. (4th) 456, 81 Man. R. (2d) 161, 30 W.A.C. 161, 145 N.R. 1, [1992] S.C.J. No. 107 (S.C.C.). In arriving at this opinion, the court referred to a report that the Law Reform Commission of Canada made in 1975. In this report, it recommended that "need", the traditional basis for support, be given a different interpretation. Need, in its view, should be defined in terms of the economic damage caused by the division of labour in the marriage, and the cost to repair this damage. The basis for support should be compensation for the economic loss incurred by the spouse who stays at home for the purpose of contributing non-monetary benefits to the marriage. It recommended that "the law should ascertain the extent to which the withdrawal from the labour force by the dependant spouse during the marriage (including loss of skills, seniority, work experience, continuity and so on) has adversely affected that spouse's ability to maintain himself or herself. The need upon which the right to maintenance is based therefore follows from the loss incurred by the maintained spouse in contributing to the marriage partnership." This recommendation seemed consistent with the court's understanding that the introduction of the objectives by the 1985 *Divorce Act* resulted in a shift away from "means and needs" as the exclusive test to "a much wider spectrum of considerations" defined by the objectives.

*Self-sufficiency is a relative concept encompassing more than the ability to meet basic expenses – Fisher v. Fisher*, 2008 CarswellOnt 43, 2008 ONCA 11, 88 O.R. (3d) 241, 232 O.A.C. 213, 47 R.F.L. (6th) 235, 288 D.L.R. (4th) 513, [2008] O.J. No. 38 (Ont. C.A.). In clarifying the definition of self-sufficiency the court states that, "self-sufficiency, with its connotation of economic independence, is a relative concept. It is not achieved simply because a former spouse can meet basic expenses on a particular amount of income; rather, self-sufficiency relates to the ability to support a reasonable standard of living. It is to be assessed in relation to the economic partnership the parties enjoyed and could sustain during cohabitation, and that they can reasonably anticipate after separation... Thus, a determination of self-sufficiency requires consideration of the parties' present and potential incomes, their standard of living during marriage, the efficacy of any suggested steps to increase a party's means, the parties' likely post-separation circumstances (including the impact of equalization of their property), the duration of their cohabitation and any other relevant factors."

*Encroaching on capital to maintain a standard of living comparable to that enjoyed during the marriage can indicate hardship from the breakdown of the marriage* — Chutter v. Chutter, 2008 CarswellBC 2661, 2008 BCCA 507, 60 R.F.L. (6th) 263, 301 D.L.R. (4th) 297, [2009] 3 W.W.R. 246, 86 B.C.L.R. (4th) 233, 263 B.C.A.C. 109, 443 W.A.C. 109, [2008] B.C.J. No. 2398 (B.C.C.A.), additional reasons at 2009 CarswellBC 1028, 2009 BCCA 177, 70 R.F.L. (6th) 1, 97 B.C.L.R. (4th) 32, [2009] 12 W.W.R. 100, 309 D.L.R. (4th) 670, 269 B.C.A.C. 206, 453 W.A.C. 206 (B.C.C.A.). Leave to appeal refused 2009 CarswellBC 1386, 2009 CarswellBC 1387, [2009] S.C.C.A. No. 41, 398 N.R. 390 (note), 284 B.C.A.C. 319 (note) (S.C.C.). The parties were married for almost 30 years and the wife was seeking spousal support. In awarding no spousal support, the Trial Judge found that the assets that the wife received could provide her with a standard of living that was comparable to that which she enjoyed during the marriage. On appeal, the court found that the Trial Judge overlooked principles underlying compensatory support where one spouse has been disadvantaged by the marriage and its breakdown. The court further noted that if the wife must encroach upon her capital to maintain a standard of living comparable to that which she enjoyed during the marriage, then arguably she is suffering hardship from the breakdown of the marriage and experiencing the loss of the marital standard of living, since her capital would deplete over time and eventually she would be in a worse position than if the marriage had continued. On appeal, spousal support was reinstated.

*Neither party entitled to spousal support; parties' circumstances relatively similar* — Beaudry v. Beaudry, 2010 CarswellAlta 289, 2010 ABQB 119, 80 R.F.L. (6th) 88, 22 Alta. L.R. (5th) 219, 489 A.R. 294 (Alta. Q.B.). The parties commenced cohabitation in 1996, married in 1997, and separated in January 2006. The husband had two children from his previous marriages and the wife had three children from her previous marriage. During the first 6 years of marriage the wife cared for the children, completed a management programme, became a licensed real estate agent in 2002 and subsequently carried on business as a self-employed agent as of 2007. The wife's income was $79,142. The husband's income was significantly reduced due to the recession and he earned less than $24,000 per year. The husband and wife brought an application for spousal support and the court found that neither party was entitled to spousal support. The relationship of 10 years was of moderate term, and the conditions, means and needs of each party were relatively similar. At the date of separation both parties were economically self-sufficient. The court found that the husband suffered health conditions affecting his ability to support himself, but he remained able to work and was economically self-sufficient. The wife was disadvantaged by the marriage in the early years of the relationship but overcame the disadvantage by establishing a successful career as a real estate agent.

*Payee cohabitation not an automatic bar to support* — B. (G.) c. G. (L.), 1995 CarswellQue 23, 1995 CarswellQue 120, EYB 1995-67821, 15 R.F.L. (4th) 201, [1995] 3 S.C.R. 370, [1995] R.D.F. 611, 127 D.L.R. (4th) 385, 186 N.R. 201, [1995] S.C.J. No. 72 (S.C.C.). Where a payee is cohabiting, he or she is not automatically disentitled to support.

*Where the payee spouse receives assets on equalization in exchange for a part of her former spouse's pension entitlement, she must use those assets in a reasonable attempt to generate income at least by the time the pension starts to pay out* — Boston v. Boston, 2001 CarswellOnt 2432, 2001 CarswellOnt 2433, REJB 2001-25002, 17 R.F.L. (5th) 4, [2001] 2 S.C.R. 413, 201 D.L.R. (4th) 1, 28 C.C.P.B. 17, 271 N.R. 248, 149 O.A.C. 50, C.E.B. & P.G.R. 8385 (headnote only), [2001] S.C.J. No. 45 (S.C.C.). She cannot save the assets that she receives upon equalization and choose instead to live on the liquidation of the former spouse's pension when he retires. If she were permitted to do so, she would accumulate an estate while the former spouse's estate is liquidating. Not having invested her assets, she should be found to have an income based on what they could reasonably produce if invested. Here the husband retired on his pension income and applied to reduce the support payments to his wife that were ordered in a consent judgement made before retirement. The judgement also equalized the net family properties of the parties which included the capitalized value of that part of the husband's pension earned during the marriage. In implementing the judgement the husband received net assets of approximately $385,000 ($333,329 being the capitalized value of his pension) and the wife received assets of approximately $370,000 ($213,000 of which was comprised of the matrimonial home and its contents). At the time of the proceedings the wife's assets had increased in value to approximately $493,000. The husband's assets were worth $7,000. Actuarial evidence showed that if the wife invested $250,000 in a life annuity, it would produce $18,025 per year for life. If she invested $500,000 it would produce $36,050 per year for life. The motions judge granted the application and reduced the amount of support from $3,433.12 per month (indexed annually to the cost of living) to $950 per month (not indexed) taking into account the ability of the wife to produce a reasonable income from her investments and the available income the husband would have from the part of his pension that was not equalized in the property division. The Ontario Court of Appeal changed the $950 to $2,000 a month. The Supreme Court of Canada allowed an appeal from the Court of Appeal and reinstated the judgement of the motions judge with the further order that the monthly amount be indexed and arrears, if any, of spousal support be paid to the wife.

*Focus under 15.2(6)(c) is not compensation but rather need — Moge v. Moge,* 1992 CarswellMan 143, 1992 CarswellMan 222, EYB 1992-67141, 43 R.F.L. (3d) 345, [1992] 3 S.C.R. 813, [1993] R.D.F. 168, [1993] 1 W.W.R. 481, 99 D.L.R. (4th) 456, 81 Man. R. (2d) 161, 30 W.A.C. 161, 145 N.R. 1, [1992] S.C.J. No. 107 (S.C.C.). Madame Justice McLachlin, in her concurring reasons, held that in the considering the question of economic hardship arising from the breakdown of the marriage the focus was "not on compensation for what the spouses have contributed to or gained from the marriage but rather on post-marital need." She states that "if the breakdown of the marriage has created economic hardship for one or the other, the judge must attempt to grant relief from that hardship."

*Spousal support reduced on appeal as the trial judge failed to impute more income to the wife and erred in assessing her actual need as her expenses were overstated — Saunders v. Saunders,* 2011 CarswellNS 620, 2011 NSCA 81, 7 R.F.L. (7th) 265, 307 N.S.R. (2d) 297, 975 A.P.R. 297 (N.S.C.A.). The parties were married in 1974 and separated in 2007. The husband was a doctor working in the United States, and the wife was a registered nurse who worked part time. By consent order, the parties had agreed to spousal support of $8,000 per month, but the wife appealed and support was increased to $9,100 per month. On appeal by the husband, the Court of Appeal spousal support was reduced to $7,500 per month.

*The condition, means and needs of the wife did not accord with the findings of trial judge, who considered the appropriate facts, but misapprehended them - appeal allowed — Smith v. Smith,* 2011 CarswellNB 377, 2011 NBCA 66, 9 R.F.L. (7th) 286, 375 N.B.R. (2d) 208, 336 D.L.R. (4th) 285, 969 A.P.R. 208 (N.B.C.A.). Section 15.2(4) of the *Divorce Act* states that courts must take the means of each spouse into consideration. In the *Smith* case, the trial judge considered the appropriate facts, but misapprehended them. He considered the husband's possible future debts to be present-day actual debts and awarded spousal support of $1,000 per month. The trial judge's decision was reviewable The appellate court allowed the appeal, set aside the order made in the court below and set the amount of spousal support payable in the amount of $1,709.50 per month. See *Gonabady-Namadon v. Mohammadzadeh,* 2009 CarswellBC 2767, 2009 BCCA 448, 74 R.F.L. (6th) 1, 98 B.C.L.R. (4th) 23, 277 B.C.A.C. 48, 469 W.A.C. 48 (B.C.C.A.) at 5.2 Means and Needs of Party from Whom Support is Sought Post-separation Increases in the Payor Spouse's Income.

*Need is a relative concept — James v. James,* 2009 CarswellBC 1490, 2009 BCCA 261, 66 R.F.L. (6th) 246, 94 B.C.L.R. (4th) 183, [2009] 10 W.W.R. 11, 273 B.C.A.C. 75, 461 W.A.C. 75

(B.C.C.A.). On a variation application, the court held that the wife was entiled to a level of support that could maintain a lifestyle not dramatically different from that which she enjoyed during the years when the parties were married. The husband had the ability to pay. Support had been set at $5,750 per month when the husband's income was estimated to be $500,000. At the variation application, the court considered that his income for 2005 to 2006 was approximately $1 million dollars. The court varied the amount of spousal support to $9,000 per month.

*Where a recipient had no reasonable expectation of self-sufficiency, support continued —* Hepburn v. Hepburn, 2013 CarswellBC 2592, 2013 BCCA 383, 34 R.F.L. (7th) 267, 48 B.C.L.R. (5th) 251, 344 B.C.A.C. 6, 587 W.A.C. 6 (B.C.C.A.). A husband sought to vary a consent order for spousal support on the basis that his income had decreased. The reduction in income occurred because he spent more time on media opportunities which were not lucrative, rather than on his primary occupation as a physician. The chambers judge found that, while the husband was free to pursue these non-remunerative opportunities, he was not able to use this decision as a basis for a reduction of spousal support. It was open to him to attempt to work more hours as a physician, and the reduction of income was a result of his preferences rather than circumstances. The original order was indefinite, and the wife was reliant on the support as there was no reasonable expectation that she would return to the workforce and attain even partial self-sufficiency.

*Spousal support should be reduced where the quantum far exceeds the stated needs of the dependant spouse —* Turner v. Turner, 1998 CarswellBC 2434, 43 R.F.L. (4th) 437, 60 B.C.L.R. (3d) 64, 114 B.C.A.C. 303, 186 W.A.C. 303, [1998] B.C.J. No. 2615 (B.C.C.A.). In this case, the trial judge set an amount of support that was four times the amount requested in the wife's material, and was based in part upon her anticipated costs of living independently, even though it was not known if the wife were capable of living on her own, and the material did not provide a basis for calculating what it would cost if she were able to so do. Spousal support was reduced from $2,000 to $1,200 per month.

*Need, in calculating support, varies in accordance with the circumstances of the parties and the family unit as a whole —* Myers v. Myers, 1995 CarswellBC 1095, 17 R.F.L. (4th) 298, 65 B.C.A.C. 226, 106 W.A.C. 226, [1995] B.C.J. No. 2300 (B.C.C.A.). Leave to appeal refused 1996 CarswellBC 3125, 1996 CarswellBC 3126, 83 B.C.A.C. 319 (note), 136 W.A.C. 319 (note), 203 N.R. 319 (note), [1995] S.C.C.A. No. 536 (S.C.C.). Need does not necessarily end when the claimant spouse achieves a subsistence level of income or any level above subsistence. It is a flexible concept and is only one factor to be considered in determining whether a support award is warranted.

*Wife's needs could be eliminated by relying on her parents and husband's income had declined precipitously — no support —* A. (P.) c. C. (S.), 1988 CarswellQue 42, 14 R.F.L. (3d) 246, 12 Q.A.C. 278, [1988] R.J.Q. 323, [1988] R.D.F. 105 (C.A. Que.). Where the husband had been ordered to pay spousal support based upon sizeable past income and his access to credit, the order was reversed on appeal. The husband had retained little or none of his past revenues and his wife, with some assistance from her parents, could meet her own needs.

*The husband's argument that wife was married twice before, and has three adult children and a brother and sister capable of supporting her, was rejected since the primary burden of support for a needy partner lies with the spouse —* Fedor v. Fedor, 2011 CarswellAlta 418, 2011 ABQB 185, 96 R.F.L. (6th) 309, 46 Alta. L.R. (5th) 221, 525 A.R. 128, [2011] A.J. No. 314 (Alta. Q.B.).

*The husband's wish to turn over his interest-earning assets to his son could not displace support obligation for needy wife —* Fedor v. Fedor, 2011 CarswellAlta 418, 2011 ABQB 185, 96 R.F.L. (6th) 309, 46 Alta. L.R. (5th) 221, 525 A.R. 128, [2011] A.J. No. 314 (Alta. Q.B.).

*The wife's entitlement to time-limited support was based on her need arising from the income disparity between the parties* — *Barraco v. Scott*, 2011 CarswellOnt 8325, 2011 ONSC 4467, 9 R.F.L. (7th) 126 (Ont. S.C.J.). The parties married in 1994, had 3 children, and separated in 2006. Prior to the marriage and for 3 years during the marriage, the wife had worked in financial services. During the marriage, she assumed primary care of the children, obtained a teaching degree and other academic qualifications and taught part-time. After the separation, she became a mortgage broker. At the time of separation, she was 38 years old and the husband, an assistant Crown Attorney, was 39 years old. The wife earned $52,000 and the husband earned $187,000. On the wife's application for retroactive and ongoing support, the court concluded that although the wife performed a somewhat greater proportion of the non-economic responsibilities, the husband participated to the extent of his abilities and time. The court further determined that although the mar-riage did not disadvantage the wife in terms of career choices, the wife's claim was based on her need arising from the fact of the parties' income disparity. Accordingly, it was or-dered that the wife receive retroactive support in the amount of $20,000, and ongoing support in the amount of $2,100 per month terminating January 2018.

*From a practical point of view, the amount of spousal support should be a reflection of recipient's reasonable needs and not exceed the payor's means* — *Phillips-Curwin v. Curwin*, 2008 CarswellNS 328, 2008 NSSC 198, [2008] N.S.J. No. 267 (N.S.S.C.). The wife, age 34, had primary care of the parties' two children while the husband, age 42, was employed as a sales representative with an income of $156,000. The court ordered the husband to pay the wife spousal support in the amount of $2,000 per month in addition to child support.

*Support payable* — *a significant disparity in the spouses' incomes resulting from their cohabitation and the functions each performed over the years, the wife is in need and the husband has an ability to provide financial assistance* — *Emery v. Emery*, 2008 CarswellOnt 1165, 51 R.F.L. (6th) 294, [2008] O.J. No. 844 (Ont. S.C.J.), additional reasons at 2008 CarswellOnt 1655 (Ont. S.C.J.), additional reasons at 2008 CarswellOnt 2924 (Ont. S.C.J.).

*A former spouse is entitled to support based on need where she has a disability that makes it difficult, if not impossible, for her to maintain permanent employment and her disability pension does not provide her with sufficient income to meet her needs* — *H. (L.M.) v. H. (G.D.)*, 2006 CarswellBC 1684, 2006 BCSC 1035 (B.C.S.C.), reversed 2008 CarswellBC 2815, 2008 BCCA 547, 61 R.F.L. (6th) 48, 86 B.C.L.R. (4th) 320, 264 B.C.A.C. 125, 445 W.A.C. 125 (B.C.C.A.). The parties' relationship had lasted 15 years. The fact that the dependant spouse did not seek interim support, that she had formed a new spousal-like relationship and that for a time was being supported by her new spouse, although he was no longer able to do so, are not necessarily bars to a later claim for support. The plaintiff asserted that her new partner was unemployed, as he was suffering from depression. However, as she provided no medical evidence to support this contention, the court was not satisfied that the former wife had established entitlement to an order for periodic spousal support.

*Need goes beyond the basic necessities of life and varies according to the circumstances of the parties* — *T. (T.) v. H. (J.M.)*, 2014 CarswellBC 725, 2014 BCSC 451 (B.C.S.C.). The parties were married for 17 years, and the wife sought indefinite spousal support. The judge found that, although the parties had a medium-term marriage, they were a close economic unit and support should reflect that the wife had a "presumptive claim to equal standards of living" on the dissolution of the marriage.

*A support recipient did not demonstrate a reason for lack of income earned at the levels projected by an original support order to demonstrate a material change in circumstances* — *Kerman v. Kerman*, 2014 CarswellBC 679, 2014 BCSC 428 (B.C.S.C.). The wife sought a retroactive increase of support. The parties were married for 17 years and had separated approximately 17 years prior to this application. An order for support was made in 2008 which anticipated the income each party would earn. The wife showed she had not earned the income anticipated by the order. The judge found she had not explained circumstances, such as an unanticipated medical condition, or demonstrated steps taken to self-sufficiency that would form a material change in circumstances. Her application was dismissed.

*Spousal support was to continue until the recipient wife had obtained self-sufficiency anticipated 4 years after a 20-year marriage when there was no evidence the husband could not afford to pay. This was consistent with the parties' previous agreement* — *C. (M.S.) v. C. (T.L.),* 2013 CarswellNS 885, 2013 NSSC 378, 337 N.S.R. (2d) 177, 1067 A.P.R. 177 (N.S.S.C.). The parties had concluded a separation agreement, which provided for spousal support at below the Guidelines range and review at any time without showing a material change in circumstances. The parties were married for 20 years, and the judge found that the wife was entitled to compensatory support, which was consistent with the original agreement for spousal support. The wife projected she would be self-sufficient within 4 years of separation, and spousal support was ordered to continue until that time. There was no evidence that the husband did not have the means to pay support.

*In determining spousal support, a court will consider inheritance as part of the recipient's means. The husband had an income that was approximately $80,000 more than that of the wife and despite her superior capital position, spousal support was ordered to continue* — *Holman v. Holman,* 2013 CarswellOnt 16472, 2013 ONSC 6988 (Ont. S.C.J.). The parties were married for 19 years prior to separation in 2002. They had two adult daughters. The wife had been a stay-at-home mother during the marriage. She had received $300,000 from an inheritance after separation, which the judge found must be considered as part of her assets and means under the *Family Law Act.* The judge also found that her means were equal to or superior to those she enjoyed during the marriage. She had attained self-sufficiency. Spousal support was not terminated because it had been paid for 10 years, and the husband had means to pay.

*An increase in the wife's income that formed more than the total amount of spousal support payable to her was a material change in circumstances. Support was terminated* — *Dodman v. Chiola,* 2012 CarswellNS 635, 2012 NSSC 272, [2012] N.S.J. No. 474 (N.S.S.C.). The husband sought to terminate spousal support which had been set by a 2010 order. The husband's income had decreased, while the wife's had increased by 70%. The judge found this change constituted a material change in circumstances, and support was terminated.

*Means of the recipient spouse do not include income from real property assets that are not currently income-producing* — *M. (P.R.) v. M. (B.J.),* 2012 CarswellBC 3748, 2012 BCSC 1795 (B.C.S.C.). The parties were married for 23 years and had four children. The wife sought spousal support. The wife had received significant assets of over $4 million through the division of property. The husband argued that the wife's income should take into account potential income received through management of real property assets, which were not currently income-producing. The judge rejected this argument, finding that to "engage in this type of exercise removes any element of finality in terms of division of property and contaminates a proper analysis of income upon which spousal support is to be calculated".

*Partner found not to be needy or helpless* — *no spousal support ordered* — *Fisher v. Fisher,* 2009 CarswellAlta 1642, 2009 ABQB 85, 74 R.F.L. (6th) 117, 456 A.R. 363 (Alta. Q.B.). In this case, Ms. Fisher sought spousal support after the breakdown of her 8 year common law relationship. In rejecting her claim, the court noted, "in summary, this is a situation in which Ms. Fisher was independent and self-sufficient prior to marriage and remained equally independent and self-sufficient when she left the marriage. She is neither needy nor helpless. She has not established that there was any pattern of marital economic dependence. The mere fact that Mr. Fisher now earns considerably more than she does is not itself a basis for spousal support."

*A spouse is not required to encroach on his/her capital to meet daily expenses — Elgner v. Elgner*, 2009 CarswellOnt 7702, 85 R.F.L. (6th) 5, [2009] O.J. No. 52691 (Ont. S.C.J.), leave to appeal refused 2010 CarswellOnt 1640, 2010 ONSC 1578, 85 R.F.L. (6th) 62, 99 O.R. (3d) 687, 267 O.A.C. 1, [2010] O.J. No. 1139 (Ont. Div. Ct.), additional reasons at 2010 CarswellOnt 3918, 2010 ONSC 2399, 85 R.F.L. (6th) 71 (Ont. Div. Ct.), affirmed 2010 CarswellOnt 6860, 2010 ONSC 3512, 92 R.F.L. (6th) 106, 103 O.R. (3d) 588, 324 D.L.R. (4th) 277, 268 O.A.C. 267 (Ont. Div. Ct.), affirmed 2011 CarswellOnt 5673, 2011 ONCA 483, 5 R.F.L. (7th) 1, 105 O.R. (3d) 721, 336 D.L.R. (4th) 159, 282 O.A.C. 28 (Ont. C.A.), leave to appeal refused 2011 CarswellOnt 12421, 2011 CarswellOnt 12421 (S.C.C.). After the parties' separation, the wife was encroaching on her capital, received as an equalization payment, to meet her daily expenses. In awarding a large spousal support award, the court noted that while the wife received generous amounts of capital, even if all of that were invested, it would never produce an income that could even meet her expenses after separation. She therefore should not have to deplete a large percentage of her capital for her daily needs.

*Wife entitled to spousal support despite high income — Gilliland v. Gilliland*, 2009 CarswellOnt 3895, 72 R.F.L. (6th) 88, [2009] O.J. No. 2782 (Ont. S.C.J.). If there is a significant income disparity, entitlement on either compensatory or non-compensatory grounds may be established despite the fact that the recipient has a relatively high income. In this case, the wife earned $93,000 as a pilot and had a number of income producing properties. The court found that although the wife earned a high income, she was still entitled to spousal support because her husband earned more than she did, and the parties were married for 17 years.

*Spousal support awarded because of disparity in income — Vlachias v. Vlachias*, 2009 CarswellBC 1647, 2009 BCSC 843 (B.C.S.C.). The parties moved in together in 1997, married in 1999, and separated in 2007. The husband earned approximately $95,000 per year and the wife earned $48,000 per year. The parties each paid their personal expenses and contributed to household expenses. The court found that the wife did not give up employment opportunities and could support herself, particularly after receiving her share of the family assets. The wife did not suffer economic loss from the marriage nor was she disadvantaged; however, the court found that the wife was entitled to a small amount of spousal support based on compensatory principles in the amount of $12,000.

*No spousal support for wife because she was a drug addict — F. (G.G.) v. F. (R.)*, 2009 CarswellBC 317, 2009 BCPC 43 (B.C. Prov. Ct.). The wife was addicted to cocaine and engaged in prostitution when the parties met and married in 1997. In 1998, the wife developed a cyst in her neck which became infected, resulting in paraplegia and use of a wheelchair. The parties separated in 2005 and the wife sought spousal support. The court found that since 2007 the wife had been in receipt of social assistance from which her rent was paid directly and what was left over was used to buy her drugs. The court dismissed her application for spousal support and stated that this was not a marriage that gave rise to a social obligation. Since separation, the wife's needs had been met by the government and the court accepted the husband's argument that if he paid her spousal support, the wife would use it to feed her drug habit.

*Dependant spouse's inability to find employment not attributable to marriage breakdown — time-limited support ordered — R. (S.M.) v. R. (P.E.)*, 2002 CarswellBC 637, 2002 BCPC 92, 25 R.F.L. (5th) 375 (B.C. Prov. Ct.). Where the wife had been selfsupporting throughout the parties' 8-year relationship and 4-year marriage, but was on welfare and unable to find work after separation, she was awarded periodic spousal support for a period of 18 months. The wife clearly had a need but, long term, her inability to find employment could not be attributed to the collapse of the marriage.

*Need was not established where the wife's financial circumstances had improved since separation — Gervasio v. Gervasio*, 1999 CarswellOnt 1061, 45 R.F.L. (4th) 342 (Ont. Gen. Div.).

Although the wife had been out of the workforce for a number of years caring for the parties' children, her bank balances and R.R.S.P. account had increased after separation, and she had been able to purchase a house. She had failed to update her financial statement. In the circumstances, she was unable to establish the need for support and her claim was dismissed.

*Payee cohabiting — no need for ongoing support, but entitled to lump sum as compensatory support — Kits v. Kits*, 1998 CarswellBC 2323, 42 R.F.L. (4th) 167, [1998] B.C.J. No. 2539 (B.C.S.C.). Where the wife would be able to maintain her standard of living with the income of her new partner, child support and an unequal property division in her favour, her application for periodic support was denied. She was, however, entitled to a lump sum to compensate her for the loss of a lucrative career.

*Where the husband suffered a shortfall in the amount needed to support himself as a result of the division of matrimonial property, his need was found to be based on an economic disadvantage properly traced to the marriage breakdown — he was accordingly entitled to support — Bracewell v. Bracewell*, 1994 CarswellAlta 379, 4 R.F.L. (4th) 183, 152 A.R. 379, [1994] A.J. No. 312 (Alta. Q.B.). The parties had cohabited for 32 years. At the time of the trial, the husband was unable to work because of ill-health and was dependant on a pension income and the benefit of sharing expenses with the woman with whom he lived and who operated a bed and breakfast business in her home. The wife was employed and earned an income that was higher than the husband's. His pensions were included in the property division whereby the payments were to be equally divided at source and one-half paid to the wife and one-half to the husband. The wife held the greater share of the balance of the matrimonial property and was ordered to pay the husband $22,828 as an equalization payment. A shortfall based on the husband's needs was found to be $350 a month, which the wife was ordered to pay so long as she was employed and the husband was not.

*Payor not to be impoverished — Flicker v. Fricker*, 1991 CarswellNS 607, 109 N.S.R. (2d) 234, 297 A.P.R. 234 (N.S.T.D.). In an application for spousal support, the needs of the claimant party must be addressed, but not at the expense of impoverishing the other.

*Fact that party squandered severance allowance relevant but he would have been in need anyway — Jering v. Jering*, 1987 CarswellMan 99, 7 R.F.L. (3d) 42, 45 Man. R. (2d) 296 (Man. Q.B.). Although the husband had squandered $20,000 of a $55,000 severance allowance after losing his job, the wife was ordered to pay periodic support to him until he found employment. Even if he had not dissipated the funds, he would have required assistance.

*Onus on claimant in a new relationship to show continuing disadvantage from first relationship — Juvatopolos v. Juvatopolos*, 2004 CarswellOnt 4423, 9 R.F.L. (6th) 147, [2004] O.T.C. 941, [2004] O.J. No. 4381 (Ont. S.C.J.), affirmed 2005 CarswellOnt 4774, 19 R.F.L. (6th) 76, 202 O.A.C. 1, [2005] O.J. No. 4181 (Ont. C.A.). Where a spouse lost the opportunity to have a successful career at an earlier age as a result of her assumed role of mother and traditional wife, the economic disadvantage continued even though at a later period, she became available for work. Where, as in this case, the wife had formed a new relationship, the onus lay with her to establish, that notwithstanding this new relationship, the economic loss resulting from the first relationship remained. The court found that from the perspective of compensatory support, the wife had discharged that onus.

*Remarriage relevant on support reduction — Savoie v. Savoie*, 1999 CarswellMan 308, 49 R.F.L. (4th) 336, [1999] 9 W.W.R. 63, 175 D.L.R. (4th) 291, 138 Man. R. (2d) 128, 202 W.A.C. 128, [1999] M.J. No. 298 (Man. C.A.). A reduction in spousal support took into account the wife's remarriage, among other factors.

*Payee cohabiting — suffered economic disadvantage, not disentitled to support, but amount is affected — Lauderdale v. Lauderdale*, 1996 CarswellAlta 43, 21 R.F.L. (4th) 17, 180 A.R. 81, [1996] A.J. No. 53 (Alta. Q.B.), reversed 1997 CarswellAlta 448, 29 R.F.L. (4th) 34, 200 A.R.

198, 146 W.A.C. 198, [1997] A.J. No. 499 (Alta. C.A.). If a spouse suffers an economic disadvantage as a result of the breakdown of the marriage, entering into a new relationship does not change that fact. Remarriage is an erroneous consideration for rejection of a periodic support model. Remarriage is only one factor to be considered. The award of lump sum spousal support was set aside and the question of the quantum of periodic support was remitted to the trial judge to be determined on the record.

*Relevance of payee cohabitation — Wettlaufer v. Wettlaufer*, 2007 CarswellBC 179, 2007 BCSC 137, [2007] B.C.J. No. 168 (B.C. Master). While the payee's cohabitation has some financial implications, it does not create a presumption against spousal support.

*Cohabitation does not disentitle a spouse to support, but economic benefits of cohabitation should be considered in relation to need for support — Bennett v. Bennett*, 2005 CarswellAlta 1994, 2005 ABQB 984, 22 R.F.L. (6th) 399, [2006] 9 W.W.R. 62, 57 Alta. L.R. (4th) 380, [2005] A.J. No. 1824 (Alta. Q.B.). What must be considered is the need for spousal support and the effect of the cohabitation or remarriage on that need. If the cohabitation or remarriage is simply transference to similar circumstances, there should not be an obligation to pay interim spousal support. If it is established that an applicant is living in cohabitation with another and yet refuses to provide the financial information of her partner, her application for interim spousal support should be dismissed. The wife received several economic advantages that mitigated her need for interim spousal support. She received extended health and dental benefits under her friend's Blue Cross coverage and a 50% waiver of tuition fees for her courses taken at the local college. She lived in her male friend's newly purchased home in which only the two of them resided. He earned a monthly gross income of $5,916.67 ($71,000 annually). The wife, at the time of the hearing, did not earn income as she attended college in order to gain self-sufficiency. The four children of the marriage were in the husband's care. The court did not accept that the wife's monthly expenses were an accurate reflection of her current need, as her male friend was assisting her financially. The court was of the opinion that the wife could undertake some employment in the summer months and income was imputed to her. The court found that the wife had a minimal need for spousal support and the husband had some ability to pay. The court ordered the husband to pay the wife $500 per month in interim spousal support.

*Fact that payee cohabiting with partner of significant income does not preclude support entitlement — R. (R.S.) v. R. (S.M.)*, 2006 CarswellBC 2295, 2006 BCSC 1404, 30 R.F.L. (6th) 339, [2006] B.C.J. No. 2109 (B.C.S.C.). Where the wife had received support pursuant to a separation agreement, was at the time of the hearing in a common law relationship with a new partner who had a significant income and was consequently not seeking support at that time, the court refused to dismiss her claim for spousal support. In the circumstances of the case, the wife was entitled to support on the basis of compensatory principles and need. If the *Spousal Support Advisory Guidelines* were followed, she would receive substantial support. The court stated that the wife's needs might change. If she stayed in the present relationship, her partner might or might not be able to support her as she was presently supported. Her own financial situation might improve, If she was not in the relationship, she might or might not need support. The question of her need would have to be assessed along with other considerations, at the time of her support application. The husband's application to dismiss the wife's claims for spousal support was refused.

*Spousal support should not be terminated where a subsequent relationship is not stable and there is no financial sharing — Gallant v. Gallant*, 2005 CarswellNS 325, 2005 NSSC 151, 234 N.S.R. (2d) 47, 745 A.P.R. 47, [2005] N.S.J. No. 297 (N.S.S.C.). The court found that the wife and her male friend were not in a common law relationship. They did not hold themselves out as a common-law couple, and he had his own residence. There was no evidence of a stable relationship, a shared commitment or a financial enmeshment. The court stated that even if it were wrong in reaching this conclusion, it would not be satisfied that support should be terminated. The only relevance of the relationship would be the extent to which the male friend contributed to the household expenses thereby reducing the wife's need.

*Where by the terms of a separation agreement a spouse is disentitled to spousal support if the wife remarries or other significant changes occur in the wife's financial circumstances, a common-law relationship should not be equated with remarriage* — Abbott v. Abbott, 2004 CarswellNfld 99, 2004 NLSCUFC 14, 236 Nfld. & P.E.I.R. 163, 700 A.P.R. 163, [2004] N.J. No. 135 (N.L.U.F.C). Further, the facts did not establish a common law relationship. Although the couple lived together when the male friend was in St. John's and although there was sexual activity, and the friend assisted minimally with household expenses, by paying to the wife roughly the same amount as previous boarders, the evidence to rebut a common-law relationship was far more persuasive. Neither party had access to the other's bank accounts. The wife introduced him to family, friends and colleagues as her "boyfriend" and he referred to her, and introduced her, as his "girlfriend". In addition, there were no references, by family, friends and acquaintances, to the couple being "partners" or being in a "common-law relationship". They began dating in February 2003 and did not start living under the same roof until December 2003. Neither party had definite long-term plans to stay with the other. Further, if the male friend, a pilot, obtained employment outside of the St. John's area, the wife did not intend to move with him. Consequently, the evidence did not support the existence of a common-law relationship. In addition, the court found that there had not been a significant change in the wife's financial circumstances.

*Payee cohabiting — no financial need for support* — Boddington v. Boddington, 2003 CarswellOnt 3914, 44 R.F.L. (5th) 13, [2003] O.J. No. 4008 (Ont. S.C.J.), additional reasons at 2003 CarswellOnt 5332, [2003] O.J. No. 5388 (Ont. S.C.J.), further additional reasons at 2003 CarswellOnt 5333, [2003] O.J. No. 5389 (Ont. S.C.J.). The wife's application for spousal support was dismissed on the ground that the wife had entered into a new spousal-type relationship and had no financial need for support. Despite the wife's claim that her new relationship was a friendship only, she had moved into her male friend's house, was shown as a co-owner on the deed to property, shared his business and had identified him as her "spouse" on her income tax return. A payee is not disentitled to support merely because she has a new relationship. However, in this case, the court would not order support, as the evidence did not demonstrate that the wife had a financial need that obligated the husband to pay support.

*Payee cohabiting — no financial need for support* — Peeples v. Peeples, 2003 CarswellNS 439, 2003 NSSF 52, [2003] N.S.J. No. 461 (N.S.S.C.). Where a spouse moves from her marriage to another interdependent relationship in which there are two incomes and her new relationship has been stable for a number of years, there is no need to order spousal support.

*No material change in circumstances — boyfriend/girlfriend relationship with third party* — H. (O.T.) v. H. (S.L.), 2003 CarswellBC 2020, 2003 BCSC 1270, [2003] B.C.J. No. 1942 (B.C Master), affirmed 2003 CarswellBC 2260, 2003 BCSC 1399, [2003] B.C.J. No. 2128 (B.C.S.C.). The court held that there was insufficient evidence to establish that the wife's relationship with her male friend was a marriage-like relationship. While the male friend stayed over occasionally, he owned and maintained his own separate residence. Even if there were such a relationship, it had not as yet lasted 2 years, the time required before he might have an obligation to her. At the most, one-half of the common costs of housing and utilities might be charged to him. However, in this case, the court found that the wife and her friend were not cohabiting and an attribution of common costs could not fairly be made to the wife's friend.

*Payee cohabiting — not disentitled to support, but amount is affected* — McNutt v. McNutt, 2000 CarswellOnt 847, 5 R.F.L. (5th) 90 (Ont. S.C.J.). Where the parties had cohabited for 37 years in a traditional marriage, and where the wife was dependant on her husband throughout that time, support was awarded at $1000 a month ($300 less than interim support). The court took into account, among other things, that she was residing with another individual and it was reasonable to assume that expenses were shared.

*Subsequent cohabitation irrelevant when support is compensatory — Uens v. Uens,* 2000 CarswellOnt 4478, 11 R.F.L. (5th) 202 (Ont. S.C.J.). In cases where support is awarded to compensate a spouse for advantages he or she conferred on a partner during their relationship, the fact that the spouse remarries or cohabits with another person should be irrelevant. Support in such cases is in the nature of relief against unjust enrichment and the second relationship is irrelevant to the benefit conferred on the prior partner. Accordingly, a payee in such cases should receive the same amount of support regardless of whether he or she remarries or cohabits with another person.

*No material change in circumstances — payee cohabiting — cohabitation does not disentitle a spouse to support — Uens v. Uens,* 2000 CarswellOnt 4478, 11 R.F.L. (5th) 202 (Ont. S.C.J.). Where the wife who was a homemaker and primarily responsible for the parties' five children, was entitled to support on a compensatory and non-compensatory basis, the fact that she was living common law with a third party was not an automatic bar to support. The wife and her current partner had a pre-nuptial agreement which provided that with the exception of rent, she was responsible for household expenses for the children and that each party waived support from the other. She was considering further education or education upgrade before seeking employment. The court found that the husband was earning $60,000 a year. It ordered spousal support in the amount of $500. However that amount was reduced to $300 per month until the child support arrears were eliminated.

*Support not varied from agreed-upon amount despite wife's new cohabitation — Osmar v. Osmar,* 2000 CarswellOnt 1927, 8 R.F.L. (5th) 375, [2000] O.J. No. 2060 (Ont. S.C.J.), additional reasons at 2000 CarswellOnt 2343, 8 R.F.L. (5th) 387, [2000] O.T.C. 979, [2000] O.J. No. 2504 (Ont. S.C.J.). The court held that while the wife's day-to-day financial needs were significantly reduced because she cohabited with a man who earned approximately $75,000 per annum, the spousal support provisions of the separation agreement clearly must have contemplated compensatory support for the roles adopted by the spouses during the marriage and the economic consequences of those roles. The marriage was a traditional one with the husband in the paid work force and the wife staying at home with the children. The court considered the factors and circumstances identified in ss. 33(8) and (9) of the *Family Law Act* and concluded that it was not appropriate to vary the spousal support provision of the separation agreement. The wife had lost ground financially by converting the child support to a tax neutral award under the Guidelines. The husband had made extravagant purchases, leasing a new $65,000 vehicle and committing himself to the purchase of a 4,000 square foot, $400,000 home during the currency of the litigation. Compensatory spousal support ought to be paid in priority to R.R.S.P. contributions and the husband's other lifestyle choices. Although the agreement contemplated future variation of spousal support, it did not refer to the wife's remarriage or cohabitation as specific factors that would trigger a variation. Such a clause is often found in such agreements. Its absence fortified the court's conclusion that the spousal support was primarily, if not exclusively, compensatory in nature. It was premature to vary it.

*No material change in circumstances — payee cohabiting — unstable relationship with a new partner, but her lifestyle to be considered — Lockyer v. Lockyer,* 2000 CarswellOnt 2805, 10 R.F.L. (5th) 318, [2000] O.J. No. 2939 (Ont. S.C.J.). The fact that the wife was enjoying a comfortable lifestyle through cohabitation with a new partner did not disentitle her to spousal support. The wife's status in her new relationship was precarious and subject to the terms of a cohabitation agreement. The wife's current lifestyle was, however, an appropriate consideration in determining the issue of quantum. The husband was ordered to pay the wife $375 per month. For a 2-year period from the date of judgement, the wife could earn $20,000 per year from employment and the husband $24,500 per year from employment without triggering a material change in circumstances. Neither party was employed at the time of judgement. The husband had retired from the Canadian army.

*Relevance of possibility of remarriage* — Lauderdale v. Lauderdale, 1999 CarswellAlta 296, 1999 ABQB 453, 50 R.F.L. (4th) 411, 241 A.R. 355 (Alta. Q.B.). The fact that a spouse may remarry is not a relevant consideration in determining whether or not that spouse suffered an economic disadvantage as a result of the marriage. Such a possibility can, however, be relevant in determining whether support should be restricted to a limited term.

*Payee cohabiting* — *relationship not permanent* — Bell v. Bell, 1998 CarswellNfld 246, 42 R.F.L. (4th) 301 (Nfld. U.F.C.). The wife was found to have been economically disadvantaged upon the dissolution of the parties 36-year traditional marriage. Although the wife was living with another man, it was not a permanent relationship. She intended to move out on her own upon resolution of the support issues. The husband was ordered to pay the wife $5,000 as lump sum spousal support and monthly spousal support of $2,000 for an indefinite period.

*Payee cohabiting* — *interim application, no need demonstrated* — Byerley v. Byerley, 1998 CarswellOnt 3649, 41 R.F.L. (4th) 50, 75 O.T.C. 73, [1998] O.J. No. 3781 (Ont. Gen. Div.). A court should deny interim spousal support where the dependant spouse fails to demonstrate, with cogent and compelling evidence, a current need for interim spousal support from the husband. In this case, the wife who was living in a common-law union, did not provide the court with information about her common-law spouse's income and expenses. She had been selfsupporting for a year and after that lived with her common-law husband for almost a year before she sought support. At the time of the hearing, the wife and her common-law husband were expecting a child.

*Payee cohabiting* — *no economic disadvantage resulting from the breakdown of the marriage* — Franken v. Franken, 1997 CarswellOnt 4150, 33 R.F.L. (4th) 264, 45 O.T.C. 205, [1997] O.J. No. 4574 (Ont. Gen. Div.). The wife's claim for spousal support was dismissed. She was living in a common law relationship with a man who earned a substantial income and contributed generously to her needs. As there was no evidence of economic hardship adduced by the wife, she did not establish the required economic disadvantage resulting from the breakdown of the marriage.

*Payee cohabiting* — *no need for support* — Carpenter v. Carpenter, 1991 CarswellNfld 146, 93 Nfld. & P.E.I.R. 279, 292 A.P.R. 279 (Nfld. T.D.). The court refused the wife's application for support because, with the training she had taken, she should be self-sufficient within a short period of time and she was already being supported by another man.

*Payee cohabiting* — *not disentitled to support, but amount is affected* — Squires v. Squires, 1988 CarswellNfld 241, 72 Nfld. & P.E.I.R. 91, 223 A.P.R. 91, [1988] N.J. No. 151 (Nfld. U.F.C.). The fact that a spouse seeking support has entered into a common-law relationship is irrelevant to the obligation to support and is only properly considered in relation to the issue of quantum. The husband's payments should be reduced by the amount of the pecuniary benefits that the wife will receive from her common-law husband. The court ordered the husband to pay spousal support of $100 per month.

*No material change in circumstances* — *payee cohabiting* — *wife's common-law relationship relevant but not automatic bar to support* — Droit de la famille - 1105, [1987] R.D.F. 293 (C.S. Que.). A wife's common-law relationship with another man does not automatically disentitle her to support, but is a factor properly considered in determining quantum.

*Payee cohabiting* — *new relationship not stable, not disentitled to support* — Key v. Key, 1986 CarswellBC 509, 1 R.F.L. (3d) 150 (B.C.S.C.). Where the wife was living with another man and benefiting financially from the relationship, she was nevertheless found entitled to maintenance in light of the fact that the new relationship was not yet settled. The marriage had lasted 25 years and the wife was awarded $700 monthly. The court was of the opinion that the matter of support should be reviewed in the future in connection with the wife's efforts to find employment and the husband's expected retirement from the military.

*Wife's new cohabitation among reasons for denying support* — *Gillis v. Gillis*, 1984 CarswellMan 44, 40 R.F.L. (2d) 145 (Man. Q.B.). The wife's claim for support for herself and her child was dismissed in light of the facts that she was living with another man who was contributing to their support and that she was earning enough to support both herself and the child. As the husband was supporting another child of the marriage who was in his custody, a maintenance award was not warranted.

*Wife's new cohabitation and probability of self-sufficiency led to denial of support despite apparently strong compensatory claim* — *Singleton v. Singleton*, 1982 CarswellBC 529, 28 R.F.L. (2d) 39 (B.C.S.C.). The wife was denied maintenance despite the fact that her husband could never have completed his medical education had she not assumed responsibility for the children and that the husband's income was markedly in excess of her own. As the wife was now living with another man and had entered into a business with him which would likely be successful it was held that she could adequately maintain herself.

*Availiability of social assistance to payee doesn't reduce her needs for purpose of spousal support* — *Harvey v. Harvey*, 1995 CarswellBC 345, 14 R.F.L. (4th) 128, 9 B.C.L.R. (3d) 83, 60 B.C.A.C. 178, 99 W.A.C. 178, [1995] B.C.J. No. 1284 (B.C.C.A.). A spouse cannot rely on the availability of social assistance to the claimant as a means of avoiding support obligations.

*Social assistance for payee* — *does not affect extent of payor's support obligation* — *Gray v. Gray*, 1986 CarswellMan 102, 3 R.F.L. (3d) 457, 45 Man. R. (2d) 156, [1986] M.J. No. 661 (Man. Q.B.), affirmed (1987), 1987 CarswellMan 109, 8 R.F.L. (3d) 147, 49 Man. R. (2d) 90 (Man. C.A.). The extent of a husband's obligation to pay maintenance to his wife should not be measured by the availability of social assistance to her.

*Social assistance for payee* — *payor still required to contribute even though payment will be deducted from payee's welfare cheque* — *Papaspirou v. Soussoudis*, 1999 CarswellOnt 2685, 2 R.F.L. (5th) 437 (Ont. S.C.J.). Even where as a result of a spousal support order, the entire amount will be deducted from the recipient's welfare cheque, the family should, where possible, bear some responsibility for a fellow member's support. In a case such as this one where both spouses have little means, there is no point in reducing both parties to a state of impoverishment. The husband earned $23,470 a year and the wife was on welfare. He was ordered to contribute $250 per month in spousal support.

*Social assistance for payee* — *fact that award quantum would be deducted from assistance received not relevant* — *Duncan v. Duncan*, 1992 CarswellAlta 314, 40 R.F.L. (3d) 358, 128 A.R. 57 (Alta. Q.B.). Where the wife is receiving social assistance, the fact that she will not benefit from an award that is less than this assistance is not a fact that should be taken into account when determining the issue of support.

*Section 15.2(4) justifies consideration of factors other than compensation* — *Kloos v. Kloos*, 1996 CarswellMan 126, 21 R.F.L. (4th) 1, [1996] 5 W.W.R. 553, 110 Man. R. (2d) 129, 118 W.A.C. 129, [1996] M.J. No. 146 (Man. C.A.). A wife's multiple sclerosis, in remission during the marriage, which resurfaces after separation preventing her from working is a "condition" or one of the "other circumstances" within s. 15(5) [now 15.2(4)] that justifies an order for support for an indefinite period. There is no inconsistency between the general principles that govern an award of "compensation" and the principles applicable where a spouse has a continuing illness following the breakup of the marriage. "The relevance of the medical circumstances of the spouse seeking support is mandated by an analysis of the factors to be taken into account pursuant to sec. 15(5) of the Act, namely, the "condition" and the "other circumstances" of the parties." When dealing with a sick or disabled spouse, a court should consider all the circumstances and hardships that result from the breakdown of the marriage, however caused.

*Investment income from accident settlement helps reduce wife's need for spousal support —* Hepp v. Hepp, 1990 CarswellBC 434, 24 R.F.L. (3d) 367, 67 D.L.R. (4th) 470 (B.C.C.A.). The investment income earned from an accident settlement should be taken into account in determining the spouse's means and needs.

*Earning capacity of recipient to be considered —* Ewing v. Ewing, 1987 CarswellSask 562, 56 Sask. R. 263 (Sask. C.A.), varying 1986 CarswellSask 613, 51 Sask. R. 51 (Sask. Q.B.). Where a payee's considerable earning capacity as a lawyer was not considered at trial, spousal support will be reduced on appeal.

*Support applicant's income would exceed that of the support respondent — no support —* Cartier v. Cartier, 2007 CarswellOnt 7869, 47 R.F.L. (6th) 436, [2007] O.J. No. 4732 (Ont. S.C.J.). The wife's application for spousal support was dismissed. After equalization the wife would still have assets valued in excess of $500,000 and her annual employment income would exceed the husband's.

*Parties would have similar standards of living without support — no support ordered —* Elias v. Elias, 2006 CarswellBC 163, 2006 BCSC 124, [2006] B.C.J. No. 146 (B.C.S.C.), additional reasons at 2006 CarswellBC 1710 (B.C.S.C.). Support was not granted where the parties' incomes were not so disparate that either party would have a significantly different standard of living from the other.

*See also re subsequent relationship for the payee —* Levandusky v. Levandusky, 2003 CarswellOnt 2615, 39 R.F.L. (5th) 134, [2003] O.J. No. 2783 (Ont. S.C.J.), additional reasons at 2003 CarswellOnt 2613, [2003] O.J. No. 2786 (Ont. S.C.J.).

*Where both parties had extensive assets which would return a good investment income and the wife could resume her career, no spousal support was payable —* Laxton v. Coglon, 2003 CarswellBC 12, 2003 BCSC 11, 37 R.F.L. (5th) 156, [2003] B.C.J. No. 14 (B.C.S.C.). As both parties had assets of over $3,000,000, the wife's application for spousal support was dismissed. Her investments would return an annual income of $90,000 and the fact that she had stopped working during the marriage would not be particularly detrimental to her career.

*Claimant misrepresenting and unnecessarily reducing her means in attempt to establish need — support denied —* Grant v. Grant, 1997 CarswellBC 261, 27 R.F.L. (4th) 372 (B.C.S.C.). A spouse is not entitled to spousal support where she intends to wind up a family business of which she is the sole owner mainly for the purpose of increasing her chances of obtaining support. She had also misrepresented her resources and purpose-fully made it impossible to assess her financial situation. The allocation of assets upon separation and her income prospects did not support her claim of need.

*Where the payee's purported disability was not supported in the evidence, the court attributed potential employment income to the wife —* Labron v. Labron, 1996 CarswellAlta 332, 21 R.F.L. (4th) 385, 183 A.R. 251 (Alta. Q.B.). The wife had failed to present medical evidence supporting her claim that a disability prevented her from working. The court attributed income to her considering her employment income potential in determining the quantum of support payable to her.

*Spouse not restricted to frugal lifestyle imposed by husband during cohabitation —* Katay v. Katay, 1995 CarswellAlta 627, 168 A.R. 31, [1995] A.J. No. 317 (Alta. Q.B.). The parties were married for 23 years. It was a traditional marriage with the husband working, and the wife managing the household and taking care of the children. The husband controlled the finances and imposed a frugal lifestyle on the family. In divorce proceedings, the court held that the wife was entitled to support. The frugal financial regime was imposed in order to accumulate savings. This was a discretionary use of family funds and after the separation the wife should not be required to follow the same lifestyle. The court accepted her budget of $2,750 per month as being reasonable to meet her needs and awarded her spousal support in the amount of $2,500 per month for a year. Thereafter, for every additional $1 of average monthly income from employment, the spousal maintenance would decline by $0.60. There would be no adjustment should the wife's monthly income fall below $333. If the wife's monthly earned income reached $2,500, which represented an annual income of $30,000, the matter of maintenance would be reviewed, if either party requested it.

*Spousal support payable where need arose from division of matrimonial property — Bracewell v. Bracewell*, 1994 CarswellAlta 379, 4 R.F.L. (4th) 183, 152 A.R. 379, [1994] A.J. No. 312 (Alta. Q.B.). Where the husband suffered a shortfall in the amount needed to support himself as a result of the division of matrimonial property, his need was found to be based on an economic disadvantage properly traced to the marriage breakdown. He was accordingly entitled to support.

*Recipient's CPP disability benefits reduce her need — Klassen v. Klassen*, 1990 CarswellMan 38, 25 R.F.L. (3d) 277, 63 Man. R. (2d) 201 (Man. Q.B.). In determining the quantum of support payable by the husband, it is appropriate to consider Canada Pension Plan disability benefits which are being received by the wife.

*Support applicant's RRSP considered in assessing her income — Cherney v. Cherney*, 1986 CarswellSask 563, 51 Sask. R. 158 (Sask. Q.B.). The petitioner wife was ordered, in the course of quantifying her support entitlement, to deregister her R.R.S.P. in order to increase her income.

## 5.4 Length of Relationship

Section 15.2(4)(a) requires consideration of "the length of time the spouses cohabited." Along with income and the presence of children, length of relationship is one of the three key determinants of spousal support quantum and duration. It also plays a central role in the *Spousal Support Advisory Guidelines* (see Part II of this volume).

All else being equal, a longer relationship will give rise to a more generous support award, regardless of whether the objective of the award is to compensate, relieve need, or some mixture of these two objectives. The longer the relationship, the more likely it is that compensable sacrifices in income-generating potential will be made. A longer relationship may also give rise to a more substantial responsibility on the the higher-earning spouse to meet the needs of the other spouse.

*Cohabitation before marriage is counted — Bracklow v. Bracklow*, 1999 CarswellBC 532, 1999 CarswellBC 533, 44 R.F.L. (4th) 1, [1999] 1 S.C.R. 420, 169 D.L.R. (4th) 577, [1999] 8 W.W.R. 740, 63 B.C.L.R. (3d) 77, 236 N.R. 79, 120 B.C.A.C. 211, 196 W.A.C. 211, [1999] S.C.J. No. 14 (S.C.C.). In determining the duration of cohabitation for purposes of spousal support, the time before marriage is counted and given the same weight as cohabitation after the marriage.

*The longer the parties have cohabited, the greater the presumption that their standards of living should be equalized upon dissolution — Moge v. Moge*, 1992 CarswellMan 143, 1992 CarswellMan 222, EYB 1992-67141, 43 R.F.L. (3d) 345, [1992] 3 S.C.R. 813, [1993] R.D.F. 168, [1993] 1 W.W.R. 481, 99 D.L.R. (4th) 456, 81 Man. R. (2d) 161, 30 W.A.C. 161, 145 N.R. 1, [1992] S.C.J. No. 107 (S.C.C.), para. 84. Madam Justice L'Heureux Dubé, speaking for the court in that decision stated:

> Although the doctrine of spousal support which focuses on equitable sharing does not guarantee to either party the standard of living enjoyed during the marriage, this standard is far from irrelevant to support entitlement [citations omitted]. Furthermore,

great disparities in the standard of living that would be experienced by spouses in the absence of support are often a revealing indication of the economic disadvantages inherent in the role assumed by one party. As marriage should be regarded as a joint endeavour, the longer the relationship endures, the closer the economic union, the greater will be the presumptive claim to equal standards of living upon its dissolution. [citations omitted]

*Length of the marriage is only one factor to consider in determining spousal support* — *Davey v. Davey*, 2003 CarswellNS 13, 2003 NSCA 7, 36 R.F.L. (5th) 297, 211 N.S.R. (2d) 258, 662 A.P.R. 258, [2003] N.S.J. No. 12 (N.S.C.A.). Even though the parties had cohabited for only 3 years, the payor was ordered to pay support until the parties' child finished Grade 12. The trial judge properly considered the length of the marriage, while also considering the respondent's illness, which was not connected to the marriage and illness's worsening caused by the stresses inherent in the marriage breakdown, her inability to be self-sufficient and the appellant's corresponding ability to pay support, and the financial consequences of coparenting the child. The trial judge's emphasis on co-parenting was a matter entirely within his discretion.

*Medium-term marriage with close economic ties and compensatory claim* — *indefinite support* — *T. (T.) v. H. (J.M.)*, 2014 CarswellBC 725, 2014 BCSC 451 (B.C.S.C.). The parties were married for 17 years, and the wife sought indefinite spousal support. The judge found that, although the parties had a medium-term marriage, they were a close economic unit and support should reflect that the wife had a "presumptive claim to equal standards of living" on the dissolution of the marriage.

*Where no significant economic reliance was created by a short-term marriage and the payor had no earning capacity, spousal support was terminated* — *G. (C.A.) v. G. (S.)*, 2012 CarswellAlta 1619, 2012 ABQB 529, 24 R.F.L. (7th) 461, 70 Alta. L.R. (5th) 388, [2013] 2 W.W.R. 773, 548 A.R. 226 (Alta. Q.B.). The husband sought, *inter alia*, to terminate or reduce spousal support and spousal support arrears. The parties separated in 2001. The husband had been involved in a motor vehicle accident which was found to have reduced his ability to earn income. The judge considered the factors in s. 15.2(4) in determining that ongoing spousal support should be reduced to zero. The parties had a very short marriage of less than 2 years. The wife did not become economically dependent on the husband during cohabitation because the husband was unwilling or unable to work at that time and the wife was responsible for supporting the family. However, the judge found that the wife was entitled to compensatory support on the basis that she did not receive adequate compensation for her economic efforts given that she was also responsible for childcare.

*Spouse compelled to stay in another country* — *Tran v. Tran*, 2009 CarswellBC 3229, 2009 BCSC 1647 (B.C.S.C.). Where, after the parties' marriage, one party is compelled to stay in another country, the time spent in that other country is still included in the period of the marriage when determining the length of the marriage for spousal support purposes.

*A twelve-year marriage was not short particularly in light of the parties' age at the time of the marriage's commencement* — *interim spousal support ordered to be paid by 79-year-old husband to 70-year-old wife* — *Fedor v. Fedor*, 2011 CarswellAlta 418, 2011 ABQB 185, 96 R.F.L. (6th) 309, 46 Alta. L.R. (5th) 221, 525 A.R. 128, [2011] A.J. No. 314 (Alta. Q.B.).

*Despite the husband's sponsorship obligations, where a marriage is short, not consummated, and there is no economic disadvantage to the wife, no spousal support should be ordered* — *Mazloumisadat v. Zarandi*, 2010 CarswellOnt 287, 2010 ONSC 524, 81 R.F.L. (6th) 82 (Ont. S.C.J.). The parties married in 2008 in Iran and separated in 2009. The husband had sponsored his wife to come to Canada after they were married. The wife was aware in

September 2008 that the marriage was over and that the husband would commence divorce proceedings; however, she still chose to come to Canada.

*Modest amount of spousal support for short marriage* — *Abuzokkar v. Farag*, 2009 CarswellOnt 4046, [2009] O.J. No. 2915 (Ont. S.C.J.). The wife sought spousal support in this case. The husband earned $61,800 per year and the wife earned $30,000. The court found that there was no evidence that the wife stayed at home during the marriage or that she gave up jobs or education. She was not disadvantaged by the marriage and was employed full time. The court noted that the parties were only married for just over 4 years and accordingly spousal support should be for a limited period and not substantial. In this case, the Guidelines suggested spousal support in the range of $0 to $444 per month for a period of 2 to 12 years. The court awarded $200 per month for a period of 3 years. The court ordered that the amount be paid in a lump sum from the net equalization.

*While support order providing wife funds over estimated need, it seems equitable after a relationship of 11 years which has resulted in two children* — *Phillips-Curwin v. Curwin*, 2008 CarswellNS 328, 2008 NSSC 198, [2008] N.S.J. No. 267 (N.S.S.C.).

*Despite short marriage, wife entitled to time-limited support given role she performed including two moves to accommodate husband's career possibilities and care given to husband's child of a prior union* — *Campbell v. Campbell*, 2008 CarswellOnt 3270, 55 R.F.L. (6th) 405, [2008] O.J. No. 2168 (Ont. S.C.J.), additional reasons at 2008 CarswellOnt 5110, 63 R.F.L. (6th) 170 (Ont. S.C.J.).

*The existence of an immigration sponsorship agreement is a relevant factor in determining entitlement to spousal support regardless of the length of the marriage* — *Gidey v. Abay*, 2007 CarswellOnt 6145, [2007] O.J. No. 3693 (Ont. S.C.J.). The husband and wife were married in Ethiopia and the husband was a Canadian citizen. Upon his return to Canada, after the marriage, the husband sponsored his wife to come to Canada, which she did 3 years later. The parties separated shortly after the wife became a permanent resident. The Sponsorship Agreement showed that the husband agreed to sponsor his wife for 3 years after the wife becomes a permanent resident. Although the parties were only married for a short duration, and their time of cohabitation was even shorter, the court found that the husband had a responsibility to fulfill his immigration sponsorship obligations and awarded the wife support above the high end of the spousal support range to generate an amount that would meet the wife's basic needs and preclude resort to social assistance.

*In awarding spousal support, the preferable approach is to make a correlation between the duration of the cohabitation and the duration of the support award* — *Simpson v. Grignon*, 2007 CarswellOnt 3095, 39 R.F.L. (6th) 329, [2007] O.J. No. 1915 (Ont. S.C.J.). "The quantum is not so directly affected by the duration of the cohabitation, as it would be if the *Spousal Support Advisory Guidelines* were applied. The payee spouse should receive an amount of support which is affordable by the payor spouse and at the same time be sufficient to meet her basic needs. In this case, this could not be achieved even by restructuring the SSAG award except for an extremely short duration, such as for a further 18 months. The court held that an award of such a short duration would not meet the objectives set out above in the *Divorce Act*. The length of cohabitation was 4.5 years. The husband could not afford to pay an appropriate amount of spousal support and continue to pay his own rent and all the carrying costs of the matrimonial home. Therefore, I urge the wife to apply for ODSP coverage immediately for necessary additional support over and above what the husband will be ordered to pay her." The husband was ordered to pay $600 per month spousal support commencing on May 1st, 2007 and continuing on June 1st and July 1st, 2007. In addition, the husband was to continue to pay the mortgage, taxes, insurance and utilities with respect to the matrimonial home during that period.

*Cohabitation before marriage is counted* — *Anderson v. Anderson*, 2000 CarswellPEI 79, 2000 PESCTD 79, 11 R.F.L. (5th) 1, 2 P.E.I.R. 355, 195 Nfld. & P.E.I.R. 150, 586 A.P.R. 150, [2000] P.E.I.J. No. 102 (P.E.I.T.D.). Although the parties, ages 25 and 27, had been married for only a very few years, in awarding the wife spousal support for a term of 1 year, the court considered the fact that they had actually cohabited for a period of 6 and one-half years.

*Emigration to marry* — *loss of employment* — *Weichholz v. Weichholz*, 1987 CarswellAlta 472, 81 A.R. 236, [1987] A.J. No. 331 (Alta. Q.B.). Where a 66-year-old Canadian man convinced his 35-year-old Polish niece to come to Canada and marry him, the wife was awarded periodic support although the couple separated only weeks after marrying. The wife spoke no English, had left a good paying job in Poland and was in failing health.

*24-month support after 13-month marriage* — *claimant suffering from economic disadvantages of marriage* — *Baeza v. Strange-Zelaya*, 2001 CarswellMan 371, 2001 MBCA 86, 18 R.F.L. (5th) 1, 156 Man. R. (2d) 166, 246 W.A.C. 166 (Man. C.A.). The court, on appeal, affirmed the award of 24 months of spousal support awarded to the wife upon the dissolution of the parties' 13-month marriage. The marriage appeared to be one of convenience, given that the husband left the wife shortly after obtaining his landed immigrant status. The wife had entered the marriage with no debt but left it with considerable debt after supporting the husband throughout. The wife had been economically disadvantaged by the marriage and was entitled to spousal support.

*3-month marriage* — *support denied* — *Yakimovich v. Yakimovich*, 1997 CarswellBC 563, 29 R.F.L. (4th) 449, 34 B.C.L.R. (3d) 303 (B.C.S.C.), additional reasons at 1997 CarswellBC 1168 (B.C.S.C.), affirmed 1998 CarswellBC 2752, 43 R.F.L. (4th) 402, 116 B.C.A.C. 299, 190 W.A.C. 299 (B.C.C.A.). Where there is no change in an applicant payee's lifestyle or earning capacity after separation, no support should be granted. The parties' marriage had lasted 3 months.

*Marriage of short duration* — *duty to become self-sufficient* — *Solomon v. Solomon*, 1991 CarswellNS 64, 35 R.F.L. (3d) 113, 106 N.S.R. (2d) 28, 288 A.P.R. 28, [1991] N.S.J. No. 346 (N.S.C.A.). Where the dependant spouse was 35 and had been married for approximately 7 years, she had a duty to become self-sufficient in light of her age and the length of the marriage.

*Marriage of short duration produces child* — *fixed term deleted because time needed to become self-sufficient* — *Droit de la famille - 487*, 1988 CarswellQue 44, 15 R.F.L. (3d) 149, [1988] R.D.F. 205, 23 Q.A.C. 323 (note) (C.A. Que.). The appellate court held that the trial judge, in limiting support to a fixed term, exaggerated the importance of the short duration of the marriage. The parties were married and lived together for a little over a year and had a child. The fixed term of support should be struck from the judge's order as the wife, although young, required a reasonable time to become self-sufficient.

*Short second marriage occurring late in life should not result in long-term support* — *Rezansoff v. Rezansoff*, 2007 CarswellSask 23, [2007] S.J. No. 37, 2007 SKQB 32, 291 Sask. R. 139, [2007] 5 W.W.R. 366, [2007] S.J. No. 37 (Sask. Q.B.). The parties were married for 6 years. The court ordered what amounted in total to 4 years of spousal support. Both parties' working careers were over or in their closing stage. They each provided care and companionship for each other during their cohabitation. The court concluded that the respondent did not and should not be held responsible for the petitioner's support indefinitely. It stated that cohabitation and marriage was a healthy, social way of life and that the courts should not deter persons at this later stage in their lives from seeking the enjoyment and benefits of such companionship. The order was in keeping with the *Divorce Act* and the *Spousal Support Advisory Guidelines*.

*Marriage of short duration* — *support applicant not entitled to marital standard of living* — *Eng v. Eng*, 2006 CarswellBC 2237, 2006 BCSC 1353, 31 R.F.L. (6th) 407, [2006] B.C.J. No. 2044 (B.C.S.C.). The brief 3-year duration of the parties' marriage was a key factor in setting the quantum of her spousal support. Although she was entitled to live comfortably, she could not expect to be maintained at the higher level enjoyed during the marriage, given its brevity.

*Where there is a short marriage, but the payee spouse has moved to Canada in order to marry and the payor spouse has signed a sponsorship agreement, the payee spouse should receive support — Yadollahi v. Ghahferokhi*, 2005 CarswellMan 60, 2005 MBQB 36, 16 R.F.L. (6th) 420, 204 Man. R. (2d) 1, [2005] M.J. No. 53 (Man. Q.B.), additional reasons at 2005 CarswellMan 267, 2005 MBQB 137, 197 Man. R. (2d) 9, [2005] M.J. No. 257 (Man. Q.B.). The parties cohabited for 23 months, although most of that time they were physically apart from one another.

*There should be brief limited spousal support where there is a very short marriage and the dependant spouse had a pre-existing medical condition — Pedersen v. Pedersen*, 2004 CarswellBC 3279, 2004 BCSC 1627, [2004] B.C.J. No. 2593 (B.C.S.C.). The marriage lasted 2 months. The wife suffered from depression.

*Relocation and short marriage — Millward v. Millward*, 2003 CarswellOnt 1403, 48 R.F.L. (5th) 294, [2003] O.T.C. 312, [2003] O.J. No. 1517 (Ont. S.C.J.). Where the wife had left her native United States to marry the husband in Canada, and the marriage lasted barely a year, she was awarded modest periodic support for a 1-year period. The husband was obliged to contribute since he had asked the wife to leave the U.S., knowing that she would be financially dependent on him.

*Short marriage — effect on quantum — Croll v. Croll*, 2003 CarswellBC 3214, 2003 BCSC 1912, [2003] B.C.J. No. 2937 (B.C.S.C.). A short marriage weighs against a claim to equal standards of living.

*Marriage of short duration — support applicant not entitled to marital standard of living — Postrasija v. Postrasija*, 2002 CarswellOnt 1286, 27 R.F.L. (5th) 148, [2002] O.J. No. 1274 (Ont. S.C.J.). In the case of the relatively brief marriage, spousal support cannot be expected at the same level as upon the termination of a long-term traditional marriage. Such situations do not demand the equality of income, nor should the support applicant expect to enjoy the standard of living experienced during the marriage.

*Marriage of short duration — no ecomomic disadvantage — Luce v. Luce*, 1997 CarswellNB 267, 30 R.F.L. (4th) 196, 188 N.B.R. (2d) 363, 480 A.P.R. 363 (N.B.Q.B.). The wife's claim for support was dismissed upon dissolution of the parties' 3-year marriage. Since she had continued to work during the marriage and had not compromised any career aspirations or opportunities, the wife failed to prove any economic disadvantage.

*Marriage of short duration — very short, and claimant benefitted from economic advantages — Robichaud v. Harvey*, 1989 CarswellNB 267, 98 N.B.R. (2d) 135, 248 A.P.R. 135, [1989] N.B.J. No. 616 (N.B.Q.B.). Where the parties had actually lived together for only 10 weeks during their 26-month marriage, the wife's claim for spousal support was dismissed. In addition to the fact that the marriage was so brief, the wife had also reaped other financial benefits during the marriage.

*Marriage of short duration — very short, but support required under sponsorship agreement, and claimant suffered from economic disadvantages — Johnson v. Johnson*, 2005 CarswellOnt 7695, 2005 ONCJ 325, 23 R.F.L. (6th) 46, [2005] O.J. No. 5641 (Ont. C.J.). The wife was awarded ongoing spousal support upon the termination of the parties' 1-month marriage. The wife had left a good career in Russia to move to Canada to marry the husband, who had executed a government sponsorship agreement under which he was obliged to support her for 10 years. The fact that the marriage was of very short duration was more than off-set by the fact that the wife had gone from a position of self-sufficiency and independence to one of reliance and dependency as a direct result of the marriage.

*Marriage of short duration — claimant suffered from economic disadvantages — Abbott v. Abbott*, 2001 CarswellBC 420, 2001 BCSC 323, 13 R.F.L. (5th) 233, 89 B.C.L.R. (3d) 68, [2001] B.C.J. No. 371 (B.C.S.C.). The wife was awarded spousal support even though the parties had cohabited for less than a year. The parties had still managed to have two children and the wife bore the brunt of the marriage breakdown, having to interrupt her career to care for the children. The order was to be reviewed after 2 years or earlier in the event of a material change in circumstances.

*Long marriage likely to call for rough equivalency of standards of living — W. v. W.*, 2005 CarswellBC 1614, 2005 BCSC 1010, 19 R.F.L. (6th) 453, 47 B.C.L.R. (4th) 348, [2005] B.C.J. No. 1481 (B.C.S.C.). In British Columbia, the reference in *Moge* to the significance of relationship length has been viewed as meaning that "in long marriages the result will likely be a rough equivalency of standards of living. Doing so recognizes that the longer a marriage lasts, the more intertwined the economic and non-economic lives of the spouses become."

*See also re significance of marital standard of living in a long marriage — McEachern v. McEachern*, 2006 CarswellBC 2750, 2006 BCCA 508, 33 R.F.L. (6th) 315, [2007] 3 W.W.R. 471, 62 B.C.L.R. (4th) 95, 232 B.C.A.C. 185, 385 W.A.C. 185, [2006] B.C.J. No. 2917 (B.C.C.A.).

*Greater support where marriage is of long duration — significant weight to be given to long marriage — Vint v. Vint*, 1998 CarswellNS 414, 44 R.F.L. (4th) 145, 172 N.S.R. (2d) 172, 524 A.P.R. 172 (N.S.C.A.). The court held that the evidence did not support the trial judge's finding that the respondent husband had no ability to pay spousal support. The court found that the parties had had a long-term marriage of 23 years. The wife had little education and had worked at low paying part-time jobs and the husband had provided an outdated statement of expenses. The court granted the wife's appeal and ordered a new hearing.

*See also re greater support where marriage is of long duration — Penner v. Penner*, 1996 CarswellBC 2182, 24 R.F.L. (4th) 448, 82 B.C.A.C. 232, 133 W.A.C. 232 (B.C.C.A.).

*See also re greater support where marriage is of long duration — Stroud v. Stroud*, 1996 CarswellBC 723, 20 R.F.L. (4th) 392, 22 B.C.L.R. (3d) 183, 75 B.C.A.C. 48, 123 W.A.C. 48, [1996] B.C.J. No. 727 (B.C.C.A.).

*Greater support where marriage is of long duration — Waterman v. Waterman*, 1995 CarswellNfld 117, 16 R.F.L. (4th) 10, 133 Nfld. & P.E.I.R. 310, 413 A.P.R. 310, [1995] N.J. No. 295 (Nfld. C.A.). A long-term relationship engenders long-term spousal support.

*Equalization of incomes not necessarily appropriate even after long marriage — Ross v. Ross*, 1995 CarswellNB 160, 16 R.F.L. (4th) 1, 168 N.B.R. (2d) 147, 430 A.P.R. 147, [1995] N.B.J. No. 463 (N.B.C.A.). While a long relationship will create a stronger "presumptive claim to equal standards of living upon dissolution of the marriage" (see *Moge v. Moge*, [1992] 3 S.C.R. 813 (S.C.C.), at 870) spousal support is not intended to achieve equalization of incomes after divorce. After a marriage of 30 years, support for the 47-year-old wife was reduced from $1,700 to $1,250 per month. The compensatory element of spousal support should not negate the promotion of self-sufficiency. Evidence supported the lower court's finding that the support award should be indefinite.

*Marriage of long duration — claimant suffering from economic disadvantages of marriage — Brace v. Brace*, 1991 CarswellOnt 318, 35 R.F.L. (3d) 263 (Ont. C.A.). The Ontario Court of Appeal upheld the trial judge's decision that the applicant was entitled to support as there was a causal connection between the wife's economic condition and the marriage. There was sufficient evidence in the medical evidence and, considering the 17-year marriage generally, to support the trial judge's conclusion.

*Greater support where marriage is of long duration — Pearce v. Pearce*, 1999 CarswellBC 2214, 1 R.F.L. (5th) 402, 21 B.C.T.C. 383, [1999] B.C.J. No. 2278 (B.C.S.C.). The wife was entitled to spousal support to restore her to a more equitable position after the breakdown of a 31-year traditional long-term marriage.

*Greater support where marriage is of long duration — separation after retirement — Adie v. Adie*, 1994 CarswellNS 58, 7 R.F.L. (4th) 54, 134 N.S.R. (2d) 60, 383 A.P.R. 60, [1994] N.S.J. No. 395 (N.S.S.C.). The fact that the parties had been married for over 15 years and that the separation had occurred after their retirement were found to favour the wife's claim to support.

*There is no mandatory amount of support for a middle-range marriage without children — A. (N.) v. B. (R.)*, 2004 CarswellQue 575, REJB 2004-55544, [2004] R.D.F. 257, [2004] Q.J. No. 2778 (C.A. Que.). In such cases, the effect of *Moge v. Moge* and *Bracklow v. Bracklow* requires courts to be flexible and to avoid formulaic approaches to spousal support applications. The analysis is discretion driven. "[A]ccording to the jurisprudence and to doctrine, the length or duration of a marriage is only one of several factors to be considered by the trial judge."

## 5.5 Functions Performed by Each Spouse During Cohabitation

The second factor enumerated within s. 15.2(4) is "functions performed by each spouse during cohabitation." The home-making and child-rearing functions performed by the claimant spouse are often recognized under this section of the statute. Childrearing functions involving children of the marriage performed *after* the cohabitation ends are not technically relevant to this factor. However, they are certainly germane to spousal support law and are admissible as a "condition" or "other circumstance" per s. 15.2(4) or under either of the first two objectives (s. 15.2(6)).

*Functions performed by spouses may give rise to compensatory support — Bracklow v. Bracklow*, 1999 CarswellBC 532, 1999 CarswellBC 533, 44 R.F.L. (4th) 1, [1999] 1 S.C.R. 420, 169 D.L.R. (4th) 577, [1999] 8 W.W.R. 740, 63 B.C.L.R. (3d) 77, 236 N.R. 79, 120 B.C.A.C. 211, 196 W.A.C. 211, [1999] S.C.J. No. 14 (S.C.C.). The requirement to consider the functions performed by the spouses during cohabitation is one of the provisions in the *Divorce Act* that gives rise to the compensatory basis for support. Another basis is the general requirement to consider the "condition, means, needs and other circumstances" of the spouses, which may encompass lack of ability to support oneself due to foregoing career opportunities during the marriage.

*Functions performed during marriage relevant to determining economic consequences resulting from marriage or its breakdown — Moge v. Moge*, 1992 CarswellMan 143, 1992 CarswellMan 222, EYB 1992-67141, 43 R.F.L. (3d) 345, [1992] 3 S.C.R. 813, [1993] R.D.F. 168, [1993] 1 W.W.R. 481, 99 D.L.R. (4th) 456, 81 Man. R. (2d) 161, 30 W.A.C. 161, 145 N.R. 1, [1992] S.C.J. No. 107 (S.C.C.). The division of labour between the spouses in the marriage should be taken into account in determining whether there have been any economic advantages or disadvantages as a result of the marriage or its breakdown. Madam Justice L'Heureux-DubeÇ observed that the roles of the partners to a marriage should be considered in a spousal support order where "both partners make economic sacrifices and share domestic responsibilities, or where one spouse has suffered economic losses in order to enable the other spouse to further a career."

*Wife entitled to spousal support — childcare responsibilities had negatively affected wife's career — Gonabady-Namadon v. Mohammadzadeh*, 2009 CarswellBC 2767, 2009 BCCA 448, 74 R.F.L. (6th) 1, 98 B.C.L.R. (4th) 23, 277 B.C.A.C. 48, 469 W.A.C. 48 (B.C.C.A.). In this case, the parties were married for 13 years and had two children. The wife was a physician. At trial, the trial judge found that the wife was not entitled to spousal support due to her annual income of $150,000. On appeal, the court found that the trial judge erred in not finding entitlement. In reversing the decision, the court noted that although the parties had domestic help, nevertheless child care responsibilities had an impact on the wife's advancement and options. She was unable to pursue lucrative work at a hospital since the associated shift work was incompatible with her family obligations. Accordingly, given the wife's professional income and future prospects, spousal support was ordered at the low end of the range, being $2,300 monthly for 6 years and the order was made retroactive to May 14, 2008, the date of the trial judge's order.

*On appeal, spousal support awarded to wife, as domestic help in child care was a benefit to both spouses, wife had to reduce her employment activities after first child was born, and later when she had primary care of the children she was unable to pursue more lucrative work in her field as shift work was incompatible with her family obligations* — Gonabady-Namadon v. Mohammadzadeh, 2009 CarswellBC 2767, 2009 BCCA 448, 74 R.F.L. (6th) 1, 98 B.C.L.R. (4th) 23, 277 B.C.A.C. 48, 469 W.A.C. 48 (B.C.C.A.). The parties married in 1993 in Iran and had 2 children. They moved to Canada in 2001 and separated in 2006. The husband had a successful business and the wife had become a doctor in Iran. She obtained re-qualification in Canada, but the medical clinic she established in Canada failed. The husband returned to Iran and the children remained with the wife. At trial, the husband who did not make full disclosure was imputed to have an income of $250,000 and the claim of the wife, who had an income of $156,000, was dismissed. On appeal, the income imputed to the husband was $350,000 and the wife was awarded spousal support of $2,300 a month for 6 years.

*Where the husband performs functions that hone marketable skills while the wife does not, the obligation to provide support shifts to the husband* — Russell v. Russell, 1999 CarswellSask 648, 1 R.F.L. (5th) 235, 179 D.L.R. (4th) 723, [2000] 1 W.W.R. 619, 180 Sask. R. 196, 205 W.A.C. 196, [1999] S.J. No. 645 (Sask. C.A.). The husband was the principal driving force behind the generation of income from the parties' joint property before separation and he remained so after. The marriage generated a pattern of dependency which continued after separation. The court held that this dependency has to be addressed upon marriage breakdown to prevent the wife from suffering economic disadvantage arising from the marriage. The parties had agreed that the husband would perform functions which honed marketable skills and his wife would not. There was an economic consequence arising from the roles the parties adopted in marriage which justified shifting the responsibility to support from one spouse to the other.

*Failure to contribute to the development of the marriage may be a factor in limiting support* — Grohmann v. Grohmann, 1991 CarswellBC 321, 37 R.F.L. (3d) 73, 86 D.L.R. (4th) 741, 62 B.C.L.R. (2d) 264, 5 B.C.A.C. 277, 11 W.A.C. 277, [1991] B.C.J. No. 3820 (B.C.C.A.). The fact that the wife did not significantly divert her talents to the development of the marriage was a circumstance, among others, that persuaded the British Columbia Court of Appeal to affirm a support award limited to a fixed term of 5 months. Other circumstances were the duration of the marriage of 6 years, the economic advantages to the wife of the marriage, the disadvantages caused by her quitting her full-time job and the fact that, at the time of the trial, she was economically independent.

*The amount of support should take into account the payee's contribution to the marriage* — Fedon v. Fedon, 1978 CarswellMan 34, 1 R.F.L. (2d) 357, [1978] 2 W.W.R. 723 (Man. C.A.), at 378 [R.F.L.]. "The award of maintenance should not be limited to the amount of maintenance which would be enough to keep her off the welfare rolls, but should be enough to take into account the contribution which the wife has made to the marriage, not only to the acquisition of the assets of the husband, but to the health and welfare of the family unit itself", per O'Sullivan J.A.

*Where the parties had a traditional relationship, in which the wife did not work outside the home but provided childcare, and the wife was unable to support herself, a change in circumstances will not be found when no evidence showed that her circumstances had changed, despite the fact that the husband had retired since the granting of the original order* — *Gaudet v. Mainville*, 2014 CarswellNB 195, 2014 CarswellNB 196, 2014 NBQB 88, 418 N.B.R. (2d) 273, 1087 A.P.R. 273 (N.B.Q.B.). The husband sought to vary, *inter alia*, his spousal support obligation, which had been determined by a 2009 order. The parties had cohabited for 28 years. The wife did not work outside the home during that time and at the time of the original order was found to have little possibility of becoming self-sufficient. This situation had not changed by the time the husband sought to vary, and spousal support was ordered to continue at a somewhat reduced amount to reflect the fact that the wife had pension entitlement.

*Compensatory support indicated when recipient spouse suffered economic disadvantage because of the role she played during the relationship* — *T. (T.) v. H. (J.M.)*, 2014 CarswellBC 725, 2014 BCSC 451 (B.C.S.C.). The wife sought indefinite spousal support. The judge considered the role played by the wife during the marriage, finding that her role in running the household and caring for the children caused her to abandon her public relations career and she assisted the husband with his business. The judge found she had a compensatory claim for spousal support.

*Spousal support was not varied when the recipient remarried, but her remarriage did not result in overcoming the disadvantages that arose as a result of the role she had played during her first marriage in being the primary parent* — *Anderson v. Anderson*, 2014 CarswellNS 23, 2014 NSSC 7, 339 N.S.R. (2d) 244, 1073 A.P.R. 244 (N.S.S.C.). The parties were married for 5 years and had two children. The husband had sought to terminate spousal support on the basis of the wife's remarriage. A 2012 order granted spousal support for 4 years to terminate in 2015.

*Where a wife was financially disadvantaged because of her own choices rather than the role played during cohabitation, and has not taken steps towards self-sufficiency, support was terminated* — *Acker v. Acker*, 2014 CarswellNS 136, 2014 NSSC 5, 41 R.F.L. (7th) 166 (N.S.S.C.). The husband sought the termination of spousal support in this review application. The wife sought to increase spousal support based on the husband's post-separation increase in income. The parties were married for 23 years, and support was paid pursuant to Minutes of Settlement incorporated into a Corollary Relief Order. The wife had not been employed for 10 years prior to separation. The judge considered the roles played by the parties during the relationship and found that the wife had not been economically disadvantaged by the marriage, which was non-traditional. The judge found that the husband's income had increased, but was now roughly equivalent to its level at the time of separation. The wife's financial situation was found to be a result of her own choices rather than her role during the marriage. Spousal support was not increased, and a step-down order was made.

*Long-term marriage with stay-at-home spouse* — *support granted with review date given advanced age of parties and uncertain financial situation* — *Shepherd v. Shepherd*, 2013 CarswellBC 1998, 2013 BCSC 1173 (B.C.S.C.). The parties were married for 37 years. The wife had been a stay-at-home mother. The husband had lost all of his investments in the stock market after separation. The judge found that, ordinarily, the role the wife played during the marriage would make her support indefinite. However, given the parties' financial situations, he ordered a review date in 2 years.

*Where no significant economic reliance was created by a short-term marriage and the payor has no earning capacity, spousal support will terminate* — *G. (C.A.) v. G. (S.)*, 2012 CarswellAlta 1619, 2012 ABQB 529, 24 R.F.L. (7th) 461, 70 Alta. L.R. (5th) 388, [2013] 2 W.W.R. 773, 548 A.R. 226 (Alta. Q.B.). The husband sought, *inter alia*, to terminate or reduce spousal support and spousal support arrears. The parties separated in 2001. The husband had been involved in a motor vehicle accident which was found to have reduced his ability to earn income. The judge considered the factors in s. 15.2(4) in determining that ongoing spousal support should be reduced to zero. The parties had a very short marriage of less than 2 years. The wife did not become economically dependent on the husband during cohabitation because the husband was unwilling or unable to work at that time and the wife was responsible for supporting the family. However, the judge found that the wife was entitled to compensatory support on the basis that she did not receive adequate compensation for her economic efforts given that she was also responsible for childcare.

*Where a recipient has compromised her career due to the role played during the marriage, spousal support will be ordered* — Karges v. Karges, 2012 CarswellOnt 13169, 2012 ONSC 6033 (Ont. S.C.J.). The parties separated 7 years previously and had two children. No spousal support had been ordered at separation. The judge found that the wife was entitled to spousal support based on the role she played during the marriage, where her work hours were reduced because of her childcare responsibilities. The couple intended the husband to be the primary income earner. Spousal support was ordered.

*Performing the functions of homemaking and child care may result in economic consequences to be accounted for in the award of spousal support* — Kopelow v. Warkentin, 2005 CarswellBC 2636, 2005 BCCA 551, 21 R.F.L. (6th) 78, 261 D.L.R. (4th) 129, 218 B.C.A.C. 209, 359 W.A.C. 209, [2005] B.C.J. No. 2412 (B.C.C.A.), additional reasons at 2006 CarswellBC 1306, 2006 BCCA 271, 268 D.L.R. (4th) 274, 227 B.C.A.C. 176, 374 W.A.C. 176 (B.C.C.A.). The court held that the wife was entitled to spousal support in order to achieve the objectives set out the *Divorce Act* because she bore the primary responsibility for the homemaking and child-rearing functions during the marriage. As a result, she was out of the workforce for a lengthy period of time during which she had foregone such benefits as accumulated seniority, possible promotions, and access to fringe benefits, including a pension and life, disability, and health insurance. She had re-entered the workforce at the late age of 53 and consequently suffered from the effects of competitive disadvantages and an earning capacity that has been diminished by disuse. Further, she had the custodial responsibility for the children of the marriage, which would affect her economic welfare in an indirect way that would not be completely redressed by payment of child support and special expenses. These economic consequences arising out of the marriage and its breakdown should be equitably shared by the parties.

*Although husband's employment success was a consequence of his efforts, it would not have been possible if not for the wife working part-time and therefore being available to care for children* — Phillips-Curwin v. Curwin, 2008 CarswellNS 328, 2008 NSSC 198, [2008] N.S.J. No. 267 (N.S.S.C.). The wife, age 34, had primary care of the children while the husband, age 42, was employed as a sales representative with an income of $156,000. The court ordered that the husband pay the wife spousal support in the amount of $2,000 per month in addition to child support.

*Despite short marriage, wife entitled to time-limited support given role she performed including two moves to accommodate husband's career possibilities and care given to husband's child of a prior union* — Campbell v. Campbell, 2008 CarswellOnt 3270, 55 R.F.L. (6th) 405, [2008] O.J. No. 2168 (Ont. S.C.J.), additional reasons at 2008 CarswellOnt 5110, 63 R.F.L. (6th) 170 (Ont. S.C.J.).

*Functions performed during the marriage resulting in an economic disadvantage justify an award of spousal support* — Kuryliak v. Kuryliak, 1998 CarswellOnt 2534, 68 O.T.C. 13, [1998] O.J. No. 2343 (Ont. Gen. Div.), additional reasons at 1998 CarswellOnt 2535, [1998] O.J. No. 2344 (Ont. Gen. Div.), further additional reasons at 1998 CarswellOnt 2536, [1998] O.J. No. 2357 (Ont. Gen. Div.). The husband was the primary breadwinner, and the wife was the primary homemaker and care provider for the children throughout their 22-year marriage. Although the wife worked on a part-time basis during many years of the marriage her work was seen as being of less significance than that of the husband and was pursued in great measure just to supplement the family's income. The fact that the husband was able to devote all of his energies to his work and could leave responsibility for his children and home to his wife was of significant economic advantage to him, an advantage that would last him for the rest of his working life. The fact that the wife gave up her chosen career to be predominantly a homemaker and mother resulted in an economic disadvantage to her that would last the rest of her working life. She was not able to generate the same as she would have been able to generate had she stuck with her career. The equalization of net family properties did not fully address the economic consequences resulting from the functions she performed during the marriage. There was a continuing disadvantage that required an ongoing award of spousal support.

## 5.6 Order, Agreement, or Arrangement Relating to Support

Section 15.2(4)(c) requires the court to take into consideration "any order, agreement or arrangement relating to support of either spouse." If there is a court order in effect, changing it requires a variation application (s. 17 of the *Divorce Act*; s. 4.3 of this volume). The judgement of the Supreme Court in *Miglin* (below) establishes that the same law is applicable regardless of whether or not the parties had their separation agreement issued as a court order. The meaning of the word "arrangement" in this section is not entirely clear, and little discussed in the case law. It may refer to support payments being voluntarily made in the absence of an agreement or court order.

The focus of this section is prior agreements between the parties which pertain to spousal support entitlements. A "separation agreement" is one formed at the time of relationship breakdown. A "cohabitation" or "pre-nuptial" agreement is one formed while the relationship was still intact. As will be explained below, somewhat different legal principles apply to these two types of agreements.

Factors 15.2(4)(a) and (b) describe forms of evidence which are harmonious with the four statutory objectives of spousal support listed in section 15.2(6). Factor 15.2(4)(c), by contrast, is best understood as a counterpoint to the four objectives. Even if a proposed spousal support order would be perfectly in tune with the four objectives, it can be resisted on the grounds that a prior agreement provides to the contrary. However, agreements which stray too far from the *Divorce Act* objectives will not necessarily be binding. Case law establishes that the effects of domestic contracts are more easily avoided than those of commercial contracts. The power to override the support provisions of an agreement gives the court a choice. It may, in its discretion, find that it should not interfere in the arrangement made and dismiss the claim for support, or that it should ignore the agreement and make a support order on other terms.

The exercise of discretion calls for a balancing of two conflicting policies. On the one hand, the court has a responsibility to see that support arrangements are made according to the principles in the *Divorce Act*. On the other, the parties have a right to make their own arrangement. How should the conflict in these two policies be resolved? How can the court give weight to the agreement and, at the same time, discharge its responsibility to consider the other factors and implement the support objectives set out in the Act? What is the proper balance between freedom of contract and the duty of the court in support matters? To refuse jurisdiction whenever there is a valid and enforceable agreement settling support matters is to give full weight to the agreement, but may be a dereliction of judicial responsibility. On the other hand, to assess support in every case and then, if the agreement falls short, make an order in the amount assessed, gives no weight to the agreement. Nor would such a policy be practicable. The courts simply could not handle all the cases. Although an administrative concern should not determine the issue, it does put pressure on the courts to be sure of their ground when ignoring agreements.

Some restricting principle or test must be applied "so that all final separation agreements are not the subject of application to the court to ascertain the extent to which the agreement reflects the objectives of the *Divorce Act*." Some principle or test must be found to cut between the two conflicting policies, and to control the flood of litigation. The "threshold test" is such a device. If the test is not met, the court does not exercise its overriding jurisdiction and the support provisions in the agreement are allowed to stand; if it is met, the jurisdiction is exercised and support is assessed according to the principles in the *Divorce Act*. The power to "override" an agreement for support should be distinguished from the power to "vary" a previous order. When a court exercises its power to override an agreement, it does not amend the agreement itself but, instead, makes an original support order that stands apart from the agreement. When a court varies an order, on the other hand, it does amend the actual order.

The power to override an agreement has a respected history at common law. The House of Lords in *Hyman v. Hyman*, [1929] All E.R. 245 (U.K.H.L.) held that the existence of a covenant in a deed of separation does not preclude a wife from making an application to the court for maintenance. The parties cannot agree not to invoke the jurisdiction of the court, or to control the powers of the court, once its jurisdiction is invoked. The power to provide for a wife on the dissolution of her marriage is a necessary incident of the power to decree such dissolution, an action which is done not only in the interests of the wife but also in the interests of the public.

Madam Justice Wilson in *Pelech v. Pelech*, 1987 CarswellBC 147, 1987 CarswellBC 703, EYB 1987-80055, 7 R.F.L. (3d) 225, [1987] 1 S.C.R. 801, 14 B.C.L.R. (2d) 145, 17 C.P.C. (2d) 1, 38 D.L.R. (4th) 641, [1987] 4 W.W.R. 481, 76 N.R. 81, [1987] R.D.F. 264, [1987] S.C.J. No. 31 (S.C.C.), at 269 [R.F.L.], stated the position in Canada:

> the *Hyman* principle that parties cannot by contract oust the jurisdiction of the court in matters of spousal maintenance, is an established tenet of Canadian law...
>
> [...]
>
> ... where the parties have negotiated their own agreement, freely and on the advice of independent legal counsel, as to how their financial affairs should be settled on the breakdown of their marriage, and the agreement is not unconscionable in the substantive law sense it should be respected.

The common law position has been carried forward to the *Divorce Act*, 1985, s. 15.2(4)(c). The effect of this position and the legislation is that an agreement providing for support is entitled to weight, but does not preclude the court from dealing with an inadequate support provision by making an order on better terms.

When a party seeks a spousal support order which is contrary to a prior agreement, the leading authority is the judgement of the Supreme Court of Canada in *Miglin v. Miglin*, 2003 CarswellOnt 1374, 2003 CarswellOnt 1375, 2003 SCC 24, REJB 2003-40012, 34 R.F.L. (5th) 255, [2003] 1 S.C.R. 303, 66 O.R. (3d) 736, 224 D.L.R. (4th) 193, 302 N.R. 201, 171 O.A.C. 201, [2003] S.C.J. No. 21 (S.C.C.). Where the negotiations are unimpeachable, the court should exercise its discretion to set aside an agreement only when it fails to be in substantial compliance with the objectives of the *Divorce Act*. The objectives set out in s. 15.2(a) to (d) of the Act are to "recognize any economic advantages or disadvantages to the spouses arising from the marriage or its breakdown;" to "apportion between the spouses any financial consequences arising from the care of any child of the marriage over and above any obligation for the support of any child of the marriage;" to "relieve any economic hardship of the spouses arising from the breakdown of the marriage; and . . . in so far as practicable, [to] promote the economic self-sufficiency of each spouse within a reasonable period of time." In addition to these express objectives, the objectives of certainty, finality and autonomy implied from the language of the Act and found in the cases interpreting the Act are to be considered. Substantial compliance, rather than strict compliance with the other objectives, is permitted by the objective of autonomy. In commenting on this objective, the court held that in exercising their autonomy, separating or divorcing parties must be allowed some latitude to pursue their own objectives and need only be in substantial compliance with the law's objectives as reasonably understood by them in a subjective sense.

In determining whether it should override an agreement, the court should take a two-stage approach; the first relating to the time of the negotiation and execution of the agreement, and the second, to the time of the application for spousal support. In the first stage, the court must satisfy itself that the negotiation of the agreement was unimpeachable and that the agreement itself, at this time, was in substantial compliance with the overall objectives of the *Divorce Act*. In reviewing the negotiations, the court should consider the duration of cohabitation and the functions performed by each spouse during cohabitation (s. 15.2(4)(a) and (b)), the circumstances existing at the time of the negotiations and the conditions affecting the parties, including whether there was oppression, pressure, or other vulnerabilities that were taken advantage of, the conditions of the negotiations themselves such as the time over which they extended and whether they were conducted with the assistance of lawyers working on their own or with other professionals. It is not necessary to "look for 'unconscionability' as it is understood in the common law of contract . . . . There may be persuasive evidence brought before the court that one party took advantage of the vulnerability of the other party in separation or divorce negotiations that would fall short of evidence of the power imbalance necessary to demonstrate unconscionability in a commercial context between, say, a consumer and a large financial institution." But the court should not "presume that the apparently stronger party took advantage of any vulnerability on the part of the other. Rather, there must be evidence to warrant the court's finding that the agreement should not stand on the basis of a fundamental flaw in the negotiation process." It must be recognized that the emotional stress generally associated with separation and divorce does not give rise to a presumption that the parties are incapable of making agreements that it would be fair to enforce. In the same vein, vulnerabilities in and of themselves do not justify the court's intervention as professional assistance can often overcome "any systemic imbalances between the parties." However, "where the power imbalance did vitiate the bargaining process, the agreement should not be read as expressing the parties' notion of equitable sharing in their circumstances and the agreement will merit little weight."

In this first stage, after determining that the agreement was negotiated under satisfactory conditions the court must next consider the substance of the agreement. It "must determine the extent to which the agreement takes into account the factors and objectives listed in the Act, thereby reflecting an equitable sharing of the economic consequences of marriage and its breakdown. Only a significant departure from the general objectives of the Act will warrant the court's intervention on the basis that there is not substantial compliance with the Act." The agreement must be scrutinized in its totality, but the whole agreement will not necessarily be set aside if intervention is necessary. Setting aside part of it may serve to address the inequity.

At the second stage, relating to the time of the application, the court should assess the extent to which the agreement remains in substantial compliance with the overall objectives. Not all changes in circumstances since the execution of the agreement will result in the agreement, or part of it, being set aside. Changes that will not affect the enforceability of the agreement are such things as changes in the job market, more onerous parenting responsibilities than were contemplated, and a challenging transition to the workforce. Moreover, "negotiating parties should know that each person's health cannot be guaranteed as a constant" and that values of assets distributed in a property division could change. Housing prices and business prospects may fluctuate. A spouse may decide not to work. On the other hand, a judge is not required to follow the high *Pelech* standard to set aside a support provision only when a change is shown to be "radical". Similarly, it is unnecessary for the spouse claiming support to demonstrate that the change in circumstances from the time of the execution of the agreement is causally connected to the marriage or its breakdown. The test is not foreseeability but rather "the extent to which the unimpeachably negotiated agreement can be said to have contemplated the situation before the court at the time of the application". The court should focus on the "agreement's continued correspondence to the parties' original intentions as to their relative positions and the overall objectives of the Act, not on whether a change occurred *per se*." The court must be convinced that the intervention of the court and the degree of intervention are warranted before the agreement, or a provision in it, is set aside.

Parties must take responsibility for their contracts, as well as for their own lives. The court should give their agreement little weight only when the parties' circumstances at the time of the application depart significantly from the range of reasonable outcomes anticipated by the parties in a manner that puts them at odds with the objectives of the Act.

On the facts of the case, the court found that the evidence did not show that the circumstance at the time of the negotiation and execution of the agreement contained vulnerabilities. The parties negotiated their agreement over a 15-month period and were assisted by several professionals including experienced and expert counsel. The parties received sophisticated advice in tax planning and income projections. As to the substance of the agreement, there was nothing to indicate that there was a significant departure from the overall objectives of the *Divorce Act*. The assets that the parties received were of equal value. The wife received $60,000 in child support per year and indicated that it was her preference to release the husband from spousal support, provided her economic needs were met through child support. The wife was also provided with a 5-year consulting contract. Accordingly, the court found that the separation agreement was in substantial compliance with the *Divorce Act* at the time of its formation.

The court found that the only real changes in circumstances at the time of the application from the time of formation of the agreement were that the eldest child now resided with the father and the variation of the child support award was now in accordance with the *Child Support Guidelines*. The wife did not intend to work at the time she executed the agreement. She contemplated a drop in income when the consulting agreement ended. The change in her child care obligations did not take her current position beyond the reasonable range of circumstances that the parties anticipated at the time that the agreement was signed. The court, in granting the husband's appeal, held that the wife's "evidence and argument regarding her circumstances at the time of her support application fail to demonstrate that the agreement fairly negotiated and substantially compliant with the objectives of the 1985 Act at its formation should not continue to govern the parties' post-divorce obligations towards each other."

While the two-stage test in *Miglin* has become the standard approach to cases involving separation agreements, somewhat less deference is paid to cohabitation or pre-nuptial agreements reached before the relationship breakdown. The Supreme Court in *Hartshorne v. Hartshorne*, 2004 CarswellBC 603, 2004 CarswellBC 604, 2004 SCC 22, REJB 2004-55588, 47 R.F.L. (5th) 5, [2004] 1 S.C.R. 550, 25 B.C.L.R. (4th) 1, 236 D.L.R. (4th) 193, [2004] 6 W.W.R. 1, 194 B.C.A.C. 161, , 317 W.A.C. 161, 318 N.R. 1, [2004] S.C.J. No. 20 (S.C.C.), chose not to establish a "hard and fast" rule regarding the deference to be afforded to marriage agreements as compared with separation agreements. However, the court would not wish to interfere with an agreement unless it was convinced that the agreement did not substantially comply with the overall objectives of the Act in question, such as the *Family Relations Act* (British Columbia). It would be unlikely that a court would disregard an agreement in its entirety, unless there was a significant change in the parties' circumstances from what could reasonably have been anticipated at the time of negotiation. The change would be that the terms of the agreement no longer reflected the parties' intentions at the time of execution and did not comply with the objectives of the Act. To have the agreement set aside, it would be necessary to establish that these new circumstances were not reasonably anticipated by the parties, and that they led to a situation which could not be condoned.

The test is not strict forseeability. Instead, the question is the extent to which the unimpeachably negotiated agreement can be said to have contemplated the situation before the court at the time of the application. Although this case was decided under the British Columbia *Family Relations Act*, it has important implications for cases determined under the federal *Divorce Act*. Moreover, although the issue in *Hartshorne* was division of matrimonial property, it has been found applicable to pre-nuptial and co-habitation agreement terms about spousal support.

The parties entered into a marriage agreement on their wedding day. The husband had arranged for the preparation of the agreement. It provided that the parties would not share their property, but that the wife would be entitled to a 3% interest in the family home for each year of the marriage to a maximum of 49%. The husband brought assets valued at approximately $1.6 million into the marriage. The wife had no assets on the date of the marriage and was, in fact, heavily in debt. Both parties obtained independent legal advice. The wife's lawyer advised her that the agreement was unfair and that the courts would likely set it aside if the parties separated. The parties cohabited for twelve and a half years, nine of which were under the marriage. They had two children. While both parents were lawyers, the wife left her law practice to take maternity leave and remained at home to look after the children. After the separation, she obtained a position as an associate in a law firm at a salary of $52,000 a year. The main policy objective guiding the courts' role in a division of property on marital breakdown in British Columbia is fairness. This is derived from the *Family Relations Act* (British Columbia) which provides that to be enforceable, any agreement to govern a division of property upon the dissolution of marriage must operate fairly at the time of distribution of the property. If it does not, the court may reapportion the property.

To determine whether a marriage agreement in British Columbia operates fairly the court in *Hartshorne*, above, held that as a first step, it must consider the financial entitlements under the agreement, and all other entitlements for the spouses outside the agreement including spousal and child support. Second, the court must consider the factors listed in s. 65(1) of the FRA. These factors are (a) the duration of the marriage; (b) the duration of the period during which the spouses have lived separate and apart; (c) the date when property was acquired or disposed of; (d) the extent to which property was acquired by one spouse through inheritance or gift; (e) the needs of each spouse to become or remain economically independent and self-sufficient; and (f) any other circumstances relating to the acquisition, preservation, maintenance, improvement or use of property or the capacity or liabilities of a spouse. In order for the agreement to be set aside, a court must find that by reason of these factors, taken together, the economic consequences of the marriage breakdown as found in the first step were not shared equitably in all of the circumstances. What matters is whether the agreement was unfair in the circumstances present at the time of distribution. In the present case, the marriage agreement, at the wife's insistence, expressly preserved a right to spousal support which gave rise to an understanding on her part that, in light of the provisions with respect to property, her future needs could be met through support. Only if her needs could not be met, and self-sufficiency could not be attained through an order of spousal support, should it be concluded that an agreement operated unfairly. The Supreme Court of Canada reversed the trial judge's reapportionment of the division of property, which gave the wife a 40% share or all the assets, on the understanding that she had the right to apply for spousal support. Any economic disadvantage that the respondent suffered could be addressed on such an application. Considering the provisions of the *Family Relations Act*, the provisions of the agreement, and the circumstances of the parties at the time of separation, the agreement was fair at the time of the distribution under the agreement, and it should be left intact. Courts should not conclude that agreements are unfair only because they deviate from the statutory matrimonial property regime. Fairness must be considered in light of the realistic contemplation of the parties, the attention they give to changes in circumstances or unrealized implications, their true circumstances, and whether the discrepancy is such, given the s. 65 factors, a different apportionment should be made. (The court also held that where a party has been advised that an agreement is "grossly unfair" and that a court would "easily find" that a provision could be set aside, the party should not be allowed to avoid his or her contractual obligations on the basis that he or she believed from the outset that the contract was void or unenforceable.)

*On appeal of Chamber Judge's denial of interim support, Appeal Court held that wife had established a reasonable prospect of success at trial, that Agreement was impeachable on basis of the circumstances of its execution, and its substance, and as such the Agreement on an interim basis should not be given deference — Evashenko v. Evashenko*, 2011 CarswellSask 162, 2011 SKCA 22, 96 R.F.L. (6th) 247, [2011] 4 W.W.R. 410, 366 Sask. R. 228, 506 W.A.C. 228, [2011] S.J. No. 152 (Sask. C.A.). In 2003, following 14 years of marriage and 3 children, the parties separated and the court ordered the husband, who operated a trucking company, to pay to the wife, a stay-at-home mother, $1,200 per month interim support, which term, *inter alia*, was subsequently incorporated into Minutes of Settlement. The wife was represented by counsel throughout this period. The wife was suffering extreme stress, depression and drank. The children had returned to live with their father and the wife wanted reconciliation. In 2005, the husband met with his lawyer and drew up a new inter-spousal agreement, which the wife signed in front of a lawyer who did not have any financial information or a copy of the prior settlement. Six months later, the parties reconciled for 4 years, but subsequently separated. Following the separation, because of the Agreement, the wife was left with no support or property. Her 2010 application to a Chambers Judge for interim spousal support pending trial of her spousal support application was dismissed because of the Agreement. On appeal, following a *Miglin* analysis, the appeal was allowed and the issue of quantum of interim support sent back for determination.

*Parties cannot preclude court from ordering support — Zimmerman v. Shannon*, 2006 CarswellBC 2715, 2006 BCCA 499, 34 R.F.L. (6th) 32, [2007] 4 W.W.R. 35, 62 B.C.L.R. (4th) 255, 276 D.L.R. (4th) 659, 232 B.C.A.C. 122, 385 W.A.C. 122 (B.C.C.A.), reversing 2004 CarswellBC 2132, 2004 BCSC 1246, 11 R.F.L. (6th) 230 (B.C.S.C.). The court is entitled to order support under the *Divorce Act* inconsistent with contractual support obligations because the parties cannot preclude courts from ordering statutory support. Parliament did not, however, intend to confer discretion on judges to vary contractual promises to pay support.

*Despite change in circumstances which left wife destitute, agreement remains binding — Marks v. Tokarewicz*, 2004 CarswellOnt 97, 1 R.F.L. (6th) 282, 181 O.A.C. 11, [2004] O.J. No. 92 (Ont. C.A.). Leave to appeal refused 2004 CarswellOnt 1949, 2004 CarswellOnt 1950, 330 N.R. 397 (note), 197 O.A.C. 199 (note), [2004] S.C.C.A. No. 91 (S.C.C.). Although the trial judge decided the case before the *Miglin* decision at the Supreme Court of Canada, the Court of Appeal in the *Marks v. Tokarewicz* case held that her findings were dispositive of the issues on appeal. After the parties' separation, the husband paid interim spousal support to the wife pursuant to a consent order to enable her to study medicine outside the country. After completing her degree, she returned to Canada and entered into a separation agreement, whereby the husband agreed to continue paying spousal support for over a year and a half and the wife released all claims to further support. The wife did not qualify to practice medicine in Canada and, when she became destitute and was relying on social assistance, applied for spousal support under the *Divorce Act*. As the husband was earning between $500,000 and $550,000 a year, there was no question that the he had the ability to pay. The appellate court, following the procedure described in the *Miglin* decision, found that the agreement was negotiated and executed in satisfactory circumstances and that at the time when the parties entered into the agreement, it was in substantial compliance with the considerations in s. 15.2 *Divorce Act*, and with the Act's more general objectives of certainty, finality and autonomy. Both parties had independent legal advice, exchanged sworn financial statements, and the major assets were independently valued. Each party had full disclosure of the other's financial circumstances. The court considered whether the agreement still reflected the original intention of the parties and the extent to which it was still in substantial compliance with the objectives of the act. The trial judge had considered that a material change in circumstances had occurred, as the parties had anticipated that the wife would qualify to practice medicine in Canada, which she did not do. The appellate court upheld that trial court's ruling that despite the change of circumstances, a support order should not be made. The trial judge had properly assessed the parties conflicting objectives of autonomy, finality and certainty versus a plan for the equitable resolution of the financial and property issues arising from the marriage and its breakdown, in the context of the intervening events.

*According to the* Miglin *case, general principles of contract are not intended to govern the applicability of private contractual arrangements for spousal support* – *Katz v. Katz*, 2004 CarswellMan 226, 2004 MBCA 85, 4 R.F.L. (6th) 25, 184 Man. R. (2d) 271, 318 W.A.C. 271, [2004] M.J. No. 206 (Man. C.A.). In this case, the husband appealed and the wife cross-appealed from an order varying a consent judgement. The judgement provided that spousal support would be terminated if the wife were in default for more than 10 days of her obligation to pay one-half of her monthly portion of the couple's debt. The wife missed making a payment, but the husband did not give the wife notice that support would be terminated if the default were not remedied. "Had such notice been given by the husband, it is a reasonable inference to draw from the evidence that the wife would promptly have remedied the default, so as to avoid the disproportionate and disastrous consequences of the complete termination of her spousal support. In-deed, the wife argued that such a result would be so disproportionate as to constitute a penalty and thus be unenforceable, but that argument need not be resolved on these facts." The court agreed with the motions judge that spousal support did not terminate as a result of the missed payment and it dismissed the husband's appeal. The wife's cross-appeal was allowed in part with the court holding that she was entitled to apply for an increase in spousal support, as the husband had declared bankruptcy and there was a change of circumstances. The motions judge erred when he limited that increase to the amount required to permit the wife to service the debt payment. The words of the separation agreement and the objectives of s. 17 of the Act did not support such a limited consideration. The appellate court ordered a greater quantum of spousal support, with the increase to take effect on the same date as the increase ordered by the motions court.

*A wife's waiver of spousal support in a separation agreement was enforced* – *McGeachy v. McGeachy*, 2003 CarswellOnt 3793, 42 R.F.L. (5th) 415, [2003] O.J. No. 3881 (Ont. C.A.). Where the court found that in the circumstances surrounding the signing of the agreement, there was no basis for ignoring it. The wife had received independent legal advice; she was aware of her right to seek spousal support; she provided a full and final release of that support; and the original agreement at the time of the execution was in general compliance with the objectives of the *Divorce Act*. The court further found that the agreement remained in compliance with the objectives of the Act and that there had been no significant change in the parties' circumstances from what could reasonably have been anticipated at the time they negotiated the agreement. (The court did not comment on the matters which made the agreement in compliance with the objectives of the Act). The court set aside the lower court's order for spousal support and ordered that the funds paid into court were to be paid to the husband. In addition, the wife was to reimburse the husband (without interest) for spousal support that had been paid to her pursuant to an earlier order.

*Motion for summary judgement poorly suited for application of* Miglin *test — Kelly v. Kelly,* 2003 CarswellOnt 3521, 45 R.F.L. (5th) 403, [2003] O.J. No. 3611 (Ont. S.C.J.), reversed 2004 CarswellOnt 3074, 7 R.F.L. (6th) 301, 72 O.R. (3d) 108, 242 D.L.R. (4th) 677, 189 O.A.C. 305, [2004] O.J. No. 3108 (Ont. C.A.). On a motion for summary judgement, the court found that in view of the level of professional legal advice involved and the principles as set out by the Supreme Court of Canada in *Miglin v. Miglin,* the husband had discharged the onus of establishing that there was no genuine issue to be tried and dismissed the wife's action for support. Two separation agreements had been entered into with the wife receiving independent legal advice at the time of the first agreement. Both agreements contained a waiver of spousal support. At the appellate level, the court held that a motion for summary judgement is poorly suited to dispose of claims that must be resolved by applying the detailed analysis in *Miglin,* which typically requires the court to draw inferences, determine credibility, and find facts in the face of disputed evidence. In this case, the Court of Appeal set aside the order of the motions judge and dismissed the husband's motion for summary judgement.

*Although spousal support payments and the provision of other financial arrangements in a separation agreement may be in substantial compliance with the general objectives of the Act at the time of execution, expected self-sufficiency and a time-limited award may not be in compliance with those objectives at the time of execution of the agreement — Lang v. Lang,* 2003 CarswellMan 527, 2003 MBCA 158, 46 R.F.L. (5th) 200, [2004] 6 W.W.R. 454, 234 D.L.R. (4th) 525, 180 Man. R. (2d) 223, 310 W.A.C. 223, [2003] M.J. No. 463 (Man. C.A.). At the time of execution of the agreement, the wife had primary care of all of the children, two of whom had special needs requiring an extraordinary amount of her time. Considering these circumstances and the fact that she had stayed home with her children and had limited marketable skills, it was unreasonable to anticipate that she would be self-sufficient in 5 years time as contemplated by the agreement. While it is important to consider that certainty, finality and autonomy are significant objectives of the Act, they must be balanced with other objectives. The 5-year limit for spousal support did not take into account the "condition, means, needs and other circumstances" (*Divorce Act,* s. 15.2(4)) of the wife as the primary caregiver to the children and the effect her responsibilities would have on her ability to become self-sufficient. Nor did it take into account the objective to "apportion between the spouses any financial consequences arising from the care of any child of the marriage over and above any obligation for the support of any child" (s. 15.2 (b)). It also disregarded the "reasonable period of time" aspect in the objective that a spousal support order should "in so far as practicable, promote the economic self-sufficiency of each spouse within a reasonable period of time" (s. 15.296)(d)). Since the 5-year limit did not comply substantially with the overall objectives of the Act at the time the agreement was executed, the weight given to the agreement should be significantly discounted. The same reasons for deciding that the 5-year limit on spousal support was not in compliance with the overall objectives of the Act at the time of the execution of the agreement also applied with equal force at the time of the trial. Accordingly, the provision in the agreement to limit spousal support to 5 years could not stand.

*Parties cannot oust jurisdiction of the court — Cohn v. Leboff,* 1987 CarswellQue 30, 11 R.F.L. (3d) 379, [1987] R.D.F. 449 (C.A. Que.). In Quebec, a provision in an agreement whereby support would terminate when the payee began to live with someone else is invalid since spouses cannot renounce a future right to support.

*Effect of written agreement executed by parties — Newman v. Newman,* 1980 CarswellMan 43, 19 R.F.L. (2d) 122, 114 D.L.R. (3d) 517, 4 Man. R. (2d) 50 (Man. C.A.) at 125 [R.F.L.] . "The hands of the court cannot be fettered by a written agreement executed by the parties. It is clear, though, that in order to encourage at all times this type of settlement, rather than to encourage litigation between the spouses, the court should not lightly disturb the terms of a duly negotiated contract," per Monnin J.A. The court followed *Dal Santo v. Dal Santo*, 1975 CarswellBC 45, 21 R.F.L. 117 (B.C.S.C.); *Stern v. Sheps*, 1966 CarswellMan 69, 4 R.F.L. Rep. 179, 58 W.W.R. 612, 61 D.L.R. (2d) 343 (Man. C.A.), affirmed 1968 CarswellMan 26, [1968] S.C.R. 834, 64 W.W.R. 749, 69 D.L.R. (2d) 76 (S.C.C.). It did not follow *Hyman v. Hyman*, [1929] A.C. 601, [1929] All E.R. 245 (U.K.H.L.) and *Horoshok v. Horoshok*, 1965 CarswellMan 50, 53 W.W.R. 482, 54 D.L.R. (2d) 615 (Man. Q.B.).

*Court not necessarily bound by separation agreement* — *Tanenbaum v. Tanenbaum*, 1976 CarswellOnt 140, 26 R.F.L. 83, 14 O.R. (2d) 208 (Ont. C.A.), at 87 [R.F.L.] and 211 [O.R.]. "Even if the [separation] agreement is found to constitute a valid contract upon the trial of the issue, the law regarding the effect of the existence of the agreement upon the discretion of the court is not entirely clear except that the court need not consider itself bound by its provisions," per Lacourcière J.

*Agreement cannot oust jurisdiction of court to grant support* — *Morrow v. Morrow*, 1974 CarswellNS 83, 8 N.S.R. (2d) 149, 44 D.L.R. (3d) 711 (N.S.C.A.), at 153 [N.S.R.]. "[T]he law is well settled that a covenant by a spouse in a separation agreement not to invoke the jurisdiction of the court to order financial relief if a divorce is afterward granted does not bar an application for the granting of maintenance", per MacDonald J.A. See also *Cameron v. Cameron*, 1970 CarswellNS 38, 2 R.F.L. 339, 12 D.L.R. (3d) 378, 2 N.S.R. (2d) 50 (N.S.T.D.), at 346 [R.F.L.]; *Daly v. Daly*, 1980 CarswellMan 136, 19 R.F.L. (2d) 247, [1980] 6 W.W.R. 680, 4 Man. R. (2d) 63, 114 D.L.R. (3d) 435 (Man. C.A.); and *Martini v. Martini*, 1974 CarswellBC 22, 16 R.F.L. 162 (B.C.S.C.).

*Two-stage analysis* — *M. (S.) c. K. (St.)*, 2006 CarswellQue 590, 2006 CarswellQue 14248, 2006 QCCA 142, EYB 2006-100821, 34 R.F.L. (6th) 98, [2006] R.D.F. 32 (C.A. Que.), reversing 2005 CarswellQue 3654, EYB 2005-91571 (C.S. Que.). When an agreement entered into by the spouses during divorce proceedings is contested, the court should undertake a twostage analysis. The first stage of the test is two-tiered. a review of the circumstances surrounding the conclusion of the agreement and a review of the contents of the agreement to determine whether it is in substantial compliance with all of the *Divorce Act*'s general objectives, not just those of s. 15.2. The second stage of the test is to determine whether the agreement should be modified. The two-stage analysis should always be completely performed by the merits judge who is in the best position to conduct it.

*Where an order recognizes economic consequences of the marriage and breakdown of the marriage, is not time limited, and does not impose conditions, retirement will not form a material change in circumstances sufficient to vary* — *Gaudet v. Mainville*, 2014 CarswellNB 196, 2014 CarswellNB 196, 2014 NBQB 88, 418 N.B.R. (2d) 273, 1087 A.P.R. 273 (N.B.Q.B.). The husband sought to vary, *inter alia*, his spousal support obligation, which had been determined by a 2009 order. The husband had subsequently retired. The judge determined that the wife, who had been a traditional spouse, had little or no hope of attaining self-sufficiency at the time of the 2009 order.

*Spousal support was to continue until the recipient wife had obtained self-sufficiency 4 years after a 20-year marriage when there was no evidence the husband could not afford to pay. This was consistent with the parties' previous agreement* — *C. (M.S.) v. C. (T.L.)*, 2013 CarswellNS 885, 2013 NSSC 378, 337 N.S.R. (2d) 177, 1067 A.P.R. 177 (N.S.S.C.). The parties had concluded a separation agreement, which provided for spousal support at below the Guidelines range and review at any time without showing a material change in circumstances. The parties were married for 20 years, and the judge found that the wife was entitled to compensatory support, which was consistent with the original agreement for spousal support. The wife projected she would be self-sufficient within 4 years of separation, and spousal support was ordered to continue until that time. There was no evidence that the husband did not have the means to pay support.

*Means and needs that differ considerably from those anticipated by a previous order will be considered in a variation application* — Peever v. Peever, 2013 CarswellBC 486, 2013 BCSC 299 (B.C.S.C.). The husband sought to vary spousal support and extinguish support arrears because he was previously ordered responsible for the matrimonial debt, which was far higher than anticipated by the previous order. The wife did not oppose variation and recognized the husband's limited means in oral argument. Spousal support and arrears were terminated.

*Payor's income increased after separation, but this change was contemplated at the time of the original order and no material change was found* — Fargey v. Fargey, 2013 CarswellBC 510, 2013 BCSC 331, 28 R.F.L. (7th) 115 (B.C.S.C.). The wife applied to reinstate spousal support based on the husband's increase in income. Support had been paid under the terms of a separation agreement, which provided for support to expire in 2012. The judge found that, based on the evidence available at the time of the signing of the separation agreement, the success of the husband's company was reasonably foreseeable and there were no grounds to set aside the agreement.

*Where the parties have concluded minutes of settlement that provide for ongoing spousal support and retirement is not mentioned as a change in circumstances, the husband's retirement will not constitute such a change where the husband's financial situation is much improved since the signing of the minutes of settlement* — Graca v. Graca, 2012 CarswellOnt 8535, 2012 ONSC 3934 (Ont. S.C.J.). The husband sought to terminate spousal support on the basis that he had retired for medical reasons at age 58. The parties had concluded minutes of settlement at separation that provided for spousal support until either party died and the spousal support was terminated by a court order. The support was secured by a life insurance policy. The judge considered the means and needs of the parties and found that the husband was better off than he had been at the time of the signing of the minutes of settlement. The wife continued to be in need of support. Retirement was not set out as a material change in circumstances by the minutes of settlement.

*A consent order will not be enforced when the payor had the expectation that his support obligation was at an end and arrears were reduced to reflect ability to pay* — Yerex v. Yerex, 2012 CarswellBC 2356, 2012 BCSC 1181 (B.C.S.C. [In Chambers]). The husband sought to terminate spousal support retroactively. The parties were married for 26 years prior to separation and had no children. In 2002, they entered into a consent order which was neither enforced nor abided by the payor. The wife registered the separation agreement with the enforcement agency in 2011, by which time some $49,000 of arrears had accumulated. The judge found that the accrual of arrears constituted a material change of circumstances and that the husband had made the decision to retire without knowledge of the wife's intention to enforce the consent order. The husband had limited income and no accumulated assets, and the judge found he did not have the means to pay the arrears or ongoing support. Arrears were reduced to $6,000 and were payable periodically in a step-down arrangement.

*Prenuptial agreement held not to exclude wife's claim for interim spousal support as the structure, words and tenor of agreement show it was intended to deal with rights to property (real and personal), not personal support claims* — Fedor v. Fedor, 2011 CarswellAlta 418, 2011 ABQB 185, 96 R.F.L. (6th) 309, 46 Alta. L.R. (5th) 221, 525 A.R. 128, [2011] A.J. No. 314 (Alta. Q.B.). The parties, each of whom had been previously married and had adult children, were married in 1998 and separated 12 years later. The wife was 70 and the husband was 79 years old at the time of separation. The wife who had health difficulties and an annual income of $17,105.77 resided with her brother who had loaned her $12,000. The husband's income was

$64,500 and he owned his home outright. Prior to the marriage, the parties had executed a prenuptial agreement, which the husband argued excluded the wife's claim to spousal support as it exempted pre-marital assets including his income earning pensions and investments.

*Separation agreement upheld as bar to spousal support application under s. 15 — factors as evidence led inadequate to establish inability to work and consequent need* — Neate v. Neate, 2009 CarswellAlta 1213, 2009 ABQB 475 (Alta. Q.B.). Following a 20-year marriage with two children, parties executed a Separation Agreement in which wife released right to spousal support, but reserved right to claim spousal support if by reason of material change in circumstances she was unable to support herself. Husband bought out wife's half interest in matrimonial home and assumed responsibility for the two children. At the time, the wife had trained as a nursing assistant and was working. At trial, wife relied on report from pastoral counsellor that she was unable to work because of anxiety due to multiple stresses. Court did not accept this evidence as sufficient to establish wife's need due to an inability to work and accordingly no material change in circumstances had been established to open the door to a consideration of her support application.

*A separation agreement is based on the spouses living separate and apart, when this situation ends, the agreement at least as to support cannot stand* — Emery v. Emery, 2008 CarswellOnt 1165, 51 R.F.L. (6th) 294, [2008] O.J. No. 844 (Ont. S.C.J.), additional reasons at 2008 CarswellOnt 1655 (Ont. S.C.J.), further additional reasons at 2008 CarswellOnt 2924 (Ont. S.C.J.). The parties married in 1989, had 2 children, separated in 2004, reconciled and separated again in 2005. During the first separation, they executed a separation agreement by which the wife received the net proceeds of the matrimonial in exchange for her release of spousal support and the husband's pension. On an application for ongoing and retroactive spousal support *inter alia*, the court held that although the wife's release of the husband's pension survived, the wife's release of spousal support was terminated on reconciliation.

*Given that a prior agreement is a factor in determining appropriate amount of spousal support, court held that amount agreed to in separation agreement rendered void by brief reconciliation, should be paid by husband for finite period although higher than amounts in SSAG range* — Campbell v. Campbell, 2008 CarswellOnt 3270, 55 R.F.L. (6th) 405, [2008] O.J. No. 2168 (Ont. S.C.J.), additional reasons at 2008 CarswellOnt 5110, 63 R.F.L. (6th) 170 (Ont. S.C.J.). The parties lived together for 3 years, married and then separated for the first time one year later. A year and a half after that, they executed a separation agreement in which the husband agreed to pay spousal support of $500 per month. Shortly thereafter, they resumed cohabitation for several months until the wife had the husband forcibly removed. On application by the wife to enforce the agreement for spousal support, the court held that the separation agreement had been rendered void by the reconciliation, but was an indication of what the parties considered a proper support amount which the court ordered the husband to pay from the date of separation to February 2006 when she had found employment.

*No weight given to terms of agreement* — Gauthier v. Gauthier, 2004 CarswellOnt 4747, 9 R.F.L. (6th) 312, [2004] O.T.C. 1020, [2004] O.J. No. 4698 (Ont. S.C.J.). The court gave no weight to the spousal support terms of the parties' separation agreement which allowed for very modest limited term support for the wife. At the time of execution, the wife had no income, was receiving public assistance, was in poor health, had no education and had been totally dependant upon the husband throughout the parties' 22-year traditional marriage.

*A cohabitation agreement is subject to the same tests that Miglin provides for separation agreements* — Salzmann v. Salzmann, 2004 CarswellOnt 169, 50 R.F.L. (5th) 181, [2004] O.J. No. 166 (Ont. S.C.J.). On an interim application for spousal support, the court following the tests set out in *Miglin*, found that with respect to the first stage, the applicant raised an arguable case that the negotiations of the parties' cohabitation agreement were not unimpeachable. While the parties acknowledged in the agreement that the respondent was providing support to the applicant and that she was not able to provide for her own support, the period for support was "only during the relationship." Support after that was waived. There was no provision for a review of support or a possible variation if the parties married and had children. They did, in fact, marry and had one child. It appeared that the applicant was "taken advantage of" by the respondent and did not have a proper understanding of what she was "waiving" or 'releasing". In addition, there were serious doubts about whether she received adequate professional assistance before she executed the agreement. Following the *Miglin* analysis, the court found that the agreement totally failed to be in compliance with the spousal support objectives of the *Divorce Act*. The spousal support provision, once the parties married became a provision in a marriage contract by operation of the *Family Law Act* (Ontario) and constituted a factor to be considered in a claim for support under the *Divorce Act*. The waiver attempted to exclude the applicant's claim for spousal support regardless of any change in the parties' situation. The wife was not working, as the husband had terminated her employment with his company. He was found to have an imputed income of $225,000 a year. The court held that in the circumstances, and in light of the *Divorce Act* objectives, the applicant was entitled to interim spousal support. There were new circumstances that the parties had not anticipated. Consequently, the court was to give little weight, if any, to the agreement on the spousal support issue.

A *separation agreement will be set aside after applying the tests set out in the* Miglin *decision, where the circumstances surrounding the execution of the agreement are suspect and the agreement does not meet the objectives of the* Divorce Act — *Slipak v. Slipak*, 2004 CarswellOnt 13, [2004] O.J. No. 25 (Ont. S.C.J.). The husband made inadequate disclosure to his wife, a person not involved in the business aspects of the marriage, and informed her that unless she signed the agreement, she would receive nothing whatsoever. The wife knew of the contentious nature of the husband's litigation with his first wife and that he had been taking a course on separation for several weeks. She saw no alternative but to sign the agreement. Although there was independent legal advice, there was no evidence as to the quality of that advice. The agreement was not fair at the time it was made and did not meet the objectives of the *Divorce Act*. On the question of fairness, the court stated, "The Agreement provided for no spousal support whatsoever. There had been an eight-year marriage where the wife was the primary caregiver for the children and held a limited part-time job during that time period. The parties had actually resided together for two years before that. Accordingly, spousal support should have been payable under the Agreement in the circumstances".

A *separation agreement will be given no weight where at the time of its execution the dependant spouse does not receive legal advice, was not aware of her legal entitlements and received almost nothing under the agreement after a lengthy marriage (17 years), which involved raising two children* — *Rogerson v. Rogerson*, 2004 CarswellNS 154, 2004 NSSF 37, 5 R.F.L. (6th) 151, 222 N.S.R. (2d) 324, 701 A.P.R. 324, [2004] N.S.J. No. 152 (N.S.S.C.). The wife could not afford to retain counsel and did not know that Legal Aid was available to her. Although the stress that she was under at the time of the signing of the agreement may not have been severe enough, in itself, to amount to sufficient circumstances of oppression or vulnerabilities to invalidate the agreement under the first stage of the test set out in *Miglin*, this stress combined with the other circumstances at the time, principally her lack of independent legal advice, her limited education and low-paying employment, did invalidate the agreement. In view of this finding, it was unnecessary to proceed further with the *Miglin* analysis. However, the court held that if it were wrong in its assessment of the circumstances at the time of execution, the agreement was invalid on the ground that it was not in substantial compliance with the *Divorce Act*. The court observed that *Miglin* was a situation where the principal issue related to spousal support, whereas in the case at bar spousal support was an issue, but the principal issues related to matrimonial property, particularly the husband's military pension.

*Agreement applied — clause allowed reduction in support if income declined but payor failed to adduce sufficient evidence of this* — *Girard v. Girard*, 2004 CarswellBC 756, 2004 BCSC 467, [2004] B.C.J. No. 692 (B.C.S.C.). The court held that the provisions of the parties' separation agreement were within the objectives set out in s. 15.2(6) of the *Divorce Act* and in substantial compliance with the overall objectives of the Act, which included certainty, finality and autonomy. The court observed that the parties had received independent legal advice and acknowledged there had been full and complete disclosure of each of their financial circumstances; the agreement took into account that the marriage was for a long term in which the husband was the primary breadwinner and the wife, the primary caregiver and homemaker. The provision for the acquisition of a house by the wife, time-limited spousal support for her for 5 years, and a continuing contribution towards the mortgage for another 5 years recognized her dependency. This provision together with a commitment that she would make reasonable efforts to find employment to become self-supporting, and the provision that spousal support could be reduced in the event of a material reduction in the husband's yearly income, demonstrated the context within which the agreement was made. The change since the execution of the agreement was the sudden and substantial decrease in the husband's income, which was a risk that the parties understood and accepted at the time of the execution of the agreement and for which they provided a right to adjust spousal support. Since the agreement substantially complied with the objectives of the Act when it was made and continued to reflect the original intention of the parties and remained in substantial compliance with the objectives of the Act, and since the current circumstances were not a significant departure from the range of prospective circumstances that the parties could expect, the court should give the agreement significant weight. The effect in doing so was that the agreement "must be interpreted and, if appropriate, applied including the provision that spousal support may be reduced in the event of a material reduction in the plaintiff's yearly income." However, in applying these principles to the evidence, the court declined to reduce the husband's support obligation as requested because he had not produced his last income tax return, nor the banking documents or financial statements concerning the company for which he was an officer. "In order for the plaintiff to rely upon the separation agreement to reduce his obligation to pay the defendant spousal support, he must offer proof that his annual income has been materially reduced. Similarly, the plaintiff has the same obligation of putting forward a body of evidence when he asks the court to enforce the agreement." He was given leave to bring an application to vary, supported by evidence consisting at least of his personal income tax returns for the last 2 years, as well as the corporate tax returns for the same years.

*A time-limited provision for spousal support may be enforced even though the spouse develops health problems and, at the time of the application, is on welfare* — *Lyster v. Lyster*, 2003 CarswellOnt 5008, 49 R.F.L. (5th) 139, [2003] O.J. No. 4952 (Ont. S.C.J.). The wife had developed knee problems and was on welfare at the time of her application for support beyond the 3-year provision in the agreement. She submitted that at its formation, the substance of the agreement represented a significant departure from the *Divorce Act*'s general objective of autonomy and also from all the s. 15.2 objectives. The court held that as the spousal support amounted to 30% of the husband's gross annual income for 3 years, it was a generous amount that recognized her economic vulnerability and relative lack of work experience and extra childcare responsibilities. They would have considered that their marriage was relatively short, that their one child would be enrolled fulltime in day care and/or school, and that there was no reason that the wife could not be fully employed. At the time that it was signed, the agreement reflected the general objectives of the Act and consequently, it should be given great weight.

*There is no requirement for a finding of a material change in circumstances as a condition precedent for setting aside the spousal support provisions in an agreement* — Fitzgerald v. Gerlich, 2003 CarswellOnt 1816, 40 R.F.L. (5th) 84, [2003] O.T.C. 425, [2003] O.J. No. 1946 (Ont. S.C.J.). The court, relying on the *Miglin* decision, held that where there is a separation agreement in which spousal support provisions are included, and the issue of spousal support is to be decided under s. 15.2 of the *Divorce Act*, it is raised by an application of first instance, not a variation application. Before a court can set aside the spousal support provisions in an agreement, there is no requirement for a finding of a material change in circumstances. The court quoted from the *Miglin* decision, stating ". . . it is not the existence of change *per se* that matters but whether, at the time of the application, all the circumstances render continued reliance on the pre-existing agreement unacceptable."

*Agreement upheld, applying* Miglin — Wigle v. Wigle, 2003 CarswellOnt 1672, 39 R.F.L. (5th) 233, [2003] O.J. No. 1771 (Ont. S.C.J.). The court held that the general rule from the *Miglin* decision is that a court should be loathe to interfere with a separation agreement that shows a mutual intent to finalize the terms of the parties' separation agreement, and indicates their substantive intentions. The court found that the *Wigle* case fell within the general rule in *Miglin*. Each party was represented by counsel. The former wife's self-sufficiency is outweighed by the aspects of finality and autonomy. The agreement was substantially in compliance with the support provisions of the Act, and the philosophy of the Act that the parties settle their affairs. There were no new circumstances which indicate that the agreement no longer reflects the parties' intentions at the time the agreement was executed. It still reflects the philosophy of the *Divorce Act*. The agreement was upheld.

*A provision in a separation agreement that support will terminate if the wife cohabited in a conjugal relationship may be enforced against the wife* — Bakes v. Bakes, 2003 CarswellNS 220, 2003 NSSC 130, 40 R.F.L. (5th) 1, 215 N.S.R. (2d) 1, 675 A.P.R. 1, [2003] N.S.J. No. 202 (N.S.S.C.). The separation agreement provided that spousal support would be terminated if the wife were living in a common law relationship. She entered into such a relationship and applied for a continuation of spousal support. At the first stage, as set out in the *Miglin* decision, the court found that any concerns about oppression at the time of the execution of the agreement were on the side of the husband in that an unduly heavy financial burden had been placed on him. He was, however, prepared to live with it. The negotiation of the agreement did not lead to an unduly harsh or oppressive agreement for the wife. At the second stage, following the procedure in *Miglin*, the court assessed the substance of the agreement and held that an application of the terms of the agreement did not represent a significant departure from the range of reasonable expectations as anticipated by the parties so as to put them out of step with the objectives of the act. Both parties had developed health problems. The *Miglin* case specifically stated that "Negotiating parties should know that each persons (sic) health cannot be guaranteed as a constant." The husband's illness stemmed from his increased work load in fulfilling his obligations under the agreement. The wife received very generous support immediately after the marriage breakdown. The court held that it was appropriate that the terms of the separation agreement be respected and that support should be terminated as of the date when the court found that the wife was living in a common law relationship.

*Agreement upheld* — Collins v. Collins, 2003 CarswellNfld 168, 2003 NLSCTD 102, 42 R.F.L. (5th) 273, 229 Nfld. & P.E.I.R. 1, 679 A.P.R. 1, [2003] N.J. No. 169 (N.L.T.D.). The court upheld the parties' agreement as it had been negotiated in good faith. It was a fair and equitable division of their matrimonial and business assets and liabilities and corollary relief issues had been determined reasonably. The agreement continued to deal with all issues between the parties and there had been no changes in the parties' circumstances since the separation agreement so it could still govern the parties' post-divorce obligations to each other.

*Parties' intention was that material change in circumstances would justify variation —* Deneweth v. *Deneweth,* 2003 CarswellMan 431, 2003 MBQB 236, 44 R.F.L. (5th) 368, 179 Man. R. (2d) 4, [2003] M.J. No. 392 (Man. Q.B.), additional reasons at 2004 CarswellMan 101, 2004 MBQB 60, 50 R.F.L. (5th) 341, 183 Man. R. (2d) 67, [2004] M.J. No. 106 (Man. Q.B.). Where there is no reason to discount the weight of the agreement because of the circumstances surrounding the negotiation and execution of an agreement, and the substance of the agreement takes into account the factors and objectives in s. 15.2 of the *Divorce Act,* the court should then assess the extent to which the agreement still reflects the original intention of the parties, and the extent to which it is still in substantial compliance with the objectives of the act. In this case, the parties' original intention was that the spousal support provisions could be varied if either party had a material change in his or her circumstances. The court found that there had been a material change in the parties' circumstances, as the husband's income had decreased from $59,992 per annum to an expected income of $49,500. The wife's income from employment increased from $3,000 to $11,900. The court held that a reduction in spousal support must be limited in recognition of the factors and objectives set out in s. 15.2 of the *Divorce Act.* The reduction in the husband's income reduced his obligation for child support, which in turn placed further stress on the wife. In all the circumstances, the court ordered spousal support reduced from $800 to $700 per month.

*Agreement upheld despite increase in payor's income —* Bellingham v. *Bellingham,* 2003 CarswellMan 396, 2003 MBQB 221, 44 R.F.L. (5th) 357, 178 Man. R. (2d) 60, [2003] M.J. No. 348 (Man. Q.B.), additional reasons at (2004), 2004 CarswellMan 100, 2004 MBQB 75, 1 R.F.L. (6th) 11, [2004] M.J. No. 113 (Man. Q.B.), further additional reasons at 2004 CarswellMan 191, 2004 MBQB 115, 13 R.F.L. (6th) 237, [2004] M.J. No. 186 (Man. Q.B.). Where the parties' separation agreement provided for a review of spousal support if there were a substantial increase in the husband's income, the application should be dismissed when the increase in income was caused by a transaction referred to in the agreement and consequently contemplated by the parties. Pursuant to the terms of the parties' agreement, the husband purchased the wife's shares in a company and subsequently received all the company dividends. At the time the agreement was executed, the parties assumed that the entire company income, which had been split between the parties during the marriage, would be attributable to the husband following the share purchase transaction.

*The same reasoning applied in* Miglin *to separation agreements apply equally to prenuptial agreements —* Culen v. *Culen,* 2003 CarswellAlta 716, 2003 ABQB 480, 37 R.F.L. (5th) 300, 338 A.R. 308 (Alta. Q.B.). Here, with respect to the first stage, there was no evidence to indicate that the agreement should be discounted. The fact that the plaintiff was pregnant and therefore vulnerable is undermined by the fact that the agreement was negotiated at her insistence. Both parties had previous experience with separation and divorce and each was represented by counsel. The agreement was in substantial compliance with the overall objectives of the *Divorce Act.* At the second stage, the court found that the current circumstances of the parties did not represent a significant departure from the range of the reasonable outcomes which the parties would have anticipated. The pre-nuptial agreement continued to reflect the parties' original intentions with respect to their finances and provided certainty and finality. There was evidence throughout the 9-year cohabitation of the intention of the parties to be self-sufficient or autonomous and the court should take this factor into account. The court must take into account the objectives of spousal support. There was no evidence of any economic disadvantage to the plaintiff arising from the marriage or its breakdown. While the plaintiff received disability payments at the time of the hearing, as she was epileptic, she began receiving these payments prior to separation. There was no evidence that the parties established an interdependent relationship at any point in time. The parties were not in circumstances that they did not contemplate would occur. The court dismissed the plaintiff's application for spousal support.

*An agreement that released each party from claims to support from the other was upheld —* Merke v. Merke, 2003 CarswellBC 1708, 2003 BCSC 1070, 39 R.F.L. (5th) 339, [2003] B.C.J. No. 1607 (B.C.S.C.). The court found nothing in the circumstances of the negotiation and execution of the agreement to discount it, and at that time it was in substantial compliance with the principles in the *Divorce Act*. In assessing the extent to which enforcement of the agreement at the time of the hearing still reflected the original intention of the parties and the extent to which the agreement was still in substantial compliance with the objectives of the Act, the court considered whether the parties' circumstances had changed. The main change was the liquidation of the wife's business. The court found that although the wife had liquidated her restaurant business for substantially less than she had expected, the agreement had anticipated its sale or liquidation. The agreement continued to reflect the intention of the parties when they originally made the agreement. It was in substantial compliance with both the *Divorce Act* and the *Family Relations Act*.

*"No change in circumstances" clause cannot oust court's jurisdiction on variation —* Wilkinson v. Wilkinson, 1996 CarswellOnt 693, 22 R.F.L. (4th) 46 (Ont. Gen. Div.). The fact that the support provisions in a separation agreement contain a no "change of circumstances" clause does not prevent the court from entertaining an application for variation of support. See also *re effect of support order on earlier agreement —* Evermon v. Evermon, 1988 CarswellBC 583, 15 R.F.L. (3d) 10 (B.C. Co. Ct.).

*Support order supersedes earlier agreement —* H. (C.A.) v. N. (B.D.), 1987 CarswellOnt 243, 10 R.F.L. (3d) 317, [1987] O.J. No. 1864 (Ont. Fam. Ct.), affirmed 1987 CarswellOnt 273, 11 R.F.L. (3d) 429 (Ont. Dist. Ct.). An order respecting support supersedes prior arrangements in a domestic contract and prevents later recourse to the agreement. Accordingly, where a court dismisses a wife's claim for support she is not entitled to enforce the support provisions under an earlier separation agreement.

*Significance of support waiver in agreement —* Martini v. Martini, 1974 CarswellBC 22, 16 R.F.L. 162 (B.C.S.C.). The existence of a separation agreement does not prevent a court from awarding maintenance even in situations where there is a provision in the separation agreement that the wife shall not seek maintenance. It is, however, a major circumstance to be considered, particularly where a wife covenants not to take proceedings for maintenance.

*Rationale for not allowing agreement to oust court's jurisdiction —* McClelland v. McClelland, 1971 CarswellOnt 133, 6 R.F.L. 91, [1972] 1 O.R. 236, 22 D.L.R. (3d) 624 (Ont. H.C.), at 95 [R.F.L.]. "It is for these reasons, and these reasons only, that public policy dictates that an agreement made during the marriage cannot oust the court of its divorce jurisdiction to award maintenance. Once the parties are divorced and living apart, the situation is entirely changed. Status is no longer an issue. The wife is a feme sole and is free of the potentially prejudicial atmosphere of the marriage. There are, effectively, two independent parties before the court, and the court is concerned solely with determining the rights between the parties. Public policy disappears," per Lacourcie're J. See also *Woods v. Woods*, 1975 CarswellOnt 217, 22 R.F.L. 370 (Ont. H.C.), at 377 [R.F.L.]; *DiTullio v. DiTullio*, 1974 CarswellOnt 135, 16 R.F.L. 148, 3 O.R. (2d) 519, 46 D.L.R. (3d) 66 (Ont. Co. Ct.), at 150-151 [R.F.L.]; *Smith v. Smith*, 1955 CarswellOnt 73, [1955] O.R. 695, [1955] 3 D.L.R. 808 (Ont. C.A.); *Stevens v. Stevens*, 1940 CarswellOnt 10, [1940] 3 D.L.R. 283, [1940] O.R. 243, [1940] O.W.N. 249 (Ont. C.A.).

*Relevance of independant legal advice —* McGeachy v. McGeachy, 2003 CarswellOnt 3793, 42 R.F.L. (5th) 415, [2003] O.J. No. 3881 (Ont. C.A.). One of the circumstances considered by the court in upholding the parties' separation agreement was that the respondent had independent legal advice.

*Agreement allowed for variation in the event of a change in circumstances — husband misrepresented finances — Marinangeli v. Marinangeli*, 2003 CarswellOnt 2691, 38 R.F.L. (5th) 307, 228 D.L.R. (4th) 376, 66 O.R. (3d) 40, 174 O.A.C. 76, [2003] O.J. No. 2819 (Ont. C.A.). Prior to the signing of the parties' settlement agreement, the husband indicated at a pretrial conference that he anticipated a decrease in his income. In fact, he received over a million dollars when he exercised stock options within 14 months of signing the parties' settlement agreement. The case centered on the issue of whether or not the increase in the appellant's income was a change in circumstances. The wife sought to enforce the provision in the agreement that support could be revised where there had been a material change of circumstances. The appellant argued that there had not been a change in circumstances as described in *Miglin v. Miglin*, 2003 CarswellOnt 1374, 2003 CarswellOnt 1375, 2003 SCC 24, REJB 2003-40012, 34 R.F.L. (5th) 255, [2003] 1 S.C.R. 303, 66 O.R. (3d) 736, 224 D.L.R. (4th) 193, 302 N.R. 201, 171 O.A.C. 201, [2003] S.C.J. No. 21 (S.C.C.), meaning a change that was not foreseeable as part of the ordinary course of living at the time the settlement agreement was signed. In the *Marinangeli* case, Madam Justice Weiler wrote, at para. 45:

> The comments of the Supreme Court in *Miglin, supra* were intended to address the situation where the parties chose to release one another from all future support obligations by a one-time payment of lump sum support. Since no future adjustments were envisaged, the parties were expected to consider such foreseeable future changes in the ordinary course of living as an increase or decrease in income before arriving at the amount of the one time payment.

She distinguished the *Marinangeli* case from *Miglin*, since in *Marinangeli*, the parties envisaged that the amount of support would change, if there were a material change in circumstances in a party's income. The court held that the provision in the separation agreement relating to a material change in circumstances, read in its context and as a whole, did not exclude foreseeable events such as an increase or decrease in income, but the opposite.

The appellant was unsuccessful in arguing that the exercise of his options was not a material change in circumstances as defined in *Willick v. Willick*, 1994 CarswellSask 48, 1994 CarswellSask 450, EYB 1994-67936, 6 R.F.L. (4th) 161, [1994] 3 S.C.R. 670, 119 D.L.R. (4th) 405, 173 N.R. 321, [1994] R.D.F. 617, 125 Sask. R. 81, 81 W.A.C. 81, [1994] S.C.J. No. 94 (S.C.C.), that is, had the alleged change been known, the support provision would not likely have been different. As the appellant did not know the value of his options at the time the agreement was signed, the respondent could not be assumed to know their value at that time. In addition, the respondent was not told the parameters for the exercise of the options and consequently she had no way of ascertaining the value of the options in relation to the price of the underlying stock. The respondent was dependant upon the appellant for information about the value of the options.

A change in circumstances must be something that has some measure of continuity. The court did not accept the appellant's argument that the exercise of the options was not a material change in circumstances because their exercise lacked continuity. There is continuity in the frequency with which the options are awarded and continuity in that the options may be exercised over a period of time. The increase in a payor's salary and bonus by nearly 20 per cent over the previous year is a material change in circumstances that entitled the trial judge to consider the profit from the options in determining the quantum of support.

*Relevance of presence of legal counsel — Lang v. Lang*, 2003 CarswellMan 527, 2003 MBCA 158, 46 R.F.L. (5th) 200, [2004] 6 W.W.R. 454, 234 D.L.R. (4th) 525, 180 Man. R. (2d) 223, 310 W.A.C. 223, [2003] M.J. No. 463 (Man. C.A.). Whether a party has legal counsel throughout the negotiation and execution of a separation agreement is relevant to determining the weight that should be given to an agreement. However, there is no requirement that a party to a separation agreement must have legal counsel.

*Agreement set aside — wife did not understand it and had no independent legal advice — Chandra v. Chandra*, 1999 CarswellNfld 99, 45 R.F.L. (4th) 181, 174 Nfld. & P.E.I.R. 136, 533 A.P.R. 136, [1999] N.J. No. 101 (Nfld. C.A.), affirming 1997 CarswellNfld 27, 27 R.F.L. (4th) 114, 150 Nfld. & P.E.I.R. 333, 470 A.P.R. 333, [1997] N.J. No. 17 (Nfld. U.F.C.). The court refused the husband's appeal from an order setting aside the parties' marriage agreement. The husband had drafted the agreement without consultation with the wife who signed the document without understanding its contents and without benefit of independent legal advice.

*Wife had legal counsel — agreement upheld — Droit de la famille - 1601*, 1992 CarswellQue 612, EYB 1992-55792, [1992] R.D.F. 346 (C.A. Que.). Where it was evident that the wife had had the benefit of legal counsel on numerous occasions throughout the parties' matrimonial proceedings, the court refused an appeal from an order that upheld the parties' separation agreement, despite the wife's allegations that she had lacked independent legal advice. It appeared that the wife's true intentions were merely to aggravate her husband.

*Agreement set aside — lawyer who prepared it was in conflict of interest — Droit de la famille - 1532* (1991), [1992] R.D.F. 89 (C.S. Que.), reversed in part 1993 CarswellQue 335, [1993] R.J.Q. 2712, 59 O.A.C. 151, 59 Q.A.C. 151, [1993] R.D.F. 720, [1993] J.Q. No. 2001 (C.A. Que.). The court, in the context of a divorce proceeding, set aside a separation agreement on the grounds that the lawyer who prepared it had done so in a conflict of interest situation. The lawyer worked for a firm that had represented the husband for a number of years and therefore the wife had lacked independent legal advice. The agreement was clearly unreasonable and had to be annulled.

*Agreement created hastily and intended to be provisional — Droit de la famille - 598*, 1989 CarswellQue 635, EYB 1989-57104, [1989] R.D.F. 15 (C.A. Que.). The court should uphold the support provisions in a separation agreement only when they were intended to be final, binding and permanent, and not when the agreement was drawn in haste and designed to deal only with provisional measures.

*Choice of legal counsel gave rise to conflict of interest — agreement set aside support provision — Brosseau v. Brosseau*, 1989 CarswellAlta 162, 23 R.F.L. (3d) 42, 70 Alta. L.R. (2d) 247, [1990] 2 W.W.R. 34, 63 D.L.R. (4th) 111, 100 A.R. 15, [1989] A.J. No. 924 (Alta. C.A.). Leave to appeal to the S.C.C. refused (1990), 23 R.F.L. (3d) xli (note), 70 Alta. L.R. (2d) lii (note), 65 D.L.R. (4th) vii (note) (S.C.C.). Where, in negotiating a separation agreement, the husband consulted his brother and the wife consulted her husband's niece, who was an associate of the husband's brother, the court set aside a clause whereby the wife agreed not to pursue support. There had been a clear conflict of interest which had not been dispelled by a cursory review of the agreement on the wife's behalf by a second solicitor.

*Party who had independent legal advice not able to later challenge competence of lawyer — Brosseau v. Brosseau*, 1988 CarswellAlta 387, 85 A.R. 385 (Alta. Q.B.), varied 1989 CarswellAlta 162, 23 R.F.L. (3d) 42, 63 D.L.R. (4th) 111, 100 A.R. 15, 70 Alta. L.R. (2d) 247, [1990] 2 W.W.R. 34, [1989] A.J. No. 924 (Alta. C.A.). Leave to appeal refused (1990), 70 Alta. L.R. (2d) lii (note), 23 R.F.L. (3d) xli (note), 65 D.L.R. (4th) vii (note) (S.C.C.). Where the wife obtained independent legal advice prior to settling the issue of support, it was held that she could not later challenge the competence of that advice in seeking increased support in a subsequent divorce action.

*Relevance of wife's lack of experience in business matters — Brockie v. Brockie*, 1987 CarswellMan 93, 5 R.F.L. (3d) 440, 46 Man. R. (2d) 33, [1987] M.J. No. 56 (Man. Q.B.), affirmed 1987 CarswellMan 115, 8 R.F.L. (3d) 302, [1987] M.J. No. 295 (Man. C.A.). Where the wife, inexperienced in business matters, had agreed to child and spousal support which resulted in living at the poverty line, the agreement was overridden in subsequent divorce proceedings. The agreement was bordering on improvidence and failed to meet the criteria set out in s. 15 of the *Divorce Act*, 1985.

*Agreement unconscionable, already breached by respondent to support application* — *McVeetors v. McVeetors*, 1985 CarswellOnt 227, 43 R.F.L. (2d) 113, 49 O.R. (2d) 225, 7 O.A.C. 1 (Ont. C.A.). Leave to appeal to the Supreme Court of Canada refused (1985), 49 O.R. (2d) 225 (note), 15 D.L.R. (4th) 105 (note), 8 O.A.C. 320 (note) (S.C.C.). It was held that a separation agreement did not bar an award of lump sum maintenance to the wife where the husband had himself breached the agreement and the agreement itself was unconscionable. The agreement was found to be unconscionable on the evidence that the wife had executed the agreement while under great stress, the husband had failed to disclose material facts prior to its execution and the wife's standard of living had deteriorated drastically since the separation.

*Intimidation at time of negotiation* — *Ross v. Ross*, 1984 CarswellMan 35, 39 R.F.L. (2d) 51, 6 D.L.R. (4th) 385, 26 Man. R. (2d) 122 (Man. C.A.). Leave to appeal refused (1984), 6 D.L.R. (4th) 385n, 39 R.F.L. (2d) xxxviii, 55 N.R. 238n (S.C.C.). The presence of a separation agreement is an important circumstance for the court to take into account in awarding maintenance. However, in a case where there exists an unfair and unbalanced settlement arrived at in circumstances where the wife was subject to intimidation by the husband and where her independent legal advisor did not anticipate enforcement difficulties, judicial intervention is justified.

*Whether professional assistance to applicant before signing was adequate is relevant* — *Salzmann v. Salzmann*, 2004 CarswellOnt 169, 50 R.F.L. (5th) 181, [2004] O.J. No. 166 (Ont. S.C.J.). An agreement may not be negotiated in unimpeachable circumstances where, among other concerns, there are serious doubts regarding whether the applicant received adequate professional assistance before she signed the agreement.

*No evidence regarding quality of independent legal advice* — *Slipak v. Slipak*, 2004 CarswellOnt 13, [2004] O.J. No. 25 (Ont. S.C.J.). The court held that a separation agreement should be set aside where, among other considerations, there was no evidence as to the quality of the independent legal advice that was given.

*Relevance of receiving legal advice* — *Rogerson v. Rogerson*, 2004 CarswellNS 154, 2004 NSSF 37, 5 R.F.L. (6th) 151, 222 N.S.R. (2d) 324, 701 A.P.R. 324, [2004] N.S.J. No. 152 (N.S.S.C.). A separation agreement may be found to be unenforceable where at the time of its execution, among other circumstances, one spouse does not receive legal advice.

*Relevance of disclosure* — *suitability of summary judgement motion to apply* Miglin *analysis* — *Leinburd v. Leinburd*, 2004 CarswellMan 194, 2004 MBQB 113, 10 R.F.L. (6th) 398, [2004] 9 W.W.R. 635, 185 Man. R. (2d) 215, [2004] M.J. No. 185 (Man. Q.B.). A court should consider evidence of lack of disclosure as part of the overall vulnerability issue when determining whether an agreement met all of the objectives of the *Divorce Act* at the time of its formation. In its assessment, a court would weigh many factors, including the taking of professional advice. If the agreement is not set aside at this formation stage, the court must proceed to the second stage to decide whether the applicant has established that the agreement no longer reflects the parties' intention or is no longer in substantial compliance with the objectives of the *Divorce Act*. The court held that the issue of whether the wife's position was vulnerable because of inadequacies in the husband's disclosure could not be determined on a motion for summary judgement and would have to be resolved at a trial.

*Absence of independent legal advice is not a ground in itself to set aside a contract at common law* — *Phillips-Renwick v. Renwick Estate*, 2003 CarswellOnt 3107, 41 R.F.L. (5th) 337, 229 D.L.R. (4th) 158, [2003] O.J. No. 3156 (Ont. S.C.J.). Although a lawyer gave the wife a general summary of the nature and consequences of the cohabitation agreement, which became a marriage contract upon the parties' marriage, and ascertained that she understood the terms, this procedure did not amount to independent legal advice as to the wisdom of the contract, nor provide any recommendation to the client that she should sign it or refrain from doing so. Lack of independent legal advice may be relevant to one or more of the common law grounds available to set aside the contract. However, the wife was not able to establish the existence of any such ground. Further, she initiated the agreement and understood its nature and effect. Consequently, she was bound by the agreement.

*Wife had been misled regarding husband's finances — agreement set aside — Dubin v. Dubin*, 2003 CarswellOnt 534, 34 R.F.L. (5th) 227, [2003] O.J. No. 547 (Ont. S.C.J.). The court set aside the parties' marriage contract under which the wife had forfeited her right to spousal support. Although the agreement made reference to financial disclosure, the wife had been misled about the husband's true financial circumstances and had no realistic understanding of his assets and liabilities as of the date of the agreement.

*Stress and anxiety at time of negotiation do not give rise to presumption of incapacity to consent to agreement — McGregor v. Van Tilborg*, 2003 CarswellBC 1488, 2003 BCSC 918, [2003] B.C.J. No. 1427(B.C.S.C. [In Chambers]). Following *Miglin*, the court held that where a payee spouse is suffering stress and anxiety at the time of the execution of a separation agreement, there is no presumption that the parties are incapable of assenting to a binding agreement. In this case, the wife claimed to be suffering from a mental condition and under psychiatric care when she negotiated a separation agreement. The mental problems were related to some form of historical sexual abuse and did not appear to be related to the divorce.

*A separation agreement will be set aside when there has been material misrepresentation of a party's assets — Souder v. Wereschuk*, 2003 CarswellAlta 358, 2003 ABQB 258, 38 R.F.L. (5th) 185, [2003] A.J. No. 362 (Alta. Q.B.). In this case, the parties married in 1989 and separated in 1994. In 1995, the husband won $500,000 in the lottery and did not disclose his win to his wife. The parties executed a separation agreement in 1997 and were divorced in 2001. In the agreement, the wife, who was disabled, waived her claim for spousal support. The court found that the husband had materially misrepresented his assets at the time that the agreement was being negotiated. The wife claimed a matrimonial property order reflecting all the assets of the husband and spousal support. The court considered that the 5-year length of the marriage was a factor. As the lottery prize was acquired 10 months after the parties' separation, there was not a significant degree of separation. The parties were nearly 2 years short of entering into a separation agreement and the plaintiff began receiving interim spousal maintenance a few months later. The court awarded the wife one quarter of the lottery proceeds but she did not receive any spousal support. The court considered the three different models of marriages set out in *Bracklow v. Bracklow*, 1999 CarswellBC 532, 1999 CarswellBC 533, 44 R.F.L. (4th) 1, [1999] 1 S.C.R. 420, 169 D.L.R. (4th) 577, 63 B.C.L.R. (3d) 77, [1999] 8 W.W.R. 740, 236 N.R. 79, 120 B.C.A.C. 211, 196 W.A.C. 211, [1999] S.C.J. No. 14 (S.C.C.) and held that the wife had not established entitlement for support under any of the models.

*Both parties had misrepresented incomes for tax purposes — agreement upheld — Merke v. Merke*, 2003 CarswellBC 1708, 2003 BCSC 1070, 39 R.F.L. (5th) 339, [2003] B.C.J. No. 1607 (B.C.S.C.). In upholding the parties' agreement, the court found nothing in the circumstances of the negotiation and execution of the agreement to discount it. The objectives of finality, certainty, and the general interest of the parties determining their own affairs were important factors in upholding the agreement, especially where, as here, the parties both had a history of misrepresenting their incomes in order to live essentially on a tax-free basis.

*Where parties enter into an agreement through counsel, the courts tend to uphold the agreements except in the clearest of cases, and in exceptional circumstances — P. (M.L.) v. P. (G.W.)*, 2000 CarswellOnt 3937, 12 R.F.L. (5th) 434, [2000] O.T.C. 762, [2000] O.J. No. 4059

(Ont. S.C.J.). This case did not meet the requirements for such exceptional circumstances and the wife's motion for judgement in accordance with the settlement was granted. The case did involve stressful litigation but the issues raised were not gratuitously or tactically created. The husband negotiated actively up to the signing of the agreement and after it was finalized. These circumstances make it difficult to find that he lacked free will in his conduct. The allegation of false accusations of sexual abuse was not a new issue at the time of execution of the settlement agreement. Another forum could deal with this issue rather than in the context of a hearing for divorce. To enforce the agreement would not prejudice either party; rather, it would benefit both by ending the litigation, providing emotional and financial relief.

*Threat to cut off support unless other spouse signed agreement does not necessarily constitute duress* — Roberts v. Roberts, 2000 CarswellBC 784, 2000 BCSC 611, 6 R.F.L. (5th) 407 (B.C.S.C.). A single instance of one party telling the other that he would cut off support payments if she did not sign a separation agreement does not constitute duress. The agreement was comprehensive and, in the opinion of the court, fair. The wife was represented by counsel throughout the negotiations and preparation of the agreement and had independent legal advice. The wife had accepted benefits under the agreement for at least 2 years before challenging the validity of the agreement.

*Husband had not made full disclosure* — Underwood v. Underwood, 1994 CarswellOnt 394, 3 R.F.L. (4th) 457, 113 D.L.R. (4th) 571 (Ont. Gen. Div.), varied 1995 CarswellOnt 88, 11 R.F.L. (4th) 361, [1995] O.J. No. 4335 (Ont. Div. Ct.). Where the husband, during settlement negotiations, had failed to advise the wife that his financial circumstances had recently improved, the portion of the agreement under which the wife had waived her right to support was set aside and her support claim was allowed to go forward.

*Party informed of right to independent legal advice but refused it* — Sartor v. Sartor, 1993 CarswellNWT 6, 45 R.F.L. (3d) 250, [1993] N.W.T.R. 102, [1993] N.W.T.J. No. 18 (N.W.T.S.C.). Where a signatory to a separation agreement has been advised of the right to independent legal advice but chooses not to pursue it, that party cannot later rely upon the inequality of bargaining power as a reason for setting aside the agreement.

*Relevance of independent legal advice* — Durocher v. Durocher, 1991 CarswellNS 559, 106 N.S.R. (2d) 215, 288 A.P.R. 215, [1991] N.S.J. No. 393 (N.S.T.D.). The court refused to set aside the support provisions of the parties' separation agreement executed upon the dissolution of their 29-year marriage. The parties had obtained independent legal advice before signing the agreement, and the wife's allegations of undue influence, duress and unconscionability were not supported by the evidence. Furthermore, the wife had experience in handling the parties' financial affairs and, considering the property provisions of the agreement, the arrangement as a whole was not unfair.

*Agreement reached the previous day found not to be binding* — Macdonald v. Macdonald, 1986 CarswellNS 71, 4 R.F.L. (3d) 463, 79 N.S.R. (2d) 58, 196 A.P.R. 58 (N.S.T.D.). The court refused to hold the wife to a divorce settlement to which she had agreed the previous day. The wife had been under considerable strain during the negotiations and the husband would not be prejudiced by the repudiation.

*Party under psychiatric care at time of agreement* — Helmes v. Helmes, 1984 CarswellOnt 253, 40 R.F.L. (2d) 319 (Ont. H.C.). The wife was awarded monthly maintenance of $1,000 despite the fact that under earlier minutes of settlement she had agreed to accept the monthly sum of only $600. Although the husband had not exerted any pressure on the wife at the time of the settlement, she had been under psychiatric care and was in no condition to understand fully the future implications of the agreement she signed.

*Husband had misrepresented nature of agreement, wife had no legal advice* — Grossmann v. Grossmann, 1982 CarswellOnt 309, 29 R.F.L. (2d) 300 (Ont. H.C.). The court set aside a separation agreement upon which the husband relied in defence to his wife's maintenance claim. The agreement had been entered into at the instigation of the husband who had represented that it was for tax purposes only and was not intended otherwise to affect their relationship. As the wife had not had legal advice and as the agreement was not fair to her, it was ordered set aside in its entirety and transactions arranged under it were ordered unwound. See also *Bengston v. Bengston*, 1976 CarswellBC 106, 28 R.F.L. 208 (B.C.S.C.); *Beach v. Beach*, 1977 CarswellAlta 203, [1977] 3 W.W.R. 274, 2 A.R. 561 (Alta. T.D.), at 282-83 [W.W.R.]; *Woods v. Woods*, 1975 CarswellOnt 217, 22 R.F.L. 370 (Ont. H.C.), at 377 [R.F.L.]; *Nador v. Nador*, 1977 CarswellOnt 1169, 19 O.R. (2d) 728, 86 D.L.R. (3d) 463 (Ont. H.C.), at 735 [O.R.], affirmed 1977 CarswellOnt 587, 22 O.R. (2d) 685, 97 D.L.R. (3d) 161 (Ont. C.A.); *Thompson v. Thompson*, 1974 CarswellSask 23, 16 R.F.L. 158 (Sask. Q.B.).

*Agreement upheld despite lack of legal advice — Sherren v. Sherren*, 1981 CarswellNfld 88, 33 Nfld. & P.E.I.R. 526, 93 A.P.R. 526 (Nfld. T.D.). Where the petitioner wife executed a separation agreement without first obtaining legal advice, she was nevertheless estopped from denying its validity in her application for maintenance in an action for divorce. The wife was highly intelligent and had accepted benefits under the agreement and had not been deceived into accepting the terms. See also. *Armstrong v. Armstrong*, 1980 CarswellSask 278, 5 Sask. R. 435 (Sask. Q.B.), at 436 [Sask. R.]; *Acorn v. Acorn*, 1980 CarswellBC 480, 15 R.F.L. (2d) 257, [1980] B.C.J. No. 1531 (B.C.S.C.); *Methe v. Methe*, 1973 CarswellOnt 217, 9 R.F.L. 320 (Ont. H.C.); *Curtin v. Curtin*, 1976 CarswellOnt 143, 20 R.F.L. 140 (Ont. H.C.); *Dempster v. Dempster*, 1976 CarswellBC 89, 26 R.F.L. 337 (B.C.S.C.), at 338-39 [R.F.L.]; *Divinsky v. Divinsky*, 1970 CarswellBC 53, 2 R.F.L. 372, [1971] 1 W.W.R. 389, 13 D.L.R. (3d) 717 (B.C.S.C.), at 375-76 [R.F.L.].

*Agreement upheld despite lack of legal advice — Biscutti v. Biscutti*, 1977 CarswellOnt 161, 4 R.F.L. (2d) 60 (Ont. H.C.). The fact that the wife entered into the separation agreement without any independent legal advice did not preclude the husband from utilizing the agreement as a defence to her claim for maintenance where she understood the agreement and no undue influence was brought to bear. Upon a consideration of the conduct of the parties and the terms of the agreement, it was the intention of the parties that there was to be a division of the property and the wife was to be on her own.

*Where spousal support provisions in a separation agreement allow for variation if there is any change in circumstances, material or not, support may be terminated if payment necessitates an encroachment on capital — Burroughs v. Burroughs*, 2004 CarswellBC 17, 2004 BCSC 7, [2004] B.C.J. No. 29 (B.C.S.C.). The parties separated, an interim order was granted and then the parties entered into a separation agreement. The court held that the support set out in the interim order and in accordance with the separation agreement be terminated. Although the petitioner was in need of support, the respondent could not pay it unless he encroached upon his capital. The parties' assets had already been divided and the wife had not used her assets or income prudently to plan for her retirement and consequently had declared bankruptcy.

*Where a separation agreement provides that spousal support should be paid if there is a material change of circumstances, spousal support may be ordered upon a finding that there is a large disparity in standards of living as well as changes in the spouses' incomes — Innes v. Innes*, 2003 CarswellOnt 2884, 44 R.F.L. (5th) 113, [2003] O.T.C. 686, [2003] O.J. No. 3039 (Ont. S.C.J.). The court held that termination of child support constituted a material change in circumstances, as set out in the separation agreement. Further, the decline in the wife's standard of living from the time of marriage, and in particular from the time that child support ceased, as well as maintenance or improvement in the husband's standard of living and in his income, constituted material changes. The parties were married for 26 years and had four children who were adults at the time of the trial. The wife did not work for 12 years. For a further 7 years, she worked part-time and started working full time only 2 years before separation. The separation agreement provided for child support of $1,647.00 per month based on the husband's 1999 income of $101, 914.44. At that time, the wife was earning $56,900.00. In the separation agreement, the parties agreed to pay each other $1.00 per year with the right to claim further support based on a material change of circumstance. The husband had ceased to pay child support and the wife applied for spousal support. At the time of trial, the husband was expected to have an income of $138,000 a year and the wife an income of $63,500. The husband's new wife had an income of $99,000 a year, but that amount was unchanged since the execution of the parties' separation agreement. The court stated that a difference of incomes of the spouses should not automatically lead to an order of spousal support. However, that difference should not exist where there is a significant disparity in the standards of living between two spouses after a long marriage and in particular if a short time has transpired since the execution of the agreement. The court held that as it should encourage self-sufficiency and also recognize the husband's new family commitments, spousal support should be less than a 50/50 equalization of incomes, and it should be based on the husband's base salary of $128,000. The court did not take the husband's yearly bonuses into account, as the wife had started to upgrade her qualifications which would result in her moving to a higher salary level. The wife was awarded spousal support of $2,000 per month retroactive to the date when the husband stopped paying child support. This obligation was to be secured by insurance on the husband's life because of his history of terminating child support and resisting spousal support.

*Agreement called for variation if material change occurred — material change found, all factors in 15.2 relevant in fixing new quantum — Deneweth v. Deneweth*, 2003 CarswellMan 431, 2003 MBQB 236, 44 R.F.L. (5th) 368, 179 Man. R. (2d) 4, [2003] M.J. No. 392 (Man. Q.B.), additional reasons at 2004 CarswellMan 101, 2004 MBQB 60, 50 R.F.L. (5th) 341, 183 Man. R. (2d) 67, [2004] M.J. No. 106 (Man. Q.B.). The parties' original intention was that the spousal support provisions could be varied if either party had a material change in his or her circumstances. The court found that there had been a material change in the parties' circumstances, as the husband's income had decreased from $59,992 per annum to an expected income of $49,500. The wife's income from employment increased from $3,000 to $11,900. The court held that a reduction in spousal support must be limited in recognition of the factors and objectives set out in s. 15.2 of the *Divorce Act*. The reduction in the husband's income reduced his obligation for child support, which in turn placed further stress on the wife. In all the circumstances, the court ordered spousal support reduced from $800 to $700 per month.

*Support reduced pursuant to separation agreements — Kemick v. Kemick*, 1990 CarswellSask 540, 85 Sask. R. 189 (Sask. Q.B.). The court allowed the husband's application for termination of support payable pursuant to the terms of the parties' separation agreements. The husband had suffered serious financial setbacks, owing creditors in excess of $100,000, while the wife had an income of $2,500 monthly.

*Agreement allowed reduction if payor's income declined — income decline occurs with career change — support reduced — Bucher v. Bucher*, 1990 CarswellMan 339, 67 Man. R. (2d) 233 (Man. Q.B.). Where the quantum of spousal and child support payable by the husband pursuant to the parties' agreement was based on his income level, the court allowed the husband's application for a reduction in support when, upon his change of careers, his income decreased substantially. Both parties intended the obligation to be based upon the husband's ability to pay, and there was no suggestion that the career change was motivated by a desire to frustrate the wife's support rights.

*Agreement calls for variation in the event of a material change — s. 17 test applicable — Corkum v. Corkum*, 1988 CarswellOnt 247, 14 R.F.L. (3d) 275 (Ont. H.C.). Where a final settlement agreement includes a clause permitting variation in the event of a material change in circumstances, the court can vary the agreed amount of support whenever it would be able to vary under s. 17 of the *Divorce Act*.

*Marriage contract not necessarily a bar to interim support* — Chaitas v. *Christopoulos*, 2004 CarswellOnt 4956, 12 R.F.L. (6th) 43, [2004] O.J. No. 907 (Ont. S.C.J.). A marriage contract in which both spouses waive the right to spousal support is not necessarily a bar to an application for interim support. If serious issues to be tried have been raised with respect to the circumstances under which the contract was negotiated and executed, it will not act as a bar to an interim application.

*Interim support ordered despite separation agreement* — Bailey v. *Plaxton*, 2000 CarswellOnt 1194, 6 R.F.L. (5th) 29, 47 O.R. (3d) 593, [2000] O.T.C. 243, [2000] O.J. No. 1187 (Ont. S.C.J.). The court held that the former wife was entitled to interim spousal support pursuant to s. 15.2 of the *Divorce Act* despite a separation agreement which provided for spousal support for 3 years ending 10 years before the judgement. The court considered all factors required pursuant to s. 15.2, including the separation agreement, and concluded that in the circumstances it was warranted and reasonable to make an interim support order in the amount of $5000 per month pending the determination of the application under s. 15.2(1).

*Interim support ordered despite separation agreement* — Kennedy v. *Kennedy*, 2000 CarswellOnt 3622, 11 R.F.L. (5th) 150, [2000] O.J. No. 3742 (Ont. S.C.J.). A court may award interim spousal support despite a written separation agreement where the waiver of support provision does not meet the objectives of the spousal support provisions of the *Divorce Act*.

*See also re interim support contrary to separation agreement* — Taimoori v. *Fanaian*, 2000 CarswellOnt 2847, [2000] O.J. No. 2997 (Ont. S.C.J.).

*Interim support ordered despite separation agreement where significant changes had occured* — Pineault v. *Pineault*, 1993 CarswellOnt 358, 49 R.F.L. (3d) 411 (Ont. Gen. Div.). A court may award interim spousal support under the *Divorce Act* notwithstanding a full contractual release, where significant changes have occurred since the agreement was made and where it is in the public interest for the court to exercise its inherent jurisdiction to override the agreement.

*Effect of interim agreement* — Tancock v. *Tancock*, 1990 CarswellBC 436, 24 R.F.L. (3d) 389 (B.C.S.C.). Where the interim agreement under which the husband paid support to the wife was stated to be "without prejudice", the court was nevertheless required to consider the agreement under s. 15(5)(c) of the *Divorce Act* in order to determine final support.

*Effect of interim draft separation agreement* — Fejes v. *Fejes*, 1988 CarswellMan 44, 13 R.F.L. (3d) 267, 51 Man. R. (2d) 132 (Man. Q.B.). An interim draft separation agreement may properly be considered in a support application as an indication of the parties' intentions.

*Agreement reached through mediation constitutes contract despite failure to agree on wording of consent order* — E. (C.R.) v. E. (K.L.), 2003 CarswellBC 2585, 2003 BCSC 1570, 44 R.F.L. (5th) 65, [2003] B.C.J. No. 2417 (B.C.S.C.), additional reasons at 2003 CarswellBC 2585, 2003 BCSC 1570, 44 R.F.L. (5th) 65, [2004] B.C.J. No. 1219 (B.C.S.C.). Where the parties reached an agreement concerning custody and access through mediation but later disagreed on the wording of the consent order, the husband successfully applied for a stay of the proceedings which the wife was attempting to re-institute. The agreement reached through mediation was sufficiently certain to constitute an enforceable contract. The inability of the parties to agree on wording did not impact the formation of the agreement.

*Relevance of agreement which stated "without prejudice"* — Tancock v. *Tancock*, 1990 CarswellBC 436, 24 R.F.L. (3d) 389 (B.C.S.C.). Where the interim agreement under which the husband paid support to the wife was stated to be "without prejudice", the court was nevertheless required to consider the agreement under s. 15(5)(c) of the *Divorce Act* in order to determine final support.

*Wife unable to accept offer after she made counter-offer* — Leslie v. Leslie, 1988 CarswellMan 354, 55 Man. R. (2d) 215 (Man. Q.B.). Where, in the course of negotiations to settle a variation of support dispute, the wife rejected the husband's offer to settle and made an unacceptable counter-offer, it was held that it was subsequently no longer open to her to accept the husband's original offer.

*Document not binding where spouse denied recollection thereof and there were no witnesses and no legal advice* — Butler v. Butler, 1987 CarswellNfld 31, 9 R.F.L. (3d) 70, 66 Nfld. & P.E.I.R. 42, 204 A.P.R. 42 (Nfld. U.F.C.), additional reasons at 1988 CarswellNfld 17, 18 R.F.L. (3d) 180 (Nfld. U.F.C.). The court refused to allow the wife to rely upon a document which she had her husband sign whereby he purportedly agreed to share his disability pension equally with her. As the husband did not remember signing the document, it was not witnessed and no legal advice had been sought, it was found not to be the type of document usually protected by the courts.

*Husband had agreed to pay 2/3 of salary as spousal support — agreement upheld* — G. (M.) c. B. (M.), 1994 CarswellQue 787, REJB 1994-28725, [1994] R.D.F. 436 (C.A. Que.), affirming Droit de la famille - 799, 1990 CarswellQue 1441, EYB 1990-76584, [1990] R.J.Q. 1053, [1990] R.D.F. 319 (C.S. Que.). Where the husband agreed to pay two-thirds of his salary as spousal support, the court, on appeal, refused to set aside the agreement. Although the husband may have miscalculated the fiscal impact of the settlement, he had entered into the agreement freely with benefit of counsel and without any undue pressure from the wife.

*Agreement upheld despite spouse's threat to move away with the children* — Newman v. La Porta, 2008 CarswellBC 944, 2008 BCSC 522, 55 R.F.L. (6th) 328 (B.C.S.C.). The court rejected the husband's application, on the grounds of duress, to have the parties' separation agreement set aside. While the husband was vulnerable at the time the agreement was signed and the wife had threatened to move with the children if he did not sign, the power imbalance had not led to a substantial unfairness. The husband understood what he was agreeing to and had taken significant and effective steps to advance his own interests in the negotiations.

*Parties' conduct over 10 years indicated resolution of issues — argument that signature was forged rejected* — Stemmler v. May, 2007 CarswellOnt 6254, 43 R.F.L. (6th) 218 (Ont. S.C.J.), additional reasons at 2008 CarswellOnt 137, 49 R.F.L. (6th) 431 (Ont. S.C.J.). The court rejected the wife's claim that her signature on the parties' separation agreement was a forgery. In the more than 10 years since the agreement had been signed, the parties' conduct clearly demonstrated a resolution of issues consistent with the terms of the separation agreement. Accordingly, the wife's claim for retroactive child and spousal support, both of which were inconsistent with the agreement, were dismissed.

*Husband' insistence that wife sign agreement was a misuse of a stronger bargaining position* — Johnson v. Johnson, 2005 CarswellOnt 7695, 2005 ONCJ 325, 23 R.F.L. (6th) 46, [2005] O.J. No. 5641 (Ont. C.J.). The court declared the parties' marriage contract, under which the wife purportedly waived her right to spousal support, to be invalid. The wife had resigned a good position in Russia and had moved with her children to Canada, to marry the husband. His insistence that her executing the contract was a prerequisite to the marriage was, giving her vulnerable position, a misuse of his far stronger bargaining position.

*Agreement upheld despite spouse's threat to revoke immigration sponsorship at time of negotiation* — Gregory v. Brown, 2005 CarswellOnt 6799, 2005 ONCJ 284, 21 R.F.L. (6th) 289, [2005] O.J. No. 4565 (Ont. C.J.). Where the husband had signed a separation agreement on the threat that the wife withdraw her immigration sponsorship of him if he failed to do so, the agreement was nevertheless upheld. The husband had been advised not to sign by both his brother and immigration counsel and had the opportunity to seek further legal advice. The evidence fell short of establishing an unconscionable use of power by the wife over the husband.

*Wife had no lawyer and husband failed to disclose information* — agreement invalid — *Davis v. Davis*, 2003 CarswellOnt 2800, 44 R.F.L. (5th) 56, [2003] O.T.C. 666, [2003] O.J. No. 2938 (Ont. S.C.J.). The court found that the parties' separation agreement was invalid and allowed the wife's claim for spousal support to proceed. While the husband had been receiving legal advice, the wife signed the document without benefit of counsel. The husband had failed to disclose his financial information and the separation date clearly favoured the husband over the evidence. Ultimately, the agreement reflected neither the parties' intentions nor the objectives of the *Divorce Act* as relating to the wife's economic disadvantage.

*Negotiation process fair but spousal support provision not binding due to radical change in circumstances* — *Mucha v. Mucha*, 2001 CarswellSask 712, 2001 SKQB 505, 212 Sask. R. 1 (Sask. Q.B.), reversed in part on other grounds 2003 CarswellSask 264, 2003 SKCA 38, 232 Sask. R. 78, 294 W.A.C. 78, [2003] S.J. No. 251 (Sask. C.A.). A pre-nuptial contract was found to be valid where there was no evidence that the husband dominated the wife. His precondition for marriage that she sign the agreement was reasonable, given his experience of an earlier divorce. There was no urgency to meet a deadline and no evidence that he took advantage of her or that there were stressful circumstances. The husband was the more powerful of the two parties, but the wife was not under his power because of need or distress and she fully understood his financial circumstances. She had competent legal advice. Further, the contract was not grossly unfair at the time that it was made between the parties. However, the spousal support provision in which the parties waived the right to seek support was severed from the rest of the agreement and was declared unenforceable, as there had been a radical change of circumstances since the execution of the contract. The parties had lived together for 16 years; they had two sons; they moved and sold the husband's business. Further, the contract was focused on property, not support. The court ordered spousal support of $1,000 monthly for 8 months to assist the wife in her transition from part-time to full-time employment.

*Agreement upheld despite spouse's assertion that she signed it because she believed she had to do so* — *Bailey v. Plaxton*, 2001 CarswellOnt 925, 15 R.F.L. (5th) 16, [2001] O.T.C. 191, [2001] O.J. No. 1111 (Ont. S.C.J.). The court found that all the requirements existed to constitute an enforceable settlement. There was both an offer and an acceptance, which were clear and unambiguous as to their terms. They represented a complete agreement, without any other terms to be concluded. The plaintiff's lawyer had clear authority and instructions to make the offer, as the plaintiff signed it. The court should not exercise its discretion and refuse to grant judgement in accordance with the accepted offer where, as in this case, the plaintiff asserts a mistaken impression that she made the offer because she believed that she had to.

*Spouse consented to amendment but refused to sign it* — *Hennessey v. Hennessey*, 1993 CarswellNS 326, 122 N.S.R. (2d) 220, 338 A.P.R. 220 (N.S. Fam. Ct.). Where the wife had consented on the basis of a misunderstanding to an amendment to the support provisions of the decree *nisi* but refused to sign the consent upon discovery of the mistake, the court refused to incorporate the amendment. The wife's mistake was an honest one and not a factor to be considered on the husband's variation application.

*Letter agreement signed without advice of solicitor upheld* — *Remillard v. Remillard*, 1990 CarswellAlta 263, 24 R.F.L. (3d) 156, 103 A.R. 110, [1990] A.J. No. 11 (Alta. Q.B.). Where the wife had executed a letter, without the advice of her solicitor, which allowed for the variation of the support terms in the parties' separation agreement, the letter was found to be a valid collateral agreement. The separation agreement was, in fact, executed later by the wife in the presence of her solicitor, thereby giving her the opportunity of discussing the significance of the letter with him and thereby curing any defect in its execution.

*Informal agreement to support not analogous to contractual obligation* — *Botterill v. Botterill*, 1986 CarswellSask 51, 1 R.F.L. (3d) 267, 48 Sask. R. 49 (Sask. Q.B.). An informal agreement between the parties whereby the husband was to support the wife through her studies after she had done the same for him was not analogous to a contractual obligation which should be considered when determining the wife's maintenance.

*Fact that wife had sought social assistance justifies new support order despite agreement —* Doepel v. Doepel, 1983 CarswellOnt 335, 36 R.F.L. (2d) 316 (Ont. H.C.). The court awarded periodic maintenance to the wife despite the fact that she had earlier executed a separation agreement restricting her maintenance rights to a 1-year period. The fact that the wife had been forced to seek public assistance shocked the conscience of the court to the extent that it was appropriate to relieve against the matrimonial settlement.

*Agreement drafted to give rise to arrears as tactic to defeat husband's other creditors — agreement void as contrary to public policy —* Myers v. Hawco, 2004 CarswellNfld 286, 2004 NLSCUFC 38, 11 R.F.L. (6th) 291, 243 D.L.R. (4th) 726, 240 Nfld. & P.E.I.R. 248, 711 A.P.R. 248, [2004] N.J. No. 324 (N.L.U.F.C.), reversed in part on other grounds 2005 CarswellNfld 342, 2005 NLCA 74, 22 R.F.L. (6th) 17, 262 D.L.R. (4th) 719, 252 Nfld. & P.E.I.R. 121, 756 A.P.R. 121, [2005] N.J. No. 378 (N.L.C.A.). The court refused to enforce the substantial arrears owing under the parties' separation agreement. The intent of the parties in drafting the agreement was to gain priority over the husband's creditors and therefore the agreement was found to be contrary to public policy.

*Agreement drafted by lawyer husband but wife had her own independent legal advice — agreement upheld —* Haughn v. Haughn, 2008 CarswellNS 450, 2008 NSSC 256, 58 R.F.L. (6th) 50, [2008] N.S.J. No. 363 (N.S.S.C.). The court refused to set aside the wife's waiver of spousal support contained in the parties' separation agreement. The agreement had been drafted by the lawyer husband, but the wife had independent legal advice prior to signing and had disregarded her lawyer's concerns over the support waiver. The wife understood what she was signing and the substance of the agreement was in substantial compliance with support objectives under s. 15 of the *Divorce Act.*

*Health problem which predated agreement and which was known to parties at time of negotiation is not a basis for setting aside a separation agreement —* Hambuch v. Hambuch, 2003 CarswellBC 1584, 2003 BCSC 1001, [2003] B.C.J. No. 1511 (B.C.S.C.). A separation agreement will not be set aside where the payee spouse has health concerns that predated the agreement and were in the parties' minds when they reached their agreement on spousal support.

*10% change from a party's projected income does not trigger an agreement clause allowing variation in the event of a material change —* Slaughter v. McCormick, 2003 CarswellBC 1029, 2003 BCSC 692, [2003] B.C.J. No. 1030 (B.C.S.C.). A material change in circumstances with respect to child support occurred when the Guidelines came into force that entitled the trial judge to consider the profit from the options in determining the quantum of support. The court held that 10% more or less in income from what a party anticipates at the time of signing a separation agreement, is not a material change in circumstances justifying setting aside a separation agreement.

*Where an agreement contemplates a variation in child and spousal support in the event of a material increase in a party's income, there is an implied duty on the party to disclose that increase at the time it is received — failure to disclose is a ground for making the variation retroactive to the time of the increase —* Marinangeli v. Marinangeli, 2003 CarswellOnt 2691, 38 R.F.L. (5th) 307, 66 O.R. (3d) 40, 228 D.L.R. (4th) 376, 174 O.A.C. 76, [2003] O.J. No. 2819 (Ont. C.A.). Here, the parties married in 1973 and separated in 1992 after a 19-year marriage. The wife, employed as a secretary, supported the husband in the early years of the marriage, while he attended university. He completed his B.A., M.B.A. and obtained his C.A. designation. The wife stopped working outside the home after 10 years of marriage and the following year the parties' only child was born. The parties separated in 1992 and began litigation in 1993. At a pre-trial conference in May,

1996, the husband maintained that he expected a decrease in his income. In October, 1996, just prior to trial, the parties signed minutes of settlement. They provided that spousal and child support could be varied if there were a material change in circumstances. A financial statement sworn immediately prior to execution of the minutes disclosed the husband's income and showed that his property included stock options and phantom stock units, that is, notional units of stock taxed at full rates based on underlying stock performance. Although certain terms were incorporated in a judgement, the provisions for spousal support, child support and life insurance were not, with the parties relying on the minutes, or their agreement as evidenced in the minutes, to record their rights and obligations with respect to them.

The day after the minutes were signed, the husband cashed in $27,850 worth of stock options, and in the 14 months from the time of the execution of the agreement, he realized a gain from his options of over $1,000,000. He also received a substantial increase in his compensation. He did not inform his wife of these changes in his financial circumstances. After the Guidelines came into force, the wife's lawyer contacted the husband's lawyer with respect to the effect the Guidelines might have on the husband's child support obligations. Eventually the parties exchanged tax returns and the wife claimed an increase in spousal and child support on the basis of the increase in the husband's income.

The trial judge ordered increased spousal and child support retroactive to the year in which the agreement came into force. He found that the profit the husband realized on his options and the substantial increase in his employment income were material changes in circumstances, and that the husband had an implied duty to disclose them to his wife. The variation was made retroactive, because he failed to disclose the changes at the time they were effective. The husband appealed.

The Court of Appeal held that the profit realized from the exercise of his stock options was income to the husband, and found that it amounted to a material change in circumstances within the meaning of the minutes. The *Miglin* case was distinguished on the ground that there the parties executed a separation agreement intending it to be a full and final release of all future obligations, whereas here the parties agreed in the minutes of settlement that if there were a change in circumstances, spousal and child support could be varied. It was within the trial judge's discretion to award retroactive support since the criteria for making such an award was met. The court did allow the appeal with respect to the award of retroactive child support at the Guideline level for the period prior to the enactment of the Guidelines.

The Court of Appeal held that where an agreement states that spousal and child support could be varied in the event of a material change in circumstances, the payor husband, whose income had increased, had an obligation to disclose the exercise of his options and increase in salary. (See paragraphs 4 and 57.) The court also held that where, in minutes of settlement, there is a clear intention that spousal and child support could be varied if there were a material changes in the circumstances of the parties, and a material change in income occurs, the party whose income changes has an implicit obligation to disclose the change to the other party at the time it occurs. (See paragraphs 59 and 60.) The trial judge did not err in finding that the husband had an implied duty to disclose to the wife changes in his financial circumstances. In this case, the payor spouse's representations and the almost immediate improvement in his finances were the factual basis upon which to ground such a duty. The appellant had an implicit obligation to disclose his change in circumstances so as to give business efficacy to the agreement. It was reasonable and equitable to imply a term relating to disclosure. The implication of the implied term was capable of clear expression and was not contrary to any express term in the agreement. Thus, the implication by the trial judge of a term relating to disclosure met the requirements for implying a term in an agreement on ordinary contract principles.

*Disclosure issues cannot be relitigated if they are res judicata* — *Coady v. Boyle*, 2003 CarswellOnt 5074, 47 R.F.L. (5th) 283, [2003] O.T.C. 1086, [2003] O.J. No. 5161 (Ont. S.C.J.), additional reasons at 2004 CarswellOnt 938 (Ont. S.C.J.). The wife's application to set aside the parties' settlement agreement based upon the husband's alleged fraud was dismissed. The wife was basing her claim on the inadequacy of the husband's disclosure, an issue which had been decided against her in numerous earlier proceedings. Accordingly, further proceedings in respect of the issue were barred on the basis of res judicata.

*Argument that a spouse failed to disclose requires evidence of the real value of the assets or income* — *Trick v. Trick*, 2003 CarswellOnt 1103, 39 R.F.L. (5th) 418, [2003] O.T.C. 248, [2003] O.J. No. 1263 (Ont. S.C.J.). A separation agreement will not be set aside on the basis of failure to disclose where there is no evidence at trial to verify the value or the extent of a respondent's assets either at the date of marriage or at the time the contract was executed. It is therefore not possible to conclude that the respondent failed to disclose significant assets existing when the contract was made. At the time the agreement was entered into, the husband did not provide any formal financial disclosure. There was no valuation of his pension, nor were any documents produced to disclose his investments, bank accounts or RRSP's. In 1991, the parties signed the separation agreement which was incorporated into a divorce judgement in 1992, with the exception that the judgement was silent as to spousal support.

*Agreement requiring recalculation in the event of a material change created an implied disclosure obligation which was breached* — *agreement set aside* — *Murray v. Murray*, 2003 CarswellOnt 3258, 40 R.F.L. (5th) 244, 66 O.R. (3d) 540, [2003] O.T.C. 780, [2003] O.J. No. 3350 (Ont. S.C.J.), additional reasons at 2003 CarswellOnt 3862 (Ont. S.C.J.). Where a separation agreement provides that the payor spouse was to recalculate his support obligations, if there were a material change in his income and such a change occurred and he did not inform his spouse of this change, nor recalculate his support obligations, the court held that there was an implied disclosure obligation on the payor spouse arising from the agreement. Following *Miglin* and *Marinangelli*, the court was of the opinion that in light of the payor's nondisclosure of his increased income as well as other factors, it should set aside the agreement. It held that the wife could no longer be considered bound by the release of spousal support in the agreement.

*Arbitration clause in agreement* — *effective only for the purpose identified in the agreement* — *Range v. Bremner*, 2003 CarswellBC 3099, 2003 BCCA 675, 47 R.F.L. (5th) 394, 192 B.C.A.C. 186, 315 W.A.C. 186, [2003] B.C.J. No. 2820 (B.C.C.A.). Where the husband unilaterally stopped paying spousal support to the wife after losing his job, he could not rely upon an arbitration clause in the parties' separation agreement to stay the wife's application to enforce arrears. Under the agreement, the scope of matters available for arbitration was clear and limited to the narrow issue of where a change in the husband's circumstances limited his ability to pay support. The husband had stopped paying support arbitrarily and that was outside the scope of the arbitration clause.

*Husband unilaterally paid less than agreement called for* — *husband required to pay arrears* — *Sloss v. Forget*, 2004 CarswellOnt 3923, 8 R.F.L. (6th) 380, [2004] O.J. No. 3960 (Ont. S.C.J.). Where the husband had unilaterally reduced the spousal support payable by him under the parties' separation agreement because of a reduction in his income, the reduction was subsequently ordered to be paid to the wife as arrears.

*Agreement called for termination upon wife's cohabitation* — *she cohabited but that relationship ended* — *no change in circumstances found and support not reinstated* — *Svarckopf v. Svarckopf*, 2002 CarswellOnt 1342, 27 R.F.L. (5th) 193, [2002] O.J. No. 1347 (Ont. S.C.J.). Where the wife had agreed to the termination of her spousal support entitlement upon entering into a new cohabitation arrangement, she could not rely upon the ending of her common law relationship as a "change of circumstances" warranting an award of spousal support.

*Support extended contrary to agreement because circumstances had changed* — Baker v. Baker, 1996 CarswellAlta 188, 22 R.F.L. (4th) 13, 182 A.R. 41, [1996] A.J. No. 228 (Alta. Q.B.). Where the limited term spousal support provided for in the parties' separation agreement was based upon a premise that the wife would achieve self-sufficiency, she was later granted an upward variation and extension of support in view of her deteriorating financial circumstances. Changes in the economy which had negatively impacted the wife's prospects had not been contemplated when the agreement was signed and given that the wife continued to suffer economic hardship as a result of the marriage, she was entitled to the variation.

*Payor's dramatic income drop does not justify downward variation from agreed-upon level* — Rondeau v. Rondeau, 1995 CarswellNB 501, 157 N.B.R. (2d) 142, 404 A.P.R. 142 (N.B.Q.B.). Where the quantum of spousal support payable by the husband had been tied in the parties' agreement to issues such as custody, access, matrimonial property and the negative economic effects of the marriage upon the wife, the court refused the husband's application for a reduction of spousal support, although his annual income had declined from $150,000 to $46,000. To make any changes would likely have resulted in inequities and would have required the reopening of the entire agreement.

*Agreement says support terminates only upon recipient's remarriage* — *recipient's new full-time employment not basis to terminate* — Wohlfahrt v. Wohlfahrt, 1990 CarswellOnt 251, 26 R.F.L. (3d) 181, [1990] O.J. No. 770 (Ont. H.C.). Where the parties' separation agreement specified termination of the wife's support upon remarriage only, the husband could not rely upon her finding full-time employment as a basis upon which to terminate her support.

*Change in circumstance contemplated at time of agreement not basis for subsequent variation* — MacMillan v. MacMillan, 1988 CarswellNS 65, 18 R.F.L. (3d) 149, 88 N.S.R. (2d) 368, 225 A.P.R. 368 (N.S.T.D.). Changes in circumstances which were in the contemplation of the parties at the time a support agreement was entered into cannot later be used as the basis for a variation of spousal support.

*Facts that children became independent and wife found employment rendered agreement invalid* — Matthews v. Matthews, 1988 CarswellNfld 10, 11 R.F.L. (3d) 431, 68 Nfld. & P.E.I.R. 91, 209 A.P.R. 91 (Nfld. T.D.). A separation agreement negotiated when the wife was unemployed and the parties' children were living with her is no longer valid after the children achieve economic independence and the wife finds employment.

*Support extended beyond agreed-upon period but not to be permanent* — McIntyre v. McIntyre, 2007 CarswellSask 13, 2007 SKCA 5, 36 R.F.L. (6th) 243, 289 Sask. R. 255, 382 W.A.C. 255, [2007] S.J. No. 8 (Sask. C.A.). The wife's claim for permanent spousal support beyond the 2-year period specified in the parties' agreement was dismissed. She had in the agreement acknowledged that she was adequately compensated for any economic disadvantage sustained by her as a result of the marriage, support for the children was not in issue, and she had not established entitlement to permanent support on the basis of failure to reach economic self-sufficiency. The onus was upon her, as the proponent of that position, to establish that she was entitled to permanent support and she had failed to do so. The only evidence of the wife's lack of self sufficiency was that her claimed expenses exceeded her income by a large amount. However, the husband's claimed expenses also exceeded his income, but by a much smaller amount. If the expenses were correct, the parties' joint incomes were insufficient to support them both. In fact, the wife had received an additional 15 months of support and the court granted her an additional 9 months of support, deciding that 4 years of spousal maintenance would be a practicable way to promote the wife's economic self-sufficiency and to fulfill the terms of the agreement.

*Support continued after agreed-upon date in light of difficulty of finding job* — Matthews v. Matthews, 1991 CarswellNS 60, 34 R.F.L. (3d) 201, 104 N.S.R. (2d) 140, 283 A.P.R. 140 (N.S.C.A.). The court was of the opinion that, considering the factors set out in s. 15 of the

*Divorce Act* and, particularly, the respective means and needs of the parties, their circumstances and the existence of undisclosed income, the support order must be varied upwards to provide for the children. Spousal support was extended beyond the 1-year cut-off date in light of the difficulty of finding a job in the poor economy. If the wife remained unsuccessful in finding a job at the end of that time she could apply to vary to extend the time. However, as both parties have a joint responsibility to provide for the children pursuant to s. 15(8) and a court must promote self-sufficiency where practical, pursuant to s. 15(7), the wife could not continue to be unemployed and be granted support unless she could show that it was impossible to find employment.

*Court retains discretion to review issue of support again even if it had previously been terminated* — *Droit de la famille - 382*, 1988 CarswellQue 46, 16 R.F.L. (3d) 379, [1988] R.J.Q. 2408, [1988] R.D.F. 482 (C.A. Que.). A prior termination of support rights does not prevent the court from reviewing the issue of support at a later time.

*Health problems did not originate in the marriage* — *agreed-upon release of support claims not overcome* — *Pilon v. Pilon*, 1988 CarswellOnt 284, 16 R.F.L. (3d) 225, 66 O.R. (2d) 1, 53 D.L.R. (4th) 130, 29 O.A.C. 306, [1988] O.J. No. 1568 (Ont. C.A.). Leave to appeal to S.C.C. refused (1989), 19 R.F.L. (3d) xxxv, 66 O.R. (2d) xi (note), 34 O.A.C. 400 (note), 100 N.R. 237 (note) (S.C.C.). Where the wife had released support claims in a separation agreement, but was later prevented from working because of further aggravation of existing health problems, her claim for support was disallowed on appeal. The wife's economic dependency flowed from her illness and did not have its genesis in the marriage.

*Radical change in circumstances found* — *agreed-upon amount varied* — *Marshall v. Marshall*, 1988 CarswellOnt 228, 13 R.F.L. (3d) 337 (Ont. C.A.). Leave to appeal to SCC refused (1988), 31 O.A.C. 160 (note) (S.C.C.). A causal connection between the economic hardship of the wife and the dependent relationship arising from the marriage was found in *Marshall v. Marshall*. In that decision, the majority of the court was of the opinion that inflation and the wife's decline in income, which was aggravated by her fragile health, had created a radical change in circumstances, justifying an increase in support from that provided in the parties' separation agreement. The parties had separated in 1970 after a 23-year marriage. The wife had developed cancer in 1977 and was in financial need. The husband had the ability to pay. The Court of Appeal dismissed the husband's appeal from an increase in maintenance from $728 per month to $1,228 per month.

*"Radical change in circumstances" test* — *Fyffe v. Fyffe*, 1988 CarswellOnt 205, 12 R.F.L. (3d) 196, 63 O.R. (2d) 783, 48 D.L.R. (4th) 759, 25 O.A.C. 219, [1988] O.J. No. 132 (Ont. C.A.). Where the parties have executed a valid settlement agreement that is incorporated in an order of the court, the agreement will only be overturned where there is a radical change in circumstances flowing from a pattern of economic dependency engendered by the marriage. A very large decline in interest rates did not constitute such a change, as the decline was reasonably foreseeable and was not related to the marriage.

*Sexual relations not sufficient proof of common law relationship justifying support reduction under parties' agreement* — *Alves v. Alves*, 2005 CarswellAlta 1828, 2005 ABQB 911 (Alta. Q.B.). To establish that a spouse is in a common law relationship, it is incumbent on the husband to establish something more than the fact that the couple was living together and having sexual relations. Under the terms of the parties' separation agreement, the husband was entitled to a reduction in spousal support, if the wife was in a common law relationship.

*If agreement refers to remarriage, common law relationship not to be equated therewith* — *Abbott v. Abbott*, 2004 CarswellNfld 99, 2004 NLSCUFC 14, 236 Nfld. & P.E.I.R. 163, 700 A.P.R. 163, [2004] N.J. No. 135 (N.L.U.F.C.). Support was therefore not cut off, the result called for by the parties' agreement if the recipient were to remarry.

*Agreed-upon amount which reflected all objectives of* Divorce Act *did not preclude further compensatory support at a later date* — *Levandusky v. Levandusky*, 2003 CarswellOnt 2615, 39 R.F.L. (5th) 134, [2003] O.J. No. 2783 (Ont. S.C.J.), additional reasons at 2003 CarswellOnt 2613 (Ont. S.C.J.). After the separation, the parties negotiated a settlement which formed the basis of an order. At that time, the equalization and spousal and child support settlement arrangements addressed all of the objectives of the *Divorce Act*, including compensatory support that recognized the economic realities of the family partnership. However the wife, after 26 years of commitment to her first husband and family, remained entitled to some continued compensatory spousal support, despite the fact that she was living with a third party. Spousal support was reduced by two-thirds to $460 per month, plus $80 for one-half of that portion of the wife's pension not previously equalized, for a monthly support total of $540 from and including January 4, 2003 until the husband attained age 65 or until the wife's mother died, whichever event first occurred. Thereafter, compensatory spousal support would continue monthly, in an amount representing one-half of that portion of the husband's unequalized pension, namely $186.50. The court in determining support took into account that the wife would be entitled to one-half of her elderly mother's estate, which was presently valued at between $430,000 to $440,000 and perhaps an additional $118,000 for the value of the cottage which the wife's brother did not want, nor use.

*After 3 years of support paid on consent, wife not entitled to further compensatory lump sum* — *Janakowski v. Janakowski*, 2000 CarswellOnt 2478, 7 R.F.L. (5th) 117, [2000] O.J. No. 2650 (Ont. S.C.J.). The court denied the wife's claim for lump sum spousal support because such an award would be inequitable having regard to the relevant circumstances of the relationship of the parties, the choices made by the wife after the separation, and a consent order whereby the husband provided support to the wife for 3 years. At separation, the wife was not employed and, therefore, was dependent upon the husband. The separation clearly disadvantaged her, since she could no longer rely on the husband's income from employment to cover her living expenses. The consent order helped to address this economic disadvantage. There was no evidence to indicate that the wife gave up any employment or educational opportunities as a result of her role in the household. She made minimal efforts to secure employment since separation as she preferred not to work. The court held that the present inability of the wife to be self-sufficient was unrelated to the marriage or its breakdown. She had sporadic part-time employment, which indicated that she was physically capable of performing some type of work. She could not simply expect the husband to support her indefinitely because she had a need for support.

*Agreement contemplated future variation but did not mention cohabitation* — *support not varied despite wife's new cohabitation* — *Osmar v. Osmar*, 2000 CarswellOnt 1927, 8 R.F.L. (5th) 375, [2000] O.J. No. 2060 (Ont. S.C.J.), additional reasons at 2000 CarswellOnt 2343, 8 R.F.L. (5th) 387, [2000] O.T.C. 979, [2000] O.J. No. 2504 (Ont. S.C.J.). The court held that while the wife's day-to-day financial needs were significantly reduced because she cohabited with a man who earned approximately $75,000 per annum, the spousal support provisions of the separation agreement clearly must have contemplated compensatory support for the roles adopted by the spouses during the marriage and the economic consequences of those roles. The marriage was a traditional one with the husband in the paid work force and the wife staying at home with the children. The court considered the factors and circumstances identified in ss. 33(8) and (9) of the *Family Law Act* and concluded that it was not appropriate to vary the spousal support provision of the separation agreement. The wife had lost ground financially by converting the child support to a tax neutral award under the Guidelines. The husband had made extravagant purchases, leasing a new $65,000 vehicle and committing himself to the purchase of a 4,000 square foot, $400,000 home during the currency of the litigation. Compensatory spousal support ought to be paid in priority to RRSP contributions and the husband's other lifestyle choices. Although the agreement contemplated future variation of spousal support, it did not refer to the wife's remarriage or cohabitation as specific factors that would trigger a variation. Such a clause is often found in such agreements. Its absence fortified the court's conclusion that the spousal support was primarily, if not exclusively, compensatory in nature. It was premature to vary it.

*Support terminates per agreement upon remarriage — second marriage fails — Scheel v. Henkelman,* 1999 CarswellOnt 1156, 45 R.F.L. (4th) 419, [1999] O.J. No. 1372 (Ont. Gen. Div.). Where the husband stopped paying spousal support under the parties' separation agreement after the wife remarried, the court refused the wife's application to re-instate support after her second marriage failed. The agreement specifically called for termination of spousal support, if the wife remarried and any economic hardship suffered by the wife was the result of the failure of her second marriage and not the first one.

*Separation agreement not final and conclusive regarding support; therefore order under s. 15 available — Vaandering v. Vaandering,* 1990 CarswellBC 449, 25 R.F.L. (3d) 310 (B.C.S.C.). Where the parties signed a separation agreement which provided support for the wife for 1 year and any continuing support according to a further agreement between the spouses, or according to a court order, such an agreement is not final and conclusive regarding support and the court could make an originating order under s. 15 and not a variation order under s. 17. The order was not then subject to the provisions set out in the *Pelech* Trilogy.

*Wife's need caused by illness and economy — negotiated terms re spousal support still binding — Tremblay v. Tremblay,* 1988 CarswellOnt 325, 18 R.F.L. (3d) 337, 67 O.R. (2d) 76, 32 E.T.R. 110 (Ont. H.C.). Where there was no formal separation agreement, but where the parties had negotiated the terms of settlement that were incorporated into the decree *nisi,* the settlement was binding. The former wife's misfortune, caused by her illness (bursitis) and the loss of her job after separation, was not related to the marriage or to any dependency arising out of the marriage, but was related to the economic climate and lack of employment opportunities. The former wife's application to increase the support order was dismissed.

## Additional Cases

*Where a separation agreement dealing with child and spousal support is not incorporated into an order, and a party seeks to change the amount of support payable, a court should consider the application as an initial application for support under s.15.2 — Peel v. Peel,* 2012 CarswellOnt 6115, 2012 ONSC 761, 22 R.F.L. (7th) 299 (Ont. S.C.J.). The payor had made an application to reduce spousal and child support payable under a separation agreement. The court found that the agreement met the test in *Miglin* and did not change the quantum of support. The court stated that although the SSAG were not in place at the time of the agreement, the amount of spousal support was within the range that the parties had agreed to.

*Flawed execution of a domestic contract through inadequate financial disclosure and duress will be grounds to set aside the spousal support provisions of a marriage contract — McCain v. McCain,* 2012 CarswellOnt 16853, 2012 ONSC 7344, 34 R.F.L. (7th) 82 (Ont. S.C.J.). The parties were exceptionally wealthy. The wife did not work during the parties' 26-year marriage, and the parties had five children. The parties had a lavish lifestyle. The husband's father had a very successful business. The wife sought to overturn the provisions of a domestic contract and sought interim spousal support. The parties had been married for 16 years when the husband's father informed all his children that they must enter into domestic contracts with their spouses or be disinherited. The wife claimed that she had to sign the contract under duress and that there was improper financial disclosure. The judge found that, although the husband did provide disclosure about his circumstances at the time the contract was signed, the husband did not provide conjecture about his future earnings or expected lifestyle changes. The husband's net worth at the time of separation was approximately $500,000,000. This, together with the judge's finding that there was duress and an unconscionable result from the contract, caused the judge to set aside the spousal support provisions of the contract.

*Where the recipient spouse has significant assets but no liquidity, and a marriage contract is found not to provide adequately for her needs, a waiver of spousal support will be set aside* — *McCain v. McCain*, 2012 CarswellOnt 16853, 2012 ONSC 7344, 34 R.F.L. (7th) 82 (Ont. S.C.J.).

# CHAPTER 6

## OBJECTIVES

This chapter is divided into the following subsections:

### 6.1 Objectives — General

Spousal support is a remedy which serves two purposes in Canadian law. Firstly, it provides compensation when a relationship has increased the earning power of one spouse at the expense of the other spouse. Secondly, it serves to relieve the financial need which a spouse experiences after a relationship.

These two purposes animate the four objectives listed in s. 15.2(6) and s. 17(7) of the *Divorce Act*. In the *Spousal Support Advisory Guidelines* ("SSAG"), the strength of the compensatory and needs-based claims to spousal support both (i) influence the amount chosen within the range, and (ii) help define the exceptional fact patterns in which the SSAG ranges are inappropriate. In Supreme Court of Canada jurisprudence, *Moge v. Moge* firmly established the compensatory rationale for spousal support. In *Bracklow v. Bracklow, infra,* the Supreme Court made it clear that, even in the absence of a compensatory claim, need for and corresponding ability to pay spousal support can be sufficient to ground a claim.

*Bracklow* identifies *three* "conceptual grounds for entitlement to spousal support. "(1) compensatory; (2) contractual; and (3) non-compensatory." This dictum is at first difficult to reconcile with the statement above that there are two purposes of spousal support — compensation and the relief of financial need. However, this is, in fact, no more than a difference of terminology. *Bracklow*'s "contractual" ground for spousal support entitlement means simply that, if the parties have made a contract requiring spousal support to be paid, the court will enforce it unless there are sufficient reasons to set it aside. Unlike compensation and the relief of need, the enforcement of such contracts cannot be considered a definitional purpose of spousal support law under the *Divorce Act,* insofar as these contracts could be enforced by courts in the absence of any statutory authority (see s. 5.6 of this volume). What *Bracklow* refers to as the "non-compensatory" conceptual ground for entitlement to spousal support is referred to in this text, and in much of the jurisprudence, as the "needs-based" purpose of spousal support law. The common elements in all support awards based in whole or in part on non-compensatory reasoning are. (i) the financial need of the support claimant, and (ii) the ability to pay of the other spouse. The phrase "needs-based" is used in this volume as a synonym for "non-compensatory" in order to identify this distinguishing feature.

While compensation and the relief of need are conceptually distinct, in many if not most cases the award is meant to perform both of these functions. The cases annotated in this section identify legal principles relevant to the interaction between the two rationales. The following four sections of this chapter consider the four subsections of s. 15.2(6), identifying for each the relevant compensatory and needs-relieving factors.

Section 17(7) of the *Divorce Act* enumerates the four objectives of an order varying spousal support; these are identical to the four objectives of an initial spousal support order. This chapter therefore includes both initial and variation cases which are relevant to one of the objectives. Please refer to Chapter 10 for material pertaining to other aspects of spousal support variation applications.

*Frequency of conflicts between objectives indicates parliamentary intent to vest "significant discretion" in judges, objectives not meant to determine the terms of any agreement between parties about spousal support* — Miglin v. Miglin, 2003 CarswellOnt 1374, 2003 CarswellOnt 1375, 2003 SCC 24, REJB 2003-40012, 34 R.F.L. (5th) 255, [2003] 1 S.C.R. 303, 66 O.R. (3d) 736, 224 D.L.R. (4th) 193, 302 N.R. 201, 171 O.A.C. 201, [2003] S.C.J. No. 21 (S.C.C.). The judgement of Bastarache and Arbour JJ. made the following comments about the objectives listed in s. 15.2(6).

> That these objectives can and do often conflict and compete suggests an intention on the part of Parliament to vest in trial judges a significant discretion to assess the weight to be given each objective against the very particular backdrop of the parties' circumstances. These objectives are not intended to dictate by themselves the precise terms of an enforceable negotiated agreement dealing with spousal support, distribution of assets and child support, the spousal support objectives should not operate so as to preclude parties from bringing their own concerns, desires and objectives to the table in negotiating what they view as a mutually acceptable agreement, an agreement they consider to comply substantially with the objectives of the Act.

*Exclusive focus on self-sufficiency not consistent with Supreme Court case law* — Miglin v. Miglin, 2003 CarswellOnt 1374, 2003 CarswellOnt 1375, 2003 SCC 24, REJB 2003-40012, 34 R.F.L. (5th) 255, [2003] 1 S.C.R. 303, 66 O.R. (3d) 736, 224 D.L.R. (4th) 193, 302 N.R. 201, 171 O.A.C. 201, 66 O.R. (3d) 736 (note), [2003] S.C.J. No. 21 (S.C.C.). The emphasis on self-sufficiency in the Pelech v. Pelech, 1987 CarswellBC 147, 1987 CarswellBC 703, EYB 1987-80055, 7 R.F.L. (3d) 225, [1987] 1 S.C.R. 801, 14 B.C.L.R. (2d) 145, 17 C.P.C. (2d) 1, 38 D.L.R. (4th) 641, [1987] 4 W.W.R. 481, 76 N.R. 81, [1987] R.D.F. 264, [1987] S.C.J. No. 31 (S.C.C.), is inconsistent with both the compensatory model of support developed in Moge v. Moge, 1992 CarswellMan 143, 1992 CarswellMan 222, EYB 1992-67141, 43 R.F.L. (3d) 345, [1992] 3 S.C.R. 813, 99 D.L.R. (4th) 456, [1993] 1 W.W.R. 481, 145 N.R. 1, [1993] R.D.F. 168, 81 Man. R. (2d) 161, 30 W.A.C. 161, [1992] S.C.J. No. 107 (S.C.C.), and the noncompensatory model of support developed in Bracklow v. Bracklow, 1999 CarswellBC 532, 1999 CarswellBC 533, 44 R.F.L. (4th) 1, [1999] 1 S.C.R. 420, 63 B.C.L.R. (3d) 77, 169 D.L.R. (4th) 577, [1999] 8 W.W.R. 740, 236 N.R. 79, [1999] R.D.F. 203, 120 B.C.A.C. 211, 196 W.A.C. 211, [1999] S.C.J. No. 14 (S.C.C.). It is also inconsistent with the point in both cases that no single objective in s. 15.2(6) is paramount, per Bracklow, at para. 35; and Moge, at 852 [S.C.R.].

*When a court is assessing whether an agreement substantially complies with the objectives of the* Divorce Act, *the effect of the agreement need not be explicitly compared to the results indicated under the SSAG. Parties can legitimately negotiate valid agreements that depart from the Guidelines, particularly when other issues are being resolved* — Estephan v. Estephan, 2013 CarswellBC 3796, 2013 BCCA 41 R.F.L. (7th) 28, 540, 56 B.C.L.R. (5th) 20, 370 D.L.R. (4th) 470, 348 B.C.A.C. 113, 595 W.A.C. 113 (B.C.C.A.). A comparison with support under the agreement and under the Guidelines "does illuminate, in broad terms, the degree to which this agreement shows a significant variation from what the SSAG suggests as an appropriate award" (para. 42). The appellate court found that the trial judge erred in his conclusion that the agreement was in substantial compliance with the objectives of the *Divorce Act*, since the trial judge failed to test the agreement against the principles set out in *Moge v. Moge, supra,* and s. 15.2 of the *Divorce Act.* The failure was particularly important as the wife had arguably a strong compensatory support claim. The trial judge's order was set aside, and the matter remitted for a new hearing in the Supreme Court.

*The court must consider the objectives of spousal support when varying a support order —* Walters v. Walters, 2011 CarswellBC 2021, 2011 BCCA 331, 9 R.F.L. (7th) 1, 338 D.L.R. (4th) 421, 308 B.C.A.C. 282, 521 W.A.C. 282 (B.C.C.A.). The parties separated in 2005 after 23 years of marriage. The wife had been a homemaker and the (now adult) children's primary caregiver during the marriage and she had significant health issues. The original divorce order granted the wife indefinite spousal support of $1,850, a figure that was not based on the SSAG. She appealed a variation of the order that decreased the amount. At the time of the proceedings the wife was running a cleaning business and boarding international students. The husband's income had ranged from $49,000 to $89,000, but his business closed and he unilaterally decreased support to $474 per month. At the variation hearing in 2010, the chambers judge found that the business closing was a material change in circumstances. The judge determined the husband's income to be $30,000, imputed $21,000 to the wife, and used the SSAG ranges for these incomes to set support at $474 per month, to be further reduced to $318. The Court of Appeal found that the chambers judge had failed to consider relevant evidence when determining the parties' incomes and had failed to consider the objectives of spousal support when varying the support order. The matter was remitted to the court below for a new hearing.

*Interim support ordered where a wife establishes a reasonable prospect of success at trial that an inter-spousal agreement is impeachable given that it does not comply with the objectives set out in s. 15.2 of the Divorce Act and on the basis of the circumstances of its execution —* Evashenko v. Evashenko, 2011 CarswellSask 162, 2011 SKCA 22, 96 R.F.L. (6th) 247, [2011] 4 W.W.R. 410, 366 Sask. R. 228, 506 W.A.C. 228, [2011] S.J. No. 152 (Sask. C.A.), reversing 2010 CarswellSask 103, 2010 SKQB 45, 81 R.F.L. (6th) 325, [2010] 7 W.W.R. 471, 354 Sask. R. 74 (Sask. Q.B.). In 2003, following 14 years of marriage and three children, the parties separated and the court ordered the husband, who operated a trucking company, to pay to the wife, a stay-at-home mother, $1,200 per month interim support, which, *inter alia,* was subsequently incorporated into Minutes of Settlement. The wife was represented by counsel throughout this period. The wife suffered from extreme stress and depression, and had a history of alcoholism and mental illness. The children had returned to live with their father and the wife wanted a reconciliation. In 2005, the husband met with his lawyer and drew up a new inter-spousal agreement, which the wife signed in front of a lawyer who did not have any financial information or a copy of the prior settlement. Six months later, the parties reconciled for 4 years, but subsequently separated. Following the second separation, because of the inter-spousal agreement, the wife was left with no support or property. The wife's 2010 application to a chambers judge for interim spousal support pending trial of her spousal support application was dismissed because of the inter-spousal agreement. On appeal, following a *Miglin* analysis, the appeal was allowed and the issue of quantum of interim support was sent back for determination.

*Finding upheld on appeal, that wife was not entitled to support after a 20-year marriage because this is one of those rare cases when none of the four objectives under s. 15.2 was relevant to the facts —* Mills v. Mills, 2010 CarswellNB 126, 2010 CarswellNB 127, 2010 NBCA 20, 82 R.F.L. (6th) 247, 319 D.L.R. (4th) 183, 356 N.B.R. (2d) 351, 919 A.P.R. 351, [2010] N.B.J. No. 83 (N.B.C.A.). Following a 2-year cohabitation and 20-year marriage, the parties separated in 2003. There were no children of the marriage, but the wife had three children who were supported by their natural father. The husband, a lawyer, aged 61 at trial, had owned an outfitters business and had a sole practice, and had earned an average income of $6,600. The wife, aged 57 at trial, received during the marriage gifts and an inheritance from her wealthy family, child support from their natural father, and she had worked in various occupations including the husband's business. In 2004, the husband declared bankruptcy and began working as a government lawyer. The court found that the parties had been in a non-traditional marriage where they each looked after their own financial interests, and neither suffered economic disadvantages as a result of the marriage itself. In addition, the wife had poorly managed the majority of the matrimonial assets and interim spousal support she had received, and did not have disabling health issues.

*Failure in trial reasons to address the precondition entitlement directly, except for need which is only one of the factors and objectives to entitlement, is an error in principle requiring the Court of Appeal to satisfy itself as to spousal support entitlement* — Cassidy v. McNeil, 2010 CarswellOnt 1637, 2010 ONCA 218, 99 O.R. (3d) 81, 266 O.A.C. 62, [2010] O.J. No. 1158 (Ont. C.A.), reversing in part 2008 CarswellOnt 110, [2008] O.J. No. 112 (Ont. S.C.J.), affirming 2009 CarswellOnt 8859 (Ont. S.C.J.), was additional reasons to 2008 CarswellOnt 110, [2008] O.J. No. 112 (Ont. S.C.J.).

*Compensatory and non-compensatory objectives together justify support order* — W. (M.R.) v. W. (C.M.U.), 2004 CarswellBC 2695, 2004 BCCA 577, 7 R.F.L. (6th) 187, [2004] B.C.J. No. 2353 (B.C.C.A.). The appellate court upheld the lower court's decision to award compensatory and noncompensatory support on the basis that the wife stayed home as homemaker and primary caregiver to the children during the marriage. The court concluded that the wife required, and that the husband was able to pay $600 per month in spousal maintenance.

*Variation — after a change in circumstances is found, the court should make an order that satisfies the objectives under s. 17 of the* Divorce Act — Katz v. Katz, 2004 CarswellMan 226, 2004 MBCA 85, 4 R.F.L. (6th) 25, 184 Man. R. (2d) 271, 318 W.A.C. 271, [2004] M.J. No. 206 (Man. C.A.). In this case, the husband appealed and the wife cross-appealed from an order varying a consent judgement. The judgement provided that spousal support would be terminated if the wife were in default for more than 10 days on her obligation to pay one-half of her monthly portion of the couple's debt. The wife missed making a payment, but the husband did not give the wife notice that support would be terminated, if the default were not remedied. "Had such notice been given by the husband, it is a reasonable inference to draw from the evidence that the wife would promptly have remedied the default, so as to avoid the disproportionate and disastrous consequences of the complete termination of her spousal support. Indeed, the wife argued that such a result would be so disproportionate as to constitute a penalty and thus be unenforceable, but that argument need not be resolved on these facts." The court agreed with the motions judge that spousal support did not terminate as a result of the missed payment and it dismissed the husband's appeal. The wife's cross-appeal was allowed in part with the court holding that she was entitled to apply for an increase in spousal support, as the husband had declared bankruptcy and there was a change of circumstances. The motions judge erred when he limited that increase to the amount required to permit the wife to service the debt payment. The words of the separation agreement and the objectives of s. 17 of the Act did not support such a limited consideration. The appellate court ordered a greater quantum of spousal support, with the increase to take effect on the same date as the increase ordered by the motions court.

*Variation — the court should have regard to the objectives and factors underlying a consent judgement when considering an application to vary the judgement* — Comrie v. Comrie, 2001 CarswellSask 130, 2001 SKCA 33, 17 R.F.L. (5th) 271, 197 D.L.R. (4th) 223, [2001] 7 W.W.R. 294, 203 Sask. R. 164, 240 W.A.C. 164, [2001] S.J. No. 136 (Sask. C.A.). Accordingly, in the appropriate case, the negotiations leading up to the consent judgement may properly be considered as evidence in the variation application.

*Variation — weighing self-sufficiency against other statutory factors — Shurson v. Shurson,* 2008 CarswellNS 465, 2008 NSSC 264, 59 R.F.L. (6th) 154, 268 N.S.R. (2d) 176, 857 A.P.R. 176 (N.S.S.C.). Where the husband applied to vary the spousal support order which had been made for $3500 a month to his wife, to whom he had been married for 28 years and with whom he had raised three children, the court granted his application and reduced the amount of support to $2500 a month, indefinitely. The court held that because of the obligations of the family, the wife had not developed a career, and her current employment as an educational assistant was not secure. The wife had a significant compensatory claim that had not been satisfied by the support paid to date. While she could reduce her debt and expenses, self-sufficiency considerations must not be given more weight than her claim for spousal support based on the pattern of dependency, her contribution to the marriage to the detriment of her own independent earning potential, the lifestyle/income deferential, and her need for time to adjust to a standard of living based solely on her income sources.

*Variation — payee entitled to a modest standard of living where both parties' incomes had increased since initial order and child support terminated — support increased — Nelson v. Weber,* 2008 CarswellNS 256, 2008 NSSC 116, 265 N.S.R. (2d) 228, 848 A.P.R. 228, [2008] N.S.J. No. 205 (N.S.S.C.). The wife applied for a variation of a corollary relief judgement to increase spousal support. A number of changes occurred in the parties' situation since their divorce, including the fact that there was no longer a dependent child and, additionally, the fact that both parties enjoyed a higher annual income. The husband also had a new common law spouse who the court found could contribute to at least a portion of the couple's household and other living expenses. In light of these changes, the court found that there had been a material change in circumstances warranting a variation. The parties made a joint decision to have the wife remain home to raise their children that they must have felt was in their children's best interests. The wife must not bear all the financial and economic consequences resulting from that decision. She was entitled to enjoy a modest standard of living taking into consideration the condition, means, needs and other circumstances of each former spouse. The court ordered an increase in spousal support from $400 to $1000 a month retroactive to January 1, 2008.

*Variation — self-sufficiency only one factor to be considered —economic advantages and disadvantages to be considered — Farrah v. Farrah,* 2008 CarswellNB 434, 2008 NBQB 176, 58 R.F.L. (6th) 162, 339 N.B.R. (2d) 11, 870 A.P.R. 11 (N.B.Q.B.). Promoting economic self-sufficiency of a former spouse is not the only factor to be considered by the court when making a variation order. The circumstances of each case must be considered in light of the several sub-sections. In particular, a support order must recognize the economic advantages and disadvantages arising from the marriage or its breakdown.

*Transfer of property justified termination of support order — O. (C.) v. C. (O.N.),* 2005 CarswellNfid 16, 2005 NLTD 12, 11 R.F.L. (6th) 309, [2005] N.J. No. 18 (N.L.T.D.). Where, since the date of the original interim spousal support order, the husband had transferred considerable assets to the wife, the court granted the husband's application to terminate the order. As the assets transferred would generate income in excess of the order, a change in circumstances had occurred of such a nature and magnitude as to make the original order no longer appropriate.

*Compensatory amount added to non-compensatory amount, then grossed up to produce award — McLean v. McLean,* 2004 CarswellOnt 4234, [2004] O.J. No. 4261 (Ont. S.C.J.), additional reasons at 2004 CarswellOnt 4412 (Ont. S.C.J.). Compensatory support addresses the economic advantage or disadvantage arising from the marriage, the roles adopted in marriage, and the breakdown of the marriage. Non-compensatory support is based on needs and means, and a pattern of economic dependence that developed during the marriage. Compensatory and non-compensatory components of spousal support to be paid to the wife were assessed equally at $350 monthly. Grossed up for the income tax the wife would be required to pay, the court found that the appropriate monthly award was $1,000. The parties cohabited under the marriage for 20 years. They had two children. The wife earned approximately $72,300 a year and the husband earned $160,000. The wife's ability to earn a good income while looking after home and children allowed the husband time and flexibility to change careers and to succeed in what he chose to do. Also, she was placed in a position of some financial dependency during the marriage by the husband's contribution of his income to the whole of the family unit.

*Compensatory entitlement of one spouse offset by non-compensatory entitlement of the other* — Kennedy v. Kennedy, 2004 CarswellOnt 3192, 8 R.F.L. (6th) 155, [2004] O.J. No. 3222 (Ont. S.C.J.). Where one spouse is entitled to compensatory support, and the other is entitled to non-compensatory support, the entitlement to compensatory support acts as a shield or set-off to the other spouse's entitlement to non-compensatory support. The wife was entitled to compensatory support since she dropped out of high school to be a full-time wife and mother. She stayed at home for the first 7 years of the marriage. Even after she began working outside the home in 1967, she remained primarily responsible for the care of the children during their dependency. The husband frittered away tens of thousands of dollars on farming operations in the years 1995 to 2002 and was able to exclude from sharing with his wife $30,000 that he loaned their daughter and son-in-law. The wife's inherited funds were entirely shared with the husband in the net family property equalization. The wife was the only breadwinner in the family from 1999 to 2002. At the time of the application, the wife earned $45,000 to $50,000. The husband had pension income of about $17,000. Given the length of marriage and disparity in income at the time of separation, the husband was entitled to at least transitional spousal support. The husband's need for additional money was not the result of any role he played in the marriage but the result of voluntary decisions he made independent of his marital role and responsibilities, notably his decision to become a farmer. The wife had paid interim spousal support of $500 per month since the order of July 2002. The court ordered that she continue to pay this amount until the end of 2004. The court stated "She is not an insurer of his self-created need."

*Future possibilities to be considered* — Lacharite v. Lacharite, 2003 CarswellOnt 939, 39 R.F.L. (5th) 119, [2003] O.J. No. 1027 (Ont. S.C.J.). In assessing a claim for compensatory spousal support, the court must consider all existing financial realities as well as all that might befall the parties.

*Award quantum consists of $500 for compensation plus $4000 to relieve need* — Rothenburg v. Rothenburg, 2003 CarswellOnt 1380, 40 R.F.L. (5th) 363, [2003] O.T.C. 327, [2003] O.J. No. 1551 (Ont. S.C.J.). A spouse was entitled to compensatory support where there was a lengthy 28-year marriage and she had health problems. Additional factors in making such an award were her involvement in the husband's education and his consulting business, as well as the time she devoted to child care and the care of his parents. Further, given the ages of the parties, there must be some consideration to allowing the wife to save for retirement given the likelihood of a support variation on his retirement. The court awarded the wife support in the monthly sum of $4,500 which was $500 a month more than the strictly needs based model provided.

*Where the husband on a variation application shows that the wife does not require support on the basis of need, she may still be entitled to it on a compensatory basis* — Provost v. Provost, 1999 CarswellAlta 1067, 2 R.F.L. (5th) 442 (Alta. Q.B.). The wife received $4,000 a month in support for 4 years with a provision that it be reviewed at the end of that period. At the time of the review, the husband applied to extinguish or reduce the support. The wife, because of her own assets, a disability and a small annuity payment, was not entitled to continued support on a needs-based approach. However, as a result of the breakdown of the marriage, she lost the benefit of the income stream generated by her husband. On a needs-based approach, the support would be reduced to $1,800 a month. However, the husband was earning an income of $300,000 a year, and so long as he was earning a substantial income, the reduction should be less to reflect a support amount of $2,500 a month taking into account an increase in her assets since the original order was made and an income of $850 a month that she did not have at that time.

*Variation — relevant factors identified and balanced — Balcom v. Balcom*, 1999 CarswellNS 426, 2 R.F.L. (5th) 39, 181 N.S.R. (2d) 151, 560 A.P.R. 151 (N.S.S.C.). In determining whether a prior order of spousal support should be varied or terminated, the court should consider all relevant statutory factors including "the 'objectives' of a variation order listed in s. 17(7)(a)(d) and other factors such as 'the length of the marriage', continuing child caring obligations, 'the relative independence of the parties throughout the marital relationship' and 'the amount of support' already paid." The parties cohabited under the marriage for approximately 17 years. They had three children, ages 13, 11 and 8 years, who were primarily in the wife's custody. The wife obtained a better paying job after agreeing to $550 a month in a settlement that had been incorporated in a court order. The husband applied to vary or terminate the order. However, the wife had not yet achieved self-sufficiency and had been constrained from earlier career advancement by her child-care obligations, thus suffering an economic disadvantage. In the circumstances, the court held that spousal support should not be terminated, but should be reduced from $550 a month to $300 a month retroactive to the date of the application.

*After Moge the Pelech trilogy is inapplicable in the absence of an agreement — Moura v. Moura*, 1998 CarswellOnt 4919, 43 R.F.L. (4th) 344, 83 O.T.C. 321, [1998] O.J. No. 5351 (Ont. Gen. Div.). In light of *Moge v. Moge, supra*, the *Pelech* trilogy, above, is not applicable to cases where spousal support has not been determined by agreement. Consequently, entitlement to support is no longer dependant on a causal connection between a spouse's need and the marriage. Instead it is governed by the divorce legislation and in particular the four objectives contained within the legislation.

*Needs-based and compensatory rationales for support both applicable — Burnett v. Burnett*, 1997 CarswellOnt 3282, 33 R.F.L. (4th) 356, [1997] O.J. No. 3676 (Ont. Gen. Div.). Where the wife had been out of the labour force for several years and was still recovering from a long-term abusive relationship, she was entitled to both needs-based and compensatory support. Until the equalization payment was made and the wife's share of joint assets was purchased, her only income was from rent which provided her with little income. She was not ready to go back into the work force for about a year. The court granted the wife's modest request for spousal support of $100 a month.

*Reasonable expectation of support — Sheldon v. Sheldon*, 1996 CarswellAlta 291, 21 R.F.L. (4th) 422, 182 A.R. 131 (Alta. Q.B.). The wife was not obliged to establish a causal connection between her economic disadvantage arising from her illness and the marriage or its breakdown, just the reasonable expectation of support arising from the marriage.

*Variation — factors are of equal importance — Smyth v. Smyth*, 1993 CarswellAlta 449, 48 R.F.L. (3d) 280, 142 A.R. 132 (Alta. Q.B.). The prescribed objectives in ss. 15 and 17 of the *Divorce Act* are of equal importance and must be considered in every case but their relative significance will vary depending upon the circumstances.

*Variation — all objectives must be considered — Swift v. Swift*, 1992 CarswellOnt 317, 44 R.F.L. (3d) 250, 61 O.A.C. 225 (Ont. Div. Ct.). In an application for variation of support, the court should properly consider all of the objectives outlined in s. 17(7) of the *Divorce Act*.

*Quantum selected to compensate wife and bring her to marital standard of living — Sywyk v. Sywyk*, 1991 CarswellOnt 1335 (Ont. Gen. Div.). In awarding spousal support following a divorce trial, the court, after considering the property division that had been made and the 18 years of cohabitation, found that $1,000 a month would bring the wife's personal income to the $29,000 a year range, which would compensate her for the 10 years she spent at home as well as bring her up to her accustomed standard of living.

There should be some consistency between the initial and variation orders — "Where the parties stand beyond mere necessity and ability to pay, any adjustment must be made with due regard for and in harmony with the arrangements that have already been prescribed" — per Burchell J. in *Taylar v. Taylar*, 1981 CarswellNS 55, 22 R.F.L. (2d) 96, 44 N.S.R. (2d) 367, 83 A.P.R. 367 (N.S.T.D.).

*Change of circumstances does not necessarily open entire order* — *Tobin v. Tobin*, 1974 CarswellOnt 199, 19 R.F.L. 18 (Ont. H.C.). Justice Zuber observed: "I can vary that award at this stage in the light of changed circumstances but I do not concede that a change in circumstances necessarily reopens the entire issue. In other words, the change that is to be made or the variation in the decree *nisi*, should reflect the changed circumstances. A changed circumstance is not the key that unlocks the door to a reconsideration of the whole matter from the very beginning. To a certain extent, this is what the petitioner invites me to do — to say now that circumstances have changed somewhat, let us go back to the starting line and reconsider the whole matter. I decline to do that".

## 6.2 Economic Advantages or Disadvantages Arising from the Marriage or its Breakdown

Section 15.2(6)(a) of the *Divorce Act* states that a spousal support order should "recognize any economic advantages or disadvantages to the spouses arising from the marriage or its breakdown." This is the clearest and broadest statement in the statute of the compensatory purpose of spousal support. Spousal support should account for sacrifices in earning power made by the applicant during the course of the relationship. In the archetypal case of a "traditional marriage," the applicant has left the workforce during the relationship in order to care for the couple's children. After the relationship ends, regardless of whether there are ongoing childcare responsibilities, the applicant will continue to experience a loss due to having curtailed her employment. Had she been working outside the home, she would probably have received raises and upgraded her skills, enhancing her income-generating potential. Her absence from the workforce may have led to erosion of employment skills and therefore earning power. Conversely, the respondent has benefitted from the applicant's curtailed employment. Freed from childcare responsibilities, he was able to focus on his job and thereby increase his ability to earn income. Spousal support can be used to remedy the injustice which would result were the respondent allowed to receive the entire benefit of this situation, and the applicant required to bear the entire burden.

The compensatory rationale has been applied in a broad array of fact patterns. The case law is clear that compensatory support can be appropriate even if the claimant was employed throughout the marriage. The time and energy she had available for her career, and therefore the rewards, may have been reduced by domestic responsibilities. Nor is compensatory support impossible in childless marriages, insofar as disproportionate contributions to household chores or the attainment of education may justify compensation. On the other hand, a number of cases have held that a single decision to turn down a job does not necessarily entitle the claimant to an accounting of the financial consequences of that decision. All of the factors and objectives of the *Divorce Act* must be considered.

The compensatory theory of spousal support was advanced by a 1975 Law Reform Commission of Canada working paper, and was sometimes mentioned in the case law thereafter. However, it was the 1992 decision of the Supreme Court of Canada in *Moge v. Moge* which solidified the compensatory rationale as one of the two foundational pillars of spousal support law.

In 1999, Bracklow affirmed the importance of compensation, while broadening the bases for support.

What is the relevance of the compensatory rationale to the *Spousal Support Advisory Guidelines* (SSAG)? The SSAG produce suggested ranges for spousal support awards based on quantifiable, conceptually simple inputs — the length of the parties' relationship, the presence of children, and the differential between the parties' incomes. They do not require an assessment of the compensable elements in a given fact pattern in order to produce guideline ranges for amount and duration. However, the nature of the compensable elements is significant under the SSAG for two reasons. Firstly, the strength or weakness of the compensatory claim is a reason to choose a higher or lower amount within the SSAG range (SSAG s. 9.1). For example, if there is especially strong evidence that the claimant would have been earning a very high income had she not curtailed her employment during the relationship, that fact would tend to push the award to the higher end of the range. The second way in which compensatory analysis is significant under the SSAG is in justifying the "compensatory exception in short marriages without children," which is explained in s. 11.6.

*The purpose of spousal support is to relieve economic hardship that results from the "marriage or its breakdown", and the focus of the assessment of spousal support must be on the effect of the marriage in either impairing or improving each party's economic prospects — Moge v. Moge*, 1992 CarswellMan 143, 1992 CarswellMan 222, EYB 1992-67141, 43 R.F.L. (3d) 345, [1992] 3 S.C.R. 813, 99 D.L.R. (4th) 456, [1993] 1 W.W.R. 481, 81 Man. R. (2d) 161, 145 N.R. 1, [1993] R.D.F. 168, 30 W.A.C. 161, [1992] S.C.J. No. 107 (S.C.C.). Marriage is, among other things, an economic unit which generates financial benefits, and the Act reflects the fact that marriage partners should expect, and are entitled to share in those benefits. A sharing of benefits can be achieved in several ways: by child and spousal support, by the division of property, or by a combination of support and property division. The absence of accumulated assets may require that one spouse pay support to the other in order to effect an equitable distribution of resources. The Act embodies a theory of spousal support based on principles of compensation. A foundation for these principles is found in the first three of the four objectives. They deal with a broad range of economic and financial consequences. Self-sufficiency, the fourth objective, remains relevant, but is not given pre-eminence. After divorce, spouses would still have an obligation to contribute to their own support in a manner commensurate with their abilities. Compensatory spousal support would not always be awarded, or if awarded would not necessarily be granted in substantial amounts. "In cases where relatively few advantages have been conferred or disadvantages incurred, transitional support allowing for full and unimpaired reintegration back into the labour force might be all that is required to afford sufficient compensation. However, in many cases compensatory spousal support would require long-term support or an alternative settlement which provides an equivalent degree of assistance in light of all the objectives of the Act." Women have tended to suffer economic disadvantages and hardships from marriage or its breakdown because of the traditional division of labour within that institution. A diminished earning capacity resulting from long interruptions in employment to take on parenting or domestic responsibilities is a fact that has been demonstrated in a number of studies. Often difficulties in returning to the work force are exacerbated by the continuing responsibility for the care of children after divorce. The spouse who has made economic sacrifices in the marriage usually becomes the custodial parent. This responsibility further reduces her economic choice by requiring her to do such things as remain within proximity to schools, refuse to work late, and to stay at home when the children are ill. There may be some cases where, because the spouses have made economic sacrifices equally, there will be no call for compensation. But these cases will be rare. The economic consequences must be shared by both partners. The difficulty in attaining an equitable sharing of the consequences is in finding a balance between the ability of the debtor spouse to pay, and the limit to which a support order can go to achieve fair compensation for the disadvantaged spouse. The four objectives set out in the Act are an attempt to achieve an equitable sharing of the economic consequences of marriage or marriage breakdown. But the courts have an overriding discretion when ordering support which will depend on the particular facts of each case. The exercise of this discretion requires an examination of all four objectives involving a broad approach incorporating any significant element of the marriage or its termination which adversely affects the economic prospects of the disadvantaged spouse. Not all such elements will be equally important. Some of the most common compensable advantages and disadvantages which the Act envisages are:

- Loss of future earning power including such things as loss of seniority, missed promotions, lack of benefits like pension plans, and life, disability, dental and health insurance; employer-paid job-retraining and skills upgrading programmes.
- Economic disadvantage from curtailing paid employment in order to care for the children. (Usually, the most significant economic consequence of marriage or marriage breakdown arises from the birth of children.)
- Other financial consequences arising from the care of a child which are not reflected in the direct costs of support.
- In a childless marriage where the couple decides that one of them is to remain at home, any economic disadvantage to that spouse flowing from their decision.
- Where both spouses work full-time and one of them incurs economic loss by declining a promotion, refusing a transfer, leaving a position to allow the other spouse to take advantage of an opportunity for advancement, or by otherwise curtailing employment opportunities in the interest of the family.
- Contributions to the other spouse's business such as the provision of secretarial, entertainment or bookkeeping services.
- Assuming increased domestic and financial responsibilities to enable the other spouse to pursue licenses, degrees or other training and education.

In her additional comments made after concurring in the judgement of her colleague, Madame Justice McLachlin summarized her view of the first objective by saying that it is compensatory in nature allowing the judge "to compensate one spouse for sacrifices and contributions made during the marriage and benefits which the other spouse has received."

*Statutory basis for compensatory support — Bracklow v. Bracklow*, 1999 CarswellBC 532, 1999 CarswellBC 533, 44 R.F.L. (4th) 1, [1999] 1 S.C.R. 420, 63 B.C.L.R. (3d) 77, 169 D.L.R. (4th) 577, [1999] 8 W.W.R. 740, 120 B.C.A.C. 211, 236 N.R. 79, 196 W.A.C. 211, [1999] S.C.J. No. 14 (S.C.C.). The first two objectives in s. 15.2(6) of the *Divorce Act* are primarily related to compensation.

*Compensation for foregone careers and opportunities — Bracklow v. Bracklow, supra*, at 16 [R.F.L.], McLachlin J. (as she then was). "It is now well-settled law that spouses must compensate each other for foregone careers and missed opportunities during the marriage upon the breakdown of their union".

*The Appeal Court affirmed finding that a mutual decision by future spouses that the husband give up dream job in Mexico to move to Vancouver because of the wife's greater earning capacity and stability in employment was grounds for compensatory support for husband for 48 months subject to review, but scope of review provision varied to limit it to non-compensatory support related directly to the ability of husband to financially meet his parenting role under joint custody order — S. (R.M.) v S. (F.P.C.)*, 2011 CarswellBC 170, 2011 BCCA 53, 90 R.F.L. (6th) 1, 14 B.C.L.R. (5th) 84, 299 B.C.A.C. 186, 508 W.A.C. 186, [2011] B.C.J. No. 174 (B.C.C.A.), reversing 2009 CarswellBC 2597?2009 BCSC 1323, 4 R.F.L. (6th) 376 (B.C.S.C.). The parties were married in 2004, had two children, and separated in 2007 when the wife ended the marriage. The wife was an anaesthetist and the husband had been employed as sports director for a Club Med in Mexico where the parties met. In light of the wife's higher earnings potential, they agreed he would give up his position and join her in Vancouver. After the birth of their first son, they both stayed home for a period. The wife returned to work at the hospital and when the child went to day care the husband obtained work. Following the birth of their daughter, the wife again stopped work and later returned to work part-time. In 2007, the parties separated. The trial judge noting that the economic disadvantage to the husband was disproportionate to the duration of the marriage, and that his ability to obtain work was restricted by his education, experience, and language difficulties, ordered, among other relief, that the wife pay to the husband spousal support in an amount and duration that exceeded the SSAG range, subject to a 48 month review. On appeal the court held that the income imputed to the wife of $225,000 for purposes of paying support did not constitute an error in law and that the quantum of spousal support ensures that the payee spouse who was to have 35% time with the children would have the financial resources he would need to fulfil his parenting role. The scope of the review restriction however was narrowed to a review on entitlement and quantum for non-compensatory support related directly to the ability of the husband to financially meet his parenting role under the joint custody order.

*In a traditional marriage where the family moves frequently to accommodate the husband's career, spousal support should be awarded to the wife and the amount should be reduced once she is able to increase her income post-separation* — Scott v. Scott, 2010 CarswellMan 260, 2010 MBQB 139 (Man. Q.B.); affirmed 2011 CarswellMan 52, 2011 MBCA 21, 97 R.F.L. (6th) 119, 262 Man. R. (2d) 237, 507 W.A.C. 237 (Man. C.A.). The husband was in the military.

*Lump sum awarded to compensate wife for economic disadvantage arising from the marriage and its breakdown* — Hartshorne v. Hartshorne, 2009 CarswellBC 1398, 2009 BCSC 698, 70 R.F.L. (6th) 106, [2009] B.C.J. 1050 (B.C.S.C.); reversed in part 2010 CarswellBC 1618, 2010 BCCA 327, 82 R.F.L. (6th) 1, 6 B.C.L.R. (5th) 58, 289 B.C.A.C. 244, 489 W.A.C. 244 (B.C.C.A.). The wife, a lawyer, experienced an economic disadvantage during her lengthy absence form the legal profession as she fell behind her contemporaries in terms of earnings, client base, networking, professional skills, and seniority. If she had not had this interruption during the formative years of her career, she would have had opportunities to establish her practice, to provide significantly more lucrative opportunities for her, either as an associate or as a partner. In addition, her career opportunities after the parties' separation and divorce were adversely influenced by both her late age at reentry into the workforce and her role as a custodial parent.

*Although the wife came out of marriage as a person of considerable means, the court ordered support in recognition of the disparity in the parties' earning capacity due to the roles each party played in marriage; while the wife was home caring for the family, the husband was at the workplace honing his business skills* — Taylor v. Taylor, 2009 CarswellAlta 1701, 2009 ABCA 354, 72 R.F.L. (6th) 249, 15 Alta. L.R. (5th) 303, 312 D.L.R. (4th) 448, 464 A.R. 245, 467 W.A.C. 245 (Alta. C.A.), varying 2009 CarswellAlta 20, 2009 ABQB 7, 1 Alta. L.R. (5th) 74 (Alta. Q.B.). Following an 18-year marriage and two children, the parties separated in 2005. The husband who had worked for the wife's family business throughout the marriage left following the separation, although buy-out arrangements were inconclusive. He then purchased a company using 100% borrowed funds. The parties had joint custody of the children. At the time of trial, the wife was earning $33,937. The court, questioning the appropriateness of the husband's business decisions, awarded the wife spousal support based on an income of $124,000 imputed to the husband. The husband paid child support in accordance with the Guidelines. On appeal, the court, indicating that the trial judge failed to consider the financial impact of joint custody, and that it was an error to import wrongful dismissal principles into support, and that it is rarely unreasonable for someone to leave employment controlled by former in-laws, varied the husband's imputed income to $75,000 and reduced spousal support from $2,300 to $1,000 per month for six years.

*Where the wife managed the household, cared for the child, and worked part-time which left her economically disadvantaged by the breakdown of the marriage, she was entitled to support —* Rioux v. Rioux, 2009 CarswellOnt 4077, 2009 ONCA 569, 66 R.F.L. (6th) 256, 97 O.R. (3d) 102, 252 O.A.C. 126 (Ont. C.A.), reversing in part 2007 CarswellOnt 9916 (Ont. S.C.J.). The parties were married for 21 years and were both 45 at the time of separation. They had one child aged 19. Although the wife had obtained interim orders prior to trial for spousal and child support, inter alia, the husband made no payments and the wife paid the child's university expenses. At trial, the court ordered the husband to pay child support in the amount of $916 per month in full satisfaction of his obligations to the child. The court further ordered that the husband pay a lump sum for spousal support of $100,000. The trial judge further stated that the prior orders were terminated by this order, and that the wife was to continue to satisfy her obligation to be self-supporting. The Court of Appeal, noting that the equalization payment due to the wife was itself $90,000, found it unclear whether spousal support had been ordered, and if it was the amount was insufficient. At this time, the husband earned $105, 000 and the wife $16,000. The appeal court held that the trial judge failed to adequately address the wife's needs and ordered that the husband pay $1,500 per month spousal support for five years, at which time support to be the subject of review.

*Party entitled to spousal support where she had been disadvantaged by the loss of the standard of living her husband's income provided and currently there was a considerable difference in the parties' incomes —* Bell v. Bell, 2009 CarswellBC 1588, 2009 BCCA 280, 69 R.F.L. (6th) 21, 97 B.C.L.R. (4th) 55, [2010] 1 W.W.R. 98, 272 B.C.A.C. 207, 459 W.A.C. 207 (B.C.C.A.). The husband's income was $649,959 and the wife's income was $140,000. The parties divorced in 2006, after reaching an agreement on an equal division of their property, valued at $12 million. The court recognized that the wife had sufficient capital and income to meet her needs and was economically self-sufficient. However, without spousal support, she would not be compensated in terms of her lower standard of living, caused by the breakdown of the marriage. Neither party should be required to encroach on capital to deal with the difference in his or her standard of living compared to that of a spouse. The husband's current income was half the amount of his income at the time of the parties' agreement, predicated largely on his 2005 income. Consequently, the court reduced spousal support from $10,000 a month to $5,000 a month. The SSAG were not useful in this case, particularly as the husband's income was well in excess of $300,000.

*No evidence of negative impact of marriage on career — no support ordered — B. (S.M.) v. B. (L.M.),* 2006 CarswellAlta 235, 2006 ABQB 141, [2006] A.J. No. 210 (Alta. Q.B.); affirmed 2007 CarswellAlta 966, 2007 ABCA 232 (Alta. C.A.). A spouse is not entitled to spousal support where she failed to obtain a degree as anticipated, but she was already receiving the top hourly rate available for her profession. When the litigation ceased, she would be able to earn more. There is no evidence that the wife has suffered any loss of career opportunity by the marriage or its breakdown. There is no evidence that the wife sustained any compromise of her economic future by the marriage or its breakdown. The parties leave the marriage having achieved their goal of pursuing and maintaining their own careers throughout the marriage. There is no evidence that the husband did or failed to do anything which adversely affected the wife's career path; indeed there is evidence that he assisted her both financially and domestically in pursuing her career. In addition, she had failed to prove that she was disabled.

*Long-term marriage will require compensation even if both parties remained employed —* Thomas v. Thomas, 2004 CarswellAlta 41, 2004 ABQB 27, 50 R.F.L. (5th) 226, 22 Alta. L.R.

(4th) 46, 350 A.R. 58 (Alta. Q.B.); affirmed 2005 CarswellAlta 97, 2005 ABCA 24, 14 R.F.L. (6th) 170, 37 Alta. L.R. (4th) 4, 363 A.R. 159, 343 W.A.C. 159, [2005] A.J. No. 61 (Alta. C.A.). In terms of spousal support compensatory objectives, a long-term traditional marriage is certain to involve some form of economic disadvantage and resulting hardships. Even if both parties remain in the workplace, decisions made by the family may result in some form of economic disadvantage. Economic self-sufficiency may never be possible.

*Support quantum selected to share decline in lifestyles equally — Brophy v. Brophy*, 2004 CarswellOnt 23, 45 R.F.L. (5th) 56, 180 O.A.C. 389, [2004] O.J. No. 17 (Ont. C.A.); additional reasons at 2004 CarswellOnt 584 (Ont. C.A.). A party is entitled to compensatory support for economic disadvantage suffered on the breakdown of a marriage. The parties separated after 23 years of marriage. At the time of separation, the husband was 52 and the wife was 57 years old. They had three adult sons who all had special needs. This was a marriage of long duration and the wife had been out of the workforce for many years while caring for the children and managing the household. The wife was not working at the time of the appeal. The trial judge also took into account the wife's imputed investment income of $8,000 to $10,000 annually. The amount the trial judge ordered properly reflected a relatively equal sharing of the decline in the parties' lifestyles. The court upheld the lower court's award of $8,000 per month based on the husband's income of $242,000 annually.

*Absence from employment — Support awarded at reduced level — Cadigan v. Cadigan*, 2004 CarswellMan 533, 2004 MBQB 283, 189 Man. R. (2d) 245 (Man. Q.B.); affirmed 2007 CarswellMan 72, 2007 MBCA 28, 212 Man. R. (2d) 291, 389 W.A.C. 291 (Man. C.A.). The wife's childbearing and subsequent childcare responsibilities took her away from her active dental practice and caused her to suffer economic advantages and disadvantages arising from the marriage and its breakdown. Her husband's desire to have her out of their dental office most of the time in later years, as well as his behaviour with other female staff, which made working at the office unpleasant, further disadvantaged her in terms of career, skill, and practice development. Consequently the wife was entitled to the husband's continued economic support, although at a reduced level in order to promote her self-sufficiency.

*Claimant's return to similar employment does not mean compensation unnecessary — T. (J.G.) v. N. (T.)*, 2003 CarswellAlta 868, 2003 ABCA 195, 42 R.F.L. (5th) 208, 330 A.R. 187, 299 W.A.C. 187, [2003] A.J. No. 786 (Alta. C.A.). The mere fact that the mother was able to return to the same type of employment she had before assuming primary responsibility for the parties' children was no reason not to award her compensatory support. To adopt a contrary approach would be to ignore the reality of career progression and advancement.

*Claimant postponed her education to facilitate that of the other spouse — long-term support ordered despite her self-sufficiency — Allaire v. Allaire*, 2003 CarswellOnt 1002, 35 R.F.L. (5th) 256, 170 O.A.C. 72, [2003] O.J. No. 1069 (Ont. C.A.). Where the wife had supported the husband through his completion of two university degrees, her compensatory support award was upheld on appeal. The fact that she had to postpone her own secondary education resulted in a permanent economic detriment to her. In situations such as in the present case where a former spouse will continue to suffer financial disadvantages of the marriage and its breakdown and the other spouse will continue to obtain financial advantages, long-term compensatory support is appropriate, even if the disadvantaged spouse is self-sufficient. In the 3 years prior to the trial, the husband earned between $207,721 and $176,689. The wife was presently enrolled in a Masters programme and anticipated that with the completion of this degree, her income would increase to $68,793. The appellate court upheld a spousal award of $2,500 per month without time limitation.

*Courts to look at overall advantages and disadvantages arising from marriage and not perform minute accounting — Roseneck v. Gowling*, 2002 CarswellOnt 4396, 35 R.F.L. (5th)

177, 62 O.R. (3d) 789, 167 O.A.C. 203, 223 D.L.R. (4th) 210 (Ont. C.A.); additional reasons at 2003 CarswellOnt 159, 223 D.L.R. (4th) 229 (Ont. C.A.); further additional reasons at 2003 CarswellOnt 649, 38 R.F.L. (5th) 180 (Ont. C.A.). Compensatory support should not be awarded where a spouse in a relatively short marriage claims to be economically disadvantaged because she did not make R.R.S.P. and pension contributions during 3 years of the marriage. She did not have regular employment outside the home during that time. Fair distribution does not require a minute accounting of the financial details of the parties. In terms of compensatory support, the courts should be looking at a wide view of the advantages and disadvantages of the spouses caused by their roles in the marriage. In this case, both parties had a relatively equal earning power before and after the marriage.

*Both parties out of the workforce — both parties have childcare responsibilities — step-down compensatory support ordered — Phinney v. Phinney*, 2002 CarswellNS 525, 2002 NSCA 168, 33 R.F.L. (5th) 211, 211 N.S.R. (2d) 135, 662 A.P.R. 135, [2002] N.S.J. No. 540 (N.S.C.A.). In compensatory support cases, where spouses have been out of the workforce and have on-going childcare responsibilities, limited term spousal support orders should be an exception. But an exception was made in this case where the dependant spouse in such a relationship had suffered economic disadvantage and hardship resulting from the marriage breakdown (s. 15.2(6) (a), (b) and (c)). The court awarded spousal support of $750 monthly for a year and then declining amounts for 3 years.

*Economic disadvantage — only one objective — no support — Corbeil v. Corbeil*, 2001 CarswellAlta 1138, 2001 ABCA 220, 21 R.F.L. (5th) 1, 98 Alta. L.R. (3d) 38, [2002] 3 W.W.R. 60, 286 A.R. 330, 253 W.A.C. 330, [2001] A.J. No. 1144 (Alta. C.A.). The court upheld the trial judge's refusal to grant the wife spousal support, even though she sustained an economic disadvantage on account of the marriage. The fact that one party is able to prove the existence of one objective such as economic disadvantage does not establish entitlement to support. A court must consider all of the objectives of spousal support and all of the circumstances of the parties. In this case, spousal support for the wife was rejected although the marriage lasted for 20 years. The appellate court held that the trial judge was wrong in not taking into account the wife's care of the children in considering spousal support. However, taking all the objectives and the circumstances into consideration, the wife's income after imputing some income, her potential for income growth, the fact that she works only part time, the fact that the husband also raised the children for a period of time when she left the home without significant contribution from her, their ages and the security of their positions and her asset advantage and the rejection of her evidence by the trial judge on relevant issues, and that significantly more of the assets received on the distribution are subject to tax as income, the court held that it would uphold the trial court's decision not to provide spousal support.

*Dependant spouse has given up employment upon marriage — the age of the dependant spouse is relevant — Gabb v. Gabb*, 2001 CarswellMan 68, 2001 MBCA 19, 13 R.F.L. (5th) 391, 153 Man. R. (2d) 157, 238 W.A.C. 157, [2001] M.J. No. 55 (Man. C.A.). A spouse is clearly economically disadvantaged by the parties' traditional marital relationship where the wife had given up her job upon marriage, the marriage lasted 8 years and wife was 53 at the time of the marriage breakdown.

*Compensatory rationale in a "traditional" marriage — Schnell v. Schnell*, 2001 CarswellSask 744, 2001 SKCA 123, 21 R.F.L. (5th) 197, 213 Sask. R. 174, 260 W.A.C. 174, [2001] S.J. No. 704 (Sask. C.A.). A spouse is entitled to compensatory support where she has been economically disadvantaged by the marriage through giving up her career in order to stay home with the children, and where she has been economically disadvantaged by the marriage breakdown by no longer being able to benefit from her husband's significant income, and where the other spouse has received economic advantages as a result of the marriage. The husband had an average income of $191,472 for 1996 to 1998. The appellate court upheld the trial judge's award of $2,500 per month in spousal support. The order was made for a 9-month period and was reviewable at the end of that time on the application by either party.

*Claimant entitled to compensation for economic disadvantage – period of award lengthened on appeal to allow continuation of studies – Baldwin v. Ward*, 1999 CarswellSask 355, 2 R.F.L. (5th) 56, 180 Sask. R. 124, 205 W.A.C. 124 (Sask. C.A.). An order for partial spousal support confirms that the dependant spouse had suffered economic disadvantage from the marriage or its breakdown. On appeal, the duration of spousal support was lengthened from 10 months to 3 years to permit the wife to continue with her studies. The parties separated after 18 years of marriage.

*Variation – support will be granted for future need where a spouse has suffered economic disadvantage because of the marriage, even though there was no current need – Savoie v. Savoie*, 1999 CarswellMan 308, 49 R.F.L. (4th) 336, [1999] 9 W.W.R. 63, 175 D.L.R. (4th) 291, 138 Man. R. (2d) 128 (Man. C.A.). Where the wife had a future need for support which arose because of her economic disadvantage suffered as a result of the long-term traditional marriage, her appeal was allowed in part and spousal support was set at $300 per month, even though she did not have any current economic need (Man. C.A.). This amount of $300 was half of what the wife had previously received under the parties' separation agreement and at trial. The reduction took into account her remarriage and the setting aside of the separation agreement.

*Variation – support extended where wife had suffered economic disadvantage as a result of the marriage and its breakdown – Wooldridge v. Wooldridge*, 1999 CarswellAlta 320, 1999 ABCA 124, 45 R.F.L. (4th) 308, 172 D.L.R. (4th) 637, 237 A.R. 64 (Alta. C.A.); additional reasons at 1999 CarswellAlta 620, 49 R.F.L. (4th) 445, 250 A.R. 168 (Alta. C.A.). The court held that where the wife has not worked outside the home for 20 years and she and two of her four children have suffered severe psychological difficulties since separation, there have been economic disadvantages to the wife as a result of the marriage and its breakdown, spousal support should not be terminated. Under these circumstances, self-sufficiency for the wife might not be possible for some time, if ever. The husband was ordered to pay $2,500 per month in spousal support. Once the husband has ceased to pay child support, the spousal support, if necessary, could be increased.

*Claimant spouse moves for other's career but finds comparable jobs – Leitch v. Leitch*, 1999 CarswellOnt 3942 (Ont. S.C.J.); affirmed 2001 CarswellOnt 3289 (Ont. C.A.). A spouse who consents to moves initiated by the other spouse which necessitate her changing to comparable jobs, is disadvantaged but only to a small extent and is thereby entitled to a small amount of compensatory support. Although the wife was not, at the time of the appellate hearing, working as a qualified nurse, a position for which she was qualified, she was working in an associated field at the top of her pay scale. She had not shared her earnings with the family over the course of the marriage, but had enjoyed the lifestyle provided by the husband. She had also upgraded her skills by taking a 2-year full-time university programme during the marriage.

*Absence from workforce – Martin v. Martin*, 1998 CarswellNfld 298, 42 R.F.L. (4th) 251, 517 A.P.R. 181, 168 Nfld. & P.E.I.R. 181, [1998] N.J. No. 323 (Nfld. C.A.). The wife's award of lump-sum support was upheld on appeal, where she had given up a permanent job and was out of the workforce for 16 years. The order had awarded her a lump sum of $10,000 for retraining and was not to be interfered with on appeal merely because she changes her mind about retraining and saved the money instead.

*Claimant qualified as teacher but had left work – award reduced to prevent her from having more disposable income than the husband – Rea v. Rea*, 1998 CarswellMan 440, 42 R.F.L. (4th) 92, 166 D.L.R. (4th) 443, 131 Man. R. (2d) 95, 187 W.A.C. 95 (Man. C.A.). Support may be awarded to compensate an economic disadvantage arising from the breakdown of the marriage. The wife in a traditional marriage of 36 years assumed the role of homemaker, raised their three children, and assisted her husband in his career. She was a qualified teacher, but because of her domestic duties, taught only in the first year of the marriage and for 7 years after the birth of their first child. The trial judge ordered the husband to pay support to the wife of $1,000 a month until his retirement and $850 a month thereafter. On appeal, the amount payable on retirement was reduced to $500 a month. In making the reduction the Court of Appeal observed that the original order would have given the husband less disposable income on retirement than the wife would have. However, she was entitled to compensation for economic disadvantage, and the husband was able to continue paying that compensation into his retirement. Although the wife may not have suffered an economic disadvantage as a result of the marriage, she did suffer an economic disadvantage as a result of the martial breakdown.

*Compensatory and needs-based factors both present — support justified — Taylor v. Taylor,* 1998 CarswellBC 547, 38 R.F.L. (4th) 408, 50 B.C.L.R. (3d) 212, 157 D.L.R. (4th) 701, 104 B.C.A.C. 217, 170 W.A.C. 217, [1998] B.C.J. No. 586 (B.C.C.A.). A wife who is disadvantaged by the marriage in circumstances where her husband is advantaged, and who, because of illness is disadvantaged by the breakdown of the marriage, may be awarded support for an indefinite period. The husband and wife cohabited for 3 years and were married for 6 years. With the consent of the husband, the wife did not seek employment outside the marriage. She cared for the husband's daughter and supported him in his business by entertaining customers and associates, and by traveling with him. She began to develop medical problems during cohabitation and after separation became permanently disabled. The trial judge ordered the husband to pay support of $3,000 a month to her for an indefinite period. An appeal to the British Columbia Court of Appeal was dismissed. The trial judge's findings based on compensatory principles that the wife had been economically disadvantaged, and the husband economically advantaged as a result of the marriage, should not be disturbed. Nor should his finding that the wife was economically disadvantaged by the marriage breakdown, principally because her illness had intervened to render her unemployable. The husband did not suffer a similar disadvantage arising from the marriage breakdown, having survived a bankruptcy, paid down his debt to his employer, and set up a new beginning for himself in California, with the advantage of ongoing, remunerative employment. In addition to applying compensatory principles, the trial judge viewed this as a case in which the wife's need for support, and the husband's corresponding ability to meet that need without undue hardship. The need in this case arose largely, but not solely, as a result of the wife's illness, which was not causally connected to the marriage. However, the fact that a spouse's illness and consequent inability to become self-sufficient was not causally connected to the marriage does not necessarily justify the denial of support, or the limitation of support. In any event, the 9-year period of cohabitation and the specific findings of economic disadvantage to the wife arising from the marriage and its breakdown fully justified the trial judge's conclusion that the husband should continue to pay support to her at the rate of $3,000 a month.

*Dependant spouse — chose to work part time — Daoust c. Leboeuf,* 1998 CarswellOnt 76, 35 R.F.L. (4th) 143, 107 O.A.C. 73 (Ont. C.A.). The Court of Appeal upheld the trial judge's award of spousal support as, in the circumstances, he gave sufficient consideration to the economic advantages and disadvantages arising from the marriage. The wife had chosen to work part time. Her cross-appeal of spousal support award was dismissed.

*Marriage had not interfered with claimant's employment and she had not furthered husband's career — no support — Jonasson v. Jonasson,* 1997 CarswellBC 1505, 30 R.F.L. (4th) 20, 95 B.C.A.C. 94, 154 W.A.C. 94, [1997] B.C.J. No. 1704 (B.C.C.A.). Where the trial judge's findings that the marriage had not interfered with the wife's finding of employment and that she had not furthered the husband's career were both reasonable, the appellate court upheld the dismissal of the wife's claim for compensatory support.

*Statutory authority for compensatory support — Stuart v. Stuart*, 1996 CarswellBC 517, 22 R.F.L. (4th) 26, 21 B.C.L.R. (3d) 65, 73 B.C.A.C. 30, 120 W.A.C. 30, [1996] B.C.J. No. 526 (B.C.C.A.). There is no separate head of relief in the *Divorce Act* for compensatory spousal support.

*Need not related to disadvantage caused by marriage — support denied — Woloshyn v. Woloshyn*, 1996 CarswellMan 170, 22 R.F.L. (4th) 129, 109 Man. R. (2d) 35, [1996] M.J. No. 153 (Man. Q.B.); affirmed 1997 CarswellMan 116, 28 R.F.L. (4th) 70, 115 Man. R. (2d) 225, 139 W.A.C. 225 (Man. C.A.). Where, throughout the marriage, the wife had been an equal and, at times, the primary breadwinner, her claim for spousal support was denied despite the fact that she was at the time of trial unemployed. The wife's current difficulty was the result of illness and industry changes and was not related to any economic disadvantage suffered as a result of the marriage.

*Economic advantages received during marriage to be considered as well as disadvantages — Huisman v. Huisman*, 1996 CarswellOnt 2470, 21 R.F.L. (4th) 341, 30 O.R. (3d) 155, 91 O.A.C. 293, 137 D.L.R. (4th) 41 (Ont. C.A.); varying 1994 CarswellOnt 456, 8 R.F.L. (4th) 145 (Ont. U.F.C.). The court allowed the husband's appeal from the wife's award of indefinite spousal support and imposed a 6-year limitation. The trial judge had failed to consider that throughout the parties' 8-year marriage a number of economic advantages had also accrued to the wife.

*Loss of future earnings, loss of seniority, missed promotions, loss of benefits — Messer v. Messer*, 1996 CarswellSask 662, 26 R.F.L. (4th) 352, 150 Sask. R. 23, [1996] S.C.J. No. 699 (Sask. Q.B.); reversed in part 1997 CarswellSask 595, 33 R.F.L. (4th) 426, 163 Sask. R. 101, 165 W.A.C. 101, [1997] S.J. No. 645 (Sask. C.A.). Where a spouse sacrifices a career to remain in the home, the court, in assessing that spouse's entitlement to spousal support should look beyond simple loss of future earnings. Factors such as loss of seniority, missed promotions and lack of access to pension plans and insurance should also be considered. The order was set aside and the court had grave doubts about the quantum of $800 per month. The matter was remitted to the lower court.

*How to calculate compensation — Crandall v. Crandall*, 1996 CarswellNB 233, 23 R.F.L. (4th) 387, 179 N.B.R. (2d) 59, 455 A.P.R. 59 (N.B.C.A.). Compensatory support will not be awarded on the basis that a party contributed to the development of a spouse's ability which enabled the spouse to earn income. The court held that there was no possibility of fixing a value on the development of an ability, or of finding any merit in the notion that each ability developed should be valued as a distinct asset. The compensatory aspect of a support award is related to the economic hardship resulting from the lack of opportunity of a party to develop his or her own potential during the marriage. However, the fact that the husband was able to pursue a career and to develop other skills is evidence of the fact that the wife was in a less advantageous position, and has a right to claim compensatory support.

*Economic disadvantages should not be borne by support payor alone — measure of support should be the actual loss of income suffered by the payee — Ross v. Ross*, 1995 CarswellNB 160, 16 R.F.L. (4th) 1, 168 N.B.R. (2d) 147, 430 A.P.R. 147, [1995] N.B.J. No. 463 (N.B.C.A.). The court on appeal found no error in the trial judge giving weight to the length of time the marriage lasted and the functions performed by the spouses during the marriage. He was correct in finding that the wife had "organized her life to prioritize the needs of the family to the detriment of her own career" and had "suffered an economic disadvantage arising from the marriage and its breakdown". He was correct, also, in concluding that her earnings were "clearly insufficient to achieve self-sufficiency" and that the future attainment of this objective did not appear to be reasonably possible. However, in awarding support of $1,700 a month, the trial judge erred by shifting the full burden of the economic disadvantages of the marriage and its breakdown to the husband, and ignored the wife's responsibility to make an effort to increase her earning capacity and contribute to the promotion of her self-sufficiency. He should have related the amount of support to the respondent's actual loss of income and the resulting reduction in her standard of living. The sum of $1,250 a month better reflected this reality. This amount, in addition to the respondent's salary and investment income, would meet her needs and provide adequate compensation for the economic disadvantages resulting from the marriage and its breakdown.

*Recognize advantages of marriage as well as disadvantages — Waterman v. Waterman,* 1995 CarswellNfld 117, 16 R.F.L. (4th) 10, 133 Nfld. & P.E.I.R. 310, 413 A.P.R. 310, [1995] N.J. No. 295 (Nfld. C.A.). After the termination of a long-term traditional marriage, the court, in determining spousal support, should not concentrate solely on identifying losses which have resulted from the marriage. The court should also recognize the social and financial effects of marriage on the claimant's ability to be self-sufficient after the termination of the marriage.

*Economic advantages received during marriage to be considered as well as disadvantages — Mason v. Mason,* 1995 CarswellMan 3, 10 R.F.L. (4th) 249, 104 Man. R. (2d) 81 (Man. Q.B.); affirmed 1995 CarswellMan 498, 18 R.F.L. (4th) 134, 102 Man. R. (2d) 239, 93 W.A.C. 239 (Man. C.A.). Although the wife had given up her career to raise the children, her claim for spousal support was dismissed on the ground that the advantages flowing to her from the marriage outweighed the disadvantages. She had received substantial assets and cash which would provide her with sufficient income to support herself

*Contributions of spouses need not be precisely calculated — McGrath v. Holmes,* 1995 CarswellNWT 1, 10 R.F.L. (4th) 161 (N.W.T.C.A.). In determining entitlement to spousal support, the court is required to take into account advantages and disadvantages resulting from the marriage and to weigh whether there is a net loss or gain which should be compensated by a support order. The court need not calculate with precision the financial contributions of each party and award support to offset any inequality of contribution to living costs and expenses..

*Variation — on an application for termination of spousal support, the court should examine the economic consequences resulting from the breakdown of the marriage — C. (N.) c. L. (Y.),* [1994] R.D.F. 205 (C.A. Que.).

*Variation — economic consequences of abusive conduct towards spouse — Martin v. Martin,* 1993 CarswellSask 57, 50 R.F.L. (3d) 77, 113 Sask. R. 316, 52 W.A.C. 316 (Sask. C.A.). It is appropriate for a court to take into account the detrimental economic consequences that one spouse's abusive conduct has created for the other spouse. On this basis, the appellate court would not interfere with the trial judge's award of spousal maintenance.

*Variation — economic disadvantage of marriage not overcome, support extended — Walker v. Walker,* 1992 CarswellBC 156, 39 R.F.L. (3d) 305, 68 B.C.L.R. (2d) 92, 12 B.C.A.C. 137, 23 W.A.C. 137 (B.C.C.A.), where the wife has been economically disadvantaged by the marriage by remaining at home and she has not overcome those disadvantages, the trial court did not err in respect to the recognition of the promotion of self-sufficiency. She was still in need and support should not be reduced.

*Loss of career — Purcell v. Purcell,* 1995 CarswellOnt 82, 11 R.F.L. (4th) 181, [1995] O.J. No. 980 (Ont. Gen. Div.); additional reasons at 1995 CarswellOnt 4429, 11 R.F.L. (4th) 181 at 200 (Ont. Gen. Div.); varied 1996 CarswellOnt 2305, 26 R.F.L. (4th) 267, [1996] O.J. No. 2404 (Ont. C.A.); additional reasons at 1996 CarswellOnt 4007, 26 R.F.L. (4th) 272 (Ont. C.A.). Where the husband had, with the wife's consent, left his employment, in part to attend to family concerns, he was found entitled to spousal support. The husband had suffered an economic disadvantage as a result of the marriage breakdown and he was entitled to support until he was re-established in the workforce.

*Career not developed during marriage — Lasalle v. Lasalle,* 1994 CarswellAlta 387, 7 R.F.L. (4th) 100, [1994] A.J. No. 661 (Alta. C.A.). The court upheld the wife's spousal support award that was made after the divorce and the failure of the wife's business. The wife had sacrificed her own career throughout the parties' 16-year marriage and may well otherwise have established herself financially.

*Fact that support claimant benefitted from other spouse's education or career does not preclude it serving as basis for spousal support* — *Colletta v. Colletta*, 1993 CarswellOnt 359, 50 R.F.L. (3d) 1, [1993] O.J. No. 2537 (Ont. C.A.). A support award under the *Divorce Act* should reflect any assistance given by a dependant to his or her spouse's education or professional advancement, despite the fact that the dependant may have shared in the increased income that resulted for some considerable time.

*Claimant may not be entitled to entire mathematically calculated compensation* — *Elliot v. Elliot*, 1993 CarswellOnt 348, 48 R.F.L. (3d) 237, 65 O.A.C. 241, 106 D.L.R. (4th) 609, 15 O.R. (3d) 265, [1993] O.J. No. 2308 (Ont. C.A.). The wife left her employment with Bell Canada in 1981 when the first child was born and remained at home to care for him and their second child until 1989. She returned to work at Bell Canada, but her prospects were not as good as when she was last there. The trial judge relying on opinion evidence offered by an economist found that the present value of the wife's income loss calculated from the date of the trial to her retirement was $158,205.90. He discounted this amount for income tax and divided the result in two holding that the husband should assume half the risk. In the result, he awarded the wife "as lump sum maintenance on her claim for lost future economic opportunity, the sum of $52,735.80." The husband appealed and the wife cross-appealed contending that the lump sum should be $236,384. The appeal was allowed and the cross-appeal dismissed. The objective in the *Divorce Act* that a spousal support order is to "recognize" an economic disadvantage, does not mean that the claimant has a right to full compensation. The objective involves compensating for an economic disadvantage as much as is reasonably possible "but, equally obviously, lack of resources may well stand in the way of full compensation." It is no answer to a lack of resources to say that the lump sum for compensation could be paid by installments at interest over a number of years. This pays no attention to the husband's means or to the principle of equitable sharing of the consequences of the marriage. It is not reasonably possible to apply these considerations where the compensation is in the form of a lump sum. Also, in ordering spousal support the court must take into account all the consequences to the parties. There should be an equal sharing of both the advantages and the disadvantages. "The basic flaw in the [economist's] approach is that it isolates one event or decision in the history of the marriage, the decision of the Elliots that Mrs. Elliot would leave the workforce to care for the children until the last of them was in school full-time, and treats it as the only event on which to focus in determining the amount of the award of spousal support." And "he treated it in much the same way as if her career interruption had been caused by injuries suffered in a motor vehicle accident. He calculated all of the damages flowing from that event.." In so doing, he did not properly determine the full effect of the advantages and disadvantages arising from the breakdown of the marriage. In addition, the tort approach of a motor vehicle accident does not treat the means of the payor to be a relevant consideration which is contrary to the requirement in the *Divorce Act* when determining spousal support. Another problem in the economist's approach of present valuing the loss as a lump sum is that it is unnecessarily speculative when compared to periodic support which can be varied if there is a change in circumstances. In this case, an order for periodic support would be a more appropriate method of providing for the equitable sharing of the available resources. The court allowed the husband's appeal and varied the trial judgement by setting aside the orders made and substituting an order for periodic support of $2,000 a month, allocated $1,000 a month for spousal support and $500 a month for each of the two children.

*Marriage, in part, is an economic unit and on marriage breakdown the parties are entitled to share in the benefits produced by the unit according to the functions performed* — *Elliot v. Elliot, supra.* The wife's earned income was less than what she might reasonably have expected it to be had she remained in the workforce resulting in an economic disadvantage upon the breakdown of the marriage. The wife contended that she gave up her business career to stay at home and look after the children while her husband became the sole "breadwinner" and thereby enjoyed an uninterrupted business career path. By assuming these roles, she was economically disadvantaged and he was economically advantaged upon the breakdown of the marriage. The court held that marriage, among other things, is an economic unit which generates financial benefits and spouses should expect and are entitled to share in those financial benefits. Here, the financial benefit created by the unit was the husband's income stream from his career. The appropriate sharing was for him to pay the wife support of $1,000 a month.

*Lower court judgment requiring payment as compensation overturned as it was too narrowly based on economist's evidence quantifying wife's loss — Elliot v. Elliot, supra.* The court struck on appeal an order requiring the husband to pay lump sum support as compensation to the wife for surrendering her career during the marriage. The order had been based solely on an economist's report which specified the wife's loss of future income because of the marriage but totally disregarded the husband's lack of ability to pay. Further, the report considered the effect of only one decision made during the marriage, instead of balancing the advantages and disadvantages accruing to both parties as a result of the marriage relationship.

*Absence from workforce, relocation for spouse's employment — Walton v. Walton,* 1993 CarswellSask 47, 46 R.F.L. (3d) 137, 110 Sask. R. 263 (Sask. Q.B.); affirmed 1993 CarswellSask 33, 1 R.F.L. (4th) 93, 108 D.L.R. (4th) 704, 59 W.A.C. 129, 116 Sask. R. 129, 23 C.B.R. (3d) 315, [1993] S.J. No. 637 (Sask. C.A.); additional reasons at (1993), 23 C.B.R. (3d) 315 at 320 (Sask. C.A.). Where the wife was employed at the time of separation, but had earlier left the workforce to care for the children, and at another time had obtained a job transfer for family purposes, she was found entitled to limited term support to allow her to complete university. The wife had been economically disadvantaged by the marriage.

*Economically disadvantaged — support based on current and predictable needs — Best v. Best,* 1993 CarswellOnt 367, 50 R.F.L. (3d) 120, [1993] O.J. No. 2444, 1 C.C.P.B. 8 (Ont. Gen. Div.); additional reasons at 1994 CarswellOnt 4781, [1994] O.J. No. 1241 (Ont. Gen. Div.); affirmed 1997 CarswellOnt 3499, 31 R.F.L. (4th) 1, 103 O.A.C. 344, 35 O.R. (3d) 577, 156 D.L.R. (4th) 717, 15 C.C.P.B. 170, [1997] O.J. No. 4007, 1997 C.E.B. & P.G.R. 8329 (headnote only) (Ont. C.A.); reversed on the issues 1999 CarswellOnt 1995, 1999 CarswellOnt 1996, 49 R.F.L. (4th) 1, [1999] 2 S.C.R. 868, 174 D.L.R. (4th) 235, 43 O.R. (3d) 740 (headnote only), 242 N.R. 1, 123 O.A.C. 1, 21 C.C.P.B. 1, [1999] S.C.J. No. 40, 1999 C.E.B. & P.G.R. 8361 (headnote only) (S.C.C.). Where the court found that the 57-year-old wife had been economically disadvantaged by the marriage, but found it difficult to assess the extent of the disadvantage, she was awarded spousal support based upon her current and predictable circumstances.

*Absence from work force; indefinite periodic support — Ross v. Ross,* 1993 CarswellOnt 301, 45 R.F.L. (3d) 230, 12 O.R. (3d) 705, 62 O.A.C. 384, [1993] O.J. No. 662 (Ont. C.A.). The court was of the opinion that in a long-term traditional marriage where the payee spouse has manifestly limited career skills, it is not appropriate that a spouse be given a 3-year declining support order. Such an award does not take into account the specific objectives set out in the *Divorce Act* and, in particular, does not recognize the economic disadvantages to the appellant caused by the marriage breakdown and her 23-year absence from the paid workforce. The Court of Appeal ordered indefinite periodic support in the amount of $1,850 per month.

*Claimant contributed to spouse's career at the expense of her own — Caratun v. Caratun,* 1992 CarswellOnt 287, 42 R.F.L. (3d) 113, 10 O.R. (3d) 385, 96 D.L.R. (4th) 404, 47 E.T.R. 234, 58 O.A.C. 140 (Ont. C.A.). Where the wife had contributed to her husband's career at the expense of her own, she was found entitled to a compensatory allowance.

*Lesser career — Patrick v. Patrick*, 1991 CarswellBC 315, 35 R.F.L. (3d) 382, 62 B.C.L.R. (2d) 188 (B.C.S.C.); additional reasons at 1991 CarswellBC 2027 (B.C.S.C.); affirmed 1993 CarswellBC 320, 49 R.F.L. (3d) 453, 85 B.C.L.R. (2d) 303, [1993] B.C.J. No. 1963 (B.C.C.A.). The pharmacist wife was awarded spousal support upon dissolution of her 10-year marriage. Although employed, the result of the marriage breakdown and her continuing childrearing role rendered the wife financially and professionally disadvantaged in comparison with what her circumstances would have been had the marriage continued or had it never occurred. On appeal, the court found no basis for imposing a time limit on the payment of support. There was nothing to prevent the appellant from applying for a variation of maintenance if there were a change in circumstances.

*Marriage of short duration — claimant benefitting from economic advantages of marriage and current economic independence — Grohmann v. Grohmann*, 1991 CarswellBC 321, 37 R.F.L. (3d) 73, 62 B.C.L.R. (2d) 264, 5 B.C.A.C. 277, 86 D.L.R. (4th) 741, 11 W.A.C. 277, [1991] B.C.J. No. 3820 (B.C.C.A.). The trial judge's decision to award maintenance for a fixed term of 5 months was affirmed on appeal, taking into account the 6 years of marriage, the fact that the wife did not significantly divert her talents to the development of the marriage, the economic advantages to the wife of the marriage, the disadvantages caused by her quitting her full-time job and the fact that the wife was now economically independent.

*Wife had acted as homemaker and developed problems which precluded employment — indefinite support — Brace v. Brace*, 1988 CarswellOnt 286, 16 R.F.L. (3d) 287 (Ont. H.C.); varied 1991 CarswellOnt 318, 35 R.F.L. (3d) 263 (Ont. C.A.). The wife had assumed the role of a traditional homemaker during the marriage and had developed serious physical and emotional problems that prevented her from seeking employment. Her economic need was found to be causally connected to the marriage, and support for an indefinite term was ordered.

*Consequence of husband's professional qualification for compensatory support analysis — Johnson v. Johnson*, 1988 CarswellBC 301, 16 R.F.L. (3d) 113, 29 B.C.L.R. (2d) 359, 1988 CarswellBC 301 (B.C.C.A.). Compensatory maintenance was not granted where the wife's claim was founded on the ground that she gave up her goals in order to support the appellant in becoming an ophthalmologist, and that the his ability to earn a substantial income was due in part to her contribution. The wife did receive benefits from her husband's training, and during the marriage she had a higher standard of living and, afterwards, higher maintenance. Most of the husband's present income was attributable to his hard work, some to his qualifications.

*Relevance of causal connection test in different types of relationship — Linton v. Linton*, 1988 CarswellOnt 198, 11 R.F.L. (3d) 444, 64 O.R. (2d) 18, 29 E.T.R. 14, 49 D.L.R. (4th) 278 (Ont. H.C.); affirmed 1990 CarswellOnt 316, 30 R.F.L. (3d) 1, 1 O.R. (3d) 1, 41 E.T.R. 85, 42 O.A.C. 328, 75 D.L.R. (4th) 637 (Ont. C.A.). The Ontario Court of Appeal in *Linton v. Linton* held that the causal connection principles are relevant only to the extent that a causal connection requirement or objective may be taken to emerge from the *Divorce Act*, 1985. Osborne J.A., writing for the court, found that the specific references to a causal connection in s. 17(10) and to elements of causal connection in s. 15 indicate some relevancy and that to a limited extent the causal connection requirement is applicable both on original support claims and on applications to vary support orders. Generally, the courts consider that there should not be any responsibility for spousal support in a marriage of short duration, especially where both spouses have been employed and where there are no children. In such situations, there is no causal connection between economic need and the marriage relationship. For support applications following the dissolution of these relationships, the principle of self-sufficiency rather than the principle of causal connection should be given priority. However, courts were likely to find a causal connection between a spouse's economic need and the marriage where the parties had had a long traditional marriage. The objective of self-sufficiency is clearly qualified by Parliament's expression "insofar as practicable".

*Assisting in spouse's education* — Berry v. Murray, 1982 CarswellBC 665, 30 R.F.L. (2d) 310, [1983] 1 W.W.R. 561 (B.C.C.A.). The husband's appeal against an order requiring him to pay monthly maintenance of $900 to his wife was dismissed. As the wife had supported her husband through medical school, she could not be expected to be self-sufficient when she had sacrificed her own development to further his ability to earn a substantial income.

*Medium-term marriage with close economic ties and compensatory claim* — *indefinite support* — T. (T.) v. H. (J.M.), 2014 CarswellBC 725, 2014 BCSC 451 (B.C.S.C.). The parties were married for 17 years and the wife sought indefinite spousal support. The judge found that, although the parties had a medium-term marriage, they were a close economic unit and support should reflect that the wife had a "presumptive claim to equal standards of living" on the dissolution of the marriage.

*Self-sufficiency did not result in termination of support after 8 years when entitlement was compensatory* — Holman v. Holman, 2013 CarswellOnt 16472, 2013 ONSC 6988 (Ont. S.C.J.). The parties were married for 19 years prior to separation in 2002. They had two adult daughters. The wife had been a stay-at-home mother during the marriage. She had received $300,000 from an inheritance after separation, which the judge found must be considered as part of her assets and means under the *Family Law Act*. The judge also found that her means were equal to or superior to those she enjoyed during the marriage. She had attained self-sufficiency. Spousal support was not terminated because it had been paid for 10 years.

*Where no significant economic reliance was created by a short-term marriage and the payor has no earning capacity, spousal support will terminate* — G. (C.A.) v. G. (S.), 2012 CarswellAlta 1619, 2012 ABQB 529, 24 R.F.L. (7th) 461, 70 Alta. L.R. (5th) 388, [2013] 2 W.W.R. 773, 548 A.R. 226 (Alta. Q.B.). The husband sought, *inter alia*, to terminate or reduce spousal support and spousal support arrears. The parties separated in 2001. The husband had been involved in a motor vehicle accident which was found to have reduced his ability to earn income. The judge considered the factors in s. 15.2(4) in determining that on-going spousal support should be reduced to zero. The parties had a very short marriage of less than 2 years. The wife did not become economically dependent on the husband during cohabitation because the husband was unwilling or unable to work at that time and the wife was responsible for supporting the family. However, the judge found that the wife was entitled to compensatory support on the basis that she did not receive adequate compensation for her economic efforts given that she was also responsible for childcare.

*Negating arguments raised by 79-year-old husband that wife's medical and financial position no worse than prior to marriage, that she had relatives available to assist her, and that he wished to give assets to his son, not alter his obligation to provide non-compensatory support* — Fedor v. Fedor, 2011 CarswellAlta 418, 2011 ABQB 185, 96 R.F.L. (6th) 309, 525 A.R. 128, 46 Alta. L.R. (5th) 221, [2011] A.J. No. 314 (Alta. Q.B.). Following a 12-year marriage, the wife age 70 and the husband age 79 separated. The wife had suffered from fibromyalgia and arthritis before and during the marriage. Following the separation, the wife had an income of $17,105.77 and resided with her brother as she had done prior to the marriage. The husband earned $116,625.48 per year from his pensions and investments. On the wife's application for interim spousal support, the husband raised the fact of a prenuptial agreement, but it was held that it did not address the issue of support. The husband also argued that the wife who had been married twice before with three children, was being assisted by her brother, and that her health and financial position had not deteriorated during the marriage. The court awarded the wife interim support in the amount of $1,500 per month. The court stated that the primary burden of support takes precedence over the possible availability of support from relatives which is consistent with the recognition of the economic disadvantages and hardship sustained by the wife arising from the marriage breakdown within the meaning of sections 15.2 (6) (a) and (c) of the *Divorce Act*. While she may be situated similarly to her pre-marriage position, she is disadvantaged in comparison to the position she enjoyed while married. Nor did the fact that she had left the marriage alter the obligation. Further the husband's wish to give interest-earning assets to his son did not displace his obligation to the wife.

*[15.2(6)(a) and (b)] Husband's application for compensatory spousal support, relatively short period of cohabitation — Adams v. Adams,* 2011 CarswellAlta 948, 2011 ABQB 306, 5 R.F.L. (7th) 258, 53 Alta. L.R. (5th) 20 (Alta. Q.B). The husband, an airline pilot, and the wife, a doctor, cohabited four and one half years of a nine-year marriage. They had two children. At the time of the marriage, the husband was 37 and the wife was 35 years old. The husband sought spousal support on the basis of his claims that he contributed to her education in qualifying as a gastroenterologist, that he was a homemaker during the marriage, and that his career was stalled for reasons associated with the marriage. On the evidence, the court stated that the husband was more similar to someone in semi-retirement than a homemaker, that the parties' incomes had little connection to the marriage and that the husband had not been disadvantaged in his career other than by his own lack of initiative, and choices, except for a relatively short period of time. The husband was awarded two years compensatory support of $24,000, but was also ordered to pay three years of retroactive child support.

*Sixteen years of spousal support is not unreasonable after an almost 20-year marriage, given the disparity in the parties' incomes during the marriage and since separation — Dishman v. Dishman,* 2010 CarswellOnt 7700, 2010 ONSC 5239, 94 R.F.L. (6th) 217, 2010 C.E.B. & P.G.R. 8406 (Ont. S.C.J.).

*Reduced career achievements — childcare — Duff v. Duff,* 2007 CarswellNB 342, 2007 NBQB 222, 322 N.B.R. (2d) 219, 829 A.P.R. 219 (N.B.Q.B.). Where the wife was economically disadvantaged at the time of the breakdown of the marriage, as she had only worked part-time so that she could look after the children, she was entitled to spousal support. Her current work record combined with her Certified Management Accountant designation would have led probably to significant financial security and benefits had she remained in the workplace full time. Probably, upon her return to the workplace she would become self sufficient. Parties had agreed to use figures of $35,856 for wife's income and $83,000 for husband's income. Monthly support of $1,000 for 18 months was appropriate. The marriage had lasted 15 years.

*Education interrupted — move to Canada — review order for support — Damian v. Damian,* 2007 CarswellOnt 3468 (Ont. S.C.J.); additional reasons at 2007 CarswellOnt 3169 (Ont. S.C.J.). Where the mother's education was interrupted by the parties move to Canada and later by their separation, she was entitled to spousal support at least until she could retrain. The order was to be reviewed in 3 years' time.

*No conventional career path — entitled to support — Colquhoun v. Colquhoun,* 2007 CarswellOnt 18 (Ont. S.C.J.). The wife was entitled to support where she had given up a conventional career path to pursue entrepreneurial pursuits, the separation left her without an established career path or the means to pursue further entrepreneurial ventures, and she, at 49, was of an age where it would be difficult for her to recover. The wife was dependent on the husband during the marriage, as he was able to maintain his career in sales while working on their entrepreneurial businesses when it was convenient for him to do so. The wife had established need and the husband had the means to provide and to earn more income. The situation was not going to change and consequently the spousal support should not be time-limited.

*Wife employed during marriage but entitled to compensation — Marshall v. Marshall,* 2007 CarswellNS 618, 2008 NSSC 11, 47 R.F.L. (6th) 327, 835 A.P.R. 18, 261 N.S.R. (2d) 18 (N.S.S.C.). Where the wife had been employed during the marriage, but her employment had been secondary to her role as a homemaker, she was granted spousal support. The husband had been the primary wage earner throughout the marriage and, although the wife was employed, it was only on a casual basis and with no seniority. Accordingly, the wife was suffering the most negative financial consequences of the marriage breakdown.

*Where the economic hardship after the breakdown of a short marriage does not fall more heavily on the support applicant, no support should be awarded* — McKee v. Priestlay, 2007 CarswellBC 1375, 2007 BCSC 852 (B.C.S.C.). The parties cohabited for less than 3 years. The plaintiff did not interrupt career plans to enter the relationship or to raise the defendant's family. She benefitted economically from the marriage. If anyone suffered economically from the marriage, it was the defendant.

*Despite income differential, no compensatory support awarded* — Lamothe v. Lamothe, 2006 CarswellOnt 8150, 35 R.F.L. (6th) 148 (Ont. S.C.J.). The husband's application for spousal support was dismissed. Although the husband had been unemployed throughout many years of the marriage and the wife's income was considerably higher, the husband had failed to prove an economic disadvantage resulting from the marriage. The husband had suffered from a medical issue, but that had been long resolved and the evidence supported the conclusion that the husband had consciously decided to remain at home and not seek employment or training for a number of years.

*Claimant unemployed at time of proceedings but had worked through marriage — no support* — Lambton v. Lambton, 2004 CarswellBC 2606, 2004 BCSC 1400, 9 R.F.L. (6th) 400 (B.C.S.C.); additional reasons at 2004 CarswellBC 3062, 2004 BCSC 1725 (B.C.S.C.). The wife's claim for spousal support was dismissed upon the termination of the parties' 5-year marriage. Although unemployed at the time of the proceedings, the 48-year-old wife had worked throughout the marriage and had not suffered any economic disadvantage as a result of the marriage or its breakdown.

*Absence from workforce — compensated — no entitlement to support* — McCorriston v. McCorriston, 2006 CarswellSask 265, 2006 SKQB 217 (Sask. Q.B.). If a dependant spouse, on account of a marriage, loses no skills, seniority or pension benefits and leaves the marriage with more assets than she had upon entering the marriage, and her husband supported her children from a prior marriage, the economic advantages she received from the marriage more than compensate for any economic loss she may have suffered as a result of being out of the workforce.

*Debt for re-training — relocating for spouse's employment — economic disadvantage* — Traversy v. Glover, 2006 CarswellOnt 4380, 30 R.F.L. (6th) 372, [2006] O.J. No. 2908 (Ont. S.C.J.). Where, after separation, the wife had to borrow money to finance her retraining, her application for lump sum support as partial reimbursement for the loan was allowed. The wife had given up her employment to relocate with the husband and had then remained in the home for a number of years to care for the parties' children. The wife's debt could be properly characterized as an economic disadvantage resulting from the breakdown of the marriage.

*Both disadvantaged but one spouse having greater difficulty in recovering* — Coxworthy v. Coxworthy, 2006 CarswellNS 308, 2006 NSSC 205 (N.S.S.C.). Where both parties were disadvantaged by the breakdown of the marriage, but it would be more difficult for the wife to recover from those disadvantages because of her disability, which made her unable to work, the court ordered the husband to pay spousal support of $200 per month.

*Absence from workforce — entitled to spousal support* — Crawford v. Crawford, 2006 CarswellBC 2754, 2006 BCSC 1664 (B.C.S.C.). The wife gave up a career in the public service and despite her best efforts is not able to re-enter the job market at anywhere close to the level she would have achieved had she remained in the workforce. She also lost her pension and benefits, even though she received, in partial recognition of this fact, about 62% of the family assets and non-spousal support but she needs spousal support in order to live in the modest way she lived during the marriage. She was found entitled to spousal support. The court considered both the factors and the objectives under the *Divorce Act*.

*Assisted in spouse's career — entitled to 2 years spousal support — Al Hosseini v. Kazemi*, 2006 CarswellBC 1077, 2006 BCSC 693 (B.C.S.C.); additional reasons at 2006 CarswellBC 1966, 2006 BCSC 1154 (B.C.S.C.). Where the dependant spouse devoted herself to the furtherance of her husband's career goals, without completely setting aside her own career objectives, she was entitled to 2 years' support to pursue establishing a private occupational therapy practice. Following this period, there would be an automatic review of both issues of entitlement and quantum of support.

*Support entitlement after "traditional" marriage — McAuley v. McAuley*, 2006 CarswellBC 2711, 2006 BCSC 1643 (B.C.S.C.). Where the parties were married for a lengthy period of time during which the wife had the primary responsibility for the children and home and the husband was the main wage earner, the wife was awarded spousal support.

*Support awarded given length of marriage and its highly traditional nature — wife had been largely absent from the job market and had not obtained qualifications — Tsurugido v. Romero*, 2006 CarswellBC 2904, 2006 BCSC 1754 (B.C.S.C.). The parties had been married for 21 years and the wife had been a stay-at-home mother throughout the marriage.

*Wife's relocations to support husband's career were not a basis for compensatory support but debt arising from his bankruptcy was a basis — Romaniuk v. Romaniuk*, 2005 CarswellOnt 1779, 17 R.F.L. (6th) 272 (Ont. S.C.J.); additional reasons at 2005 CarswellOnt 1780 (Ont. S.C.J.). The court dismissed the wife's claim for compensatory support where, after being laid off by her employer, she voluntarily moved from the city in which she lived to another city to pursue a relationship with the respondent. She later moved to yet another city to pursue her career and the respondent followed her. Subsequently, she left that employment and moved to Ottawa with the respondent. She had had employment in a number of different fields, and was pursuing a career as a dispatcher. She was, in fact, unemployed when she finally did move to Ottawa. The facts of the case do not support a compensatory order for support in terms of any loss of career opportunity on the part of the applicant. However, the applicant was entitled to compensatory support on account of her debt which arose from his declaration of bankruptcy.

*No economic dependence during marriage — spouse leaves employment — no support — Charbonneau v. Charbonneau*, 2004 CarswellOnt 5211, 9 R.F.L. (6th) 67 (Ont. S.C.J.). Where the wife had never been financially dependant on the husband during the parties' 5-year marriage and had voluntarily left her full-time employment after separation, her claim for spousal support was dismissed.

*Nature of entitlement to compensatory support — Taylor v. Taylor*, 2004 CarswellOnt 4851, 10 R.F.L. (6th) 202, [2004] O.J. No. 4802 (Ont. S.C.J.). There are three different thresholds for compensatory support found in clauses 15.2(6)(a), (b) and (c) of the *Divorce Act*. (1) an "economic disadvantage" to a spouse which arises from "the marriage or its breakdown" (clause 15.2(6)(a)); or (2) "financial consequences [to a spouse] arising from the care of any child of the marriage" that needs apportioning (clause 15.2(6)(b)); or (3) some "economic hardship" to a spouse flowing from "the breakdown of the marriage" (clause 15.2(6)(c)). Although subsection 15.2(6) is phrased conjunctively, a party need only cross one of the thresholds to be entitled to compensatory support. Under clause 15.2(6)(a), fairness is a test that may be used. In other words, the court should act on a proven economic disadvantage where the disadvantage is of such a degree that it would be unfair to ignore. In this case, the wife sought compensatory support to reflect her share of "the financial losses" sustained as a consequence of the marriage, the separation and the conduct of the husband. The husband had become extremely depressed after his daughter's murder and eventually he had a mental breakdown and declared bankruptcy. The court held that the wife had suffered an unfavourable condition and therefore an economic disadvantage arising from the marriage or its breakdown and was entitled to specific compensatory support in the sum of $10,517.

*Joint decision that wife leave employment to care for children is a basis for compensatory support — Skrivanek v. Pow*, 2004 CarswellBC 2949, 2004 BCSC 1609 (B.C.S.C.). The wife was entitled to compensatory support to recognize her lost economic opportunity through a joint decision for many years that she not work full-time so she could care for the children.

*Purpose of compensatory support — relocation — Walkden v. Walkden*, 2004 CarswellAlta 1799, 2004 ABQB 823 (Alta. Q.B.). The purpose of compensatory support is to compensate a spouse who has given up his or her own economic security for the purpose of caring for children and supporting his or her spouse's career. In this case, the wife was working full time and had her own career before marriage. After the parties' marriage, she followed the husband to Saudi Arabia where, as a woman, she was technically not able to work. However, she did work from time to time in order to keep herself busy rather than to earn an income. When her first child was born in 1980, she left the work force entirely to stay at home with the children. Since returning to Canada she had taken additional upgrading courses and was now working full time. She would never be able to replace the income and positions she would have received had they not gone to Saudi Arabia. She was the classic case for which compensatory spousal support was intended. The court awarded her a lump sum of $300,000 in compensatory support.

*Relocating for spouse's employment — Kaluza v. Kaluza*, 2003 CarswellBC 3132, 2003 BCSC 1879, 50 R.F.L. (5th) 71 (B.C.S.C.). Where the wife remained employed throughout the marriage, but had moved several times to support the husband's career, she was found to have suffered an economic disadvantage and was awarded limited term support for a period of 5 years. The wife's career had suffered as she had less seniority and experience as a result of the moves and her childcare responsibilities.

*Evidence of exceptional contribution beyond household management and childcare required for compensatory support — DeCicco v. DeCicco*, 2003 CarswellOnt 4364, 45 R.F.L. (5th) 147 (Ont. S.C.J.); additional reasons at 2003 CarswellOnt 4937, 47 R.F.L. (5th) 312 (Ont. S.C.J.). A claim for compensatory support arises when one spouse confers on the other a benefit that would unjustly enrich the other, if he or she were allowed to retain the benefit without some form of accounting made to the conferring spouse. Generally, there must be something more than the assumption of household management and child-care to justify an award of compensatory support. There should be evidence of an exceptional contribution.

*Compensation for husband's failure to provide promised employment to wife — Collins v. Collins*, 2003 CarswellNfld 168, 2003 NLSCTD 102, 42 R.F.L. (5th) 273, 229 Nfld. & P.E.I.R. 1, 679 A.P.R. 1, [2003] N.J. No. 169 (N.L.T.D.). The husband had agreed to provide his wife with employment for a certain period and was ordered to pay $1,000 as compensatory support for failure to do so.

*Neither party economically disadvantaged by marriage — no support — Voiculescu v. Voiculescu*, 2003 CarswellNS 252, 2003 NSSF 29, 42 R.F.L. (5th) 215 (N.S.S.C.); additional reasons at 2003 CarswellNS 564, 2003 NSSF 46, 2 R.F.L. (6th) 228 (N.S.S.C.). Where the wife's income actually exceeded that of the husband, her application for spousal support was dismissed. While both parties suffered financial setbacks during marriage, neither had been more economically disadvantaged by the marriage than the other.

*Absence from employment — Hill v. Magee*, 2002 CarswellBC 522, 2002 BCSC 353, 26 R.F.L. (5th) 95, [2002] B.C.J. No. 516 (B.C.S.C.). The wife was awarded periodic spousal support without any time limitation upon dissolution of the parties' 23-year marriage. Although she was employed, she had been out of the workforce for 10 years when rearing the children. She had achieved the highest level of full-time employment to which she could aspire given her education and experience and her income was insufficient to meet even a modest standard of living.

*Variation — support increased where wife adversely affected by the marriage and her dependence on the marriage — Eccles v. Eccles*, 2002 CarswellOnt 1284, 27 R.F.L. (5th) 47 (Ont. S.C.J.), the wife had, for 10 years during the parties' marital cohabitation, sublimated her own career development and for 10 years following separation had devoted herself to the care of the children. Eventually custody was transferred to the husband, which further aggravated the wife's fragile mental state and limited her employment opportunities. The court dismissed the husband's application to terminate her spousal support and upwardly adjusted the support payable and included a lump sum award. There was a wide disparity between the employment abilities of the parties resulting directly from the marriage and the wife's financial dependence on the marriage was a complete one.

*Disadvantage to spouse claiming support not necessary to justify compensation if other spouse received advantage from marriage — Shaw v. Shaw*, 2002 CarswellOnt 2333, [2002] O.J. No. 2782 (Ont. S.C.J.). In order to establish entitlement to spousal support based on compensatory grounds, it is not essential that the court find that the applicant was economically disadvantaged by the role she played in the relationship. The objectives of the *Divorce Act* speak of "economic advantages or disadvantages to the spouses". Even if the applicant did not experience a disadvantage, the fact that her spouse experienced an advantage gives rise to an entitlement to spousal support. In this case, the wife who worked full time was found to be the mainstay of the household during much of the marriage, relieving the childcare provider and managing the childcare needs. Her assumption of responsibility for those two aspects of household management relieved the husband of those responsibilities and allowed him to make his career his priority. It followed that applicant established on the balance of probabilities that she was entitled to compensatory spousal support. For the first 2 years of their marriage, the wife made more money than the husband. After that time, his income significantly increased and thereafter the gap between their incomes widened dramatically. While the wife's ability to contribute to a R.R.S.P. was interrupted by her maternity leaves and her change of jobs, the husband's contribution to a spousal R.R.S.P. compensated for this disadvantage. The wife became less career oriented once she had children. The court found that there was no evidence that the wife refused any opportunities or declined to pursue any educational programmes which would have enhanced her marketability. There was no independent evidence from the wife's superiors at her former employer's as to her value as an employee and whether her commitment to her family undermined or precluded promotion. Nor was there any evidence whether her innate abilities would have limited her prospects of advancement. The court was not prepared to find that the disadvantage which the wife experienced as a result of her role in the relationship was significant. However, the fact that the husband did receive an advantage led to the wife's entitlement to compensatory support.

*Reduced earning capacity — Higgins v. Higgins*, 2001 CarswellOnt 2729, 19 R.F.L. (5th) 300, [2001] O.T.C. 576, [2001] O.J. No. 3011 (Ont. S.C.J.). The wife was awarded $1,000 monthly support upon the breakdown of the parties' 18-year marriage. Although the wife had failed to adduce sufficient evidence that her health prevented her from working, there was evidence that she had been economically disadvantaged by her role in the marriage and its breakdown. She would never have the same earning capacity as the husband and would never, on her own, be able to regain her pre-separation standard of living.

*Dependant spouse discouraged from working for same firm as other spouse — West v. Marche*, 2001 CarswellNfld 117, 17 R.F.L. (5th) 458, 200 Nfld. & P.E.I.R. 341, 603 A.P.R. 341, [2001] N.J. No. 115 (Nfld. T.D.). Where the husband had discouraged the wife from seeking employment with the same company for which he worked, he could not, after the parties' separation, claim that he had no obligation to support her, at least to some degree, until she became self-supporting. The wife would have been in a better position to become self-sufficient, but for the husband's insistence that she not work and was accordingly entitled to periodic support.

*Small compensatory award made in absence of much evidence of loss — Beaton v. Beaton,* 2001 CarswellNS 419, 2001 NSSF 30, 20 R.F.L. (5th) 252, 199 N.S.R. (2d) 271, 623 A.P.R. 271 (N.S.S.C.). The wife was granted very limited compensatory support where she was absent from the workforce for approximately 4 years and the court had little or no evidence quantifying her "loss of seniority, promotion opportunities, training and pension contributions". She had received $1,100 per month for 13 months and was entitled to a further $1,000 per month for a period of 1 year and $725 per month in spousal support for an additional year.

*Claimant had been encouraged by spouse to take early retirement but was not in need — no compensatory support — Launchbury v. Launchbury,* 2001 CarswellOnt 1384, 15 R.F.L. (5th) 106 (Ont. S.C.J.); affirmed 2005 CarswellOnt 1335, 12 R.F.L. (6th) 393 (Ont. C.A.). A court will not award compensatory support to a party whose spouse induced her to take early retirement so that they could purchase and run a business together where, at the time of the hearing, the party was earning close to her previous income and had a significant net worth ($500,000) and did not require support.

*Wife moved and abandoned business — no children — compensatory support justified — Tabata v. Smith,* 2001 CarswellAlta 1294, 2001 ABQB 776, 21 R.F.L. (5th) 451, 297 A.R. 168 (Alta. Q.B.). Where there is a short marriage of 5 years, a spouse is still entitled to compensatory support, where she left her business which she co-owned and helped to build, and relocated to another province to be with her husband. As a result of her leaving, the company experienced financial difficulties and eventually failed. The parties did not have children. Both were employed at the time of the hearing and the wife was becoming self sufficient. The court found that had the wife not married, she would have stayed in the province where her business was located and would have continued to run her business which would have been a successful enterprise. She was required to forgo this business opportunity because of the marriage and therefore was entitled to lump sum compensatory support.

*Compensatory support calculated to equal lost income plus assist in start-up costs for new business — Dunn v. Menear,* 2000 CarswellOnt 4778, 14 R.F.L. (5th) 293 (Ont. S.C.J.). Support should be ordered to compensate a spouse for loss of income for the time (6 months) that he was prevented from carrying on his old law practice and to provide some assistance in financing the start-up costs of a new practice. The husband was unable to carry on his old law practice, as he was convicted of assaulting his wife and spent some time in jail, followed by time on probation where he was forbidden from being in the city where his old practice was situated. The wife was required to pay a lump sum payment of support based upon the husband's average monthly billings in a total amount of $9,000. That sum was reduced to allow for the fact that the lump sum payment would not be deductible to the applicant and would not be taxable in the hands of the respondent. The husband had given up his job in Toronto to work in Orillia where the wife was employed.

*Variation — support continued where wife economically dependant after a lengthy traditional marriage — Krill v. Krill,* 2000 CarswellAlta 136, 4 R.F.L. (5th) 249 (Alta. Q.B.), the court refused the husband's application for a downward variation of the spousal support payable by him. At the time of the divorce, the wife had been enrolled in university with the intent of upgrading her skills. She had, however, voluntarily dropped out and was unemployed, although attempting to start a career. Given the parties' long-term traditional marriage, it was found that it was not unreasonable for the wife to remain economically dependent on the husband 2 1/2 years after the divorce and 5 1/2 years after the parties' separation. Accordingly, the wife's support was extended for a further 2 years.

*Wife had found new work in the same field but still entitled to compensatory support —* *Halloran v. Hotte*, 2000 CarswellOnt 3997, 12 R.F.L. (5th) 57 (Ont. S.C.J.). The wife was granted spousal support for 3 years upon dissolution of the parties' 9-year marriage. The wife had left her civil service job during the marriage to care for the parties' children. Although she was once again employed as a civil servant, her salary was much lower than it could have been if she had not given up her job. The wife was 33 years old and her salary would likely increase over time, eliminating her need for spousal support.

*Claimant had worked while doing most household labour, allowing husband to develop* *career — Weir v. Weir*, 2000 CarswellBC 1892, 2000 BCSC 1391, 11 R.F.L. (5th) 223, 80 B.C.L.R. (3d) 342, [2000] B.C.J. No. 1900 (B.C.S.C.). Where, throughout the parties' 21-year marriage, the wife had performed the bulk of household and family duties while continuing to work full-time, she was awarded both lump sum and limited term periodic support, which together would promote her eventual self-sufficiency. The wife's efforts had freed the husband to pursue more lucrative career and business opportunities.

*No loss or hardship resulting from marriage — support denied — Stewart v. Stewart*, 2000 CarswellNS 316, 12 R.F.L. (5th) 218 (N.S.S.C.). The court refused the husband's application for spousal support upon dissolution of the parties' 38-year marriage. The husband had retired from the military and his health impeded his ability to work, while the wife continued to be employed as a nurse. Although the wife could afford to pay, the husband could not point to any economic loss or hardship resulting from the marriage, which justified his claim.

*Variation — importance of loss of other spouse's income stream as an economic* *disadvantage to the wife — Provost v. Provost*, 1999 CarswellAlta 1067, 2 R.F.L. (5th) 442 (Alta. Q.B.). The loss on marriage breakdown of an income stream generated by her husband is an economic disadvantage to the wife which should be considered in favour of the wife on the husband's application to reduce spousal support where there is a great disparity in their incomes.

*Foregone career — Schmuck v. Reynolds-Schmuck*, 1999 CarswellOnt 2424, 50 R.F.L. (4th) 429, [1999] O.J. No. 3104 (Ont. S.C.J.); additional reasons at 2000 CarswellOnt 202, 46 O.R. (3d) 702, [2000] O.J. No. 247 (Ont. S.C.J.). Where the wife had made sacrifices in foregoing her own career as a secretary, had suffered economic hardship because of the marriage and its breakdown, had need and the husband had the ability to pay, then the wife was entitled to spousal support.

*Absence from workforce — moving for spouse's work — entitled to 9 months support —* *Weekes v. Weekes*, 1998 CarswellMan 32, 36 R.F.L. (4th) 323, 124 Man. R. (2d) 317 (Man. Q.B.). Where the wife moved with the husband from New York to Winnipeg to further his career with the result that she severely limited her own, she was awarded 9 months' spousal support. But for the marriage and the move, the wife would have been self-sufficient.

*Lesser careers — Moura v. Moura*, 1998 CarswellOnt 4919, 43 R.F.L. (4th) 344, [1998] O.J. No. 5351 (Ont. Gen. Div.). The court held that secondary-earner wives who continue to work during the marriage while assuming the responsibility of the primary child caregiver, but whose employment is subordinated to those of their husbands, are disadvantaged in terms of career advancement and should be entitled to spousal support. The wife in this case was awarded $400 monthly support for an indeterminate period.

*Variation — spousal support terminated where frequent separations did not cause wife's* *need and did not flow from marriage — Kurbegovich v. Kurbegovich*, 1998 CarswellOnt 267, 36 R.F.L. (4th) 220 (Ont. Gen. Div.). The court allowed the husband's application to terminate the wife's spousal support 7 years after the parties' divorce. The parties had separated frequently throughout their marriage with the result that the wife's need did not flow from a pattern of dependency created by the marriage. In addition, the 39-year-old wife could have returned to employment similar to that held prior to marriage, but had failed to do so.

*Absence from workforce — moving for spouse's work — entitled to support — Timms v. Timms*, 1997 CarswellAlta 439, 29 R.F.L. (4th) 392, 51 Alta. L.R. (3d) 99, [1997] 7 W.W.R. 392, 203 A.R. 81, [1997] A.J. No. 463 (Alta. Q.B.); additional reasons at 1997 CarswellAlta 574, [1998] 4 W.W.R. 458, 204 A.R. 398, 55 Alta. L.R. (3d) 138 (Alta. Q.B.). Where the wife had emigrated to Canada to improve the husband's job security and had thereby negatively affected her own career, the court found she was entitled to support with no specified termination date. During the 13-year marriage the wife had remained in the home to raise the parties' child and had always put her own needs after those of the husband and son.

*Long-term traditional marriage — support awarded to wife employed full time — Blair v. Blair*, 1997 CarswellOnt 4908, 34 R.F.L. (4th) 370, [1997] O.J. No. 4949 (Ont. Gen. Div.). Where the parties had cohabited in a traditional, long-term marriage of 22 years in which the husband advanced his career and the wife stayed at home to care for the family, time-limited spousal support would not compensate her for the economic disadvantage she suffered, nor would it pay for the economic advantage it gave to the husband. Although the wife at the time of the proceedings was employed nearly full-time, she was awarded spousal support of $300 per month for an indefinite period.

*Decision to give up teaching career not a basis for support in light of other factors — R. (W.H.) v. R. (J.M.)*, 1997 CarswellOnt 3178, [1997] O.J. No. 2795 (Ont. Gen. Div.). The court dismissed a claim for lump sum compensatory support, based primarily on the loss to the wife arising from the fact she gave up her teaching career when the family moved from Quebec to Ontario in 1983. The court held that the Ontario Court of Appeal has been critical of lump sum compensatory support to redress alleged economic loss claimed to be caused by one decision made during the marriage. Considering an order for support compensatory or otherwise the *Divorce Act* directed that consideration of the condition, means, needs and other circumstances of each spouse be taken into account. Financially the parties were relatively equal. Each had property of approximately $100,000 and earning power of $45,000 per annum. The wife had a better education including musical talent. She had superior living skills, resiliency, and health and was clearly the stronger person. The husband had had an unfortunate life experience and except for finances, had less than his wife in every category. The court held that the compensatory lump sum and child support claims were more than satisfied by the value the wife had enjoyed in the use of the equalization payment ($100,500) for the last 7 years.

*Relevance of fact that wife had chosen to re-train rather than seek immediate employment — Worst v. Worst*, 1997 CarswellBC 1985 (B.C.S.C.). The court denied a claim for compensatory spousal support in the following circumstances. (1) There had already been an equitable sharing of the economic consequences of the marriage and its breakdown with the reapportionment of the matrimonial home. (2) The wife had not suffered an economic disadvantage in the relationship such as to trigger a right to compensatory support. (3) The husband did not continue to reap economic advantages from the relationship. (4) The wife had chosen not to pursue employment with her existing qualifications but, instead, decided to attend retraining courses. A court should not place responsibility for that economic decision on the respondent. The court stated that of the two, upon completing her studies, the wife likely faced the more secure future.

*Absence from workforce — now employed — no evidence of disadvantage — not entitled to support — Begin v. Begin*, 1996 CarswellNS 521, 156 N.S.R. (2d) 253, 461 A.P.R. 253 (N.S.S.C.). Where the wife herself had chosen to abandon her career after becoming pregnant, but was employed at the time of separation, her application for spousal support was dismissed. There was no evidence that she had been disadvantaged by the marriage or its breakdown.

*Marriage and breakdown justify compensatory support for re-training — Lanctot v. Lanctot*, 1996 CarswellOnt 2518, 6 O.T.C. 161 (Ont. Gen. Div.). The court held that because of the marriage and its breakdown, the wife was cast out on her own with no work experience. She was entitled to compensatory support sufficient to enable her to retrain. The husband had been a chaplain in the military and had taken various postings in Canada and Europe. The military terminated the husband's employment. He eventually obtained employment on a contract basis. Shortly after the husband told the wife that he wished to end their marriage, she was admitted to hospital, depressed and suicidal and she continued to suffer from depression at the time of the proceedings.

*Relocated to further spouse's career; husband entitled to support*— Stefanyk v. Clancy, 1996 CarswellNS 509, 27 R.F.L. (4th) 256, 156 N.S.R. (2d) 161, 461 A.P.R. 161 (N.S.S.C.).

*Absence from workforce — assisting in spouse's education — quantum —* Keyes v. Keyes, 1996 CarswellNS 45, 17 R.F.L. (4th) 201, 148 N.S.R. (2d) 239, 429 A.P.R. 239 (N.S.S.C.). The wife was found to have been economically disadvantaged by the marriage even though she had resumed full-time employment many years prior to separation. The wife had withdrawn from the workforce for a period of 12 years to raise the children and allow the husband to complete his education from which he derived an economic advantage. Given the 24-year duration of the marriage prior to separation and the fact that, despite the wife's employment, the husband remained the primary provider, the wife was entitled to a lifestyle equal to his.

*Marriage of long duration — claimant suffering from economic disadvantages of marriage —* Burke v. Burke, 1996 CarswellNS 302, 153 N.S.R. (2d) 1, 450 A.P.R. 1 (N.S.S.C.). The court awarded spousal support to the wife taking into account the length of the marriage of 23 years. She had suffered economic hardship because of the marriage. Her lack of income was directly related to her assuming the role of a home making spouse and mother. By giving priority to the raising of the children she lost many of the skills required in her profession of nursing. She was awarded spousal support of $1,600 a month for the life of the parties, and a lump sum support payment of $2,500.

*Support applicant's contribution to unremunerative business not a basis for compensatory support —* French v. French, 1996 CarswellNB 385, [1996] N.B.R. (2d) (Supp.) No. 39, [1996] N.B.J. No. 386 (N.B.Q.B.). Where a party undertakes work and expense to assist his or her spouse through training and helps in a business, no compensatory support is payable where the business is based almost entirely on the spouse's ability and will probably only be a hobby, depending a great deal on the respondent's incentive and interest in doing the work involved. In this case, the spouse did return to his former employment where he worked until retirement. The applicant wife was not entitled to compensatory support.

*Support even though spouse had earned reasonable income during marriage —* O'Hara v. O'Hara, 1995 CarswellNB 43, 15 R.F.L. (4th) 408, 421 A.P.R. 295, 164 N.B.R. (2d) 295 (N.B.Q.B.). The wife was found to have been disadvantaged by the breakdown of the parties' 8-year marriage and was awarded support for a period of 2 years, although she had worked and earned a reasonable income throughout the marriage.

*Absence from workforce, loss of benefits — some advantages —* Stebbins v. Stebbins, 1995 CarswellNS 67, 14 R.F.L. (4th) 226 (N.S.S.C.). Where the parties agreed that the wife would not work during the marriage, she was found entitled to spousal support. Although the wife had benefitted through extensive travel and the furtherance of her education, she had also suffered adverse economic effects such as the loss of earning powers and benefits which she would have obtained if she had entered the workforce at an earlier age.

*Loss of financial security of marriage not in of itself a relevant factor regarding compensatory support —* Kernahan v. Skworoda, 1995 CarswellBC 2669 (B.C.S.C.). It was held that the wife's loss of the financial security created by the marriage was not a factor to be considered in determining her entitlement to compensatory support.

*Claimant unable to work but no disadvantage from marriage or breakdown — no support —* Noseworthy v. Noseworthy, 1995 CarswellNfld 128, 17 R.F.L. (4th) 21, 136 Nfld. & P.E.I.R. 64,

423 A.P.R. 64, [1995] N.J. No. 360 (Nfld. U.F.C.). The husband's claim for spousal support was dismissed upon termination of the parties' 2-year marriage. Although he was no longer able to work because of a medical condition and could not achieve self-sufficiency, he had suffered no economic disadvantage from the marriage or its breakdown.

*Claimant in better position than other spouse at end of marriage, her reduced income due to personal choice — no support — Stich v. Stich,* 1995 CarswellBC 1094, 17 R.F.L. (4th) 178 (B.C.S.C.). Compensatory support is only justified on the basis of recognizing any economic advantages or disadvantages caused by the marriage. Where the wife was actually in a better position than the husband at the end of the marriage and any decrease in her earnings was the result of her own decision not to return to her more lucrative earlier career, her application for support was dismissed.

*Wife moved for husband's career but found a new job — loss of income not proven — no compensable loss — Prince v. Prince,* 1995 CarswellNS 201, 16 R.F.L. (4th) 236, 144 N.S.R. (2d) 47, 416 A.P.R. 47 (N.S.S.C.); additional reasons at (1996), 153 N.S.R. (2d) 356, 450 A.P.R. 356, 1996 CarswellNS 329 (N.S.S.C.); appeal allowed in part on other grounds; cross-appeal dismissed (1997), 163 N.S.R. (2d) 28, 487 A.P.R. 28, 35 R.F.L. (4th) 328, 1997 CarswellNS 444, [1997] N.S.J. No. 433 (N.S.C.A.). The wife's claim for lump sum support for "lost opportunity" because of an interruption of her career was dismissed in light of the finding that she had not suffered an economic disadvantage from the marriage in terms of her career. Although she had been forced to give up well-paying employment to move with the husband, she had located another lucrative position and her claim that had she stayed in her original job her salary would be higher was purely speculative. There was no compensable loss as a result of the wife leaving her employment.

*Wife had worked part-time during marriage but no economic disadvantage — Mullins v. Mullins,* 1995 CarswellNfld 8, 12 R.F.L. (4th) 461 (Nfld. U.F.C.). The fact that the parties had mutually decided that the wife should only pursue her nursing career part-time during the parties' 6-year marriage was found insufficient to establish that she had been economically disadvantaged. She was a trained and self-sufficient professional and she was only entitled to interim periodic support for a 6-month period to assist her in reentering the workforce.

*Claimant fails to prove that marriage prevented pursuing education — no support — Ho v. Ho,* 1993 CarswellOnt 287, 1 R.F.L. (4th) 340, [1993] O.J. No. 2919 (Ont. Gen. Div.). Where the wife had withdrawn from nursing school shortly before the marriage, contrary to the husband's wishes, her claim for support was refused. The wife was unable to prove that the marriage prevented her from returning to nursing school; accordingly, no economic disadvantage had been established.

*Economic disadvantage — loss of pooled income — support — Harris v. Harris,* 1994 CarswellBC 678, 7 R.F.L. (4th) 91 (B.C.S.C.). Where as a result of the marriage breakdown the wife lost the advantage of pooled income with her husband, she was found entitled to periodic support for a 3-year-period. Throughout the parties' 26-year marriage, both had worked and had pooled their incomes for family purposes and, absent that pooled income, the wife lacked sufficient resources to meet her needs.

*Decision to turn down teaching job not a basis for support in light of other factors — Cerget v. Cerget,* 1994 CarswellOnt 445, 7 R.F.L. (4th) 322 (Ont. Gen. Div.); additional reasons at 1994 CarswellOnt 446, 7 R.F.L. (4th) 343 (Ont. Gen. Div.); affirmed 1994 CarswellOnt 3496 (Ont. Gen. Div.). Where the wife claimed compensatory support based solely on her decision to turn down a teaching job during her engagement believing it would be detrimental to her future family life, her claim was dismissed. That approach was found to be flawed as it isolated one event in the parties' marriage and treated it as the only one to be determined by the court in determining the issue of spousal support.

*Quantum and duration connected to extent of economic disadvantage — Tully v. Tully,*
1994 CarswellOnt 475, 9 R.F.L. (4th) 131 (Ont. Gen. Div.); additional reasons at 1994
CarswellOnt 2333 (Ont. Gen. Div.). Entitlement to support depends on proof of some economic
disadvantage arising from marriage or its breakdown. The quantum and duration of the support
should bear some relation to the extent of the economic disadvantage.

*Absence from workforce — Reilly v. Reilly,* 1994 CarswellBC 645, 10 R.F.L. (4th) 6, [1994]
B.C.J. No. 2482 (B.C.S.C.); additional reasons at 1994 CarswellBC 3032, 10 R.F.L. (4th) 6 at 23
(B.C.S.C.); additional reasons at 1995 CarswellBC 2857 (B.C.S.C.); additional reasons at (1996),
1996 CarswellBC 1279 (B.C.S.C.). Although the 60-year-old wife was qualified to teach French,
she was nevertheless found entitled to support because of her age and the role of homemaker she
had performed throughout the parties' lengthy marriage.

*Absence from workforce — changes in industry — no compensatory support — Zander v.
Zander,* 1994 CarswellOnt 452, 8 R.F.L. (4th) 35, [1994] O.J. No. 4003 (Ont. Gen. Div.). The
court refused the wife's claim for compensatory support arising from the fact that she had left a
position with an airline early in the marriage to assume the role of a traditional homemaker.
Structural changes occurring in the airline industry over the years would undoubtedly have
affected the wife's career and a report which ignored these changes could not be used to
substantiate the considerable lump-sum compensation sought.

*Variation — to reduce support there must be a material change and evidence that the
economic disadvantage had been overcome — Patrick v. Patrick,* 1994 CarswellBC 221, 92
B.C.L.R. (2d) 50, [1994] 7 W.W.R. 441 (B.C.S.C.); additional reasons at 1994 CarswellBC 2894
(B.C.S.C.). In order to vary downward a compensatory support order, the payor must establish
that not only had there been a significant change in financial circumstances but also that the factors
which resulted in economic disadvantage no longer existed and that the lost advantage had been
recovered.

*Economist's evidence regarding compensable loss had too many contingencies — Petley-
Jones v. Petley-Jones,* 1993 CarswellBC 621, 48 R.F.L. (3d) 166. (B.C.S.C.) The British
Columbia Supreme Court refused to award lump sum support based upon an economist's report,
citing the number of contingencies inherent in the statistical analysis.

*Claimant's income same after marriage as it was before and assets had increased — no
support — Kessel v. Kessel,* 1993 CarswellOnt 286, 1 R.F.L. (4th) 324 (Ont. Gen. Div.); additional
reasons at 1994 CarswellOnt 3069 (Ont. Gen. Div.). Where the wife's income, both before and
after marriage, was relatively equal and her asset base had increased in value during the parties'
relationship, her claim for spousal support was dismissed.

*Substantial income differential but claimant failed to prove disadvantage from marriage —
no support — Bakken v. Bakken,* 1992 CarswellAlta 520, 132 A.R. 356 (Alta. Q.B.). The
husband's application for support was dismissed. The husband had lost his job and between
working sporadically and receiving social assistance, had maintained a monthly income of $1,500.
Although the wife had a substantial income as a medical doctor, the husband had not suffered any
economic disadvantage as a result of the marriage. The marriage had not restricted his ability to
work or to maintain and upgrade his qualifications.

*Claimant gave up career to attempt reconciliation — support awarded — Stunt v. Stunt,*
1990 CarswellOnt 329, 30 R.F.L. (3d) 353 (Ont. Gen. Div.). Where the wife voluntarily gave up
her career to attempt a reconciliation between the parties, she was awarded periodic support for a
period of 2 years to allow her to re-establish herself. She would be able to become self-sufficient,
but her career had lost its directness of path and stability because of the marriage and its
breakdown.

*Need not caused by marriage but rather by profligacy — support denied — Ryan v. Ryan,*
1989 CarswellOnt 217, 18 R.F.L. (3d) 435 (Ont. H.C.). Where the wife returned to work after

the birth of the parties' child, but lived beyond her means, her application for support was dismissed. There was no causal connection between the wife's perceived need and the marriage.

*Contribution to husband's career was helpful but not crucial — no compensatory support — McDonell v. McDonell*, 1988 CarswellBC 596, 16 R.F.L. (3d) 174 (B.C.S.C.). Where the wife's contribution to the husband's career was helpful, but not crucial, and the husband would have no doubt succeeded on his own and the wife did not delay or give up her career ambitions so as to advance his career, there was no factual or legal basis for an award of compensatory maintenance.

*Variation — support not granted on basis of economic disadvantage where wife's income diminished by marital situation — support terminated — Tingley v. Tingley*, 1993 CarswellNB 611, 49 R.F.L. (3d) 87, 141 N.B.R. (2d) 86, 361 A.P.R. 86 (N.B.Q.B.). Where income the wife derives from a job is not less than it would have been had she not been married, the wife has not suffered any economic disadvantage because of the marriage or its breakdown and support should not be granted on the basis of economic disadvantage. On a motion to vary or terminate support, the court ordered that spousal support should be terminated.

*Both disadvantaged — spouse with lower income entitled to support — Amaral v. Amaral*, 1993 CarswellOnt 372, 50 R.F.L. (3d) 364, [1993] O.J. No. 2712 (Ont. Gen. Div.); additional reasons at 1993 CarswellOnt 373, 50 R.F.L. (3d) 384 (Ont. Gen. Div.). Where both parties have suffered an economic disadvantage from the marriage breakdown in the form of the loss of the other spouse's income, the spouse with the smaller income is entitled to have the disadvantage addressed through a support award.

*Claimant's financial position same as before marriage — support denied — Gawley v. Gawley*, 1993 CarswellMan 52, 48 R.F.L. (3d) 104, 86 Man. R. (2d) 317 (Man. Q.B.). The husband's application for interim support was refused although the wife had throughout the parties' brief marriage supported the alcoholic husband and paid his debts. As the husband's financial position was about the same as it had been before the marriage, he could not point to any economic disadvantage suffered.

*Only some of claimant's problems predated the marriage — Morison v. Morison*, 1993 CarswellAlta 442, 47 R.F.L. (3d) 34, 139 A.R. 124 (Alta. Q.B.). Where some of the wife's current problems were attributable to her first marriage, this did not remove from her second husband the responsibility for the continued and exacerbated economic disenfranchisement which she experienced as a result of the second marriage. The wife was accordingly entitled to support.

*Consider both advantages and disadvantages of marriage to support claimant — Rosin v. Rosin*, 1993 CarswellAlta 439, 46 R.F.L. (3d) 242 (Alta. Q.B.). When determining whether an award of compensatory support should be made, the court must also examine the economic advantages flowing to the claimant as a result of the marriage. Compensatory support should not be awarded unless the economic disadvantages resulting from the marriage outweigh the economic advantages and non-economic rewards of the relationship.

*Statutory basis for compensatory entitlement — Zanyk v. Zanyk*, 1993 CarswellSask 48, 46 R.F.L. (3d) 169, 110 Sask. R. 112 (Sask. Q.B.). The support provisions in the *Divorce Act*, pursuant to *Moge v. Moge*, 1992 CarswellMan 143, 43 R.F.L. (3d) 345, [1992] 3 S.C.R. 813 are to be seen as having a compensatory aspect where there is evidence of economic disadvantage arising from the marital relationship.

*Spouse financially disadvantaged — disadvantage not quantifiable — Petley-Jones v. Petley-Jones*, 1993 CarswellBC 621, 48 R.F.L. (3d) 166 (B.C.S.C.). When making or varying an order for spousal maintenance, the court must consider whether the decisions made during the marriage have had the effect of economically disadvantaging one spouse or benefitting the other upon its dissolution. The court considered that the wife, a nurse, in this case had, to some extent, been financially disadvantaged because her commitment to her husband, her children, and their home prevented her from developing a career, particularly in the early years of the marriage. The decisions in this regard were perhaps more the wife's than the husband's but were largely for the benefit of the husband. These decisions led to an economic disadvantage but one that could not be quantified.

*Absence from workforce — Jenkins v. Jenkins,* 1993 CarswellBC 171, 47 R.F.L. (3d) 219, 81 B.C.L.R. (2d) 133 (B.C.S.C.). The court, in considering the objectives in the *Divorce Act* and the *Moge* decision, was of the opinion that where the wife leaves her profession to be a homemaker, raises the parties' family, causing her qualifications to become stale and at 47 has little training for remunerative work, she has sustained a substantial economic disadvantage from the marriage and its breakdown and indefinite spousal support should be granted to supplement her own earnings.

*Variation — economic disadvantage to wife after long-term traditional marriage likely to persist, support extended — Burmeister v. Burmeister,* 1993 CarswellMan 49, 47 R.F.L. (3d) 186 (Man. Q.B.). The court refused the husband's application to terminate the spousal support which had been awarded at the end of the parties' 28-year traditional marriage. The wife had never been self-supporting and, given her health problems, was never likely to be. The economic disadvantage suffered by her as a result of the marriage continued and was likely to continue. Accordingly, the case was one in which support should be considered permanent.

*Husband's absence from workforce — Leek v. Lightfoot,* 1993 CarswellAlta 438, 45 R.F.L. (3d) 364, 136 A.R. 235 (Alta. Q.B.). Where the parties were content that the husband remain in the home while the wife worked, with the result that he was virtually unemployable when the marriage ended, the wife was ordered to pay him periodic support. The husband had been economically disadvantaged as a result of the marriage and was entitled to support while he studied to upgrade his qualifications.

Wife employed but still entitled to compensatory support for lost opportunities to advance — *Lee v. Lee,* 1992 CarswellOnt 298, 42 R.F.L. (3d) 445 (Ont. Gen. Div.). Where the wife had given up her career and had relocated several times when her husband, who was in the armed forces, was transferred, she was found to be entitled to support to compensate her for lost economic advantages. Although the wife was employed, she had lost the opportunities for advancement which would have arisen had she not given up her career.

*Wife remained home during early part of marriage — economic disadvantage found — Crook v. Crook,* 1992 CarswellNS 75, 42 R.F.L. (3d) 297, 115 N.S.R. (2d) 258, 314 A.P.R. 258 (N.S. T.D.). Where the wife had remained in the home to care for the children during the early part of the marriage and had only a modest income at the time of separation, she was found to be entitled to spousal support. The wife had suffered an economic disadvantage from the homemaker role she had adopted through much of the parties' 25-year traditional marriage.

*Acquiescence of husband in wife's withdrawal from workforce — Droit de la famille - 1486,* [1991] R.D.F. 592 (C.S. Que.). The court granted support to the 61-year-old wife on the basis that the husband had acquiesced in her not working throughout the parties' 30-year marriage and that it was unlikely, at her age, that she would find full-time employment.

*Wife moved to Canada for very short marriage — 6 months of support ordered — Sadilkova v. Sadilkova,* 1991 CarswellBC 579, 38 R.F.L. (3d) 441 (B.C.S.C.). Where the wife had moved from Czechoslovakia to Canada to marry, but the marriage disintegrated very quickly, she was awarded support for a 6-month period only. Although the wife had made no effort to achieve self-sufficiency in Canada, there was employment for her in Czechoslovakia. The 6-month period would allow the wife to plan for her future and to make the appropriate arrangements.

*Absence from workforce — lengthy and traditional marriage — full-time employment — entitled to support — Christian v. Christian,* 1991 CarswellOnt 343, 37 R.F.L. (3d) 26, 7 O.R. (3d) 441 (Ont. Gen. Div.). The wife was awarded periodic support upon the breakdown of the parties' long-term traditional marriage, despite the fact that she had retrained and had obtained full-time employment. The wife had, throughout the marriage, put the family first and, even with her employment, she would not be able to maintain a reasonable standard of living from her own resources.

*Lesser career role because of marriage — entitled to support for 2 years — Balcombe v. Balcombe*, 1990 CarswellOnt 322, 30 R.F.L. (3d) 177, 42 O.A.C. 150 (Ont. Div. Ct.). Where the wife forfeited a promotion in an attempt to salvage the marriage, the court awarded her support in the amount of $400 per month for 2 years.

*Lesser career role because of marriage — entitled to support — Jukosky v. Jukosky*, 1990 CarswellOnt 336, 31 R.F.L. (3d) 117, [1990] O.J. No. 2470 (Ont. Gen. Div.). There is an entitlement to support where, as a result of the duties of a marriage, a spouse loses his or her place on the labour market ladder. However, although the husband's convincing of the wife to move had cost her over $22,000 in lost seniority benefits, her application for support was refused in subsequent divorce proceedings. As the wife had re-established a stable career and was now earning more than the husband, there was no basis for an award.

*Employment throughout marriage not a bar to support — Rodrigues v. Rodrigues*, 1990 CarswellOnt 325, 30 R.F.L. (3d) 231 (Ont. Gen. Div.). The wife was awarded periodic support despite the fact that she had been employed throughout the marriage. The wife could not be viewed as a "career woman" and realistically required support.

*Compensatory rationale produces lump sum support entitlement — Ormerod v. Ormerod*, 1990 CarswellOnt 270, 27 R.F.L. (3d) 225 (Ont. U.F.C.). The court, in determining the quantum of support, took evidence into account of the wife's future economic losses, attributable to the fact that she had interrupted her nursing career in order to look after the parties' children and home. She had no present need for support. Implicit in this approach is the idea that the wife should be compensated for losses that are causally connected to the marriage. The evidence the court received was a report, prepared by an economist, that addressed future economic loss in earnings by the wife because of the interruption of her career, and a second report, prepared by an actuary, that responded to the first report. The wife was awarded $103,000 lump sum support to compensate her for future economic loss from the time of her return to nursing until her retirement. She did not receive compensation for her losses between the date of separation and the date of trial. The court concluded that there was a mutual aspect to this loss for the husband and wife. While the wife retrained, she did without the income she would have received if she had instead returned to work. At the same time, the husband paid support and did not receive occupational rent for the matrimonial home.

*Career sacrifices during marriage — support ordered during claimant's period of retraining — Tancock v. Tancock*, 1990 CarswellBC 436, 24 R.F.L. (3d) 389 (B.C.S.C.). Where the wife had given up her nursing career to work in her husband's office, he was ordered to pay support while she returned to school to retrain as a dental hygienist.

*Career interruption — Deroo v. Deroo*, 1990 CarswellOnt 281, 28 R.F.L. (3d) 86 (Ont. H.C.). Where the wife has interrupted her career for family purposes, she is entitled to reasonable spousal support for 1 year until she is working full-time.

*Compensatory support orders must be based on need — Baker v. Baker*, 1989 CarswellOnt 291, 22 R.F.L. (3d) 346 (Ont. U.F.C.). Courts may only grant compensatory support orders based on need. The orders should take into account one spouse's contribution to the other's career enhancement as an element of such orders.

*Compensatory principles apply even if claimant employed during marriage — Faint v. Faint*, 1989 CarswellBC 408, 21 R.F.L. (3d) 65 (B.C.S.C.). This case concerned a long-term marriage, this time one of approximately 17 years. The court followed the *Bast* decision and added at p. 71 [R.F.L.] that "where a wife is employed during the marriage there should be taken into account the limitations on the equality of the employment necessarily brought about by the demands of the marriage, and family duties."

*Marriage relationship led to withdrawal from workforce which led to economic need — Le Breton v. Le Breton,* 1989 CarswellMan 49, 21 R.F.L. (3d) 254, 60 Man. R. (2d) 234 (Man. Q.B.). The wife was entitled to support where she had an economic need, established in her evidence, as a result of her inability to earn any more than she was presently earning. The inability was caused by her long-standing withdrawal from the workforce due to the marriage relationship.

*Brief marriage, claimant had quit job but not to become a homemaker — support denied — Green v. Green (La Montagne),* 1989 CarswellNS 65, 23 R.F.L. (3d) 386 (N.S.T.D.); affirmed 1989 CarswellNS 66, 23 R.F.L. (3d) 398 (N.S.C.A.). Where, during the course of the parties' brief marriage, the wife quit her job of her own accord and did not assume the role of homemaker, her application for support was refused. She was capable of full-time employment and her need was not causally connected to the marriage.

*Absence from work force — moving with spouse — entitled to support — Norris v. Norris,* 1988 CarswellNfld 12, 13 R.F.L. (3d) 307, 70 Nfld. & P.E.I.R. 327, 215 A.P.R. 327 (Nfld. U.F.C.). Where the wife had left her employment to accompany the husband to the United States in furtherance of his education and later postponed her own education while the parties built a house, she was awarded support on divorce to assist her with her university studies. As the wife had contributed significantly to the parties' financial well-being and the husband's educational endeavours, it was equitable that he contribute to her education.

*Support to continue for 2 further years although claimant employed — Bast v. Bast,* 1988 CarswellOnt 216, 13 R.F.L. (3d) 98 (Ont. H.C.). The court found that the wife's 21 years outside the workforce created a causal connection between the marriage and the wife's dependency. The trial judge continued the wife's support of $500 per month for 2 years even though she was working at the time.

*Assisting in spouse's education — education did not increase spouse's income — no entitlement to support — Bodnar v. Bodnar,* 1987 CarswellOnt 289, 6 R.F.L. (3d) 66 (Ont. H.C.). Although a spouse may be entitled to support in recognition of the fact that she contributed to her husband's support while he attended university, this will not be the case where it was unlikely that the husband's degree would provide him with more employment income than he would have earned without it.

*Variation — no statutory requirement to eliminate economic disadvantages by means of support — Droit de la famille - 341,* 1987 CarswellQue 1140, EYB 1987-78326, [1987] R.J.Q. 416, [1987] R.D.F. 51 (C.S. Que.). Although under s. 17(7)(a) of the *Divorce Act* the court should recognize the economic disadvantages of a spouse which have resulted from the failure of the marriage, the Act does not require the court to eliminate those disadvantages through a support award.

*Loss of competitiveness in the job market — entitlement to support — Primeau v. Primeau,* 1986 CarswellOnt 267, 2 R.F.L. (3d) 113 (Ont. H.C.). Where, as a result of her role in the marriage, the wife had lost some degree of competitiveness in the job market and her subsequent efforts to become self-sufficient had been fruitless, she was found to be entitled to periodic maintenance.

*Contribution to the husband's career is a significant factor — Trifts v. Trifts,* 1984 CarswellNB 339, 54 N.B.R. (2d) 147, 140 A.P.R. 147 (N.B.Q.B.). Where the wife had contributed substantially to the realization of her husband's career potential so that he was earning an annual salary of $86,000, she was awarded annual maintenance of $27,600 to support herself and her three children.

*Spouse married at mature age — unemployment not attributable to marriage — Spicer v. Spicer,* 1980 CarswellNfld 9, 14 R.F.L. (2d) 180, 25 Nfld. & P.E.I.R. 133, 68 A.P.R. 133 (Nfld. T.D.). Where the respondent was a mature woman when she married the petitioner, the fact that she had no job experience or training could not be attributed to the marriage. In the circumstances, it was appropriate for the petitioner to pay a modest amount of periodic maintenance for a limited period of time.

## 6.3 Financial Consequences Arising From the Care of Any Child of the Marriage

Section 15.2(6)(b) provides that a spousal support order should "apportion between the spouses any financial consequences arising from the care of any child of the marriage over and above any obligation for the support of any child of the marriage." This subsection is compensatory in nature, and may be considered an elaboration or example of subsection 15.2(6)(a). The financial consequences of child care are the most common example of "economic advantages or disadvantages ... arising from the marriage or its breakdown" justifying compensation.

This section is often cited when the support claimant's child care activities during the relationship justify support, as in the *Moge* case. However, it also calls attention to the consequences of child care performed *after* the relationship's end. In the archetypal case the spousal support claimant will have sole custody of the children of the marriage, and caring for them will continue to affect her ability to earn income. For example, shift work and overtime are likely to be impossible for a single parent, and having any job whatsoever depends on arranging child care. These financial consequences are not likely to be adequately compensated by child support, and are therefore to be remedied by spousal support. As the concurring judgment of McLachlin J. in *Moge* put it, "if a spouse, *either before or after separation*, has or continues to incur financial disadvantage as a result of caring for a child of the marriage, he or she should be compensated" (emphasis added).

*Diminished earning capacity — interruptions from employment to undertake childcare responsibilities continuing after separation — Moge v. Moge*, 1992 CarswellMan 143, 1992 CarswellMan 222, EYB 1992-67141, 43 R.F.L. (3d) 345, [1992] 3 S.C.R. 813, 99 D.L.R. (4th) 456, [1993] 1 W.W.R. 481, 145 N.R. 1, [1993] R.D.F. 168, 81 Man. R. (2d) 161, 30 W.A.C. 161, [1992] S.C.J. No. 107 (S.C.C.). Women have tended to suffer economic disadvantages and hardships from marriage or its breakdown because of the traditional division of labour within that institution. A diminished earning capacity resulting from long interruptions in employment to take on parenting or domestic responsibilities is a fact that has been demonstrated in a number of studies. Often difficulties in returning to the work force are exacerbated by the continuing responsibility for the care of children after divorce. The spouse who has made economic sacrifices in the marriage usually becomes the custodial parent. This responsibility further reduces her economic choice by requiring her to do such things as remain within proximity to schools, refuse to work late, and to stay at home when the children are ill.

*Responsibility for child care before or after separation may require compensation through spousal support — Moge v. Moge, supra.* The Supreme Court of Canada found that Mrs. Moge should be compensated by way of spousal support, in part, because her ability to earn income had been diminished by assuming responsibility for the care of the children. Madam Justice L'Heureux-Dubé writing for the majority was of the view that compensation may be indicated if "due to childcare responsibilities one spouse declines a promotion, refuses a transfer, leaves a position to allow the other spouse to take advantage of an opportunity for advancement or otherwise curtails employment opportunities and thereby incurs economic loss." If child care responsibilities continue after divorce, the disadvantages attached to those responsibilities also continue. To be a custodial parent involves adopting a lifestyle which places many limitations upon that parent. She must find accommodation suited to the needs of the child, including play space, closeness to day care, schools and recreational facilities. She is seldom free to accept shift work, is restricted in any overtime work by the day care arrangements available, and must be prepared to give priority to the needs of a sick child over the demands of an employer. After a full day's work, the custodial parent faces a full range of homemaking responsibilities including cooking, cleaning and laundry, as well as the demands of the child himself for the parent's attention. Madame Justice McLachlin (as she then was) concurred with Madame Justice L'Heureux-Dubé in holding that the *Divorce Act* raised compensatory considerations based on childcare responsibilities. She stated that "if a spouse either before or after separation, has or continues to incur financial disadvantages as result of caring for a child of the marriage, he or she should be compensated."

*Where parties agreed that husband would give up job in order to assist the wife in the care of their son following the birth was grounds for compensatory support to the husband subject to review in 48 months as to entitlement and quantum* — *S. (R.M.) v. S. (F.P.C.),* 2011 CarswellBC 170, 2011 BCCA 53, 90 R.F.L. (6th) 1, 14 B.C.L.R. (5th) 84, 299 B.C.A.C. 186, 508 W.A.C. 186, [2011] B.C.J. No. 174 (B.C.C.A.), reversing 2009 CarswellBC 2597, 2009 BCSC 1323, 74 R.F.L. (6th) 376 (B.C.S.C.). The parties were married in 2004, had two children, and separated in 2007 when the wife ended the marriage. The wife was an anaesthetist and the husband had been employed as sports director for a Club Med in Mexico where the parties met. In light of the wife's higher earnings potential, they agreed he would give up his position and join her in Vancouver. After the birth of their first son, they both stayed home for a period. The wife returned to work at the hospital and when the child went to day care the husband obtained work. Following the birth of their daughter, the wife again stopped work and later returned to work part-time. In 2007, the parties separated. The trial judge, noting that the economic disadvantage to the husband was disproportionate to the duration of the marriage, and that his ability to obtain work was restricted by his education, experience, and language difficulties, ordered, among other relief, that the wife pay to the husband spousal support in an amount and duration that exceeded the SSAG range, subject to a 48-month review. On appeal the court held that the income imputed to the wife of $225,000 for purposes of paying support did not constitute an error in law and that the quantum of spousal support ensures that the payee spouse who was to have 35% time with the children would have the financial resources he would need to fulfil his parenting role. The scope of the review restriction, however, was narrowed to a review on entitlement and quantum for noncompensatory support related directly to the ability of the husband to financially meet his parenting role under the joint custody order.

*Husband's application for compensatory spousal support, relatively short period of cohabitation* — *Adams v. Adams,* 2011 CarswellAlta 948, 2011 ABQB 306, 5 R.F.L. (7th) 258, 53 Alta. L.R. (5th) 20 (Alta. Q.B.), additional reasons at 2011 CarswellAlta 2177, 2011 ABQB 812, 5 R.F.L. (7th) 289, 53 Alta. L.R. (5th) 51 (Alta. Q.B.). The husband, an airline pilot, and the wife, a doctor, cohabited 4Ï years of a 9-year marriage. They had two children. At the time of the marriage, the husband was 37 and the wife was 35 years old. The husband sought spousal support on the basis of his claims that he contributed to her education in qualifying as a gastroenterologist, that he was a homemaker during the marriage, and that his career was stalled for reasons associated with the marriage. On the evidence, the court stated that the husband was more similar to someone in semi-retirement than a homemaker, that the parties' incomes had little connection to the marriage and that the husband had not been disadvantaged in his career other than by his own lack of initiative, and choices, except for a relatively short period of time. The husband was awarded 2 years compensatory support of $24,000, but was also ordered to pay 3 years of retroactive child support.

*Wife's career severely disadvantaged by becoming a full-time mother* — *Davies v. Quantz,* 2010 CarswellOnt 9748, 2010 ONCA 896, 100 R.F.L. (6th) 176, [2010] O.J. No. 5629 (Ont. C.A.), affirming 2010 CarswellOnt 10064, 2010 ONSC 416, 100 R.F.L. (6th) 156 (Ont. S.C.J.).

The parties cohabitated for 18 years before they separated. They were both highly educated and for the first 9 years of the relationship the parties were "equals". After the birth of their children, the wife gave up her successful career to become the primary caregiver, at which point the parties transitioned into a traditional marriage. The wife's application for spousal support was granted. The husband's annual income was $428,000. The wife's career was severely disadvantaged by her assuming the role of full-time mother and by moving from Quebec to Ontario to advance the husband's career. The wife was aware that the husband expected her to resume her career once the children were in school full-time. The wife was entitled to support on a compensatory basis and because of need. She was awarded $9,440 per month based on the amount at the lowest end of the *Spousal Support Advisory Guidelines* range for a payor earning $428,000 a year. As the children were both in school full-time, the wife was in a position to seek work. A time-limited support order was made for 8 years, at which point the wife was expected to be self-supporting. The spousal support order was upheld on appeal with the Court of Appeal noting that the wife could seek variation of the order in the future, if the circumstances permitted.

*Although wife came out of marriage as a person of considerable means, the court ordered support in recognition of the disparity in the parties' earning capacity due to the roles each party played in marriage — while the wife was home caring for the family, the husband was at the workplace honing his business skills* — Taylor v. Taylor, 2009 CarswellAlta 1701, 2009 ABCA 354, 72 R.F.L. (6th) 249, 15 Alta. L.R. (5th) 303, 312 D.L.R. (4th) 448, 464 A.R. 245, 467 W.A.C. 245, [2009] A.J. No. 1162 (Alta. C.A.), additional reasons at 2010 CarswellAlta 556, 2010 ABCA 103, 76 R.F.L. (6th) 259, 21 Alta. L.R. (5th) 275, 482 A.R. 387, 490 W.A.C. 387, [2010] A.J. No. 334 (Alta. C.A.), varying 2009 CarswellAlta 20, 2009 ABQB 7, 1 Alta. L.R. (5th) 74 (Alta. Q.B.). Leave to appeal refused 2010 CarswellAlta 744, 2010 CarswellAlta 745, 493 A.R. 254 (note), 502 W.A.C. 254 (note), 407 N.R. 386 (note), (S.C.C.). Following an 18-year marriage and two children, the parties separated in 2005. The husband, who had worked for the wife's family business throughout the marriage, left following the separation, although buy-out arrangements were inconclusive. He then purchased a company using 100% borrowed funds. The parties had joint custody of the children. At the time of trial, the wife was earning $33,937. The court, questioning the appropriateness of the husband's business decisions, awarded the wife spousal support based on an income of $124,000 imputed to the husband. The husband paid child support in accordance with the Guidelines. On appeal, the court, indicating that the trial judge failed to consider the financial impact of joint custody, and that it was an error to import wrongful dismissal principles into support, and that it is rarely unreasonable for someone to leave employment controlled by former in-laws, varied the husband's imputed income to $75,000 and reduced spousal support from $2,300 to $1,000 per month for 6 years.

*Wife entitled to spousal support — childcare responsibilities had negatively affected wife's career* — Gonabady-Namadon v. Mohammadzadeh, 2009 CarswellBC 2767, 2009 BCCA 448, 74 R.F.L. (6th) 1, 98 B.C.L.R. (4th) 23, 277 B.C.A.C. 48, 469 W.A.C. 48 (B.C.C.A.). In this case, the parties were married for 13 years and had two children. The wife was a physician. At trial, the trial judge found that the wife was not entitled to spousal support due to her annual income of $150,000. On appeal, the court found that the trial judge erred in not finding entitlement. In reversing the decision, the court noted that although the parties had domestic help, nevertheless child care responsibilities had an impact on the wife's advancement and options. She was unable to pursue lucrative work at a hospital since the associated shift work was incompatible with her family obligations. Accordingly, given the wife's professional income and future prospects, spousal support was ordered at the low end of the range, being $2,300 monthly for 6 years and the order was made retroactive to May 14, 2008, the date of the trial judge's order.

*Compensatory spousal support awarded where wife was primary caregiver to parties' child during marriage and after separation, and thereby permitted spouse to engage in his employment*

— *H. (L.M.) v. H. (G.D.)*, 2008 CarswellBC 2815, 2008 BCCA 547, 61 R.F.L. (6th) 48, 86 B.C.L.R. (4th) 320, 264 B.C.A.C. 125, 445 W.A.C. 125 (B.C.C.A.). The husband's work required him to travel outside the family's community. He could only do so because of the wife's undertaking of the childcare role.

*Ongoing absence from work force to care for children — support — Kopelow v. Warkentin*, 2005 CarswellBC 2636, 2005 BCCA 551, 21 R.F.L. (6th) 78, 261 D.L.R. (4th) 129, 218 B.C.A.C. 209, 359 W.A.C. 209, [2005] B.C.J. No. 2412 (B.C.C.A.), additional reasons at 2006 CarswellBC 1306, 2006 BCCA 271, 268 D.L.R. (4th) 274, 227 B.C.A.C. 176, 374 W.A.C. 176 (B.C.C.A.), reversing in part 2002 CarswellBC 2706, 2002 BCSC 1546, [2002] B.C.J. No. 2534 (B.C.S.C.). The wife's spousal support was increased on appeal from $1,500 monthly to $3,500. The parties had been married for 12 years during which the wife had to remain out of the work force to care for the children, a duty which would likely last for another 6 or 7 years. The marriage was a long one and the wife was entitled to enjoy a similar status of living as the husband without having to liquidate assets.

*Variation — appeal granted where insufficient weight given to role of father as sole support for three children — Imrie v. Imrie*, 1999 CarswellOnt 3266, 1 R.F.L. (5th) 65 (Ont. C.A.). The appellate court granted the father's appeal from an order increasing spousal support. The Court of Appeal presumed that the motions court decision was based on the fact that the appellant's income from the time of the initial order was sufficient to constitute a change in the appellant's "means" within s. 17(4) of the *Divorce Act*. The Court of Appeal was of the opinion that the motions judge did not give appropriate weight to all the objectives in s. 17(7) of the Act, specifically s. 17(7)(b), as the appellant was the sole financial support for three teenage daughters.

*Variation — where the wife was unable to be self-sufficient because of child care obligations, support granted — Wooldridge v. Wooldridge*, 1999 CarswellAlta 320, 1999 ABCA 124, 45 R.F.L. (4th) 308, 172 D.L.R. (4th) 637, 237 A.R. 64, 197 W.A.C. 64, [1999] A.J. No. 433 (Alta. C.A.), additional reasons at 1999 CarswellAlta 620, 1999 ABCA 208, 49 R.F.L. (4th) 445, 250 A.R. 168, 213 W.A.C. 168 (Alta. C.A.). Where the wife has not worked outside the home for 20 years and two of her four children had suffered severe psychological difficulties since separation, there had been financial consequences to the wife of caring for the children of the marriage, spousal support should not be terminated. Considering all of the circumstances, self-sufficiency for the wife might not be possible for some time, if ever. The husband was ordered to pay $2,500 per month in spousal support. Once the husband has ceased to pay child support, the spousal support, if necessary, could be increased.

*Variation — support extended as wife's duties as custodial parent interfered with her education and thereby her employment — Poohkay v. Poohkay*, 1997 CarswellAlta 604, 30 R.F.L. (4th) 9, 200 A.R. 211, 146 W.A.C. 211 (Alta. C.A.), additional reasons at 1997 CarswellAlta 987, 33 R.F.L. (4th) 140 (Alta. C.A.). The wife successfully appealed from an order dismissing her application for lifting of the time limitation on her spousal support order. At the time of the original order, the parties had not anticipated the extent to which the mother's duties as a custodial parent would interfere with her educational upgrading efforts. Had the parties known that their assumptions were incorrect at the time the original order was made, a different order would likely have resulted. As the wife would likely be able to enter the workforce in the near future, a lump sum award was preferable to an indefinite periodic one.

*Diminished earning capacity — ongoing care of children — Patrick v. Patrick*, 1991 CarswellBC 315, 35 R.F.L. (3d) 382, 62 B.C.L.R. (2d) 188 (B.C.S.C.), additional reasons at 1991 CarswellBC 2027 (B.C.S.C.), affirmed 1993 CarswellBC 320, 49 R.F.L. (3d) 453, 85 B.C.L.R. (2d) 303, [1993] B.C.J. No. 1963 (B.C.C.A.),. The pharmacist wife was awarded indefinite spousal support upon dissolution of her 10-year marriage. Although employed, the result of the marriage breakdown and her continuing child-rearing role rendered the wife financially and professionally disadvantaged in comparison with what her circumstances would have been had the marriage continued or had it never occurred. On appeal, the court found no basis for imposing a time limit on the payment of support. There was nothing to prevent the appellant from applying for a variation of maintenance if there were a change in circumstances.

*Ongoing childcare responsibilities cause diminished ability to work* — *Piller v. Piller*, 1975 CarswellBC 107, 17 R.F.L. 252, 54 D.L.R. (3d) 150, [1975] 4 W.W.R. 342 (B.C.C.A.), at 345-46 [W.W.R.]. "[T]he wife has custody of the children and not only does the husband consent to her devoting part of her time [to] looking after them, he insists upon it. Under these circumstances, the diminution of her income makes it fit and just that the husband should contribute to her maintenance., the court shall make an appropriate order for the maintenance of the wife and the children by the payment of periodic sums, having regard, *inter alia*, to the diminution in the income of the wife that is reasonably attributable to her caring for the children during usual working hours", per Farris C.J.B.C.

*Where the parties had a traditional marriage in which the wife did not work outside the home but provided childcare, and the wife was found unable to support herself, a change in circumstances will not be found when no evidence showed that the situation had changed* — *Gaudet v. Mainville*, 2014 CarswellNB 195, 2014 CarswellNB 196, 2014 NBQB 88, 418 N.B.R. (2d) 273, 1087 A.P.R. 273 (N.B.Q.B.). The husband sought to vary, *inter alia*, his spousal support obligation, which had been determined by a 2009 order. The husband had subsequently retired. The judge determined that the wife, who had been a traditional spouse, had little or no hope of attaining self-sufficiency at the time of the 2009 order. The parties cohabited for 28 years, and the wife did not work outside the home during that time. At the time of the original order she was found to have little possibility of becoming self-sufficient. This situation had not changed by the time the husband sought to vary, and spousal support was ordered to continue at a somewhat reduced amount to reflect the fact that the wife had pension entitlement.

*Spousal support award for a stay-at-home father* — *Jacobs v. Dingee-Jacobs*, 2010 CarswellNB 380, 2010 NBQB 114, 89 R.F.L. (6th) 286, 360 N.B.R. (2d) 40, 930 A.P.R. 40 (N.B.Q.B.). The parties had a 24-year marriage. For the majority of the marriage the husband acted as the children's primary caregiver and did not work outside the home. The parties moved a number of times in order to advance the wife's career. The husband was awarded spousal support on a compensatory and non-compensatory basis. The husband remained at home, with the wife's agreement, to care for the children and the home. The benefit of outside assistance, such as a part-time nanny and a cleaner, did not make redundant the parties' objective of having the husband stay home. Although the husband's efforts to secure work were limited, his age, health issues and time away from the workforce would make finding work difficult. The husband suffered economic hardship as a result of the marriage and was entitled to compensatory support. He was also entitled to non-compensatory support on the basis that he had no income and could not be self-sufficient. A time-limited support order was not appropriate as it was unresolved as to when the husband might achieve self-sufficiency. Spousal support was set at the mid-point of the *Spousal Support Advisory Guidelines* range.

*Absence from workforce* — *child with illness* — *entitled to support* — *Oddi v. Oddi*, 2000 CarswellOnt 1772, 7 R.F.L. (5th) 164, [2000] O.J. No. 1778 (Ont. S.C.J.). A wife who gives up her job to care for the parties' child who has Down's Syndrome is entitled to spousal support. She could not be expected to work, given her son's special needs.

*Fact that husband maintaining children among reasons for dismissing wife's claim for support* — *Frouws v. Frouws*, 2007 CarswellBC 301, 2007 BCSC 195, [2007] B.C.J. No. 282 (B.C.S.C.). The husband had maintained the parties' three children since separation, without any contribution from the wife. All of the children, because of medical difficulties, would continue to need support. Consequently, the wife's claim for spousal support was dismissed. The husband had provided her with minimal support until she had entered her current marriage-like relationship and he had financed her upgrading course which enabled her to improve her employment skills. She had received the advantage of a $15,000 retroactive payment of child tax benefits and ongoing monthly tax benefit payments.

*Care of child with medical condition — support — diminished working capacity — Murphy v. Paulin*, 2001 CarswellBC 1553, 2001 BCSC 842, 18 R.F.L. (5th) 339, [2001] B.C.T.C. 842 (B.C.S.C.). The wife was awarded periodic spousal support upon the dissolution of the parties' 15-year marriage. Their youngest child remained in the care of the wife and suffered from a serious medical condition. Although the wife did manage to work part-time, the requirement that she take time away from work to tend to the child's needs affected both her employment opportunities and the security of her employment.

*Care of child with medical condition — support — spouse unable to work — Oddi v. Oddi*, 2000 CarswellOnt 1772, 7 R.F.L. (5th) 164, [2000] O.J. No. 1778 (Ont. S.C.J.). Where the wife had given up her job to care for the parties' child who had Down's Syndrome, her application for spousal support was granted. The wife could not be expected to work, given the need to maintain the home for the children and look after her son's special needs.

*Fact that respondent to support claim had sole custody of children among reasons for denying spousal support claim — Kenning v. Kenning*, 1995 CarswellBC 83, 11 R.F.L. (4th) 216 (B.C.S.C.). The husband had assumed full responsibility for the children after the separation. The wife had suffered no economic disadvantage from the marriage or its breakdown and was capable of caring for herself.

*Care of child with medical condition — support — diminished working capacity — Droit de la famille - 1568*, 1992 CarswellQue 1641, EYB 1992-74916, [1992] R.D.F. 240 (C.S. Que.). Where the wife had to care for the parties' asthmatic son, it was not reasonable to expect her to work full-time to achieve self-sufficiency.

*Ongoing care of child with medical condition — support — diminished working capacity — Keane v. Keane*, 1980 CarswellOnt 267, 17 R.F.L. (2d) 299 (Ont. H.C.), at 300 [R.F.L.]. The petitioner wife sought substantial maintenance upon divorce for the parties' severely disabled child in her custody. The petitioner, who was otherwise able to work to support herself, was unable to take full-time employment because of the care this child required. Per Winter L.J.S.C. awarding $600 per month for the child. "As is usual in most cases where both partners are not gainfully employed, there is just not enough money earned to take care of the full requirements of the separated homes. This, however, is an unusual case because of the necessity of almost constant care for the infant child of the marriage. Care of the child is the first responsibility of the parents and the respondent husband and father will have to rearrange his priorities to make provision for the child.. The life expectancy of the child is not long and accordingly the emergency for funds will be of relatively short lived duration but must be a responsibility accepted by the father during that period."

*Choice of part-time work and work in unrelated fields during marriage due to child care responsibilities is a basis for compensatory support — Bell v. Bell*, 1998 CarswellNS 486, 1998 NSCA 213, 44 R.F.L. (4th) 77, [1998] N.S.J. No. 466 (N.S.C.A.). A wife suffers an economic disadvantage because of the marriage where, unlike her husband who was able to pursue his career on a continuous basis, she did not work when their three children were young, or worked at jobs unrelated to her career as a nurse; and when the children were older, instead of working in a hospital, worked in a nursing home so she could work part-time and be with them when needed. She was entitled to support of $800 a month after a 30-year marriage on top of her earnings of $37,000 a year in view of her husband's earnings of $66,500 a year.

*Children plus household responsibilities provide basis for compensatory support — Gray v. Gray*, 1998 CarswellAlta 117, 1998 ABCA 60, 35 R.F.L. (4th) 456 (Alta. C.A.). Where the wife had raised the children and tended to all household responsibilities throughout the parties' 23-year marriage, she was found to have suffered disadvantages from the marriage entitling her to spousal support.

*Once youngest child is in school full-time, review to occur* — *Duits v. Duits,* 2006 CarswellOnt 8582 (Ont. S.C.J.). A spouse is entitled to support to supplement her income from part-time work until the youngest child is in school full-time, at which time there should be a review of the spousal support order.

*Care of children and relocations created dependence* — *support* — *Rutherford v. Rutherford,* 2004 CarswellNS 301, 2004 NSSC 148, 7 R.F.L. (6th) 344, 225 N.S.R. (2d) 293, 713 A.P.R. 293, [2004] N.S.J. No. 291 (N.S.S.C.). Where the wife had moved several times during the parties' 20-year marriage to facilitate the husband's military career and had cared for the parties' two children, an economic dependence upon him had been created. She had no income, no prospect of income and was accordingly entitled to spousal support.

*Career not compromised by marriage* — *Roberts v. Roberts,* 2003 CarswellNS 268, 2003 NSSC 146, 42 R.F.L. (5th) 135, [2003] N.S.J. No. 246 (N.S.S.C.). Where the wife had worked throughout the marriage and continued to advance the career she had begun prior to the marriage, her application for spousal support was dismissed. Although she had also been the primary caregiver to the parties' children, her employment situation had never been compromised.

*11-year absence from work-force to raise children* — *1-year of support ordered* — *N. (T.A.) v. N. (R.G.),* 2003 CarswellAlta 1622, 2003 ABQB 920, 3 R.F.L. (6th) 121 (Alta. Q.B.), additional reasons at 2003 CarswellAlta 1722, 2003 ABQB 988, 3 R.F.L. (6th) 129 (Alta. Q.B.), additional reasons at 2004 CarswellAlta 66, 2004 ABQB 48, 3 R.F.L. (6th) 131 (Alta. Q.B.). A spouse is entitled to compensatory support where she was a stay-at-home mother caring for young children for 11 years. Although there was no evidence of any opportunities which actually existed that were foregone by the wife during the course of their marriage, the court acknowledged that the husband did gain as a result of the wife being at home looking after the children. The court held that the wife was entitled to some compensatory support following the separation given her limited financial means, and the problems she faced in the transition after a long-term marriage, many of the debts of which she was still paying at the time of the hearing. The court awarded compensatory support of $750 per month for the first year following the parties' separation. After that point the court concluded that the wife became sufficiently self-supporting and no further support was owed.

*Wife's medical treatment required due to stress of dealing with challenging child-husband required to contribute to cost*: *Y. (A.L.) v. Y. (L.M.),* 2001 CarswellAlta 491, 2001 ABQB 311, 17 R.F.L. (5th) 233, [2001] 9 W.W.R. 141, 92 Alta. L.R. (3d) 347, 294 A.R. 274, [2001] A.J. No. 506 (Alta. Q.B.). The *Divorce Act* allows the court, through compensatory support, to apportion between the spouses financial consequences arising from the care of a child over and above the obligation for child support. Accordingly, the husband was ordered to contribute to the doctor-ordered respite case for the mother which had been the result of the stress relating to her care of the parties' emotionally challenged child.

*Illness of child required interruption of wife's career* — *Heal v. Heal,* 1998 CarswellOnt 4468, 43 R.F.L. (4th) 88, 82 O.T.C. 188, [1998] O.J. No. 4828 (Ont. Gen. Div.). The wife had been forced to leave her employment for a 3-year period during the parties' 29-year marriage to care for the parties' seriously ill child. Upon returning to work, she had to accept a less lucrative position. The interruption of her career was found to be compelling evidence of an economic disadvantage arising from the marriage entitling her to support.

*Economic disadvantage from long marriage and 11 children* — *Tracey v. Tracey,* 1998 CarswellOnt 3477, 41 R.F.L. (4th) 278, 73 O.T.C. 64, [1998] O.J. No. 3494 (Ont. Gen. Div.).

Where the 60-year-old dependant spouse in a traditional 34-year marriage gave birth to 11 children, she was economically disadvantaged as a result of the breakdown of the marriage and suffered economic hardship. She was entitled to spousal support and was awarded $500 a month.

*See also re consequences of child care — Moura v. Moura,* 1998 CarswellOnt 4919, 43 R.F.L. (4th) 344, 83 O.T.C. 321, [1998] O.J. No. 5351 (Ont. Gen. Div.).

*Support denied where other spouse had custody of children — Dunn v. Dunn,* 1995 CarswellNS 64, 14 R.F.L. (4th) 50 (N.S.S.C.). The fact that the husband had retained custody of the children was among the reasons for denying the wife's spousal support claim.

*Applicant who voluntarily leaves employment and care of children to return to university not entitled to support — Kenning v. Kenning,* 1995 CarswellBC 83, 11 R.F.L. (4th) 216 (B.C.S.C.). Where, subsequent to separation, the wife gave up her nursing job to return to university, leaving the father to care and provide for the children, her application for spousal support was dismissed. As the husband had assumed the full care and support of the children on his labourer's salary, he could not be expected to finance the wife's education as well.

*Left employment — loss of business opportunities — Belliveau-Williamson v. Williamson,* 1989 CarswellNB 22, 21 R.F.L. (3d) 142, 97 N.B.R. (2d) 186, 245 A.P.R. 186 (N.B.Q.B.). Where it was found that the wife would likely have had a successful business career had she not given up opportunities to care for the parties' children, she was awarded periodic support for a 7-year term to enable her to educate herself and secure a position commensurate with her abilities and lifestyle.

*Payor assumes full financial responsibility for child — Head v. Johnson,* 1989 CarswellMan 303, 61 Man. R. (2d) 267, [1989] M.J. No. 367 (Man. Q.B.). Where the husband assumed full responsibility for the support of the parties' child, a university student, the wife's claim for spousal support was dismissed. Any claim by the wife was more than offset by the husband's sole assumption of child support.

*1-year marriage which produced a child justified a 3-year spousal support order — Wagener v. Wagener,* 1988 CarswellMan 65, 17 R.F.L. (3d) 308, 55 Man. R. (2d) 91 (Man. Q.B.). Where there has been a short-term marriage and where the parties have a child, the courts may find a causal connection between one spouse's need and the marriage. In this decision, the wife had remained in the home and cared for the parties' child. Support for 3 years was awarded despite the fact that the marriage had lasted for only 1 year.

*Variation — support continued where wife was in her mid-fifties and had focused on raising the parties' five children —Droit de la famille - 1091,* [1987] R.D.F. 174 (C.S. Que.). The court refused to grant the husband's application to terminate his 54-year-old wife's support. The wife had, throughout the 26-year marriage, devoted herself to raising the partner's five children and it was not reasonable to expect her now to achieve self-sufficiency.

## 6.4 Economic Hardship of the Spouses Arising From the Breakdown of the Marriage

Section 15.2(6)(c) states that a spousal support order should "relieve any economic hardship of the spouses arising from the breakdown of the marriage." This has been held to include hardship caused by the way in which the marriage broke down, for example depression or stress caused by marital discord. However, it also includes hardship which was not caused by the marriage, but which would have been less onerous had the marriage survived. A common fact pattern involves the support claimant's illness or disability. The law assumes that, had the marriage continued, the claimant spouse would have been financially supported by the other party.

Therefore the breakdown of the marriage has made the illness or disability a source of increased hardship, and thus support is justified by section 15.2(6)(c).

Section 15.2(6)(c) is the key statutory authority for *needs-based support*, which along with compensation is one of the two central rationales for the remedy. Spousal support on this basis does not require a demonstration that the need or hardship was caused by the other spouse or by anything which happened during the marriage. The fact that the spouse claiming support is in need (provided that the other spouse has the ability to pay) may justify support even if there is no compensatory rationale for it. It may also justify a support award greater than that justified by the compensatory rationale alone.

A claimant may be experiencing "hardship" or "need" even though she has a standard of living well in excess of objective standards such as the poverty line or the income threshold for social assistance. Hardship and need are usually established by reference to the marital standard of living. However, the Supreme Court's judgment in *Bracklow* made it clear that the support payor will not necessarily be required to maintain the support claimant at the marital standard or meet her entire need. After a long marriage, a realistic goal for support applicants is to receive enough spousal support to permit the same standard of living as that enjoyed by the payor after the separation. The payor's ability to pay must be considered along with the recipient's need (see sections 5.2 and 5.3 of this volume regarding the means and needs of the claimant and respondent).

*A spouse who experiences need may be entitled to spousal support regardless of whether there is a compensatory rationale for it* — Bracklow v. Bracklow, 1999 CarswellBC 532, 1999 CarswellBC 533, 44 R.F.L. (4th) 1, [1999] 1 S.C.R. 420, 63 B.C.L.R. (3d) 77, 169 D.L.R. (4th) 577, [1999] 8 W.W.R. 740, 236 N.R. 79, 120 B.C.A.C. 211, 196 W.A.C. 211 (S.C.C.), at 16 [R.F.L.], McLachlin J. (as she then was). A spouse who is unable to work because of a debilitating illness may be entitled to support on the "social obligation model" where there are no compensatory or contractual elements present. The social obligation model gives rise to non-compensatory support, which is the third conceptual basis for spousal support; the other two being the compensatory and the contractual bases. Non-compensatory support predicated on this model may be awarded by establishing only the fact of marriage and need. Entitlement to spousal support in circumstances such as where the spouse is incapacitated by illness does not depend on finding an economic disadvantage caused by the marriage. Entitlement may flow from the marriage breakdown; that is, it may flow from the fact that on breakdown the spouse no longer receives the benefits of a common household.

The parties cohabited for 7 years; 4 years before marriage and 3 years after. For the first 2 years, the wife paid two-thirds of their living expenses because she was earning more than her husband and because her two children were living with them. After this initial period, they shared expenses equally. About a year before the separation, the wife suffered from health problems causing her to quit her employment, and she was unable to work from that time on. The marriage breakdown caused the wife to be in a state of economic hardship as contemplated by s. 15.2(6)(c) of the *Divorce Act*, that is, an "economic hardship of the spouses arising from the breakdown of the marriage." The wife was eligible for support on the basis of this hardship, the length of cohabitation, her need and the husband's financial ability to pay. Although a potential for a lifelong obligation was involved in the serious commitment of marriage, full payment for the indefinite future, in the circumstances of this case, may be unfair. The determination of the quantum and duration of support was referred back to the trial judge. All relevant statutory factors were to be considered, together with the amount of support already paid. The trial judge's determination on this referral, reported at 1999 CarswellBC 2978, was that the husband should continue to pay support of $400 a month for a period of 5 years from when support was first ordered. This determination created arrears of $16,000 for payments that should have been made in this period. To satisfy the arrears, the husband was ordered to pay a further $400 a month starting at the end of the 5-year period and continuing until the full amount of the arrears had been paid.

*Insofar as economic circumstances permit, the Act seeks to put the remainder of the family in as close a position as possible to the household before the marriage breakdown — Moge v. Moge,* 1992 CarswellMan 143, 1992 CarswellMan 222, EYB 1992-67141, 43 R.F.L. (3d) 345, [1992] 3 S.C.R. 813, 99 D.L.R. (4th) 456, [1993] 1 W.W.R. 481, 81 Man. R. (2d) 161, 145 N.R. 1, [1993] R.D.F. 168, 30 W.A.C. 161, [1990] S.C.C.A. No. 249 (S.C.C.). Per Madame Justice L'Heureux-Dubé, although the doctrine of spousal support which focuses on equitable sharing does not guarantee to either party the standard of living enjoyed during the marriage, this standard is far from irrelevant to support entitlement. Furthermore, great disparities in the standard of living that would be experienced by spouses in the absence of support are often a revealing indication of the economic disadvantages inherent in the role assumed by one party. As marriage should be regarded as a joint endeavour, the longer the relationship endures, the closer the economic union, the greater will be the presumptive claim to equal standards of living upon its dissolution. Madame Justice McLachlin, in her concurring judgment, held that the focus in the consideration of economic hardship arising from the breakdown of the marriage was "not on compensation for what the spouses have contributed to or gained from the marriage but rather on post-marital need." She stated that "if the breakdown of the marriage has created economic hardship for one or the other, the judge must attempt to grant relief from that hardship."

*The wife's entitlement to non-compensatory support, based on her ill health on her inability to support herself or to replace the benefits experienced during the marriage was affirmed on appeal — Rockall v. Rockall,* 2010 CarswellAlta 1859, 2010 ABCA 278, 90 R.F.L. (6th) 317, 35 Alta. L.R. (5th) 1, 490 A.R. 135, 497 W.A.C. 135 (Alta.C.A.), reversing in part 2010 CarswellAlta 291?2010 ABQB 124, 24 Alta. L.R. (5th) 37 (Alta Q.B.). The parties cohabited for a year, were married for five years, separated and were divorced. The husband was an oilrig manager. The wife had lived a high-risk lifestyle and the husband knew she was HIV positive prior to their marriage. The wife had completed some post secondary education during the marriage. She had drug debts and was addicted to gambling. She was diagnosed with AIDS during the proceedings. Following the separation, she was living in a women's shelter. The Court of Appeal confirmed the trial judge's finding of the wife's entitlement to non-compensatory support, but stated that since the general rule is to order periodic support, it was an error that no reasons were given for the retroactive and perspective lump sum orders. The Court of Appeal substituted the lump sum orders with periodic support orders.

*Non-compensatory support awarded where wife had been financially dependent upon the husband, was unable to work because of her medical condition and no longer shared in the income from the family business — H. (L.M.) v. H. (G.D.),* 2008 CarswellBC 2815, 2008 BCCA 547, 61 R.F.L. (6th) 48, 86 B.C.L.R. (4th) 320, 264 B.C.A.C. 125, 445 W.A.C. 125 (B.C.C.A.). The wife's failure to provide a medical report outlining her partner's prognosis for recovery should not have been the basis for rejecting a claim for non-compensatory support. The trial judge had not made any adverse findings of credibility regarding the partner's evidence concerning his inability to work. The wife had shown at trial that she had a clear financial need for support. The appellate court allowed the appeal from the order dismissing the wife's entitlement to spousal support and remitted the issue of the quantum and duration of the award to the trial court for determination.

*Need not established, no entitlement to support — Katz v. Nimelman,* 2007 CarswellOnt 7659, 46 R.F.L. (6th) 392 (Ont. S.C.J.); additional reasons at 2008 CarswellOnt 1917, 54 R.F.L. (6th) 177 (Ont. S.C.J.); affirmed 2009 CarswellOnt 2971, 2009 ONCA 445 (Ont. C.A.). At trial, the court concluded that the wife had undisclosed assets and income. She also had the ability to earn income. She was required to maximize her income before seeking support from her husband. If she did not wish to generate rental income, she could also reduce her expenses by obtaining less costly housing. The court anticipated that the wife would revive her wrongful dismissal claims with the expectation of obtaining money through them. On appeal, the court held that the trial judge had assessed the wife's claim on the basis that she was disabled but that, considering the assets that she held, she failed to demonstrate need. The decision involved findings of fact and the exercise of discretion and the trial judgement was supported by the evidence.

*Equalization of incomes not justified by wife's contributions to marriage — Martin v. Martin*, 2004 CarswellOnt 5438, 12 R.F.L. (6th) 415, [2004] O.T.C. 1139 (Ont. S.C.J.); additional reasons at 2005 CarswellOnt 1437 (Ont. S.C.J.); affirmed 2006 CarswellOnt 4876, 40 R.F.L. (6th) 32, 81 O.R. (3d) 503, 81 O.R. (3d) 495, 272 D.L.R. (4th) 666, 214 O.A.C. 140 (Ont. C.A.). The court dismissed the wife's claim for an almost equal share in the husband's income for spousal support. The husband had earned a substantial income as a professional hockey coach and equating the parties contribution to the marriage to earned income ignored the husband's talent.

*Where a payee spouse leaves a marriage with considerable assets which would generate significant income, together with her own potential income, she would be entitled to support until she re-establishes herself in her career — Hodgkinson v. Hodgkinson*, 2003 CarswellBC 2461, 2003 BCSC 1538, 44 R.F.L. (5th) 82, [2003] B.C.J. No. 2296 (B.C.S.C.); varied 2006 CarswellBC 767, 2006 BCCA 158, 25 R.F.L. (6th) 235, 267 D.L.R. (4th) 357, 53 B.C.L.R. (4th) 52 (B.C.C.A.). The 44-year-old wife had received over $3,000,000 after division of the parties' assets. At the time of marriage the wife's assets had been minimal and she had benefitted considerably from the marriage in terms of property acquisition. Although she had not worked during the 9-year marriage, she had marketable skills. The court awarded the wife $150,000 in lump sum support. It held that it was necessary to consider the parties' standard of living during the marriage and the standard of living after separation that was still reasonably available to them, although they were in two residences.

*Marital lifestyle relevant in justifying lump sum spousal support award — Tauber v. Tauber*, 2001 CarswellOnt 2842, 18 R.F.L. (5th) 384, 203 D.L.R. (4th) 168, [2001] O.T.C. 625, [2001] O.J. No. 3259 (Ont. S.C.J.); affirmed 2003 CarswellOnt 1009, 34 R.F.L. (5th) 450, 64 O.R. (3d) 229, 225 D.L.R. (4th) 186, 170 O.A.C. 1, [2003] O.J. No. 1083 (Ont. C.A.). The wife was awarded lump sum support of $500,000 upon the breakdown of the parties' 18-month marriage. The husband was extremely wealthy and his conditions, means, needs and circumstances had not changed since the time of the marriage. The wife on the other hand had given birth to the parties' child. Accordingly, her needs were greater than before the marriage, particularly as the child was now entitled to a lifestyle commensurate with being the son of a wealthy father. Although the wife had already been paid $100,000 pursuant to the parties' marriage contract, the payment was in the nature of a property settlement and not in satisfaction of the husband's spousal support obligation. Affirming this judgement, the court of appeal held that the payment would assist the wife to provide a lifestyle comparable to the one which the child had enjoyed when he lived with both parents, a lifestyle to which the husband was readily able to contribute. The payment would enable the wife to enhance her self-sufficiency and help her to purchase a permanent home for herself and the parties' child. While the amount was a substantial one, it should be seen in the context of the husband's assets which were worth between $19 and $20 million, his undisputed ability to pay, and the parties' lifestyle during the marriage.

*It is inconsistent with the overall scheme of the* Divorce Act *that economic hardship should be equated with a subsistence standard of living — Giraud v. Giraud*, 1997 CarswellBC 2575, 34 R.F.L. (4th) 255, 44 B.C.L.R. (3d) 98, 155 D.L.R. (4th) 112, 100 B.C.A.C. 27, 163 W.A.C. 27

(B.C.C.A.). According to dictionary definitions what is economic hardship, similar to what constsitutes need, will vary with the circumstances of the parties.

*Replicating marital lifestyle is a goal of support only if means clearly available* — *Escaravage v. Escaravage*, 1995 CarswellBC 420, 14 R.F.L. (4th) 256, 59 B.C.A.C. 113, 98 W.A.C. 113 (B.C.C.A.). Support at such a level as to support the marital lifestyle should only be ordered where the means are clearly available.

*Significance of marital standard of living* — *Linton v. Linton*, 1990 CarswellOnt 316, 30 R.F.L. (3d) 1, 1 O.R. (3d) 1, 42 O.A.C. 328, 75 D.L.R. (4th) 637, 41 E.T.R. 85 (Ont. C.A.). The court was of the view that the appropriate standard of living is a reasonable standard of living, having in mind the circumstances of the marriage. Where there is a long marriage and an ability to pay support according to this standard, reasonable standard of living should be assessed in the context of the marital standard of living. The amount to be awarded should take into account the effect of the property disposition.

*Continuation of marital lifestyle not guaranteed* — *Caspick v. Caspick*, 1990 CarswellNB 24, 27 R.F.L. (3d) 337, 71 D.L.R. (4th) 411, 106 N.B.R. (2d) 249, 265 A.P.R. 249 (N.B.C.A.). Support is awarded to redress economic disadvantages attributable to the marriage and not to guarantee a continuation of the marital lifestyle.

*Wife entitled to marital standard of living after 46-year marriage* — *Lynk v. Lynk*, 1989 CarswellNS 60, 21 R.F.L. (3d) 337, 92 N.S.R. (2d) 1, 237 A.P.R. 1 (N.S.C.A.). In a more traditional decision concerning a marriage of 46 years, the appellate division of the Nova Scotia Supreme Court decided that the standard of living to which the wife was entitled, having regard to the husband's ability to pay, was equal to that which she would have enjoyed had this long-lasting marriage continued through the husband's retirement years.

*Relevant factors for appropriate standard of living* — *Heinemann v. Heinemann*, 1989 CarswellNS 56, 20 R.F.L. (3d) 236, 91 N.S.R. (2d) 136, 233 A.P.R. 136, 60 D.L.R. (4th) 648 (N.S.C.A.). The appropriate standard of living for a dependent spouse in a traditional marriage is the approximate standard she would have had if she had followed her own career objectives rather than those of the marriage. However, it should not be wholly unrelated to that which she enjoyed prior to the dissolution of the marriage.

*Payee entitled to reasonable and adequate standard of living* — *Marshall v. Marshall*, 1988 CarswellOnt 228, 13 R.F.L. (3d) 337 (Ont. C.A.). The Ontario Court of Appeal affirmed a decision which had stated that, while the wife was not expected to retain the standard of living which she had had before separation, she was intended to have a reasonable and adequate standard of living.

*Inflation among factors amounting to radical change in circumstances* — *Marshall v. Marshal, supral.* The majority of the Court of Appeal was of the opinion that because of inflation, which resulted in a decline in the value of money between the date of the separation and the date of the trial, the consequent decline in the wife's own income was a radical change in her circumstances generated by her previous pattern of dependency and aggravated by her fragile health. The required causal connection between the hardship experienced by the wife and the dependent relationship arising from the marriage was established. There was no error in principle in increasing the wife's support from $728 per month to $1,228 per month.

*Where a wife was financially disadvantaged because of her own choices rather than the role played during cohabitation, and had not taken steps towards self-sufficiency, support was terminated* — *Acker v. Acker*, 2014 CarswellNS 136, 2014 NSSC 5, 41 R.F.L. (7th) 166 (N.S.S.C.). The husband sought the termination of spousal support in this review application. The wife sought to increase spousal support based on the husband's post-separation increase in income. The parties were married for 23 years, and support was paid pursuant to Minutes of Settlement incorporated into a Corollary Relief Order. The wife had not been employed for 10 years prior to separation. The judge considered the roles played by the parties during the relationship and found that the wife had not been economically disadvantaged by the marriage, which was nontraditional. The judge found that the husband's income had increased, but was now roughly equivalent to its level at the time of separation. The wife's financial situation was found to be a result of her own choices rather than her role during the marriage. Spousal support was not increased, and a step-down order was made.

*Husband ordered to pay wife non-compensatory temporary spousal support as wife's income is significantly lower than husband's since she should be in position to maintain a reasonable standard of living in recent aftermath of breakdown of marital relationship involving a high joint income — Perry v. Fujimoto*, 2011 CarswellOnt 4180, 2011 ONSC 3334 (Ont. S.C.J.). The parties had been married for 18 years and had two children. They were to have joint custody. The husband was a corporate executive with a fixed income of $353,000 in 2010, and the wife was an optometrist with an income fixed at $113,000 for 2010. The wife had had a motor vehicle accident causing her to see fewer patients a day. The husband had a net worth of $400,000 and the wife had a net worth of $1,406,000. Following calculation of temporary child support, and considering the means, needs and circumstances, including the difference in the spouses net worth, the husband was ordered to pay temporary spousal support in the amount of $4,000 per month.

*Negating arguments raised by 79-year-old husband that wife's medical and financial position no worse than prior to marriage, that she had relatives available to assist her, and that he wished to give assets to his son, not alter his obligation to provide non- compensatory support — Fedor v. Fedor*, 2011 CarswellAlta 418, 2011 ABQB 185, 96 R.F.L. (6th) 309, 525 A.R. 128, 46 Alta. L.R. (5th) 221, [2011] A.J. No. 314 (Alta. Q.B.). Following a 12-year marriage, the wife age 70 and the husband age 79 separated. The wife had suffered from fibromyalgia and arthritis before and during the marriage. Following the separation, the wife had an income of $17,105.77 and resided with her brother as she had done prior to the marriage. The husband earned $116,625.48 per year from his pensions and investments. On the wife's application for interim spousal support, the husband raised the fact of a prenuptial agreement, but it was held that it did not address the issue of support. The husband also argued that the wife who had been married twice before with three children, was being assisted by her brother, and that her health and financial position had not deteriorated during the marriage. The court awarded the wife interim support in the amount of $1,500 per month. The court stated that the primary burden of support takes precedence over the possible availability of support from relatives which is consistent with the recognition of the economic disadvantages and hardship sustained by the wife arising from the marriage breakdown within the meaning of sections 15.2 (6) (a) and (c) of the *Divorce Act*. While she may be situated similarly to her pre-marriage position, she is disadvantaged in comparison to the position she enjoyed while married. Nor did the fact that she had left the marriage alter the obligation. Further the husband's wish to give interest-earning assets to his son did not displace his obligation to the wife.

*Spousal support award for a stay-at-home father — Jacobs v. Dingee-Jacobs*, 2010 CarswellNB 380, 2010 NBQB 114, 89 R.F.L. (6th) 286, 360 N.B.R. (2d) 40, 930 A.P.R. 40 (N.B.Q.B.). The parties had a 24-year marriage. For the majority of the marriage the husband acted as the children's primary caregiver and did not work outside the home. The parties moved a number of times in order to advance the wife's career. The husband was awarded spousal support on a compensatory and non-compensatory basis. The husband remained at home, with the wife's agreement, to care for the children and the home. The benefit of outside assistance, such as a part-time nanny and a cleaner, did not negate the parties' objective of having the husband stay home. Although the husband's efforts to secure work were limited, his age, health issues and time away from the workforce would make finding work difficult. The husband suffered economic hardship as a result of the marriage and was entitled to compensatory support. He was also entitled to non-compensatory support on the basis that he had no income and could not be self-sufficient. A time-limited support order was not appropriate as it was unresolved as to when the husband might achieve self-sufficiency. Spousal support was set at the mid-point of the *Spousal Support Advisory Guidelines* range.

*A spouse who was disabled and would remain unemployable is entitled to a time limited spousal support award — Haggerty v. Haggerty*, 2010 CarswellNS 6, 2010 NSSC 9, 80 R.F.L. (6th) 227 (N.S.S.C.). The parties lived as common-law partners for 3 years and were married for 7 years. They had no children. During the course of the marriage the wife became disabled and would remain unemployable. The wife was awarded spousal support on a non-compensatory basis for 7 years. The parties had lived as mutually dependent partners who had accepted the responsibility of supporting one another. Although the wife's disability occurred during the marriage, it was not caused by the marriage or the circumstances of the marriage. Consequently, the award of spousal support for an indefinite period would cause an imbalance between the parties' mutual obligations and the clean-break model. The wife's likely failure to be able to attain economic self-sufficiency did not automatically result in the husband's continuing obligation for spousal support. The court determined that 7 years of spousal support was appropriate given that the marriage was of a medium length.

*Marital standard of living is point of reference, not payor's post-separation income — Chalifoux v. Chalifoux*, 2006 CarswellAlta 907, 2006 ABQB 535, [2006] A.J. No. 883 (Alta. Q.B.); additional reasons at 2007 CarswellAlta 230, 2007 ABQB 111 (Alta. Q.B.). A payee spouse is entitled to a reasonable standard of living having regard to the family income during the marriage and not to the payor spouse's increased income since marriage ended.

*See also re loss of standard of living justifying support — Sweeney v. Sweeney*, 2004 CarswellNB 363, 2004 NBQB 267, 8 R.F.L. (6th) 424 (N.B.Q.B.).

*Husband not responsible through support for wife's extravagant post-separation lifestyle choices — Bradley v. Bradley*, 2003 CarswellSask 688, 2003 SKQB 415, 45 R.F.L. (5th) 237, 240 Sask. R. 193 (Sask. Q.B.). Where the wife had made some extravagant lifestyle choices subsequent to separation, she could not reasonably expect her husband to finance them without having to draw upon some of her own financial resources. She was perfectly entitled to make these choices but she was also required to live with the consequences.

*Wife not entitled to sufficient support to allow continuation of lavish marital lifestyle — Cook v. Cook*, 2002 CarswellNS 198, 2002 NSSC 124, 27 R.F.L. (5th) 12, 204 N.S.R. (2d) 167, 639 A.P.R. 167 (N.S.S.C.). Where the wife chose to remain in a large five bedroom home and eat all of her meals in restaurants, she could not realistically expect the husband to subsidize the same through spousal support, despite the affluence of both parties and lavish lifestyle that they enjoyed together.

*Wife had used luxury cars during marriage — lesser car not a substitute — Bennett v. Bennett*, 2001 CarswellOnt 168, 13 R.F.L. (5th) 325 (Ont. S.C.J.). Where as a result of the husband's car business the wife had habitually had the use of a luxury car the court rejected the husband's application to replace the vehicle currently in the wife's possession with one of significantly less value. The husband could not attempt, through court orders, to create a "new, less lavish reality" for the wife. Especially when his own would significantly increase if he was not required to maintain hers.

*Long-term marriage — presumption that payor and recipient should have equal standards of living — Labron v. Labron*, 1996 CarswellAlta 332, 21 R.F.L. (4th) 385, 183 A.R. 251 (Alta. Q.B.). In a long-term traditional marriage where the wife has generally fulfilled the role of caregiver for the family while the husband has developed a career, there is a strong presumption that both parties should share an equal standard of living upon dissolution of the marriage.

*Relevance of marital standard of living — Droit de la famille - 2132*, 1995 CarswellQue 203, EYB 1995-84547, [1995] R.D.F. 116, 11 C.C.P.B. 272 (C.S. Que.). Where the wife had sufficient income to support herself in a style which would have been sufficient for most Canadians, she had throughout the parties' 25-year marriage been used to a lavish lifestyle. She was therefore found entitled to periodic support up until the husband's retirement.

*Husband had required parties to live substantially below means when married — wife not required to continue this frugality — Katay v. Katay*, 1995 CarswellAlta 627, 168 A.R. 31 (Alta. Q.B.). Where the husband had, throughout the parties' 23-year traditional marriage, imposed a frugal lifestyle on the family in order to accumulate savings, the quantum of spousal support to which the wife was entitled was not limited to a continuation of that lifestyle.

*See also re significance of marital standard of living — Row v. Row*, 1991 CarswellAlta 144, 35 R.F.L. (3d) 237, 82 Alta. L.R. (3d) 237, 123 A.R. 324 (Alta. Q.B.).

*Where payee's earnings are more than before a 4-year marriage, spousal support should be denied — Murray v. Murray (No. 2)*, 1992 CarswellNfld 276, 98 Nfld. & P.E.I.R. 297, 311 A.P.R. 297 (Nfld. U.F.C.). The employment obtained by the wife after separation paid more than her job prior to the parties' 4-year marriage. The marriage had not caused the wife any economic hardship.

*Support justified by illness may be time limited or indefinite — Rayvals v. Rayvals*, 2004 CarswellBC 2870, 2004 BCCA 630, 11 R.F.L. (6th) 125, 37 B.C.L.R. (4th) 374, 205 B.C.A.C. 267, 337 W.A.C. 267, 248 D.L.R. (4th) 262 (B.C.C.A.); reversing in part 2002 CarswellBC 304, 2002 BCSC 128, 25 R.F.L. (5th) 399, [2002] B.C.J. No. 201 (B.C.S.C.). Where a person is ordered to make payments pursuant to s. 15.2 of the *Divorce Act* to a former spouse who, as a result of having developed a devastating physical illness during the marriage, was unable to be gainfully employed, the amount and duration of support varies with the circumstances and practical and policy issues affecting the particular case. While the payor should not be obligated to pay in perpetuity, a time limit may not be appropriate either.

*Wife's clinical depression resulted from marriage breakdown — Haldone v. Haldone*, 1999 CarswellBC 735, 1999 BCCA 200, 45 R.F.L. (4th) 285, 122 B.C.A.C. 280, 200 W.A.C. 280 (B.C.C.A.). Where the wife suffered from clinical depression resulting from the breakdown of the marriage, her spousal support award was upheld on appeal. Although the wife had worked throughout the marriage her health problems now prevented her from doing so. As there was a link between the wife's depression, her economic disadvantage and the marriage breakdown, spousal support was appropriate.

*Need arising from physical or emotional disabilities can be grounds for support — McKean v. McKean*, 1992 CarswellMan 28, 38 R.F.L. (3d) 172, 75 Man. R. (2d) 318, 6 W.A.C. 318 (Man. C.A.). A spouse is not disqualified from support under the *Divorce Act* because his or her need arises from physical or emotional disabilities, at least where the condition arose during the marriage.

*Medical condition related to marriage insofar as husband knew of it at time of marriage — Droit de la famille - 803*, [1990] R.J.Q. 957, [1990] R.D.F. 317 (headnote only) (C.A. Que.). Where the wife had suffered from epilepsy, which prevented her from working full-time, the husband was obliged to pay spousal support. The wife's inability to achieve self-sufficiency was related to the marriage in as much as the husband was aware of the wife's condition at the time of the marriage and had accepted it.

*Husband had given disabled wife the impression during marriage that he would support her for life — Eng v. Eng*, 2006 CarswellBC 2237, 2006 BCSC 1353, 31 R.F.L. (6th) 407, [2006] B.C.J. No. 2044 (B.C.S.C.). The court refused to put a time limit on the wife's spousal support upon termination of the parties' 3-year marriage. The wife was disabled at the time of the marriage and the husband had from the outset created the impression that he would support her for life.

Although she had derived some benefit from the marriage, these were offset by the lack of medical benefits and support from her former spouse.

*Claimant unfit to work — indefinite support awarded — Lovich v. Lovich*, 2006 CarswellAlta 1312, 2006 ABQB 736, 31 R.F.L. (6th) 140, 64 Alta. L.R. (4th) 231 (Alta. Q.B.); additional reasons at 2006 CarswellAlta 1419, 2006 ABQB 797, 68 Alta. L.R. (4th) 182 (Alta. Q.B.). If a dependant spouse is declared unfit to work on the uncontradicted evidence of her psychiatrist, no income should be attributed to her and she is entitled to support. This was a 25-year marriage during which the wife essentially did not work outside the home after the children were born. The court ordered spousal support of indefinite duration, subject to any change of circumstances.

*Claimant unfit to work — indefinite support awarded — Fraser v. Fraser*, 2004 CarswellOnt 3343, 8 R.F.L. (6th) 125 (Ont. S.C.J.). Where the husband was diagnosed with leukemia after separation and was unable to work, he was found to have suffered an economic disadvantage from the breakdown of the marriage and was awarded spousal support.

*Claimant had numerous ailments — support ordered with review in 4 years — Leonard v. Leonard*, 2002 CarswellOnt 367, 26 R.F.L. (5th) 146 (Ont. S.C.J.). Where the breakdown of the marriage, compounded with the wife's numerous physical ailments, severely curtailed her ability to work, she was awarded periodic support, subject to review in four-year's time.

*Injuries from post-separation accidents justified support — Riberdy v. Riberdy*, 2001 CarswellOnt 2400, 18 R.F.L. (5th) 161 (Ont. S.C.J.); additional reasons at (2001), 2001 CarswellOnt 2920 (Ont. S.C.J.). The wife was awarded spousal support on the basis of the need arising from injuries she had suffered in two post-separation accidents.

*Husband would have paid for wife's medical treatments had marriage continued — support justified — Winfield v. Winfield*, 1998 CarswellOnt 134, 35 R.F.L. (4th) 393, [1998] O.J. No. 175 (Ont. Gen. Div.); additional reasons at 1998 CarswellOnt 855 (Ont. Gen. Div.). A wife in a marriage of 30 years who had multiple sclerosis was found to have suffered economic disadvantages as a result of the end of the marriage. Because of the marriage break-up, she was required to spend money for services that she was unable to perform and which her husband would have undertaken if the parties had remained married. She was awarded periodic support for an indefinite term.

*Relocated to further spouse's career — illness after separation — Dillon v. Dillon*, 1997 CarswellNB 4, 27 R.F.L. (4th) 197, 184 N.B.R. (2d) 371, 469 A.P.R. 371 (N.B.Q.B.). Where the wife had given up her career to move with the husband to further his career and later developed a debilitating mental illness, which prevented her from working, she was found entitled to spousal support. The breakdown of the marriage had resulted in economic hardship to her.

*Causal link not required between illness and marriage — Ashworth v. Ashworth*, 1995 CarswellOnt 489, 15 R.F.L. (4th) 379 (Ont. Gen. Div.). There is no requirement that a spouse establish a causal link between a debilitating illness and the marriage as a prerequisite to support. Such an illness can properly constitute a "condition" or "other circumstance" that affects the spouse's economic prospects.

*Hardship largely caused by medical condition which predated marriage — Morrison v. Morrison*, 1995 CarswellBC 2674 (B.C.S.C.). Where the wife's economic problems were largely the result of a neurological disorder which existed before the marriage, but her post-separation depression could be traced in part to the marriage breakdown, she was found entitled to limited term support.

*Causal link not required between alcoholism and marriage — Day v. Day*, 1994 CarswellNS 133, 129 N.S.R. (2d) 169, 362 A.P.R. 169 (N.S.S.C.); additional reasons at 1994 CarswellNS 48, 3 R.F.L. (4th) 432, [1994] G.S.T.C. 26, 129 N.S.R. (2d) 186, 362 A.P.R. 186 (N.S.S.C.). Where the wife's ability to work was affectd by her alcoholism it was found that proof of a causal connection between her alcoholism and the marriage was not a prerequisite to the granting of her claim for spousal support.

*Blindness predated marriage — economic hardship not therefore entirely attributable to marriage — Garbutt v. Garbutt*, 1993 CarswellMan 172, 84 Man. R. (2d) 237 (Man. Q.B.). The court found, in assessing the wife's support, that her economic disability could not be totally attributed to the marriage. The wife had been blind at the date of the marriage and her disability would have affected her functioning in a work environment whether or not she had married.

*Causal link not required between illness and marriage if other spouse has ability to pay — Parish v. Parish*, 1993 CarswellOnt 316, 46 R.F.L. (3d) 117 (Ont. Gen. Div.). Where the husband's continuing health problems prevented him from being self-sufficient, the wife, who had the ability to pay, was ordered to contribute to his support. The fact that the husband's need was not related to the marriage did not disentitle him to support.

*Causal link need not be proven between psychiatric condition and marriage — Ivans v. Ivans*, 1992 CarswellMan 51, 42 R.F.L. (3d) 270, 82 Man. R. (2d) 101 (Man. Q.B.). Where it was unclear whether the wife's debilitating psychiatric disorder was related to the marriage, the husband was ordered to pay spousal support. The wife was in desperate need of support and the husband had the ability to pay.

*Claimant's illness not caused by other spouse — support reduced by amount she would have earned in the absence of illness — Jerowsky v. Jerowsky*, 1990 CarswellAlta 292, 32 R.F.L. (3d) 188, 114 A.R. 381 (Alta. Q.B.). Where the wife became ill after separation and was unable to work, it was held that the husband was not responsible for any economic disadvantage flowing from this post-separation disability. Accordingly, the support otherwise ordered payable was reduced by an amount which the wife could have earned had she not been ill.

*Husband had supported wife during marriage, therefore she was more vulnerable afterwards and therefore hardship resulted from marriage breakdown — Henton v. Henton*, 1990 CarswellBC 483, 28 R.F.L. (3d) 383 (B.C.S.C.). Where the wife had had an aneurism that caused her to be unable to live independently, the court found that she was entitled to support. During the marriage, the husband had absorbed the wife's disadvantages and the resulting hardship; since the end of the marriage she was more vulnerable, a direct result of the marriage breakdown.

*Depression not caused by marriage but husband aware of it at time of marriage — Deane v. Deane*, 1989 CarswellSask 572, 81 Sask. R. 171 (Sask. Q.B.). The wife's prospects of becoming self-sufficient were hampered by bouts of depression. Although her condition was not causally connected to the marriage, the husband was aware of it before he married her. The husband was ordered to pay support to the wife for a 2-year period.

*Health problems caused by pregnancy and therefore by marriage — nominal support ordered — McAfee v. McAfee*, 1989 CarswellBC 409, 21 R.F.L. (3d) 75 (B.C.S.C.). Where the wife's health problems and her resulting inability to work were related to complications that arose during her pregnancy, her need upon the parties' separation was found to be causally connected to the marriage and she was found to be entitled to support. Since the husband claimed to have no assets and no income, he was ordered to pay the wife maintenance of $1 annually until there was a material change in the circumstances of either of the parties as contemplated by s. 17 of the *Divorce Act*, 1985.

*Health problems partially caused by pregnancy — Fairall v. Fairall*, 1989 CarswellAlta 378, 20 R.F.L. (3d) 107, 93 A.R. 224 (Alta. Q.B.); additional reasons at 1990 CarswellAlta 272, 26 R.F.L. (3d) 126, 106 A.R. 277 (Alta. Q.B.). The wife's health problems could be traced in part to the birth of the parties' children; consequently, her economic needs were found to be related to the marriage. The husband was ordered to pay $200 per month to the wife for 3 years.

*Arthritis developed during marriage, need not have been caused by it — White v. White*, 1989 CarswellOnt 215, 18 R.F.L. (3d) 216 (Ont. H.C.). *White* followed *Smith v. Smith*, 1987

CarswellOnt 269, 11 R.F.L.(3d) 214 (Ont. H.C.), in holding that the husband was responsible for the wife's support, since her illness, rheumatoid arthritis, developed during the marriage, even if there was no causal connection between the illness and the marriage.

*Illness which predates marriage more likely to be unrelated to it — Droit de la famille - 1170*, [1988] R.D.F. 180 (C.S. Que.). If a dependent spouse's illness exists prior to the marriage, it may also be seen as unrelated to the marriage. Consequently, support may be terminated.

*Onus on support claimant to demonstrate connection between health problems and marriage or else become self-supporting in 6 years — Francis v. Francis*, 1988 CarswellOnt 280, 16 R.F.L. (3d) 149 (Ont. H.C.). Where the wife's severe hypertension together with her anginal syndrome and consequent inability to work might have had its genesis in the marriage, she must prove this link or otherwise become self-supporting within a reasonable time which, in this case, would be 6 years from the date of separation. The parties had been married for 23 years, had two children, and were in their mid-forties.

*Injury suffered after marriage not a basis for support — Miller v. Miller*, 1988 CarswellOnt 272, 15 R.F.L. (3d) 366 (Ont. H.C.). The wife was injured in a car accident after the marriage and was denied support.

*Illness and hardship not caused by marriage — support limited to 2 years — Goering v. Goering*, 1988 CarswellOnt 231, 13 R.F.L. (3d) 383 (Ont. H.C.). The wife suffered from high blood pressure and asthma and was undergoing psychiatric treatment. She was on welfare prior to the marriage, did not work during cohabitation, and had not sought employment after she lost custody of the parties' child. The husband applied to vary the wife's support order. The husband discharged the burden of proof to establish that the connection between the wife's economic dependency and her marriage no longer existed. In light of the wife's past employment history, the standard of living to which she had been accustomed prior to marriage, her lack of formal education, and the short duration of the marriage, the wife was entitled to 2 years' support from the date of the divorce in order to retrain for employment.

*Disease not caused by marriage — no support — Williams v. Williams*, 1988 CarswellNfld 13, 13 R.F.L. (3d) 321, 70 Nfld.& P.E.I.R. 331, 215 A.P.R. 331 (Nfld. T.D.). The court held that where, after separation, the wife had developed Parkinson's disease and was therefore unable to work, her application for support was dismissed. The wife's economic hardship was not connected to the marriage; it resulted from the disease.

*Illness arose during marriage but not caused by it — Winterle v. Winterle*, 1987 CarswellOnt 236, 10 R.F.L. (3d) 129 (Ont. H.C.). The court also denied support to a former husband on the basis of an absence of causal connection between his need and the marriage. In this case, the parties had cohabited for 9 years and the husband suffered from manic depression and chronic schizophrenia diagnosed during the marriage.

*There should be brief limited spousal support where there is a very short marriage and the dependant spouse had a pre-existing medical condition — Pedersen v. Pedersen*, 2004 CarswellBC 3279, 2004 BCSC 1627 (B.C.S.C.). The marriage lasted 2 months. The wife suffered from depression.

*Approximate equal standard of living — Cadigan v. Cadigan*, 2004 CarswellMan 533, 2004 MBQB 283, 189 Man. R. (2d) 245 (Man. Q.B.); affirmed 2007 CarswellMan 72, 2007 MBCA 28, 212 Man. R. (2d) 291, 389 W.A.C. 291 (Man. C.A.). Spousal support was reduced in order to promote the wife's self-sufficiency and to encourage her to take this objective seriously. The reduced amount was intended to relieve her economic hardship sufficiently that together with her employment and a reasonable financial plan, she could enjoy a lifestyle and standard of living approximating that of the husband.

*Change in circumstances from marriage breakdown sufficient basis for non-compensatory support award — Fisher v. Fisher*, 2001 CarswellNS 31, 2000 NSCA 18, 12 R.F.L. (5th) 348, 190

N.S.R. (2d) 144, 594 A.P.R. 144 (N.S.C.A.); varying 2000 CarswellNS 101, 7 R.F.L. (5th) 45 (N.S.S.C.). The court allowed the wife's appeal from the dismissal of her claim for spousal support. The trial judge erred in finding that spousal support was not warranted because of the wife's lack of effort to achieve self-sufficiency after the collapse of her long-term traditional marriage. Given the wife's age and background she could at best, be expected only to attain a limited degree of self-sufficiency. Furthermore, there should have been some recognition of the change in the wife's economic circumstances resulting from the marriage breakdown. There is no basis for awarding support on compensatory principles where the wife's career potential had not suffered as a result of the marriage or the traditional role she played in it. However, non-compensatory support may be awarded on the ground that she suffered economic disadvantage as a result of the breakdown of the marriage.

*Entitlement established on the basis of economic hardship* — *Gabb v. Gabb*, 2001 CarswellMan 68, 2001 MBCA 19, 13 R.F.L. (5th) 391, 153 Man. R. (2d) 157, 238 W.A.C. 157, [2001] M.J. No. 55 (Man. C.A.). Entitlement to spousal support may be established on any combination of three bases, contract, compensation for the disadvantages arising out of the marriage or its breakdown, or support required to relieve the economic hardships arising from the marriage breakdown. In the *Gabb* case, given the duration (9 years) and circumstances of the marriage combined with the age of the wife at the time of the marriage breakdown (53), the wife was undoubtedly economically disadvantaged as a result of the nature of the relationship itself. The court, in upholding the trial court's spousal support award of $500 per month, stated that the support award was justifiable in all of the circumstances, on the ground of relieving economic hardship alone. In the year following separation the wife's income was just over $10,000 and the husband's income remained between $40,000 and $45,000. The wife was debt-free and the husband owed $75,000 in income tax. The court dismissed the husband's appeal.

*Provision for future need* — *Savoie v. Savoie*, 1999 CarswellMan 308, 49 R.F.L. (4th) 336, [1999] 9 W.W.R. 63, 175 D.L.R. (4th) 291, 138 Man. R. (2d) 128 (Man. C.A.). Where the wife had a future need for support which arose because of her economic disadvantage suffered as a result of the long-term traditional marriage, her appeal was allowed in part and spousal support was set at $300 per month, even though she did not have a current economic need. This amount of $300 was half of what the wife had previously received under the parties' separation agreement and at trial. The reduction took into account her remarriage and the setting aside of the separation agreement.

*Support ordered based on hardship arising from breakdown of traditional marriage* — *Greener v. Greener*, 1997 CarswellNB 528, 35 R.F.L. (4th) 179, 194 N.B.R. (2d) 376, 496 A.P.R. 376 (N.B.C.A.). Where the wife suffered from economic hardship that resulted from the breakdown of the traditional marriage between the parties, she was entitled to spousal support. The trial judge properly considered the wife's employment history, her present circumstances, and her attempts at self-sufficiency. The order was upheld on appeal.

*Wife's disability worsened during marriage* — *spouses agreed that she would quit her job* — *Giraud v. Giraud*, 1997 CarswellBC 2575, 34 R.F.L. (4th) 255, 44 B.C.L.R. (3d) 98, 155 D.L.R. (4th) 112, 100 B.C.A.C. 27, 163 W.A.C. 27 (B.C.C.A.). The wife had a disability before marriage and that disability worsened during marriage. She had cancelled her disability insurance when, according to the parties' agreement, she quit her job upon her marriage to the respondent. The appellant was 57 and the respondent 76 years of age.

*Quantum of support based on reliance interest* — *Giraud v. Giraud*, 1997 CarswellBC 2575, 34 R.F.L. (4th) 255, 44 B.C.L.R. (3d) 98, 155 D.L.R. (4th) 112, 100 B.C.A.C. 27, 163 W.A.C. 27, [1997] B.C.J. No. 2717 (B.C.C.A.). The court held that the appropriate order would have guaranteed that the appellant could maintain a lifestyle equivalent to that which she would have enjoyed had she not accepted the respondent's promises to provide financial security for her when she married him. The court ordered that the appellant should receive $2,500 per month as support during the parties' joint lives. The appellant was 57 and the respondent 76 years of age.

*Marriage breakdown meant that illness led to economic disadvantage — Snyder v. Snyder,* 1993 CarswellAlta 441, 47 R.F.L. (3d) 13, 138 A.R. 255 (Alta. Q.B.); affirmed (September 23, 1994), Foisy J.A., Irving J.A., Lieberman J.A. (Alta. C.A.). Where the wife was prevented from working as a result of an illness which she developed after separation, she was nevertheless found entitled to support. If it had not been for the marriage breakdown, the illness from which she suffered would not have resulted in her economic disadvantage.

*Claimant's economic difficulties due to recession and not to marriage breakdown therefore support application dismissed — B. (N) v. C. (N.),* 1993 CarswellQue 255, 57 Q.A.C. 1 (C.A. Que.). Where the wife had previously been self-sufficient, but at the time of separation was unemployed, her application for support was dismissed. The wife's economic difficulties were not related to the breakdown of the marriage but rather to the recession.

*Marriage of long duration — claimant suffering from economic disadvantages of marriage — Yaschuk v. Logan,* 1992 CarswellNS 64, 39 R.F.L. (3d) 417, 110 N.S.R. (2d) 278, 299 A.P.R. 278, [1992] N.S.J. No. 99 (N.S.C.A.); reversing 1991 CarswellNS 59, 33 R.F.L. (3d) 316, 103 N.S.R. (2d) 371, 282 A.P.R. 371 (N.S.T.D.). Where the husband's abuse of the wife during the course of a long-term traditional marriage could be linked to her health problems, an award of periodic support made in the wife's favour was upheld on appeal. The wife could not work because of her health and she was entitled to have the economic disadvantage flowing from the marriage redressed.

*Continuation of marital lifestyle not guaranteed to support claimant — Caspick v. Caspick,* 1988 CarswellNB 50, 17 R.F.L. (3d) 295, 93 N.B.R. (2d) 63, 238 A.P.R. 63 (N.B.Q.B.); varied 1990 CarswellNB 24, 27 R.F.L. (3d) 337, 71 D.L.R. (4th) 411, 106 N.B.R. (2d) 249, 265 A.P.R. 249 (N.B.C.A.). Support is awarded to redress an economic disadvantage attributable to the marriage and not to guarantee a continuation of the marital lifestyle. Accordingly, where the wife could not establish that her inability to maintain her pre-separation lifestyle was causally connected to the marriage, she was found not to have any general right to support. In that case, the parties had been married for 9 years and the wife had worked part-time as a bookkeeper in the husband's business. There was no evidence that the marriage diminished her earning potential. At the time of the divorce hearing, the wife was earning $1,500 per month.

*Wife employed full-time — support awarded due to her loss of benefit of husband's higher income — Reinhardt v. Reinhardt,* 2004 CarswellOnt 3275, 8 R.F.L. (6th) 34 (Ont. S.C.J.); additional reasons at 2004 CarswellOnt 4374 (Ont. S.C.J.). The wife was awarded periodic spousal support although she was employed full time. The husband's annual salary was considerably more than the wife's, who accordingly had suffered an economic disadvantage because of the loss to her of a standard of living enjoyed by her as a beneficiary of combined incomes.

*14 years of support had satisfied compensatory rationale but need persisted and therefore support entitlement did too — Stier v. Stier,* 2004 CarswellBC 2615, 2004 BCSC 1458 (B.C.S.C. [In Chambers]). Where compensatory grounds of support do not exist or have been satisfied, a support obligation may still exist because one of the parties has an economic need. The court found that 14 years of support payments satisfied any obligation the husband may have had to provide compensatory support, but that the wife was entitled to non-compensatory support.

*Support varied downward to leave payor with 57% of net disposable income — Snjaric v. Snjaric,* 2003 CarswellOnt 4033, 48 R.F.L. (5th) 193 (Ont. S.C.J.). The court held that notwithstanding a long marriage of 27 years and an entitlement to compensatory and non-compensatory support, it was equitable to leave the payor spouse with more of the parties' combined net disposable income. In this case, the husband had to work full-time; twice the number of actual and imputed hours that the wife would work. In the equalization of property, he was required to include the capitalized value of his future pension, affording the wife the ability to use those funds right away towards the purchase of a home, and thus a smaller mortgage payment. The original order made the wife's support conditional upon her making her best efforts to develop her proficiency in English. Her diligence in this matter was questionable. Spousal support was varied from $1,200 monthly to $1,000 monthly. She would continue to have 43% of the combined net disposable income of the parties and the husband 57%.

*Income disparity alone not enough to justify support* — *M. (D.G.) v. M. (K.M.)*, 2002 CarswellAlta 289, 2002 ABQB 225, 26 R.F.L. (5th) 152 (Alta. Q.B.). The fact that the husband had a substantially larger income than the wife was not, in itself, evidence that the wife suffered career inequalities as a result of the marriage or its breakdown. The wife's annual income had more than doubled since the date of the marriage and there was no evidence that her living standard had declined. Accordingly, her claim for spousal support was dismissed.

*Disparity in income justifies support* — *Stang v. Stang*, 2001 CarswellBC 1526, 2001 BCSC 975, 19 R.F.L. (5th) 187 (B.C.S.C.). The wife's economic disadvantage was found to have arisen partially from injuries suffered in a post-separation automobile accident for which she had recovered damages. However, as a substantial difference existed between the allocated income to the wife in the damage award and the husband's income, she was entitled to the ongoing spousal support. The disparity between her income and the husband's was a direct result of the marriage and its breakdown.

*Husband's abuse causes stress-related illnesses* — *Kennedy v. Kennedy*, 2000 CarswellOnt 3622, 11 R.F.L. (5th) 150, [2000] O.J. No. 3742 (Ont. S.C.J.). Where the wife's stress-related illnesses, which prevented her from working, were the result of emotional and psychological abuse by the husband, the court found she suffered an economic disadvantage related to the marriage and was entitled to interim spousal support.

*Non-compensatory support ordered to allow time to return to reasonable lifestyle and self-sufficiency* — *Hoxford v. Hoxford*, 1999 CarswellOnt 2300, 2 R.F.L. (5th) 257 (Ont. S.C.J.). The wife was entitled to non-compensatory spousal support to assist her to adjust to the marriage breakdown and to reorganize her financial affairs. The parties had a modern marriage in which both of them worked and they were not dependent upon each other. The only disadvantage that the wife suffered was that she would have to return to a reasonable lifestyle by herself, with the necessary changes to achieve self-sufficiency without the advantages of both parties pooling their resources. The husband was ordered to pay lump sum spousal support of $10,800, payable in the amount of $450 a month over 24 months.

*Fibromyalgia developed before relationship ended* — *Stuart v. Stuart*, 1997 CarswellNB 265, 30 R.F.L. (4th) 204 (N.B.Q.B.). Where the wife had developed fibromyalgia 6 years before the parties separated, her condition was found to be a factor in determining spousal support to alleviate the economic disadvantages caused by the marriage.

*Claimant's prescription drug addiction and limited income not related to marriage-support denied* — *MacDonald v. Rasmussen*, 1997 CarswellSask 362, 29 R.F.L. (4th) 310 (Sask. Q.B.). Where both the parties were physicians, but the wife worked only part time, to some degree because of illness and an addiction to prescription drugs, her application for support was refused. The wife's claims of debilitating pain were already exaggerated so as to ensure her supply of prescription drugs. Her dependency was not related to the marriage and her limited practice was largely the result of her own choice. No support was awarded.

*Poor health not caused by marriage but hardship caused by breakdown* — *Clifford v. Clifford*, 1995 CarswellSask 15, 13 R.F.L. (4th) 374 (Sask. Q.B.). Where the wife's poor health was not related to the marriage, but her economic hardship could be traced to the marriage breakdown, she was awarded spousal support until further order of the court.

*Husband had co-signed loans for wife's failed business therefore hardship shared equally —* Pope v. Pope, 1995 CarswellNfld 7, 12 R.F.L. (4th) 391 (Nfld. U.F.C.). The court rejected the wife's claim for support based upon her assertion that her business had faltered as a result of the trauma from the marriage breakdown. The husband had co-signed the wife's business loans and had suffered more post-separation economic hardship than she did.

*Parties' incomes not necessarily to be equalized —* Chalmers v. Chalmers, 1994 CarswellBC 656, 2 R.F.L. (4th) 446 (B.C.S.C.). Economic disadvantage or the sacrifice of a career by one spouse, in conjunction with the advancement of the other's career, will not justify the equalization of the parties' incomes through a support award.

*Claimant's health had deteriorated during marriage — support justified —* Sand v. Sand, 1994 CarswellBC 651, 2 R.F.L. (4th) 136 (B.C.S.C.). Where the parties married in their later years and the wife's health had deteriorated during the marriage so that she could not work, she was found to have suffered economic hardship as a result of the marriage breakdown.

*Illness aggravated by marriage breakdown —* Roy v. Roy, 1993 CarswellOnt 282, 1 R.F.L. (4th) 170 (Ont. Gen. Div.). Where the wife's illness, which limited her working ability, was not directly related to the marriage but was aggravated as a result of the marriage breakdown, she was found entitled to indefinite periodic support.

*Illness not caused by marriage but failure to become self-sufficient caused by homemaker role —* Klassen v. Klassen, 1990 CarswellMan 38, 25 R.F.L. (3d) 277, 63 Man. R. (2d) 201 (Man. Q.B.). Where the wife had developed health problems during the course of a long traditional marriage and was accordingly unable to support herself, the husband was ordered to pay support. Although the wife's illness was not caused by the marriage, the husband could not thereby evade his support responsibility to the wife. The wife's rheumatoid arthritis had caused her to leave several jobs over the years. The wife's economic plight was also causally connected to the marriage. She had failed to become self-sufficient as a direct result of the many years she had devoted to being a homemaker and primary childcare giver. She was awarded $250 bi-weekly for an indefinite term.

*Wife employed throughout marriage — husband not expected to finance retraining for a different profession —* Droit de la famille - 1236, [1989] R.D.F. 241 (C.S. Que.). Where the wife had been employed as a secretary throughout the marriage, it was found not to be reasonable to expect the husband to finance her retraining as a nurse after the parties' separation. The wife was accordingly allowed spousal support for a period of 5 months only.

*Support terminated after 17 years because recipient's poor health not related to marriage —* Droit de la famille - 1194, [1988] R.D.F. 406 (C.S. Que.). The court terminated the wife's support after 17 years since the wife's poor health, which prevented her from working, had developed long after separation and was not related to the marriage.

*Disease diagnosed during but not caused by marriage not a basis for long-term support —* Schroeder v. Schroeder, 1987 CarswellMan 89, 45 D.L.R. (4th) 632, 11 R.F.L. (3d) 413, 52 Man. R. (2d) 219 (Man. Q.B.). The wife, who was suffering from multiple sclerosis diagnosed during the marriage and who was unable to work, was denied support. The court was of the opinion that, where the economic hardship of a spouse has its genesis in the disabling effects of a disease which affects him or her and which has nothing to do with the marriage or its breakdown, the support obligation becomes the communal responsibility of the state and not that of the other spouse. The wife was granted support for 6 months to adjust to her new situation.

*Injury suffered before marriage less likely to be a basis for support —* Huber v. Huber, 1987 CarswellOnt 267, 11 R.F.L. (3d) 208, 63 O.R. (2d) 201 (Ont. U.F.C.). If a dependent spouse's illness exists prior to the marriage, it may also be seen as unrelated to the marriage. Consequently, support may be terminated.

*Variation — divorced spouse may share in the increased income of payor — Marcus v. Marcus*, 1977 CarswellBC 377, [1977] 4 W.W.R. 458 (B.C.C.A.), at 463-64 [W.W.R.]." I have no doubt that cases will arise in the exercise of the discretion given under s. 11(2) [now s. 17] of the *Divorce Act* where it will be fit and just to order additional maintenance so a divorced wife may share in the increased standard of living of her former husband. I do not say that such cases will be limited only to those where need can be shown. Without doubt many cases will arise where, because of the wife's limited means, her health, the existence of dependent children, past contributions made by the wife or other circumstances, an increase in the fortune or income of the husband occurring after the divorce will justify an order enlarging maintenance payments to the wife. I reject, however, the argument that such a result must follow automatically in all cases", per McIntyre J.A.

*Variation — divorced spouse may share in the increased income of payor — Clark v. Clark*, 1974 CarswellBC 210, 16 R.F.L. 214, [1974] 6 W.W.R. 424, 47 D.L.R. (3d) 149, [1974] B.C.J. No. 651 (B.C.S.C.). There is no authority for the proposition that a decree of divorce which incorporates an agreement for maintenance already entered into between the parties may only be varied if the wife demonstrates need; the discretion vested in the court by s. 11(2) [now s. 17] of the *Divorce Act* is not so limited. Where the earnings of the husband substantially increase in the years following the decree the wife may, in a proper case, be granted increased maintenance even though she cannot prove actual need; she is entitled to an increase in her standard of living commensurate with the increase in the means of the husband.

## 6.5 Promotion of Economic Self-Sufficiency

An award of spousal support should "in so far as practicable, promote the economic self-sufficiency of each spouse within a reasonable period of time" (s. 15.2(6)(d)). There are two ways in which a spousal support award might do so. Firstly, the additional funds might permit the recipient to increase his or her earning potential, typically through education or job training. Secondly, the award can be time-limited, as opposed to indefinite in duration. An award which is expected to end at a particular point in time can act as an incentive to secure an alternative source of income by that point.

The concept of self-sufficiency is also used by respondents as an argument *against* spousal support. If it can be proven that the support claimant either (i) has the ability to be self-sufficient, or (ii) *ought to* have the ability to be self-sufficient, such a finding will weaken the claimant's arguments for support on the basis of the first three objectives. A claimant who is or ought to be self-sufficient is less likely to be suffering disadvantage from the marriage or its breakdown (15.6(2)(a)). The financial consequences of her child care efforts must not be so severe as to require total dependency on support (15.6(2)(b)). Finally, if she is capable of supporting herself, the hardship arising from marriage breakdown (15.6(2)(c)) must not be of the most extreme variety.

It is often noted that Parliament made this objective, unlike the other three, subject to the limiting clause "in so far as practicable." This is among the reasons for which self-sufficiency reasoning now has limited utility as a defence to a support claim, particularly in longer marriages. However, if either party is not making sufficient efforts to generate income, there is ample precedent for imputing it when determining the means of the parties. (See ss. 5.2 and 5.3 of this volume.)

*The Divorce Act does not impose a duty upon former spouses to become self-sufficient. Section 15.2(6)(d) of the Divorce Act merely states that an order should "in so far as practicable, promote the economic self-sufficiency" of the parties — Droit de la famille - 091889*, 2011

CarswellQue 13698, 2011 CarswellQue 13699, 2011 SCC 64, 6 R.F.L. (7th) 1, 339 D.L.R. (4th) 624, [2011] 3 S.C.R. 775, 424 N.R. 341, [2011] S.C.J. No. 64 (S.C.C.). See **10.3 Variation – Change in Circumstances – meaning** for a detailed discussion of the case.

*No duty to become self-sufficient – Leskun v. Leskun,* 2006 CarswellBC 1492, 2006 SCC 25, 34 R.F.L. (6th) 1, [2006] 1 S.C.R. 920, 349 N.R. 158, 226 B.C.A.C. 1, 268 D.L.R. (4th) 577, 373 W.A.C. 1, 62 B.C.L.R. (4th) 197, [2006] S.C.J. No. 25 (S.C.C.). The court held that failure to achieve self-sufficiency is not a breach of a duty. Self-sufficiency is simply one factor amongst others to be taken into account. Where incapacity to support oneself is alleged, independent evidence is highly desirable, but not essential.

*Lack of self-sufficiency may not be caused by marriage – Bracklow v. Bracklow,* 1999 CarswellBC 532, 1999 CarswellBC 533, 44 R.F.L. (4th) 1, [1999] 1 S.C.R. 420, 63 B.C.L.R. (3d) 77, 169 D.L.R. (4th) 577, [1999] 8 W.W.R. 740, 236 N.R. 79, [1999] R.D.F. 203, 120 B.C.A.C. 211, 196 W.A.C. 211, [1999] S.C.J. No. 14 (S.C.C.). The fourth objective – *to promote economic self-sufficiency – is not necessarily tied to compensation for disadvantages caused by the marriage or its breakup. A spouse's lack of self-sufficiency may arise from sources that have nothing to do with the marriage and are non-compensatory like the disappearance of the kind of work the spouse was trained to do, or ill-health.*

*Variation – self-sufficiency is only one of four objectives that should be considered in making a variation of support order – Moge v. Moge,* 1992 CarswellMan 143, 1992 CarswellMan 222, EYB 1992-67141, 43 R.F.L. (3d) 345, [1992] 3 S.C.R. 813, 99 D.L.R. (4th) 456, [1993] 1 W.W.R. 481, 145 N.R. 1, [1993] R.D.F. 168, 81 Man. R. (2d) 161, 30 W.A.C. 161, [1992] S.C.J. No. 107 (S.C.C.). The Supreme Court of Canada considered that self-sufficiency was a relevant objective in making variation orders together with the other objectives set out in s. 17(7). Self-sufficiency, however, should not be given pre-eminence. After divorce, parties should contribute to their own support according to their abilities.

*Where there was no expectation of self-sufficiency when the original order was made, spousal support was ordered to continue on a variation application – Hepburn v. Hepburn,* 2013 CarswellBC 2592, 2013 BCCA 383, 34 R.F.L. (7th) 267, 48 B.C.L.R. (5th) 251, 344 B.C.A.C. 6, 587 W.A.C. 6 (B.C.C.A.). A husband sought to vary a consent order for spousal support on the basis that his income had decreased. The original order was indefinite, and the wife was reliant on the support as there was no reasonable expectation that she would return to the workforce and attain even partial self-sufficiency. The Court of Appeal found that there was evidence to support the chambers judge finding that the husband had reduced his hours as a physician to accommodate his unpaid media initiatives and upheld the finding that there was no material change in circumstances. However, the judge found he did lose some income through factors beyond his control, and this was found to be a material change sufficient to recalculate support.

*Palpable and overriding error in trial judge's view of wife's circumstances as to whether wife was able to be self sufficient – Smith v. Smith,* 2011 CarswellNB 377, 2011 CarswellNB 378, 2011 NBCA 66, 9 R.F.L. (7th) 286, 336 D.L.R. (4th) 285, 375 N.B.R. (2d) 208, 969 A.P.R. 208, [2011] N.B.J. No. 245 (N.B.C.A.). The parties cohabited for 2 years and were married for 29 years with two children. At the time of the trial, the wife, aged 52, was working as a bookkeeper earning $15,600 and the husband was earning $62,500. On appeal by the wife, the Court of Appeal set aside the spousal support order of $1,000 per month and ordered spousal support payable by the husband to the wife in the amount of $ 1,709.50 indefinitely. The husband conceded that quantum of support was the only outstanding issue at trial. The trial judge focused primarily on the husband's ability to pay and made a palpable and overriding error in considering the husband's possible future debts to be present day actual debts. By misapprehending the wife's means and needs, the trial judge erred in the determination that the wife should be self-sufficient. Spousal support was ordered at the mid-range of the *Spousal Support Advisory Guidelines.* The case turned on an error of fact so the court did not need to consider whether or not the "common law should be adapted to provide that a spousal support award which does not follow the Guidelines gives rise to an error of law."

*Indefinite support awarded in long term marriage where dependency on lifestyle is established and spouse's age at separation is relevant to person's ability to become self-supporting* — *Cassidy v. McNeil*, 2010 CarswellOnt 1637, 2010 ONCA 218, 99 O.R. (3d) 81, 266 O.A.C. 62 (Ont. C.A.); affirming 2009 CarswellOnt 8859 (Ont. S.C.J.); reversing in part 2008 CarswellOnt 110 (Ont. S.C.J.). Following a 23-year marriage and three children the parties separated for the final time. The three children resided with the husband following separation. Two of the children were adults at the time of trial. At the time of marriage, the wife was a teacher and the husband was in doctoral studies in Electrical Engineering. During the marriage, the parties moved three times due to the husband's education and employment circumstances with the result that at times the wife's employment was limited to part-time and substitute teaching. For three years, the wife stayed home to look after the parties' two children and to set up their new house after a move. The wife indicated that she wished to pursue graduate studies, but was obliged to forego this plan for financial reasons. The wife ultimately obtained part time, then full time employment at a private school, which permitted the children to attend the school at a reduced cost. Her teaching hours, however, were long and her non-union teaching contract was subject to annual renewal. The husband's position as a university professor was tenured. The wife had suffered health issues during the marriage including miscarriages and a breakdown in 2002. At the time of trial, the husband was earning $137,656.30 and the wife was earning $85,000.00. The trial judge dismissed the wife's claim for retrospective spousal support, and allowed her claim for prospective spousal support awarding her $1,200 monthly for five years on the basis she should be paying child support for the younger child and that she had established a need for spousal support at least during the period until the child had completed her education or was on her own. On appeal, the Court of Appeal noted that the trial judge's exclusive reference to need was an error in principle. The appeal court stated that the wife would have benefited from the parties' joint incomes and their interdependency over 23 years of marriage and that interdependency would have evolved into an economic merger of their interests. Such a merger, together with the wife's somewhat compromised career path, met the threshold of entitlement. The wife was age 48 at the time of separation. The appeal court noted that duration of marriage and age at separation are relevant to a person's ability to be self-supporting, Where the trial judge had ordered spousal support of $1,500 per month for five years, on appeal support was varied to $950 per month indefinitely.

*While one of the purposes of spousal support is to promote economic self-sufficiency,t this may not be possible in certain circumstances* — *Baradoy v. Baradoy*, 2010 CarswellAlta 137, 2010 ABCA 33 (Alta. C.A.). The Court of Appeal affirmed the findings at a review hearing that the wife had applied herself to efforts to become self-sufficient and found that the trial judgement of ongoing support was reasonable in light of the parties' traditional, 25-year marriage.

*Self sufficiency is a relative concept* — *a court tries to provide for a reasonable standard of living taking into account the lifestyle that the couple enjoyed during their marriage* — *Rioux v. Rioux*, 2009 CarswellOnt 4077, 2009 ONCA 569, 66 R.F.L. (6th) 256, 97 O.R. (3d) 102, 252 O.A.C. 126 (Ont. C.A.). In this case, at the time of separation, the parties anticipated a shared income of about $125,000. At the time of trial, the husband earned approximately $100,000 and the wife earned approximately $26,000. The court held that the wife was entitled to spousal support beyond that which she received up to the time of trial. The parties had had a traditional marriage which had lasted over 20 years. The husband worked full time and the wife had managed the home and worked part time. The wife's role in the family had resulted in her being economically disadvantaged by the breakdown of the marriage. The court held that while the wife remained in the work force and was relatively young (45 at the date of separation), she needed some time to become self-sufficient. The court ordered further non-compensatory transitional support to soften the impact of the decrease in the standard of living caused by the marriage breakup. The court ordered spousal support in the amount of $1,500 per month (which was within the Guidelines), for a further 5 years, commencing April 1, 2007 to March 1, 2012, at which time spousal support would be subject to review by either party.

*Spousal support denied — wife had ability to earn income — Katz v. Nimelman*, 2007 CarswellOnt 7659, 46 R.F.L. (6th) 392 (Ont. S.C.J.); additional reasons at 2008 CarswellOnt 1917, 54 R.F.L. (6th) 177 (Ont. S.C.J.); affirmed 2009 CarswellOnt 2971, 2009 ONCA 445 (Ont. C.A.). At trial, the court concluded that the wife had undisclosed assets and income. She also had the ability to earn income. She was required to maximize her income before seeking support from her husband. If she did not wish to generate rental income, she could reduce her expenses by obtaining less costly housing. The court anticipated that the wife would revive her wrongful dismissal claims with the expectation of obtaining money by these means. On appeal, the court held that the trial judge had assessed the wife's claim on the basis that she was disabled but that, considering the assets that she held, she failed to demonstrate need. The decision involved findings of fact and the exercise of discretion and the trial judgment was supported by the evidence.

*Trial judge failed to consider whether wife could realistically achieve self-sufficiency, even with full time employment, given that self-sufficiency does not mean subsistence level, but the ability to support one self in keeping with the standard of living enjoyed during the marriage. — Heimsoth v. Heimsoth*, 2009 CarswellAlta 478, 2009 ABCA 129, 65 R.F.L. (6th) 27, 457 A.R. 22, 457 W.A.C. 22 (Alta. C.A.), reversing in part 2007 CarswellAlta 1147, 2007 ABQB 539 (Alta. Q.B.). At the ages of 19 and 21 respectively the husband and wife cohabited for one year and then married. Following a marriage of 24 years, with two children, the parties separated in 1999. After the birth of the second child, the parties had decided that the wife would stay home to care for the children and household. Over the course of the marriage the family moved cities seven times to accommodate the husband's employment. The husband's argument that they agreed she would only remain out of the workforce until the younger child was aged 10 was rejected as the family moved four times after this time to accommodate the husband's employment. At the time of separation, the husband was earning in excess of $100,000 and the wife earned $5,000 as she had been working for two months a year for several years. At the time of the separation, the wife was suffering from depression and an order was made granting her spousal support of $4,000 per month, subject to review in five years. In 2007, the trial judge held that the spousal support be reduced over two years and then terminated because the wife was no longer suffering from depression, was underemployed, and had exaggerated her symptoms. The wife's appeal was allowed in part. The Court of Appeal, noting the finding that she was now able to work, stated that nothing suggested that she was capable of achieving self-sufficiency, or that she could support herself at a level in keeping with the standard of living she enjoyed during the marriage. The appeal court attributed an income of $24,000 to the wife and $140,000 to the husband with support payable to the wife in the amount of $2,000 per month with a review, at the instance of either party, when the husband turned 65 or in the event of a material change.

*Self-sufficiency is a relative concept that relates to achieving a reasonable standard of living having regard to the lifestyle the couple enjoyed during their marriage. — Rioux v. Rioux*, 2009 CarswellOnt 4077, 2009 ONCA 569, 66 R.F.L. (6th) 256, 97 O.R. (3d) 102, 252 O.A.C. 126 (Ont. C.A.), reversing in part 2007 CarswellOnt 9916 (Ont. S.C.J.). By the time of separation, the parties anticipated sharing an income of about $125,000. While the wife remained in the workforce and was relatively young, she needed time to reach a goal of sufficiency and was entitled to non-compensatory traditional support to soften the impact of the separation.

*An order pursuant to s. 17(7) of the Divorce Act varying an order for support is intended to encourage self-sufficiency as far as practicable — however, the provision was not intended to impose an obligation on a spouse to become self-sufficient — Gray v. Gray*, 1986 CarswellMan 102, 3 R.F.L. (3d) 457, 45 Man. R. (2d) 156 (Man. Q.B.); affirmed 1987 CarswellMan 109, 8 R.F.L. (3d) 147, 49 Man. R. (2d) 90 (Man. C.A.).

*Support order should promote self-sufficiency and allow recipient period to habituate herself to less affluent lifestyle — Bast v. Bast*, 1988 CarswellOnt 216, 13 R.F.L. (3d) 98 (Ont. H.C.). The court commented that the wife, who was in her mid-fifties and who had been married for 21 years, was unlikely to achieve, through her own economic efforts, the kind of lifestyle she had enjoyed during the marriage. Salhany LJ.S.C. stated that this fact was not the husband's fault. The court was of the view that an order for support should attempt to promote self-sufficiency and, at the same time, recognize that the wife would need a period of time to gear down from her former standard of living. Support was continued for another 2 years; support would therefore end 3 years after the divorce.

*Self-sufficiency not to outweigh other factors — time-limited order inappropriate — Tedham v. Tedham*, 2005 CarswellBC 2346, 2005 BCCA 502, 20 R.F.L. (6th) 217, 47 B.C.L.R. (4th) 254, [2006] 3 W.W.R. 212, 261 D.L.R. (4th) 332, [2005] B.C.J. No. 2186 (B.C.C.A.); additional reasons at 2005 CarswellBC 2699, 2005 BCCA 553, 47 B.C.L.R. (4th) 276, [2006] 3 W.W.R. 234, 261 D.L.R. (4th) 332 at 359, 217 B.C.A.C. 250, 358 W.A.C. 250 (B.C.C.A.). While the wife was able to contribute to her support, she was unable to be self-sufficient as she was not capable of earning anything resembling the income which would permit her to live in accordance with the standard of living of the parties during marriage. Consequently, a time-limited order was inappropriate. With a time-limited order, the other objectives of a support order, which were significant were overshadowed by the objective of self-sufficiency and the failure to recognize fully that the objective of self-sufficiency is qualified by the words, "in so far as is practicable". The previous time-limited order which was under appeal did not address the compensatory factors arising from the marriage, her need in relation to the standard of living enjoyed by the parties during the marriage, or her contribution to his income.

*When a support recipient had not taken reasonable steps towards self-sufficiency, and there was no demonstrated reason for lack of income earned at the levels projected by an original support order, the recipient's motion for a retroactive increase was dismissed — Kerman v. Kerman*, 2014 CarswellBC 679, 2014 BCSC 428 (B.C.S.C.). The wife sought a retroactive increase of support. The parties were married for 17 years and had separated approximately 17 years prior to this application. An order for support was made in 2008 which anticipated the income each party would earn. The wife showed she had not earned the income anticipated by the order. The judge found she had not explained circumstances, such as an unanticipated medical condition, or demonstrated steps taken to self-sufficiency that would form a material change in circumstances. Her application was dismissed.

*Spousal support was to continue until the recipient wife had obtained self-sufficiency anticipated 4 years after a 20-year marriage when there was no evidence the husband could not afford to pay. This was consistent with the parties' previous agreement — C. (M.S.) v. C. (T.L.)*, 2013 CarswellNS 885, 2013 NSSC 378, 337 N.S.R. (2d) 177, 1067 A.P.R. 177 (N.S.S.C.). The parties had concluded a separation agreement, which provided for spousal support at below the Guidelines range and review at any time without showing a material change in circumstances. The parties were married for 20 years, and the judge found that the wife was entitled to compensatory support, which was consistent with the original agreement for spousal support. The wife projected she would be self-sufficient within 4 years of separation, and spousal support was ordered to continue until that time. There was no evidence that the husband did not have the means to pay support.

*A spouse will be considered to have reached self-sufficiency where her means are equal or superior to those she enjoyed during the marriage, even if much of her wealth arises from a legacy received after the parties separated* — Holman v. Holman, 2013 CarswellOnt 16472, 2013 ONSC 6988 (Ont. S.C.J.). The parties were married for 19 years prior to separation in 2002. They had two adult daughters. The wife had been a stay-at-home mother during the marriage. She had received $300,000 from an inheritance after separation, which the judge found must be considered as part of her assets and means under the *Family Law Act*. The judge also found that her means were equal to or superior to those she enjoyed during the marriage. She had attained self-sufficiency. The wife had been disadvantaged by the marriage. The husband had the means to pay. He was obliged to pay support for a total of eleven years, at which point it would be terminated.

*Support recipient found still entitled to support because she was not yet self-sufficient* — Bockhold v. Bockhold, 2010 CarswellBC 369, 2010 BCSC 214, [2010] B.C.J. No. 283 (B.C.S.C. [In Chambers]). The parties were married for 17 years and had two children. Pursuant to a consent order entered into in 2003, the husband agreed to pay the wife spousal and child support with spousal support subject to review upon cessation of child support. The court found that the wife was not self-sufficient despite entering into a new relationship and receiving spousal support for 10 years because she had been out of work during most of the marriage and was diagnosed with a disability. The husband was ordered to pay an increased amount of ongoing spousal support indefinitely.

*Spousal support terminated because wife found to be self-sufficient* — Mills v. Eglin, 2009 CarswellBC 3133, 2009 BCSC 1595 (B.C.S.C.). The parties were married for 15 years and had three children. The husband brought a variation application due to his reduced income. In terminating spousal support, the court found that the wife had become self-sufficient despite only receiving spousal support for 6 years.

*Failure to become self-sufficient does not result in permanent spousal support* — *payor was custodial parent* — Fraser v. Puddifant, 2005 CarswellNS 593, 2005 NSSC 340, 240 N.S.R. (2d) 33, 763 A.P.R. 33, [2005] N.S.J. No. 340, [2005] N.S.J. No. 558 (N.S.S.C.). The parties were married for 14 years. The husband was ordered to pay support of $600 per month. The wife suffered from a mental illness and was unable to become self-sufficient. The husband also had custody and sole financial responsibility for the child. The husband applied to vary support. The court reduced spousal support to $300 per month, payable for another 3 years. The court stated that failure to attain self-sufficiency did not result in permanent entitlement to support and the duration of support should not exceed the length of marriage despite the wife's illness.

*Support would allow completion of teacher's college which would foster self-sufficiency after career interruption to care for children* — Gregory v. Ball, 2004 CarswellAlta 1450, 2004 ABQB 789, 9 R.F.L. (6th) 338 (Alta. Q.B.); reversed 2005 CarswellAlta 1526, 2005 ABCA 354, 21 R.F.L. (6th) 42 (Alta. C.A.). The wife was awarded spousal support for 4 years to allow her to complete her teacher's college programme. The wife had remained at home with the parties' children during the 6-year marriage and the consequent disadvantages that she had suffered could best be overcome if she became financially self-sufficient.

*Lack of effort to become self-sufficient leads to reduction in support* — Juvatopolos v. Juvatopolos, 2004 CarswellOnt 4423, 9 R.F.L. (6th) 147, [2004] O.T.C. 941 (Ont. S.C.J.); affirmed 2005 CarswellOnt 4774, 19 R.F.L. (6th) 76, 202 O.A.C. 1 (Ont. C.A.). Since she offered very little by way of genuine effort to become self-sufficient, the quantum of spousal support was reduced substantially. In addition, her failure to invest at least some of her inheritance of $56,000 as a continuing source of income was an exacerbating factor in reducing support. At the present time she was receiving approximately $31,000 per year with the contribution received from her partner. The court held that the order should be varied and the spousal support should be reduced to from $1,200 to $400 per month.

*Loss of economic security — retraining — Coupar v. Coupar*, 1998 CarswellBC 2540, 43 R.F.L. (4th) 443, 57 B.C.L.R. (3d) 161, 186 W.A.C. 255, 114 B.C.A.C. 255, [1998] B.C.J. No. 2673 (B.C.C.A.). Where the marriage breakdown took economic security away from the wife, the appellate court upheld the lower court's decision to award the wife spousal support during the time that she attended school on a full-time basis in her effort to be self-sufficient.

*Variation — where a payee spouse among other reasons, refuses to take any active steps to become employed, spousal support should cease — Ungerer v. Ungerer*, 1998 CarswellBC 670, 37 R.F.L. (4th) 41, 158 D.L.R. (4th) 37, 105 B.C.A.C. 250, [1998] 7 W.W.R. 469, 48 B.C.L.R. (3d) 188 (B.C.C.A.).

*Variation — award of indefinite support granted where payee not self-sufficient as not able to advance career — Reid v. Reid*, 1997 CarswellNB 450, 33 R.F.L. (4th) 145, 192 N.B.R. (2d) 156, 489 A.P.R. 156 (N.B.C.A.). Where the payee has changed jobs following her husband's career relocations, and she has not been able to advance her career or obtain seniority rights or pension or health benefits, and post separation she has moved with the parties' child to an area close to her family and friends, but where she had not been able to obtain employment, the court held that she did not have prospects for self-sufficiency and the award of indefinite spousal support was upheld.

*Variation — payee's relocation to area where she did not have employment, not grounds to terminate support — Reid v. Reid, supra*. The wife's voluntary relocation to an area where she could not readily find employment was not a sufficient reason to allow the husband's application to terminate her support. The wife's move to be closer to her family was reasonable and her employment at the time of separation had paid only minimum wages and had no prospect for advancement.

*Trial judge overemphasized self-sufficiency — Giraud v. Giraud*, 1997 CarswellBC 2575, 34 R.F.L. (4th) 255, 44 B.C.L.R. (3d) 98, 155 D.L.R. (4th) 112, 100 B.C.A.C. 27, 163 W.A.C. 27 (B.C.C.A.). The court found that the trial judge gave inappropriate emphasis to the promotion of economic self-sufficiency as an objective of an order for spousal support.

*Absence from workforce — entitled to support for retraining period which would allow self-sufficiency — McNeil v. McNeil*, 1995 CarswellSask 476, 16 R.F.L. (4th) 323, 133 Sask. R. 228 (Sask. Q.B.); reversed 1996 CarswellSask 244, 144 Sask. R. 71, 124 W.A.C. 71 (Sask. C.A.). Where the wife had suffered an injury upon her return to work as a nurse's assistant and could not work for some time in that field, she was awarded periodic spousal support for 30 months. She had been economically disadvantaged by the marriage in that she had been out of the job market for a number of years. The support award would allow her to complete her nursing degree and eventually achieve self-sufficiency.

*Duty to pursue self-sufficiency applies to a 65-year-old man — McGrath v. Holmes*, 1995 CarswellNWT 1, 10 R.F.L. (4th) 161 (N.W.T.C.A.). Where a 62-year-old unemployed man makes no effort to find employment after marriage breakdown, he is not allowed to rely merely upon his age to support his claim for spousal support.

*The functions performed in a long marriage may make self-sufficiency unattainable — Waterman v. Waterman*, 1995 CarswellNfld 117, 16 R.F.L. (4th) 10, 133 Nfld. & P.E.I.R. 310, 413 A.P.R. 310, [1995] N.J. No. 295 (Nfld. C.A.). The court observed that while spousal support is linked to the broad general criteria of needs and means in relation to each spouse's conditions and circumstances, the needs of the spouses are not given the same primacy as the needs of the children. The duration of cohabitation and the functions performed during it are additional factors that must be taken into account. These factors reflect the reality, for instance, of the difficulties encountered in attaining self-sufficiency by a wife who comes out of a long-term traditional marriage without an outside career. While self-sufficiency remains a desirable objective which should nonetheless be considered and fostered in framing a support order, this factor draws attention to its not always being attainable and requires that judicial discretion be exercised taking this possibility into account. If the duration lasts longer than 30 years, for example, such as was the situation in the case at bar, involving a wife and mother who has devoted herself to looking after the home and the children's upbringing, the functions assumed by her will necessarily result in a de-emphasizing of self- sufficiency and a greater awareness of the economic disadvantage and hardships of the marriage breakup on her.

*Persistent disadvantage justified support despite failure to achieve self-sufficiency — Fejes v. Fejes*, 1993 CarswellMan 38, 45 R.F.L. (3d) 13, 103 D.L.R. (4th) 118, 36 W.A.C. 273, 83 Man. R. (2d) 273 (Man. C.A.). The court reversed the trial judge's decision which had reduced the quantum of spousal support payable to the wife. Although the wife had obtained a university degree after separation, the trial judge had placed too much emphasis upon the wife's failure to achieve self-sufficiency. The wife had given up her career aspirations to raise the children throughout the parties' 17-year marriage and the economic disadvantage to the wife resulting from the marriage continued.

*Variation — self-sufficiency is only required where practicable — Droit de la famille - 1675*, 1993 CarswellQue 58, 46 R.F.L. (3d) 131, [1993] R.D.F. 218 (C.A. Que.). In determining an application for termination of spousal support, self-sufficiency of the payee spouse is a goal only insofar as it is practical. Where the payee continues to suffer an economic disadvantage as a result of the marriage, support should not be terminated.

*Retraining and time-limited support can fulfill purpose of compensatory spousal support — Blais c. Blais*, 1992 CarswellNB 40, 38 R.F.L. (3d) 337, 124 N.B.R. (2d) 32, 312 A.P.R. 32 (N.B.C.A.). The fact of marriage itself does not give rise to a spouse's right to support. Support is intended to return a spouse to the position in life that he or she would have enjoyed had his or her talents not been diverted by the marriage. Frequently, this end can be accomplished through retraining and re-entry into the workforce and by placing a time limit on the time needed, based on the facts of the case, to attain self-sufficiency.

*Variation — the fact that a spouse should be able to become self-sufficient in the future is not an adequate ground for revoking the support payable to that spouse — Helston v. Helston*, 1992 CarswellSask 49, 39 R.F.L. (3d) 168 (Sask. C.A.).

*Variation — support terminated where wife had made no effort to achieve self-sufficiency — Droit de la famille - 1600*, 1992 CarswellQue 740, EYB 1992-56245 (C.A. Que.). The court on appeal allowed the husband's application to terminate the wife's spousal support. Although she had not worked during the parties' 18-year marriage, the 52-year-old wife had made no effort in the 5 years following the divorce to become self-sufficient, despite the fact that she was in good health and had some education.

*Variation — no effort to become self-sufficient, 1-year limit on future support on variation application — Douthwright v. Douthwright*, 1992 CarswellNB 46, 42 R.F.L. (3d) 1, 95 D.L.R. (4th) 188, 128 N.B.R. (2d) 437, 322 A.P.R. 437 (N.B.C.A.). Where the wife had made no effort to achieve self-sufficiency during the 25 years which she received spousal support, the court, on the husband's appeal from an order increasing her support, placed a one-year limit on her future support entitlement. The marriage had not been a traditional one and the parties had only actually cohabited for a 3-year period.

*Where the 46-year-old wife had failed to achieve complete self-sufficiency 7 years after separation, the husband's application for reduced support was granted and her monthly support was reduced by half — Droit de la famille - 823*, 1990 CarswellQue 716, EYB 1990-57665, [1990] R.L. 504 (C.A. Que.).

*Variation — on an application to vary spousal support, the court must consider all of the factors outlined in s. 17(7) of the Act and not just s. 17(7)(d) — Jayatilaka c. Roussel*, 1991 CarswellNB 44, 36 R.F.L. (3d) 447, 174 N.B.R. (2d) 204, 444 A.P.R. 204 (N.B.C.A.).

*Variation — support was terminated where the wife had made no effort to obtain self-sufficiency — Droit de la famille - 978*, [1991] R.D.F. 220 (C.A. Que.), the court terminated the wife's support, which had been based upon the parties' agreement, 13 years after the parties' divorce. The wife had never made an effort to seek self-sufficiency and as a result her needs were caused by her own inactivity and not the failure of the marriage.

*Self-sufficiency reasoning not a bar to indefinite support — Brace v. Brace*, 1991 CarswellOnt 318, 35 R.F.L. (3d) 263 (Ont. C.A.). The Ontario Court of Appeal in upholding the High Court decision granting support for an indefinite term noted that "the wife's efforts to become self-sufficient should not impact negatively on her claim for support."

*Wife has duty to become self-sufficient but support to continue — Solomon v. Solomon*, 1991 CarswellNS 64, 35 R.F.L. (3d) 113, 106 N.S.R. (2d) 28, 288 A.P.R. 28 (N.S.C.A.). The wife was 35 and worked part-time in a day-care centre since a back injury prevented her from returning to her nursing career. She had custody of the parties' two children. The parties were married for approximately 7 years. The wife had a duty to become self-sufficient in light of her age and the length of the marriage. The court, considering all the circumstances, upheld the decision that the husband should pay $1,400 per month for spousal and child support payments for 2 years and thereafter $1,800 per month.

*Absence from workforce — lengthy and traditional marriage — entitled to support — Donald v. Donald*, 1991 CarswellNS 58, 33 R.F.L. (3d) 196, 81 D.L.R. (4th) 48, 103 N.S.R. (2d) 322, 282 A.P.R. 322, [1991] N.S.J. No. 214 (N.S.C.A.). In a long-standing traditional marriage, the court should not place too much emphasis on promoting the dependant spouse's self-sufficiency but should take into account the factors set out in s. 15(5), the economic advantages the dependant spouse derived from the marriage, and the disadvantages and hardship arising to the other from its breakdown. The husband, an orthodontist, was ordered to pay support for an indefinite period to his wife who had acquired a commerce degree during the marriage but who was working as a customer service clerk or teller, having failed to obtain management positions.

*Self-sufficiency principle not a basis for curtailing support after long-term traditional marriage — Matthews v. Matthews*, 1990 CarswellBC 488, 29 R.F.L. (3d) 381 (B.C.C.A.). The principle of spousal self-sufficiency should be given a restrictive interpretation in cases of long-term traditional marriages where a spouse is unable to achieve financial independence. In such cases, it cannot be relied upon as a ground for reducing or terminating spousal support.

*Claimant had pursued education to the point of self-sufficiency during the marriage — not entitled to support to enable her to pursue doctorate after separation — Oswell v. Oswell*, 1990 CarswellOnt 278, 28 R.F.L. (3d) 10, 74 O.R. (2d) 15 (Ont. H.C.); affirmed 1992 CarswellOnt 306, 43 R.F.L. (3d) 180, 12 O.R. (3d) 95 (Ont. C.A.). The wife's claim for support for a period while she completed her doctorate was dismissed. Since the wife had followed her academic aspirations during the marriage and had thereby attained a degree of self-sufficiency, it could not be said that due to the marriage she was in a worse position to earn a living than if she had never married her husband. The court ordered support for 6 months from the date of trial so that the former wife could find employment or make the adjustment to pursue her doctorate.

*Wife would never be able to become self-sufficient — support awarded — Story v. Story*, 1989 CarswellBC 237, 23 R.F.L. (3d) 225, 42 B.C.L.R. (2d) 21, 65 D.L.R. (4th) 549 (B.C.C.A.). The concept of causal relation only applies upon an application to vary a support order when the parties' rights have been finally decided by agreement or order or when a support order falls within the description contained in s. 17(10) of the *Divorce Act*. In all other cases, variation of support should be considered under the principles in the *Divorce Act*, but without considering the issue of causal relation. The court found that the wife's mental illness, lack of experience and training, and long absence from the work-force would not enable her to become self-sufficient. The husband had the ability to pay support and the wife was entitled to support without a time limitation.

*Self-sufficiency not expected of women who married with a reasonable expectation of a permanent homemaking role — Droit de la famille - 614*, 1989 CarswellQue 306, [1989] R.J.Q. 535, 33 Q.A.C. 126, [1989] R.D.F. 347 (note) (C.A. Que.). The courts do not require complete financial autonomy for wives who married at a time when marriage was a social contract under which women agreed to devote their working lives to raising a family.

*Need-based award reduced due to insufficient effort on the part of the support claimant — Robinson v. Robinson*, 1988 CarswellNS 41, 13 R.F.L. (3d) 90, 82 N.S.R. (2d) 424, 207 A.P.R. 424 (N.S.C.A.). Where the wife was in need after the parties' lengthy marriage but was not making best use of her talents, a modest support award made at trial was upheld on appeal.

*7-year childless marriage — support reduced on appeal with reference to self-sufficiency objective — Snyder v. Snyder*, 1987 CarswellNS 53, 10 R.F.L. (3d) 144, 80 N.S.R. (2d) 257, 200 A.P.R. 257 (N.S.C.A.). The Nova Scotia Court of Appeal restricted support to a wife, where the parties had both worked throughout their 7-year marriage and were capable of being self-sustaining. The husband was 39 and the wife 40, and they had not had any children. The court, in allowing the husband's appeal from a maintenance order, ruled that the trial judge had not given due consideration to the provision in the *Divorce Act* for the spouses to achieve self-sufficiency and to the fact that there was nothing in the marriage which gave rise to a condition of economic dependency. The wife was awarded $600 per month for a period of 2 years.

*Evidence of ability to support self among reasons for denying support — Fogel v. Fogel*, 1976 CarswellOnt 120, 24 R.F.L. 18 (Ont. H.C.); affirmed 1979 CarswellOnt 379, 9 R.F.L. (2d) 55, 24 O.R. (2d) 158 (Ont. C.A.). The wife's claim for maintenance was denied as the husband had been awarded custody of the children, the marriage had been of brief duration and the evidence established that the wife was able to support herself adequately.

*Although wife suffered minimal economic disadvantage arising from 12-year marriage with three children, the primary basis of wife's entitlement to support is her inability to attain self-sufficiency in light of the marital standard of living — Barraco v. Scott*, 2011 CarswellOnt 8325, 2011 ONSC 4467, 9 R.F.L. (7th) 126 (Ont. S.C.J.). The parties married in 1994, had three children and separated in 2006. Prior to the marriage and for three years during the marriage, the wife had worked in banking and financial services. During the marriage, she assumed primary care of the children, obtained a teaching degree and other academic qualifications and taught part-time. After the separation she became a mortgage broker. At the time of separation, she was 38 years old and the husband, an assistant Crown Attorney, was 39 years old. The wife earned $52,000 and the husband earned $187,000. On wife's application for retroactive and ongoing support, it was ordered that the wife receive retroactive support in the amount of $20,000, and ongoing support in the amount of $2,100 per month terminating January 2018.

*Variation — downward variation of support where wife had not maintained contract and sought limited amount of employment — Bryant v. Gordon*, 2007 CarswellBC 1613, 2007 BCSC 946, 45 R.F.L. (6th) 99, [2007] B.C.J. No. 1460 (B.C.S.C. [In Chambers]). The spousal support payable by the husband was reduced on the basis that the wife's efforts towards self-sufficiency were found wanting and income was imputed to her. She had unreasonably failed to maintain remuneration contract employment and wished to restrict her work week to 4 days with mid-afternoon endings to her work days.

*Dependent spouse gave up possibility of career to look after family — entitled to support — Jean v. Jean*, 2006 CarswellAlta 1781, 2006 ABQB 938, 410 A.R. 260, [2006] A.J. No. 1687 (Alta. Q.B.). A spouse is required to provide support for his spouse where she gave up her prospects of a career or working life to meet the needs of the family. He is at least required to help her become self-sufficient. She, in turn, is required to make a serious effort to become self-sufficient.

*Marriage not entitlement to lifelong support but support given for time required to adjust —* Cey v. Teske, 2006 CarswellSask 484, 2006 SKQB 315, 286 Sask. R. 221 (Sask. Q.B.). Marriage does not entitle a spouse to lifelong support. Where the wife is capable of retraining and re-entering the work force, she should contribute to her own support. However, the wife has been financially disadvantaged by the breakdown of the marriage and she requires time to put her financial affairs in order and it will take some time for her to receive the full value of her property division, and it will take 1 to 2 years for her to retrain and find a job. The court ordered the husband to pay the wife spousal support of $6,000 per month until she was paid in full for her interest in the husband's company. At that point, support was to be reduced to $5,000 per month until June, 2009 at which time the support shall be reviewed.

*Claimant found to be self-sufficient — no support —* Eastwood v. Eastwood, 2006 CarswellNB 655, 2006 NBQB 413, 34 R.F.L. (6th) 408, 307 N.B.R. (2d) 210, 795 A.P.R. 210 (N.B.Q.B.). Where the parties were both somewhat dependant upon the other for economic support during the marriage, the wife's application for spousal support was dismissed. The parties were both living lifestyles similar to that enjoyed during the marriage and the wife was self-sufficient.

*Variation — support terminated where wife not rigorously pursuing career opportunities —* Baker v. Baker, 2005 CarswellOnt 7067, 22 R.F.L. (6th) 209 (Ont. S.C.J.). The court allowed the husband's application for termination of his former wife's spousal support 4 years after the parties' divorce. The husband's burden of child support was substantial and would be even more so when the two youngest joined the older ones at university. The wife had not been qualified as a teacher subsequent to divorce and had not been diligent in exploring further income opportunities.

*Variation — support terminated where wife had obtained self-sufficiency, an illness then prevented her from working, but her new spouse had responsibility for her support — P.* (M.F.F.A.) v. P. (F.M.A.), 2003 CarswellBC 2447, 2003 BCSC 1502, 47 R.F.L. (5th) 170 (B.C.S.C.). The court allowed the husband's application to terminate the spousal support payable to his former wife. After the divorce, the wife had remarried, successfully completed a dental assistant's course and undertaken part-time employment. The wife then developed cancer and was unable to work. For the purposes of support, the wife had achieved "self sufficiency" upon completion of her course and her failure to secure full-time employment was the result of her own decision. The wife's new spouse now had primary responsibility for her support.

*Wife capable of supporting herself — no support —* Caron v. Caron, 2004 CarswellSask 745, 2004 SKQB 424, 9 R.F.L. (6th) 268 (Sask. Q.B.); additional reasons at 2005 CarswellSask 145, 2005 SKQB 120, 261 Sask. R. 141 (Sask. Q.B.). The wife's claim for spousal support was dismissed upon the dissolution of the parties' 16-year marriage. The wife had been employed throughout most of the marriage and was capable of supporting herself at a fairly decent wage, although had chosen not to do so. Her plans to upgrade her education were doubtful.

*Lack of effort to pursue self-sufficiency — support not to be extended after expiration of time limit —* Lyster v. Lyster, 2003 CarswellOnt 5008, 49 R.F.L. (5th) 139 (Ont. S.C.J.). Where the time limited spousal support payable to the wife pursuant to the parties' separation agreement expired, the wife's application for spousal support was refused. Since the parties' separation, the wife did not assume responsibility to become self-supporting and it was her lack of serious effort that left her financially needy. The wife had failed to fulfill her obligation to make concrete plans and serious efforts to re-enter the workplace, particularly in the face of a time-limited spousal support provision. The wife's current circumstances were reasonably foreseeable when the parties executed the agreement.

*Spousal support for wife to allow her to remain home with child with regard to whom husband had stood in loco parentis — Jorgensen v. Jorgensen*, 2003 CarswellNS 312, 2003 NSSF 32, 43 R.F.L. (5th) 386 (N.S.S.C.). The 56-year-old wife's claim for spousal support was dismissed upon the dissolution of her 10-year marriage. The wife was not financially disadvantaged by the marriage and had always found work when she wanted it. She could not expect the husband to subsidize her in her wish to remain home to care for her mentally challenged adult child. She had brought this child into the marriage, although the husband had stood *in loco parentis*.

*Variation — support terminated where wife's unemployment was by choice — Janakowski v. Janakowski*, 2000 CarswellOnt 2478, 7 R.F.L. (5th) 117 (Ont. S.C.J.). The court refused to extend the wife's spousal support entitlement beyond the period called for in the parties' consent order. The wife had been employed throughout the relationship and neither of the parties had realized any economic advantage from the marriage. The wife had preferred to remain unemployed after the parties' separation with the result that her need was not truly related to the marriage or its breakdown.

*Gradual step-down support order would allow wife to re-establish career — Dorey v. Snyder*, 1999 CarswellOnt 1492, 48 R.F.L. (4th) 67 (Ont. Gen. Div.). The wife was awarded limited term support upon dissolution of the parties' 16-year marriage. At the outset of the marriage the parties shared the same educational background and were both employed in thriving careers. However, after the wife had taken 4 years off to raise the parties' children, she returned to the workforce earning less than half of the husband's salary. The wife had proven herself capable of earning income and with gradually reducing support over 4 years, she would have the opportunity to re-establish herself.

*Variation — support terminated where wife's career prospects improved during marriage — Dorey v. Dorey*, 1998 CarswellNS 493, 44 R.F.L. (4th) 383, 172 N.S.R. (2d) 75, 524 A.P.R. 75 (N.S.S.C.). Where the husband had paid spousal support for 3 years and the court ordered further support for a year, as well as payment of the wife's home-care course, the husband's spousal support obligations had been met. The parties had been in a relatively short marriage (8 years) and the wife's career path had not been hindered by the marriage; rather, during the marriage, the wife had improved her qualifications by obtaining her Grade 12.

*Variation — increase in support where wife's plan to become self-sufficient had not occurred — Garrison v. Garrison*, 1998 CarswellOnt 2086, 38 R.F.L. (4th) 435 (Ont. Gen. Div.). The wife was allowed to rely upon the fact that her expectation that she would be able to re-train and become self-sufficient had not materialized as a change in circumstances warranting an increase in support.

*Variation — payee — failure to complete course — Therrien-Cliche c. Cliche*, 1997 CarswellOnt 1166, 30 R.F.L. (4th) 97, 99 O.A.C. 202, [1997] O.J. No. 1451 (Ont. C.A.). Where the wife's limited term support order was based on an assumption that she would complete a nursing course, the removal of the limitation upon her failure to complete the course was upheld on appeal. The wife's changed circumstances, had they existed at the time of the original order, would have resulted in a different support order.

*Variation — application for increased support dismissed where payee did not fulfill her educational goals — Lilly v. Lilly*, 1994 CarswellBC 691, 9 R.F.L. (4th) 434 (B.C.C.A.); affirming 1993 CarswellBC 634, 50 R.F.L. (3d) 329 (B.C.S.C.). Where the wife was unable to justify her failure to upgrade her education as was anticipated in her original spousal support order, the dismissal of her application for increased support was upheld on appeal. Her educational goals should have improved as her children became older and less dependant upon her as the primary care-giver.

*Variation — statement in minutes of settlement to seek employment does not bar wife from support — Erickson v. Erickson*, 1999 CarswellNS 137, 47 R.F.L. (4th) 326, 175 N.S.R. (2d) 185,

534 A.P.R. 185 (N.S.S.C.). A clause in minutes of settlement signed by the parties in which the wife agreed to "diligently seek full-time employment" and also acknowledged "her intention to make her best efforts to secure full-time employment" does not bar her from support if she is unable to find full-time work. The court found, following *Moge v. Moge*, [1992] 3 S.C.R. 813, that the court must look at all four objectives under s. 17(7) of the *Divorce Act* and not just self-sufficiency. In any event, the court also found that the wife had used her best efforts to secure full-time employment and at 56 it was unrealistic to expect her to become economically self-sufficient.

*Variation — no support where payee's lack of self sufficiency caused by intentional failure to return to work — Teeple v. Teeple*, 1998 CarswellOnt 5165, 43 R.F.L. (4th) 251 (Ont. Gen. Div.); reversed 1999 CarswellOnt 2958, 2 R.F.L. (5th) 564, 124 O.A.C. 294, 90 O.T.C. 80 (note) (Ont. Gen. Div.). Where a spouse is unable to work at the time of the variation hearing, but such inability is the result of her intentional failure to return to her employer, and is not related to the marriage, the court will not require the payor spouse to continue to pay spousal support. This is so, even though the payor spouse takes early retirement to reduce his income substantially so that he could decrease the amount of anticipated spousal support.

*Support to be paid to husband to facilitate retraining — Nock v. Nock*, 1998 CarswellOnt 3920, 43 R.F.L. (4th) 110 (Ont. Gen. Div.). The husband was found to be entitled to spousal support. After separation the husband lost his job and decided that retraining would be his best chance for re-entering the workforce. The husband suffered from a learning disability and would require tutorial assistance to complete his studies. The husband's inability to access the wife's income to cover living expenses while retraining constituted an economic hardship flowing directly from the marriage breakdown. The husband was entitled to periodic support reviewable in 18 months' time.

*Support denied despite some disadvantage from marriage — financial independence imminent — Kyle v. Kyle*, 1996 CarswellSask 101 (Sask. Q.B.). Where the wife had given up her full-time job upon marriage but had resumed full-time work after separation, her claim for spousal support was dismissed. Although somewhat disadvantaged by the marriage, she had trained and gained experience while married and would soon achieve financial independence.

*No disadvantage from marriage and claimant capable of supporting herself — no support — Kenning v. Kenning*, 1995 CarswellBC 83, 11 R.F.L. (4th) 216 (B.C.S.C.). Where after her early years as a homemaker, the wife qualified as a registered nurse, obtained a good paying job and, subsequent to separation, left that job to return to university, her application for spousal support was dismissed. Whereas the wife had improved her station considerably throughout the 21-year marriage, the husband had been confined to his job as a labourer and had assumed full responsibility for the children after the separation. The wife had suffered no economic disadvantage from the marriage or its breakdown and was capable of caring for herself.

*No forseeable expectation of self-sufficiency — indefinite support ordered — Au v. Au*, 1993 CarswellAlta 446, 47 R.F.L. (3d) 342 (Alta. Q.B.). The husband was ordered to pay to the wife periodic support for an indefinite period upon termination of their 20-year traditional marriage. Given the wife's difficulty with English and the disadvantages resulting from the marriage, it was not reasonable to expect her to achieve any form of self-sufficiency within the foreseeable future.

*Self-sufficiency is not the same as subsistence — Morison v. Morison*, 1993 CarswellAlta 442, 47 R.F.L. (3d) 34, 139 A.R. 124 (Alta. Q.B.). Where the wife had earned $20,000 annually after separation, she was nevertheless found entitled to "top up" support. She lived in a large city where living expenses were high so that her income amounted to subsistence and not self-sufficiency.

*Self-sufficiency not of primary importance after long-term traditional marriage — Prothman v. Prothman*, 1993 CarswellAlta 594, 137 A.R. 241 (Alta. Q.B.). The promotion of self-sufficiency is but one factor to be considered in assessing a spouse's entitlement to support, and may not be persuasive in the context of a long-term traditional marriage.

*Variation — in an application for a variation of spousal support, the factors set out in s. 17(7) of the* Divorce Act *should be reviewed not only from the date of the original order but from the inception of the marriage — Adam v. Adam,* 1993 CarswellMan 63,, 50 R.F.L. (3d) 216, 89 Man. R. (2d) 275 (Man. Q.B.). Applying this principle, a wife was found entitled to compensation from the husband for support that she had needed but not received in the past.

*Variation — termination of support order where wife's efforts insufficient — Furlong v. Furlong,* 1992 CarswellNS 379, 111 N.S.R. (2d) 391, 303 A.P.R. 391 (N.S.T.D.). The court allowed the husband's application to terminate the wife's support brought 4 years after the parties' divorce. The wife was only working part-time and had failed to prove that she had made every reasonable effort to achieve self-sufficiency.

*Self-sufficiency not of primary importance after long-term traditional marriage — Harris v. Harris,* 1992 CarswellBC 560, 40 R.F.L. (3d) 253 (B.C.S.C.). The principle of spousal self-sufficiency is to be given a restrictive interpretation in the case of traditional long-term marriages where the spouse in need has sacrificed a career for the family and is unlikely ever to achieve full economic independence.

*Fact that wife's lifestyle and income comparable to what she had before marriage among reasons to deny support application — Mueller v. Mueller,* 1992 CarswellBC 554, 39 R.F.L. (3d) 328 (B.C.S.C.). Where the wife's lifestyle and income were consistent with those enjoyed prior to marriage, her application for support was dismissed. Further, as the husband lacked the means to pay and as the wife had previously released her support rights in an agreement prior to a brief reconciliation, support was not appropriate.

*Although claimant had failed at various ventures, he was capable of self-sufficiency — Soyland v. Soyland,* 1992 CarswellAlta 629, 128 A.R. 89 (Alta. Q.B.). The court refused the husband's application for spousal support. Although he had failed at a number of various employment and business ventures, he had proved his ability to be self-sufficient should he choose to work and could not point to any economic hardship arising from the marriage or its breakdown.

*Variation — the principle of spousal self-sufficiency should be given a restrictive interpretation in cases of long-term marriages where a spouse is unable to achieve self-sufficiency — Harris v. Harris,* 1992 CarswellBC 560, 40 R.F.L. (3d) 253 (B.C.S.C.). In the *Harris* decision, the wife had achieved a measure of self-sufficiency but her standard of living had fallen drastically as a result of the dissolution of the marriage. The husband's income had declined significantly since trial. Consequently, the wife was awarded permanent maintenance at a reduced amount.

*Variation — application to terminate support refused where not practical for wife to sell house — Ryan v. Ryan,* 1992 CarswellNS 126, 114 N.S.R. (2d) 255, 313 A.P.R. 255 (N.S.T.D.), the court refused the husband's application to terminate the wife's spousal support. Although the wife continued to live in the matrimonial home in which there was over $70,000 in equity, it was impractical to require her to sell it to increase her self-sufficiency.

*Variation — support terminated where wife had had sufficient time to recover from her health problems — Hawker v. Hawker,* 1992 CarswellSask 483, 103 Sask. R. 247 (Sask. Q.B.). The court made a provisional order terminating the wife's support 2 years after the parties' divorce. At the time of the divorce it was anticipated that it would take the wife 2 years to complete a rehabilitation programme relating to her drug, alcohol and depression problems. The court accepted the husband's uncontested evidence that the recovery time had passed and that the wife should now take responsibility for her own self-sufficiency.

*Variation — application to terminate support set aside pending review in 6 months' time — Gillam v. Gillam,* 1991 CarswellNfld 234, 89 Nfld. & P.E.I.R. 89, 278 A.P.R. 89 (Nfld. T.D.).

The husband's application to terminate spousal support and the wife's application for increased support were both set aside pending a review of the parties' situation in 6 months' time. Although the wife had attempted to become self-sufficient she had not yet succeeded and a better picture of her prospects would be obtained after a further 6 months.

*Variation — even in the case of a traditional marriage, a wife may still be required to take reasonable steps to retrain and to decide on a suitable career — Boucher v. Boucher*, 1991 CarswellNS 66, 36 R.F.L. (3d) 179, 108 N.S.R. (2d) 96, 294 A.P.R. 96 (N.S. Fam. Ct.). Accordingly, where in the 7 years subsequent to the end of the parties' traditional marriage, the wife had not acted reasonably in pursuing self-sufficiency, the court allowed the husband's application for a variation of spousal support. The wife was granted a $4,000 lump sum to permit her to retrain together with continued periodic support for one more year only.

*Variation — where the wife was required, under the terms of the decree nisi, to raise the children in an economically depressed area, the husband could not rely upon the wife's failure to become self-sufficient as a grounds for reducing spousal support — Rebelo v. Rebelo*, 1991 CarswellNS 132, 104 N.S.R. (2d) 172, 283 A.P.R. 172 (N.S.T.D.).

*Claimant's career sacrifices during marriage justified support but she would also be required to work — Vokey v. Vokey*, 1991 CarswellMan 47, 35 R.F.L. (3d) 458, 74 Man. R. (2d) 312 (Man. Q.B.). Where the wife had moved several times in furtherance of the husband's career and had assumed the majority of child care responsibilities, a sufficient causal connection was found to justify an award of spousal support to her. However, as she had worked in the past, she was obliged to contribute to some extent to her own support, despite her frequent bouts with depression.

*Entitlement to spousal support requires demonstration that applicant is reasonably pursuing self-sufficiency — Hayes v. Hayes*, 1991 CarswellBC 542, 34 R.F.L. (3d) 274 (B.C.S.C.). The court was of the opinion that in order to be entitled to spousal support, an applicant must satisfy the court that she is taking reasonable steps to achieve financial independence. Where the wife wished to give up her present job to complete her educational qualifications to become a teacher and the evidence showed that she was likely to obtain this type of employment, she met the onus and was awarded support during her retraining period. In the event that she did not obtain employment when her course ended, the spousal support would be continued. The wife's use of the proceeds from her share of the family assets to purchase a smaller home for herself and the parties' two children was reasonable as she had reduced accommodation costs. The proceeds need not be used to finance her retraining programme.

*Claimant's mental illness not caused by the other spouse — claimant could become self-sufficient — Golini v. Golini*, 1991 CarswellOnt 246, 31 R.F.L. (3d) 289, 82 D.L.R. (4th) 255 (Ont. U.F.C.). In refusing the applicant husband's claim for spousal support, the court was of the opinion that the husband's mental illness was not caused by the wife. The illness had not prevented him from achieving significant academic success and there was no reason why he could not be self-sufficient.

*Support applicant had full-time employment but not expected to be fully self-sufficient after 25-year marriage — support ordered — LeMoine v. LeMoine*, 1991 CarswellNB 218, 118 N.B.R. (2d) 53, 296 A.P.R. 53 (N.B.Q.B.). Where the parties had separated after 25 years of marriage and the wife had devoted most of that time to maintaining the household and raising the children, her economic need was found to be causally connected to the marriage. Although the 48-year-old wife had retrained and secured full-time employment as a receptionist/secretary, it was unreasonable at this stage to expect her to become fully self-supporting.

*Part-time job and student loans made wife self-sufficient and therefore not entitled to support — Huppe v. Huppe*, 1990 CarswellMan 52, 28 R.F.L. (3d) 70, 66 Man. R. (2d) 241 (Man. Q.B.). Where the wife had returned to school and had obtained a part-time job, her application for support was dismissed. Given her part-time employment and her access to interest-free student loans, she was self-sufficient and could prove no need for support.

*Retraining would finish in 2 years but support ordered for 3 years* — Rose v. Rose, 1990 CarswellAlta 278, 27 R.F.L. (3d) 267 (Alta. Q.B.). Where the evidence indicated that the payee spouse would be able to complete her studies in 2 years, but that such a regime would be intellectually and emotionally draining, and make efforts to parent the child in her custody difficult, and so discouraging and disruptive to the wife's life as to make hope of self-sufficiency an unrealistic goal, the court ordered spousal support for 3 years.

*Variation — support extended for 2 years, followed by wife obtaining social assistance if not self-sufficient* — Droit de la famille - 886, 1990 CarswellQue 1555, EYB 1990-76712, [1990] R.D.F. 550 (C.S. Que.). Where the wife claimed that ill health had prevented her from achieving self-sufficiency in the 11 years since the parties' divorce, the husband was ordered to continue paying spousal support only for a further two-year period. If the wife had failed to achieve financial independence during that period, she would be required to seek social assistance to meet her needs.

*Variation — wife's lack of self-sufficiency arose from the marriage as she had moved numerous times and had several pregnancies* — Droit de la famille - 1354, [1990] R.D.F. 582 (C.S. Que.). Where the wife had been through several pregnancies and 13 moves during the parties' 23-year marriage, the husband could not rely upon the failure to achieve self-sufficiency as grounds for terminating her spousal support. The wife's economic hardships had resulted directly from the marriage and its failure, since her total lack of experience and training throughout the marriage prevented her from finding suitable employment.

*Variation — support terminated where wife capable of being self-sufficient* — MacAllister v. MacAllister, 1990 CarswellNB 109, 101 N.B.R. (2d) 422, 254 A.P.R. 422 (N.B.Q.B.). Where the wife's decision to work only part-time was motivated solely out of a dislike of her career or a lack of ambition, the court allowed the husband's application to terminate spousal support. As she was fully capable of becoming economically self-sufficient, it was appropriate that the husband's support obligations be brought to an end.

*Variation — support terminated after a further 6 months where wife had not exerted herself to find full-time employment* — Klaudi v. Klaudi, 1990 CarswellOnt 227, 25 R.F.L. (3d) 134 (Ont. H.C.). Where, subsequent to the termination of the parties' long term traditional marriage, the wife had shown little ambition and had made only spotty efforts to find full-time employment, the husband's application to terminate her support after a further six-month period was allowed. The husband had supported her for 5 years after the divorce and should be allowed to get on with his life.

*Variation — support terminated after 7 years where wife had not made a reasonable effort to achieve self-sufficiency* — Derkach v. Derkach, 1989 CarswellMan 57, 22 R.F.L. (3d) 423, 60 Man. R. (2d) 278 (Man. Q.B.). Where the wife had difficulty adjusting to the breakdown of the parties' traditional marriage and had accordingly not made a reasonable attempt to achieve self-sufficiency during the 7 years since the divorce, her support was ordered terminated.

*Variation — where subsequent to the parties' divorce the wife realized significant assets from the sale of the family home, had entered into a stable conjugal relationship with another man and had failed to seek employment despite her ability to do so, the court allowed the husband's application to terminate her support* — Schofield v. Schofield, 1989 CarswellAlta 28, 19 R.F.L. (3d) 165, 65 Alta. L.R. (2d) 258, [1989] 4 W.W.R. 84, 98 A.R. 150 (Alta. Q.B.).

*Variation — support continued, where wife sole support of children* — Droit de la famille - 1240, [1989] R.D.F. 262 (C.S. Que.). Where the wife had solely provided for the needs of the parties' children during the 11 years following the parties' divorce, her failure to become self-sufficient could not be cited as a ground for terminating her support.

*Wife employed before and during marriage — self-sufficiency should be encouraged —* Lewis v. Lewis, 1989 CarswellNfld 15, 23 R.F.L. (3d) 252 (Nfld. T.D.). Where the wife had worked both before and during the marriage, her application for spousal support was dismissed. She had not suffered an economic disadvantage because of the marriage and should be encouraged to be self-sufficient.

*Skills not eroded by marriage, self-sufficiency imminent — no support — Motz v. Motz*, 1989 CarswellAlta 384, 22 R.F.L. (3d) 238, 99 A.R. 339 (Alta. Q.B.). Where the wife's nursing skills had not been eroded by the marriage and where she could expect shortly to be self-sufficient through upgrading and a substantial property settlement, her application for support was refused.

*Insufficient effort to re-enter workforce — Picciano v. Picciano*, 1989 CarswellMan 54, 22 R.F.L. (3d) 196 (Man. Q.B.). Where during the 3 years after the parties' separation the wife made no real effort to re-enter the work force but was content to live on the proceeds of an interim support award, her application for support in divorce proceedings was refused. Her conduct was not consistent with her argument that she was unable to support herself.

*Wife not in need but had incurred debts to upgrade skills — Scobie v. Scobie*, 1989 CarswellSask 75, 21 R.F.L. (3d) 447, 77 Sask. R. 264 (Sask. Q.B.). Where the wife had incurred debts after separation to upgrade her skills and had achieved self-sufficiency, it was held that the husband should contribute to her self-sufficiency expenses through a limited term support order, despite her current lack of need.

*Wife should seek work immediately instead of seeking retraining given husband's insufficient ability to pay — Norlander v. Norlander*, 1989 CarswellSask 73, 21 R.F.L. (3d) 317 (Sask. Q.B.). Where the wife wished to resume her education and retrain, but the husband earned insufficient funds to support two households, it was held that the wife was required for the time being to forgo retraining and seek work.

*Wife expected to pursue self-sufficiency despite lack of work experience — Longmuir v. Longmuir*, 1989 CarswellMan 47, 21 R.F.L. (3d) 151, 59 Man. R. (2d) 122 (Man. Q.B.). The fact that the 48-year-old wife lacked work experience did not excuse her from attempting to achieve self-sufficiency. Accordingly, she was awarded periodic support which was subject to review by the court in 1 year's time.

*Although wife had worked throughout marriage, 2 years' support ordered to permit retraining — Giddings v. Giddings*, 1989 CarswellNB 80, 100 N.B.R. (2d) 224, 252 A.P.R. 224 (N.B.Q.B.). Where the wife was not self-sufficient despite the fact that she had worked throughout the marriage, the husband was ordered to pay support to her for 2 years to permit her to complete a nursing course. The *Divorce Act* recognizes spousal responsibility to promote economic self-sufficiency of the other spouse.

*Variation — support terminated after long period — Hudson v. Hudson*, 1989 CarswellNB 98, 102 N.B.R. (2d) 199, 256 A.P.R. 199 (N.B.Q.B.). The husband's application for termination of spousal support brought 16 years after the parties' divorce was allowed. The wife had had ample time to become self-sufficient.

*Variation — the wife's failure to seek self-sufficiency was a material change in circumstances justifying a variation of the support order — Smith v. Smith*, 1989 CarswellOnt 237, 20 R.F.L. (3d) 38 (Ont. H.C.). Where the wife, who was educated and capable of self-sufficiency, failed to seek employment during the 5 years subsequent to the parties' divorce, the husband's application to terminate spousal support was allowed.

*Variation — wife's support to be phased out as wife capable of being self-supporting — Droit de la famille - 1238*, [1989] R.D.F. 251 (C.S. Que.). The court granted the husband's application to phase out gradually the support payable to his 49-year-old former wife. The wife was in good health, had a university degree and her children were grown. Accordingly, her claim that it was impossible for her to find a job was not credible.

*Variation — support terminated where wife embarked on expensive educational programme — Droit de la famille - 473*, [1988] R.J.Q. 1034, [1988] R.D.F. 240 (C.S. Que.). Where the wife left a well-paying job to commence a 5-year post-graduate programme, the husband's application to terminate spousal support was allowed. The obligation did not encompass the financing of his wife's studies after having paid generous support for a 4-year period.

*No obligation to become self-sufficient given childcare functions during marriage and given other spouse's ability to pay — Elsom v. Elsom*, 1987 CarswellBC 535, 10 R.F.L. (3d) 234 (B.C.S.C.). It was found that the wife had no obligation to become self-supporting given her husband's considerable assets and the fact that she had remained in the home during the marriage to raise the parties' child.

*Variation — two-year term to encourage self-sufficiency — Oldfield v. Oldfield*, 1987 CarswellMan 114, 8 R.F.L. (3d) 297, 51 Man. R. (2d) 129 (Man. Q.B.). While s. 17 of the *Divorce Act, 1985* requires that there be a change in circumstances before a court can make a variation order, once that change is established s. 17(7) introduces far-reaching criteria that almost give the court a curative power in varying a prior order. The court can attempt to encourage self-sufficiency by refusing to award support or limiting the order. in which the court refused to increase the support payable to the wife, who was alcoholic and refused treatment, and in fact limited her future entitlement to 2 years to encourage self-sufficiency.

*Expectation that wife would become self-sufficient after retraining among reasons for denying support claim — Fahr v. Fahr*, 1986 CarswellSask 561, 50 Sask. R. 55 (Sask. Q.B.). The wife's claim for maintenance was refused in light of the substantial capital assets she had received upon the division of the matrimonial property and because her training as a registered nurse would allow her to become self-sufficient.

*Clear evidence of inability to become self-sufficient required to overcome duty to do so — Rednall v. Rednall*, 1986 CarswellBC 543, 4 R.F.L. (3d) 337 (B.C.S.C.). The duty of a spouse to become self-sufficient must be considered in the context of each individual case. The duty is extinguished only in the face of clear evidence of a spouse's inability to become self-supporting.

*Variation — wife's refusal to accept work outside immediate area grounds for terminating support — Droit de la famille - 318*, 1986 CarswellQue 1204, EYB 1986-79063, [1986] R.J.Q. 2911, [1986] R.D.F. 591 (C.S. Que.); affirmed [1990] R.D.F. 178 (C.A. Que.). The court ordered the termination of the wife's maintenance 10 years after the parties' divorce. Although the wife had since the divorce completed her Master's degree in translation, her refusal to accept work outside of the medical area greatly reduced the possibility of her achieving economic independence.

*Variation — an order pursuant to s. 17(7) of the* Divorce Act *varying an order for support is intended to encourage self-sufficiency as far as practicable — Gray v. Gray*, 1986 CarswellMan 102, 3 R.F.L. (3d) 457, 45 Man. R. (2d) 156 (Man. Q.B.); affirmed 1987 CarswellMan 109, 8 R.F.L. (3d) 147, 49 Man. R. (2d) 90 (Man. C.A.). However, the provision was not intended to impose an obligation on a spouse to become self-sufficient.

# CHAPTER 7

## TERMS AND CONDITIONS

This chapter is divided into the following subsections:

## 7.1 General

**Terms and conditions — general**

An order for spousal support may be made "for a definite or indefinite period or until a specified event occurs," and the court "may impose terms, conditions or restrictions in connection with the order as it thinks fit and just": *Divorce Act*, s. 15.2(3).

### 7.1.1 Retroactive Spousal Support

See also Volume 3, Chapter 10, section 10.7 Retroactive Variation of Support Orders and Chapter 19A Retroactive Support and the SSAG.

The Supreme Court of Canada cases of *D.B.S. v. S.R.G.; T.A.R. v. L.J.W.; Henry v. Henry; S. (D.B.) v. G. (S.R.)*, 2006 CarswellAlta 976, 2006 CarswellAlta 977, 2006 SCC 37, 31 R.F.L. (6th) 1, [2006] 2 S.C.R. 231, 61 Alta. L.R. (4th) 1, [2006] 10 W.W.R. 379, 270 D.L.R. (4th) 297, 391 A.R. 297, 377 W.A.C. 297, 351 N.R. 201, [2006] S.C.J. No. 37 (S.C.C.), discussed below, although dealing with retroactive child support, have had a significant effect upon retroactive spousal support.

*D.B.S. v. S.R.G.; T.A.R. v. L.J.W.; Henry v. Henry; Hiemstra v. Hiemstra* were four Alberta cases heard by a panel of seven judges. Bastarche J. with McLachlin C.J., LeBel and Deschamps JJ., wrote the majority judgement, and Abella J., with Fish and Charron JJ., wrote concurring reasons. The issue before the court was the nature of parents' obligations to make child support payments for periods of time when the responsibility to do so was never identified, mush less enforced. This situation arises when the parent receiving support decides that he or she should have been paid more support than he or she received, even though there was no court order or separation agreement which provided for these higher payments. While the court termed these awards retroactive awards, it pointed out that they were "retroactive" only in the sense that they were not dealing with future payments. The parents who were ordered to make these payments, were being ordered to do so because, in hindsight, it was determined that the parents should have made these payments before.

Two of the appeals before the court dealt with retroactive awards under the federal *Divorce Act* and two appeals were brought under the Alberta *Parentage and Maintenance Act*, R.S.A. 2000, c. P-1, now repealed. The parties in those cases accepted that that their cases would essentially be decided as if they fell under the federal system. Two cases dealt with claims where no support payments had ever been made and two asked for original awards to be increased. All of these cases concerned parents who failed to ask for increases in child support in a timely fashion. In each of the cases, the children lived prolonged periods without the support that they were entitled to have. Bastarache J. stated that whatever the outcome in these particular cases, the ultimate objective must be to make certain that children benefit from the support which they are owed, at the time they are owed it.

Mr. Justice Bastarache set out the particular legal principles to be considered in granting or refusing to grant retroactive child support. They are:

1. Retroactive awards are not truly retroactive. They do not hold parents to a legal standard that did not exist at the relevant time.

2. Retroactive awards should not be seen as exceptional orders to be made in exceptional circumstances. While such an order should not be presumed, it will not only be found in rare circumstances.

3. In exercising their discretion, courts should award retroactive support where fairness dictated it, but should keep in mind that certainty for payor parents was also an important principle.

4. A payor parent under the federal legislation has the obligation to increase his or her child support payments when his or her income rises.

5. Where the payor parent's income rises and the amount of child support does not, there will be an unfulfilled obligation that could later be enforced by a court.

6. An application is necessary to trigger the court's jurisdiction to make a retroactive award of child support.

7. It will not always be appropriate for a court to make a retroactive child support order. Such awards will not always conform to the purposes behind the child support regime. Such awards may cause hardship to a payor parent where prospective awards would not.

8. A court should strive for a holistic view of the matter and decide each case on the basis of its particular facts.

9. Parents have an obligation to support their children in a way commensurate with their incomes.

10. Bastarache J., at para. 50, held that "in exercising their own power to legislate matters concerning child support, the provinces need not conform to the paradigm espoused

by the *Divorce Act* and the *Guidelines*." In this decision, the parties in the *D.B.S. v. S.R.G.* and *T.A.R. v. L.J.W.* cases, which proceeded under Alberta's now repealed *Parentage and Maintenance Act*, accepted that their cases would be decided substantially as if they fell under the federal system.

11. Delay in seeking child support is not presumptively justifiable.

12. Where the delay is caused by the recipient parent's unreasonableness and not by the payor parent's blameworthy conduct, the principle of certainty will be compelling. Nonetheless, unreasonable delay by the recipient parent does not have the effect of eliminating the payor parent's obligation. Child support is the right of the child and cannot be waived by the parent.

13. Recipient parents must act promptly and responsibly in monitoring the amount of child support paid. From the child's point of view, a retroactive award is a poor substitute for past obligations not met.

14. A payor parent who knowingly avoids or diminishes his/her support obligation to his or her children should not be allowed to benefit from such conduct.

15. The conduct of the payor parent could militate against a retroactive award where the payor parent's conduct has had the effect of fulfilling his or her support obligation.

16. Courts should consider the present circumstances of the child, as a child who is currently enjoying a relatively high standard of living may benefit less from a retroactive award than a child who is currently in need. Need is an important factor when courts consider retroactive awards. It is significant to consider the child's needs at the time that the support should have been paid. A child who experienced hardship in the past may be compensated for this experience with a retroactive award. A child, who had all the advantages, is less likely to receive retroactive support.

17. Courts should try to craft retroactive awards in a way that minimizes the payor parent and his other dependants' hardship.

18. A retroactive award should be retroactive to the date when effective notice was give to the payor parent that support should be paid or that the amount being paid is inadequate.

19. It will usually be inappropriate to make a support award retroactive to a date more than 3 years before formal notice was given to the payor parent.

20. The date when increased support should have been paid will be a more appropriate date from which retroactive support should begin, when the payor parent engages in blameworthy conduct such as when he or she intimidates and lies to the recipient parent, but also when he or she withholds information. When a payor parent does not disclose a material change in circumstances, including an increase in income, the presumptive date may be moved to the time that the circumstances changed materially.

21. Undue hardship arguments under s. 10 are available in determinations of retroactive child support awards and will generally be easier to show in such cases than in determinations of prospective awards.

22. In summary, on an application for retroactive support, a court must consider:
    a. whether the recipient parent has supplied a reasonable excuse for the delay;
    b. the conduct of the payor parent;
    c. the circumstances of the children; and
    d. the hardship the retroactive award might entail.

Abella J. (with Fish, Charron JJ.) concurred in the results of the appeals, but differed in respect to Bastarache J.'s views about the presumptive starting date for the calculation of child support arrears, about the relevance of blameworthy conduct, and about the desirability of a 3-

year limitation period. Abella J.'s justification for her differing view was based on the underlying premise that parents have a free-standing joint obligation to support their children based on their ability to do so.

She agreed with Bastarache J. that these awards are not, in fact, "retroactive" awards, as they are instead compensation for what is legally owed.

She added that since only the payor parent knows when there has been a change in income that would justify an increase in child support, he or she should have the major responsibility for ensuring that a child benefits from the change as soon as is reasonably possible. To require the recipient parent to ensure that the payor parent is paying a fair amount is impractical and unrealistic. The presumptive starting point for payment of an increased amount of support should be when the change occurred, not when the change was disclosed or discovered. The need for certainty for payor parents and a child's entitlement to support in accordance with parental ability to pay are not inconsistent propositions.

There should be no role for "blameworthy conduct" in determining the date at which children can recover the support to which they are entitled. The amount of support should fluctuate with the amount of income, regardless of parental misconduct.

The recipient parent should not be required to demonstrate that the payor parent's failure to pay increased support resulted in hardship for the child. The debt remains nonetheless.

Having a presumptive date of entitlement to increased child support does not eliminate judicial discretion.

If a recipient parent has delayed in seeking increased support, it should not usually affect child support awards.

There should not be any automatic time limit on the amount of retroactive support. However, undue hardship could militate against a retroactive order being made as of the date of the change of circumstances. The 3-year rule is an unnecessary fettering of judicial discretion.

[For further discussion of these cases, see *Canadian Divorce Law and Practice*, Volume 1 at 15§85 Retroactive Child Support.]

*An order of spousal support is effective as of the date that proceedings are commenced where the recipient spouse is in need prior to trial and she has not delayed in bringing her application* — *Kerr v. Baranow*, 2011 CarswellBC 240, 2011 CarswellBC 241, 2011 SCC 10, 93 R.F.L. (6th) 1, [2011] 1 S.C.R. 269, 108 O.R. (3d) 399, 14 B.C.L.R. (5th) 203, 328 D.L.R. (4th) 577, 64 E.T.R. (3d) 1, [2011] 3 W.W.R. 575, 411 N.R. 200, 274 O.A.C. 1, 300 B.C.A.C. 1, 509 W.A.C. 1, [2011] S.C.J. No. 10 (S.C.C.).

*Support recipients are presumptively entitled to support from the time they have given notice of their intention to seek support* — *LeVan v. LeVan*, 2008 CarswellOnt 2738, 2008 ONCA 388, 90 O.R. (3d) 1, 51 R.F.L. (6th) 237, 239 O.A.C. 1, [2008] O.J. No. 1905 (Ont. C.A.), affirming [2006] O.J. No. 3584 (Ont. S.C.J.), additional reasons at 82 O.R. (3d) 1 at 76, 2006 CarswellOnt 7334, 32 R.F.L. (6th) 359, [2006] O.J. No. 4599 (Ont. S.C.J.), additional reasons at 2008 CarswellOnt 3713, 2008 ONCA 505, 51 R.F.L. (6th) 261 (Ont. C.A.). Leave to appeal refused 2008 CarswellOnt 6207, 2008 CarswellOnt 6208. [2008] S.C.C.A. No. 331 (S.C.C.).

*If a trial judge grants a retroactive spousal support order but fails to take into consideration the tax implications of such an order, there is an error and the award should be discounted* — *Mew v. Mew*, 2012 CarswellAlta 2161, 2012 ABCA 382 (Alta. C.A.). The court discounted the award by the amount of 28.6%, which would result in the amendment of the original order such that there is $40,930 payable in retroactive spousal support, representing $57,325 originally ordered minus $16,395, which is 28.6% to reduce the amount payable to $40,930.

*Retroactive support to the wife upheld from the date of the initiation of the proceedings* — *Redman v. Korchinski*, 2006 CarswellMan 436, 2006 MBCA 149, 33 R.F.L. (6th) 36, [2007] 2 W.W.R. 611, 277 D.L.R. (4th) 427, 212 Man. R. (2d) 90, 389 W.A.C. 90 (Man. C.A.). The husband had knowledge of the support claim since the initiation of proceedings and had failed to forward financial information in a timely way.

*Factors governing an award of retroactive spousal support — Bremer v. Bremer*, 2005 CarswellOnt 601, 13 R.F.L. (6th) 89, [2005] O.J. No. 608 (Ont. C.A.). The Court of Appeal identified the factors relevant to a claim for retroactive spousal support which included: i) the extent to which the claimant established past need (including any requirement to encroach on capital) and the payor's ability to pay; ii) the underlying basis for the ongoing support obligation; iii) the requirement that there be a reason for awarding retroactive support; iv) the impact of a retroactive award on the payor and, in particular, whether a retroactive order will create an undue burden on the payor or effect a redistribution of capital; v) the presence of blameworthy conduct on the part of the payor such as incomplete or misleading financial disclosure; vi) notice of an intention to seek support and negotiations to that end; vii) delay in proceeding and any explanation for the delay; and viii) the appropriateness of a retroactive order pre-dating the date on which the application for divorce was issued.

*An applicant who requests financial information preliminary to negotiations or litigation of a support claim and who then proceeds reasonably with the claim is presumptively entitled to prospective support from the date of notice that a support claim is brought — MacKinnon v. MacKinnon*, 2005 CarswellOnt 1536, 13 R.F.L. (6th) 221, 75 O.R. (3d) 175, 256 D.L.R. (4th) 385, 199 O.A.C. 353, [2005] O.J. No. 1552 (Ont. C.A.).

*Wife's claim for retroactive spousal support refused where she lacked an explanation as to why she had failed to seek interim support and she had continued to live very well after separation — Martin v. Martin*, 2004 CarswellOnt 5438, 12 R.F.L. (6th) 415, [2004] O.T.C. 1139, [2004] O.J. No. 5170 (Ont. S.C.J.), additional reasons at 2005 CarswellOnt 1437, [2005] O.J. No. 1437 (Ont. S.C.J.), affirmed 2006 CarswellOnt 4876, 40 R.F.L. (6th) 32, 81 O.R. (3d) 503, 81 O.R. (3d) 495, 272 D.L.R. (4th) 666, 214 O.A.C. 140, [2006] O.J. No. 3238 (Ont. C.A.). There was no evidence of hardship, nor had the husband participated in any blameworthy conduct.

*Delay in bringing application may result in denial of retroactive award — Horner v. Horner*, 2004 CarswellOnt 4246, 6 R.F.L. (6th) 140, 72 O.R. (3d) 561, 245 D.L.R. (4th) 410, 191 O.A.C. 28, [2004] O.J. No. 4268 (Ont. C.A.). The Court of Appeal noted that retroactive spousal support is not granted as a matter of course. A party is expected to act in her own interests to pursue an increase in support promptly. A court will deny an award of retroactive support where a party is aware of changed circumstances, but delays in bringing an application.

*Retroactive lump sum support to compensate wife for the expenses she incurred between the parties' separation and the trial — Allaire v. Allaire*, 2003 CarswellOnt 1002, 35 R.F.L. (5th) 256, 170 O.A.C. 72 (Ont. C.A.). There was no basis to interfere with the award.

*Where the wife had not claimed support immediately upon separation, but had maintained herself by drawing upon capital resources, the award of retroactive support back to the date of separation was upheld on appeal — Kloos v. Kloos*, 1996 CarswellMan 126, 20 R.F.L. (4th) 1, [1996] 5 W.W.R. 553, 110 Man. R. (2d) 129, 118 W.A.C. 129, [1996] M.J. No. 146 (Man. C.A.).

*The Divorce Act permits, in the proper circumstances, for the making of a support order which includes payment for a period which predates the petition — Lidstone v. Lidstone*, 1993 CarswellNS 44, 46 R.F.L. (3d) 203, 121 N.S.R. (2d) 213, 335 A.P.R. 213, [1993] N.S.J. No. 165 (N.S.C.A.).

*The power to award spousal support retroactively back to the date of separation should be exercised sparingly — Giguere v. Giguere*, 2003 CarswellOnt 5006, 46 R.F.L. (5th) 184, [2003] O.J. No. 5102 (Ont. S.C.J.), additional reasons at 2004 CarswellOnt 273, [2004] O.J. No. 444 (Ont. S.C.J.). Where after separation the wife had delayed bringing her support claim on the chance that the parties had incurred no debt and she had no immediate pressing need then for funds, her spousal support was made retroactive only to the date of her claim.

*Retroactive support where husband had sold his business receiving a large amount of money and had chosen to reduce his own income* — *Leeder v. Leeder*, 2002 CarswellOnt 80, 25 R.F.L. (5th) 291, [2002] O.J. No. 57 (Ont. S.C.J.), the husband was ordered to pay combined retroactive spousal and child support of $100 monthly, although his annual income was only $125,000. The husband had previously owned a business which generated an annual income of close to $500,000, but he had sold it for a considerable amount of money. Reduction of his income was the husband's own doing and he had realized a substantial profit on the sale.

*Retroactive support awarded where payor's income was considerably larger than forecasted at time of interim order* — *Vitagliano v. Di Stavolo*, 2001 CarswellOnt 1065, 17 R.F.L. (5th) 194, [2001] O.J. No. 1138 (Ont. S.C.J.). The wife was awarded retroactive lump sum spousal and child support. Whereas the interim support orders had been based on the husband's forecast income of $115,000, his actual income throughout the duration of the interim order had been in excess of $200,000. His contribution towards his children's support had, therefore, clearly been unreasonable.

*Where the wife had been unemployed and forced to encroach upon her capital to support herself and her child, a lump sum retroactive spousal support order made in her favour was upheld on appeal* — *Prince v. Prince*, 1997 CarswellNS 444, 1997 NSCA 144, 35 R.F.L. (4th) 328, 163 N.S.R. (2d) 28, 487 A.P.R. 28, [1997] N.S.J. No. 433 (N.S.C.A.).

*A lump sum for past support should only be awarded in exceptional circumstances as it is really a windfall and is not really used for past support* — *Messer v. Messer*, 1996 CarswellSask 662, 26 R.F.L. (4th) 352, 150 Sask. R. 23, [1996] S.C.J. No. 699 (Sask. Q.B.), reversed 1997 CarswellSask 595, 33 R.F.L. (4th) 426, 163 Sask. R. 101, 165 W.A.C. 101, [1997] S.J. No. 645 (Sask. C.A.). Accordingly, where the wife's spousal support order was increased substantially on appeal, the court refused her request for a lump sum equivalent to the differential over time between the appellate amount and the original amount. The wife had delayed in bringing the appeal forward, such delay resulting in a substantial differential for which the husband had no opportunity to plan.

*Section 15 of the* Divorce Act *is broad enough to entitle a judge to award support for a period predating the date of the divorce* — *Donald v. Donald*, 1991 CarswellNS 58, 33 R.F.L. (3d) 196, 81 D.L.R. (4th) 48, 103 N.S.R. (2d) 322, 282 A.P.R. 322, [1991] N.S.J. No. 214 (N.S.C.A.).

*A retroactive support order is not intended as a contribution to daily expenses but rather is a creation of a debt obligation* — *Schmuck v. Reynolds-Schmuck*, 1999 CarswellOnt 2424, 50 R.F.L. (4th) 429, [1999] O.J. No. 3104 (Ont. S.C.J.), additional reasons at 2000 CarswellOnt 202, 46 O.R. (3d) 702, [2000] O.J. No. 247 (Ont. S.C.J.). Retroactive orders are appropriate where the payor should have been paying support.

*The date for the beginning of the retroactive period should be the date when the intention to seek support was made known* — *Moro v. Miletich*, 1998 CarswellOnt 1194, 40 R.F.L. (4th) 115, 63 O.T.C. 264, [1998] O.J. No. 1799 (Ont. Gen. Div.). The court has jurisdiction under s. 15 of the *Divorce Act* to award retroactive spousal support. It should be made retroactive where the applicant expresses an intention to seek support, immediately begins sincere negotiations, conducts them expeditiously, and promptly brings the application when negotiations break down. The wife was awarded retroactive spousal support for a 13-month period during which she had legitimate need, had actively sought support and had negotiated toward that end.

*Section 15 of the Divorce Act appears to be concerned with providing support for only the present and the* future — *it does not appear to authorize a retroactive support order* — *Cerget v. Cerget*, 1994 CarswellOnt 445, 7 R.F.L. (4th) 322, [1994] O.J. No. 1633 (Ont. Gen. Div.), additional reasons at 1994 CarswellOnt 446, 7 R.F.L. (4th) 343 (Ont. Gen. Div.), further additional reasons at 1994 CarswellOnt 3496 (Ont. Gen. Div.).

*The court is entitled to award lump sum spousal support to retroactively compensate a spouse for the interim support which could have been awarded for the period between separation and trial* — Kowaluk v. Kowaluk, 1995 CarswellMan 438, 17 R.F.L. (4th) 185 (Man. Q.B.).

*No retroactive support but transitional support provided* — Fiacco v. Fiacco, 1995 CarswellSask 11, 11 R.F.L. (4th) 240, 129 Sask. R. 154 (Sask. Q.B.), the wife's application for retroactive spousal support upon the breakdown of the parties' 2-year marriage was dismissed. Although she had no job and no immediate prospects there was no justification, after such a brief marriage, for retroactive support. She was, however, entitled to periodic support to assist her in getting back on the path she was on prior to the marriage.

*Section 15 of the* Divorce Act *does not authorize the court to set maintenance retroactively* — Mannett v. Mannett, 1992 CarswellNS 373, 111 N.S.R. (2d) 327, 303 A.P.R. 327 (N.S.T.D.). The issue of retroactive maintenance is only properly addressed in the case of an existing maintenance order for which a variation is sought pursuant to s. 17.

## 7.2 Term-limited or Indefinite

### 7.2.1 Support for a Definite Period

*In the case of a long-term "traditional" marriage, the Court of Appeal will not uphold an order terminating an agreed upon limited-term spousal award unless the payor can demonstrate an adequately significant change in circumstances* — Droit de la famille - 123256, 2013 CarswellQue 8788, 2013 CarswellQue 14061, 2013 QCCA 1504, EYB 2013-226415, 37 R.F.L. (7th) 1 (C.A. Que.). The parties were married for over 20 years and separated in 2007. The wife was earning no income at separation, and the husband's salary was about $350,000. The parties signed a generous but limited-term spousal support agreement in 2007. In 2009 the parties signed a new agreement reducing support to $30,000 per year for 36 months and $15,000 per year for an additional 36 months. The new agreement limited support to those 6 years, but contained a clause that the support amount would not change regardless of the wife's income. In the following years the husband's income fluctuated, and the wife began to earn a salary. In 2011 the husband was earning about $110,000, and the wife was earning about $50,000. The husband applied to the Superior Court for a variation, and the judge terminated support based on the husband's changed circumstances. The Quebec Court of Appeal found that the change was not significant enough to justify termination given the terms of the parties' agreement.

*The Court of Appeal will terminate support where the trial judge inappropriately ordered indefinite support due to a miscalculation of the length of the parties' relationship* — Domirti v. Domirti, 2010 CarswellBC 2864, 2010 BCCA 472, 10 B.C.L.R. (5th) 281, 294 B.C.A.C. 127, 498 W.A.C. 127, [2010] B.C.J. No. 2074 (B.C.C.A.), additional reasons 2011 CarswellBC 108, 2011 BCCA 30, 13 B.C.L.R. (5th) 208 (B.C.C.A.). The trial judge miscalculated the years of marriage when calculating from the date of the trial rather than the date of separation and ordered indefinite support. The Court of Appeal terminated support as the proper calculation suggested a maximum of 16 years' support. The appeals judge stated, at para. 48:

> ... in circumstances where it is appropriate to consider the application of SSAG an award that falls substantially outside the SSAG ranges may permit appellate intervention (para. 42). In my view, that is what has occurred in this case, albeit inadvertently, by granting the respondent indefinite support.

*A party's decision to be a stay-at-home parent after a shorter-term relationship does not merit an award of indefinite support* — D. (K.) v. D. (N.), 2011 CarswellBC 3325, 2011 BCCA 513, 7 R.F.L. (7th) 44, 25 B.C.L.R. (5th) 230, [2012] 3 W.W.R. 41, 315 B.C.A.C. 12, 535 W.A.C. 12, [2011] B.C.J. No. 2406 (B.C.C.A.). The parties lived together for 7 years and separated in 2006. The husband's income was $150,000, and the wife's income had fluctuated between $30,000 and $50,000 but she left the workforce in 2004 to concentrate on fertility treatments. The wife sought indefinite support, stating that she was "not interested in working or re-training" and that she planned to be a stay-at-home mother at least until such time as the children were in school. The judge imputed income to her and awarded her limited support in the amount of $2,800 for one year. (The wife became pregnant by a third party and applied to vary support. The chambers judge found that the pregnancy was a material change in circumstances and varied the order. The Court of Appeal dismissed the husband's appeal.)

*A court may appropriately order limited-term support to compensate for loss of business income where the parties co-owned businesses but only one party operated them during separation* — C. (D.L.) v. C. (F.M.), 2011 CarswellBC 2925, 2011 BCCA 444, 4 R.F.L. (7th) 249, 25 B.C.L.R. (5th) 51 (B.C.C.A.). The parties lived together for 12 years and separated in 2005. The parties owned two cafeÇ franchises. The trial judge awarded the wife $2,017 per month in support for 4 years to compensate her for loss of income due to transitional disadvantage, as the husband earned income from the businesses during separation while the wife did not. The Court of Appeal dismissed the husband's appeal, finding that the trial judge's award of spousal support did not duplicate asset division.

*Medium-term relationships will result in limited-term support with the aim of helping the payee achieve economic self-sufficiency* — Hurst v. Gill, 2011 CarswellNS 748, 2011 NSCA 100, 13 R.F.L. (7th) 70, 342 D.L.R. (4th) 583, 309 N.S.R. (2d) 86, 979 A.P.R. 86 (N.S.C.A.). The parties lived together for 13 years. The wife's income was $80,000, and the husband's income was $25,000. The trial judge awarded the husband support of $2,200 per month for 18 months based on his earning capacity as well as the time needed to become self-sufficient. The Court of Appeal found that the trial judge did not err on this point.

*Where the wife was awarded a time-limited spousal support award* — Davies v. Quantz, 2010 CarswellOnt 9748, 2010 ONCA 896, 100 R.F.L. (6th) 176 (Ont. C.A.); affirming 2010 CarswellOnt 10064, 2010 ONSC 416, 100 R.F.L. (6th) 156 (Ont. S.C.J.). The parties cohabitated for 18 years before they separated. They were both highly educated and for the first 9 years of the relationship the parties were "equals". After the birth of their children, the wife gave up her successful career to become the primary caregiver, at which point the parties transitioned into a traditional marriage. The wife's application for spousal support was granted. The husband's annual income was $428,000. The wife's career was severely disadvantaged by her assuming the role of full-time mother and by moving from Quebec to Ontario to advance the husband's career. The wife was aware that the husband expected her to resume her career once the children were in school full-time. The wife was entitled to support on a compensatory basis and because of need. She was awarded $9,440 per month based on the lowest end of the *Spousal Support Advisory Guidelines* amount for a payor earning $428,000. As the children were both in school full-time, the wife was in a position to seek work. A time-limited support order was made for 8 years, at which point the wife was expected to be self-supporting. The spousal support order was upheld on appeal with the Court of Appeal noting that the wife could seek variation of the order in the future if the circumstances permitted.

*19-year marriage — 7-year period of spousal support* — Fisher v. Fisher, 2008 CarswellOnt 43, 2008 ONCA 11, 47 R.F.L. (6th) 235, 88 O.R. (3d) 241, 232 O.A.C. 213, 288 D.L.R. (4th) 513, [2008] O.J. No. 38 (Ont. C.A.). The Court of Appeal held that despite the parties' 19-year marriage, the order of support should be for a definite period of 7 years, in light of the wife's employment position and relative youth. The order was designed to enable the wife to become financially independent or adjust to a lower standard of living within 7 years. The wife was 45 years of age at the time of the appeal.

*Yearly payments ordered for 3 years — England v. England*, 2007 CarswellAlta 999, 2007 ABQB 494 (Alta. Q.B.). The court ordered spousal support payments of $32,500 annually until the end of December 2010.

*Support limited to 3-year period where lack of medical evidence and wife's claim for disability benefits had been rejected — Archer v. Archer*, 2005 CarswellOnt 1515, 12 R.F.L. (6th) 247, [2005] O.J. No. 1508 (Ont. C.A.), reversing 2004 CarswellOnt 4957, 10 R.F.L. (6th) 229, [2004] O.J. No. 1807 (Ont. Div. Ct.). The court, on appeal, reinstated a trial judgement limiting the wife's spousal support to a 3-year term. Although the wife was borderline mentally retarded, the trial judge's findings was supportable based upon the lack of medical evidence and the fact that the wife's application for disability benefits had been rejected.

*Application for unlimited spousal support rejected where wife had large property settlement and payor had not discouraged wife from working during the marriage — Gregory v. Ball*, 2004 CarswellAlta 1450, 2004 ABQB 789, 9 R.F.L. (6th) 338 (Alta. Q.B.), reversed in part 2005 CarswellAlta 1526, 2005 ABCA 354, 21 R.F.L. (6th) 42 (Alta. C.A.). The court refused the wife's application for unlimited spousal support upon the dissolution of the parties' 16-year marriage. Although the wife was not expected to earn income during the marriage, the husband did not discourage the wife from pursuing a career. Furthermore, the wife had received over $4 million on division of the parties' assets and was in a position to generate income.

*Appeal from time-limited support where wife fully employed and prospect of her self-sufficiency was realistic — Spencer v. Spencer*, 2002 CarswellBC 1081, 2002 BCCA 265, 27 R.F.L. (5th) 431, 212 D.L.R. (4th) 323 (B.C.C.A.), affirming 2000 CarswellBC 1391, 2000 BCSC 965, 8 R.F.L. (5th) 419 (B.C.S.C.). Where the wife had been out of the workforce for part of the marriage, but was employed full-time at the time of the parties' separation, the court dismissed her appeal from the time limitation placed upon her spousal support award. The trial judge had properly characterized the marriage as a "hybrid" one rather than a "traditional" one, and that the prospect of her achieving self-sufficiency was a realistic one.

*Support for 2-year period, health issues and short marriage — Olstead v. Olstead*, 1999 CarswellBC 895, 1999 BCCA 211, 45 R.F.L. (4th) 46, 124 B.C.A.C. 315, 203 W.A.C. 315 (B.C.C.A.). The trial judge's order that the wife pay spousal support to the husband for a two-year period was upheld on appeal where the husband suffered from depression and chronic anxiety but the parties had been married for a short time.

*Three-month support after 5-year marriage where wife taking language training — Juretic v. Ruiz*, 1999 CarswellBC 1479, 1999 BCCA 417, 49 R.F.L. (4th) 299, 126 B.C.A.C. 196, 206 W.A.C. 196, [1999] B.C.J. No. 1556 (B.C.C.A.), the court, on appeal, upheld a 3-year limited term spousal support order after the dissolution of the parties' 5-month marriage. The husband had advertised for a wife in Guatemala, and had brought her to Canada where she was taking English language training to improve her job prospects. At the time of the marriage, the husband must have been aware that the wife would need time to integrate into the language and social customs of Canada.

*Where wife had already obtained employment and a degree of self-sufficiency, the time limitation was warranted — Hopkinson v. Hopkinson*, 1997 CarswellBC 2760, 34 R.F.L. (4th) 137, 43 B.C.L.R. (3d) 232, 101 B.C.A.C. 41, 164 W.A.C. 41 (B.C.C.A.). The court refused the wife's appeal from the time limitation placed upon her spousal support award.

*Time-limited appropriate where wife at 65 would receive pension income that would replace the support income — Crawford v. Crawford*, 1997 CarswellOnt 4953, 33 R.F.L. (4th) 381, [1997] O.J. No. 5065 (Ont. C.A.). The court dismissed the wife's appeal from a limitation upon her spousal support award that would see it terminate when she reached 65. The parties' 41-year marriage had been a traditional one.

*Limited term support upheld where lack of self-sufficiency caused by abuse of prescription medication* — *Mason v. Blatt*, 2004 CarswellOnt 5440, 12 R.F.L. (6th) 115 (Ont. Div. Ct.). The time limitation placed upon the spousal support awarded to the husband was upheld on appeal. Although the husband suffered from depression, the evidence supported the finding that the husband's inability to support himself was more related to his abuse of prescription medication. The husband had done nothing to rehabilitate himself while receiving interim support and an unlimited permanent order could actually do him a disservice.

*Limited-term support is appropriate in a medium-length marriage where the payee party fails to demonstrate economic dependency* — *Depatie v. Squires*, 2012 CarswellOnt 2701, 2012 ONSC 1399 (Ont. Div. Ct.). The parties lived together for over 12 years. The husband earned $78,000, and the wife had earned $28,000 for the first 10 years of the relationship but was earning $26,000 in disability benefits at separation. The wife sought indefinite support based on her disability and economic dependency. The trial judge refused the wife's application, finding no evidence that her economic dependency arose from her disability (her disability benefit was similar to her past employment income) or that compensatory support was warranted. The judge awarded her $1,082 per month in support for 9 years from the date of separation. The Court of Appeal dismissed the wife's appeal, having found, at para. 15, "no error in the learned trial judge's finding that the time limited spousal support order was both appropriate and reasonable in the circumstances."

*A time-limited support agreement can be retroactively extended if the payee demonstrates need and the payor has the ability to pay* — *van Rythoven v. van Rythoven*, 2010 CarswellOnt 10590, 2010 ONSC 5923, 99 R.F.L. (6th) 152 (Ont. Div. Ct.), additional reasons at 2011 CarswellOnt 1688, 2011 ONSC 1369 (Ont. Div. Ct.). The parties married in 1980, separated in 1993, and entered into an agreement for time-limited spousal support in 1996. The court dismissed the wife's application to vary the order in 1998. The applications judge accepted the wife's evidence that at the time of the agreement she believed her physical and mental health would improve, allowing her to return to work, but instead her condition had worsened. She provided evidence to support her claim that she was unable to rejoin the workforce. The court ordered support in spite of the 1996 agreement, stating that the wife had established entitlement pursuant to *Bracklow* and that the agreement "did not satisfy the second branch of the test established by *Miglin*" (para. 5). The Court of Appeal dismissed the husband's appeal.

*A wife, who is disabled and would remain unemployable, may be awarded a time-limited spousal support award on a non-compensatory basis, where the marriage is of a medium length and there are no children* — *Haggerty v. Haggerty*, 2010 CarswellNS 6, 2010 NSSC 9, 80 R.F.L. (6th) 227 (N.S.S.C.). The parties lived as common-law partners for 3 years and were married for 7 years. They had no children. During the course of the marriage the wife became disabled and would remain unemployable. The wife was awarded spousal support on a non-compensatory basis for 7 years. The parties had lived as mutually dependent partners who had accepted the responsibility of supporting one another. Although the wife's disability occurred during the marriage, it was not caused by the marriage or the circumstances of the marriage. The award of spousal support for an indefinite period would cause an imbalance between the parties' mutual obligations and the clean-break model. The wife's likely failure to be able to attain economic self-sufficiency did not automatically result in the husband's continuing obligation for spousal support. The court determined that 7 years of spousal support was appropriate given that the marriage was of a medium length.

*Limited term support ordered where payee is relatively young* — *Grinyer v. Grinyer*, 2008 CarswellOnt 366, 49 R.F.L. (6th) 219, [2008] O.J. No. 290 (Ont. S.C.J.). Where the wife was still relatively young upon the dissolution of the parties' 22-year marriage, her spousal support entitlement was capped at 4 years. She was deemed capable of becoming self-sufficient within that period.

*Limited term support of 5 years so that payee could seek further training and skills development if self-sufficiency was a possibility* — *H. (G.C.) v. H. (H.E.)*, 2008 CarswellBC 1742, 2008 BCSC 1127, 57 R.F.L. (6th) 325 (B.C.S.C.). The parties had been married for 25 years. The 48-year-old wife had remained in the home throughout the marriage and had limited skills.

*Limited support for 1 year where wife had marketable skills* — *Bradley v. Bradley*, 2003 CarswellSask 688, 2003 SKQB 415, 45 R.F.L. (5th) 237, 240 Sask. R. 193 (Sask. Q.B.), the 58-year-old wife was awarded spousal support as she had marketable skills and there was no reason why she couldn't rejoin the workforce and remain gainfully employed until she was 65.

*Support for 7 years where wife young and employable but had the care of four young children* — *Rush v. Rush*, 2002 CarswellPEI 28, 2002 PESCTD 22, 27 R.F.L. (5th) 151, 211 Nfld. & P.E.I.R. 198, 633 A.P.R. 198 (P.E.I.T.D.). She would be required to provide them with full-time care for some time.

*Limited term support for 9 months where the wife had been economically self-sufficient for much of the marriage but would require some time to build up her medical practice* — *Low v. Robinson*, 2000 CarswellAlta 68, 2000 ABQB 60, 4 R.F.L. (5th) 368, 76 Alta. L.R. (3d) 238, [2000] 4 W.W.R. 663, 258 A.R. 201, [2000] A.J. No. 96 (Alta. Q.B.), additional reasons at 2000 CarswellAlta 336, 7 R.F.L. (5th) 148, 79 Alta. L.R. (3d) 137, [2000] 7 W.W.R. 509, 258 A.R. 201 at 235 (Alta. Q.B.), further additional reasons at 2000 CarswellAlta 574, 2000 ABQB 399, 82 Alta. L.R. (3d) 175, [2000] 10 W.W.R. 690, 274 A.R. 377, [2000] A.J. No. 695 (Alta. Q.B.).

*Where the husband had ended the marriage in a sudden and unconscionable way, the wife was found to be entitled to limited term support to help her cope with the hardships caused and to ease her through the transition* — *Millar v. Homenuik*, 2003 CarswellAlta 963, 2003 ABQB 570, 41 R.F.L. (5th) 322 (Alta. Q.B.).

*Wife awarded 1-year limited support where wife had worked throughout marriage* — *Jefferson v. Jefferson*, 2002 CarswellBC 298, 2002 BCSC 151, 26 R.F.L. (5th) 129 (B.C.S.C.). The wife was awarded periodic spousal for a period of 1 year upon the dissolution of the parties' 10-year marriage. Except for the immediate periods surrounding the birth of her children the wife continued to work and there was no evidence that her career aspirations had been adversely affected by the marriage. Her child rearing responsibilities had, to a small degree, impacted her economically.

*Limited term support for 18 months where wife had worked but was currently on welfare* — *R. (S.M.) v. R. (P.E.)*, 2002 CarswellBC 637, 2002 BCPC 92, 25 R.F.L. (5th) 375 (B.C. Prov. Ct.). The wife had been self-supporting throughout the parties' 8-year relationship and 4-year marriage, but was on welfare and unable to find work after separation. The wife clearly had a need but, long term, her inability to find employment could not be attributed to the collapse of the marriage.

*Limited term support where wife disadvantaged by breakdown of marriage with loss of employment* — *Erb v. Erb*, 2003 CarswellOnt 1339, 41 R.F.L. (5th) 49 (Ont. S.C.J.), additional reasons at 2003 CarswellOnt 2395 (Ont. S.C.J.). Where the wife felt obliged to leave her employment with her husband's family business after separation, she was granted limited term spousal support. The wife had suffered a disadvantage from the breakdown of the marriage because of the practical necessity of leaving the business. Where the wife remained employed throughout the marriage but had moved several times to support the husband's career, she was found to have suffered an economic disadvantage and was awarded limited term support for a period of 5 years. The wife's career had suffered as she had less seniority and experience as a result of the moves and her child care responsibilities. *Kaluza v. Kaluza*, 2003 CarswellBC 3132, 2003 BCSC 1879, 50 R.F.L. (5th) 71 (B.C.S.C.).

*Limited-term support until wife obtains full-time employment as a teacher — Balcerzak v. Balcerzak*, 1998 CarswellOnt 3785, 41 R.F.L. (4th) 13, 75 O.T.C. 1, [1998] O.J. No. 3860 (Ont. Gen. Div.). The wife was awarded $600 monthly. The wife had stayed home with the children during a 16-year marriage and had resumed her teaching career as a supply teacher, after the separation.

*Whether a spouse may remarry may be relevant in determining whether support should be restricted to a limited term — Lauderdale v. Lauderdale*, 1999 CarswellAlta 296, 1999 ABQB 453, 50 R.F.L. (4th) 411, 241 A.R. 355 (Alta. Q.B.). The fact that a spouse may remarry is not a relevant consideration in determining whether or not that spouse suffered an economic disadvantage as a result of the marriage.

*Limited-term support where wife had previously had substantial earnings — Dorey v. Snyder*, 1999 CarswellOnt 1492, 48 R.F.L. (4th) 67, [1999] O.J. No. 1820 (Ont. Gen. Div.). The wife awarded limited term support upon dissolution of the parties' 16-year-marriage. At the outset of the marriage the parties shared the same educational background and were both employed in thriving careers. However, after the wife had taken 4 years off to raise the parties' children, she returned to the workforce earning less than half of the husband's salary. The wife had proven herself capable of earning income and with gradually reducing support over 4 years, she would have the opportunity to re-establish herself.

*Support limited to 7 months where husband should have become employed during that period — Motyl v. Motyl*, 1998 CarswellSask 11, 36 R.F.L. (4th) 268, 162 Sask. R. 310 (Sask. Q.B.). The husband, who had been employed at the outset of the marriage worked for the wife during the latter part of the marriage, and lost his job when the relationship ended. The court held that the husband was entitled to spousal support, as he suffered economic hardship as a result of the breakdown of the marriage. The wife had paid 7 monthly payments to the husband before discontinuing them. As the husband was capable, the court was of the opinion that with due diligence he could have re-established himself within the 7 months. Spousal support was awarded only in the amount already paid.

*Spousal support was limited to a term of 9 months which would enable her to be self-sufficient — Baldwin v. Ward*, 1998 CarswellSask 96, 36 R.F.L. (4th) 193, 164 Sask. R. 81 (Sask. Q.B.) Where the wife had not suffered any economic disadvantages from the marriage, the court refused her application for 5 or 6 years of spousal support which would allow her to complete her doctorate. The wife would be economically self-sufficient upon completion of her Master's degree in 9 months' time and should she wish to continue her education beyond that, both scholarships and part-time employment were available to her.

*Support limited to a further 9 months where the wife had unduly restricted her job search and the parties had only been married for 2 years — Weekes v. Weekes*, 1998 CarswellMan 32, 36 R.F.L. (4th) 323, 124 Man. R. (2d) 317 (Man. Q.B.). Where the wife had limited her employment opportunities by moving with the husband from New York to Winnipeg, she was found to be entitled to support.

*Spousal support for 2 years where wife disadvantaged by moves related to husabnd's employment — Burns v. Burns*, 1997 CarswellNB 499, 33 R.F.L. (4th) 446, 194 N.B.R. (2d) 195, 496 A.P.R. 195 (N.B.Q.B.). Where the wife had been unable during the parties' troubled 12-year marriage, to establish any long-term employment as a result of frequent moves required by the husband's military career, she was awarded periodic support for a period of 2 years.

*Support limited to 1 year to encourage wife's self-sufficiency — Horvath v. Fraess*, 1997 CarswellSask 707, 36 R.F.L. (4th) 32, 161 Sask. R. 274 (Sask. Q.B.). The court refused the wife's request for a 3½ year spousal support award which would have allowed her to remain in the home until the parties' child began school. The award was limited to a year as the postponement of the wife's re-entry into the workforce for 3½ years would not promote her economic self-sufficiency and would make it very difficult for the husband to establish an independent life.

*Limited support with the timing related to the payment of the wife's equalization payment — Russell v. Russell*, 1997 CarswellSask 246, 29 R.F.L. (4th) 370, [1997] 7 W.W.R. 443, 155 Sask. R. 213 (Sask. Q.B.). Where the parties had no children and the wife had a grade 12 education and job skills, she was granted limited term support, upon dissolution of the 22-year marriage. As the wife had suffered no economic disadvantage from the marriage, termination of her support was linked with the payment to her of her equalization entitlement.

*Limited-term support of 3 years, as the wife had obtained a degree of self-sufficiency and given that the wife was considerably younger than the husband — Bellman v. Bellman*, 1999 CarswellBC 1122, 46 R.F.L. (4th) 414, 11 B.C.T.C. 187, [1999] B.C.J. No. 1196 (B.C.S.C.), additional reasons at 1999 CarswellBC 1749 (B.C.S.C.). The parties had a traditional marriage for 15 years during which the wife agreed to stay in the home with the children. In the 7 years since separation the wife had achieved a certain degree of self-sufficiency and given that the husband was now 60 and the wife only 50, 3 years' worth of support was appropriate.

*The wife's support was limited to 2 years upon the dissolution of the parties' 21-year traditional marriage — the order was intended to promote economic independence on the wife's part and to give her an opportunity to retrain to achieve that end — Gosset v. Gosset*, 1997 CarswellBC 1626, 30 R.F.L. (4th) 221, 38 B.C.L.R. (3d) 289 (B.C.S.C.).

*Where the wife had the ability over time to improve her employment position, she was awarded decreasing term support which would promote self-sufficiency — Hashem v. Hashem*, 1993 CarswellNfld 23, 46 R.F.L. (3d) 303 (Nfld. U.F.C.). Her support would terminate upon her husband's retirement at which time she would share in his pension income.

*Support for 3 years granted where it was highly likely that the payee would regain employment as a nurse during that period — Woolgar v. Woolgar*, 1995 CarswellNfld 3, 10 R.F.L. (4th) 309, [1995] N.J. No. 188 (Nfld. U.F.C.). Where after the breakdown of the parties' 28-year marriage, the wife quit her nursing position because of stress associated with the divorce; she was awarded spousal support in declining amounts over a 3-year period.

*Where the wife had worked throughout the marriage, but had left her job as a result of the emotional stress resulting from the marriage breakdown, she was awarded periodic support for a period of 9 months — Swirhun v. Swirhun*, 1993 CarswellBC 591, 1 R.F.L. (4th) 53 (B.C.S.C.). By the date of trial, the wife was able to once again seek employment. The limited term support would give her the opportunity to re-establish herself to her former income level.

*Where the husband's unemployment was due, in part, to the marriage he was awarded spousal support for a 2-year period — it was probable that the husband would be able to find employment within 2 years, failing which he could seek an extension of the support order — Purcell v. Purcell*, 1995 CarswellOnt 82, 11 R.F.L. (4th) 181, [1995] O.J. No. 980 (Ont. Gen. Div.).

*Fixed term of support to give wife time to increase her ability to be self-supporting — Walton v. Walton*, 1993 CarswellSask 33, 1 R.F.L. (4th) 93, 23 C.B.R. (3d) 315, 108 D.L.R. (4th) 704, 116 Sask. R. 129, 59 W.A.C. 129, [1993] S.J. No. 637 (Sask. C.A.), affirming 1993 CarswellSask 47, 46 R.F.L. (3d) 137, 110 Sask. R. 263 (Sask. Q.B.). A fixed-term spousal support award in favour of the wife was upheld on appeal. During the marriage both parties had worked and pooled their resources until the time the wife had returned to school. In light of their pooling arrangement and the fact that the husband's income had substantially exceeded that of the wife, it was not unreasonable to expect the husband to support the wife for the brief period required for her to improve her ability to be self-supporting.

*Limited support as transitional support* — Hopkinson v. Hopkinson, 1996 CarswellBC 357, 21 R.F.L. (4th) 285, 20 B.C.L.R. (3d) 254 (B.C.S.C.), affirmed 1997 CarswellBC 2760, 34 R.F.L. (4th) 137, 43 B.C.L.R. (3d) 232, 101 B.C.A.C. 41, 164 W.A.C. 41 (B.C.C.A.). Where the wife had entered the marriage with some university education and job experience and since separation was close to achieving self-sufficiency, she was awarded support for a period of 30 months to allow her to adapt to a life without the income and other benefits that formerly flowed into the household she had maintained with her husband.

*Wife given limited support for 6 months whereupon it was assumed she would be employed — husband had supported wife while she took a re-training course* — St. Germaine v. St. Germaine, 1996 CarswellAlta 151, 21 R.F.L. (4th) 244, [1996] A.J. No. 163 (Alta. C.A.). The court allowed the husband's appeal from an indefinite support award in the wife's favour. Although the wife had suffered an economic disadvantage from the marriage, the husband had supported the wife during a re-training programme which gave her the potential to be self-sufficient and it was now time for her to realize that potential.

*Wife granted support for 3 years in short-term marriage where she had ability to earn greater income than currently* — Hunter v. Hunter, 1998 CarswellMan 126, 37 R.F.L. (4th) 453, 127 Man. R. (2d) 199 (Man. Q.B.). The parties had only been married for 5 years. The wife had a university degree and should pursue more remunerative employment prospects than as an administrative clerk with the government.

*Wife given 1-year support to give the wife an opportunity to upgrade her education or obtain full-time employment* — Scott v. Scott, 1996 CarswellAlta 306, 183 A.R. 103, 21 R.F.L. (4th) 436, [1996] A.J. No. 337 (Alta. Q.B.). The court imposed a 1-year limitation on the wife's spousal support award upon the termination of the parties' 16-year marriage. As the wife had left her employment to move with the husband to further his career the wife had been economically disadvantaged by the marriage and its breakdown. However, in the 3 years since the parties had separated the wife had not taken any steps towards upgrading her education or obtaining full-time employment. The 1 year's worth of support would allow her the opportunity to do so.

*Where the wife had left her employment on several occasions during the parties' 4-year marriage and vast discrepancies existed between the parties' incomes, the wife was found to have suffered an adverse financial consequence from the marriage and was found entitled to support for a period of 30 months* — Turcotte v. Turcotte, 1996 CarswellOnt 1507, 22 R.F.L. (4th) 364, 1 O.T.C. 156, [1996] O.J. No. 1327 (Ont. Gen. Div.).

*Support limited to 1 year where wife refused to take medication* — Droit de la famille - 1696, [1992] R.D.F. 686 (C.S. Que.), affirmed (20 May 1993), Doc. Montreal 500-09-001916-923 (C.A. Que.). Where the wife refused to take medication which would alleviate the symptoms of her manic depressive condition and allow her to live a normal life, her spousal support was limited to a 1-year period. The wife had to accept the consequences of her own choice.

*Limited support until spouse had finished training* — Boyd v. Boyd, 1992 CarswellBC 169, 41 R.F.L. (3d) 182, 68 B.C.L.R. (2d) 201, 13 B.C.A.C. 148, 24 W.A.C. 148 (B.C.C.A.), the court overturned a support award requiring the husband to pay spousal support to his wife until she had discharged the student loans incurred while she was retraining. The correct principle to be applied was that spousal support should terminate within 6 months to a year after the spouse has completed retraining.

*Spousal support to end 2 years after child support where failure to become self-sufficient not caused by marriage* — Rouleau v. Rouleau, 1992 CarswellNS 505, 111 N.S.R. (2d) 162, 303 A.P.R. 162 (N.S. Fam. Ct.). Where the wife's failure to become self-sufficient after the parties' divorce was largely the result of personal and emotional problems that were not related to the marriage, the court ordered that her spousal support payments were to cease 2 years after the last of her child support payments. Although it was not reasonable to expect the husband to support her for life, he had benefited from her home and child care responsibilities and should support her for a further limited time.

*3-year limitation placed on support – Rice v. Rice*, 1992 CarswellNS 541, 113 N.S.R. (2d) 444, 309 A.P.R. 444 (T.D.). A 3-year limitation was placed upon the wife's right to spousal support upon termination of the parties' 16-year marriage. Although the wife suffered from serious psychological problems which prevented her from working, the condition arose after separation and there was no evidence that it was related to the marriage.

*Time limit inappropriate where husband knew of wife's medical condition at time of marriage – Droit de la famille - 1420*, [1991] R.D.F. 293 (C.S. Que.). Where the husband was aware at the time of the marriage of the serious ailments which the wife suffered, it was inappropriate to set any time limit upon her spousal support entitlement.

## 7.2.2 Support for an Indefinite Period

*The Court of Appeal will defer to the trial judge regarding indefinite support orders provided that the correct principles were considered – Werner v. Werner*, 2013 CarswellNS 20, 2013 NSCA 6, 325 N.S.R. (2d) 175, 1031 A.P.R. 175 (N.S.C.A.). The wife requested indefinite support in her cross-appeal. The Court of Appeal judge, at para. 61, stated: "She makes good arguments –but these were considered by the trial judge. We cannot substitute our own discretion for his, provided he considered correct principles ."

*Non-disclosure of early retirement means the payor party cannot use the retirement to try to have an order for indefinite support rescinded – MacLanders v. MacLanders*, 2012 CarswellBC 3736, 2012 BCCA 482, 24 R.F.L. (7th) 24, 39 B.C.L.R. (5th) 255 (B.C.C.A.). The husband took early retirement just before the initial proceedings without notice. The lower court awarded the wife indefinite support, and the husband appealed partly on the grounds that the award of indefinite support to the wife amounted to double recovery of her interest in his pension. The Court of Appeal found that the trial judge had not erred, stating at paras. 22 and 23:

> [T]he husband, through his non-disclosure of material information, limited the possibility of a substantial reapportionment of the family assets in favour of the wife because an award of indefinite spousal support for the wife was available to redress the economic consequences to her of the marriage breakdown.

> In these circumstances, the *Willick* test precludes the husband from relying on his retirement as a material change in circumstances to support an order rescinding his spousal support obligation.

The appeal was denied.

*If an order does not expressly limit the duration of support, the order will not be interpreted as limiting it – Kelly v. Kelly*, 2011 CarswellBC 842, 2011 BCCA 173, 18 B.C.L.R. (5th) 99, 303 B.C.A.C. 209, 512 W.A.C. 209 (B.C.C.A.). The parties separated in 2001, and the children stayed with the husband. The court ordered him to pay the wife $300 in spousal support until her return to work. When the husband asked about a review, the judge mentioned the wife going back to work "next year" as an example of a material change. The husband applied to terminate support when the wife obtained employment in 2009. The chambers judge did not find that the trial judge's statement suggested limited-term support.

*A court should not include a fixed exchange rate in an award for indefinite support – Saunders v. Saunders*, 2011 CarswellNS 620, 2011 NSCA 81, 7 R.F.L. (7th) 265, 307 N.S.R. (2d) 297, 975 A.P.R. 297 (N.S.C.A.). The trial judge erred in not considering the fluctuations in exchange rates when awarding a fixed amount of support for an indefinite period.

*The trial judge should not limit the duration of support in the case of a lengthy marriage which caused the parties significant economic advantage and disadvantage, respectively* — *Cassidy v. McNeil*, 2010 CarswellOnt 1637, 2010 ONCA 218, 99 O.R. (3d) 81, 266 O.A.C. 62, [2010] O.J. No. 1158 (Ont. C.A.). The parties were married for 23 years, during which the wife worked part-time. The wife earned $85,000, and the husband earned $137,000. The court awarded the wife $1,200 in support but limited it to 5 years, stating that this would give her enough time to complete her education. The husband appealed, requesting that the order be set aside. In her cross-appeal the wife asked for an extension of the duration. The Ontario Court of Appeal found that the trial judge had erred in restricting the duration of support based on the wife's education, as need should be the only relevant factor. The court granted the wife's crossappeal, stating at para. 71: "Given the 'economic merger' between the parties, the uncertainties surrounding the wife's employment, and the husband's security of employment, I see no basis to time-limit spousal support."

*The court may consider indefinite support to be no longer appropriate 17 years after separation due to the expectation of self-sufficiency* — *Aspe v. Aspe*, 2010 CarswellBC 3077, 2010 BCCA 508, 89 R.F.L. (6th) 245, 11 B.C.L.R. (5th) 309, 327 D.L.R. (4th) 231, 294 B.C.A.C. 290, 498 W.A.C. 290 (B.C.C.A.).

*It is appropriate to rely on the SSAG to order indefinite duration* — *Michaud v. Kuszelewski*, 2009 CarswellNS 646, 2009 NSCA 118, 75 R.F.L. (6th) 3, 312 D.L.R. (4th) 598, 284 N.S.R. (2d) 310, 901 A.P.R. 310 (N.S.C.A.), affirming 2008 CarswellNS 498, 2008 NSSC 276, 269 N.S.R. (2d) 35, 860 A.P.R. 35 (N.S.S.C.). The parties began cohabiting in 1991. The woman had a child from a previous relationship born in 1990, and the parties had a child together who was born in 1992. They separated in 1998. Despite the existence of an interim order for child and spousal support, the husband had paid very little during a period of 6 years. The wife thereafter obtained an upward variation of the order for spousal support. The Nova Scotia Court of Appeal found that it was "appropriate in the circumstances of this case for the trial judge to rely on the *Spousal Support Advisory Guidelines*" in ordering an award with indefinite duration as a result of continuing care of dependent children. The appeal was dismissed.

*Indefinite support where wife unlikely to become self-sufficient* — *Milton v. Milton*, 2007 CarswellNB 537, 2007 NBQB 363, 44 R.F.L. (6th) 429, 326 N.B.R. (2d) 324, 838 A.P.R. 324, [2007] N.B.J. No. 414 (N.B.Q.B.), affirmed 2008 CarswellNB 591, 2008 CarswellNB 592, 2008 NBCA 87, 62 R.F.L. (6th) 286, 338 N.B.R. (2d) 300, 866 A.P.R. 300, [2008] N.B.J. No. 467 (N.B.C.A.). Where the parties had a long traditional marriage of over 20 years during which the wife had been out of the workforce for much of the time, no time limit was placed upon her award of spousal support. It was unlikely that the wife could become self-sufficient and would continue to require financial support from the husband. Where the wife gave up a conventional career path to pursue entrepreneurial pursuits, the separation left her without an established career path or the means to pursue further entrepreneurial ventures, and she, at 49, was of an age at which it would be difficult for her to recover. She was entitled to support.

*Similar considerations as those set out in child support cases are also relevant to deciding whether retroactive spousal support should be granted* — *Kerr v. Baranow*, 2011 SCC 10, 2011 CarswellBC 240, 2011 CarswellBC 241, 93 R.F.L. (6th) 1, [2011] 1 S.C.R. 269, 108 O.R. (3d) 399, 14 B.C.L.R. (5th) 203, 328 D.L.R. (4th) 577, 64 E.T.R. (3d) 1, [2011] 3 W.W.R. 575, 411 N.R. 200, 274 O.A.C. 1, 300 B.C.A.C. 1, 509 W.A.C. 1, [2011] S.C.J. No. 10 (S.C.C.). In a case concerning unmarried parties, the court stated the following factors in considering whether or not to grant retroactive spousal support:

1. the needs of the recipient;
2. the conduct of the payor;

3.   the reason for the delay in seeking support; and

4.   any hardship the retroactive award may occasion on the payor spouse.

"However, in spousal support cases, these factors must be considered and weighed in light of the different legal principles and objectives that underpin spousal as compared with child support," at paragraph 207.

There is a different legal foundation for spousal support and child support. Unlike child support, there is no presumptive entitlement to spousal support and, in general, the spouse usually is not under a legal obligation to protect the separated spouse's legal interests. Consequently, issues of notice, delay and misconduct generally are more significant in respect to claims for spousal support.

Where, as in this case, the payor argues that support should have been sought earlier, there are two underlying concerns:

1.   The first relates to the certainty of the payor's legal obligations; the fact that such an order may reach back into the past and make it more difficult to make one's financial arrangements and the fact that a significant and unexpected "retroactive' award may impose financial hardship.

2.   The second concerns putting proper incentives on the claimant so that he or she will proceed with his or her claims as soon as possible. Neither of these matters is of much significance in this case.

The court held that the decision about ordering retroactive spousal support is a matter for judicial discretion in light of the particular circumstances. If an order is sought effective from the commencement of proceedings, this fact will often be a significant factor in how the relevant considerations are weighed.

The conduct at issue must be conduct 'broadly relevant' to the support obligation, for example, concealing assets or failing to make appropriate disclosure.

A consideration of the circumstances of the spouse seeking support relates to the needs of that spouse, both at the time the support should have been paid and at present. A spouse who has experienced hardship in the past may be compensated through retroactive support. Whereas if a spouse enjoyed all the advantages in the past, his or her argument for retroactive support will be less compelling. There is a risk that a retroactive spousal support order will be crafted without taking into account what the payor can currently afford and thus may destabilize his or her finances. It is important to be flexible and to take a holistic view in these matters.

The Supreme Court of Canada in the *Kerr* appeal found that the Court of Appeal erred in finding that the appellant, Ms. Kerr, who suffered from a serious disability, was not in need prior to trial. She, in fact, was in need of support from the respondent from the date she started her proceedings and remained so at the time of trial. Her need was constant throughout this period. The Court of Appeal erred in principle in setting aside the judge's order effective as of the date of commencement of proceedings on the ground that Ms. Kerr had no need during that period while upholding the judge's findings of need in circumstances that were no different from those existing at the time proceedings were commenced. The Court of Appeal was wrong to find fault with Ms. Kerr in not bringing an interim application. The claimant was of limited means and interim applications may prolong rather than expedite proceedings. There was virtually no delay in applying for maintenance. Further, there was no inordinate delay between the date of application and the date of trial. The court concluded that the Court of Appeal was in error in setting aside the portion of the judge's order for support between the commencement of proceedings and the beginning of trial. It restored the trial judge's order making support effective as of the commencement of the proceedings.

*An award of indefinite support does not mean infinite or permanent support — Such an award is variable under appropriate circumstances pursuant to the* Divorce Act — *Cadigan v. Cadigan,* 2004 CarswellMan 533, 2004 MBQB 283, 189 Man. R. (2d) 245 (Man. Q.B.), affirmed 2007 CarswellMan 72, 2007 MBCA 28, 212 Man. R. (2d) 291, 389 W.A.C. 291 (Man. C.A.).

*Where the wife had supported the husband through two university degrees and therefore the marriage had a long-term impact on her career advancement and earning capacity, support for an indefinite time was granted — Allaire v. Allaire,* 2003 CarswellOnt 1002, 35 R.F.L. (5th) 256, 170 O.A.C. 72 (Ont. C.A.). The trial judge's refusal to put a time limitation on the wife's spousal support award was upheld on appeal.

*Where a spouse has been out of the workforce and has on-going childcare responsibilities, limited term spousal support orders should not be the norm — Phinney v. Phinney,* 2002 CarswellNS 525, 2002 NSCA 168, 33 R.F.L. (5th) 211, 211 N.S.R. (2d) 135, 662 A.P.R. 135 (N.S.C.A.). However, the court in the Phinney case awarded spousal support of $750 monthly for a year and then declining amounts for 3 years.

*Where the payee has not worked outside of the home for several years, since the birth of the eldest child, and she has been a full-time mother and homemaker with a grade 12 education, spousal support should not be time-limited — Bildy v. Bildy,* 1999 CarswellOnt 497, 44 R.F.L. (4th) 81, 42 O.R. (3d) 737, 127 O.A.C. 44, [1999] O.J. No. 501 (Ont. C.A.). This was a 13-year marriage and the children would still need supervision for a number of years. The court held that as the support payments were not overly generous in the first place and were subject to the obligation of the appellant to pay the equalization payment for 5 years, spousal support payments of $30,000 should be continued for 5 years to give adequate recognition to the need to encourage the wife to take some positive steps towards self-sufficiency by finding employment. At that time, either party should have the right to review the quantum of the support payments.

*Support will not be ordered to be time-limited because of concern that the payee will not try to become self-sufficient — Choquette v. Choquette,* 1998 CarswellOnt 2939, 39 R.F.L. (4th) 384, [1998] O.J. No. 3024 (Ont. C.A.), the court dismissed the husband's appeal from an indefinite support award in the wife's favour. The husband sought either reduction in support on a defined schedule or review at a specified time out of concern that the wife would not attempt self-sufficiency. It was held that these circumstances would be better dealt with a variation application after they occurred rather than anticipating them in the current order.

*Indefinite support imposed on variation — Schmidt v. Schmidt,* 1998 CarswellBC 55, 36 R.F.L. (4th) 1, 44 B.C.L.R. (3d) 223, 156 D.L.R. (4th) 94, [1998] 6 W.W.R. 624, 102 B.C.A.C. 124, 166 W.A.C. 124, [1998] B.C.J. No. 42 (B.C.C.A.). The court, on appeal removed a time limitation imposed in the wife's application for a variation of spousal support which would have terminated her support payments upon the husband's retirement. The wife would continue to be in need after the husband's retirement and although his income would be reduced it would still significantly exceed that of the wife. The husband's pension income should have properly been considered in the wife's variation application although the fact of the pension had been a factor in the parties' earlier property division.

*Appeal from limited term support granted where wife after 30-year marriage unable to achieve self-sufficiency — Sitwell v. Sitwell,* 1998 CarswellBC 1118, 38 R.F.L. (4th) 401, 50 B.C.L.R. (3d) 205, 108 B.C.A.C. 278, 176 W.A.C. 278, [1998] B.C.J. No. 1172 (B.C.C.A.). Where the wife, after separation, had been unable to seek employment because of depression relating to the marriage breakdown, the court allowed her appeal from a limited term spousal support order. The wife, throughout the parties' 30-year marriage, had periodically pursued studies and some part-time employment. Given the wife's personality and life experiences it was unlikely that she would be able to achieve self-sufficiency during the term of the 18-month spousal support order. Accordingly, a permanent support order was substituted, requiring the wife periodically to provide the husband with copies of job applications and responses, reports on her health and copies of her income tax returns.

*Spousal support orders made for an indefinite period of time do not need to contain dates by which a review is to take place, nor must they contain financial disclosure requirements on the part of the spouse receiving support* — Flewwelling v. Flewwelling, 1997 CarswellNB 483, 33 R.F.L. (4th) 390, 194 N.B.R. (2d) 100, 496 A.P.R. 100 (N.B.C.A.).

*The wife successfully appealed a time-limited spousal support award of 3 months duration and was granted periodic support of $800 per month for an indefinite period* — Clarke v. Clarke, 1997 CarswellBC 2833, 34 R.F.L. (4th) 382, 46 B.C.L.R. (3d) 37, 101 B.C.A.C. 225, 164 W.A.C. 225, [1997] B.C.J. No. 2869 (B.C.C.A.). The division of assets in this case was not of such a nature that the need for periodic support was eliminated. The parties had had a traditional marriage and the wife had been out of the workforce for many years. However, she did acquire full-time employment, but her future earning prospectus were limited. The trial judge recognized that she had suffered an economic disadvantage because of the role she assumed in the marriage. She was 50 years of age at the time of trial.

*Time limit deleted where wife had not achieved full-time employment* — Kent v. Frolick, 1996 CarswellOnt 91, 19 R.F.L. (4th) 152, [1996] O.J. No. 130 (Ont. Gen. Div.), varied 1996 CarswellOnt 3580, 23 R.F.L. (4th) 1, [1996] O.J. No. 3356 (Ont. C.A.). Where 2 years prior to the termination of the parties' 15-year marriage the homemaker wife had returned to school and was earning $4,000 as a part-time supply teacher. At trial, spousal support was limited to a 20-month period. Given her training, the wife was well positioned to obtain full-time employment within that time-frame. However, the court varied the order as the appellant at time of trial had only achieved part-time employment and it was not reasonable to limit her support. The time limitation was deleted.

*The court should not impose a limitation on spousal support simply because the need arose from health problems which predated the marriage* — Kloos v. Kloos, 1996 CarswellMan 126, 20 R.F.L. (4th) 1, [1996] 5 W.W.R. 553, 110 Man. R. (2d) 129, 118 W.A.C. 129, [1996] M.J. No. 146 (Man. C.A.).

*Wife's ability to become self-sufficient limited by health problems* — no time limit on support — Devernichuk v. Devernichuk, 1993 CarswellSask 43, 45 R.F.L. (3d) 328, 109 Sask. R. 297, 42 W.A.C. 297 (Sask. C.A.). It is improper to limit spousal support after the breakdown of a long-term traditional marriage where the wife's inability to support herself has been complicated by health problems which she developed during the marriage.

*Wife remained home for 23 years during marriage* — unlimited support ordered — Droit de la famille - 1566 , 1992 CarswellQue 1027, EYB 1992-59356, [1992] R.D.F. 222 (C.A. Que.). Where the wife had remained in the home for 23 years during the marriage to tend to the household, her economic need was found to be causally connected to the marriage. Accordingly, she was found entitled to periodic support without any time limitation.

*Indefinite support where wife had no previous employment and it was premature to determine that her need would not extend beyond graduation* — Fox v. Fox, 1994 CarswellNB 28, 153 N.B.R. (2d) 1, 8 R.F.L. (4th) 257, 392 A.P.R. 1, [1994] N.B.J. No. 415 (N.B.C.A.), varying 1993 CarswellNB 390, 133 N.B.R. (2d) 361, 341 A.P.R. 361 (N.B.Q.B.). It would be inappropriate to limit the support of the 42-year-old wife, who had returned to university, to the period up to her graduation.

*The court will not award indefinite support in the case of a medium-length marriage where the wife is still young and the parties shared household duties* — MacDonald v. MacDonald, 2012 CarswellOnt 15337, 2012 ONSC 6657, [2012] O.J. No. 5757 (Ont. S.C.J.), additional reasons at 2013 CarswellOnt 191, 2013 ONSC 287 (Ont. S.C.J.). The parties were in a relationship for 12 years and married for 10. The court noted that an indefinite spousal order was inappropriate and the wife did not seek it.

*Indefinite spousal support — spousal support award for a stay-at-home father — Jacobs v. Dingee-Jacobs*, 2010 CarswellNB 380, 2010 NBQB 114, 89 R.F.L. (6th) 286, 360 N.B.R. (2d) 40, 930 A.P.R. 40 (N.B.Q.B.). The parties had a 24-year marriage. For the majority of the marriage, the husband acted as the children's primary caregiver and did not work outside the home. The parties moved a number of times in order to advance the wife's career. The husband was awarded spousal support on a compensatory and non-compensatory basis. The husband remained at home, with the wife's agreement, to care for the children and the home. The benefit of outside assistance, such as a part-time nanny and a cleaner, did not make redundant the parties' objective of having the husband stay home. Although the husband's efforts to secure work were limited, his age, health issues and time away from the workforce would make finding work difficult. The husband suffered economic hardship as a result of the marriage and was entitled to compensatory support. He was also entitled to non-compensatory support on the basis that he had no income and could not be self-sufficient. A time-limited support order was not appropriate as it was unresolved as to when the husband might achieve self-sufficiency. Spousal support was set at the mid-point of the *Spousal Support Advisory Guidelines* range.

*Indefinite spousal support — spousal support award for a stay-at-home father — Jacobs v. Dingee-Jacobs*, 2010 CarswellNB 380, 2010 NBQB 114, 89 R.F.L. (6th) 286, 360 N.B.R. (2d) 40, 930 A.P.R. 40 (N.B.Q.B.). The parties had a 24-year marriage. For the majority of the marriage, the husband acted as the children's primary caregiver and did not work outside the home. The parties moved a number of times in order to advance the wife's career. The husband was awarded spousal support on a compensatory and non-compensatory basis. The husband remained at home, with the wife's agreement, to care for the children and the home. The benefit of outside assistance, such as a part-time nanny and a cleaner, did not make redundant the parties' objective of having the husband stay home. Although the husband's efforts to secure work were limited, his age, health issues and time away from the workforce would make finding work difficult. The husband suffered economic hardship as a result of the marriage and was entitled to compensatory support. He was also entitled to non-compensatory support on the basis that he had no income and could not be self-sufficient. A time-limited support order was not appropriate as it was unresolved as to when the husband might achieve self-sufficiency. Spousal support was set at the mid-point of the *Spousal Support Advisory Guidelines* range.

*Indefinite support where wife unlikely to become self-sufficient — Milton v. Milton*, 2007 CarswellNB 537, 44 R.F.L. (6th) 429, 2007 NBQB 363, 326 N.B.R. (2d) 324, 838 A.P.R. 324, [2007] N.B.J. No. 414 (N.B.Q.B.), affirmed 2008 CarswellNB 591, 2008 CarswellNB 592, 2008 NBCA 87, 62 R.F.L. (6th) 286, 305 D.L.R. (4th) 94, 338 N.B.R. (2d) 300, 866 A.P.R. 300, [2008] N.B.J. No. 467 (N.B.C.A.). Where the parties had a long traditional marriage of over 20 years during which the wife had been out of the workforce for much of the time, no time limit was placed upon her award of spousal support. It was unlikely that the wife could become self-sufficient and would continue to require financial support from the husband. Where the wife gave up a conventional career path to pursue entrepreneurial pursuits, the separation left her without an established career path or the means to pursue further entrepreneurial ventures, and she, at 49, was of an age where it would be difficult for her to recover, she was entitled to support.

*Indefinite support where wife had need and husband had the means to pay — Colquhoun v. Colquhoun*, 2007 CarswellOnt 18 (Ont. S.C.J.). The wife was dependent on the husband during the marriage, as he was able to maintain his career in sales while working on their entrepreneurial businesses when it was convenient for him to do so. The wife had established need and the husband had the means to provide and to earn more income. The situation was not going to change and consequently the spousal support should not be time-limited.

*Indefinite support where wife dependant upon husband — Huck v. Huck,* 2004 CarswellOnt 3607, 9 R.F.L. (6th) 362, [2004] O.J. No. 3652 (Ont. S.C.J.). Where the wife had no real prospect of obtaining work other than in retail sales, no time limit was placed on her spousal support. The wife was emotionally and economically dependant on the husband, lacked self-confidence and self-reliance and had a severely diminished capacity to earn income.

*Indefinite support granted where wife had worked so that husband could study and had later cared for parties' children — Rozen v. Rozen,* 2003 CarswellBC 1564, 2003 BCSC 973, 37 R.F.L. (5th) 205, [2003] B.C.J. No. 1486 (B.C.S.C.). The court refused to put a time limitation on the wife's support following the breakdown of the parties' 20-year marriage. The wife had, in the early stages of the marriage, entered into the workplace to allow the husband to continue his studies full time. She had also, throughout the marriage, been the primary caregiver to the parties' children. Taking into account the wife's contribution to the marriage, the economic advantages obtained by the husband as a result of the marriage, and the economic hardships which befell her in not being able to pursue her own professional aspirations, permanent support was appropriate.

*Indefinite support granted where wife supported husband and then cared for children — Doherty v. Doherty,* 2001 CarswellOnt 2238, 19 R.F.L. (5th) 46, [2001] O.T.C. 463 (Ont. S.C.J.). The court refused to place a time limitation on the wife's spousal support upon the dissolution of the parties' 23-year marriage. The wife had supported the husband through the first 5 years of marriage as he completed medical studies and thereafter had remained at home to raise the parties' children. Now 46 years of age, she suffered from osteo-arthritis. The wife was found to have sacrificed her own career and had experienced a serious economic disadvantage from the breakdown of the marriage. Given her age, the time out of the workplace and, to some extent, her health, her prospects for employment and self-sufficiency were quite limited.

*No time limit for qualified professional working part-time — Johnston v. Johnston,* 2001 CarswellNB 235, 2001 NBQB 52, 19 R.F.L. (5th) 154 (N.B.Q.B.), the court refused to put a time limitation on the spousal support awarded to the wife, despite the fact that she had maintained her professional status as a nurse throughout the marriage and worked on a part-time basis.

*Indefinite support where wife had cared for child and could only obtain a low paid job — Schmuck v. Reynolds-Schmuck,* 1999 CarswellOnt 2424, 50 R.F.L. (4th) 429, [1999] O.J. No. 3104 (Ont. S.C.J.), additional reasons at 2000 CarswellOnt 202, 46 O.R. (3d) 702, [2000] O.J. No. 247 (Ont. S.C.J.). The court refused to place a time limitation on the wife's spousal support award. The wife had left her secretarial job 2 years into the parties' 12-year marriage to care for the parties' child. Although she had attempted to upgrade her skills during the marriage, she could never aspire to employment beyond a relatively low paid clerical position.

*No time limit where payee had disabling illness — Winfield v. Winfield,* 1998 CarswellOnt 134, 35 R.F.L. (4th) 393, 52 O.T.C. 166, [1998] O.J. No. 175 (Ont. Gen. Div.). Where the wife was suffering from multiple sclerosis at the time of the parties' separation and was likely never to return to work, the court found it to be an inappropriate case for imposing a time limit on the wife's spousal support.

*No time limit where wife's career restricted because of child and home care — Dick v. Dick,* 1993 CarswellOnt 320, 46 R.F.L. (3d) 219, [1993] O.J. No. 140 (Ont. Gen. Div.), additional reasons at 1993 CarswellOnt 4128 (Ont. Gen. Div.). Where the wife's opportunity for career advancement had been significantly curtailed because of her home and child care responsibilities, and the husband's career had thereby been advanced, it was inappropriate to place a time limit on the wife's periodic support.

*Indefinite support where wife had childcare responsibilities, including caring for a seriously challenged child — Stretch v. Stretch,* 1996 CarswellAlta 523, 186 A.R. 26 (Alta. Q.B.). The wife was found entitled to indefinite spousal support upon the breakdown of the parties' 15-

year traditional marriage. There were 6 children of the marriage, ranging from ages 6 to 17 and the youngest, who suffered from cerebral palsy, required the mother to provide 24-hour care. As a result, the wife's ability to return to the workforce after a 20-year absence would have to be delayed.

*Indefinite support where wife left her career to care for children* — Horvath v. Horvath, 1996 CarswellMan 171, 22 R.F.L. (4th) 279, 109 Man. R. (2d) 20 (Man. Q.B.). Where the wife had abandoned her career as a dental assistant to raise the parties' children throughout the parties' 14-year marriage, she was found to have suffered an economic disadvantage from the marriage entitling her to support without time limitation. The wife's lack of job experience, seniority and opportunity for advancement made it unlikely that she would ever become self-sufficient.

*Indefinite support, not until payor's retirement* — Chalmers v. Chalmers, 1994 CarswellBC 656, 2 R.F.L. (4th) 446, [1994] B.C.J. No. 570 (B.C.S.C.). The court refused the husband's request that spousal support be ordered only until his retirement. The court should not, in setting support, anticipate the future. Variation proceedings are available to allow for later adjustments should circumstances warrant.

*Indefinite support* — *payor had serious illness* — Laurence v. Laurence, 1993 CarswellBC 329, 50 R.F.L. (3d) 26, 85 B.C.L.R. (2d) 378, 33 B.C.A.C. 81, 54 W.A.C. 81 (B.C.C.A.). An indefinite award of spousal support made in favour of the 48-year-old wife, who suffered from muscular dystrophy and was unable to work, was upheld on appeal.

*Indefinite support where wife lost job with husband's business* — Droit de la famille - 1968, [1994] R.D.F. 301 (C.S. Que.). Where the wife had been employed by the husband's business throughout much of the parties' 22-year-marriage and her employment had ceased upon the parties' separation, she was awarded unlimited periodic support. The ending of the marriage had resulted in the wife's economic hardship.

*Indefinite support appropriate after long-term traditional marriage* — Stevens v. Stevens, 1992 CarswellOnt 275, 41 R.F.L. (3d) 212, 93 D.L.R. (4th) 311 (Ont. U.F.C.). It was held that the lack of causal connection between the wife's illness, which inhibited her from becoming self-sufficient, and the marriage did not justify a time limitation on her support award. As the parties' marriage was a long-term traditional one, the wife had suffered economic disadvantage justifying ongoing support even without taking her illness into account.

*Applicant's time out of workforce and health problems* — *no time limit on award* — Lenner v. Lenner, 1991 CarswellAlta 508, 118 A.R. 99 (Alta. Q.B.), affirmed 1991 CarswellAlta 789, 125 A.R. 231, 14 W.A.C. 231 (Alta. C.A.). Leave to appeal refused (1992), 145 N.R. 391 (note), 141 A.R. 316 (note), 46 W.A.C. 316 (note) (S.C.C.). Where the 45-year-old wife had not been employed outside of the home for 19 years and had severe psychiatric problems, the court refused to place a time limit on her support award.

*Indefinite support after 10-year marriage* — *possibility of variation sufficient to do justice to payor* — Patrick v. Patrick, 1991 CarswellBC 315, 35 R.F.L. (3d) 382, 62 B.C.L.R. (2d) 188 (B.C.S.C.), additional reasons at 1991 CarswellBC 2027 (B.C.S.C.), affirmed 1993 CarswellBC 320, 49 R.F.L. (3d) 453, 85 B.C.L.R. (2d) 303, [1993] B.C.J. No. 1963 (B.C.C.A.). The Court of Appeal found no basis for imposing a time limit on the payment of support. There was nothing to prevent the appellant from applying for a variation of maintenance if there were a change in circumstances.

## 7.2.3  Support after Termination of Support Order

*A prior termination of support rights does not prevent the court from reviewing the issue of support at a later time* — *Droit de la famille - 382*, 1988 CarswellQue 46, 16 R.F.L. (3d) 379, [1988] R.J.Q. 2408, [1988] R.D.F. 482 (C.A.).

*An application for support upon the expiration of the support obligations in the parties' separation agreement should be treated as an original application for support under s. 15 of the Divorce Act and not an application to vary under s. 17(10) of the Act* — *Vaandering v. Vaandering*, 1990 CarswellBC 449, 25 R.F.L. (3d) 310 (B.C.S.C.).

## 7.2.4  Terms and Conditions — Support Until Specified Event

*Trial judge's ruling that support ordered until particular income level reached disapproved of at the Supreme Court of Canada* — *Hartshorne v. Hartshorne*, 2004 CarswellBC 603, 2004 CarswellBC 604, 2004 SCC 22, REJB 2004-55588, 47 R.F.L. (5th) 5, [2004] 1 S.C.R. 550, 25 B.C.L.R. (4th) 1, 236 D.L.R. (4th) 193, [2004] 6 W.W.R. 1, 194 B.C.A.C. 161, 318 N.R. 1, 317 W.A.C. 161, [2004] S.C.J. No. 20 (S.C.C.). The trial judge had ordered the husband to pay $2,500 in support until wife earned $2,000 per month, at which time it was to be reduced to $1,500 per month. At the Supreme Court of Canada, at para. 101, Bastarache J. wrote:

> The trial judge should have realized that it was inappropriate to deprive the appellant of 40 percent of his interest in his main source of income if he was to pay $2,500 per month to the respondent as spousal support. On the one hand, taken together, Beames J.'s orders for spousal support and for reapportionment of the law firm constituted "double-dipping" and are thus anomalous; on the other hand, the remaining family assets considered together can properly be viewed as respondent's fair share. This conclusion does not prejudice any variation application that the respondent might bring for a reevaluation of her need for spousal support following this decision.

The court allowed the appeal in part to the extent that the appellant's law firm should not have been reapportioned in favour of the respondent.

*A term in a separation agreement providing for the cessation of maintenance payments upon remarriage or cohabitation by the wife is a valid term* — *Caron v. Caron*, 1987 CarswellYukon 8, 1987 CarswellYukon 43, EYB 1987-67973, 7 R.F.L. (3d) 274, [1987] 1 S.C.R. 892, 14 B.C.L.R. (2d) 186, 38 D.L.R. (4th) 735, [1987] 4 W.W.R. 522, 75 N.R. 36, [1987] R.D.F. 263, 2 Y.R. 246, [1987] S.C.J. No. 32 (S.C.C.). The non obstante language in another paragraph of the agreement does not empower the court to reinstate maintenance for the former wife where it has been validly discontinued as a result of the wife's cohabitation.

*Where a separation agreement provides for specific events signalling the termination of support, the courts will respect these terms in the absence of a material change in circumstances* — *Chase v. Chase*, 2013 CarswellAlta 258, 2013 ABCA 83, 24 R.F.L. (7th) 21, [2013] A.J. No. 145 (Alta. C.A.). The parties' separation agreement provided for termination of spousal support upon the wife's remarriage or the husband reaching the age of 60. Neither event had yet occurred when the husband decided to retire early, claiming that his health prevented him from working. The court denied the husband's application to vary the order, finding that voluntary retirement did not constitute a material change in circumstances. The Court of Appeal upheld the decision.

*The court awarded support until the wife turned 60 because the husband was absent from the children's lives, the wife was ill and the children had medical issues* — *Caldwell v. Caldwell*, 2013 CarswellAlta 1241, 2013 ABCA 268, 33 R.F.L. (7th) 285 (Alta. C.A.). The parties separated after 12 years of marriage. The chambers judge awarded the wife spousal support in the amount of $790 per month until her 60th birthday, subject to variation in the case of a significant change in circumstances. The husband appealed, citing the relatively short length of the marriage and the 18 years he had been paying support. The Court of Appeal noted that while long-term spousal support is unusual after a medium-length marriage, it was appropriate in these circumstances because the husband had been and continued to be completely absent from the children's lives, the wife had chronic physical and mental health difficulties of a serious nature, and the children had medical issues.

The court ordered the husband to pay support until the wife's return to the workforce — *Kelly v. Kelly*, 2011 CarswellBC 842, 2011 BCCA 173, 18 B.C.L.R. (5th) 99, 303 B.C.A.C. 209, 512 W.A.C. 209 (B.C.C.A.). The parties separated in 2001, and the children stayed with the husband. The court ordered the husband to pay the wife $300 in spousal support until her return to work.

The court will grant a request for an extension of support in the case of a specific event if the event will occur within the timeframe suggested by the SSAG — *Jens v. Jens*, 2008 CarswellBC 2091, 2008 BCCA 392, 57 R.F.L. (6th) 31, 84 B.C.L.R. (4th) 250, 300 D.L.R. (4th) 136, 260 B.C.A.C. 185, 439 W.A.C. 185, [2008] B.C.J. No. 1886 (B.C.C.A.). The parties were married for 8 years and separated in 2004. The court awarded the wife 3 years' spousal support. The wife applied for an extension of support because she was scheduled to undergo surgery. The court noted that she had voluntarily deferred the procedure, and she responded that this was due to stress. The court extended spousal support for 3 months. On appeal, the wife presented evidence of further health problems and requested an extension of support in the amount of $2,750 per month until she became "employed and self-sufficient, at which time the order may be reviewed" (para. 42). The Court of Appeal noted that her "ability to achieve economic self-sufficiency at this point in her life is doubtful" (para. 46) and, using the SSAG, ordered $2,000 per month in support for 5 additional years. [Authors' Note: In *Jens*, the court gave 5 years' support, NOT till a specific event].

Agreements regarding payment until a specific event must comply with the Divorce Act's objectives — *Mirza v. Mirza*, 2006 CarswellBC 1899, 2006 BCCA 362, 31 R.F.L. (6th) 301, 269 D.L.R. (4th) 259, 229 B.C.A.C. 186, 379 W.A.C. 186, [2006] B.C.J. No. 1756 (B.C.C.A.), additional reasons at 2007 CarswellBC 313, 2007 BCCA 106, 237 B.C.A.C. 104, 392 W.A.C. 104 (B.C.C.A.). The parties were married in 1969 and separated after 30 years of marriage. They executed a separation agreement in 2000. At about that time the husband had lost his $65,000 per year job, and the wife's income was $23,700. The agreement provided that the husband was to pay the wife $700 per month in support for life, unless she remarried or began living in a common-law relationship. The wife sought to void the separation agreement on the basis that she was vulnerable when she signed the agreement (she had had no independent legal advice), that the agreement was unfair under the *Family Relations Act*, and that it failed to meet objectives of the *Divorce Act*. At this time the husband was earning $78,000 per year, while the wife was earning $36,000. The court ordered the husband to pay $1,600 per month indefinitely, regardless of when he retired. The appeals judge found that the separation agreement did not anticipate the husband's employment and increased income, and therefore failed to comply substantially with the objectives of the *Divorce Act*. The wife was only entitled to share in the husband's income so long as he remained employed. The court ordered the husband to continue paying $1,600 per month in support until retirement (even if it were early retirement), upon which spousal support obligation would revert to the terms set out in separation agreement.

Support until remarriage or court orders otherwise — *Dutchak v. Dutchak*, 2007 CarswellSask 668, 2007 SKCA 138, 45 R.F.L. (6th) 41, 302 Sask. R. 310, 411 W.A.C. 310 (Sask. C.A.), affirming 2006 CarswellSask 834, 2006 SKQB 543, 36 R.F.L. (6th) 189, 291 Sask. R. 238 (Sask. Q.B.). The parties married in 1954 and separated in 1983. The husband entered into a contract agreeing to pay the wife $400 in support "until she remarries or a court of competent jurisdiction otherwise orders". She began living with a romantic partner (whom she did not marry) in 2003, and the payments stopped. The husband brought an application to terminate support in 2006, and the wife sought support from the second partner. The court ordered the husband to pay $100 per month in support given the wife's need and his income. The Court of Appeal upheld the decision.

*Support until youngest child reaches the age of majority* — *Kopelow v. Warkentin*, 2005 CarswellBC 2636, 2005 BCCA 551, 21 R.F.L. (6th) 78, 261 D.L.R. (4th) 129, 218 B.C.A.C. 209, 359 W.A.C. 209, [2005] B.C.J. No. 2412 (B.C.C.A.), additional reasons at 2006 CarswellBC 1306, 2006 BCCA 271, 268 D.L.R. (4th) 274, 227 B.C.A.C. 176, 374 W.A.C. 176 (B.C.C.A.). The parties were married for almost 12 years and separated in 1998. The trial judge ordered the husband to pay $1,995 per month in child support and $1,500 per month in spousal support until the younger child reached the age of majority.

*Support until payee obtained full-time employment* — *Balcerzak v. Balcerzak*, 1998 CarswellOnt 3785, 41 R.F.L. (4th) 13, 75 O.T.C. 1, [1998] O.J. No. 3860 (Ont. Gen. Div.). Payee was awarded $600 monthly until she obtained full-time employment as a teacher. The wife had stayed home with the children during a 16-year marriage and had resumed her teaching career as a supply teacher, after the separation.

*Support until payor had paid amount for payee's course* — *Armstrong v. Armstrong*, 1997 CarswellOnt 4268, 34 R.F.L. (4th) 38, 46 O.T.C. 274, [1997] O.J. No. 4137 (Ont. Gen. Div.), additional reasons at (November 12, 1997), Doc. Ottawa 23545/96 (Ont. Gen. Div.). Where the wife was required to pay off $14,000 resulting from courses she had taken, the husband was barred from seeking a variation of spousal support until such time as he had paid her that amount in periodic support.

*Account cannot be frozen until obligation honoured* — *Poitras c. Poitras*, 1994 CarswellNB 21, 3 R.F.L. (4th) 111, 149 N.B.R. (2d) 211, 381 A.P.R. 211 (N.B.C.A.). The court has no jurisdiction to order that a payor spouse's bank accounts be frozen until that spouse honours his or her spousal support obligation. Enforcement mechanisms are available to the payee spouse if required.

*Support awarded only until division of matrimonial property* — *Mailhot v. Mailhot*, 1989 CarswellBC 381, 19 R.F.L. (3d) 140 (B.C.S.C.). Where the wife was found, following separation, to have suffered an economic downturn that flowed from a pattern of economic dependency created by the marriage, she was awarded support until such time as the parties' matrimonial property was distributed. The parties in this case had experienced a long marriage lasting 16 years.

### 7.2.5 Terms and Conditions — Specific Awards of Support

### Terms and conditions — fluctuating awards

*Quantum to vary depending on wife's income* — *Katay v. Katay*, 1995 CarswellAlta 627, 168 A.R. 31, [1995] A.J. No. 317 (Alta. Q.B.). The court accepted the wife's budget of $2,750 per month as being reasonable to meet her needs and awarded her spousal support in the amount of $2,500 per month for a year. Thereafter, for every additional $1 of average monthly income from employment, the spousal maintenance would decline by $0.60. There will be no adjustment should the wife's monthly income fall below $333. If the wife's monthly earned income reaches $2,500, which represented an annual income of $30,000, the matter of maintenance would be reviewed, if either party requested it.

*Fluctuating awards depending on whether payor working or not — Champion v. Champion,* 1994 CarswellPEI 13, 2 R.F.L. (4th) 455, 115 Nfld. & P.E.I.R. 175, 360 A.P.R. 175 (P.E.I.T.D.). Where it was anticipated that the father would experience future periods of unemployment, he was ordered to pay $400 monthly child support while working and only $200 when not.

*Payor to pay percentage of income as spousal support — Auger v. Auger,* 1991 CarswellMan 400, 77 Man. R. (2d) 196 (Man. Q.B.). Where the husband was unemployed at the time of the divorce hearing but had previously enjoyed a substantial income, a spousal support order was made in the wife's favour requiring the husband to pay to the wife one-half of his gross monthly income in excess of $1,000 up to a maximum of $500.

*Not proper to order automatic reinstatement of payments if payor became employed — Edwards v. Edwards,* 1990 CarswellNS 43, 26 R.F.L. (3d) 142, 97 N.S.R. (2d) 11, 258 A.P.R. 11 (N.S.T.D.). Where the husband had lost his business and his support obligations were suspended, a provision in the order requiring the automatic reinstatement of the support payments upon the husband's finding of employment was deleted upon appeal. The husband was entitled to have his support obligation determined on the basis of actual means and needs and not on the basis of any future earnings which were unknown and speculative.

## Terms and conditions — indexed awards

*The court may deny a payee's claim for unpaid support relating to accrued indexing amounts in order to offset a decision not to terminate support retroactively — Lawder v. Windsor,* 2013 CarswellOnt 13517, 2013 ONSC 5948, 37 R.F.L. (7th) 417 (Ont. S.C.J.). The parties separated in 1997 after 16 years of marriage. In 2000 the court ordered the husband to pay $800 per month in spousal support to be indexed annually. The husband paid support minus the indexed increases. The husband applied to terminate support retroactively, and the wife argued that she should receive the accumulated amount as a lump sum. The court terminated ongoing support but found that terminating support retroactively would "create unacceptable hardship" for the wife. The court denied the wife's claim for the accrued indexing amount to offset the decision not to terminate support retroactively.

*If the payee party does not actively pursue payment of indexed increases for a long period of time, the court will not grant the amount retroactively — Droit de la famille - 122828,* 2012 CarswellQue 11488, 2012 QCCS 5442, EYB 2012-213411 (C.S. Que.). The parties were in a "traditional" marriage for 30 years. Their separation agreement stipulated that the husband pay $7,760 per month in spousal support with indexation, to decrease to $4,200 per month in 12 years' time. The wife sued for over $42,000 in retroactive indexing. The husband claimed that the wife did not ask him for this amount during the 7-year period in question and in fact told him not to worry about it. The court found at para. 69 that, "the Wife, by her inertia and tacit consent, renounced her right to receive the indexation. Her claim will consequently be dismissed."

*Claims for accrued indexing-related amounts are variation claims for retroactive support rather than for arrears regarding cost-of-living increases — S. (J.R.G.) v. S. (J.A.),* 2011 CarswellBC 3290, 2011 BCSC 1612 (B.C.S. [In Chambers]). The court stated at para. 63:

> Section 6 of the Separation Agreement provided that the support payments would be increased or decreased by the lesser of the Consumer Price Index or the husband's annual increase in income. However, the orders of Sigurdson J. did not provide for cost of living increases. As a result, Ms. J. cannot make a claim for arrears regarding cost of living increases. Instead, her claim would be for variation and retroactive support.

*Failure to index spousal support in agreement not unreasonable given spouse's other advantages — indexing on an ongoing basis was, however, granted* — Misumi v. Misumi Estate, 2003 CarswellOnt 957, 39 R.F.L. (5th) 150, [2003] O.T.C. 235, [2003] O.J. No. 1094 (Ont. S.C.J.)), additional reasons at 2003 CarswellOnt 3085, 42 R.F.L. (5th) 428, [2003] O.T.C. 235, [2003] O.J. No. 3189 (Ont. S.C.J.). Where the spousal support payable to the wife pursuant to the parties' agreement was not indexed, her application for increased spousal support based on retroactive indexing brought 20 years later against the husband's estate was dismissed. The parties, at the time of the settlement, had carefully contemplated the wife's future needs and the failure to index was not unreasonable given the other advantages achieved by the wife in the settlement. The wife had failed to apply for a variation for decades and, in light of all the circumstances, it was inappropriate now to reopen the settlement.

*Indexing of spousal support ordered* — Smith v. Smith, 1998 CarswellOnt 676, 36 R.F.L. (4th) 419, 58 O.T.C. 269, [1998] O.J. No. 617 (Ont. Gen. Div.), additional reasons at 1998 CarswellOnt 1319, 36 R.F.L. (4th) 419, 58 O.T.C. 269 (Ont. Gen. Div.), further additional reasons at 1998 CarswellOnt 2781, [1998] O.J. No. 2671 (Ont. Gen. Div.), the spousal support payable by the husband was ordered to be indexed. Although there is no specific authority for indexing in the *Divorce Act*, jurisdiction was found under s. 15.2(4) and the criteria applied in determining the order was borrowed from s. 38 of the *Family Law Act*, R.S.O. 1990, c. F.3.

*The language of s. 15(4) of the* Divorce Act *(1985) is sufficiently broad to provide jurisdiction to index a support order* — Linton v. Linton, 1990 CarswellOnt 316, 30 R.F.L. (3d) 1, 1 O.R. (3d) 1, 75 D.L.R. (4th) 637, 41 E.T.R. 85, 42 O.A.C. 328, [1990] O.J. No. 2267 (Ont. C.A.).

*Court refused to index support awards, given economic conditions* — Kent v. Frolick, 1996 CarswellOnt 91, 19 R.F.L. (4th) 152, [1996] O.J. No. 130 (Ont. Gen. Div.), additional reasons at 1996 CarswellOnt 2200, 3 O.T.C. 122, [1996] O.J. No. 1899 (Ont.Gen.Div.), further additional reasons at 1996 CarswellOnt 2596, [1996] O.J. No. 130 (Ont. Gen. Div.), varied on other grounds 1996 CarswellOnt 3580, 23 R.F.L. (4th) 1, [1996] O.J. No. 3356 (Ont. C.A.). Where both of the parties earned their income from publicly funded institutions, the court refused to order indexation of the spousal and child support payable by the husband. Given the economic climate, it was inappropriate for the support orders to be indexed.

*The court declined to index the wife's spousal support order until such time as a freeze on the husband's income was lifted* — Simms v. Simms, 1996 CarswellNB 21, 20 R.F.L. (4th) 147, 173 N.B.R. (2d) 161, 441 A.P.R. 161, [1996] N.B.J. No. 46 (N.B.Q.B.).

*The court has the authority to index support obligations in divorce proceedings notwithstanding the lack of express authority to do so in the* Divorce Act — Payne v. Short, 1995 CarswellOnt 71, 10 R.F.L. (4th) 257 (Ont. Gen. Div.).

*Support order indexed* — Yamniuk v. Yamniuk, 1991 CarswellBC 530, 33 R.F.L. (3d) 86, [1991] B.C.J. No. 933 (B.C.S.C.). Where the 57-year-old wife had been away from the workforce during the parties' 21-year marriage, the 61-year-old husband was ordered to pay spousal support. Such order was to be indexed and subject to review upon the parties' retirement.

*Indexing ordered based on the Consumer Price Index* — Kerr v. Kerr, 1989 CarswellSask 299, 22 R.F.L. (3d) 221, [1990] 1 W.W.R. 93, 62 D.L.R. (4th) 694, 79 Sask. R. 52, [1989] S.J. No. 480 (C.A.). Under the broad "terms and conditions" language of s. 15(4) of the *Divorce Act*, the court has power to include in an order for support a clause for automatic increase or decrease based upon the Consumer Price Index.

*Where it was determined that the wife would likely require support indefinitely, the support order was indexed to the lesser of the Consumer Price Index or the percentage increase in the husband's income* — Vogel v. Vogel, 1988 CarswellOnt 329, 18 R.F.L. (3d) 445 (Ont. H.C.).

A separation agreement providing for cost of living increases may be incorporated into the decree nisi to avoid the necessity of repeated variation applications — *Rice v. Pask*, 1982 CarswellSask 227, [1983] 2 W.W.R. 302 (Sask. Q.B.).

Where the parties do not have an escalator clause in their settlement agreement, a trial judge cannot insert one in the decree nisi where there is no change in circumstances of the kind required to justify a variation of the minutes of settlement — *Richardson v. Richardson*, 1987 CarswellOnt 315, 1987 CarswellOnt 963, EYB 1987-67464, 7 R.F.L. (3d) 304, [1987] 1 S.C.R. 857, 17 C.P.C. (2d) 104, 38 D.L.R. (4th) 699, 77 N.R. 1, 22 O.A.C. 1, [1987] S.C.J. No. 30 (S.C.C.).

## Terms and conditions — matrimonial home

Where the matrimonial home is offered to the payee party in lieu of spousal support, the court will not allow the other party to charge a notional real estate commission in order to bring down the price — *Willie v. Willie*, 2013 CarswellBC 2026, 2013 BCCA 318, 31 R.F.L. (7th) 1, 46 B.C.L.R. (5th) 113, 32 R.P.R. (5th) 48, 339 B.C.A.C. 294, 578 W.A.C. 294 (B.C.C.A.). The parties agreed that the wife would forgo her claim to spousal support in return for an unequal division of family assets. This was to be accomplished by an "adjustment payment" of $1,013,000 to the wife, which the husband was to pay in an immediate installment of $350,000, with the balance to come from his interest in the net sale proceeds of the matrimonial home. In the case of a shortfall due to a poor real estate market, the husband was to make this up with a further payment. If the net sale proceeds exceeded the amount required for the adjustment payment, the husband was to receive the balance. The parties had trouble selling the house, and the wife relisted the property. The wife offered to purchase it and the husband refused, after which the wife brought an application for an order that the home be sold to her for $1,140,100. The chambers judge refused to deduct the notional real estate commission from the purchase price. The Court of Appeal dismissed the appeal, stating at para. 21 that, "it was inappropriate to deduct a notional commission derived from a fictional sale of the matrimonial home to third party" given that one of the parties would continue to reside there with no plans of reselling.

The non-owning party's exclusive possession of the matrimonial home after separation cannot be characterized as a lifetime interest in the property — *Kedmi v. Korem*, 2012 CarswellNS 957, 2012 NSCA 124, 323 N.S.R. (2d) 259, 1059 A.P.R. 259 (N.S.C.A.). A separation agreement gave the wife a lifetime interest in the matrimonial home. The court noted she did not have a "lifetime interest" in the matrimonial home, but rather had exclusive possession.

Inheritance to be used to discharge mortgage on matrimonial home — *Polson v. Polson*, 1998 CarswellOnt 2181, 38 R.F.L. (4th) 449, [1998] O.J. No. 2112 (Ont. Gen. Div.). Where the husband's income was insufficient to meet the wife's and children's interim spousal support needs, but he had inherited $170,000, the husband was ordered to pay that amount to discharge the mortgage on the family home and thus considerably reduce the wife's expenses. When the house was eventually resold, the proceeds were to be used to repay the husband.

Terms may include an inducement to payor to permit rest of family to live in home — *Van Zyderveld v. Van Zyderveld*, 1976 CarswellAlta 104, 1976 CarswellAlta 158, 23 R.F.L. 200, [1977] 1 S.C.R. 714, [1976] 4 W.W.R. 734, 68 D.L.R. (3d) 364, 1 A.R. 14, 9 N.R. 413. In awarding maintenance, a court has power to impose terms and conditions even if the terms and conditions are intended as an inducement to the owner of a matrimonial home to allow his wife and children to continue to reside in the home; an order directing the payment of $400 maintenance for the wife with such payment being satisfied to the extent of $300 by the husband owner making the mortgage, tax and insurance payments on the house so long as the wife and children remain in the house, is not a division of property.

*It is improper for a trial judge to order the husband to pay an amount representing the weekly value of the wife's interest in the matrimonial home as long as he remains there* — *Richards v. Richards*, 1978 CarswellNB 68, 22 N.B.R. (2d) 107, 39 A.P.R. 107 (N.B.C.A.). The wife has the same right as the husband to occupy and to obtain an order for partition and sale of the property.

*Payee can apply for additional support if she and children deprived of exclusive possession of the matrimonial home* — *McConnell v. McConnell*, 1975 CarswellNB 80, 57 D.L.R. (3d) 268, 11 N.B.R. (2d) 19 (N.B.C.A.), at 271 [D.L.R.]. "In the event of the petitioner [wife] and/or her minor children being deprived of the exclusive occupancy of the matrimonial home at any time because of any act, omission or failure on the part of the appellant [husband] the petitioner shall be at liberty to apply for an increase in the amount of the periodic payments hereby confirmed or as subsequently may be ordered," per Limerick J. See also *Storm v. Storm*, 1977 CarswellNB 64, 19 N.B.R. (2d) 359, 30 A.P.R. 359 (C.A.), at 360 [N.B.R.].

*Spousal support could be increased if the payee and children did not have exclusive possession of the matrimonial home* — *Chamberlain v. Chamberlain*, 1977 CarswellNB 319, 18 N.B.R. (2d) 55 (N.B.Q.B.). The husband was ordered to pay maintenance in the sum of $60 a week for the wife and children on the condition that he allow them to have exclusive occupation of the matrimonial home. If he refused to allow them to occupy the matrimonial home exclusively he would have to pay maintenance of $500 a month.

*A term of a support order is broad enough to encompass a term or condition that [the wife] be permitted the use of a dwelling* — *Huff v. Huff*, 1971 CarswellMan 7, 4 R.F.L. 258, 16 D.L.R. (3d) 584 (Man. C.A.), per Seaton J. in *Gomes v. Gomes*, below.

*Conveyance of the home cannot be a term or condition of a support order* — *Gomes v. Gomes*, 1972 CarswellBC 73, 6 R.F.L. 398, 24 D.L.R. (3d) 112, [1972] 3 W.W.R. 151 (B.C.S.C.), at 400 [R.F.L.], per Seaton J.

## Terms and conditions — remarriage or common-law unions

*Where a separation agreement provides for specific events signalling the termination of support, the courts will respect these terms in the absence of a material change in circumstances* — *Chase v. Chase*, 2013 CarswellAlta 258, 2013 ABCA 83, 24 R.F.L. (7th) 21, [2013] A.J. No. 145 (Alta. C.A.). The parties' separation agreement provided for termination of spousal support upon the wife's remarriage or the husband reaching the age of 60. Neither event had yet occurred when the husband decided to retire early, claiming that his health prevented him from working. The court denied the husband's application to vary the order, finding that voluntary retirement did not constitute a material change in circumstances. The Court of Appeal upheld the decision.

*When a separation agreement specifies that continued spousal support hinges on whether the payee party is in a new conjugal relationship, the trial judge is best placed to determine credibility in this regard* — *Hatchard v. Hatchard*, 2003 CarswellNS 352, 2003 NSCA 100, 45 R.F.L. (5th) 357, [2003] N.S.J. No. 346 (N.S.C.A.), affirming 2002 CarswellNS 622 (N.S.S.C.). The parties were married for 12 years and separated in 1997. In 2008 they entered into a separation agreement which provided that the husband was to pay the wife $750 per month until she remarried or began a common-law relationship. The trial judge found that the wife's current relationship was a common-law relationship, and the wife appealed. The court discussed the test set out in *Soper v. Soper*, 1985 CarswellNS 46, 67 N.S.R. (2d) 49, 44 R.F.L. (2d) 308, 155 A.P.R. 49, [1985] N.S.J. No. 10 (N.S.C.A.) and determined that the trial judge both considered the relevant factors and was best placed to determine credibility. The trial judge's opinion of the wife was clear:

> I think, really, what you have got here is a mask and it is a mask that is set up not to appear as a common law relationship with rent and all those things, but when you lift that mask there is no question in my mind [...] a common law relationship has been proven in this particular case and I would direct that all payments due her under the agreement would automatically cease at this time. (para. 4)

The Court of Appeal dismissed the appeal.

*The court may strike restrictive conditions regarding remarriage if it finds them to be unconscionable* — *V. (D.) c. F. (J.A)*, 2002 CarswellQue 1361, 2002 CarswellQue 3890, REJB 2002-32177, [2002] R.J.Q. 1309, 220 D.L.R. (4th) 121, [2002] R.D.F. 511 (C.A. Que.). The parties were married for 35 years and separated in 1998. The wife signed a separation agreement weighted heavily in the husband's favour which included a stipulation that, "The wife hereby irrevocably renounces to any alimentary pension or maintenance for herself after her remarriage or cohabitation as defined herein or after March 1st, 2001." The court struck this and other provisions given the wife's vulnerability.

*Where the wife has need and the husband has the ability to pay, the court may interpret a remarriage clause very broadly* — *Dutchak v. Dutchak*, 2007 CarswellSask 668, 2007 SKCA 138, 45 R.F.L. (6th) 41, 302 Sask. R. 310, 411 W.A.C. 310 (Sask. C.A.). The parties married in 1954 and separated in 1983. The husband entered into a contract agreeing to pay the wife $400 in support "until she remarries or a court of competent jurisdiction otherwise orders". She began living with a romantic partner (whom she did not marry) in 2003, and the husband stopped making payments. The husband brought an application to terminate support in 2006, and the wife sought support from the second partner. The court found that she had been in a common-law relationship with her second partner rather than a marriage. The court ordered the (first) husband to pay $100 per month in support given the wife's need and his income. The Court of Appeal upheld the decision.

## Support — payment to third parties

*The court has jurisdiction to order a husband to make maintenance payments to a government welfare agency* — the Divorce Act *does not require that maintenance payments be made to a party to the marriage* — *Hamelin v. Ladouceur*, 1985 CarswellAlta 335, 43 R.F.L. (2d) 420, 61 A.R. 241 (Alta. Q.B.).

*Payor may be ordered to pay support to the Public Trustee where the recipient spouse may not be able to manage her financial affairs* — *Raffin v. Raffin*, 1971 CarswellOnt 114, 5 R.F.L. 274, [1972] 1 O.R. 173, 22 D.L.R. (3d) 497 (Ont. C.A.). A lump sum payment was awarded to the respondent wife but the trial judge was doubtful of her ability to manage or administer a relatively large sum of money without assistance. Accordingly, he ordered that her husband pay the sum of $5,000 to the Public Trustee to be disbursed by him for the benefit of the respondent.

*The court may order that child maintenance payments be made to the registrar of the Supreme Court, Family Division* — *MacKenzie v. MacKenzie*, 1975 CarswellPEI 8, 25 R.F.L. 354, 9 Nfld. & P.E.I.R. 176 (P.E.I.S.C.). See also *Proctor v. Proctor*, 1975 CarswellMan 17, 22 R.F.L. 217, 57 D.L.R. (3d) 766 (Man. Q.B.), where payment of child maintenance was through the Family Court.

*Lump sum payment made to the support recipient and her solicitor jointly where the solicitor could provide financial management* — *Bates v. Bates*, 1971 CarswellNB 11, 7 R.F.L.

344, 4 N.B.R. (2d) 174 (N.B.Q.B.), at 349 [R.F.L]. "While it is not necessary that the decree *nisi* itself so provide I direct that payment of the lump sum aforesaid shall be made to the petitioner and her solicitor jointly. I have full in the latter's ability to see that the moneys are, at least initially, properly invested and that some appropriate scheme is set up for their management to ensure, as far as possible, that they will be of enduring value to the petitioner", per Dickson J.

## Terms and conditions — support orders binding against estates

*In order to ensure that support obligations are binding on the payor's estate, the court will not terminate support or life insurance payments absent a demonstrated material change in circumstances — Rondeau v. Rondeau,* 2011 CarswellNS 15, 2011 NSCA 5, 90 R.F.L. (6th) 328, 330 D.L.R. (4th) 559, 299 N.S.R. (2d) 244, 947 A.P.R. 244, [2011] N.S.J. No. 10 (N.S.C.A.). The parties separated after 28 years of marriage. The husband, who earned $223,578 annually, had supported the family financially since the children were born. The husband agreed to pay $3,400 per month pursuant to the parties' separation agreement, which was incorporated into an order in 2003. The agreement also required him to "maintain a $400,000 life insurance policy and provide through the provisions of his will that his estate could honour his spousal support obligations". In 2009 the court granted the husband's application to reduce support and also reduced the amount of life insurance based on the husband's demonstration of a material change in circumstances. The wife appealed. The Court of Appeal found that the mere passage of time did not constitute a material change in circumstances and ordered the husband to continue to pay support and maintain life insurance in the amount of $133,000 to ensure that his obligation would be met in the event of his death.

*When a party, prior to his death, failed to obtain insurance to cover support obligations pursuant to the parties' separation agreement, the court will not find that there was a constructive trust allowing the other party to collect from insurers not contemplated in the agreement — Ladner v. Wolfson,* 2011 CarswellBC 2364, 2011 BCCA 370, 24 B.C.L.R. (5th) 43, 341 D.L.R. (4th) 299, [2012] 1 W.W.R. 466, 310 B.C.A.C. 225, 526 W.A.C. 225, [2011] B.C.J. No. 1692 (B.C.C.A.). Leave to appeal refused 2012 CarswellBC 1134, 2012 CarswellBC 1135, 328 B.C.A.C. 319 (note), 435 N.R. 390 (note), 558 W.A.C. 319 (note) (S.C.C.). In the parties' separation agreement, the husband agreed to arrange life insurance payable to the wife in order to cover his spousal support obligations. He failed to do so but he had other life insurance payable to his estate. His estate was insolvent, and the wife claimed a "good conscience" constructive trust over the insurance proceeds so as to gain priority over his other creditors. The question was whether a constructive trust could be imposed over insurance proceeds when there was no proprietary nexus between the life insurance contemplated in the separation agreement and the other life insurance payable to the husband's estate on his death. The Court of Appeal found that there was no fiduciary relationship between the parties and therefore a constructive trust could not be established.

*Support order not binding against estate — Schwartz Estate v. Schwartz,* 1998 CarswellOnt 302, 36 R.F.L. (4th) 110, 21 E.T.R. (2d) 9, 52 O.T.C. 72, [1998] O.J. No. 378 (Ont. Gen. Div.). It takes clear, specific and unequivocal language before a spousal support order will be construed as surviving the death of the payor spouse. An award which is stated to be "for an indefinite period" does not meet the test and is insufficient to bind the estate of the payor spouse.

*A court will not make a support order binding upon the payor spouse's estate where the wife is not in extremely necessitous circumstances, nor is the husband in relatively affluent circumstances — Reilly v. Reilly,* 1999 CarswellBC 1537, 50 R.F.L. (4th) 424 (B.C.S.C.), varied

2000 CarswellBC 361, 2000 BCCA 130, 5 R.F.L. (5th) 116, 26 B.C.T.C. 318, 137 B.C.A.C. 151, 223 W.A.C. 151 (B.C.C.A.).

*The court held that it was without jurisdiction to make a support order binding on the payor's estate* — *Carmichael v. Carmichael*, 1992 CarswellNS 80, 43 R.F.L. (3d) 145, 96 D.L.R. (4th) 685, 115 N.S.R. (2d) 45, 314 A.P.R. 45 (N.S.C.A.).

*It is unclear whether the court has any power to make a divorce support order binding on the payor's estate* — *Hillhouse v. Hillhouse*, 1992 CarswellBC 359, 43 R.F.L. (3d) 266, 74 B.C.L.R. (2d) 230, 20 B.C.A.C. 28, 35 W.A.C. 28, [1992] B.C.J. No. 2409 (B.C.C.A.). In any case, such an order is inappropriate where the payor has limited means and a likely modest estate.

*The court refused to make an order for support binding on the estate of the payor spouse where, although the wife was in necessitous circumstances, they were not extreme and the husband was not a wealthy man and had other financial obligations* — *Ripley v. Ripley*, 1991 CarswellBC 2, 30 R.F.L. (3d) 41, 52 B.C.L.R. (2d) 362, [1991] B.C.J. No. 4 (B.C.C.A.).

*An originating order for support under s. 15 of the Act cannot be made after the potential payor has died* — *British Columbia (Public Trustee) v. Price*, 1990 CarswellBC 42, 25 R.F.L. (3d) 113, 43 B.C.L.R. (2d) 368, [1990] 4 W.W.R. 52, 67 D.L.R. (4th) 481, [1990] B.C.J. No. 580 (B.C.C.A.).

*Limited-term spousal support order binding on estate* — *Brubacher v. Brubacher Estate*, 1997 CarswellOnt 2374, 30 R.F.L. (4th) 276, 18 E.T.R. (2d) 296, 33 O.T.C. 241, [1997] O.J. No. 2466 (Ont. Gen. Div.). Where the payor spouse dies before expiration of a limited term support order, the divorce judgement constitutes a charge against the estate because of its temporal specificity. Open-ended orders would terminate on death, requiring the payee spouse to pursue a claim under provincial succession legislation.

*A court may make a support obligation binding upon a payor spouse's estate* — *Linton v. Linton*, 1990 CarswellOnt 316, 30 R.F.L. (3d) 1, 1 O.R. (3d) 1, 75 D.L.R. (4th) 637, 41 E.T.R. 85, 42 O.A.C. 328, [1990] O.J. No. 2267 (Ont. C.A.), at 39 [R.F.L.]. "In a traditional marriage, making a support order binding on the payor's estate is consistent with s. 15(7)(a) of the *Divorce Act*. It recognizes, in the particular circumstances, the economic disadvantages arising from the marriage and its breakdown", per Osborne J.A. He also writes, at p. 38 [R.F.L.]:

> Although the *Divorce Act* has no specific provision making a support order an obligation of the payor's estate, there is ample authority to support the conclusion that [a] trial Judge [has] jurisdiction to make the support order an obligation of the husband's estate.

See *Snively v. Snively*, 1971 CarswellOnt 132, 6 R.F.L. 75, [1971] 3 O.R. 132, 19 D.L.R. (3d) 628 (Ont. Co. Ct.); *Connelly v. Connelly*, 1974 CarswellNS 38, 16 R.F.L. 171, 47 D.L.R. (3d) 535, 9 N.S.R. (2d) 48 (N.S.C.A.); *Katz v. Katz*, 1983 CarswellMan 46, 33 R.F.L. (2d) 412, 21 Man. R. (2d) 1 (Man. C.A.), additional reasons at 1983 CarswellMan 254, 25 Man. R. (2d) 57 (Man. C.A.); *Chadderton v. Chadderton*, 1972 CarswellOnt 175, 8 R.F.L. 374, [1973] 1 O.R. 560, 31 D.L.R. (3d) 656 (Ont. C.A.); *Krause v. Krause*, 1975 CarswellAlta 127, 23 R.F.L. 219, [1976] 2 W.W.R. 622, 64 D.L.R. (3d) 352 (Alta. C.A.); and *Huff v. Huff*, 1971 CarswellMan 7, 4 R.F.L. 258, 16 D.L.R. (3d) 584 (Man. C.A.); *Hemming v. Hemming*, 1983 CarswellNS 57, 33 R.F.L. (2d) 157, 145 D.L.R. (3d) 699, 58 N.S.R. (2d) 65, 123 A.P.R. 65 (N.S.C.A.), leave to appeal to SCC refused (1983), 145 D.L.R. (3d) 699n, 57 N.S.R. (2d) 346n, 120 A.P.R. 346n, 51 N.R. 80 (S.C.C.); *Lesser v. Lesser*, 1985 CarswellOnt 240, 44 R.F.L. (2d) 255, 49 O.R. (2d) 794, 16 D.L.R. (4th) 312 (Ont. H.C.), affirmed 1985 CarswellOnt 1664, 51 O.R. (2d) 100, 19 D.L.R. (4th) 575 (Ont. C.A.); *Swalm v. Swalm*, 1973 CarswellOnt 146, 12 R.F.L. 181 (Ont. H.C.); *Burns v. Burns*, 1981 CarswellAlta 89, [1981] 6 W.W.R. 685, 17 Alta. L.R. (2d) 30, 129 D.L.R. (3d) 178, 32 A.R. 367 (Alta. Q.B.).

*Where separation agreement is silent concerning duration, support order terminated upon payor's death* — *Despot v. Despot Estate*, 1992 CarswellBC 566, 42 R.F.L. (3d) 218, 46 E.T.R. 169, 95 D.L.R. (4th) 62, [1992] B.C.J. No. 1902 (B.C.S.C.). The wife was not entitled to continued support against her late husband's estate although a term in the parties' separation agreement had entitled her to support for life or until she remarried. Although the financial terms of the agreement had been incorporated into the decree *nisi*, the decree was silent concerning the duration of the order. Accordingly, the support order terminated upon the husband's death and, as she had elected to take support under the *Divorce Act*, the wife could not revive the agreement.

*An insurance policy upon payor's life rather than support secured against his estate* — *Van de Sande v. Van de Sande*, 1994 CarswellAlta 484, 148 A.R. 30 (Alta. Q.B.). The court refused the wife's application that her spousal support be secured against the husband's estate. It was held that if the wife, who was incapacitated, wished security, she was free to take out an insurance policy on his life.

*Where the payee spouse required support from the payor in order to supplement her income and to raise it above the poverty level, a support order will be a charge on the husband's estate in the event that he predeceases her* — *Rodrigues v. Rodrigues*, 1990 CarswellOnt 325, 30 R.F.L. (3d) 231 (Ont. Gen. Div.).

*Support as permanent obligation of the payor's estate* — *Katz v. Katz*, 1983 CarswellMan 46, 33 R.F.L. (2d) 412, 21 Man. R. (2d) 1 (Man. C.A.), reversing in part 1983 CarswellMan 254, 15 Man. R. (2d) 435 (Man. Q.B.). Where it was held on the wife's application for an upward variation of maintenance that the amount was still adequate but may not be so in the future, a variation was granted rendering the wife's maintenance a permanent obligation of the husband's estate.

*Payment of unpaid balance of support ordered if payor died before full payment made* — *Buydens v. Buydens*, 1983 CarswellMan 44, 33 R.F.L. (2d) 134, 20 Man. R. (2d) 344 (Man. Q.B.). Where the 67-year-old husband was ordered to pay $12,000 maintenance to his wife in $250 monthly instalments, it was further ordered that the husband's estate be fixed with the payment of any unpaid balance should the husband die before the full award was satisfied.

*Order against husband's estate for support* — *Swalm v. Swalm*, 1973 CarswellOnt 146, 12 R.F.L. 181 (Ont. H.C.). Galligan J. made an order charging the husband's estate with periodic monthly payments and therefore did not include in the order an amount to enable the wife to set aside money to secure herself in the case of the husband's early death. See also *Krause v. Krause*, 1974 CarswellAlta 186, 19 R.F.L. 230, [1975] 4 W.W.R. 738 (Alta. T.D.), varied 1975 CarswellAlta 127, 23 R.F.L. 219, [1976] 2 W.W.R. 622, 64 D.L.R. (3d) 352 (Alta. C.A.).

*The court cannot make an order fixing the husband's estate with a liability not imposed during the husband's lifetime* — *Ducharme v. Ducharme*, 1981 CarswellMan 73, 21 R.F.L. (2d) 309, [1981] 3 W.W.R. 336, 6 Man. R. (2d) 367, 119 D.L.R. (3d) 478 (Man. Q.B.). Unless the decree or an agreement between the parties extended the husband's maintenance obligation beyond his death, the obligation to pay is extinguished on the death of the payor unless the order states otherwise, except with respect to arrears.

*Support binding against husband's estate* — *Wells v. Davidson*, 1981 CarswellSask 72, 24 R.F.L. (2d) 358, 12 Sask. R. 115 (Sask. U.F.C.). "I am satisfied that if an order survives the death of the payor, it, in the proper circumstances may be varied", per Gagne J., allowing the wife's application for a variation of maintenance subsequent to the payor husband's death.

*The wife's application to vary maintenance was allowed subsequent to the death of the payor husband* — *Burns v. Burns*, 1981 CarswellAlta 89, [1981] 6 W.W.R. 685, 17 Alta. L.R. (2d) 30, 32 A.R. 367, 129 D.L.R. (3d) 178 (Alta. Q.B.).

*Where the husband is not a wealthy man it is not appropriate to make an order for maintenance extending beyond his lifetime because it would unduly encumber what is likely to be* a *relatively modest estate* — *Jackh v. Jackh*, 1980 CarswellBC 202, 18 R.F.L. (2d) 310, 22 B.C.L.R. 182, [1981] 1 W.W.R. 481, 113 D.L.R. (3d) 267, [1980] B.C.J. No. 1987 (B.C.S.C.).

*Payee likely to survive payor* — *order made binding on estate* — *Brickman v. Brickman*, 1987 CarswellMan 116, 8 R.F.L. (3d) 318, 51 Man. R. (2d) 6 (Man. Q.B.). Where the wife was likely to survive the husband and the husband owed a continuing obligation to the wife given the long-term traditional nature of the marriage, the support order was varied so as to be binding upon his estate.

### Terms and conditions — designating beneficiary

*The court found that the wife was entitled to the husband's death benefit as a designated beneficiary even though she and the husband were separated and he had been living with another partner at the time of his death* — *Carrigan v. Quinn*, 2012 CarswellOnt 13522, 2012 ONCA 736, 24 R.F.L. (7th) 199, 2 C.C.P.B. (2nd) 227, 356 D.L.R. (4th) 686, 112 O.R. (3d) 161, 2012 C.E.B. & P.G.R. 8007, 298 O.A.C. 281 (Ont. C.A.). Leave to appeal refused 2013 CarswellOnt 3406, 2013 CarswellOnt 3407, 453 N.R. 389 (note), 320 O.A.C. 396 (note) (S.C.C.). The parties were married for over 20 years. After they separated, the husband, now deceased, entered into a new relationship but remained legally married to the wife, whom he had named as sole beneficiary of his life insurance policies and residue of his estate. Upon the husband's death in 2008, the wife brought an action regarding her entitlement to his pre-retirement death benefit. The trial judge found that both the wife and the current partner were spouses and dismissed the wife's claim. The Court of Appeal allowed the wife's appeal, finding that while the wife was not entitled to the death benefit because she was not living with the husband at the time of his death (and the current partner was not entitled to it because she was not a legally married spouse), the wife was entitled to his death benefit as a designated beneficiary. The court noted at that, "Section 1 of the [*Pension Benefits Act*] recognizes both categories of relationships in which the deceased was involved at the time of his death — his legally married spouse and his common law spouse — as spousal relationships. However, s. 48 cannot be interpreted as being capable of applying to two co-existing spousal relationships."

*A clause in a separation agreement renouncing and waiving any claim to the other party's estate does not affect a will or life insurance policy* — *Morrell Estate v. Robinson*, 2009 CarswellNS 683, 2009 NSCA 127, 76 R.F.L. (6th) 1, 315 D.L.R. (4th) 255, 52 E.T.R. (3d) 1, 285 N.S.R. (2d) 185, 905 A.P.R. 185, [2009] N.S.J. No. 597 (N.S.C.A.), affirming 2008 CarswellNS 530, 2008 NSSC 295, 60 R.F.L. (6th) 185, 45 E.T.R. (3d) 46, 269 N.S.R. (2d) 58, 860 A.P.R. 58, [2008] N.S.J. No. 434 (N.S.S.C.). The parties were married in 2001. The husband's will left his estate to the wife, and he named her as the beneficiary on his life insurance policy. The parties separated in 2005 and signed a separation agreement in 2006 which provided that the parties "renounce and waive any claim in the estate of the other and any right to share in the estate of the other, whether such claim or right arises under statute or otherwise". In 2008 the husband died without having changed his will or his insurance policy. The chambers judge stated at para. 16: "Section 20 of the separation agreement does not, in my view, affect the right of [the wife] to be the sole beneficiary under the will." The deceased husband's mother appealed. The court dismissed the appeal.

*Designated beneficiary* — *Parsons v. Parsons*, 1995 CarswellOnt 1087, 17 R.F.L. (4th) 267, [1995] O.J. No. 3225 (Ont. Gen. Div.). Where the husband had previously cancelled certain life insurance policies which had named his wife as beneficiary, he was ordered to secure his wife's spousal support by designating her irrevocably as beneficiary of all supplementary death benefits accruing to him under the *Canadian Forces Superannuation Act*.

## Terms and conditions — interest on support award

*Pre-judgement interest granted on lump sum award, despite wife's 8-year delay in seeking support* — *Kopunovic v. Cukotic-Kopunovic*, 1996 CarswellOnt 107, 19 R.F.L. (4th) 137, [1996] O.J. No. 82 (Ont. Gen. Div.), additional reasons at 1996 CarswellOnt 1238 (Ont. Gen. Div.). The wife was awarded substantial pre-judgement interest on a lump sum spousal support claim brought 8 years after the parties' separation. The interest was not properly reduced despite the wife's delay, as it was the result of her psychological problems and a dependency which had been fostered by the husband. Furthermore, the husband had continued to benefit from the wife after separation and had not altered his financial position in reliance upon the absence of a claim.

*No automatic interest on arrears* — *G. (L.) v. B. (G.)*, 1996 CarswellQue 323, EYB 1996-87585, 21 R.F.L. (4th) 234, [1996] R.J.Q. 381, [1996] R.D.F. 187 (C.S. Que.). There is nothing in the *Divorce Act* nor in the *Civil Code of Quebec* on alimentary obligations that suggests that interest is automatically payable on arrears of support. The requirement to pay interest must accordingly be explicit in the case of an alimentary order.

## Terms and conditions — maintaining benefits

*Where the deceased party failed to obtain insurance to cover support obligations pursuant to the parties' separation agreement, the court will not find that there was a constructive trust allowing the other party to collect from insurers* — *Ladner v. Wolfson*, 2011 CarswellBC 2364, 2011 BCCA 370, 24 B.C.L.R. (5th) 43, 341 D.L.R. (4th) 299, [2012] 1 W.W.R. 466, 310 B.C.A.C. 225, 526 W.A.C. 225, [2011] B.C.J. No. 1692 (B.C.C.A.). Leave to appeal refused 2012 CarswellBC 1134, 2012 CarswellBC 1135, 328 B.C.A.C. 319 (note), 435 N.R. 390 (note), 558 W.A.C. 319 (note) (S.C.C.). In the parties' separation agreement, the husband agreed to arrange life insurance payable to the wife in order to cover his spousal support obligations. He failed to do so but he had other life insurance payable to his estate. His estate was insolvent, and the wife claimed a "good conscience" constructive trust over the insurance proceeds so as to gain priority over his other creditors. The question was whether a constructive trust could be imposed over insurance proceeds when there was no proprietary nexus between the life insurance contemplated in the separation agreement and the other life insurance payable to the husband's estate on his death. The Court of Appeal found that there was no fiduciary relationship between the parties and therefore a constructive trust could not be established.

*Where a husband fails to maintain the amount of life insurance provided for in the parties' separation agreement, the court will award the wife the amount she would have received* — *Turner v. DiDonato*, 2009 CarswellOnt 1389, 2009 ONCA 235, 63 R.F.L. (6th) 251, 95 O.R. (3d) 147, 311 D.L.R. (4th) 146, 46 E.T.R. (3d) 1, 247 O.A.C. 116 (Ont. C.A.). The parties signed a separation agreement which set out that the husband was to pay spousal support until the wife reached the age of 65. The agreement required the husband to designate the wife as sole beneficiary of his $100,000 of life insurance and to maintain that insurance for as long as he was obligated to support her. If the husband died without insurance in effect, his obligation to contribute to wife's support was to be first charge on his estate. The husband had remarried and when he died the wife had not yet reached age 65 and the life insurance only had coverage of $43,507.15. The wife's action for shortfall was allowed. The court dismissed the second wife's appeal, finding that the trial judge had correctly interpreted the agreement, the language of which was inconsistent with the second wife's contention that the policy was merely intended to be security for the husband's diminishing spousal support obligations at the time of his death.

*Maintaining benefits where wife's employment difficulties arose from the marriage* — *Eccles v. Eccles*, 2002 CarswellOnt 1284, 27 R.F.L. (5th) 47, [2002] O.J. No. 1346 (Ont. S.C.J.), reversed in part 2003 CarswellOnt 3235, 43 R.F.L. (5th) 321, 175 O.A.C. 394 , [2003] O.J. No. 3300 (Ont. C.A.), additional reasons at 2003 CarswellOnt 4098, 47 R.F.L. (5th) 4, [2003] O.J. No. 4124 (Ont. C.A.). Where the wife's inability to find meaningful employment flowed directly out of the marriage, the husband was ordered to maintain for the benefit of the wife all extended health, dental and medical benefits available to him through his employment, or alternatively to pay costs of a similar plan for the wife until she may be covered herself by a future employer.

## Terms and conditions — provisional awards

*Lump sum award ordered provisionally if property award set aside* — *Noel v. Noel,* 1998 CarswellAlta 409, 1998 ABQB 402, 39 R.F.L. (4th) 214, 62 Alta. L.R. (3d) 376, [1998] 10 W.W.R. 605, 217 A.R. 201, [1998] A.J. No. 1483 (Alta. Q.B.). The husband won a prize of $5.47 million in a lottery 14 months after the parties' final separation, but before their divorce. At the time of the hearing there were approximately $8 million of lottery winnings and earnings. The parties had been married for over 15 years and the wife was in poor health. The court ordered that the husband pay the wife approximately $2 million and in the event that that order was set aside, provisional spousal support in a lump sum to be calculated at the rate of $2,500 per month for 20 years, beginning on the date of this judgement using a discount rate of 5%. Support was ordered on the basis of the economic interdependency of the parties, the lengthy duration of the marriage, the functions each spouse performed during cohabitation, the wife's present condition, means and needs and, most significantly, the husband's vast financial resources.

## Terms and conditions — other

*No jurisdiction to require disclosure on originating application* — *Poitras c. Poitras,* 1994 CarswellNB 21, 3 R.F.L. (4th) 111, 149 N.B.R. (2d) 211, 381 A.P.R. 211 (N.B.C.A.). In determining support, the court lacks the jurisdiction to order the payor to advise his former spouse and the court of any changes in his or her financial situation. Before an obligation to disclose arises, it is necessary for the payee to commence proceedings for variation.

*Decree must be consistent with order* — *Roschuk v. Roschuk,* 1980 CarswellMan 29, 15 R.F.L. (2d) 196 (Man. C.A.). A decree *nisi* was altered, on appeal, to delete conditions limiting the wife's entitlement to maintenance which were included when the husband's solicitor prepared the decree *nisi* but were not imposed in the reasons for judgement.

## 7.3 Spousal Support — Method of Payment — Lump Sum or Periodic

In awarding support, the court may "make an order requiring a spouse to secure or pay, or to secure and pay, such lump sum or periodic sums, or such lump sum and periodic sums, as the court thinks reasonable for the support of the other spouse": *Divorce Act,* s. 15.2(1). The term "spouse" in this subsection includes a former spouse: *Divorce Act,* s. 15.

In the usual case, courts make periodic awards of support. In exceptional circumstances, courts will make lump sum awards. See *Kowaluk v. Kowaluk* (1996), 1996 Carswell Man 198 (Man. Q.B.), below; and *Leblond v. Grenier* (12 février 1992), C.A. Québec 200-09-00369-907 (C.A. Que.).

Lump sum awards are generally made to satisfy real and immediate needs. Such orders may be made to provide a home for the payee spouse, to retire a payee's debts, to reach a conclusive settlement, or to provide transitional funding while the payee spouse retrains or for other reasons.

The power to "secure" support has two meanings: to post an income producing security with the income to be used as support, and, secondly, to post security as a guarantee of payment. The two meanings come from the two similar phrases used in the subsection "to secure *or* pay" and "to secure *and* pay" [emphasis added]. If the subsection contained only the first phrase, to secure or pay, the court would have no jurisdiction to order payment of support and the posting of security to be realized in default of payment. This, in fact, was the case with the 1968 *Divorce Act*. The comparable subsection in this early version of the Act contained only the power to "secure or pay" the support amount and the judicial interpretation of this phrase at the Supreme Court of Canada clarified the distinction between the two meanings.

The subsequent addition of the second phrase "to secure *and* pay" (emphasis added) allows the court to order a spouse to pay support, and at the same time order the spouse to post security to guarantee payment in the sense that if the spouse defaults in the obligation to pay, the security could be realized, at least to the extent of the deficiency.

The combination of the two phrases in the present Act. "to secure *or* pay, or to secure *and* pay" (emphasis added) leads to the possibility of three kinds of orders, and not merely two as existed under the old statute:

(i) order to pay support;

(ii) order to secure support where the security yields periodic payments such as interest payments and the benefitting spouse is entitled to these payments and nothing more; and

(iii) order to secure payment of support where the order is collateral to a concurrent order to pay support and the security can be realized if there is default in payment.

*The phrase "secure or pay" was not broad enough to permit the court to make both an order to pay periodic sums and concurrently to order the posting of security which could be realized if there were default under the order to pay — Nash v. Nash*, 16 R.F.L. 295, [1975] 2 S.C.R. 507, 47 D.L.R. (3d) 558, 2 N.R. 271, and *Van Zyderveld v. Van Zyderveld*, 23 R.F.L. 200, [1977] 1 S.C.R. 714, [1976] 4 W.W.R. 734, 9 N.R. 413. The court had no power under this single phrase, it was held, to order security to stand as a guarantee of payment. An order to pay and an order to secure are two distinct and independent orders. An order to pay periodic support creates a personal obligation and a debtor creditor relationship. Under the Act of 1968 an order to secure, on the other hand, did not impose such an obligation. If ordered to secure periodic payments, the only obligation of the spouse against whom the order was made, was to provide the security and nothing more. There was no personal obligation to pay, and the spouse never became a debtor in respect of the payments. The other spouse had the benefit of the security and was required to look to it alone. If it did not yield the expected payments, the spouse putting up the security could not be called upon to make good the deficiency.

*Order requiring payor to do what is necessary to make the security effective — Switzer v. Switzer* (1969), 1 R.F.L. 262, 70 W.W.R. 161, 7 D.L.R. (3d) 638 (Alta. C.A.). See also *Dexter v. Dexter* (1975), 11 N.B.R. (2d) 11 at 13, 7 A.P.R. 11 (C.A.). "The wording in [s. 11 of the *Divorce Act*, 1968] . . . is the court may make an order 'requiring the husband to secure'. The section to my mind contemplates that the court shall direct the husband to do the things that are necessary to make the security effective and may order him to execute an instrument whereby the sum ordered to be paid is effectively secured on the property. The husband, however, is not personally liable to pay the periodic sums where he has been ordered to secure such sums. In respect of any sum ordered to be paid by the court but not secured he is, of course, personally liable to pay such sums", per McDermid J.A.

*The court, when ordering periodic payments or a lump sum amount and at the same time providing for security of payment, must direct that the payments be paid out of the security — Van*

*Zyderveld v. Van Zyderveld*, [1977] 1 S.C.R. 714, 23 R.F.L. 200, [1976] 4 W.W.R. 734, 68 D.L.R. (3d) 364, (sub nom. *Zyderveld v. Zyderveld*) 9 N.R. 413, 1 A.R. 14. See also Law v. Law (1978), 23 N.B.R. (2d) 114, 44 A.P.R. 114 (C.A.); and *Foy v. Foy* (1979), 14 R.F.L. (2d) 12 (Ont. C.A.). Therefore, where the maintenance is ordered to be secured against a house which is further ordered to be sold, the order must show that it is the proceeds of any sale from which payment of the lump sum is to be made without attaching additional conditions for the time of sale.

*Where the trial judge did not explicitly discuss the inherent income tax law implications of an award of spousal support, his conduct was not unreasonable nor an error* — Edgar v. Edgar, 2012 CarswellOnt 11952, 2012 ONCA 646 (Ont. C.A.). The trial judge had calculated arrears of periodic payments based on the *Spousal Support Advisory Guidelines* and provided that the credits due to the husband for spousal and child support were to be set off against his obligation to the appellant for ongoing child support. The wife argued that the trial judge had erred in failing to consider the different income tax treatments applicable to child and spousal support. The court held that "the tax treatment arises by virtue of the *Income Tax Act* which is not susceptible to change by court order. The fact that the periodic payments are quantified at a point in time and that a set off is ordered by the court as a collection mechanism does not change the nature of the underlying legal character of the periodic spousal support payments." This ground of appeal was dismissed.

*A court has no jurisdiction to secure maintenance payments against the interest in property of a trustee in bankruptcy as neither a claim for maintenance nor a claim for arrears of maintenance is provable in bankruptcy proceedings* — Kutschenreiter v. Kutschenreiter (1983), 46 C.B.R. (N.S.) 1 (Ont. H.C.); see also *Switzer v. Switzer* (1970), 1 R.F.L. 262, 70 W.W.R. 161, 7 D.L.R. (3d) 638 (Alta.); J. v. J. (1969), 8 D.L.R. (3d) 760 (Sask.); *Pugh v. Pugh* (1970), 4 R.F.L. 213 at 221, 2 N.S.R. (2d) 409, 16 D.L.R. (3d) 318 (T.D.).

*Personal guarantee not required from payor where support is secured* — Bastarache v. Bastarache (1975), 25 R.F.L. 72 at 74, 11 N.B.R. (2d) 564, 7 A.P.R. 564 (Q.B.). "I have considered the possibility of requiring a personal guarantee from the respondent as well but the decision in the Nash case [[1975] 2 S.C.R. 507, 16 R.F.L. 295, 47 D.L.R. (3d) 558, 2 N.R. 271] makes it clear that, when a sum for maintenance is secured, the party providing the security is free from any further obligation in respect of the sum secured so long as the security remains in force without variation", per Stevenson J.

### 7.3.1 Lump Sum — Jurisdiction

In awarding support, the court may "make an order requiring a spouse to secure or pay, or to secure and pay, such lump sum or periodic sums, or such lump sum and periodic sums, as the court thinks reasonable for the support of the other spouse": *Divorce Act*, s. 15.2(1). The term "spouse" in this subsection includes a former spouse: *Divorce Act*, s. 15.

The Divorce Act and the Ontario Family Law Act "*contain provisions conferring a broad discretion on judges to make an award of periodic or lump sum spousal support or to make an award comprising both forms of support*" — Davis v. Crawford, 2011 CarswellOnt 2512, 2011 ONCA 294, 95 R.F.L. (6th) 257, 106 O.R. (3d) 221, 332 D.L.R. (4th) 508, 277 O.A.C. 200, [2011] O.J. No. 1719 (Ont. C.A.), additional reasons at 2009 CarswellOnt 2612, 71 R.F.L. (6th) 54, [2009] O.J. No. 1959 (Ont. S.C.J.). Nonetheless, these provisions do indicate factors which should be considered in deciding whether lump sum spousal support is appropriate. [This decision was decided under the Ontario *Family Law Act*. However the Divorce Act was discussed, and the case may be useful for cases under the *Divorce Act.*]

*An award of lump sum support is discretionary and case specific, and requires weighing the advantages against the disadvantages of a lump sum award —* Aksman v. Shenderey, 2011 CarswellOnt 14461, 2011 ONCA 816, 8 R.F.L. (7th) 192 (Ont. C.A.). The payor husband appealed, *inter alia*, an award of lump sum spousal support. The Court of Appeal upheld the award of lump sum support, finding that an award of lump sum support is discretionary and case specific. The judge was found to have given adequate reasons for his decision, including the payor's frequent lateness with his payments, and weighed the advantages versus the disadvantages of a lump sum award as required by *Davis v. Crawford, supra.*

*A court has authority to make a lump sum award even when none has been sought —* Phillips v. Phillips, 1995 CarswellAlta 381, 14 R.F.L. (4th) 113, 174 A.R. 11, 102 W.A.C. 11 (Alta. C.A.). A judge should always consider whether to make a retroactive award to account for any shortfall in an interim order based on the evidence heard at trial. Here, it was not clear that there was any shortfall. The order was varied with the lump sum award deleted and periodic support reduced.

*On an application for support, the objective is proper support —* Osborne v. Osborne, 1973 CarswellSask 31, 14 R.F.L. 61, [1973] S.J. No. 236 (Sask. Q.B.), varied 1974 CarswellSask 38, 23 R.F.L. 358 (Sask. C.A.). Wide as the court's discretion is on applications for maintenance, including the power to order payment of a lump sum, the court's discretion must be exercised for the attainment of one purpose only, namely, the provision of proper maintenance. In arriving at the amount of such a lump sum, care must be taken not to do so on any basis of working out what might be an equitable division of assets between the husband and the wife, having regard to their respective contributions to its accumulation, and then to fix a lump sum arrived at on that basis.

*A trial judge is entitled to consider and award lump sum support where the claimant asserts the claims orally during trial but the documents contain only a general claim for support —* Mosher v. Mosher, 1995 CarswellNS 11, 13 R.F.L. (4th) 385, 140 N.S.R. (2d) 40, 399 A.P.R. 40, [1995] N.S.J. No. 133 (N.S.C.A.), reversing in part 1993 CarswellNS 391, 126 N.S.R. (2d) 367, 352 A.P.R. 367 (N.S.S.C.).

*Although the court lacks jurisdiction to order the transfer of the matrimonial home from the husband to the wife in a divorce proceeding, an order awarding lump sum maintenance to the wife, which sum could be satisfied by the husband's transfer of the home, is within the court's jurisdiction —* Widrig v. Widrig, 1981 CarswellNS 67, 24 R.F.L. (2d) 379, 48 N.S.R. (2d) 269, 92 A.P.R. 269 (N.S.T.D.).

*"Section 11(1) [now s. 15.2(1)] does not authorize the court to enter into the area of divisions of property for any purpose" —* Rathwell v. Rathwell, 1974 CarswellSask 26, 16 R.F.L. 387 (Sask. Q.B.), at 390-91 [R.F.L.]. The reason is plain. The BNA Act, 1867, c. 3, s. 92(13), gives exclusive jurisdiction to the provinces in the realm of 'property and civil rights in the Province'. It is only when the court grants a divorce that s. 11 [now s. 15] empowers the court to make an order for maintenance, and such is then made solely as consequential relief accompanying the divorce itself. When a divorce is refused no order can be made under said s. 11 [now s. 15.2(1)], because such would not be relief corollary to a divorce but would be an order affecting the property and civil rights of a husband and wife, inter se, and such an order would be outside the legislative authority of the Parliament of Canada.

## 7.3.2 Lump Sum — General

See also **Chapter 15 Restructuring — Lump Sum.**

Lump sum awards are usually made to satisfy real and immediate needs. Such orders may be made to provide a home for the payee spouse, to retire a payee's debts, to reach a conclusive settlement, or to provide transitional funding while the payee spouse retrains. A court may find a lump sum warranted where the payor spouse has a history of non-payment, late payment or it is anticipated that he or she will not pay in the future or when there is a high conflict situation or for other reasons. Lump sum support has been awarded where the parties are of modest means or the parties are of widely disparate incomes and sufficient assets, the payor spouse is intending to live or is living outside the country, particularly where the payor has no assets within Canada, or where the payee has relocated to Canada or a province where the payor lives. Since *Davis v. Crawford*, below, courts have held that lump sum spousal support awards are not restricted to "very unusual circumstances". However, most spousal support awards are in the form of periodic payments.

Periodic spousal support payments are taxable in the hands of the payee and deductible in the hands of the payor. Lump sum spousal support payments, in contrast, are tax neutral.

It is important to note that some awards are not lump sum awards, but instead periodic support awards being the aggregate of unpaid monthly payments. See, for example, *Rockall v. Rockall*, 2010 CarswellAlta 1859, 2010 ABCA 278, 90 R.F.L. (6th) 317, 35 Alta. L.R. (5th) 1, 490 A.R. 135, 497 W.A.C. 135, [2010] A.J. No. 1064 (Alta. C.A.); and also *Edgar v. Edgar*, 2012 CarswellOnt 11952, 2012 ONCA 646 (Ont. C.A.). In some cases, this fact will have important tax implications. [See the paragraph immediately above.]

*In deciding the proper form of an order, the courts, pursuant to the* Divorce Act *and the provincial support statutes, are intended to deal with the economic consequences of the marriage breakdown for both parties and to provide a fair and equitable distribution of resources to alleviate these consequences, regardless of gender — Bracklow v. Bracklow*, 1999 CarswellBC 532, 1999 CarswellBC 533, 44 R.F.L. (4th) 1, [1999] 1 S.C.R. 420, 63 B.C.L.R. (3d) 77, 169 D.L.R. (4th) 577, [1999] 8 W.W.R. 740, 236 N.R. 79, [1999] R.D.F. 203, 120 B.C.A.C. 211, 196 W.A.C. 211, [1999] S.C.J. No. 14 (S.C.C.).

*If a court wishes to fix lump sum support, it is obliged to fix it with reference to the principles applicable to such an award — Young v. Young*, 1993 CarswellBC 264, 1993 CarswellBC 1269, EYB 1993-67111, 49 R.F.L. (3d) 117, [1993] 4 S.C.R. 3, 84 B.C.L.R. (2d) 1, 108 D.L.R. (4th) 193, [1993] 8 W.W.R. 513, 18 C.R.R. (2d) 41, 160 N.R. 1, [1993] R.D.F. 703, 34 B.C.A.C. 161, 56 W.A.C. 161, [1993] S.C.J. No. 112 (S.C.C.). See also *MacNeil v. MacNeil*, 1994 CarswellNS 42, 2 R.F.L. (4th) 432, 113 D.L.R. (4th) 218, 129 N.S.R. (2d) 284, 362 A.P.R. 284, [1994] N.S.J. No. 105 (N.S.C.A.). McLachlin J., as she then was, stated in the *Young* decision, at para. 58:

> The trial judge did not express any jurisprudential or evidentiary basis for awarding the lump sum maintenance. The goal was no doubt to achieve the end of conveying the entire interest in the matrimonial home to the wife. But this justification does not support an award of lump sum maintenance; more is required.

*While lump sum spousal support awards do not have to be limited to "very unusual circumstances", as a matter of principle, most spousal support orders will be in the form of periodic payments — Davis v. Crawford*, 2011 CarswellOnt 2512, 2011 ONCA 294, 95 R.F.L. (6th) 257, 106 O.R. (3d) 221, 332 D.L.R. (4th) 508, 277 O.A.C. 200, [2011] O.J. No. 1719 (Ont. C.A.), additional reasons at 2011 CarswellOnt 4562, 2011 ONCA 423, [2011] O.J. No. 2637 (Ont. C.A.). Largely, this is so for very practical reasons: (1) In many cases, there will not be enough money available to fund a lump sum support award, either to replace or to supplement an award of periodic support. (2) Where a married spouse has received an equalization payment, this payment will remove a dependent spouse's need for transitional capital. (3) There may not be any considerations favouring a lump sum award from the perspective of either spouse. (4) In some cases, where circumstances may favour a lump sum award, the demands of life, including the possibility that the parties' means and needs will change, will outweigh the considerations favouring a lump sum award. In *Davis v. Crawford*, the parties were common law spouses who cohabited for 23 years and separated when the woman was 64 years of age and the man was 66. While the man claimed his only sources of income would be his RRSP (valued at $435,871, as of March 2008) and CPP plus Old Age Security, the trial judge considered that he had greater assets and means than he had acknowledged. This finding was not overturned on appeal. The woman's income was $2,250 per month. The court upheld an award of lump sum spousal support of $135,000. [This decision was decided under the Ontario *Family Law Act*. However the *Divorce Act* was discussed, and the case may well be useful for cases under the *Divorce Act*.]

"[T]he ability to pay is an important consideration in making an award of spousal support, including lump sum spousal support" — *Davis v. Crawford, supra.*

A lump sum award should not be made in the guise of support for the purpose of redistributing assets — *Davis v. Crawford, supra* [95 R.F.L. (6th) 257], which cites, at paras. 60-61, *Mannarino v. Mannarino*, 1992 CarswellOnt 308, 43 R.F.L. (3d) 309, [1992] O.J. No. 2730 (Ont. C.A.); and *Willemze-Davidson v. Davidson*, 1997 CarswellOnt 700, 98 O.A.C. 335, [1997] O.J. No. 856 (Ont. C.A.), at para. 32 for this proposition. Redistribution of assets is not one of the purposes of a spousal support award under the governing legislation. However a lump sum order can be made to "relieve [against] financial hardship, if this has not been done by [means of property] orders". It is commonly accepted that a lump award can only be granted where the payor "has the ability to make a lump sum payment without undermining the payor's future self-sufficiency" (para. 63).

In considering an award of lump sum spousal support, a court must evaluate the advantages against the disadvantages of such an award — *Davis v. Crawford, supra*; amd see *Aksman v. Shenderey*, 2011 CarswellOnt 14461, 2011 ONCA 816, 8 R.F.L. (7th) 192 (Ont. C.A.); *Murphy v. Murphy*, below.

The ability to pay is one of the factors to consider in making any award for spousal support — there is no provision in the Ontario Pension Benefits Plan or the Ontario Family Law Act that would allow for the immediate transfer of a lump sum out of a pension plan to satisfy a support order — *Decaen v. Decaen*, 2013 CarswellOnt 3922, 2013 ONCA 218, 303 O.A.C. 261, [2013] O.J. No. 1549 (Ont. C.A.).

Failure to consider advantages and disadvantages of a lump sum award will be a reversible error of law — *Murphy v. Murphy*, 2013 CarswellOnt 17352, 2013 ONSC 7015, 39 R.F.L. (7th) 320, 117 O.R. (3d) 749 (Ont. S.C.J.). The payor husband asked for leave to appeal, *inter alia*, an arbitrator's award of $250,000 in lump sum spousal support to the wife. The judge found that the arbitrator's reasons for awarding lump sum support were insufficient. A clean break from disclosure issues was found not to be a legitimate reason for awarding lump sum support, especially as the arbitrator had ruled that there was sufficient disclosure to proceed with the arbitration. The award would not relieve issues of tax implications of the award. Further, the arbitrator did not consider the advantages or disadvantages of a lump sum award, which the judge found were critical legal principles arising from *Davis v. Crawford*. The award of lump sum support was struck.

A large spousal support amount awarded to a party may not be a lump sum, but rather a calculation of periodic spousal support payments due to the party in the specified periods of time — *Edgar v. Edgar*, 2012 CarswellOnt 11952, 2012 ONCA 646 (Ont. C.A.). The trial judge had calculated arrears of periodic payments based on the *Spousal Support Advisory Guidelines* and provided that the credits due to the respondent husband for spousal and child support were to be set off against his obligation to the appellant wife for ongoing child support. The husband was awarded $28,000 in spousal support.

*Lump sum spousal support was justifiable where the payor spouse had obtained a significant economic advantage by having the payee spouse take on the bulk of domestic and financial responsibilities, thus enabling the payor spouse to regain his health and ability to return to work; the magnitude of his wealth justified a considerable award of compensatory spousal support; and there was no difficulty in identifying the economic advantages and disadvantages arising from the relationship with sufficient accuracy to award a lump sum — Greenberg v. Daniels*, 2005 CarswellOnt 84, 20 R.F.L. (6th) 287, 194 O.A.C. 115, [2005] O.J. No. 87 (Ont. C.A.). A clean break was appropriate. The husband had assets in excess of $6.5 million dollars and a salary in excess of $500,000 annually. The wife had received interim support of approximately $70,000 net and was awarded lump sum support of $400,000.

*Lump sum payment to ensure child's lifestyle and help wife's self-sufficiency — Tauber v. Tauber*, 2003 CarswellOnt 1009, 34 R.F.L. (5th) 450, 64 O.R. (3d) 229, 225 D.L.R. (4th) 186, 170 O.A.C. 1, [2003] O.J. No. 1083 (Ont. C.A.). The appellate court upheld a lump sum payment of $500,000 for spousal support. The payment would assist the wife to provide a lifestyle comparable to the one which the child had enjoyed when he lived with both parents, a lifestyle to which the husband was readily able to contribute. The payment would enable the wife to enhance her self-sufficiency and help her to purchase a permanent home for herself and the parties' child. While the amount was a substantial one, it should be seen in the context of the husband's assets which were worth between $19 and $20 million, his undisputed ability to pay, and the parties' lifestyle during the marriage.

*Rationale for lump sum award — Topolnitsky v. Topolnitsky*, 1997 CarswellMan 525, 32 R.F.L. (4th) 196, 118 Man. R. (2d) 276, 149 W.A.C. 276, [1997] M.J. No. 529 (Man. C.A.). A lump sum spousal support in favour of the wife was found to be justified by the following factors: (1) the wife's inability to work because of her health; (2) the resistance of the husband in the past to provide any support for the wife; (3) the parties' advancing years; (4) the husband's interest in a successful company; (5) the lack of any real chance of improvement in the wife's financial circumstances; and (6) the existence of a financial pool from which the husband could draw to pay the lump sum.

*Lump sum support should be awarded only in very unusual circumstances, where there is a real risk that periodic payments will not be made — Mannarino v. Mannarino*, 1992 CarswellOnt 308, 43 R.F.L. (3d) 309, [1992] O.J. No. 2730 (Ont. C.A.). Lump sum spousal support was not granted as the husband had always been a good provider and there was no evidence to suggest that he was unable to manage his finances, unless the failure of his franchise muffler business indicated an inability to manage his finances. Awarding lump sum spousal support would result in a substantial redistribution of family property and would make it impossible for the husband to apply for a reduction of support if there were a significant change in his future personal circumstances. Lump sum spousal support was set aside and replaced with periodic support. (However, see *Davis v. Crawford*, above [95 R.F.L. (6th) 257].)

*Lump sum awards intended to compensate for inadequate interim awards are the exception rather than the rule — Andries v. Andries*, 1998 CarswellMan 180, 36 R.F.L. (4th) 175, 159 D.L.R. (4th) 665, [1998] 7 W.W.R. 536, 126 Man. R. (2d) 189, 167 W.A.C. 189, [1998] M.J. No. 196 (Man. C.A.).

*Courts usually make periodic awards of support. In exceptional circumstances, courts will make lump sum awards. See Kowaluk v. Kowaluk*, 1996 CarswellMan 198, 24 R.F.L. (4th) 261, 110 Man. R. (2d) 184, 118 W.A.C. 184, [1996] M.J. No. 247 (Man. C.A.); and Droit de la famille - 1542, below; contra, *Davis v. Crawford*, above.

*Circumstances in which lump sum rather than periodic support is appropriate — Sharpe v. Sharpe*, 1997 CarswellOnt 227, 27 R.F.L. (4th) 206, 22 O.T.C. 298, [1997] O.J. No. 336 (Ont. Gen. Div.). The circumstances are:

(a) where difficulties enforcing periodic payments are anticipated;

(b) where the possibility exists that the payor's livelihood is or will become precarious;

(c) where sufficient assets are available from which a lump sum could be paid;

(d) where the payor is about to leave or has left the jurisdiction;

(e) where it is desirable to terminate personal contact between the spouses;

(f) where the dependant spouse is taking job retraining;

(g) to provide a "nest egg" for the contingencies of life;

(h) to compensate for the dependant spouse's lost pension benefits;

(i) where the marriage is of a short duration;

(j) where the dependant spouse has established a new relationship;

(k) to effect a retroactive award of spousal support;

(l) to enable the dependant spouse to discharge a debt.

*"Lump sum support orders should not be made to achieve a more equitable division of capital assets, including real property ... The purpose of a lump sum support order must, however, be distinguished from its effect. Any lump sum support order will result in a transfer of capital from the payor to the payee equal to the lump sum order to be paid. To justify a lump sum child or spousal support order, there should be a valid reason for not making a periodic support order which usually will be paid from the payor's income"* — Willemze-Davidson v. Davidson, 1997 CarswellOnt 700, 98 O.A.C. 335, [1997] O.J. No. 856 (Ont. C.A.). A lump sum child support order was made in light of the husband's attitude, financial circumstances, his consistent record of non-payment and his new family responsibilities which made it highly unlikely that he would pay periodic child support. See also Mannarino v. Mannarino, 1992 CarswellOnt 308, 43 R.F.L. (3d) 309, [1992] O.J. No. 2730 (Ont. C.A.).

*Lump sum awards are the exception and not the rule* — Lauderdale v. Lauderdale, 1996 CarswellAlta 43, 21 R.F.L. (4th) 17, 180 A.R. 81, [1996] A.J. No. 53 (Alta. Q.B.), reversed 1997 CarswellAlta 448, 29 R.F.L. (4th) 34, 200 A.R. 198, 146 W.A.C. 198, [1997] A.J. No. 499 (Alta. C.A.). Lump sum awards of spousal support remained the exception rather than the rule. This was due to the difficulty of disentangling the economic lives of the divorcing spouses, which difficulty mitigated in favour of periodic sharing of the income stream of the employed spouse.

*Lump sum support should only be granted in exceptional circumstances* — Kowaluk v. Kowaluk, 1995 CarswellMan 438, 17 R.F.L. (4th) 185 (Man. Q.B.), reversed, 1996 CarswellMan 198, 24 R.F.L. (4th) 261, 110 Man. R. (2d) 184, 118 W.A.C. 184, [1996] M.J. No. 247 (Man. C.A.). The wife sought lump sum support for the period from the separation to the trial. She was granted periodic support, but not lump sum support. There was no evidence that she made any attempt to obtain interim support, nor was there any evidence that she maintained her right to such interim support during the course of the proceedings. The circumstances were not exceptional.

*A lump sum award should only be awarded in exceptional circumstances where economic need is demonstrated* — Droit de la famille - 1542, 1992 CarswellQue 570, EYB 1992-55749 (C.A. Que.).

*An award of lump sum support will be based on principles for spousal support rather than the redistribution of property* — Morrison v. Morrison, 2013 CarswellNS 830, 2013 NSSC 358, 337 N.S.R. (2d) 98, 1067 A.P.R. 98 (N.S.S.C.). The wife sought lump sum spousal support in the amount of one-half of the equity in the matrimonial home because the husband had a limited ability to pay periodic support. The judge found that the parties had similar income and that an award of lump sum spousal support should be based on spousal support principles, rather than as a means of redistributing property. The wife was found to have no entitlement to either periodic or lump sum spousal support.

*Lump sum support will not be ordered when the recipient spouse cannot meet the onus of demonstrating how such an award would be satisfied* — *Peel v. Peel*, 2012 CarswellOnt 6115, 2012 ONSC 761, 22 R.F.L. (7th) 299 (Ont. S.C.J.).

*As a general rule, lump sum support as a method of paying retroactive support should only be made in the exceptional case* — *Hovorka v. Hovorka*, 1996 CarswellSask 100, 140 Sask. R. 36 (Sask. Q.B.). A lump sum in satisfaction of prior support obligations is simply a windfall for the claimant in reimbursement for funds notionally spent.

*Lump sum interim support should be awarded only in the most exceptional of circumstances* — *Droit de la famille - 1613*, [1992] R.D.F. 404 (C.S. Que.).

*Where a spouse has an immediate or specific need, such as paying the extraordinary expenses of furthering her education, a court will award lump sum support* — *McGuigan v. McGuigan*, 1991 CarswellNS 57, 33 R.F.L. (3d) 183, 105 N.S.R. (2d) 170, 284 A.P.R. 170 (N.S.T.D.).

*A court should not give a lump sum support award a "property" appearance by setting it off against a property entitlement unless no other reasonable alternative exists* — *Glazier v. Glazier*, 1991 CarswellOnt 325, 36 R.F.L. (3d) 84, 5 O.R. (3d) 183, [1991] O.J. No. 1552 (Ont. Gen. Div.).

*The wife was granted a lump sum award of $7,000 which represented the payments that should have been made under the parties' voluntary agreement and which the husband unilaterally stopped* — *Magne v. Magne*, 1990 CarswellMan 44, 26 R.F.L. (3d) 364, 65 Man. R. (2d) 241 (Man. Q.B.).

*A lump sum payment should only be ordered where periodic payments have not provided proper maintenance* — *Osborne v. Osborne*, 1973 CarswellSask 31, 14 R.F.L. 61, [1973] S.J. No. 236 (Sask. Q.B.), at 70-71 [R.F.L.], varied 1974 CarswellSask 38, 23 R.F.L. 358 (Sask. C.A.)."In my opinion, when the court finds that a petitioner is entitled to a maintenance order the court should first order periodic payments, and then, when it is necessary to provide proper maintenance, order a lump-sum payment in addition to the periodic payments. There will be, of course, special cases where in their circumstances a lump sum in lieu of periodic payments would be justified", per Disbery J.

*Lump sum maintenance is not to be used indirectly to effect a division of property* — *Droit de la famille - 49*, [1983] C.S. 996 (C.S. Que.). See also *Dieser v. Dieser*, 1977 CarswellAlta 378, 6 A.R. 298 (Alta. T.D.). The purpose of lump sum maintenance is to provide for some particular purpose, such as the purchase of a home or to guarantee maintenance payments in an unstable situation. The award is not to be used to affect a division of family assets.

*The wife was not entitled to an award of lump sum maintenance on the sole basis that the husband had accrued sizeable assets during the course of the marriage* — *Laflamme v. Laplante*, 1981 CarswellQue 698, [1981] C.S. 1031 (C.S. Que.).

*The purpose of lump sum maintenance is not to divide or redistribute the husband's capital* — *Rathwell v. Rathwell*, 1974 CarswellSask 26, 16 R.F.L. 387 (Sask. Q.B.); *Ferguson v. Ferguson*, 1974 CarswellBC 59, 19 R.F.L. 331 (B.C.S.C.), at 334-35 [R.F.L.].

*Lump sum support should generally be granted only to cover costs and expenses which are of an alimentary nature* — *Droit de la famille - 1229*, [1989] R.D.F. 152 (C.S. Que.).

### 7.3.3 Lump Sum — Granted — Examples

See *Davis v. Crawford*, 2011 CarswellOnt 2512, 2011 ONCA 294, 95 R.F.L. (6th) 257, 106 O.R. (3d) 221, 332 D.L.R. (4th) 508, 277 O.A.C. 200, [2011] O.J. No. 1719 (Ont. C.A.), above.

*Where the wife was a part-time practicing lawyer, a court could take into account her ability to support herself and her substantial "non-family" assets when it concluded that a lump sum payment of $150,000 for spousal support would reasonably compensate the wife for being unable to earn what her husband could earn in the practice of law, having devoted much of her time to raising the children during and after the marriage* — Q. *(R.E.) v. K. (G.J.)*, 2012 CarswellBC 887, 2012 BCCA 146, 17 R.F.L. (7th) 255, 31 B.C.L.R. (5th) 264, 348 D.L.R. (4th) 622, [2012] 8 W.W.R. 270, 319 B.C.A.C. 98, 542 W.A.C. 98 (B.C.C.A.), additional reasons at 2012 CarswellBC 1774, 2012 BCCA 267, 17 R.F.L. (7th) 291, 31 B.C.L.R. (5th) 300, [2012] 8 W.W.R. 306 (B.C.C.A.).

*It is appropriate to award lump sum spousal support where the payor parent has not been regularly meeting his child support obligations under the current order and it appears that his sense of responsibility toward his child and his spouse is dwindling as time passes, and that he views their well-being as lower priorities than some of the other demands on his financial and personal resources* — *Stace-Smith v. Lecompte*, 2011 CarswellBC 573, 2011 BCCA 129, 97 R.F.L. (6th) 91, 16 B.C.L.R. (5th) 119, 302 B.C.A.C. 250, 511 W.A.C. 250 (B.C.C.A.). The parties were common law spouses who had lived together for 4 years and had a child. The court found that the woman was entitled to lump sum compensatory and non-compensatory spousal support in the amount of $18,000.

*Chronic lateness in support payments will be considered when determining the appropriateness of a lump sum award of spousal support* — *Aksman v. Shenderey*, 2011 CarswellOnt 14461, 2011 ONCA 816, 8 R.F.L. (7th) 192 (Ont. C.A.). The payor husband appealed, *inter alia*, an award of lump sum spousal support. The Court of Appeal upheld the award of lump sum support, finding that an award of lump sum support is discretionary and case specific. The judge was found to have given adequate reasons for his decision, including the payor's chronic lateness with his payments, and weighed the advantages versus the disadvantages of a lump sum award as required by *Davis v. Crawford*.

*A lump sum award is justified where the application judge has before him evidence of the husband's abusive behaviour, intention not to pay spousal support and probable non-compliance with a court order* — *Zenteno v. Ticknor*, 2011 CarswellOnt 13822, 2011 ONCA 722 (Ont. C.A.). At the time of the appeal, the husband's pleadings were struck and the matter proceeded as a default judgement hearing because the husband did not fulfill certain undertakings. The application judge awarded the wife a lump sum payment for spousal support of $193,385 to be secured by a charge on the property owned by the husband and a 2002 automobile to be transferred to her absolutely in the amount of $6,615 which was to be deducted from the lump sum award. The appellate court would not interfere in the support order, as there was no error in principle, significant misapprehension of the evidence or the award was not clearly wrong.

*A lump sum spousal support award will be upheld on appeal where it had been granted to give the wife the opportunity to perhaps pursue a programme or course towards re-entry into the workforce, and to acknowledge that the wife was entitled to receive some compensation from her husband of 7 years, as non-compensatory support* — *Young v. Young*, 2011 CarswellNB 241, 2011 CarswellNB 242, 2011 NBCA 46, 374 N.B.R. (2d) 350, 965 A.P.R. 350 (N.B.C.A.). The trial judge undertook a proper analysis with regard to spousal support, including a review of the *Spousal Support Advisory Guidelines*.

*An award of lump sum support which will assist the recipient to remain in the matrimonial home with the child will be found to be reasonable* — *Karisik v. Chow*, 2010 CarswellBC 3272, 2010 BCCA 548, 94 R.F.L. (6th) 70, 12 B.C.L.R. (5th) 107, 301 B.C.A.C. 133, 510 W.A.C. 133 (B.C.C.A.), leave to appeal refused 2011 CarswellBC 1436, 2011 CarswellBC 1437, 305 B.C.A.C. 320 (note), 425 N.R. 390 (note), 515 W.A.C. 320 (note), [2011] S.C.C.A. No. 59 (S.C.C.). The wife appealed a trial decision which awarded her lump sum spousal support based on a monthly periodic amount. The trial judge used the *Spousal Support Advisory Guidelines* in order to determine an appropriate amount and duration of support. The wife objected to the award of lump sum, rather than periodic, support. The Court of Appeal held that the trial judge reasonably exercised his discretion in awarding lump sum support on the basis that this would assist the wife in retaining the matrimonial home.

*Order for lump sum spousal support granted where the husband had a history of nonpayment and his unemployment jeopardized future payments —* Vanos v. Vanos, 2009 CarswellOnt 6420, 77 R.F.L. (6th) 123, [2009] O.J. No. 4217 (Ont. S.C.J.), reversed in part on other grounds 2010 CarswellOnt 9680, 2010 ONCA 876, 94 R.F.L. (6th) 312, 271 O.A.C. 222, [2010] O.J. No. 5539 (Ont. C.A.). The wife was entitled to spousal support for an indefinite period. The husband was ordered to make monthly payments of $1,489, which was the middle figure of the SSAG range. Given the husband's history of non-payment of support orders and his current unemployment, an order for a lump sum payment and a vesting order were justified. The lump sum support payment for future spousal support was $121,500. The order for lump sum spousal support was upheld on appeal.

*Lump sum support is preferable to avoid re-filing of 10 years of income tax returns —* Hartshorne v. Hartshorne, 2009 CarswellBC 1398, 2009 BCSC 698, 70 R.F.L. (6th) 106, [2009] B.C.J. No. 1050 (B.C.S.C.), reversed in part 2010 CarswellBC 1618, 2010 BCCA 327, 82 R.F.L. (6th) 1, 6 B.C.L.R. (5th) 58, 320 D.L.R. (4th) 398, 289 B.C.A.C. 244, 489 W.A.C. 244, [2010] B.C.J. No. 1271 (B.C.C.A.). A periodic award is taxable in the hands of the recipient and deductible from the taxable income of the payor. Lump sum payments are tax neutral as they are not taxable in the hands of the recipient, nor deductible for the payor. In this case, it was agreed that the court should structure the spousal support award as a lump sum payment to avoid the necessity of both parties refiling a decade of income tax returns.

*Lump sum awarded to compensate wife for economic disadvanage arising from the marriage and its breakdown —* Hartshorne v. Hartshorne, 2009 CarswellBC 1398, 2009 BCSC 698, 70 R.F.L. (6th) 106, [2009] B.C.J. No. 1050 (B.C.S.C.). The wife, a lawyer, experienced this disadvantage during her lengthy absence from the legal profession as she fell behind her contemporaries in terms of earnings, client base, networking, professional skills, and seniority. If she had not had this interruption during the formative years of her career, she would have had opportunities to establish her practice, to provide significantly more lucrative opportunities for her, either as an associate or as a partner. In addition, her career opportunities after the parties' separation and divorce were adversely influenced by both her late age at re-entry into the workforce and her role as a custodial parent.

*Lump sum spousal support may be granted, regardless of whether there is a risk of non-payment of support —* Vynnyk v. Baisa, 2007 CarswellOnt 403, 38 R.F.L. (6th) 344, [2007] O.J. No. 274 (Ont. S.C.J.), additional reasons at 2007 CarswellOnt 9218, 52 R.F.L. (6th) 328 (Ont. S.C.J.), affirmed 2008 CarswellOnt 5629, 2008 ONCA 657, 55 R.F.L. (6th) 239, [2008] O.J. No. 3747 (Ont. C.A.).

*Payor spouse's reluctance to disclose income — payee forced to encroach on capital —* Pettigrew v. Pettigrew, 2005 CarswellNS 676, 2005 NSSC 219, 34 R.F.L. (6th) 184, [2005] N.S.J. No. 616 (N.S.S.C.), affirmed 2006 CarswellNS 349, 2006 NSCA 98, 30 R.F.L. (6th) 7, 246 N.S.R. (2d) 298, 780 A.P.R. 298, [2006] N.S.J. No. 321 (N.S.C.A.). Where the husband had been reluctant to disclose his total income to the wife and she had been forced to encroach on capital to support herself after separation, she was awarded lump sum support of $30,000.

*Lump sum to purchase home —* Tauber v. Tauber, 2003 CarswellOnt 1009, 34 R.F.L. (5th) 450, 64 O.R. (3d) 229, 225 D.L.R. (4th) 186, 170 O.A.C. 1, [2003] O.J. No. 1083 (Ont. C.A.). The appellate court upheld a lump sum payment of $500,000 for spousal support, which would enable the wife to enhance her self-sufficiency and help her to purchase a permanent home for herself and the parties' child. The payment would assist her to provide a lifestyle comparable to the one which the child had enjoyed when he lived with both parents, a lifestyle to which the husband was readily able to contribute. While the amount was a substantial one, it should be seen in the context of the husband's assets which were worth between $19 and $20 million, his undisputed ability to pay, and the parties' lifestyle during the marriage.

*Lump sum as conclusive settlement — Kennedy v. Sinclair*, 2001 CarswellOnt 1634, 18 R.F.L. (5th) 91, [2001] O.J. No. 1837 (Ont. S.C.J.), affirmed 2003 CarswellOnt 2507, 42 R.F.L. (5th) 46, [2003] O.J. No. 2678 (Ont. C.A.). Where the husband had a history of failing to comply with court orders as well as a history of violence towards the wife, it was determined that a clean break between the parties was the best result. Accordingly, lump sum spousal support was appropriate.

*Lump sum compensatory support — De Beeld v. De Beeld*, 1999 CarswellBC 2084, 1999 BCCA 515, 2 R.F.L. (5th) 162, 179 D.L.R. (4th) 186, 10 B.C.T.C. 79, 129 B.C.A.C. 101, 210 W.A.C. 101, [1999] B.C.J. No. 2157 (B.C.C.A.). The appellate court, in affirming the lower court decision, awarded the wife $40,000 lump sum compensatory support. During the marriage, the wife had supported her husband through university and during the time he qualified as a chartered accountant and she had later suffered a serious injury in a car accident which prevented her from working fulltime.

*Lump sum to purchase home — Vermeulen v. Vermeulen*, 1999 CarswellNS 171, 2 R.F.L. (5th) 140, [1999] N.S.J. No. 193 (N.S.C.A.). While lump sum spousal support payments may be made to provide funds towards the purchase of a house in certain circumstances, it is an error in law to make a lump sum award without specifics required to determine the amount and without an immediate need being shown.

*Lump sum to compensate for payee's loss of economic opportunity and support — DeFaveri v. Toronto Dominion Bank*, 1999 CarswellOnt 773, 45 R.F.L. (4th) 141, [1999] O.J. No. 822 (Ont. C.A.), additional reasons at 1999 CarswellOnt 1828 (Ont. C.A.). In a long term traditional marriage where the wife did not work for many years but at the time of the hearing had obtained employment, the wife was entitled to a lump sum of $39,000 on account of loss of economic opportunity and support. This was the same amount owing by the wife to the husband in the property calculation, so no exchange of funds needed to take place.

*"[T]he contingency that the wife will require support in the future is a factor to be considered in making a lump sum award of support" — DeFaveri v. Toronto Dominion Bank, supra.*

*Support previously paid only under compulsion — arrears — McClure v. McClure*, 1999 CarswellBC 734, 1999 BCCA 199, 45 R.F.L. (4th) 31, 9 B.C.T.C. 80, 123 B.C.A.C. 231, 201 W.A.C. 231 (B.C.C.A.). A lump sum award of support was upheld on appeal where support has not been paid even though ordered, except under compulsion, and support was substantially in arrears.

*Considering all the assets of the parties — their acquisition, disposal of some of these assets, their income, the respondent's interest in the matrimonial home which the appellant brought into the marriage, and the need for both parties to become economically independent — Richardson v. Richardson*, 1998 CarswellBC 2086, 41 R.F.L. (4th) 137, 112 B.C.A.C. 262, 182 W.A.C. 262 (B.C.C.A.). The trial judge awarded the respondent $60,000 as lump sum support and her interest in the matrimonial home, a decision which was upheld on appeal.

*Failure to make timely interim spousal support payments — concealment of assets — Gray v. Gray*, 1998 CarswellAlta 117, 1998 ABCA 60, 35 R.F.L. (4th) 456 (Alta. C.A.). Where the evidence indicated that the husband had failed to make timely interim spousal support payments and that he had attempted to make off with and conceal assets because of his animosity towards his wife, the wife was granted lump sum spousal support on appeal.

*Wife gave up employment and moved out of the country — Roberts v. Shotton*, 1997 CarswellNS 8, 1997 NSCA 197, 156 N.S.R. (2d) 47, 461 A.P.R. 47 (N.S.C.A.). Where the wife had given up her job as a waitress and speculative plans to start a catering business to move with her husband to Italy to permit him to take an employment opportunity, she was found entitled to a lump sum payment of $5,000 in spousal support on dissolution of the parties' brief marriage, less the gross amount of periodic support, if any, paid by the husband between the trial and the judgement. This payment was made out of abundance of caution and in order to allow the wife to adjust to her post-marital situation.

*Lump sum support is appropriate in cases where it is needed to fund retraining and to meet immediate needs — Mosher v. Mosher*, 1995 CarswellNS 11, 13 R.F.L. (4th) 385, 140 N.S.R. (2d) 40, 399 A.P.R. 40, [1995] N.S.J. No. 133 (N.S.C.A.), reversing in part 1993 CarswellNS 391, 126 N.S.R. (2d) 367, 352 A.P.R. 367 (N.S.S.C.). It should not be awarded to cover legal fees nor is it appropriate to provide for future security where the claimant is also receiving periodic support.

*The court awarded the wife periodic and lump sum maintenance to promote her self-sufficiency, providing her with funds for a car, driving lessons and possibly for training to return to the workforce — the lump sum payment could be satisfied by the husband conveying to the wife his interest in the matrimonial home — McDonald v. McDonald*, 1988 CarswellNS 53, 15 R.F.L. (3d) 268, 85 N.S.R. (2d) 118, 216 A.P.R. 118 (N.S.T.D.).

*Disparity in wealth — Waterman v. Waterman*, 1995 CarswellNfld 117, 16 R.F.L. (4th) 10, 133 Nfld. & P.E.I.R. 310, 413 A.P.R. 310, [1995] N.J. No. 295 (Nfld. C.A.). The dismissal of the wife's claim for retroactive lump sum support was reversed on appeal. The wife had delayed in seeking support primarily because of her health problems. Further, the husband had not paid any support after separation with the result that he acquired additional assets while the wife was forced to seek welfare.

*Wife moved for husband's career but found a new job — loss of income not proven — no compensable loss but lump sum awarded — Prince v. Prince*, 1995 CarswellNS 201, 16 R.F.L. (4th) 236, 144 N.S.R. (2d) 47, 416 A.P.R. 47, [1995] N.S.J. No. 334 (N.S.S.C.), additional reasons at 1996 CarswellNS 329, 153 N.S.R. (2d) 356, 450 A.P.R. 356 (N.S.S.C.); appeal allowed in part on other grounds; cross-appeal dismissed 1997 CarswellNS 444, 35 R.F.L. (4th) 328, 163 N.S.R. (2d) 28, 487 A.P.R. 28, [1997] N.S.J. No. 433 (N.S.C.A.). The wife was awarded a lump sum of $8,000 as compensation for the economic disadvantage she suffered as a result of the marriage breakdown. After the separation, she encroached on her capital as a result of the husband's inadequate payment of child support for a period of 6 months.

*Lump sum for future needs, given wife's poor health — Theberge v. Theberge*, 1995 CarswellOnt 1082, 17 R.F.L. (4th) 196, [1995] O.J. No. 2828 (Ont. C.A.). The court upheld on appeal the wife's lump sum support order which was granted in anticipation of her future needs. Evidence clearly established the likelihood of a decline in the wife's income given her poor health and the order therefore fell within the broad ambit of the trial judge's discretion.

*Lump sum to retire payee's debts — M. (F.) v. G. (S.)*, 1994 CarswellQue 1055, EYB 1994-57439, [1994] R.D.F. 625 (C.A. Que.). A $1,000,000 lump sum support award made in favour of the wife was upheld on appeal where the court was satisfied that it was needed by the wife to maintain her standard of living and to pay off accumulated debts.

*Husband used wife's assets to pay down his debts — lump sum justified — Henderson v. Sharma-Henderson*, 1993 CarswellOnt 338, 47 R.F.L. (3d) 388, [1993] O.J. No. 1074 (Ont. Gen. Div.), affirmed 1994 CarswellOnt 444, 7 R.F.L. (4th) 317, [1994] O.J. No. 1919 (Ont. C.A.). Where the husband had dissipated the wife's assets to pay off his debts and the wife, because of her age, lack of education and the depression resulting from the marriage breakdown, was unable to find fulltime employment for a number of years, the wife was found entitled to lump sum compensatory support. The marriage had left her at an economic disadvantage and had given the husband an advantage at her expense.

*Lump sum support is justifiable in the case of immediate needs such as home repairs and professional upgrading — MacNaughton v. MacNaughton,* 1991 CarswellNS 54, 32 R.F.L. (3d) 312, 103 N.S.R. (2d) 356, 282 A.P.R. 356 (N.S.C.A.). See also *Matthews v. Matthews,* below.

*Wife had need and limited earning power — Droit de la famille - 974,* 1991 CarswellQue 2191, [1991] R.L. 278 (C.A. Que.). The 60-year-old wife received lump sum support of $10,000 upon dissolution of the parties' 32-year marriage. The wife had need and limited earning capacity and, although the husband was retired, he had accumulated significant pension assets.

*To provide security for the future — Droit de la famille - 1206,* [1990] R.D.F. 354 (C.A. Que.), reversing in part [1988] R.D.F. 435 (C.S. Que.). The $25,000 lump sum awarded to the 60-year-old wife at trial was increased to $75,000 on appeal. Although the husband had always fulfilled his obligations toward his wife in the past, she was entitled to a certain degree of security for the future.

*In awarding lump sum maintenance, the court is entitled to consider the lifestyle enjoyed by the claimant during a period of cohabitation prior to marriage — Droit de la famille - 805,* 1990 CarswellQue 45, 26 R.F.L. (3d) 198, [1990] R.L. 267 (C.A. Que.).

*Compensatory lump sum payment — husband increased assets — wife had not received salary — Droit de la famille - 873,* [1990] R.D.F. 616 (C.A. Que.). Where the husband had enriched his assets at the wife's expense and where the wife had never received a salary for all the years she had worked in the family business, a compensatory lump sum payment to her of $90,000 was upheld on appeal.

*Lump sum to retire payee's debts, including legal fees — T. (M.) v. G. (G.),* [1989] R.L. 614 (C.A. Que.).

*Payor an alcoholic — wife awarded a lump sum where it was feared that the husband's alcoholism could interfere with his payment of periodic support — Droit de la famille - 467,* 1988 CarswellQue 353, [1988] R.J.Q. 633, 25 Q.A.C. 130, [1988] R.D.F. 73 (C.A. Que.).

*Where the wife had given up her own aspirations to assist her husband through his medical training she was found entitled, upon divorce, to lump sum support to allow her to pursue her educational goals — Morris v. Morris,* 1988 CarswellNS 187, 85 N.S.R. (2d) 307, 216 A.P.R. 307, [1988] N.S.J. No. 235 (N.S.T.D.), affirmed 1988 CarswellNS 61, 17 R.F.L. (3d) 179, 86 N.S.R. (2d) 378, 218 A.P.R. 378 (N.S.C.A.). See also *Drummond v. Smith,* 1988 CarswellAlta 340, 18 R.F.L. (3d) 120 (Alta. Q.B.).

*Lump sum to cover re-training period — after move from foreign country — Mroz v. Mroz,* 1987 CarswellAlta 351, 7 R.F.L. (3d) 66, 77 A.R. 159 (Alta. C.A.).

*Lump sum as conclusive settlement — reduce conflict — contact not advisable — likelihood of failure to pay periodic support — Currie v. Currie,* 1986 CarswellNS 79, 5 R.F.L. (3d) 192, 75 N.S.R. (2d) 439, 186 A.P.R. 439 (N.S.C.A.).

*Where the husband's means did not permit payment to his wife of sufficient periodic maintenance, a lump sum was awarded to her in an amount equal to the husband's interest in the matrimonial home — Pennington v. Pennington,* 1985 CarswellBC 584, 49 R.F.L. (2d) 113, [1985] B.C.J. No. 2553 (B.C.C.A.).

*Lump sum awarded to meet emergencies and unexpected contingencies — Kudlowich v. Kudlowich,* 1984 CarswellMan 75, 44 R.F.L. (2d) 111 (Man. C.A.).

*Lump sum justifiable for capital requirements — Ciarniello v. Ciarniello,* 1981 CarswellBC 585, 21 R.F.L. (2d) 410, [1981] 3 W.W.R. 146 (B.C.C.A.), at 414-15 [R.F.L.].

*Lump sum payment where situation fraught with bitterness — Ratcliffe v. Ratcliffe,* 1976 CarswellBC 95, 27 R.F.L. 227 (B.C.S.C.), at 232 [R.F.L.]. See also *Helfrich v. Helfrich,* 1976 CarswellAlta 219, 1 A.R. 595 (C.A.), at 596 [A.R.].

*Lump sum to provide home for wife and where payor has failed to make periodic payments* — Carmichael v. Carmichael, 1976 CarswellBC 100, 27 R.F.L. 325, 69 D.L.R. (3d) 297 (B.C.C.A.), at 330 [R.F.L.].

*Lump sum for capital or education or where payor may dissipate capital* — Krause v. Krause, 1975 CarswellAlta 127, 23 R.F.L. 219, 64 D.L.R. (3d) 352, [1976] 2 W.W.R. 622 (Alta. C.A.), at 228 [R.F.L.].

*Where because of the husband's age and inclination it appeared that he would not long continue to be employed, it was held that an award of lump sum maintenance to the wife was appropriate* — Weir v. Weir, 1976 CarswellNS 11, 26 R.F.L. 345, 14 N.S.R. (2d) 539 (N.S.C.A.).

*Lump sum to provide home* — Osborne v. Osborne, 1973 CarswellSask 31, 14 R.F.L. 61, [1973] S.J. No. 236 (Sask. Q.B.), at 71 [R.F.L.], varied 1974 CarswellSask 38, 23 R.F.L. 358 (Sask. C.A.).

*Lump sum awarded where parties of modest means* — Raffin v. Raffin, 1971 CarswellOnt 114, 5 R.F.L. 274, [1972] 1 O.R. 173, 22 D.L.R. (3d) 497 (Ont. C.A.). The use of the lump sum payment is not confined to cases of large estates or large estates and special circumstances. If anything, it may well be more applicable to safeguard the needs of members of a family entitled to maintenance where the people are of modest means.

*Where a creditor party plans to make an assignment in bankruptcy, a charge of lump sum support may be made against the matrimonial home* — Zouganelis-Fobert v. Fobert, 2013 CarswellOnt 18063, 2013 ONSC 7909 (Ont. S.C.J.). The husband was self-employed and had significant debts. He stated to the court that he planned to make an assignment in bankruptcy. The judge noted that, due to the husband's self-employment, it would be difficult to collect support owing and granted the wife an order of a charge against the matrimonial home for the lump sum support that was ordered.

*Lump sum support may be awarded on account of the husband's behaviour and the wife's circumstances in addition to the husband's ability to pay, despite the wife having waived her right to spousal support* — Cuffe v. Desjardins, 2013 CarswellOnt 7934, 2013 ONSC 4044, 37 R.F.L. (7th) 219, [2013] O.J. No. 2706 (Ont. S.C.J.), additional reasons at 2013 CarswellOnt 11489, 2013 ONSC 5275 (Ont. S.C.J.). The parties' marriage contract included a waiver of spousal support, and their separation agreement gave the wife a payment of $130,000 in return for the release of all claims against the husband. The court took the husband's conduct and the wife's situation into account and awarded her a lump sum payment of $60,000 in retroactive support in addition to ongoing indefinite support, which fell within the high end of the range. The court stated, at para. 70: "Here, I consider a lump sum suitable to address the importance placed on savings and debt reduction during this marriage and the disparate situations of the parties in this regard after the termination of marriage."

*Where a party has need based on the breakdown of the relationship, lump sum support will be ordered which would allow the wife to purchase the husband's interest in the matrimonial home* — Coles v. Coles, 2013 CarswellNfld 303, 2013 NLTD(F) 23 (N.L.T.D.). The parties were married for 18 years and had one son. The husband's income had dramatically increased since separation. The judge found that the wife was not economically disadvantaged by the marriage, but she had been economically disadvantaged by the breakdown of the marriage and was receiving social assistance. The judge held she was entitled to needs-based support in a lump sum, which would allow her to purchase the husband's interest in the matrimonial home.

*When there is a significant reapportionment of the proceeds of the family home whereby the payee receives approximately $600,000 more than the payor spouse, there is no need for spousal support for the next 28 months* — Kvarnstrom v. Kvarnstrom, 2013 CarswellBC 2565, 2013 BCSC 1566 (B.C.S.C.). The payor has a history of non-payment of support as well as unstable future income. [Authors' comment: Effectively, the reapportionment acted as lump sum spousal support.]

*Lump sum support will be ordered when the payor's ability to pay is based on net worth rather than income and he does not have the ability to pay periodic support* — *Davis v. Tatton*, 2013 CarswellBC 3554, 2013 BCSC 2126 (B.C.S.C.). The wife sought, *inter alia*, lump sum spousal support. The husband's pleadings had been struck. The parties had a brief marriage in which they cohabited for less than a year. The wife had given up a well-paying job upon marriage at the request of the husband, and the judge found she had suffered economic disadvantage from the marriage despite its short duration sufficient to ground an award of spousal support. The judge considered the factors in *Davis v. Crawford* and awarded lump sum support on the basis that it was a short-term marriage and the wife required spousal support in order to support her while she found suitable employment. The husband's ability to pay stemmed from his net worth rather than his income, as he was retired, and he could have difficulty in paying an order for periodic support. The wife's ability to enforce an award for periodic support was also unknown.

*Where the payor spouse has shown reluctance to pay needed support and was contemplating an inter-provincial move, lump spousal support will be ordered* — *Marsh v. Marsh*, 2012 CarswellBC 3330, 2012 BCSC 1597 (B.C.S.C.), additional reasons at 2013 CarswellBC 813, 2013 BCSC 567 (B.C.S.C.). The parties had a 24-year marriage, and the husband had a new partner with whom he wished to move to Alberta. The court found that the husband's "parsimonious attitude" toward the wife since separation, as well as the fact that if he moved to Alberta periodic support would be difficult to enforce, indicated that a clean break would be preferable. Lump sum spousal support on a compensatory and non-compensatory basis was ordered.

*Where the parties have little or no ability to communicate, a lump sum award of spousal support will be made* — *Grimba v. Bossi*, 2012 CarswellOnt 2934, 2012 ONSC 1386, [2012] O.J. No. 956 (Ont. S.C.J.), additional reasons at 2012 CarswellOnt 5840, 2012 ONSC 2290 (Ont. S.C.J.). The parties had very little ability to communicate. They had two adult dependent children. The judge found that, given their inability to communicate, a lump sum award of spousal support on a compensatory basis was required.

*Where a payor has no ability to pay periodic support, but does have assets available to satisfy a lump sum award, lump sum spousal support will be ordered* — *Waldick v. Waldick*, 2011 CarswellNS 503, 2011 NSSC 257 (N.S.S.C.). The husband had voluntarily terminated his employment. Lump sum spousal support was awarded to the wife, to be paid out of the husband's matrimonial assets.

*Where a recipient spouse has experienced a finite term of incapacity, a lump sum may be awarded to reflect that time* — *Polich v. Polich*, 2011 CarswellBC 1931, 2011 BCSC 949 (B.C.S.C.). The parties separated in 2009. The judge found the wife had suffered an emotional collapse after the breakdown of the marriage and had not worked since that time. The judge found that the wife had required a period of time in order to recover from the separation, but had sufficiently recovered after 9 months. The wife was awarded a lump sum award of spousal support reflecting a 9-month entitlement because of her incapacity to work. There was no medical evidence of ongoing disability.

*Where the parties have disparate incomes, lump sum support will be awarded to assist in the transitional period where the recipient spouse has suffered economic loss as a result of the breakdown of the marriage* — *Kretschmer v. Terrigno*, 2011 CarswellAlta 564, 2011 ABQB 221 (Alta. Q.B.), affirmed 2012 CarswellAlta 2064 , 2012 ABCA 345, 26 R.F.L. (7th) 296, 77 Alta. L.R. (5th) 300, [2013] 6 W.W.R. 701, 539 A.R. 212, 561 W.A.C. 212 (Alta. C.A.), additional reasons at 2013 CarswellAlta 989, 2013 ABCA 210, 88 Alta. L.R. (5th) 64, [2014] 1 W.W.R. 826, 553 A.R. 244, 583 W.A.C. 244 (Alta. C.A.). Leave to appeal refused 2013 CarswellAlta 420,

2013 CarswellAlta 421 (S.C.C.). The parties had a relatively short, 18-month marriage and a 38-month cohabitation. The wife suffered economic hardship as a result of the breakdown of the marriage. The judge award $15,000 lump sum support to compensate the wife during the transitional period after the breakdown of the marriage. The parties had disparate incomes. The decision was affirmed by the Court of Appeal.

Lump sum spousal support will be awarded where it will assist the recipient in attaining self-sufficiency by allowing her to purchase the payor's interest in the matrimonial home — Lee v. Lee, 2011 CarswellBC 514, 2011 BCSC 286 (B.C.S.C.). The wife was entitled to 24 months of lump sum spousal support.

Where lump sum spousal support, in accordance with SSAG, was appropriate to address a multitude of complex support issues — M. (A.A.) v. K. (R.P.), 2010 CarswellOnt 1139, 2010 ONSC 930, 81 R.F.L. (6th) 370, [2010] O.J. No. 807 (Ont. S.C.J.). The parties, who were both veterinarians, had a 9-year relationship and had two children. The husband had an estimated income of $189,900 and the wife had an estimated income of $100,000 in 2009. The parties entered a separation agreement that included a mutual release of spousal support. They did not discuss the spousal support clause, thereby failing to focus on the circumstances in which the agreement was executed and departing significantly from the overall objectives of the Divorce Act. The wife was entitled to compensatory and non-compensatory support. A lump sum payment, as a form of restructuring in accordance with the SSAG, was appropriate. The lump sum payment would address the various complex issues of the commencement date, delay, post-separation increases in income and the balance of compensatory and noncompensatory aspects of the order. The wife was awarded a lump sum of $44,000, netted down for tax purposes.

Non-compensatory claim for spousal support awarded as a lump sum and later reduced to reflect the tax consequences — Arnold v. Arnold, 2009 CarswellBC 2684, 2009 BCSC 1384 (B.C.S.C.), additional reasons at 2010 CarswellBC 278, 2010 BCSC 166 (B.C.S.C.). The wife had a reasonable claim for non-compensatory spousal support at the low end of the SSAG range. She was awarded support of $1,365 per month for a period of 3.5 years. In accordance with the parties' preference, a lump sum award of $57,330 was made. In additional reasons, the court reduced the support order by 30% to reflect the tax consequences of a lump sum award.

Lump sum spousal support award for mid-length marriage — Venco v. Lie, 2009 CarswellBC 1639, 2009 BCSC 831 (B.C.S.C.). Following the breakdown of a 9-year marriage, the wife had made efforts to become self-sufficient, but was not yet completely so. She was entitled to time-limited spousal support on a compensatory and non-compensatory basis. The SSAG range was from nil to $98 per month for 4.5 to 11 years. The wife was awarded a lump sum payment of $5,000. The lump sum payment was prudent given the husband's hostility towards the wife, his stated intention to prevent her from receiving any monetary compensation following the divorce, and his history of non-payment of spousal support.

Lump sum ordered to affect a clean break — Fountain v. Fountain, 2009 CarswellOnt 6342, 77 R.F.L. (6th) 255 (Ont. S.C.J.). The court found that the parties needed a clean-break and that the husband was able to pay the wife a lump sum spousal support amount. The court ordered support for 15 years which totalled $90,000. It reduced this amount by 22% for tax, 6% for a discount rate, and then finally 25% for negative contingencies.

Modest amount of spousal support for short marriage paid as lump sum — Abuzokkar v. Farag, 2009 CarswellOnt 4046, [2009] O.J. No. 2915 (Ont. S.C.J.). The wife sought spousal support in this case. The husband earned $61,800 per year and the wife earned $30,000. The court found that there was no evidence that the wife stayed at home during the marriage or that she gave up jobs or education. She was not disadvantaged by the marriage and was employed full-time. The court noted that the parties were married for just over 4 years and accordingly spousal support should be for a limited period and not be substantial. In this case, the Guidelines suggested spousal support of a range of $0 to $444 per month for a period of 2 to 12 years. The court awarded $200 per month for a period of 3 years, to be paid in a lump sum from the net equalization.

*Lump sum to establish new residence — A. (J.H.) v. A. (C.G.)*, 2008 CarswellMan 126, 2008 MBQB 62, 58 R.F.L. (6th) 327, [2008] M.J. No. 94 (Man. Q.B.). The husband was ordered to pay lump sum spousal support in the amount of $6,400 to help the wife with immediate transition costs while she established a new residence for herself and the children.

*Spousal support may be awarded in a lump sum in part because of the payor's history of erratic support payments and the likelihood that he will leave the jurisdiction — Lou v. Lou*, 2008 CarswellBC 784, 2008 BCSC 490, [2008] B.C.J. No. 702 (B.C.S.C.).

*Lump sum for vehicle — Marshall v. Marshall*, 2007 CarswellNS 618, 2008 NSSC 11, 47 R.F.L. (6th) 327, 261 N.S.R. (2d) 18, 835 A.P.R. 18, [2007] N.S.J. No. 552 (N.S.S.C.). The wife was awarded $8,000 lump sum support to satisfy her real and immediate need to buy a vehicle to allow her to work and transport the children.

*Lump sum granted where wife stayed home with children during parties' 5-year union — Hodder v. Hodder*, 2007 CarswellNfld 361, 2007 NLTD 202, 47 R.F.L. (6th) 84, 272 Nfld. & P.E.I.R. 236, 830 A.P.R. 236 (N.L.T.D.). The wife stayed at home during the marriage to care for her own children and her husband's children from a previous relationship. The fact that they had another child together further delayed the 37-year-old wife's re-entry into the workforce. She had, as a result, lost critical time during which she could work towards self-sufficiency, such pursuits generally being easier when a person is younger.

*Lump sum to retire payee's debts — Traversy v. Glover*, 2006 CarswellOnt 4380, 30 R.F.L. (6th) 372, [2006] O.J. No. 2908 (Ont. S.C.J.). Where, after separation, the wife had to borrow money to finance her retraining, her application for lump sum support as partial reimbursement for the loan was allowed. The wife had given up her employment to relocate with the husband and had then remained in the home for a number of years to care for the parties' children. The wife's debt could be properly characterized as an economic disadvantage resulting from the breakdown of the marriage.

*Lump sum ordered to compensate wife for disadvantage — Taylor v. Taylor*, 2004 CarswellOnt 4851, 10 R.F.L. (6th) 202, [2004] O.T.C. 1053, [2004] O.J. No. 4802 (Ont. S.C.J.). The court should act on a proven economic disadvantage where the disadvantage is of such a degree that it would be unfair to ignore. In this case, the wife sought compensatory support to reflect her share of "the financial losses" sustained as a consequence of the marriage, the separation and the conduct of the husband. The husband had become extremely depressed after his daughter's murder and eventually he had a mental breakdown and declared bankruptcy. The court held that the wife had suffered an unfavourable condition and therefore an economic disadvantage arising from the marriage or its breakdown and was entitled to specific compensatory support in the sum of $10,517.

*Lump sum for transitional period after marriage breakdown — McKay v. McKay*, 2004 CarswellAlta 1801, 2004 ABQB 974, 12 R.F.L. (6th) 118 (Alta. Q.B.), additional reasons at 2005 CarswellAlta 43, 2005 ABQB 25, 12 R.F.L. (6th) 125 (Alta. Q.B.). The wife was awarded lump sum support of $5,000 to compensate her retroactively for the brief period after the marriage breakdown during which she was getting back on her feet in terms of employment and living circumstances.

*Husband had no assets in Ontario — Aunger v. Aunger*, 2004 CarswellOnt 4677, 9 R.F.L. (6th) 29, [2004] O.T.C. 1010, [2004] O.J. No. 4679 (Ont. S.C.J.), additional reasons at 2005 CarswellOnt 1235, 15 R.F.L. (6th) 6 (Ont. S.C.J.). The wife was awarded lump sum spousal support of $200,000 upon her divorce from her wealthy husband. As the husband lived abroad and had no assets in Ontario, the wife was not going to receive any equalization payment to assist her in her financial adjustment because of the marriage breakdown. The lump sum was reflective of the limited term support to which she would otherwise be entitled.

*Compensation for relocation and other sacrifices — lump sum awarded — Walkden v. Walkden*, 2004 CarswellAlta 1799, 2004 ABQB 823 (Alta. Q.B.). The purpose of compensatory support is to compensate a spouse who has given up his or her own economic security for the purpose of caring for children and supporting his or her spouse's career. In this case, the wife was working full time and had her own career before marriage. After the parties' marriage, she followed the husband to Saudi Arabia where, as a woman, she was technically not able to work. However, she did work from time to time in order to keep herself busy rather than to earn an income. When her first child was born in 1980, she left the work force entirely to stay at home with the children. Since returning to Canada she had taken additional upgrading courses and was now working full time. She would never be able to replace the income and positions she would have received had they not gone to Saudi Arabia. She was the classic case for which compensatory spousal support was intended. The court awarded her a lump sum of $300,000 in compensatory support.

*Claimant deserved compensation but was not in need — lump sum awarded — Koch v. Koch*, 2001 CarswellOnt 3460, 22 R.F.L. (5th) 114, [2001] O.J. No. 3840 (Ont. S.C.J.). The court awarded the wife compensatory spousal support where she had suffered some economic disadvantage as a result of the marriage breakdown. She was the main caretaker of the children, looked after her mother and father in their failing health and experienced the emotional wear and tear of the lawsuit which contributed to part of her loss of her earnings for some of the years following separation. The court did find, however, that another, perhaps larger, component of the decrease in income in the later years was the availability of the children's trust money into which the wife dipped. This lessened her motivation to work as hard as she had previously. The court accepted the wife's evidence that the disadvantage would be removed after the conclusion of the parties' litigation and awarded her lump sum support of $25,000, which was not taxable and which would bring some final resolution to the case. The marriage, while of a reasonably lengthy duration, enabled the wife to become qualified and able to support herself. She had some significant assets and would have more liquid capital from the disposition of the jointly-held property. Importantly, she had no demonstrable need, even if there was no particular emphasis placed on the monetary assistance from her boyfriend who had helped her for the prior 2 years.

*Short time period, means of payor, clean break — Tabata v. Smith*, 2001 CarswellAlta 1294, 2001 ABQB 776, 21 R.F.L. (5th) 451, 297 A.R. 168, [2001] A.J. No. 1196 (Alta. Q.B.). Because of the very short term during which periodic spousal support payments would be warranted, the means of the husband to pay a lump sum award, and the clear need for these parties to put this process behind them and move on, the court found that it was an appropriate case for a lump sum spousal support award.

*Non-compensatory support — Lump sum promotes a clean break — Hoxford v. Hoxford*, 1999 CarswellOnt 2300, 2 R.F.L. (5th) 257 (Ont. S.C.J.). The wife was entitled to non-compensatory spousal support to assist her to adjust to the marriage breakdown and to reorganize her financial affairs. The parties had had a modern marriage in which both of them worked and they were not dependent upon each other. The only disadvantage that the wife suffered was that she would have to return to a lifestyle by herself, with the necessary changes to achieve self-sufficiency without the advantages of both parties pooling their resources. The husband was ordered to pay lump sum spousal support of $10,800, payable in the amount of $450 a month over 24 months.

*Provisional lump sum award based on economic interdependency, lengthy marriage and most importantly the payor's vast financial resources — Noel v. Noel*, 1998 CarswellAlta 409, 1998 ABQB 402, 39 R.F.L. (4th) 214, 62 Alta. L.R. (3d) 376, [1998] 10 W.W.R. 605, 217 A.R. 201,

[1998] A.J. No. 1483 (Alta. Q.B.). The husband won a prize of $5.47 million in a lottery 14 months after the parties' final separation, but before their divorce. At the time of the hearing there were approximately $8 million of lottery winnings and earnings. The parties had been married for over 15 years and the wife was in poor health. The court ordered that the husband pay the wife approximately $2 million and in the event that that order was set aside, provisional spousal support in a lump sum to be calculated at the rate of $2,500 per month for 20 years, beginning on the date of this judgement using a discount rate of 5%.

*Clean break can be better served by lump sum* — Baranec v. Baranec, 1998 CarswellOnt 2350, 67 O.T.C. 153, [1998] O.J. No. 2289 (Ont. Gen. Div.).

*Wife gave up career to look after children — no need for periodic support — wife had entered new relationship with affluent partner who could support her* — Kits v. Kits, 1998 CarswellBC 2323, 42 R.F.L. (4th) 167, [1998] B.C.J. No. 2539 (B.C.S.C.).

*Lump sum as conclusive settlement* — Sagl v. Sagl, 1997 CarswellOnt 2144, 31 R.F.L. (4th) 405, [1997] O.J. No. 2837 (Ont. Gen. Div.), additional reasons at 1997 CarswellOnt 4984, 35 R.F.L. (4th) 107 (Ont. Gen. Div.). The wife was granted lump sum spousal support in order to facilitate a clean break between the parties. The relationship between the parties was a bitter one and the husband had a history of ignoring previous periodic support orders.

*Where the marriage had delayed the wife's development of employment skills and the marriage breakdown had impaired her ability to pursue a career because of a diminished psychological capacity, she was awarded a lump sum as a compensatory allowance* — Kopunovic v. Cukotic-Kopunovic, 1996 CarswellOnt 107, 19 R.F.L. (4th) 137, [1996] O.J. No. 82 (Ont. Gen. Div.), additional reasons at 1996 CarswellOnt 1238 (Ont. Gen. Div.).

*Lump sum as conclusive settlement* — Droit de la famille - 1995, 1994 CarswellQue 2019, EYB 1994-75659, [1994] R.D.F. 247 (C.S. Que.).

*Where the wife's current level of self-support and provisions for her retirement were affected by the interruption of her career as a registered nurse to raise the children, she was awarded lump sum compensatory support* — Jorden v. Jorden, 1995 CarswellNB 31, 14 R.F.L. (4th) 97, 162 N.B.R. (2d) 241, 415 A.P.R. 241 (N.B.Q.B.).

*To encourage husband in obtaining employment* — Andrews v. Andrews, 1995 CarswellBC 82, 11 R.F.L. (4th) 117, [1995] B.C.J. No. 194 (B.C.S.C.). Where an award of periodic support to the unemployed husband would possibly discourage him from actively seeking employment, lump sum support was found to be appropriate.

*Lump sum as conclusive settlement* — Droit de la famille - 2123 (1994), [1995] R.D.F. 90 (C.S. Que.). The parties had a 15-year marriage. The wife had given up her career to care for the parties' children and was therefore economically disadvantaged. However, her decision not to return to her former teaching career somewhat compromised her claim and resulted in a smaller lump sum than claimed.

*Re-training allowance* — Leek v. Leek, 1994 CarswellBC 657, 3 R.F.L. (4th) 63, [1994] B.C.J. No. 659 (B.C.S.C.).

*Unreliable payor* — Battaglini v. Battaglini, 1994 CarswellOnt 401, 4 R.F.L. (4th) 235 (Ont. Gen. Div.).

*Lump sum set off against amount payable by support payee to support payor* — Newstone v. Newstone, 1994 CarswellBC 202, 2 R.F.L. (4th) 129, 91 B.C.L.R. (2d) 246, 39 B.C.A.C. 223, 64 W.A.C. 223 (B.C.C.A.). The court could properly award lump sum support to a wife by setting the sum off against funds which the wife would otherwise be required to pay to the husband. Such an order does not amount to an improper redistribution of capital.

*Lump sum awarded where husband unemployed but expected to return to work — wife in need* — Poisson v. Poisson, 1993 CarswellOnt 315, 46 R.F.L. (3d) 105, [1993] O.J. No. 705 (Ont. Gen. Div.).

*Payors income limited* — *Amaral v. Amaral*, 1993 CarswellOnt 372, 50 R.F.L. (3d) 364, [1993] O.J. No. 2712 (Ont. Gen. Div.), additional reasons at 1993 CarswellOnt 373, 50 R.F.L. (3d) 384 (Ont. Gen. Div.). Where the husband's income was limited and a periodic spousal support award would strain his ability to support himself and meet his child support obligations, a modest lump sum was awarded to the wife which would allow both parties to become self-sufficient within a reasonable time.

*Lump sum as compensatory award* — *Monks v. Monks*, 1993 CarswellMan 37, 44 R.F.L. (3d) 459, 84 Man. R. (2d) 268, [1993] M.J. No. 85 (Man. Q.B.).

*Lump sum as conclusive settlement* — *contact not advisable* — *Parish v. Parish*, 1993 CarswellOnt 316, 46 R.F.L. (3d) 117, [1993] O.J. No. 741 (Ont. Gen. Div.).

*Lump sum to retire payee's post-separation debts* — *compensation for lack of pension* — *Droit de la famille - 1633*, [1992] R.D.F. 657 (C.S. Que.).

*Assistance for payee achieving self-sufficiency paid out of the husband's share of the proceeds of sale of the matrimonial home* — *Horner v. Horner*, 1992 CarswellAlta 647, 132 A.R. 106 (Q.B.), additional reasons at 1992 CarswellAlta 724, 136 A.R. 241 (Alta. Q.B.).

*To cover period of learning English* — *Bhatti v. Bhatti*, 1992 CarswellBC 556, 40 R.F.L. (3d) 161 (B.C.S.C.). Where the wife was employed but required training to become proficient in English she was awarded a lump sum of $7,500 upon termination of her 30-year marriage.

*Agreement found disadvantageous to wife* — *second lump sum ordered* — *Droit de la famille - 1560*, 1992 CarswellQue 1632, EYB 1992-74902, [1992] R.D.F. 186 (C.S. Que.).

*Compensation for loss of earnings while tending to family responsibilities* — *Ormerod v. Ormerod*, 1990 CarswellOnt 270, 27 R.F.L. (3d) 225, [1990] O.J. No. 1035 (Ont. U.F.C.). Where because of her family responsibilities, the wife interrupted her nursing career for a number of years, the husband was ordered to pay her a lump sum of $103,000 as compensation for her loss of future income resulting from the interruption. The lump sum was based upon the report of an economist and his projection of the wife's loss of future income, which was both relevant and probative to the issues at hand.

*Compensation for loss of earnings while tending to family responsibilities* — *Katz v. Katz*, 1989 CarswellOnt 260, 21 R.F.L. (3d) 167 (Ont. U.F.C.). Where the wife had given up her career as a pharmacist to care for the children, but was able after separation to resume her career at a salary between $25,000 and $50,000, she was awarded a lump sum of $15,000 to assist her with the adjustment.

*A court may make a lump sum award from assets for child and spousal support where the husband is likely to fritter away the capital* — *Stricker v. Stricker*, 1991 CarswellAlta 332, 118 A.R. 138, 33 R.F.L. (3d) 367, [1991] A.J. No. 617 (Alta. Q.B.).

*Lump sum as conclusive settlement* — *contact not advisable* — *Droit de la famille - 1532* (1991), [1992] R.D.F. 89 (C.S. Que.). The wife was awarded lump sum support where it was found that the future frequent contact between the parties which would result from periodic support was not advisable.

*Lump sum granted where wife stayed home with parties' four children and helped finance husband's education* — *Smithson v. Smithson*, 1991 CarswellMan 388, 72 Man. R. (2d) 174, [1991] M.J. No. 173 (Man. Q.B.).

*Lump sum as conclusive settlement* — *compensatory support* — *payee spouse experienced economic loss from frequent moves* —*Kearley v. Kearley*, 1991 CarswellNfld 276, 94 Nfld. & P.E.I.R. 171, 298 A.P.R. 171 (Nfld. U.F.C.).

*Lump sum payment to establish wife in new career* — *MacLean v. MacLean*, 1990 CarswellBC 476, 28 R.F.L. (3d) 103, [1990] B.C.J. No. 1472 (B.C.S.C.).

*Lump sum to retire payee's debts, legal fees* — *Droit de la famille - 840*, 1990 CarswellQue 1487, [1990] R.J.Q. 1565, [1990] R.D.F. 510 (C.S. Que.). The wife was awarded lump sum support to allow her to purchase a new car and discharge her legal fees and to provide her with some financial stability.

*Lump sum as compensatory award for supporting family* — Droit de la famille - 859, 1990 CarswellQue 1760, EYB 1990-83796, [1990] R.J.Q. 1891, [1990] R.D.F. 498 (headnote only) (C.S. Que.).

*Lump sum as compensatory award for supporting family* — Droit de la famille - 1327, [1990] R.D.F. 347 (C.S. Que.). Where the wife had supported the husband and the family during the husband's medical studies, the wife was awarded a $10,000 compensatory allowance.

*Lump sum compensates wife for acquisition of assets* — Droit de la famille - 1349, [1990] R.D.F. 562 (C.S. Que.). Where evidence established that the wife had assisted the husband in accumulating $240,000 in assets, the wife was awarded a compensatory lump sum of $30,000. Where the wife had assisted the husband in his business and had borne household and child care responsibilities by herself, she was granted lump sum support of $5,000 as compensation for her contribution.

*A lump sum award is justifiable to meet expenses created by moving to a new residence and to pay for tuition at a post-secondary institution* — MacDonald v. MacDonald, 1990 CarswellNS 325, 98 N.S.R. (2d) 229, 263 A.P.R. 229 (N.S.T.D.).

*Lump sum as conclusive settlement* — Droit de la famille - 1352, [1990] R.D.F. 576 (C.S. Que.). See also Droit de la famille - 1326, [1990] R.D.F. 602 (C.S. Que.).

*As compensation for unpaid periodic payments* — Magne v. Magne, 1990 CarswellMan 44, 26 R.F.L. (3d) 364, 65 Man. R. (2d) 241 (Man. Q.B.). Where the husband had unilaterally terminated voluntary support payments prior to the divorce hearing, the wife was awarded lump sum support to compensate for the periodic payments not received.

*Wife relocated to Canada, economically disadvantaged by marriage* — Bhatthal v. Bhatthal, 1990 CarswellAlta 104, 28 R.F.L. (3d) 152, 74 Alta. L.R. (2d) 307, 107 A.R. 70 (Alta. Q.B.). The wife was awarded lump sum support even though her income exceeded that of the husband. The husband had forced her to give up her teaching job in India and move to Canada, where he proceeded to dissipate her property. As a result, the wife had been severely economically disadvantaged by the marriage. See also Babek v. Babek, 1988 CarswellOnt 259, 15 R.F.L. (3d) 168, [1988] O.J. No. 718 (Ont. H.C.).

*Lump sum maintenance should not be awarded merely to equalize earnings between the parties* — Kiesman v. Kiesman, 1986 CarswellMan 247, 42 Man. R. (2d) 78 (Man. Q.B.). In an application for lump sum maintenance, the following factors should be considered, the duration of the marriage; the conduct of the parties during marriage; the division of responsibilities both during marriage and after separation; the assets of each party; and the means of each party.

*Where the wife had raised the parties' four children and had worked for the husband during the marriage without salary, she was awarded lump sum maintenance* — Droit de la famille - 1013, [1986] R.D.F. 109 (C.S. Que.). See also Droit de la famille - 1009, [1986] R.D.F. 91 (C.S. Que.).

*Lump sum — reservation of award* — Stack v. Stack, 1978 CarswellNfld 8, 4 R.F.L. (2d) 215 (Nfld. T.D.), at 224 [R.F.L.]. "As the respondent [husband] has no assets now, nor did he have any after he transferred virtually all that he had to the petitioner pursuant to the agreement between them, I am less certain as to her right to lump sum maintenance. I reserve to her the right to apply for lump sum maintenance, but this is not to be taken as a finding that she is so entitled. That will have to be decided then", per Mahoney J.

*Lump sum — reservation of award* — Gross v. Gross, 1977 CarswellAlta 311, 2 A.R. 440 (Alta. T.D.), at 445 [A.R.]. Where there was no satisfactory evidence before the court as to whether payment by the Armed Forces for the wife's retraining would cease upon divorce, nor was there adequate evidence of the actual cost of retraining, the court reserved the question of a lump sum award.

*Lump sum — reservation of award* — *Elligott v. Elligott*, 1977 CarswellAlta 181, 3 R.F.L. (2d) 61, 6 A.R. 282 (Alta. T.D.), at 66 [R.F.L.]. "If all of the information was available to the court, it may have been possible to determine whether or not the respondent [wife] was entitled to receive an award of a lump sum by way of maintenance. A great deal more information is required to determine this issue. In the result, the matter of the lump sum award is reserved, the respondent to have the right to make an application to the court for the determination of this issue as and when she may be advised, upon proper notice to the petitioner", per Greschuk J.

## 7.3.4 Lump Sum — Refusal of Awards

*The ability to pay is one of the factors to consider in making any award for spousal support — there is no provision in the* Ontario Pension Benefits Plan *or the Ontario* Family Law Act *that would allow for the immediate transfer of a lump sum out of a pension plan to satisfy a support order —* Decaen v. Decaen, 2013 CarswellOnt 3922, 2013 ONCA 218, 303 O.A.C. 261, [2013] O.J. No. 1549 (Ont. C.A.). Without evidence from the mother that the the pension plan would allow for an immediate transfer to satisfy a spousal support award, the appellate court did not find any error in the trial judge's assessment that the father would have no ability to immediately satisfy an order for lump sum support in the amount of $54,000.

*Where the trial judge failed to ascertain the amount of a lump sum payment in a contested separation agreement, the Court of Appeal may find the facts insufficient for analysis and remit the matter to trial —* Estephan v. Estephan, 2013 CarswellBC 3796, 2013 BCCA 540, 41 R.F.L. (7th) 28, 56 B.C.L.R. (5th) 20, 370 D.L.R. (4th) 470, 348 B.C.A.C. 113, 595 W.A.C. 113 (B.C.C.A.). The parties' separation agreement included the wife's release of spousal support in exchange for a lump sum. The wife applied to set aside the agreement. The trial judge analyzed the agreement according to the principles set out in *Miglin* and found that the separation agreement was valid and binding, but failed to ascertain the exact amount of the lump sum. The wife appealed. The Court of Appeal found that the trial judge erred in failing to consider the principles set out in *Moge* and s. 15.2 of the *Divorce Act.* The appeal judge found that the facts were insufficient for analysis without the amount of the wife's lump sum, as without this information it was not clear whether the agreement complied with the objectives of the Act in light of the wife's claim to compensatory support. The Court of Appeal ordered a new trial.

*A $1.3 million capital gain should not be included in a payor parent's annual income as it would result in a transfer of wealth to the dependent spouse or provide her with additional lump sum spousal support —* McNeil v. McNeil, 2013 CarswellNB 606, 2013 CarswellNB 607, 2013 NBCA 65, 40 R.F.L. (7th) 382, 369 D.L.R. (4th) 79, 412 N.B.R. (2d) 303, 1070 A.P.R. 303 (N.B.C.A.).

*Reasons must be given for an award of lump sum support — periodic support awarded, being the aggregate of unpaid monthly payments —* Rockall v. Rockall, 2010 CarswellAlta 1859, 2010 ABCA 278, 90 R.F.L. (6th) 317, 35 Alta. L.R. (5th) 1, 490 A.R. 135, 497 W.A.C. 135 (Alta. C.A.). The parties were married for approximately 5 years. The trial judge found that the wife was entitled to non-compensatory, needs-based support. She had AIDS, a fact of which the husband was aware prior to the marriage, and her condition prevented her from working as she was frequently hospitalized. The Court of Appeal held that the trial judge erred in failing to provide reasons for his award of lump sum support, since the general rule is to order periodic support barring exceptional circumstances. There was no authority justifying a lump sum award based on concerns that the payee spouse may have a shortened lifespan due to illness, as had been argued by the wife. Without reasons, the appellate court could not determine the basis of the exercise of the trial judge's discretion. Since spousal support in this case was non-compensatory and related to her ongoing needs and circumstances, periodic support was more appropriate. Since the failure to give reasons amounted to an error, the lump sum arrears award was set aside and replaced with an order for periodic support totalling the same amount.

*A lump sum spousal support award will not be granted where the court does not accept that there is a real risk that the respondent will not comply with an award for periodic spousal support* — Beck v. Beckett, 2011 CarswellOnt 8467, 2011 ONCA 559, 4 R.F.L. (7th) 48, 341 D.L.R. (4th) 69, 283 O.A.C. 109, [2011] O.J. No. 3752 (Ont. C.A.). The parties had cohabited for 22 years and had two children. The Court of Appeal found that while the man had not paid a costs order, the order was relatively small and pending trial. Otherwise the man had complied with court orders. In addition, although the man was not making the court-ordered child support payments, his counsel had explained that the man did not have sufficient funds to pay child support since his share of the house sale proceeds remained in trust and his only income was from his pension. Given his history prior to trial, once the man had access to the funds held in trust, it was reasonable to believe it would not be difficult to enforce a periodic support order. The lower court was entitled to refuse to make a lump sum spousal support award. The appellate court made an order for spousal support at the rate of $433 per month retroactive to November 2010, when the younger child was no longer dependent; this amount stood at the mid-range of the *Spousal Support Advisory Guidelines.* The woman had submitted that as a common law spouse, she would not be entitled to a share of the man's pension. The Court of Appeal noted that this spousal support would likely be paid out of the man's pension.

*Lump sum — refusal of award, court cannot specify support payment from a particular source* — Gallant v. Gallant, 1998 CarswellMan 477, 42 R.F.L. (4th) 353, 166 D.L.R. (4th) 79, 131 Man. R. (2d) 15, 187 W.A.C. 15, [1998] M.J. No. 481 (C.A.). The court allowed the husband's appeal from an order requiring him to transfer $25,000 from his RRSP to the wife as lump sum support. By specifying the payment from a particular source the order amounted to "back-door equalization" rather than spousal support.

*Lump sum support not to be used to indirectly redistribute property* — Kent v. Frolick, 1996 CarswellOnt 91, 19 R.F.L. (4th) 152, [1996] O.J. No. 130 (Ont. Gen. Div.), additional reasons at 1996 CarswellOnt 2200, 3 O.T.C. 122, [1996] O.J. No. 1899 (Ont. Gen. Div.), further additional reasons at 1996 CarswellOnt 2596, [1996] O.J. No. 130 (Ont. Gen. Div.), varied 1996 CarswellOnt 3580, 23 R.F.L. (4th) 1, [1996] O.J. No. 3356 (Ont. C.A.).

*Lump sum support should not be awarded to cover legal fees nor is it appropriate to provide for future security where the claimant is also receiving periodic support* — Mosher v. Mosher, 1995 CarswellNS 11, 140 N.S.R. (2d) 40, 13 R.F.L. (4th) 385, 399 A.P.R. 40, [1995] N.S.J. No. 133 (N.S.C.A.), reversing in part 1993 CarswellNS 391, 126 N.S.R. (2d) 367, 352 A.P.R. 67 (N.S.S.C.). Lump sum support is appropriate in cases where it is needed to fund retraining and to meet immediate needs.

*Lump sum refusal of award, redistributing property not proper basis for lump sum order* — Russell v. Russell, 1995 CarswellAlta 291, 16 R.F.L. (4th) 229, 33 Alta. L.R. (3d) 170, 175 A.R. 225 (Alta. C.A.). The court rejected the wife's claim for lump sum support. The wife's claim was to redress the perceived deficiency resulting from the parties' property division order and, as a veiled attempt to redistribute property, was not a proper basis for a lump sum order.

*Lump sum support is not properly used to compensate a spouse for a perceived inadequacy of interim support earlier ordered* — Hauff v. Hauff, 1994 CarswellMan 40, 5 R.F.L. (4th) 419, 95 Man. R. (2d) 83, 70 W.A.C. 83, [1994] M.J. No. 287 (Man. C.A.).

*A lump sum order blending pension entitlement, spousal and child support should not be made without clear apportionment* — Hanna v. Hanna, 1994 CarswellNS 51, 4 R.F.L. (4th) 148 (N.S.C.A.).

*Lump sum refusal of award, no economic disadvantage established* — MacNeil v. MacNeil, 1994 CarswellNS 42, 2 R.F.L. (4th) 432, 129 N.S.R. (2d) 284, 362 A.P.R. 284, 113 D.L.R. (4th) 218, [1994] N.S.J. No. 105 (N.S.C.A.). The court allowed the husband's appeal from an award of lump sum support made in the wife's favour. Although she had at one time during the marriage put her nursing career on hold to care for the family, she had returned full-time prior to separation and was earning at the top of the pay scale. Accordingly, she had not established that she was economically disadvantaged and the order amounted more to an improper redistribution of capital between the spouses.

*Lump sum spousal support is not appropriate where the payor's ability was in question* — the lower court had not taken into account the principle of equitable sharing of the consequences of the marriage, and the order involved speculation — Elliot v. Elliot, 1993 CarswellOnt 348, 48 R.F.L. (3d) 237, 15 O.R. (3d) 265, 106 D.L.R. (4th) 609, 65 O.A.C. 241, [1993] O.J. No. 2308 (Ont. C.A.). Leave to appeal refused 1994 CarswellOnt 5818, 1994 CarswellOnt 5819, 3 R.F.L. (4th) 290 (note), 18 O.R. (3d) xvi (note), 112 D.L.R. (4th) vii (note), 175 N.R. 324 (note), 74 O.A.C. 159 (note), [1993] S.C.C.A. No. 522 (S.C.C.). The wife had sacrificed her career for the family. The lower court had based the lump sum award on an expert's report. The lump sum order was replaced with periodic support.

*Lump sum refusal of award* — no expectation of compensation for contribution to husband's political campaign — DaCosta v. DaCosta, 1990 CarswellOnt 314, 29 R.F.L. (3d) 422, 74 D.L.R. (4th) 491, [1990] O.J. No. 1916 (Ont. Gen. Div.), affirmed (1992), 1992 CarswellOnt 257, 40 R.F.L. (3d) 216, 7 O.R. (3d) 321, 44 E.T.R. 196, 53 O.A.C. 354, 89 D.L.R. (4th) 268, [1992] O.J. No. 384 (Ont. C.A.). The court refused the wife's claim for compensatory support based upon her contributions to her husband's political campaign. She had not expected to be compensated for her political contributions and he had not been financially enriched thereby.

*Lump sum refusal of award, spouse could not use award to set up pension fund for himself* — Droit de la famille - 1661, 1992 CarswellQue 1749, EYB 1992-75079, [1992] R.J.Q. 2479 (C.S. Que.). The husband could not claim a lump sum to compensate for that which the division of family assets did not give him.

*Lump sum support is not an appropriate remedy where the claimant wishes only to avoid future possible harrassment from the payor spouse* — D. (D.) c. B. (J.), 1991 CarswellQue 256, 43 Q.A.C. 105, [1991] R.D.F. 661 (C.A. Que.).

*Where a party seeks a lump sum in order to obtain a division of assets in the guise of a support payment, it will not be granted* — Matthews v. Matthews, 1991 CarswellNS 60, 104 N.S.R. (2d) 140, 34 R.F.L. (3d) 201, 283 A.P.R. 140 (N.S.C.A.), citing Hemming v. Hemming, 1983 CarswellNS 57, 33 R.F.L. (2d) 157, 145 D.L.R. (3d) 699, 58 N.S.R. (2d) 65, 123 A.P.R. 65 (N.S.C.A.). To be entitled to support a party must show she has an immediate need. In the Matthews case, the court was of the opinion that there was no immediate need justifying an order for lump sum support.

*Lump sum not allowed in order to pay a family debt* — Guemili v. Guemili, 1989 CarswellMan 42, 19 R.F.L. (3d) 347 (Man. C.A.). The wife had waived the right to support and the husband had agreed to pay $815 towards a family debt. When the husband declared bankruptcy and the debt was unpaid, the wife successfully obtained in divorce proceedings, a lump sum support order for $815. The husband's appeal from the order was allowed, given that the payment could not be properly characterized as support.

*Lump sum award struck where no specific or immediate need* — Moore v. Moore, 1987 CarswellNS 68, 6 R.F.L. (3d) 438, 77 N.S.R. (2d) 267, 191 A.P.R. 267 (N.S.C.A.).

*An award of lump sum spousal support will be struck where the court failed to consider the advantages and disadvantages of a lump sum award. Such a failure is a reversible error of law* — Murphy v. Murphy, 2013 CarswellOnt 17352, 2013 ONSC 7015, 39 R.F.L. (7th) 320, 117 O.R. (3d) 749 (Ont. S.C.J.). The payor husband asked for leave to appeal, *inter alia*, an arbitrator's award of $250,000 in lump sum spousal support to the wife. The judge found that the arbitrator's reasons for awarding lump sum support were insufficient. A clean break from disclosure issues was found not to be a legitimate reason for awarding lump sum support, especially as the arbitrator had ruled that there was sufficient disclosure to proceed with the arbitration. The award would not relieve issues of tax implications of the award. Further, the arbitrator did not consider the advantages or disadvantages of a lump sum award, which the judge found were critical legal principles arising from *Davis v. Crawford*. The award of lump sum support was struck.

*Financial hardship of the recipient spouse is a relevant factor in awarding lump sum support — lump sum support may be ordered in non-exceptional cases* — Peel v. Peel, 2012 CarswellOnt 6115, 2012 ONSC 761, 22 R.F.L. (7th) 299 (Ont. S.C.J.) The wife sought lump sum spousal support. The husband sought to terminate spousal support. The judge noted that lump sum support was not only limited to exceptional circumstances but also to situations where the recipient spouse was facing financial hardship. Periodic support was awarded as the wife had not adequately demonstrated financial hardship.

*Where a party does not have sufficient funds available to pay a lump sum award, it will not be ordered* — Brandl v. Rolston, 2012 CarswellBC 1809, 2012 BCSC 902 (B.C.S.C.), affirmed 2013 CarswellBC 1273, 2013 BCCA 235, 31 R.F.L. (7th) 296, 362 D.L.R. (4th) 439, 338 B.C.A.C. 141, 577 W.A.C. 141 (B.C.C.A.). The parties had divided their assets 5 years before the hearing, and any lump sum amount would be a redistribution of capital assets. The husband had made full disclosure.

*Lump sum support will not be ordered when the payor does not have the ability to pay such an order and where it will be tantamount to using support to redistribute assets* — Stafford v. Stafford, 2013 CarswellOnt 16838, 2013 ONSC 7452, 38 R.F.L. (7th) 188, [2013] O.J. No. 5514 (Ont. S.C.J.). The wife, with the permission of the court, amended her pleadings after learning of the husband's assignment in bankruptcy and requested, *inter alia*, lump sum spousal support.

*Lump sum support will not be appropriate on an interim basis where the payor has demonstrated a willingness to pay support and when lump sum support may compromise his ongoing ability to be self-supporting* — Chin v. Chin, 2012 CarswellOnt 10909, 2012 ONSC 4971, [2012] O.J. No. 4172 (Ont. S.C.J.). The parties had three children. The husband was suffering serious financial difficulties, including lawsuits against him and there was a possibility of bankruptcy. The judge found the husband had shown a willingness to participate in the court process and to support his family, and there were no issues with disclosure. The judge noted that *Davis v. Crawford* stated that the effect of an award of lump sum support on the ability of a payor to continue to be financially self-sufficient was an important factor in determining the appropriateness of lump sum support. An award of lump sum support could force the husband into bankruptcy, and the judge found it was premature to order lump sum support on an interim basis.

*Lump sum support will not be ordered when the recipient spouse cannot meet the onus of demonstrating how such an award would be satisfied* — Peel v. Peel, 2012 CarswellOnt 6115, 2012 ONSC 761, 22 R.F.L. (7th) 299 (Ont. S.C.J.). The wife sought lump-sum spousal support. The husband sought to terminate spousal support. The parties had separated 6 years previously and periodic spousal and child support had been paid since that time under a separation agreement that had not been turned into a court order. The judge found that the parties had not agreed to lump sum support and the wife had not established financial hardship sufficient to make such an order. The judge also found that such an order would require the husband to sell assets or borrow against them and the wife had not met her onus of demonstrating how that could be accomplished. Periodic support was ordered.

*Lump sum — refusal of award, payee not allowed to keep all proceeds of sale of matrimonial home — Mondino v. Mondino*, 2004 CarswellOnt 3513, 9 R.F.L. (6th) 170, [2004] O.J. No. 3572 (Ont. S.C.J.). The court refused the wife's claim for lump sum spousal support in the form of allowing her to keep all the proceeds from the sale of the family home. Although there was evidence that the husband might be inclined to put his own financial interests before those of his family, the order requested would be a disguised form of property transfer and accordingly unfair.

*Lump sum spousal support was not awarded where the effect of the order would primarily amount to a shifting of assets — Dababneh v. Dababneh*, 2003 CarswellOnt 5004, 48 R.F.L. (5th) 55, [2003] O.T.C. 1088, [2003] O.J. No. 5103 (Ont. S.C.J.), additional reasons at 2004 CarswellOnt 654, [2004] O.J. No. 575 (Ont. S.C.J.).

*Decision to give up job unilateral — no lump sum compensatory support but periodic support ordered — Halloran v. Hotte*, 2000 CarswellOnt 3997, 12 R.F.L. (5th) 57 (Ont. S.C.J.). The wife's claim for lump sum compensatory support was dismissed. Although she had given up her job to care for the parties' children, her decision had been a unilateral one. However, she was granted periodic support of $400 per month for 3 years.

*Lump sum — refusal of award, payee's temporary loss of Indian treaty status — Laflamme v. Laflamme*, 1998 CarswellAlta 253, 38 R.F.L. (4th) 335, [1998] A.J. No. 292 (Alta. Q.B.). The court rejected the wife's claim for lump sum spousal support based upon her temporary loss of Indian treaty status during the parties' 1-year marriage. The marriage was of very short duration and the wife had been aware of the status loss during marriage.

*Lump sum — refusal of award — economic hardship caused by calling loan against wife only a possibility — Graham v. Platt*, 1996 CarswellMan 44, 19 R.F.L. (4th) 32, 108 Man. R. (2d) 62 (Man. Q.B.). The wife's request for lump sum support was refused. The wife had cosigned a business loan for the husband, whose business subsequently failed and the loan had been called against him. Any economic hardship as a result of the loan remained only a possibility for the wife and as such could not be the basis for a spousal support award.

*The discretion to award lump sum spousal support under s. 15 of the Divorce Act should not be used to redistribute property or to compensate a spouse for contingent liabilities — Graham v. Platt, supra.*

*Lump sum not for distant retirement needs — Coady v. Coady*, 1995 CarswellNS 486, 144 N.S.R. (2d) 106, 416 A.P.R. 106 (N.S.S.C.). An immediate and specific need must be established before a lump sum will be awarded.

*Lump sum refusal of award, husband had taken early retirement as a result of illness and lacked the capital to pay lump sum spousal support — Deane v. Deane*, 1995 CarswellOnt 428, 14 R.F.L. (4th) 55, [1995] O.J. No. 1150 (Ont. Gen. Div.). Although the wife had left her employment to care for the parties' child, this one factor could not be considered in isolation as a rationale for ordering lump sum support.

*Lump sum refusal of award — Sword v. Sword*, 1994 CarswellNfld 88, 118 Nfld. & P.E.I.R. 69, 369 A.P.R. 69 (Nfld. U.F.C.). The wife's claim for lump sum support was dismissed in the absence of evidence that she had suffered an economic disadvantage of a type warranting lump sum compensatory support. The disadvantage resulting from her remaining in the home with the children could be adequately addressed through periodic support.

*Lump sum refusal of award — would deplete payor's only asset — Zabiegalowski v. Zabiegalowski*, 1992 CarswellOnt 260, 40 R.F.L. (3d) 321 (Ont. U.F.C.). The court refused the wife's application for lump sum support upon the collapse of a marriage in which the parties had cohabited for only 14 months. The lump sum would have depleted the 57-year-old husband's only asset and would have amounted to an unequal division of property.

*Lump sum refusal of award — where the unemployed husband's only asset was his equity in the family home,* a lump sum support award in the wife's favour was found not to be appropriate — *Auger v. Auger,* 1991 CarswellMan 400, 77 Man. R. (2d) 196 (Man. Q.B.).

*Lump sum refusal of award — wife had not established her need — McWilliam v. McWilliam,* 1989 CarswellAlta 395, 23 R.F.L. (3d) 265, 100 A.R. 65, [1989] A.J. No. 1014 (Alta. Q.B.). Where the wife had use of $40,000 more than her share of matrimonial property after separation and had been re-instated to the same employment position that she had held prior to marriage, her claim for lump sum support was dismissed. Having an annual income of $63,000, the wife was unable to establish any need.

*Lump sum — refusal of award — payee had not consulted payor before leaving employment and returning to school — payor had no other assets — Krohn v. Krohn,* 1987 CarswellMan 263, 47 Man. R. (2d) 58 (Q.B.). Where the wife had quit her job to return to school, her claim for lump sum support to discharge her debts accumulated during her schooling was dismissed. She had voluntarily taken on the debts by not consulting her husband before quitting her job, and further, the husband had no assets beyond the family home out of which to pay a lump sum.

*Lump sum — refusal of award — a court ought not to award support based upon speculation on possibility — Riley v. Riley,* 1987 CarswellNS 57, 11 R.F.L. (3d) 105 (N.S. Fam. Ct.). A wife's claim for lump sum support to finance the parties' son's university education was dismissed as it was based on the presumption that the son would complete school.

## 7.3.5 Spousal Support — "To Secure or Pay"

In awarding support, the court may "make an order requiring a spouse to secure or pay, or to secure and pay, such lump sum or periodic sums, or such lump sum and periodic sums, as the court thinks reasonable for the support of the other spouse": *Divorce Act,* s. 15.2(1). The term "spouse" in this subsection includes a former spouse: *Divorce Act,* s. 15.

The power to "secure" support has two meanings: firstly, to post an income producing security with the income to be used as support; and, secondly, to post security as a guarantee of payment. The two meanings come from the two similar phrases used in the subsection "to secure *or* pay" and "to secure *and* pay" [emphasis added]. If the subsection contained only the first phrase, to secure or pay, the court would have no jurisdiction to order payment of support and the posting of security to be realized in default of payment. This, in fact, was the case with the 1968 *Divorce Act.* The comparable subsection in this early version of the Act contained only the power to "secure or pay" the support amount, and the judicial interpretation of this phrase at the Supreme Court of Canada clarified the distinction between the two meanings.

The subsequent addition of the second phrase "to secure *and* pay" [emphasis added] allows the court to order a spouse to pay support and, at the same time, order the spouse to post security to guarantee payment in the sense that if the spouse defaults in the obligation to pay, the security could be realized, at least to the extent of the deficiency.

The combination of the two phrases in the present Act — "to secure *or* pay, or to secure *and* pay" [emphasis added] — leads to the possibility of three kinds of orders and not merely two, as existed under the old statute:

(i) order to pay support;
(ii) order to secure support where the security yields periodic payments such as interest payments and the benefitting spouse is entitled to these payments and nothing more; and
(iii) order to secure payment of support where the order is collateral to a concurrent order to pay support and the security can be realized if there is default in payment.

287

*The phrase "secure or pay" was not broad enough to permit the court to make both an order to pay periodic sums and concurrently to order the posting of security which could be realized if there were default under the order to pay —* Nash v. Nash, 1974 CarswellOnt 140, 1974 CarswellOnt 224, 16 R.F.L. 295, [1975] 2 S.C.R. 507, 47 D.L.R. (3d) 558, 2 N.R. 271 (S.C.C.); and *Van Zyderveld v. Van Zyderveld,* 1976 CarswellAlta 104, 1976 CarswellAlta 158, 23 R.F.L. 200, [1977] 1 S.C.R. 714, 68 D.L.R. (3d) 364, [1976] 4 W.W.R. 734, 1 A.R. 14, 9 N.R. 413 (S.C.C.). The court had no power under this single phrase, it was held, to order security to stand as a guarantee of payment. An order to pay and an order to secure are two distinct and independent orders. An order to pay periodic support creates a personal obligation and a debtor-creditor relationship. Under the Act of 1968, an order to secure, on the other hand, did not impose such an obligation. If ordered to secure periodic payments, the only obligation of the spouse against whom the order was made was to provide the security and nothing more. There was no personal obligation to pay, and the spouse never became a debtor in respect of the payments. The other spouse had the benefit of the security and was required to look to it alone. If it did not yield the expected payments, the spouse putting up the security could not be called upon to make good the deficiency.

*Order requiring payor to do what is necessary to make the security effective —* Switzer v. Switzer, 1969 CarswellAlta 53, 1 R.F.L. 262, 7 D.L.R. (3d) 638, 70 W.W.R. 161 (Alta. C.A.). Per McDermid J.A., at para. 16:

> The wording in [s. 11 of the *Divorce Act,* 1968] is the court may make an order "requiring the husband to secure." The section to my mind contemplates that the court shall direct the husband to do the things that are necessary to make the security effective and may order him to execute an instrument whereby the sum ordered to be paid is effectively secured on the property. The husband, however, is not personally liable to pay the periodic sums where he has been ordered to secure such sums. In respect of any sum ordered to be paid by the court but not secured he is, of course, personally liable to pay such sums.

See also *Dexter v. Dexter,* 1975 CarswellNB 79, 11 N.B.R. (2d) 11 (N.B.C.A.).

*The court, when ordering periodic payments or a lump sum amount and at the same time providing for security of payment, must direct that the payments be paid out of the security —* Van Zyderveld v. Van Zyderveld, supra. See also *Law v. Law,* 1978 CarswellNB 206, 23 N.B.R. (2d) 114, 44 A.P.R. 114 (N.B.C.A.); and *Foy v. Foy,* 1979 CarswellOnt 356, 14 R.F.L. (2d) 12 (Ont. C.A.). Therefore, where the maintenance is ordered to be secured against a house which is further ordered to be sold, the order must show that it is the proceeds of any sale from which payment of the lump sum is to be made without attaching additional conditions for the time of sale.

*Personal guarantee not required from payor where support is secured —* Bastarache v. Bastarache, 1975 CarswellNB 17, 25 R.F.L. 72, 11 N.B.R. (2d) 564 (N.B.Q.B.). "I have considered the possibility of requiring a personal guarantee from the respondent as well but the decision in the *Nash* case [1974 CarswellOnt 140] makes it clear that, when a sum for maintenance is secured, the party providing the security is free from any further obligation in respect of the sum secured so long as the security remains in force without variation," per Stevenson J. at para. 12.

*Support is not to be a sharing of assets —* Krause v. Krause, 1975 CarswellAlta 127, 23 R.F.L. 219, [1976] 2 W.W.R. 622, 64 D.L.R. (3d) 352 (Alta. C.A.), at 227 [R.F.L.]. "In my opinion Parliament has a jurisdiction to authorize a maintenance order as an incident to a decree of divorce. Parliament may not have the power to redistribute capital assets acquired during the marriage. It is only when a lump sum is a proper way to provide maintenance or when a lump sum is necessary t put a person in a particular position that a lump sum award should be made. Granting a lump sum to reduce periodic maintenance — because capital will produce income — is really redistributing capital. Maintenance has always had a particular meaning in the law — as is shown by the English and Australian decisions — as well as our own. It does not mean a sharing of capital assets. It is doubtful that Parliament could legislate such a division", per Moir J.A.

*A court has no jurisdiction to secure maintenance payments against the interest in property of a trustee in bankruptcy as neither a claim for maintenance nor a claim for arrears of maintenance is provable in bankruptcy proceedings — Kutschenreiter v. Kutschenreiter,* 1983 CarswellOnt 174, 46 C.B.R. (N.S.) 1, [1983] O.J. No. 302 (Ont. H.C.); see also *Switzer v. Switzer, supra; J. v. J.,* 1969 CarswellSask 126, 8 D.L.R. (3d) 760 (Sask. Q.B.); *Pugh v. Pugh,* 1970 CarswellNS 49, 4 R.F.L. 213, 2 N.S.R. (2d) 409, 16 D.L.R. (3d) 318 (N.S.T.D.), at 221 [R.F.L.].

## Periodic Support — Payment Secured Against Payor's Property

*Support order secured against payor's corporate entities — Wildman v. Wildman,* 2006 CarswellOnt 6042, 33 R.F.L. (6th) 237, 25 B.L.R. (4th) 52, 273 D.L.R. (4th) 37, 82 O.R. (3d) 401, 215 O.A.C. 239, [2006] O.J. No. 3966 (Ont. C.A.), the court, on appeal, upheld an order securing the husband's support obligations against his corporate entities. The separate legal personality of a corporate entity can be disregarded in appropriate family law cases where it is completely dominated and controlled by a spouse and being used as a shield for improper conduct.

*Lump sum secured on matrimonial home — Bhatthal v. Bhatthal,* 1990 CarswellAlta 104, 28 R.F.L. (3d) 152, 74 Alta. L.R. (2d) 307, 107 A.R. 70 (Alta. Q.B.). Where the relationship between the parties was acrimonious and where the wife feared that the husband would abandon the family and return to India, the lump sum child and spousal support that the husband was ordered to pay was further ordered to be secured against the husband's interest in the family home.

*Support secured against proceeds of sale of the husband's property — Sukhram v. Sukhram,* 1987 CarswellMan 101, 7 R.F.L. (3d) 453, 47 Man. R. (2d) 126 (Man. Q.B.). Where the husband had expressed his intention never to pay spousal or child support, the wife was awarded lump sum spousal support as well as periodic child support, 15 months of which were ordered secured from the proceeds of sale of the husband's property.

*Support secured against payor's property in Ontario — Gilbert v. Gilbert,* 1972 CarswellOnt 134, 7 R.F.L. 188 (Ont. H.C.). The evidence indicated that the respondent husband had not supported his wife. Her health, as indicated by a doctor's report and the petitioner's own evidence was such that she had suffered more than one heart attack. The petitioner was 59 years of age. The respondent lived in Florida and had disposed of all assets within the jurisdiction of the court save and except a one-third interest as a tenant-in-common in a farm having an estimated value of between $500,000 and $600,000. The respondent had refused to pay any alimony or support to the petitioner because of the petitioner's refusal to bar her dower in the aforementioned farm. Periodic payments of $650 per month were secured against the husband's interest in this property. See also *Harasyn v. Harasyn,* 1970 CarswellSask 13, 2 R.F.L. 105, 13 D.L.R. (3d) 635 (Sask. Q.B.); *Grypiuk v. Grypiuk,* 1970 CarswellSask 14, 2 R.F.L. 280 (Sask. Q.B.); *Bangert v. Bangert,* 1977 CarswellNB 313, 18 N.B.R. (2d) 327 (N.B.Q.B.); *Sullivan v. Sullivan,* 1973 CarswellNB 18, 18 R.F.L. 298, 8 N.B.R. (2d) 690 (N.B.Q.B.), at 300 [R.F.L.]; *Vickers v. Vickers,* 1973 CarswellNB 21, 18 R.F.L. 338, 9 N.B.R. (2d) 96, 1 A.P.R. 96 (N.B.Q.B.), at 339 [R.F.L.]; *Golightly v. Golightly,* 1972 CarswellOnt 193, 9 R.F.L. 212 (Ont. H.C.); *Calder v. Calder,* 1974

CarswellOnt 119, 15 R.F.L. 265 (Ont. H.C.), at 267 [R.F.L.]; *Lyman v. Lyman*, 1973 CarswellNB 19, 18 R.F.L. 326, 9 N.B.R. (2d) 89, 1 A.P.R. 89 (Q.B.); and *J. v. J.*, supra.

*Periodic payments were secured by a mortgage on the equity of redemption of the husband's lands* — *Neville v. Neville*, 1980 CarswellNfld 171, 30 Nfld. & P.E.I.R. 176, 84 A.P.R. 176 (Nfld. U.F.C.), the petitioner sought an order of maintenance for herself and her children, who were receiving social assistance. The respondent gave evidence, under oath, which in effect amounted to his having no income, no savings, no prospects of work, nor was he in a position to provide any maintenance to his wife and children. However, in view of the fact that the respondent husband had a $4,000 equity in some parcels of land, periodic payments were secured by a mortgage on the equity of redemption in the husband's lands.

## Lump Sum — Securing Awards

*Lump sum — jurisdiction to secure awards* — *Morrison v. Morrison*, 1971 CarswellBC 24, 4 R.F.L. 399 (B.C.S.C.). See also *Olynyk v. Olynyk*, 1932 CarswellAlta 24, [1932] 1 W.W.R. 825, 26 Alta. L.R. 485, [1932] 2 D.L.R. 785 (B.C.C.A.). The court lacks jurisdiction to order a husband's property to be registered in the wife's name under the guise of securing maintenance to the wife. See also *Brickman v. Brickman*, 1982 CarswellOnt 274, 27 R.F.L. (2d) 391 (Ont. C.A.).

*Lump sum — jurisdiction to secure awards* — *Hind v. Hind*, 1975 CarswellOnt 157, 20 R.F.L. 331 (Ont. Div. Ct.). Where the parties have sold the jointly owned matrimonial home, there is no jurisdiction in a District Court judge to order the husband to pay his share of the proceeds into court as security for a possible maintenance order in favour of the wife in a future divorce hearing.

*Lump sum — corporate property not subject to charge* — *Adams v. Adams*, 1970 CarswellNB 167, 3 N.B.R. (2d) 451 (N.B.C.A.). The husband transferred two properties, which constituted his main assets, to a holding company in order to put them out of the reach of the wife who was claiming maintenance. The court held that there was no authority to support an order securing maintenance payments by making them a charge upon property not belonging to the husband but to a company which the husband owns or controls. See also *Minty v. Minty*, 1977 CarswellBC 194, 4 R.F.L. (2d) 1, 5 B.C.L.R. 119 (B.C.S.C.), at 2 [R.F.L.]; *Lister v. Lister*, 1970 CarswellOnt 161, 3 R.F.L. 194, [1971] 1 O.R. 149, 14 D.L.R. (3d) 641 (Ont. H.C.).

*Lump sum secured on matrimonial home* — *Andrews v. Andrews*, 1980 CarswellOnt 339, 21 R.F.L. (2d) 348, [1980] O.J. No. 1503 (Ont. C.A.). A judge has no power under the *Divorce Act* to direct the sale of a matrimonial home. However, a trial judge may order that one spouse secure payment to the other of a lump sum, charged together with interest on the payor's share of the matrimonial home. Consequently, upon the sale of the home, all maintenance arrears would be a charge upon the payor's share of the proceeds.

*Lump sum secured on matrimonial home* — *payment deferred until matrimonial home sold* — *Lachance v. Lachance*, 1976 CarswellMan 15, 28 R.F.L. 186 (Man. C.A.), at 187 [R.F.L.]. "There have been many cases . . . where a husband has been ordered to pay a lump sum equivalent to the value of his equity in the family home. But the amount to be paid should be specified. It is often provided that a husband may satisfy payment by transferring his equity or an appropriate part of it to the wife. Here, payment was to be deferred until the property would be sold. There is no way of knowing now what the value of the equity would be when that event occurs. In our view, this is not an order for payment of a lump sum. In our opinion, an appropriate order, under all the circumstances here, would be to require a lump sum payment of $5,000 to be secured against the husband's equity in the home, the lump sum to be payable when the property is sold", per Monnin J.A.

*Lump sum payment against matrimonial home set aside — payor to secure to payee lump sum payment by way of mortgage against matrimonial home — McConnell v. McConnell*, 1975 CarswellNB 80, 57 D.L.R. (3d) 268, 11 N.B.R. (2d) 19 (N.B.C.A.), at 22 [N.B.R.]. "With this in mind I would vary the order of the trial Judge and set aside the lump sum payment of $25,000 as creating too great a hardship on the appellant [husband] which could affect his ability to make the periodic payments. In lieu thereof I would order the appellant to secure to the petitioner, the payment of $25,000 by way of a mortgage on the matrimonial home, and 1 acre of land including that on which the house is situate and access to the highway road and a chattel mortgage on the household effects, furniture and fixtures in the matrimonial home subject to any mortgage or mortgages now in effect thereon, without interest and without recourse against the appellant, payable in two years from the date of this judgement", per Limerick J.A.

*Lump sum secured on matrimonial home on certain conditions — Chadderton v. Chadderton*, 1972 CarswellOnt 175, 8 R.F.L. 374, [1973] 1 O.R. 560, 31 D.L.R. (3d) 656 (Ont. C.A.). The Court of Appeal held that a judge in Ontario has no authority under the *Divorce Act* to order one spouse to transfer real estate or specific assets to the other spouse, although Arnup J.A., said he thought there ought to be such a provision. It seems clear, then, that I have no authority to order directly the result which I think would be fair in this case. I think that I can accomplish that result indirectly, however, by varying the form of the order made in the *Chadderton* case. There will be an order requiring the husband to secure in favour of the wife the lump sum of $36,000, upon certain conditions. See also *Gloude v. Gloude*, 1976 CarswellOnt 562, 14 O.R. (2d) 571, 74 D.L.R. (3d) 405 (Ont. H.C.), at 407-08 [D.L.R.]; *Schell v. Schell*, 1976 CarswellBC 444, 29 R.F.L. 349 (B.C.S.C.), at 351 [R.F.L.]; *Davis v. Davis*, 1979 CarswellAlta 359, 23 A.R. 440 (Q.B.); *Vosper v. Vosper*, 1981 CarswellMan 279, 7 Man. R. (2d) 92 (Man. Q.B.); *Leitch v. Leitch*, 1978 CarswellAlta 341, 12 A.R. 65 (Alta. T.D.), at 72 [A.R.]; *Stevens v. Stevens*, 1977 CarswellNB 304, 17 N.B.R. (2d) 656 (N.B.Q.B.), at 662 [N.B.R.]; *Ottho v. Ottho*, 1974 CarswellBC 61, 20 R.F.L.1 (B.C.S.C.), at 2 [R.F.L.]; *Johnson v. Johnson*, 1975 CarswellAlta 9, 23 R.F.L. 293 (Alta. T.D.), at 302 [R.F.L.]; *Bandura v. Bandura*, 1977 CarswellAlta 447, 6 A.R. 478 (Alta. T.D.), at 484 [A.R.]; *Wagner v. Wagner*, 1970 CarswellAlta 85, 73 W.W.R. 474 (Alta. S.C.); and *Schulte v. Schulte*, 1972 CarswellOnt 115, 6 R.F.L. 164 (Ont. S.C.); *Secord v. Secord*, 1978 CarswellPEI 16, 2 R.F.L. (2d) 97, [1978] P.E.I.J. No. 111  (P.E.I.T.D.); *Kinshella v. Kinshella*, 1976 CarswellAlta 68, 30 R.F.L. 297 (Alta. T.D.).

*Lump sum — grounds for securing or refusing to secure awards — no evidence that payor will not comply with the order — Guberman v. Guberman*, 1976 CarswellMan 88, 27 R.F.L. 15, [1977] 2 W.W.R. 1 (Man. C.A.), at 21 [R.F.L.]. "On the issue of the appellant [husband] providing security, I am unable to find any evidence or real or apprehended concern that the appellant will not comply with the maintenance order. It is true that the respondent has taken up residence in California and that the appellant's business interests are in Manitoba and Canada, but that is her choice. . . Should the circumstances change, making the provision of security essential, that can be appropriately obtained", per Hall J.A.

*Lump sum — grounds for securing or refusing to secure awards — payor failed to pay support for 17 years — Bradshaw v. Bradshaw*, 1975 CarswellOnt 245, 24 R.F.L. 200 (Ont. C.A.), at 200-01 [R.F.L.]. "The evidence is clear that the respondent ... [husband] deserted the petitioner in 1959, leaving her with two daughters. From that time until the present, the petitioner supported not only herself, but the two daughters without any assistance from the respondent. There was an order in the Family Court for payment, but it appears that this order was not productive. ... The petitioner now wishes a lump sum award to be made, and that lump sum to be secured against the property. The end product of this sought-after lump sum award is to, in effect, make the petitioner the sole owner of the property. In our opinion, this is a fit case for the making of such an order in view of the efforts expended by the petitioner in the past. The decree *nisi* will be varied by adding an order that the respondent pay the petitioner a lump sum in the amount of $25,000, this lump sum award to be secured against the property in question", per Zuber J.A.

*Lump sum — grounds for securing or refusing to secure awards — payor failed to pay support — Garratt v. Garratt*, 1974 CarswellBC 223, 16 R.F.L. 168, [1974] 6 W.W.R. 659 (B.C.S.C.), at 171 [R.F.L.]. "[The husband] is unwilling to pay his former wife anything. He left his salaried job last July and took work as a commission salesman for a building supply company. At the time of the second hearing he was out of work. He has established a relationship with another woman and she and her two children live with him. ... [The wife] is working at two jobs and has had to carry the burden of the support of the children. The Registrar has recommended that the respondent pay $50 per month for each of the three children, and I confirmed that part of the recommendation on 17th April 1974. With respect, I think that the Registrar has come to the correct conclusion on the maintenance for the petitioner in his recommendation that the respondent pay a lump sum of $10,000 which, when paid, will end the obligations of the respondent for the maintenance and support of the petitioner. I propose to adopt the procedure that was followed by the Court of Appeal of Ontario in *Chadderton v. Chadderton, supra*, to require the respondent to secure in favour of the petitioner the lump sum of $10,000", per Hutcheon L.J.S.C. See also *Redding v. Redding*, 1976 CarswellNfld 117, 13 Nfld. & P.E.I.R. 214, 29 A.P.R. 214 (Nfld. T.D.), at 216 [Nfld. & P.E.I.R.].

*Lump sum — grounds for securing or refusing to secure awards — wife could not claim a charge against the half interest registered in the name of the trustee in bankruptcy in an application for maintenance — Sundholm v. Sundholm*, 1980 CarswellOnt 273, 17 R.F.L. (2d) 365 (Ont. H.C.). A trustee in bankruptcy obtained title to the husband's interest in the matrimonial home by virtue of the operation of a court order, which was registered on title after the petition was issued but before the matter came on for trial. See also *Kutschenreiter v. Kutschenreiter, supra; Brocklebank v. Brocklebank*, 1975 CarswellBC 72, 25 R.F.L. 53 (B.C.S.C.), at 70 [R.F.L.]; *Mesrobian v. Mesrobian*, 1978 CarswellOnt 260, 4 R.F.L. (2d) 341 (Ont. H.C.), at 346 [R.F.L.]; *Jacyk v. Jacyk*, 1970 CarswellOnt 106, 1 R.F.L. 274 (Ont. H.C.), at 275 [R.F.L.], reversed 1970 CarswellOnt 138, 2 R.F.L. 412 (Ont. C.A.); *Jackson v. Jackson*, 1976 CarswellOnt 125, 24 R.F.L. 109 (Ont. H.C.), at 118 [R.F.L.]; *Dart v. Dart*, 1974 CarswellOnt 88, 14 R.F.L. 97 (Ont. H.C.), at 100-01 [R.F.L.]; *J. v. J., supra*, at 763 [D.L.R.]; *Holewa v. Holewa*, 1977 CarswellAlta 77, 6 A.R. 476, 3 Alta. L.R. (2d) 253 (Alta. T.D.).

### 7.3.6 Lump Sum — In Addition to Periodic Sums

*Lump sum and periodic support ordered — lump sum spousal support may be granted, regardless of whether there is a risk of non-payment of support — Vynnyk v. Baisa*, 2007 CarswellOnt 403, 38 R.F.L. (6th) 344, [2007] O.J. No. 274 (Ont. S.C.J.), additional reasons at 2007 CarswellOnt 9218, 52 R.F.L. (6th) 328 (Ont. S.C.J.), affirmed 2008 CarswellOnt 5629, 2008 ONCA 657, 55 R.F.L. (6th) 239, [2008] O.J. No. 3747 (Ont. C.A.). The court stated at paras. 125-26:

> ... If the element of risk of non-payment were always required, however, there would be no way a Court could make a combined periodic and lump sum award since each is based on a different premise. Periodic support is based on the premise the payor will pay but lump sum would have to be based on the premised the payor would not.

> That would be inconsistent with the *Divorce Act*, R.S.C. 1997, c. 1, s.2, which clearly contemplates situations where both forms of support are awarded. Section 15.2 of the *Divorce Act* reads: "A court ... may ... make an order requiring one spouse to secure or

pay, or to secure and pay, such lump sum or periodic sums, or *such lump sum and periodic sums*, as the court thinks reasonable ... [Emphasis added].

The court ordered lump sum support of $75,000 in addition to the periodic support, taking the tax implications into account.

*Lump sum and ongoing periodic spousal support ordered* — *Card v. Card*, 2009 CarswellBC 1696, 2009 BCSC 865 (B.C.S.C.), additional reasons at 2009 CarswellBC 2484, 2009 BCSC 1268 (B.C.S.C.). The parties were married for 18 years and had three children. The wife was a traditional stay-at-home mother for the majority of the marriage. The wife brought an application for spousal support. The court ordered that the husband pay the wife $60,000 in lump sum and $500 per month in periodic spousal support for an indefinite period (the court allowed for a review after 6 years). The wife needed the $60,000 to pay for the husband's share of the matrimonial home. The court noted that the combination of lump sum and ongoing spousal support was warranted, based on the 18-year marriage which significantly disadvantaged the wife economically.

*Lump sum — in addition to periodic sums* — *Wolch v. Wolch*, 1981 CarswellMan 25, 20 R.F.L. (2d) 325 (Man. C.A.). Where the husband was ordered to pay the wife periodic maintenance from the date of petition, the court, on an appeal of the maintenance provision, varied the decree *nisi* to provide for periodic payments payable from the date of hearing and a lump sum payable in lieu of arrears of interim maintenance accruing from the date of petition.

*Lump sum — in addition to periodic sums* — *Maillet v. Maillet*, 1975 CarswellNB 19, 25 R.F.L. 126, 13 N.B.R. (2d) 330 (N.B.Q.B.), at 127-28 [R.F.L.]. "The monthly sum agreed to be paid by the husband could not in any way be considered adequate even for the maintenance of the children, although it would not appear desirable for practical purposes to fix that amount any higher. I am satisfied that these are proper circumstances in which to require the respondent to pay to the petitioner, in addition to the periodical payments for the maintenance of the children, a lump sum in respect of the future maintenance of the wife", per Dickson J. See also *Van Snick v. Van Snick*, 1978 CarswellNS 202, 27 N.S.R. (2d) 127, 41 A.P.R. 127 (N.S.C.A.).

*Lump sum — in addition to periodic sums* — *Eisenhauer v. Eisenhauer*, 1975 CarswellNS 162, 14 N.S.R. (2d) 164 (N.S.C.A.). When a lump sum is awarded as maintenance, the monthly allowance which otherwise would be granted must be appropriately reduced or even eliminated. See also *Dexter v. Dexter*, 1975 CarswellNB 79, 11 N.B.R. (2d) 11 (N.B.C.A.), where the wife was awarded two lump sums in lieu of a single lump sum and periodic maintenance.

*Lump sum — in addition to periodic sums* — *Rathwell v. Rathwell*, 1974 CarswellSask 26, 16 R.F.L. 387 (Sask. Q.B.), at 394-95 [R.F.L.]. "Lump-sum payments are given when such are necessary in order to provide reasonable maintenance in the light of the particular circumstances, because the giving of periodic payments alone would not result in providing such maintenance. ... Generally reasonable maintenance can be provided by ordering periodic payments alone, and by so doing the court maintains the power to vary its order from time to time in order to do justice to both parties whenever a change in circumstances requires that such be done ... when the court finds that a petitioner is entitled to a maintenance order the court should, generally speaking, first order periodic payments, and then, when it is necessary in order to provide proper maintenance, to order a lump-sum payment in addition to the periodic payments", per Disbery J. See also *Juby v. Juby*, 1977 CarswellOnt 156, 3 R.F.L. (2d) 323 (Ont. H.C.); *Lawrence v. Lawrence*, 1981 CarswellNS 52, 20 R.F.L. (2d) 414, 45 N.S.R. (2d) 541, 86 A.P.R. 541 (N.S.T.D.), at 418-19 [R.F.L.], where the circumstances warranted both a lump sum award and periodic payments; and *Van Mehren v. Van Mehren*, [1970] 1 All E.R. 153, [1970] P. 185, [1970] 1 W.L.R. 56 (Eng. C.A.); *Hutchinson v. Hutchinson*, 1972 CarswellMan 29, 6 R.F.L. 353, [1972] 3 W.W.R. 59, 25 D.L.R. (3d) 23 (Man. Q.B.), at 357 [R.F.L.].

## 7.3.7 Lump Sum — Calculations

Where the wife was a part-time practicing lawyer, a court could take into account her ability to support herself and her substantial "non-family" assets when it concluded that a lump sum payment of $150,000 for spousal support would reasonably compensate the wife for being unable to earn what her husband could earn in the practice of law, having devoted much of her time to raising the children during and after the marriage — Q. (R.E.) v. K. (G.J.), 2012 CarswellBC 887, 2012 BCCA 146, 17 R.F.L. (7th) 255, 31 B.C.L.R. (5th) 264, 348 D.L.R. (4th) 622, [2012] 8 W.W.R. 270, 319 B.C.A.C. 98, 542 W.A.C. 98 (B.C.C.A.), additional reasons 2012 CarswellBC 1774, 2012 BCCA 267, 17 R.F.L. (7th) 291, 31 B.C.L.R. (5th) 300, [2012] 8 W.W.R. 306 (B.C.C.A.). It was not reasonable for the trial judge to choose the sum of $150,000, which is approximately mid-way between the amounts sought by the respective parties.

Where a court awards lump sum spousal support instead of periodic support, it is preferable that the court consider whether the amount awarded is in keeping with the Spousal Support Advisory Guidelines. If it is not, some reasons should be provided for why the Guidelines do not provide an appropriate result — Davis v. Crawford, 2011 CarswellOnt 2512, 2011 ONCA 294, 95 R.F.L. (6th) 257, 106 O.R. (3d) 221, 332 D.L.R. (4th) 508, 277 O.A.C. 200, [2011] O.J. No. 1719 (Ont. C.A.), additional reasons at 2011 CarswellOnt 4562, 2011 ONCA 423, [2011] O.J. No. 1719, [2011] O.J. No. 2637 (Ont. C.A.). The court cited Fisher v. Fisher, 2008 CarswellOnt 43, 2008 ONCA 11, 47 R.F.L. (6th) 235, 88 O.R. (3d) 241, 288 D.L.R. (4th) 513, 232 O.A.C. 213, [2008] O.J. No. 38 (Ont. C.A.), at para. 103. The trial judge had awarded lump sum spousal support of $135,000. The Court of Appeal concluded that the trial judge awarded an amount of support that she concluded would generate an income stream of $1,000 per month for 15 years using a 4% interest rate. Although the trial judge did not specifically refer to the income tax consequences of a lump sum award, as the trial judge was an experienced family law judge, the appellate court considered that the trial judge would have taken income tax consequences into her calculations. Given the woman's age of 66 and no evidence that she was not in good health, it was not unreasonable to use a 15-year income stream projection. There had been a 23-year relationship with no children. The lump sum award was upheld on appeal. [This decision was decided under the Ontario Family Law Act. However the Divorce Act was discussed, and the case may well be useful for cases under the Divorce Act.]

Where restructuring does not result in a lump sum amount that is consistent with the Divorce Act, an exception to the SSAG will be found in determining quantum of the lump sum where the payor has serious health issues — support award calculation software is not helpful for lump sum awards based on restructured support — Robinson v. Robinson, 2011 CarswellBC 3271, 2011 BCSC 1489, 14 R.F.L. (7th) 141 (B.C.S.C.), affirmed 2012 CarswellBC 3789, 2012 BCCA 497, 25 R.F.L. (7th) 47, 40 B.C.L.R. (5th) 108 (B.C.C.A.). The trail judge awarded lump sum spousal support under the without child formula. The parties were married for 28 years and had two adult, independent children. The trial judge found that the wife had a claim for compensatory support and used the SSAG in order to determine monthly support of $6,000, or a mid-range amount. She then found that lump sum spousal support was indicated given the possible difficulty of collecting payments as the husband had moved to Germany, the husband's poor health, and his income. However, the trial judge found that the lump sum indicated by the computer analysis did not meet the objectives of the Divorce Act and the trial judge preferred another method of calculation. Consequently, the trial judge made an order based on "the factors of relative tax situations, an appropriate discount rate for the present value, and a contingency rate where necessary". Given the poor health of the husband, the lump sum award was less than it would have been otherwise. The judge found that this case fell within the exceptions of the SSAG found at s. 3.4.2. The decision was upheld by the Court of Appeal.

*Determining the correct lump sum is not a simple mathematical exercise* — *Hartshorne v. Hartshorne*, 2009 CarswellBC 1398, 2009 BCSC 698, 70 R.F.L. (6th) 106, [2009] B.C.J. No. 1050 (B.C.S.C.), reversed in part 2010 CarswellBC 1618, 2010 BCCA 327, 82 R.F.L. (6th) 1, 6 B.C.L.R. (5th) 58, 320 D.L.R. (4th) 398, 289 B.C.A.C. 244, 489 W.A.C. 244, [2010] B.C.J. No. 1271 (B.C.C.A.), additional reasons at 2011 CarswellBC 107, 2011 BCCA 29, 95 R.F.L. (6th) 14, 330 D.L.R. (4th) 503, 14 B.C.L.R. (5th) 33, 299 B.C.A.C. 6, 508 W.A.C. 6, [2011] B.C.J. No. 107 (B.C.C.A.). The court considered the award it would have made without the assistance of SSAG, the quantums generated by the wife's counsel, and the quantum the court calculated using 2 years of SSAG monthly support plus an 8-year lump sum. It found that the wife was entitled to lump sum retroactive spousal support in the amount of $350,000 payable on February 28, 2001, the date of Beames J.'s second and final judgement. The court decided that the amount was not too high considering the standard of living that the parties had during their marriage.

*The Spousal Support Advisory Guidelines will be used to determine the amount of a lump sum award of spousal support* — *Karisik v. Chow*, 2010 CarswellBC 3272, 2010 BCCA 548, 94 R.F.L. (6th) 70, 12 B.C.L.R. (5th) 107, 301 B.C.A.C. 133, 510 W.A.C. 133 (B.C.C.A.). Leave to appeal refused 2011 CarswellBC 1436, 2011 CarswellBC 1437, 305 B.C.A.C. 320 (note), 425 N.R. 390 (note), 515 W.A.C. 320 (note), [2011] S.C.C.A. No. 59 (S.C.C.). The wife appealed a trial decision which awarded her lump sum spousal support based on a monthly periodic amount. The trial judge used the *Spousal Support Advisory Guidelines* in order to determine an appropriate amount and duration of support. The wife objected to the award of lump sum, rather than periodic, support. The Court of Appeal held that the trial judge reasonably exercised his discretion in awarding lump sum support on the basis that this would assist the wife in retaining the matrimonial home.

*Conversion to lump sum by comparison of cost-to-payor or versus value-to-recipient* — *Roach v. Dutra*, 2009 CarswellBC 487, 2009 BCSC 229, [2009] B.C.J. No. 353 (B.C.S.C.), additional reasons at 2009 CarswellBC 1375, 2009 BCSC 693, 70 R.F.L. (6th) 410 (B.C.S.C.), affirmed 2010 CarswellBC 1267, 2010 BCCA 264, 82 R.F.L. (6th) 42, 87 C.P.C. (6th) 239, 5 B.C.L.R. (5th) 95, 288 B.C.A.C. 141, 488 W.A.C. 141 (B.C.C.A.). An appropriate periodic award was determined through reference to the SSAG. The court then found that the cost to the payor of paying the global amount as a lump sum would be between $25,000 and $34,000, while the value of the benefit to the recipient would be between $31,000 and $43,000. The lump sum owing was fixed at $30,000.

*Lump sum spousal support will include calculations of tax repercussions and contingencies including early retirement* — *Marsh v. Marsh*, 2012 CarswellBC 3330, 2012 BCSC 1597 (B.C.S.C.), additional reasons 2013 CarswellBC 813, 2013 BCSC 567 (B.C.S.C.). The parties had a 24-year marriage, and the husband had a new partner with whom he wished to move to Alberta. Lump sum spousal support on a compensatory and non-compensatory basis was ordered. Support was based on Divorcemate calculations or a formulaic approach with contingencies and tax repercussions included.

*Lump sum support will be based on the entitlement of the spouse to periodic support* — *Grimba v. Bossi*, 2012 CarswellOnt 2934, 2012 ONSC 1386, [2012] O.J. No. 956 (Ont. S.C.J.), additional reasons at 2012 CarswellOnt 5840, 2012 ONSC 2290 (Ont. S.C.J.). The parties had very little ability to communicate. They had two adult dependent children. They were married for 19 years. The judge found that the wife was entitled to compensatory spousal support for a further 10 years and based the calculation of the lump sum payment on that time period.

*Time value of money considered in converting periodic award to lump sum* — *Freeman v. Freeman*, 2008 CarswellBC 1366, 2008 BCSC 857, [2008] B.C.J. No. 1247 (B.C.S.C.), additional reasons at 2008 CarswellBC 2386, 2008 BCSC 1462, [2008] B.C.J. No. 2065 (B.C.S.C.). The appropriate periodic payments, calculated using the *Spousal Support Advisory*

*Guidelines*, totaled $11,550. Taking into account that the recipient would have immediate access to the money, a lump sum of $10,000 was ordered. (This equates to a discount of approximately 8.85% per year).

*Non-compensatory claim for spousal support awarded as a lump sum and later reduced to reflect the tax consequences* — Arnold v. Arnold, 2009 CarswellBC 2684, 2009 BCSC 1384 (B.C.S.C.), additional reasons at 2010 CarswellBC 278, 2010 BCSC 166 (B.C.S.C.). The wife had a reasonable claim for non-compensatory spousal support at the low end of the SSAG range. The wife was awarded support of $1,365 per month for a period of 3.5 years. In accordance with the parties' preference, a lump sum award of $57,330 was made. In additional reasons, the court reduced the support order by 30% to reflect the tax consequences of a lump sum award.

*Lump sum reduced by 50% to account for future contingencies* — Raymond v. Raymond, 2008 CarswellOnt 7939, 64 R.F.L. (6th) 160, [2008] O.J. No. 5294 (Ont. S.C.J.). Having chosen the mid-range SSAG figure as appropriate and having decided to order a lump sum, the judge calculated the lump sum. The SSAG quantum of $3,246 per month was reduced to a net amount of $2,240. This amount was multiplied by the number of months in the mid-range SSAG duration, and then reduced by 6% to account for the time-value of money. Finally, it was reduced by 50% "to take into account future contingencies."

*Lump sum ordered — no adjustment for tax implications* — Reavie v. Heaps, 2008 CarswellBC 1624, 2008 BCSC 1038, 58 R.F.L. (6th) 111, [2008] B.C.J. No. 1461 (B.C.S.C.). The trial judge found that the SSAG quantum range was $2,175 to $2,900 per year, and that the duration range was 0.5 to 1.0 years. A lump sum of $2,900 was ordered, without any adjustment for tax implications.

*Lump sum ordered with specified reductions* — Durakovic v. Durakovic, 2008 CarswellOnt 5329, [2008] O.J. No. 3537 (Ont. S.C.J.). The court summarized when lump sum awards should be awarded and then determined that the wife was entitled to a lump sum award. The court awarded the wife spousal support of $3,500 for 28 months, reduced 30% for income tax, 3% for present value, and 25% for negative contingencies.

*Conversion to lump sum with tax adjustment* — Martin v. Martin, 2007 CarswellOnt 683, [2007] O.J. No. 467 (Ont. S.C.J.), additional reasons at 2007 CarswellOnt 1574 (Ont. S.C.J.). This case offers an example of conversion of a SSAG-based periodic support award being converted to a lump sum. See also *Smith v. Smith*, 2006 CarswellBC 2761, 2006 BCSC 1655, [2006] B.C.J. No. 2920 (B.C.S.C.).

*Lump sum awarded where husband unemployed but expected to return to work — wife in need* — Poisson v. Poisson, 1993 CarswellOnt 315, 46 R.F.L. (3d) 105, [1993] O.J. No. 705 (Ont. Gen. Div.). Where the husband was unemployed because of health reasons, but the wife required financial support, the court ordered him to pay lump sum support. The lump sum was calculated on the assumption that the husband would return to work and the gross sum determined by calculating the periodic support which would otherwise be payable until the date of the husband's retirement. The amount was discounted to reflect the tax payable on the funds, the present value of the funds and for negative contingencies such as remarriage or loss of employment.

See also McLeod, Mamo, *Annual Review of Family Law 2012*, at pages 558-59, which provides:

> In order to approximate the benefit to the recipient and the cost to the payor, to the value of periodic time limited order, the calculation of the lump sum has to include an adjustment for the following factors
>
> > (i) The difference in tax treatment: Periodic payments are tax deductible/tax includable, a lump sum is tax neutral ...

(ii) Present value discount. The value of having all of the money paid at once, up front rather than over time. Most courts are using a formulaic method to discounting ...

(iii) Future contingencies, relating to changes in financial circumstances of each party or significant life events with financial consequences, such as changes in income, marital status, mortality retirement, disability etc. ...

## 7.3.8 Miscellaneous

*Where the husband, the payor spouse, argued that lump sum spousal support was granted to enable the wife, the payee spouse, to complete the requirements for her teaching degree and she did not do so, she will not be ordered to re-pay the award* — Foster v. Foster, 2013 CarswellBC 1134, 2013 BCCA 205 (B.C.C.A.). The appellate court affirmed the reasons of the trial judge that when the payor was before the Court of Appeal, he was aware that his wife was working and that she had not continued her post-secondary education in Canada. The appellate court informed the husband that he would need to bring an application to vary the spousal support award at the Supreme Court. He acted to his own detriment in waiting three years to do so.

*The payment of a global sum representing both a lump sum spousal support award and an unequal division of matrimonial assets cannot stand as they have different prerequisites, functions and consequences* — Werner v. Werner, 2013 CarswellNS 20, 2013 NSCA 6, 325 N.S.R. (2d) 175, 1031 A.P.R. 175 (N.S.C.A.). The court varied the $125,000 award by ascribing $30,000 to a division of matrimonial property and $95,000 as a lump sum for spousal support.

*Reasons must be given for an award of lump sum support; periodic support awarded, being the aggregate of unpaid monthly payments* — Rockall v. Rockall, 2010 CarswellAlta 1859, 2010 ABCA 278, 90 R.F.L. (6th) 317, 35 Alta. L.R. (5th) 1, 490 A.R. 135, 497 W.A.C. 135, [2010] A.J. No. 1064 (Alta. C.A.). Since the failure to give reasons amounts to an error, the lump sum arrears award was set aside and replaced with an order for periodic support totalling the same amount.

*Lump sum set off against amount payable by support payee to support payor* — Newstone v. Newstone, 1994 CarswellBC 202, 2 R.F.L. (4th) 129, 91 B.C.L.R. (2d) 246, 39 B.C.A.C. 223, 64 W.A.C. 223, [1994] B.C.J. No. 139 (B.C.C.A.). The court could properly award lump sum support to a wife by setting the sum off against funds which the wife would otherwise be required to pay to the husband. Such an order does not amount to an improper redistribution of capital.

*An unmarried spouse may be required to pay lump sum spousal support from assets not subject to the provincial property regime* — Davis v. Crawford, 2009 CarswellOnt 2612, 71 R.F.L. (6th) 54, [2009] O.J. No. 1959 (Ont. S.C.J.), affirmed 2011 CarswellOnt 2512, 2011 ONCA 294, 95 R.F.L. (6th) 257, 106 O.R. (3d) 221, 332 D.L.R. (4th) 508, 277 O.A.C. 200, [2011] O.J. No. 1719 (Ont. C.A.), additional reasons at 2011 CarswellOnt 4562, 2011 ONCA 423, [2011] O.J. No. 2637 (Ont. C.A.).

*No review of support will be ordered when a lump sum award of support is made* — Marsh v. Marsh, 2012 CarswellBC 3330, 2012 BCSC 1597 (B.C.S.C.), additional reasons 2013 CarswellBC 813, 2013 BCSC 567 (B.C.S.C.). The parties had a 24-year marriage, and the husband had a new partner with whom he wished to move to Alberta. Lump sum spousal support on a compensatory and non-compensatory basis was ordered. The judge found a clean break was required and declined to order a review at age 65, finding that lump sum support was a one-time payment and to order a review would defeat the purpose of the clean break.

*Husband not required to sell farm to fund support* — *Knoth v. Knoth*, 2003 CarswellBC 579, 2003 BCSC 417, 38 R.F.L. (5th) 123, [2003] B.C.J. No. 615 (B.C.S.C.). The court refused the wife's application for an order compelling the husband to sell his farm to make funds available for the payment of spousal support. The farm was the only source of the husband's income, and the sale would prevent him from earning anything in the traditional way he had.

*Division of pension not contrary to* Pension Benefits Act — *Nicholas v. Nicholas*, 1998 CarswellOnt 1828, 37 R.F.L. (4th) 13, 17 C.C.P.B. 130, 61 O.T.C. 371, 1998 C.E.B. & P.G.R. 8339 (headnote only), [1998] O.J. No. 1750 (Ont. Gen. Div.). An order requiring that the entirety of the husband's pension be transferred to the wife, 50% to be paid as a registered retirement savings and the other 50% as pension in pay on a monthly basis, does not contravene the *Pension Benefits Act*, R.S.O. 1990, c. P.8.

See also McLeod, Mamo, *Annual Review of Family Law 2012*, at pages 558-59.

## 7.4 Review Terms

**Terms and conditions** — *support orders specifying review*

See also **Chapter 10, section 10.17 Review Proceedings**.

## 7.5 Support Order as an Obligation of the Payor's Estate

*Although there is no express provision in the Divorce Act obliging the payor's estate to pay a spousal support order, there is authority for a trial judge to make a support payor's estate pay a support order* — *Linton v. Linton*, 1988 CarswellOnt 198, 11 R.F.L. (3d) 444, 64 O.R. (2d) 18, 49 D.L.R. (4th) 278, 29 E.T.R. 14 (Ont. H.C.), affirmed 1990 CarswellOnt 316, 30 R.F.L. (3d) 1, 1 O.R. (3d) 1, 75 D.L.R. (4th) 637, 41 E.T.R. 85, 42 O.A.C. 328 (Ont. C.A.). The court noted that s. 34(4) of the Ontario *Family Law Act, 1986* "provides that a support order is binding on the payor's estate if no order to the contrary is made." The court considered that making a support order binding on the payor's estate is consistent with s. 15(7)(a) of the *Divorce Act* in cases where there has been a traditional marriage. Such an order takes account of the economic disadvantages arising from the marriage and its breakdown. The court held, among other things, that the husband's estate should be bound by the spousal support order.

*A court does not have the jurisdiction on the granting of a divorce to order the payor's estate to pay periodic spousal support if the payor predeceases the payee* — *Black v. Black*, 1981 CarswellNS 397, 123 D.L.R. (3d) 499, 46 N.S.R. (2d) 361, 89 A.P.R. 3 (N.S.T.D.).

# CHAPTER 8
## DETERMINATION OF INCOME

The incomes of both parties are of central importance in determining appropriate spousal support, as the SSAG are income-based guidelines. Income is the most important, although not the only, relevant element in the financial "means" and "needs" to which s. 15.2(4) makes reference. See ss. 5.2 and 5.3 of this volume for commentary and cases about the means and needs of the party from whom support is sought and the party who seeks support, respectively.

The *Federal Child Support Guidelines*, P.C. 1997-469 and the provincial equivalents (collectively, CSG) only have legal effect with regard to child support. However, the income calculation provisions found in ss. 15 through 20 and Schedule III of the CSG are commonly used to calculate the parties' incomes for spousal support purposes as well, especially if both child support and spousal support are at issue, courts routinely do so without comment. These portions of the CSG, which are reproduced below, are also the starting point for the definition of income under the *Spousal Support Advisory Guidelines* (SSAG). See also Carol Rogerson and Rollie Thompson, "Spousal Support Advisory Guidelines, July 2008" at 6.1; *M. (P.R.) v. M. (B.J.)*, 2013 CarswellBC 2204, 2013 BCCA 327, 34 R.F.L. (7th) 1, 340 B.C.A.C. 198, 579 W.A.C. 198, [2013] B.C.J. No. 1530 (B.C.C.A.); *Brandl v. Rolston*, 2013 CarswellBC 1273, 2013 BCCA 235, 31 R.F.L. (7th) 296, 362 D.L.R. (4th) 439, 338 B.C.A.C. 141, 577 W.A.C. 141 (B.C.C.A.); *Ouellette v. Ouellette*, 2012 CarswellBC 904, 2012 BCCA 145, 16 R.F.L. (7th) 39, 32 B.C.L.R. (5th) 67, 319 B.C.A.C. 160, 542 W.A.C. 160 (B.C.C.A.); *Smith v. Smith*, 2012 CarswellOnt 3113, 2012 ONSC 1116, [2012] O.J. No. 800 (Ont. S.C.J.), at para.76; and *Ludmer v. Ludmer*, 2013 CarswellOnt 1625, 2013 ONSC 784, 33 R.F.L. (7th) 331, [2013] O.J. No. 699 (Ont. S.C.J.), at para. 151.

However, there are certain salient distinctions between income calculation methods for child support and spousal support. Chapter 11.3 describes a number of alterations which must be made to the FCSG calculations when the SSAG are being used. In one sense, income is less important in spousal support law than in child support law. While determination of income is often effectively dispositive of a child support dispute, it is only one component of needs and means analysis in a spousal support dispute. On the other hand, income determination can be seen as more important in spousal support law in the sense that two incomes (that of the recipient and that of the payor) are always in issue.

Some courts may be less willing to impute income for the purpose of spousal support than they are for the purpose of child support. This reflects the idea that children have a more compelling claim on a payor's income than former spouses do, a principle which is reflected in s. 15.3 of the *Divorce Act*. For commentary on s. 15.3 and a general discussion of the relationship between spousal support and child support, see s. 9.3 of this volume. Note that income from stock options or income which can arguably be characterized as capital property may also be included for child support but not spousal support.

[See User's Guide, March 31, 2010, section 5(a).] However, the approach to income imputation may not be the same for child and spousal support purposes. Scott Booth in *The Spousal Support Advisory Guidelines; Avoiding Errors and Unsophisticated Use* (2009), 28 C.F.L.Q. 339, writes:

> Another area of difficulty that may arise in practice is with income imputation to a support recipient who either has sole or shared custody of children. According to the

Advisory Guidelines, imputing income pursuant to CSG s. 19(1) is the appropriate way to address self-sufficiency issues. However, how difficult is it going to be to convince a court to impute income where there is a significant negative impact on children. In shared custody situations this problem is exacerbated by the "usual" set off approach for determination of child support. That is, not only would the recipient who is being imputed income have a consequent reduction in spousal support, they would also have a reduction in child support if "Guidelines" income is the same for both child and spousal support. Will this deter imputation for spousal support purposes even where it is clear that a spouse is intentionally underemployed?

Support payors may make claims to have income "imputed" to support recipients.

The author also notes that there have been difficulties with the computer software in imputing income.

See **Chapter 11, section 11.3 Income**.

Finally, Schedule III, s. 3 of the CSG states that "to calculate income for the purpose of determining an amount under an applicable table, deduct ... the spousal support received from the other spouse." In determining income for child support purposes, this provision has effect when the party paying child support is receiving spousal support from the other. When using the CSG to vary spousal support, this section should not be applied in fixing the income of the spousal support recipient.

*Impute income if recipient spouse received assets from pension division and did not invest them for income — professional actuarial advice required — Boston v. Boston*, 2001 CarswellOnt 2432, 2001 CarswellOnt 2433, 2001 SCC 43, REJB 2001-25002, 17 R.F.L. (5th) 4, [2001] 2 S.C.R. 413, 28 C.C.P.B. 17, 201 D.L.R. (4th) 1, 149 O.A.C. 50, 271 N.R. 248, 2001 C.E.B. & P.G.R. 8385 (headnote only), [2001] S.C.J. No. 45 (S.C.C.). The majority judgement of Major J. (at para. 66) gave the following example of a circumstance in which income should be imputed in the process of fixing a spousal support quantum. "If the payee spouse receives assets in exchange for a share of the capitalized value of the other spouse's pension and she does not invest those assets in an attempt to produce an income, the court should impute an income to the payee spouse based on what those assets could reasonably produce if invested." With regard to the method by which this imputation should be made, the judgement did not refer to the FCSG. Instead, it stated that the imputation "should not be based on artificial assumptions but on professional actuarial advice."

*Under the* Spousal Support Advisory Guidelines *income is calculated as in the* Federal Child Support Guidelines — *s. 19(1) of the* Federal Child Support Guidelines *allows the court to impute income — M. (P.R.) v. M. (B.J.)*, 2013 CarswellBC 2204, 2013 BCCA 327, 34 R.F.L. (7th) 1, 340 B.C.A.C. 198, 579 W.A.C. 198, [2013] B.C.J. No. 1530 (B.C.C.A.). The Court of Appeal upheld the reasons of the trial judge ruling that it is not an error to fail to impute income on non-income-earning assets. When the husband received a larger share of the assets, the wife received valuable assets without income. The appellate court was of the opinion that the trial judge's view that it is undesirable to "impute income on the strength of appreciation of an asset because to do so would erode the finality of the division of assets" (para. 23) has considerable force, especially here where assets were awarded to the wife with the understanding that they did not generate income. Further, an increase in value of the matrimonial home is merely an increase on paper with no benefit until sale. As for other properties, there was no viable plan for realizing the hypothetical return. The court noted that "a housing choice may so exceed the needs of a party that, considering the marital standard, it is appropriate to reflect the mismatch in setting spousal support" (para. 26). This is a consideration that engages the exercise of judgement at the trial court level. There is not such a mismatch of residence to reasonable family needs and marital standard that it can be said the judge erred in failing to impute some income to that asset. Upon separation, the husband received over $8.5 million in assets, and the wife received assets of just over $4 million in the distribution of all family assets.

*Section 6.1 of the* Spousal Support Advisory Guidelines *refers to the* Federal Child Support Guidelines *framework to determine income — Brandl v. Rolston,* 2013 CarswellBC 1273, 2013 BCCA 235, 31 R.F.L. (7th) 296, 362 D.L.R. (4th) 439, 338 B.C.A.C. 141, 577 W.A.C. 141 (B.C.C.A.). The imputation of income to a spouse is a finding of fact to which an appellate court should pay considerable deference.

*The* Spousal Support Advisory Guidelines *at 6.1 provide that the same income measure should be used in calculating spousal support as child support — Ouellette v. Ouellette,* 2012 CarswellBC 904, 2012 BCCA 145, 16 R.F.L. (7th) 39, 32 B.C.L.R. (5th) 67, 319 B.C.A.C. 160, 542 W.A.C. 160 (B.C.C.A.). The trial judge had awarded retrospective and prospective spousal support to the wife at the mid-range level of the *Spousal Support Advisory Guidelines,* taking into account the parties' disparate incomes. The appellate court, although not referring to the SSAG, upheld the spousal support part of the judgment and affirmed the appropriateness of the court emphasizing the disparity in the parties' standards of living after separation in a determination of spousal support. Also, the fact that the wife received significant assets was not a bar to support.

*Income determination after pension division — avoiding double recovery — Boston v. Boston, supra.* The majority stated the following at para. 64 about how to determine spousal support after a pension division: "To avoid double recovery, the court should, where practicable, focus on that portion of the payor's income and assets that have not been part of the equalization or division of matrimonial assets when the payee spouse's continuing need for support is shown." No reference was made to the *Child Support Guidelines.* In *Le Bel v. Chartrand,* 2007 CarswellOnt 7598, [2007] O.J. No. 4586 (Ont. S.C.J.), this passage was used by a payor who convinced the court to use a lower income figure to calculate spousal support than that which was used for child support.

*Banked vacation pay received upon retirement should be included in income for the calculation of spousal support — Emery v. Emery,* 2010 CarswellBC 1170, 2010 BCCA 229, 85 R.F.L. (6th) 251, 287 B.C.A.C. 116, 485 W.A.C. 116 (B.C.C.A.). The Court of Appeal modified a trial judgement which suspended spousal support upon the early retirement of the husband, where it was reasonably expected he would find some other remunerative employment. The Court of Appeal substituted a reduced spousal support obligation which took into account banked vacation pay.

*Where a payor's income steadily increases, the court should use the payor's most recent income in determining spousal support — Jakob v. Jakob,* 2010 CarswellBC 599, 2010 BCCA 136, 80 R.F.L. (6th) 264, 6 B.C.L.R. (5th) 212 (B.C.C.A.). The wife appealed a variation order that increased the amount of spousal support payable by the payor husband from a previous order. In making the variation order, the lower court had averaged the payor's income over the previous 3 years. In fact, his income had steadily increased. The appellate court granted the appeal finding that the chambers judge had erred in law by calculating the payor's income based on an average of the past 3 years' annual income.

*It is inappropriate to average income for support where income is steadily increasing — Jakob v. Jakob, supra.* The primary issue in this case was whether it is appropriate to average a payor's income where that income has been steadily increasing. The parties were married for 16 years and there were no children. At trial, the wife was awarded $1,000 per month in spousal support. This was reduced to $475 per month in 2003, and reduced further to $200 per month in 2005. The wife sought increased spousal support and the trial judge awarded her $350 per month by averaging the husband's income. The Court of Appeal stated that it was inappropriate to average incomes for the purpose of support and awarded the wife spousal support of $600 per month.

*When imputing income for spousal support, no reason not to use FCSG method — Myers v. Hawco*, 2005 CarswellNfld 342, 2005 NLCA 74, 22 R.F.L. (6th) 17, 62 D.L.R. (4th) 719, 252 Nfld. & P.E.I.R. 121, 2756 A.P.R. 121, [2005] N.J. No. 378 (N.L.C.A.). The Court held, at para. 42, that "if income is imputed for purposes of determining child support, there is no basis in principle for using a different income to ascertain spousal support."

*Appropriate to use FCSG to determine income for spousal support — Murray v. Murray*, 2003 CarswellOnt 3258, 40 R.F.L. (5th) 244, 66 O.R. (3d) 540, [2003] O.T.C. 780, [2003] O.J. No. 3350 (Ont. S.C.J.), additional reasons at 2003 CarswellOnt 3862 (Ont. S.C.J.), reversed 2005 CarswellOnt 3900, 17 R.F.L. (6th) 248, 76 O.R. (3d) 548, 257 D.L.R. (4th) 320, 201 O.A.C. 254, [2005] O.J. No. 3563 (Ont. C.A.), additional reasons at 2005 CarswellOnt 7278, 79 O.R. (3d) 147, 205 O.A.C. 107, [2005] O.J. No. 5379 (Ont. C.A.), leave to appeal refused 2006 CarswellOnt 1033, 2006 CarswellOnt 1034, 221 O.A.C. 399 (note), 352 N.R. 198 (note) (S.C.C.), Croll J. held at para. 57 of the trial judgement that "the income calculation provisions found in sections 15 through 19 of the Guidelines should apply to the calculation of . . . income for spousal support purposes as well." See also *Wells v. Wells*, 2003 CarswellOnt 4791, [2003] O.J. No. 5033 (Ont. S.C.J.), additional reasons at 2003 CarswellOnt 4642, [2003] O.J. No. 4899 (Ont. S.C.J.).

*Appropriate to apply FCSG pre-tax corporate income provisions — Brophy v. Brophy*, 2002 CarswellOnt 3163, 32 R.F.L. (5th) 1, [2002] O.J. No. 3658 (Ont. S.C.J.), affirmed 2004 CarswellOnt 23, 45 R.F.L. (5th) 56, 180 O.A.C. 389, [2004] O.J. No. 17 (Ont. C.A.), additional reasons at 2004 CarswellOnt 584 (Ont. C.A.). The court found it appropriate to apply the FCSG provision to include pre-tax corporate income to this spousal support case because both child support and spousal support "relate to a paying spouse's ability to provide support to a dependent" (para. 35).

*The* Child Support Guidelines *apply to a determination of income for spousal support purposes — Smith v. Smith*, 2012 CarswellOnt 3113, 2012 ONSC 1116, [2012] O.J. No. 800 (Ont. S.C.J.), at paras. 76-78. Note that Justice Chappel states at para. 78: The determination of income for the purposes of applying the *Spousal Support Advisory Guidelines* differs than for child support cases, in that social assistance is not treated as income for the purposes of the *Spousal Support Advisory Guidelines*, and the Child Tax Benefit and other government child benefits are included in income under the "with child" formula.

*Where a trial judge bases his or her order upon the parties' current incomes at the time of the order, there is no error in his or her approach — Tomio v. Armorer*, 2011 CarswellOnt 11144, 2011 ONSC 5757 (Ont. S.C.J.). The parties had separated in 2005, but continued to reside under the same roof until June 2008. When he made his order of January 13, 2009, Murray J. apparently based his temporary order upon the parties' then current income. The court relied on the following statement from the *Spousal Support Advisory Guidelines* (July 2008) which states: "The Advisory Guidelines start from the practical position that the relevant time for determining the incomes of the spouses is the date of the hearing or the date of the agreement, at both interim and initial stages."

"*The Advisory Guidelines are of limited use in cases ... where a court is being asked to fix an amount of support that will commence many years after separation*" — *Donnelly v. Descoteaux*, 2011 CarswellOnt 12648, 2011 ONSC 5796 (Ont. S.C.J.). See also *Racki v. Racki*, 2011 CarswellOnt 13385, 2011 ONSC 6733 (Ont. S.C.J.) for a similar comment. Rollie Thompson discusses this statement in his article, "Fifteen Spousal Support Errors, and Fifteen "Corrections": How to Avoid SSAG Screwups, *Miglin* Moments and Changing Variations", *National Family Law Program, 2012,* commenting:

That's just plain wrong. Whether support must be determined shortly after separation or many years after separation, a court still has to decide what incomes should be used for the payor and the recipient. A delayed claim does not justify returning to the old discretionary, "dart-at-dartboard" approach to spousal support. In these cases, we find judges being very vague about incomes, with little analysis and much of that "in all the circumstances" language. These "delayed claim" cases do require careful analysis of post-separation income increases, and the SSAG ranges for alternative payor incomes, but the SSAG should still be applied.

*Treatment of deferred income — Ross v. Ross*, 2010 CarswellOnt 4398, 2010 ONSC 3590, 92 R.F.L. (6th) 159 (Ont. S.C.J.). The structure of the father's income was that he received a base annual salary followed by a performance bonus paid pursuant to a stock bonus/ deferred compensation arrangement, which was dependent on a number of factors. The deferred compensation portion of his income could account for up to 50% or more of his annual income, dependent on a range of factors. The father's position was that in any current year, only his base salary plus his cash bonus should be taken into account for the purpose of calculating income to establish child and spousal support. Then, the value of the stock vesting in any particular year should be included in income for the support calculations for that year. The court noted that the question was not whether the deferred income was income for support purposes, but how that might affect when the father might satisfy that obligation. The court concluded that "the legislation and case law to date suggests that, except where an employee voluntarily defers compensation for the specific purpose of minimizing a support obligation, no part of such deferred compensation should be included as current income for support purposes until the compensation is actually realized. This is not a case where an employee is voluntarily deferring income for the specific purpose of minimizing support, in which case some or all of that deferred income could be imputed for support purposes."

*Treatment of Child Tax Benefit as Income — Bigelow v. Downie*, 2009 CarswellBC 381, 2009 BCSC 205 (B.C.S.C.). In the with child support formula, the Child Tax Benefit, the Universal Child Care Benefit, the child portion of the GST credit and any other child benefits for the children of the marriage are treated as income for spousal support purposes.

*Different income used for spousal and child support — Dickson v. Dickson*, 2009 CarswellMan 515, 2009 MBQB 274, 247 Man. R. (2d) 56 (Man. Q.B.); additional reasons at 2010 CarswellMan 388, 2010 MBQB 164, 256 Man. R. (2d) 251 (Man. Q.B.). Where the payor's income exceeds the "ceiling" of $350,000 per year, a court will usually order the formulaic table amount of child support for payor incomes up to $1 million per year, but a lower income can be used for purposes of the SSAG. In this case, the court used the father's actual income of $520,872 to calculate child support, but used $350,000 as the income to calculate spousal support because this amount was more appropriate.

*Where a wife is entitled to both retroactive and ongoing spousal support, the husband's 2007 retirement incentive should not be considered in determining the appropriate quantum of support payable — Hurst v. Hurst*, 2008 CarswellOnt 5707, 58 R.F.L. (6th) 377 (Ont. S.C.J.). The parties separated in 2000 after a 36-year marriage. In 2003, the divorce judgement incorporating their minutes of settlement provided for periodic support for the wife until the husband's 65th birthday. Thereafter, variation would be limited to pension income not already taken into account in the equalization payment and any post-retirement income.

*The post-separation gratuitous, non-contributory retirement incentives received by the husband should not be added to his income to determine his spousal support obligations — the spousal support for the wife is not compensatory in nature — Gammon v. Gammon*, 2008 CarswellOnt 802, [2008] O.J. No. 603 (Ont. S.C.J.); additional reasons at 2008 CarswellOnt

6319, 60 R.F.L. (6th) 208, [2008] O.J. No. 4252 (Ont. S.C.J.). The parties separated following a 7-year marriage. Three years later, the husband received, from Ford Canada, an enhanced retirement package for workers who elected retirement and a $30,000 new car voucher. This motion was brought subsequent to trial to determine costs, the amount of spousal support given the husband's retirement and the incentives, and the issue of support termination.

*Stock options excluded from income used for spousal support – Le Bel v. Chartrand*, 2007 CarswellOnt 7598 (Ont. S.C.J.). The payor conceded that his income for the purpose of child support calculations should be $345,596, the amount stated on his 2006 income tax return. This amount included $118,000 in stock options. The recipient argued that spousal support should also be based on this income. The court instead used the figure $281,480, the payor's projected 2007 income exclusive of stock options. At para. 30, the court mentioned the following three factors leading to this decision: "the variability in Mr. Le Bel's income over the past four years, the uncertainty whether option income will form part of his 2008 income, and the problems created when one treats stock options as both capital and income."

*On an interim application for spousal support, a court should be wary about making determinations which would reclassify expenses for the purposes of determining income for spousal support purposes; it should only be done in cases of dire need as there is often insufficient information – Drapak v. Drapak*, 2008 CarswellSask 897, 2008 SKQB 505, 64 R.F.L. (6th) 421, 328 Sask. R. 317 (Sask. Q.B.). At the time of separation, the parties were living on and running a farming operation. The wife maintained that the husband in each of 2005, 2006 and 2007 deducted an average of $25,750 in non-cash expenses such as depreciation of capital cost allowance and optional inventory adjustments. She had argued that these amounts or a portion of them should be added back into the husband's income to determine his income for the purposes of spousal support. AS the husband had leased out his land and received rental income, as well as his income from farming, his income may be similar to that of the wife. She was not clearly in dire need. The calculation of farming income, especially for interim applications is a difficult endeavor. In this case, there was insufficient information to reclassify expenses in determining spousal support.

*Do not include in recipient's income social assistance which she will no longer receive once spousal support is paid – Lawrence v. Lawrence*, 2006 CarswellBC 228, 2006 BCSC 167, 24 R.F.L. (6th) 112, [2006] B.C.J. No. 210 (B.C.S.C.). Counsel for the payor provided a calculation under the *Spousal Support Advisory Guidelines* which included, within the recipient's income, social assistance she was receiving from the government. The court held at para. 84 that this was inappropriate because she would no longer qualify for social assistance were she to receive spousal support.

*Appropriate to use FCSG intentional underemployment provision in spousal support income determination – Rilli v. Rilli*, 2006 CarswellOnt 6335, [2006] O.J. No. 4142 (Ont. S.C.J.). After reviewing the case law and the SSAG, the court found at para. 16 that the child support guidelines and their jurisprudence are "tools that a judge may use in his/her discretion in determining the 'condition, means and needs' of the parties under section 15.2(4) of the *Divorce Act*." The court proceeded to apply an appellate case about intentional underemployment under the child support guidelines to the parties' spousal support dispute.

*Advantages of imputing income per FCSG s. 19 – Jean v. Jean*, 2006 CarswellAlta 1781, 2006 ABQB 938, 410 A.R. 260, [2006] A.J. No. 1687 (Alta. Q.B.). Greckol J. noted with approval that many cases have used an income imputed under FCSG s. 19 for spousal support purposes. The court held at para. 107 that this technique avoids "an inconsistent and awkward outcome where two different incomes are ascribed to a payor spouse in the course of the same application or trial." It also found statutory authority for considering imputed income in the use of the word "means" in s. 15.2(4) of the *Divorce Act*.

# Federal Child Support Guidelines, Can. Reg. 97-175

*(excerpts: ss. 15-20 and Schedule III)*

## INCOME

**Determination of annual income**

**15.** (1) Subject to subsection (2), a spouse's annual income is determined by the court in accordance with sections 16 to 20.

**Agreement**

(2) Where both spouses agree in writing on the annual income of a spouse, the court may consider that amount to be the spouse's income for the purposes of these Guidelines if the court thinks that the amount is reasonable having regard to the income information provided under section 21.

**Calculation of annual income**

**16.** Subject to sections 17 to 20, a spouse's annual income is determined using the sources of income set out under the heading "Total income" in the T1 General form issued by the Canada Revenue Agency and is adjusted in accordance with Schedule III.

SOR/2007-59, s. 4(a)

**Pattern of income**

**17.** (1) If the court is of the opinion that the determination of a spouse's annual income under section 16 would not be the fairest determination of that income, the court may have regard to the spouse's income over the last three years and determine an amount that is fair and reasonable in light of any pattern of income, fluctuation in income or receipt of a non-recurring amount during those years.

**Non-recurring losses**

(2) Where a spouse has incurred a non-recurring capital or business investment loss, the court may, if it is of the opinion that the determination of the spouse's annual income under section 16 would not provide the fairest determination of the annual income, choose not to apply sections 6 and 7 of Schedule III, and adjust the amount of the loss, including related expenses and carrying charges and interest expenses, to arrive at such amount as the court considers appropriate.

**Shareholder, director or officer**

**18.** (1) Where a spouse is a shareholder, director or officer of a corporation and the court is of the opinion that the amount of the spouse's annual income as determined under section 16 does not fairly reflect the money available to the spouse for the payment of child support, the court may consider the situations described in section 17 and determine the spouse's annual income to include

(a) all or part of the pre-tax income of the corporation, and of any corporation that is related to that corporation, for the most recent taxation year; or

(b) an amount commensurate with the services that the spouse provides to the corporation, provided that the amount does not exceed the corporation's pre-tax income.

305

## Adjustment to corporation's pre-tax income

(2) In determining the pre-tax income of a corporation for the purposes of subsection (1), all amounts paid by the corporation as salaries, wages or management fees, or other payments or benefits, to or on behalf of persons with whom the corporation does not deal at arm's length must be added to the pre-tax income, unless the spouse establishes that the payments were reasonable in the circumstances.

## Imputing income

**19.** ropriate in the circumstances, which circumstances include the following:

(a) the spouse is intentionally under-employed or unemployed, other than where the under-employment or unemployment is required by the needs of a child of the marriage or any child under the age of majority or by reasonable educational or health needs of the spouse;

(b) the spouse is exempt from paying federal or provincial income tax;

(c) the spouse lives in a country that has effective rates of income tax that are significantly lower than those in Canada;

(d) it appears that income has been diverted which would affect the level of child support to be determined under these Guidelines;

(e) the spouse's property is not reasonably utilized to generate income;

(f) the spouse has failed to provide income information when under a legal obligation to do so;

(g) the spouse unreasonably deducts expenses from income.

(h) the spouse derives a significant portion of income from dividends, capital gains or other sources that are taxed at a lower rate than employment or business income or that are exempt from tax; and

(i) the spouse is a beneficiary under a trust and is or will be in receipt of income or other benefits from the trust.

## Reasonableness of expenses

(2) For the purpose of paragraph (1)(g), the reasonableness of an expense deduction is not solely governed by whether the deduction is permitted under the *Income Tax Act*.

## Non-resident

**20.** Subject to subsection (2), where a spouse is a non-resident of Canada, the spouse's annual income is determined as though the spouse were a resident of Canada.

## Non-resident taxed at higher rates

(2) Where a spouse is a non-resident of Canada and resides in a country that has effective rates of income tax that are significantly higher than those applicable in the province in which the other spouse ordinarily resides, the spouse's annual income is the amount that the court determines to be appropriate taking those rates into consideration.

## SCHEDULE III
(Section 16)

## ADJUSTMENTS TO INCOME

**1.** Where the spouse is an employee, the spouse's applicable employment expenses described in the following provisions of the *Income Tax Act* are deducted:

(a) [Repealed SOR/2000-337, s. 8(1)]

(b) paragraph 8(1)(d) concerning expenses of teacher's exchange fund contribution;

(c) paragraph 8(1)(e) concerning expenses of railway employees;

(d) paragraph 8(1)(f) concerning sales expenses;

(e) paragraph 8(1)(g) concerning transport employee's expenses;

(f) paragraph 8(1)(h) concerning travel expenses;

(f.1) paragraph 8(1)(h.1) concerning motor vehicle travel expenses;

(g) paragraph 8(1)(i) concerning dues and other expenses of performing duties;

(h) paragraph 8(1)(j) concerning motor vehicle and aircraft costs;

(i) paragraph 8(1)(l.1) concerning *Canada Pension Plan* contributions and *Employment Insurance Act* premiums paid in respect of another employee who acts as an assistant or substitute for the spouse;

(j) paragraph 8(1)(n) concerning salary reimbursement;

(k) paragraph 8(1)(o) concerning forfeited amounts;

(l) paragraph 8(1)(p) concerning musical instrument costs; and

(m) paragraph 8(1)(q) concerning artists' employment expenses.

**2.** Deduct any child support received that is included to determine total income in the T1 General form issued by the Canada Revenue Agency.

SOR/2007-59, s. 4(c)

### Spousal support and universal child care benefit

**3.** To calculate income for the purpose of determining an amount under an applicable table, deduct

(a) the spousal support received from the other spouse; and

(b) any universal child care benefit that is included to determine the spouse's total income in the T1 General form issued by the Canada Revenue Agency.

### Special or extraordinary expenses

**3.1** To calculate income for the purpose of determining an amount under section 7 of these Guidelines, deduct the spousal support paid to the other spouse and, as applicable, make the following adjustment in respect of universal child care benefits:

(a) deduct benefits that are included to determine the spouse's total income in the T1 General form issued by the Canada Revenue Agency and that are for a child for whom special or extraordinary expenses are not being requested; or

(b) include benefits that are not included to determine the spouse's total income in the T1 General form issued by the Canada Revenue Agency and that are received by the spouse for a child for whom special or extraordinary expenses are being requested.

SOR/2007-59, s. 3

**4.** Deduct any amount of social assistance income that is not attributable to the spouse.

**5.** Replace the taxable amount of dividends from taxable Canadian corporations received by the spouse by the actual amount of those dividends received by the spouse.

**6.** Replace the taxable capital gains realized in a year by the spouse by the actual amount of capital gains realized by the spouse in excess of the spouse's actual capital losses in that year.

**7.** Deduct the actual amount of business investment losses suffered by the spouse during the year.

**8.** Deduct the spouse's carrying charges and interest expenses that are paid by the spouse and that would be deductible under the *Income Tax Act*.

**9.** Where the spouse's net self-employment income is determined by deducting an amount for salaries, benefits, wages or management fees, or other payments, paid to or on behalf of persons with whom the spouse does not deal at arm's length, include that amount, unless the spouse establishes that the payments were necessary to earn the self-employment income and were reasonable in the circumstances.

**10.** Where the spouse reports income from self-employment that, in accordance with sections 34.1 and 34.2 of the *Income Tax Act*, includes an additional amount earned in a prior period, deduct the amount earned in the prior period, net of reserves.

**11.** Include the spouse's deduction for an allowable capital cost allowance with respect to real property.

**12.** Where the spouse earns income through a partnership or sole proprietorship, deduct any amount included in income that is properly required by the partnership or sole proprietorship for purposes of capitalization.

**13.** (1) Where the spouse has received, as an employee-benefit, options to purchase shares of a Canadian-controlled private corporation, or a publicly traded corporation that is subject to the same tax treatment with reference to stock options as a Canadian-controlled private corporation, and has exercised those options during the year, add the difference between the value of the shares at the time the options are exercised and the amount paid by the spouse for the shares and any amount paid to acquire the options to purchase the shares, to the income for the year in which the options are exercised.

(2) If the spouse has disposed of the shares during a year, deduct from the income for that year the difference determined under subsection (1).

**14.** If a spouse is deemed to have received a split-pension amount under paragraph 60.03(2)(b) of the *Income Tax Act* that is included in that spouse's total income in the T1 General form issued by the Canada Revenue Agency, deduct that amount.

**Practice Tip – Foreign Tax Rates:** When representing payors who reside and work outside of Canada, counsel should be cognizant of the fact that the SSAG does not take into account higher effective tax rates in foreign jurisdictions. The premises upon which the SSAG amounts are based include assumptions relating only to Canadian taxation rates and government benefits and credits. Section 20 of the Child Support Guidelines ("CSGs") was amended on May 1, 2006 to allow the court to take higher effective tax rates in foreign jurisdictions into account. Section 20(2) of the CSGs provides that where a spouse is a non-resident of Canada and resides in a country that has effective rates of income tax that are significantly higher than those applicable in the province in which the other spouse ordinarily resides, the spouse's annual income is the amount that the court determines to be appropriate taking those rates into consideration. Thus, the amendment to the non-resident provision of the CSGs allows a court to reduce a spouse's foreign income in determining income for support purposes to account for situations where that spouse lives outside Canada and has to pay a higher effective rate of tax in the other country. In such cases, a spouse has a reduced ability to pay, when compared with Canadian residents with similar income. The Ontario Superior Court in *Rilli v. Rilli*, 2006 CarswellOnt 6335 (Ont. S.C.J.) found that the income determination provisions of the CSGs apply to the determination of a payor's income for spousal support. Section 20(2) forms part of the income determination provisions of the CSGs. Accordingly, on an interim motion for spousal support, the motions judge has the discretion to determine the appropriate income for support purposes, taking into account the payor's higher effective foreign tax rate. The complicating factor for counsel is that the SSAG software will not calculate a range of support using the higher tax rate. In a foreign jurisdiction with high tax rates, the amount of support may be disproportionate in relation to the payor's overall income. A formulaic approach should be designed to address the increasingly common situation where a payor resides in a foreign jurisdiction with higher effective tax rates. Until this formulaic approach is designed and the software is updated, it is necessary for counsel and the court to balance the tax positions of both parties on the interim motion. In the circumstances, it would be reasonable for a support recipient to seek a support amount that is lower than the range of support under SSAG on the motion to account for higher tax rates, as was the case in *Boju v. Corr*, 2009 CarswellOnt 563 (Ont. S.C.J.).

**Practice Tip – Determining a Payor's Income for Support Purposes:** When determining a payor's income for support purposes, counsel should be cognizant of the fact that a payor's post-separation increased income may not be relevant or relied on by the court. Too often counsel simply presume that the parties' current incomes are to be considered when determining the quantum of support. Chequemate spousal support calculations are accordingly prepared based on the current income of the parties. The clear appellate jurisprudence on this issue should not be ignored. In *Fisher v. Fisher*, the Ontario Court of Appeal made clear that a spousal support award will be based on the parties' respective incomes as at the date of separation. In that case, the Court of Appeal averaged the payor's increasing income in the last 3 years before separation, as well as his increased income in the year of separation, to determine his income for support purposes. The payor's post-separation income was not considered.

Counsel for the recipient must first marshal evidence to prove that the recipient contributed to the payor's post-separation increased income in some substantive way before the increased income will be considered by the court. The case law is clear that in order for the support recipient to share in the payor's post-separation increased income, s/he must first show that s/he contributed to the skills or the credentials which the payor acquired that led to his or her ability to earn his now increased income (*Moge v. Moge*, [1992] 3 S.C.R. 813; *Dextraze v. Dextraze* (2004), 2004 CarswellBC 287, 2004 BCSC 215 (B.C.S.C.)).

Being a supportive spouse, without more, is not enough. The support recipient will share in post-separation income where s/he contributed to the acquisition by the payor of his/her education or credentials, or in some other "tangible" way to the advancement of his/her career. In *C. (D.B.) v. W. (R.M.)*, 2006 CarswellAlta 1723 (Alta. Q.B.), the wife was a supportive spouse and a good mother, but "there was no credible evidence to show that [the husband]'s post-separation success was in any way attributable to the wife's contributions". As a result, the court refused to allow the wife to share in the increased income. In *Rozen v. Rozen*, (2003) 37 RFL (5th) 205 (B.C.S.C.), the wife of 20 years was disentitled from sharing in post-separation increased income because it was not attributable to her efforts or sacrifices, but rather to a business reorganization and the husband's additional work.

In *Robinson v. Robinson*, (1993) 66 OAC 381 (Ont. C.A.), the Ontario Court of Appeal refused the wife's application to share in a post-separation income increase. The parties were married for 13 years. The wife was acknowledged to be a good mother and homemaker who attended social functions with the husband and entertained in their home. The court observed that the evidence did not show that she had assisted in any other important way to advance the husband's career. In *Chalifoux v. Chalifoux*, 2006 ABQB 535 (Alta. Q.B.), Justice Read found an insufficient connection between the husband's increased post-separation income and the marriage to warrant a significant sharing. In *Fletcher v. Fletcher*, 2003 ABQB 890 (Alta. Q.B.), the court ruled that the portion of the husband's increased income attributable to his relationship with his employer was not linked to the wife and was unavailable for sharing through support. Accordingly, the recipient must prove that his or her efforts and sacrifices directly contributed to the payor's increased income before the increased income will be taken into account by the court.

Gary S. Joseph, Partner, & Michael J. Stangarone, Partner, MacDonald & Partners LLP

# CHAPTER 9

## OTHER ISSUES

This chapter is divided into the following sections:

### 9.1 Disclosure

Disclosure is a crucial matter for family law: *Ewing v. Ewing*, 1987 CarswellSask 85, 7 R.F.L. (3d) 168, 56 Sask. R. 260 (Sask. C.A.); *Zarepour v. Jamshidi*, 2013 CarswellOnt 6647, 2013 ONSC 2952 (Ont. S.C.J.); and *Silverstein v. Silverstein*, 1978 CarswellOnt 216, 20 O.R. (2d) 185, 87 D.L.R. (3d) 116, 1 R.F.L. (2d) 239, 1 F.L.R.A.C. 20 (Ont. H.C.). Disclosure should be full and frank, meaning complete, detailed and timely: *Rizzo v. Rizzo*, 2001 CarswellOnt 275, 14 R.F.L. (5th) 177, [2001] O.J. No. 303 (Ont. S.C.J.); approved of in *Emery v. Emery*, 2008 CarswellOnt 1165, 51 R.F.L. (6th) 294, [2008] O.J. No. 844 (Ont. S.C.J.), at para.40. Disclosure is important in order for the parties to understand their financial circumstances and make well-informed decisions. Failure to provide timely disclosure delays the litigation process and increases costs. This failure can undermine possible settlement or lead to an unfair settlement which may ultimately be set aside. However, it is difficult to strike the right balance between non-disclosure and excessive disclosure. While full and frank disclosure is an essential part of family law litigation, exhaustive disclosure is not necessarily appropriate; courts and parties must consider the relevance of the disclosure sought, as well as the costs and time to acquire the disclosure in relation to its importance: *Kovachis v. Kovachis*, 2013 CarswellOnt 15040, 2013 ONCA 663, 36 R.F.L. (7th) 1, 367 D.L.R. (4th) 189, 311 O.A.C. 228, [2013] O.J. No. 4954 (Ont. C.A.). Before a court imposes sanctions, it must consider "the clarity of the disclosure request, the continued relevance of the requested disclosure and the probative value of the missing disclosure weighed against the difficulty of obtaining the disclosure": *Chernyakhovsky v. Chernyakhovsky*, 2005 CarswellOnt 942, [2005] O.J. No. 944 (Ont. S.C.J.), at para. 15. In order to determine whether disclosure is required, the test is whether the information has a "semblance of relevancy" in regard to the material issues in the case. It is a low legal threshold. See *Bensuro Holdings Inc. v. Avenor Inc.*, 2000 CarswellOnt 1215, 186 D.L.R. (4th) 182, [2000] O.J. No. 1188 (Ont. S.C.J.), at paras. 8, 11 and 13; and *Boyd v. Fields*, 2006 CarswellOnt 8675, [2006] O.J. No. 5762 (Ont. S.C.J.), at para. 11.

The SSAG indicate that the same definition of "income" is used for SSAG purposes as for child support purposes. See *Spousal Support Advisory Guidelines*, July 2008 at 6.1.Where the "with child support formula" applies, there is no issue. However, where there are no children of the marriage, most jurisdictions require disclosure of income and expenses if there is a spousal support claim, so the same information should be disclosed. To be precise, the provincial family rules, not the CSGs, are the source of the disclosure obligation in either instance for spousal support purposes.

It is a given that the parties must make disclosure. It is less clear if and when third parties must make disclosure. A party's second spouse may be required to provide financial disclosure in proceedings related to the party's first marriage: *Cox v. Cox*, 2007 CarswellAlta 127, 2007 ABCA 37, 34 R.F.L. (6th) 329 (Alta. C.A.). If the husband seeks to make a case for termination of spousal support based on the means of the wife's new partner, the husband should make similar disclosure: *Ballegeer v. Ballegeer*, 2013 CarswellMan 332, 2013 MBQB 162, 293 Man. R. (2d) 263 (Man. Q.B.). Financial disclosure of a party's common law spouse may not be required: *Bodman v. Bodman*, 1998 CarswellMan 48, 38 R.F.L. (4th) 210, 127 Man. R. (2d) 1, [1998] M.J. No. 62 (Man. Master). Requests for disclosure of a trust's financial statements must be directly relevant to the claim for spousal support from the beneficiary: *Clapp v. Clapp*, 2014 CarswellOnt 10739, 2014 ONSC 4591, 48 R.F.L. (7th) 329 (Ont. S.C.J.). See also *Ludmer v. Ludmer*, 2009 CarswellQue 740, 2009 QCCA 1414, EYB 2009-161845, 87 R.F.L. (6th) 42, [2009] R.J.Q. 1988, [2009] Q.J. No. 7381 (C.A. Que.), for consideration of the disclosure requirements from a party's father who was the trustee of a trust established for the benefit of the trustee's three children. The trustee had implemented an estate freeze. Disclosure may also be obtained from third party corporations where a party is a shareholder or officer: *Reisman v. Reisman*, 2007 CarswellOnt 3849 (Ont. S.C.J.). In *Reisman*, the husband was ordered to produce disclosure pertaining to a third party company in which he had a non-controlling interest. See also *Loeb v. Loeb*, 2013 CarswellOnt 3247, 2013 ONSC 1730, 34 R.F.L. (7th) 149 (Ont. S.C.J.), at paras. 13, 14, 39 and 54.

Disclosure is required at every stage of the litigation process. Provincial legislation such as the Ontario *Family Law Act*, s. 56(4)(a) clearly provides that a court may set aside a domestic contract or a provision in it where there is a lack of financial disclosure. In settlement negotiations, there is "a duty to make full and honest disclosure of all relevant financial information . . . to protect the integrity of the result of negotiations undertaken in these uniquely vulnerable circumstances": *Rick v. Brandsema*, 2009 CarswellBC 342, 2009 CarswellBC 343, 2009 SCC 10, 62 R.F.L. (6th) 239, [2009] 1 S.C.R. 295, 90 B.C.L.R. (4th) 1, 303 D.L.R. (4th) 193, [2009] 5 W.W.R. 191, 266 B.C.A.C. 1, 449 W.A.C. 1, 385 N.R. 85, [2009] S.C.J. No. 10 (S.C.C.). "[F]ull and complete financial disclosure is necessary in the family law context, particularly when parties have entered into domestic contracts": *Turk v. Turk*, 2014 CarswellOnt 10364, 2014 ONSC 4490 (Ont. S.C.J.). Disclosure is required at the interim stage: *Droit de la famille - 131908*, 2013 CarswellQue 6882 (C.A. Que.). Documents and communications involved in a collaborative family law process are subject to disclosure and production in order to determine income for spousal support: *A. (D.) v. A. (L.)*, 2014 CarswellNB 342, 2014 CarswellNB 343, 2014 NBCA 39, 45 R.F.L. (7th) 31, 54 C.P.C. (7th) 40, 420 N.B.R. (2d) 133, 1091 A.P.R. 133, [2014] N.B.J. No. 187 (N.B.C.A.). Provincial family law rules may set out specific financial disclosure requirements. For instance in Ontario, see Family Law Rules, Ont. Reg.69/15, Rules13, 15(21.1), 17(14.2) 19(1.1) and 19(3).

A court may employ a wide range of sanctions where it finds that disclosure is inadequate or non-existent. Provincial family rules set out the sanctions for failure to disclose relevant information. In Ontario, where a party does not obey an order or comply with the *Family Law Rules*, the party may find himself or herself the object of the court's wide power to "deal with the failure by making any order that it considers necessary for a just determination of the matter." See for example *Family Law Rules*, Ont. Reg. 69/15 R. 1(7.1) and *Family Law Rules*, Ont. Reg. 114/99, R. R.1(8) and R. 1(8.1) and (8.2).

Case law provides examples of sanctions which have been ordered. Improper disclosure by the payor spouse may result in an order for lump sum spousal support so as to ensure that adequate support is paid: *Davis v. Crawford*, 2011 CarswellOnt 2512, 2011 ONCA 294, 95 R.F.L. (6th) 257, 106 O.R. (3d) 221, 332 D.L.R. (4th) 508, 277 O.A.C. 200, [2011] O.J. No. 1719 (Ont. C.A.). A court may impute income where there is inadequate disclosure: *Bodine-Shah v. Shah*, 2014 CarswellBC 1354, 2014 BCCA 191, 61 B.C.L.R. (5th) 50, 355 B.C.A.C. 255, 607 W.A.C. 255 (B.C.C.A.); *Gagne v. Gagne*, 2011 CarswellOnt 1476, 2011 ONCA 188, 99 R.F.L. (6th) 1, [2011] O.J. No. 1015 (Ont. C.A.); *Poursadeghian v. Hashemi-Dahaj*, 2010 CarswellBC 2740, 2010 BCCA 453, 88 R.F.L. (6th) 278, 10 B.C.L.R. (5th) 102, 292 B.C.A.C. 239, 493 W.A.C. 239 (B.C.C.A.). Special damages may be awarded: *Rozen v. Rozen*, 2002 CarswellBC 2224, 2002 BCCA 537 (B.C.C.A.). See also *S. (J.D.) v. P. (D.Y.C.)*, 2014 CarswellBC 2475, 2014 BCSC 1577 (B.C.S.C.). A recipient spouse's inadequate financial disclosure may result in retroactive variation of a spousal support order: *Z. (A.B.) v. A. (A.L.F.)*, 2014 CarswellBC 2276, 2014 BCSC 1453 (B.C.S.C.). An award of costs is a very common sanction. See *Rana v. Rana*, 2014 CarswellBC 839, 2014 BCSC 530 (B.C.S.C.); and *Mondino v. Mondino*, 2014 CarswellOnt 1953, 2014 ONSC 1102 (Ont. S.C.J.). The court will dismiss a payor party's motion for summary judgement where the payee spouse has not provided adequate financial disclosure: *Patrick v. Beitz*, 2013 CarswellOnt 14074, 2013 ONSC 6397 (Ont. S.C.J.).

For a practical guide to information required for disclosure purposes in a basic family law matter, see Vivian Alterman, MBA, CPA, CA, CBV, *Family Law Toolkit 2014, The Disclosure Challenge in Family Law Matters*, LSUC, September 9, 2014.

## 9.1.1 Case Law

*A judge's failure to assess a spouse's additional submission of financial information after that party's initial failure to disclose income is a material error* — Bodine-Shah v. Shah, 2014 CarswellBC 1354, 2014 BCCA 191, 61 B.C.L.R. (5th) 50, 355 B.C.A.C. 255, 607 W.A.C. 255 (B.C.C.A.). Due to the husband's failure to disclose his income adequately, the trial judge imputed income of $90,000, based on the husband's evidence of a typical return of 10% on gross revenue from his business, and awarded the wife spousal support of $2,500 a month retroactive to 2011. The appeal judge found that the husband's lack of disclosure and other financial chicanery formed an evidentiary basis for imputing an income that was substantially higher than what he claimed at trial. The appeal judge, however, noted that the trial judge did not appear to have assessed the husband's evidence in support of his 2013 application to determine whether the imputed income continued to reflect his income after 2011. The husband's additional evidence was that he had ceased his business, retrained to become a truck driver, and was earning an annual income of approximately $77,000. The Court of Appeal found that this evidence, if accepted by the trial judge, was capable of demonstrating a reduction in the appellant's income for the purpose of spousal support and that the trial judge's apparent failure to consider potentially relevant evidence was a material error. The court held, *inter alia*, that the support issue be remitted to the trial judge for redetermination of amount (and duration if relevant).

*Where the wife does not disclose her new partner's income, financial circumstances and contribution to household expenses, the husband's spousal support obligation should be primarily based on the wife's entitlement to limited compensatory support* — Qaraan v. Qaraan, 2014 CarswellOnt 6276, 2014 ONCA 401 (Ont. C.A.). The trial judge found that the wife was entitled to support on both a compensatory and a non-compensatory basis. However, because of the wife's lack of disclosure regarding her new husband's financial circumstances, the trial judge awarded her the relatively modest sum of $500 per month in compensatory support only. The Court of Appeal found no reason to interfere with the trial judge's decision, noting that the determination of spousal support is highly discretionary.

*The court may find a payor spouse's credible explanation for missing disclosure adequate for the purpose of determining spousal support* — *F. (R.) v. B. (M.G.),* 2014 CarswellBC 945, 2014 BCCA 143, 41 R.F.L. (7th) 1, 59 B.C.L.R. (5th) 221, 354 B.C.A.C. 49, 605 W.A.C. 49 (B.C.C.A.). The husband provided extensive disclosure, but some expense claims information was missing. (The trial judge noted that there were six binders of joint documents filed at trial which comprised primarily the husband's documents.) While the husband acknowledged that he had not produced invoices in support of all his expense claims, he provided a credible oral explanation of how he had determined his annual income and business expenses. The trial judge found that the husband had made full financial disclosure and therefore based spousal support on the husband's line 150 income and imputed income to the wife. The wife appealed, requesting that the court attribute income to the husband as a result of his failure to make full disclosure. The wife argued that she had strong compensatory and non-compensatory claims for spousal support as a result of her role in the marriage. She gave up career opportunities to be a stay-at-home mother and teacher to the parties' five children. The Court of Appeal noted that her arguments had to be contextualized. Pursuant to an interim order, the wife had received spousal support in excess of her entitlement according to the husband's income and further support by way of the husband's mortgage payments. The Court of Appeal agreed with the trial judge that the husband had provided extensive income disclosure and declined to order additional spousal support, but concluded the decision with a strong caution lest its finding be interpreted as condoning non-disclosure.

"*Non-disclosure of relevant information that is in the possession and control of a party, and is necessary for the determination of an issue in the litigation, is a risky strategy. It has typically attracted adverse consequences to that party*" — *Weintz v. Weintz,* 2014 CarswellBC 855, 2014 BCCA 118, 60 B.C.L.R. (5th) 282, 41 R.F.L. (7th) 93, 353 B.C.A.C. 185, 603 W.A.C. 185 (B.C.C.A.).

*Documents and communications involved in a collaborative family law process are subject to disclosure and production in order to determine income for spousal support* — *A. (D.) v. A. (L.),* 2014 CarswellNB 342, 2014 CarswellNB 343, 2014 NBCA 39, 45 R.F.L. (7th) 31, 54 C.P.C. (7th) 40, 420 N.B.R. (2d) 133, 1091 A.P.R. 133, [2014] N.B.J. No. 187 (N.B.C.A.). The parties' marriage contract was drawn up following a collaborative family law (CFL) process and included a spousal support provision. The husband's payment of $653,013 purported to include lump sum spousal support. The wife sought to have the contract set aside on a number of grounds, including non-disclosure. The husband filed a Notice of Motion seeking disclosure from the lawyers involved in the CFL process. The motion judge determined that while class privilege applied to that process, all documents compellable pursuant to the *Marital Property Act,* S.N.B. 2012, c. 107l; the *Divorce Act,* R.S.C. 1985, c. 3 (2nd Supp.); the *Federal Child Support Guidelines;* and the *Rules of Court,* as well as documents produced to verify the financial information, were subject to disclosure and production. The judge added, however, that disclosure orders should not be overly broad and that all communications regarding the CFL process would remain privileged. The lawyers appealed the disclosure order on the grounds that the CFL materials were protected from disclosure and that the relevant financial information was available by other means. The Court of Appeal noted that the extent of disclosure under the Guidelines is broad and depends upon a party's sources of income and the nature of any business or corporate holdings. The appeals court disagreed with the motion judge's limitation of disclosure to compellable documents under family law and other legislation. The Court of Appeal stated that, "no privilege stands in the way of the respondents' discovery of communications, discussions, proposals, whether written or oral, and documents created during the collaborative law process." See also *Ramsden v. Ramsden*, 2013 CarswellBC 1602, 2013 BCSC 949, [2013] B.C.J. No. 1123 (B.C.S.C.), in which the court made a similar finding regarding deceptive document disclosure in family law mediation.

*While full and frank disclosure is an essential part of family law litigation, exhaustive disclosure is not necessarily appropriate* — Kovachis v. Kovachis, 2013 CarswellOnt 15040, 2013 ONCA 663, 367 D.L.R. (4th) 189, 36 R.F.L. (7th) 1, 311 O.A.C. 228, [2013] O.J. No. 4954 (Ont. C.A.). The husband appealed from a decision granting the wife's motion to strike the husband's pleadings for failure to comply with previous disclosure orders. Mr. Justice Laskin found that the husband had provided substantial disclosure, the motion judge and the wife had failed to list what disclosure the husband had not made, there was an absence of evidence that the husband had willfully disobeyed any of the previous disclosure orders, and the principle of proportionality should be considered. All of these findings led to the conclusion that the husband's pleadings should be reinstated. The judge noted R. 1.04(1.1)\ of the Ontario *Rules of Civil Procedure*, which provides: "In applying these rules, the court shall make orders ... that are proportionate to the importance and complexity of the issues ... in the proceeding." He stated, at para. 34:

> Although full and frank disclosure is a necessary component of family law litigation, exhaustive disclosure may not always be appropriate. Courts and parties should consider the burden that disclosure requests bring on the disclosing party, the relevance of the requested disclosure to the issues at hand, and the costs and time to obtain the disclosure compared to its importance: see *Chernyakhovsky v. Chernyakhovsky* (2005), 137 A.C.W.S. (3d) 988 (Ont. S.C.J.) [2005 CarswellOnt 942 (Ont. C.J.)] at paras. 8, 15, *Boyd v. Fields* (2006), [2007] W.D.F.L. 2449 (Ont. S.C.J.) [2006 CarswellOnt 8675 (Ont. S.C.J.)] at paras. 12-14. Disclosure orders must be fair to both parties and appropriate to the case.

The judge allowed the appeal, set aside the order of the motion judge and reinstated the father's pleadings.

*The court may order disclosure for the purpose of determining spousal support before trial at any stage of the proceedings, including the interim stage* — Droit de la famille - 131908, 2013 CarswellQue 6882 (C.A. Que.). The Supreme Court of Canada's reasoning in *Leskun* regarding the requirement for full and honest financial disclosure applies to spousal support issues. The court noted that while there was at present "no agreement in sight" between the parties regarding the issue of support, full financial disclosure was nevertheless required in order to allow for the possible agreement, as well as to enable the court to establish the quantum of support. The court noted that disclosure must not wait until a trial on the merits of a divorce case, as this would "completely undermine the principle of disclosure."

*Where a party knowingly fails to disclose relevant information, he or she is precluded from relying on that information as a material change in circumstances in order to try to rescind his or her spousal support obligation* — MacLanders v. MacLanders, 2012 CarswellBC 3736, 2012 BCCA 482, 24 R.F.L. (7th) 24, 39 B.C.L.R. (5th) 255 (B.C.C.A.). The husband's decision not to disclose his planned retirement limited the possibility of substantial reapportionment of the family assets in the wife's favour because of the availability of indefinite spousal support. In refusing to consider the husband's retirement as a material change in circumstances with regards to spousal support, the court stated that the Willick test precluded the husband from relying on the previously omitted information as a material change in circumstances, as the event was "known, foreseeable, and specifically within his contemplation" before trial and not disclosed to the judge. The court rejected this ground of appeal.

Where it is a party's interpretation of his or her disclosed documents that is at issue rather than actual failure to disclose income for the purpose of determining spousal support, the Court of Appeal will allow the payor spouse's appeal on the issue of support — Armstrong v. Armstrong, 2012 CarswellBC 1095, 2012 BCCA 166, 33 B.C.L.R. (5th) 86, 350 D.L.R. (4th) 186, 320 B.C.A.C. 94, 543 W.A.C. 94, [2012] B.C.J. No. 770 (B.C.C.A.).

Improper disclosure by the payor spouse may result in an order for lump sum spousal support in order to ensure that adequate support is paid — Davis v. Crawford, 2011 CarswellOnt 2512, 2011 ONCA 294, 95 R.F.L. (6th) 257, 106 O.R. (3d) 221, 332 D.L.R. (4th) 508, 277 O.A.C. 200, [2011] O.J. No. 1719 (Ont. C.A.).

Where the payor spouse provides inadequate disclosure, the Court of Appeal may impute income in order that the husband continues to pay spousal support in the high range despite ordering that he pay more in child support — Gagne v. Gagne, 2011 CarswellOnt 1476, 2011 ONCA 188, 99 R.F.L. (6th) 1, [2011] O.J. No. 1015 (Ont. C.A.). The trial judge had departed from the Child Support Guidelines by awarding a lower amount of child support and higher amount of spousal support. The Court of Appeal adjusted the figures so that the child support was the CSG table amount with spousal support remaining at the high end of the range. This reconfiguration was possible due to the husband's lack of full financial disclosure as the court attributed income to the husband.

Where the husband fails to make full financial disclosure and in other ways attempts to evade his support obligation and it appears his behaviour is unlikely to change, the Court of Appeal will uphold the trial judge's decision to award lump sum spousal support — Vanos v. Vanos, 2010 CarswellOnt 9680, 2010 ONCA 876, 94 R.F.L. (6th) 312, 271 O.A.C. 222, [2010] O.J. No. 5539 (Ont. C.A.). The trial judge found this was a case for lump sum support for several reasons. Besides failing to accurately disclose his income, the court found that the husband tended to put his own financial interest above that of the wife and children, and that he resented, and would continue in future to resent, paying spousal support because he was estranged from the children. The court ordered support retroactive to the date the husband received the wife's notice of claim.

The court may draw an adverse inference against a spouse who fails to provide adequate disclosure and may impute income to that party as a result — Poursadeghian v. Hashemi-Dahaj, 2010 BCCA 453, 2010 CarswellBC 2740, 88 R.F.L. (6th) 278, 10 B.C.L.R. (5th) 102, 292 B.C.A.C. 239, 493 W.A.C. 239 (B.C.C.A.). The trial judge imputed income to the husband, who did not provide the requisite financial information. See also Li v. Wong, 2010 CarswellAlta 1982, 2010 ABCA 296 (Alta. C.A.), where the husband's appeal from a chambers judge imputation of income for spousal support purposes was dismissed. The court held that proceedings addressing further financial disclosure were upcoming and the result might give the parties an opportunity to change the order of the chambers judge in either direction. Also in Martin v. Orris, 2010 CarswellMan 246, 2010 MBCA 59, 255 Man. R. (2d) 126, 486 W.A.C. 126, [2010] M.J. No. 180 (Man. C.A.), affirming 2009 CarswellMan 522, 2009 MBQB 290, 246 Man. R. (2d) 262 (Man. Q.B.), the husband appealed from a judgement requiring him to pay interim spousal support based on income that was imputed to him. The appeal was dismissed as there were no grounds to merit appellate intervention at the interim stage of the proceedings. In Pedro v. Pedro, 2011 CarswellOnt 4969, 2011 ONCJ 299 (Ont. C.J.), on an interim child and spousal support motion, income was imputed to the husband on the basis that he had failed to comply with financial disclosure orders and failed to provide required medical evidence to support his position that his health needs justified the reduction of work hours. The court made an adverse inference against the husband based on his conduct and made an interim spousal support order based on both a compensatory and non-compensatory basis in the mid-range under the SSAG which would leave the husband with 47.1% of the family's total net disposable income.

*Financial disclosure by husband's second wife required* — *Cox v. Cox*, 2007 CarswellAlta 127, 2007 ABCA 37, 34 R.F.L. (6th) 329 (Alta. C.A.). The court, on appeal, upheld an order requiring the husband's second wife to disclose her corporate financial statements within the context of the wife's spousal support review. The husband's corporate activities were closely related to those of his second wife, and disclosure had been sought as a prerequisite to determining the husband's income. However, the order compelling the second wife to disclose her personal financial records was stayed.

*Where the husband had been reluctant to disclose his total income to the wife and she had been forced to encroach on capital to support herself after separation, she was awarded lump sum support of $30,000* — *Pettigrew v. Pettigrew*, 2005 CarswellNS 676, 2005 NSSC 219, 34 R.F.L. (6th) 184, [2005] N.S.J. No. 616 (N.S.S.C.), affirmed 2006 CarswellNS 349, 2006 NSCA 98, 30 R.F.L. (6th) 7, 246 N.S.R. (2d) 298, 780 A.P.R. 298, [2006] N.S.J. No. 321 (N.S.C.A.).

*Husband's disclosure deemed inadequate in light of his lifestyle* — *Hum v. Man*, 1998 CarswellOnt 3764, 42 R.F.L. (4th) 382 (Ont. C.A.). The court allowed the wife's appeal from her spousal support award and ordered a new trial. The trial judge had rejected the wife's claim that the husband falsified financial records and participated in questionable business practices to conceal income. The husband's lifestyle simply was not consistent with his claimed income, which was below the poverty level.

*In proceedings for support, the parties have an obligation to make full disclosure and to produce all relevant documents, in the absence of such disclosure the court may, inter alia, draw adverse inference or order disclosure* — *Ewing v. Ewing*, 1987 CarswellSask 85, 7 R.F.L. (3d) 168, 56 Sask. R. 260 (Sask. C.A.).

*A party's misleading failure to provide financial disclosure in family law proceedings is one form of reprehensible conduct that may result in an award of special damages* — *Rozen v. Rozen*, 2002 CarswellBC 2224, 2002 BCCA 537, 30 R.F.L. (5th) 207, 173 B.C.A.C. 102, 283 W.A.C. 102, [2002] B.C.J. No. 2192 (B.C.C.A.). See also *S. (J.D.) v. P. (D.Y.C.)*, 2014 CarswellBC 2475, 2014 BCSC 1577 (B.C.S.C.).

*Requests for disclosure of a trust's financial statements must be directly relevant to the claim for spousal support from the beneficiary* — *Clapp v. Clapp*, 2014 CarswellOnt 10739, 2014 ONSC 4591, 48 R.F.L. (7th) 329 (Ont. S.C.J.). The parties both claimed spousal support. The husband sought disclosure of information about a trust in which the wife had a beneficial interest in part to determine each party's entitlement to support from the other. The wife provided a deed of settlement of the trust and its financial statement. The husband sought further disclosure regarding the trust during the period spanning 1995 to the present, including financial statements, income tax returns, the schedule of distributions, amendments and resolutions, the number of the wife's mother's grandchildren, a statement of benefits paid to the wife, and any loans the wife may have received from the trust. The husband also requested disclosure dating back to 1995 of the wife's and/or the trust's interest in a company, as well as a list of all shareholders of that or any other company in which the trust owned shares. The trustee produced the trust's financial statements from 2010 to 2013. The wife stated that the trustee refused her request for further information. The court found the disclosure adequate, as the statements disclosed the trust's assets and distributions, and would have stated whether there were additional distributions beyond those already included in the family property and divided with the husband. The court did not require evidence that there were no amendments to the trust beyond the wife's statement, unless the husband should require a sworn statement to that effect. The court found no relevance regarding the request for the number of the wife's mother's grandchildren and made no order in that regard. The court determined that the amounts the wife received should not be regarded as her own income, and there were no emergency circumstances to justify an order requiring her to use capital to pay spousal support to the husband. The court did order the wife to produce documents including her written confirmation that she had no beneficial interest in any other trust from 1995 to the present. The judge stated that additional information would not be relevant and that, without relevance, further disclosure would be an unwarranted intrusion on the privacy of the trust's other beneficiaries.

*The court is unlikely to order disclosure of gifts prior to three years before separation when determining income for the purpose of spousal support — Clapp v. Clapp, supra.* In support of his spousal support claim, the husband sought disclosure from the wife dating from 1995 to the present, including the wife's income tax returns, notices of assessment, her mother's will and distribution of assets, a schedule of the mother's gifts to the wife, and confirmation that the wife did not have a beneficial interest in any trust other than the one the husband knew of. The judge ordered both parties to disclose gifts of a value over $1,000 during the three years prior to their separation, as well as to disclose the grantor and estimated value of each gift during this time. The court ordered the wife to produce an estate inventory, a list of distributions, and any undistributed portion of her mother's estate. The court concluded, however, that any gifts granted prior to the past three years had minimal relevance and that requiring disclosure of these gifts would impose a burden disproportionate to its relevance.

*The corporate veil should be pierced where a party uses the corporation as a vehicle to disguise his or her true income — Walsh v. Walsh,* 2014 CarswellOnt 10753, 2014 ONSC 4588 (Ont. S.C.J.). The husband was the sole owner of a corporation and declared as the corporation's employee an annual income of $84,000, the amount upon which the husband proposed the court base spousal and child support. The judge found that the income earned by the husband's corporation rather than the employment earnings declared represented his actual income and that he was therefore responsible for substantial arrears through his failure to disclose his true income. The court calculated the husband's income for 2011 at $194,258, for 2012 at $242,188, for 2013 at $320,000, and for 2014 at $320,000. The court ordered arrears and ongoing mid-range spousal support as well as disclosure updates.

*A recipient spouse's inadequate financial disclosure may result in retroactive variation of a spousal support order — Z. (A.B.) v. A. (A.L.F.),* 2014 CarswellBC 2276, 2014 BCSC 1453 (B.C.S.C.). The recipient wife's income increased significantly, but she did not disclose this increase on her income tax returns and failed to provide the information at trial. The court varied the original interim order in accordance with the new evidence of her financial circumstances. See also *M. (T.L.) v. M. (D.P.),* 2014 CarswellBC 2175, 2014 BCSC 1386 (B.C.S.C.), which addresses this issue similarly.

*"The jurisprudence makes it abundantly clear that full and complete financial disclosure is necessary in the family law context, particularly when parties have entered into domestic contracts" — Turk v. Turk,* 2014 CarswellOnt 10364, 2014 ONSC 4490 (Ont. S.C.J.). The wife sought to have spousal support and other provisions of the parties' separation agreement set aside in part due to the husband's inadequate financial disclosure. The court required a full factual record in order to determine whether disclosure had been adequate and rejected the husband's arguments that the disclosure requested was extensive and onerous to compile, that it would be more cost-effective to refrain from requiring further disclosure, or, without supporting evidence, that such disclosure would be prejudicial. The court ordered the husband to produce a financial statement with supporting documentation.

*The court is unlikely to calculate income for spousal support based on alleged undisclosed income without documentation supporting such an allegation — Mason v. Mason,* 2014 CarswellOnt 9899, 2014 ONSC 4290, 47 R.F.L. (7th) 173 (Ont. S.C.J.). Before separation, the parties enjoyed a high standard of living that was substantially supported by undisclosed cash income. The wife gave the court to understand that the husband continued to earn significant undeclared income and requested that the court include this income in his declared income for the purpose of calculating spousal support. The judge stated that it would be inappropriate to base support on an estimate of undisclosed income as this could be interpreted as condonation of non-disclosure.

"If the basis for the application to vary the amount of spousal support is a decrease in income, the evidence must be sufficient to allow for a comparison between the ability to pay at the time of the impugned support order and the present ability" — FitzGerald v. Lee, 2014 CarswellOnt 9015, 2014 ONSC 4011 (Ont. S.C.J.).

The court will strike from the record any disclosure of without prejudice communications made in the context of settlement negotiations where such disclosure violates settlement privilege — Kaytor v. Unser, 2014 CarswellSask 388, 2014 SKQB 181 (Sask. Q.B.). The wife sought interim spousal support and other relief and included information from the parties' settlement negotiation in her affidavit. The court noted, at para. 7:

> [S]ettlement privilege exists to allow for full and frank discussion as between the parties and to ensure that a party is not prejudiced in the litigation because of a settlement position which may be taken. This in turn encourages resolution of disputes and obviously allows for comments to be made which would not be part of the litigation process.

The court ordered $300 in costs in respect of the privilege violation.

Where the recipient spouse fails to disclose child support payments from a third party, the court may consider this financial information relevant when determining the time limit for an award of spousal support — A.B. v. C.D., 2014 CarswellBC 1707, 2014 BCSC 1081 (B.C.S.C.). In part due to information that emerged regarding the wife's receipt of $20,000 in child support payments from the child's biological father, the court limited spousal support to six years. The court did not specify exactly how the information was relevant to the order, but the judge made it clear that the wife's non-disclosure of this income was a factor in the decision.

"Arguably, the court should promote greater rather than lesser document disclosure in a family law context, particularly with respect to financial issues" — Doman v. Ciccozzi, 2014 CarswellBC 1361, 2014 BCSC 866 (B.C.S.C.). Spousal support was one of the issues the parties planned to resolve at trial. The payor husband made three requests for disclosure from the recipient wife. The wife eventually complied, but her disclosure was incomplete; the husband brought an application for disclosure seeking production of 31 types of documents or information. The court agreed that this documentation and information was relevant to financial issues to be determined at trial, but found that some of the requests either did not relate to document production or had to await the outcome of the examinations for discovery.

Parenting issues are not an adequate explanation for over a year's delay respecting a recipient party's disclosure of documents — Doman v. Ciccozzi, supra.

The court is likely to vary a spousal support provision retroactively in the parties' domestic agreement where there was inadequate and misleading financial disclosure — Seed v. Desai, 2014 CarswellOnt 6616, 2013 ONSC 3329 (Ont. S.C.J.). The parties' separation agreement included a review provision for spousal support. When the husband asked the court to review the issue of spousal support, the wife requested that the agreement be set aside on the basis that the husband's financial disclosure had been incomplete and inaccurate. The husband testified that the annual income of $85,000 he had imputed to himself was not actually an income figure, but rather a sum upon which he had decided he could afford to base support payments. He had not explained this process to the wife at the time. This self-imputed income did not correspond to the income he declared on his tax return, which was $136,374, an amount which also did not accurately reflect his income according to a Canada Revenue Agency audit. The wife asked that spousal and child support be retroactively increased from the date of separation in keeping with the amount revealed by the CRA audit as well as a report. The court found that the amount of spousal support the parties had agreed to could not stand in light of the husband's misleading disclosure, but that weight could be given to the intention to pay and review spousal support at a high level by retroactive order. The court awarded support at the high end of the SSAG range based on the husband's tax return information.

When making an interim order for spousal support, the court may draw an inference of business profitability from a party's failure to disclose relevant information and assume that the party has the means to pay the support ordered — Durston v. Durston, 2014 CarswellMan 144, 2014 MBQB 68, 304 Man. R. (2d) 166 (Man. Q.B.).

The court does not have jurisdiction to dismiss a motion to vary spousal support on the basis of non-disclosure in the absence of an order to disclose — FitzGerald v. Lee, supra. The wife requested that the court dismiss the husband's motion to vary spousal support in part on the basis that he failed to disclose his updated financial information. The court stated that its jurisdiction to dismiss a case on such grounds was predicated on a party's failure to obey a court order compelling disclosure rather than simply on the failure to disclose. In the absence of such a disclosure order, the court had no authority to dismiss the husband's motion to vary.

Where a party has not complied with disclosure orders and owes spousal and child support as well as costs, the court may hold proceeds from the sale of that party's home in trust until further order of the court — Wentges v. Faiz, 2014 CarswellOnt 8184, 2014 ONSC 3583 (Ont. S.C.J.).

A costs award based on delay due to one party's non-disclosure may be reduced in part by the other party's flawed arguments and unreasonable offers — McCombe v. McCombe, 2014 CarswellOnt 7700, 2014 ONSC 3278 (Ont. S.C.J.). The court observed that the disclosure issues in the case regarding income determination for spousal support did not justify a blanket order for substantial indemnity costs.

A finding of deliberate or willful non-disclosure is not necessary for making an order under s. 213 of the B.C. Family Law Act — Doman v. Ciccozzi, supra. The wife's entitlement to spousal support was at issue, and she had failed to produce documents that the husband had requested. The court stated that remedies now available under the Family Law Act with respect to delayed or inadequate document disclosure place an even greater emphasis on a party's disclosure obligations. The court cited G. (J.D.) v. V. (J.J.), 2013 CarswellBC 2161, 2013 BCSC 1274, 33 R.F.L. (7th) 56 (B.C.S.C.), in this regard.

Where the parties have been involved in protracted, emotionally charged litigation and both allege incomplete financial disclosure for spousal support purposes, the court may intervene and make a final order based on rough but sufficient figures as well as forbid further applications absent full and frank financial disclosure according to the court's terms — Clarke v. Clarke, 2014 CarswellBC 1307, 2014 BCSC 824 (B.C.S.C.).

"[O]nce the claimant has provided an evidentiary basis for the imputation of income, the responding party must provide some clarity as to whether the expenses can be reasonably deducted for child or spousal support purposes" — Sobiegraj v. Sobiegraj, 2014 CarswellOnt 4049, 2014 ONSC 2030, [2014] O.J. No. 1588 (Ont. S.C.J.).

Deliberate lack of disclosure in an attempt to frustrate the other party's claim for spousal support and other relief may lead to an award of special costs — Rana v. Rana, 2014 CarswellBC 839, 2014 BCSC 530 (B.C.S.C.).

The court may characterize a lack of timely disclosure regarding spousal support as adding to the complexity and difficulty of a case under R. 24(11) of the Family Law Rules when determining costs — Dupuis v. Desrosiers, 2014 CarswellOnt 4351, 2014 ONCJ 157 (Ont. C.J.).

The court will award only partial indemnity costs for the payor party's non-disclosure regarding spousal support at a prior stage in the proceedings when it is apparent that ongoing spousal support was not a reasonable possibility — Mondino v. Mondino, 2014 CarswellOnt 1953, 2014 ONSC 1102 (Ont. S.C.J.).

Where a recipient spouse fails to disclose her income fully and knowingly accepts spousal support monies to which she is not entitled, the court may order repayment to the payor spouse — Orlando v. Jepsen, 2013 CarswellOnt 13594, 2013 ONSC 6033, 36 R.F.L. (7th) 340 (Ont. S.C.J.). The wife failed to disclose her financial circumstances fully and subsequently resisted termination of spousal support and attempted to prolong support. The court found that she had knowingly accepted monies she was not entitled to receive despite her awareness of the husband's financial problems. The court stated that it would create a dangerous precedent to permit the wife to retain monies obtained by breaching the parties' consent order disclosure requirements and that not making a restitution order would be tantamount to condoning and encouraging unacceptable conduct. On the other hand, the court observed that the wife was the primary caregiver of the parties' children and had a considerably lower income than the husband. The court stated that it would be "troubling" to order repayment of monies already spent, particularly the portions spent on the children. However, the court concluded that the wife should be required to repay $24,629 in spousal support to which, in light of proper disclosure, it was clear she had not been entitled. The court left it to the parties to determine the method of repayment, noting that the sum could not be offset by child support payments.

If the husband seeks to make a case for termination of spousal support based on the means of the wife's new partner, the husband should make similar disclosure; otherwise the court "would be shooting in the evidentiary dark" — Ballegeer v. Ballegeer, 2013 CarswellMan 332, 2013 MBQB 162, 293 Man. R. (2d) 263 (Man. Q.B.).

"Full financial disclosure is a fundamental, basic and early requirement of family law litigants so that issues of need, ability to pay, division of assets and overall fairness in all of the circumstances can be properly assessed and determined by the parties and by the court" — Zarepour v. Jamshidi, 2013 CarswellOnt 6647, 2013 ONSC 2952 (Ont. S.C.J.).

The remedy of termination of support for a party's failure to file a reply to notice to disclose is a substantive rather than a procedural issue, as such a remedy affects the payee spouse's substantive right to support — Scully v. Scully, 2013 CarswellSask 297, 2013 SKQB 169, 418 Sask. R. 315 (Sask. Q.B.).

Where the recipient spouse's imperfect disclosure does not prevent resolution of the support provision in the parties' separation agreement, the court will not order further disclosure where the agreement obliges the payor to continue to pay support — S. (H.J.) v. S. (K.C.), 2013 CarswellBC 1698, 2013 BCSC 998 (B.C.S.C.).

While undisclosed gifts and inheritances would not normally be subject to equalization, they may be relevant to determination of the payee spouse's support claim — Kerzner v. Kerzner, 2013 CarswellOnt 278, 2013 ONSC 361, [2013] O.J. No. 187 (Ont. S.C.J.).

The court will dismiss a payor party's motion for summary judgement where the payee spouse has not provided adequate financial disclosure — Patrick v. Beitz, 2013 CarswellOnt 14074, 2013 ONSC 6397 (Ont. S.C.J.). The court noted that the wife's non-disclosure could be dealt with appropriately by way of costs as well as an order for disclosure including specific dates, failing which the husband could bring a motion to strike her pleading and/or find her in contempt.

Where the husband has had ample time to make financial disclosure, the court may decline his request to adjourn the matter in lieu of having income imputed for the purpose of determining interim spousal and child support — Stockwell v. Dalcin, 2013 CarswellOnt 4326, 2013 ONSC 2179 (Ont. S.C.J.). The court ordered interim support based on imputed income and ordered that the husband produce the requested financial disclosure within 30 days.

*When attempting to rescind arrears of spousal and child support by a motion to change after having income imputed, the payor spouse must go beyond establishing subsequent declared income and, rather, demonstrate evidence of a change in circumstances —* Trang v. Trang, 2013 CarswellOnt 4069, 2013 ONSC 1980, 29 R.F.L. (7th) 364, [2013] O.J. No. 1618 (Ont. S.C.J.). "When a court imputes income, that's a determination of a fact. It's not an estimate. It's not a guess. It's not a provisional order awaiting better disclosure, or further review. If 'declared income' automatically prevailed on a motion to change support, it would defeat the purpose of imputing income in the first place. It might even be a disincentive for payors to participate in the initial process" (paras. 51, 53).

*Where the payor's non-disclosure is particularly egregious, the court may award solicitor-client costs to the other party —* Dickson v. Dickson, 2012 CarswellMan 264, 2012 MBQB 152, 16 R.F.L. (7th) 96, 279 Man. R. (2d) 135 (Man. Q.B.). The husband provided "false, misleading and incomplete" financial disclosure throughout the proceedings. The interim claim for spousal support and other relief was not complex, and there had been no need for protracted litigation. The court observed that the husband's conduct, including non-disclosure, unnecessarily consumed the wife's financial resources as well as prevented her from stopping proceedings to resolve her claims through settlement. The court awarded the wife solicitor-client costs in the amount of $35,000, inclusive of fees, disbursements and taxes in keeping with the factors specified in Court of Queen's Bench R. 57.01(1). The court noted that income disclosure for both parties is essential in determining spousal support and other issues, and that non-disclosure undermines the objectives of the *Divorce Act.*

*It would be unfair to the wife to proceed without disclosure and information from the husband on the basis that her business valuator required the information to complete his retainer —* Bailey v. Bailey, 2012 CarswellOnt 5038, 2012 ONSC 2486 (Ont. S.C.J.), per Justice Mulligan.

*While the payor spouse's non-disclosure of financial information may justify a spousal support award at the upper range of the SSAG, the court will weigh this principle against the need to create a self-sufficiency incentive for the recipient spouse —* Bourgeois v. Bourgeois, 2011 CarswellOnt 6571, 2011 ONSC 4421 (Ont. S.C.J.).

*It is well established that the court has inherent jurisdiction to vary an interim support order under the Divorce Act when the assumptions on which the order was made later prove to have been clearly understated —* Lahanky v. Lahanky, 2011 CarswellNB 421, 2011 NBQB 220, 375 N.B.R. (2d) 370, 969 A.P.R. 370, [2011] N.B.J. No. 271 (N.B.Q.B.). The court varied spousal support on a motion initiated by the wife where the husband had previously failed to disclose his full income. The court referred to Dumont v. Dumont, 1987 CarswellNB 118, 86 N.B.R. (2d) 183, 219 A.P.R. 183, [1987] N.B.J. No. 1054 (N.B.Q.B.), in its decision.

*The court may order retroactive support where the husband underpaid support due to non-disclosure of income and assets —* Eva v. Eva, 2011 CarswellOnt 9025, 2011 ONSC 5217 (Ont. S.C.J.), additional reasons at 2011 CarswellOnt 13251, 2011 ONSC 7092 (Ont. S.C.J.).

*The court may order retroactive support at the high range of the SSAG in light of delay and underpayment due to the husband's inadequate disclosure of income and assets —* Beltran v. Folkesson, 2011 CarswellBC 1665, 2011 BCSC 866 (B.C.S.C.).

*The husband's failure to disclose financial information may lead to the court backdating entitlement from the date the husband ceased to contribute to support, rather than from the initiation of proceedings —* Taylor v. Taylor, 2011 CarswellOnt 8825, 2011 ONSC 3690 (Ont. S.C.J.). The husband consistently failed to comply with his disclosure obligations after court orders to that effect were issued. The court held that the usual commencement date for spousal support entitlement was the initiation of the proceedings. However, the court noted that the spouse who had undergone hardship may be compensated by a retroactive award and consequently awarded support from the date the husband ceased to pay support.

*The husband's disclosure was deemed inadequate in light of the significant assets he had accumulated* — Grinyer v. Grinyer, 2008 CarswellOnt 366, 49 R.F.L. (6th) 219, [2008] O.J. No. 290 (Ont. S.C.J.). An annual income of $108,000 was imputed to the husband for spousal support purposes, despite his claim that his business was in financial difficulty. Since separation, the husband had accumulated significant assets which were inconsistent with his claim of impecuniosity. Furthermore, he had failed to produce solid financial information for his business.

*Where the wife's delay in seeking support is due to the husband's lack of disclosure, the court may backdate the review period and order lump sum retroactive spousal support* — Kerman v. Kerman, 2008 CarswellBC 1358, 2008 BCSC 852, 58 R.F.L. (6th) 157 (B.C.S.C.). The original order contained a review clause. The court noted that review clauses are usually prospective, but because the husband failed to disclose his employment status and assets to the wife at the time, the court backdated the review by the period of the wife's delay in bringing her claim, which was 38 months. The court awarded the wife $97,321 plus interest free of tax as a retroactive lump sum award. The husband argued that he was worse off by needing to provide the sum to the wife free of tax. The court responded that by having caused the wife's delay in seeking support due to his non-disclosure, the husband could not now complain that he would have been better off had he paid the support amounts periodically over time. While the court characterized the order as one for retroactive lump sum support, the court also noted that, to its knowledge, "this is the first case where a court in this province has notionally backdated a review. The resulting award therefore does not fit neatly into any existing category."

*While disclosure is a given in family law, the probative value of the evidence must be considered* — Chernyakhovsky v. Chernyakhovsky, 2005 CarswellOnt 942, [2005] O.J. No. 944 (Ont. S.C.J.). The mother brought a motion to change seeking additional support. The father responded with an amended motion to change, including a motion to strike the applicant mother's pleadings for failure to disclose items ordered to be disclosed in an endorsement dated May 17, 2004. The parties had both worked in franchise arrangements. The mother currently worked in two dental offices as a salaried employee. The court found that some of the request for disclosure was confusing and too imprecise to be enforceable. Further, some of the request was for relevant information concerning the income of a franchise operator, but the mother at the time of the motion to vary worked in a dental office. Justice Rogers described the nature of the disclosure process in family law cases as follows at paras. 6, 7, 8 and 15:

> [6] The new approach to fact finding under the Family Law Rules has been to make disclosure a given. Fact-finding is not to be a battleground. There ought to be an orderly, prompt request for disclosure with an organized speedy reply. The process is not to go on forever and the case is to move on because the facts point to a resolution or to the necessity of a trial. Obtaining the factual evidence is no longer a game of hide and seek.

> [7] The rules provide a number of tools to create this approach. Rules 19 and 20 set up the process. Sanctions for failure to comply with a disclosure order are found in Rules 1(8), 13(7), 14(23) and 19(10). These sanctions are severe. A litigant may find his or her pleadings struck and the case proceeding without his or her participation. The severity of the sanctions serves to emphasize the importance of disclosing the necessary information in a file quickly.

> [8] The courts must, however, be clear that the disclosure process cannot be used to cause delay or to reap tactical advantage. The court must consider the burden certain disclosure requests bring for the disclosing party. Is the probative value of the sought-after disclosure so great in relation to the difficulty of obtaining the disclosure that said disclosure would be ordered and sanctions imposed for failure to comply? How does

the disclosure request fit into the overall context of the case? Is the issue for which disclosure is requested a central issue in the case? Or is it peripheral? Does the cost of obtaining the disclosure outweigh the value of the issue in the case? Is there a more expeditious and cheaper way of getting the same information? As the case develops, is the disclosure still related to an important issue in the case? As always, the court must balance these competing interests to ensure fairness.

[...]

[15] Before imposing sanctions the court must consider the clarity of the disclosure request, the continued relevance of the requested disclosure and the probative value of the missing disclosure weighed against the difficulty of obtaining the disclosure.

*Failure to provide timely disclosure may be grounds for awarding retroactive support —* Leinburd v. Leinburd, 2004 CarswellMan 194, 2004 MBQB 113, 10 R.F.L. (6th) 398, [2004] 9 W.W.R. 635, 185 Man. R. (2d) 215, [2004] M.J. No. 185 (Man. Q.B.). Improper conduct regarding timely disclosure of improvements to a payor's financial position may, in certain circumstances, give rise to retroactive spousal support despite the parties' agreement to the contrary.

*Where both parties had demonstrated a lack of cooperation in producing the documents required to reach conclusions about each party's rights, neither party was awarded costs at the conclusion of their divorce proceedings —* Lamarche c. Crevier, 2000 CarswellOnt 28, 4 R.F.L. (5th) 88, [2000] O.J. No. 45 (Ont. S.C.J.), additional reasons at 2000 CarswellOnt 1142 (Ont. S.C.J.).

*Financial disclosure of husband's common law spouse not required —* Bodman v. Bodman, 1998 CarswellMan 48, 38 R.F.L. (4th) 210, 127 Man. R. (2d) 1, [1998] M.J. No. 62 (Man. Master). The court rejected the wife's application to compel the husband to provide financial disclosure of the affairs of his common law wife. The application for disclosure had not been served on the common law wife, and there was no evidence that the husband had access to her financial information.

*The court's disapproval of a party misleading it concerning finances should be dealt with through costs —* Chisholm v. Chisholm, 1997 CarswellBC 324, 32 B.C.L.R. (3d) 20 (B.C.S.C.). Spousal support is not to be awarded as a means of punishing one spouse and rewarding another. Accordingly, where a spouse misleads the court concerning assets, the court's disapproval is more appropriately expressed through a cost award and not through an enhanced support award.

*Disclosure requirements waived where husband was willing to pay any reasonable amount —* Zwingenberger v. Zwingenberger, 1995 CarswellOnt 1084, 17 R.F.L. (4th) 239, [1995] O.J. No. 3402 (Ont. Gen. Div.). Where the husband claimed that full disclosure of his financial position would hurt his company's financial position and he indicated his ability and willingness to pay any reasonable increase in spousal support ordered, the requirement that he make full financial disclosure was waived. The finding would only have added unnecessarily to the length and cost of the proceedings.

*Effect of non-disclosure in family law —* Cunha v. Cunha, 1994 CarswellBC 509, 99 B.C.L.R. (2d) 93, [1994] B.C.J. No. 2573 (B.C.S.C.), at para. 9:

> Non-disclosure of assets is the cancer of matrimonial property litigation. It discourages settlement or promotes settlement which are inadequate. It increases the time and expense of litigation. The prolonged stress of unnecessary battle may lead weary and drained women simply to give up and walk away with only a share of the assets they know about, taking with them the bitter aftertaste of a reasonably-based suspicion that justice was not done.

Quoted with approval in *Leskun v. Leskun*, 2006 CarswellBC 1492, 2006 CarswellBC 1493, 2006 SCC 25, 34 R.F.L. (6th) 1, [2006] 1 S.C.R. 920, 62 B.C.L.R. (4th) 197, 268 D.L.R. (4th) 577, 226 B.C.A.C. 1, 373 W.A.C. 1, 349 N.R. 158, [2006] S.C.J. No. 25 (S.C.C.), at para. 34.

*Where the evidence in an interim support application indicates that the husband's income exceeds that specified in his declaration, the court is not bound by such declaration in quantifying the support payable* — *Droit de la famille - 1231*, [1989] R.D.F. 189 (C.S. Que.).

*Even where a settlement is negotiated by the parties, it is desirable that the means of the payor be disclosed so that the court can satisfy itself of the propriety of the settlement* — *Cumisky v. Cumisky*, 1974 CarswellSask 75, 18 R.F.L. 182, [1974] 5 W.W.R. 544 (Sask. Q.B.).

*A record of 3 years of financial disclosure on the part of a claimant is generally sufficient in a claim for spousal support* — *Forbes v. Forbes*, 1994 CarswellMan 365, 99 Man. R. (2d) 280 (Man. Master).

*Incomplete disclosure will not disentitle a recipient spouse to support where the court has some expenses evidence from which to extrapolate an income that falls within entitlement range* — *Bennett v. Reeves*, 2014 CarswellOnt 3920, 2014 ONCJ 145 (Ont. C.J.).

*There is no basis to set aside a domestic agreement regarding spousal support and other family law issues for non-disclosure of assets where both parties knowingly entered into the agreement without providing financial disclosure* — *Strifler v. Strifler*, 2014 CarswellOnt 1559, 2014 ONCJ 69 (Ont. C.J.).

*A payor spouse seeking a retroactive variation of spousal support must fully disclose his or her financial circumstances* — *Boland v. Boland*, 2012 CarswellOnt 2748, 2012 ONCJ 102, [2012] O.J. No. 925 (Ont. C.J.), additional reasons at 2012 CarswellOnt 5050, 2012 ONCJ 239, 22 R.F.L. (7th) 368 (Ont. C.J.). The husband was diagnosed with cancer and consequently sought retroactive reduction and termination of spousal support. The court found that the husband had not provided any financial disclosure, failed to provide evidence regarding the reason for delaying commencing the motion, and was not fully forthright about his business plans in the future. The court declined to order a retroactive decrease, finding that the husband had not established need.

*In deciding whether to order retroactive support, a court should apply a disclosure/due diligence model whereby a dependant must exercise due diligence in pursuing support rights when the dependant learns the facts entitling him or her to (increased) support* — *Hayes v. Hayes*, 2005 CarswellOnt 3385, 2005 ONCJ 241, 18 R.F.L. (6th) 340, [2005] O.J. No. 3301 (Ont. C.J.) (wife entitled to retroactive support where husband failed to disclose increase in income and wife instituted proceedings without delay); *Boland v. Boland*, 2006 CarswellNfld 208, 2006 NLUFC 37, 259 Nfld. & P.E.I.R. 60, 781 A.P.R. 60, [2006] N.J. No. 206 (N.L.U.F.C.) (husband was not credible and failed to meet legal obligations with respect to declaration of his income and payment of spousal support, retroactive lump sum amount was ordered). A payor should not expect any judicial sympathy if he or she withheld material information or tried to avoid support: *Marinangeli v. Marinangeli*, 2003 CarswellOnt 2691, 38 R.F.L. (5th) 307, 66 O.R. (3d) 40, 174 O.A.C. 76, 228 D.L.R. (4th) 376, [2003] O.J. No. 2819 (Ont. C.A.) (retroactive support because of payor's failure to disclose); *Redman v. Korchinski*, 2006 CarswellMan 436, 2006 MBCA 149, 33 R.F.L. (6th) 36, [2007] 2 W.W.R. 611, 277 D.L.R. (4th) 427, 212 Man. R. (2d) 90, 389 W.A.C. 90 (Man. C.A.) (husband failed to forward relevant financial information in a timely fashion, retroactive spousal support order was upheld on appeal).

## 9.2 Delay in Bringing Application

*Effect of delay on support claim* — *C. (Y.J.) v. C. (Y.D.)*, 2001 CarswellOnt 3514, 56 O.R. (3d) 150, 150 O.A.C. 247 (Ont. C.A.); *M. (K.) v. M. (H.)*, 1992 CarswellOnt 998, 1992

CarswellOnt 841, EYB 1992-67549, [1992] 3 S.C.R. 6, 14 C.C.L.T. (2d) 1, 96 D.L.R. (4th) 289, 142 N.R. 321, 57 O.A.C. 321, [1992] S.C.J. No. 85 (S.C.C.). Mere delay as with the equitable doctrine of *laches* is not a defence to a claim for spousal support. In addition, there must be acquiescence on the part of the plaintiff, or the plaintiff's conduct must have either caused the defendant to alter his position in reasonable reliance on the appellant's acceptance of the *status quo* or permitted a situation which it would be unjust to disturb. Ultimately, the issue of delay or laches is a matter of justice as between the parties.

*A relevant consideration is whether the delay is prejudicial to the payor — Marinangeli v. Marinangeli*, 2003 CarswellOnt 2691, 38 R.F.L. (5th) 307, 66 O.R. (3d) 40, 228 D.L.R. (4th) 376, 174 O.A.C. 76, [2003] O.J. No. 2819 (Ont. C.A.). While there was some delay on the part of the respondent in requesting increased spousal support once she became aware of the appellant's income, this delay occasioned no prejudice. The major portion of the delay after the Minutes were signed arose prior to the respondent becoming aware of the appellant's circumstances and was due to his non-disclosure.

*Modest award where 18 years since divorce — Brown v. Brown*, 1996 CarswellAlta 651, 187 A.R. 156, 127 W.A.C. 156, [1996] A.J. No. 658 (Alta. C.A.). The Chambers Judge, without giving reasons, awarded the wife spousal support, despite the fact that the parties had been divorced for approximately 18 years and despite the fact that at that time the former wife had received legal advice that she was entitled to seek support. When the parties were divorced, spousal support was reserved. The wife cared for the parties' severely disabled child and prior to seeking support, developed various illnesses. The former husband agreed that spousal support was payable, but disputed the amount. The wife had assisted the husband with his education and had suffered much of the economic hardship arising from the breakdown of the marriage. It was unlikely that she would ever be able to achieve economic self-sufficiency. The Chambers Judge ordered the appellant to pay the respondent $1500/month by way of spousal support, a lump sum of $3,700, and costs. The appellant court granted the appeal and substituted an award of $500 a month in place of the award granted by the Chambers Judge. Hunt J.A. stated at para. 17:

> There is nothing in the very unusual facts of this case that provides a method of setting the quantum of spousal support with any degree of mathematical certainty. However, the long delay in seeking spousal support and the short duration of the marriage are key factors militating against the amount awarded by the chambers judge. In our view, that award was excessive. The respondent's circumstances make it unlikely that she will ever enjoy a comfortable level of income. On the other hand, although the appellant is more economically secure than she is, he is not wealthy and he has a new child to support. In this situation, all that can be accomplished with a spousal award is a modest alleviation of the impoverished circumstances of the respondent.

*Delay reasonable in light of circumstances — Lautermilch v. Lautermilch*, 2005 CarswellNB 294, 2005 CarswellNB 295, 2005 NBCA 59, 286 N.B.R. (2d) 46, 748 A.P.R. 46, [2005] N.B.J. No. 215 (N.B.C.A.). The court quoted from the judgement of the trial judge who considered the reasonableness of the former wife's 8½ year delay in seeking spousal support. The judge stated:

> Delay is not a concept that is evaluated in a vacuum. All of the circumstances of the case require consideration. I have taken into consideration the case law outlined by [Mr. Lautermilch] in his brief, as well as the case law outlined in the brief submitted on behalf of [Mrs. Lautermilch]. Of importance in this case are [Mrs. Lautermilch's] financial circumstances throughout rendering her incapable of seeking legal advice, her emotional condition, of living with her physical limitations, her use of medication and

the emotional trauma of living with a very sick child and coping with her untimely death. Taking all of those circumstances into consideration, I am satisfied that the pursuit of her legal rights was the bottom end of priorities throughout. She should not be deprived of pursuing her claim in all of the circumstances of this case. I therefore conclude that the delay in this case was both adequately explained and in my view justified.

The former husband asserted that in the circumstances "there was an agreement between the parties that no spousal support would be claimed." In the alternative, he sought a reduction of the $700 per month support payment and a limited term for payment of it. Further, he claimed that the trial judge erred "in determining that the former wife was able to work only thirty five hours per week in the absence of medical evidence." The appellate court held that there was no basis in law on which to interfere with the trial judge's decision; deference must be accorded. The appeal was dismissed.

*Claimant unaware of right to seek support at time of divorce 20 years beforehand —* Hillhouse v. Hillhouse, 1992 CarswellBC 359, 43 R.F.L. (3d) 266, 74 B.C.L.R. (2d) 230, 20 B.C.A.C. 28, 35 W.A.C. 28, [1992] B.C.J. No. 2409 (B.C.C.A.), reversing 1990 CarswellBC 1794 (B.C.S.C. [In Chambers]). Where the wife was unaware of her right to seek permanent support at the time of the parties' divorce, her subsequent claim for support was not barred by the fact that 20 years had elapsed since the date of the divorce. Her continuing need was still causally connected to the parties' long-term traditional marriage.

*There is no entitlement to support where the claimant did not have a need until 6 years after the parties' separation —* Rezel v. Rezel, 2007 CarswellOnt 2313, 37 R.F.L. (6th) 445, [2007] O.J. No. 1460 (Ont. S.C.J.).

*Separation had occurred 13 years beforehand — ongoing spousal support ordered — Friend* v. Paul, 2006 CarswellOnt 8549, [2006] O.J. No. 5315 (Ont. S.C.J.). Where the parties were married for 17 years, the wife stayed home with the children for 12 years and, notwithstanding her attempts to become self-sufficient, there was a significant gap in her earnings and those of the husband, the wife was awarded ongoing spousal support, despite the fact that it was 13 years since separation.

*Delay in wife's claim plus husband's having taken on responsibilities lead to denial of claim — Lerner v. Lerner,* 2008 CarswellSask 496, 2008 SKQB 308, 56 R.F.L. (6th) 105, 321 Sask. R. 78 (Sask. Q.B.). The wife's claim for spousal support, brought to light years after the parties' separation, was dismissed. The husband had assumed full financial responsibility for the parties' children and had taken responsibility for a large family debt. In light of this, the wife's late claim for spousal support defied logic.

*Delay explained by pre-nuptial agreement and separation agreement — B. (B.A.) v. B.(S.S.),* 2005 CarswellBC 945, 2005 BCSC 593, 15 R.F.L. (6th) 247, [2005] B.C.J. No. 882 (B.C.S.C.). Where the wife did not seek spousal support for 11 months after the parties' separation, the delay was explained by two agreements, a pre-nuptial agreement and a separation agreement, which precluded the wife from seeking spousal support unless she moved to set them aside. The court found that there was no evidence that a retroactive lump sum award would impose an unfair burden on the husband at this time. The award would have the effect of redistributing capital, but that would not be its purpose. Its purpose would be to compensate the wife for the extent to which she depleted her resources during a time in which she should have been receiving spousal support. The wife had received social assistance for 11 months after separation, but was currently employed and earning $51,000 per year. The court found that the separation agreement was negotiated in a rush and should be somewhat discounted. The husband was ordered to pay the wife lump sum spousal support of $17,500.

*In exceptional circumstances, support can be awarded despite delay* — Gearin v. Gearin, 1999 CarswellNfld 87, 45 R.F.L. (4th) 333, 176 Nfld. & P.E.I.R. 76, 540 A.P.R. 76, [1999] N.J. No. 97 (Nfld. U.F.C.). In a determination of whether spousal support should be granted, the *Divorce Act* and the case law support the conclusion that a delay is an important circumstance to be considered, but it can, in certain exceptional circumstances, be superseded by putting forth a reasonable explanation for the delay, so that that a court can exercise its discretion to allow a consideration of entitlement to spousal support. The court considered that delay was *one* critical circumstance in the determination but that it was generally accepted that a court does have discretion to permit a party to make a claim for permanent maintenance years after a divorce was granted without an original order. It cited *Provost v. Provost*, 1997 CarswellBC 159, 27 R.F.L. (4th) 184 (B.C.S.C.) for this proposition and also stated that the delay is not an "unexplained delay". See *K. (H.J.) v. B. (J.E.)*, 1997 CarswellBC 2558, 33 R.F.L. (4th) 409, 44 B.C.L.R. (3d) 77, 100 B.C.A.C. 1, 163 W.A.C. 1 (B.C.C.A.).

In the *Gearin* case, the parties were divorced in 1990 and there was a consent order, without reference to spousal support in 1992. The wife brought an application for interim spousal support in 1998. Although she sought support in her divorce counter petition, it was not dealt with in the consent order following the divorce. She considered that the $990 monthly payments of child support to her supplemented her own income. She believed that it would have been pointless to attempt to also get spousal support from the husband at that time because he did not have the resources to pay spousal support in addition to $990 in monthly child support. She also considered that if she were denied spousal support in 1992, and she subsequently applied, this could prove detrimental because her entitlement to spousal support *could* then be deemed to be *res judicata*.

The court quoted with approval from *Janes v. Janes*, 1985 CarswellNfld 32, 47 R.F.L. (2d) 378, 54 Nfld. & P.E.I.R. 310, 160 A.P.R. 310 (Nfld. U.F.C.), where Cameron J. stated at p. 313 [Nfld. & P.E.I.R.]:

> ... time lags are appropriate factors for consideration in determining if maintenance should be awarded. . . . The applicant must demonstrate exceptional circumstances to satisfy the court that the marriage having been dissolved and issues having been resolved between the parties, the court should disturb that arrangement and grant an order for maintenance. One critical circumstance to be considered is the delay in bringing the application.

The court found that the wife had provided reasonable explanations for her long delay in seeking spousal support. It exercised its discretion and allowed the wife to have her entitlement to interim spousal support considered at this time.

*For purposes of interim relief the court found that a delay in applying for support 8½ years after support had ended was sufficiently explained by the efforts the wife made to become self-supporting and to live off her capital in order to avoid bringing the application* — Bailey v. Plaxton, 2000 CarswellOnt 1194, 6 R.F.L. (5th) 29, 47 O.R. (3d) 593, [2000] O.T.C. 243, [2000] O.J. No. 1187 (Ont. S.C.J.).

*Separation 18 years earlier — support awarded* — Droit de la famille - 1321, [1990] R.D.F. 233 (C.S. Que.). The court refused the husband's claim that the wife be denied spousal support. Although the parties had been separated for 18 years, the wife had carried the burden of raising the children herself, which, combined with her health problems, had impeded her opportunity to become self-sufficient.

*Parties separated 10 years earlier — support entitlement found due to decline in health* — Droit de la famille - 1229, [1989] R.D.F. 152 (C.S. Que.). The court awarded support to the wife despite the fact that the parties had been separated for over 10 years. The wife had attempted self-sufficiency but a decline in her health had prevented her from working, with the result that the court was unable to conclude that she could be self-sufficient.

## 9.3 Relationship between Spousal Support and Child Support

Subsections 15.3(1) and (2) of the *Divorce Act* give express priority to an application for child support over an application for spousal support. In keeping with the general tenor of the amendments, the *Guidelines* amount would be ordered for child support even if the amount left over would be inadequate for spousal support. There would be no *pro rata* allocation of the available fund between the two applicants with both receiving less than they need. The child would receive his or her full share, and the spouse less than his or her full share in the allocation. Subsection 15.3(3) provides that if spousal support is inadequate because of the payor spouse's child support obligations, and child support is reduced or terminated, that change would constitute a change in circumstances for the purposes of applying for spousal support or a variation of spousal support.

*Where the husband lacked the ability to afford spousal support after taking into account his child support obligations and the lower end of the range under SSAG was zero, the court did not make an order for spousal support — MacFarland v. MacFarland*, 2009 CarswellOnt 2949, 70 R.F.L. (6th) 196, [2009] O.J. No. 2149 (Ont. S.C.J.). The court stated that when child support was no longer payable, the provisions of the *Divorce Act*, s. 15.3(3) might become applicable.

*Spousal support claim dismissed where parties in shared custody situation and had comparable net disposable incomes — Neeteson v. Neeteson*, 2007 CarswellOnt 7125, 45 R.F.L. (6th) 164 (Ont. S.C.J.), additional reasons at 2007 CarswellOnt 7942, 50 R.F.L. (6th) 29 (Ont. S.C.J.). Where the result of child support order in a shared parenting situation left the father with 49% of net disposable income and the wife with 51%, the wife's claim for spousal support was dismissed. Given the shared custody arrangement, it was equitable that the parties ought to retain comparable net disposable incomes.

*Increase in spousal support when child support ended — Friend v. Paul*, 2006 CarswellOnt 8549, [2006] O.J. No. 5315 (Ont. S.C.J.). Where the husband would have more funds available to him when the child support obligation ended, the court held that it would be appropriate that the net disposable income division between the parties be closer to 50%, and consequently the husband was ordered to pay $300 in spousal support until child support ended and then $500 per month.

*Effect of child support on interim spousal support — Lane v. Lane*, 1996 CarswellOnt 506, 19 R.F.L. (4th) 168 (Ont. Gen. Div.). Where the husband, who was awarded custody of the parties' daughter, could no longer work overtime because of his child care responsibilities, the decrease in his income was considered in determining the quantum of interim spousal support to be paid by him.

*Voluntary payments to children cannot take precedence over spousal support in circumstances where the children are living independently and earning income — Tedham v. Tedham*, 2005 CarswellBC 2346, 2005 BCCA 502, 20 R.F.L. (6th) 217, 47 B.C.L.R. (4th) 254, 261 D.L.R. (4th) 332, [2006] 3 W.W.R. 212, [2005] B.C.J. No. 2186 (B.C.C.A.), additional reasons at 2005 CarswellBC 2699, 2005 BCCA 553, 47 B.C.L.R. (4th) 276, 261 D.L.R. (4th) 332 at 359, [2006] 3 W.W.R. 234, 217 B.C.A.C. 250, 358 W.A.C. 250 (B.C.C.A.).

*Judge does not quantify spousal support due to effect of child support on ability to pay — Hunt v. Smolis-Hunt*, 2001 CarswellAlta 1357, 2001 ABCA 229, 20 R.F.L. (5th) 409, 97 Alta. L.R. (3d) 238, 205 D.L.R. (4th) 712, [2001] 11 W.W.R. 233, 286 A.R. 248, 253 W.A.C. 248, [2001] A.J. No. 1170 (Alta. C.A.). The payee is clearly entitled to compensatory support where she changed her work to respond to the career plans and goals of her husband and to the needs of the children. Her sacrifices were made in order for him to achieve his goal of becoming a lawyer. By assisting her husband with his goals, she bestowed a great economic advantage on him and a disadvantage on herself and an economic hardship, both short and long-term. The court held that the trial judge complied with the requirements of s. 15.3 (terms and conditions of spousal support orders) of the *Divorce Act* by giving reasons why she could not quantify the award. She did not do so because she found that the payor would be unable to pay any periodic or lump sum other than through his equity in the matrimonial assets which had been extinguished by the child support awards.

*Retroactive and ongoing spousal support will be granted where previous awards did not adequately take into account the economic hardship caused by the marriage because of the priority of child support obligations* — *Danby v. Danby*, 2008 CarswellOnt 5512, [2008] O.J. No. 3659 (Ont. S.C.J.). The husband sought a variation lowering his support obligations after he retired. At the time of the prior support order, two of the parties' children were considered dependents. The judge found that the husband's spousal support obligations should continue, given the ongoing need and the fact that previous spousal support payments "did not meet the appropriate support objectives but, rather, were slightly more than nominal" in order to allow the payment of child support, which is given precedence when means are limited. Therefore, the obligation to support was ongoing, and as the older child was no longer dependent, money was now available for spousal support. The judge found that the wife was entitled to compensatory and non-compensatory support and that economic hardship had not been adequately addressed in the previous order. He granted retroactive and ongoing support.

*Lower spousal support award, given payor's child support obligations* — *Peters v. Peters*, 2002 CarswellNS 389, 2002 NSSF 40, [2002] N.S.J. No. 413 (N.S.S.C.). The husband was ordered to pay an amount of spousal support that was less than that to which the payee spouse was entitled, because of the husband's obligations to pay child support. Under s. 15.3 of the *Divorce Act*, the priority of the child support payments requires the court to make an order for spousal support "less than it otherwise would have been". In the *Peters* case, if the husband paid the full amount of child and spousal support, he would be in a deficit position. The wife was disabled. She was awarded $1,500 per month, rather than the $2,500 to which she was entitled. The wife could revisit the issue of spousal support, if the husband's obligation to pay child support was decreased or terminated.

*Spousal support and child support should be dealt with separately and not set-off one against the other* — *Y. (H.) v. Y. (D.)*, 1999 CarswellPEI 43, 49 R.F.L. (4th) 450, 175 Nfld. & P.E.I.R. 85, 537 A.P.R. 85 (P.E.I. T.D. [In Chambers]). The husband was not allowed to set-off his monthly child support obligation against a spousal support over-payment owed by the wife. Child support and spousal support obligations should not be intermingled. It is unfair to the child and contrary to the spirit of the legislation to excuse a parent from paying child support on the basis of dealings between the spouses.

*Child support not payable* — *Bourque v. Phillips*, 2000 CarswellNB 17, 223 N.B.R. (2d) 242, 572 A.P.R. 242, [2000] N.B.J. No. 13 (N.B.Q.B.), an application for child support by the child's grandmother against his biological parents was successfully opposed by the father. The father pleaded undue hardship resulting from his obligations under a separation agreement for the support of his spouse and two children of his second marriage. The court was satisfied that the payment of support for three children (total combined child and spousal support payments of approximately $24,000 per year) on an income of $34,000 per year was "excessive" or "disproportionate" and consequently permitted the father to succeed on his claim up to and inclusive of the date when he was no longer required to pay spousal support for his second wife.

*Child support helps to relieve need, this is relevant to support entitlement* — *Kits v. Kits*, 1998 CarswellBC 2323, 42 R.F.L. (4th) 167, [1998] B.C.J. No. 2539 (B.C.S.C.). The wife's receipt of child support which reduced her need was among the reasons for denying her application for periodic support. However, a lump sum was awarded on compensatory principles.

*While child support takes priority to spousal support, a payee spouse should not be left destitute, if possible* — *Kaderly v. Kaderly*, 1997 CarswellPEI 85, [1997] P.E.I.J. No. 74 (P.E.I.T.D.). Jenkins J. stated that while s. 15.3(1) of the *Divorce Act* stated that child support is to take priority over spousal support, Parliament did not intend this to operate so as to provide everything a child may need or which may benefit a child and leave the mother, who is a spouse, destitute. For purposes of the *Guidelines*, the payor earned $111,000. He was ordered to pay $850 per month in spousal support until October 31, 2007, subject to specific conditions for variation and $1 per year from November 2007 to October 2012. He was also ordered to pay child support to the mother of $1,800 per month and upon the child enrolling in university, the father was instead required to pay the portion of child support applicable to that child, *i.e.*, $450 per month for the 8month period from September to May, directly to that child or to the university in which the child was enrolled.

*Where the husband lacked sufficient funds to pay both child and spousal support, it was held that the needs of the child must take priority* — *Hiller v. Hiller*, 1995 CarswellAlta 618, 167 A.R. 81 (Alta. Q.B.).

*Child support reduced amount of spousal support because of indirect benefit of child support* — *R. v. R.*, 2000 CarswellOnt 2744, 10 R.F.L. (5th) 88, [2000] O.T.C. 596, [2000] O.J. No. 2830 (Ont. S.C.J), additional reasons at 2001 CarswellOnt 797, 15 R.F.L. (5th) 163 (Ont. S.C.J.). The court took into account that the wife would benefit indirectly from substantial child support payments in quantifying her own spousal support entitlement.

*Effect of child support on spousal support* — *M. (S.B.) v. M. (N.)*, 2002 CarswellBC 989, 2002 BCSC 529, 27 R.F.L. (5th) 363, [2002] B.C.J. No. 951 (B.C.S.C.). The court, in quantifying the wife's spousal support entitlement, considered the fact that the custodial husband's childcare expenses were likely to be reduced considerably over the next 5 years, given the ages of the children.

*Effect of child support on interim spousal support* — *Lane v. Lane*, 1996 CarswellOnt 506, 19 R.F.L. (4th) 168 (Ont. Gen. Div.). Where the husband, who was awarded custody of the parties' daughter, could no longer work overtime because of his child care responsibilities, the decrease in his income was considered in determining the quantum of interim spousal support to be paid by him.

*Non-custodial parent who applied for spousal support* — *unable to contribute to child support* — *Reyher v. Reyher*, 1993 CarswellMan 54, 48 R.F.L. (3d) 111 (Man. Q.B.). The fact that the wife was unable to contribute to the support of the child in the husband's custody was found to be a relevant factor in determining the quantum of spousal support payable to her. The husband was entitled to some consideration for the child-care costs which he carried.

*In determining child support, the children's needs should be given priority over those of the parents* — *King v. King*, 1990 CarswellNS 39, 25 R.F.L. (3d) 338, 95 N.S.R. (2d) 409, 251 A.P.R. 409, [1990] N.S.J. No. 114 (N.S.T.D.). In this case, the children's needs were paramount to those of the father, the payor parent. The wife had not made out any case for lump sum maintenance. The application of the husband for reduced periodic maintenance was refused. The court held that the husband could elect either to continue as he had in the past to pay the amount of $750 per month tax-free to his wife, or to pay an equivalent amount with respect to which the wife would pay the income tax.

## 9.4 Effects of Property on Spousal Support

*Capital assets acquired after the parties' separation should be taken into account in deciding spousal support* — Leskun v. *Leskun*, 2006 CarswellBC 1492, 2006 CarswellBC 1493, 2006 SCC 25, 34 R.F.L. (6th) 1, [2006] 1 S.C.R. 920, 62 B.C.L.R. (4th) 197, 268 D.L.R. (4th) 577, 226 B.C.A.C. 1, 373 W.A.C. 1, 349 N.R. 158, [2006] S.C.J. No. 25 (S.C.C.). In determining spousal support, a court can take into account a payor spouse's capital assets acquired after the marital break-up. Since the capital assets at issue did not exist at the time of the initial division, there was no question of "double dipping".

*Where entitlement and ability to pay were present, a recipient spouse should not have to live on capital assets acquired in the matrimonial property division* — Bergquist v. *Bergquist*, 2014 CarswellSask 112, 2014 SKCA 20, 39 R.F.L. (7th) 251, 433 Sask. R. 173, 602 W.A.C. 173, [2014] S.J. No. 108 (Sask. C.A.). The wife was granted substantial property in the equalization process. She was 63 and had never worked outside the family businesses. The trial judge declined to impute income to her and also declined to impute income to her based on her assets. The Court of Appeal upheld this decision, finding that, following the decision of *Goeldner v. Goeldner*, 2005 CarswellOnt 83, 15 R.F.L. (6th) 272, 194 O.A.C. 129, [2005] O.J. No. 86 (Ont. C.A.), where entitlement and ability to pay was present, a spouse should not have to live on capital.

*Income of a spousal support recipient will not include non-income earning assets* — M. *(P.R.) v. M. (B.J.)*, 2013 CarswellBC 2204, 2013 BCCA 327, 34 R.F.L. (7th) 1, 340 B.C.A.C. 198, 579 W.A.C. 198, [2013] B.C.J. No. 1530 (B.C.C.A.). The parties married in 1983, had four children, and separated in 2006. The husband was the sole income earner. On separation, the husband received over $8.5 million in assets, and the wife received assets of just over $4 million. The trial judge calculated the wife's income for 2012 at $55,000 based on interest income and imputed employment income. This amount excluded non-income-earning assets. The Court of Appeal dismissed the husband's appeal, finding that the trial judge did not err in failing to impute income on non-income-earning assets. The Court of Appeal stated that, "[t]he possibility that upon a sale of the assets, or putting them to different use, may earn income, in my view, does not mandate those actions" and, further, agreed with the trial judge about "the undesirability of seeking to impute income on the strength of appreciation of an asset because to do so would erode the finality of the division of assets."

*Where stock options were purchased using funds from the property division, and the payor had made reasonable efforts to produce income using matrimonial assets, income was not imputed to him. Income was imputed to the wife for failing to generate any income from her marital assets* — Lane v. *Lane*, 2012 CarswellAlta 67, 2012 ABCA 2 (Alta. C.A.). The Court of Appeal upheld a trial decision in which income was imputed to the wife for failing to generate any income at all from her marital assets, which the court found "could easily have earned income."

*Support award may be reduced in light of property award, however, the fact that a court has reapportioned property under s. 65 of the* Family Relations Act *does not mean that there should not be an award of spousal support* — Tedham v. *Tedham*, 2005 CarswellBC 2346, 2005 BCCA 502, 20 R.F.L. (6th) 217, 47 B.C.L.R. (4th) 254, 261 D.L.R. (4th) 332, [2006] 3 W.W.R. 212, [2005] B.C.J. No. 2186 (B.C.C.A.), additional reasons at 2005 CarswellBC 2699, 2005 BCCA 553, 47 B.C.L.R. (4th) 276, 261 D.L.R. (4th) 332 at 359, [2006] 3 W.W.R. 234, 217 B.C.A.C. 250, 358 W.A.C. 250 (B.C.C.A.). Where a property award has compensated the other spouse to some extent for the disadvantages she suffered as a result of the marriage and its breakdown, an award of spousal support, whether the Advisory Guidelines are taken into account or not, should be lower than it otherwise would have been. The court considered the appropriate order for spousal support where there was a 16-year marriage and the court was utilizing the "without child support formula" which would yield a support order in the range of $6,300 to $8,500 per month with a duration of between 8 and 16 years, assuming the husband's income was in the range of $343,000 per year and the wife's was in the range of $30,000 per year. The court ordered indefinite spousal support of $6,000 per month, less than amounts provided in the range in the Advisory Guidelines since it held that an award must take into account the reapportionment of property ordered by the court. Such cases are determined on the extent to which the reapportionment has adequately compensated for the economic dislocation caused to a spouse flowing from the marriage or its breakdown, and any continuing need the spouse may have for support.

*The general rule against double dipping does not apply to phantom stock bonuses where a significant portion of the profit from the phantom stock arose after separation* — Marinangeli v. Marinangeli, 2003 CarswellOnt 2691, 38 R.F.L. (5th) 307, 66 O.R. (3d) 40, 228 D.L.R. (4th) 376, 174 O.A.C. 76, [2003] O.J. No. 2819 (Ont. C.A.). The appellant's income had increased. The respondent was not hoarding her capital at the expense of the appellant. Most of what she received in the equalization process was the matrimonial home which is not an income-producing asset. The respondent was not able to contribute to her own support in a significant way and she was in debt. She demonstrated need and suffered economic hardship from the marriage or its breakdown. There was no error on the part of the trial judge in including a phantom stock bonus in the appellant's income. The receipt of payment when stock options are exercised is the taking of deferred income at a particular time and the value should be brought into income in the year that the options are exercised. The value of the options which have been exercised are an appropriate factor for the trial judge to consider in making an order for spousal support.

*In circumstances where economic hardship from a marriage or its breakdown exists, it may not be possible to avoid drawing upon assets for support which have already been the subject of property equalization between the spouses* — MacPherson v. Auld, 2007 CarswellOnt 6555, 44 R.F.L. (6th) 364 (Ont. S.C.J.), additional reasons at 2008 CarswellOnt 5642, 60 R.F.L. (6th) 429 (Ont. S.C.J.).

*The wife's spousal support was structured to reduce gradually over time with each installment of the sizable equalization payment to which she was entitled* — LeVan v. LeVan, 2008 CarswellOnt 2738, 2008 ONCA 388, 51 R.F.L. (6th) 237, 90 O.R. (3d) 1, 239 O.A.C. 1, [2008] O.J. No. 1905 (Ont. C.A.), additional reasons at 2008 CarswellOnt 3713, 2008 ONCA 505, 51 R.F.L. (6th) 261 (Ont. C.A.); affirming 2006 CarswellOnt 5393, 32 R.F.L. (6th) 291, 82 O.R. (3d) 1, [2006] O.J. No. 3584 (Ont. S.C.J.), additional reasons at 2006 CarswellOnt 7334, 32 R.F.L. (6th) 359, 82 O.R. (3d) 1 at 76, [2006] O.J. No. 4599 (Ont. S.C.J.); leave to appeal refused 2008 CarswellOnt 6207, 2008 CarswellOnt 6208, [2008] 3 S.C.R. viii (note), 391 N.R. 391 (note), 256 O.A.C. 394 (note), [2008] S.C.C.A. No. 331 (S.C.C.).

*Substantial inheritance could fund spousal support* — Pecore v. Pecore, 2004 CarswellOnt 748, 48 R.F.L. (5th) 89, 6 E.T.R. (3d) 113, 7 E.T.R. (3d) 113, [2004] O.T.C. 188, [2004] O.J. No. 695 (Ont. S.C.J.), affirmed 2005 CarswellOnt 4043, 17 R.F.L. (6th) 261, 19 E.T.R. (3d) 162, 202 O.A.C. 169, [2005] O.J. No. 3712 (Ont. C.A.), affirmed 2007 CarswellOnt 2752, 2007 CarswellOnt 2753, 2007 SCC 17, 37 R.F.L. (6th) 237, [2007] 1 S.C.R. 795, 279 D.L.R. (4th) 513, 32 E.T.R. (3d) 1, 224 O.A.C. 330, 361 N.R. 1, [2007] S.C.J. No. 17 (S.C.C.). Where both parties were prohibited from working because of health issues, and the husband particularly so, the wife was nevertheless required to pay spousal support to the husband. The wife had received a substantial inheritance which would generate an annual income of approximately $35,000. Accordingly, the wife was in a financial position to pay support.

*Wife receives spousal support partially funded by equalized share of pension* — Meiklejohn v. Meiklejohn, 2001 CarswellOnt 3480, 19 R.F.L. (5th) 167, 150 O.A.C. 149, [2001] O.T.C. 323, 2001 C.E.B. & P.G.R. 8395 (note), [2001] O.J. No. 3911 (Ont. C.A.), additional reasons at 2001

CarswellOnt 4050 (Ont. C.A.). Where most of the value in the wife's assets was reflected in the matrimonial home and RRSPs, it was not unreasonable for her to retain them and still be awarded spousal support even if part of it came from the husband's equalized share of his pension. She had no entitlement to survivor benefits if the husband cancelled his life insurance and predeceased her.

*Spousal support should be reduced where the equalization payment has a significant effect on income* — Munro v. Munro, 1997 CarswellOnt 3905, 33 R.F.L. (4th) 464, [1997] O.J. No. 4194 (Ont. C.A.). The wife's spousal support awarded upon dissolution of the parties' 18-year marriage was reduced on appeal. Although the length of the marriage and the fact that the wife had been primary caregiver to the husband's children entitled her to support, the quantum awarded at trial was too high given the impact of the equalization payment upon the parties' incomes.

*British Columbia Family Relations Act — matrimonial home remedy does not preclude spousal support* — Penner v. Penner, 1996 CarswellBC 2182, 24 R.F.L. (4th) 448, 82 B.C.A.C. 232, 133 W.A.C. 232 (B.C.C.A.). A reapportionment of the matrimonial home under the *Family Relations Act* (British Columbia) in favour of the wife is not an order for a lump sum or compensatory support. Therefore, an order for periodic support that comes close to equalizing the parties' incomes and that is made in addition to the reapportionment is not double recovery.

*If support linked to property, new trial on property issues necessitates reconsideration of support* — Wunsche v. Wunsche, 1994 CarswellOnt 838, 18 O.R. (3d) 161, 114 D.L.R. (4th) 314, 70 O.A.C. 380, [1994] O.J. No. 816 (Ont. C.A.). Where spousal support had been linked to equalization of net family property, a new trial ordered on the issue of equalization required that the issue of support be reconsidered also.

*Reapportionment of property must be decided before spousal support will be determined. Reapportionment of property was found to have fully met the objectives and factors in a spousal support award, and no spousal support was ordered* — G. (M.S.) v. R. (S.K.), 2014 CarswellBC 2095, 2014 BCSC 1344 (B.C.S.C.). Economic self-sufficiency was found to be a factor in both property reapportionment and in spousal support awards. The judge considered other factors for reapportionment and found that an equal division would be unfair to the wife. The reapportionment changed the conditions, means and needs of the parties. As a result, because the reapportionment fully met the objectives and factors considered in a spousal support award, no support was ordered.

*Relevance of ongoing pension contributions* — Krell v. Krell, 2008 CarswellBC 262, 2008 BCSC 158 (B.C.S.C.). The payor argued that his spousal support entitlement should be less than it would otherwise be because he was contributing $450 per month to a pension plan which would benefit the recipient in the future. The trial judge stated that he saw "some merit" in this submission.

*Support awarded for limited term after long marriage because recipient was soon to receive pension and RRSP income* — England v. England, 2007 CarswellAlta 999, 2007 ABQB 494 (Alta. Q.B.). A court will award limited term support, subject to review, in a long-term marriage where the payee spouse will receive pension benefits in a few years and would also be able to draw on her RRSPs, and she had not taken significant steps to manage her medical condition. The court ordered spousal support payments of $32,500 annually for the wife to the end of December 2010. The support order was to be reviewed at that time.

*The quantum of spousal support should not be reduced because of the matrimonial property division, where there is entitlement and an ability to pay, as the wife should not be expected to live on her equity* — Callahan v. Callahan, 2007 CarswellNS 72, 2007 NSSC 46 (N.S.S.C.).

*Set off of support agasint the disproportionate amount of property payee spouse received* — Kuszka v. Kuszka, 2006 CarswellAlta 403, 2006 ABQB 169 (Alta. Q.B.). Where a dependant spouse has received a disproportionate share of the parties' assets, the payor spouse has paid most of the children's expenses since separation, he has assumed the family debt and relinquished the family vehicle to the dependant spouse, the court will set off the amount of retroactive support from the date of separation to the date of trial (6 years) against the disproportionate amount of property which the dependant had received.

*Spousal support will be denied where the dependant spouse has received her equalization payment and if she invested it at a reasonable rate of interest, she would be self-sufficient* — Bolt *v.* Bolt, 2006 CarswellOnt 1490 (Ont. S.C.J.), additional reasons at 2006 CarswellOnt 1734 (Ont. S.C.J.).

*Support denied where wife had received significant assets* — Manna *v.* Manna, 2008 CarswellBC 1641, 2008 BCSC 1046, 56 R.F.L. (6th) 372 (B.C.S.C.), additional reasons at 2008 CarswellBC 2177, 2008 BCSC 1365, 62 R.F.L. (6th) 393 (B.C.S.C.). The court dismissed the 55-year-old wife's claim for spousal support against her long-retired former husband. The wife had retrained late in life as a teacher and was capable of earning $600 monthly as a tutor, if she applied herself diligently. She had also received significant assets by way of reapportionment of family assets.

*A party will not be doubly compensated by receiving spousal support and there apportionment of family assets where spousal support is necessary in certain cases* — G. (R.L.) *v.* G. (R.G.), 2006 CarswellBC 498, 2006 BCSC 348 (B.C.S.C.), additional reasons at 2006 CarswellBC 2153, 2006 BCSC 1299 (B.C.S.C.). In this case, (a) the parties cohabited for approximately 25 years; (b) the marriage was a "traditional" one — the husband was the primary income earner and the wife was the primary homemaker and child care provider; (c) by agreement, the wife left the workforce to raise the children, during which time the husband advanced his career; (d) the husband's income is approximately three times that of the wife; (e) the wife's health problems will limit her ability to earn income, and could end her ability to earn income; (f) the wife has health issues that cannot be ignored; (g) the wife's age makes it more difficult for her to advance her career, if her health permits, than if she were a younger woman; and (h) the husband has a greater income than the wife, and will continue to have greater income, and consequently, is able to meet the compensatory needs of the wife, as well as assist her in attempting to achieve self sufficiency. The court ordered support of $750 per month, assuming that her health would permit her to return to work immediately. While it may be unrealistic for a dependant spouse who is 56 and who has been out of the work force for many years to become employed, there is an obligation to generate investment income from assets, including assets obtained as a result of equalization.

*Conservative rate of return from invested equalization imputed to recipient* — Serra *v.* Serra, 2007 CarswellOnt 665, 36 R.F.L. (6th) 66, [2007] O.J. No. 446 (Ont. S.C.J.), reversed 2009 CarswellOnt 513, 2009 ONCA 105, 61 R.F.L. (6th) 1, 93 O.R. (3d) 161, 246 O.A.C. 37 (Ont. C.A.), additional reasons at 2009 CarswellOnt 2475, 2009 ONCA 395, 66 R.F.L. (6th) 40, [2009] O.J. No. 1905 (Ont. C.A.). In this case, the court held that the wife was entitled to a sizeable equalization payment. The earnings that those funds could generate if conservatively invested should be imputed to her.

*Property award should generate income* — Cey *v.* Teske, 2006 CarswellSask 484, 2006 SKQB 315, 286 Sask. R. 221 (Sask. Q.B.). In determining the quantity of support, the court took into account that the wife had received a substantial property settlement which went a long way to compensating her for economic disadvantages she had suffered during the marriage. She would be able to generate income from that settlement. The court also considered that the husband's ability to pay spousal support would be negatively affected by the property division. He would need to borrow to pay out his wife's interest.

*Indefinite support not given where wife had received very significant assets* — *Gregory v. Ball*, 2004 CarswellAlta 1450, 2004 ABQB 789, 9 R.F.L. (6th) 338 (Alta. Q.B.), reversed in part 2005 CarswellAlta 1526, 2005 ABCA 354, 21 R.F.L. (6th) 42 (Alta. C.A.). The court refused the wife's application for unlimited spousal support upon the dissolution of the parties' 16-year marriage. Although the wife was not expected to earn income during the marriage, the husband did not discourage the wife from pursuing a career. Furthermore, the wife had received over $4 million on division of the parties' assets and was in a position to generate income.

*Spousal support granted despite property award and waiver of support* — *N. (D.K.) v. O. (M.J.)*, 2003 CarswellBC 2290, 2003 BCCA 502, 41 R.F.L. (5th) 142, 18 B.C.L.R. (4th) 247, 232 D.L.R. (4th) 323, 187 B.C.A.C. 129, 307 W.A.C. 129 (B.C.C.A.), the wife was awarded spousal support despite the fact that she had waived her support rights by agreement. Although the reapportionment of family assets under the agreement went someway towards meeting the wife's needs, spousal support was also needed in the short term.

*Transfer of property justified termination of support order* — *O. (C.) v. C. (O.N.)*, 2005 CarswellNfld 16, 2005 NLTD 12, 11 R.F.L. (6th) 309 (N.L.T.D.). Where, since the date of the original interim spousal support order, the husband had transferred considerable assets to the wife, the court granted the husband's application to terminate the order. As the assets transferred would generate income in excess of the order, a change in circumstances had accrued of such a nature and magnitude as to make the original order no longer appropriate.

*No support in light of property award and personal injury settlement* — *Boel v. Boel*, 1994 CarswellBC 387, 4 R.F.L. (4th) 266, 95 B.C.L.R. (2d) 375, 45 B.C.A.C. 261, 72 W.A.C. 261 (B.C.C.A.). Where the wife, as a result of a motor vehicle accident, had negotiated a settlement which guaranteed her a lifetime income indexed for inflation, she was found not to qualify for support. The settlement, combined with a property award, weighted in her favour rendered support unnecessary.

*Property and support issues should be dealt with separately in making orders in respect of either issue* — *first, property rights should be determined and then spousal and child support* — *Hanna v. Hanna*, 1994 CarswellNS 51, 4 R.F.L. (4th) 148 (N.S.C.A.).

*Property award sufficient for wife's needs* — *Droit de la famille - 1990*, 1994 CarswellQue 2062, EYB 1994-73357, [1994] R.D.F. 463 (C.S. Que.). The wife was granted only limited term spousal support as the parties' marriage had lasted only 8 years, and was childless. Furthermore, the wife's share of family assets was sufficient to allow her time to find suitable employment.

*Excluded capital does not affect spousal support* — *Shepley v. Shepley*, 2006 CarswellOnt 382, 24 R.F.L. (6th) 422, [2006] O.J. No. 293 (Ont. S.C.J.). The court held that a spouse ought not to be made to use his non-equalized excluded capital to support his former spouse.

*Support reduced over time in line with property judgement also paid over time* — *Rosenau v. Rosenau*, 2004 CarswellSask 462, 2004 SKQB 275, 6 R.F.L. (6th) 372, 267 Sask. R. 1 (Sask. Q.B.), the husband was ordered to pay periodic spousal support decreasing over time in accordance with the percentage of the property judgement that was also payable over time to the wife.

*No support in light of property award* — *Hodgkinson v. Hodgkinson*, 2003 CarswellBC 2461, 2003 BCSC 1538, 44 R.F.L. (5th) 82, [2003] B.C.J. No. 2296 (B.C.S.C.). Where the 44-year-old wife had received over $3,000,000 after division of the parties' assets, her claim for spousal support was dismissed. At the time of marriage the wife's assets had been minimal and she had benefited considerably from the marriage in terms of property acquisition. The wife, although she had not worked during the 9-year marriage, had marketable skills and her potential employment income, in combination with her investment income, was sufficient to meet her needs.

*Payor spouse not required to ensure that wife's property retain purchasing power — Spiers v. Spiers*, 2003 CarswellAlta 1413, 2003 ABQB 830, 48 R.F.L. (5th) 198, 25 Alta. L.R. (4th) 131, [2004] 9 W.W.R. 371, [2003] A.J. No. 1223 (Alta. Q.B.), it was held that the disadvantage suffered by the wife as a result of the breakdown of the marriage did not obligate the husband to ensure that the wife's matrimonial property package would retain its purchasing power.

*Spousal support, despite substantial property award — Metzner v. Metzner*, 2001 CarswellBC 1923, 2001 BCSC 1288, 22 R.F.L. (5th) 149 (B.C.S.C. [In Chambers]). On an application for review of spousal support payable to the wife in the court awarded the wife additional spousal support of $5,000 a month for a further 2 years to complete her law degree in order to assuage continuing need and to reflect the husband's ability to pay, even though the wife had received $7,000 in spousal support for 7 years, which, according to the order, was to cease after the 7-year period. She had also left the marriage with substantial assets worth $817,000. The husband's income had increased from $250,000 at the time of separation to over $1,700,000 for purposes of the *Child Support Guidelines* at the time of the application.

*Assets should be considered according to their income-earning capacity — Corbeil v. Corbeil*, 2001 CarswellAlta 1138, 2001 ABCA 220, 21 R.F.L. (5th) 1, [2002] 3 W.W.R. 60, 98 Alta. L.R. (3d) 38, 286 A.R. 330, 253 W.A.C. 330, [2001] A.J. No. 1144 (Alta. C.A.). Although the Supreme Court in the *Boston* case, above, focused on whether spousal support should be varied when the payor retires and his income is from a pension that was capitalized and included in an earlier property division, the principle that assets must be considered from the perspective of their income earning capacity has a more general application.

*Pension — already included in the division of property — Meiklejohn v. Meiklejohn*, 2001 CarswellOnt 3480, 19 R.F.L. (5th) 167, 150 O.A.C. 149, [2001] O.T.C. 323, C.E.B. & P.G.R. 8395 (note), [2001] O.J. No. 3911 (Ont. C.A.), additional reasons at 2001 CarswellOnt 4050 (Ont. C.A.). The Court of Appeal held that the wife was entitled to support, even if part of it came from the husband's equalized share of his pension. Most of the value in the wife's assets was reflected in the matrimonial home and RRSPs and it was not unreasonable for her to retain them in this form. She would have no entitlement to survivor benefits if the husband cancelled his life insurance and predeceased her.

*No spousal support will be granted where the applicant has substantial assets which can generate sufficient income — Fields v. Fields*, 2000 CarswellMan 225, 2000 MBQB 32, 6 R.F.L. (5th) 148 (Man. Q.B.). The wife's application for interim support should be dismissed where she had 1.3 million dollars in income-generating assets, a house valued at $240,000, and a cottage worth $160,000. A person with substantial assets should not be allowed to organize them is such a way "as to virtually insure the need for support." This is especially the case with respect to interim support.

*Liability for debts relevant — Cantwell v. Cantwell*, 2000 CarswellOnt 4391, 12 R.F.L. (5th) 33 (Ont. S.C.J.). In considering the disadvantages to a spouse arising from the marriage or its breakdown, a court may consider a spouse's potential liability for debts, particularly if the other spouse will have funds available to him in the near future.

*Fact that claimant brought inheritance into marriage and spent portion during it on parties' lifestyle not a basis for support — Hoskins v. Hoskins*, 1998 CarswellSask 38, 36 R.F.L. (4th) 44 (Sask. Q.B.). The fact that the wife, who had inherited a large estate from her first marriage, had expended considerable sums which had benefitted both herself and her current husband did not give rise to an economic disadvantage resulting from the marriage. The wife had made the expenditure voluntarily and she maintained the bulk of the exempt property with which she had entered the marriage. Her application for support upon termination of the parties' 5-year marriage was dismissed.

*Support to be reduced once equalization payment received — Loiselle v. Loiselle*, 2000 CarswellOnt 3488, 12 R.F.L. (5th) 400 (Ont. S.C.J.). The wife was awarded monthly periodic spousal support of $1,500, which was to reduce to $900 once she had received her equalization entitlement.

*Spousal support granted despite large capital payment — Bailey v. Plaxton*, 2000 CarswellOnt 1194, 6 R.F.L. (5th) 29, 47 O.R. (3d) 593, [2000] O.T.C. 243, [2000] O.J. No. 1187 (Ont. S.C.J.). The court, on an interim application ordered the husband to pay increased spousal support of $5,000, in the face of a separation agreement, which provided for spousal support for 3 years ending in 1990, and despite the fact that the wife had received a large capital payment. The husband had argued that the wife's current financial problems were the direct result of poor investment decisions on her part and that she had made "some lifestyle decisions that were profligate." The court held that it could not decide this matter at an interim stage. However, it did decide to award her interim spousal support, pending the determination of an application under section 15.2(1) of the *Divorce Act*. The court was satisfied that the wife was in severe financial circumstances. She was in need. The husband's net worth had greatly increased since separation and was now over $5 million dollars. He had the ability to pay support.

*Limited-term support where the payee had received a large capital payment — Cavanagh v. Cassidy*, 2000 CarswellOnt 1658, 7 R.F.L. (5th) 282, [2000] O.J. No. 1658 (Ont. S.C.J.). The husband had provided the wife with a fully paid home, all of the household furniture and a van, by using assets which were "excluded" assets under the *Family Law Act*, namely his inheritance from his mother and the insurance proceeds from the parties' child's death to pay off credit card debt, the van and the mortgage on the home, for a value of approximately $135,000. He had paid support to the wife for 6 years, and he had abandoned any claim for equalization. In light of the husband's provisions for the wife, the court held that he had discharged his obligations to the wife for "non-compensatory" factors. Any need on the part of the wife would be nominal. Further, the court doubted if the husband had the ability to continue to pay spousal support, based on his income and budget and in light of his responsibilities to the parties' other child and to the husband's new family. The court considered that the wife must contribute to her own support. The parties' union lasted 5 years, three of which occurred when they were married. The husband was required to pay the wife $750 for a 3-month period, $500 for a 4-month period and $300 for a 5-month period.

*Ordering the payment of spousal support from funds from previously equalized property could be considered "double dipping" — however, such payment could be justified where the payor's assets have increased in value since separation — Caldwell v. Caldwell*, 1999 CarswellOnt 1491, 46 R.F.L. (4th) 446 (Ont. Gen. Div.).

*No support where wife received all of the proceeds from matrimonial home — Rains v. Rains*, 1994 CarswellNS 61, 9 R.F.L. (4th) 141, 5 C.C.P.B. 258, 137 N.S.R. (2d) 250, 391 A.P.R. 250 (N.S.S.C.). Where the husband was totally and permanently disabled and in receipt of long-term disability benefits, the wife's claim for support was denied. In matrimonial property proceedings, the wife had already been awarded the entire proceeds from the ordered sale of the matrimonial home, which would provide her with funds with which to support herself.

*Support may not be payable in light of division of marital assets — Newson v. Newson*, 1993 CarswellBC 84, 45 R.F.L. (3d) 115, 78 B.C.L.R. (2d) 35, 25 B.C.A.C. 24, 43 W.A.C. 24, [1993] B.C.J. No. 438 (B.C.C.A.). In determining entitlement to support, the court should strive to promote the equitable sharing of the economic consequences of marital separation. This can be achieved, however, through the division of marital assets in which case a support order may not be required.

*Periodic payments received by a spouse as a share of the other spouse's pension are properly characterized as property and not as support* — Lavoie v. Lavoie, 1991 CarswellNS 51, 32 R.F.L. (3d) 77, 101 N.S.R. (2d) 65, 275 A.P.R. 65 (N.S. Fam. Ct.).

*Where a trial court fixes support subsequent to dividing matrimonial property, an appellate court is entitled to revisit the support issue, if the division of property was altered on appeal* — Tibbetts v. Tibbetts, 1992 CarswellNS 85, 44 R.F.L. (3d) 281, 119 N.S.R. (2d) 26, 330 A.P.R. 26, 98 D.L.R. (4th) 609 (N.S.C.A.), additional reasons at 1993 CarswellNS 475, 102 D.L.R. (4th) 767 (N.S.C.A.).

*Property issues should be determined before support issues* — Kowalewich v. Kowalewich, 1998 CarswellBC 767, 38 R.F.L. (4th) 282, 108 B.C.A.C. 12, 176 W.A.C. 12, 50 B.C.L.R. (3d) 12, [1998] B.C.J. No. 8 (B.C.C.A.), additional reasons at 1998 CarswellBC 2438 (B.C.C.A.); varied 2001 CarswellBC 1418, 2001 BCCA 451, 19 R.F.L. (5th) 348, 92 B.C.L.R. (3d) 56, [2001] 9 W.W.R. 644 (B.C.C.A.). Both the issues of child and spousal support were deferred and to be considered afresh after the property arrangements between the spouses had been finalized and paid out.

*Equalization payment among reasons given to deny application for support* — R. (W.H.) v. R. (J.M.), 1997 CarswellOnt 3178, [1997] O.J. No. 2795 (Ont. Gen. Div.). The court held that the compensatory lump sum and child support claims were more than satisfied by the value the wife had enjoyed in the use of the equalization payment ($100,500) for the last 7 years.

*Bankruptcy does not relieve from spousal support obligation* — Bronson v. Bronson, 1997 CarswellOnt 2411, 47 C.B.R. (3d) 142, 31 O.T.C. 312 (Ont. Gen. Div.). An order requiring the defendant to pay compensatory support based on the plaintiff's contributions to the support of the family, the realization of the defendant's career potential as well as his substantial earning capacity which significantly exceeded the plaintiff's capacity, constituted a debt or liability under a support order within the meaning of s. 178(1)(c) of the *Bankruptcy and Insolvency Act*. Accordingly, the defendant was not released from this debt as a result of his bankruptcy. An order was made declaring that subsequent to his discharge from bankruptcy, the sum of $10,400 remained owing by the defendant to the plaintiff as a debt or liability under a support order together with post-judgement interest and costs.

*Relevance of reapportionment of matrimonial home* — Worst v. Worst, 1997 CarswellBC 1985 (B.C.S.C.). Among the reasons why the court denied a claim for compensatory spousal support was the fact that there had already been an equitable sharing of the economic consequences of the marriage and its breakdown with the reapportionment of the matrimonial home.

*Payor's heavy debt load not sufficient reason to restrict spousal support* — Turcotte v. Turcotte, 1996 CarswellOnt 1507, 22 R.F.L. (4th) 364, 1 O.T.C. 156, [1996] O.J. No. 1327 (Ont. Gen. Div.). The husband was not allowed to rely upon his heavy debt load as a reason for restricting the wife's spousal support. His situation was largely the result of deliberate choice and as he was a highly intelligent man, it was up to him to find solutions to his financial problems.

*Share of property provides sufficient compensation — no spousal support* — Miller v. Miller, 1996 CarswellSask 187, 22 R.F.L. (4th) 103, 142 Sask. R. 149, [1996] S.J. No. 212 (Sask. Q.B.). Where the wife received a sizable share of the parties' matrimonial property, her application for spousal support was refused. The value of her share of property was sufficient compensation for any economic disadvantage arising from the marriage.

*Matrimonial assets and assets exempt from division are both relevant in deciding spousal support* — Labron v. Labron, 1996 CarswellAlta 332, 21 R.F.L. (4th) 385, 183 A.R. 251 (Alta. Q.B.). In determining the issue of spousal support, the assets of the parties are a relevant consideration regardless of whether they are matrimonial assets or assets exempt from division.

*No spousal support where insufficient assets without depleting payor's capital and payee previously careless with finances* — *Melnychuk v. Melnychuk*, 1995 CarswellSask 224, 16 R.F.L. (4th) 366, [1995] 9 W.W.R. 764, 133 Sask. R. 299 (Sask. Q.B.). The wife's claim for spousal support was dismissed. Neither party was able to work for health reasons. Although the husband had investments in excess of $250,000, he lacked sufficient assets to support both himself and his wife without dipping into his capital. As the wife had been careless in the previous management of her resources, her claim was properly denied.

*Dependant spouse* — *substantial assets* — *no limitation on spousal support* — *MacIsaac v. MacIsaac*, 1995 CarswellNS 491, 144 N.S.R. (2d) 354, 416 A.P.R. 354 (N.S.S.C.), reversed 1996 CarswellNS 177, 21 R.F.L. (4th) 358, 150 N.S.R. (2d) 321, 436 A.P.R. 321, [1996] N.S.J. No. 185 (N.S.C.A.). Where the wife received substantial assets upon dissolution of the parties' 25-year traditional marriage, she was granted spousal support without any time limitation. It would be inappropriate to emphasize self-sufficiency to the exclusion of other *Divorce Act* objectives, but it was necessary that she be encouraged to become self-sufficient.

*Relevance of spouse having assumed responsibility for debts* — *Dunn v. Dunn*, 1995 CarswellNS 64, 14 R.F.L. (4th) 50 (N.S.S.C.). The fact that the husband had assumed responsibility for the family debts was among the reasons for denying the wife's spousal support claim.

*Relevance of property division to spousal support entitlement* — *Sneddon v. Sneddon*, 1993 CarswellAlta 342, 46 R.F.L. (3d) 373, 9 Alta. L.R. (3d) 311, 139 A.R. 167 (Alta. Q.B.). According to the compensatory support model established by the Supreme Court of Canada in *Moge*, spousal support is intended to relieve economic hardship resulting from the marriage or its breakdown. In determining the appropriate support, the effect of any property divisions should also be taken into account.

*Economic disadvantage* — *consider property as well as support* — *Messer v. Messer*, 1993 CarswellSask 51, 47 R.F.L. (3d) 4, 108 Sask. R. 155, [1993] S.J. No. 255 (Sask. Q.B.), reversed 1996 CarswellSask 131, 22 R.F.L. (4th) 8, 141 Sask. R. 163, 114 W.A.C. 163 (Sask. C.A.). In determining the economic disadvantage to a party resulting from marriage, the benefits received from a matrimonial property division should also be considered. On appeal, the court held that the trial court had erred in law in imposing a time limit on the duration of support. The order was set aside and the court had grave doubts about the quantum of $800 per month. The matter was remitted to the lower court.

*Proceeds from sale of family assets need not be used to fund re-training* — *spousal support should do so* — *Hayes v. Hayes*, 1991 CarswellBC 542, 34 R.F.L. (3d) 274, [1991] B.C.J. No. 2450 (B.C.S.C.). The wife's use of the proceeds from her share of the family assets to purchase a smaller home for herself and the parties' two children was reasonable as she had reduced accommodation costs. The proceeds need not be used to finance her retraining program and spousal support could be awarded for that purpose.

*No considereation of equalization payment used to purchase necessaries when considering support* — *Anderson v. Anderson*, 1990 CarswellMan 50, 27 R.F.L. (3d) 358, 66 Man. R. (2d) 248 (Man. Q.B.), affirmed 1991 CarswellMan 43, 35 R.F.L. (3d) 223, 75 Man. R. (2d) 235, 6 W.A.C. 235 (Man. C.A.). In determining a spouse's need for support, the court should not take into consideration an equalization payment ordered under a provincial property division statute where such payment is required by the spouse to purchase or replace assets necessary for daily life.

*RRSP not generating income not relevant to means* — *Ellis v. Ellis*, 1990 CarswellSask 61, 26 R.F.L. (3d) 184, 84 Sask. R. 272 (Sask. Q.B.). An RRSP that is not generating income should not be taken into account in determining the parties' "means and needs" for support purposes.

*Relevance of payee's exclusive possession of matrimonial home — Francis v. Francis*, 1989 CarswellOnt 329, 24 R.F.L. (3d) 265 (Ont. C.A.), varying 1987 CarswellOnt 338, 8 R.F.L. (3d) 460 (Ont. H.C.). Where the wife was awarded $1,000 monthly child support, as well as exclusive possession of the family home, the support award was reduced to $750 on appeal. In light of the advantage accruing to the wife through the exclusive possession order, and the corresponding detriment to the husband, the support award was too high.

*Spousal support awarded only until property entitlement received — Goodfield v. Goodfield*, 1989 CarswellOnt 332, 24 R.F.L. (3d) 429, 71 O.R. (2d) 457 (Ont. H.C.). Where the income from the wife's pending property award would enable her to be self-sufficient, she was awarded periodic support only until such time as she received her property entitlement.

*Unequal property division used to remedy wife's need in lieu of spousal support — Smithson v. Smithson*, 1988 CarswellBC 403, 15 R.F.L. (3d) 393, 32 B.C.L.R. (2d) 241, 53 D.L.R. (4th) 136 (B.C.S.C.). The wife's need, which arose out of health problems that existed before marriage and that eventually disabled her, was found not to be causally connected to the marriage. Accordingly, although the husband was not required to pay support, the bulk of the parties' property was awarded to the wife.

*Where payee received equalization payment and payor paid payee's student loan — no spousal support — Cline v. Cline*, 1988 CarswellNB 531, 12 R.F.L. (3d) 289, 84 N.B.R. (2d) 301, 214 A.P.R. 301 (N.B.Q.B.). The court dismissed the wife's claims for support in divorce proceedings to end her 5-year marriage. As the wife had received an equalization payment and the husband had assumed responsibility for her student loan, a support order could not be justified given the brief duration of the marriage.

*Spousal support reduced where a property payment was not wisely invested — Cherney v. Cherney*, 1987 CarswellSask 94, 9 R.F.L. (3d) 133, 60 Sask. R. 69 (Sask. C.A.), reversing 1986 CarswellSask 563, 51 Sask. R. 158 (Sask. Q.B.). Where the wife had refused to make full use of the income opportunities resulting from her property award, the $765 monthly maintenance allowance granted on divorce was reduced on appeal to $450 monthly. With more effort and a more realistic management of her assets, she could realize a greater income without encroaching on her capital.

*Wife's receipt of capital assets among reasons for denying support claim — Fahr v. Fahr*, 1986 CarswellSask 561, 50 Sask. R. 55 (Sask. Q.B.). The wife's receipt of substantial capital assets upon the division of the matrimonial property was among the reasons for denying her support claim.

## Pensions and spousal support

*Double recovery in cases with pension division — Boston v. Boston*, 2001 CarswellOnt 2432, 2001 CarswellOnt 2433, 2001 SCC 43, REJB 2001-25002, 17 R.F.L. (5th) 4, [2001] 2 S.C.R. 413, 28 C.C.P.B. 17, 201 D.L.R. (4th) 1, 271 N.R. 248, 149 O.A.C. 50, 2001 C.E.B. & P.G.R. 8385 (headnote only), [2001] S.C.J. No. 45 (S.C.C.). In cases where support is mainly compensation-based and not primarily based on needs, care should be taken to avoid double recovery. Where a pension is involved, double recovery occurs where the pension, equalized as property, is also treated as income from which the pension-holding spouse makes spousal support payments. However, sometimes double recovery cannot be avoided. In certain circumstances, a pension which has been equalized previously can also be viewed as a maintenance asset. Double recovery may be permitted where the payor spouse has the ability to pay, and where the payee-spouse has made a reasonable effort to use the equalized assets in an income-producing way but, despite this, an economic hardship from the marriage or its breakdown persists. Double recovery may also be permitted in spousal support orders/agreements based mainly on need as opposed to compensation, which was not the case in this appeal (at para. 65).

*Where, in the property division at the time of separation, the husband's pension plan was not divided according to agreement and instead the wife chose to make a smaller equalization payment to the husband than otherwise required, to demand that the husband pay spousal support 16 years later is permissible since the wife continued to have need and the situation is an exception to the rule against double recovery* — Senek v. Senek, 2014 CarswellMan 287, 2014 MBCA 67, 46 R.F.L. (7th) 1 (Man. C.A.).The husband appealed a motion to terminate spousal support. Without continued support, the wife would be living well below the poverty line. The husband, upon his retirement, had an income of $38,472.

*Spousal support was ordered where the payor's income was pension income, even when the pension had been included in matrimonial property division, where the payor had the ability to pay and the recipient had ongoing need* — Vaughan v. Vaughan, 2014 CarswellNB 41, 2014 CarswellNB 42, 2014 NBCA 6, 44 R.F.L. (7th) 20, 372 D.L.R. (4th) 579, 415 N.B.R. (2d) 286, 1076 A.P.R. 286, [2014] N.B.J. No. 35 (N.B.C.A.). The Court of Appeal upheld a trial decision awarding spousal support to a wife based on the husband's pension income. The wife had ongoing need, and the husband had the ability to pay. The exception to "double-dipping" applied.

*Where the objectives of the* Divorce Act *can only be met by "double-dipping", spousal support will be ordered when the payor's income is pension-based and the pension has been divided between the parties* — Flieger v. Adams, 2012 CarswellNB 219, 2012 CarswellNB 220, 2012 NBCA 39, 18 R.F.L. (7th) 28, 387 N.B.R. (2d) 322, 1001 A.P.R. 322, [2012] N.B.J. No. 137 (N.B.C.A.). The parties were married for 35 years. In 2010, the husband retired and applied to vary spousal support. Prior to the hearing, he unilaterally reduced spousal support to $405 biweekly. The motion judge found that the retirement constituted a material change in circumstances and reduced spousal support to $405 bi-weekly, finding that the husband had the means to pay some support and the situation fell into the exception to the presumption against "double-dipping" into pension income found in Boston. The Court of Appeal found that double-dipping was permissible when necessary to meet the objectives of s. 17(7) where both a compensatory and a needs-based entitlement to support had been found.

*Where a recipient spouse had reasonably invested pension income and made steps to reenter the workforce, spousal support was awarded despite the retirement of the payor* — MacQuarrie v. MacQuarrie, 2012 CarswellPEI 5, 2012 PECA 3, 18 R.F.L. (7th) 1, 319 Nfld. & P.E.I.R. 246, 992 A.P.R. 246, [2012] P.E.I.J. No. 5 (P.E.I.C.A.). The wife had received her pension equalization and placed it in a locked-in RRSP that she was unable to access until aged 65. The trial judge had ordered the husband to continue to pay spousal support despite his retirement. The judge found that she was entitled to compensatory support and had made reasonable steps to re-enter the workforce and capitalize on the assets awarded to her.

*Where neither party had income other than from marital assets, spousal support was not awarded, as to do so would be "double-dipping"* — Puiu v. Puiu, 2011 CarswellBC 3174, 2011 BCCA 480, 10 R.F.L. (7th) 108, 313 B.C.A.C. 76, 533 W.A.C. 76, [2011] B.C.J. No. 2308 (B.C.C.A.). The husband was 66 and had been laid off from his employer. He was unable to find a new job. The wife had not worked outside the home during the marriage. The Court of Appeal upheld a trial judge's decision not to award spousal support. Neither party had any income outside of that from pension and assets, which had already been divided. The Court of Appeal held that to award support in these circumstances would amount to "double-dipping".

*Where pension assets are "locked-in" until a certain age as contemplated by a separation agreement, they will not be considered as income when determining spousal support* — Emery v. Emery, 2010 CarswellBC 1170, 2010 BCCA 229, 85 R.F.L. (6th) 251, 287 B.C.A.C. 116, 485 W.A.C. 116 (B.C.C.A.). The wife had received a portion of the husband's pension and had rolled it into "locked-in" RRSPs, which she was not able to access for another 2 years. The Court of Appeal found that it was not an error to assess her income for spousal support excluding that income, to which she had no access.

*Collapsed RRSPs were not taken into account as income for spousal support purposes when marital assets had already been divided* — *B. (P.M.) v. B. (M.L.)*, 2012 CarswellNB 71, 2012 CarswellNB 72, 2012 NBCA 11, 22 R.F.L. (7th) 15, 347 D.L.R. (4th) 547, 382 N.B.R. (2d) 380, 988 A.P.R. 380, [2012] N.B.J. No. 44 (N.B.C.A.). The Court of Appeal found it was inappropriate to include collapsed RRSPs as income for support purposes. The husband had collapsed them due to difficult financial circumstances. It was held that the husband's choice to take his share of the matrimonial property as RRSPs was not relevant.

*Generally, double recovery should be avoided* — *Chamberlain v. Chamberlain*, 2003 CarswellNB 208, 2003 CarswellNB 209, 2003 NBCA 34, 36 R.F.L. (5th) 241, 226 D.L.R. (4th) 272, 259 N.B.R. (2d) 309, 681 A.P.R. 309, [2003] N.B.J. No. 168 (N.B.C.A.). As a general rule, whenever practicable, the courts, for purposes of spousal support, should not resort to an asset, such as a pension, that has already been used in the division of property.

*Spousal support, despite release of interest in payor spouse's pension, did not constitute double dipping* — *Bertrim v. Bertrim*, 2004 CarswellOnt 10, 49 R.F.L. (5th) 1, 180 O.A.C. 372, [2004] O.J. No. 3 (Ont. Div. Ct.). Where the wife had released all interest in the husband's pension, his continuing obligation to provide spousal support after his retirement did not offend the principle of "double dipping". The wife continued to experience economic hardship as the result of the marriage or its breakdown and she had a continuing need for support. Furthermore, the husband had the ability to pay and the wife had been responsible with her finances.

*No double dipping* — *Pacheco v. Pacheco*, 2001 CarswellOnt 798, 13 R.F.L. (5th) 442, [2001] O.J. No. 1122 (Ont. S.C.J.). Where it was assumed that the husband would retire with full pension within 3 years, the wife's spousal support was to be subject to review at that time. The wife would receive a substantial lump sum when the pension was divided and it would be unfair to require the husband to continue to pay support from the half pension remaining to him.

*Consideration that pension had been included in determining equalization claim* — *Dolman v. Dolman*, 1998 CarswellOnt 2082, 38 R.F.L. (4th) 362, 63 O.T.C. 351, [1998] O.J. No. 1976 (Ont. Gen. Div.), additional reasons at 1998 CarswellOnt 2884 (Ont. Gen. Div.). Where the husband's only income was from his pension, the court was required, in determining the quantum of the wife's spousal support, to consider the fact that the husband's pension had been included in calculating the equalization payment payable by him.

*To avoid double dipping in respect to payor's pension* — *Shadbolt v. Shadbolt*, 1997 CarswellOnt 3544, 32 R.F.L. (4th) 253, 45 O.T.C. 124, [1997] O.J. No. 3666 (Ont. Gen. Div.). In order to avoid double-dipping in cases where a spouse is awarded a share in the other's pension plan and proceeds from that plan are also used to determine the other spouse's ability to pay spousal support, the portion of the pension that has not been equalized or compensated for should be considered for support purposes.

*It is not improper to divide a payor's pension as property and to include pension income in calculating the payor's ability to pay spousal support upon retirement* — *Rivers v. Rivers*, 1993 CarswellOnt 330, 47 R.F.L. (3d) 90 (Ont. Gen. Div.).

*Although a party's pension may have already been divided in matrimonial property proceedings, it may still be considered in determining the pensioner's ability to pay support* — *Inverarity v. Inverarity*, 1993 CarswellAlta 456, 50 R.F.L. (3d) 251, 146 A.R. 389 (Alta. Q.B.), varied 1996 CarswellAlta 51, 182 A.R. 1 (Alta. Q.B.).

*Even though pension divided, pension income can be considered part of payor's mean* — *Vennels v. Vennels*, 1993 CarswellBC 17, 45 R.F.L. (3d) 165, 76 B.C.L.R. (2d) 69, [1993] B.C.J. No. 378 (B.C.S.C.). Where the court has divided family assets, including the husband's pension, before determining the amount of spousal support payable by him, he has no cause to complain of "double dipping". The husband has suffered no injustice from having his pension income treated as "means" for support purposes.

*Pension — already included in the division of property* — *Strang v. Strang*, 1992 CarswellAlta 70, 1992 CarswellAlta 468, EYB 1992-66872, 39 R.F.L. (3d) 233, [1992] 2 S.C.R. 112, 3 Alta. L.R. (3d) 1, 92 D.L.R. (4th) 762, 137 N.R. 203, 125 A.R. 331, 14 W.A.C. 331, [1992] S.C.J. No. 55 (S.C.C.). There is no double recovery where the pension was inadequately capitalized in the property division and it cannot be said that the pension income is from property that has already been divided. In these circumstances, the issue of double recovery simply does not arise.

*Pension — already included in the division of property* —*Flett v. Flett*, 1992 CarswellOnt 300, 43 R.F.L. (3d) 24, [1992] O.J. No. 2214 (Ont. U.F.C.). Even though a spouse's pension value may be included in equalization proceedings, it is not improper to consider pension income received by that spouse when determining his or her ability to pay support.

*Pension benefits are not a substitute for spousal support payment* — *Lavoie v. Lavoie*, 1991 CarswellNS 51, 32 R.F.L. (3d) 77, 101 N.S.R. (2d) 65, 275 A.P.R. 65 (N.S. Fam. Ct.). The wife was receiving payments from the husband's pension plan pursuant to an earlier order. These were to be characterized as property and were not a substitute for support. The husband was ordered to pay $100 per month in spousal support.

## 9.5 Conduct

Section 15.2(5) provides that in making an order, or an interim order for spousal support, "the court shall not take into consideration any misconduct of a spouse in relation to the marriage."

While under the *Divorce Act* misconduct is not a factor in a determination of entitlement to support, the leading case of *Leskun v. Leskun*, below, has indicated that the financial consequences of misconduct can be taken into account for support purposes. *Leskun* and cases that have discussed it indicate that the consequences will need to be severe in order for the courts to take them into consideration.

Provincial legislation may take misconduct into account in determining spousal support. For instance, s. 33(10) of the Ontario *Family Law Act* provides that "the obligation to provide support for a spouse exists without regard to the conduct of either spouse, but the court may in determining the amount of support have regard to a course of conduct that is so unconscionable as it constitutes an obvious and gross repudiation of the relationship."

*While misconduct is not a relevant consideration in determining support, the consequences of misconduct are relevant considerations* — *Leskun v. Leskun*, 2006 CarswellBC 1492, 2006 CarswellBC 1493, 2006 SCC 25, 34 R.F.L. (6th) 1, [2006] 1 S.C.R. 920, 62 B.C.L.R. (4th) 197, 268 D.L.R. (4th) 577, 349 N.R. 158, 226 B.C.A.C. 1, 373 W.A.C. 1, [2006] S.C.J. No. 25 (S.C.C.). The matter of misconduct cannot be viewed in isolation. The lower court judgement to continue spousal support should be sustained on the basis of factors other than misconduct. In this particular case, the wife had various family difficulties. In addition, she and her family had medical problems, all of which were exacerbated by the breakdown of the marriage. Further, the narrowness of the wife's work experience and the difficulty for someone approaching 60 years of age to re-enter the workforce after a lengthy absence with few marketable skills outside of her former job, which had been eliminated, were factors in determining whether she could support herself. Mr. Justice Binnie delivered the unanimous judgement of a 7-member panel of the Supreme Court of Canada which affirmed the Court of Appeal decision to continue the wife's spousal support. The parties had been married for 20 years. The wife worked most of the marriage and assisted the husband financially in obtaining his education. She had serious back surgery. Shortly before separation, she learned that her employment would be terminated. The wife had expected to move with the husband to Chicago, but he informed her that she would not be going, and that he wanted a divorce, as he wished to marry someone else. Southin J.A. in the British Columbia Court of Appeal described the wife as "bitter to the point of obsession with [the husband's] misconduct and in consequence [she] has been unable to make a new life. Her life [was] this litigation."

*Section 15.2(5) does not prohibit consideration of relevant misconduct occurring outside the marriage which has financial consequences for the parties — Racco v. Racco,* 2014 CarswellOnt 5377, 2014 ONCA 330, 44 R.F.L. (7th) 348, 373 D.L.R. (4th) 240, 318 O.A.C. 374, [2014] O.J. No. 2000 (Ont. C.A.). The husband appealed, *inter alia,* the award of spousal support in a lump sum to the wife and in doing so argued that the trial judge incorrectly considered his misconduct in awarding support in contravention of s. 15.2(5). The Court of Appeal held that s. 15.2(5) referred to misconduct in relation to the marriage and that it was open to the trial judge to consider misconduct which occurred outside of the marriage. In this case, the appellant's criminal conduct, leading to a conviction for sexual assault which had a large impact on his income, had led to economic hardship for the wife. The trial judge was able to use his discretion in considering this conduct.

*Emotional consequences flowing from marital misconduct were considered in a spousal support award — G. (M.S.) v. R. (S.K.),* 2014 CarswellBC 2095, 2014 BCSC 1344 (B.C.S.C.). The judge held that he must consider s. 15.2(5) when making a spousal support order. While marital conduct could not be considered under s. 15.2(5), he held, at para. 209:

> the emotional consequences that flow from such misconduct, as distinct from the misconduct itself, may be "highly relevant" to the factors that are to be considered in determining the entitlement, duration and amount of support, particularly the spouse's ability to earn income and achieve economic self-sufficiency.

However, the property had been reapportioned, and consequently the wife's claim for support was dismissed despite the harmful conduct of the husband and its consequences.

*Where a spouse advanced a civil tort claim for battery, s. 15.2(5) dictated that the spousal support claim and damages for the tort were to be analyzed separately — Hildebrant v. Hildebrant,* 2014 CarswellBC 1894, 2014 BCSC 1189 (B.C.S.C.). The husband had been convicted of assault against the wife. The judge found the assault was not relevant to a spousal support analysis, and damages for the civil tort of battery, which the wife had advanced as a claim at trial, were to be analyzed separately.

*Where hardship is not related to spousal support, it should not be considered — Denis v. Ostrowalker,* 2014 CarswellOnt 1386, 2014 ONSC 578 (Ont. S.C.J.). The judge found that the spousal misconduct in the marriage was "irrelevant to the awarding of spousal support." The wife's hardship was found to be a result of her own conduct, and the judge found she was on a path to self-destruction prior to the parties' marriage, which had a duration of less than 2 years. The wife admitted to being a non-functioning alcoholic who was unable to hold a job due to her illness.

*Financial ramifications of misconduct were considered in a decision not to award retroactive spousal support — Godin v. Godin,* 2013 CarswellNS 1059, 2013 NSSC 316, 340 N.S.R. (2d) 24, 1077 A.P.R. 24 (N.S.S.C.). The wife claimed retroactive spousal support from the date of separation. The judge found it was not an appropriate case for retroactive spousal support, given that the husband had serviced a high level of matrimonial debt post-separation and the wife had failed to disclose her financial situation and her misconduct relating to the children. The judge underlined that the wife's misconduct was not considered in the decision not to order retroactive spousal support order, but the financial ramifications of her misconduct were considered. The mother had fraudulently claimed to be dying of cancer, which led the family to relocate to Nova

Scotia where the wife then resided with her former husband. The mother subsequently moved to British Columbia and planned the relocation of the children to that province in contravention of a custody order.

*Where consequences of spousal misconduct were not relevant, they were not considered in a spousal support award* — Smith v. Smith, 2013 CarswellOnt 13918, 2013 ONSC 6261 (Ont. S.C.J.). The husband alleged that the wife had had an extra-marital relationship. Evidence was inconclusive, and the judge found the consequences of such misconduct were not relevant.

*Needs-based spousal support was awarded to a husband who had been convicted of assault against the payor wife* — Wang v. Song, 2013 CarswellOnt 204, 2013 ONSC 42 (Ont. S.C.J.). The parties were married for 16 years and had one child. The relationship breakdown included a series of assaults by the husband against the wife, from which criminal convictions resulted. Expert evidence demonstrated that the husband suffered from mental illness. The husband was no longer able to practise his profession because of his mental illness, and the judge awarded him needs-based spousal support.

*While the Supreme Court of Canada in* Leskun v. Leskun *qualified s. 15(5) of the* Divorce Act *in a narrow manner allowing consideration of misconduct which has a detrimental and emotional affect upon an aggrieved spouse regaining financial independence, the evidence of the wife was not of that character or degree* — Bilinski v. Bilinski, 2009 CarswellSask 460, 2009 SKQB 285, 336 Sask. R. 61 (Sask. Q.B.). The wife had come from the Ukraine to marry the husband. When she left him, he did not support her after the date of her return ticket to the Ukraine. He withheld professional documents from her until the court compelled him to turn them over.

*Husband awarded temporary spousal support, even though he had assaulted wife* — Takhar v. Takhar, 2009 CarswellOnt 5847 (Ont. S.C.J.). In 2005, the parties executed a marriage contract. In 2006, they signed an amendment to their marriage contract. Six months later the husband was arrested for assault and threatening to cause death. He later pleaded guilty and was given a suspended sentence. The wife was a physician who earned over $400,000 a year. The husband, an engineer, claimed to earn $45,000 a year. The wife contended that the husband earned $120,000 a year. This matter was better left to trial. The court did not determine entitlement to support under the *Divorce Act* or the Ontario *Family Law Act*, but rather under the contract. The court noted that the wife could raise the argument on a hearing of the application that s. 15.2(5) of the *Divorce Act* prevents the court in making an order for spousal support from taking into consideration "any misconduct of a spouse", but that this prohibition relates only to "misconduct of a spouse in relation to the marriage" and arguably at least some of the husband's conduct did not relate to the marriage. The court ordered the wife to pay the husband $6,000 a month as set out in the parties' agreement.

*Wife's claim that she could not work as a a real estate salesperson because her husband's misconduct embarrassed her was not substantiated and not accepted by the court* — Brant v. Brant, 2008 CarswellBC 2909, 2008 BCSC 1706 (B.C.S.C.), additional reasons at 2009 CarswellBC 1108, 2009 BCSC 566 (B.C.S.C.). The wife, among other matters, referred to the husband being arrested in times past, and she referred to search warrants being executed on property that they owned. The wife called no psychological or psychiatric evidence to support this claim. The court did not find the defendant's submission that she could not work because of the plaintiff's misconduct convincing. The court held that there was no factual basis in this case to support a claim for spousal maintenance on the *Leskun* principle to increase her hours, upgrade her education, or look for additional or other employment that would materially improve her financial circumstances.

*Case distinguished from* Leskun v. Leskun — Georgiou v. Georgiou, 2007 CarswellOnt 3551 (Ont. S.C.J.). Whereas in *Leskun* "the wife had family problems, medical difficulties, narrow work experience, few marketable skills and was having difficulty re-entering the labour force and Ms. Leskun argued that her husband's adulterous conduct left her emotionally devastated and ill equipped to become self-supporting," the wife in the *Georgiou* case assumed that the husband would not seek a review of support and did not increase her hours, upgrade her education, or look for additional or other employment to improve her financial circumstances significantly. The court concluded that the husband was entitled to some relief in the payment of spousal support to encourage the wife to fulfil her contractual undertaking to use her best efforts to become self-supporting as set out in the parties' agreement in 2003. Spousal support was reduced from $2,000 per month currently to $1,500 per month, reviewable after December 1, 2008.

*Conduct is not a factor in determination of spousal support — Gainer v. Gainer*, 2006 CarswellOnt 2443, 24 R.F.L. (6th) 18, [2006] O.J. No. 1631 (Ont. S.C.J.). A case decided before the Supreme Court of Canada judgement in *Leskun v. Leskun*, above, the court held that while the wife had sustained a life-altering emotional injury from the husband's hidden past and his current behaviour, conduct was not a factor in determining quantum of support payable from one spouse to another. Conduct, according to the *Divorce Act*, was not a factor. Case law indicated that conduct will now rarely, if ever, affect support under provincial legislation. Further, a payor spouse who has behaved badly cannot be punished by requiring him or her to pay inordinately high support because of his or her conduct. After 34 years of marriage, the husband had disclosed to the wife that he had had a number of affairs during the last 10 years of their marriage, in addition to a current ongoing relationship. The wife's pre-existing depressive condition worsened on learning of her husband's conduct. The wife was awarded interim spousal support. The court was required to take into account the wife's medical evidence. However, it did not believe on the basis of that evidence that the wife's medical condition was so severe as to cause her to be disabled and incapable of reintegrating into the workforce. The court exhorted the wife to take steps to become an income earner within at least 22 months. If she were unable to show that she had taken these steps, then the husband would be at liberty to bring a motion to reduce spousal support.

*Physical abuse did affect wife's ability to work — Anthony v. Anthony*, 2007 CarswellSask 45, 2007 SKQB 21 (Sask. Q.B.), additional reasons at 2007 CarswellSask 131, 2007 SKQB 92 (Sask. Q.B.). While the court found that a spouse's ability to perform on the job was adversely affected by the husband's physical abuse of the wife, the court did not find that her ability to be self-supporting at the present time was diminished by the husband's conduct during the marriage.

*Claimant had deliberately destroyed other spouse's business interests — Sibbet v. Sibbet*, 2001 CarswellMan 204, 2001 MBQB 40, 17 R.F.L. (5th) 424, [2001] 10 W.W.R. 241, 157 Man. R. (2d) 33, [2001] M.J. No. 181 (Man. Q.B.). The court rejected the wife's claim for compensatory support. The wife, who suffered from a number of emotional problems, had maliciously and deliberately set out on a course of conduct designed to undermine the husband's business interests. The businesses were, in the end, destroyed and her claim for compensatory support was lost as a result of her economic misconduct.

*Husband's apparent misconduct in marrying in order to facilitate immigration should not be taken into account in determining support — Imani v. Imani*, 1999 CarswellBC 1369, 48 R.F.L. (4th) 118 (B.C.S.C.). The wife's application for spousal support upon termination of her 2-year marriage was dismissed. Although it appeared that the husband entered the marriage solely to facilitate his immigration to Canada and left the wife for no reason when his status allowed him to work, the wife's income still exceeded that of the husband. The husband's apparent misconduct could not be considered.

*Disability caused in part by husband's conduct — support ordered with review provision — Epp v. Epp*, 1998 CarswellBC 1346, 40 R.F.L. (4th) 137 (B.C.S.C. [In Chambers]). The wife was awarded periodic spousal support reviewable upon her attaining age 45. She had worked as a nurse throughout most of the marriage, but had developed a disability caused in part by the husband's conduct. Her disability pension amounted to half her former income and, as she had been economically disadvantaged by the marriage, she was entitled to support.

*Although a judge may not properly consider marital fault in fixing support, he or she is entitled to take into account the economic effects of one spouse's conduct on the other — Martin v. Martin*, 1999 CarswellSask 57, 50 R.F.L. (3d) 77, 113 Sask. R. 316, 52 W.A.C. 316 (Sask. C.A.).

*During marriage respondent to support claim had supported alcoholic claimant and paid his debts — support denied for this among other reasons — Gawley v. Gawley*, 1993 CarswellMan 52, 48 R.F.L. (3d) 104, 86 Man. R. (2d) 317 (Man. Q.B.). The husband's application for interim support was refused although the wife had throughout the parties' brief marriage supported the alcoholic husband and paid his debts. As the husband's financial position was about the same as it had been before the marriage, he could not point to any economic disadvantage suffered.

*Husband abused wife during lengthy marriage — illness — entitled to support — Yaschuk v. Logan*, 1991 CarswellNS 59, 33 R.F.L. (3d) 316, 103 N.S.R. (2d) 371, 282 A.P.R. 371 (N.S.T.D.), reversed 1992 CarswellNS 64, 39 R.F.L. (3d) 417, 110 N.S.R. (2d) 278, 299 A.P.R. 278, [1992] N.S.J. No. 99 (N.S.C.A.). The court was of the opinion that where the wife gave up a career to marry and developed health problems, mostly attributable to the mental and physical abuse during a 27-year marriage, the spouse had an obligation to support her up to a reasonable standard of living. The wife had need and the husband had the ability to pay support. It was in his best interests to assist her to become rehabilitated into the workforce and financially self-sufficient.

*Husband's conduct led to wife's inability to become self-sufficient — Anderson v. Anderson*, 1990 CarswellMan 50, 27 R.F.L. (3d) 358, 66 Man. R. (2d) 248, [1990] M.J. No. 365 (Man. Q.B.). Where the wife's inability to be economically self-sufficient could be directly traced to the husband's aggressive conduct and its detrimental effect upon the wife's self-esteem and mental health, her need was found to have been causally connected to the marriage.

*Health problems caused in part by husband's conduct establish entitlement to support — Vogel v. Vogel*, 1988 CarswellOnt 329, 18 R.F.L. (3d) 445 (Ont. H.C.). Where the 51-year-old wife had been out of the work-force throughout the parties' 20-year marriage and where health problems prevented her from working full-time, she was found to be entitled to support. As some of her health problems, particularly her emotional instability and lack of confidence, were causally connected to her treatment by the husband, her entitlement to support was established.

*Where a spouse repudiates the spousal relationship to live with someone else, that fact alone does not disentitle that spouse to support if need is established — Robichaud v. Robichaud*, 1988 CarswellBC 608, 17 R.F.L. (3d) 285 (B.C.C.A.).

*Conduct not to be taken into account — Droit de la famille - 487*, 1988 CarswellQue 44, 15 R.F.L. (3d) 149, [1988] R.D.F. 205, 23 Q.A.C. 323 (note) (C.A. Que.). In determining support, s. 15(6) [now s. 15.2(5)] prevents a trial judge from taking into account the conduct of the parties (such as finding on the basis of their conduct that the marriage from the outset was doomed to failure) in determining the amount of support.

*Misconduct causing a financial loss to the other spouse can be compensated — Jukosky v. Jukosky*, 1990 CarswellOnt 336, 31 R.F.L. (3d) 117 (Ont. Gen. Div.). While according to s. 15(6) [now s. 15.2(5)], moral misconduct no longer results in financial punishment *per se*, nevertheless, where duplicitous conduct by one spouse to save his own ends leads to a quantifiable financial loss by the other spouse, a spousal support order should roughly compensate the wife for her loss of income. However, spousal support was not awarded because the wife's career was stable and her disclosed income was higher than her husband's.

*Wife's lack of commitment to marriage a factor in not granting support — Cole v. Cole*, 1991 CarswellNfld 175, 91 Nfld. & P.E.I.R. 301, 286 A.P.R. 301 (Nfld. T.D.). The court refused the wife's application for support upon the failure of their 5-year marriage. She had made little effort to provide for herself since the separation and, furthermore, her lack of commitment had been largely responsible for the dissolution of the parties' relationship.

## 9.6 Income Tax Issues

See *Canadian Divorce Law and Practice*, Volume 2.

*Retroactive spousal support awards may be paid in a lump sum, and the lump sum reduced by a percentage to adjust for the lost tax deductibility to the payor* — *Samoilova v. Mahnic*, 2014 CarswellAlta 224, 2014 ABCA 65, 41 R.F.L. (7th) 83, [2014] A.J. No. 154 (Alta. C.A.). The parties had agreed that the SSAG should form the basis of any award. The trial judge made an award of lump sum, retroactive support. After the reasons were released, but prior to the entry of the order, the husband's counsel wrote a letter to the judge noting that the judge had not taken into account the tax ramifications of the order, which was not taxable in the hands of the recipient, nor deductible by the payor. Husband's counsel asked that the tax ramifications be considered. The wife's counsel took the position that any change to the order would result in hardship. The judge subsequently reduced the amount of the lump sum to reflect the fact that the parties had agreed the SSAG would apply, and the presumption in the SSAG is that support will be taxable in the hands of the recipient and deductible by the payor. In order to achieve fairness, the lump sum was reduced by 30%. The appellate court upheld this decision, ruling that it would likely be an error not to consider tax consequences once raised as an issue.

*Where the trial judge did not explicitly discuss the inherent income tax law implications of an award of spousal support, his conduct was not unreasonable, nor an error* — *Edgar v. Edgar*, 2012 CarswellOnt 11952, 2012 ONCA 646 (Ont. C.A.). The trial judge had calculated arrears of periodic payments based on the *Spousal Support Advisory Guidelines* and provided that the credits due to the husband for spousal and child support were to be set off against his obligation to the appellant for ongoing child support. The wife argued that the trial judge had erred in failing to consider the different income tax treatments applicable to child and spousal support. The court held at para. 12 that "the tax treatment arises by virtue of the *Income Tax Act* which is not susceptible to change by court order. The fact that the periodic payments are quantified at a point in time and that a set off is ordered by the court as a collection mechanism does not change the nature of the underlying legal character of the periodic spousal support payments." This ground of appeal was dismissed.

*Failure to state the tax implications of a spousal support order correctly constituted reversible error* — *Patton-Casse v. Casse*, 2012 CarswellOnt 14417, 2012 ONCA 709, 29 R.F.L. (7th) 210, 298 O.A.C. 111 (Ont. C.A.). The arbitrator was found by an appeals judge to have incorrectly interpreted the tax implications of awarding a retroactive, lump sum, spousal support payment. The appeals judge calculated support afresh because neither party requested the matter be returned to the arbitrator. The appeals judge calculated support at midway between the amounts proposed by the parties as no adjustment to the lump sum amount was able to "place both parties in the position they would have been in had the payment been deductible and taxable." The Court of Appeal upheld the decision.

*Spousal support payments are required to be paid to the spouse, rather than to a child, in order to be tax-deductible* — *Ofori-Nimako v. R.*, 2005 CarswellNat 1400, 2005 CarswellNat 3820, 2005 FCA 195, [2005] 3 C.T.C. 164, 2005 D.T.C. 5264 (Eng.), [2005] F.C.J. No. 902 (F.C.A.). The appellant had paid the spousal support amount to the adult child instead of to his former spouse. The Federal Court of Appeal found this changed the character of the payment and it was no longer deductible as a "support amount" under s. 56.1(4).

*Tax deductibility of costs was not considered when determining the amount of a costs award* — *Stevens v. Stevens*, 2012 CarswellOnt 15385, 2012 ONSC 6881, 29 R.F.L. (7th) 19 (Ont. S.C.J.). The judge considered recent legal writings (Epstein's Newsletter) in finding that the CRA now made costs awards taxable in the hands of the recipient in cases where the recipient had claimed a deduction for those costs. Therefore, the court found that it would be inappropriate to consider tax deductibility when determining costs quantum.

*Spousal support ordered as a lump sum to be paid in three instalments was found to be taxable as capital, rather than being characterized as a "support amount" under the* Income Tax Act — *Bergeron c. R.*, 2012 CarswellNat 1298, 2012 CarswellNat 4087, 2012 TCC 143, 2012 D.T.C. 1157 (Fr.), 2013 D.T.C. 1004 (Eng.) (T.C.C. [Informal Procedure]). The husband paid $19,200 to the wife as the result of a spousal support award made to her pursuant to a judgement for a lump sum award. He had paid the amount in three installments. The tax court judge found that, in order for the husband to deduct this amount from his income for tax purposes, it had to be characterized as a support amount by s. 56.1(4) of the *Income Tax Act*. Because the amounts were not payable periodically, the judge found these amounts were not deductible. Rather they were found to be a capital payment:

> [8] ... A lump sum paid during a taxation year is admissible as an allowance on a periodic basis when it can be shown that the lump sum payment represents amounts payable periodically, which are payable only after the date of the order or written agreement and which are outstanding.

See also *Bennett v. R.*, 2010 CarswellNat 3595, 2010 CarswellNat 4573, 2010 FCA 249, 91 R.F.L. (6th) 63, 2010 D.T.C. 5163 (Eng.) (F.C.A.).

*Where an amount paid specifically for a car lease was considered by the parties to be spousal support and was paid periodically, it was allowed as a deduction* — *Krpan v. R.*, 2006 CarswellNat 6138, 2006 CarswellNat 3517, 2006 TCC 595, [2007] 1 C.T.C. 2347, 2006 D.T.C. 18 (Eng.) (T.C.C. [General Procedure]). The husband appealed the CRA's decision to disallow inclusion of amounts paid for the lease of his former wife's car. The husband paid $4,000 in spousal support monthly and $500 to the wife specifically for her to lease a car. After evidence by the parties' family lawyers, the Tax Court found that the $500 was intended to form part of the spousal support payment and allowed the deduction.

*Tax deductibility of legal costs was found to be an applicable criterion in determining costs awards* — *Pollitt v. Pollitt*, 2011 CarswellOnt 5873, 2011 ONSC 3162, 3 R.F.L. (7th) 151, [2011] O.J. No. 3029 (Ont. S.C.J.). The judge considered tax deductibility of legal costs for the successful recipient spouse and held that such consideration was proper under the R. 24 factors and the exercise of his discretion under s. 131 of the *Courts of Justice Act*. Including tax deductibility as a factor was found to work towards the goals of costs awards, including partial indemnification for the successful party.

*An unsigned draft separation agreement is insufficient to support alimony deduction under the* Income Tax Act — *McIntosh v. R.*, 2000 CarswellNat 221, 2000 CarswellNat 4507, 5 R.F.L. (5th) 417, [2000] 2 C.T.C. 2423, 2003 D.T.C. 894 (T.C.C. [Informal Procedure]).

*Lump sum support award "grossed down"* — *Dunn v. Menear*, 2000 CarswellOnt 4778, 14 R.F.L. (5th) 293 (Ont. S.C.J.). The $9,000 lump sum support order was reduced to allow for the fact that the payment would not be deductible to the applicant and would not be taxable in the hands of the respondent.

*Where the husband had been ordered to pay interim spousal support in the form of monthly mortgage payments, subsequent amending orders that deemed the payments retroactively to be "maintenance" for income tax purposes were found to render the amounts deductible by the husband* — *Larsson v. R.*, 1996 CarswellNat 1618, 25 R.F.L. (4th) 384, [1996] 3 C.T.C. 2430, 98 D.T.C. 2213, [1996] T.C.J. No. 723 (T.C.C.).

*Payments by payor spouse to third party* — *Veilleux c. R.*, 2002 CarswellNat 1083, 2002 CarswellNat 2577, 2002 CAF 201, 27 R.F.L. (5th) 450, [2003] 1 C.T.C. 138, 294 N.R. 323, [2002] F.C.J. No. 737 (Fed. C.A.). Section 60.1 (2) of the *Income Tax Act*, R.S.C. 1985, c. 1 (5th Supp.) creates a presumption that payments made by one spouse to a third party on behalf of the other spouse constitute a periodic payment to be used at the beneficiary's discretion, and is therefore properly characterized as a "support amount".

*Lump sum does not qualify for a tax deduction* — *Low v. Robinson*, 2000 CarswellAlta 336, 7 R.F.L. (5th) 148, 79 Alta. L.R. (3d) 137, [2000] 7 W.W.R. 509, 258 A.R. 201 at 235 (Alta. Q.B.), additional reasons to 2000 CarswellAlta 68, 2000 ABQB 60, 4 R.F.L. (5th) 368, 76 Alta. L.R. (3d) 238, [2000] 4 W.W.R. 663, 258 A.R. 201, [2000] A.J. No. 96 (Alta. Q.B.). The spousal support paid by the husband was found not to be tax deductible in his hands. Although the husband was ordered to pay periodic support for 9 months, the court further ordered that he pay it in a lump sum given his limited cash flow. Revenue Canada, in its interpretation of "periodic payments" had stated that an amount paid as a single lump sum in place of several periodic payments not yet due did not qualify for deduction.

*What constitutes a written agreement for tax purposes* — *Simpson v. R.*, 1996 CarswellNat 1350, 25 R.F.L. (4th) 443, [1996] 2 C.T.C. 2687, [1996] T.C.J. No. 391 (T.C.C.), a jointly signed letter of instruction to the wife's solicitor to prepare the parties' separation agreement was found to constitute "a written agreement" within the meaning of the *Income Tax Act*. The fact that the wife had written "without prejudice" on the document did not change its character. Accordingly, support paid by the husband pursuant to the letter was properly deducted by him.

*It is the responsibility of counsel to place before the court the information necessary to calculate the tax implications for both parties of a particular support award* — *Millar v. Millar*, 1996 CarswellPEI 27, 22 R.F.L. (4th) 238, 139 Nfld. & P.E.I.R. 91, 433 A.P.R. 91 (P.E.I.C.A.).

*The court, in a divorce action, lacks jurisdiction to make an order granting retroactive tax deductibility under the* Income Tax Act *for support payments* — *Short v. Short*, 1996 CarswellBC 893, 21 R.F.L. (4th) 429, [1996] B.C.J. No. 910 (B.C.S.C.). Furthermore, retroactivity of tax treatment under the *Divorce Act* can extend only back to the date of the divorce petition.

*Spouses are entitled to enter into arrangements between themselves which effectively set aside the application of ss. 56(1)(b) and 60(b) of the* Income Tax Act, *R.S.C. 1985, c. 1 (5th Supp)* — *Pelletier c. R.*, 1994 CarswellNat 1199, 1994 CarswellNat 1960, 4 R.F.L. (4th) 287, [1995] 1 C.T.C. 2327, [1994] T.C.J. No. 200 (T.C.C.).

*Any money that the husband was to give to the wife over and above his required support obligation should also qualify as tax deductible support* — *Godinek v. Godinek*, 1992 CarswellOnt 255, 40 R.F.L. (3d) 78, [1992] O.J. No. 726 (Ont. Gen. Div.).

*Payments without an agreement cannot be deducted from the payor's income* — *Teevens v. R.*, 1994 CarswellNat 952, 3 R.F.L. (4th) 212, [1994] 1 C.T.C. 2848 (T.C.C.). Where in anticipation of separation and divorce, the husband had deposited funds in a joint bank account and the wife, over 4 months, had withdrawn in excess of $4,000, the husband was not allowed for tax purposes to treat the funds withdrawn as support. At the time, the husband's support obligation was moral rather than legal and absent an agreement or court order he could not properly deduct the amount.

*A transfer of property in settlement of support arrears may be properly deducted from the transferor's income pursuant to s. 60(b) or (c) of the* Income Tax Act — *Gibson v. R.*, 1994 CarswellNat 1514, 5 R.F.L. (4th) 209, [1996] 1 C.T.C. 2105, 95 D.T.C. 749 (T.C.C.). Cash payment is not required provided that an agreement or binding determination of the cash value of the transferred property exists.

*What constitutes a written agreement for tax purposes* — *Nelson v. R.*, 1993 CarswellNat 1214, 1 R.F.L. (4th) 1, [1994] 1 C.T.C. 2031, 94 D.T.C. 1003 (T.C.C.). A letter from the wife's solicitor to the husband specifying a proposed settlement of all outstanding issues between the parties, including spousal support, was found to constitute a "separation agreement" for the purposes of the *Income Tax Act*. The husband, who was not represented, had written his acceptance of the proposed settlement and had signed and returned it to the wife's solicitor, evidencing the parties' mutual intention to live separate and apart and to be bound by the terms of the agreement.

*The court lacks jurisdiction to declare that a support order is not subject to tax consequences* — *Green v. Green*, 1993 CarswellBC 592, 1 R.F.L. (4th) 130 (B.C.S.C. [In Chambers]). The court may, however, decline to make an interim support order for a brief time to allow the payor the opportunity to make voluntary payments that will not attract tax consequences.

*A support order in which the amount payable was stipulated as "excluding tax" does not prevent the Minister of National Revenue from treating as taxable the amount received by the payee spouse* — *Arshinoff v. R.*, 1994 CarswellNat 953, 3 R.F.L. (4th) 221, [1994] 1 C.T.C. 2850 (T.C.C.). If the intent of the order was that the specified amount was to be received after taxes, the base amount should have been grossed up accordingly.

*Procedure for court to follow in order for payor to receive the tax deduction* — *Pallotto v. R.*, 1993 CarswellNat 1135, 48 R.F.L. (3d) 116, [1993] 2 C.T.C. 3024 (T.C.C.). If a court intends to invoke the remedial power in s. 60(1), (3) of the *Income Tax Act*, it should follow the wording of the provision as closely as possible and should indicate the amount paid in the taxation year or the immediately preceding taxation year. In addition, it should clearly provide that these amounts are to be considered as having been paid and received pursuant to the order or written agreement. See also: *Family Law Act* of Ontario, vol. 2, Income Tax Aspects of Income and Property Sharing. ¶1, Alimony and Maintenance.

*Legal fees* — *Meisels v. R.*, 1993 CarswellNat 1151, 50 R.F.L. (3d) 45, [1993] 2 C.T.C. 3108, 95 D.T.C. 358 (T.C.C.). Money spent on legal fees to establish a support right under the *Divorce Act* is not deductible by the payee in calculating his or her income for tax purposes.

*Tax implications for periodic and lump sum spousal support* — *Hartshorne v. Hartshorne*, 2009 CarswellBC 1398, 2009 BCSC 698, 70 R.F.L. (6th) 106, [2009] B.C.J. 1050 (B.C.S.C.), reversed 2010 CarswellBC 1618, 2010 BCCA 327, 82 R.F.L. (6th) 1, 6 B.C.L.R. (5th) 58, 320 D.L.R. (4th) 398, 289 B.C.A.C. 244, 489 W.A.C. 244, [2010] B.C.J. No. 1271 (B.C.C.A.). Periodic spousal support payments are taxable in the hands of the recipient and deductible from the taxable income of the payor. Lump sum payments are not taxable in the hands of the recipient, nor deductible for the payor. In this case, counsel for both parties agreed that the court should structure the spousal support award as a lump sum payment to avoid the necessity of both parties re-filing a decade of income tax returns.

## 9.7 Nominal Awards

### 9.7.1 General

*Nominal support awarded* — *Mannervelli v. Mannervelli*, 1998 CarswellOnt 3738, 41 R.F.L. (4th) 117, 75 O.T.C. 365, [1998] O.J. No. 3859 (Ont. Gen. Div.). The husband in was ordered to pay $1 per year nominal spousal support where the parties had been married for 25 years, raised these children and the wife had a full-time job as a bus driver.

*Nominal ordes not needed — Folga v. Folga*, 1986 CarswellOnt 279, 2 R.F.L. (3d) 358, [1986] O.J. No. 1487 (Ont. H.C.). As the *Divorce Act* permits a subsequent support application, there is no need for a nominalorder.

*Nominal orders not needed — Filbert v. Filbert*, 1985 CarswellMan 59, 48 R.F.L. (2d) 101, 35 Man. R. (2d) 294 (C.A.). Future entitlement to maintenance is not foreclosed by the absence of a protective order. Accordingly, it is preferable to avoid the use of a nominal maintenance order when it is clearly unnecessary.

*Nominal order not proper — Nelson v. Nelson*, 1984 CarswellNS 54, 43 R.F.L. (2d) 189, 65 N.S.R. (2d) 210, 147 A.P.R. 210 (N.S.C.A.), reversing 1984 CarswellNS 335, 64 N.S.R. (2d) 30, 143 A.P.R. 30 (N.S.T.D.). The failure to make a nominal maintenance award at the time of a divorce does not bar a subsequent application for maintenance. Therefore a nominal award made only to preserve a spouse's right to maintenance in the future is not proper.

## 9.7.2 Case Law

*Nominal award struck on appeal — Vickers v. Vickers*, 2001 CarswellNS 194, 2001 NSCA 96, 18 R.F.L. (5th) 431, 201 D.L.R. (4th) 65, 194 N.S.R. (2d) 268, 606 A.P.R. 268, [2001] N.S.J. No. 218 (N.S.C.A.). When there was no evidence that the wife had ever been financially dependent on the husband, a nominal support award made in her favour was struck on appeal.

*Nominal award made where unclear if wife could achieve self-sufficiency — Dobranski v. Dobranski*, 1998 CarswellBC 234, 35 R.F.L. (4th) 403, 46 B.C.L.R. (3d) 248, 103 B.C.A.C. 214, 169 W.A.C. 214, [1998] B.C.J. No. 295 (B.C.C.A.). Where the trial judge dismissed the wife's claim for spousal support, despite the fact that it was unclear whether she would be able to achieve self-sufficiency once the children were grown, a nominal support order was made in her favour on appeal.

*Nominal support was ordered where entitlement was made out but the payor had no ability to pay — Martin v. Martin*, 2014 CarswellNS 471, 2014 NSSC 236, 45 R.F.L. (7th) 300 (N.S.S.C.). The parties were married for 22 years and cohabited for 8 years prior to marriage. Both parties' only income was disability payments from the Workers' Compensation Board. Both disabilities were found to be permanent. Nominal support of $1 per year was ordered to reflect the wife's entitlement on needs-based grounds and reflect the husband's inability to pay.

*Nominal support was ordered where entitlement was made out but the payor had no ability to pay — R. (D.C.H.) v. R. (J.)*, 2013 CarswellBC 2345, 2013 BCSC 1407 (B.C.S.C.). See also *G. (M.R.) v. L. (A.)*, 2013 CarswellBC 319, 2013 BCSC 173 (B.C.S.C.).

*A spousal support order of nil dollars will be made with the possibility of variation where the payor lacks the ability to pay — Goodine v. Goodine*, 2013 CarswellNS 211, 2013 NSSC 98 (N.S.S.C.). The parties had significant matrimonial debts. The judge found that the husband did not have sufficient income to pay spousal support and service the matrimonial debts for which he was responsible. The wife had not demonstrated any effort towards self-sufficiency. A spousal support order of nil dollars was ordered with the possibility of variation within 4 years after separation.

*Where a payor was expected to declare bankruptcy, nominal spousal support was ordered — Reece v. Reece*, 2013 CarswellNS 104, 2013 NSSC 33 (N.S.S.C.). The husband was found to have no ability to pay spousal support because of his expected bankruptcy. The wife was found to have entitlement, and nominal support of $1 annually was ordered "to preserve the entitlement so that the amount might be varied upward if there is this [sic] a change in circumstance within an appropriate period of time that would justify such variation" (para. 73).

*A nominal award was not required in order to secure future entitlement where a lump sum spousal award had been made* — Traversy v. Glover, 2006 CarswellOnt 4380, 30 R.F.L. (6th) 372, [2006] O.J. No. 2908 (Ont. S.C.J.). A judge made a lump sum spousal support award but concluded that "this is not in full and final settlement of the wife's claim and since no releases are being exchanged, the dismissal of the wife's support claim does not bar her from reapplying should future circumstances so warrant." A nominal periodic award was not made.

*Nominal award to ensure the possibility of variation in the future* — Dababneh v. Dababneh, 2003 CarswellOnt 5004, 48 R.F.L. (5th) 55, [2003] O.T.C. 1088, [2003] O.J. No. 5103 (Ont. S.C.J.), additional reasons at 2004 CarswellOnt 654, [2004] O.J. No. 575 (Ont. S.C.J.), the wife was awarded nominal support of $1.00 per year. The husband had health and alcohol-related problems which inhibited him from working and he could not be ordered to work just to create income for support. The nominal order left open the possibility of variation in the future.

*Nominal support awarded where wife concerned about her financial status if children no longer receiving child support* — Wolfe v. Wolfe, 2002 CarswellNS 129, 2002 NSSF 18, 26 R.F.L. (5th) 447, 202 N.S.R. (2d) 386, 632 A.P.R. 386 (N.S.S.C.). The wife acknowledged that she would have financial difficulty if child support was awarded in accordance with Guideline amounts. However, her concern about her financial status should the children no longer qualify for support was legitimate.

*Where the wife's dependency on the marriage had increased over the parties' 16-year marriage, but the husband's resources were limited, she was awarded nominal spousal support of 1 dollar per year* — Young v. Young, 1999 CarswellNS 24, 49 R.F.L. (4th) 455, 175 N.S.R. (2d) 113, 534 A.P.R. 113 (N.S.S.C.).

*Nominal support where wife entitled to more support but payor had limited resources* — Davies v. Davies, 1999 CarswellBC 1505, 50 R.F.L. (4th) 353, [1999] B.C.J. No. 1578 (B.C.S.C.). The wife was awarded annual spousal support of $1.00 following the dissolution of the parties 35-year traditional marriage. Although the wife was entitled to more, the husband had retired at age 55, had no source of income other than his pension and was unable to locate employment. The order could be reviewed should either parties' circumstances change.

*Nominal support where wife had been economically advantaged by the marriage* — Davidson v. Davidson, 1998 CarswellAlta 879, 42 R.F.L. (4th) 154, 230 A.R. 151, [1998] A.J. No. 1040 (Alta. Q.B.). The wife was granted only nominal interim support. The wife had substantial assets, considerable rental income and had obtained two university degrees during the marriage. The parties had amassed a sizable fortune and the wife had actually been economically advantaged by the marriage by her entitlement to a share in these assets.

*Nominal support so that wife could seek support if her circumstances deteriorated* — Bosomworth v. Bosomworth, 1997 CarswellBC 2270, 34 R.F.L. (4th) 71 (B.C.S.C.), additional reasons at 1997 CarswellBC 2587 (B.C.S.C.). Where the 52-year-old wife had done contract work from her home throughout the marriage but was in poor health and could lose the ability to work in the future, she was granted nominal support which would allow her to seek a variation should her circumstances deteriorate. The husband's pension income was insufficient to allow payment of spousal support at the time of the order.

*Nominal support to provide for wife if her circumstances worsened* — Davis v. Davis, 1994 CarswellMan 42, 6 R.F.L. (4th) 121, 94 Man. R. (2d) 175, [1994] M.J. No. 340 (Man. Q.B.), the wife was awarded nominal support to protect her right to apply for greater support in the future. Although at the time of the trial she had sufficient resources to meet her own needs, she was legally blind and suffered from emotional and psychiatric problems which could impact her in the future.

*Where the wife would require re-training to achieve self-sufficiency, but the husband was without means, the wife was nevertheless awarded nominal support* — Peer v. Peer, 1989 CarswellOnt 230, 19 R.F.L. (3d) 388, [1989] O.J. No. 658 (Ont. H.C.).

*Nominal support where the husband had limited means* — McTaggart v. McTaggart, 1993 CarswellOnt 366, 50 R.F.L. (3d) 110 (Ont. Gen. Div.). The husband was required to pay the wife a substantial equalization payment over a 10-year period, he was required to pay spousal support of only $50 monthly, despite the wife's unquestionable need for support.

*Nominal support to preserve support rights* — Ghidoni v. Ghidoni, 1992 CarswellBC 557, 40 R.F.L. (3d) 184, [1992] B.C.J. No. 610 (B.C.S.C.). Where at the time of the hearing the wife was working and was self-sufficient, but had the potential of developing serious health problems, the court ordered support of $1 to preserve her support rights should a future need arise.

*Where the husband had lost his career and business but had prospects of a career revival, the wife was awarded nominal support* — McAfee v. McAfee, 1989 CarswellBC 409, 21 R.F.L. (3d) 75, [1989] B.C.J. No. 1134 (B.C.S.C.).

*Where the wife lacked current economic need but was likely to have need in the future given her inability to set aside funds for future security, she was awarded nominal support* — Johnston v. Johnston, 1989 CarswellOnt 272, 21 R.F.L. (3d) 399 (Ont. H.C.).

*Where the wife had no need for ongoing spousal support, the husband's obligation to pay spousal support was reduced to $1 per month* — Taber v. Taber, 2010 CarswellOnt 3760, 2010 ONCJ 81, 87 R.F.L. (6th) 227 (Ont. C.J.), additional reasons at 2010 CarswellOnt 7378, 2010 ONCJ 201, 87 R.F.L. (6th) 239, [2010] O.J. No. 4159 (Ont. C.J.). Upon separation, the husband was ordered to pay the wife $1,200 per month in spousal support. In their separation agreement, the parties agreed that the retirement of either party would constitute a material change in circumstances. After taking early retirement at the age of 55, the husband brought a motion to terminate spousal support. With the assistance of independent legal advice and full financial disclosure, the parties had entered a comprehensive separation agreement. The matrimonial property, including the husband's pension, had been valued and equalized at the time of the separation agreement. However, the increased value of the pension that resulted from the husband's early retirement had not been equalized and was to be considered income for the purposes of determining the husband's obligation for spousal support. The husband and wife had approximately the same level of income. The wife was also in a relationship that resembled marriage. The court found she had no need for spousal support. The husband was ordered to pay the wife $1 per month in spousal support. By not terminating spousal support, the wife could apply to vary it again should there be another material change in circumstances.

## 9.8 Retroactive Support

See **Chapter 7, section 7.1.1 Retroactive Spousal Support.**

# CHAPTER 10

# VARIATION AND REVIEW*

The following provisions in s. 17 of the *Divorce Act* are relevant to the variation of spousal support orders:

**Order for variation, rescission or suspension**

17. (1) A court of competent jurisdiction may make an order varying, rescinding or suspending, prospectively or retroactively,

(a) a support order or any provision thereof on application by either or both former spouses; or

**Terms and conditions**

(3) The court may include in a variation order any provision that under this Act could have been included in the order in respect of which the variation order is sought.

**Factors for spousal support order**

(4.1) Before the court makes a variation order in respect of a spousal support order, the court shall satisfy itself that a change in the condition, means, needs or other circumstances of either former spouse has occurred since the making of the spousal support order or the last variation order made in respect of that order, and, in making the variation order, the court shall take that change into consideration.

[1997, c. 1, s. 5(1)]

**Conduct**

(6) In making a variation order, the court shall not take into consideration any conduct that under this Act could not have been considered in making the order in respect of which the variation order is sought.

**Objectives of variation order varying spousal support order**

(7) A variation order varying a spousal support order should

(a) recognize any economic advantages or disadvantages to the former spouses arising from the marriage or its breakdown;

(b) apportion between the former spouses any financial consequences arising from the care of any child of the marriage over and above the obligation for the support of any child of the marriage;

(c) relieve any economic hardship of the former spouses arising from the breakdown of the marriage; and

---

* The authors wish to acknowledge the assistance of Rosemary Masemann in the preparation of this chapter.

(d) insofar as practicable, promote the economic self-sufficiency of each former spouse within a reasonable period of time.

[1997, c. 1, s. 5(3), (4)]

## Limitation

(10) Notwithstanding subsection (1), where a spousal support order provides for support for a definite period or until a specified event occurs, a court may not, on an application instituted after the expiration of that period or the occurrence of that event, make a variation order for the purpose of resuming that support unless the court is satisfied that

(a) a variation order is necessary to relieve economic hardship arising from a change described in subsection (4.1) that is related to the marriage; and

(b) the changed circumstances, had they existed at the time of the making of the support order or the last variation order made in respect of that order, as the case may be, would likely have resulted in a different order. [1997, c. 1, s. 5(6)]

## Copy of order

(11) Where a court makes a variation order in respect of a support order or a custody order made by another court, it shall send a copy of the variation order, certified by a judge or officer of the court, to that other court.

---

**17 History.** The only substantial change to these provisions since the enactment of the *Divorce Act* in 1985 was the addition of s. 17(4.1). There were also a few other minor changes in s. 17 which reflected the differentiation of child support from spousal support. This differentiation was less pronounced in the statute as originally enacted.

---

For the variation of child support orders, see *Canadian Divorce Law and Practive*, Volume 1, s. 17§49.

For variation − objectives, see Chapter 6.

A variation proceeding is a proceeding by either or both former spouses to vary, rescind or suspend, prospectively or retroactively, any provision in an order previously made in a corollary relief proceeding for support or custody: s. 2(1) (variation proceeding), and s. 17(1). The power to vary retroactively allows the court to adjust any arrears of support as well as ongoing payments to meet new circumstances.

The proceeding may be taken in a court in any province in which either former spouse is ordinarily resident at the commencement of the proceeding, or in a province where both former spouses accept the jurisdiction of the court: ss. 5(1)(a) and (b). The right to take a proceeding in the court of a province in which the parties are not ordinarily resident, but "accept" the jurisdiction of the court in that province, is an exception to the rule that jurisdiction cannot be based on the parties' consent.

A limitation imposed on the choice of jurisdiction arises in the case of a variation proceeding that joins a claim to vary a custody order with the claim to vary spousal support. If the claim to a variation of the custody order is opposed and the child involved is most substantially connected with another province, the court having original jurisdiction may, on application by the former spouse or on its own motion, transfer the entire proceeding to the court in that other province (s. 6(3)) and that court will then have exclusive jurisdiction: s. 6(4).

Where, because the parties have re-established themselves in different provinces and one of them would either have to travel a long distance or conduct the proceeding from afar, the alternative is to proceed by way of a provisional order. See ss. 18 and 19.

The payee may assign a support order to a government minister or agency and in that event the assignee "is entitled to the payments due under the order, and has the same right to be notified of, and to participate in, proceedings under this Act to vary, rescind, suspend or enforce the order as the person who would otherwise be entitled to the payments." (S. 20.1(1) and (2).) Such an assignment is often made where the payee is in receipt of social welfare benefits and the responsible ministry or agency seeks to recoup some of the cost by enforcing the order against the payor.

This chapter is divided into the following sections:

## 10.1  Variation — General

A judge does not need to make a detailed assessment of each of the factors in s. 17(7) of the Divorce Act on a motion to vary — LeBlanc c. LeBlanc, 2013 CarswellNB 122, 2013 CarswellNB 123, 2013 NBCA 22, 401 N.B.R. (2d) 334, 1041 A.P.R. 334, [2013] N.B.J. No. 79 (N.B.C.A.). The parties were married for 18 years. After his retirement, the husband applied to vary spousal support on the basis of income of $35,000. The judge varied spousal support on an imputed income of $50,000 annually. The husband appealed. The Court of Appeal found the motion judge did not make a detailed assessment of each of the objectives of s. 17(7) of the Divorce Act, but found that she was not required to do so. She did refer to s. 17(7) at the beginning of her reasons, and there was no evidence that she disregarded these criteria.

Where a previous motion to vary occurred prior to a review date set in an order, a second motion will be allowed when the review date has occurred to take into account the different onus on a review versus a variation application — Brooks v. Brooks, 2012 CarswellNB 332, 2012 CarswellNB 333, 2012 NBCA 50, 390 N.B.R. (2d) 94, 1011 A.P.R. 94 (N.B.C.A.). The parties were married for almost 20 years and had two children. They had a consent order for corollary relief which dealt with spousal and child support. Three years after the order, the wife applied to vary retroactive and ongoing spousal support. The motion judge found that the wife, who had previously moved for such an order, had already been heard and was attempting to relitigate issues that had been decided. The Court of Appeal found that, because the wife's first application to vary was made prior to the time she was allowed to seek review under the consent order, she had not been heard on the issue of review. The second motion did not require a material change in circumstances. The Court of Appeal ordered a new hearing.

In order to ensure that support obligations are binding on the payor's estate, the court will not terminate support or life insurance payments absent a demonstrated material change in circumstances — Rondeau v. Rondeau, 2011 CarswellNS 15, 2011 NSCA 5, 90 R.F.L. (6th) 328, 330 D.L.R. (4th) 559, 299 N.S.R. (2d) 244, 947 A.P.R. 244, [2011] N.S.J. No. 10 (N.S.C.A.). The parties separated after 28 years of marriage. The husband, who earned $223,578 annually, had supported the family financially since the children were born. The husband agreed to pay $3,400 per month pursuant to the parties' separation agreement, which was incorporated into an order in 2003. The agreement also required him to "maintain a $400,000 life insurance policy and provide through the provisions of his will that his estate could honour his spousal support obligations". In 2009 the court granted the husband's application to reduce support and also reduced the amount of life insurance based on the husband's demonstration of a material change in circumstances. The wife appealed. The Court of Appeal found that the mere passage of time did not constitute a material change in circumstances and ordered the husband to continue to pay support and maintain life insurance in the amount of $133,000 to ensure that his obligation would be met in the event of his death.

A material change in circumstance,s such as pregnancy, may delay a reduction of support — D. (K.) v. D. (N.), 2011 CarswellBC 3325, 2011 BCCA 513, 7 R.F.L. (7th) 44, 25 B.C.L.R. (5th) 230, [2012] 3 W.W.R. 41, 315 B.C.A.C. 12, 535 W.A.C. 12, [2011] B.C.J. No. 2406 (B.C.C.A.). The parties were married for 7 years and separated in 2006. The husband earned $150,000 annually, and the wife had left the workforce to undergo fertility treatments. Using the SSAG, the trial judge awarded the wife spousal support of $2,800 per month for 1 year, to be reduced to $1,900 to reflect the wife's imputed income, to be reviewed in 2013 when the younger child entered kindergarten. In a second trial, the judge found that the wife's pregnancy arising from a relationship with a third party after separation was a material change in circumstances that justified postponing a reduction of support.

*Whether a final spousal support order is described as "permanent" or "indefinite", the order is subject to variation upon establishing a material change of circumstances — Jakob v. Jakob*, 2010 CarswellBC 599, 2010 BCCA 136, 80 R.F.L. (6th) 264, 6 B.C.L.R. (5th) 212 (B.C.C.A.).

*Where reasons are not given in the original order for a set term of spousal support, variation is possible — Cassidy v. McNeil*, 2010 CarswellOnt 1637, 2010 ONCA 218, 99 O.R. (3d) 81, 266 O.A.C. 62, [2010] O.J. No. 1158 (Ont. C.A.). Given the "economic merger" between the parties, the uncertainties surrounding the wife's employment, and the husband's security of employment, the court found there was no basis for time-limited spousal support. Indefinite spousal support was ordered.

*Where a party seeks only to interpret, not vary, a support provision in a corollary relief judgement, the party is not required to plead a request to vary and is not confined to a s. 17 application — Riding v. Nova Scotia (Attorney General)*, 2009 CarswellNS 411, 2009 NSCA 82, 281 N.S.R. (2d) 275, 893 A.P.R. 275 (N.S.C.A.). A corollary relief judgment provided that spousal support ends when payor's income "[fell] below $80,000 per annum". The payor retired on September 30, 2007 and claimed that his support obligation ended on that day. It was found that the obligation to support extended until the end of the calendar year (December 31, 2007).

*Monthly payments to replace lost pension benefits were support payments which could be varied — McCowan v. McCowan*, 1995 CarswellOnt 435, 14 R.F.L. (4th) 325, 24 O.R. (3d) 707, 84 O.A.C. 125, [1995] O.J. No. 2245 (Ont. C.A.). Where the husband was ordered to make monthly payments to the wife to replace pension benefits lost on the dissolution of the marriage, it was held that such payments could properly be characterized as "support payments" which could be varied under s. 17 of the *Divorce Act*.

*Where the husband agreed to purchase, through instalments, the wife's share of the family business, such payments could not be characterized as support payments and accordingly could not be varied as such — Craig (Bassett) v. Craig*, 1989 CarswellNS 40, 24 R.F.L. (3d) 341, 78 C.B.R. (N.S.) 97, 65 D.L.R. (4th) 106, 94 N.S.R. (2d) 196, 247 A.P.R. 196, [1989] N.S.J. No. 401 (N.S.C.A.). The fact that the payment had been classified as support payments in the husband's bankruptcy proceedings did not render the issue *res judicata*.

*A material chang>e of circumstances may be on account of a change in living arrangements, not only income — T. (C.J.) v. T. (G.A.)*, 2012 CarswellAlta 506, 2012 ABQB 193, 12 R.F.L. (7th) 402, [2012] A.J. No. 333 (Alta. Q.B.). The parties were married for 16 years. The parties entered a separation agreement, under which the husband was required to pay the wife $1,302 per month in spousal support until March 2016. The spousal support award was based on the husband's income of $84,000 and the wife's income of $9,000. On the husband's application, spousal support was reduced to $700 per month. Based on the evidence available, the husband's 2011 income was determined to be $101,408 and the wife's was $33,174. The fact that the *Spousal Support Advisory Guidelines* now existed, and that $1,302 exceeded the upper limit for support payable under the Guidelines, did not constitute a material change in circumstances. It was not sufficient to just consider a material change to the financial circumstances of the parties. More expansively, a material change was to have been made in the circumstances, including living arrangements, incomes or expenses, of the parties. A material change had taken place in the incomes and expenses of both parties, and the wife's living arrangements had changed where she received a $2,000 monthly contribution to living expenses by her common-law partner. If the parties had known the current circumstances in 2006, the separation agreement would have contained different terms. The Guidelines were notionally applied and a mid-range award of $700 per month was appropriate.

### Relationship between *Divorce Act* and provincial legislation

*The trial judge, in the context of divorce proceedings, was without jurisdiction to vary orders made earlier under provincial legislation — Kosendiak v. Kosendiak*, 1992 CarswellBC 1293 (B.C.C.A.).

*An order for support made under the Divorce Act is not properly varied under provincial enforcement legislation — Newfoundland v. Reid*, 1989 CarswellNfld 13, 19 R.F.L. (3d) 385, 79 Nfld. & P.E.I.R. 338, 246 A.P.R. 338 (Nfld. C.A.).

*Provincial legislation restricting the jurisdiction to cancel support arrears is not applicable on divorce — in the case of a conflict, the federal law is paramount — Droit de la famille - 356*, 1987 CarswellQue 34, 8 R.F.L. (3d) 349, [1987] R.J.Q. 764, 8 Q.A.C. 142 (C.A. Que.).

*A court, in divorce proceedings, lacks the jurisdiction under s. 17 to vary support if the original order was made pursuant to provincial legislation or if the parties had entered into a separation agreement — Champion v. Champion*, 1994 CarswellPEI 13, 2 R.F.L. (4th) 455, 115 Nfld. & P.E.I.R. 175, 360 A.P.R. 175 (P.E.I.T.D.).

*There is no conflict between s. 140 of the* Courts of Justice Act, R.S.O. 1990, c. C.43 *and s. 17 of the* Divorce Act, R.S.C. 1985, c. 3 (2nd Supp.) *as the statutes have different purposes — Ballentine v. Ballentine*, 2003 CarswellOnt 2492, 37 R.F.L. (5th) 9, 65 O.R. (3d) 481, 35 C.P.C. (5th) 209, 228 D.L.R. (4th) 570, 173 O.A.C. 368, [2003] O.J. No. 2589 (Ont. C.A.). Section 17 of the *Divorce Act* provides statutory authority to a judge to vary, rescind or suspend support and custody orders. In contrast, s. 140 of the *Courts of Justice Act* does not deal in pith and substance with divorce, support or custody and is intended to prevent abuses of the court's processes.

*Variation of support should be sought under the Divorce Act, not provincial enforcement legislation — Prince Edward Island (Director of Maintenance Enforcement) v. Callaghan*, 1991 CarswellPEI 16, 32 R.F.L. (3d) 117, 96 Nfld. & P.E.I.R. 271, 305 A.P.R. 271 (P.E.I.C.A.). Section 11(5) of the *Maintenance Enforcement Act*, R.S.P.E.I. 1988, c. M-1, does not authorize variation of a *Divorce Act* support order in enforcement proceedings under the *Maintenance Enforcement Act*. Variation must be sought under the *Divorce Act* itself.

### Objectives of variation order

The objectives of a variation order are set out in s. 17(7) which provide that a variation order varying a spousal support order should:

(a) recognize any economic advantages or disadvantages to the former spouse arising from the marriage or its breakdown;

(b) apportion between the former spouses any financial consequences arising from the care of any child of the marriage over and above any obligation for the support of any child of the marriage;

(c) relieve any economic hardship of the former spouses arising from the breakdown of the marriage; and

(d) in so far as practicable, promote the economic self-sufficiency of each former Spouse within a reasonable period of time.

The objectives of a variation order are substantially the same as the objectives of an initial order. For a commentary and case law on the objectives of a variation order, see Chapter 6.

### Factors for a variation of a spousal support order

Section 17(4.1) of the *Divorce Act* provides:

(4.1) Factors for spousal support order — Before the court makes a variation order in respect of a spousal support order, the court shall satisfy itself that a change in the condition, means, needs or other circumstances of either former spouse has occurred since the making of the spousal support order or the last variation order made in respect of that order, and, in making the variation order, the court shall take that change into consideration. [1997, c. 1, s. 5(1)]

Thus, before varying a spousal support order, a court must satisfy itself that a change in condition, means, needs or other circumstances of either spouse has occurred since the original order, or the last variation order, was made. The court must take the change of circumstances into consideration in making the present variation order.

It is important to note that factors in a variation order for spousal support are different than factors for an initial spousal support order. See chapter 5 Factors.

## 10.2 Variation and Delay in Enforcement

*Claim for arrears of support barred because of delay* — *McMullen v. McMullen*, 1994 CarswellNB 26, 5 R.F.L. (4th) 444, 150 N.B.R. (2d) 277, 385 A.P.R. 277, [1994] N.B.J. No. 308 (N.B.C.A.), reversing 1993 CarswellNB 378, 141 N.B.R. (2d) 297, 361 A.P.R. 297 (N.B.Q.B.). Where the wife, 4 years after the termination of an 8-year common law relationship, attempted to enforce 12 years of support arrears against her former husband, the court found that her claim for that period was barred by the doctrine of laches.

*Claim for arrears of support barred because of delay* — *Payee spouse had other means of support and had not attempted to enforce her award* — *Dutchak v. Dutchak*, 2007 CarswellSask 668, 2007 SKCA 138, 45 R.F.L. (6th) 41, 302 Sask. R. 310, 411 W.A.C. 310 (Sask. C.A.), affirming 2006 CarswellSask 834, 2006 SKQB 543, 36 R.F.L. (6th) 189, 291 Sask. R. 238 (Sask. Q.B.). The court dismissed the wife's appeal from an order cancelling over 10 years of spousal support arrears owed by the husband. The wife had throughout those years been involved in a common law relationship with another man who supported her and she had pointedly made no effort to enforce her support award.

*Where the parties had tacitly agreed to disregard a second support order and continue to abide by an earlier order, the payee spouse was stopped by her conduct from enforcing arrears under the second order* — *Kimpton v. Kimpton*, 2003 CarswellOnt 2552, 41 R.F.L. (5th) 99, [2003] O.J. No. 2626 (Ont. S.C.J.).

*Spousal support granted despite 17-year delay, as change of circumstance with reoccurrence of payee's illness* — *Richardson v. Normand*, 2000 CarswellMan 420, 2000 MBQB 110, 8 R.F.L. (5th) 185, [2000] 9 W.W.R. 360, 151 Man. R. (2d) 12 (Man. Q.B.). The wife was granted spousal support 17 years after the parties' uncontested divorce, since the court found that there was a change in circumstances as the wife's cancer had reoccurred, thus preventing her from continuing her employment. At the time of the divorce, the wife was granted nominal spousal support of $1.00 per year, and that award, according to the court, kept the door open for support. While the court found the wife's delay troubling, it accepted her argument that the illness left her without the strength or will to pursue her legal rights. Her explanation for the delay was credible and the application for variation was granted.

## 10.3 Variation — Change in Circumstances

### When variation order may be made — change of circumstances — meaning

A spousal support order for an obligation continuing indefinitely (i.e., not for a limited duration) may be varied, rescinded or suspended, "prospectively or retroactively" at any time (s. 17(1)(a)) if the court is satisfied "that a change in the condition, means, needs or other circumstances of either former spouse has occurred since the making of the spousal support order or the last variation order made in respect of that order" (s. 17(4.1)). The *Divorce Act* uses the terms "spouse" and "former spouse" inter-changeably. To avoid any confusion by this usage, the Act provides that "'spouse' includes a former spouse" (s. 15). A support order under the Act is corollary to an order for divorce and is granted as a second step after the divorce order is made. So at the point in time of the support order, the parties are former spouses.

However, where the obligation to provide spousal support is limited to "a definite period or until a specified event occurs," restrictions are placed on the right to vary after the period has expired or the event has occurred putting an end to the obligation. In these cases, "a court may not, on an application instituted after the expiration of that period or the occurrence of the event, make a variation order for the purpose of resuming that support unless the court is satisfied that ... (a) a variation order is necessary to relieve economic hardship arising from a change described in subsection (4.1) *that is related to the marriage*; and ... (b) the changed circumstances, had they existed at the time of the making of the spousal support order or the last variation order made in respect of that order, as the case may be, would likely have resulted in a different order" (s. 17(10)(a) and (b)). (Emphasis added.) See Variation after support for limited term expires, below.

This section creates a different and apparently higher threshold for a specific type of variation application — one which seeks to resume support after the expiry of a time-limited order. It does not apply to applications to *reduce* the quantum or duration of support provided for by a prior order. Nor does it apply to an application to extend the length of a time-limited support arrangement if the variation application is brought before the original date of expiry. Thus, a support recipient who makes an unsuccessful effort to achieve self-sufficiency after the expiration of a support order faces the steeper s. 17(10) threshold, whereas one who seeks to extend the period while payments are still being made does not.

The test for determining whether there has been a change of circumstances was articulated by the Supreme Court of Canada in *Willick v. Willick*, 1994 CarswellSask 48, 1994 CarswellSask 450, EYB 1994-67936, 6 R.F.L. (4th) 161, [1994] 3 S.C.R. 670, 119 D.L.R. (4th) 405, 173 N.R. 321, [1994] R.D.F. 617, 125 Sask. R. 81, 81 W.A.C. 81, [1994] S.C.J. No. 94 (S.C.C.). The court accepted as "common ground that the change must be a material change of circumstances." And it went on to hold:

> This means a change, such that, if known at the time, would likely have resulted in different terms. The corollary to this is that if the matter which is relied on as constituting a change was known at the relevant time, it cannot be relied on as the basis for variation.

*Willick* dealt with a child support order, but subsequently in *B. (G.) c. G. (L.)*, 1995 CarswellQue 23, 1995 CarswellQue 120, EYB 1995-67821, 15 R.F.L. (4th) 201, [1995] 3 S.C.R. 370, 127 D.L.R. (4th) 385, 186 N.R. 201, [1995] R.D.F. 611, [1995] S.C.J. No. 72 (S.C.C.), the court extended the test to apply to the variation or change of spousal support orders as well.

Support orders often have their origin in minutes of settlement or separation agreements where the support obligation is set out and then further formalized by being incorporated in a court order made on consent. The right to vary such an order was considered by the Supreme

Court of Canada in *Miglin v. Miglin*, 2003 CarswellOnt 1374, 2003 CarswellOnt 1375, 2003 SCC 24, REJB 2003-40012, 34 R.F.L. (5th) 255, [2003] 1 S.C.R. 303, 66 O.R. (3d) 736, 224 D.L.R. (4th) 193, 302 N.R. 201, 171 O.A.C. 201, [2003] S.C.J. No. 21 (S.C.C.), which elaborated on the material circumstances test. In *Miglin*, the court dealt with a prior agreement in relation to an original application for spousal support, but said that the test it developed had equal application to motions to vary consent orders — "it would be inconsistent if a different test applied to change an agreement in the form of an initial order under s. 15.2 [of the *Divorce Act*] and to variation of an agreement incorporated into an order under s. 17. In our view, the Act does not create such inconsistency." The test consists of two stages. In the first stage "the court should first look to the circumstances in which the agreement was negotiated and executed to determine whether there is any reason to discount it." In assessing the circumstances, "the court should be alive to the conditions of the parties, including whether there were any circumstances of oppression, pressure, or other vulnerabilities, taking into account all of the circumstances, including those set out in s. 15.2(4)(a) [the length of time the spouses cohabited] and (b) [the functions performed by each spouse during cohabitation] and the conditions under which the negotiations were held, such as their duration and whether there was professional assistance." .... "Where vulnerabilities are not present, or are effectively compensated by the presence of counsel or other professionals or both, or have not been taken advantage of, the court should consider the agreement as a genuine mutual desire to finalize the terms of the parties' separation and as indicative of their substantive intentions. Accordingly, the court should be loathe to interfere. In contrast, where the power imbalance did vitiate the bargaining process, the agreement should not be read as expressing the parties' notion of equitable sharing in their circumstances and agreement will merit little weight."

If satisfied that the conditions under which the agreement was negotiated were satisfactory, the court must then go on to the second stage to consider whether the substance of the agreement, when viewed as a whole, takes into account the factors and objectives listed in the *Divorce Act* and, in doing so, reflects an equitable sharing of the economic consequences of the marriage and its breakdown. This stage recognizes that although an agreement has been negotiated in substantial compliance with the objectives of the Act the "parties may find themselves down the road of their post-divorce life in circumstances not contemplated. Accordingly, on the bringing of an [application for a spousal support determination that differs from the agreement], the court should assess the extent to which enforcement of the agreement still reflects the original intention of the parties and the extent to which it is still in substantial compliance with the objectives of the Act." At this stage, the applicant for a support order must "clearly show that, in light of the new circumstances, the terms of the agreement no longer reflect the parties' intentions at the time of execution and the objectives of the Act. Accordingly, it will be necessary to show that these new circumstances were not reasonably anticipated by the parties, and have led to a situation that cannot be condoned." ... "The test here is not strict foreseeability" because "virtually no change [is] entirely unforeseeable. The question, rather, is the extent to which the unimpeachably negotiated agreement can be said to have contemplated the situation before the court at the time of the application." (Emphasis added.)

*Miglin* does not alter the requirement that to change an order or an agreement (filed under the *Family Law Act*) there must first be a finding that a material change in circumstances has occurred. *Miglin* comes into play only after that finding has been made.

The Supreme Court in *Miglin* holds that on an application to vary an order based on an agreement, it must be shown that the "new circumstances were not reasonably anticipated by the parties." This, the court points out, does not challenge the parties with "strict foreseeability." However, forsee ability at some level is part of the material change principle. If, in the court's view, at the time of the original disposition the parties foresaw, or ought to have foreseen the new circumstances, the court cannot find the required change of circumstances. This is made clear in *B. (G.) v. G. (L.), supra*:

> Here, the trial judge found as a fact that at the time of the agreement the respondent knew that the appellant was "seeing" the third party and that it was *foreseeable* that they would co-habit. In view of this finding, the trial judge correctly concluded that there was no material change of circumstances. [Emphasis added.]

The Ontario Divisional Court in *Innes v. Innes*, 2005 CarswellOnt 1835, 15 R.F.L. (6th) 187, 199 O.A.C. 69, [2005] O.J. No. 1839 (Ont. Div. Ct.), leave to appeal refused 2005 CarswellOnt 8389, 25 R.F.L. (6th) 27 (Ont. C.A.), considered the question of a material change and foreseeability as determined in *Willick* and *Miglin*:

> [25] The test for a material change of circumstances set out in the decisions of the Supreme Court of Canada in *Willick* and *Miglin* is not the objective foreseeability of a change in circumstances. The issue for a court to determine is whether the parties, in negotiating their agreement, have anticipated the situation before the court, so that the court can conclude that the terms of their agreement contemplated the situation before it. To answer this question, the court must consider the terms of the agreement, as well as the circumstances of the parties at the time that the agreement was made, and ask whether the terms of the agreement would likely have been different had the changed circumstances been in existence at the time of the agreement (Marinangeli, 2003 CarswellOnt 2691 (Ont. C.A.) at para. 47).

> [26] Thus, while the cessation of child support was foreseeable here, that fact alone is not determinative in this case. The court must still look at the parties' agreement to determine whether this event was contemplated by its terms with respect to the obligation to pay spousal support.

> [27] Here, the parties acknowledged an entitlement to spousal support. However, in their agreement, they did not finally determine the issue of quantum. In this case, as in *Marinangeli*, the parties contemplated that a material change in circumstances could occur despite the foreseeability of certain events, such as a change in the parties' income. Therefore, a pure foreseeability test for a material change of circumstances is not appropriate.

On December 21, 2011, the Supreme of Court of Canada released two companion decisions, *Droit de la famille - 091889*, 2011 SCC 64, 2011 CarswellQue 13698, 2011 CarswellQue 13699, 6 R.F.L. (7th) 1, [2011] 3 S.C.R. 775, 339 D.L.R. (4th) 624, 424 N.R. 341, [2011] S.C.J. No. 64 (S.C.C.). The majority judgments were co-authored by Justices Abella and Rothstein. Both cases dealt with variation of spousal support orders under s. 17 (4.1) of the *Divorce Act* and in both cases the court ordered that earlier spousal support orders should be restored.

*Droit de la famille – 091889, supra,* concerns a former husband's cross-application to vary a court order requiring him to pay spousal support to his former wife. The issue before the courts was the determination of the approach on an application for variation of a spousal support order under s. 17(4.1) (factors for spousal support order) of the *Divorce Act*, where the support terms of an agreement had been incorporated into an order. The court was also required to consider if the approach were different from initial applications for spousal support under s. 15.2 (spousal support order). The wife appealed the decision of the trial court and of the Quebec Court of Appeal, which had varied the amount of support in an original 2003 order and held that the husband's support obligations would cease as of August 31, 2010. The trial and appeal courts had ruled that spousal support should be terminated because the wife was capable of working and had an obligation to become self-sufficient. The Supreme Court of Canada, allowed the appeal, as it found that there had been no material change of circumstances since the order was made and that there was therefore no basis on which to vary the order under s. 17(4.1) of the *Divorce Act*.

The wife, soon after the parties' marriage in 1988, learned that she had multiple sclerosis. The husband, both during and after the parties' marriage, was aware of her condition. The wife had not been employed outside the home since her diagnosis, and had been receiving permanent disability benefits from her former employer's health insurance plan. In the course of the marriage, the husband worked outside the home, while the wife cared for the household and the children. The parties separated in April 2002 and were divorced on May 13, 2003. On April 30, 2003, the parties entered into a "Consent to Judgment on Provisional Measures and Accessory Measures," a comprehensive agreement which dealt with the issues arising from the parties' separation. Each party had independent legal advice when they executed the agreement. The agreement was incorporated into an order. In its terms, the order included a provision for indexed spousal support payable by the husband to the wife in the initial amount of $3,688 per month. The preamble to the order stated that the parties took into account the criteria set out in s. 15.2(4) (factors) of the *Divorce Act* and those set out in s. 15.2(6) (objectives). The order did not set out a termination date for the payment of spousal support and did not make any reference to the wife seeking employment. In 2007, the wife applied under s. 17 of the *Divorce Act* to vary the order, as she sought a retroactive increase in child support in accordance with the Quebec *Child Support Guidelines*. The husband, in response, brought a motion to vary under s. 17 of the *Divorce Act*, as he sought a reduction and subsequent termination of spousal support, based on a change in his financial circumstances. He also argued that the wife was able to work outside the home and could have done so even during the parties' marriage. The trial judge concluded that the wife was able to work outside the home and ordered reduced spousal support in a step down order, which would eventually terminate support. The wife was unsuccessful on appeal. The appeal court held that "the passage of time, accompanied by a failure to become (or to attempt to become) self-sufficient can give rise to a material change of circumstances." In this case, a material change of circumstances could be inferred.

The Supreme Court of Canada held that in determining whether the conditions for variation exist, the threshold that must be met before a court may vary a prior spousal support order is articulated in s. 17(4.1). A court must consider whether there has been a change in the conditions, means, needs or other circumstances of either former spouse *since the making of the spousal support order*. Following *Marinangeli v. Marinangeli*, 2003 CarswellOnt 2691, 38 R.F.L. (5th) 307, 66 O.R. (3d) 40, 228 D.L.R. (4th) 376, 174 O.A.C. 76, [2003] O.J. No. 2819 (Ont. C.A.), at para. 49, the court stated that generally "a material change must have some degree of continuity, and not merely be a temporary set of circumstances." The court added that there were other factors which could help a court in deciding whether a particular change were material. Referring to MacPherson J.A., dissenting in part, in *P. (S) v. P. (R.)*, 2011 CarswellOnt 2839, 2011 ONCA 336, 1 R.F.L. (7th) 269, 332 D.L.R. (4th) 385, 281 O.A.C. 263 (Ont. C.A.), at paras. 54 and 63, the court considered that one such factor as to whether they considered a particular change to be material was the subsequent conduct of the parties.

The court held that the threshold variation question is the same whether or not a spousal support order incorporates an agreement: Has a material change of circumstances occurred since the making of the order? See *Leskun v. Leskun*, 2006 CarswellBC 1492, 2006 CarswellBC 1493, 2006 SCC 25, 34 R.F.L. (6th) 1, [2006] 1 S.C.R. 920, 62 B.C.L.R. (4th) 197, 268 D.L.R. (4th) 577, 226 B.C.A.C. 1, 349 N.R. 158, 373 W.A.C. 1, [2006] S.C.J. No. 25 (S.C.C.). An incorporated agreement is not irrelevant. It "may address future circumstances and predetermine who will bear the risk of any changes that might occur. And it may well specifically provide that a contemplated future event will or will not amount to a material change."

The court considered that there were three ways that the parties might in their agreements deal with changes that might or might not give rise to variation. They were:

1. Parties may either contemplate in an agreement incorporated in an order that a specific type of change will or will not give rise to variation. In such cases the answer to whether a material change in circumstances has occurred since the making of the order may be found in the terms of the order itself. As the agreement has been incorporated into a court order, the terms can therefore be presumed, as of that time, to have been in compliance with the objectives of the *Divorce Act* when the order was made.

2. "An agreement incorporated into an order may include a general provision stating that it is subject to variation upon a material change of circumstances." As there is no specific information, the court will need to examine the terms of the s. 15.2 order and the circumstances of the parties at the time that order was entered into to decide what amounts to a material change.

3. "An agreement incorporated into a s. 15.2 order may simply include a general term providing that it is final, or finality may be necessarily implied." However, even in these circumstances, the court's jurisdiction under s. 17 cannot be ousted (*Leskun, supra*). A provision indicating that an order is final in fact means that the order of the court is final *subject to* s. 17 of the *Divorce Act*. Consequently, courts will always apply the *Willick* inquiry to determine if a material change of circumstances exists. [See paras. 39 to 41.]

The consideration of the change in circumstances is the same for an order that incorporates a prior spousal support agreement as for one that does not. [See para. 46.]

Where the s. 17 threshold for variation of a spousal support order has been reached, a court must determine what variation to the order needs to be made in light of the change in circumstances. The court then considers the material change, and should restrict itself to making only the variation justified by that change. As Justice L'Heureux-Dubé, concurring in *Willick*, observed: "A variation under the Act is neither an appeal of the original order nor a *de novo* hearing" (p. 739). A fresh order unrelated to the existing one should not be made, unless circumstances require the rescission, rather than a mere variation of the order." See Bastarache and Arbour JJ. s in *Leskun, supra*, at para. 62.

In *Droit de la famille – 091889, supra*, the Supreme Court of Canada held that the spousal support order should not have been varied under s. 17. "The trial judge conducted a *de novo* hearing on the issue of the wife's ability to work and concluded that the wife was 'capable of working outside the home and that she should seek to become economically self-sufficient.'" The trial judge made no finding about whether there had been a material change in the wife's circumstances since the 2003 order was made. The Court of Appeal was of the opinion that the trial judge's factual determination of the wife's capacity to work, combined with the passage of time, constituted a material change of circumstances. However, the Supreme Court of Canada held that these findings were unsustainable. The husband who had always been fully aware of his wife's health and "made representations, before and after the separation, to her disability insurer, to pension personnel, and to tax authorities that she was unable to work. At trial he changed his position, claiming that she could, at that point, work." Expert evidence indicated that there had been no change in the wife's medical condition in 19 years. The husband argued on the basis of factors in s. 15.2(6) of the *Divorce Act* that the wife had a duty to seek employment. In particular, he relied on the objective that "insofar as practicable" there should be economic self-sufficiency. Consequently, the wife's failure to seek employment was a material change of circumstances. However, the Supreme Court of Canada rejected this submission, as there was nothing in the order stipulating that the wife was expected to seek employment. Spousal support, in the wife's case, was intended to be for an indeterminate period. Further, the *Divorce Act* does not impose a duty upon former spouses to become self-sufficient. Section 15.2(6)(d) of the *Divorce Act* merely states that an order should "in so far as practicable, promote the economic self-sufficiency" of the parties.

Considering the actual circumstances of the parties at the time the order was made, and the terms of the order, there was no material change of circumstances since the making of the order. The wife's failure to seek employment was not something that "if known at the time, would likely have resulted in different terms" in the order. When the order was granted, the wife had multiple sclerosis and was not expected to seek employment outside the home; her medical condition had not changed since that time. Consequently, the husband's application for variation was unsuccessful, as he had failed to meet the threshold required by s. 17(4.1). The Supreme Court of Canada allowed the wife's appeal and ordered that the indexed spousal support in the original order was to continue, effective retroactively to the date that the trial court varied it.

In *Droit de la famille — 091889, supra*, the former wife sought to have the court reverse the judgment of the Court of Appeal which varied a 1991 spousal support order, requiring her former husband, to pay spousal support. This appeal dealt with a variation application under s. 17(4.1) of the *Divorce Act*. The court, relying on its analysis in *Droit de la famille —091889*, supra, allowed the appeal. The parties married in 1958 and divorced in 1984, at which time, the husband was ordered to pay spousal and child support in the amount of $1,950 per month. The husband remarried in 1985 and the husband and his second wife had a son. In 1987, the husband applied for a reduction in the amount of support, as the children no longer lived with their mother. His application was amended in 1988 to request a termination of both child and spousal support. There was a cross-application for increased spousal support. The husband was successful on his application. However, in 1991, the Court of Appeal allowed the wife's appeal and ordered the husband to pay her $2,000 per month (indexed) in spousal support, the "1991 Order." The wife had never been able to become financially independent, despite her best efforts, because of her domestic responsibilities. Following the 1991 Order, the parties executed an agreement to substitute a surety which was incorporated into a consent judgment (the "Surety Order"). The Surety Order replaced hypothecs the wife had registered against the husband's property with an irrevocable banking letter of credit. Both parties were represented by counsel when they entered into that agreement. In the Surety Order, the husband gave up his right to request a reduction or cancellation of spousal support based on a change in the wife's circumstance. In 2006, the husband closed his business and retired. In 2008, the husband applied to terminate his spousal support obligations under the 1991 Order, based on the fact that there had been a material change in his circumstances, as he no longer had employment income due to his retirement, and the market downturn had a negative impact on his assets. He argued that these factors, plus his financial assistance to his son who was in university, meant that he was no longer able to pay support. The trial judge accepted that at the time of trial, the husband had investments worth over half a million dollars. At trial in January 2009, the husband was 71 and his former wife was 80.

In the trial judge's view, the combined facts of the husband's most recent retirement and the difficult economic climate represented a material change in circumstances justifying a variation of the amount of spousal support ordered in 1991 from a $2,000 indexed monthly amount ($2,911 per month by the time of trial) to $1,500 per month, unindexed. The wife appealed, arguing that there was no material change of circumstances justifying a variation in spousal support. The husband cross-appealed, arguing that the trial judge had erred by not taking the wife's financial circumstances into account when determining the appropriate variation. The Court of Appeal dismissed the wife's appeal and allowed the husband's cross-appeal. Considering the parties' financial situation, the appellate court concluded that given their ages and assets, support should be terminated. Without trial findings about the wife's full financial situation and without updated information about the husband's assets, the appellate court concluded that the parties had roughly equal assets, and that it would be inequitable not to take into account the value of the wife's home which the wife had retained on divorce in 1984. In the court's opinion, part of the wife's expenses arose from the costs of living alone in her home worth $344,600. The wife could not force the husband to continue to pay her spousal support on the basis of where she chose to live. Many of her expenses would be eliminated, if she sold her home.

The Supreme Court of Canada held that the husband has failed to establish that there had been a material change in his circumstances. There was no evidence as to the husband's financial circumstances at the time of the 1991 Order. In addition, there was no evidence about whether the husband sold any of his investments and thereby realized his loss and the resulting value of his marketable assets, when they declined in value in late 2008 as a result of the economic climate. These gaps in evidence meant that the court could not assess how the husband's economic circumstances compared to those in 1991. There was therefore no way of measuring whether there was any material change that would entitle him to a variation of spousal support. The husband was required by the *Divorce Act* and the Rules of Practice of the Superior Court of Quebec in family matters ("R.F.P.") "to identify the change relied on and to provide sufficient evidence to enable a court to decide whether a material change in his circumstances had in fact occurred since the making of the 1991 Order." [See paragraph 43.] The Court of Appeal erred in accepting the trial court's view that the husband had shown a material change. This error was worsened by the Court of Appeal's unilateral determination of the financial situation, deciding that in light of the wife's expenses, she should sell her home and rent instead. Consequently, the appellate court had terminated her support. The Supreme Court of Canada held that the indexed spousal support in the 1991 Order was to continue, effective retroactively to the date it was varied by the trial court.

When a payor retires with a full pension after completing a full term of service in the Armed Forces and when suffering from increasing ill health, these changes will constitute a material change in circumstances — Powell v. Levesque, 2014 CarswellBC 186, 2014 BCCA 33, 38 R.F.L. (7th) 261, 57 B.C.L.R. (5th) 132, 370 D.L.R. (4th) 370, 350 B.C.A.C. 43, 598 W.A.C. 43 (B.C.C.A.). The parties, who were women, cohabited for 8 years between 1990 and 1998. After paying support for 12 years, the appellant applied to vary spousal support on the basis of her early retirement. She had retired at 44, and the judge at first instance found the medical reasons for her retirement were not compelling. The Court of Appeal held that the motions judge had erred in not finding a material change in circumstances. The appellant had retired from the Armed Forces with a full pension after completing her full term of service in the face of mounting health issues, which the Court of Appeal found was not unreasonable.

Where a payor earns less income because of personal preferences rather than factors beyond his control, no change in circumstances will be found — Hepburn v. Hepburn, 2013 CarswellBC 2592, 2013 BCCA 383, 34 R.F.L. (7th) 267, 48 B.C.L.R. (5th) 251, 344 B.C.A.C. 6, 587 W.A.C. 6 (B.C.C.A.). A husband sought to vary a consent order for spousal support on the basis that his income had decreased. It had decreased because of more time being spent on media opportunities, which were not lucrative, rather than on the husband's primary occupation as a physician. He had changed clinics at the request of his employer, which led to reduced hours. The chambers judge found that, while the husband was free to pursue these non-remunerative opportunities, he was not able to use this fact as a basis for a reduction in spousal support. It was open to him to attempt to work more hours as a physician, and the reduction in income was as a result of his preferences, rather than circumstances. The chambers judge also found the relocation was voluntary. The original order was indefinite, and the wife was reliant on the support as there was no reasonable expectation she would return to the workforce and attain even partial self-sufficiency. The Court of Appeal found that there was evidence to support the chambers judge finding that the husband had reduced his hours as a physician to accommodate his unpaid media initiatives. The court upheld the finding that there was no material change in circumstances. However, the judge found the husband did lose some income through a factor beyond his control (loss of part-time employment), and this was found to be a material change sufficient to recalculate support.

*Termination of employment will be found to be a material change in circumstances when it was not contemplated at the time of the separation agreement* — Campbell v. Campbell, 2012 CarswellNS 594, 2012 NSCA 86, 320 N.S.R. (2d) 223, 1014 A.P.R. 223 (N.S.C.A.). The parties were married for 28 years and had three children. During the marriage, the wife was a stay-at-home mother who suffered from severe emphysema that prevented her from working. The husband had been paying support pursuant to a separation agreement when he was terminated from his employment. The wife appealed the decision of a trial judge to reduce spousal support to reflect the husband's capacity to pay income. He had previously paid spousal support from his severance pay, which was now exhausted. The Court of Appeal upheld a trial decision to vary spousal support, finding that, although the trial judge had not explicitly mentioned Step 2 of the *Miglin* test (current circumstances leading to noncompliance with the objectives of the *Divorce Act*), he had considered the relevant factors.

*Change in circumstances will be found when the payor retires* — Flieger v. Adams, 2012 CarswellNB 219, 2012 CarswellNB 220, 2012 NBCA 39, 18 R.F.L. (7th) 28, 387 N.B.R. (2d) 322, 1001 A.P.R. 322, [2012] N.B.J. No. 137 (N.B.C.A.). The parties were married for 35 years. In 2010, the husband retired and applied to vary spousal support. Prior to the hearing, he unilaterally reduced spousal support to $405 bi-weekly. The motions judge found that the retirement constituted a material change in circumstances and reduced spousal support to $405 bi-weekly, finding that the husband had the means to pay some support and the situation fell into the exception to the presumption against "double dipping" into pension income found in *Boston*.

*A finding of fact will not be varied unless there is palpable error by the finder of fact according to the applicable standard of review found in* — Housen v. Nikolaisen, 2002 CarswellSask 178, 2002 CarswellSask 179, 2002 SCC 33, REJB 2002-29758, [2002] 2 S.C.R. 235, 10 C.C.L.T. (3d) 157, 211 D.L.R. (4th) 577, 30 M.P.L.R. (3d) 1, [2002] 7 W.W.R. 1, 286 N.R. 1, 219 Sask. R. 1, 272 W.A.C. 1, [2002] S.C.J. No. 31 (S.C.C.) — Mills v. Mills, 2010 CarswellNB 126, 2010 CarswellNB 127, 2010 NBCA 20, 356 N.B.R. (2d) 351, 319 D.L.R. (4th) 183, 82 R.F.L. (6th) 247, 919 A.P.R. 351, [2010] N.B.J. No. 83 (N.B.C.A.). The court had made a finding of fact that the parties' were not involved in a traditional marriage and that consequently there was no obligation to provide support. Despite the long length of the marriage and the interim support given by the husband, there was no error found in this case. The parties did not have commingled finances and the wife did not support the growth of her husband's career (which was non-existent).

*Where there is no material change in circumstances, a court does not have jurisdiction to vary support* — Bemrose v. Fetter, 2007 CarswellOnt 5819, 2007 ONCA 637, 42 R.F.L. (6th) 13, 228 O.A.C. 311, [2007] O.J. No. 3488 (Ont. C.A.). The motion judge had given three reasons for finding a change in circumstance: a "material" change in the husband's income; a change in the child's residence; and a change in the wife's financial situation. The court held that the motion judge erred in finding that these reasons met the threshold of a material change in circumstance. The motion judge had held that the income of the husband, who was a clergyman, had increased materially. However, at the time of the variation application, the husband was performing the same job with only a modest increase in salary. It could not be said to be a change that, if known, would have resulted in different terms. The motion judge found a material increase because of the income he imputed to the husband based on the clergy residence deduction. However, in the circumstances of this case, it was not open to him to depart from the methodology that had been used by the trial judge. A change in the child's residence could not, in this case, be a material change of circumstance, since the possibility that the child might choose to reside with the husband was a matter which was fully known to the trial judge. Even if a child were residing with the wife at the time of the motion, that fact could not be relied on as the basis for a variation in spousal support. There was no change in the wife's financial situation that had not been contemplated by the trial judge. The issue of imputed income was *res judicata* and her imputed income remained at $40,000 per year. As there was no material change in circumstances, the motion judge did not have jurisdiction to vary spousal support. Consequently, the court set aside those parts of the motion order that varied spousal support and restored the relevant parts of the trial order. The review provision was retained.

*Where there is a variation of a final order which incorporates an agreement for support, the test in Miglin must be satisfied — establishing a change in circumstances is not enough — Jeffrey v. Jeffrey*, 2007 CarswellOnt 7401, [2007] O.J. No. 4412 (Ont. S.C.J.). The applicant husband made a motion to change a final order which incorporated the parties' agreement for support. The court, after referring to s. 17(4.1) of the *Divorce Act*, which sets out the requirement for a change in circumstances, continued:

> A party who seeks to vary a final order with respect to support which incorporates the parties' agreement respecting support and other matters must satisfy the test set out by the Supreme Court of Canada in *Miglin v. Miglin*, [2003] 1 S.C.R. 303 (S.C.C.). It is not sufficient to establish a material change in circumstances; rather, the court is to focus on "the totality of the circumstances, of which a change in the parties' circumstances will likely be an element". The issue is "whether, at the time of the application, all the circumstances render continued reliance on the pre-existing agreement unacceptable" (*Miglin*, at para. 63).

Where the order that the applicant seeks to change has been judicially determined after a hearing, the court must assume that the order conforms to the factors and objectives of the *Divorce Act*, and that there is no reason, in *Miglin* language, to "discount" it.

*An application to vary a support order is not an appeal from the order, and its merits or lack of them cannot be revisited — Witzel v. Witzel*, 2008 CarswellOnt 2549, 55 R.F.L. (6th) 275 (Ont. S.C.J.). Where the court observed that a variation motion is not to be considered as an appeal of an original order and should be granted only if there is a material change in circumstances.

*In terms of the Miglin test, only stage two has any relevance where the initial order was judicially determined — consent orders incorporating the terms of an agreement may enjoy the same deference as orders judicially determined after a hearing — Dolson v. Dolson*, 2004 CarswellOnt 4164, 7 R.F.L. (6th) 25, [2004] O.T.C. 890, [2004] O.J. No. 4197 (Ont. S.C.J.), *Loit v. Gove*, 2006 CarswellOnt 488, [2006] O.J. No. 347 (Ont. S.C.J.), and *Kemp v. Kemp*, 2007 CarswellOnt 1774, [2007] O.J. No. 1131 (Ont. S.C.J.). Therefore, applying *Willick* and *Miglin* on a motion to vary a court order (certainly where it has been judicially determined and possibly where it is made on consent), means the applicant must show only (1) a material change in circumstances, and (2) the second part of the *Miglin* test, that the order no longer conforms to the factors and objectives of the *Divorce Act*, or no longer reflects an equitable sharing of the economic consequences of the marriage and its breakdown. (These may not be two distinct elements so much as an evolution of the meaning of a change in circumstances.)

*There is little difference in the treatment of a s. 17 application and a s. 15.2 application, the necessary characteristics of a "change in circumstances" will be the same in either case — Dolson v. Dolson*, 2004 CarswellOnt 4164, 7 R.F.L. (6th) 25, [2004] O.T.C. 890, [2004] O.J. No.

4197 (Ont. S.C.J.), the parties entered into minutes of settlement for the purpose of resolving all issues in their ongoing litigation. The minutes of settlement were incorporated into a consent divorce judgement shortly after they were executed. In the minutes, the wife agreed to accept lump sum spousal support equivalent to the husband's equity in the matrimonial home, along with spousal support of $600 per month for the first year, and $500 per month for the next 4 years. Spousal support was to terminate as of the final payment on January 1, 2004, and was not to be varied or extended despite any change in their circumstances, catastrophic or otherwise. The wife applied to set aside or vary the spousal support provisions of the settlement. Justice Heeney held that if it were found that a variation were justified, the court must then start from the proposition that the initial order was fit and just. In the *Dolson* case, the court stated at para. 70:

> To the extent that any differential treatment is to be accorded s. 17 applications as compared with s. 15(2) applications it appears to be confined to the remedy to be granted by the court. Assuming that the judge has found a variation to be justified he or she must start from the proposition that the initial order was fit and just and fashion an order that takes account of the changed circumstances in a way that still gives due weight to the original order which reflects the parties understanding of what constitutes an equitable sharing of the economic consequences of the marriage.

At para. 74, the court stated:

> The court hearing a s. 17 application must embark on the two-stage analysis prescribed in *Miglin* but if a variation is warranted the variation order must start from the proposition that the original order was fit and just and the court must give consideration to the fact that the initial order and agreement reflected the parties understanding of what constitutes an equitable sharing of the economic consequences of the marriage.

The court concluded that as there was little difference in the treatment of a s. 17 application and a s. 15.2 application; the necessary characteristics of such a "change" will be the same in either case. The "unforeseeability" element is still found in the approach set out in *Miglin* for s. 17 applications. In fact, the test is probably more stringent than in the *Pelech* test. The change must be significant. *Miglin* suggests that written agreements between spouses should generally be upheld. The court found that the wife's fragile economic situation did not constitute a change in circumstances, but rather a series of choices on her part that amounted to a failure to carry out the plans for becoming self-sufficient that are apparent in the minutes of settlement. In the *Dolson* decision, the court held that no change in circumstances, meeting the criteria in s. 17(10), had been proven. Therefore it was not necessary to further pursue the second stage of the *Miglin* analysis.

"*A party who seeks to vary a final order with respect to support which incorporates the parties' agreement respecting support and other matters must satisfy the test set out by the Supreme Court of Canada in* Miglin" — *Jeffrey v. Jeffrey*, 2007 CarswellOnt 7401, [2007] O.J. No. 4412 (Ont. S.C.J.). The husband brought a motion for a temporary order varying spousal support retroactively and prospectively. The court stated in the *Jeffrey* case that it is not sufficient to establish a material change in circumstances; rather, the court is to focus on "the totality of the circumstances, of which a change in the parties' circumstances will likely be an element". The issue is "whether, at the time of the application, all the circumstances render continued reliance on the pre-existing agreement unacceptable"(*Miglin*, at para. 63)." The husband argued that there had been a material change in both his income and the respondent's prospects for employment that would justify a substantial reduction in his support obligations. The court held that the husband had not met the burden of establishing that there had been a material change in the financial or other circumstances of the parties that would not have been contemplated at the time the final order was made. There is no indication that there has been any change since the time of the consent order in the husband's lifestyle or in the manner in which he had structured his affairs. The husband had been cavalier with respect to his obligations to the wife. There was no reason to grant the temporary order that he was seeking and accordingly the decision was affirmed, except for the termination of child support on consent.

*How the* Miglin *analysis relates to the threshold test of material change is unclear, but that test must be met on a variation application* — *Kemp v. Kemp,* 2007 CarswellOnt 1774, [2007] O.J. No. 1131 (Ont. S.C.J.). The parties signed minutes of settlement in 2002 whereby they agreed to a mutual waiver of spousal support. The minutes of settlement were incorporated in a final order. The wife subsequently brought an application to vary the spousal support order. Justice Blishen held that while the court does have jurisdiction to vary a final order denying spousal support, there was no basis for variation in this case. The court observed that the Supreme Court of Canada's comments do not provide a great deal of guidance to trial judges concerning the application of the *Miglin* analysis on variation applications. How that analysis relates to the threshold test of material change remains unclear in the jurisprudence. The court ruled that the procedural and substantive fairness of an agreement incorporated into a final order would not be an issue, unless the agreement could be set aside under the common law. The wife was not arguing that the agreement should be set aside. Although it is unclear how the *Miglin* stage two analysis relates to the material change test under s. 17(4.1) of the *Divorce Act,* the statutorily imposed requirement to find a material change of circumstances is a threshold test which must be met. The court in *Kemp* held that there was no material change in the wife's circumstances as both parties were in debt, the husband's income had increased only marginally (by $4000 annually) and the wife's health and income among other factors were unchanged since the order. The court cited the requirement that a material change in circumstances be found and referred to the test as set out in *B. (G.) c. G. (L.)* and *Willick.*

In *Kemp,* Justice Blishen commented as follows (at paras. 74 and 75):

> Even if Mrs. Kemp had been able to establish on a balance of probabilities that there had been a material change in circumstances with respect to the waiver of spousal support in the final Order, I do not find that she has met the criteria in stage two of *Miglin,* which is a more stringent test. As stated at para. 91 of *Miglin:*
>
> > ... an order made under the Act has already been judicially determined to be fit and just. The objectives of finality and certainty noted above caution against too broad a discretion in varying an order that the parties have been relying on in arranging their affairs. ... Where the order at issue incorporated the mutually acceptable agreement of the parties, that order reflected the parties' understanding of what constituted an equitable sharing of the economic consequences of the marriage.

In essence, the wife in this case was required to prove a significant change in the parties' circumstances from what could reasonably be anticipated at the time of the negotiation. The wife must clearly show that in light of the new circumstances, the agreement to waive spousal support and the court's order denying spousal support, no longer reflected the parties' intentions and were no longer in substantial compliance with the *Divorce Act* objectives. The Supreme Court of Canada in *Miglin* stresses that a certain degree of change is foreseeable most of the time and lists an extensive number of post separation changes which the parties would be presumed to have contemplated.

*Payee's present circumstances were not within the reasonable contemplation of the parties* — *Ambler v. Ambler,* 2004 CarswellBC 2255, 2004 BCCA 492, 5 R.F.L. (6th) 229, 36 B.C.L.R.

(4th) 10, [2004] B.C.J. No. 2076 (B.C.C.A.). The court applied the *Miglin* tests in a case where the wife had failed to become economically self-sufficient by the time her support ended. There was no issue that the negotiations which led to the consent order met the first stage test in *Miglin*. The issue was whether the case met the second stage of the *Miglin* inquiry that is "whether the wife's present circumstances were within the reasonable contemplation of the parties at the time of the consent order." The Court of Appeal found that the consent order only stated that at the end of the 48 months "the [husband's] obligation to pay maintenance will cease absolutely as will the [wife's] entitlement to maintenance", unlike the open-ended release in the *Miglin* separation agreement. The fact that the husband was able to vary his support payments based on his reduced income from his forced change of employment suggests that only limited changes in economic circumstances were contemplated. The 48-month term implied that the parties expected the wife to obtain self-sufficiency in that period of time. The parties knew of the wife's career objectives at the time of the consent order and circumstances beyond the wife's control prevented her from reaching those objectives. The court held that as the circumstances had not been reasonably contemplated, it could not be said that the circumstances were condoned by the consent order and precluded variation. The appeal was dismissed.

*The principles outlined in* Miglin v. Miglin *apply to applications to vary brought under s. 17 of the* Divorce Act, *if the order or judgement in issue incorporates the provisions of an agreement — Spencer v. Spencer*, 2005 CarswellSask 148, 2005 SKQB 116, 14 R.F.L. (6th) 460, 261 Sask. R. 150, [2005] S.J. No. 150 (Sask. Q.B.). The former husband applied to vary the terms of a spousal support agreement incorporated into a judgement. The husband relied on his loss of employment as the change in circumstance justifying variation of support. The court applied the two-stage *Miglin* test. The agreement clearly met the first stage of the test. The husband relied on his job loss as a material change in circumstances justifying a variation in spousal support. The court posed the question, "whether his job loss is a significant departure from the range of reasonable outcomes that could have been anticipated by the parties." The court held that if the husband did not consider the possibility of his job loss, he should have, as a job loss could reasonably have been anticipated as a possible future event. The husband could have insisted on the inclusion of a material change provision in the parties' agreement to protect him in the event of unemployment. The court found that the husband had resources from which to pay spousal support. The fact that he might be required to use some portion of his share of the family property to satisfy his support obligation did not lead to an inequity. The husband's application was dismissed.

*Change of circumstances not foreseen at the time of the divorce judgement — Wilansky v. Wilansky*, 2008 CarswellNfld 246, 2008 NLSCUFC 27, 280 Nfld. & P.E.I.R. 4, 859 A.P.R. 8 (N.L.U.F.C.). The husband sought a provisional order which would vary his child support and spousal support obligations retroactively and prospectively. The court found that if the husband's bankruptcy had been known at the time that spousal support was consented to, the husband would not have, because he could not have, agreed to the amount of support. His materially changed circumstances were not within the reasonable contemplation of the parties. Further, this change satisfied the requirement for a material change in circumstances as required in the divorce judgement. The wife had knowledge of the husband's bankruptcy when it occurred. The court agreed to vary spousal support retroactively effective from the date of bankruptcy. At the provisional hearing, the court held that spousal support should be terminated as the husband has been deemed to be unable to pay any spousal support since the date of bankruptcy. The order to terminate support did not, however, preclude future variation applications or variations to this provisional order after the wife tendered her evidence at the confirmation hearing. Consequently, there was no change in circumstances that could be relied upon as the basis for variation. In addition, the current slowdown in the lumber industry had been anticipated for several years and in other years the husband's secondary business had either operated at a loss or generated very little income. The court assumed that the husband could earn additional income from other sources other than his main type of employment. The wife's slight improvement in her employment due to an increase in the minimum wage was not a substantial or significant change which would warrant a departure from the amount of spousal support the parties agreed to in the consent order.

*The test for foreseeability is a subjective test* — Stones v. Stones, 2004 CarswellBC 404, 2004 BCCA 99, 48 R.F.L. (5th) 223, 195 B.C.A.C. 41, 319 W.A.C. 41, [2004] B.C.J. No. 378 (B.C.C.A.). The court stated, at paras. 15 and 16:

> ... the question of what is a material change of circumstance may vary from one case to another. That is particularly so in relation to foreseeability. There are a group of cases which decide that retirement from employment, even at the retirement age set by the employer, or by collective agreement, can be a material change of circumstances, although clearly it would be foreseeable ... the question should really be asked in each case of whether the circumstance in question was one which the parties must have had in contemplation and built into the framing of their agreement. Perhaps it is a change that the parties were prepared to leave out of contemplation in the agreement because of complexity or some other reason, so that when it occurs it is a material change of circumstances, even though the parties knew it must be going to happen at some time or another.

The husband was self-employed at the time that the agreement was signed. The court stated that it "would have been a very complicated and unreliable process to try to set down in advance what would be the kind of change that should be one that the parties did contemplate or should be one which the parties did not contemplate." The court held that in this particular consent order, the husband's subsequent unemployment was a material change in circumstances. The wife's appeal from an order retro actively reducing spousal support and determining her entitlement to interest on spousal support arrears was dismissed.

*Facts which are known at the time support order was made cannot later be relied upon to prove a change of circumstances justifying a variation of the order* — B. (G.) c. G. (L.), 1995 CarswellQue 23, 1995 CarswellQue 120, EYB 1995-67821, 15 R.F.L. (4th) 201, [1995] 3 S.C.R. 370, 127 D.L.R. (4th) 385, 186 N.R. 201, [1995] R.D.F. 611, [1995] S.C.J. No. 72 (S.C.C.). Where the court at the time the wife's support order was made acknowledged that she was seeing another man and it was foreseeable that they could eventually cohabit, the later fact of that cohabitation did not justify a reduction in support.

*When determining whether a change of circumstances exists, on which to base a variation of a spousal support order, the guiding principle is the determination of whether, if known at the time of the original order, the change would have resulted in a different order* — Read v. Read, 2000 CarswellNS 52, 2000 NSCA 33, 4 R.F.L. (5th) 126, 183 N.S.R. (2d) 181, 568 A.P.R. 181, [2000] N.S.J. No. 54 (N.S.C.A.).

*Variation refused, matters considered on appeal* — Cosper v. Cosper, 1997 CarswellNS 388, 1997 NSCA 155, 32 R.F.L. (4th) 241 (N.S.C.A.). An application to vary a spousal support award was refused when the bulk of the wife's arguments centered on the unfairness of the original order, which had already been the basis for an unsuccessful appeal.

*Original order on consent not a bar to variation* — Benoît v. Reid, 1995 CarswellNB 239, 171 N.B.R. (2d) 161, 131 D.L.R. (4th) 346, 18 R.F.L. (4th) 136, 437 A.P.R. 161, [1995] N.B.J. No. 553 (N.B.C.A.). The fact that an original order is made on consent does not bar an application for variation.

*Change in circumstances must be material and substantial* — *Mullin v. Mullin*, 1993 CarswellPEI 17, 48 R.F.L. (3d) 322, 108 Nfld. & P.E.I.R. 61, 339 A.P.R. 61, [1993] P.E.I.J. No. 69 (P.E.I.C.A.), the court held that it was settled law that there must be a material and substantive change in the circumstances before a variation order will be granted under the provisions of s. 17(4) of the Act.

*Change in circumstances must be significant* — *Oldham v. King*, 1987 CarswellMan 83, 11 R.F.L. (3d) 75, 51 Man. R. (2d) 177 (Man. Q.B.). In variation applications, s. 17(4) does not contemplate consideration by the court of every little change in a party's financial circumstances. The changes must be significant for a finding that a variation is warranted.

*A court on a support variation application should not respond by ordering minor or temporary changes or changes which were within the contemplation of the judge at the original hearing* — *Michel v. Michel*, 1988 CarswellOnt 320, 18 R.F.L. (3d) 182, 67 O.R. (2d) 60, 55 D.L.R. (4th) 636, [1988] O.J. No. 2058 (Ont. H.C.).

*A "material" change in circumstances is one which likely would have resulted in different terms if known at the time of the original orders* — *Hayes v. Hayes*, 1995 CarswellNB 33, 14 R.F.L. (4th) 296, 166 N.B.R. (2d) 1, 425 A.P.R. 1, [1995] N.B.J. No. 242 (N.B.C.A.). Leave to appeal refused (1996), 18 R.F.L. (4th) 89n, [1995] S.C.C.A. No. 377 (S.C.C.).

*Issues relating to a change in circumstances may be dealt with only as they arise* — *although a spouse's concerns about his or her economic future may be justified, they cannot support an application for increased support* — *Murphy v. Murphy*, 1994 CarswellMan 181, 10 R.F.L. (4th) 102, 120 D.L.R. (4th) 215, [1995] 2 W.W.R. 457, 97 Man. R. (2d) 247, 79 W.A.C. 247 (Man. C.A.).

*The mere passing of time in itself does not constitute a "change in circumstances" justifying a variation in support* — *Droit de la famille - 1187*, [1988] R.D.F. 290 (C.S. Que.). See also *Droit de la famille - 1230* (1988), [1989] R.D.F. 193 (C.S. Que.); *Vigneault c. Cloutier*, 1989 CarswellQue 288, 1989 CarswellQue 1826, 65 D.L.R. (4th) 598, 32 Q.A.C. 161, [1989] R.D.F. 686 (C.A. Que.).

*Changes in circumstances which must have been contemplated by the parties at the time a support order was made cannot later be relied upon as a basis for varying that order* — *Gaudet v. Gaudet*, 1988 CarswellPEI 14, 15 R.F.L. (3d) 65, 70 Nfld. & P.E.I.R. 107, 215 A.P.R. 107, [1988] P.E.I.J. No. 56 (P.E.I.C.A.).

*The "material change in circumstances" required to justify a variation in spousal support need not be a catastrophic event* — *Innes v. Innes*, 2003 CarswellOnt 2884, 44 R.F.L. (5th) 113, [2003] O.T.C. 686, [2003] O.J. No. 3039 (Ont. S.C.J.), reversed 2005 CarswellOnt 1835, 15 R.F.L. (6th) 187, 199 O.A.C. 69, [2005] O.J. No. 1839 (Ont. Div. Ct.). Leave to appeal refused 2005 CarswellOnt 8389, 25 R.F.L. (6th) 27 (Ont. C.A.).

*The change contemplated by s. 17(4.1) is a material change of circumstances* — *that is, a change which, if known at the time of the original order, would likely have resulted in different terms* — *Sequens v. Sequens*, 1999 CarswellBC 1114, 48 R.F.L. (4th) 53 (B.C.S.C.). Here it was found that the wife's failure to make a reasonable effort to become partially or wholly self-sufficient, and the husband's termination of his employment, were both material changes. Neither change required a rescission of the order, however. The original support order should be varied by suspending the obligation to make payments prospectively with the right of the wife to apply for a review upon the husband obtaining employment or in 1 year, whichever is earlier.

*Foreseeability of declining health with age may not prevent finding of change in circumstances* — *Kerwood v. Kerwood*, 1999 CarswellBC 780, 48 R.F.L. (4th) 127, 9 B.C.T.C. 227, [1999] B.C.J. No. 830 (B.C.S.C. [In Chambers]). The court allowed the 83-year-old wife's application for an increase to her 30-year-old spousal support order. The wife's health had declined as she grew older and she required near-daily home care. The fact that declining health with age is foreseeable did not alter that the wife had experienced a change in circumstances. As the husband's income had actually increased over the years, he was in a position to pay the increased amount.

*The change in circumstances required to be proved as a condition precedent to a variation of a support order need not arise from the marriage or its breakdown* — *Tully v. Tully*, 1994 CarswellOnt 475, 9 R.F.L. (4th) 131 (Ont. Gen. Div.), additional reasons at 1994 CarswellOnt 2333 (Ont. Gen. Div.).

*Applicant not required to exhaust capital before seeking increased support* — *Brickman v. Brickman*, 1987 CarswellMan 116, 8 R.F.L. (3d) 318, 51 Man. R. (2d) 6 (Man. Q.B.). The court increased the support payable to the wife although she had maintained a $35,000 capital fund intact since the time of the divorce. It was held that, particularly in the case of a "traditional" marriage, the payee spouse should not be required to render herself penniless before seeking increased support based on changed circumstances.

*The coming into force of the Divorce Act, 1985, and in particular the provisions regarding spousal support, was not in itself a "change of circumstances" justifying a variation of the maintenance provisions contained in a decree nisi granted under the Divorce Act, 1970* — *Derkach v. Derkach*, 1986 CarswellSask 79, 5 R.F.L. (3d) 335, 55 Sask. R. 78, [1986] S.J. No. 669 (Sask. Q.B.).

*On an application to vary support, the court is restricted to considering changes in circumstances occurring subsequent to the date of the order and is not entitled to consider events occurring between the time when minutes of settlement were executed and the order made* — *Thombs v. Thombs*, 1988 CarswellOnt 256, 15 R.F.L. (3d) 83, [1988] O.J. No. 650 (Ont. U.F.C.).

*In an application for an upward variation of maintenance, the test is not that the claiming spouse be enduring hardship, but rather what is reasonable in the circumstances* — *Katz v. Katz*, 1983 CarswellMan 46, 33 R.F.L. (2d) 412, 21 Man. R. (2d) 1 (Man. C.A.), additional reasons at 1983 CarswellMan 254, 25 Man. R. (2d) 57 (Man. C.A.), reversing 1982 CarswellMan 167, 15 Man. R. (2d) 435 (Man. Q.B.).

*The mere passage of time from the date of a decree nisi is not in itself sufficient justification for a decrease in spousal maintenance* — *Lawson v. Kroitor*, 1984 CarswellSask 73, 43 R.F.L. (2d) 326, 37 Sask. R. 306 (Sask. Q.B.).

*"It is neither possible nor desirable to approach the resolution of an application ... [for variation of maintenance] on the basis of any mathematical formula related either to the husband's income or by applying to the present time and facts ratio extracted from the maintenance and income amounts at the time of the decree nisi"* — *Wilson v. Wilson*, 1982 CarswellBC 528, 27 R.F.L. (2d) 424 (B.C.S.C.), reversed 1983 CarswellBC 617, 37 R.F.L. (2d) 205 (B.C.C.A.).

*The fact that a payee spouse has managed to make ends meet does not necessarily equate with having achieved financial independence, so as to justify the termination of a support award* — *Droit de la famille - 901*, [1990] R.J.Q. 2771 (C.A. Que.).

*The fact that the parties resumed cohabitation prior to the granting of the decree absolute does not remove from a spouse the right to seek variation of corollary relief granted at the time of the decree nisi* — *Droit de la famille - 665*, 1989 CarswellQue 266, 30 Q.A.C. 216, [1989] R.D.F. 429 (C.A. Que.).

*Section 17(7)(d) of the Divorce Act, 1985 indicates a policy which will, in many cases, require spousal support to be cut off at some point* — *Martin v. Martin*, 1988 CarswellBC 197, 14 R.F.L. (3d) 388, 26 B.C.L.R. (2d) 390, [1988] B.C.J. No. 1001 (B.C.C.A.). The court must decide when that point in time is reached.

*The support variation provisions of the Divorce Act are not intended to reduce a payee spouse's lifestyle immediately to one which is as modest as possible as soon as that spouse makes significant efforts at achieving self-sufficiency — Petrocco v. von Michalofski*, 1998 CarswellOnt 336, 36 R.F.L. (4th) 278, [1998] O.J. No. 200 (Ont. Gen. Div.), affirmed (1998), 1998 CarswellOnt 4813, 43 R.F.L. (4th) 372, 120 O.A.C. 193 (Ont. Div. Ct.).

*Variation where one or both parties below the poverty line — Younker v. Younker*, 1991 CarswellPEI 17, 32 R.F.L. (3d) 138 (P.E.I.T.D.). In a variation application, the court stated that, in general, a person paying support should not have his or her income lowered to the extent that he or she is forced below the poverty line. However, if the person being supported is below the poverty line, then the supporting person should be required to pay support even it that results in the supporting person being placed below the poverty line.

*Temporary decline in payor's income was insufficient for variation of support — Gresham v. Gresham*, 1988 CarswellSask 62, 16 R.F.L. (3d) 108 (Sask. Q.B.). Where the husband's business was cyclical in nature, a temporary decline was found insufficient ground on which to base an application for reduced support.

*Once a bona fide reconciliation has occurred, any existing support order is of no force and effect — Smith v. Smith*, 1989 CarswellOnt 294, 22 R.F.L. (3d) 393, [1989] O.J. No. 3019 (Ont. H.C.). The onus of proving that a reconciliation is not *bona fide* rests on the person so alleging.

*A payor is not entitled to have support arrears rescinded simply because the amount is substantial — Greve v. Greve*, 1987 CarswellOnt 264, 11 R.F.L. (3d) 180 (Ont. H.C.). In the absence of proof of prior inability to pay, unreasonable delay in enforcement or laches, arrears should not be reduced.

*A variation order will not be granted where the only proposed change was a change of court — Grunewald v. Grunewald*, 1990 CarswellBC 471, 27 R.F.L. (3d) 101 (B.C.S.C.). Where the husband sought a variation of the custody, access, and support provisions under s. 17 of the Act only to the extent of changing the court in which the issues would be considered, the application was dismissed. As he did not propose changing the actual terms of the order, it was not a proper case for variation under s. 17.

*Payments of high legal fees not change in circumstances justifying variation — Caufield v. Caufield*, 1986 CarswellOnt 323, 4 R.F.L. (3d) 312 (Ont. H.C.). Where the wife had managed to spend or dissipate $183,000 subsequent to the divorce, her application for increased maintenance was refused. The husband could not be expected to subsidize her bad judgement.

*Reconciliation does not, in itself, expunge support arrears accumulated during the period of separation — Norris v. Norris*, 1991 CarswellOnt 253, 32 R.F.L. (3d) 103, [1991] O.J. No. 222 (Ont. U.F.C.). An earlier line of cases considered reconciliation to be a condonation of marital fault. However, the concept of fault having been effectively removed from family law, it would be anachronistic if the existence of a valid support order depended upon marital conduct.

*The variation provisions of the Divorce Act, 1985 merely codify the principles that have developed through the case law as it relates to the obligation of a former spouse to become self-supporting — Single v. Single*, 1986 CarswellNS 80, 5 R.F.L. (3d) 287 (N.S. Fam. Ct.).

*Once the payee spouse was free from economic disadvantage from the marriage, support could be terminated — Sookocheff v. Sookocheff*, 1988 CarswellSask 59, 15 R.F.L. (3d) 303, 70 Sask. R. 178 (Sask. Q.B.). Where, having received support payments for 2 years after the parties' divorce, the wife achieved self-sufficiency and had emerged from the marriage free from any related economic disadvantage, the support order was terminated.

*Dismissal of a prior application to vary a support order does not render the variation issue res judicata — Gessner v. Gessner*, 1990 CarswellSask 54, 24 R.F.L. (3d) 308, 82 Sask. R. 223, [1990] S.J. No. 78 (Sask. Q.B.). The *Divorce Act* expressly allows for variation applications to be brought when and as often as the specified pre-conditions for the applications exist.

## 10.3.1 Change of Circumstances — Onus of Proving Change

*There must be evidence to substantiate a claim of a material change in circumstances to establish financial circumstances at the time of trial and at the time of the variation application so that a court can compare the economic circumstances and determine if there has been a material change that would entitle an applicant to a variation of spousal support — Droit de la famille - 09668*, 2011 CarswellQue 13700, 2011 CarswellQue 13701, 2011 SCC 65, 6 R.F.L. (7th) 68, [2011] 3 S.C.R. 819, 339 D.L.R. (4th) 658, 425 N.R. 1 (S.C.C.). See **10.3 Variation – Change in Circumstances – meaning** for a detailed discussion of the case.

*When a fixed- and short-term order of spousal support has been awarded previously, whose purpose is to allow the recipient the time needed to become self-sufficient, the burden rests on the applicant for variation to show an inability to become self-sufficient — Williams v. Williams*, 2010 CarswellSask 213, 2010 SKCA 52, 83 R.F.L. (6th) 11, [2010] S.J. No. 206 (Sask. C.A.). The lower court had ordered spousal support for the wife for a 1-year period. She had applied to vary the period of support. The applicant had not shown that she was unable to become self-sufficient during the 1-year period of spousal support; rather, she had not demonstrated that she had even attempted to become self-sufficient.

*Onus of proving change of circumstances lies with applicant — Walker v. Walker*, 1992 CarswellBC 156, 39 R.F.L. (3d) 305, 68 B.C.L.R. (2d) 92, 12 B.C.A.C. 137, 23 W.A.C. 137 (B.C.C.A.). On a variation application, the onus of showing that the circumstances have changed lies with the applicant.

*Onus lies with applicant — Harris v. Harris*, 1992 CarswellBC 560, 40 R.F.L. (3d) 253 (B.C.S.C.). The onus is on an applicant to show that the change in circumstances is such that it warrants a variation of the original support order.

*Onus lies with applicant — Pardy v. Pardy*, 1986 CarswellNB 29, 3 R.F.L. (3d) 317, 73 N.B.R. (2d) 340, 184 A.P.R. 340 (N.B.Q.B.). The onus is on a party seeking variation of a support order to satisfy the court that the "change" specified in s. 17(4) of the *Divorce Act* is a material and substantive break with the past situation of the parties. The altered circumstances must render the existing order of support irreconcilable with the current conditions, means, needs and other circumstances of either former spouse or child.

*If no reason to expect review at time of original order — Story v. Story*, 1989 CarswellBC 237, 23 R.F.L. (3d) 225, 42 B.C.L.R. (2d) 21, 65 D.L.R. (4th) 549, [1989] B.C.J. No. 2238 (B.C.C.A.). "When a support order is made where there is no reason to expect that it will be reviewed upon certain events occurring or facts becoming known, as upon the hearing of a trial, there will be a heavier onus upon a party seeking a variance to establish a substantial economic change in the circumstances of at least one of the parties which, even if recognized as a possibility, was not taken into account at the trial, and which results in serious economic disadvantage to one party which can be accommodated without serious disadvantage to the other," per McEachern C.J.B.C.

*Failure to disclose — Alexander v. Alexander*, 1997 CarswellOnt 1343, 31 R.F.L. (4th) 131, 25 O.T.C. 103, [1997] O.J. No. 1092 (Ont. Gen. Div.), additional reasons at 1998 CarswellOnt 2836, [1998] O.J. No. 2924 (Ont. Gen. Div.), further additional reasons at 1998 CarswellOnt 4318, 43 R.F.L. (4th) 166, 80 O.T.C. 71, [1998] O.J. No. 4540 (Ont. Gen. Div.), affirmed 2000 CarswellOnt 241, 133 O.A.C. 395, [2000] O.J. No. 154 (Ont. C.A.). Where the husband had failed to make a complete and frank disclosure of his assets on his application to terminate his wife's spousal support, he was not found to have established the required material change in circumstances.

## 10.3.2 Change of Circumstances — Facts Known at Time of Order

*Facts known at time of original order cannot be relied upon* — *B. (G.) c. G. (L.)*, 1995 CarswellQue 23, 1995 CarswellQue 120, EYB 1995-67821, 15 R.F.L. (4th) 201, [1995] 3 S.C.R. 370, 127 D.L.R. (4th) 385, 186 N.R. 201, [1995] R.D.F. 611, [1995] S.C.J. No. 72 (S.C.C.). Facts which are known at the time support order was made cannot later be relied upon to prove a change of circumstances justifying a variation of the order. Accordingly, where the court at the time the wife's support order was made acknowledged that she was seeing another man and it was foreseeable that they could eventually cohabit, the later fact of that cohabitation did not justify a reduction in support.

*The threshold condition to be met by an applicant who seeks to vary a support order is a material change in circumstances from the date of the order sought to be varied — where the husband knew that he planned to retire before the summary trial but did not disclose the information to the trial judge, the threshold condition has not been met and the spousal support award should not be varied* — *MacLanders v. MacLanders*, 2012 CarswellBC 3736, 2012 BCCA 482, 24 R.F.L. (7th) 24, 39 B.C.L.R. (5th) 255 (B.C.C.A.). His application to vary on the basis of a decline in his health also failed due to a scarcity of evidence on that issue as a result of the dismissal of his fresh evidence application on appeal.

*Where no medical evidence of inability to work has been given, and the parties have contemplated triggering events for termination of support that have not occurred, support will not be terminated and no change in circumstances will be found* — *Chase v. Chase*, 2013 CarswellAlta 258, 2013 ABCA 83, 24 R.F.L. (7th) 21, [2013] A.J. No. 145 (Alta. C.A.). The husband applied to vary a support order to terminate support. The chambers judge had found there was no change in circumstances. The parties had a separation agreement providing for termination of support when the wife remarried or the husband reached age 60. Neither triggering event had occurred. The husband had decided to retire after his employment was terminated, citing ill health, but he had provided no medical evidence. The judge found that the husband had chosen to retire and that the parties had contemplated what would constitute a change in circumstances when drafting the separation agreement. Consequently, there was no change in circumstances.

*The move of a child from the recipient parent's home to that of the paying parent does not necessarily constitute changed circumstances for the determination of the suitability of a variation in spousal support if the change was reasonably foreseeable at the time of the original support order* — *Pustai v. Pustai*, 2010 CarswellOnt 1960, 2010 ONCA 251, [2010] O.J. No. 1336 (Ont. C.A.). Here, the trial judgement that the child's move from the mother's to the father's residence was reasonably foreseeable and therefore not a material change in the circumstances was upheld on the grounds that such a move was reasonably foreseeable at the time of the original order for support.

*Where circumstances which were not contemplated at the time of the signing of minutes of settlement come to pass, a variation order should be granted* — *Turpin v. Clark*, 2009 CarswellBC 3149, 2009 BCCA 530, 80 R.F.L. (6th) 239, 4 B.C.L.R. (5th) 48, 313 D.L.R. (4th) 452, [2010] 6 W.W.R. 613, 278 B.C.A.C. 220, 471 W.A.C. 220, [2009] B.C.J. No. 2328 (B.C.C.A.). Leave to appeal refused 2010 CarswellBC 1055, 2010 CarswellBC 1056, 297 B.C.A.C. 320 (note), 407 N.R. 396 (note), 504 W.A.C. 320 (note), [2010] S.C.C.A. No. 5 (S.C.C.). The parties, in their agreement anticipated that the wife would be able to earn upwards of $25,000, rather than the significantly smaller sum she actually earned because of her health problems.

*Acrimony between the parties that was present at the time of the original order will not be sufficient to re-open issues of support* — *Litman v. Sherman*, 2008 CarswellOnt 3542, 2008 ONCA 485, 52 R.F.L. (6th) 239, 238 O.A.C. 164 (Ont. C.A.). The parties had an extremely acrimonious relationship from the time of their marriage onward. The trial judge refused to re-open the support issue as the wife was unable to show a material change in circumstances based on the parties' acrimonious relationship and her changed financial circumstance. Deference was given by the Court of Appeal to the trial judge's finding that the wife's financial circumstances were unchanged, and that the parties' relationship had been acrimonious at the first trial in which support was not awarded.

*New facts would have led to different order originally — Read v. Read*, 2000 CarswellNS 52, 2000 NSCA 33, 4 R.F.L. (5th) 126, 183 N.S.R. (2d) 181, 568 A.P.R. 181, [2000] N.S.J. No. 54 (N.S.C.A.). When determining whether a change of circumstances exists, on which to base a variation of a spousal support order, the guiding principle is the determination of whether, if known at the time of the original order, the change would have resulted in a different order.

*New facts would have led to different order originally — Poohkay v. Poohkay*, 1997 CarswellAlta 604, 30 R.F.L. (4th) 9, 200 A.R. 211, 146 W.A.C. 211 (Alta. C.A.), additional reasons at 1997 CarswellAlta 987, 33 R.F.L. (4th) 140 (Alta. C.A.). In this case, the wife successfully appealed from an order dismissing her application for lifting of the time limitation on her spousal support order. At the time of the original order, the parties had not anticipated the extent to which the mother's duties as a custodial parent would interfere with her educational upgrading efforts. Had the parties known that their assumptions were incorrect at the time the original order was made, a different order would likely have resulted. As the wife would likely be able to enter the workforce in the near future, a lump sum award was preferable to an indefinite periodic one.

*New facts would have led to different order originally — MacDonald v. MacDonald*, 1997 CarswellAlta 566, 30 R.F.L. (4th) 1, 200 A.R. 193, 146 W.A.C. 193 (Alta. C.A.). A 20% increase in the husband's salary 4 years after the parties' divorce constituted a sufficient change in circumstances to warrant an increase in the wife's spousal support. If the pending increase had been known at the time of the original order, it would likely have resulted in an award of support to be increased at the time the salary change was anticipated.

*New facts would have led to different order originally — Tees v. Tees*, 1997 CarswellNWT 29, 31 R.F.L. (4th) 290, [1997] N.W.T.R. 315, [1997] N.W.T.J. No. 65 (N.W.T.S.C.). Where subsequent to the divorce the wife's existing multiple sclerosis condition deteriorated to the extent that she could no longer work, the court extended her limited term support award. But for the marriage breakdown, she would not have to bear the economic consequence which flowed from her disability. If the total disability had existed at the time of the original order, it would likely have resulted in an indeterminate order for a higher amount.

*Application refused — applicant's inability to find work not due to marriage — L. (H.) v. L. (M.H.)*, 2003 CarswellBC 2206, 2003 BCCA 484, 44 R.F.L. (5th) 388, 19 B.C.L.R. (4th) 327, 232 D.L.R. (4th) 52, 186 B.C.A.C. 264, 306 W.A.C. 264, [2003] B.C.J. No. 2098 (B.C.C.A.). The parties entered into a separation agreement which included terms relating to spousal support, giving the wife $3,000 per month for 2 years. These terms were incorporated into an order for divorce. Before the end of the 2 years, the wife brought an application to extend the payment of spousal support indefinitely. The wife had developed significant health problems. Support was extended for another 10 months. At a second variation hearing, the wife was granted further support retroactive to when support under the first variation ceased and that order was reviewable after 3 years. The husband appealed from this order. Since the original order, as varied, had expired, s. 17(10) of the *Divorce Act* applied. Section 17(10) provides that where a spousal support order is for a definite period or until a specified event occurs, a court cannot make a variation order resuming support on an application after the expiration of the period or occurrence of the event, unless the court is satisfied that a variation order is needed to relieve economic hardship related to the marriage and the changed circumstances since the making of the order or last variation order would have resulted in a different order. The court held in a two to one decision, that the chambers judge, not having the benefit of the *Miglin* judgement, erred in her overall approach to the problem of variation. The court must look at the objectives of support set out in the Act as a whole, including the policy goals of certainty, autonomy and finality. The fact that the wife was not able to obtain work was not sufficient reason to find that the agreement should no longer continue to govern the parties' post-divorce obligations towards each other. The court noted that the first variation was based on a delay in seeking employment because of illness, whereas the second variation was based on the inability to find employment. The reason for the inability was not disclosed to the court. The court was of the opinion that the absence of evidence connecting the inability to find work with something that occurred in the marriage was fatal to the wife's claim for further support. The alleged change in circumstances was not related to the marriage. There was no reason to interfere with the agreement between the parties. The husband's appeal was allowed.

*Application refused — applicant merely attempting to relitigate — Cosper v. Cosper*, 1997 CarswellNS 388, 32 R.F.L. (4th) 241 (N.S.C.A.). An application to vary a spousal support award was refused when the bulk of the wife's arguments centred around the unfairness of the original order, which had already been the basis for an unsuccessful appeal.

*New facts would have led to different order originally — Therrien-Cliche c. Cliche*, 1997 CarswellOnt 1166, 30 R.F.L. (4th) 97, 99 O.A.C. 202, [1997] O.J. No. 1451 (Ont. C.A.). Where the wife's limited term support order was based on an assumption that she would complete a nursing course, the removal of the limitation upon her failure to complete the course was upheld on appeal. The wife's changed circumstances, had they existed at the time of the original order, would have resulted in a different support order.

*Change need not be unforseeable to be material — Kerwood v. Kerwood*, 1999 CarswellBC 780, 48 R.F.L. (4th) 127, 9 B.C.T.C. 227, [1999] B.C.J. No. 830 (B.C.S.C. [In Chambers]). Declining health with advancing age, which is forseeable in a general way, may constitute a material change in circumstances. A change to be "material" does not have to be "unforeseeable". The Supreme Court of Canada in *Willick v. Willick*, 1994 CarswellSask 48, 1994 CarswellSask 450, EYB 1994-67936, 6 R.F.L. (4th) 161, [1994] 3 S.C.R. 670, 119 D.L.R. (4th) 405, 173 N.R. 321, [1994] R.D.F. 617, 125 Sask. R. 81, 81 W.A.C. 81, [1994] S.C.J. No. 94 (S.C.C.) and *B. (G.) c. G. (L.)*, 1995 CarswellQue 23, 1995 CarswellQue 120, EYB 1995-67821, 15 R.F.L. (4th) 201, [1995] 3 S.C.R. 370, 127 D.L.R. (4th) 385, 186 N.R. 201, [1995] R.D.F. 611, [1995] S.C.J. No. 72 (S.C.C.) does not equate materiality with unforseeability. Not all objectively foreseeable changes are necessarily within the contemplation of the parties at the time of the original order. In addition, the standard of judicial discretion must be flexible so that it does not artificially limit the adaptability of the language of s. 17(4.1) of the *Divorce Act*. To hold that a change must be unforeseeable to be material would result in an artificial limitation of s. 17(4.1). The parties were divorced in 1976, and the husband paid $425 a month as spousal support pursuant to a court order since the divorce. The former wife, age 83, applied to increase the amount of support to enable her to pay for home care. She suffered from several health problems due to age. She was 50 at the time of the original order. Mr. Justice Macaulay, increasing the support to $850 a month, stated. "If these circumstances had been known at the time of the hearing in 1976, the order made would likely have differed. I accept that it is foreseeable that health declines with age, but I do not accept that the court would have ordered identical support for a 50-year-old woman, without debilitating illness, as the court would have [ordered] had it been known that the woman would suffer from such an illness 20 years later. The specific change in circumstances was not known at the relevant time. I am satisfied that it is material".

## 10.3.3 Change in Payor's Circumstances

### General

When a payor retires with a full pension after completing a full term of service in the Armed Forces and when suffering from increasing ill health, these changes will constitute a material change in circumstances — *Powell v. Levesque*, 2014 CarswellBC 186, 2014 BCCA 33, 38 R.F.L. (7th) 261, 57 B.C.L.R. (5th) 132, 370 D.L.R. (4th) 370, 350 B.C.A.C. 43, 598 W.A.C. 43 (B.C.C.A.). The parties, who were women, cohabited for 8 years between 1990 and 1998. After paying support for 12 years, the appellant applied to vary spousal support on the basis of her early retirement. She had retired at 44, and the judge at first instance found the medical reasons for her retirement were not compelling. The Court of Appeal held that the motions judge had erred in not finding a material change in circumstances. The appellant had retired from the Armed Forces with a full pension after completing her full term of service in the face of mounting health issues, which the Court of Appeal found was not unreasonable.

Where a payor earns less income because of personal preferences rather than factors beyond his control, no change in circumstances will be found — *Hepburn v. Hepburn*, 2013 CarswellBC 2592, 2013 BCCA 383, 34 R.F.L. (7th) 267, 48 B.C.L.R. (5th) 251, 344 B.C.A.C. 6, 587 W.A.C. 6 (B.C.C.A.). A husband sought to vary a consent order for spousal support on the basis that his income had decreased. It had decreased because of more time being spent on media opportunities, which were not lucrative, rather than on the husband's primary occupation as a physician. He had changed clinics at the request of his employer, which led to reduced hours. The chambers judge found that, while the husband was free to pursue these non-remunerative opportunities, he was not able to use this fact as a basis for a reduction in spousal support. It was open to him to attempt to work more hours as a physician, and the reduction in income was as a result of his preferences, rather than circumstances. The chambers judge also found the relocation was voluntary. The original order was indefinite, and the wife was reliant on the support as there was no reasonable expectation she would return to the workforce and attain even partial self-sufficiency. The Court of Appeal found that there was evidence to support the chambers judge finding that the husband had reduced his hours as a physician to accommodate his unpaid media initiatives. The court upheld the finding that there was no material change in circumstances. However, the judge found the husband did lose some income through a factor beyond his control (loss of part-time employment), and this was found to be a material change sufficient to recalculate support.

Where no medical evidence of inability to work has been given, and the parties have contemplated triggering events for termination of support that have not occurred, support will not be terminated and no change in circumstances will be found — *Chase v. Chase*, 2013 CarswellAlta 258, 2013 ABCA 83, 24 R.F.L. (7th) 21, [2013] A.J. No. 145 (Alta. C.A.). The husband applied to vary a support order to terminate support. The chambers judge had found there was no change in circumstances. The parties had a separation agreement providing for termination of support when the wife remarried or the husband reached age 60. Neither triggering event had occurred. The husband had decided to retire after his employment was terminated, citing ill health, but he had provided no medical evidence. The judge found that the husband had chosen to retire and that the parties had contemplated what would constitute a change in circumstances when drafting the separation agreement. Consequently, there was no change in circumstances.

Termination of employment will be found to be a material change in circumstances when it was not contemplated at the time of the separation agreement — *Campbell v. Campbell*, 2012 CarswellNS 594, 2012 NSCA 86, 320 N.S.R. (2d) 223, 1014 A.P.R. 223 (N.S.C.A.). The parties were married for 28 years and had three children. During the marriage, the wife was a stay-at-home mother who suffered from severe emphysema that prevented her from working. The husband had been paying support pursuant to a separation agreement when he was terminated from his employment. The wife appealed the decision of a trial judge to reduce spousal support to reflect the husband's capacity to pay income. He had previously paid spousal support from his severance pay, which was now exhausted. The Court of Appeal upheld a trial decision to vary spousal support, finding that, although the trial judge had not explicitly mentioned Step 2 of the *Miglin* test (current circumstances leading to noncompliance with the objectives of the *Divorce Act*), he had considered the relevant factors.

## Change of circumstances — payor's bankruptcy

*Agreement entitled the recipient to periodic payments in exchange for releasing interest in business which then went bankrupt* — *Craig v. Bassett*, 1988 CarswellNS 29, 15 R.F.L. (3d) 461, 70 C.B.R. (N.S.) 83 (N.S.T.D.), affirmed 1988 CarswellNS 31, 17 R.F.L. (3d) 225, 1 C.B.R. (N.S.) 82, 53 D.L.R. (4th) 465, 87 N.S.R. (2d) 216, 7222 A.P.R. 216, [1988] N.S.J. No. 374 (N.S.C.A.). Where the parties' decree *nisi* incorporated a settlement whereby the wife released her interest in the husband's business in exchange for money to be paid in instalments, the wife's right to those funds was not affected by the husband's subsequent bankruptcy. The money owing to the wife was basically for her support and was accordingly protected by s. 148 of the *Bankruptcy Act*.

*Unimpeded earning capacity despite bankruptcy* — *Richards v. Richards*, 1986 CarswellSask 461, 48 Sask. R. 131 (Sask. C.A.). The court dismissed the husband's appeal from an order refusing to cancel arrears and reduce maintenance payable after his assignment in bankruptcy. The husband was a young, able-bodied man who continued to operate a business in spite of the bankruptcy.

*Payor's bankruptcy plus recipient's wealth justifies termination* — *Bargh v. Bargh*, 2003 CarswellBC 740, 2003 BCSC 489, 37 R.F.L. (5th) 235 (B.C.S.C.). Where the husband was unexpectedly assessed a sizable tax debt and had to declare bankruptcy to clear it, his application to cancel the spousal support payable to his former wife was allowed. The assignment into bankruptcy constituted a material change justifying the cancellation. Furthermore, the wife had sizable assets and was not entitled to further support.

## Change of circumstances — payor cohabiting

*Income from payor's new spouse relevant* — *Chevalier v. Chevalier*, 1993 CarswellNS 406, 128 N.S.R. (2d) 112, 359 A.P.R. 112 (N.S.S.C.). The father's ability to pay, on an application by the mother for increased child support, was calculated on the premise that the father's common-law spouse contributed one-half of the couple's rent and utilities.

*Income from payor's new spouse relevant* — *McLean v. McLean*, 1975 CarswellNB 23, 26 R.F.L. 115, 14 N.B.R. (2d) 64, 15 A.P.R. 64 (N.B.Q.B.). Where the former husband is living with another woman who is employed, that woman is expected to help pay his household expenses, thereby freeing more of his funds for the payment of maintenance.

## Change of circumstances — remarriage of payor

*Payor's remarriage not necessarily a bar to continued support obligation* — *Bracklow v. Bracklow*, 1999 CarswellBC 532, 1999 CarswellBC 533, 44 R.F.L. (4th) 1, [1999] 1 S.C.R. 420,

63 B.C.L.R. (3d) 77, 169 D.L.R. (4th) 577, [1999] 8 W.W.R. 740, 236 N.R. 79, [1999] R.D.F. 203, 120 B.C.A.C. 211, 196 W.A.C. 211, [1999] S.C.J. No. 14 (S.C.C.). The payor had remarried, and, in obiter, the court observed that a reduction may be called for due to "obligations arising from new relationships in so far as they have an impact on means." However, in light of all the facts the wife's application for continued support was granted.

*Payor's remarriage is not necessarily a bar to continued support* – Moge v. Moge, 1992 CarswellMan 143, 1992 CarswellMan 222, EYB 1992-67141, 43 R.F.L. (3d) 345, [1992] 3 S.C.R. 813, 99 D.L.R. (4th) 456, [1993] 1 W.W.R. 481, 145 N.R. 1, [1993] R.D.F. 168, 81 Man. R. (2d) 161, 30 W.A.C. 161, [1992] S.C.J. No. 107 (S.C.C.). The payor husband had remarried since the original support order; the recipient had not. The fact of the husband's remarriage was not a bar to continuance of spousal support. On an application to vary, the court must take into account all the factors in s. 17(7), not merely need and ability to pay.

*Benefits maintenance for recipient – new payor relationship* – Kenny v. MacDougall, 2007 CarswellNS 561, 2007 NSCA 126, 47 R.F.L. (6th) 55 (N.S.C.A.). Where the husband had fulfilled his support obligations toward his former wife, the court struck a provision requiring the husband to maintain medical and dental insurance coverage for her. The husband had remarried and the wife was in a new relationship and continuation of the insurance requirement was inconsistent with the discharge of support obligations.

*Probable support obligation to second spouse is relevant* – Harvey v. Harvey, 1995 CarswellBC 345 14 R.F.L. (4th) 128, 60 B.C.A.C. 178, 9 B.C.L.R. (3d) 83, 99 W.A.C. 178, [1995] B.C.J. No. 1284, (B.C.C.A.). Where the husband had separated from his second wife and would likely face a substantial support claim, his support obligation toward his first wife was terminated. Combined with other factors, the husband's circumstances had been significantly changed.

*Marriage to third party with whom payor cohabiting at time of original order* – Smith v. Smith, 1989 CarswellMan 59, 23 R.F.L. (3d) 89, 62 Man. R. (2d) 93 (Man. Q.B.); varied 1990 CarswellMan 47, 27 R.F.L. (3d) 32, 66 Man. R. (2d) 181, 71 D.L.R. (4th) 612 (Man. C.A.). Where at the time the parties' spousal support order was made the husband was supporting his cohabitant, his subsequent marriage to the cohabitant could not be relied upon as a change in circumstances warranting a variation of the support order.

*Remarriage of payor plus recipient's ongoing need justify increase* – Leonard v. Leonard, 2008 CarswellOnt 5708 (Ont. S.C.J.); additional reasons at 2008 CarswellOnt 6516 (Ont. S.C.J.). See *Leonard*, in s. **10.3.4**.

*Payor's new spouse plus recipient's medical conditions justified increase* – Foster v. Foster, 2000 CarswellOnt 4082, 13 R.F.L. (5th) 61 (Ont. S.C.J.). The court rejected the husband's application to terminate the wife's spousal support and allowed her application for an increase. The wife's medical conditions resulted in her classification as "disabled" under the Canada Pension Plan. The husband could afford to pay more, given an increase in his salary and the fact that he had remarried and had a new wife with whom to share expenses.

*Payor's new family obligations plus his low income* – Wolfe v. Wolfe, 1995 CarswellBC 609, 15 R.F.L. (4th) 86 (B.C.S.C.). Where the husband was only employed seasonally, was reliant on social assistance and had a second family to support, his application to terminate spousal support was allowed.

*Payor's new family obligations plus relative financial positions of parties justify termination* – Wolfe v. Wolfe, 1995 CarswellBC 609, 15 R.F.L. (4th) 86. The court allowed the husband's application to terminate the spousal support payable to the wife. Although the award had been a modest one and did little to redress the economic imbalance which flowed from the marriage, it was a substantial burden to the husband. The continuation of the award threatened the continued economic viability of the husband's second family and, given the imminent ability of the wife to rejoin the workforce, the termination was justifiable.

*Income from payor's new spouse relevant — no reduction — Hachey v. Hachey*, 1994 CarswellNB 268, 9 R.F.L. (4th) 71 (N.B.Q.B.). The husband's application for a reduction in the spousal support payable by him pursuant to a 9-month old consent order was dismissed. The husband was splitting the income from a catering business with his common law wife, whose income was also properly considered in determining his ability to pay. Although the common law wife was not obligated to contribute towards support of the first wife, it did affect the husband's funds.

*Not enough to go around — Smith (Arsenault) v. Smith*, 1992 CarswellNS 68, 40 R.F.L. (3d) 316, 113 N.S.R. (2d) 226, 309 A.P.R. 226 (N.S. Fam. Ct.). It is difficult, if not impossible, to develop a set of rules governing the effect of second families on first family support obligations that will apply in all cases. In many instances, the court can do little more than try to make life liveable where there is not enough money to go around.

*Payor's new marriage and debts do not automatically justify termination — Droit de la famille - 1672*, [1992] R.D.F. 566 (C.S. Que.); affirmed (June 22, 1994), no C.A. Montréal 500-09-001698-927 (C.A. Que.). The court refused the husband's application to terminate spousal support 3 years after the termination of their 23-year marriage. Although the husband had considerable debts and new family obligations, his financial problems could be attributable largely to his mismanagement of his sizeable income. The wife had made genuine efforts to achieve self-sufficiency and, given the lavish lifestyle the parties had enjoyed, she could not be expected to do just anything to earn a living.

*Income from payor's new spouse relevant — Watson v. Watson*, 1991 CarswellBC 548, 35 R.F.L. (3d) 169, [1991] B.C.J. No. 2604 (B.C.S.C.). Where, as a result of remarriage and the sharing of expenses, the husband had more disposable income, the quantum of child support which he was required to pay was increased.

*Payor's new marriage does not justify termination — Greco v. Levin*, 1991 CarswellOnt 291, 33 R.F.L. (3d) 405 (Ont. Gen. Div.). A payor spouse who remarries is not permitted to rely upon his obligations to his second family as justification for an inability to pay support for a child from the first family. Second family obligations are undertaken with full knowledge of the first family obligations.

*Payor's new marriage and obligations do not automatically justify termination — Jacobs v. Jacobs*, 1990 CarswellOnt 310, 29 R.F.L. (3d) 320 (Ont. Gen. Div.). The remarriage of the payor spouse, in itself, will not justify a reduction in support payable absent proof of actual economic effect.

*Payor's new family obligations may justify reduction — Burt v. Burt*, 1990 CarswellNfld 13, 25 R.F.L. (3d) 92, 81 Nfld. & P.E.I.R. 241, 255 A.P.R. 241 (Nfld. T.D.). Where a payor has insufficient income and resources to maintain two families, the support payable to his first family should be reduced, thereby giving the new family unit the opportunity to flourish.

*Disclosure required re finances of new spouse — Mense v. Mense*, 1988 CarswellMan 330, 54 Man. R. (2d) 228, [1988] M.J. No. 335 (Man. Q.B.). The husband was ordered to disclose financial information about his new wife in the context of an application for variation of support brought by his former wife.

*Both remarried, payor had new twin children — Underwood v. Underwood*, 1987 CarswellNS 74, 7 R.F.L. (3d) 447 (N.S. Fam. Ct.). Where both parties had remarried and the husband had, since the divorce, parented twins, his application to rescind spousal support was allowed.

*Balancing the needs of two families — Northcott v. Northcott*, 1986 CarswellNfld 11, 1 R.F.L. (3d) 216, 59 Nfld. & P.E.I.R. 199, 178 A.P.R. 199 (Nfld. T.D.). In an application to reduce maintenance, the needs of the first family must be balanced against the desirability of giving the payor spouse's new family the opportunity to succeed. (Ruling made under the *Divorce Act*, 1968.)

## Change of circumstances — payor's future contingencies

*Payor's retirement merely anticipated, not realized – therefore variation order premature –* Renwick v. Renwick, 2007 CarswellBC 2697, 2007 BCCA 521, 43 R.F.L. (6th) 286, 73 B.C.L.R. (4th) 12, 247 B.C.A.C. 274, 409 W.A.C. 274 (B.C.C.A.); reversing 2006 CarswellBC 2489, 2006 BCSC 1502 (B.C.S.C.). Where the husband's stated intention to operate his business for 6 months without remuneration and then retire did not trigger a term in the parties' consent order terminating his obligation to pay spousal support after retirement. An order made in these circumstances was accordingly rescinded as premature.

*Payor's retirement merely anticipated, not realized – LeBlanc v. LeBlanc,* 1995 CarswellNB 36, 14 R.F.L. (4th) 414, 163 N.B.R. (2d) 192, 419 A.P.R. 192 (N.B.Q.B.); affirmed 1995 CarswellNB 193, 14 R.F.L. (4th) 414n, 167 N.B.R. (2d) 375, 427 A.P.R. 375 (N.B.C.A.). The husband's application for termination of the wife's spousal support brought in anticipation of his retirement was dismissed. The husband had not yet suffered a reduction in income and, in fact, since the date of the last variation his income had increased substantially.

*Termination date set for point in the future when payor planned to retire – Epstein v. Epstein,* 1991 CarswellNB 240, 115 N.B.R. (2d) 418, 291 A.P.R. 418 (N.B.Q.B.); affirmed 1991 CarswellNB 290, 122 N.B.R. (2d) 176, 306 A.P.R. 176 (N.B.C.A.). Where the wife had been awarded sizeable assets upon the dissolution of the parties' marriage, the court allowed the husband's application to set a termination date for the wife's spousal support 5 years hence. The husband planned to retire at that time and sought the order to facilitate his financial planning.

*Original order based on payor's anticipated income – August v. August,* 1989 CarswellMan 43, 21 R.F.L. (3d) 1, 57 Man. R. (2d) 128, 58 D.L.R. (4th) 459, [1989] M.J. No. 184 (Man. C.A.). Where a support order had been based upon the husband's anticipated income, the husband's failure to reach such anticipated income was found to be a sufficient change of circumstances to justify a variation of the support order.

*Original order made in cognizance of potential for increased payor income – Benson v. Benson,* 1987 CarswellNfld 28, 8 R.F.L. (3d) 43, 63 Nfld. & P.E.I.R. 35, 194 A.P.R. 35 (Nfld. C.A.). The fact that a trial judge, in setting maintenance, recognized that a dependant spouse might in the future receive income from employment does not preclude that income, when received, from being recognized as a change of circumstances justifying a variation.

*Payor loses job but receives severance and consulting contract income – no reduction at time of trial – Sasonow v. Sasanow,* 2000 CarswellOnt 1085, 6 R.F.L. (5th) 415 (Ont. S.C.J.). In a case under the Ontario *Family Law Act*, the court held that where a payor has been terminated but receives salary under a severance package and also receives consulting contract payments, his plea of reduced income relates only to the future. The husband's application to vary spousal support was dismissed.

*Reasonable for payor to anticipate retirement, which would reduce ability to pay – Andrew v. Andrew,* 1999 CarswellOnt 2056 (Ont. Gen. Div.). See *Andrew,* below, in s. **10.3.4.**

*Payor's retirement contemplated but not yet a reality – Tatomir v. Tatomir,* 1989 CarswellSask 440, 78 Sask. R. 49 (Sask. Q.B.). The fact that a payor spouse may be contemplating retirement should not be considered on the payee's application for increased support. The payor is free to raise the issue in future variation applications after the retirement has actually taken place.

## Change of circumstances — payor's retirement

*Where a party alleged that his retirement was the basis for a reduction of spousal support, but at the time of his retirement he did not seek a variation, his own actions suggest he did not view his retirement as a material change and the retirement cannot later be used a s a basis for reducing support — Droit de la famille - 09668*, 2011 CarswellQue 13700, 6 R.F.L. (7th) 68. For a detailed discussion of the case, see **10.3 Variation – Change in Circumstances – Meaning.**

*Payor's involuntary retirement — "change of circumstances" — Strang v. Strang*, 1990 CarswellAlta 271, 26 R.F.L. (3d) 113, 107 A.R. 111 (Alta. C.A.); affirmed 1992 CarswellAlta 70, 1992 CarswellAlta 468, EYB 1992-66872, 39 R.F.L. (3d) 233, [1992] 2 S.C.R. 112, 3 Alta. L.R. (3d) 1, 92 D.L.R. (4th) 762, 137 N.R. 203, 125 A.R. 331, 14 W.A.C. 331, [1992] S.C.J. No. 55 (S.C.C.). The forced retirement of a payor spouse is a "change of circumstances" within the meaning of s. 17 of the *Divorce Act* which may justify a reduction in support.

*Reduction of spousal support based on payor's retirement and reviewable anytime after approximately 6 months — Emery v. Emery*, 2010 CarswellBC 1170, 2010 BCCA 229, 85 R.F.L. (6th) 251, 287 B.C.A.C. 116, 485 W.A.C. 116 (B.C.C.A.); additional reasons at 2010 CarswellBC 2137, 2010 BCCA 376, 100 R.F.L. (6th) 154 (B.C.C.A.). The Court of Appeal modified a trial judgment which suspended spousal support upon the early retirement of the husband, where it was reasonably expected he would find some other remunerative employment. The Court of Appeal substituted a reduced spousal support obligation which took into account banked vacation pay. In its additional reasons, the Court of Appeal further reduced the spousal support payable in light of the payor's debt load and inability to obtain employment. The court set spousal support for 2009 at $1139 per month which was at the low end of the Advisory Guidelines range.

*Where the payor spouse retires, the other spouse is not required to draw on the payor spouse's pension at that time — Swales v. Swales*, 2010 CarswellAlta 1946, 2010 ABCA 292, 90 R.F.L. (6th) 314 (Alta. C.A.); reversing 2010 CarswellAlta 507, 2010 ABQB 187, 26 Alta. L.R. (5th) 341, 2010 C.E.B. & P.G.R. 8382 (Alta. Q.B.). The parties separated after a long-term traditional marriage. The husband was paying $1,200 per month in spousal support. The wife had also received a one-half interest in the husband's pension, valued at $99,000. The husband retired at age 55 and began drawing on his pension income. The wife did not start drawing on her pension income on the grounds she would not be able to retire until she was 65. The husband's application to terminate spousal support was dismissed. In the minutes of settlement the parties had agreed to a review of quantum when the husband reached age 55. There was a considerable portion of the husband's pension that had not been equalized and could be used to pay spousal support, if required, without "double dipping". No authority existed that former spouses were required to start drawing on their pension income at the same time. Using a subjective test, the chambers judge found that, given her limited ability to earn income and her modest assets, it was not reasonable for the wife to start drawing on her pension income. The Court of Appeal allowed the husband's appeal and remitted the matter to be reheard. The reasonableness of how a spouse deals with his or her assets is an objective test. The Court of Appeal could not apply the objective test in this case without evidence, inter alia, of the wife's enhanced pension entitlement should she wait until age 65 to start to draw it down.

*A variation order based on a change in financial circumstances that will occur after retirement should not be made speculatively before the actual circumstances are known — Dufresne v. Dufresne*, 2009 CarswellOnt 5617, 2009 ONCA 682 (Ont. C.A.). Although the Court of Appeal agreed the parties' financial circumstances would likely change upon retirement, this was not sufficient grounds to vary support, specifically concerning the husband's life insurance policy, before the actual change occurred.

*Payor's retirement merely anticipated, not realized — therefore variation order premature —* Renwick v. Renwick, 2007 CarswellBC 2697, 2007 BCCA 521, 43 R.F.L. (6th) 286, 73 B.C.L.R. (4th) 12, 247 B.C.A.C. 274, 409 W.A.C. 274 (B.C.C.A.); reversing 2006 CarswellBC 2489, 2006 BCSC 1502 (B.C.S.C.). The husband's stated intention to operate his business for 6 months without remuneration and then retire did not trigger a term in the parties' consent order terminating his obligation to pay spousal support after retirement. An order made in these circumstances was accordingly rescinded as premature.

*Early retirement plus new and employed spouse balanced by new payor obligations — support reduced —* Meiklejohn v. Meiklejohn, 2001 CarswellOnt 3480, 19 R.F.L. (5th) 167, 150 O.A.C. 149, [2001] O.T.C. 323, 2001 C.E.B. & P.G.R. 8395 (note), [2001] O.J. No. 3911 (Ont. C.A.); additional reasons at 2001 CarswellOnt 4050 (Ont. C.A.); reversing 2000 CarswellOnt 1190, 6 R.F.L. (5th) 360 (Ont. S.C.J.). The court allowed the husband's appeal from the dismissal of his application to reduce the quantum of spousal support payable by him. The 40% reduction in his income that occurred upon his early retirement was significant and had to be acknowledged. Although he had remarried and his new wife was employed, the trial court had placed too much emphasis on the new wife's income, disregarding the fact that the combined resources of the husband and his wife had to support a household of four people.

*Retirement reduces ability to pay —* Cramer v. Cramer, 2000 CarswellBC 908, 2000 BCCA 272, 6 R.F.L. (5th) 107, 75 B.C.L.R. (3d) 125, [2000] 6 W.W.R. 47, 186 D.L.R. (4th) 704, 139 B.C.A.C. 34, 227 W.A.C. 34, [2000] B.C.J. No. 873 (B.C.C.A.). At trial, the parties' assets had been split slightly in the wife's favour and a generous award of maintenance had been granted to enable her to pursue her educational and vocational objectives. To continue support at the present time would be effectively redistributing the parties' assets. Like her husband, the wife should realize on her remaining capital asset and live on the resulting income until she is eligible for an old age pension. The husband's retirement no longer enabled him to support the wife and consequently the appeal court upheld the trial judgment terminating spousal support.

*Retirement not entirely justified — imputation of income —* Teeple v. Teeple, 1999 CarswellOnt 2958, 2 R.F.L. (5th) 464, 124 O.A.C. 294, 90 O.T.C. 80 (note) (Ont. C.A.). Where the payor takes early retirement contrary to his intention at the time of a property settlement made between the parties, and the court finds that the early retirement is for the purpose of avoiding the payment of spousal support, the court may impute an income to the payor in an amount that is more than his retirement income. In this case, the payor's income was $80,000 a year prior to retirement and $27,000 a year afterwards. By reasons of the early retirement, his pension increased in value from $51,000 to $145,000. The wife was 53 years of age and he was 50. In the circumstances, the court, without stating the amount, imputed an income that was less than he was earning before he retired. Monthly support of $1,000 a month "represents a fair compromise and we so order." The $1,000 a month was to be indexed in accordance with the Consumer Price Index and made binding on the payor's estate.

*Retirement reduces ability to pay — but support made a first charge on payor's estate —* Doe v. Doe, 1999 CarswellOnt 2111, 126 O.A.C. 168, [1999] O.J. No. 2564 (Ont. C.A.). The husband appealed from a judgment dismissing his application to vary spousal support. The parties had been married for 20 years, separated in 1977 and divorced in 1981. On a variation application in 1987, spousal support had been increased from $3000 to $4,500 per month and the appellant acknowledged that he would have to support the respondent after his retirement. In 1999, the former husband withdrew from his law practice and took a lump sum payment and 2 years of salary before retiring at age 65. The appellant had re-married. The respondent's net worth was $550,000. The court was of the opinion that the appeal should be allowed and spousal support reduced. The appellant's retirement gave rise to a material change of circumstances, which warranted a reduction in spousal support from $4,500 to $2,500 per month. Further, support payments were ordered to be a first charge on the appellant's estate for the rest of the respondent's life.

*Payor's retirement merely anticipated, not realized* — *LeBlanc v. LeBlanc,* 1995 CarswellNB 36, 14 R.F.L. (4th) 414, 163 N.B.R. (2d) 192, 419 A.P.R. 192 (N.B.Q.B.); affirmed 1995 CarswellNB 193, 14 R.F.L. (4th) 414n, 167 N.B.R. (2d) 375, 427 A.P.R. 375 (N.B.C.A.). The husband's application for termination of the wife's spousal support brought in anticipation of his retirement was dismissed. The husband had not yet suffered a reduction in income and, in fact, since the date of the last variation his income had increased substantially.

*Retirement reduces ability to pay* — *Capuska v. Capusaka,* 1993 CarswellMan 47, 46 R.F.L. (3d) 37 (Man. C.A.). The husband appealed from an order which had reduced support from $500 to $150 per month. On appeal, the court eliminated maintenance since, as a practical reality, the husband, who since trial had taken early retirement, had barely sufficient funds to meet his own needs.

*Retirement reduces income but wife's need continuing* — *Hodgert v. Hodgert,* 1993 CarswellAlta 445, 47 R.F.L. (3d) 216, 141 A.R. 347, 46 W.A.C. 347 (Alta. C.A.). In light of the wife's continuing need, the fact that the husband had retired was insufficient to justify a termination of the spousal support payable by him.

*Involuntary retirement* — *Pick v. Pick,* 1991 CarswellSask 455, 92 Sask. R. 171 (Sask. Q.B.); affirmed (September 5, 1991), Gerwing, Vancise, Wakeling JJ.A. (Sask. C.A.). Although the husband's financial condition had changed because of his forced retirement at age 65, the change was not related to the marriage. The court refused the husband's application for an order terminating his spousal support obligations under a separation agreement.

*Retirement reduces income and parties' child had become self-sufficient* — *C. (J.R.) c. L. (L.),* 1992 CarswellQue 247, 48 Q.A.C. 239 (C.A. Que.). The wife's spousal support was reduced in light of the facts that the husband's income had been reduced significantly upon his retirement and that the parties' child, who had been living with the wife, had achieved self-sufficiency.

*Foreseeability of retirement at time of original order* — *Droit de la famille - 1138,* [1990] R.D.F. 216 (C.A. Que.); affirming (1987), [1988] R.D.F. 29 (C.S. Que.). The court refused, after the husband's retirement, to reduce significantly the support payable to the wife. The trial judge, at the time of the divorce, had considered the husband's retirement when establishing the quantum of alimony payable.

*Where the wife was entitled to continue receiving spousal support for 7 years following the husband's early retirement* — *Dishman v. Dishman,* 2010 CarswellOnt 7700, 2010 ONSC 5239, 94 R.F.L. (6th) 217, 2010 C.E.B. & P.G.R. 8406 (Ont. S.C.J.). After separation, the husband was ordered to pay the wife $750 per month in spousal support. The husband's employer faced bankruptcy and the husband, aged 52.5, accepted early retirement that included a $125,000 retirement incentive. The husband's motion to terminate spousal support was dismissed. Equalization of the matrimonial property, which included the valuation of the husband's pension, was based on the assumption that the husband would retire when he was 59-and-a-half years old. The husband's early retirement was a material change in circumstances that permitted the court to consider a change to spousal support. Several exceptions to the rule against "double dipping" existed in this case. The wife had reason to expect support for an additional 7 years and had demonstrated need for the support. The value of the husband's pension upon earlier retirement at 52-and-a-half was significantly higher than if he had retired at 59-and-a-half. The wife was not expected to bear all of the negative financial consequences that arose from the husband's early retirement. The husband had the means to continue paying, and was capable of seeking full-time employment. Spousal support was ordered for 7 years after the date of the husband's retirement.

*Where the husband was not entitled to terminate spousal support on the grounds that his voluntary early retirement was taken for personal reasons* — Szczerbaniwicz v. Szczerbaniwicz, 2010 CarswellBC 759, 2010 BCSC 421, 84 R.F.L. (6th) 166 (B.C.S.C.). The parties separated after a 31-year traditional marriage. The husband was paying $3,300 per month in interim spousal support, based on an annual salary of $118,000. The husband decided to retire early at age 52 to pursue a Ph.D. The wife's application for spousal support was granted. The husband's decision to take early retirement was entirely personal and did not relieve him of his obligation to pay spousal support. The court inferred that early retirement was taken in part so that the husband could avoid paying the court-ordered support. For support purposes, the court found the husband was reasonably capable of earning $90,000 per year. The wife, who neither intended nor was able to retire until age 65, was not required to draw from her equalized portion of the husband's pension income. Spousal support was ordered on both a compensatory and non-compensatory basis. The husband was ordered to pay $2,300 per month. A review was to occur when the husband reached 60, the age at which he would have been required to retire.

*Voluntary early retirement forms a material change in circumstances where the retirement is done in good faith and not to frustrate support obligations* — Hoar v. Toner, 2010 CarswellNB 220, 2010 NBQB 167, 84 R.F.L. (6th) 404, 361 N.B.R. (2d) 94, 931 A.P.R. 94 (N.B.Q.B.). Where continuing need existed, the pension income was taken into account as available income for spousal support purposes irrespective of a previous division of property which included the husband's pension. The judge awarded ongoing, although reduced, spousal support to the wife because of her continuing need and her reasonable efforts at self-sufficiency after a 25-year marriage.

*Payor's voluntary retirement results in termination of spousal support* — Lewis v. Lewis, 2009 CarswellAlta 1491, 2009 ABQB 539, 73 R.F.L. (6th) 410 (Alta. Q.B.). After separation, the parties agreed that the husband would pay the wife $2,500 per month in spousal support. Subsequently, the husband retired from the RCMP, after 27 years and sought to terminate spousal support. The husband was 58. The husband argued that he found his employment stressful and he had recently suffered a knee injury. The court noted that, "the decision of when to retire from a life-long career is a personal matter into which the court should not interfere except in exceptional circumstances. Given the husband no longer has children of the marriage to support, has provided all spousal support payments thus far required, and entered a settlement of matrimonial property far more favourable to the Respondent than himself, there is nothing to justify the court's review of this Applicant's decision."

*Early retirement is an applicable factor for determining variation in support when it does not seem to be a way to avoid support payments* — Gajdzik v. Gajdzik, 2008 CarswellBC 233, 2008 BCSC 160, 50 R.F.L. (6th) 390 (B.C.S.C. [In Chambers]). The husband's income was nonetheless imputed to include continued part-time work in his field. The wife was receiving support because of her low level of education and the fact that she was a housewife for the duration of the marriage (25 years). The husband wished to retire early. This was found to be acceptable to the trial judge.

*Payor retires but ability to pay unaffected* — Leonard v. Leonard, 2008 CarswellOnt 5708 (Ont. S.C.J.); additional reasons at 2008 CarswellOnt 6516 (Ont. S.C.J.). See s. **10.3.4**.

*Retirement incentive distinguished from severance* — Hurst v. Hurst, 2008 CarswellOnt 5707, 58 R.F.L. (6th) 377 (Ont. S.C.J.). The separation agreement required the payor to transfer a portion of his pension to the recipient and pay support until a projected retirement date. After that date support would cease, unless the payor received income other than pension payments. Subsequently, the payor received a $70,000 retirement incentive. Given that the recipient had reached normal retirement age, given that the retirement incentive was available for a limited time, and given that it could not have been contemplated at the time of the parties' agreement, his decision to accept it and retire was reasonable and not designed to defeat the recipient's support entitlement. The payment was not, therefore, a material change justifying a departure from the terms of the parties' agreement. While there was other new income which did justify a variation, the retirement incentive was not included in the payor's income for the purpose of calculating his new obligation to the recipient.

*A material change in circumstances may be found, even when the payor triggers his own retirement as an independent businessman* — *Fishlock v. Fishlock*, 2007 CarswellOnt 2235, 46 R.F.L. (6th) 254 (Ont. S.C.J.). The parties had minutes of settlement that provided for spousal support to continue at a certain level barring remarriage or retirement. The husband, who had owned a company, sold it upon retirement. The wife had used much of her capital since the dissolution of the marriage 12 years previously. Consideration was given to the provision in the minutes of settlement, but this did not preclude variation because of changed circumstances.

*Early retirement reasonable given disability* — *Bishop v. LaCroix*, 2004 CarswellNB 563, 2004 NBQB 401, 12 R.F.L. (6th) 1, 276 N.B.R. (2d) 75, 724 A.P.R. 75 (N.B.Q.B.). The fact that the husband had taken early retirement as a result of a disability was found to warrant a reduction in the spousal support payable to the wife. The decision to retire was reasonable in the circumstances and as the wife had voluntarily consented to a reduction in child support as a result of the retirement, she could not reasonably expect a different treatment for spousal support.

*Retirement early or by choice* — *Bullock v. Bullock*, 2004 CarswellOnt 919, 48 R.F.L. (5th) 253, [2004] O.J. No. 909 (Ont. S.C.J.). The court refused the husband's application to terminate spousal support. Despite the claim that the 62-year-old husband had been forced to close down his business as a result of a downturn in business, the evidence supported the view that he had voluntarily retired and was living comfortably on his second wife's income.

*Retirement early or by choice* — *Sisk v. Sisk*, 2003 CarswellNS 245, 2003 NSSF 28, 41 R.F.L. (5th) 409, 216 N.S.R. (2d) 144, 680 A.P.R. 144 (N.S.S.C.). Where the husband had agreed to pay spousal support annually of $28,800 until he retired at age 65, but had unilaterally reduced the support to $12,000 annually when he had unexpectedly taken early retirement at 55, the court awarded the wife monthly support of $600 until she was 65. The wife's anticipated support was significantly reduced by the husband's early retirement and, despite his reduced income, she was still entitled to support that addressed her need for financial security.

*Pension — double-dipping allowed given recipient's ongoing need — support reduced upon payor's retirement* — *Stone v. Stone*, 2003 CarswellNS 237, 2003 NSSC 131, 37 R.F.L. (5th) 435 (N.S.S.C.). Where the wife had been awarded a share in the husband's pension, her spousal support was reduced to $1 per month subsequent to his retirement. While his pension income was now his only source of revenue, the wife continued to be employed earning $13,000 per annum. As the wife's income was now higher than the husband's and considering the fact that she shared in his pension, the reduction was appropriate. Given her age, tenuous health, her job security and the fact that she could not yet access the husband's pension, her right to spousal support should not be completely eliminated.

*Retirement foreseeable at time of agreement therefore agreement not varied* — *Pearson v. Pearson*, 2000 CarswellSask 378, 2000 SKQB 232, 8 R.F.L. (5th) 396, 194 Sask. R. 284 (Sask. Q.B.). The retirement of one of the parties and the consequent reduction of income are reasonably foreseeable circumstances at the time that parties execute a separation agreement. The husband's application for a variation of spousal support pursuant to a separation agreement signed 25 years before, which was incorporated in the divorce decree, was dismissed.

*Early retirement reasonable given disability and not originally foreseen* — *Gowan v. Gowan*, 2000 CarswellOnt 3567, 11 R.F.L. (5th) 101 (Ont. S.C.J.). Where physical problems necessitated a decision by the husband to take early retirement, it was found that a change in circumstances had occurred sufficient to warrant a downward variation of the spousal support payable by him. There was nothing in the husband's decision which, in the circumstances, would make a variation unreasonable. Furthermore, the prospect of the husband's early retirement was neither known or contemplated when the order had been made 10 years earlier.

*Foreseeability of retirement at time of original order — Allen v. Allen,* 1999 CarswellBC 876, 47 R.F.L. (4th) 218 (B.C.S.C.). The retirement of one of the parties would be a material change in circumstances if the retirement was not known at the relevant time and not taken into account by the trial judge. In this decision, the husband's retirement was foreseen and considered at the time of the support order. The wife's economic disadvantage was not addressed by reapportionment of the main family asset, but was specifically to be addressed by spousal support. The husband's application to vary spousal support was dismissed.

*Retirement not entirely justified — Doe v. Doe,* 1999 CarswellOnt 679, 44 R.F.L. (4th) 105, 90 O.T.C. 297 (Ont. Gen. Div.); reversed 1999 CarswellOnt 2111, 126 O.A.C. 168, [1999] O.J. No. 2564 (Ont. C.A.). The court should refuse to consider a reduced income resulting from retirement to be a material change in circumstances where it is apparent that the payor spouse has intentionally organized his financial affairs to frustrate a support obligation.

*Reasonable for payor to anticipate retirement, which would reduce ability to pay — Andrew v. Andrew,* 1999 CarswellOnt 2056 (Ont. Gen. Div.). See *Andrew,* below, in s. **10.3.4**.

*Semi-retired payor still had ability to pay — Kerwood v. Kerwood,* 1999 CarswellBC 780, 48 R.F.L. (4th) 127, 9 B.C.T.C. 227, [1999] B.C.J. No. 830 (B.C.S.C. [In Chambers]). The former wife, aged 83, was successful in increasing her support from her 82-year-old husband where she had health problems due to aging. It was immaterial that her physical decline was foreseeable. The former husband had reduced his work load as a doctor but this reduction was not considered significant as he continued to see patients and had a considerable investment fund. The parties married in 1942, separated in 1964 and divorced in 1976.

*Payor's pension — double-dipping — Dick v. Dick,* 1999 CarswellOnt 3243, 4 R.F.L. (5th) 54 (Ont. S.C.J.); additional reasons at 2000 CarswellOnt 1551 (Ont. S.C.J.). The court allowed the husband's application for a reduction in child support payable after his retirement. As the husband had made an equalization payment based upon the capitalization of his pension, that portion of his pension that had been capitalized was not properly included in his income after retirement.

*Payor's pension — double-dipping — MacLeod v. MacLeod,* 1999 CarswellSask 931, 1999 SKQB 267, 3 R.F.L. (5th) 401, 190 Sask. R. 90, [1999] S.J. No. 891 (Sask. Q.B.). Where the payor spouse has retired from employment and double recovery of the payor's pension in property division and support cannot be proved, spousal support will be reduced on the basis of the parties' changed financial circumstances. The husband had separated from his second wife and the first wife's capital and income positions had improved.

*Foreseeability of retirement at time of original order — Doe v. Doe,* 1999 CarswellOnt 679, 44 R.F.L. (4th) 105, 90 O.T.C. 297 (Ont. Gen. Div.). See *Doe,* above.

*Retirement alone does not justify variation — Allen v. Allen,* 1999 CarswellBC 876, 47 R.F.L. (4th) 218 (B.C.S.C.). In *Allen v. Allen,* unlike *Andrew v. Andrew, supra,* the court refused to vary support where there had been a traditional marriage and the husband had retired. The court held that a spouse is not entitled to a variation based solely on the fact of retirement. The parties had been married for 24 years, had had four children and the wife had not worked outside the home during the marriage. The husband had re-married and his second wife was employed. The husband had a long-standing obligation to pay spousal support and could afford to do so. Until recently, the first wife, who was presently employed at substantially less than her husband's pre-retirement earnings, had suffered significant economic hardship as a result of the breakdown of the marriage.

*Retirement reduces ability to pay — Hutchison v. Hutchison*, 1998 CarswellOnt 2867, 38 R.F.L. (4th) 377, [1998] O.J. No. 3027 (Ont. Gen. Div.). The court allowed the husband's application for a reduction in the spousal support payable by him after his retirement. A substantial portion of the husband's income was derived from his pension, an asset which had already been equalized in the wife's favour. The retirement represented a material change in circumstances justifying a reduction in support.

*Retirement reduces ability to pay — Roller v. Roller*, 1997 CarswellSask 732, 35 R.F.L. (4th) 373, 161 Sask. R. 149 (Sask. Q.B.). If there is no change in circumstances, the passage of time does not end a spousal support obligation. Where a payor's income has dropped significantly (44%) from the date of the order due to retirement, there is a significant change of circumstances and spousal support should be terminated. The husband had supported his wife for 27 years, from the time she was stricken with multiple sclerosis. The court also took into account the fact that the husband had an obligation to support a dependant common-law spouse of 25 years, who was also ill.

*Legitimacy of retirement — factors — Haramis v. Haramis*, 1997 CarswellOnt 5837, 44 R.F.L. (4th) 207, 28 O.T.C. 203, [1997] O.J. No. 518 (Ont. Gen. Div.). Early retirement voluntarily taken without justification cannot be relied upon as a reason to reduce support obligations. However, retirement is justified where the applicant pays the agreed spousal support for 13 years, retires at age 58 from a strenuous job in a company which is downsizing, and, as an incentive, receives severance pay at two and one-half times the normal amount together with a substantial pension supplement. The court, on the husband's application, terminated the support obligation, but ordered him to pay to the wife a lump sum amount of 14% of his severance pay.

*Retirement reduces ability to pay — retirement not factored in to original order — Rousseau v. Rousseau*, 1995 CarswellBC 1175, 18 R.F.L. (4th) 292, [1995] B.C.J. No. 2460 (B.C.S.C. [In Chambers]). Where the husband's annual income was reduced upon his retirement from $422,000 annually to under $120,000 the court allowed his application for a downward variation of the $6,300 monthly spousal support payable by him. The retirement constituted a change of circumstances which would have a substantial and continuing effect. Furthermore, it had not been foreseen at the original trial as the trial judge had not considered the effect of the husband's pending retirement when setting the quantum of support.

*Retirement did not reduce ability to pay — Hannon v. Brennan*, 1995 CarswellNfld 80, 18 R.F.L. (4th) 407, 138 Nfld. & P.E.I.R. 62, 431 A.P.R. 62 (Nfld. U.F.C.). The court refused the husband's application for a decrease in the spousal support payable by him. Although the husband had retired, he continued to have the means of paying the support ordered. Furthermore, the wife's economic disadvantage resulting from the marriage was continuing.

*Retirement did not reduce ability to pay — Bartlett v. Bartlett*, 1994 CarswellNfld 27, 2 R.F.L. (4th) 202, 115 Nfld. & P.E.I.R. 245, 360 A.P.R. 245 (Nfld. U.F.C.). The imposition of an obligation to pay support requires an ability to meet the order by a reasonable apportionment of available means. The nature or source of those means, whether salary, pension, other income or salary is not material. Accordingly, the court refused the husband's application for a decrease in the spousal support payable based on the fact that he had retired and his salary was replaced by pension income.

*Involuntary retirement — significant drop in income — Smyth v. Smyth*, 1993 CarswellAlta 449, 48 R.F.L. (3d) 280, 142 A.R. 132 (Alta. Q.B.). Mandatory retirement with a concurrent significant drop in income constitutes a change in circumstances justifying a review of a spousal support obligation.

*Whether retirement justified — relevance — Vennels v. Vennels*, 1993 CarswellBC 17, 45 R.F.L. (3d) 165, 76 B.C.L.R. (2d) 69, [1993] B.C.J. No. 378 (B.C.S.C.). Where a payor has taken voluntary early retirement, the court should assess the facts of the case carefully to ensure that the retirement was not motivated by a desire to defeat the payor's support obligations.

*Retirement reduces ability to pay* — *Allen v. Allen*, 1992 CarswellNB 101, 127 N.B.R. (2d) 390, 319 A.P.R. 390 (N.B.Q.B.). The court allowed the husband's application for a termination of the support contained in the parties' 1984 divorce decree. As the husband had recently retired and his pension income was now less than the wife's employment income, a clean break was appropriate. Considering the wife's employment income at the time of the divorce, it was arguable that, had the present *Divorce Act* been in force then, she would not have received any support.

*Retirement early or by choice* — *Levesque v. Levesque*, 1992 CarswellSask 429, 99 Sask. R. 11 (Sask. Q.B.). Where the husband had chosen early retirement and had thus reduced his ability to pay spousal support, the court allowed his application to terminate periodic support payments provided he pay $18,000 to his wife by way of lump sum. While the choice of early retirement is not a change of circumstances to consider in reducing support, the fact the husband could no longer pay required resolution.

*Retirement early or by choice* — *contrary to payor's indication to recipient* — *Campbell v. Campbell*, 1991 CarswellOnt 333, 36 R.F.L. (3d) 284 (Ont. U.F.C.). The court dismissed the husband's application for termination of spousal support to his wife based upon the fact that he had taken early retirement. The husband had earlier confirmed to the wife in writing his intention not to retire for several more years. As the wife had arranged her affairs accordingly, the doctrine of promissory estoppel applied and the husband was estopped from adducing evidence of changed circumstances until the indicated retirement date.

*Whether retirement justified* — *relevance* — *Molnar v. Molnar*, 1991 CarswellSask 71, 35 R.F.L. (3d) 424, 98 Sask. R. 187 (Sask. Q.B.). Where the husband's early retirement at age 51 was justified for medical reasons, his application for termination of spousal support to his former wife was allowed. His sole income was derived from a pension, the monthly amount of which was equaled by the former wife's employment income.

*Retirement reduces ability to pay* — *Droit de la famille - 1344*, [1990] R.D.F. 529 (C.S. Que.). Where the husband's income had been reduced drastically upon his retirement, the court allowed his application to terminate spousal support. Although the wife would have to sell her home and continue to work part-time after turning 65, she could, on the basis of these occurrences, be said to have achieved financial independence.

*Retirement reduces ability to pay* — *reduction granted but not termination* — *Petersen v. Petersen*, 1989 CarswellMan 273, 59 Man. R. (2d) 119 (Man. Q.B.). Where the husband's income had decreased upon his retirement and his former wife's had increased as a result of pension benefits, the spousal support payable by him was reduced. Although he sought termination of all support payable, this was not possible as long as the wife's need and the husband's ability to pay remained.

*Retirement early or by choice plus illness of payor's second wife* — *support not reduced* — *Morse (Rand) v. Morse*, 1991 CarswellNS 586, 108 N.S.R. (2d) 133, 294 A.P.R. 133 (N.S. Fam. Ct.). The court refused the husband's application for reduced spousal support which he based upon a reduction of income resulting from his early retirement and the illness of his second wife. Both changes cited by the husband had been taken on voluntarily and could not be relied upon by him as changes in circumstances.

*Retirement early or by choice* — *at age 61* — *support terminated* — *Droit de la famille - 1526* (1991), [1992] R.D.F. 81 (C.S. Que.). The court allowed the husband's application for termination of spousal support after his retirement at age 61. The husband's decision was reasonable and it would not be proper to require the husband to draw upon his assets to support his former wife when her own assets remained untouched.

*Retirement early or by choice — not a ground for terminating support — Droit de la famille -*
*1446*, [1991] R.D.F. 370 (C.S. Que.). The husband was not allowed to rely upon his voluntary
early retirement as a ground for terminating the spousal support specified in the parties'
agreement. The wife, who had been a homemaker throughout the parties' 25-year marriage,
continued to suffer from the economic consequences of the marriage.

*Termination date set for point in the future when payor planned to retire — Epstein v.*
*Epstein*, 1991 CarswellNB 240, 115 N.B.R. (2d) 418, 291 A.P.R. 418 (N.B. Q.B.); affirmed 1991
CarswellNB 290, 122 N.B.R. (2d) 176, 306 A.P.R. 176 (N.B.C.A.). See *Epstein*, noted earlier in
this section.

*Retirement not entirely justified — Tatomir v. Tatomir*, 1989 CarswellSask 83, 24 R.F.L.
(3d) 282, 81 Sask. R. 173 (Sask. Q.B. [In Chambers]). Where the husband had voluntarily taken
early retirement and could no longer afford to pay the $350 monthly spousal support required,
the support order was reduced by a minimum amount only on his variation application.

## Change of circumstances — involuntary loss of, or reduction in payor's income

*Involuntary employment loss is a change in circumstances warranting variation — Strang*
*v. Strang*, 1989 CarswellAlta 389, 23 R.F.L. (3d) 17, 100 A.R. 208 at 210, [1989] A.J. No. 1239
(Alta. Q.B.); affirmed 1990 CarswellAlta 271, 26 R.F.L. (3d) 113, 107 A.R. 111 (Alta. C.A.);
affirmed 1992 CarswellAlta 70, 1992 CarswellAlta 468, EYB 1992-66872, 39 R.F.L. (3d) 233,
[1992] 2 S.C.R. 112, 3 Alta. L.R. (3d) 1, 92 D.L.R. (4th) 762, 137 N.R. 203, 125 A.R. 331, 14
W.A.C. 331, [1992] S.C.J. No. 55 (S.C.C.). A non-voluntary loss of employment by the payor is a
change in circumstances sufficient to warrant a variation of a support order.

*Termination of employment will be found to be a material change in circumstances when it*
*was not contemplated at the time of the separation agreement — Campbell v. Campbell*, 2012
CarswellNS 594, 2012 NSCA 86, 320 N.S.R. (2d) 223, 1014 A.P.R. 223 (N.S.C.A.). The parties
were married for 28 years and had three children. During the marriage, the wife was a stay-at-
home mother who suffered from severe emphysema that prevented her from working. The
husband had been paying support pursuant to a separation agreement when he was terminated
from his employment. The wife appealed the decision of a trial judge to reduce spousal support
to reflect the husband's capacity to pay income. He had previously paid spousal support from his
severance pay, which was now exhausted. The Court of Appeal upheld a trial decision to vary
spousal support, finding that, although the trial judge had not explicitly mentioned Step 2 of the
*Miglin* test (current circumstances leading to non-compliance with the objectives of the *Divorce*
*Act*), he had considered the relevant factors.

*Reduction in professional practice income — LeBlanc v. LeBlanc*, 2000 CarswellNB 45, 5
R.F.L. (5th) 76, 225 N.B.R. (2d) 235, 578 A.P.R. 235, [2000] N.B.J. No. 61 (N.B.C.A.). Where a
trial court has varied the amount of spousal support downwards so that both former spouses have
approximately the same income, taking into account the reduction in the payor's income, an
appellate court will not interfere in the quantum of support. In this case, the parties, who were
both in their 70s, had been divorced for 23 years. The wife was not self-sufficient and the husband
had a diminished capacity to earn his livelihood as a lawyer. He had spent all his RRSPs and RIFs
to try to meet his expenses.

*Reduction in professional practice income justified reduction in support — Reilly v. Reilly*,
2000 CarswellBC 361, 2000 BCCA 130, 5 R.F.L. (5th) 116, 137 B.C.A.C. 151, 223 W.A.C. 151
(B.C.C.A.). Where a trial judge found that the payor's evidence that his income from his law
practice had been reduced from $200,000 to $150,000 and then to almost nil was
"incomprehensible and not believable", the appellate court was of the opinion that this

reduction constituted a change of circumstances that would justify a reduction in the amount of support from $3,000 to $2,000 a month.

*Reduction in income justifies reduction in support but both parties have duty to work — Wyman v. Wyman,* 1999 CarswellNS 49, 49 R.F.L. (4th) 447 (N.S.C.A.). A trial judge erred in placing the onus on a wife to seek employment while the husband should also be employable and seek work. The appellate court granted the wife's appeal from a decision reducing the amount of spousal support paid by the husband after his job was eliminated. The spousal support, which had been reduced from $1000 to $500 per month, was increased to $700 per month.

*Reduction in payor's income did not make him unable to pay — Oyen v. Oyen,* 1994 CarswellBC 80, 9 R.F.L. (4th) 454, 2 B.C.L.R. (3d) 166, 52 B.C.A.C. 277, 86 W.A.C. 277 (B.C.C.A.). Where the payor's income was considerable, little weight was placed on the decline in the payor's income since he was clearly in a position to pay increased monthly maintenance for the children and given that an increase was otherwise justified in the circumstances.

*Income from payor's new spouse relevant — Hersey v. Hersey,* 1993 CarswellNB 18, 47 R.F.L. (3d) 117, 135 N.B.R. (2d) 67, 344 A.P.R. 67, [1993] N.B.J. No. 278 (N.B.C.A.). While the income of a child support payor's new spouse cannot be used directly to support the payor's children, it is properly taken into account in determining the income available to meet the payor's household expenses.

*Reduction in income plus recipient's increased self-sufficiency justifies reduction in support — Brassard c. Beaulieu* (3 juin 1992), no C.A. Québec 200-09-000121-928 (C.S. Que.). A reduction in the husband's annual income from $38,000 to $32,000 was found to be a sufficient change in circumstances to warrant a downward variation of his wife's support from $100 weekly to $250 monthly. The court allowed the husband's appeal from an order refusing to annul his ongoing spousal support obligations. The husband had experienced an economic downturn, having to sell off some of his assets to discharge support arrears, where the wife had practically achieved financial independence.

*Loss of employment due to health problems did not make husband unable to pay — Smith v. Smith,* 1989 CarswellMan 59, 23 R.F.L. (3d) 89, 62 Man. R. (2d) 93 (Man. Q.B.); varied 1990 CarswellMan 47, 27 R.F.L. (3d) 32, 66 Man. R. (2d) 181, 71 D.L.R. (4th) 612 (Man. C.A.). The husband's application for a decrease in the support payable to his wife was dismissed. Although he had lost his employment because of health problems and was living on disability benefits, he could continue to make his support payments by rationalizing his expenses and his debts.

*Loss of business income partially the fault of the payor — support reduced by amount proportionate to his share of the blame — Craig (Bassett) v. Craig,* 1989 CarswellNS 51, 20 R.F.L. (3d) 66, 91 N.S.R. (2d) 236, 233 A.P.R. 236 (N.S. T.D.); reversed 1989 CarswellNS 40, 24 R.F.L. (3d) 341, 78 C.B.R. (N.S.) 97, 65 D.L.R. (4th) 106, 94 N.S.R. (2d) 196, 247 A.P.R. 196 (N.S.C.A.). Where the husband's reduced resources were the result of a business failure for which he was 50% responsible, his application at trial for a variation of his spousal support obligation was only allowed in part. Support was reduced by 50%, being the amount inversely proportional to the degree that the business failure could be attributed to the husband, but was overturned on appeal. The appellate court held that the parties' intention was that the purchase money payable for the wife's share of the business was maintenance within s. 178 of the *Bankruptcy Act.* These purchase moneys were for her maintenance. However, she gave up maintenance pursuant to the *Divorce Act.* Consequently, there was no order pursuant to the *Divorce Act* to vary. The appeal was allowed and the order set aside.

*Reduction in income justifies reduction in support — R. c. D.,* [1989] R.D.F. 58 (C.A. Que.). Where as a result of losing his job it appeared that the husband would have to liquidate his assets to provide for his own needs, his application to terminate spousal support over a period of time was allowed.

*Reduction in income plus recipient's new cohabitation justifies reduction in support — Eddy v. Eddy*, 1986 CarswellBC 568, 5 R.F.L. (3d) 418 (B.C.C.A.). Where subsequent to the maintenance award the husband had lost his job, the wife had moved in with another man and the parties shared custody of their child despite a custody award in the wife's favour, the husband's application for a reduction in the quantum of maintenance payable by him was granted.

*A temporary reduction in income may result in a retroactive variation of spousal support, but does not constitute a material change in circumstances when the payor's income regains its former level — Pandya v. Pandya*, 2010 CarswellOnt 2475, 2010 ONSC 2026 (Ont. S.C.J.). The husband was ordered to pay spousal support according to the guidelines consistent with the consent order of 2007 when his income was similar to what it was in 2009. The intervening dip in income because of health problems and professional disputes resulted in an overpayment of support which was deducted in ten installments from the wife's support.

*A material reduction in the payor's income is a relevant factor in determining the amount of ongoing spousal support — Stewart v. Stewart*, 2007 CarswellOnt 999, 35 R.F.L. (6th) 427 (Ont. S.C.J.). The relative net worth of the parties, as well as the impossibility of the wife finding a job that would support her led to an ongoing support order despite the husband's reduced circumstances.

*Reduction in income plus recipient's squandering of assets justify reduction in support — Balaban v. Balaban*, 2006 CarswellOnt 8452, 35 R.F.L. (6th) 139 (Ont. S.C.J.); additional reasons at 2007 CarswellOnt 1518 (Ont. S.C.J.). See *Balaban*, below s. **10.3.4.**

*Reduction in professional practice income plus recipient's employment potential — Hanson v. Hanson*, 2003 CarswellSask 573, 2003 SKQB 370, 43 R.F.L. (5th) 119 (Sask. Q.B.). Where the husband's hearing deteriorated to the point that he was compelled to close his medical practice, his application for a reduction in the spousal support payable by him was granted. In addition, the wife had also proven herself capable of generating revenue.

*Reduction in income justifies reduction in support — Loiselle v. Loiselle*, 2000 CarswellOnt 3488, 12 R.F.L. (5th) 400, [2000] O.J. No. 3610 (Ont. S.C.J.). The court reduced spousal support from $2,500 to $1,500 per month, and $900 per month upon equalization, as the husband's business had declined. The court made its determination after taking into account the monies that are available to the wife from assisting her elderly mother and from selling Avon products. The court did not take into account the interest on the wife's RRSPs, which were unrealized.

*Reduction in income justifies reduction in support — Fleury v. Fleury*, 2000 CarswellOnt 2833, 11 R.F.L. (5th) 71 (Ont. C.J.). The court reduced the amount of support payable from $722 to $350 per month where the husband's projected gross annual income for 2000 was $33,200 down from his 1999 gross annual income of $64,196.

*Payor loses job but receives severance and consulting contract income — no reduced ability to pay at time of trial — Sasonow v. Sasanow*, 2000 CarswellOnt 1085, 6 R.F.L. (5th) 415 (Ont. S.C.J.). In a case under the Ontario *Family Law Act*, the court held that where a payor has been terminated but receives salary under a severance package and also receives consulting contract payments, his plea of reduced income relates only to the future. The husband's application to vary spousal support was dismissed.

*Reduction in income foreseeable at time of original order — Harris v. Harris*, 2000 CarswellOnt 2703, 10 R.F.L. (5th) 45, 135 O.A.C. 312, [2000] O.J. No. 2794 (Ont. C.A.). The court dismissed an appeal by the husband from a lower court judgment dismissing his application to vary spousal support in a divorce judgment. The court was of the opinion that the applicant did not meet the threshold test that there had been a change in circumstances, because the circumstances were known when the minutes of settlement were signed. The husband sought to reduce spousal support on the basis of his own reduced income owing to the substantial drop in activity in the international construction business in which he worked. The husband claimed to have no business income in 1998. The court relied on *B. (G.) c. G. (L.)*, 1995 CarswellQue 23, 1995 CarswellQue 120, EYB 1995-67821, 15 R.F.L. (4th) 201, [1995] 3 S.C.R. 370, 127 D.L.R. (4th) 385, 186 N.R. 201, [1995] R.D.F. 611, [1995] S.C.J. No. 72 (S.C.C.), at 271 [R.F.L.], in stating that a material change is a change which, if known at the time, would likely have resulted in different terms. The court was of the view that the swings in the economy, particularly in the construction industry, were foreseeable. It was also foreseeable that the husband would at some point no longer be employed. He would have believed that he could find support from other sources than income. The husband was an accountant and businessman and was assumed to have considered these possibilities.

*Reduction in professional practice income temporary — temporary variation granted — Young v. Young*, 1999 CarswellOnt 1332, 47 R.F.L. (4th) 214 (Ont. S.C.J.). The court reduced the husband's spousal support payments from $2,000 to $500 per month for a time-limited period, since, subsequent to minutes of settlement, the husband's ill health had prompted him to work part-time as a lawyer which greatly reduced his income and at the same time, the wife's income from employment and investments had increased. The parties had been married for 34 years and the court was of the opinion that the parties should be placed on an equal financial basis, as much as possible. There had been no "material" change in the parties' net worth since the time of settlement.

*Reduction in income justifies reduction in support — reduction in support proportionate to loss of income — Kurbegovich v. Kurbegovich*, 1998 CarswellOnt 267, 36 R.F.L. (4th) 220 (Ont. Gen. Div.). Where the husband's income had decreased by 24% since the making of a spousal support order, the court allowed his application to reduce the arrears owing under that order by the same 24%.

*Loss of full-time employment justifies reduction in support — recipient had remarried and not in need — Ferrigan v. Ferrigan*, 1998 CarswellOnt 901, 36 R.F.L. (4th) 206 (Ont. Gen. Div.). Where the husband had been forced to retire from full-time employment, but kept working part-time to meet his spousal support obligations, although it adversely affected his health, his application to terminate spousal support was allowed. The husband had suffered undue hardship and the wife, who had remarried, actually enjoyed a higher standard of living than the husband.

*Loss of job countered by severance and likelihood of future employment — Gillard v. Gillard*, 1998 CarswellAlta 173, 36 R.F.L. (4th) 209 (Alta. Q.B.). The court refused the husband's application to terminate the spousal support payable by him after he had lost his employment. The husband had received a substantial severance package and was not likely to remain unemployed for long.

*Loss of job due to wrongdoing — insufficient disclosure by payor — Pavlicevic v. Pavlicevic*, 1998 CarswellBC 522, 37 R.F.L. (4th) 107 (B.C.S.C.). Where the payor spouse loses his job because of wrongdoing, there is a change of circumstance which would permit a court to vary or rescind a support order. However, the payor had not met the onus to show that, because of this change, a variation of periodic permanent maintenance should be made. The payor had not made full disclosure of his means and financial circumstances.

*Reduction in income justifies reduction in support — reduction temporary, for period of unemployment only — Williams v. Williams*, 1997 CarswellNS 504, 35 R.F.L. (4th) 387, 165 N.S.R. (2d) 188, 495 A.P.R. 188, [1997] N.S.J. No. 540 (N.S.S.C.). The court refused the husband's application to terminate the spousal support payable to his disabled wife. Since the husband had previously experienced periods of unemployment, there had been no radical change in circumstances. The wife's need was continuing and would likely never abate. The order was, however, amended to allow the husband to reduce spousal support payments to $1.00 when he was unemployed.

*Reduction of income does not reduce ability to pay* — *Bettles v. Wright*, 1997 CarswellPEI 56, 30 R.F.L. (4th) 256, 153 Nfld. & P.E.I.R. 350, 475 A.P.R. 350, [1997] 1 P.E.I.R. 222 (P.E.I.T.D. [In Chambers]). See *Bettles*, in s. **10.3.4**, below.

*Loss of job countered by severance and likelihood of future employment* — *Garner v. Garner*, 1997 CarswellSask 727, 35 R.F.L. (4th) 262, [1998] 5 W.W.R. 443, 160 Sask. R. 95 (Sask. Q.B.). It was held that the husband's loss of employment was an insufficient change in circumstances to relieve him from his spousal support obligations contained in minutes of settlement to which both parties had agreed. Although payment under the minutes was qualified specifically by the condition that the husband remain employed, the 72-week severance package received by him resulted in no immediate change to his financial position. As the 72-week period had not expired, the husband could conceivably still find alternate employment before his financial situation truly changed.

*Loss of employment plus new family obligations justified termination* — *Roller v. Roller*, 1997 CarswellSask 732, 35 R.F.L. (4th) 373, 161 Sask. R. 149 (Sask. Q.B.). The court allowed the husband's application to terminate spousal support for his wife who had permanently entered a nursing home 13 years into their 31-year marriage. The husband had entered into a common law relationship that had endured for over 25 years and with a 44% reduction in his income after a health-induced forced retirement, the husband could not meet the needs of both his former wife and his common law wife. This was an appropriate case in which the public purse should take up the support burden as it related to the former wife.

*Loss of job still mitigated by severance therefore application premature* — *Wilkinson v. Wilkinson*, 1996 CarswellOnt 693, 22 R.F.L. (4th) 46 (Ont. Gen. Div.). Where husband was still receiving severance payments relating to his job loss, his application for a decrease in his support obligation resulting from that job loss was dismissed as premature.

*Loss of job mitigated by severance* — *Kattler v. Kattler*, 1996 CarswellSask 209, 22 R.F.L. (4th) 274, 145 Sask. R. 5 (Sask. Q.B.). Where the husband had lost his job but received a 1-year severance package, the job loss was found not to constitute a sufficient change in circumstances justifying a variation of the support payable by the husband. The severance award still enabled the husband to pay.

*Loss of income did not make husband unable to pay* — *Peters v. Karr*, 1994 CarswellMan 253, 93 Man. R. (2d) 222 (Man. Q.B.). Where the husband owned his own company and set his own salary, his application for reduced spousal support based upon the effect of the recession on his business was dismissed. If he chose not to reduce further the retained earnings in his company, he had ample additional resources which he could draw upon to meet his support obligations.

*Reduction in income plus recipient's lack of efforts to become self-sufficient* — *Leet v. Leet*, 1994 CarswellNS 377, 131 N.S.R. (2d) 19, 371 A.P.R. 19 (N.S.S.C.). The court allowed the husband's application to terminate support to his former wife of 19 years in light of the fact that he had lost his job and had an uncertain future and that she had made little effort to achieve self-sufficiency. A lump sum award equivalent to 2 years' support was substituted in recognition of the wife's continuing need.

*Reduction in income justifies reduction in support* — *Tingley v. Tingley*, 1993 CarswellNB 611, 49 R.F.L. (3d) 87, 141 N.B.R. (2d) 86, 361 A.P.R. 86 (N.B.Q.B.). The court granted the husband's application for a termination of spousal support 12 years after the original order. In the intervening time, the husband's financial situation had deteriorated and the wife's had improved. Furthermore, the wife failed to adduce any evidence that she had suffered any economic disadvantages arising from the marriage or its breakdown.

*Reduction in income justifies reduction in support but term still not limited* — *Wood v. Wood*, 1993 CarswellOnt 296, 45 R.F.L. (3d) 85 (Ont. Gen. Div.). The reduction in the husband's annual income from $500,000 to $75,000 justified a reduction in the spousal support payable to the wife from $7,000 to $2,500. Limiting the term of spousal support could not be justified given the wife's continuing economic disadvantage which resulted from the marriage.

*Payor's new family obligations — Kerr v. Kerr*, 1992 CarswellOnt 277, 41 R.F.L. (3d) 264 (Ont. Gen. Div.). Where a father has remarried and started a new family but has not made any effort to adjust his lifestyle to accommodate the child support order made in relation to the children of his first marriage, the court may refuse the application to completely expunge the arrears owing under a court order for support of the children of the first marriage.

*Reduction in income justifies reduction in support and term limited to 1 year — Johnston v. Johnston*, 1992 CarswellMan 193, 84 Man. R. (2d) 12 (Man. Q.B.). Where the husband who had been earning $88,000 at the time of the support order lost his job, the court allowed his application and reduced his spousal support obligation from $1,000 to $400 monthly with a limit of 1 year. The change in the husband's financial circumstances was dramatic and justified a variation

*Reduction in income justifies reduction in support — Ewert v. Ewert*, 1991 CarswellSask 492, 91 Sask. R. 311 (Sask. Q.B.). Where the husband's income had been reduced by 22% since the date of the decree *nisi* and the wife had since found employment, the payor husband's application for a reduction in the spousal support payable was allowed.

*Reduction in payor's income means no increase in support — Hasting v. Hastings*, 1986 CarswellMan 228, 42 Man. R. (2d) 215 (Man. Q.B.). Where the husband was involuntarily unemployed and consequently decided to return to school, the wife's application for an upward variation in maintenance was refused.

*Reduction in payor's income probably temporary and did not make him unable to pay — Mullin v. Mullin*, 1993 CarswellPEI 17, 48 R.F.L. (3d) 322, 108 Nfld. & P.E.I.R. 61, 339 A.P.R. 61, [1993] P.E.I.J. No. 69 (P.E.I.C.A.). In *Mullin v. Mullin*, the court refused the husband's application for a termination of his wife's support based, inter alia, on his decline in income. There was no evidence that the husband's income decline was a permanent situation and, in all likelihood, it was a temporary aberration.

*Lack of means to pay must be proven — Kollinger v. Kollinger*, 1995 CarswellMan 207, 14 R.F.L. (4th) 363, 102 Man. R. (2d) 296, 93 W.A.C. 296 (Man. C.A.). Where the husband had sought a downward variation of spousal support payable by him on the basis of a disability, the variation was refused. His appeal was likewise dismissed on the basis that the trial judge was entitled to find that the husband had failed to prove that he lacked the means to make the support payments.

*Payor's health problems balanced against presence of his new, employed spouse — Kearney v. Kearney*, 1988 CarswellMan 338, 54 Man. R. (2d) 42 (Man. Q.B.). Where the husband had suffered a stroke, but was in receipt of disability benefits, his application to reduce spousal and child support was dismissed. As the husband's new wife was also employed, the means currently available to the husband were equal to those available when the order had originally been made.

### Change of circumstances — payor voluntarily reducing own income

*Voluntary transfer of assets to second spouse — Reilly v. Reilly*, 1999 CarswellBC 1537, 50 R.F.L. (4th) 424 (B.C.S.C.); varied 2000 CarswellBC 361, 2000 BCCA 130, 5 R.F.L. (5th) 116, 137 B.C.A.C. 151, 223 W.A.C. 151 (B.C.C.A.). The husband's claim of impecuniosity following the transfer of all of his assets to his new wife could not be relied upon as a change in circumstances justifying a reduction in the spousal support payable by him.

*Payor voluntarily quit job — Droit de la famille - 884*, [1990] R.D.F. 546 (C.A. Que.). Where the husband had quit his job specifically to avoid his support obligations, his application to annul all arrears owing was successful at trial but was reversed on appeal. His decision to live on unemployment benefits instead of earning a salary did not release him from his support obligations.

*Payor quit job in order to share childcare with payee — payor not intentionally underemployed — Huntly v. Huntly*, 2008 CarswellMan 50, 2008 MBQB 42, 224 Man. R. (2d) 185 (Man. Q.B.). The parties each brought motions to vary a final spousal support order, along with a child support order, which required the husband to pay $650 a month to the wife in spousal support. The husband at that time was employed as a machinist and earned $46,676 a year. He had since quit his job to enable him to work "straight" days and to permit him to spend more time with the children and take them to their various activities as the parties now shared custody of the children. His annual income for 2006 and 2007 was accepted to be approximately $29,300. The wife argued that the spousal support should remain as was ordered on the basis that the husband was intentionally underemployed. The court found that it was reasonable for the husband to no longer work evening shifts. He was not intentionally underemployed, but his underemployment was necessitated by the needs of the children of the marriage. The court declined to vary the spousal support for 2004 and 2005, the years the husband was still employed as a machinist, but ordered $377 a month in spousal support in 2006. No spousal support was ordered payable for 2007 onwards on the basis that the *Spousal Support Advisory Guidelines* suggest that none should be paid, as once the husband pays the child support and other extraordinary expenses of the children, he simply could not afford to make any further payment of spousal support.

*Circumstances leading to decline in income within payor's control — Coolen v. Coolen*, 2002 CarswellNS 300, 2002 NSSF 34 (N.S.S.C.). Where the change in circumstances resulting in a reduction in the husband's income was wholly within his control and was neither necessary nor sufficient to support a change in his support obligations, the court declined to grant retroactive variation of the interim spousal award.

*Self-induced reduction of ability to pay — Harris v. Harris*, 1992 CarswellBC 560, 40 R.F.L. (3d) 253 (B.C.S.C.). If a person's circumstances change through choice or by voluntary conduct, an applicant spouse cannot take advantage of those circumstances and hope to seek a variance of the original support order.

*Self-induced reduction of ability to pay — Hildebrandt v. Hildebrandt*, 1991 CarswellSask 67, 34 R.F.L. (3d) 373, 94 Sask. R. 215 (Sask. Q.B.). Where the payor spouse's decline in income is the result of his or her own deliberate actions, it cannot be relied upon as a basis for an application to reduce the amount of support payable.

*Self-induced reduction in ability to pay — Callison v. Callison*, 1992 CarswellBC 561, 40 R.F.L. (3d) 451 (B.C.S.C.). The court may deny a variation in support where the payor spouse has failed to honour commitments that he or she has the capacity to fulfill. If a payor's reduced ability to pay is the result of circumstances which are self-induced, it would be unfair to the payee to reduce support.

*Reduction in employment income mala fides — Irvine v. Irvine*, 1990 CarswellMan 49, 27 R.F.L. (3d) 199, 67 Man. R. (2d) 205, [1990] M.J. No. 392 (Man. Q.B.). Where the husband had quit his employment and later accepted a lower paying job in an effort to undermine his wife and children's support entitlement, his application to cancel arrears and spousal support and reduce child support was dismissed. Any change in the husband's circumstances was self-induced and *mala fides*.

*Payor's choice of "lifestyle"* — *Anderson v. Anderson*, 1989 CarswellNS 464, 92 N.S.R. (2d) 333, 237 A.P.R. 333 (N.S. Fam. Ct.). The fact that a husband has adopted a "back-to-earth" stress-free lifestyle does not relieve him of the obligation to support his children.

### Change of circumstances — payor deceased

*Support terminated on motion by payor's estate* — *Droit de la famille - 324*, 1986 CarswellQue 626, EYB 1986-83342, [1987] R.J.Q. 149, [1987] R.D.F. 48 (C.S. Que.). The court allowed an application by the executors of the late husband's estate to terminate the wife's maintenance. During the 20 years since the parties' separation, the wife had sufficient time to achieve financial independence and had managed to improve her financial position considerably.

*Support not varied despite death of payor* — *Banks v. Banks*, 1985 CarswellYukon 4, 47 R.F.L. (2d) 450 (Y.T.S.C.). The court has jurisdiction to vary a maintenance award, even though the payor spouse has died.

### Change of circumstances — payor — increase in income after separation

### See 5.2 Means and Needs of Party from Whom Support is Sought

### Change of circumstances — payor — other changes

*Child's change of residence to live with payor not a material change* — *Pustai v. Pustai*, 2010 CarswellOnt 1960, 2010 ONCA 251, [2010] O.J. No. 1336 (Ont. C.A.). The parties entered into a consent order which provided that one of the children was to live with the mother while the other three children were to live with the father. That order also provided that the father would pay the mother $3,000 in spousal support, and that either party could seek a review of the quantum of support upon a material change of circumstances. After the consent order, the one child who was to reside with the mother moved and went to live with his father. The father then sought to change spousal support, arguing that his deteriorating financial position and the child's move into his care constituted a material change of circumstances in relation to the spousal support order. The court found that the child's move was not a material change for the purpose of a spousal support variation, and further, did not accept that there had been a deterioration in the father's income. In rejecting the father's application to vary spousal support, the court also noted that the father would no longer have to pay the child support in relation to the fourth child now living with him.

*Adverse tax ruling not a material change* — *Ravka v. Ravka*, 2001 CarswellOnt 1642, 18 R.F.L. (5th) 155 (Ont. S.C.J.); reversed 2002 CarswellOnt 3081, 35 R.F.L. (5th) 176, 165 O.A.C. 44, [2002] O.J. No. 3636 (Ont. C.A.). The fact that the husband, as a result of an *Income Tax Act* ruling, was required to bring certain income tax reserves into his income, did not justify a reduction in the spousal support payable by him pursuant to the parties' separation agreement. The assessment did not constitute a material change in circumstances.

*Increased debt load of payor* — *Stordy v. Stordy*, 2000 CarswellPEI 34, 2000 PESCAD 7, 6 R.F.L. (5th) 436, 186 Nfld. & P.E.I.R. 142, 564 A.P.R. 142 (P.E.I.C.A.). The increased debt load of the payor does not constitute a change in the condition, means, needs or other circumstances which justify reduction in the amount of monthly spousal support payments. The wife's appeal from a variation order to decrease spousal support payments made to her by her husband was granted.

*Payee originally intending to live independently, in fact moved in with parents — Martin v. Martin*, 1993 CarswellSask 57, 50 R.F.L. (3d) 77, 113 Sask. R. 316, 52 W.A.C. 316 (Sask. C.A.). Where the intended state of affairs at the time when an interim maintenance order was made does not materialize, an order should be made cancelling the arrears. In the *Martin* decision, the wife had expected to live independently, but, in fact, moved in with her parents and thus reduced expenses.

*Original order made based on payee's estimate of budget, after which more accurate figures become available — MacDonald v. MacDonald*, 1993 CarswellAlta 5, 46 R.F.L. (3d) 1, 10 Alta. L.R. (3d) 20, [1993] A.J. No. 312 (Alta. C.A.). Where one party was just about to move at the time of trial and was only estimating her budget, once she had become settled in her new home, her circumstances will have changed, and the other party may apply at any time to vary the maintenance order made by the trial judge on the ground of a change in circumstances.

*Payor's erroneous belief that support obligation had been settled with lump sum — Douthwright v. Douthwright*, 1991 CarswellNB 45, 38 R.F.L. (3d) 48, 122 N.B.R. (2d) 36, 306 A.P.R. 36 (N.B.Q.B.); varied 1992 CarswellNB 46, 42 R.F.L. (3d) 1, 95 D.L.R. (4th) 188, 128 N.B.R. (2d) 437, 322 A.P.R. 437 (N.B.C.A.). In circumstances where the husband erroneously believed, on the advice of his lawyer, that his ongoing spousal support obligation had been settled through the payment of a lump sum, it was found that this alone was insufficient to justify a termination of his wife's periodic support.

*Discovery of non-disclosure by payor — Miller v. Miller*, 1992 CarswellSask 60, 42 R.F.L. (3d) 278, [1992] S.J. No. 426 (Sask. C.A.). The absence of full financial disclosure by the payor spouse may not, in itself, constitute a change of circumstances justifying the variation of an order setting the quantum of spousal arrears owing.

*Misrepresentation of value of assets and liabilities — Psaila v. Psaila*, 1987 CarswellBC 6, 6 R.F.L. (3d) 141, 10 B.C.L.R. (2d) 336 (B.C.C.A.). The fact that a spouse misrepresented the value of assets and liabilities where maintenance was originally determined may justify a later variation of maintenance payable.

*Lower sale price of matrimonial home, to the detriment of support payor — Bolger v. Bolger*, 1983 CarswellNB 46, 36 R.F.L. (2d) 184, 50 N.B.R. (2d) 3, 131 A.P.R. 3 (N.B.C.A.). Where the ordered sale of the marital home brought less than anticipated, with the result that the husband was left to pay family debts out of his own resources rather than out of the proceeds of sale, it was held that a sufficient change of circumstances had occurred to justify a reduction in the quantum of maintenance payable by him to his wife.

*Where the husband failed to show his ability to earn income was permanently impaired, no material change in circumstances existed — Samson v. Metail*, 2012 CarswellOnt 4579, 2012 ONSC 2393 (Ont. S.C.J.). The parties had a 16-year, traditional marriage. When spousal support was first determined in 1993, the wife was in the process of completing qualifications to become a teacher's aide. Spousal support was ordered at $750 per month, which was reduced to $500 per month once the wife's income reached $25,000. The husband paid $500 in spousal support from 1994 to the current motion. The husband's motion to terminate spousal support was dismissed and the wife's motion to vary spousal support was also dismissed. The husband failed to show his ability to earn income was permanently impaired, or that he had significantly depleted capital to reduce debt. The wife suffered continued economic disadvantage and termination of support was not warranted. The wife also failed to show a material change in circumstances, or to justify increase in spousal support based on initial failure in 1993 to index support.

*Even if a material change of circumstances had not occurred, the husband's income had decreased and support was decreased accordingly — Barnes v. Barnes*, 2012 CarswellNS 57, 2012 NSSC 21 (N.S.S.C.). The parties lived together for 20 years, and were married for 11 years. The parties entered a separation agreement, which included terms for spousal support of $300 per year, indefinitely. In agreement the husband's income was $50,000. The husband's motion to terminate spousal support was dismissed, but support was reduced to $225 per month. The husband's estimated income for 2011 was $30,200. The wife's 2011 income was estimated at $32,000. In the years since the agreement was registered, the husband's income did not exceed $36,000. Although it was not possible to determine if a change of circumstances existed related to the husband's expenses, his income had decreased by 25 to 30 percent. The husband's monthly support obligation was reduced accordingly. The parties clearly intended in the agreement that the wife would receive support payments indefinitely.

*Where the conditions set out in a separation agreement were not met, there was no variation of spousal support* — *Greffe v. Greffe*, 2012 CarswellOnt 1401, 2012 ONSC 858, 19 R.F.L. (7th) 181, [2012] O.J. No. 551 (Ont. S.C.J.). The parties were married 25 years and had a largely traditional marriage. Under the separation agreement the wife accepted child support of $2,000 per month for nine years. Given that the husband's annual income was approximately $150,000, the wife had foregone spousal and child support payments of approximately $5,000 per month. The husband was terminated from his employment and his income decreased significantly. The husband's motion to vary spousal support was dismissed. None of the conditions set out in the agreement under which spousal support would be varied and reduced to $1,000 were met. The loss of the husband's employment was not unforeseeable and was anticipated in the agreement. The husband was therefore expected to plan for potential economic difficulties.

*Where the payor wife's final income was not yet known, it was not possible to determine if a material change of circumstances had occurred* — *S. (V.) v. S. (G.)*, 2011 CarswellAlta 2221, 2011 ABQB 818 (Alta. Q.B.). The parties were married for 17 years and had two children. The wife was a family physician and the husband was a millwright. The wife's 2010 income was 290,000 and the husband's income was $53,000. Under an interim order the wife was ordered to pay the husband $5,623 per month in spousal support. The wife paid $4,500 per month in spousal support as there was set-off of $763 per month in child support payable by the husband. The wife's application to reduce spousal support was dismissed. The wife claimed her 2011 income was estimated to be $167,500. Reasons for decease were the wife's decision to work fewer hours and her secretary's decision to book fewer patients on the grounds the wife was stressed. Without knowing the wife's final 2011 income it was not possible to determine if a change in circumstance had occurred.

*Retroactive and ongoing spousal support will be granted when previous awards do not adequately take into account the economic hardship caused by the marriage because of the priority of child support obligations* — *Danby v. Danby*, 2008 CarswellOnt 5512, [2008] O.J. No. 3659 (Ont. S.C.J.). The husband sought a variation lowering his support obligations after he retired. At the time of the prior support order, two of the parties' children were considered dependents. The judge found that the husband's spousal support obligations should continue, given the ongoing need and the fact that previous spousal support payments "did not meet the appropriate support objectives but, rather, were slightly more than nominal" in order to allow the payment of child support, which is given precedence when means are limited. Therefore, the obligation to support was ongoing, and as the older child was no longer dependent, money was now available for spousal support. The judge found that the wife was entitled to compensatory and non-compensatory support and that economic hardship had not been adequately addressed in the previous order. He granted retroactive and ongoing support.

*Injury allegedly preventing payor from working* — *payor's evidence of in capacity not accepted by court* — *payee on cusp of achieving self-sufficiency* — *support payments terminated* — *S. (M.R.) v. S. (A.M.)*, 2008 CarswellNfld 194 (N.L. Prov. Ct.). Where the husband applied to terminate a spousal support order on the basis that his ability to pay had changed significantly since the last order was made, the court granted his application. The husband claimed that an injury prevented him from earning any income and he therefore made minimal effort to secure employment. Based on contradictory evidence called by the wife, the court concluded that the husband had, in fact, been working, and by not disclosing his income in either his testimony or financial statements the husband had engaged in a deliberate course of conduct designed solely to defeat his obligation to pay spousal support. However, on the basis of the principles enunciated under s. 39(8) of the *Family Law Act* of Newfoundland and Labrador, which the court recognized set out virtually the same principles as s. 17(7) of the *Divorce Act, 1985*, the court nevertheless found that it would be appropriate to terminate the husband's obligation to pay spousal support as of December 31, 2008.

*Payor disabled as a result of accident and no longer working — support decreased — Pratt v. Pratt*, 2008 CarswellNB 116, 2008 NBQB 94, 334 N.B.R. (2d) 22, 858 A.P.R. 22, [2008] N.B.J. No. 85 (N.B.Q.B.). The husband sought an order to vary, both retroactively from March 2003 and prospectively, the spousal support ordered to be paid by him to his wife by order made November 3, 1998 (see below, s. 10.7.1). That order required him to pay $235.00 twice monthly to his wife. In bringing his variation application, the husband alleged that there had been a change in circumstances due primarily to his being totally disabled as a result of being injured in an employment-related motor vehicle accident that occurred in March 2003. The court granted the variation application on the basis that the parties' circumstances were sufficiently different from those that existed in 1998. The parties were nearly 60 or close to it, the husband was now disabled and receiving benefits as a result of that injury along with Canada Pension Plan ("C.P.P.") benefits. The wife was also now receiving C.P.P. benefits. The wife's medical expenses, although currently covered through Social Assistance, were now almost $5,000 per year. Having considered her income and expenses, the court found that the wife's need for support continued and that the husband continued to have an ability to pay but reduced the amount of support to $300 a month starting July 1, 2007.

*Health problems only relevant if they affect income — Tait v. Tait*, 1994 CarswellOnt 451, 8 R.F.L. (4th) 18 (Ont. Gen. Div.). The deterioration of a payor's health amounts to a substantial change in circumstances warranting a variation of a spousal support order only where a concomitant impairment in the payor's income has also occurred.

*Taken together, events justified support termination — Ralph v. Ralph*, 1994 CarswellNfld 32, 7 R.F.L. (4th) 238, 122 Nfld. & P.E.I.R. 153, 379 A.P.R. 153, [1994] N.J. No. 267 (Nfld. T.D.). Where, since the date of the spousal support order, the husband had become unemployed, had lost his home to fire and had had a child with his common law partner, the court allowed his application for variation and made a provisional order terminating his obligation to pay spousal support.

*Payor inherits money — Kulcheski v. Kulcheski*, 1990 CarswellMan 330, 66 Man. R. (2d) 32 (Man. Q.B.). The wife's nominal support order was varied and a $6,500 lump sum granted after the husband had inherited $99,000.

*Payor seeks termination to enable him to return to school — Egan v. Egan*, 1990 CarswellNS 102, 100 N.S.R. (2d) 49, 272 A.P.R. 49 (N.S. Fam. Ct.). Where the husband sought to terminate the support payable to the wife in order to allow him to take a sabbatical and finish his Ph.D., his application was dismissed. As the wife was still in the home caring for the parties' child, her need for support continued.

*Payor seeks reduction to enable him to leave institution — costs and benefits to family members weighed — McGuire v. McGuire*, 1989 CarswellNS 50, 20 R.F.L. (3d) 45, 230 A.P.R. 420, 90 N.S.R. (2d) 420 (N.S.T.D. [In Chambers]). The court refused the application of the mentally ill and institutionalized husband for a reduction of child and spousal support, which would have permitted him to transfer to a residential from an institutional setting. The potential benefit to the husband from the transfer would not offset the detriment resulting to the wife and child caused by the drastic reduction in support.

*Payor working 80 hours per week allowed to reduce support payments* — *Clarke v. Clarke*, 1986 CarswellNfld 176, 62 Nfld. & P.E.I.R. 264, 190 A.P.R. 264 (Nfld. T.D.). Where the husband was working over 80 hours per week, his application for a reduction in the maintenance payable to his former spouse was allowed. As he was working in excess of the norm, it was fitting that he be allowed to enjoy some benefit from his extraordinary effort.

## 10.3.4  Change in Payee's Circumstances

### General

Where a recipient spouse has income that was not contemplated by the original order, this will constitute a material change in circumstances — *Hepburn v. Hepburn*, 2013 CarswellBC 2592, 2013 BCCA 383, 48 B.C.L.R. (5th) 251, 34 R.F.L. (7th) 267, 344 B.C.A.C. 6, 587 W.A.C. 6 (B.C.C.A.). The wife had started working and now had a stable income of $12,000, which was not contemplated by the consent order. The Court of Appeal found that this constituted a material change and adjusted spousal support accordingly.

Where a payor has received an inheritance, which has been spent, and remains economically dependent, spousal support will continue but may be reduced to reflect other changes in circumstances — *LeBlanc c. LeBlanc*, 2013 CarswellNB 122, 2013 CarswellNB 123, 2013 NBCA 22, 401 N.B.R. (2d) 334, 1041 A.P.R. 334, [2013] N.B.J. No. 79 (N.B.C.A.). The parties were married for 18 years. After his retirement, the husband applied to vary spousal support on the basis of income of $35,000. The judge varied spousal support on an imputed income of $50,000 annually. The husband appealed. The wife had received an inheritance of $90,000, which had been spent. The motions judge found that she nonetheless remained economically dependent and spousal support should continue, but reduced the quantum to reflect other changed circumstances.

*Change in circumstances will be found when the payor retires* — *Flieger v. Adams*, 2012 CarswellNB 219, 2012 CarswellNB 220, 2012 NBCA 39, 18 R.F.L. (7th) 28, 387 N.B.R. (2d) 322, 1001 A.P.R. 322, [2012] N.B.J. No. 137 (N.B.C.A.). The parties were married for 35 years. In 2010, the husband retired and applied to vary spousal support. Prior to the hearing, he unilaterally reduced spousal support to $405 bi-weekly. The motions judge found that the retirement constituted a material change in circumstances and reduced spousal support to $405 bi-weekly, finding that the husband had the means to pay some support and the situation fell into the exception to the presumption against "double dipping" into pension income found in *Boston*.

### Change of circumstances — inflation

*Passage of 13 years since original order constituted material change* — *Cymbalisty v. Cymbalisty*, 2002 CarswellMan 561, 2002 MBQB 324, 35 R.F.L. (5th) 31, 169 Man. R. (2d) 265, [2002] M.J. No. 526 (Man. Q.B.); affirmed 2003 CarswellMan 458, 2003 MBCA 138, 44 R.F.L. (5th) 27, 232 D.L.R. (4th) 718, 38 C.C.P.B. 265, [2004] 8 W.W.R. 220, 180 Man. R. (2d) 112, 310 W.A.C. 112, 2003 C.E.B. & P.G.R. 8079 (Man. C.A.). It was found that the fact that the wife's spousal support order had never been reviewed in the 13 years since it was made was in itself a material change in circumstances which supported her claim for an upward variation.

*Inflation creates material change* — *Horn v. Horn*, 1987 CarswellMan 315, 48 Man. R. (2d) 142 (Man. Q.B.); affirmed 1987 CarswellMan 82, 11 R.F.L. (3d) 23, 49 Man. R. (2d) 301

(Man. C.A.). The adverse influence of inflation upon the payee wife's circumstances was sufficient to justify a variation in support.

*Inflation may create material change — France v. France*, 1986 CarswellMan 239, 42 Man. R. (2d) 315 (Man. Q.B.); varied 1987 CarswellMan 98, 6 R.F.L. (3d) 354, 44 Man. R. (2d) 238 (Man. C.A.). Inflation over a long period of time may warrant an increase in spousal maintenance payable. (Ruling made under the *Divorce Act*, 1968.)

*Inflation plus increase in payor's income amount to material change — LeBlanc v. LeBlanc*, 1995 CarswellNB 36, 14 R.F.L. (4th) 414, 163 N.B.R. (2d) 192, 419 A.P.R. 192 (N.B.Q.B.); affirmed 1995 CarswellNB 193, 14 R.F.L. (4th) 414n, 167 N.B.R. (2d) 375, 427 A.P.R. 375 (N.B.C.A.). In *LeBlanc*, the wife's application for an increase in spousal support was allowed. Although she had $81,000 in savings and RRSP's valued at $15,900, she should not be required to use her assets to achieve an acceptable level of self-sufficiency. Over the years her means had been depleted through inflation while the husband's income had increased dramatically.

*Inflation plus higher costs to raise older child amount to material change — Marshall v. Marshall*, 1992 CarswellMan 57, 43 R.F.L. (3d) 303, 81 Man. R. (2d) 156, 30 W.A.C. 156 (Man. C.A.). In this case, an increase in the cost of living and the greater costs involved in raising an older child were found to be sufficient material changes in circumstances to warrant an increase in child support.

*Inflation plus higher costs to raise older child amount to material change — Will v. Thauberger Estate*, 1991 CarswellSask 69, 34 R.F.L. (3d) 432, 95 Sask. R. 52, 42 E.T.R. 286 (Sask. Q.B.); varied 1991 CarswellSask 87, 38 R.F.L. (3d) 68, 97 Sask. R. 97, 12 W.A.C. 97, 44 E.T.R. 266 (Sask. C.A.). The increased child care expenses resulting from inflation and the aging of the children may constitute a "material change in circumstances" justifying an increase in support.

*Cost-of-living escalator clause upheld — Lardner v. Lardner*, 1980 CarswellBC 510, 20 R.F.L. (2d) 234 (B.C.C.A.). An order by the trial judge directing that a periodic maintenance award be tied to the cost of living index and be adjusted accordingly on the 1st of January each year subsequent thereto was upheld on appeal. (Ruling made under the *Divorce Act*, 1968.)

*Cost-of-living escalator clause overruled — Ursini v. Ursini*, 1975 CarswellOnt 247, 24 R.F.L. 261 (Ont. C.A.), at 263 [R.F.L.]. "[The] judgement provided that the weekly maintenance for the wife and each of the children 'shall be increased by the percentage shown in the annual cost of living index of Statistics Canada' . . . Generally an order for maintenance must be varied by an order made upon a motion for that relief. This order cannot stand. In the circumstances of this case it was not appropriate," per Brooke J.A. (Ruling made under the *Divorce Act*, 1968.).

*Inflation did not create new need due to new sources of income for recipient — MacKean v. MacKean*, 1993 CarswellNS 561, 119 N.S.R. (2d) 252, 330 A.P.R. 252 (N.S. Fam. Ct.). The payee wife's claim for increased support was dismissed. The income which she had begun to receive from Old Age Security and Canada Pension more than off-set any inflationary erosion which had taken place since the original support award.

*Inflation creates material change — Duplak v. Duplak*, 1988 CarswellMan 340, 54 Man. R. (2d) 70 (Man. Q.B.). In this case, the inflation which had occurred in the 12 years since the parties' support order was made was found, in itself, to be a sufficient change in circumstances justifying an upward variation.

*Inflation giving rise to need for additional support creates material change — Basque v. Basque*, 1988 CarswellNB 157, 89 N.B.R. (2d) 214, 226 A.P.R. 214 (N.B.Q.B.). Although inflation by itself may constitute a "change in circumstances" within the meaning of the *Divorce Act*, there must be evidence that the inflation has brought about a need for additional support before the court will grant an application for increased support.

*Where inflation affected parties equally* — *Single v. Single*, 1986 CarswellNS 80, 5 R.F.L. (3d) 287 (N.S. Fam. Ct.). Where the effect of inflation has been relatively equal on both parties, the payee spouse cannot rely upon that factor as a grounds for an upward variation in maintenance.

## Change of circumstances — payee cohabiting

*Cohabitation foreseeable at time of original order* — *B. (G.) c. G. (L.)*, 1995 CarswellQue 23, 1995 CarswellQue 120, EYB 1995-67821, 15 R.F.L. (4th) 201, [1995] 3 S.C.R. 370, 127 D.L.R. (4th) 385, [1995] R.D.F. 611, 186 N.R. 201, [1995] S.C.J. No. 72 (S.C.C.). Where at the time that a support order was made, the payee wife acknowledged that she was seeing another man and the court found that it was foreseeable they would cohabit, their eventual cohabitation did not amount to a material change of circumstances that would be sufficient to vary the order. Consequently, the spousal support order should not be reduced.

*Cohabitation in and of itself does not disentitle recipient* — *Caron v. Caron*, 1987 CarswellYukon 8, 1987 CarswellYukon 43, EYB 1987-67973, 7 R.F.L. (3d) 274, [1987] 1 S.C.R. 892, 14 B.C.L.R. (2d) 186, 38 D.L.R. (4th) 735, [1987] 4 W.W.R. 522, [1987] R.D.F. 263, 2 Y.R. 246, 75 N.R. 36, [1987] S.C.J. No. 32 (S.C.C.), at 280 [R.F.L.]. The cases generally suggest that unless there is an explicit provision in a separation agreement dealing with the effect of remarriage or cohabitation on a spouse's right to maintenance, cohabitation in itself does not disentitle a spouse to maintenance. However, cohabitation is a relevant factor on a support application or variation. (Ruling made under the *Divorce Act*, 1968.)

*Reclaiming support entitlement after end of common-law relationship* — *Dutchak v. Dutchak*, 2007 CarswellSask 668, 2007 SKCA 138, 45 R.F.L. (6th) 41, 302 Sask. R. 310, 411 W.A.C. 310 (Sask. C.A.); affirming 2006 CarswellSask 834, 2006 SKQB 543, 36 R.F.L. (6th) 189, 291 Sask. R. 238 (Sask. Q.B.). Where the husband withheld spousal support for the payee wife for the period of over 10 years during which she was living in a common-law relationship, it was found that his obligation was temporarily suspended based on estoppel. However, upon termination of the relationship, the husband's support obligation was revised.

*Common-law relationship plus failure to enforce support obligation for 10 years justifies cancelling arrears* — *Dutchak v. Dutchak*, 2007 CarswellSask 668, 2007 SKCA 138, 45 R.F.L. (6th) 41, 302 Sask. R. 310, 411 W.A.C. 310 (Sask. C.A.). The court dismissed the wife's appeal from an order cancelling over 10 years of spousal support arrears owed by the husband. The wife had throughout those years been involved in a common-law relationship with another man who supported her and she had pointedly made no effort to enforce her support award.

*After both parties in new relationships and original support term finished, health benefits terminated* — *Kenny v. MacDougall*, 2007 CarswellNS 561, 2007 NSCA 126, 47 R.F.L. (6th) 55 (N.S.C.A.). Where the husband had fulfilled his support obligations toward his former wife, the court struck a provision requiring the husband to maintain medical and dental insurance coverage for her. The husband had remarried and the wife was in a new relationship and continuation of the insurance requirement was inconsistent with the discharge of support obligations.

*Support obligation reduced in light of new relationship* — *Juvatopolos v. Juvatopolos*, 2004 CarswellOnt 4423, 9 R.F.L. (6th) 147, [2004] O.T.C. 941 (Ont. S.C.J.); affirmed 2005 CarswellOnt 4774, 19 R.F.L. (6th) 76, 202 O.A.C. 1 (Ont. C.A.). The husband's support obligation toward the payee wife was reduced in light of her new relationship. The relationship appeared to be one of some permanence and her new partner was providing for her financially in a significant way. He was giving her $1,200 per month for living expenses, the amount the husband was required to pay under the existing spousal support order. The application judge had ordered that the quantum of support be reduced to $400 per month. The appellate court held that it should not interfere with the decision of the application judge as that decision was entitled to deference on appeal. It did not exceed the generous ambit within which reasonable disagreement was possible and was not plainly wrong.

*Common-law relationship can exist despite living apart and paying rent — Hatchard v. Hatchard*, 2003 CarswellNS 352, 2003 NSCA 100, 45 R.F.L. (5th) 357 (N.S.C.A.). The court, on appeal, affirmed the trial judge's finding that the payee wife had entered into a common law relationship. Although the wife lived on a separate floor in her new partner's house and paid rent to him, they socialized and vacationed together and partook in sexual relations.

*Unilaterally stopping support payments after recipient enters new relationship — recipient does not seek resumption of support for 12 years — McMullen v. McMullen*, 1994 CarswellNB 26, 5 R.F.L. (4th) 444, 150 N.B.R. (2d) 277, 385 A.P.R. 277, [1994] N.B.J. No. 308 (N.B.C.A.); reversing 1993 CarswellNB 378, 141 N.B.R. (2d) 297, 361 A.P.R. 297 (N.B.Q.B.). Where the husband did not pay support to the wife for a 12-year period after she had entered into a common-law relationship, the court, on appeal, reversed an order compelling the husband to recommence payments. The onus was on the wife to demonstrate that the economic loss resulting from the marriage or its breakdown continued. She had failed to do so.

*Common-law relationship may not exist despite living together and sexual relations — Gillham v. Gillham*, 1993 CarswellAlta 56, 48 R.F.L. (3d) 156, 11 Alta. L.R. (3d) 153, [1993] A.J. No. 527 (Alta. C.A.). The court reversed on appeal an order reducing the payee wife's spousal support. The husband claimed that the wife had entered into a common law relationship which, under the terms of the parties' separation agreement, entitled him to a reduction in the spousal support payable. The evidence of the wife's relationship presented at the hearing was vague and ambiguous and did not discharge the husband's onus of proving the relationship. To discharge the onus, it was incumbent on the husband to establish something more than the fact that the couple was having sexual relations while living together.

*Cohabitation in which third party does not pay disproportionate share of expenses — Walker v. Walker*, 1992 CarswellBC 156, 39 R.F.L. (3d) 305, 68 B.C.L.R. (2d) 92, 12 B.C.A.C. 137, 23 W.A.C. 137 (B.C.C.A.). While the payee's establishment of a common law relationship can constitute a substantial change in circumstances for the purposes of s. 17 of the *Divorce Act*, in certain cases, where the evidence indicates a relationship which is a matter of financial convenience and there is no evidence that the third party contributes more on significantly less than his individual share of expenses, no such material change in circumstances warranting a variation of support will be found.

*New relationship expected to lead to recipient's self-sufficiency — Droit de la famille - 1490*, 1991 CarswellQue 934, EYB 1991-58075, [1992] R.D.F. 20 (C.A. Que.). Where the payee wife had entered into a common-law relationship and it was expected that, with her new partner's assistance, she would soon be self-supporting, the court, on appeal, allowed the husband's application for termination of spousal support.

*New common-law relationship does not automatically justify variation — F. (J.) c. H. (B.)*, 1987 CarswellQue 380, 6 Q.A.C. 221 (C.A. Que.). Cohabitation by a payee with another individual does not in itself provide the basis for cancellation of a maintenance order. The relevant test continues to be the payee's need and cohabitation does not necessarily decrease these needs.

*Spousal support not terminated because of new relationship — Uberall v. Uberall*, 2010 CarswellBC 445, 2010 BCSC 251 (B.C.S.C.). The parties were together for 25 years and were married for 19 years. The parties entered into a consent order whereby the husband paid the wife $500 per month in spousal support. Subsequently, the husband brought a motion to terminate spousal support since the wife was in a new relationship. The court refused to terminate spousal support given the long relationship and the wife's needs.

*Spousal support not terminated because of payee's new relationship* — *Fritsch v. Fritsch*, 2008 CarswellOnt 7838, [2008] O.J. No. 5238 (Ont. S.C.J.). In this case, the husband brought a motion to terminate spousal support because the payee wife was in a new, permanent relationship. In dismissing the husband's motion, the court noted, "the mere fact that the Applicant is still living with her partner does not automatically constitute a material change in circumstances.. Re-partnering by a dependent spousal does not necessarily terminate entitlement, particularly when that entitlement is (in whole or in part) compensatory."

*New marriage to high-earning third party not anticipated at time of original order and justified retroactive termination* — *Redpath v. Redpath*, 2008 CarswellBC 72, 2008 BCSC 68, 48 R.F.L. (6th) 373, 79 B.C.L.R. (4th) 137, [2008] 10 W.W.R. 362 (B.C.S.C. [In Chambers]). The court allowed the husband's application to terminate the payee wife's spousal support retroactively back to the date she had begun to cohabitate with her new husband. The wife's remarriage had not been anticipated at the date of the original order and her cohabitation with her new husband, who enjoyed a very healthy income, constituted "a change in circumstances".

*Compensatory order — new relationship irrelevant* — *R. (R.S.) v. R. (S.M.)*, 2006 CarswellBC 2295, 2006 BCSC 1404, 30 R.F.L. (6th) 339, [2006] B.C.J. No. 2109 (B.C.S.C.). If a person receiving spousal support forms a new relationship, that fact is irrelevant if the initial order is compensatory in nature.

*Cohabitation plus marketable skills amount to material change* — *Ryan v. Hardy*, 2004 CarswellNS 505, 2004 NSSF 111, [2004] N.S.J. No. 467 (N.S.S.C.). Living in a common law relationship or remarriage is not an automatic bar to the receipt of spousal support from a previous partner. This is, however, a material consideration. In this case, support would terminate within 2 years as the wife's circumstances had changed. She had been in a common-law relationship for over a year. She had marketable skills and could re-train to achieve self-sufficiency.

*New common-law relationship does not automatically justify variation* — *Gallant v. Gallant*, 1999 CarswellNB 263, 50 R.F.L. (4th) 389, 214 N.B.R. (2d) 86, 547 A.P.R. 86 (N.B.Q.B.). Cohabiting with another either in a common-law relationship or in a marriage does not automatically give rise to a material change in circumstances sufficient to vary or terminate spousal support. Particularly in long-term marriages, support is composed of a number of elements. One of them is the result of dealing with the economic disadvantages of the marriage. Being a homemaker, caregiver, meal maker, not having a job or a career, pension entitlements, higher education, and other assets often leave the payee with little to show for years of dedication and sacrifice. Support covers not only living expenses, but also compensation for abandoning personal advancement or development for the general welfare of the family unit. In each case, the court must look at the length of the previous marriage and the consequences of the dissolution; the current living standards of each of the former spouses; the nature and permanence of subsequent relationships; and the economic benefits flowing to the payee as a result of the new relationships. On a variation application, all the objectives of s. 17(7) of the *Divorce Act* must be considered.

*Where original order compensatory and new relationship not significant for support* — *Tabel v. Tabel*, 1997 CarswellSask 746, 35 R.F.L. (4th) 379, 162 Sask. R. 49 (Sask. Q.B.). Where the emphasis in the original spousal support order was on the payee wife's need and the order was arguably compensatory in nature, the court refused to terminate the wife's support on the basis that she had entered into a common law relationship. The original order had been based upon the parties' agreement and although the relationship constituted a change in the wife's circumstances, it was not of a sufficient magnitude to warrant a variation in support, particularly in light of the fact that the attainment of self-sufficiency on the part of the wife was entirely illusory.

*Recipient who enters a new relationship has burden of showing continuing need — Rideout v. Rideout*, 1995 CarswellBC 87, 13 R.F.L. (4th) 191, [1995] B.C.J. No. 571 (B.C.S.C.), additional reasons at 1995 CarswellBC 3259, 13 R.F.L. (4th) 191n, [1995] B.C.J. No. 1213 (B.C.S.C.). A spouse who enters into a new relationship has the burden of demonstrating a continuing need for support.

*New cohabitation plus $20,000 inheritance not sufficient to justify variation — Gallagher v. Hogg*, 1993 CarswellMan 43, 45 R.F.L. (3d) 337 (Man. Q.B.). It was held that the payee wife's living arrangement with a male friend and her modest inheritance of $20,000 were not in themselves sufficient changes in circumstances to warrant a variation of a court order which incorporated the support provisions of a final settlement agreement. The husband had to prove a radical unforeseen change in circumstances before a variation would be granted. The reduction in the husband's income met the criterion and support was consequently reduced.

*New relationship which meets all recipient's needs justifies termination — Babington v. Babington*, 1993 CarswellNB 20, 47 R.F.L. (3d) 296, 134 N.B.R. (2d) 271, 342 A.P.R. 271 (N.B.Q.B.). Where the payee wife entered into a common-law relationship in which all of her economic needs were being met, her order for support, which was based upon the parties' separation agreement, was terminated. As the agreement contemplated variation, the court's jurisdiction was in no way affected. Support is based on need, and if no need exists, a support order should be terminated.

*Sharing expenses with new cohabitee plus increase in income justify variation — Manson v. Manson*, 1990 CarswellNS 514, 101 N.S.R. (2d) 83, 275 A.P.R. 83 (N.S. Fam. Ct.). Where, subsequent to the divorce, the payee wife's annual income had increased from $11,000 to $36,000 and she began sharing living expenses with a new common law partner, the husband's application to reduce the support payable to her was allowed.

*New relationship which decreases recipient's need justifies reduction — Trueman v. Trueman*, 1989 CarswellNB 217, 100 N.B.R. (2d) 281, 252 A.P.R. 281 (N.B.Q.B.). Where the payee wife entered into a common law relationship with a man who employed her, shared accommodation with her, and provided her with a car and trips, the husband's application for a decrease in spousal support was allowed. The parties' separation agreement allowed for support variation based upon a "material change in circumstances" and such a material change had occurred when the wife's relationship substantially reduced what she would have had to pay to maintain a similar lifestyle.

*New cohabitation does not automatically justify variation — MacDougall v. MacRae*, 1989 CarswellNB 17, 19 R.F.L. (3d) 329, 95 N.B.R. (2d) 200, 241 A.P.R. 200 (N.B.Q.B.). The fact that a payee spouse cohabits with another person is not a ground to terminate or vary support under the *Divorce Act*.

*New cohabitation does not automatically justify termination but is relevant — Thombs v. Thombs*, 1988 CarswellOnt 256, 15 R.F.L. (3d) 83 (Ont. U.F.C.). The fact that a payee spouse has begun to cohabit does not automatically disentitle that spouse to continued support. However, the impact of the living arrangement on the spouse's need is a valid consideration in determining the continued right to support.

*Financial contribution of new cohabitee plus recipient's self-sufficiency efforts justify variation — Dubois v. Dubois*, 1987 CarswellMan 104, 8 R.F.L. (3d) 48, 50 Man. R. (2d) 174 (Man Q.B.); additional reasons at 1987 CarswellMan 410, 50 Man. R. (2d) 174 at 176 (Man. Q.B.). A court has jurisdiction to vary an order for corollary support where the financial circumstances of the parties have not changed significantly from the time of the order but other circumstances have changed. A financial contribution by a cohabitee to a payee and the efforts of the payee in respect of self-sufficiency are relevant circumstances on an application to vary support.

### Change of circumstances — remarriage of payee

*Where a party knows at the time of settlement that the other party was in another relationship that was likely leading to marriage, the fact of the marriage is not a material change in circumstances — Bhupal v. Bhupal*, 2009 CarswellOnt 3662, 2009 ONCA 521, 69 R.F.L. (6th) 43, 97 O.R. (3d) 230, 251 O.A.C. 292 (Ont. C.A.). The appellant husband must be found to have taken account of the possible remarriage of the payee wife to a wealthy man when the parties negotiated support. The appellant had not requested a term that spousal support would be reviewed or reduced upon remarriage or cohabitation. The fact that the wife did marry cannot be relied upon as a basis for a variation.

*Remarriage plus new career and financial comfort justified termination — Roberts v. Beresford*, 2006 CarswellBC 337, 2006 BCCA 67, 22 R.F.L. (6th) 243, 222 B.C.A.C. 234, 368 W.A.C. 234, 50 B.C.L.R. (4th) 276 (B.C.C.A.). Where the payee wife had a new career, a new marriage and was financially comfortable, the termination of her spousal support was upheld on appeal.

*Remarriage which did not dramatically improve recipient's finances did not justify termination — Peloquin v. Peloquin*, 2004 CarswellMan 344, 2004 MBQB 193, 11 R.F.L. (6th) 111, 186 Man. R. (2d) 308, [2006] 2 W.W.R. 165 (Man. Q.B.); affirmed 2005 CarswellMan 424, 2005 MBCA 133, 22 R.F.L. (6th) 47, 201 Man. R. (2d) 93, 366 W.A.C. 93 (Man. C.A.). The court refused the husband's application to terminate spousal support upon the remarriage of the wife. The wife's financial situation had not dramatically improved with her remarriage. She and her husband had been together for 24 years in a traditional marriage and as only 4 1/2 years had elapsed since their separation, there had been insufficient time for the wife to overcome the financial disadvantage she had suffered.

*Remarriage plus increased employability of recipient — Davies v. Davies*, 2003 CarswellSask 638, 2003 SKCA 91, 44 R.F.L. (5th) 53 (Sask. C.A.). Where subsequent to the dissolution of the parties' 16-year traditional marriage the wife had remarried and graduated from teachers' college, the husband's application to terminate her spousal support was granted subject to continuation for a brief term to allow her to seek out teaching employment.

*Collapse of subsequent marriage leading to new need does not justify resumption of spousal support contrary to parties' original agreement — Ennis v. Ennis*, 2000 CarswellAlta 79, 2000 ABCA 33, 5 R.F.L. (5th) 302, 77 Alta. L.R. (3d) 289, 281 A.R. 161, 248 W.A.C. 161, [2000] A.J. No. 75 (Alta. C.A.), varying 1998 CarswellAlta 1284, 45 R.F.L. (4th) 323, [1998] A.J. No. 352 (Alta. Q.B.). The parties agreed at separation that spousal support would cease upon the remarriage of the recipient. She did remarry, separated from this second spouse 7 months later, and sought reinstatement of spousal support. The appellate court refused to reinstate the wife's original support award. Although more attention should have been paid to ss. 17(4.1) and 17(10) of the *Divorce Act*, the trial judge reached the correct conclusion in finding that the wife's economic difficulties related more to the failure of her second marriage than to the first.

*Remarriage justifies reduction but not termination — Savoie v. Savoie*, 1999 CarswellMan 308, 49 R.F.L. (4th) 336, [1999] 9 W.W.R. 63, 175 D.L.R. (4th) 291, 138 Man. R. (2d) 128 (Man. C.A.). The court was of the opinion that remarriage in and of itself does not necessarily justify termination of a spousal support order. However, in that decision, spousal support was reduced from $600 to $300 reflecting the wife's remarriage and the setting aside of the parties' separation agreement. The wife had a future need for support which arose because of her economic disadvantage suffered as a result of the long-term traditional marriage.

*Recipient's remarriage is not necessarily a bar to continuance of spousal support* — *Harris v. Gilbert*, 1997 CarswellOnt 115, 26 R.F.L. (4th) 199, 32 O.R. (3d) 139, 97 O.A.C. 14 (Ont. C.A.). Both parties had remarried, and the husband sought and obtained from the court below an order to terminate the support obligation on this basis. The Divisional Court overturned that judgment and restored the original obligation on the grounds that the trial court had not considered all the necessary factors. This was affirmed by the Court of Appeal.

*Given compensatory rationale for spousal support, remarriage is not always a bar to continued support* — *Rosario v. Rosario*, 1991 CarswellAlta 344, 37 R.F.L. (3d) 24, 120 A.R. 331, 8 W.A.C. 331 (Alta. C.A.); reversing 1989 CarswellAlta 398, 24 R.F.L. (3d) 168, 102 A.R. 234 (Alta. Q.B.). As the purpose of support is to compensate a spouse for what he or she may have given up by reason of the marriage, it is not improper, in some cases, to require a payor spouse to continue spousal support notwithstanding the fact that the payee has remarried.

*Remarriage followed quickly by death of new husband does not effect support entitlement* — *Droit de la famille - 941*, 1991 CarswellQue 200, 1 Q.A.C. 278, [1991] R.D.F. 502 (C.A. Que.); reversing (1990), [1991] R.J.Q. 412, [1991] R.D.F. 107 (C.S. Que.). Where the wife's new husband died within months of remarriage, it was held that the fact of the marriage did not effect her former husband's support obligations towards her.

*Remarriage is a relevant factor* — *Ceulemans v. Ceulemans*, 1986 CarswellSask 516, 50 Sask. R. 120 (Sask. C.A.). The remarriage of one or both of the parties should be taken into consideration when determining a change of circumstances in an application to vary maintenance. (Ruling made under the *Divorce Act*, 1968.)

*After recipient's remarriage to supportive new spouse, support obligation cancelled* — *Oxenham v. Oxenham*, 1982 CarswellOnt 249, 26 R.F.L. (2d) 161, 35 O.R. (2d) 318 (Ont. C.A.). After the recipient remarried a man who supported the parties' children and indicated willingness to adopt them, the payor's spousal support obligation was cancelled. (Ruling made under the *Divorce Act*, 1968.)

*Needs-based spousal support will be more affected by remarriage than compensatory support, because the policy reasons for awarding needs-based support dictate that the burden for supporting the needy spouse now falls on the payee's new husband or wife* — *Kelly v. Kelly*, 2007 CarswellBC 342, 2007 BCSC 227, [2007] B.C.J. No. 324 (B.C.S.C.). The husband applied for termination of spousal support because of the remarriage of his former wife. The spousal support was needs-based. It was judged that the spousal support for the wife would continue for a limited time and that the burden of supporting her would gradually shift to her new spouse.

*Recipient remarriage is not a bar to support* — *Kennedy v. Kennedy*, 2005 CarswellOnt 2296, [2005] O.J. No. 2334 (Ont. S.C.J.). The remarriage of the applicant can no longer be a bar to continued support, but merely a factor in determining if there ought to be a change to the quantum.

*Recipient remarriage is not a bar to further support, but it does constitute a change in circumstance* — *Franz v. Wilson*, 2005 CarswellOnt 3711, [2005] O.J. No. 3478 (Ont. S.C.J.). Remarriage usually constitutes a material change in circumstances sufficient to trigger a variation application. However, the remarriage of a spouse who is the recipient of spousal support does not automatically mean that support should be terminated. In this case, the court considered the article "Glass Ceilings in Spousal Support", Syrtash Collection of Family Law Articles, SFLRP/ 1998-2001 at pp. 33-34, where the author provides a list of issues that the court must consider in making a determination of whether support should be terminated. That list includes the following:

(i)    Does the spouse still need support in view of her new relationship and the income of her new partner?

(ii)    Is there a way to terminate the periodic obligation while acknowledging an ongoing entitlement (ie., by way of a final lump sum payment)?

(iii)    Did the parties specify the reason(s) why support was being paid when they signed their agreement?

(iv)    Was it foreseeable at the time of the agreement that the spouse would re-marry/cohabit?

(v)    Can it be said with any degree of certainty that the new relationship will last? Is it an enduring relationship, or is it short-lived?

(vi)    What efforts is the spouse making to achieve self-sufficiency? Is the spouse staying out of the workforce to maintain a new home for the new relationship?

(vii)    Will the new relationship ever compensate her for the economic consequences of the first marriage?

The court held that the wife continued to have need of spousal support but not at the same level as before her remarriage. Considering all the factors involved, the court ordered spousal support of $1,500 per month, (reduced from $2,000 per month).

*Recipient remarriage is not a bar to further support, but it does constitute a change in circumstance — Friesen v. Friesen*, 2004 CarswellBC 2454, 2004 BCSC 1344, [2004] B.C.J. No. 2224 (B.C.S.C.). Remarriage does not itself end a spouse's entitlement to support, but it does constitute a change in circumstances as contemplated under s. 17(4.1). The wife bears the burden of demonstrating that despite her remarriage she has a continuing need for spousal support. A variation of the existing order should meet the objectives set out in s. 17(4). The court noted that. (i) the length of the parties' marriage was 25 years; (ii) the five children of the marriage continued to reside with the wife; (iii) the wife was not permitted to undertake employment in Canada at the time of the hearing; (iv) the parties have been separated for 4 years, but the wife has not achieved economic self-sufficiency; (v) the wife's new husband was self-employed and earned income in 2002 of $58,687; (vi) the new husband had the care of two children from his first marriage who reside with him and the wife; and (vii) the parties have not yet resolved their respective claims to family assets. The court reduced spousal support from $3500 per month to $2500 per month.

*Despite term in agreement, remarriage was not a material change justifying variation — Wright v. Wright*, 2005 CarswellSask 626, 2005 SKQB 138, 261 Sask. R. 227 (Sask. Q.B.). Despite the fact that the interspousal agreement and consent order provided that the wife's remarriage would result in a reduction of spousal support, the court held that the wife's remarriage and the modest consequent change in her standard of living did not constitute a material change in circumstance sufficient to justify a variation in the spousal support order rendered 3 years previously. The parties had been married for 21 years and the wife was primarily a homemaker, responsible for caring for the home and family. She was only employed part-time during the marriage. She was 51 years old at the time of the order. The husband was retired at the time the order was made and was in receipt of his pensions. The fact that the wife was not employed at the time of the hearing and had not become self-sufficient was not a material change sufficient to warrant variation.

*Remarriage justifies reduction to nominal amount but not termination, given potential for future need — Plotz v. Boehmer-Plotz*, 2004 CarswellOnt 613, [2004] O.J. No. 587 (Ont. S.C.J.); additional reasons at 2004 CarswellOnt 1196 (Ont. S.C.J.). The payee wife accepted a variation based on the material change in circumstances resulting from her remarriage. The court held that it would be inappropriate to terminate spousal support from her first husband as it might jeopardize her in the event that her second marriage ended. The spousal support provision was varied to be a nominal annual payment of $1.00.

*Remarriage justifies reduction but not termination — Millen v. Millen,* 2004 CarswellOnt 2594 (Ont. S.C.J.); additional reasons at 2004 CarswellOnt 2571 (Ont. S.C.J.). On a variation application where the payee spouse has remarried, the financial contribution of the new spouse, or what his contribution should be, is of great significance. The former husband and the wife had been in a long-term marriage. The court held that the wife remained entitled to a support award against the former husband, although at a reduced rate, to redress the economic consequences of the marriage. Support was reduced to $900 monthly.

*Remarriage plus improved health and part-time work justified reduction — Prince v. Prince,* 2000 CarswellAlta 557, 2000 ABQB 371, 8 R.F.L. (5th) 165 (Alta. Q.B.). Where the payee had re-married and she was healthier and working part-time, the court reduced spousal support. Support was not eliminated in light of the 27-year marriage and the fact that her illnesses seemed to flow from the parties' marriage.

*Original support entitlement tied in to property settlement — McKay v. McKay,* 2000 CarswellBC 1983, 2000 BCSC 1393, 11 R.F.L. (5th) 179 (B.C.S.C.). Where the spousal support agreed to by the parties was intricately tied in to the parties' property settlement, the court refused the husband's application to vary the wife's spousal support after her remarriage. The original support order had been compensatory in nature and reflected the fact that the wife had agreed not to seek a portion of the husband's employment pension. In the circumstances, rescinding or reducing the wife's support would be unfair.

*Recipient's development of medical problems plus fact that payor's pension had not been divided constituted change in circumstances despite recipient's remarriage — Boudreau v. Bradbury,* 1998 CarswellBC 935, 38 R.F.L. (4th) 1, [1998] B.C.J. No. 1007 (B.C.S.C. [In Chambers]). The court allowed the wife's application for an upward variation of a nominal support award 17 years after the parties' divorce. The wife had developed severe medical problems which constituted the required "change in circumstances" and, although she had remarried, this fact alone did not disqualify her from support. At the time of the divorce, the husband's pension had not been a divisible asset and he had been receiving a pension benefit now for a number of years.

*Remarriage did not justify reduction given continued disadvantage from first marriage breakdown — Bettles v. Wright,* 1997 CarswellPEI 56, 30 R.F.L. (4th) 256, 153 Nfld. & P.E.I.R. 350, 475 A.P.R. 350, [1997] 1 P.E.I.R. 222 (P.E.I.T.D. [In Chambers]). Where the remarriage of the wife had not redressed the economic disadvantage to her as a result of the breakdown of her first marriage, the court refused the husband's application for a reduction in the spousal support payable by him.

*Recipient self-sufficiency does not, in and of itself, justify termination — Lamey v. Lamey,* 1996 CarswellPEI 9, 19 R.F.L. (4th) 172, 138 Nfld. & P.E.I.R. 53, 431 A.P.R. 53 (P.E.I.T.D.). More than a determination of self-sufficiency is required to reduce or terminate a spousal support award. Accordingly, where the wife had remarried and achieved a degree of self-sufficiency, her spousal support was reduced, but not terminated as the husband had requested. The wife had been a homemaker throughout the parties' 29-year traditional marriage and had foregone the accumulation of her own pension so that her husband could accumulate his own. Without continuing to pay support, the husband would have reaped all the benefits from that pension.

*Entitlement to support from second marriage does not automatically void entitlement to benefits from the first marriage — Nantais v. Nantais,* 1995 CarswellOnt 891, 16 R.F.L. (4th) 201, 26 O.R. (3d) 453 (Ont. Gen. Div.). The fact that a former spouse is entitled to support benefits from a second relationship does not relieve the first spouse from the obligation to continue to pay spousal support if need is continuing.

*Recipient remarriage is not a bar to support where need and disadvantage from first marriage continue* — *Campbell v. Rooney*, 1995 CarswellPEI 1, 10 R.F.L. (4th) 351, 129 Nfld. & P.E.I.R. 294, 402 A.P.R. 294 (P.E.I.T.D.). Remarriage does not automatically disentitle a spouse from support where that spouse continues to suffer an economic disadvantage resulting from the marriage and is in need.

*Remarriage places onus on recipient to show continued need* — *Range v. Range*, 1995 CarswellBC 416, 14 R.F.L. (4th) 11, [1995] B.C.J. No. 1248 (B.C.S.C.). Although remarriage does not automatically terminate a spouse's right to support, it does shift the onus to that spouse of proving why the second marriage does not meet his or her needs. Where the wife and her second husband maintained two homes and were short of funds to meet their needs, the first husband's application for termination of spousal support was allowed. The burden of maintaining the second home should not properly be passed on to the husband.

*Remarriage justified termination of support entitlement and cancellation of arrears given high income from new spouse* — *Wrobel v. Wrobel*, 1994 CarswellAlta 401, 8 R.F.L. (4th) 403, 160 A.R. 241, [1994] A.J. No. 688 (Alta. Q.B.). It was found that the remarriage of the wife to an individual with a good income justified the termination of her spousal support order and the cancellation of arrears owing from the date of the marriage.

*Remarriage does not place onus on recipient to prove continuing need* — *May v. May*, 1993 CarswellOnt 354, 48 R.F.L. (3d) 432 (Ont. Gen. Div.). It is no longer correct to hold that a former spouse who has entered into a new relationship must prove that he or she still has a continuing need to receive support. Self-sufficiency is only one factor for the court to consider in establishing the quantum of an award. In an application to vary support, the court must deal with all of the statutory objectives of support as specified in the *Divorce Act*. In this case, the court was of the opinion that the wife in her second marriage continued to be economically disadvantaged by her first marriage and its dissolution. The husband had also remarried and had three step-children. The court granted an order reducing the support payments.

*Remarriage did not justify termination* — *Moore v. Moore*, 1992 CarswellAlta 576, 137 A.R. 211, [1992] A.J. No. 1140 (Alta. Q.B.). The fact that the wife had remarried was found not to constitute a sufficient radical unforeseen change in circumstances to justify the termination of her support payable under a final settlement agreement.

*Remarriage is not, in and of itself, a bar to further support* — *Lever v. Lever*, 1991 CarswellNfld 48, 90 Nfld. & P.E.I.R. 266, 280 A.P.R. 266 (Nfld. U.F.C.). The remarriage of a payee spouse does not, in and of itself, constitute a change of substantial circumstances justifying a reduction in the child support paid to that spouse.

*Recipient who remarries and fails to enforce deemed to have agreed to termination and cannot seek to enforce after end of second* — *Bush v. Bush*, 1989 CarswellOnt 266, 21 R.F.L. (3d) 298 (Ont. U.F.C.). Where the wife attempted to enforce a support order against her first husband after the failure of her second marriage, the court allowed the husband's application to terminate the order. The wife's remarriage and failure to enforce support was tantamount to an agreement whereby the parties severed their prior ties and went their own ways. A similar case is *Underwood v. Underwood*, discussed above, at section **10.3.3**.

## Change of circumstances — payee no longer has primary responsibility for children

*End of recipient's obligation to support one of multiple children did not justify reduction of spousal support* — *Droit de la famille - 1867*, 1993 CarswellQue 663, EYB 1993-56426 (C.A.

Que.). The fact that the wife no longer had to support one of the children was not a ground for reduction of her own spousal support.

*Where spousal support obligation is modest, end of recipient's obligation to support children does not justify variation — Walker v. Walker,* 1992 CarswellBC 156, 39 R.F.L. (3d) 305, 68 B.C.L.R. (2d) 92, 12 B.C.A.C. 137, 23 W.A.C. 137 (B.C.C.A.). While there may be instances where a material change in circumstances results from the fact that the payee no longer has primary responsibility for the parties' children, where there is a modest amount of spousal maintenance in issue such a variation could not be supported on this basis.

*Spousal support increased; wife still not self-sufficient — Bockhold v. Bockhold,* 2010 CarswellBC 369, 2010 BCSC 214, [2010] B.C.J. No. 283 (B.C.S.C. [In Chambers]). The parties were married for 17 years and had two children. Pursuant to a consent order entered into in 2003, the husband agreed to pay the wife spousal and child support with spousal support subject to review upon cessation of child support. Child support terminated and the husband brought a motion to review. The court found that the wife was not self-sufficient despite entering into a new relationship and receiving spousal support for 10 years because she had been out of work during most of the marriage and was diagnosed with a disability. The husband was ordered to pay an increased amount of ongoing spousal support indefinitely.

*Amount payable as child support may continue to be payable as spousal support where child has become adult but amount had been used to support both child and recipient and where recipient's need would persist — Smith v. Smith,* 1998 CarswellOnt 676, 36 R.F.L. (4th) 419, 58 O.T.C. 269, [1998] O.J. No. 617 (Ont. Gen. Div.); additional reasons at 1998 CarswellOnt 1319, 36 R.F.L. (4th) 419, 58 O.T.C. 269 (Ont. Gen Div.); further additional reasons at 1998 CarswellOnt 2781, [1998] O.J. No. 2671 (Ont. Gen. Div.). Where the husband had been paying $250 directly to the wife as child support for the parties' 22-year-old son, it was held that when the child no longer qualified for support the amount was to continue to be paid to the wife as spousal support. The support had been used by the wife for her own benefit as well as that of the child and her need would continue.

*End of recipient's obligation to support children does not, in and of itself, justify variation — Gillis v. Gillis,* 1994 CarswellNS 47, 3 R.F.L. (4th) 128, 130 N.S.R. (2d) 112, 367 A.P.R. 112 (N.S.S.C.). Spousal support payable to a custodial parent should not be reduced simply because the children have left home and become self-sufficient. If spousal need continues, there is no reason to justify a reduction in support.

## Change of circumstances — property awards to payee

*Recipient who had received portion of payor's RRSP in property division not barred from receiving support payments funded by remainder RRSP — Cymbalisty v. Cymbalisty,* 2003 CarswellMan 458, 2003 MBCA 138, 44 R.F.L. (5th) 27, 232 D.L.R. (4th) 718, 38 C.C.P.B. 265, [2004] 8 W.W.R. 220, 180 Man. R. (2d) 112, 310 W.A.C. 112, 2003 C.E.B. & P.G.R. 8079 (Man. C.A.); affirming 2002 CarswellMan 561, 2002 MBQB 324, 35 R.F.L. (5th) 31, 169 Man. R. (2d) 265, [2002] M.J. No. 526 (Man. Q.B.). Where the husband lost his job and was forced to pay spousal support out of his RRSP, the fact that the wife had previously been awarded a share of his RRSP in property division proceedings did not justify the termination of his support obligation. As the wife had clearly been disadvantaged by the marriage and had a continuing need for support, the wife's situation was within the rule against double dipping. Double dipping can be justified on the basis of need and compensation.

*Where support agreement compensatory and tied into property settlement — McKay v. McKay,* 2000 CarswellBC 1983, 2000 BCSC 1393, 11 R.F.L. (5th) 179 (B.C.S.C.). Where the spousal support agreed to by the parties was intricately tied in to the parties' property settlement, the court refused the husband's application to vary the wife's spousal support after her remarriage. The original support order had been compensatory in nature and reflected the fact that the wife had agreed not to seek a portion of the husband's employment pension. In the circumstances, rescinding or reducing the wife's support would be unfair.

*Award to recipient of a portion of payor's pension after original support order was grounds for reduction* — Adams v. Adams, 1998 CarswellOnt 4427, 42 R.F.L. (4th) 285 (Ont. Gen. Div.). The court allowed the husband's application for a reduction in the spousal support payable by him pursuant to the parties' settlement. After the settlement, the wife had succeeded in an application for division of the husband's pension. The husband was accordingly entitled to a reduction equal to the monthly pension benefit received by the wife.

*Ownership of substantial income-producing assets justifies reduction* — Hansen v. Hansen, 1997 CarswellNS 260, 31 R.F.L. (4th) 384, [1997] N.S.J. No. 252 (N.S.S.C.). The wife's spousal support was ordered reduced in light of her ownership of substantial income-producing assets.

*Property award subsequent to original spousal support award justified reduction of support to nominal sum* — Weicker v. Weicker, 1986 CarswellAlta 467, 4 R.F.L. (3d) 397, 74 A.R. 16 (Alta. Q.B.). Where the wife was awarded a substantial property settlement subsequent to the parties' divorce, the earlier maintenance order made in the divorce proceeding was reduced to the nominal sum of $1. The property award constituted a material change in circumstances which, if properly invested, would allow the wife to become self-sufficient.

### Change of circumstances — payee disabled

*Extension and reduction of support* — Jens v. Jens, 2008 CarswellBC 2091, 2008 BCCA 392, 57 R.F.L. (6th) 31, 84 B.C.L.R. (4th) 250, 300 D.L.R. (4th) 136, 260 B.C.A.C. 185, 439 W.A.C. 185, [2008] B.C.J. No. 1886 (B.C.C.A.). The recipient's history of health problems included oral cancer, carpal tunnel syndrome, depression, and anxiety. These had intensified since the original order, and the recipient had no source of income apart from spousal support and disability allowance. Just after the separation 3 years beforehand, payments of $2,750 had commenced. A consent order between the parties called for this support to cease in April 2006, but on the recipient's application it was extended until June 2007. On her application for a further variation, the duration was extended for 5 years but the amount was reduced to $2,000 per month to comply with the *Spousal Support Advisory Guidelines*.

*Recipient injured 2 years after end of original award* — *no causal link to marriage* — Droit de la famille - 382, [1987] R.J.Q. 1748 (C.S. Que.); affirmed 1988 CarswellQue 46, 16 R.F.L. (3d) 379, [1988] R.J.Q. 2408, [1988] R.D.F. 482 (C.A. Que.). Where the wife was injured and unable to work two years after her support award had terminated, the court refused to reinstate her support. There was no causal link between the wife's economic difficulties and her former marriage.

*Disability undermining recipient's self-sufficiency arising after 17 years of merely nominal support justifies new support order* — Richardson v. Normand, 2000 CarswellMan 420, 2000 MBQB 110, 8 R.F.L. (5th) 185, [2000] 9 W.W.R. 360, 151 Man. R. (2d) 12 (Man. Q.B.). The wife was granted spousal support 17 years after the parties' uncontested divorce, since the court found that there was a change in circumstances as the wife's cancer had reoccurred, thus preventing her from continuing her employment. The parties had no contact for 20 years. At the time of the divorce, the wife was granted nominal spousal support of $1.00 per year, and that award acknowledged that the wife was entitled to support, but at the time of the divorce did not need it. The wife had been disadvantaged by the breakdown of the marriage as she had lost the financial assistance she would have received if the parties had remained together. She had suffered economic hardship, as she was no longer economically self-sufficient. Considering the factors for spousal support and the objectives of a variation order, the court ordered support of $250 per month.

*Deterioration of payee's health after consent order — consent order left door open for variation — Elaschuk v. Elaschuk,* 1999 CarswellOnt 2024, 1 R.F.L. (5th) 373, 123 O.A.C. 184, [1999] O.J. No. 2462 (Ont. Div. Ct.). Where a consent order provided for an award of spousal support, subject to further order of the court, the parties did not appear to view the support order as final and a variation order did not contradict this view. The wife was entitled to increased spousal support as the marriage breakdown caused a great disadvantage to her, her income was reduced, she had full custodial and most financial responsibility for the child of the marriage. She was in need and the husband could afford to pay support. At the time of the consent order, the wife had been diagnosed with multiple sclerosis but was employed full time. At the time of the variation hearing, the wife had become totally disabled and was unable to find full-time employment.

*30-year-old support order increased due to age-related deterioration in health — Kerwood v. Kerwood,* 1999 CarswellBC 780, 48 R.F.L. (4th) 127 (B.C.S.C. [In Chambers]). The court allowed the 83-year-old wife's application for an increase to her 30-year-old spousal support order. The wife's health had declined as she grew older and she required near-daily home care. The fact that declining health with age is foreseeable did not alter that the wife had experienced a change in circumstances. As the husband's income had actually increased over the years, he was in a position to pay the increased amount.

*Recipient's development of medical problems plus fact that payor's pension had not been divided constituted change in circumstances despite recipient's remarriage — Boudreau v. Bradbury,* 1998 CarswellBC 935, 38 R.F.L. (4th) 1, [1998] B.C.J. No. 1007 (B.C.S.C. [In Chambers]). See *Boudreau,* above, **Remarriage of payee.**

## Change of circumstances — payee on welfare

*Receipt of welfare benefits by recipient does not necessarily justify increase to spousal support — Richardson v. Richardson,* 1987 CarswellOnt 315, 1987 CarswellOnt 963, EYB 1987-67464, 7 R.F.L. (3d) 304, [1987] 1 S.C.R. 857, 17 C.P.C. (2d) 104, 38 D.L.R. (4th) 699, 77 N.R. 1, 22 O.A.C. 1, [1987] S.C.J. No. 30 (S.C.C.). The fact that a former spouse has been forced onto the welfare rolls is not, in and of itself, grounds for the variation of a spousal support order. In absence of a significant change in circumstances tied to economic dependency resulting from the marriage, the obligation to support a former spouse in need becomes the responsibility of the state. (Ruling made under the *Divorce Act,* 1968.)

*Recipient's dependence on social assistance insufficient reason to vary support agreement — Pelech v. Pelech,* 1987 CarswellBC 147, 1987 CarswellBC 703, EYB 1987-80055, 7 R.F.L. (3d) 225, [1987] 1 S.C.R. 801, 14 B.C.L.R. (2d) 145, 17 C.P.C. (2d) 1, 38 D.L.R. (4th) 641, [1987] 4 W.W.R. 481, [1987] R.D.F. 264, 76 N.R. 81, [1987] S.C.J. No. 31 (S.C.C.). The payor had fulfilled his support duties under the parties' maintenance agreement, which had been concluded after independent legal advice to both parties and which had been formalized as a court order. Subsequently, the payor prospered but the recipient's health deteriorated and she had to apply for social assistance. She applied for variation of the support agreement 12 years after it was issued, in order to resume support. The court upheld the trial judge's refusal to grant the relief sought.

*Termination which would leave recipient on welfare refused — Droit de la famille - 941,* (1990), [1991] R.J.Q. 412, [1991] R.D.F. 107 (C.S. Que.), reversed 1991 CarswellQue 200, 41

Q.A.C. 278, [1991] R.D.F. 502 (C.A. Que.). Where the wife would otherwise be forced onto public assistance, the court refused to grant the husband's application for termination of spousal support payable to her, despite the fact that she had remarried. Her new husband had died within a month of the marriage and, therefore, an annulment of the support obligation could not be justified.

*Recipient dependent on employment insurance — payor and recipient both destitute — Harding v. Harding*, 1991 CarswellNS 290, 109 N.S.R. (2d) 268, 297 A.P.R. 268 (N.S. Fam. Ct.). The court allowed the husband's application to terminate his wife's support although she was living on unemployment insurance and had little prospect of employment after the end of the parties 24-year traditional marriage. The husband was also destitute, suffering from depression and alcoholism, and was living on welfare. Severing the tie between the parties was the best and possibly only chance to promote the economic self-sufficiency of each.

*Fact that application might make recipient dependent on welfare does not justify adding state as party — Pearson v. Pearson*, 1990 CarswellNB 19, 25 R.F.L. (3d) 79, 105 N.B.R. (2d) 445, 264 A.P.R. 445 (N.B.Q.B.). The fact that a payee spouse may become a public charge if the payor's application for reduced support is granted is not grounds to add the state as a party to the variation application.

*Receipt by recipient of old age pension and supplement — Miles v. Miles*, 1990 CarswellNfld 14, 25 R.F.L. (3d) 348, 80 Nfld. & P.E.I.R. 333, 249 A.P.R. 333 (Nfld. T.D.). The receipt by a payee spouse of an old age pension and supplement may amount to a material change in circumstances warranting a variation of support. The supplement does not have the same connotation as welfare and does not preclude the termination of support.

*Recipient receiving welfare payments both before and after agreement about support — Droit de la famille - 390*, 1987 CarswellQue 1243, EYB 1987-78439, [1987] R.D.F. 506 (C.S. Que.). Where the wife had executed a separation agreement releasing the husband from all obligations, the fact that she was on welfare both before and after the agreement was insufficient to warrant a variation to provide support for the wife.

### Change of circumstances — payee squandering assets

*Poor administration of income and lack of determination to become independent — Droit de la famille - 783*, [1990] R.D.F. 220 (C.A. Que.). The court allowed the husband's application to annul the wife's alimony award on the basis that she had administered her income badly and had shown no determination to become financially independent.

*Recipient should have used assets to generate income — Balaban v. Balaban*, 2006 CarswellOnt 8452, 35 R.F.L. (6th) 139 (Ont. S.C.J.); additional reasons at 2007 CarswellOnt 1518 (Ont. S.C.J.). The court allowed the husband's application to terminate his spousal support obligation. The husband had, through no fault of his own, lost his employment through a restructuring and had little prospect of finding new employment. Furthermore, although the parties had almost equivalent capital bases, the wife, unlike the husband, had not utilized her investments wisely to generate income for herself.

*Property settlement should have been used for training — L. (D.L.) v. L. (D.J.)*, 1991 CarswellBC 539, 34 R.F.L. (3d) 163 (B.C.S.C.). Where it would have been more reasonable for the wife to have used her property settlement funds for her own retraining, rather than to purchase a new home, the court allowed the husband's application to reduce her spousal support and to place a time limit on her future entitlement.

*Squandering assets not obtained from payor — Gullens v. Gullens*, 1990 CarswellNS 42, 26 R.F.L. (3d) 121, 97 N.S.R. (2d) 30, 258 A.P.R. 30 (N.S. Fam. Ct.). The fact that the wife had squandered the settlement she had received in a personal injury action was found insufficient to justify a variation of the husband's support obligations contained in a final separation agreement. The funds were intended as special and general damage for personal injuries and the wife was not accountable to the husband for their expenditure.

*Poor investment didn't justify termination — Shabaga v. Shabaga*, 1987 CarswellBC 569, 6 R.F.L. (3d) 357 (B.C.S.C.). The fact that the wife had made a bad investment and lost a significant amount of money was held not to be sufficient reason to justify the termination of her support.

*Payor's means had increased but recipient had squandered assets — Kitson v. Kitson*, 1986 CarswellOnt 247, 1 R.F.L. (3d) 103 (Ont. H.C.). Where the wife squandered the property awarded to her under a provincial statute her subsequent claim for greater maintenance on divorce was dismissed despite the fact that the husband's means had increased significantly. The husband could not be expected to subsidize the wife's mistakes. (Ruling made under the *Divorce Act*, 1968.)

## Change of circumstances — payee — other

*The wife's pregnancy by a third party may be a material change in circumstances justifying variation of an order — D. (K.) v. D. (N.)*, 2011 CarswellBC 3325, 2011 BCCA 513, 7 R.F.L. (7th) 44, 25 B.C.L.R. (5th) 230, [2012] 3 W.W.R. 41, 315 B.C.A.C. 12, 535 W.A.C. 12, [2011] B.C.J. No. 240 (B.C.C.A.). The parties lived together for 7 years and separated in 2006. The husband's income was $150,000, and the wife's income had fluctuated between $30,000 and $50,000 but she left the workforce in 2004 to concentrate on fertility treatments. The wife sought indefinite support, stating that she was "not interested in working or retraining" and that she planned to be a stay-at-home mother at least until such time as the children were in school. The judge imputed income to her and awarded her limited support in the amount of $2,800 for one year. (The wife became pregnant by a third party and applied to vary support. A party's decision to be a stay-at-home parent after a shorter-term relationship does not merit an award of indefinite support. The chambers judge found that the pregnancy was a material change in circumstances and varied the order. The Court of Appeal dismissed the husband's appeal.)

*Improvement in the recipient's financial position does not necessarily constitute a material change in circumstances if there is still a demonstrated need of financial support — Fowler v. Fowler*, 2010 CarswellOnt 2647, 2010 ONCA 328 (Ont. C.A.). Although the recipient wife's financial position had improved somewhat in the years since separation, she was found to be in continued need of spousal support.

*A decision to vary or maintain spousal support amounts may take in to account the continued non-compliance of the paying spouse with previous support orders, imputed income from the payor, and the changed financial circumstances of the recipient spouse in determining whether there has been a material change in circumstances — Burley v. Burley*, 2009 CarswellOnt 54, 2009 ONCA 2, 61 R.F.L. (6th) 240, 244 O.A.C. 198 (Ont. C.A.). In this case, despite the recipient's recent return to work which was recent enough not to be apparent from tax returns, the trial judge found that the wife's unemployment was not a precondition of the original spousal support order and the payor's ongoing subterfuge regarding his income indicated ongoing support.

*Change in income differential between parties does not automatically justify variation — LeClair v. LeClair*, 2005 CarswellNB 704, 2005 CarswellNB 705, 2005 NBCA 107, 22 R.F.L. (6th) 123, 293 N.B.R. (2d) 137, 762 A.P.R. 137, [2005] N.B.J. No. 502 (N.B.C.A.). The fact that the income differential between the parties had changed does not necessarily mean that an order varying spousal support should issue. Accordingly, when the wife began to receive disability benefits subsequent to her spousal support order it was found not to constitute a sufficient material change to justify a variation of her spousal support.

*Remarriage plus increased employability of recipient* — *Davies v. Davies*, 2003 CarswellSask 638, 2003 SKCA 91, 44 R.F.L. (5th) 53 (Sask. C.A.). See *Davies*, above, **Remarriage of payee**.

*Agreement required recipient to re-train "as soon as possible" — interpretation of this phrase* — *Wooldridge v. Wooldridge*, 1999 CarswellAlta 320, 1999 ABCA 124, 45 R.F.L. (4th) 308, 172 D.L.R. (4th) 637, 237 A.R. 64 (Alta. C.A.); additional reasons at 1999 CarswellAlta 620, 49 R.F.L. (4th) 445, 250 A.R. 168 (Alta. C.A.). In an appeal by the wife from a judgment ordering the termination of spousal support and the reduction of child support, the court granted her appeal. In considering that the wife had not fulfilled her undertaking in the parties' separation agreement to retrain "as soon as possible", the chambers judge had given too narrow an interpretation of the phrase. A proper interpretation of the phrase must take into account all of the circumstances of the wife, not just her own poor health since separation, but also the fact she had taken care of two severely psychologically ill children and that she had not worked outside the home for 20 years. Under these circumstances, self-sufficiency for the wife might not be possible for some time, if ever. The husband was ordered to pay $2,500 per month in spousal support. Once the husband has ceased to pay child support, the spousal support, if necessary, could be increased.

*Recipient gave away money to third party and then sought increase* — *Murta v. Murta*, 1997 CarswellMan 561, 33 R.F.L. (4th) 429, 123 Man. R. (2d) 155, 159 W.A.C. 155, [1997] M.J. No. 547 (Man. C.A.). Where the payee gives a large sum of money to a relative and then seeks an increase in support to cover expenses which, without her gift, could have been covered by the payee, there is no material change in circumstances to warrant a variation.

*Children leave payor's home — child who was not "of the marriage" moved in with recipient* — *Canuel v. Canuel*, 1997 CarswellBC 1335, 33 R.F.L. (4th) 195, 39 B.C.L.R. (3d) 358, 94 B.C.A.C. 188, 152 W.A.C. 188, [1997] B.C.J. No. 1654 (B.C.C.A.). The court held that where the children had left the father's home and one child, who was not a child of the marriage within the meaning of the *Divorce Act*, had moved in with the mother and the other child now lived on his own, it was appropriate to increase spousal maintenance. However, doubling the amount was excessive. The appeal was allowed and spousal support, which had been $700, then doubled to $1400, was set at $1,000 a month. The lower court had not given due consideration to the fact that the payor had resigned from his employment resulting in a reduction in income, and that the family home was now in the sole possession of the payor.

*Lack of effort to achieve self-sufficiency* — *Rogers v. Rogers*, 1997 CarswellBC 1097, 28 R.F.L. (4th) 265 (B.C.S.C.); reversed 1999 CarswellBC 769, 1999 BCCA 238, 45 R.F.L. (4th) 65, 67 B.C.L.R. (3d) 315, 173 D.L.R. (4th) 449, 122 B.C.A.C. 64, 200 W.A.C. 64, [1999] B.C.J. No. 849 (B.C.C.A.). The court allowed the husband's application for a downward variation of the wife's spousal support. At the time of the original order the wife implied to the husband that her use of her qualifications as a real estate sales person would eventually minimize her support needs. However, in the 4 years since the order, she had made virtually no efforts to achieve self-sufficiency. On appeal, support was reinstated. She had an obligation to "try" to become employed not to become employed.

*Failure of good faith efforts to become self-sufficient* — *Wilson v. Wilson*, 1994 CarswellMan 36, 5 R.F.L. (4th) 75, 95 Man. R. (2d) 253, 70 W.A.C. 253 (Man. C.A.). Where the court had based a wife's spousal support on the assumption that she would become self-sufficient, the fact that she did not, despite her efforts, constituted a change in circumstances sufficient to support a variation application.

*Recipient re-enters workforce, but disadvantage from marriage continues — McGregor v. McGregor*, 1994 CarswellNB 23, 3 R.F.L. (4th) 343, 148 N.B.R. (2d) 176, 378 A.P.R. 176, [1994] N.B.J. No. 220 (N.B.C.A.), reversing 1993 CarswellNB 610, 49 R.F.L. (3d) 17, 139 N.B.R. (2d) 296, 357 A.P.R. 296 (N.B.Q.B.). Where the wife had re-entered the workforce following the termination of a long-term traditional marriage, an order ending her spousal support was upheld on appeal. Although it was unlikely that the wife would ever be as successful in her career as she would have been had the parties not married, there was insufficient evidence to justify an indefinite support award.

*Recipient loses right to widow's pension from payor's employment — Murphy v. Murphy*, 1994 CarswellMan 181, 10 R.F.L. (4th) 102, [1995] 2 W.W.R. 457, 120 D.L.R. (4th) 215, 97 Man. R. (2d) 247, 79 W.A.C. 247 (Man. C.A.). Where subsequent to the divorce, the wife discovered that she had lost the right to the widow's benefit under the husband's pension, it was held that this alone did not constitute a change of circumstances warranting an upward variation of her spousal support.

*New source of income for recipient — Droit de la famille - 1730*, 1993 CarswellQue 840, EYB 1993-58054 (C.A. Que.). In determining an application for a reduction in spousal support, the fact that the payee spouse has begun to receive old age pension benefits may properly be considered.

*Pension benefits split as matrimonial property, support recipient starts to receive benefits — Grainger v. Grainger*, 1991 CarswellSask 82, 37 R.F.L. (3d) 139 (Sask. Q.B.); affirmed 1992 CarswellSask 48, 39 R.F.L. (3d) 101, 100 Sask. R. 161, 18 W.A.C. 161 (Sask. C.A.). Where the parties' pension benefits had been settled in the course of matrimonial property proceedings, the husband could not later rely upon the fact that the wife had begun to share in his pension benefits as a reason to justify a reduction in the spousal support payable to her.

*Increase in recipient's income — Mullin v. Mullin*, 1990 CarswellPEI 104, 87 Nfld. & P.E.I.R. 1, 271 A.P.R. 1 (P.E.I.T.D.); varied 1991 CarswellPEI 21, 37 R.F.L. (3d) 142, 95 Nfld. & P.E.I.R. 73, 301 A.P.R. 73 (P.E.I.C.A.). A 400% increase in the payee's annual income is a change of circumstances warranting a reduction in support payable.

*Where it was not apparent that the wife contributed to the husband's future earning potential, the support payable under the separation agreement was not varied — Salvatore v. Etcovitch-Holley*, 2012 CarswellOnt 9678,?2012 ONSC 3996 (Ont. S.C.J.). The parties divorced in 1997 following a 20-year traditional marriage. Under a separation agreement entered in 2006 the husband was required to pay the wife $931 monthly spousal support. Support was indexed. The husband first approached the subject of variation in 2007. The wife had a disability, which was not supported by evidence, but inferred from receipt of disability pension. The husband's application to vary spousal support was dismissed. The husband was ordered to pay $1,230.72 per month, increased in accordance with indexing. The parties admitted that a material change of circumstances existed so as to contemplate variation of the divorce judgment. The wife sustained an economic disadvantage from the marriage breakdown. In the years since the divorce the wife had made a minimal effort to achieve increased self-sufficiency. The *Spousal Support Advisory Guidelines* did not apply. An indefinite spousal support order was warranted. It was not apparent that the wife contributed to the husband's future earning potential. No evidence existed to change basis on which spousal support was determined. The wife did not establish need for additional support, and budget proposed was "impossibly false".

*Where an applicant has overcome economic disadvantages caused by the separation, spousal support will not be indicated on a variation application — Antoniow v. Antoniow*, 2012 CarswellOnt 4195, 2012 ONSC 2116. The parties had a 17 year relationship and each parent had custody of one child. The judge found the applicant was no longer entitled to support as seven years had passed since the separation and she had successfully overcome any disadvantages caused by the separation.

*When self-sufficiency is delayed by family obligations such as childcare, and these obligations change in intensity, a material change in circumstances may be found* — *Kuzik v. Kuzik*, 2010 CarswellAlta 795, 2010 ABQB 272 (Alta. Q.B.). The husband in this case applied for cancellation of spousal support on the grounds that his former wife was exaggerating the amount of time required to care for their son because of his medical problems. The court refused to terminate spousal support but reduced it because of the time that had elapsed since separation (5 years), the improved health of the child and the fact that the wife was young and had the ability to become more self-sufficient.

*Recipient working at full capacity but unable to achieve reasonable standard of living* — *Leonard v. Leonard*, 2008 CarswellOnt 5708 (Ont. S.C.J.), additional reasons at 2008 CarswellOnt 6516 (Ont. S.C.J.). The parties' separation agreement required the recipient to become self-sufficient, contemplated variation in the event of a change in circumstances, and allowed for a review after 5 years. Fourteen years later, the payor had remarried, and his new spouse's contribution combined with his $55,000 pension brought his household income to $103,000. The health of the 62-year-old recipient had declined, and she had been unable to find substantial work in her chosen profession. She worked part-time as a supply teacher, and did a variety of other part-time jobs to supplement her income. The court found that the recipient was working to her full capacity, given her age and credentials. The spousal support was increased by $600 per month.

*New receipt of CPP benefits* — *original order called for change if recipient found "employment"* — *Crawford v. Kelly*, 2004 CarswellBC 1972, 2004 BCSC 1000, 9 R.F.L. (6th) 299 (B.C.S.C.). The fact that the wife received CPP benefits had no impact upon her spousal support order which specified a reduction should she find "employment". CPP benefits could not be characterized as "employment income".

*Payor's illness plus recipient's financial success amount to grounds for reduction* — *Young v. Young*, 1999 CarswellOnt 1332, 47 R.F.L. (4th) 214 (Ont. S.C.J.). The court reduced the husband's spousal support payments from $2,000 to $500 per month for a time-limited period, since, subsequent to minutes of settlement, the husband's ill health had prompted him to work part-time as a lawyer which greatly reduced his income and at the same time, the wife's income from employment and investments had increased. The parties had been married for 34 years and the court was of the opinion that the parties should be placed on an equal financial basis, as much as possible. There had been no "material" change in the parties' net worth since the time of settlement.

*Self-sufficiency achieved by recipient* — *Andrew v. Andrew*, 1999 CarswellOnt 2056 (Ont. Gen. Div.). The court held that it would be unfair to require the former husband to continue to pay support to his former wife when she had achieved a practical level of self-sufficiency and spousal support was terminated. The parties had had a 13-year marriage and the applicant had paid spousal support for 19 years. The applicant was near retirement age, but his net worth would not realistically permit retirement at an appropriate standard. The respondent had chosen to retire and had factored her support payments into her decision to do so. However, her earnings from a new post-retirement job would offset her loss of support.

*Death of recipient* — *non-entitlement of estate to support arrears* — *King Estate v. King*, 1994 CarswellNB 280, 8 R.F.L. (4th) 380, 153 N.B.R. (2d) 20, 392 A.P.R. 20 (N.B.Q.B.). Where the wife died subsequent to an order fixing the husband's substantial support arrears, the court granted the husband's application to vacate the arrears. The purpose of spousal support is to meet the ongoing expenses of the payee, a purpose which had disappeared with the wife's death.

*Recipient originally receives award due to illness, recovers enough to take part-time job, insufficient change to vary support — Stonestreet v. Stonestreet*, 1989 CarswellBC 385, 19 R.F.L. (3d) 314 (B.C.S.C.); varied 1989 CarswellBC 404, 21 R.F.L. (3d) 28 (B.C.S.C.). Where the wife had been awarded support because of her inability to work due to illness, the court refused the husband's application to reduce her support after she began working part-time. As she continued to have health problems and her employment was not secure, there was no significant change of circumstances upon which to base the variation requested.

*Recipient receives money gifts from family member — insufficient change to vary support — Sittmann v. Sittmann*, 1987 CarswellNfld 25, 6 R.F.L. (3d) 268, 62 Nfld. & P.E.I.R. 316, 190 A.P.R. 316 (Nfld. U.F.C.). It was held that the husband was not to be relieved of, or have diminished, his liability to pay support for his wife and their children because of gratuitous financial assistance provided by the wife's father which enabled them to enjoy a higher standard of living than they would ordinarily enjoy.

## 10.4 Interim Orders

### Interim orders pending variation

*Interim variation of spousal support where wife had obtained education and work since separation — Stevens v. Stevens*, 2004 CarswellSask 544, 2004 SKQB 332, 8 R.F.L. (6th) 223, [2006] 3 W.W.R. 174, 252 Sask. R. 166, [2004] S.J. No. 510 (Sask. Q.B.). The husband was granted an interim variation of the spousal support payable by him. While the wife had played a "traditional" role during the parties' 19-year marriage, in the 7 years since separation she had earned two university degrees and enjoyed an annual income in excess of $40,000.

*There is no statutory power authorizing the court to grant any interim relief once a decree nisi has been granted — MacNeil v. MacNeil*, 1982 CarswellOnt 1365, 134 D.L.R. (3d) 115 (Ont. H.C.). Therefore, in an application to vary the maintenance provisions of a decree *nisi*, the court is without jurisdiction to grant interim maintenance pending the hearing of the variation application.

### Variation of interim support orders

*Where a court has made an interim order for spousal support and the court rescinds the support arrears without the party seeking rescission making full disclosure, the order should be set aside and the arrears fixed — Vaandering v. Vaandering*, 2002 CarswellBC 48, 2002 BCCA 34, 24 R.F.L. (5th) 192, 162 B.C.A.C. 199, 264 W.A.C. 199 (B.C.C.A.).

*Interim support pending trial reduced after trial — Davignon v. Davignon*, 2000 CarswellOnt 468, 5 R.F.L. (5th) 37, 129 O.A.C. 322, 106 O.T.C. 234, [2000] O.J. No. 427 (Ont. C.A.). The husband paid $3,500 per month in spousal support on consent from the date of separation until it was reduced to $2,500, on motion, to the time of trial. At trial, the judge failed to give any reasons for his award of support. The husband sought a reduction in the outstanding interim award. While the court would normally order a new trial, the appellate court, in light of the parties' limited resources, determined the issues on the record before it. The court found that the proper amount of support was $2,500 per month.

*Court reluctant to vary interim order for support — Parsons v. Guevremont*, 1999 CarswellNS 199, 1999 NSCA 97, 48 R.F.L. (4th) 437 (N.S.C.A.). The husband's appeal from a dismissal of an application for variation of spousal support paid to him by his wife was dismissed, as there was no evidence of a material change in circumstances properly before the court and the courts are reluctant to interfere with a discretionary order at the interlocutory level.

*Court increased the amount of interim spousal support — Silk v. Silk*, 1995 CarswellNB 4, 10 R.F.L. (4th) 407, 159 N.B.R. (2d) 268, 409 A.P.R. 268 (N.B.C.A.). The appellate court increased the amount of interim spousal support, where the judge did not take into account the wife's ability to provide for herself, considered in the context of the husband's earnings. Further, the judge did not apply the same criterion to the husband as he did to the wife when determining how their standards of living would be affected by an award of interim support to the wife and did not take into account that the award would provide the husband with beneficial tax consequences.

*The doctrine of res judicata does not apply to interim orders in family law proceedings — White v. White*, 1999 CarswellNfld 67, 45 R.F.L. (4th) 100, 172 Nfld. & P.E.I.R. 233, 528 A.P.R. 233, [1999] N.J. No. 72 (Nfld. C.A.). While there is no specific provision allowing variation of interim support orders, there are numerous cases where the courts have permitted such variations. In addition, interim orders are interlocutory and consequently are always open to review by the court that made them.

*Where a judge makes clear that he is making an interim order with very little reliable evidence and that further evidence is required that can only be adduced at trial for a determination of the issues, an interim order will not be varied — Blatherwick v. Blatherwick*, 2014 CarswellOnt 2644, 2014 ONSC 1433, 44 R.F.L. (7th) 379 (Ont. S.C.J.). The parties were married for 39 years. Following their separation, they became very litigious and there were some 20 court orders made in 3 years. There were six motions before the court, *inter alia*, a motion by the husband to vary an interim order for spousal support. The husband claimed there was a material change in circumstances in that the original judge relied on a grossed up income provided by his business valuator because he had not been paying tax on his worldwide income. Subsequent to that order, the husband made a voluntary disclosure to the CRA and was required to pay tax. The motions judge dismissed this as a ground for a finding of a material change in circumstances as it was clear the first judge did not rely on the report of the business valuator. The motions judge also stated the court required *viva voce* evidence relating to a business debt as there was "very little" reliable evidence and found that a trial was required as soon as possible. He made clear it was an interim order, and the quality of the evidence had not changed since the original interim order was made. The interim order was not varied.

*The Superior Court of British Columbia has jurisdiction to vary interim support orders pursuant to its inherent jurisdiction, but will do so only in exceptional circumstances when the matter is urgent and cannot wait for trial — Janmohamed v. Janmohamed*, 2014 CarswellBC 170, 2014 BCSC 107 (B.C.S.C.). The husband was a business owner, and there was an interim order for child and spousal support where income had been imputed to him. The husband sought to vary, *inter alia*, spousal support on the basis that his income had decreased. He had unilaterally ceased paying his obligations under the interim order. The judge found that the court did have jurisdiction to vary an interim support order, but only in exceptional circumstances. This jurisdiction existed pursuant to the inherent jurisdiction of the court rather than through a statutory provision in the *Divorce Act*. The court found the burden to show exceptional circumstances was heavy.

*When a change in circumstances was contemplated by the original interim order, that order will not be varied — Clarke v. Clarke*, 2013 CarswellBC 3557, 2013 BCSC 2130 (B.C.S.C.). The wife sought variation of an interim order for spousal support on the basis that the payor husband had retired. The judge held that a material change was one which, if known at the time of the order, would have led to a different result. As the husband's future retirement was known at the time the order and was contemplated, it did not form a material change and support was not varied. The judge noted that there were other financial issues that were not yet determined which could change spousal support, which the trial judge would determine.

*Where a party consents to an interim variation in spousal support, variation will be ordered because the decision does not bind the trial judge* — *R. (L.E.) v. R. (R.A.)*, 2013 CarswellBC 3613, 2013 BCSC 2191 (B.C.S.C.). The husband sought to vary or set aside an interim order of spousal support made some 2 months previously on consent. The wife consented to a reduction in spousal support. The judge held that, absent this consent, he would not have varied the order and noted that he would not have done so but for the fact that the interim orders did not bind the decision of the trial judge.

*An interim order will be varied to reflect newly available financial disclosure* — *Rheault v. Hammond*, 2013 CarswellAlta 1766, 2013 ABQB 530, 5 Alta. L.R. (6th) 51 (Alta. Q.B.). The husband sought, *inter alia*, to vary an interim order of spousal support on the basis of reduced income. The husband had resisted financial disclosure for many years. He had finally disclosed his income, and the judge varied the interim order accordingly.

*Where income is in flux and fuller evidence is required for an accurate calculation of support, but income seems commensurate with the previous order, interim support will not be varied* — *W. (T.A.) v. W. (S.R.)*, 2013 CarswellBC 1523, 2013 BCSC 907 (B.C.S.C.). The parties were married for 4 years and had one child. The wife sought, *inter alia*, variation of spousal support. The parties had a year-old consent order for interim support, which was sought to be varied. The judge found that the difference in the husband's income from that time was only $2,000 and his income was very much in flux. Consequently, it was more prudent to wait for a full determination of financial issues at trial in order to calculate support accurately.

*Where income available for spousal support has not changed since the original order, an interim order will not be varied* — *McMillan v. McMillan*, 2013 CarswellOnt 11833, 2013 ONSC 5144 (Ont. S.C.J.). The wife sought to vary the support provisions of a consent order on the basis that the husband had misrepresented his earnings. The husband claimed he had not misrepresented his income and that the difference in income presented and that on his T4 was taxable room-and-board benefits provided by his employer, which was a gold mine in Nunavut. The judge found that room and board did not constitute income for the purposes of spousal support and declined to vary support.

*The Superior Court of British Columbia has jurisdiction to vary interim support orders, pursuant to its inherent jurisdiction, but will do so only in exceptional circumstances when the matter is urgent and cannot wait for trial* — *Janmohamed v. Janmohamed, supra*. The husband was a business owner, and there was an interim order for child and spousal support where income had been imputed to him. The husband sought to vary, *inter alia*, spousal support on the basis that his income had decreased. The judge found that the court did have jurisdiction to vary an interim support order, but only in exceptional circumstances. This jurisdiction existed pursuant to the inherent jurisdiction of the court, rather than through a statutory provision in the *Divorce Act*. The court found the burden to show exceptional circumstances was heavy.

*Where financial issues are very complex and cannot be satisfactorily determined without expert evidence at trial, interim support will not be varied* — *Janmohamed v. Janmohamed, supra*. The husband, who was a business owner, provided some financial disclosure, but the judge concluded the financial issues were complex and could only be resolved satisfactorily through trial. The application to vary was dismissed.

*An illness causing a reduction in income will be grounds to vary an interim support order* — *Biddle v. Biddle*, 2010 CarswellOnt 6279, 2010 ONSC 4611, [2010] O.J. No. 3604 (Ont. S.C.J.), additional reasons at 2010 CarswellOnt 7524, 2010 ONSC 5235 (Ont. S.C.J.). The payor husband became ill and was unable to earn the same amount of income as at the time of the original interim order. The wife alleged the husband exaggerated his illness. The judge found the illness formed a material change of circumstances and varied the interim order to reflect his new income, but noted that a determination of the reasonable impact of his illness would have to wait until trial.

*An interim order will not be varied when there is no new information or evidence presented since the last interim order* — *Lawless v. Lawless*, 2008 CarswellOnt 4632 (Ont. S.C.J.). The judge found that there was a triable issue as to the husband's income, but found that an interim order was not the place to determine income. The husband had not complied with previous disclosure requirements and, after having done so, could not re-litigate the issues pending trial.

*Interim spousal support will be varied when a material change of circumstances from the time of the original interim order is found* — *Carlton v. Carlton*, 2006 CarswellSask 308, 2006 SKQB 259 (Sask. Q.B.). The parties had an 18-year relationship and four children. The judge varied an earlier interim order which was made in anticipation of the wife being a fulltime student. As she was only a part-time student, and was also sharing household expenses with a new spouse, spousal support was varied.

*Delay of the trial combined with dire economic circumstances faced by the payor spouse will be reason to reduce interim support pending trial* — *T. (H.) v. T. (C.)*, 2006 CarswellNun 23, 2006 NUCJ 19 (Nun. C.J.). The payor husband was significantly in arrears, had lost some of his employment and had filed for bankruptcy. There had been a previous interim support order, but the trial had been delayed due to unforeseen circumstances. The husband was in "dire economic circumstances", and the judge found that this was a material change in circumstances that was sufficient to order a reduced amount of interim spousal support.

*An interim order of support will be varied under s. 17 of the* Divorce Act *when there is a material change in circumstances* — *Horan v. Horan*, 2003 CarswellBC 526, 2003 BCSC 372, [2003] B.C.J. No. 550 (B.C.S.C.).

*Court reluctant to vary interim order for support* — *West v. West*, 2001 CarswellOnt 1936, 18 R.F.L. (5th) 440, [2001] O.T.C. 422, [2001] O.J. No. 2149 (Ont. S.C.J.). The court refused the husband's application for a retroactive downward variation of the interim child and spousal support payable by him. The matter was best left to the trial judge where the court would have the best and most complete evidence available. If any inequity had resulted from the interim order, it could be redressed at trial.

*Court reluctant to vary interim order for support* — *Robertson v. Oake*, 2000 CarswellOnt 1393 (Ont. S.C.J.). Where the husband, a chiropractor, experienced a decline in income on account of his suspension from the College of Chiropractors, but he did continue to work at a reduced income level, the court granted his motion for reduced support in part by reducing the amount payable for child support. The court ordered that spousal support be maintained at the same level as in the interim order. Both parties knew of the upcoming disciplinary proceedings against the husband at the time the settlement was negotiated.

*Interim orders should only be varied when there is a compelling change of circumstances such that one or both parties would be seriously prejudiced by waiting until trial* — *Hama v. Werbes*, 1999 CarswellBC 2515, 2 R.F.L. (5th) 203, [1999] B.C.J. No. 2558 (B.C.S.C. [In Chambers]). Rather than apply for a variation, the parties should seek an early trial date and a "final" resolution of the issues in dispute. Section 17 of the *Divorce Act* and s. 14 of the *Federal Child Support Guidelines* do not apply to interim applications. The variation provisions of the *Divorce Act* are found in s. 17. The reference in s. 17(1) to support orders contemplates support orders granted under s. 15.1(1), not interim orders granted under s. 15.1(2).

*Court reluctant to vary interim order for support* — *except where hardship found or existing order absurd* — *Tremblay v. Tremblay*, 1997 CarswellOnt 3672, 39 R.F.L. (4th) 324, [1997] O.J. No. 3805 (Ont. Gen. Div.). The court's jurisdiction to vary interim orders should be exercised only in cases of hardship, or where a continuation of the existing order would be absurd due to changed circumstances since the time of making it. The variation procedure multiplies interim proceedings rather than moving straight away to a final solution. In this case the wife began living with another man and although the court on the husband's application to vary the order did not have sufficient information to conclude that the new living arrangements would disentitle her to support completely, they led the court to conclude that her financial circumstances had changed for the better since the making of the interim order, and that a reduction in interim spousal support was warranted.

*Where an application for interim support is dismissed, the court lacks jurisdiction to entertain an application for a variation of that order — France v. France,* 1996 CarswellOnt 1187, 22 R.F.L. (4th) 203, [1996] O.J. No. 1031 (Ont. Gen. Div.).

*Court allowed variation of interim support order in extreme circumstances — Renpenning v. Renpenning,* 1992 CarswellSask 445, 107 Sask. R. 23 (Sask. Q.B.). The court allowed the husband's application for a 50% reduction in interim spousal support payable where he suffered a drastic decline in income, owed substantial tax arrears, had assumed responsibility for the material debts and had developed Parkinson's disease.

*Court's jurisdiction to vary support order on an interim basis — Hannon v. Sherrett,* 1992 CarswellOnt 315, 44 R.F.L. (3d) 134 (Ont. Gen. Div.). The court lacks jurisdiction under s. 17(1) of the *Divorce Act* to vary a spousal or child support order in a divorce judgement on an interim basis. The court can, however, make such a variation of a child support order in a proper case through an exercise of its *parens patriae* jurisdiction.

*Court's jurisdiction to vary interim support order which incorporates a settlement agreement — Nein v. Nein,* 1991 CarswellSask 76, 36 R.F.L. (3d) 417 (Sask. Q.B.). An interim order for support under s. 15 of the Act may be varied under s. 17, notwithstanding that the order incorporates a settlement agreement.

*The court has jurisdiction to vary an interim support order in the face of a substantial change in circumstances — Stannard v. Stannard,* 1991 CarswellAlta 334, 34 R.F.L. (3d) 249, 123 A.R. 27, [1991] A.J. No. 679 (Alta. Q.B.).

*Variation of an interim order is generally not available where a party is dissatisfied with the order — Kolter v. Kolter,* 1990 CarswellSask 512, 88 Sask. R. 127 (Sask. Q.B.). Variation of an interim support order is not a remedy available to a party dissatisfied with the order, except where the order is obtained fraudulently or where material information is withheld or where there is a material and unanticipated change of circumstances. Otherwise, a dissatisfied party should proceed to a trial as soon as possible.

*A court generally lacks jurisdiction to vary an interim support order before a divorce is granted — Validen v. Validen,* 1990 CarswellMan 60, 30 R.F.L. (3d) 163, 71 Man. R. (2d) 213, [1990] M.J. No. 619 (Man. Q.B.). It can do so only where the order contains terms and conditions under s. 15(4) of the *Divorce Act* permitting the variation. In such a case, the individual seeking the variation bears a heavy onus.

*Although the* Divorce Act *is silent on the issue, the court has jurisdiction to vary interim support orders where warranted — Dumont v. Dumont,* 1987 CarswellNB 118, 86 N.B.R. (2d) 183, 219 A.P.R. 183, [1987] N.B.J. No. 1054 (N.B.Q.B.). The court is entitled to use its inherent jurisdiction to do justice between the parties and the absence of an express statutory authority does not deprive the court of this jurisdiction.

*Substantial long over-due arrears under an interim order enforced — Saeglitz v. Saeglitz,* 1994 CarswellOnt 389, 3 R.F.L. (4th) 244 (Ont. U.F.C.). The court enforced substantial arrears owing under an interim support order which had been accumulating over 7 years. Although the wife had not vigorously pursued them during the 7-year period, the husband, given his substantial means, was not allowed to argue that he interpreted non-enforcement as an indication that he need not pay them.

*Although the* Divorce Act *is silent on the issue, the court has jurisdiction to vary interim support orders where warranted — McLeod v. McLeod*, 1993 CarswellNS 37, 45 R.F.L. (3d) 181, 121 N.S.R. (2d) 80, 335 A.P.R. 80 (N.S. Fam. Ct.). The absence of an express power to vary an interim support order under the *Divorce Act* does not mean that interim orders cannot be varied. An interim support order under the *Divorce Act* is always subject to review, alteration, or variation. Specifically, the Nova Scotia Supreme Court has the authority to vary an interim order. A Family Court judge, on the other hand, has the jurisdiction to make recommendations to the Supreme Court with respect to variations of interim orders under R. 57.30 of the Nova Scotia *Civil Procedure Rules*. In general, though, interim orders should be brought back directly to the Supreme Court. Interim orders are intended to be temporary, and any change in circumstances warranting a variation should be addressed at trial. Exceptions to this general rule occur when there are lengthy delays in getting the matter on for trial and enforcement proceedings of support, custody, or access orders have already been commenced in the Family Court.

*An interim order can be varied to provide a necessary allowance for shelter — Spoletini v. Spoletini*, 1996 CarswellBC 1033, 22 R.F.L. (4th) 330 (B.C. Master). Where the wife's interim support order contemplated that she would reside with her mother and therefore have minimal shelter costs, she was granted an increase in support when circumstances required that she find her own apartment. To deny the wife a reasonable and necessary allowance for shelter would be absurd.

*Interim order cannot be varied under s. 17 of the* Divorce Act *— Boznik v. Boznik*, 1993 CarswellBC 22, 45 R.F.L. (3d) 354, 76 B.C.L.R. (2d) 202 (B.C.S.C.). Where the parties were divorced, but no final support order was made, it was found that an earlier interim support order continued in force. Given its interim nature, such an order is not subject to variation under s. 17 of the *Divorce Act*. But see *Dupont v. Dupont*, 1993 CarswellBC 615, 47 R.F.L. (3d) 273 (B.C.S.C.), in which the court entertains an application under s. 17 for variation of an interim support order.

## 10.5  Variation Ordered

### Variation after support for limited term expires

Where the obligation to provide spousal support is limited to "a definite period or until a specified event occurs," restrictions are placed on the right to vary after the period has expired, or the event has occurred which puts an end to the obligation. In these cases, "a court may not, on an application instituted after the expiration of that period or the occurrence of the event, make a variation order for the purpose of resuming that support unless the court is satisfied that ... (a) a variation order is necessary to relieve economic hardship arising from a change described in subsection (4.1) *that is related to the marriage*; and ... (b) the changed circumstances, had they existed at the time of the making of the spousal support order or the last variation order made in respect of that order, as the case may be, would likely have resulted in a different order." (S. 17(10)(a) and (b).) (Emphasis added.)

Section 17(10) represents a change from the 1968 *Divorce Act*. Under the 1968 Act, support orders could be varied at any time even after the expiration of a limited term. The obvious purpose of s. 17(10) is to curb this tendency, and to see limited term orders as having an attribute of finality. The restrictions were explained in the Information Paper issued by the Minister of Justice in May, 1985 on first reading of the Bill for the current Act. "While the [*Divorce Act, 1985*] gives the court the express right to make fixed-term maintenance orders in appropriate cases, having regard to all the circumstances of a specific case, it follows that such awards should not be varied or revived indefinitely. Otherwise, such orders would be meaningless. However, the Act provides for certain exceptions in order to alleviate injustices that certain situations could create. That is not to say that all conditions arising after the expiration of a fixed-term maintenance award, and the need for support which could thereby be incurred by an ex-spouse, should be the responsibility of the other spouse. In situations where it could be proved that economic hardship has arisen through changed circumstances *related to the marriage*, which would have resulted in a different original order if they had existed at the time of the original order, an application to change the conditions of the order will be received. This, for example, will encompass the incapacity of an ex-spouse to become economically self-sufficient after the expiration of a fixed-term maintenance award because of changing circumstances related to child care."

*Support extended where payee experienced precarious financial circumstances caused by the breakdown of the marriage — Wang v. Poon*, 2008 CarswellBC 2333, 2008 BCCA 442, 58 R.F.L. (6th) 235, 84 B.C.L.R. (4th) 199, 302 D.L.R. (4th) 679, [2008] B.C.J. No. 2113 (B.C.C.A.), varying 2007 CarswellBC 297, 2007 BCSC 194, 70 B.C.L.R. (4th) 120, [2007] B.C.J. No. 271 (B.C.S.C.). The court extended on appeal the period of time during which the wife was to receive spousal support. The wife was 47 years old, spoke little English and the trial award dd not properly take into account her precarious financial circumstances arising from the breakdown of the marriage. While she had obtained employment as a hairdresser, the trial award, when combined with her income, would barely meet her modest projected expenses.

*Time limit may be removed where the support recipient is unable to find work after this time despite reasonable efforts to do so — this inability constitutes a material change in circumstances sufficient to trigger variation of spousal support — McGoey v. McGoey*, 2008 CarswellOnt 6, 48 R.F.L. (6th) 174 (Ont. S.C.J.). The original support order envisaged self-sufficiency occurring within 5 years but, despite reasonable efforts to make this occur, the recipient was not yet self-sufficient. She worked 62% of available days as a supply teacher and her income was imputed at 75% of days worked, which the wife admitted was possible for her to obtain.

*Payee changed career plan — issues to be addressed at trial — Ghahrai v. Mohammad*, 2006 CarswellOnt 7325, [2006] O.J. No. 4651 (Ont. S.C.J.). Justice Fragomeni clearly set out that a variation application with respect to a time-limited spousal support order (in that case minutes of settlement which were incorporated into an order) is covered by the provisions of s. 17 of the *Divorce Act* which requires the moving party to demonstrate a material change in circumstance. The court considered the requirements for a material change of circumstances as set out in *Willick v. Willick*, 1994 CarswellSask 48, 1994 CarswellSask 450, EYB 1994-67936, 6 R.F.L. (4th) 161, [1994] 3 S.C.R. 670, 119 D.L.R. (4th) 405, [1994] R.D.F. 617, 173 N.R. 321, 125 Sask. R. 81, 81 W.A.C. 81, [1994] S.C.J. No. 94 (S.C.C.) and in *B. (G.) c. G. (L.)*, 1995 CarswellQue 23, 1995 CarswellQue 120, EYB 1995-67821, 15 R.F.L. (4th) 201, [1995] 3 S.C.R. 370, 127 D.L.R. (4th) 385, 186 N.R. 201, [1995] R.D.F. 611, [1995] S.C.J. No. 72 (S.C.C.). Fragomeni J. said the following of *Willick*:

[15] At paragraph 52 of *B. (G.) c. G. (L.)* the court states. the analysis which the court must undertake to determine the extent of the variation once the sufficiency of a change has been established was discussed in *Willick supra* where I noted in this connection (at pages 734-735):

Once a sufficient change that will justify variation has been identified the court must next determine the extent to which it will reconsider the circumstances underlying and the basis for the support order itself. For the reasons below I believe that it is artificial for a court to restrict its analysis strictly to the change which has justified variation. Moreover while a variation hearing is neither an appeal nor a trial *de novo*, where the alleged change or changes are of such a nature of magnitude as to make the original order irrelevant or no longer appropriate then an assessment of the entirety of the present circumstances of the parties is in order.

Justice Fragomeni in *Ghahrai v. Mohammad*, made the following comment at paragraph 27:

> [27] The explicit requirement that the effect of the change must be causally connected to the marriage imposes a significant limitation on the jurisdiction of this court once an order has terminated. Further the change relied upon must be of a substantial unforeseen and continuing nature.

In *Gharhai*, the facts of the case were that the parties negotiated minutes of settlement which were incorporated into an order providing that the husband would pay periodic spousal support until April 2006. The wife argued that at the time of the agreement she was planning to upgrade her high school credits but had no definite or concrete plans. She sought to vary the agreement as she later decided she wanted to pursue a nursing degree and did not have the means to do so. There is no reported trial decision but Justice Fragomeni expressed serious doubt about whether this was a material change. The court imported the two-stage *Miglin* test into the analysis for a variation application. In *Miglin*, the Supreme Court set out the requirements for variation of spousal support in a negotiated agreement. In *Ghahrai v. Mohammad*, the court ultimately dismissed the application to vary as it was brought by way of interim motion and on the basis of conflicting affidavit evidence. The judge stated that there was a serious issue as to whether the wife had established a material change and ordered that the issue be canvassed at trial.

*Wife not able to become self-sufficient* — *Ambler v. Ambler*, 2004 CarswellBC 2255, 2004 BCCA 492, 5 R.F.L. (6th) 229, 36 B.C.L.R. (4th) 10, [2004] B.C.J. No. 2076 (B.C.C.A.). The issue was whether the trial judge was correct in finding that at the time of the consent order the parties had not contemplated the fact that the wife might be unable to become economically self-sufficient. The husband, on appeal, contended that this situation was contemplated and, therefore, the fact that she did not become self-sufficient was not a change in circumstances as required by s. 17(10) in light of *Miglin*. The consent order provided that at the end of 48 months the husband's obligation to pay maintenance and the wife's entitlement to maintenance would cease absolutely. "Technically the application in *Miglin* was under s. 15.2 rather than s. 17(10) but the court emphasized (at para 91) that the same test of reasonable anticipation should apply under both provisions." The husband accepted that the wife suffered "economic hardship" from a change that "related to the marriage" as required by s. 17(10), but submitted that there was no evidence on which to find that it was unanticipated at the time of the consent order within the *Miglin* test. In applying the first stage of the test, the court on appeal found that "both parties were represented by counsel, the order was approved by the court, and there are no issues of oppression or vulnerabilities that would undermine its enforcement." Having made this finding the court continued: "The issue raised here relates to the second stage of the *Miglin* inquiry — whether the wife's present circumstances were within the reasonable contemplation of the parties at the time of the consent order." At the time of the consent order the parties anticipated that the wife would obtain full-time employment as an educational assistant and become self-sufficient. She made reasonable efforts to find employment, but was unsuccessful "because of circumstances beyond [her] control." The parties expected the wife would become self-sufficient, but "Was it reasonably anticipated at the time that the wife would fail to achieve self-sufficiency despite reasonable efforts?" In dismissing the appeal, the court found that the chambers judge applied the test of whether the failure was an unforeseen change in circumstances, which was "consistent with

*Miglin*." Having found on the evidence that the circumstances were not reasonably contemplated, it could not be said that they were condoned by the consent order and precluded variation.

*Inability of payee to find employment was not a change in circumstances warranting a variation in spousal support* — L. *(H.) v. L. (M.H.)*, 2003 CarswellBC 2206, 2003 BCCA 484, 44 R.F.L. (5th) 388, 19 B.C.L.R. (4th) 327, 232 D.L.R. (4th) 52, 186 B.C.A.C. 264, 306 W.A.C. 264, [2003] B.C.J. No. 2098 (B.C.C.A.). The parties signed a separation agreement which was incorporated into the divorce order. The court granted the husband's appeal from a judgement varying a time-limited spousal support order. The court held that the analysis in *Miglin* was equally applicable to inquiries under s. 17 (10) of the *Divorce Act* as to the role of separation agreements. Consequently, the courts on a variation application must look at whether the agreement was in substantial compliance with the objectives of the *Divorce Act* as a whole. The court outlined the two-stage test in *Miglin* and observed that under s. 17(10), there were additional hurdles relating to the requirements that there be a "change of circumstances" and that the change in circumstances be "related to the marriage". In this case, by the terms of the agreement and taking into account that the parties obtained the advice of a vocational consultant, the parties specifically considered the wife's need to become self-sufficient and the steps that were necessary to achieve that end. On that basis, they entered into a final and binding agreement. The fact that the wife was not able to find work was not a sufficient reason to conclude that the agreement should no longer continue to govern the parties' post-divorce obligations towards each other. The appeal was allowed.

*Dismissal of wife's application for extending limited-term support upheld* — *Wedsworth v. Wedsworth*, 2001 CarswellNS 218, 2001 NSCA 102, 19 R.F.L. (5th) 455, 194 N.S.R. (2d) 198, 606 A.P.R. 198 (N.S.C.A.). The court, on appeal, upheld the dismissal of the wife's application for an interim order extending the period of her limited term spousal support. Although the trial judge had misstated the threshold test for variation of a consent order, the evidence still supported the correct test as set out in s. 17(4.1) of the *Divorce Act*.

*In an application to vary and extend a limited-term spousal support award, the court cannot rely upon its parens patriae jurisdiction to grant interim support pending the hearing* — Y. *(H.) v. Y. (D.)*, 1998 CarswellPEI 104, 42 R.F.L. (4th) 418, 170 Nfld. & P.E.I.R. 44, 522 A.P.R. 44 (P.E.I.C.A.). *Parens patriae* can only be invoked in the case of adult dependants if they are mentally incompetent

*The facts that the wife could not find employment after the completion of her degree and intended to pursue further education were insufficient to warrant an extension of her time-limited support* — *Duplisea v. Duplisea*, 1995 CarswellNB 41, 15 R.F.L. (4th) 1, 164 N.B.R. (2d) 170, 421 A.P.R. 170 (N.B.C.A.).

*Extension of support for 6 months transition period after training* — *McKinney v. McKinney*, 2004 CarswellAlta 1344, 2004 ABQB 717, 9 R.F.L. (6th) 418 (Alta. Q.B.). The wife's support was ordered extended to a date 6 months after the anticipated completion of her training as a teaching assistant. The wife was entitled to support for a reasonable time after graduation as security against the possibility that she might not find employment immediately.

*No extension of support where wife had dissipated much of her assets* — *Seymour v. Seymour*, 2001 CarswellBC 1564, 2001 BCSC 777, 20 R.F.L. (5th) 139, [2001] B.C.J. No. 1091 (B.C.S.C.). The court refused the wife's application to extend her spousal support entitlement in a court ordered review of the original support order. The wife had realized significant assets upon the parties' divorce but had quit her job to move thousands of miles away to live with a man. The relationship failed after the wife had dissipated much of her money. It was held that the wife's need was largely related to events occurring after the parties' divorce and that her choices had unreasonably limited her ability to become self-sufficient. An order of permanent spousal support would have been tantamount to a redistribution of the parties' assets.

*Support cannot be extended under s. 17 in light of a full and final release of support as part of a separation agreement — Leopold v. Leopold*, 2000 CarswellOnt 4707, 12 R.F.L. (5th) 118, 51 O.R. (3d) 275, 195 D.L.R. (4th) 717, [2000] O.T.C. 868, [2000] O.J. No. 4604 (Ont. S.C.J.). Section 17 of the *Divorce Act* provides clear rules when spousal support is sought after the expiration of time-limited support. The provision, however, is not applicable to a case in which the parties executed a full and final release of support as part of their separation agreement.

*Support not extended where the wife's changed circumstances were not related to the marriage or its breakdown — Rizzo v. Rizzo*, 2000 CarswellOnt 4983, 12 R.F.L. (5th) 445 (Ont. S.C.J.). The wife's application for spousal support, brought after the expiration of the 4-year support period called for in the parties' separation agreement, was dismissed. The wife had fallen and permanently injured herself and her resulting depression inhibited her employment opportunities. Although the wife's injuries were found to be a radical unforeseen change in her circumstance, her situation was not the result of the marriage or its breakdown. The marriage had not been a long one, nor had the wife given up career opportunities as a result. She had been given adequate time to achieve self-sufficiency.

*Where the wife was unable to justify her failure to upgrade her education as was anticipated in her original spousal support award, the dismissal of her application for an extension of her limited-term support was upheld on appeal — Lilly v. Lilly*, 1994 CarswellBC 691, 9 R.F.L. (4th) 434 (B.C.C.A.), affirming 1993 CarswellBC 634, 50 R.F.L. (3d) 329 (B.C.S.C.), additional reasons at 1994 CarswellBC 663, 50 R.F.L. (3d) 341, [1994] B.C.J. No. 74 (B.C.S.C.).

*Support not extended where wife's need not related to the marriage or its breakdown — Janakowski v. Janakowski*, 2000 CarswellOnt 2478, 7 R.F.L. (5th) 117 (Ont. S.C.J.). The court refused to extend the wife's spousal support entitlement beyond the period called for in the parties' consent order. The wife had been employed throughout the relationship and neither of the parties had realized any economic advantage from the marriage. The wife had preferred to remain unemployed after the parties' separation with the result that her need was not truly related to the marriage or its breakdown.

*Support not extended where wife's need not related to the marriage — Schroder v. Schroder*, 1998 CarswellAlta 407, 38 R.F.L. (4th) 395, 221 A.R. 395 (Alta. Q.B.). The court dismissed the wife's application to vary spousal support 8 years after the expiry of her limited-term support. The wife had upgraded her education and found employment, but she had been forced to quit because of a back injury. As the wife's current financial difficulty was not connected to the marriage, the variation was not appropriate.

*Support extended where wife's injury would frustrate her attempts to be self-supporting — Marshall v. McNeil*, 1998 CarswellSask 100, 36 R.F.L. (4th) 264, 164 Sask. R. 91 (Sask. Q.B.), the court extended the 30-month limitation on the wife's spousal support after she suffered a back injury which would temporarily thwart her efforts toward self-sufficiency.

*Support not extended, payee deliberately unemployed, payee had been supported for longer time than cohabitation — Kurbegovich v. Kurbegovich*, 1998 CarswellOnt 267, 36 R.F.L. (4th) 220, [1998] O.J. No. 217 (Ont. Gen. Div.), the court found that the wife's need did not flow from a pattern of economic dependency that was generated by the marriage relationship. She was out of the work force during the marriage partly to be a full-time mother. However, by reason of the nature of her work prior to her relationship with her husband, she could have re-entered the work force after the separation in the same or similar type of work, as a waitress or factory worker. She did work briefly at a restaurant, but stayed out of the work force deliberately from the time that she was fired from that job. She stated that she did so, as she wished to stay with her children and she had received some injuries in accidents. There was no allegation in the statement of claim, the medical report filed, nor in the wife's evidence that she was totally unemployable because of health reasons. The court held that the length of cohabitation affected an award of spousal support in certain circumstances. In this case, the parties had cohabitated between 5½ to 6 years. The wife had received support for 7 years. The court found that the husband's obligation to support his wife was satisfied and no further spousal support was warranted in all of the circumstances.

*The court held that the wife had failed to establish a material change in circumstances related to the marriage relationship and its breakdown and refused to extend the wife's spousal support beyond the 3-year transition period set out in the parties' separation agreement which had been incorporated in the divorce judgement* — Symonds v. Symonds, 1997 CarswellOnt 3294 (Ont. Gen. Div.). The wife had received full and competent legal advice regarding the separation agreements and the divorce judgement. She had made an informed decision respecting the terms of spousal support. She was under no misapprehension, coercion or pressure respecting her agreement to the time-limited support provision. A court should be reluctant to set aside the negotiated agreement of the parties as to spousal support. The agreement, ratified by the divorce judgement, represented the informed intentions of the parties. Consequently, it was entitled to substantial weight in the exercise of the court's supervisory discretion to vary a support order, especially where there was no radical and unforeseen change in circumstances. In a variation proceeding, the court must assume that the original support order was correct. The court was of the opinion that the support provision of the final divorce judgement was in accord with the objectives of subsection 15(7) of the *Divorce Act* in providing spousal support for a 3-year period to allow the applicant to re-integrate into the job market. Her attempts to secure employment over the years were not well documented. However, the fact that she did secure some employment suggested that she was employable within a roughly comparable level to that which she may have enjoyed had she not devoted herself to the role she maintained during the marriage by agreement of the parties. However, she failed to pursue all available employment opportunities.

*Support extended where existing illness worsened after the divorce* — Tees v. Tees, 1997 CarswellNWT 29, 31 R.F.L. (4th) 290, [1997] N.W.T.R. 315, [1997] N.W.T.J. No. 65 (N.W.T.S.C.). Where, subsequent to the divorce, the wife's existing multiple sclerosis condition deteriorated to the extent that she could no longer work, the court extended her limited term support award. But for the marriage breakdown, she would not have to bear the economic consequences which flowed from her disability. If the total disability had existed at the time of the original order, it would likely have resulted in an indeterminate order for a higher amount. Where the result of the expiry of a time-limited spousal support award would require the wife to encroach upon capital for her living expenses, her application for an extension was allowed.

*Support extended in light of unexpected recession* — Fredrickson v. Fredrickson, 1993 CarswellSask 52, 48 R.F.L. (3d) 48, 111 Sask. R. 219 (Sask. Q.B.). The court allowed the wife's application for an extension of her spousal support beyond the term specified in the parties' separation agreement. The time frame contemplated in the agreement was based upon the wife's completion of her education and her resulting self-sufficiency. As the parties could not have anticipated the recession which frustrated the wife's ability to find employment after obtaining her teaching qualifications, it would be unfair not to provide her with additional time to make the adjustments.

*Support not extended where economic hardship unrelated to the marriage* — Hiscock v. Dickie, 1994 CarswellNB 276, 6 R.F.L. (4th) 149 (N.B.Q.B.), the court refused to extend the wife's support period as called for in the parties' consent order. Although she had been unable to find employment despite retraining, she was unable to demonstrate that her economic hardship arose from a change that was related to the marriage.

*No extension of support where economic disadvantages had been addressed through property and support* — Debacker v. Debacker, 1993 CarswellAlta 453, 49 R.F.L. (3d) 106, 143

A.R. 228 (Alta. Q.B.). Where the wife had agreed to limited term support and a substantial property settlement, her subsequent application for an extension of support was refused. The wife had the resources to achieve self-sufficiency and any benefits to the husband and disadvantages to the wife from the relationship had already been compensated through the property and support settlement.

*No extension of support where wife's circumstances primarily arose from her financial mismanagement — Droit de la famille - 1645*, [1992] R.D.F. 460 (C.S. Que.). The court refused to set aside a provision in the parties' agreement whereby the wife's support entitlement was to end on a specified date. The wife had had legal advice at the time of the agreement and her current financial problems were more related to her own mismanagement of funds than to the marriage.

*Support extended where wife's job search hampered by care of special needs child — Hack v. Hack*, 1991 CarswellMan 384, 72 Man. R. (2d) 131 (Man. Q.B.). Where the wife's efforts at job hunting had been hindered by her need to care for the parties' autistic child, who had recently been placed in a residential school, her support award was extended for a further 6-month period.

*Extension of support denied where wife did not utilize property settlement for support and husband paid support from his pension payments — Ehlers v. Ehlers*, 1991 CarswellSask 86, 38 R.F.L. (3d) 41 (Sask. Q.B.). The court refused the wife's application to extend her spousal support beyond its specified expiration date. The wife refused to use any of the property settlement to support herself and as the husband drew upon his pension to pay support, a pension which had also been divided with the wife, the ongoing support order was effectively a derogation from the proceeds of his share of the matrimonial property. Support was accordingly ordered to continue for only 3 more months.

*An application to extend support after the expiration of an existing support order is properly considered as a variation application, rather than as an original application for support — Matas v. Matas*, 1990 CarswellMan 43, 26 R.F.L. (3d) 349, 67 Man. R. (2d) 218 (Man. Q.B.), varied at 1990 CarswellMan 57, 29 R.F.L. (3d) 282, 68 Man. R. (2d) 317 (Man. C.A.).

*Support not extended where wife did not find employment, as dependency not related to the marriage — Droit de la famille - 1350*, [1990] R.D.F. 558 (C.S. Que.). Where the wife had failed to find employment within the 6-month period during which the parties had agreed that the husband would pay spousal support, the court refused to extend her support. The wife's financial dependency could no longer be related to the marriage and did not justify a modification of the parties' agreement.

*The Divorce Act does not provide for variation of fixed-term support prior to the expiration of the term — Droit de la famille - 1243*, [1989] R.D.F. 298 (C.S. Que.).

*Support extended due to mutual mistake as to date of completion of wife's studies — Iaacson v. Isaacson*, 1987 CarswellBC 532, 10 R.F.L. (3d) 121 (B.C.S.C.). The court granted the wife an extension of spousal support beyond the period specified in the parties' settlement agreement which had been incorporated into the decree *nisi*. As the wife had miscalculated the remaining duration of her studies, the agreement had been based upon the parties' mutual mistake.

## Variation ordered — change of mode of payment

*Jurisdiction to vary support — Hayre v. Hayre (No. 2)*, 1978 CarswellBC 82, 5 R.F.L. (2d) 85, 6 B.C.L.R. 390 (B.C.S.C.), at 392 [B.C.L.R.]; affirmed 1978 CarswellBC 170, 8 B.C.L.R. 161, 93 D.L.R. (3d) 766 (B.C.C.A.). "On a motion to vary under s. 11(2) [now s. 17], the court's jurisdiction is a jurisdiction to vary the maintenance, and it is not restricted to the particular mode of payment that the original order called for", per Berger J.

*Lump sum may be added to or substituted for periodic payment* — *Vance v. Vance*, 1974 CarswellOnt 85, 13 R.F.L. 378 (Ont. C.A.), at 381-82 [R.F.L.]; and see 1974 CarswellOnt 950, 13 R.F.L. 386, 2 O.R. (2d) 537, 43 D.L.R. (3d) 481 (Ont. C.A.). An order providing for the payment of periodic maintenance may be varied so as to provide for the substitution or addition of a lump sum payment.

*Jurisdiction to change mode of payment* — *Sagoo v. Sagoo*, 1987 CarswellMan 94, 6 R.F.L. (3d) 128 (Man. Q.B.). The Act gives the court the jurisdiction to convert an order for periodic support into one lump sum support.

*Lump sum awarded after payor failed to make periodic payments* — *Droit de la famille - 918*, [1990] R.J.Q. 2927 (C.S. Que.). Where, during the 20 years after the parties' divorce, the husband had paid the weekly support ordered only twice, the court allowed the wife's application for a lump sum equivalent to the husband's interest in the family home which the wife continued to occupy. Since the husband, an alcoholic, could not assist the wife in any other way, it would not have been fair if the wife were to lose the house and be forced to look to her children for support.

*Lump sum awarded after payor failed to make periodic payments and income precarious* — *Hastings v. Hastings*, 1986 CarswellMan 228, 42 Man. R. (2d) 215 (Man. Q.B.). A nominal periodic maintenance award was varied to permit a lump sum award where the husband had demonstrated an unwillness to volunteer support and his future earnings were precarious.

*Payor had not been making periodic payments but had assets and expected income* — *Rumbolt v. Rumbolt*, 1980 CarswellNfld 98, 28 Nfld. & P.E.I.R. 532, 79 A.P.R. 532 (Nfld. T.D.). A periodic award was varied to provide for a lump sum instead, where the unemployed husband had made no payments on the periodic order but was expecting insurance proceeds and owned the matrimonial home. The arrears of periodic payments owing were not affected by the lump sum award.

*Payor's failure to use best efforts to liquidate assets* — *immediate lump sum payment ordered* — *Tottrup v. Tottrup*, 1991 CarswellAlta 327, 32 R.F.L. (3d) 361, 115 A.R. 311 (Alta. C.A.). The husband had been ordered to pay periodic support, as well as lump sum support. The lump sum support was to be derived from the sale of certain assets for which the husband was to use his best efforts to sell. The wife's application to vary was allowed and an immediate lump sum ordered. The husband had not used his best efforts to dispose of the assets and had been continually delinquent in his periodic support obligations.

*No variation to lump sum from periodic payments previously agreed upon* — *Droit de la famille - 402*, [1990] R.D.F. 184 (C.A. Que.), affirming 1987 CarswellQue 489, EYB 1987-83389, [1987] R.D.F. 492 (C.S. Que.). Where the parties' agreement at the time of divorce called for periodic support, the court refused to interfere with that agreement to grant the wife's later request for a considerable lump sum.

*Payee tended to spend freely* — *Droit de la famille - 874*, 1990 CarswellQue 647, EYB 1990-57143, [1990] R.D.F. 623 (C.A. Que.). Leave to appeal refused (1991), 131 N.R. 320 (note), 40 Q.A.C. 319 (note) (S.C.C.). Where the wife had a propensity to spend freely, the court allowed the husband's appeal whereby periodic support was substituted for the earlier order of a substantial lump sum.

*Lump sum ordered to allow retraining, periodic support time-limited* — *Boucher v. Boucher*, 1991 CarswellNS 66, 36 R.F.L. (3d) 179, 108 N.S.R. (2d) 96, 294 A.P.R. 96 (N.S. Fam. Ct.). Where, after the parties' divorce, the wife had acted unreasonably in pursuing an unsuccessful real estate career, the court allowed the husband's application to vary her periodic spousal support. She was awarded a lump sum to allow her to retrain and periodic support for only 1 year further to allow her to readjust.

*Mode of payment changed to lump sum so as to bring about clean break* — *Droit de la famille - 913*, 1990 CarswellQue 49, 30 R.F.L. (3d) 83, [1990] R.D.F. 642 (C.S. Que.). Where, despite her reasonable efforts to achieve self-sufficiency, the wife had been unable to do so, her periodic support was varied to a lump sum so as to bring about a clean break between the parties.

## Variation ordered — gradual phasing out

*Step-down order — Balazsy v. Balazsy*, 2009 CarswellOnt 5982, 75 R.F.L. (6th) 315, [2009] O.J. No. 4113 (Ont. S.C.J.). The parties were married for 18 years and had 3 children. On consent, the husband paid spousal support of $750 per month. The husband's income fluctuated after the consent order was made and he brought a motion to vary. The court ordered a step-down order as follows: $650 per month for 2010, $550 per month for 2011, $450 per month for 2012, $350 per month for 2013, and $250 per month for 2014.

*Where the wife had suffered economic disadvantage arising from the breakdown of the marriage, but had received long-term support, a step down order of support was made — deJong v. deJong*, 2009 CarswellOnt 1304 (Ont. S.C.J.). When the parties separated, their four children were very young. After separation the wife looked after the children. While it was difficult for the wife to focus on her own self-improvement and financial independence while the children were young, as they grew older, she had a duty to work towards some financial independence. At the time of the hearing 18 years had passed since separation. There was no medical evidence of the wife's alleged health problems. The court held that the wife's current circumstances were related at this point neither to the marriage or to her relationship with the husband. She had received support for a reasonable amount of time for her to have moved toward economic self-sufficiency. The court made a step down order so that the wife could adjust to the concept of less support but also presumably so that she could take steps to start earning an income of her own.

*Phasing-out of payments ordered — Boucher v. Boucher*, 2006 CarswellNS 141, 2006 NSSC 88, 23 R.F.L. (6th) 432, 242 N.S.R. (2d) 286, 770 A.P.R. 286 (N.S.S.C.). The court allowed the father's application for termination of the wife's spousal support by ordering decreasing payments over a period of time. Since the parties' divorce, the children had matured and no longer required the wife's constant care and she had made no efforts towards self-sufficiency.

*Purpose of phasing out — de Gobeo v. de Gobeo*, 2005 CarswellMan 457, 2005 MBQB 261, 22 R.F.L. (6th) 228, 197 Man. R. (2d) 229, [2005] M.J. No. 441 (Man. Q.B.). Where the objectives of the *Divorce Act* may be better served by giving the spousal support payee a "softer landing" then would flow from a stark and sudden termination of support, termination after a further specified period may be appropriate.

*Phasing-out ordered because wife had failed to seek self-sufficiency — Droit de la famille - 1177*, [1988] R.D.F. 320 (C.S. Que.). Where in the 7 years subsequent to the parties' divorce the wife had made no effort to achieve self-sufficiency, the court granted the husband's application to phase out spousal support. The wife had been previously instructed by the court to seek employment and could not rely upon childcare duties as an excuse for not having done so.

*Payee's failure to seek employment justified phasing out — Deering v. Deering*, 1986 CarswellNfld 165, 60 Nfld. & P.E.I.R. 230, 181 A.P.R. 230 (Nfld. T.D.). Where the wife failed to make an effort to obtain available employment, an order was made gradually phasing out the support payable to her pursuant to the parties' decree *nisi*.

## Variation ordered — variation of lump sum awards

*Varying as yet unpaid lump sum award — Hiscock v. Hiscock*, 1987 CarswellNfld 27, 7 R.F.L. (3d) 418, 62 Nfld. & P.E.I.R. 336, 190 A.P.R. 336 (Nfld. T.D.). The court may vary a lump sum support award that has not yet been paid.

*Varying a lump sum award already paid and spent — Wyatt v. Wyatt*, 1985 CarswellNfld 25, 1 R.F.L. (3d) 252, 59 Nfld. & P.E.I.R. 124, 178 A.P.R. 124 (Nfld. T.D.). The court has jurisdiction to vary a maintenance order even after a lump sum previously awarded, has been paid and spent.

*Lump sum agreed to be paid in instalments, payor seeks to reduce amount — Connellan (Galbraith) v. Galbraith*, 1988 CarswellNS 63, 17 R.F.L. (3d) 351 (N.S. Fam. Ct.). Where the parties agreed to a lump sum payable in instalments, representing the father's past and future child support obligations, the court refused the father's application to reduce the sum. Any reduction would allow the father to bargain his way out of arrears and then, on default of the bargain, to escape responsibility for obligations he had acknowledged.

*After lump sum award, payee seeks further lump sum and periodic support — Droit de la famille - 287*, [1987] R.D.F. 37 (C.S. Que.). Where the wife had been awarded lump sum maintenance to cover future needs, her subsequent application for further periodic and lump sum maintenance was found to be *res judicata*.

## Variation ordered — variation to add lump sum awards

*New lump sum awarded to pay for retraining — causal connection found — Peckford v. Peckford*, 1989 CarswellNfld 139, 78 Nfld. & P.E.I.R. 167, 244 A.P.R. 167 (Nfld. T.D.). Where the wife was unable to find employment during the 4-year period following the parties' divorce, the husband was ordered, on a variation application, to pay a lump sum of $12,000 to the wife to permit her to retrain. A causal connection existed between the marriage and the wife's inability to find employment.

## Variation ordered — discharge of security

*Registration of an order against property does not immunize it from variation — Wiseman v. Wiseman*, 1987 CarswellBC 275, 8 R.F.L. (3d) 447, 18 B.C.L.R. (2d) 19, [1987] B.C.J. No. 1403 (B.C.S.C.). The registration of an earlier support order against property does not prevent the court from later varying support or cancelling arrears in a proceeding for divorce.

*Court would cancel judgement against matrimonial home upon payment into court of amount owed for spousal support — MacHale v. MacHale*, 1974 CarswellBC 18, 15 R.F.L. 380 (B.C.S.C.). "I would be prepared to make an order that the judgement [registered against the matrimonial home] be cancelled upon payment into Court of the sum of $20,000 which I understand to be equivalent, approximately, to the present value of the payments ordered by the decree *nisi*. If that sum is paid into Court consideration can then be given to its use for the maintenance payments," per Hutcheon L.J.S.C.

*Security interest of respondent in matrimonial home owned by applicant relevant to assessing quantum of support — Campbell, Re*, 1972 CarswellBC 47, 9 R.F.L. 323 (B.C.S.C.), at 324 [R.F.L.]. "This security, it goes without saying, is the respondent's; and the fact that the security, in addition, provided her and the children with a roof over their heads was, I think, a very real factor in assessing the quantum of money payable by the applicant for monthly maintenance," per Kirke Smith J.

*Nature of interest granted by charge on lands — Harvey v. Gould*, 1959 CarswellBC 50, 28 W.W.R. 329, 18 D.L.R. (2d) 590 (B.C.S.C.), at 332 [W.W.R.]. "What [the husband] is asking, in effect, is permission to sell what he himself describes as his "only remaining asset", the home in which his first wife and family are living, and wish to continue to live, so that the proceeds of this security can replace, for 2 years or so, his personal obligation under the maintenance order. Given this breathing space, he says, he should be in a position to make the requisite payments thereafter. These being the facts, what are the applicable legal principles? I start from the proposition that a maintenance order registered in the Land Registry Office. ... is, by its very nature, a charge on the lands until all provisions of the judgement have been fully satisfied. Such a charge is not satisfied and discharged merely by keeping payments up to date. It is a charge by way of security for future payments," per Wilson J.

### Variation ordered — support order binding payor's estate

*Payee likely to survive payor — order made binding on estate — Brickman v. Brickman*, 1987 CarswellMan 116, 8 R.F.L. (3d) 318, 51 Man. R. (2d) 6 (Man. Q.B.). Where the wife was likely to survive the husband and the husband owed a continuing obligation to the wife given the long-term traditional nature of the marriage, the support order was varied so as to be binding upon his estate.

### 10.6  Effect of Default in Payment in Variation Application

These cases pertain to the effect of default under the *Divorce Act, 1968.*

*Applicant seeking variation should have explanation for arrears — Young v. Young*, 1976 CarswellNS 18, 29 R.F.L. 391, 17 N.S.R. (2d) 375, 19 A.P.R. 375 (N.S. C.A.), at 391 [R.F.L.]. "It is the unanimous decision of this court that the respondent should either have paid the arrears or given some explanation as to why he had not done so before his application for reduction of the monthly payments was entertained", per Coffin J.A.

*Variation application not to be entertained until arrears dealt with — Gray v. Gray*, 1983 CarswellOnt 258, 32 R.F.L. (2d) 438, [1983] O.J. No. 2313 (Ont. H.C.). The court refused to entertain the husband's application for a downward variation of child maintenance until such time as accrued maintenance arrears were discharged or satisfactory arrangements to do so were made.

*Arrears forgiven due to a combination of factors — Berman v. Berman*, 1981 CarswellOnt 249, 22 R.F.L. (2d) 109 (Ont. H.C.). The court granted the husband's application to vary retroactively a decree absolute by incorporating therein the terms of the separation agreement between the parties. The husband was not required to pay the arrears accumulated to the time of his application, in view of the fact that the wife was not in urgent need, there had been a substantial change in circumstances, and both parties should have an equal right to apply for a variation.

*Variation denied because applicant was in arrears, among other reasons — Hayes v. Hayes*, 1981 CarswellNS 108, 43 N.S.R. (2d) 349, 81 A.P.R. 349 (N.S.T.D.). A husband was refused a variation in periodic payments under a decree *nisi* where he had overstated his budgetary expenses, failed to establish grounds for variation and was still in arrears on the original order.

*Applicant must demonstrate good faith before variation can be considered — Carter v. Carter*, 1977 CarswellOnt 178, 4 R.F.L. (2d) 396 (Ont. H.C.), at 400. "I think that the *Parkinson* decision [1973 CarswellOnt 124, [1973] 3 O.R. 293, 11 R.F.L. 128, 36 D.L.R. (3d) 521 (Ont. C.A.)] is also authority for the proposition that the matter of varying the existing quantum of support should not be entertained until such time as the respondent Mr. Carter had demonstrated to the court that he is acting in good faith, and that can be demonstrated by payment of the arrears which are presently outstanding", per McDermid L.J.S.C.

*Party witholding support for tactical reasons — Baker v. Baker*, 1975 CarswellOnt 272, 25 R.F.L. 328 (Ont. H.C.), at 331 [R.F.L.]. "I think it is also relevant that the applicant husband was two months in arrears in his alimony payments on the date on which the motion was argued. His resources clearly were such that he could have continued to make the alimony payments while the motion was pending and I can only infer that he chose to put economic pressure on the respondent by ignoring his obligations under the decree *nisi*, in hopes that she would thereby be compelled to agree to a settlement under which the alimony payments would be reduced. The court is most reluctant to grant relief to an applicant who will resort to such tactics and will scrutinize his claim with great care," per Southey J.

## 10.7 Retroactive Variation of Support Orders

### 10.7.1 General

See also Volume 3, Chapter 7, section 7.1.1 Retroactive Spousal Support and Chapter 19A Retroactive Support and the SSAG.

The *Divorce Act* explicitly provides for a retroactive variation of a support order:

**17.** (1) A Court of competent jurisdiction may make an order varying, rescinding or suspending, prospectively or retroactively,

(a) a support order or any provision thereof on application by either or both former spouses: *Divorce Act*, s. 17(1)(a).

*Relevant factors — Marinangeli v. Marinangeli*, 2003 CarswellOnt 2691, 38 R.F.L. (5th) 307, 66 O.R. (3d) 40, 228 D.L.R. (4th) 376, 174 O.A.C. 76, [2003] O.J. No. 2819 (Ont. C.A.). In *Marinangeli*, the Court of Appeal sets out the criteria for making or declining to make an award of retroactive support, quoting from Rowles J.A. in *S. (L.) v. P. (E.)*, 1999 CarswellBC 1402, 1999 BCCA 393, 50 R.F.L. (4th) 302, 67 B.C.L.R. (3d) 254, 175 D.L.R. (4th) 423, [1999] 12 W.W.R. 718, 126 B.C.A.C. 28, 206 W.A.C. 28, [1999] B.C.J. No. 1451 (B.C.C.A.). While these criteria in the *L.S. v. E.P.* decision were applied only to child support orders, Weiler J.A., in the *Marinangeli* case, stated that they apply both to child and spousal support orders. The court also emphasized that the decision to award retroactive support should be exercised sparingly. Rowles J.A. states:

[66] A review of the case law reveals that there are a number of factors which have been regarded as significant in determining whether to order or not to order retroactive child maintenance. Factors militating in favour of ordering retroactive maintenance include. (1) the need on the part of the child and a corresponding ability to pay on the part of the non-custodial parent; (2) some blameworthy conduct on the part of the non-custodial parent such as incomplete or misleading financial disclosure at the time of the original order; (3) necessity on the part of the custodial parent to encroach on his or her capital or incur debt to meet child rearing expenses; (4) an excuse for a delay in bringing the application where the delay is significant; and (5) notice to the non-custodial parent of an intention to pursue maintenance followed by negotiations to that end.

Factors which have militated against ordering retroactive maintenance include: (1) the order would cause an unreasonable or unfair burden to the non-custodial parent, especially to the extent that such a burden would interfere with ongoing support obligations; (2) the only purpose of the award would be to redistribute capital or award spousal support in the guise of child support; and (3) a significant, unexplained delay in bringing the application.

*It was open to a court to characterize voluntary support payments as retroactive support payments* — *Hughes v. Hughes*, 2009 CarswellAlta 1309, 2009 ABCA 282, 68 R.F.L. (6th) 134, 11 Alta. L.R. (5th) 115 (Alta. C.A.). The case management judge had the jurisdiction to make this characterization because the status of the voluntary payments was never determined.

*When retroactive variation is appropriate* — *Andries v. Andries*, 1998 CarswellMan 180, 36 R.F.L. (4th) 175, 159 D.L.R. (4th) 665, [1998] 7 W.W.R. 536, 126 Man. R. (2d) 189, 167 W.A.C. 189, [1998] M.J. No. 196 (Man. C.A.). Retroactive support should only be ordered in special or exceptional circumstances.

*When retroactive variation is appropriate* — *Trick v. Trick*, 2003 CarswellOnt 1103, 39 R.F.L. (5th) 418, [2003] O.J. No. 1263 (Ont. S.C.J.). Retroactive support should only be ordered in special or exceptional circumstances.

*Exceptional circumstances required* — *Colbert v. Andersen*, 2003 CarswellMan 29, 2003 MBQB 13, 171 Man. R. (2d) 97 (Man. Q.B.). Retroactive variation orders, whether they impose new obligations or grant relief from old obligations, are inherently unfair and should only be made where exceptional circumstances are shown to exist. In this case, where arrears under a support order had accumulated over a number of years, fairness to the payor required that the order be varied with respect to 2 years when his income was far less than the support to be paid.

*Evidence required supporting motion for retroactive variation of support* — *no income evidence provided* — *onus not discharged* — *Pratt v. Pratt*, 2008 CarswellNB 116, 2008 NBQB 94, 334 N.B.R. (2d) 22, 858 A.P.R. 22, [2008] N.B.J. No. 85 (N.B.Q.B.). In *Pratt v. Pratt* (see above, s. **10.3.3**), the court was not satisfied that a retroactive variation order was justified. The court found that the husband had not discharged the onus to support his motion for a retroactive variation of support, primarily because he had not provided sufficient evidence that his income during the time period from March 2003 (the date of the accident which rendered him disabled) to July 1, 2007 was different from that when support was initially ordered in 1998.

*Fivefold increase in payor income did not justify retroactive variation* — *Scott v. Scott*, 2004 CarswellNB 587, 2004 CarswellNB 588, 2004 NBCA 99, 10 R.F.L. (6th) 135, 278 N.B.R. (2d) 61, 728 A.P.R. 61, [2004] N.B.J. No. 468 (N.B.C.A.). Notwithstanding the substantial increase in the husband's income from $50,000 at the time of separation to an average of $258,966 in the 3 years prior to trial, the appellate court held that "while there was some evidence in the ... case which might have justified the exercise of discretion in favour of a retroactive variation, and while it would have been helpful to have the benefit of the motions judge's reasons for refusing a retroactive award, [it was] unable to conclude that the refusal was the result of either a palpable and overriding error in the motions judge's findings or an error in principle. Considering the deference owed to the motions judge, [it] would not interfere with the manner in which she exercised her discretion".

*Payee's cohabitation justifies retroactive termination* — *Redpath v. Redpath*, 2008 CarswellBC 72, 2008 BCSC 68, 48 R.F.L. (6th) 373, 79 B.C.L.R. (4th) 137, [2008] 10 W.W.R. 362, [2008] B.C.J. No. 68 (B.C.S.C. [In Chambers]). The court allowed the husband's application to terminate the wife's spousal support retroactively back to the date she had begun to cohabitate with her new husband. The wife's remarriage had not been anticipated at the date of the original order and her cohabitation with her new husband, who enjoyed a very healthy income, constituted "a change in circumstances".

*Original order based on incorrect facts* — *arrears cancelled* — *Eulenhaupt v. Eulenhaupt*, 2008 CarswellOnt 5308 (Ont. S.C.J.). At the time of the initial spousal support order in 1995, the husband did not appear at the trial. The court found that he had been mentally ill and unemployed at the time, and that the wife knew these facts, but allowed the support order to be made based on his previous income. Over the next 13 years, $75,000 was garnished from the husband's disability pension and paid to the wife. This would have left $130,000 in arrears under the original order, but after concluding that the original order was based on incorrect facts and considering what an appropriate order might have been, the court rescinded all these arrears.

*Relevance of non-disclosure — Fotheringham v. Fotheringham*, 2004 CarswellOnt 67, 2 R.F.L. (6th) 288 (Ont. S.C.J.). If the evidence established a finding of incomplete or misleading financial disclosure on the part of either or both parties, but such a finding would not be determinative of the case, the court would not order retroactive variation of the interim support orders in question.

*Payee in need but payor unable to pay more — Fraser v. Fraser*, 2004 CarswellOnt 3343, 8 R.F.L. (6th) 125 (Ont. S.C.J.). Where the husband who suffered from leukemia and was unable to work because of his ill health had need that was not addressed by spousal support payable by the wife, his claim for retro active variation of spousal support was dismissed where the wife did not have sufficient income to look after his need.

*Where making termination retroactive would force sale of RRSPs — E. (R.G.) v. B. (J.)*, 2004 CarswellQue 1358, REJB 2004-61349, [2004] R.D.F. 461 (C.S. Que.). Support payable to the wife was terminated in the circumstances, but the termination was not made retroactive since a retroactive variation (and an obligation to repay an amount to the husband) would force her to sell RRSPs which would reduce one of her future sources of income at retirement.

*Retroactivity denied where payor's income had remained steady — Kumar (Litigation Guardian of) v. McKenna*, 2003 CarswellOnt 5450, [2003] O.J. No. 5473 (Ont. S.C.J.), additional reasons at 2004 CarswellOnt 842, [2004] O.J. No. 799 (Ont. S.C.J.). The court held that there was no basis for retroactive variation of spousal support as the husband's income had varied very little over the years, but generally had remained in the $30,000 range.

*Party who had unjustifiably terminated support payments ordered to pay interest on arrears — Lawson v. Lawson*, 2004 CarswellAlta 780, 2004 ABQB 415, 7 R.F.L. (6th) 72 (Alta. Q.B.), additional reasons at 2004 CarswellAlta 1867, 2004 ABQB 922, 11 R.F.L. (6th) 273, 366 A.R. 5, [2004] A.J. No. 693 (Alta. Q.B.), reversed 2005 CarswellAlta 1005, 2005 ABCA 253, 19 R.F.L. (6th) 81, 48 Alta. L.R. (4th) 224, [2006] 1 W.W.R. 241, [2005] A.J. No. 905 (Alta. C.A.). A husband with substantial assets who unilaterally terminated spousal support requiring the wife to borrow funds to maintain the standard of living for the children was ordered to pay interest on a relatively small amount of spousal support arrears at a credit card rate of 18% per year.

*Retroactive increase ordered despite payee's improving finances — Fitzgerald v. Gerlich*, 2003 CarswellOnt 1816, 40 R.F.L. (5th) 84, [2003] O.T.C. 425, [2003] O.J. No. 1946 (Ont. S.C.J.). The former husband sought, among other things, a review and variation of the provisions for spousal support contained in a separation agreement which he had entered into with his former spouse. The husband had unilaterally reduced spousal support from $1,750 per month as set out in the agreement to $1,000 per month. Under the agreement, support provisions were subject to variation in the event of a material change in circumstances. The agreement also provided for a review of support after the wife had completed her education. The husband sought to reduce the wife's spousal support to $250 per month from May 2001 and to cease making payments in June 2005. According to the separation agreement, either party was entitled to a review of support after April 2001, and the husband argued that he was entitled to a variation of support based on his former wife's changes in circumstances, her remarriage and her move from Ontario to British Columbia. The court imputed an annual income to the former wife from September 2001 forward of $25,000 annually after the completion of her course and her move to British Columbia. It ordered an increase in child support over the amount stipulated in the agreement, noting that under the *Child Support Guidelines* child support must be given precedence to spousal support, and it retroactively varied spousal support providing the wife with

$400 per month until May 2003, after which she was entitled to $600 per month, as the husband was no longer required to pay child support for one of the parties' children. The former wife's financial circumstances improved in 2001 and 2002 but she suffered economic disadvantages that flowed from her role in the family. The former husband's income increased; he had stable secure employment, and he was sharing expenses with a partner who earned as much as he did. The court held that the termination of spousal support was not consistent with objectives under the *Divorce Act*.

*Payee's need plus payor's wealth and duplicitousness justify retroactive increase — Trick v. Trick*, 2003 CarswellOnt 1103, 39 R.F.L. (5th) 418, [2003] O.J. No. 1263 (Ont. S.C.J.). The court held that there were in this case special and exceptional circumstances which justified a retroactive order of spousal support. The husband did not disclose to the wife the dramatic increase in his income which occurred shortly after the execution of the parties' separation agreement. The wife delayed in pursuing her claim for increased support but did not know the extent of the husband's improved financial circumstances. In order to live, the applicant had completely depleted the capital she received on separation and had borrowed money from friends and family for living expenses and to provide a decent place to live for herself and her children. As the court found that the husband had misled the court throughout in the proceedings regarding his financial position, and had failed to inform his former wife of his improved financial circumstances, at trial the court found that he had financial resources and was able to make up the proper financial support for his former wife and children to make their lives reasonably comfortable. The fact that his new wife was the sole titled owner of their home, despite his significant financial contributions over the years to the equity in the home, constituted a transfer made with the intention of defeating the support claims of his former wife. The change in the method of holding title, while these proceedings were pending, was clearly an attempt to put his assets out of the first wife's reach in the event that she secured a judgement for retroactive support. The court imputed a current and prospective income of $120,000 (Can.) to him, which included the $31,000 (Can.) pension. Having regard to all of the factors and objectives noted in s. 15.2 of the *Divorce Act*, the court ordered that the husband pay the sum of $800 per month towards the wife's spousal support for a period of 3 years or until the entire retroactive child and spousal support had been paid, whichever was sooner.

*Payor's conduct not such as to justify retroactivity — Harder v. Harder*, 2001 CarswellBC 1811, 2001 BCSC 919 (B.C.S.C.). The court rejected the wife's argument that the court should make an order increasing the quantum of support retroactive to the time of an interim support hearing on the ground that, at that time, the defendant misled the court and understated his income when he applied to reduce the quantum of support. It held that at the time of the hearing the defendant provided his most current income information including a recent pay stub that clearly indicated some overtime. The court was not satisfied the defendant intentionally misled the court, nor was it satisfied that the circumstances established a degree of misconduct on the part of the defendant that would justify a retroactive variation of the amount of support that was ordered on an interim basis.

*Payor's income increases and failure to pay support balanced against payee's delay and fact that children had moved out — Mosher v. Mosher*, 1999 CarswellNS 182, 47 R.F.L. (4th) 445, 177 N.S.R. (2d) 236, 542 A.P.R. 236, [1999] N.S.J. No. 202 (N.S.S.C.). Where the husband had received huge increases in income since the granting of the corollary relief judgement which was subsequently approved by the Court of Appeal, and consequently he received a large benefit by paying less child and spousal support than he would otherwise have been required to pay, the court ordered a retroactive adjustment by way of a lump sum spousal support order. The court estimated that the husband had received a $100,000 advantage as a result of paying inadequate child support that effected the wife's spousal support, some of which she used to assist the children. The court awarded the wife $50,000, after taking into account the wife's delay in pursuing the matter and the fact that none of the children at the time of the hearing lived with their mother.

*Payee ordered to make partial repayment* — *Brown v. Brown*, 1999 CarswellOnt 2245, 2 R.F.L. (5th) 65, 45 O.R. (3d) 308, [1999] O.J. No. 2713 (Ont. S.C.J.). A support order may be varied retroactively where circumstances do not transpire as anticipated at the time of the order. The husband's income was reduced to $66,000 a year when he returned to Canada from Saudi Arabia where he earned $200,000 a year tax-free. This was a material change in circumstances that was not forseeable entitling him to a reduction in the support obligation of $3,500 a month he had agreed to in divorce proceedings. Support was reduced to $1,250 a month giving the parties equivalent standards of living. The reduction was retroactive for a period of 15 months which would require the wife to repay $33,750. But on a basis of the competing needs and equities of the parties, it would be unfair to require a repayment in this amount. The wife was ordered to repay $17,000, the amount she had saved in this period.

## 10.7.2 Retroactive Variation of Support Orders — Arrears

In s. 17(1) of the Act, the explicit power to vary support orders retroactively confirms the right to have arrears as well as ongoing future payments adjusted to meet changed circumstances.

*Retroactive variation orders, including those that cancel arrears of spousal support, must be based on a material change in circumstances during the period of retroactivity and do not involve a fault-based analysis* — *failure by the recipient spouse to enforce her rights is not a sufficient basis for cancelling the arrears* — *Brown v. Brown*, 2010 CarswellNB 30, 2010 CarswellNB 31, 2010 NBCA 5, 76 R.F.L. (6th) 33, 315 D.L.R. (4th) 293, 353 N.B.R. (2d) 323, 910 A.P.R. 323, [2010] N.B.J. No. 18 (N.B.C.A.). The court does not have a residual discretion to forgive arrears based on hardship. Arrears of more than $100,000 in child and spousal support were found to be payable.

*Jurisdiction to cancel arrears under Divorce Act* — *Lewis v. Lewis*, 1999 CarswellBC 2468, 2 R.F.L. (5th) 417 (B.C.S.C.). The "rule against hoarding" should be considered along with the provisions of s. 17 of the *Divorce Act*, and in this context the court may exercise its discretion and not enforce arrears of over 1 year. Section 17, although not specifically mentioning the right to cancel arrears, should be approached in the same way as provincial legislation, which expressly grants this right. The parties entered into a separation agreement and had the support provision incorporated in their divorce judgement. At a time when the obligation was to pay $500 a month, the former husband unilaterally reduced his payments to $250 a month. Eleven years later he applied to cancel the arrears under the judgement which were in excess of $34,000, and to vary retroactively the support order to $250 a month. In the meantime, he had remarried and both he and his second wife had retired. He had a retirement income and some registered retirement savings plans. His former wife had sold her home, used the proceeds for her living expenses until they ran out, and then relied on social assistance. In dismissing the former husband's application, the court exercised its discretion and enforced payment of the arrears for a 10-year period, the parties having agreed that by reason of the *Limitation Act* arrears of spousal support over 10 years cannot be collected. The former wife was not hoarding because she was emotionally incapable of confronting her former husband about the default. Although this lack of dissent and her subsequent silence induced the husband to believe he would not be required to pay and was free to plan his retirement accordingly, the prejudice involved was offset by the fact that his substantially superior financial position was based in part upon the financial deprivation that she suffered. The recovery of arrears is important not only to compensate the payee for what was improperly withheld, but also to demonstrate that the orders of the court are to be obeyed. The arrears were fixed at $30,000 for the 10 years payable with interest under the *Court Order Interest Act.*

*Onus is on party seeking cancellation of arrears* — *Weinstein v. Weinstein*, 1994 CarswellBC 37, 8 R.F.L. (4th) 354, 1 B.C.L.R. (3d) 174 (B.C.S.C.), reversed 1995 CarswellBC 304, 15 R.F.L. (4th) 353, 8 B.C.L.R. (3d) 23, 61 B.C.A.C. 314, 100 W.A.C. 314 (B.C.C.A.). "[T]he onus is on the applicant to show that it would be grossly unfair for his or her application not to be granted. Furthermore, when determining whether refusal of the order would be grossly unfair, the court is directed to focus on the reasons why the applicant did not comply with or seek variation of the order, with further provision for the court to consider any 'special circumstances.' Except in the case of special circumstances then, the statute focuses on the circumstances of the applicant, not the circumstances of the recipient," per Boyd J.

*Threshold for cancellation of arrears* — *Fetterley v. Fetterley*, 1988 CarswellAlta 331, 14 R.F.L. (3d) 47, 89 A.R. 350 (Alta. Q.B.), affirmed 1989 CarswellAlta 396, 24 R.F.L. (3d) 61, 102 A.R. 131, [1989] A.J. No. 1185 (Alta. C.A.). If respect for a negotiated final support settlement is to be given full accord and the support payments thereunder are to be sustained, then, absent delay amounting to *laches*, the arrears of such payments should be left intact and should not be subject to reduction or cancellation.

*Having difficulty paying is insufficient to justify cancellation* — *Newton v. Newton*, 2003 CarswellBC 497, 2003 BCSC 333, 37 R.F.L. (5th) 391, [2003] B.C.J. No. 551 (B.C.S.C.). The fact that the husband found that paying required spousal support was "difficult" did not meet the heavy burden required for the cancellation of support arrears.

*Arrears reduced but ordered to be paid in lump sum from RRSP* — *Miller v. Miller*, 2001 CarswellNS 54, 2001 NSCA 31, 14 R.F.L. (5th) 139, 196 D.L.R. (4th) 689, 193 N.S.R. (2d) 371, 602 A.P.R. 371 (N.S.C.A.). In *Miller*, the appellate court allowed the wife's appeal of an order which had forgiven the husband's payment of arrears of spousal support. At the time that the arrears accrued, the husband had an obligation to make payments and had the ability to do so. The fact that paying the arrears in monthly periodic payments would make it difficult for the husband to pay spousal support from the time of the hearing forward, was not a valid reason for completely forgiving the arrears. While he did not have sufficient employment income to pay a lump sum of $5,500 owing in arrears, he had an RRSP which could be cashed in and he could thereby make a significant payment on the arrears. The wife had a need for support. The court held that the husband was required to pay the sum of $3,000 in full satisfaction of arrears of $5,500 of spousal support.

*Arrears cancelled as of day payor became unable to pay* — *Klassen v. Klassen*, 1993 CarswellMan 34, 44 R.F.L. (3d) 433, 83 Man. R. (2d) 214, 36 W.A.C. 214 (Man. C.A.). Where the payor's inability to pay spousal support was found to predate a debilitating injury, arrears were properly remitted back to the date of the inability to pay and not merely back to the date of the injury.

*Partial arrears cancellation* — *only back to date of unemployment* — *Galan v. Galan*, 1990 CarswellMan 37, 25 R.F.L. (3d) 225, 64 Man. R. (2d) 203, 66 D.L.R. (4th) 259, [1990] M.J. No. 57 (Man. C.A.). Where the husband was unemployed and accordingly unable to pay support arrears owing, he was nevertheless not totally relieved of the obligation for the arrears. He had not made payments when he had been financially able to do so and accordingly a total cancellation of arrears would be unfair.

*Reduction of arrears made contingent on ongoing payment* — *Greco v. Greco*, 2000 CarswellOnt 3431, 11 R.F.L. (5th) 109 (Ont. S.C.J.). The court ordered both the spousal and child support arrears owing by the husband to be substantially reduced, provided that the husband regularly paid the amount of on-going support specified.

*Arrears partially cancelled — payor unemployed while payee's position had improved —* *Seon v. Molgat,* 1993 CarswellMan 286, 89 Man. R. (2d) 317 (Man. Q.B.). After the parties separated in 1988, the father had been paying $600 per month in child support, which fell into arrears. Under a consent variation order in 1990, the parties agreed to set arrears at $6,500 and child support at $300 per month for 1 year. The father failed to pay as agreed and he was currently unemployed. The father had entered a new relationship in 1988 and had two additional children. His new partner was employed and supporting him. The mother alleged that the father had unreported business income. The mother relied on her parents and had taken out $10,000 in loans. The mother had attended law school and had recently found employment as a lawyer. The father brought a motion to have child support reduced and arrears remitted. The court held it was equitable and just to remit all arrears, except for the $6,500 under the consent order, considering the father's situation, particularly both parties' continued expectation of him being able to pay, and the mother's improved prospects. The arrears under the 1990 consent order were the subject of an agreement between the parties which the court was not to vary. Payment on the arrears was ordered at $50 per month. Having considered the respective incomes of the parties, the court set ongoing child support at $200 per month.

*Payor who sought to evade obligations — Johnson v. Johnson,* 1995 CarswellBC 858, 66 B.C.A.C. 239, 108 W.A.C. 239 (B.C.C.A.). Where the husband had transferred his assets into the name of a third party, ceased paying spousal support and went to live abroad, the court refused his application to discharge the spousal support arrears owing. The husband's actions were designed to defeat the wife's claims and it would be inequitable and morally repugnant to cancel the arrears.

*Where no good reason for interruption of payments — Québec (Procureur général) c.* *Champagne,* 1992 CarswellQue 2288 (C.A. Que.). Where the husband had, without a good reason, unilaterally stopped paying spousal support, the annulment of the arrears was reversed on appeal.

*Arrears cancelled due to inability to pay — August v. August,* 1989 CarswellMan 43, 21 R.F.L. (3d) 1, 58 D.L.R. (4th) 459, 57 Man. R. (2d) 128, [1989] M.J. No. 184 (Man. C.A.). The terms of the variation order made by the trial judge reduced the arrears of $79,000 to $22,000 upon the transfer by the husband of his interest in the family home to the wife. The Court of Appeal, in allowing the appeal and rescinding the arrears, held that the provisions of the variation order were not supported by the evidence and that the terms were beyond the husband's means and abilities to meet.

*Variation of arrears accruing from provincial support order — jurisdiction — August v.* *August, supra.* Arrears accruing under a support order made pursuant to provincial legislation are beyond the court's discretion on a variation application brought under s. 17 of the *Divorce Act.*

*Having paid matrimonial home expenses without being ordered to is not a substitute for* *making payments as ordered — Kumar (Litigation Guardian of) v. McKenna,* 2003 CarswellOnt 5450, [2003] O.J. No. 5473 (Ont. S.C.J.), additional reasons at 2004 CarswellOnt 842, [2004] O.J. No. 799 (Ont. S.C.J.). The court rejected the Public Guardian and Trustee's argument to forgive the support arrears owed by the husband as, at the time in question, the husband had the ability to pay and no compelling reason not to do so. Despite an ability to pay, the husband, almost from the beginning, failed to provide the support as ordered. His conduct resulted in his wife's inability to sell the matrimonial home which tied her to a house which she could not afford. When the Public Guardian and Trustee took control of the husband's affairs, it determined that his estate could not afford to pay global support but continued to pay for expenses in relation to the matrimonial home, expenses which had not been ordered to be paid. The court rejected the Public Guardian and Trustee's request that these expenses be considered support and applied against arrears. The wife was in need of support during these years, circumstances which the husband and his representatives were in a position to alleviate. The claim to forgive arrears was dismissed.

*Onus on application to cancel arrears – Plett v. Plett*, 2002 CarswellBC 2083, 2002 BCSC 1308, [2002] B.C.J. No. 2078 (B.C.S.C. [In Chambers]). An application to cancel arrears under a support order made after a divorce has been granted is an application to vary, rescind or suspend the order under s. 17 of the *Divorce Act*. Under this section, the onus is on the payor to show that a material change of circumstances has occurred, which is a change that, if known at the time of the original order, would likely have resulted in different terms. In the case, no such change of circumstances was found.

*Adoption of parties' child by mother's new fiancé might justify cancellation of spousal support arrears – Thompson v. Dorn*, 2000 CarswellBC 334, 2000 BCSC 265, [2000] B.C.J. No. 315 (B.C. Master). The Master, in an *obiter* remark, stated that if the child were adopted by the mother's fiancé with the father's consent, it might be appropriate for the father to apply to cancel all his arrears of spousal maintenance. He would then be in a better position to support his new family. With the prospect of such an arrangement, the Master suspended the enforcement of payment of arrears of spousal support for 6 months, after which they would become payable at $500 per month. The total amount of arrears was $8,387. The father had had little contact with the child after the separation. The child was just over 3 years of age and the mother's fiancé was prepared to adopt her.

*Insufficient payor income justifies cancellation of arrears – Balaski v. Balaski*, 1999 CarswellSask 250, 45 R.F.L. (4th) 114, 178 Sask. R. 313, [1999] S.J. No. 259 (Sask. Q.B.). Where the payor's income was insufficient to sustain spousal support obligations, arrears were extinguished.

*Heart attack 13 years beforehand, plus failure of payee to enforce, justified cancellation of arrears accumulated since that date – Fawcett v. Fawcett*, 1995 CarswellBC 1178, 18 R.F.L. (4th) 450 (B.C.S.C.). Where the husband had suffered a heart attack in 1982 and had advised the wife of his inability to pay her spousal support as ordered, the court allowed the husband's 1995 application to rescind all arrears and terminate the order. The wife had never attempted in 13 years to enforce the order and the husband's heart attack, had a variation been sought at the time, would have constituted a change in circumstances.

*Payor who paid legal fees and whose finances improved held responsible for arrears – Duncan v. Duncan*, 1994 CarswellSask 560, 117 Sask. R. 274 (Sask. Q.B.). The parties were married in 1984 and separated in 1989. There were three children of the marriage and one child of the wife's prior to the marriage. The husband was a farmer whose income had increased over the past 3 years. Spousal and child support were ordered following divorce proceedings, but the husband accumulated $8,400 in arrears, although paying legal expenses of $20,000. The husband's application to extinguish payment of arrears was refused. Given the husband's payment of legal fees over his support obligations, and in view of his vastly improved financial situation, there was no justification for extinguishing the arrears.

*Reduction in employment income mala fides therefore arrears not cancelled – Irvine v. Irvine*, 1990 CarswellMan 49, 27 R.F.L. (3d) 199, 67 Man. R. (2d) 205, [1990] M.J. No. 392 (Man. Q.B.). Where the husband had quit his employment and later accepted a lower-paying job in an effort to undermine his wife's and children's support entitlement, his application to cancel arrears and spousal support and reduce child support was dismissed. Any change in the husband's circumstances was self-induced and *mala fides*.

*Arrears not cancelled where need and means to pay had continued to exist – Nykoliation v. Nykoliation*, 1989 CarswellMan 287, 60 Man. R. (2d) 307 (Man. Q.B.). Where the husband had met his support obligations for only 1 year out of the 7 since the parties' divorce, his application to vary support and cancel arrears was dismissed. The wife and the two children in her care were living near the poverty level while the husband enjoyed substantial cash flow from farming.

*Impossibility of payor paying both arrears and ongoing support* — *Tremblett v. Tremblett*, 1988 CarswellNfld 251, 75 Nfld. & P.E.I.R. 175, 234 A.P.R. 175 (Nfld. U.F.C.). The enforcement order must be one which the payor is able to perform. Thus, the payor should not be put in a position where it would be impossible to meet his obligations in respect of ongoing maintenance as well as the arrears.

*Impossibility of payor paying both arrears and ongoing support* — *Grimwood v. Grimwood*, 1988 CarswellSask 487, 68 Sask. R. 179 (Sask. Q.B.). The enforcement order must be one which the payor is able to perform. Thus, the payor should not be put in a position where it would be impossible to meet his obligations in respect of ongoing maintenance as well as the arrears.

*After many years of uncontested partial payment, enforcement of arrears denied* — *Seward v. Seward*, 1988 CarswellNS 35, 12 R.F.L. (3d) 54, 85 N.S.R. (2d) 30, 216 A.P.R. 30 (N.S. Fam. Ct.). Where the wife had for many years accepted less support than that specified in the divorce decree, the court allowed the husband's application for an order rescinding the arrears. The wife had not incurred debt from not receiving the arrears and to allow enforcement would constitute a windfall.

*Powers of court* — *Englar v. Englar*, 1978 CarswellOnt 225, 2 R.F.L. (2d) 237, 19 O.R. (2d) 561, 85 D.L.R. (3d) 609 (Ont. C.A.), at 247 [R.F.L.]. The court has power to cancel or reduce arrears of maintenance ordered to be paid under a decree *nisi* and, where necessary, to give directions as to how the remaining arrears shall be paid.

*Case with review of authorities prior to 1976* — *R. v. MacDonald*, 1976 CarswellOnt 146, 26 R.F.L. 204, 14 O.R. (2d) 409, 74 D.L.R. (3d) 57 (Ont. H.C.). This case offers a thorough review of the authorities dealing with the variation of maintenance arrears.

## 10.7.3 Delay Inducing Belief Arrears Would not be Enforced

In cases where spousal support arrears have accumulated over time, the law will in some cases limit the ability of the payee to enforce the debt. In these cases it is said that the payee's delay in seeking enforcement constituted "waiver" or "acquiescence," that the defense of *laches* is made out, or that a policy against "hoarding" support prevents enforcement. The passage of time has been used as a defense even if nothing happened during that time to affect the payor's ability to pay or the payee's need. However, in many cases, the parties' circumstances are found to have changed during the period as well. An explanation by the payee for her delay in seeking enforcement is naturally helpful to her cause. It may also be relevant evidence that she has been forced into debt or, conversely, been able to balance her budget despite the failure to pay.

Judges seeking a compromise reaction to delay can enforce some, but not all, of the arrears. Courts occasionally enforce a "one-year rule," whereby arrears more than a year old are not enforced. This position was especially prevalent in the 1970's and 80's. However, this "rule" has now been explicitly renounced by several courts and is inconsistent with limitations statutes in a number of jurisdictions. Delay is much less likely to impede enforcement of child support arrears than it is of spousal support arrears. (See *Canadian Divorce Law and Practice*, Volume 1, s. 17§65.)

Judges will sometimes waive arrears due to enforcement delay on the grounds that the payor has been lulled into believing that he would not have to pay. In other cases, it is observed that a debt for the entire amount of the arrears would have no chance of being paid. A more questionable rationale which sometimes appears is that if the payee did not pursue enforcement during a given period then she must not have really needed the money. If she did not really need it, then she should not be entitled to collect it. There are two grave flaws in this reasoning. Firstly, after the Supreme Court of Canada decisions in *Moge* and *Bracklow*, it is clear that spousal support can serve a compensatory purpose. To the extent that an ex-spouse has been awarded support in order to account for sacrifices made during the relationship, the extent to which she "needs" the money is irrelevant. Secondly, the practical barriers to seeking enforcement are often formidable. These barriers include the cost of litigation in time and money and, in some cases, the payee's justifiable reluctance to confront an abusive payor in court. A payor who intimidates a payee into foregoing enforcement for a certain period should not thereby escape the debt, and it would seem that a payee who takes time to overcome systemic barriers to enforcement it would seem should not be punished.

*Test for cancelling arrears under British Columbia's* Family Relations Act — *C. (L.K.) v. C. (M.I.)*, 1993 CarswellBC 46, 44 R.F.L. (3d) 229, 77 B.C.L.R. (2d) 52, 100 D.L.R. (4th) 68, 22 B.C.A.C. 53, 38 W.A.C. 53, [1993] B.C.J. No. 155 (B.C.C.A.). In British Columbia, when an application is brought under the *Family Relations Act* for an order cancelling arrears of maintenance, the court may do so "only if it is satisfied that it would be grossly unfair not to do so" (now s. 96(2)).

*Test for cancelling arrears under Manitoba* Family Maintenance Act — *Galan v. Galan*, 1990 CarswellMan 37, 25 R.F.L. (3d) 225, 66 D.L.R. (4th) 259, 64 Man. R. (2d) 203, [1990] M.J. No. 57 (Man. C.A.). Where a payor seeks relief from an obligation to pay arrears of support which have accumulated under an order made pursuant to the provisions of the Manitoba *Family Maintenance Act*, R.S.M. 1987, c. F.20, the applicable section is s. 61(4) of that Act rather than s. 54 of the *Court of Queen's Bench Act*, S.M. 1988-89, c. 4. Subsection 61(4) of the *Family Maintenance Act* sets out a two-pronged test for the court to apply in determining whether a payor should be relieved from having to pay all or some of the arrears. Under the first branch of the test in s. 61(4), a court must be satisfied that, having regard to the interests of the payor or the payor's estate, it would be grossly unfair and inequitable not to rescind or reduce the arrears. If, and only if, the court is satisfied that the first branch of the test has been met is it then required to consider the second branch of the test in s. 61(4) of the Act. Under the second branch of the test, the court must determine whether rescission or reduction of arrears is justified, having regard to the "interests of the person entitled to the payments or the estate of that person." In the case at bar, there had been no formal assignment of the support order by the wife to the Director, and words "interests of the person" in s. 61(4)(b) referred to the wife's interest and not to the Director's.

*Enforcing a judgement for arrears under provincial legislation in Saskatchewan* — *Jungaro v. Wannamaker*, 1990 CarswellSask 63, 26 R.F.L. (3d) 292, 84 Sask. R. 64, 68 D.L.R. (4th) 636 (Sask. C.A.), varying 1989 CarswellSask 78, 23 R.F.L. (3d) 50, 63 D.L.R. (4th) 497, 79 Sask. R. 56 (Sask. Q.B.). Section 53 of the *Enforcement of Maintenance Orders Act* applies to "final" foreign orders registered in Saskatchewan for the purposes of enforcement under the *Reciprocal Enforcement of Maintenance Orders Act*, S.S. 1983, c. R-4.1.

*Jurisdictional issues regarding 1-year rule* — *August v. August*, 1989 CarswellMan 43, 21 R.F.L. (3d) 1, 58 D.L.R. (4th) 459, 57 Man. R. (2d) 128, [1989] M.J. No. 184 (Man. C.A.). The disinclination of the court in the *Remillard* case to apply the "1-year rule" to "federal arrears" was questioned in *August v. August*. Philp J.A. (Monnin C.J.M. concurring) expressed the view at p. 11 [R.F.L.] that although the "1-year rule" was a development of the common law, "its abrogation ought to be found in direct statutory enactment, if for no other reason than the fact that the [*Divorce Act*] is national in its application." The court further stated that it was beyond the jurisdiction of a provincial superior court to say that the broad discretion permitted under the *Divorce Act* was to be restricted in that particular province.

*1-year rule still applicable in 1989* — *August v. August, supra.* It was held that the "1-year rule" was still applicable to variation proceedings under the *Divorce Act.*

*1-year rule a guide but not a rule of law* — *Lake v. Lake,* 1988 CarswellNS 34, 11 R.F.L. (3d) 234, 82 N.S.R. (2d) 357, 207 A.P.R. 357, [1988] N.S.J. No. 23 (N.S.C.A.). The Nova Scotia Supreme Court (Appeal Division) held that the "1-year rule" was not a rule of law and should be considered merely as a guide.

*Practice in 1978* — *1-year cap on arrears enforcement* — *Septon v. Septon,* 1978 CarswellMan 12, 3 R.F.L. (2d) 26 (Man. C.A.). The court has jurisdiction to deal with arrears of maintenance. A practice has grown up under which the court will generally not enforce arrears of maintenance beyond a period of 1 year.

*1-year rule applied to prevent "hoarding"* — *Hampton v. Carrier,* 1994 CarswellOnt 2020 (Ont. Gen. Div.). The court opined that in all but very exceptional circumstances, arrears, particularly when not pursued in a timely fashion, should not reach backward in time beyond 1 year. Child support, like spousal support, is intended to provide for monthly present needs. No exceptional circumstances existed here, and, accordingly, all the arrears that had accumulated during the last 4 years were to be stayed except for those arrears which had accrued in the past year, less the amount that the payor had voluntarily paid and less the amount which he had likely spent on the children while they were in his care.

*13-year delay* — *1-year rule applied* — *Labrecque c. Dupuis,* 1992 CarswellNB 345 (N.B.Q.B.). In 1978, in Quebec, pursuant to a divorce order, the husband was ordered to pay child and spousal support of $50 a week. In 1991, the wife applied to enforce the order reciprocally in New Brunswick. Arrears were approximately $37,000. As the children were now adults and the wife had not previously attempted to enforce the arrears, arrears of 1 year were ordered, together with a lump sum of $3,000 in satisfaction of all further spousal support obligations.

*Under 1-year rule, onus is on payee to justify enforcement* — *Patry v. Patry,* 1974 CarswellOnt 143, 16 R.F.L. 332 (Ont. Fam. Ct.). The 1-year limit, while not to be considered a hard and fast rule, is a means by which the onus of proof may be assigned in enforcement proceedings; the onus to show why the court might enforce more than 1 year's arrears would be upon the wife or child or other payee seeking to enforce the order.

*1-year rule does not restrict enforcement of maintenance under Manitoba's provincial legislation* — *Flamand v. Flamand,* 1987 CarswellMan 105, 8 R.F.L. (3d) 51, 48 Man. R. (2d) 33 (Man. C.A.). The "1-year rule" no longer restricts enforcement of maintenance arrears under the Manitoba *Family Maintenance Act,* S.M. 1978, c. 25. Such arrears are held to be a vested debt subject to divestment pursuant to s. 31.3(4) of the Act where it can be shown that it would be "grossly unfair and inequitable not to do so", and that such divestment is justified having regard to the interests of the payee. The onus is on the payor to establish the conditions set out in s. 31.3(4), on the balance of probabilities.

*No 1-or 2-year rule under Manitoba's provincial legislation* — *Kent v. Kent,* 1985 CarswellMan 38, 44 R.F.L. (2d) 263, 16 D.L.R. (4th) 712, 31 Man. R. (2d) 244 (Man. C.A.). Leave to appeal granted (1985), 46 R.F.L. (2d) xxxv (note), 21 R.F.L. (3d) xxxiv (note), 35 Man. R. (2d) 238 (note), 62 N.R. 322 (note) (S.C.C.). The court held that when the Legislature, in 1980, enacted provisions in the *Family Maintenance Act,* specifying that no limitation as to time existed for the recovery of maintenance arrears (subject to the power of the court to relieve the payor of the obligation to pay the arrears for the reasons set out in s. 31.3(4) of the Act), the so-called "1-year rule" or "2-year rule" was no longer relevant.

*"Fairness" is the test, not 1-year rule* — *payee had knowingly allowed payor to believe that support not required* — *MacKinnon v. Duffy,* 2000 CarswellOnt 2752, 10 R.F.L. (5th) 336, [2000] O.J. No. 2948 (Ont. S.C.J.). Because spousal-support orders are made to satisfy the

financial need of the payee spouse, there is good reason for the court to be vigilant against hoarding. But this should be accomplished on a case-by-case basis and not through the application of a rigid rule, such as the "1-year" rule. Justice prevails if the court uses simple fairness (or unfairness) as the test in determining whether arrears of spousal support should be varied. The husband was ordered to pay the wife $750 a month for spousal support and the same amount for child support. He immediately fell into arrears. His lawyer wrote to the wife setting out his understanding that she was remarrying and moving to the United States and that, therefore, the husband would no longer be under an obligation to pay support. Thirteen years later, without any contact in the meantime, the wife filed the support orders with Family Responsibility Office for enforcement. The arrears at that time were $241,500. The husband applied to vary the orders retroactively. The court granted the application in part finding, on the facts, that it was fair to allow the wife to enforce $25,000 of the arrears of spousal support. The balance should be rescinded. Too much time had passed to allow post-judgement interest. The husband's income had decreased and the wife, who was unemployed at the time of the orders, was earning income, a situation which satisfied the requisite test of a material change in circumstances. The wife did not adequately explain her delay in enforcing the orders. The husband was not guilty of bad faith, and his belief that his obligation had ceased was not unreasonable.

*1-year rule not applied — Remillard v. Remillard*, 1986 CarswellMan 328, 2 R.F.L. (3d) 215, [1986] 4 W.W.R. 721, 42 Man. R. (2d) 151 (Man. Q.B.). The court declined to apply the judge-made "1-year rule" in respect of an order made under the *Divorce Act*. Since it had been held that the rule was inapplicable in respect of orders made under provincial statutes, it would be incongruous for a payor spouse to be in a better position should his arrears happen to be "federal."

*Payee dies after arrears accumulate for 9 years — arrears not extinguished — Hennings v. Hennings Estate*, 1999 CarswellOnt 1541, 27 E.T.R. (2d) 251, 48 R.F.L. (4th) 346, [1999] O.J. No. 1740 (Ont. S.C.J.), additional reasons at 1999 CarswellOnt 1780, 49 R.F.L. (4th) 295, 98 O.T.C. 300 (Ont. S.C.J.). In 1988, the husband was ordered to pay $250 monthly in spousal support. At the time of the wife's death in 1997, the husband had paid only $611.60 through garnishments by the Family Responsibility Office and arrears of $44,000 had accumulated. The husband's application for an order extinguishing the arrears on the basis of material change in circumstances was dismissed. Support arrears constituted a valid judgement debt enforceable by the payee's estate. The failure by the applicant to make support payments contributed significantly to the depletion of assets in the wife's estate. There was no "1-year" rule which limited enforcement of arrears to 1 year especially in light of provincial schemes of governmental enforcement of support orders. There has been no material change in circumstances. A mere accumulation of arrears, without reliable evidence of a past inability to pay, is neither a change of circumstances under the statutes, nor a special circumstance.

*1-year rule no longer law in Alberta — Belcourt v. Belcourt*, 1987 CarswellAlta 349, 6 R.F.L. (3d) 396, 77 A.R. 347 (Alta. Q.B.). It was held that it is no longer the law in Alberta to prevent enforcement of arrears beyond a 1-year period.

*1-year rule not a binding limitation in Saskatchewan — Perrault (Unger) v. Unger*, 1986 CarswellSask 432, 52 Sask. R. 70, [1986] S.J. No. 593 (Sask. Q.B.). The "1-year rule," whereby payment of arrears is not enforceable beyond a 1-year period, is not a binding limitation in Saskatchewan. The *Enforcement of Maintenance Orders Act*, S.S. 1984-85-86, c. E-9.2, provides that 15 arrears owing for up to 10 years are enforceable.

*1-year rule not applied because remedies had been pursued and there was no "hoarding" — Cassidy v. Cassidy*, 1985 CarswellOnt 298, 47 R.F.L. (2d) 106 (Ont. Fam. Ct.). Where there was no suggestion that the enforcement remedies were not actively pursued and there was no hoarding, the court held that there was no justification for applying the "1-year rule" even if such a rule did exist.

*Payee who had misunderstood court order entitled to enforce arrears — McDonald v. McDonald*, 1983 CarswellNS 404, 61 N.S.R. (2d) 341, 133 A.P.R. 341 (N.S. Fam. Ct.). In *McDonald*, the "1-year rule" was not applied. The wife's delay in seeking enforcement was not motivated by a desire to hoard 3 years' worth of maintenance arrears; rather, the delay arose from the wife's misunderstanding of a previous verbal instruction from the court that no further maintenance applications were to be made until the husband's income had increased.

*1-year rule too arbitrary — Tulik v. Tulik*, 1983 CarswellSask 407, 28 Sask. R. 150 (Sask. Q.B.). As the "1-year rule" was found to be too arbitrary, the court declined to apply this rule in abating maintenance arrears.

*Delay in seeking enforcement combined with payor's obligations to support his new family justified reduction in arrears — Young v. Konkle*, 1993 CarswellAlta 436, 1 R.F.L. (4th) 211 (Alta. Q.B.). The parties married in 1975, separated in 1980 and divorced in 1982. The father was ordered to pay child support of $50 a month for each of the two children of the marriage. He rarely paid. Both parties remarried and the father had three more children. He was unemployed from 1980 to 1984 and occasionally employed until 1989, after which he had a full-time job. The mother left the province in 1984, returning in 1988. While away, she had no contact with the father and made no demands for support. The parties' older child was no longer a child of the marriage and the younger child would only be so for a few more months. The court held that the father's liability for supporting the older child was to cease immediately. The arrears of $10,650 were reduced to $4,500, and the father was ordered to pay reduced arrears and support of $100 per month in respect of the younger child, while he remained a child of the marriage. After child support ended, the father was to pay the mother $100 a month towards the reduced arrears. In exercising its discretion regarding the cancellation or reduction of arrears, the court had to consider the reality of the payor's present financial circumstances, including the right of a second family to support. In this case, the father had little means to pay support until 1989. It was unfair of the mother to wait until the children were almost independent to demand child support.

*Payor would be entirely unable to pay arrears if enforced after 10-year delay — Spedding v. Spedding*, 1989 CarswellBC 389, 19 R.F.L. (3d) 368, [1989] B.C.J. No. 153 (B.C.S.C.). In many cases dealing with the "1-year rule", not only is there a delay by the payee spouse in enforcing the support order, but the evidence often reveals that the payor spouse has no reasonable prospect of ever being able to pay the accumulated arrears. For instance, in *Spedding*, the wife delayed 9 years in enforcing the order, and the husband was lulled into believing she would never enforce the order, with the result that he made no provision for maintenance payments in his budget and saved nothing. However, the evidence also indicated that the husband never had much money and certainly did not now have any prospect of earning sufficient moneys to pay ongoing maintenance as well as the full amount of arrears. The court held that it was reasonable for the respondent to expect that the petitioner would never enforce a 1979 support order.

*Inability of support payor to pay arrears — Steeves v. Steeves*, 1988 CarswellNB 248, 87 N.B.R. (2d) 400, 221 A.P.R. 400 (N.B.Q.B.). The payor's inability to ever be able to pay the accumulated arrears was as important as the delay by the payee spouse in enforcing the arrears.

*Impossibility of the payor ever paying arrears — Barnesky v. Barnesky*, 1988 CarswellMan 60, 16 R.F.L. (3d) 450, 53 Man. R. (2d) 212, [1988] M.J. No. 357 (Man. Q.B.). The payor's inability to ever be able to pay the accumulated arrears was as important as the delay by the payee spouse in enforcing the arrears.

*Arrears reduced but not cancelled due to delay — Newman v. Newman*, 1990 CarswellMan 42, 26 R.F.L. (3d) 313, 65 Man. R. (2d) 294 (Man. Q.B.). Where as a result of the wife's inaction to enforce a support order, arrears had accumulated in the sum of $30,000, the arrears were ordered reduced to $5,000. As the husband had also not acted reasonably in failing to bring a variation application earlier, both parties were required to assume some responsibility for their inaction.

*5-year delay balanced against failure of husband to seek variation — arrears for 12 months ordered to be paid — Vine v. Vine*, 1986 CarswellOnt 258, 1 R.F.L. (3d) 425, 54 O.R. (2d) 580 (Ont. H.C.). The failure of the wife to do anything about the arrears that had accumulated since 1980 was taken by the court to be strong evidence of a lack of need on her part. However, arrears for a period of 12 months were ordered paid, as the husband had unilaterally ceased paying support without first obtaining an order to vary the decree *nisi*. Such conduct was not to be condoned nor encouraged by the court.

*Parties jointly responsible for accumulation of arrears — partial payment orders — Beauchemin v. Beauchemin*, 1981 CarswellNS 168, 47 N.S.R. (2d) 594, 90 A.P.R. 594 (N.S. Fam. Ct.). Where both parties' actions had contributed to the accumulation of arrears over a 23-month period and the husband's circumstances had changed so that he was no longer in as good a financial position to pay, the Nova Scotia Family Court ordered him to pay maintenance for only 12 of the 23 months' worth of arrears.

*After 5-year delay, only 1 year of arrears enforced — Ruth v. Ruth*, 1981 CarswellNS 165, 47 N.S.R. (2d) 357, 90 A.P.R. 357 (N.S. Fam. Ct.). The court limited recovery of arrears to a period of 1 year only, where the wife had allowed the arrears to accrue for 5 years before she sought to enforce payment. The court ruled that the wife had waited too long to bring her action.

*Support payee seeks writ of seizure and sale after 3-year delay — Ballentine v. Ballentine*, 1999 CarswellOnt 2591, 50 R.F.L. (4th) 211, 45 O.R. (3d) 706, 107 O.T.C. 133, [1999] O.J. No. 3103 (Ont. S.C.J.), affirmed 2000 CarswellOnt 2768, 10 R.F.L. (5th) 11, 135 O.A.C. 276, [2000] O.J. No. 2870 (Ont. C.A.). The parties divorced in 1976 after a 20-year marriage. The husband was ordered to make spousal support payments of $1,447.31 per month, subject to the cost-of-living adjustments. After 1995, the husband began to default on support obligations. The wife applied for a writ of seizure and sale against the husband's property to enforce the arrears, more than 3 years after the default began. Pursuant to rule 60.07(2) of the *Rules of Civil Procedure*, leave was required. The application for leave was granted. There is no "1-year" rule for enforcement of support arrears. The 1-year rule is compatible with neither the provisions nor the spirit of family law legislation. Delay in enforcement is only a factor to be considered where, and to the extent that, it supports a finding of waiver or acquiescence or a finding that it would otherwise be inequitable to enforce the claim. Delay is only a factor to be considered along with others including evidence of detrimental reliance or change of position. Enquiry into the application of the provisions of s. 17 of the *Divorce Act* is not automatically called for whenever an application for leave is made under r. 60.07(2). Such an enquiry should be made only when the payor has moved to cancel arrears and has the onus of proving that the factual conditions for rescinding or varying an order have satisfied. The evidence in this case did not show that the husband reasonably believed that the wife was abandoning her right to support or that he was misled in any way or to any extent. The wife's conduct was consistent with her continuing intention to enforce the right to support.

*After 12-year delay, onus placed on support payee to show continuing loss from marriage — McMullen v. McMullen*, 1994 CarswellNB 26, 5 R.F.L. (4th) 444, 150 N.B.R. (2d) 277, 385 A.P.R. 277, [1994] N.B.J. No. 308 (N.B.C.A.). After a 12-year marriage, the parties divorced in 1979. The husband was ordered to pay the wife monthly spousal support. The husband unilaterally stopped paying spousal support in 1981 after becoming aware that the wife had entered into a common-law relationship. The wife's common-law relationship ended in 1989. Subsequently, the wife had full-time employment until she was disabled in an automobile accident in 1991. As the injuries prevented her from working, the wife began receiving social assistance benefits. In early 1993, following a dispute with the husband concerning their child, the wife applied to have the spousal support resumed and to collect the arrears. The husband applied to have the support terminated and the arrears eliminated. Citing the delay on the part of both parties, the trial judge eliminated the arrears but refused to terminate the support. Arguing that the wife had achieved self-sufficiency and was no longer entitled to support, the husband appealed. The court was of the opinion that, considering the length of the wife's common-law relationship, her failure to enforce the support obligation for 12 years and the circumstances which eventually led her to attempt to enforce it, the trial judge should have placed the onus on the wife to establish that the economic loss resulting from the marriage continued. As that onus was never placed on the wife, the husband's appeal was allowed.

*Having received reduced amount for 3 years without protest amounted to waiver of entitlement to full amount — D. (S.) v. R. (G.),* [1994] R.D.F. 209 (C.A. Que.). In 1988, a divorce decree ratified the parties' agreement, which provided that the wife would have custody of the children and the husband would pay her $1,100 in monthly support. The parties had also agreed that, should the wife move to Vancouver, child support would be reduced to $1,000 per month. After the divorce, the wife moved to Vancouver, but, in 1989, she returned to Montreal. After her return, the husband continued to pay her $1,000 per month. In 1991, the wife moved for variation of support and claimed the arrears for the period after she came back to Montreal. The motion was allowed in part on other grounds. The trial judge concluded that the wife had waived her right to arrears. The wife's appeal of the trial judge's decision on the motion was allowed in part on other grounds. The wife received the reduced amount of support during 3 years without protest which amounted to a waiver of her right to claim arrears.

*Delay not amounting to laches does not justify reduction or cancellation — Fetterley v. Fetterley,* 1988 CarswellAlta 331, 14 R.F.L. (3d) 47, 89 A.R. 350 (Alta. Q.B.), affirmed 1989 CarswellAlta 396, 24 R.F.L. (3d) 61, 102 A.R. 131, [1989] A.J. No. 1185 (Alta. C.A.). If respect for a negotiated final support settlement is to be given full accord and the support payments thereunder are to be sustained, then, absent delay amounting to *laches*, the arrears of such payments should be left intact and should not be subject to reduction or cancellation.

*6 years' arrears from Illinois judgement enforced — Stark v. Stark,* 1978 CarswellAlta 288, 8 R.F.L. (2d) 254, [1979] 1 W.W.R. 748, 13 A.R. 339, 94 D.L.R. (3d) 556 (Alta. C.A.). Where a husband was substantially in arrears of maintenance pursuant to an Illinois maintenance order, the Alberta court awarded the wife arrears going back approximately 6 years. The Alberta court also dismissed the husband's appeal of the award, stating that it was not against public policy to enforce a foreign maintenance award for arrears past 1 year, and that the Illinois judgement was final and conclusive under Illinois law.

*After 12-year delay, arrears not enforced — Delaney v. Elkins,* 2004 CarswellNS 269, 2004 NSSF 63, 224 N.S.R. (2d) 168, [2004] N.S.J. No. 263 (N.S.S.C.). Where the husband no longer paid combined child and spousal support after a child had become 19, but the wife did not try to enforce the order until approximately 12 years after the payment had stopped, the court found that the doctrine of *laches* and the "hoarding" principle barred the wife from retroactively collecting payments for spousal support.

*10 years arrears ordered to be paid, plus interest — Lewis v. Lewis,* 1999 CarswellBC 2468, 2 R.F.L. (5th) 417 (B.C.S.C.). The "rule against hoarding" should be considered along with the provisions of s. 17 of the *Divorce Act,* and in this context the court may exercise its discretion and not enforce arrears of over 1 year. Section 17, although not specifically mentioning the right to cancel arrears, should be approached in the same way as provincial legislation, which expressly grants this right. The parties entered into a separation agreement and had the support provision incorporated in their divorce judgement. At a time when the obligation was to pay $500 a month, the former husband unilaterally reduced his payments to $250 a month. Eleven years later he applied to cancel the arrears under the judgement which were in excess of $34,000, and to vary retroactively the support order to $250 a month. In the meantime, he had remarried and both he and his second wife had retired. He had a retirement income and some registered retirement savings plans. His former wife had sold her home, used the proceeds for her living expenses until they ran out, and then relied on social assistance. In dismissing the former husband's application, the court exercised its discretion and enforced payment of the arrears for a 10-year period, the parties having agreed that by reason of the *Limitation Act* arrears of spousal support over 10 years cannot be collected. The former wife was not hoarding because she was emotionally incapable of confronting her former husband about the default. Although this lack of dissent and her subsequent silence induced the husband to believe he would not be required to pay and was free to plan his retirement accordingly, the prejudice involved was offset by the fact that his substantially superior financial position was based in part upon the financial deprivation that she suffered. The recovery of arrears is important not only to compensate the payee for what was improperly withheld, but also to demonstrate that the orders of the court are to be obeyed. The arrears were fixed at $30,000 for the 10 years payable with interest under the *Court Order Interest Act*.

*Heart attack 13 years beforehand, plus failure of payee to enforce, justified cancellation of arrears accumulated since that date* — Fawcett v. Fawcett, 1995 CarswellBC 1178, 18 R.F.L. (4th) 450 (B.C.S.C.). Where the husband had suffered a heart attack in 1982 and had advised the wife of his inability to pay her spousal support as ordered, the court allowed the husband's 1995 application to rescind all arrears and terminate the order. The wife had never attempted in 13 years to enforce the order and the husband's heart attack, had a variation been sought at the time, would have constituted a change in circumstances.

*Payor found to have ability to pay and ordered to pay entire amount in arrears* — Saeglitz v. Saeglitz, 1994 CarswellOnt 389, 3 R.F.L. (4th) 244 (Ont. U.F.C.). The husband was ordered to pay $300 per week interim support to his wife. Subsequently, arrears of $45,400 accumulated. Upon separation, the wife had commenced an action in the Supreme Court which was transferred to the Unified Family Court 2 years later but did not find its way into that court's administration until 4 years after that. Both parties had not pursued their claims. The wife's action included a claim for arrears of support with pre-judgement interest. The court found that the husband's argument that he was induced by the delay in enforcement into believing that he would not be required to pay had no merit, and that he had the ability to pay the arrears. In determining that pre-judgement interest was allowed from the date at which the case was transferred to the United Family Court, the court considered that s. 140 of the *Courts of Justice Act*, 1984, S.O. 1984, c. 11 permitted consideration of the parties' conduct when determining the appropriate rate of interest. While neither party moved this case along, the bulk of the delay was attributed to the wife, whose responsibility it was to move the case forward in a timely fashion. The court found that if the wife had pursued her right sex peditiously, she would not have been deprived of her funds for such a long time. While interest was not to be awarded as punishment, it was appropriate to account for the wife's conduct and to consider the unfairness that would arise to the husband if he were made responsible for pre-judgement interest from the date of separation.

*Arrears reduced due to failure of husband's business and delay in enforcement* — Delorme v. Woodham, 1993 CarswellMan 275, 89 Man. R. (2d) 16 (Man. Q.B.). The husband had been ordered to pay $150 per month support for his wife and their son. The wife subsequently remarried and, on his own initiative, the husband ceased making the support payments. The wife took no steps to claim payment of arrears for a lengthy period of time, during which period the husband suffered business losses culminating in bankruptcy. The husband owed support arrears of $15,000. On application for the cancellation of arrears, the husband's arrears were reduced to $4,000 which was to be repaid at the rate of $25 per month. The court found that there had been a change in the condition, means, needs and other circumstances of the parties. It was inferred that if the husband had brought an application to vary the maintenance based on his wife's remarriage, or based on his business difficulties, his obligation to pay would likely have been reduced.

*11-year delay — arrears not cancelled — Bulych v. Bulych*, 1993 CarswellSask 502, 117 Sask. R. 157 (Sask. Q.B.). In 1980, the father was ordered to pay the mother $150 per month in child support and $100 per month in spousal support. Nothing was paid until the mother registered her order with the Maintenance Enforcement Office 11 years later. The father's income was then garnished to pay arrears of $35,550. The father brought an application for a reduction in child support payable and a cancellation of arrears, asserting that he was unable to pay because he had been living in poverty. Arrears of child support were to be forgiven only if the court was satisfied that the payor could not have paid and there was no possibility that he would ever be able to pay. The father should have detailed his situation and the steps he took to remedy his alleged decrease in income. The court was left to conclude that he could have paid his modest obligation but chose not to, and there was no doubt that he presently had the ability to pay. The application was therefore dismissed.

*Arrears cancelled due to 5-year delay and due to changed circumstances of parties — McGean v. McGean*, 1992 CarswellNS 74, 42 R.F.L. (3d) 251, 116 N.S.R. (2d) 209, 320 A.P.R. 209, [1992] N.S.J. No. 353 (N.S.T.D.). The court retroactively rescinded spousal support back to when the last support order was made in August, 1987 on the basis of changed circumstances of both parties. In the alternative, the court stated that if it were necessary, it would have found that any arrears of support which had accumulated to date should be terminated by virtue of the doctrine of *laches*. The court rejected the former wife's explanation that the reason for her delay in enforcing support was discomfort or reluctance to pursue the instant litigation and the "stress" of pursuing her former husband. While there is no general rule of a 1-year limit on the enforcement of spousal arrears, the court stated that it had the discretion to decline to enforce all or a portion of the amount owing in order to relieve against hoarding or because of *laches*.

*2-year delay — arrears ordered to be paid — McKinnon v. McKinnon*, 1991 CarswellNS 515 (N.S.T.D.). Where the husband interpreted the maintenance provisions of the minutes of settlement to mean that he did not have to pay child maintenance, and the wife did not apply to enforce the maintenance provisions for 2 years, the court ordered maintenance paid, including arrears.

*6-year delay — arrears cancelled — Strowbridge v. Strowbridge*, 1989 CarswellNfld 203, 80 Nfld. & P.E.I.R. 111, 249 A.P.R. 111, [1989] N.J. No. 252 (Nfld. T.D.). Arrears that had been accumulating for 6 years were ordered cancelled because of the payee's failure to seek enforcement.

*6-year delay explained by payor being in a different province — Martin v. Martin*, 1989 CarswellSask 82, 24 R.F.L. (3d) 150, 81 Sask. R. 98 (Sask. Q.B.). The husband's application to rescind arrears was dismissed in circumstances where he relied not only on an inability to pay but on the wife's failure to enforce the arrears for 6 years even though she knew of his whereabouts. A cancellation of arrears under the *Divorce Act* requires a change of circumstances. A delay in enforcement did not warrant cancellation of the arrears. In any event, the court found that there had not been any unreasonable and unexplained delay by the former wife since she was unable to pursue her husband, who lived in another province, until 1987 when inter-provincial enforcement services were made available to her and she could garnish his salary.

*Delay in enforcement alone insufficient to justify cancellation — Martin v. Martin*, 1989 CarswellSask 82, 24 R.F.L. (3d) 150, 81 Sask. R. 98 (Sask. Q.B.). The mere fact of delay in the enforcement of support does not justify the cancellation of arrears, particularly where the payor had the means to pay support and also the means to discharge the arrears.

*20 years since last attempt to enforce combined order for spousal and child support, children now all grown adults* — *Cormier v. Cormier*, 1988 CarswellNB 169, 90 N.B.R. (2d) 431, 228 A.P.R. 431 (N.B.Q.B.), reversed 1989 CarswellNB 335, 102 N.B.R. (2d) 13, 256 A.P.R. 13, [1989] N.B.J. No. 1037 (N.B.C.A.). The application of the so-called "1-year rule" was held to be appropriate. In this case, the former wife sought to enforce maintenance arrears which had accumulated under a 1958 divorce order. She had attempted to enforce the order once in 1968. The youngest of the four beneficiaries under the order was now 37 years of age, and the oldest was 44. The court held that the support order should not be enforced beyond 1 year given that the applicant had sat idly by and had taken no steps to enforce her rights, given the paucity of evidence in general, and given that the children were now all adults.

*Relevant factors included fact that there was no explanation for delay in enforcement* — *Caissie v. Caissie*, 1988 CarswellNB 159, 89 N.B.R. (2d) 313, 226 A.P.R. 313 (N.B.Q.B.). A factor militating against full recovery of the arrears was the wife's inability to offer a satisfactory explanation for her delay in enforcing the support provisions of an Ontario decree *nisi* when she knew the whereabouts of her former husband and his financial circumstances.

*5-year delay — payor lulled into sense of security* — *Tremblett v. Tremblett*, 1988 CarswellNfld 251, 75 Nfld. & P.E.I.R. 175, 234 A.P.R. 175 (Nfld. U.F.C.). The fact that the delay in some cases has caused payors to be lulled into believing falsely that the payee would not enforce the order has also been considered by the courts as a reason why the full amount of the arrears should not be enforced. Thus, where the amount of the payor's wages being attached, on consent, was less than the amount of support set out in the court order, and where no action was taken by the wife for 5 years to recover the balance, it was not unreasonable for the payor to be lulled into a certain sense of security that the wife was prepared to accept the lesser amount.

*8-year delay — Grimwood v. Grimwood*, 1988 CarswellSask 487, 68 Sask. R. 179 (Sask. Q.B.). A provisional order pursuant to s. 8(8) of the *Saskatchewan Reciprocal Enforcement of Maintenance Orders Act* was made substantially reducing the arrears under a registered British Columbia order. The court considered the fact that the wife had made no efforts to enforce the order from the time it was made in 1978 to 1986 when she registered the order in Saskatchewan even though she knew of the husband's whereabouts.

*Delay by state agency in enforcing assigned support entitlement* — *Barnesky v. Barnesky*, 1988 CarswellMan 60, 16 R.F.L. (3d) 450, 53 Man. R. (2d) 212, [1988] M.J. No. 357 (Man. Q.B.). Where, in order to receive social assistance, the payee spouse has assigned the support order to a government department, that department must act in a timely manner to enforce any arrears accumulating under the order. In the *Barnesky* decision, where the Department of Employment Services and Economic Security sat on its rights to enforce the support order for 5 or 6 years and offered no explanation as to why no efforts were made to enforce the order, the court granted the husband's application to rescind all of the arrears. Prompt action by the Department would have alerted the husband that the support order, which he and his spouse believed was no longer in effect because they had reconciled briefly after the order was made, was still existing and in effect. The unexplained *laches* was alone sufficient to justify the remission of arrears, although the court also noted that the husband had no ability to pay during the period when the arrears were accumulating.

*Payee who accepted partial payment for 7 years not allowed to enforce arrears for the unpaid portions* — *Seward v. Seward*, 1988 CarswellNS 35, 12 R.F.L. (3d) 54, 85 N.S.R. (2d) 30, 216 A.P.R. 30 (N.S. Fam. Ct.). Where the wife accepted funds diverted to her from the Canadian Armed Services for 7 years, without pursuing any of the legal remedies available to her to enforce the difference in amount between what she received and what she was entitled to receive under the order, the court concluded that all outstanding arrears should be cancelled. There was no justification for applying the "1-year rule" since the former wife was obviously satisfied with the amount that was being diverted to her, as evidenced by her having done nothing about the arrears. The court was of the opinion that *laches* applied to arrears that were for the benefit of the children as well as the spouse. Moreover, the former wife had no debts arising from not having received the arrears. Accordingly, to enforce the payment of arrears now would result in a windfall for the wife. A windfall was against public policy, as maintenance was to be used to maintain a person and not to be hoarded.

*Enforcement sought via order for seizure and sale denied after delay greater than 1 year —* Wood v. Wood, 1986 CarswellNB 130, 68 N.B.R. (2d) 219, 175 A.P.R. 219 (N.B.Q.B.). Leave to issue an order for seizure and sale in respect of arrears of child support, which had become due more than 12 months before the proceedings, was refused to a wife where she had made no effort to enforce payment, had by her conduct led her husband to believe she would not enforce her rights, and had been able to meet all her obligations during the period in question. These arrears were cancelled.

*Payee had misled payor into belief that payment would not be required —* Rollins v. Kutash, 1982 CarswellAlta 35, 26 R.F.L. (2d) 444, 18 Alta. L.R. (2d) 322 (Alta. Prov. Ct.). Where the wife failed for 6 years to enforce arrears of child support ordered pursuant to a decree *nisi*, and the husband had, in fact, been forbidden by the wife's second husband to pay, the court applied the "1-year rule." The conduct of the wife had misled the husband into believing that she was not going to require payment.

*Payee had agreed not to enforce order —* Foley v. Foley, 1981 CarswellNS 152, 46 N.S.R. (2d) 475, 89 A.P.R. 475 (N.S. Fam. Ct.). The court dismissed the wife's application to enforce a foreign maintenance order where she had agreed not to enforce the order and had abided by this agreement for 6 years.

*Previous efforts to enforce arrears and payee's expenses, plus payor's ability to pay, justified enforcement —* Harris v. Harris, 1980 CarswellBC 1, 21 B.C.L.R. 145, 110 D.L.R. (3d) 483 (B.C.S.C.). Where the respondent's wife had been faced with many expenses during the period in which the arrears had accumulated, an order for payment of the arrears was held not to constitute hoarding. Moreover, the respondent had diligently pursued her claim and the petitioner had sufficient assets to pay the accumulated arrears.

*Payee had good reasons to delay action — enforcement allowed —* S. v. S., 1974 CarswellSask 37, 18 R.F.L. 373 (Sask. Q.B.). The applicant was allowed to enforce arrears which had accumulated under a support order in a decree *nisi* for a period beyond 1 year in circumstances where (a) the applicant had left the collection of maintenance with the Family Court which did not deal expeditiously with the matter, and (b) the respondent husband had notified the applicant that he would be going to university for a number of years and that it would be impossible for him to pay any substantial sums for maintenance.

*Under 1-year rule, onus is on payee to justify enforcement —* Mihalic v. Mihalic, 1973 CarswellOnt 121, 11 R.F.L. 102 (Ont. H.C.). In *Mihalic*, the court expressed the view that the effect of the "1-year rule" was one of onus. Accordingly, where a person was attempting to enforce arrears beyond 1 year, there was an onus on that person to satisfy the court that such discretion should be exercised in his or her favour.

## 10.7.4 Retroactive Variation of Support Orders — Tax Credits

*Alleged agreement between parties must be enforced by a separate suit —* Meltzer v. Meltzer, 1992 CarswellMan 48, 41 R.F.L. (3d) 257, 93 D.L.R. (4th) 435, 78 Man. R. (2d) 299, 16 W.A.C. 299 (Man. C.A.). The court overturned, on appeal a retro active variation of a support award intended to give tax relief to the payor husband. A purported agreement between the spouses that moneys paid voluntarily by the husband to the wife would attract tax consequences in the wife's hands should be enforced by suit, and not by varying a prior support order.

*Jurisdiction to make order to allow income tax credit regarding support — Gallo v. Gallo,* 1990 CarswellAlta 273, 26 R.F.L. (3d) 217 (Alta. Q.B.). The court has, in the proper case, jurisdiction to make an order varying an earlier support order or rectifying a separation agreement to allow for retroactive income tax credit for payments made.

## 10.8  Variation — Interference with Access Rights

*Denial of access justifies termination of support — Ungerer v. Ungerer,* 1998 CarswellBC 670, 37 R.F.L. (4th) 41, 48 B.C.L.R. (3d) 188, 158 D.L.R. (4th) 47, [1998] 7 W.W.R. 469, 105 B.C.A.C. 250, 171 W.A.C. 250, [1998] B.C.J. No. 698 (B.C.C.A.). Where the wife had, for over 5 years, thwarted the husband's access to their child, even after having been imprisoned for contempt, the court ordered the termination of her spousal support. The wife's breach of the access order in itself was sufficiently reprehensible to justify termination and her further refusal to seek employment was also inexcusable.

## 10.9  Variation — Consent Orders for Support

See *Willick v. Willick,* 1994 CarswellSask 48, 1994 CarswellSask 450, EYB 1994-67936, 6 R.F.L. (4th) 161, [1994] 3 S.C.R. 670, 119 D.L.R. (4th) 405, 173 N.R. 321, [1994] R.D.F. 617, 125 Sask. R. 81, 81 W.A.C. 81, [1994] S.C.J. No. 94 (S.C.C.).

*The doctrines of res judicata and issue estoppel do not apply to an agreement which is incorporated into an order for spousal maintenance made under the* Divorce Act *— the jurisdiction of the court has not been ousted — D. (B.G.) v. D. (R.W.),* 2003 CarswellBC 1192, 2003 BCCA 259, 35 R.F.L. (5th) 315, 226 D.L.R. (4th) 378, 181 B.C.A.C. 312, 298 W.A.C. 312, [2003] B.C.J. No. 1098 (B.C.C.A.). The parties separated, and signed a separation agreement, whereby they agreed that the husband would pay spousal support for 2 years and either party could apply for continued support or termination of support. After 2 years, the wife applied for spousal support. The parties reached an agreement which was incorporated into a consent order, whereby the wife was awarded support which was duly paid. The wife subsequently applied to vary the consent order to provide support.

"*A consent order is similar to a separation agreement — principles analogous to those set out by the Supreme Court of Canada in* Miglin *apply to determine whether a person who has consented to an order should be allowed to ask for relief which is inconsistent with the terms of the existing consent order.*" *— Ordano v. Moore,* 2003 CarswellAlta 576, 2003 ABQB 362, 39 R.F.L. (5th) 361 (Alta. Q.B.). This case dealt with access.

*In family law, the courts, for obvious policy reasons, encourage parties to settle their affairs in order to prevent unnecessary litigation and the unnecessary dissipation of assets and, consequently, courts are reluctant to later interfere with consensual arrangements reached between the parties, except where substantial grounds are demonstrated — Huculak v. Huculak,* 2000 CarswellBC 2546, 2000 BCCA 662, 12 R.F.L. (5th) 107, [2000] B.C.J. No. 2530 (B.C.C.A.). Such substantial grounds were not found. There was not a proper evidentiary basis for the variation sought by the appellant. In this case, a spousal support order was made following a settlement conference.

*Agreement varied to take account of husband's change of employment — Murta v. Murta,* 1991 CarswellMan 54, 38 R.F.L. (3d) 92, 77 Man. R. (2d) 131, 85 D.L.R. (4th) 501 (Man. Q.B.), reversed 1992 CarswellMan 60, 98 D.L.R. (4th) 445, 44 R.F.L. (3d) 70, 83 Man. R. (2d) 170, 36

W.A.C. 170 (Man. C.A.). Where the parties had entered a consent agreement after divorce whereby the husband would pay an additional 5% increase in spousal support each year that he continued in a specified position, his voluntary retirement from that position was found to be a circumstance that the parties had not contemplated at the time of the agreement. Accordingly, the court had jurisdiction to vary the agreement and found that, as the husband's current salary was roughly the equivalent of his former one, it was reasonable that the annual increase continue as long as that circumstance continued. On appeal, the Court found that as the agreement was not a final one, it could be varied if there was a material change in circumstances. There had been such a change. The financial needs of the wife had increased and her medical condition was deteriorating. The husband's income had more than doubled in the past few years. Support was increased to $1,800 per month.

*Support continued despite husband's remarriage and contemplated early retirement —* Brown v. Brown, 1988 CarswellNB 49, 17 R.F.L. (3d) 281 (N.B.Q.B.). The fact that the husband had remarried and contemplated early retirement was found insufficient to justify a downward variation in spousal support where the original sum had been established through minutes of settlement.

*Material change in circumstances, consent order inapplicable —* Lee v. Lee, 1998 CarswellBC 2031, 41 R.F.L. (4th) 303, [1998] B.C.J. No. 2201 (B.C.S.C.). The husband in a consent decree had been ordered to pay spousal support payments until he retired, at which time the wife would receive an interest in her husband's pension. The legislation changed and the wife elected to receive a lump sum payment of the pension. The husband stopped making spousal support payments. A lower court set aside the spousal support order but, on appeal at 1997 CarswellBC 2845, 35 R.F.L. (4th) 200, [1997] B.C.J. No. 2947 (B.C.C.A.), the court referred the matter of spousal support back to the court below. The B.C. Supreme Court, at 41 R.F.L. (4th) 303, ruled that a material change had occurred and the consent order was inapplicable. The court was of the opinion that the husband no longer had an obligation to pay support once the wife had obtained her lump sum pension, but since the husband had delayed in applying for maintenance and as a result the wife had incurred debts, the husband should be required to pay an additional 6 months of support from the time that the wife received her share of the pension.

*Great deference to consent orders —* Friedman v. Friedman, 1987 CarswellBC 580, 8 R.F.L. (3d) 83 (B.C.S.C.). On an application to vary support, the court should take the amount originally ordered as correct and consider the extent of any changes since that order. In particular, consent orders made with legal advice ought not to be lightly disturbed.

*Pension payments could be considered as support and could be varied —* McCowan v. McCowan, 1995 CarswellOnt 435, 14 R.F.L. (4th) 325, 24 O.R. (3d) 707, 84 O.A.C. 125, [1995] O.J. No. 2245 (Ont. C.A.). Where the wife, in a consent judgement, agreed to forego spousal support in exchange for payments by the husband to replace pension benefits lost on the dissolution of the marriage, it was held that the wife could properly seek variation of the payments under s. 17 despite the dismissal of the wife's support claim in the consent judgement. The pension payments could properly be characterized as support.

*Changes which were not radical nor unforeseen not basis for variation of support —* Mason v. Mason, 1989 CarswellNS 249, 93 N.S.R. (2d) 428, 242 A.P.R. 428 (N.S. Fam. Ct.). The husband's application for a reduction in support, brought 2 months after the parties had agreed to a consent support order, was dismissed. The factors upon which the husband based the claim, namely his poor health and failing real estate business, were neither radical changes nor unforeseen at the time of the consent order.

## 10.10  Variation — Suspension of Support Payments

*Suspension of spousal support does not relieve a payor spouse of the obligation to pay spousal support forever, but rather constitutes a temporary relief measure — McDermott v. McDermott*, 2008 CarswellBC 767, 2008 BCCA 166, 254 B.C.A.C. 176, 426 W.A.C. 176 (B.C.C.A.). The husband was ordered to pay outstanding spousal support after the suspension period had ended.

Section 17(1) provides that a court may suspend a support order or any provision in a support order on an application by either or both former souses. The order can be suspended prospectively or retroactively.

*Support order suspended while payor attempted to overcome a drug problem — Freund v. Dent*, 1995 CarswellMan 206, 14 R.F.L. (4th) 251, 102 Man. R. (2d) 316, 93 W.A.C. 316 (C.A.). The court allowed the husband's appeal and ordered that enforcement proceedings respecting the support arrears owed by him be suspended for 4 months. The husband was attempting to overcome a drug problem and find steady employment. The four-month suspension would permit him to find employment without risk of losing it because of enforcement proceedings.

*Where the husband lost his employment and the evidence indicted that the wife had not made sufficient efforts to find employment since the divorce, the wife's spousal support order was suspended — Sequens v. Sequens*, 1999 CarswellBC 1114, 48 R.F.L. (4th) 53 (B.C.S.C.). Although there had been a change in circumstances, it was not sufficient to warrant rescission of the order. The wife was, therefore, free to seek re-instatement when the husband found employment.

*Support payments suspended when payor injured in an accident — Dupont v. Dupont*, 1993 CarswellBC 615, 47 R.F.L. (3d) 273 (B.C.S.C.), it was found that an accident suffered by a payor spouse justified a suspension of child support obligations pending settlement of the accident claim, but did not justify a cancellation of the order.

*Support suspended until payee completed drug dependency programme — Robertson v. Robertson*, 1988 CarswellNS 292, 84 N.S.R. (2d) 303, 213 A.P.R. 303 (N.S. Fam. Ct.). Where the wife lost her employment because of her unreasonable refusal to seek assistance for alcohol dependency, the husband's obligation to pay spousal support was suspended until the wife completed certain drug dependency programmes.

*Support order suspended only while payor unemployed — Sobstyl v. Sobstyl*, 1989 CarswellAlta 443, 100 A.R. 178 (Alta. Q.B.). Although the court may temporarily reduce a support award based upon a settlement agreement where the payor is out of work, such an order should not be interpreted as meaning that the original settlement will not be upheld once the payor is again employed.

## 10.11  Variation — Jurisdiction to Override Domestic Contracts — Radical Change and Causal Connection

Since the decision of the Supreme Court of Canada in *Miglin v. Miglin*, 2003 CarswellOnt 1374, 2003 CarswellOnt 1375, 2003 SCC 24, REJB 2003-40012, 34 R.F.L. (5th) 255, [2003] 1 S.C.R. 303, 66 O.R. (3d) 736, 224 D.L.R. (4th) 193, 302 N.R. 201, 171 O.A.C. 201, [2003] S.C.J. No. 21 (S.C.C.), the trilogy of *Pelech*, [1987] 1 S.C.R. 801, *Richardson*, [1987] 1 S.C.R. 857, and *Caron*, [1987] 1 S.C.R. 892, cannot be considered as applying to the exercise of the court's discretion under the *Divorce Act* 1985 to override support agreements. See discussion of the *Miglin* case in Chapter 5, s. 5.6.

## 10.12 Variation — Order Incorporating Spousal Support Provisions of Agreements

[*Author's Note*: Cases decided before *Miglin v. Miglin* should be read with caution].

The test is the same in variation to change an agreement in the form of an initial order and variation of an agreement incorporated into a variation order — *Miglin v. Miglin*, 2003 CarswellOnt 1374, 2003 CarswellOnt 1375, 2003 SCC 24, REJB 2003-40012, 34 R.F.L. (5th) 255, [2003] 1 S.C.R. 303, 66 O.R. (3d) 736, 224 D.L.R. (4th) 193, 171 O.A.C. 201, 302 N.R. 201, [2003] S.C.J. No. 21 (S.C.C.), discussed in detail in Chapter 5, s. 5.6. Bastarache Arbour JJ., writing for the majority, said at para. 91:

> ... it would be inconsistent if a different test applied to change an agreement in the form of an initial order under s. 15.2 and to variation of an agreement incorporated into an order under s. 17. In our view the Act does not create such an inconsistency. ... The objectives of finality and certainty noted above caution against too broad a discretion in varying an order that the parties have been relying on in arranging their affairs. Consideration of the overall objectives of the Act is consistent with the non-exhaustive direction in s. 17(7) that a variation order "should" consider the four objectives listed there. More generally, a contextual approach to interpretation, reading the entire Act, should indicate that the court would apply those objectives in light of the entire statute. Where the order at issue incorporated the mutually acceptable agreement of the parties, that order reflected the parties' understanding of what constituted an equitable sharing of the economic consequences of the marriage. In our view, whether acting under s. 15.2 or under s. 17, the Court should take that into consideration.

The threshold variation question of whether there has been a material change in circumstances since the making of the order is the same whether or not a spousal support order incorporates an agreement — the examination of the change in circumstances is the same for an order that incorporates a prior separation agreement as for one that does not — *Droit de la famille - 091889*, 2011 CarswellQue 13698, 2011 CarswellQue 13699, 2011 SCC 64, 6 R.F.L. (7th) 1, [2011] 3 S.C.R. 775, 339 D.L.R. (4th) 624, 424 N.R. 341, [2011] S.C.J. No. 64 (S.C.C.). For a detailed discussion of the case, see **10.3 Variation — Change in Circumstances — Meaning**.

The parties in an agreement cannot oust the court's jurisdiction under s. 17 — *Droit de la famille - 091889*, supra; *Droit de la famille - 09668*, 2011 CarswellQue 13700, 2011 CarswellQue 13701, 2011 SCC 65, 6 R.F.L. (7th) 68, [2011] 3 S.C.R. 819, 339 D.L.R. (4th) 658, 425 N.R. 1 (S.C.C.). For a detailed discussion of the case, see **10.3 Variation — Change in Circumstances — Meaning**.

Where the parties' support order is based on a separation agreement that specifies what may and may not constitute a material change, the court should apply the analytic framework from L.M.P. v. L.S. rather than Miglin to s. 17 variation applications — *Droit de la famille - 132380*, 2013 CarswellQue 14061, 2013 CarswellQue 8788, 2013 QCCA 1504, EYB 2013-226415, 37 R.F.L. (7th) 1 (C.A. Que.). The wife applied to vary a support order arising from the parties' separation agreement. Justice Kasirer noted that varying orders based on agreements is particularly problematic where the agreement sets out the parameters for variation regarding what constitutes a material change. The trial judge had found the husband's decreased income and the wife's increased and stabilized income to be a material change and consequently varied support. The trial judge, however, did not take the parties' agreement into account, which stated that changes in the wife's income would not be a factor in a variation application and would therefore not constitute a material change. A *Miglin* framework applied to s. 15.2 of the *Divorce Act* and was not appropriate for s. 17 of the Act. Further, *Miglin* dealt with definitive settlements, which did not fit the facts here.

*Once the support terms of the parties' separation agreement are incorporated into the divorce judgement, the parties must be considered to have elected to pursue their statutory remedies under s. 17 of the* Divorce Act — *Loit v. Gove*, 2006 CarswellOnt 488, [2006] O.J. No. 347 (Ont. S.C.J.). The wife brought a motion to dismiss the husband's application to vary support payments. The parties had signed a separation agreement which was attached as a schedule to their divorce judgement. The support provisions were not incorporated into the order. The agreement provided that support was variable in the event of a material change in circumstances. The parties set out lists of various circumstances which would not constitute a material change in circumstances and those which would. Subsequently, the parties entered into an amending agreement, which, on consent, was incorporated into an order of the court. Spousal support was reduced and the material change in circumstances clause was deleted from the parties' arrangements and a further provision incorporated which provided that variation of spousal support could only occur where the wife did not receive payment provided in the employment agreement between her and a specified company or the company was insolvent and either party could rely on this provision as creating an absolute bar to any application to vary support other than the fact that the wife was not receiving payment provided in the said employment agreement. The wife remarried. The court considered that the motion was brought as the wife was seeking summary judgement dismissing the variation application, given the limitations on the husband's right to apply to vary. The court held that once the support terms of the parties' separation agreement were incorporated into the divorce judgement, the parties must be considered to have elected to pursue their statutory remedies under s. 17 of the *Divorce Act*. The court at para. 37 stated that the first question to ask was whether the judge who made the initial support order was authorized under s. 15.2(3) to impose a restriction on future variation. A further question, raised at para. 46 is what effect should the intentions of the parties referred to in their negotiated agreement have on the variation application. The court reviewed a number of authorities, particularly in *Miglin*, a case which was not referred to by counsel in *Loit v. Gove*. It quoted the following passage:

> [44] ... Where the order at issue incorporated the mutually acceptable agreement of the parties, that order reflected the parties' understanding of what constituted an equitable sharing of the economic consequences of the marriage. In our view, whether acting under s. 15.2 or under s. 17, the court should take that into consideration.

*Support terminated where, while the wife had need, the respondent did not have the means to pay* — *Burroughs v. Burroughs*, 2004 CarswellBC 17, 2004 BCSC 7 (B.C.S.C.). In the *Burroughs* case, the parties separated, an interim order was granted and then the parties entered into a separation agreement. The court held that the support set out in the interim order and in accordance with the separation agreement be terminated. The petitioner was in need of support but the respondent did not have the means to provide that support unless he were to encroach upon his capital. Their assets had already been divided and the wife had not used her assets or income prudently to plan for her retirement.

*The former husband had not met the onus on him of establishing that his current circumstances represented a significant departure from the range of reasonable outcomes anticipated by the parties at the time their support order, which incorporated their separation agreement, was made* — *Venables v. Venables*, 2004 CarswellSask 85, 2004 SKQB 29 (Sask. U.F.C.). In such a case, a court is unable to proceed to the next step and examine whether the circumstances place the parties at odds with the objectives of the act, so that the agreement should be given little weight. Consequently, the application to vary spousal support was dismissed.

*Support varied downward where husband retired and wife had new partner — Levandusky v. Levandusky*, 2003 CarswellOnt 2615, 39 R.F.L. (5th) 134 (Ont. S.C.J.), additional reasons at 2003 CarswellOnt 2613 (Ont. S.C.J.). Where the husband had retired and the wife had begun to live with a new partner, the husband was successful in reducing the amount of spousal support payable to her pursuant to the parties' earlier minutes of settlement.

*Variation refused where husband would have known that changes could occur in his industry and that such changes would not affect his ability to pay support — Harris v. Harris*, 2000 CarswellOnt 2703, 10 R.F.L. (5th) 45, 135 O.A.C. 312 (Ont. C.A.). The court refused, on appeal, to interfere with the dismissal of the husband's application to vary the spousal support payable by him. The original support order was based upon the parties' settlement agreement in which the husband specifically agreed not to seek a variation. Although the husband had experienced a reduction in income from his construction business, he was well aware when he agreed to the support terms that the construction industry was sensitive to swings in the economy. The husband was an astute businessman and when he entered into the agreement he obviously believed that changes in his ability to earn income were not material to his support obligations.

*Support not varied downwards where husband took earlier than expected retirement — Meiklejohn v. Meiklejohn*, 2000 CarswellOnt 1190, 6 R.F.L. (5th) 360 (Ont. S.C.J.), spousal support was not reduced even though the payor spouse's income declined when he took earlier than expected retirement from his teaching position. The court was of the opinion that the change in the payor's income, when considered in the context of the shared economic consequences of the marriage and its breakdown, and in light of the parties' overall economic circumstances, did not warrant a variation in his support obligation to his former wife. At the time of the trial, he paid less in tax and saved in contributions. He was entitled to CPP benefits to age 65 without "clawback" which added $7000 - $8000 to his income, if he earned less than $8,000 per year from other sources. His current wife presumably assisted him in many of his expenses. Consequently his income was close to the income he received when the separation agreement was negotiated.

*The Miglin analysis would be applicable in some variation proceedings — Kehler v. Kehler*, 2003 CarswellMan 270, 2003 MBCA 88, [2003] 8 W.W.R. 429, 39 R.F.L. (5th) 299 (Man. C.A.). The court in an *obiter* remark stated that in some circumstances involving consent orders based on separation agreements, *Miglin* would be applicable in variation proceedings. The court referred to para. 91 of that decision which stated "it would be inconsistent if a different test applied to change an agreement in the form of an initial order under s. 15.2 and to a variation of an agreement incorporated into an order under s. 17." The Supreme Court had held that the *Divorce Act* does not create such inconsistency.

*The incorporation of a spousal support agreement into a divorce judgement implies that the parties recognize that variation of the amount of support is possible if there is compliance with the variation provisions of the* Divorce Act — *MacDonald v. MacDonald*, 1997 CarswellAlta 566, 30 R.F.L. (4th) 1, 200 A.R. 193, 146 W.A.C. 193 (Alta. C.A.).

*A support order which incorporates the provisions of a separation agreement may be varied under s. 17 of the Act where such agreement contemplates future variation — Barrington v. Barrington*, 1991 CarswellSask 88, 38 R.F.L. (3d) 77 (Sask. C.A.).

*Temporary health issues anticipated at time of agreement were not grounds for reducing support — Chant v. Chant*, 1990 CarswellBC 493, 30 R.F.L. (3d) 271, [1990] B.C.J. No. 2564 (B.C.C.A.). Where the husband was forced to cease work for a 6-month period because of hip surgery, the court, on appeal, reversed an order reducing his monthly support obligation from $4,000 to $3,000. The quantum of support had been settled by the parties, and the husband's decline in income was not substantial in any permanent sense and could have been anticipated at the time of the parties' agreement.

*Where the husband had voluntarily changed jobs and accepted a lower salary, his application to vary support was refused* — Fetterly v. Fetterly, 1989 CarswellAlta 396, 24 R.F.L. (3d) 61, 102 A.R. 131, [1989] A.J. No. 1185 (Alta. C.A.). The order had been based upon the parties' minutes of settlement and the change in the husband's circumstances could not be characterized as material, let alone radical and unforeseen as required by the Supreme Court of Canada trilogy for varying an award based upon a final settlement.

*Variation granted on the basis of payor's loss of employment* — Mendelssohn v. Anderson, 1998 CarswellOnt 3287 (Ont. Gen. Div.). The parties had entered into a separation agreement which had been incorporated into a divorce judgement. The husband had ceased making support payments. The husband sought a variation or termination of support. At the time of the separation, the husband had an income of $250,000. Four years later, his employment was terminated and he received $1,000,000 as a settlement. At the time of the variation application, he had an imputed income of $65,000. The former husband had remarried. The court found that there had been a change in the husband's circumstances and reduced support to $2,000 a month. Arrears of spousal support could be satisfied by redeeming RRSP savings.

*Nature of change required, parties knew of the disease but not its seriousness at the time of the original order* — Fraser v. Fraser, 1998 CarswellAlta 568, 227 A.R. 389 (Alta. Q.B.). The court considered whether the threshold test set out in s. 17(4.1) of the *Divorce Act* had been met and considered that the appropriate standard is that the court must be satisfied that there has been a material change in circumstances between the time of the prior order and the time of the application before the court. The change would be some unknown matter that arises or changes to a known matter that the parties knew were unable to anticipate with a requisite degree of certainty. In this case, the parties knew that the wife had developed multiple sclerosis but they did not know the degree to which the disease would effect her in the future. The wife's application was allowed and her support increased to $1,200 per month.

*Where the payor spouse developed a terminal illness which necessitates substantial health costs after the separation agreement has been executed and a consent order at the time of divorce has reduced the amount of support, a "radical change in circumstances" which was not foreseen at the time of divorce had occurred* — Carson v. Carson, 1998 CarswellNB 120, [1998] N.B.J. No. 145 (N.B.Q.B.). In varying the order and reducing spousal support from $350 to $200 per month, the court found that the fact that the husband was seriously ill with cancer constituted a material change in circumstances as required for a variation under s. 17(1) of the *Divorce Act*.

*Where there is a change of circumstances clause, the test of unforseeablity does not apply* — Bradley v. Bradley, 1997 CarswellOnt 2016, 29 R.F.L. (4th) 151, 43 O.T.C. 122, [1997] O.J. No. 2349 (Ont. Gen. Div.). The parties signed a separation agreement which precluded variation proceedings except for a catastrophic change in either party's circumstances. At the time the agreement was signed the parties knew that the applicant wife was suffering from multiple sclerosis. The court was of the opinion that even though the parties knew of the wife's illness, the court was not prevented from considering her illness on an application to vary. The court held that where, as in this case, the parties had agreed to a provision permitting an application to the courts based on a change in circumstances, the prerequisite test of unforseeability did not apply. The wife proved that her deterioration in health in the 2 years before the application amounted to a "catastrophic change". The court in determining spousal support considered the appropriate amount based on the respondent's ability to pay. In balancing the interests of the first wife with those of the respondent's second family, particularly to his children who were 12 and 14, the court was of the opinion that the respondent could not meet all of the first wife's financial needs and she might be required to look to government and community resources to assist her with her remaining medical expenses. Spousal support was increased by a further $393 per month.

*If a matter is known at the time of the execution of the agreement, it cannot be relied upon as a basis for variation* — Robinson v. Robinson, 1997 CarswellOnt 2437, 33 O.T.C. 297 (Ont. Gen. Div.). The court upheld a divorce judgement which incorporated minutes of settlement whereby the husband was required to pay $1,300 monthly for the support of the wife. The court relied on *Willick v. Willick*, 1994 CarswellSask 48, 1994 CarswellSask 450, EYB 1994-67936, 6 R.F.L. (4th) 161, [1994] 3 S.C.R. 670, 119 D.L.R. (4th) 405, [1994] R.D.F. 617, 173 N.R. 321, 125 Sask. R. 81, 81 W.A.C. 81, [1994] S.C.J. No. 94 (S.C.C.) in holding that in order to grant a variation, there must be a change in circumstances which, if known at the time, would have resulted in different terms. Conversely, if a matter were known at the relevant time, it could not be relied on as a basis for variation. The parties' incomes had both increased since the divorce judgement, but those increases were clearly anticipated at the time of separation. The parties were aware of the wife's impending inheritance at the time they executed the minutes of settlement. Further, the wife's present income of $64,851.22 did not render her self-sufficient within the meaning of s. 17(7) of the *Divorce Act*. The wife's employment was uncertain, given her health and lack of education and skills.

*Husband not required to pay support, as consent order binding* — Wilson v. Pollard, 1997 CarswellOnt 757, 31 O.T.C. 206, [1997] O.J. No. 1017 (Ont. Gen. Div.). The parties had executed a separation agreement in which each released the other from any claims against his or her respective pension or retirement savings plans and subsequently they signed a consent order for spousal support which was indexed to the applicant's net employment income. The former husband was forced to retire from his employment and claimed that he was no longer required to pay spousal support. The court found that the separation agreement was a valid binding agreement and that the consent order was a final order which expressed the real intention of the parties. When the former husband was forced to retire, his employment income was reduced to zero and his pension income was not available to the wife as she had released her interest in his pension by signing the separation agreement. The husband was no longer required to pay spousal support.

*The husband's loss of employment was an insufficient change in circumstances to relieve him from his spousal support obligations contained in minutes of settlement to which both parties had agreed* — Garner v. Garner, 1997 CarswellSask 727, 35 R.F.L. (4th) 262, [1998] 5 W.W.R. 443, 160 Sask. R. 95 (Sask. Q.B.). Although payment under the minutes was qualified specifically by the condition that the husband remain employed, the 72-week severance package received by him resulted in no immediate change to his financial position. As the 72-week period had not expired, the husband could conceivably still find alternate employment before his financial situation truly changed.

*Parties' changes, including wife's mental illness and husband's responsibilities for new family were insufficient to warrant variation of spousal support* — Sneideman v. Sneideman, 1998 CarswellMan 141, 125 Man. R. (2d) 214 (Man. Q.B.). The husband's application for termination of spousal support and the wife's cross-application for an increase in spousal support were both dismissed. The parties entered into a separation agreement in which the husband agreed to pay the wife spousal support consisting of the difference between her earnings and $1,000 per month. The parties agreed that all of the terms of the agreement would survive divorce. The parties had one daughter whom the husband supported. The decree *nisi* provided that the husband pay the wife $1,000 per month. The husband had remarried and had two very young children. The first wife developed mental illness during the marriage and continued to suffer from this disability. The court was of the opinion that all of the changes in the parties' circumstances were not sufficient to warrant a variation of spousal support as required by s. 17(4)(1) of the *Divorce Act*. The court considered s. 17(7) of the *Divorce Act* and found that the first wife had been economically disadvantaged both by the marriage and its breakdown. Further, because of her mental illness she had, so far as was practicable, done all she could to become economically self-sufficient. Following *Moge v. Moge*, 1992 CarswellMan 143, 1992 CarswellMan 222, EYB 1992-67141, 43 R.F.L. (3d) 345, [1992] 3 S.C.R. 813, 99 D.L.R. (4th) 456, [1993] 1 W.W.R. 481, [1993] R.D.F. 168, 145 N.R. 1, 81 Man. R. (2d) 161, 30 W.A.C. 161, [1992] S.C.J. No. 107 (S.C.C.) and *Kloos v. Kloos*, 1996 CarswellMan 126, 20 R.F.L. (4th) 1, [1996] 5 W.W.R. 553, 110 Man. R. (2d) 129, 118 W.A.C. 129, [1996] M.J. No. 146 (Man. C.A.), the court was of the opinion that the model for support under the *Divorce Act* was compensatory in nature, providing an equitable sharing of economic consequences of the marriage and its break-up.

*Where the parties sign a comprehensive separation agreement which is incorporated in a consent order, the person seeking to vary the order must demonstrate a radical and unforeseen change in circumstances — the wife's remarriage was insufficient — Knechtel v. Knechtel*, 1997 CarswellBC 1857, [1997] B.C.J. No. 1928 (B.C.S.C.). The fact that the former wife had remarried did not constitute such a change. Her remarriage ought to have been in the contemplation of both parties as they negotiated a final settlement of their own marriage. Further, while the wife's current husband had a significant income, marriages do not necessarily represent life-long security. The wife's remarriage is neither radical nor unforeseen and she does not have income on which she may rely as a matter arising from her own capacity. The parties' agreement that the respondent was to provide the petitioner with a university education falls squarely within the statutory objectives of a spousal support award, as a means of providing the spouse with a new career.

*The husband's application to rescind spousal support and the wife's cross-application to vary spousal maintenance awards were both dismissed — Shephard v. Fancy*, 1998 CarswellNS 105 (N.S.S.C. [In Chambers]). As the payor spouse's financial circumstances had deteriorated and the payee spouse's mental and physical condition had also deteriorated, there would be no change in the amount of support from that amount set out in the parties' separation agreement which was subsequently incorporated in a corollary relief judgement. The parties' changes in circumstances had cancelled each other out. The court considered the factors set out in s. 17(7) and found that it did not assist the wife but at the same time the husband could not eliminate his obligation to support the wife as set out in the agreement.

*Change must be substantial, unforeseen and of a continuing nature — the wife's leaving her employment to care for a sick child was such a change — L. (E.C.H.) v. L. (G.L.)*, 1998 CarswellBC 1486, 41 R.F.L. (4th) 108 (B.C.S.C.). The court held that where the parties have entered into a final separation agreement in which they agreed that no spousal maintenance would be payable beyond a limited period and the parties signed a consent order, a variation will only be granted when the test of a change of circumstances within the meaning of s. 17 of the *Divorce Act* has been met. The change must be a material change which is substantial, unforeseen and of a continuing nature. In this decision, the parties at the time of signing the separation agreement knew that their daughter needed counselling. Therefore, the test, if applied to the daughter, would have indicated that no such change could be said to have occurred. However, there were changes in a different sense. The wife upgraded her education, but with the deterioration in the health of her daughter, she left her employment and cared for the daughter for 2 years. The court found that the wife was justified in making her decisions relating to her daughter. The change in the wife's plans for re-introduction into the work force to remaining at home to care for a sick child was a material change and one not known or foreseen at the time of entering into the separation agreement. It was substantial and unforeseen and of a continuing nature as it caused the wife to be economically dependent. The court awarded an additional year of support but reduced the amount from $3,000 provided in the separation agreement to $2,000 per month.

*Where wife was to be supported until economically self-sufficient, but possessed assets such as a registered retirement savings plan and inherited rental property which could provide her with income, her support could be reduced* — Hansen v. Hansen, 1997 CarswellNS 260, 31 R.F.L. (4th) 384, [1997] N.S.J. No. 252 (N.S.S.C.). The parties signed a separation agreement which was incorporated in the decree *nisi* with certain modifications and was amended again after divorce. The parties had been married for 35 years and the wife had been a traditional stay-at-home wife and mother for the first 16 years. She later upgraded her education and obtained employment. According to the agreement amended after divorce, the wife was to receive spousal support until she was economically self-sufficient. The wife had inherited rental property, her share of which was valued at between $127,000 and $137,000. The court was of the opinion that where a spouse remains economically dependent on the spousal support provided by their separation agreement, the spouse is entitled to such support. Where, however, as in this decision, the spouse has valuable assets, such as registered retirement savings plans and an interest in the real property from her mother's estate, both of which are income producing assets which could provide her with income which would approximately equal her present income including support, her spousal support should not necessarily be continued. The agreement provided for a review of maintenance and to consider " . . . any change in the conditions, means or other circumstances of . . . the parties." The court found that the wife was in some measure dependent on the husband but reduced spousal maintenance from $1,230 monthly under the agreement to $410 monthly.

*Change must be substantial, unforeseen and of a continuing nature* — *the wife's leaving her employment to care for a sick child was such a change* — Verbrugge v. Verbrugge, 1997 CarswellBC 559, 28 R.F.L. (4th) 35 (B.C.S.C.). The parties had executed a separation agreement which provided for spousal support for 1 year and thereafter $1 each year and either party could apply to change the quantum of support, if there were a material change in his or her circumstances, the court held that the wife had met the threshold test for which the parties had contracted as well as the test as to whether or not the parties' changes were material as well as the test of a change of a substantial, unforeseen and a continuing nature as set out in *Carter v. Carter*, 1991 CarswellBC 170, 34 R.F.L. (3d) 1, 58 B.C.L.R. (2d) 45, 2 B.C.A.C. 241, 5 W.A.C. 241, [1991] B.C.J. No. 2209 (B.C.C.A.).

*Where the parties' separation agreement allowed the husband to vary the quantum of spousal support payable in accordance with fluctuations in his income, he was required to include severance pay received on termination of his position as income* — Richard v. Richard, 1994 CarswellNB 270, 2 R.F.L. (4th) 395, 145 N.B.R. (2d) 383, 372 A.P.R. 383 (Q.B.). The husband had reduced the amount paid to his wife after receiving severance and finding new employment. He was accordingly ordered to pay increased support as well as support arrears.

*Where a support provision of a separation agreement is incorporated into a decree nisi, an application to vary support relates to the decree and not to the original agreement* — King Estate v. King, 1994 CarswellNB 280, 8 R.F.L. (4th) 380, 153 N.B.R. (2d) 20, 392 A.P.R. 20 (Q.B.).

*Variation allowed where husband forced to retire* — Smyth v. Smyth, 1993 CarswellAlta 449, 48 R.F.L. (3d) 280, 142 A.R. 132 (Alta. Q.B.). The court allowed for a reduction in the quantum of spousal support payable to the wife pursuant to minutes of settlement. The agreement had been predicated on the understanding that the husband would work to his normal retirement age and that the wife would obtain employment. The husband's forced early retirement was a radical unforeseen change in circumstances which permitted the variation, even in the absence of a specific clause in the minutes allowing for variation. In setting the new support payable, the failure of the wife to seek employment commensurate with her education and experience was also properly considered.

*A drastic decline in the payor's income justified a reduction in support* — Gallagher v. Hogg, 1993 CarswellMan 43, 45 R.F.L. (3d) 337 (Man. Q.B.). The facts that the payee wife had commenced to live with another man, had received a modest inheritance and an increase in salary were not sufficient grounds to vary a support order based upon the parties' final settlement agreement. However, a drastic decrease in the husband's salary did meet the "unforeseen change in circumstances" test and a reduction in spousal support was justified.

*Timing of change — Huey v. Huey*, 1991 CarswellOnt 357, 39 R.F.L. (3d) 14 (Ont. Gen. Div.). Where the support provisions of the parties' agreement are incorporated into a decree *nisi*, a party seeking a variation of support need prove a change in circumstances from the date of the order and not from the date of the agreement.

*Where the husband had lost his job and suffered a decline in income, his application to vary the agreement-based spousal support was refused — Smith v. Smith*, 1991 CarswellOnt 266, 32 R.F.L. (3d) 353 (Ont. Gen. Div.). The husband's circumstances were not connected to the marriage and could properly be considered as part of the normal "ups and downs" of life that the parties had in mind when they negotiated the settlement.

*In a variation application dealing with a consent order based upon the support provision of the parties' separation agreement, the court must be guided by the relevant provisions of the Divorce Act and by the nature of the parties' bargain — if the agreement is found to have been unfair to the payee spouse from its inception, the court's decision on the variation application is not fettered by the agreement — Davies v. Davies*, 1991 CarswellOnt 250, 32 R.F.L. (3d) 14, [1991] O.J. No. 660 (Ont. Gen. Div.).

*Where the parties' minutes of settlement anticipate a future variation of support, the radical unforeseen change of circumstances onus is not applicable — Jerowsky v. Jerowsky*, 1990 CarswellAlta 292, 32 R.F.L. (3d) 188, 114 A.R. 381 (Alta. Q.B.).

*A court will vary a spousal support order based on an agreement when there is a change in circumstances of a certain kind — that change is the same change that the court requires to enable it to override an agreement and make an original support order under s. 15 — Richardson v. Richardson*, 1987 CarswellOnt 315, 1987 CarswellOnt 963, EYB 1987-67464, 7 R.F.L. (3d) 304, [1987] 1 S.C.R. 857, 17 C.P.C. (2d) 104, 38 D.L.R. (4th) 699, 77 N.R. 1, 22 O.A.C. 1, [1987] S.C.J. No. 30 (S.C.C.); see also *Santosuosso v. Santosuosso*, 1997 CarswellOnt 369, 27 R.F.L. (4th) 234, 32 O.R. (3d) 143, 97 O.A.C. 42, 48 O.T.C. 240, [1997] O.J. No. 501 (Ont. Div. Ct.); and *Large v. Large*, 1997 CarswellBC 1165, 29 R.F.L. (4th) 188, [1997] B.C.J. No. 1171 (B.C.S.C.).

*Where a final separation agreement is incorporated into the decree nisi, the wording of the decree providing for the payment of spousal support "until further order" cannot alter the final effect of the agreement for the purposes of a variation application — Masters v. Masters*, 1991 CarswellSask 59, 84 D.L.R. (4th) 253, 34 R.F.L. (3d) 34, 93 Sask. R. 241, 4 W.A.C. 241, [1991] S.J. No. 376 (Sask. C.A.), affirmed 1994 CarswellSask 42, 1994 CarswellSask 449, [1994] 1 S.C.R. 883, 114 D.L.R. (4th) 575, 4 R.F.L. (4th) 1, 168 N.R. 11, 120 Sask. R. 318, 68 W.A.C. 318, [1994] S.C.J. No. 33 (S.C.C.).

*A court may vary a support order based upon a final settlement agreement where there is a radical unforeseen reduction in the payor's ability to pay — a reduction in the payor's ability caused by a stroke qualifies as valid grounds for variation — Smith v. Smith*, 1990 CarswellMan 47, 71 D.L.R. (4th) 612, 27 R.F.L. (3d) 32, 66 Man. R. (2d) 181, [1990] M.J. No. 350 (Man. C.A.). Leave to appeal refused (1991), 79 D.L.R. (4th) vii (note), 32 R.F.L. (3d) 159 (note), 78 Man. R. (2d) 88 (note), 135 N.R. 160 (note), 16 W.A.C. 88 (note) (S.C.C.).

*Minutes of settlement upheld — Carrigan v. Carrigan*, 1987 CarswellNS 175, 80 N.S.R. (2d) 276, 200 A.P.R. 276 (T.D.). Where by minutes of settlement the husband had agreed to pay specified maintenance to his wife, his subsequent application to vary the sum was dismissed. The husband had freely entered into the agreement and no change of circumstances had occurred.

*Support agreed to in minutes of settlement terminated* — *Goddard v. Goddard,* 1988 CarswellOnt 293, 16 R.F.L. (3d) 453 (Ont. H.C.). Where the husband had agreed to pay spousal support by minutes of settlement, his obligation was later terminated in face of his retirement and the wife's confinement to a nursing home. The husband's ability to pay was limited and as the wife was able to cover her living arrangements from her own resources, she no longer had need of support.

*Retirement is not sufficient grounds for varying support* — *LaPierre v. LaPierre,* 1995 CarswellNS 9, 10 R.F.L. (4th) 327, 137 N.S.R. (2d) 189, 391 A.P.R. 189 (N.S.S.C.). Where the husband had, through minutes of settlement, agreed to the quantum of spousal support payable, his subsequent retirement was found not to constitute sufficient grounds for a reduction of the amount. As the minutes of settlement were intended to be final, they could only be varied in the face of a radical change in circumstances. As the parties must have contemplated the husband's eventual retirement, the radical change threshold had not been met.

*The court has jurisdiction to incorporate a separation agreement into a divorce judgement and to vary it retroactively* — *there is no general principle that a party seeking such incorporation or variation must first pay all arrears outstanding under the agreement* — *Pousette v. Pousette,* 1993 CarswellBC 602, 46 R.F.L. (3d) 152, [1993] B.C.J. No. 1105 (B.C.S.C.).

*Cohabitation clause could not be relied upon to terminate wife's support* — *Cooper v. Cooper,* 1998 CarswellNfld 254, 42 R.F.L. (4th) 317, 168 Nfld. & P.E.I.R. 58, 517 A.P.R. 58, [1998] N.J. No. 289 (Nfld. U.F.C.), affirmed 2001 CarswellNfld 17, 2001 NFCA 4, 13 R.F.L. (5th) 29, 198 Nfld. & P.E.I.R. 1, 595 A.P.R. 1, [2001] N.J. No. 19 (Nfld. C.A.). The husband was not allowed to rely upon a cohabitation clause in the parties' separation agreement to justify termination of the wife's spousal support. The agreement allowed for termination if the wife lived with another man as husband and wife. Although the wife shared a home with her boyfriend in Florida for several months of the year, she maintained separate financial arrangements and paid for her own food. She also maintained a separate residence during the balance of the year.

## 10.13 Variation — Order to Dismiss or Terminate Support

*Spousal support will not be terminated where the recipient has borne all responsibility for raising the children with disabilities and the recipient has medical issues* — *Caldwell v. Caldwell,* 2013 CarswellAlta 1241, 2013 ABCA 268, 33 R.F.L. (7th) 285 (Alta. C.A.). The parties were married for 12 years and separated in 1995. They had four children. The husband applied to terminate spousal support, which application was dismissed by the chambers judge. The original order provided for support until the wife turned 60. The chambers judge considered variation, but found that it was not warranted. The wife had had sole care of the children with no access by the father; she had medical issues, and the children had learning, emotional and physical disabilities. The Court of Appeal upheld the decision and held that the chambers judge had properly considered the factors in the *Divorce Act.*

*Where no medical evidence of inability to work has been given, and the parties have contemplated triggering events for termination of support that have not occurred, support will not be terminated and no change in circumstances will be found* — *Chase v. Chase,* 2013 CarswellAlta 258, 2013 ABCA 83, 24 R.F.L. (7th) 21, [2013] A.J. No. 145 (Alta. C.A.). The husband applied to vary a support order to terminate support. The chambers judge had found there was no change in circumstances. The parties had a separation agreement providing for termination of support when the wife remarried or the husband reached age 60. Neither triggering event had occurred. The husband had decided to retire after his employment was terminated, citing ill health, but he had provided no medical evidence. The judge found that the husband had chosen to retire and that the parties had contemplated what would constitute a change in circumstances when drafting the separation agreement. Consequently, there was no change in circumstances.

*A court has jurisdiction under the Divorce Act to vary an order that dismissed or terminated spousal support* — Tierney-Hynes v. Hynes, 2005 CarswellOnt 2632, 75 O.R. (3d) 737, 256 D.L.R. (4th) 193, 200 O.A.C. 251, [2005] O.J. No. 2661 (Ont. C.A.). Leave to appeal refused 2005 CarswellOnt 7437, 2005 CarswellOnt 7438, 349 N.R. 394 (note), 215 O.A.C. 394 (note), [2005] S.C.C.A. No. 424 (S.C.C.). While under earlier versions of the *Divorce Act*, a court did not have this jurisdiction, legislative changes and the expansive language of the 1997 *Divorce Act* provide that a court has jurisdiction to vary under these circumstances. Some of the changes are the following:

> [53] ... a new provision in the current Act, s. 15.3, specifically contemplates an application for support made after an earlier dismissal of spousal support. [A]lthough the current Act distinguishes between child and spousal support, it does not distinguish between the two types of support when addressing variation applications. [T]he structure and terms of the 1997 Act, particularly ss. 15 and 17, differ in significant ways from the 1970 Act and in significant respects from the Revised 1985 Act.

In addition, self-sufficiency became only one of the objectives of the *Divorce Act*. Divorce and corollary relief proceedings were separated, so that a spouse was no longer limited to claiming support at the time of divorce, but could seek it later. A court was no longer restricted to varying a positive order for support. In this case, the court specifically noted the distinction between cases of dismissal of support and cases of extending time-limited support. Lang, J. writes at para. 71:

> [71] In restructuring the Act, Parliament could have chosen language that would have precluded any variation of a dismissal of spousal support, or limited such variations to specific situations, as it did with respect to time limited support in s. 17(1)). It chose not to do so.

It does not follow that the finding in this case will lead to the opening of the floodgates in variation of spousal support orders. In order to vary previous dismissals of spousal support, applicants will still be required to meet the threshold tests necessary to establish a meritorious claim.

*A time-limited award of support is justified when the supported party has the wherewithal to achieve self-sufficiency, and need not be reconsidered when the recipient has taken no steps to achieve this self-sufficiency under s. 17(7)(d)* — Walsh v. Walsh, 2007 CarswellOnt 1718, 2007 ONCA 218, 36 R.F.L. (6th) 262 (Ont. C.A.). Leave to appeal refused 2007 CarswellOnt 5948, 2007 CarswellOnt 5949, 378 N.R. 394 (note), 245 O.A.C. 399 (note) (S.C.C.). The trial judge terminated the husband's support of the wife, based on her lack of attempts to achieve self-sufficiency despite a capacity to do so. The trial judge's emphasis on self-sufficiency was not unreasonable and was therefore upheld on appeal.

*Orders should not be drawn to preclude a subsequent order for support, where a claim for support had been dismissed* — Gill-Sager v. Sager, 2003 CarswellBC 104, 2003 BCCA 46, 36 R.F.L. (5th) 369, 222 D.L.R. (4th) 595, 177 B.C.A.C. 155, 291 W.A.C. 155, [2003] B.C.J. No. 121 (B.C.C.A.). The law was unsettled as to whether a spouse, whose claim, pursuant to the *Divorce Act* for "support" was dismissed by the judgement in the court below, was precluded from ever succeeding on a subsequent application, no matter what the change in his or her circumstances. The court held that a plain reading of the *Divorce Act* did not lead to one seeing its plain purpose. Only the Supreme Court of Canada could provide a definitive answer. The court stated that orders should not be drawn so as to preclude a subsequent application. In this case, the wife appealed from a judgement granting the husband's motion to dismiss the wife's spousal support claim. The wife who had been blinded in an accident shortly after the marriage and who contracted Hepatitis C in a disabling form, but had recovered, was at the time of the hearing not in need of support. Her position was that if her Hepatitis C returned in a disabling form and if the health care system would not pay for all the costs of her treatment, her present means of support might cease to be adequate. If this were to happen, she wished to bring a fresh application for support founded on that change of circumstances. The court held that the order should leave the possibility open that the wife could return to court to seek support if needed. However, it did not mean that a fresh application for support could be brought immediately. The appeal was allowed.

*Spousal support may be terminated when the parties have similar asset bases and the payor's income has been drastically reduced* — Reilly v. Reilly, 2010 CarswellBC 976, 2010 BCSC 543 (B.C.S.C.).

*Depleting capital combined with insufficient employment does not constitute self-sufficiency which would justify the termination of spousal support* — Syms v. Syms, 2010 CarswellOnt 2815, 2010 ONSC 1735 (Ont. S.C.J.). The husband's motion to terminate spousal support was refused as he could not demonstrate a change in circumstances or self-sufficiency on the part of his former wife. Rather, his income remained the same and his former wife continued to experience financial need resulting from the marriage. While she was not receiving spousal support, she depleted her savings such that they dropped from approximately $20,000 to $5,000.

## 10.14 Variation and Rescission of Support Orders

### Practice — evidence

*Expert evidence not required* — Moge v. Moge, 1992 CarswellMan 143, 1992 CarswellMan 222, EYB 1992-67141, 43 R.F.L. (3d) 345, [1992] 3 S.C.R. 813, 99 D.L.R. (4th) 456, [1993] 1 W.W.R. 481, 81 Man. R. (2d) 161, 145 N.R. 1, [1993] R.D.F. 168, 30 W.A.C. 161, [1992] S.C.J. No. 107 (S.C.C.). The court considered the evidence required for a court's determination of spousal support. Madame Justice L'Heureux-Dubé noted the difficulty of the analysis, but stated, at p. 390 [R.F.L], that "this complexity does not excuse judges from hearing relevant evidence or from fully applying the law. There are no easy recipes, nor are there neat compartments on which to rely, as families and family relationships are not simple. But there are few matters more important before the courts, given the repercussions on the future of the parties themselves and in particular, their children." She added, at p. 391 [R.F.L.], that "in some cases, such evidence might come in the form of highly specific expert evidence which enables parties to present an accurate picture of the economic consequences of marriage breakdown in their particular circumstances. . . . Although of great assistance in assessing the economic consequences of marriage breakdown in a particular marriage, such evidence will not be required, nor will it be possible, in most cases. For most divorcing couples, both the cost of obtaining such evidence and the amount of assets involved are practical considerations which would prohibit or at least discourage its use. Therefore, to require expert evidence as a *sine qua non* to the recovery of compensation would not be practical for many parties, not to mention the use of court time which might be involved. It would be my hope, therefore, that different alternatives be examined."

*Where expert evidence not given, the court should use the doctrine of judicial notice* — Moge v. Moge, supra. Where expert evidence was not given, Madame Justice L'Heureux-Dubé considered a proposal of legislative guidelines for support, but seemed to prefer the use of the doctrine of judicial notice in determining spousal support. The court was of the opinion, at p. 393 [R.F.L.], that "the general economic impact of divorce on women is a phenomenon, the existence of which cannot reasonably be questioned and should be amenable to judicial notice."

*Where a party wishes to give evidence on the issue of spousal support, the court should ensure that his or her evidence is heard, no matter if it is lengthy — Moge v. Moge, supra.* Madame Justice L'Heureux-Dubé writes, at p. 394 [R.F.L.]. "This being said, even if a major portion of the time of the civil courts in this country is taken by family law matters, and the efficient and speedy disposition of affairs before the court is a valuable goal, the paramount goal is to render justice to the parties in accordance with the Act."

## Variation and recission of spousal support orders — practice — miscellaneous

*Arrears accumulating under a Divorce Act order cannot be cancelled or reduced in an application under a provincial statute — Weinstein v. Weinstein,* 1995 CarswellBC 304, 15 R.F.L. (4th) 353, 8 B.C.L.R. (3d) 23, 61 B.C.A.C. 314, 100 W.A.C. 314 (B.C.C.A.), reversing 1994 CarswellBC 37, 8 R.F.L. (4th) 354, 1 B.C.L.R. (3d) 174 (B.C.S.C.).

*Statutory right of review — Lidstone v. Lidstone,* 1993 CarswellNS 44, 46 R.F.L. (3d) 203, 121 N.S.R. (2d) 213, 335 A.P.R. 213, [1993] N.S.J. No. 165 (N.S.C.A.). Where an order for support provides for a fixed period and then states that at the end of that period, the payor may apply for a review, a former spouse is not precluded at any time from exercising his statutory right of review of support under s. 17(1), in the event of a material change in circumstances.

*Payment formula — Klassen v. Klassen,* 1993 CarswellMan 34, 44 R.F.L. (3d) 433, 83 Man. R. (2d) 214, 36 W.A.C. 214 (Man. C.A.). In allowing a motion for a reduction in support payable, the court has jurisdiction to set a payment formula which takes into account the contingency that the payor's circumstances may improve, thus eliminating the need for the payee to seek a further variation.

*Severance of entitlement and quantum issues dismissed — Zwingenberger v. Zwingenberger,* 1995 CarswellOnt 1084, 17 R.F.L. (4th) 239, [1995] O.J. No. 3402 (Ont. Gen. Div.). Where the evidence on entitlement in the wife's application for increased support would take only half a day or less, the husband's application to sever the determination of entitlement from quantum was dismissed.

*A party seeking variation of a support order is not required to establish a prima facie entitlement to variation before being authorized a notice to disclose to issue to other party — Rosin v. Rosin,* 1994 CarswellAlta 396, 8 R.F.L. (4th) 315, 158 A.R. 14 at 19, [1994] A.J. No. 663 (Alta. Q.B.).

*Support payments increased by husband's cost of living increases — Van de Sande v. Van de Sande,* 1994 CarswellAlta 484, 148 A.R. 30 (Alta. Q.B.). The court allowed a variation to the wife's spousal support award whereby her support payments were to be increased annually by the actual percentage of any cost of living increase granted to the husband.

*Variation recommendations — Lewin v. Lewin,* 1992 CarswellNS 140, 115 N.S.R. (2d) 145, 314 A.P.R. 145, [1992] N.S.J. No. 294 (N.S.T.D.). The Nova Scotia Family Court lacks jurisdiction to order a variation of a divorce decree or a corollary relief judgement. The court is restricted to making variation recommendations for consideration by the Supreme Court.

*Although the Civil Code restricts cost awards to divorce proceedings and does not include subsequent variation proceedings, the Divorce Act itself permits the court to determine cost issues on variation applications — Droit de la famille - 605,* 1989 CarswellQue 196, [1989] R.J.Q. 505, 28 Q.A.C. 106, [1989] R.D.F. 342 (C.A. Que.).

*Where variation proceedings are commenced in two different provinces, exclusive jurisdiction belongs to the province where such proceedings were first commenced — Droit de la famille - 541,* 1988 CarswellQue 357, [1988] R.J.Q. 2386, (sub nom. R. v. S.) 25 Q.A.C. 284, [1988] R.D.F. 484 (C.A. Que.).

*Payee's support reduced on enforcement proceedings which she had brought — Wilson v. Wilson*, 1987 CarswellBC 551, 11 R.F.L. (3d) 244 (B.C.C.A.). The court dismissed the wife's appeal from an order in which her maintenance had been reduced in the course of enforcement proceedings which she had initiated. Although there had been no application for variation, the judge's actions were realistic and his conclusion supportable in the circumstances.

*A husband's petition for termination of spousal support cannot be disposed of through the wife's motion for dismissal — the matter must be dealt with at trial — Droit de la famille - 1265*, [1989] R.D.F. 501 (C.S. Que.).

*It is impossible for a party to present an application to vary an original award where an appeal from that award has not yet been decided — Droit de la famille - 338*, 1986 CarswellQue 766, EYB 1986-78322, [1987] R.J.Q. 426, [1987] R.D.F. 28 (C.S. Que.).

*A party is still entitled to seek variation of a support order under the* Divorce Act *even after the order has been filed with the Director under the* B.C. Family Maintenance Enforcement Act *— McKinney v. Polston*, 1992 CarswellBC 564, 42 R.F.L. (3d) 141 (B.C.S.C.).

*Where the decree nisi is silent on the issue of support, only the court which granted the decree has jurisdiction to entertain a subsequent support application — such a proceeding is an application for corollary relief and cannot be characterized as a variation application — Evans v. Evans*, 1987 CarswellBC 564, 6 R.F.L. (3d) 166 (B.C.S.C.).

## 10.15 Variation and Foreign Divorces

See also Volume 1, 4§1 Jurisdiction to grant corollary relief.

*Variation of a support order made in another jurisdiction and varied under the* Interjurisdictional Support Orders Act, S.A. 2002, c. I-3.5 *is permissible and must, as always, consider the consequences flowing from the marriage — Warren v. Warren*, 2009 CarswellAlta 1781, 2009 ABCA 370, [2009] A.J. No. 1216 (Alta. C.A.). In this case, the appellate court found that the chambers judge in making the variation order, which was a time-limited step down order, had adequately considered the economic consequences of the marriage and its breakdown. The chambers judge had ample evidence of the factual basis pertaining of marriage to evaluate the effect of the duration of the marriage, the role and contributions of each partner and their prospects for the future.

## 10.16 Variation Order by Affidavit

**17.1** Where both former spouses are ordinarily resident in different provinces, a court of competent jurisdiction may, in accordance with any applicable rules of the court, make a variation order pursuant to subsection 17(1) on the basis of the submissions of the former spouses, whether presented orally before the court or by means of affidavits or any means of telecommunication, if both former spouses consent thereto.

---

**17.1** History. Enacted S.C. 1993, c. 8, s. 2.

---

**17.1 Variation order by affidavit**. Section 17.1 provides for a variation proceeding where both former spouses are ordinarily resident in different provinces. A court may make a variation order under s. 17.1 based on the submissions of the former spouses. These submissions may be made orally before the court or subject to the consent of both former spouses by means of affidavits or any means of telecommunication.

*There is no requirement that a parties' consent to a proceeding under s. 17.1 of the Divorce Act be in writing or be expressed in any formal way — Consent can be inferred from the parties' actions — Attrill v. Green*, 1994 CarswellAlta 753, 7 R.F.L. (4th) 176, 34 Alta. L.R. (3d) 32, 154 A.R. 334, [1994] A.J. No. 448 (Alta. Q.B.).

*Variation of a support order is provisional only where the respondent is ordinarily resident in another province and has not accepted the jurisdiction of the court, or where both spouses have not consented to the application of s. 17.1 of the* Divorce Act — *A final variation is not available even where the respondent is served with the application — Martell v. Height*, 1993 CarswellSask 45, 45 R.F.L. (3d) 344, 111 Sask. R. 279, [1993] S.J. No. 198 (Sask. Q.B.).

## 10.17 Review Proceedings

Section 15.2 (3) of the *Divorce Act* allows a court to include terms and conditions in a spousal support order. The common law has extended this provision to provide a court with jurisdiction to make "review" orders. A review order, in contrast to a variation order, does not require a change in circumstances. The Supreme Court of Canada case of *Leskun v. Leskun*, discussed in detail below, stated that courts should, where possible, decide the issues before them and make an order which is permanent, subject only to change under s. 17 where there is a change of circumstances. *Leskun* established that review orders have a limited role. They should only be granted where there is a genuine and material uncertainty at the time of the original trial. If an issue is to be decided on a future review, the issue should be clearly delineated.

[*Author's Note*: Cases decided before *Leskun*, below, should be viewed with caution.]

*Review orders under s. 15.2 have a useful, but very limited role — Leskun v. Leskun*, 2006 CarswellBC 1492, 2006 CarswellBC 1493, 2006 SCC 25, 34 R.F.L. (6th) 1, [2006] 1 S.C.R. 920, 62 B.C.L.R. (4th) 197, 268 D.L.R. (4th) 577, 226 B.C.A.C. 1, 349 N.R. 158, 373 W.A.C. 1, [2006] S.C.J. No. 25 (S.C.C.). The husband appealed from a chambers ruling denying his application to discontinue support payments. The husband had agreed to pay the wife interim spousal support of $2,250 per month. At trial, the husband was ordered to continue spousal support payments of $2,250 until the wife returned to full employment, at which time entitlement and quantum would be reviewed. The court stated that review orders are useful, for example, where there is a need to establish a new residence, start a programme of education, train or upgrade skills, or obtain employment. Where possible, courts should resolve the controversies before them and make an order which is permanent, subject only to change under s. 17 on proof of a change of circumstances. If, as in this case, the s. 15.2 court considers it essential to identify an issue for future review, the issue should be tightly circumscribed in the s. 15.2 order. This should be done because on a "review", neither party bears an onus to show changed circumstances. If the issue is not tightly limited, one of the parties will see the hearing as an opportunity to reargue his or her case. The lower court had made a review order, which was justified by serious doubt at the time of trial as to the true financial situation and prospects of the wife and what support would be needed. At the date of the trial, there were outstanding issues which the trial judge anticipated would be resolved in a relatively short time. On the facts of this case, whether the application was treated as brought under s. 15.2 (review application) or under s. 17 (variation application), it made no difference to the outcome. The application was not decided on the matter of the onus. The court found that the husband's application was properly characterized as a review application. It was not necessary for him to demonstrate a change in circumstances. Nevertheless, while certain financial issues had been resolved between the time of the trial decision and the date of the application to discontinue support, the wife's failure to become self-sufficient had not changed. The husband's appeal was dismissed.

A review provision triggered by the retirement of the payor shifting the onus to the recipient was found to be an error — Frank v. Linn, 2014 CarswellSask 510, 2014 SKCA 87, 48 R.F.L. (7th) 34, [2014] 10 W.W.R. 215, 442 Sask. R. 126, 616 W.A.C. 126, [2014] S.J. No. 458 (Sask. C.A.). The trial judge ordered a review of support to occur when the payor husband retired and for the wife to bear the onus of demonstrating continued need and ability of the husband to pay. The Court of Appeal found this was an error as such an order would exempt the husband from demonstrating the reasonableness of his decision to retire. The shift in onus was an error.

A review date does not preclude a party from returning to court to seek variation prior to a review date when there is a material change in circumstances — Jendruck v. Jendruck, 2014 CarswellBC 2375, 2014 BCCA 320, 50 R.F.L. (7th) 23, 62 B.C.L.R. (5th) 139, 376 D.L.R. (4th) 523, 360 B.C.A.C. 55, 617 W.A.C. 55, [2014] B.C.J. No. 2086 (B.C.C.A.). The Court of Appeal upheld a trial decision which provided for a review of spousal support when the parties turned 65. The Court of Appeal noted that this did not preclude a return to the court for variation by either party under s. 17 of the Divorce Act when change in means, needs or circumstances occurred prior to the review date.

A review provision for the date when the parties turned 65 that anticipated a downturn in income was reasonable — Jendruck v. Jendruck, supra. The Court of Appeal upheld a trial decision, which provided for a review of spousal support when the parties turned 65. The Court of Appeal found that this was reasonable, as it "avoids argument on an application for a variation consequent on retiring at age 65, that Mr. Jendruck's retirement was contemplated when the support order was made."

Where the parties had anticipated in their separation agreement that the wife would be self-sufficient by the review date and there were good policy reasons for upholding the agreement, an order to terminate support after 24 months will be upheld on appeal — Strecko v. Strecko, 2014 CarswellNS 448, 2014 NSCA 66, 44 R.F.L. (7th) 1, 347 N.S.R. (2d) 61, 1098 A.P.R. 61 (N.S.C.A.). The parties were married for 23 years. In 2010, they concluded a separation agreement which provided for spousal support for the wife to be reviewed in 2012. At the review hearing, the wife sought indefinite spousal support. The judge held that the wife had a continuing obligation to become self-sufficient and ordered support to terminate after an additional 24 months. The wife appealed. The Court of Appeal found that the parties had agreed to a review and policy dictated that agreements between parties should be encouraged. The parties stated in their agreement that they were optimistic the wife would be self-sufficient by the review date and created an obligation for her to make reasonable efforts to become self-sufficient. The Court of Appeal found that there was no error made by the judge at first instance, who had considered what the parties themselves had intended in the agreement.

An order for a specific review date will be in the discretion of the judge and failure to order a specific date for review is not an error in cases where indefinite support has been ordered — D. (K.) v. D. (N.), 2014 CarswellBC 430, 2014 BCCA 70, 350 B.C.A.C. 282, 598 W.A.C. 282 (B.C.C.A.). The parties had a 7-year marriage, which ended in 2006, and two children. A 2009 order provided for indefinite spousal support, inter alia. The order was varied in 2011; and in 2013 the husband applied to review the original order. The husband appealed the new order, which imputed income to the wife. He appealed on the basis that the review judge had erred in not ordering a specific review date to occur in the future. The Court of Appeal found that there was no error. The judge had given reasons for his failure to order a specific date of review and had noted that the parties could apply to vary should circumstances change.

A review must consider fully factors in s. 15.2 such as the parties' respective contributions to the relationship, means and needs — Morck v. Morck, 2013 CarswellBC 1032, 2013 BCCA 186,

28 R.F.L. (7th) 279, 44 B.C.L.R. (5th) 235, 337 B.C.A.C. 125, 576 W.A.C. 125, [2013] B.C.J. No. 803 (B.C.C.A.). The parties separated in 2005 after almost 25 years of marriage. The wife had mental health issues that were well known to the husband. In 2006, the Court awarded the wife support, reviewable after 2 years. The wife applied for a review, and the husband appealed the decision. The Court of Appeal found that the trial judge had treated the wife's application for review as an application for variation and noted that the review must be based on the parties' present circumstances rather than those of the original order. The trial judge had not adequately considered the parties' present circumstances, and the Court of Appeal sent the case back down to trial.

*Where a previous motion to vary occurred prior to a review date set in an order, a second motion will be allowed when the review date has occurred to take into account the different onus on a review versus a variation application* — Brooks v. Brooks, 2012 CarswellNB 332, 2012 CarswellNB 333, 2012 NBCA 50, 390 N.B.R. (2d) 94, 1011 A.P.R. 94 (N.B.C.A.). The parties were married for almost 20 years and had two children. The parties had a consent order for corollary relief which dealt with spousal and child support. Three years after the order, the wife applied to vary retroactive and ongoing spousal support. The motion judge found that the wife, who had previously moved for such an order, had already been heard and was attempting to re-litigate issues that had been decided. The Court of Appeal found that, because the wife's first application to vary was made prior to the time she was allowed to seek review under the consent order, she had not been heard on the issue of review. The second motion did not require a material change in circumstances. The Court of Appeal ordered a new hearing.

*The court must ensure that a review application is not treated as a variation application* — Morck v. Morck, supra. The parties separated in 2005 after almost 25 years of marriage. The wife had medical and mental health issues that were well known to the husband. In 2006 the court awarded the wife support, reviewable after 2 years. The wife applied for review, and the husband appealed the decision. The Court of Appeal found that the trial judge had treated the wife's application for review as an application for variation and noted that the review must be based on the parties' present circumstances rather than those of the original order. The husband's appeal was allowed. See also Domirti v. Domirti, 2010 CarswellBC 2864, 2010 BCCA 472, 10 B.C.L.R. (5th) 281, 294 B.C.A.C. 127, 498 W.A.C. 127, [2010] B.C.J. No. 2074 (B.C.C.A.); and Norton v. Norton, 2011 CarswellBC 2505, 2011 BCSC 1307 (B.C.S.C.).

*A fresh application must not masquerade as a review, which should be conducted in the same court that made the order* — Ballinger v. Ballinger, 2012 CarswellBC 1362, 2012 BCCA 205, 16 R.F.L. (7th) 1, 34 B.C.L.R. (5th) 182, 350 D.L.R. (4th) 116, 322 B.C.A.C. 45, 549 W.A.C. 45 (B.C.C.A.). The parties separated in 2000 after 23 years of marriage. Their separation agreement mandated a review of spousal support in 4 years. The Provincial Court increased support at review. In 2011 the husband requested an interim variation of the order pending a review. The Supreme Court decided that the Provincial Court, which had made the order, was the appropriate forum for review and that otherwise the husband should make a fresh application. The Court of Appeal dismissed the husband's appeal from this decision.

*Because a review provision should only be made when the parties' circumstances are uncertain, a lengthy review period is inappropriate* — Armstrong v. Armstrong, 2012 CarswellBC 1095, 2012 BCCA 166, 33 B.C.L.R. (5th) 86, 350 D.L.R. (4th) 186, 320 B.C.A.C. 94, 543 W.A.C. 94, [2012] B.C.J. No. 770 (B.C.C.A.). In 2010 the court made a support order subject to review only in 7 years' time. The Court of Appeal, at para. 71, found that this was too long a period: "in my view the imposition of a review provision seven years after the 'Final Order' does not fall within the parameters for such orders as outlined in Leskun at paras. 36 and 37. As discussed in that case, review orders play a very limited role and are restricted to situations where there is genuine uncertainty about the effect the breakdown of the marriage will have on the future economic circumstances of the parties."

*Review provisions must be specific, otherwise the review effectively becomes a variation —* Westergard v. Buttress, 2012 CarswellBC 360, 2012 BCCA 38, 14 R.F.L. (7th) 1, 318 B.C.A.C. 108, 541 W.A.C. 108, [2012] B.C.J. No. 255 (B.C.C.A.). The parties were in a common-law relationship for 15 years and separated in 2004. In 2005, the court granted the wife spousal support with an option to review as of 2009 to allow her time to become economically self-sufficient. The wife applied for the review in 2010. The new order, which continued the support, was reviewable in 2013 with the onus on the wife to establish that support should continue further. The Court of Appeal, at para. 23, found this second review provision was "not fully in keeping with the general rule that judges should, where possible, fully and finally determine support obligations." The Court of Appeal judge limited the reviewable issues to the wife's entitlement to support based on her progress towards self-sufficiency.

*A motions judge should not reject a review application provided for in a consent order without a "fresh adjudication of spousal support issues" —* Brooks v. Brooks, 2012 CarswellNB 332, 2012 CarswellNB 333, 2012 NBCA 50, 390 N.B.R. (2d) 94, 1011 A.P.R. 94 (N.B.C.A.). The parties' consent order provided for a review of spousal support. In 2009 the wife applied for a review, and the husband sought a review in response. The motions judge rejected the application without re-reviewing the issue. The Court of Appeal found this was an error in law and remitted the matter to the Court of Queen's Bench.

*A variation of a support order that originally contained a review condition should include another review clause, unless there is sufficient evidence of a material change in circumstances —* Walters v. Walters, 2011 CarswellBC 2021, 2011 BCCA 331, 9 R.F.L. (7th) 1, 338 D.L.R. (4th) 421, 308 B.C.A.C. 282, 521 W.A.C. 282 (B.C.C.A.). The parties were married for 23 years and separated in 2005. In 2007 a divorce order granted the wife indefinite support, subject to review in the event of a change in circumstances. In 2010 the lower court varied the order, reducing the amount of support without including a review condition. The wife appealed in 2011. The Court of Appeal found that the husband had not sufficiently demonstrated the change in circumstances required for the court to vary the order without adding a new review clause.

*The court should not order a review without justifiable reason —* Aspe v. Aspe, 2010 CarswellBC 3077, 2010 BCCA 508, 89 R.F.L. (6th) 245, 11 B.C.L.R. (5th) 309, 327 D.L.R. (4th) 231, 294 B.C.A.C. 290, 498 W.A.C. 290 (B.C.C.A.). The parties were married for 12 years and separated in 1993. The wife was awarded indefinite support. In 2009 the wife applied to the Supreme Court for a variation of the order. The chambers judge granted her support and included a review condition in the order, while noting that reviews should only be available in the event of a material change in circumstances because of the risk that the parties will see it as an opportunity to reargue the case. The Court of Appeal found that a review clause was unwarranted in the circumstances, which were not uncertain at the time of the order. The appeals judge stated, at paras. 52 and 53, that the wife had indeed used the review clause as "an opportunity to present a more convincing case for ongoing support, rather than an assessment of her steps toward self-sufficiency. ... [The wife had] 17 years since the marriage breakdown to take the steps necessary to attain self-sufficiency. Her failure to do so [was] due solely to her own improvident choices." The court set aside the order for review.

*Appropriate approach was to impute income to wife — limited-term support —* Heimsoth v. Heimsoth, 2009 CarswellAlta 478, 2009 ABCA 129, 65 R.F.L. (6th) 27, 457 A.R. 22, 457 W.A.C. 22, [2009] A.J. No. 371 (Alta. C.A.). The parties were married for 24 years. In 2002, when the parties divorced, the court ordered that the husband pay the wife $4,000 per month in spousal support. At the review hearing in 2007, the court held, in essence, that while the wife was entitled to compensatory support, this support was limited by the fact that she only really contributed for about 10 years during the marriage, namely, the 10 years she was at home full time. The court ordered spousal support for a further 18 months followed by termination of support. The Court of Appeal found that the trial judge on the review erred in limiting the wife's period of contribution to the marriage to 10 years, as the wife continued to look after the children and the household throughout the marriage. The appropriate approach would have been to impute income to the wife.

*The court should only order a review if it is truly warranted — review orders should be "the exception, not the norm"* — Fisher v. Fisher, 2008 CarswellOnt 43, 2008 ONCA 11, 47 R.F.L. (6th) 235, 88 O.R. (3d) 241, 288 D.L.R. (4th) 513, 232 O.A.C. 213, [2008] O.J. No. 38 (Ont. C.A.). The parties were married for over 18 years. In 2006 the trial judge awarded support to the wife subject to review in 3 years, speculating, at para. 69, that by this time the wife would "perhaps enter into a new relationship." The wife appealed, and the Court of Appeal found that reviews should only be ordered where there is uncertainty and a review was therefore unwarranted in the circumstances. The appeals judge further noted that reviews are to be discouraged, as they may come with high financial and emotional costs. The order was set aside.

*Review order should not be granted where the review would take place close to the time of the originating order; a review hearing should have a clearly delineated set of facts subject to consideration* — Fishery. Fisher, supra. The parties had had a 19-year marriage. There were no children. At the time of trial in 2006, the husband earned $140,000. The wife, on average, earned $30,000. The trial judge had ordered a step-down award of support over 3 years. The order also provided that either party could "seek a review of both entitlement and/or quantum ... without the need to establish a material change in circumstances." It stated, at para. 63, "[A] review, particularly one relatively proximate to the time of the originating order, causes unnecessary and significant expense for the parties, not only emotionally, but also financially." It continued, at para. 70, "Review orders, in effect, turn an initial order into a long-term interim order made after trial. Accordingly, they should be the exception, not the norm. They are appropriate when a specified uncertainty about a party's circumstances at the time of trial will become certain within an identifiable timeframe. When one is granted, it should include specifics regarding the issue about which there is uncertainty and when and how the trial judge anticipates that uncertainty will be resolved." In other circumstances, a court should issue a final order which would always be subject to variation. In a review order the burden is placed on the applicant, although it is in the context of an initial application. In the *Fisher* case, the trial evidence was that the appellant was making reasonable efforts at self-sufficiency. There was little evidence that her finances would change at any clearly marked point in time. Consequently, there was no basis for the review date provided in the trial judgement. Also, the order did not provide for the *Leskun* requirement for a clearly delineated set of the facts subject to review. The court concluded that the imposition of the review order constituted an error in principle on the facts of the case. The court allowed the appeal and set aside those parts of the divorce order dealing with the quantum of spousal support and the review order. It ordered spousal support in the amount of $3,000 monthly beginning October 1, 2004, then stepped down spousal support on April 1, 2008 to $1,500, with support terminating on September 1, 2011. This would provide the appellant with 7 years of spousal support, subject to any variation order made in accordance with s. 17 of the *Divorce Act*.

*Once the agreed conditions precedent to a review of support have been met, the court should apply s. 15(2) of the* Divorce Act, *taking into account the agreement as a relevant consideration as to quantum and duration of support* — Scott v. Scott, 2008 CarswellBC 2439, 2008 BCCA 457, 58 R.F.L. (6th) 256, 58 B.C.L.R. (4th) 314, 85 B.C.L.R. (4th) 314, 262 B.C.A.C. 102, 441 W.A.C. 102 (B.C.C.A.). In November 2006, the parties settled their family law dispute midtrial, and a consent order was made reflecting the settlement. The order provided, among other matters, that the husband would pay spousal support to the wife in the amount of

$8,000 per month. They agreed that their annual incomes for purposes of child support were, for the husband $445,150, and for the wife $96,000.The consent order provided for a review of spousal support upon the husband leaving his employment with his then employer. At the time the consent order was made, the husband had already tendered his resignation from his position effective June 29, 2007. The husband applied on August 9, 2007, for a review of the quantum of spousal support, saying his income was much reduced from what it had been at the time of the order. At the time of his application, the husband had not obtained new employment. The appellate court stated that the wife did know that the husband was leaving his employment. Whether he anticipated that he would find replacement income is of no consequence, provided the review term continued in force. As there was no basis upon which to set the review term aside, the proper approach was for the court to apply s. 15 (2) of the *Divorce Act*, taking the agreement into account. The appellate court concluded that the judge was led into error by the collateral attack upon the review clause. By embarking on that enquiry, the judge placed the review, to which husband was entitled, on the wrong foundation. The Court of Appeal set aside the order of the Chambers judge and remitted the husband's application for review back to the trial court for a new hearing.

*A court can order variation of spousal support before the review date* — Bemrose v. Fetter, 2007 CarswellOnt 5819, 2007 ONCA 637, 42 R.F.L. (6th) 13, 228 O.A.C. 311, [2007] O.J. No. 3488 (Ont. C.A.). Under s. 17(4.1) of the *Divorce Act*, a judge has jurisdiction to order a variation in spousal support on the basis of a material change in circumstances before the review date. The trial order specified that no review was to take place until 3 years after the date of the trial order. It did not purport to oust the court's jurisdiction to vary spousal support nor, in the court's view, could it.

*The right to apply for a variation exists independently of review provisions* — Bemrose v. Fetter, supra. The parties separated in 2000 after 13 years of marriage. The 2003 support order contained a provision allowing a review in no sooner than 3 years. One year later, a motions judge varied the order on the basis of a material change in circumstances. The Court of Appeal found that the motions judge did not exceed his jurisdiction in varying the order because the right to apply for a variation of support is entirely separate from a review application, which is a provision in an order or agreement.

*Although it is not necessary to establish a material change in circumstances when making an application for review provided for in a separation agreement, the onus is on the applicant to show entitlement* — McIntyre v. McIntyre, 2007 CarswellSask 13, 2007 SKCA 5, 36 R.F.L. (6th) 243, 289 Sask. R. 255, 382 W.A.C. 255, [2007] S.J. No. 8 (Sask. C.A.). The parties were together for 18 years. During the marriage, the wife left the workforce in order to become a homemaker. In 2003 the parties signed a separation agreement that provided for a review of spousal support. In 2007 the husband appealed a review decision awarding the wife ongoing support. The Court of Appeal disagreed with the lower court and found that the wife was not "contractually entitled to ongoing support" according to the separation agreement. She was entitled to the 2 years' support provided for in the agreement, subject to review, and no more.

*Once the agreed conditions precedent for a review of support have been met, the court should apply s. 15(2) of the Divorce Act, taking into account the agreement as a relevant consideration to quantum and duration of support* — McEachern v. McEachern, 2006 CarswellBC 2750, 2006 BCCA 508, 33 R.F.L. (6th) 315, 62 B.C.L.R. (4th) 95, [2007] 3 W.W.R. 471, 232 B.C.A.C. 185, 385 W.A.C. 185, [2006] B.C.J. No. 2917 (B.C.C.A.), reversing in part 2005 CarswellBC 497, 2005 BCSC 301, [2005] B.C.J. No. 460 (B.C.S.C.).

*A review order is appropriate in the case where a serious issue is foreseeable* — Tedham v. Tedham, 2005 CarswellBC 2346, 2005 BCCA 502, 20 R.F.L. (6th) 217, 47 B.C.L.R. (4th) 254, 261 D.L.R. (4th) 332, [2006] 3 W.W.R. 212, [2005] B.C.J. No. 2186 (B.C.C.A.), additional reasons at 2005 CarswellBC 2699, 2005 BCCA 553, 47 B.C.L.R. (4th) 276, 261 D.L.R. (4th) 332 at 359, [2006] 3 W.W.R. 234, 217 B.C.A.C. 250, 358 W.A.C. 250 (B.C.C.A.). The difficulty with review orders is that if they are made as a matter of course, they have the potential for unduly increasing the expense of litigation and suspending the ability of the parties from getting on with their lives. However, in this case, since the husband's problems with his eyesight could seriously affect his income-earning ability and/or work-related expenses and this was a foreseeable event which may not meet the test for a variation under s. 17(1) of the Act, the spousal support order should be subject to review.

A review hearing for spousal support, as distinct from an application to vary, does not require a demonstration of a change in circumstances — Phinney v. Phinney, 2002 CarswellNS 525, 2002 NSCA 168, 33 R.F.L. (5th) 211, 211 N.S.R. (2d) 135, 662 A.P.R. 135, [2002] N.S.J. No. 540 (N.S.C.A.). Thus, the governing section of the Divorce Act is s. 15.2.

Support reviewable after 9-month period, giving time for re-training and seeking employment — Arvai v. Arvai, 1999 CarswellOnt 4848, 12 R.F.L. (5th) 1 (Ont. S.C.J.), additional reasons at 1999 CarswellOnt 4847 (Ont. S.C.J.), varied 2001 CarswellOnt 432, 14 R.F.L. (5th) 223, 52 O.R. (3d) 481, 141 O.A.C. 343, [2001] O.J. No. 561 (Ont. C.A.). The wife was granted spousal support reviewable after a 9-month period. Given that her only experience throughout the parties' 17-year marriage was helping the husband farm, she was entitled to support during a period of retraining and while seeking employment. The marriage had caused the wife to lose the ability to support herself, as it was not reasonable to expect that she could find employment in farming.

When a review order is made, the quantum of support on the review is to be determined in light of all the circumstances then existing and with regard to the factors and objectives for spousal support orders contained in the Divorce Act — Munn v. Munn, 1999 CarswellOnt 671, 44 R.F.L. (4th) 179 (Ont. C.A.). The parties had a traditional marriage of 17 years where the husband made financial provision and the wife managed the home and raised their two children. On appeal from the order of the trial judge that the husband pay spousal support of $700 a month for 18 months, the Court of Appeal increased the order to $1,100 a month for 5 years with the provision that on or before the end of the 5 years, either party could apply to the court to reconsider the wife's entitlement and any continuation of support.

Review after 7 years in light of the factors and objectives in the Divorce Act — Bildy v. Bildy, 1999 CarswellOnt 497, 44 R.F.L. (4th) 81, 42 O.R. (3d) 737, 127 O.A.C. 44, [1999] O.J. No. 501 (Ont. C.A.). The parties separated after 13 years of marriage. The wife was a full-time mother of their two children and a homemaker. She had not worked outside the home for 8 years. She was experienced in secretarial work and the highest income she had earned was $27,000 a year. Her husband was a lawyer with an income of $240,000 a year. She owed an equalization payment to him of $43,165, which was to be paid in installments of $500 a month. By agreement made prior to May 1, 1997, her husband was paying $60,000 a year for the support of the two children and $30,000 a year for her support for total support payments of $90,000 a year. Because the agreement was made before May 1, 1997, the full $90,000 was deductible from the husband's income for tax purposes, and includible in the wife's. The issue was whether the spousal support under the agreement should be time limited. The trial judge found that it should be, and ordered that the payments terminate after 5 years. On appeal, the court held that the spousal support should be paid for a further 2 years giving a term of 7 years with the right of either party at the end of that term to reconsider the wife's entitlement to support for herself and any continuation of it. "The quantum of support, if any, should be decided in light of all the circumstances as may then exist and upon the application of ss. 15(5) [factors] and (7) [objectives] of the Divorce Act..."

In a review hearing, it is not necessary to establish a change in circumstances since the making of the order — Schmidt v. Schmidt, 1999 CarswellBC 2764, 1999 BCCA 701, 1 R.F.L.

(5th) 197, 71 B.C.L.R. (3d) 113, 132 B.C.A.C. 36, 16 B.C.T.C. 320, 215 W.A.C. 36, [1999] B.C.J. No. 2757 (B.C.C.A.). Review orders "are considered particularly useful in circumstances where there is some doubt as to whether spousal maintenance should be continued and, if so, in what amount. Rather than force the parties to go through a variation proceeding with its strict threshold test of change in circumstances, the court provides that maintenance shall be reviewed. In some cases, the court also states how the proceedings will be conducted and the nature of the evidence to be called. Pending review, the order remains in effect" (see para. 9.) A review order should not be confused with an order for limited time maintenance or an order for the payment of maintenance until the happening of a specific event. Where the payee spouse has not achieved self-sufficiency, but is striving to do so and in other circumstances, a spousal support order that was declared subject to review may be continued. In the *Schmidt* case, in April 1996, the husband was ordered to pay the wife $1000 in spousal support. In June 1997, the wife sought a review of spousal support. At the review, spousal support was increased to $1,750. The husband appealed. As this was a review hearing, it was not necessary for the wife to establish that there had been a material change in circumstances since the order of April 1996. The court at the review hearing did not err in increasing the quantum of maintenance to $1,750 per month. The husband now has the advantage of sharing expenses with his current wife and receiving monetary gifts from his parents from time to time. The court must take these benefits into account as they are part of the husband's economic circumstances which cannot be ignored. However, the wife was not able to supplement her income. She was suffering from a medical condition which presently made her unemployable. In addition, she was 50 years of age and had been out of the active workforce since 1970 raising children. Consequently, it seemed unlikely that she would become employed in the near future, if ever. She did not share expenses with a partner, although she had received occasional loans from her parents. The appellate court held that the court at the review hearing had erred in increasing spousal maintenance to $1,750.

*A review order will not be granted because of concern that the payee will not try to be self-sufficient* — Choquette v. Choquette, 1998 CarswellOnt 2939, 39 R.F.L. (4th) 384, [1998] O.J. No. 3024 (Ont. C.A.). The trial judge fully considered the objectives set out in s. 15(7) (a) through (d) of the *Divorce Act* as they applied to the facts of this case. He specifically addressed the issue of self-sufficiency and was satisfied on the evidence that the wife would "return to the workplace and move relatively quickly toward self-sufficiency". In the absence of a material error, this court should not intervene. In these circumstances, the husband's concerns that the wife might not become self-sufficient as quickly as anticipated by the trial judge are better dealt with on a variation application brought if in fact she does not become self-sufficient at the expected time.

*A support order specifying a review after a certain period of time is not a limited-term order and the review hearing is not a variation proceeding to which s. 17(10) of the* Divorce Act *applies* — Haigh v. Haigh, 1991 CarswellBC 531, 33 R.F.L. (3d) 161, 5 B.C.A.C. 109, 11 W.A.C. 109, [1991] B.C.J. No. 4030 (B.C.C.A.).

*A discussion of spousal support in a hearing does not necessarily mean that the support order was reviewed* — Brown v. Brown, 2012 CarswellAlta 1655, 2012 ABQB 597, 20 R.F.L. (7th) 119 (Alta. Q.B.). The parties separated in 2003, and the court granted the wife spousal support in 2006. The wife stated that a 2010 hearing was a spousal support review, but the court disagreed. The husband brought a review application based in part on the wife's alleged new relationship, and the court granted him leave to proceed.

*Review provisions will be appropriate when a specific element of the original order should be reconsidered* — T. (T.) v. H. (J.M.), 2014 CarswellBC 725, 2014 BCSC 451 (B.C.S.C.). The parties were married for 17 years prior to separation. The marriage was traditional, and the wife's main activity was homemaking, although she worked part-time on various projects which did not result in much income. Indefinite support was ordered. Neither party had asked for a review provision, and the judge found that review provisions were appropriate only when a specific aspect of the original order should be reconsidered. In this case, variation upon retirement by the husband was considered more appropriate.

*Where a recipient's future ability to work was unknown and the recipient was relatively young, a review provision may be ordered* — *Knapp v. Knapp*, 2014 CarswellOnt 3156, 2014 ONSC 1631 (Ont. S.C.J.). The parties cohabited for 12.5 years. The wife, aged 36, had a mental illness, was incapable of managing her property, and was represented by the Public Guardian. She had not worked since 2011 because of her illness. Both parties sought to include a review provision in the spousal support order. The judge noted, at para. 50, that review provisions should only be included exceptionally, but said:

> in this case, however, because of the uncertainty of the future course of Ms. Knapp's mental illness, the issue of medications which may control her illness, her relatively young age and the fact that both parties worked during the marriage with relatively similar incomes and relatively similar roles in the marriage, I am prepared to accept the joint submission for a review.

A review was ordered 6.5 years after separation, which was the minimum duration of support suggested by the SSAG.

*Considerations which bind the court on a review application are the same as criteria for an originating application* — *MacKay v. MacLean*, 2014 CarswellNS 254, 2014 NSSC 127 (N.S.S.C.). The husband sought a review of a spousal support obligation found in a corollary relief judgment, which provided for review after 5 years. He sought to terminate support. The judge found the corollary relief judgment contemplated support as transitional, and the wife had not made any efforts towards self-sufficiency or retraining since separation some 8 years previously. Support was terminated.

*Where a wife is financially disadvantaged because of her own choices rather than the role played during cohabitation and has not taken steps towards self-sufficiency, support was terminated* — *Acker v. Acker*, 2014 CarswellNS 136, 2014 NSSC 5, 41 R.F.L. (7th) 166 (N.S.S.C.). The husband sought the termination of spousal support in this review application. The wife sought to increase spousal support based on the husband's post-separation increase in income. The parties were married for 23 years, and support was paid pursuant to minutes of settlement incorporated into a corollary relief order. The wife had not been employed for 10 years prior to separation. The judge considered the roles played by the parties during the relationship and found that the wife had not been economically disadvantaged by the marriage, which was non-traditional. The judge found that the husband's income had increased, but was now roughly equivalent to its level at the time of separation. The wife's financial situation was found to be a result of her own choices rather than her role during the marriage. Spousal support was not increased, and a step-down order was made.

*Where a review provision is made in an order that has not been appealed, it will be valid despite a possible error in law under the principle of preventing collateral attack on the validity of orders* — *Lochhead v. Lochhead*, 2014 CarswellBC 1490, 2014 BCSC 962 (B.C.S.C.). The parties were married for 23 years prior to separation. They divorced in 2002, and a corollary relief order was made granting spousal support to the wife on the basis that she required compensatory support as she had been partially economically disadvantaged by the marriage. In 2005, a variation of the 2002 order was made. In 2010, an application for review of the 2002 order was made. The 2010 order found that the judge in 2002 had set a review date with the expectation that the wife would achieve self-sufficiency. Instead, she had become permanently disabled, but had received a substantial inheritance. Time-limited spousal support was awarded below Guidelines amounts with a review date. In this application, the husband sought to terminate support. The wife argued that the fact that the 2005 order was a variation rather than a review of the 2002 order made the 2010 review a nullity. The judge accepted the husband's argument that as no appeal was taken from the 2010 order, it must be considered valid. In any case, there was significant uncertainty at the time of the 2010 order regarding the wife's future ability to work.

*Where an indefinite order of spousal support was made partly on a compensatory basis, a review provision will not be included* — A. (S.L.) v. A. (B.A.), 2013 CarswellNB 744, 2013 CarswellNB 745, 2013 NBQB 372, 413 N.B.R. (2d) 318, 1072 A.P.R. 318 (N.B.Q.B.). The parties were married for 17 years. The husband sought to include a review provision in the order for spousal support, which was indefinite. The judge declined to do so, finding that the wife's entitlement to support was both needs-based and compensatory in nature and the compensatory element would not change and thus a review was not indicated. It was not reasonable to assume the wife would be able to achieve self-sufficiency in the limited amount of time prior to the review suggested by the husband. She was in poor health and had very limited education and work experience.

*Where material uncertainties existed as to the level of self-sufficiency that the recipient would be able to attain, a review provision was included* — Cochrane v. Cochrane, 2013 CarswellBC 3535, 2013 BCSC 2114 (B.C.S.C.). The wife was found to be entitled to indefinite spousal support. The judge included a provision for a review in an order for spousal support because there was material uncertainty as to how long the child would remain a child of the marriage and how self-sufficient the wife would be able to be in that time.

*Where the recipient's income was based on a full-time salary, a review provision was not included in an order for support which was time-limited* — C. (C.E.) v. C. (S.W.), 2013 CarswellBC 3103, 2013 BCSC 1879, 38 R.F.L. (7th) 418 (B.C.S.C.). This was an original application for spousal support. Income was imputed to the wife based on full-time employment. The husband sought to include a review provision in the order. The judge declined to do so, finding that there was no duty on the wife to achieve self-sufficiency, but rather to take reasonable steps to do so. A time-limited order of support was made.

*A review will consider the factors set out in s. 15.2(4)* — Bradford v. Bradford, 2013 CarswellBC 2774, 2013 BCSC 1700 (B.C.S.C.). The husband sought to review spousal support after a previous order had elapsed. The judge considered the s. 15.2(4) factors when determining that the wife continued to be entitled to compensatory spousal support. The previous order had been for compensatory support and was made subject to review because it was unknown how long it would take the wife to become self-sufficient. The judge at the review hearing found that the wife had made reasonable efforts, but was still entitled to compensatory support.

*The single issue giving rise to the review hearing was the prospect of the wife's economic self-sufficiency within the meaning of s. 15.2(6)(d) of the Divorce Act — "Ability to pay" was not an issue within the scope of the review* — L. (R.) v. L. (N.), 2012 CarswellNB 258, 2012 NBQB 123, 22 R.F.L. (7th) 82, 388 N.B.R. (2d) 220, 1006 A.P.R. 220 (N.B.Q.B.). At the time of trial, the wife was enrolled as a full-time student in university, with an expected graduation date in 2010. Her future employment was uncertain. She also had health issues. At the review hearing, the court found the wife was unable to become self-sufficient as she had not been able to find meaningful employment and had continuing health issues. The husband's application to terminate spousal support was dismissed. The husband was ordered to pay the wife spousal support of $950 per month until August 1, 2020. A further review was not appropriate. If there were a significant change, a variation application could be made.

*The court will respect the parameters of a separation agreement and interpret provisions according to their "plain and ordinary meaning"* — Holaday v. Holaday, 2012 CarswellSask 362, 2012 SKQB 211, 397 Sask. R. 164 (Sask. Q.B.). The parties' separation agreement stated that the spousal support order would be reviewable upon the husband's retirement. When he retired early, he applied for a review. The court found that the plain and ordinary meaning of the clause meant the expected age of retirement and did not grant a review.

Where a separation agreement provides that spousal support could be reviewed on an annual basis, and the payor applies to determine his spousal support obligation under s. 15.2(1) of the Divorce Act, there being no previous order capable of variation, the agreement is but one factor to consider in setting spousal support — there should be no retrospective determination of the support obligation — Norton v. Norton, 2011 CarswellBC 2505, 2011 BCSC 1307 (B.C.S.C.). In the application, there was no reference to a review of spousal support as contemplated in the agreement. "Neither the wording of the Agreement nor logic invites a retrospective assessment of [the payor's] obligation [for support]" (para. 43).

Where the marriage is a traditional one and the recipient spouse is negatively affected economically by the marriage, spousal support should continue after a review — Pollock v. Pollock, 2011 CarswellOnt 10125, 2011 ONSC 5150 (Ont. S.C.J.), additional reasons at 2011 CarswellOnt 13965, 2011 ONSC 6255 (Ont. S.C.J.). The parties were married for 22 years. The payor husband sought to terminate spousal support paid as a result of an order arising from minutes of settlement. The order contained a provision that support should be indefinite or until the recipient earned more than $20,000. Consequently, this application was for a review. The judge applied the Miglin principles in order to determine that the wife should continue to receive spousal support as her income had not been "substantially more" than the $20,000 threshold set out in the original order. The marriage was traditional, and she had not been intentionally under-employed.

It is not necessary to establish a material change in circumstances when applying for a spousal support review — Warke v. Wildeman, 2010 CarswellBC 3115, 2010 BCSC 1632 (B.C.S.C.). The 2004 order awarding the wife spousal support was reviewable in 2007, and the husband brought a review application in 2010. The court found that it was not necessary for him to establish a material change in circumstances.

A review hearing is not appropriate where the costs of a review hearing can be a financial burden on parties, especially where, as in this case, there is no material issue of uncertainty — Sawchuk v. Sawchuk, 2010 CarswellAlta 32, 2010 ABQB 5, 79 R.F.L. (6th) 135, 22 Alta. L.R. (5th) 383, 485 A.R. 183, [2010] A.J. No. 18 (Alta. Q.B.). The parties were married for 24 years and their lives had evolved together. At the time of separation in 2005, the wife was 43 and the husband was 48. Both were working full-time. There was a presumption that their standards of living would be equalized, based upon the parties' standard of living at separation. The court directed the husband to pay spousal support of $1,000 per month, commencing March 1, 2009, for a period of 8 years. This period of time was chosen on the basis that it anticipated a reduction in the husband's earning capacity due to age, physical demands of employment and potential retirement.

Where there are review provisions in an initial order, the support issue is to be determined as a review, that is, as an initiating application requiring a rehearing of everything from entitlement to quantum — Krane v. Krane, 2010 CarswellOnt 1471, 2010 ONSC 1488, [2010] O.J. No. 1009 (Ont. S.C.J.). The parties had a traditional marriage of over 20 years. They did not have a marriage contract. There have been several orders since separation. The husband received an economic advantage from the marriage. But for the marriage, the wife would have had greater job seniority and stability and possibly greater security for her retirement. Without support the wife would have felt greater disadvantage than the husband from the breakup of the marriage. The wife's assumption of the day-to-day care of the children, both during the marriage and after separation, had negative financial consequences for her. Both parties had suffered economic hardship as a result of the breakdown of their marriage. In the circumstances of this case, the court was not persuaded that the economic hardship of either party had been more or less than the other, except to the extent that the husband has enjoyed a significant increase in his income which was not disclosed to the wife and had not, until this hearing, been the subject of consideration in the support payable by him. Having regard to these principles and the circumstances of these parties, the court found that the goal of self-sufficiency for the wife based on her income-earning capacity was not practicable in a reasonable time. After reviewing the evidence and applying the factors and objectives, the court held that the wife was entitled to continue to receive spousal support. The court ordered retroactive support and effective January 1, 2010, spousal support of $1,050 per month.

An additional review order was made where there was uncertainty as to the parties' income prospects — Bianchin v. Bianchin, 2010 CarswellBC 534, 2010 BCSC 295 (B.C.S.C.). It was unclear whether the wife would obtain regular employment and, if so, whether she would earn in excess of $2,000 per month (the amount at which her spousal support would be affected) and there was also considerable uncertainty as to what income the husband would be able to earn in the future. A review of the order was to take place in 2 years' time.

A review order was made where there were uncertainties relating to the husband's income and the special needs of one of the parties' children — Martin v. Martin, 2010 CarswellBC 453, 2010 BCSC 261 (B.C.S.C.).

Where there are uncertainties relating to the wife's income and the changes that might occur once the youngest child graduated from high school, a review should be permitted — Judd v. Judd, 2010 CarswellBC 246, 2010 BCSC 153, 83 R.F.L. (6th) 314, [2010] B.C.J. No. 177 (B.C.S.C.). The Court stated that by making a review order it would remove the burden of having to establish a change in circumstances and also the risk that under a variation application "the applicant may have his or her application dismissed on the basis that the circumstances at the time of the variation application were contemplated at the time of the original order and, therefore, that there had been no change in circumstances." (Leskun, at para. 37). The parties were married for 17 years and had two teenage children. The wife had a commerce degree, but had not worked full time since 2003. She intended to establish a career selling real estate in her community on the Sunshine Coast. The court ordered that spousal maintenance be paid until further order of the court. Either party could apply for a review after June 30, 2013.

Where there is no uncertainty about the future prospects of either party, a review order should not be made — Purdue v. Purdue, 2009 CarswellNB 538, 2009 NBQB 303, 351 N.B.R. (2d) 215, 904 A.P.R. 215 (N.B.Q.B.). In this case, there was certainty. The wife intended to continue as a teacher's assistant and the husband intended to continue as a valued employee of the company for which he had worked for many years.

Where there is a review condition in a consent order, a material change in circumstances will not be required in order to change the amount of support — Balazsy v. Balazsy, 2009 CarswellOnt 5982, 75 R.F.L. (6th) 315, [2009] O.J. No. 4113 (Ont. S.C.J.). The parties were married in 1982 and had three children before they separated in 2000. They signed a consent order in 2005 providing for $750 in spousal support monthly. The husband brought a motion in 2006 asking for termination of support. Both parties had begun to cohabit with new partners. Because there was a review condition in the consent order, the judge did not need to find a material change in circumstances in order to change the amount of support. He examined the SSAG in determining that a "step-down" order would be appropriate. The wife had been disadvantaged by the marriage, but was finding her way to self-sufficiency.

Spousal support for an indefinite period was granted with a review after 4 years — Vanos v. Vanos, 2009 CarswellOnt 6420, 77 R.F.L. (6th) 123, [2009] O.J. No. 4217 (Ont. S.C.J.). The Court stated that it would expect the wife to have obtained at least part-time employment soon after the receipt of its judgement. On the review date, the court would expect her to be in a position to report specifically her progress and plans for upgrading her qualifications and enhancing her education. The court observed that the wife would also have the responsibility for the care of the children which must take priority over her obtaining part-time employment and upgrading her qualifications. The wife was to be paid spousal support in the mid range amount of $1,489 per month commencing July 1, 2009.

A review hearing should be ordered where the court has genuine and material uncertainty as to whether the support recipient will be able to secure better-paying permanent employment — Beck v. Beck, 2009 CarswellNfld 136, 2009 NLUFC 23 (N.L.U.F.C.). The wife was 45 years of age. She wanted to further her education so that she would not need spousal support or, at least, have it decreased. The court considered that the most sensible approach would be for the wife to obtain a "specialty" which would enable her to teach. If she followed this approach or embarked on another realistic area of study, the court still had genuine and material uncertainly as to whether she would, in fact, be able to secure better-paying, permanent employment. The review order was limited to an analysis of the wife's educational success and her efforts to obtain permanent, better-paying employment. This review hearing could be heard any time after June 15, 2012.

A review of spousal support will be ordered where the court has a very real doubt as to whether spousal support should be continued indefinitely — Barry v. Barry, 2009 CarswellNfld 67, 2009 NLUFC 13 (N.L.U.F.C.). In 2005, the wife had been awarded $900 in monthly interim spousal support. The parties had been married for 22 years. She was 46 and he was 49. The wife lived with another man, but claimed that the relationship was not intimate. She planned to move to Pasadena. There was no evidence that she would continue to share expenses with the man with whom she currently lived. Her expenses would be more than at present, which would not enable her to have a decent lifestyle, in any event. Her future health could not be determined at this time and her success at being able to complete her schooling, which she could not complete in the past, could also prevent her from getting back into the workforce. She was certainly not self-sufficient at this time and whether she could become partially, or fully, self-sufficient was uncertain. In 2005, she had been awarded $900 monthly interim spousal support. The court ordered spousal support payable in equal installments of $800 on the first and fifteenth of each month commencing April 1, 2009. A review hearing tightly circumscribed as to the wife's efforts and ability to become partially or wholly self-sufficient could be heard after April 1, 2011.

Where the parties had not delineated in their separation agreement what was to happen between the time of the original hearing and the review hearing the court considered the two live issues between the parties — the wife's ability to become self-sufficient and the husband's income — Cassaday v. Krpan, 2009 CarswellOnt 808 (Ont. S.C.J.). The court considered the factors and objectives set out in ss. 15.2(4) and (6) of the Divorce Act, regarding an order for support. The court ordered 3 more years of support from December 1, 2004 up to and including December 1, 2007. The court stated that the duration of the order was somewhat arbitrary, but was also reasonable in the circumstances. It gave the wife court-ordered support for a total of 6 years from December 1, 2001; that is the mid-range of the length of time for support suggested in the Spousal Support Guidelines. It was a reasonable length of time, given the length of the marriage (7½ years), the wife's age (44), at the time of separation and her ability to re-enter the work force. The court also recognized that the wife probably received some support between 1998 and December 2001. She was presently working and earning $40,000 gross per annum. At the time of the execution of the separation agreement, her tax return suggested that she was earning approximately $11,000. The wife was clearly making considerably more than that at the time of the review hearing and she had replaced her support income of $27,000 per annum. The court stated that there was no evidence or jurisprudence to suggest that the father was to "top up" the wife's full-time income indefinitely.

*Where a payee spouse has received compensatory support, there are no facts on which it would be appropriate to make another, further review order* — *Holmes v. Holmes,* 2009 CarswellOnt 87 (Ont. S.C.J.). The parties were married for 16 years and had two children. The divorce order granted in 2005 provided for spousal support in the amount of $1,000 per month with a mandatory review "three years from the date of this Order," that being February, 2008. In the 2009 judgement, the court stated that at the time that the review order was made, it was not clear what uncertainty existed which required a mandatory review in 3 years. The court ordered spousal support of $1,000 per month, a slight restructuring, as in *Fisher v. Fisher,* of the mid-point amount of $960 per month in accordance with the Advisory Guidelines, based on the incomes of the parties, with a termination date of December 31, 2014.

*Further review ordered* — *Wagg v. Wagg,* 2008 CarswellNS 604, 2008 NSSC 315 (N.S.S.C.). The parties married in 1981, had two children, separated in 1998 and divorced in 2004. They agreed in minutes of settlement signed in 2004 that the husband, who at the time earned approximately $160,000, would pay spousal support of $1,070 per month to the wife. The minutes contained a review clause providing that the amount was not to be reviewed earlier than two years from the date of the agreement. Since the parties' separation in 1998, the wife began part-time employment in 2003 earning $25,000 per year, and she obtained higher paying employment in October 2007, but lost her job less than a year later due to factors beyond her control. The husband, whose income had increased significantly since settlement and whose total income in 2007 was $316,788 (US), applied for an order terminating spousal support. The support was increased to $1,070 per month through the remainder of 2008, $1,500 per month in 2009, and $1,200 per month for the next two years. The court found that the wife, who had been the full-time caregiver of the couple's two children until the date of separation and whom the husband had discouraged from obtaining employment until the date of separation, had diligently attempted to be employed and to move towards self-sufficiency after the separation. Her re-entry into the workforce after 17 years of being out of the workforce was a significant barrier to her self-sufficiency. The husband had also impeded the wife's self-sufficiency by failing to live up to the terms of disclosure and by participating in her son's unexpected departure without consultation or notice. Full self-sufficiency must be sufficient to sustain existence and not necessarily a minimal existence. The wife planned to begin taking courses to attain her CGA status. In order to do so and to address the wife's current income instability, spousal support was ordered for three years at which time her financial situation should be reviewed and the onus would be on the wife to prove ongoing need. While it was unusual to order an increase in support payments after 10 years, the court held that the combination of special circumstances justified such an increase.

*Given the wife's age, degree of experience, training and length of time outside the workforce, it was purely speculative to address a measurable period of time in the foreseeable future when the wife would be self-sufficient* — *monthly spousal support of $775 was awarded and continued until further order of the court was reviewable on either party's motion after 3 years* — *Maber v. Maber,* 2007 CarswellNB 171, 2007 NBQB 99, 313 N.B.R. (2d) 208, 809 A.P.R. 208, [2007] N.B.J. No. 128 (N.B.Q.B.).

*Where the 43-year-old wife had failed to prove how her various ailments affected her current and future ability to work, her spousal support was made subject to a review in 2 years time* — *Rea v. Rea,* 2007 CarswellOnt 8257, 47 R.F.L. (6th) 351, [2007] O.J. No. 4990 (Ont. S.C.J.), additional reasons at 2008 CarswellOnt 151, 47 R.F.L. (6th) 365, [2008] O.J. No. 128 (Ont. S.C.J.).

*The factors and considerations which bind a court on a review hearing are identical to those which apply on an originating application* — *Cavanaugh v. Cavanaugh,* 2008 CarswellNB 590, 2008 NBQB 387, 77 R.F.L. (6th) 355, 341 N.B.R. (2d) 166, 876 A.P.R. 166, [2008] N.B.J. No. 464 (N.B.Q.B.), reversed 2008 CarswellNB 630 (N.B.C.A.). The Court noted that in this case the issues were not tightly delineated in the s. 15.2 order. To a great degree, the parties used the review hearing to relitigate their case. As there were no reasons for the consent order, the court conjectured that the only reason for another review would be because of the wife's intention to establish a home based business. The parties' circumstances had not changed since the last order. The court held that a continuation of support would provide the wife with additional financial support, while permitting her to try to establish her business. Spousal support was to continue in the amount of $1,450 per month, retroactive to November 2007.The order provided for a review no earlier than May 2010, 8 years post-separation. The purpose of the review would be to hear evidence regarding the wife's efforts to generate or find employment and how those efforts might have been affected by her health, among other matters. If her health had had a negative effect upon her employment, she might consider calling evidence other than her own concerning that issue. The parties had been married for 18 years and at the time of the hearing the wife was 53 years old. The husband was 55 years old. His Line 150 income for each of 2005, 2006 and 2007 was $95,684, $95,056 and $94,132.78, respectively. In 2007, the wife's Line 150 income was $34,315.85, inclusive of spousal support.

*Where a review hearing was limited to the payee spouse's need for spousal support and the payor spouse's ability to pay, the court ordered that keeping the wife's monthly spousal support obligation was justified* — Allen v. Whelan, 2008 CarswellNfld 244, 2008 NLUFC 23, [2008] N.J. No. 269 (N.L.U.F.C.). The wife was entitled to support on both a compensatory and non-compensatory basis. She had been a homemaker and out of the work force since 1988 and had severe medical problems. The quantum of support was justified because of a number of circumstances which included: the husband's current ability to pay into the Canada Pension Plan and his regular contributions to a Registered Retirement Savings Plan over the past 3 years. In addition, the husband no longer had to pay off a substantial dental bill, had been able to put money aside for a vacation, had been able to pay $1,200 annually for clothes and footwear, $960 yearly for life insurance, as well as owning a non-encumbered vehicle.

*A spousal support order subject to review in 5 years is not appropriate where the payor spouse intends to discontinue his business and retire within that time frame* — Van Herweghe v. Van Herweghe, 2008 CarswellSask 613, 2008 SKQB 369, 321 Sask. R. 8, [2008] S.J. No. 582 (Sask. Q.B.). The basis for such an order would not be because of any articulated uncertainty as to the wife's future financial circumstances, except to the extent that the husband hopes that the wife may attain some degree of self-sufficiency within that time. This situation cannot be differentiated from any other case where a payor spouse is approaching the age of retirement and anticipates a reduction in income. In light of *Leskun*, above, there is not sufficient justification to depart from the norm and, following trial, make a temporary support order subject to review, rather than a permanent order subject to variation. The wife was entitled to indefinite support. She was entitled to compensatory and non-compensatory support. The court ordered the husband to pay the wife spousal support of $6,000 per month, beginning on the first day of the month after which she vacated the family home, and continuing until further order.

*A review order was denied as the circumstances were not exceptional, even though there was uncertainty as to how long it would take the wife to become self-sufficient and the youngest child would reach 12 years of age in approximately 2 years, at which time the* Spousal Support Advisory Guidelines *recommended that a review be conducted* — Austin v. Austin, 2008 CarswellOnt 548, [2008] O.J. No. 421 (Ont. S.C.J.). The parties were married for 9 years and separated on May 8, 2002. The father earned $81,475 per year and the mother had imputed income of $15,000 per year. The father initially paid spousal support of $750 per month for 3 years ending in 2005. The court found that there was an expectation of a change in the wife's income in the future, but that there was no clear expectation of change at an identifiable point in time. The husband was ordered to pay ongoing spousal support in the amount of $800 per month which was slightly below the midrange and slightly above the previous agreed amount of $750 per month, commencing on February 1, 2008 for an indefinite period, subject to a variation in the event of a material change in circumstances. The court also ordered retroactive support.

*A review order is appropriate where there is uncertainty about the support recipient's ability to earn more income* — *Peterson v. Peterson*, 2007 CarswellSask 496, 2007 SKQB 316, 301 Sask. R. 37 (Sask. Q.B.). The wife was in need of spousal support to supplement her earned income. Her inability to earn more income was the result of her anxiety and depression. The court considered that in this case, while it was uncertain, the resolution of these proceedings, and the passage of another year, could well enable the wife to earn more income once freed of her health issues. This uncertainty overrode making an indefinite order and warranted a review order pursuant to s. 15.2 of the *Divorce Act*. The husband was ordered to pay the wife spousal support in the sum of $500 per month commencing August 1, 2007, and thereafter on the first day of each of the next 11 months. Thereafter, either party could have leave to seek a review of the spousal support order, which review would include the presentation of medical evidence of the wife's future state of health. If the wife had not made progress to overcome her anxiety/depression, and her low self-esteem, it could be that the disability was chronic and the consequences of this finding, including the objective of self-sufficiency, would not to be the responsibility of the husband.

*On a motion to vary support, the* Divorce Act *is clear that both prospective and retroactive orders are available to a court* — *see s. 17 of the Act* — *there is no corresponding provision with respect to review orders* — *MacPherson v. MacPherson*, 2007 CarswellNB 506, 2007 NBQB 230, 320 N.B.R. (2d) 386, 825 A.P.R. 386 (N.B.Q.B.). The husband was on the verge of bankruptcy. The wife's finances were stable. Since the basis for, and the terms of any review can only be found in the order, it is the order which must be looked to in determining whether any retroactive effect is available. Since the husband's right to request the review was not given by statute, but by court order; and existing orders are presumed to be correct in law; the husband chose not to pursue the review until October 2006; the order does not provide for "retroactive" effect; the earliest date for any adjustment to the support can only be the month in which the motion was filed. Consequently, the support was terminated as of October 2006.

*Review not granted, but instead court ordered a time-limited award where the parties could ill afford the expense of further litigation* — *S. (J.L.W.) v. S. (J.L.)*, 2007 CarswellBC 873, 2007 BCSC 174, [2007] B.C.J. No. 247 (B.C.S.C.), additional reasons at 2007 CarswellBC 589, 2007 BCSC 361 (B.C.S.C.). The parties were married for 2 years and had a child. The court ordered that the father pay the mother interim monthly spousal support of $1,624 for the months of February through December 2007. The *Spousal Support Guidelines* indicated a range of $1,128 to $1,642 in this case.

*A review order should be made where it is unclear when the support recipient will reach the maximum lifetime limit of coverage for her health expenses or what her health expenses will be at that time* — *Eng v. Eng*, 2006 CarswellBC 2237, 2006 BCSC 1353, 31 R.F.L. (6th) 407, [2006] B.C.J. No. 204 (B.C.S.C.). Counsel for the wife had asked that the spousal support award be reviewable when the wife reached the $100,000 maximum lifetime limit for the private insurance coverage the husband was obligated to provide. The court granted the order as requested. The court also made this order reviewable on the wife reaching 65 years of age, at which time she would be entitled to higher pension benefits. Although it was currently known that the wife would become entitled to those benefits, the order was made because it was impossible to know what her needs would be at that time. The court stated, however, that if one of the parties wanted to seek an increase or decrease to spousal support on any other basis, the applicant would have to meet the applicable test for a variation.

*A review order might not be granted, even though both parties suggest it* — *Parker v. Vik,* 2006 CarswellBC 1939, 2006 BCSC 1193, [2006] B.C.J. No. 1794 (B.C.S.C.). In light of *Leskun v Leskun,* above, the courts should only order reviews of spousal support where "there is a genuine and material uncertainty with regard to a particular matter at the time of the original trial." This was not such a case. The court made an order for permanent spousal support in the sum of $1,000 per month for an indefinite period.

*A review order was appropriate considering the wife's age, her medical condition, her lack of upgraded skills and education and her absence from the workforce for over 17 years* — *Smith v. Smith,* 2006 CarswellNfld 117, 2006 NLTD 65, 27 R.F.L. (6th) 101, 256 Nfld. & P.E.I.R. 148, 773 A.P.R. 148 (N.L.T.D.). The wife was 52. Her doctor suggested there was only a 50-50 chance that she could be well enough to seek employment. The parties were married for 27 years and had 4 children. The parties had a traditional marriage with the husband being the primary breadwinner and the wife the primary caregiver. The court ordered spousal support of $1,700 per month on an indefinite basis, but subject to a review in 3 years' time. The purpose of the review was to ascertain her progress in terms of her medical condition, employment and upgrading of her skills.

*Review orders functioning as medical updates on wife's condition* — *Lovich v. Lovich,* 2006 CarswellAlta 1312, 2006 ABQB 736, 31 R.F.L. (6th) 140, 64 Alta. L.R. (4th) 231 (Alta. Q.B.), additional reasons at 2006 CarswellAlta 1419, 2006 ABQB 797, 68 Alta. L.R. (4th) 182 (Alta. Q.B.). Although the wife's depressive illness warranted a spousal support order with no time limitation, the husband was entitled to receive medical updates on her condition at 2-year intervals. The wife's psychiatrist anticipated gradual improvement to a point where the wife could possibly work.

*Forum for review hearing where parties had lived together, had signed agreement and where the local law was applicable* — *Low v. Henderson,* 2001 CarswellBC 482, 2001 BCSC 357, 17 R.F.L. (5th) 111, [2001] B.C.T.C. 357 (B.C.S.C. [In Chambers]). The parties, in the context of their divorce, signed an agreement which required that the wife's spousal support provided therein be reviewed by the court in 2 years' time. At the time, the parties were both resident in British Columbia and the specified review was to be conducted by a British Columbia court. The wife had moved to Ontario shortly after the divorce and had registered the agreement there. After the husband had commenced review proceedings in British Columbia, the wife sought an order that the British Columbia court decline jurisdiction in favour of an Ontario court. The court refused the wife's request as all factors favoured British Columbia as the forum. The parties had lived there, the agreement was signed there and British Columbia law was to be applicable.

*Review order appropriate where wife's ability to be self-supporting uncertain* — *Kozun v. Kozun,* 2001 CarswellSask 475, 2001 SKQB 329, 18 R.F.L. (5th) 115, [2001] S.J. No. 441 (Sask. Q.B.). The husband was ordered to pay periodic spousal support, the order to be reviewed in 3 years' time. The wife, as a result of family duties, had been out of the workforce for 20 years and, although she had found some part-time employment, the extent of the wife's ability to become self-sufficient was unknown.

*Hardship not caused by marriage but rather by illness* — *support ordered with review in 1 year* — *C. (D.M.) v. C. (S.J.),* 2001 CarswellAlta 666, 2001 ABQB 419, 18 R.F.L. (5th) 17, 292 A.R. 281 (Alta. Q.B.), additional reasons at 2001 CarswellAlta 851, 2001 ABQB 540 (Alta. Q.B.). Where the wife developed a debilitating mental condition 5 years into the parties' marriage with the result that the husband supported her throughout the remaining 17 years of marriage, she was awarded periodic support subject to review in 1 year's time. Although the wife's economic circumstances were the result of her illness and not the marriage, the effect of the marriage breakdown was to deprive her of her sole means of support.

*Spousal support reviewable in 3 years time as transitional support — payee working but was economically dependent* — Perron v. Perron, 2000 CarswellMan 524, 2000 MBQB 166, 13 R.F.L. (5th) 162, 151 Man. R. (2d) 161, [2000] M.J. No. 476 (Man. Q.B.). The 49-year-old wife was granted a spousal support order, which was reviewable in 3 years, upon the dissolution of the parties' 18-year marriage. The wife had worked continually throughout the marriage and, in fact, had acquired considerable economic advantage from it. However, a pattern of economic dependence had developed and the wife would require some time to establish a financial plan that would maximize her investment income.

*A review order under s. 15.2 of the Divorce Act, in contrast to a variation order under s. 17 of the Divorce Act, is a determination of support in the first instance and does not require proof of a material change in circumstances* — Bergeron v. Bergeron, 1999 CarswellOnt 2712, 2 R.F.L. (5th) 57, 105 O.T.C. 371, [1999] O.J. No. 3167 (Ont. S.C.J.). In situations where a dependant spouse needs time to re-educate, upgrade skills or otherwise find suitable employment, a review order is especially appropriate. In the Bergeron decision, the court ordered an additional review in order that there would be a time limit on the wife's efforts to reeducate or re-train.

*Review order where husband needed to be retrained* — Nock v. Nock, 1998 CarswellOnt 3920, 43 R.F.L. (4th) 110, 74 O.T.C. 300, [1998] O.J. No. 4045 (Ont. Gen. Div.). The husband was found to be entitled to spousal support. After separation, the husband lost his job and decided that retraining would be his best chance for re-entering the workforce. The husband suffered from a learning disability and would require tutorial assistance to complete his studies. The husband's inability to access the wife's income to cover living expenses while retraining constituted an economic hardship flowing directly from the marriage breakdown. The husband was entitled to periodic support reviewable in 18 months' time.

*Review order to consider whether wife could be self supporting* — Epp v. Epp, 1998 CarswellBC 1346, 40 R.F.L. (4th) 137 (B.C.S.C. [In Chambers]). A wife who, during the marriage, became unable to work because of illness was awarded $800 a month to be reviewed at age 45 on the strength of a reasonable prospect that she would attain greater self-sufficiency by that time.

*Support to be reviewed after 1 year when wife's financial circumstances more certain* — Harman v. Harman, 1997 CarswellBC 2711, 34 R.F.L. (4th) 121, [1997] B.C.J. No. 2836 (B.C.S.C.), additional reasons at 1998 CarswellBC 996 (B.C.S.C.). Where the wife had put her career on hold to care for the children but intended to return to full-time work when the youngest child began school in less than a year, the husband was ordered to pay $950 in monthly spousal support, subject to review when the wife's financial situation became clearer.

*The court's jurisdiction to grant support orders which are subject to review in a specified time is supported by the broad language of s. 15(4) of the Divorce Act concerning terms and conditions of support orders* — Baggs v. Baggs, 1997 CarswellOnt 1012, 28 R.F.L. (4th) 185, [1997] O.J. No. 1636 (Ont. Gen. Div.).

*Review to occur if support recipient's income climbed to a specified level* — Katay v. Katay, 1995 CarswellAlta 627, 168 A.R. 31, [1995] A.J. No. 317 (Alta. Q.B.). If the wife's monthly earned income were to reach $2,500, which represented an annual income of $30,000, the matter of maintenance would be reviewed, if either party requested it.

*Review order appropriate where wife's medical condition unpredictable* — Anderson v. Anderson, 1990 CarswellMan 50, 27 R.F.L. (3d) 358, 66 Man. R. (2d) 248, [1990] M.J. No. 365 (Man. Q.B.), affirmed 1991 CarswellMan 43, 635 R.F.L. (3d) 223, 75 Man. R. (2d) 235, 6 W.A.C. 235 (Man. C.A.). Where it was inappropriate to restrict the wife's support entitlement to a specified period because of the unpredictability of her mental condition, the court nevertheless ordered that either party could seek a review in 3 years' time without the need to prove a material change in circumstances.

*Where the court was not satisfied that the wife was doing all that she could do to become self-sufficient, it made "a review order," granting spousal support for 2 years and then requiring a review of the order —* Magne v. Magne, 1990 CarswellMan 44, 26 R.F.L. (3d) 364, 65 Man. R. (2d) 241 (Man. Q.B.).

*A low amount of spousal support ordered as well as the benefits of finality to the parties prevented a judge from inserting a review provision in an order for spousal support —* Bennett v. Reeves, 2014 CarswellOnt 3920, 2014 ONCJ 145 (Ont. C.J.). The judge considered whether to include a review provision in an order for spousal support. The amount paid by the mother subtracting the child support paid by the father was $102 after tax for a duration of 9 years. The judge held that the low amount, as well as the need for finality for the parties, precluded a review provision, which was only to be ordered in exceptional circumstances.

# PART II

## SPOUSAL SUPPORT ADVISORY GUIDELINES

## EXPLANATORY NOTE

The following text consists of:

- Extracts from the final version of the Spousal Support Advisory Guidelines ("SSAG"), published in July of 2008. This document was prepared by Professor Carol Rogerson of the University of Toronto, Faculty of Law, and Professor Rollie Thompson of Dalhousie Law School. It was presented to the Family, Children and Youth Section of Department of Justice Canada. The portions included here are those required by practitioners to use the SSAG properly. Please see the full text for a comprehensive account of the rationale for and history of the SSAG, as well as examples of its application in various factual contexts: http://www.westlawecarswell.com/familysource/spousal/
- Extracts from the SSAG User's Guide, prepared by Professors Rogerson and Thompson and available in its entirety at: http://www.westlawecarswell.com/NR/rdonlyres/A0E76C84-9ADF-48C1-8E04-B097CE10C0A1/0/SSAGUserGuide.pdf
- Commentary and summaries of leading cases which explain the SSAG and their application to spousal support law, prepared by Ann Wilton and Noel Semple.

# CHAPTER 11

## INTRODUCTION

This chapter is divided into the following sections:

11.1 Entitlement
11.2 Application
11.3 Income

### 11.1 Entitlement

*To be established before applying SSAG*

> The Advisory Guidelines do not deal with entitlement, just amount and duration once entitlement has been found. A mere disparity of income that would generate an amount under the Guidelines does not automatically lead to entitlement. As is set out in Chapter 4, there must be a finding (or an agreement) on entitlement, on a compensatory or non-compensatory or contractual basis, before the formulas and the rest of the Guidelines are applied. The basis of entitlement is important, not only as a threshold issue, but also to determine location within the formula ranges or to justify departure from the ranges as an exception. Entitlement issues also arise frequently on review and variation, especially applications to terminate support. (SSAG Executive Summary)
>
> [E]ven if entitlement is established, a determination of the basis of entitlement will inform the appropriate application of the Guidelines. [User's Guide, March 31, 2010, section 2, Entitlement]
>
> [T]he *without child support* formula is based on a mix of compensatory and non-compensatory entitlement. . . [T]he *with child support* formula is largely compensatory, responding to the economic consequences of both past and on-going child-rearing responsibility, but there is also an element of non-compensatory support. [User's Guide, March 31, 2010, section 2, Entitlement]

Section 15.2 of the *Divorce Act* is the main provision governing entitlement to spousal support. *Bracklow v. Bracklow*, 1999 CarswellBC 532, 1999 CarswellBC 533, 44 R.F.L. (4th) 1, [1999] 1 S.C.R. 420, 63 B.C.L.R. (3d) 77, 169 D.L.R. (4th) 577, [1999] 8 W.W.R. 740, 120 B.C.A.C. 211, 236 N.R. 79, [1999] R.D.F. 203, 196 W.A.C. 211, [1999] S.C.J. No. 14 (S.C.C.) identifies three "conceptual grounds for entitlement to spousal support: (1) compensatory; (2) contractual; and (3) non-compensatory" grounds. [See discussion of these grounds at **Chapter 6, section 6.1, Objectives — General**]. Entitlement may be on more than one basis. Usually where there is a significant income disparity, spousal support will be awarded.

Entitlement may also be an issue on a variation or review. In addition, there may be applications for an increase in spousal support where the recipient's income has decreased or the payor's income has increased post-separation.

*Apply SSAG only after determining entitlement to spousal support* — M. (J.A.) v. M. (D.L.), 2008 CarswellNB 24, 2008 CarswellNB 25, 2008 NBCA 2, 289 D.L.R. (4th) 37, 326 N.B.R. (2d) 111, 838 A.P.R. 111, [2008] N.B.J. No. 9 (N.B.C.A.). The Court of Appeal remitted this matter to the trial court for reconsideration. In so doing, it included the following instruction regarding the use of SSAG at para. 45: "A judge must first determine entitlement, and then, if entitlement exists, should apply the federal Spousal Support Advisory Guidelines."

"*The Advisory Guidelines do not deal with entitlement to support but are only relevant to issues of quantum and duration of support once entitlement has been resolved*" — Yemchuk v. Yemchuk, 2005 CarswellBC 1881, 2005 BCCA 406, 16 R.F.L. (6th) 430, 44 B.C.L.R. (4th) 77, 257 D.L.R. (4th) 476, [2005] 10 W.W.R. 634, 215 B.C.A.C. 193, 355 W.A.C. 193, [2005] B.C.J. No. 1748 (B.C.C.A.), additional reasons at 2005 CarswellBC 2540, 2005 BCCA 527, 22 R.F.L. (6th) 60, [2005] B.C.J. No. 2319 (B.C.C.A.).

For examples of cases in which entitlement is assessed, before the SSAG are considered, see *Chutter v. Chutter*, 2008 CarswellBC 2661, 2008 BCCA 507, 60 R.F.L. (6th) 263, 86 B.C.L.R. (4th) 233, 301 D.L.R. (4th) 297, [2009] 3 W.W.R. 246, 263 B.C.A.C. 109, 443 W.A.C. 109, [2008] B.C.J. No. 2398 (B.C.C.A.), additional reasons at 2009 CarswellBC 1028, 2009 BCCA 177, 70 R.F.L. (6th) 1, 97 B.C.L.R. (4th) 32, 309 D.L.R. (4th) 670, [2009] 12 W.W.R. 100, 269 B.C.A.C. 206, 453 W.A.C. 206 (B.C.C.A.). Leave to appeal refused 2009 CarswellBC 1386, 2009 CarswellBC 1387, [2009] 1 S.C.R. vi (note), 284 B.C.A.C. 319 (note), 398 N.R. 390 (note), [2009] S.C.C.A. No. 41 (S.C.C.) and *Fisher v. Fisher*, 2008 CarswellOnt 43, 2008 ONCA 11, 47 R.F.L. (6th) 235, 88 O.R. (3d) 241, 288 D.L.R. (4th) 513, 232 O.A.C. 213, [2008] O.J. No. 38 (Ont. C.A.).

## 11.2 Application

*SSAG — Advisory only, used to determine quantum and duration*

> The *Spousal Support Advisory Guidelines* are very different from the *Federal Child Support Guidelines*. They **have not been legislated** by the federal government. They are informal guidelines that will operate on **an advisory basis only**. The Advisory Guidelines will be used to determine the amount and duration of spousal support within the existing legal framework of the *Divorce Act* and the judicial decisions interpreting its provisions. The Guidelines are not legally binding and their adoption and use will be voluntary. They are intended as a practical tool to assist spouses, lawyers, mediators and judges in determining the amount and duration of spousal support in typical cases. The various components of the Guidelines — the basic formulas, restructuring, and exceptions — are intended to build upon current practice, reflecting best practices and emerging trends across the country. (SSAG Executive Summary)

*Where a spousal support lump sum award is not outside what would be generated by the Guidelines, it will be upheld on appeal* — Davis v. Crawford, 2011 CarswellOnt 2512, 2011 ONCA 294, 95 R.F.L. (6th) 257, 106 O.R. (3d) 221, 332 D.L.R. (4th) 508, 277 O.A.C. 200, [2011] O.J. No. 1719 (Ont. C.A.). The trial judge had awarded lump sum spousal support of $135,000. It was a 23-year relationship with no children. The lump sum amount was upheld on appeal.

*SSAG relied upon unsuccessfully to challenge reapportionment* — Young v. Young, 2009 CarswellBC 3587, 2009 BCCA 518, 76 R.F.L. (6th) 75, 278 B.C.A.C. 129, 471 W.A.C. 129 (B.C.C.A.), affirming 2008 CarswellBC 1048, 2008 BCSC 672 (B.C.S.C.). The trial judge had found the wife entitled to spousal support, but that the husband lacked the means to pay it. Therefore, relying on s. 65 of the British Columbia *Family Relations Act*, he reapportioned the matrimonial home 64/36 in favour of the wife. The husband challenged this order, in part, on the basis that the reapportionment was "disproportionate to the spousal support indicated by the *Spousal Support Advisory Guidelines*." However, the appeal was dismissed, with Mackenzie J.A. stating at para. 12 that this comparison did not undermine the reapportionment.

*Trial courts not required to explain all deviations from SSAG, but doing so would be "best practice"* — Beninger v. Beninger, 2009 CarswellBC 2963, 2009 BCCA 458, 77 R.F.L. (6th) 56, 277 B.C.A.C. 36, 469 W.A.C. 36, [2009] B.C.J. No. 2197 (B.C.C.A.), affirming 2008 CarswellBC 2896, 2008 BCSC 1806, [2008] B.C.J. No. 2612 (B.C.S.C. [In Chambers]). Huddart J.A., speaking for the court, stated at para. 28: "while it is preferable for a court to organize its analysis by reference to the Guidelines as well as the statutory requirements and authorities applying them, neither the *Divorce Act* nor the authorities require justification for deviation from them.... As their name indicates, they are advisory and without statutory effect. That said, they provide helpful advice and this Court has been clear that their advice must be taken seriously and that best practice would include an explanation of any deviation from them."

*Trial judge did not err by failing to refer to SSAG* — Taylor v. Taylor, 2009 CarswellAlta 1701, 2009 ABCA 354, 72 R.F.L. (6th) 249, 15 Alta. L.R. (5th) 303, 464 A.R. 245, 467 W.A.C. 245, 312 D.L.R. (4th) 448 (Alta. C.A.), additional reasons at 2010 CarswellAlta 556, 2010 ABCA 103, [2010] A.J. No. 334, 76 R.F.L. (6th) 259, 21 Alta. L.R. (5th) 275 (Alta. C.A.); varying 2009 CarswellAlta 20, 2009 ABQB 7, 1 Alta. L.R. (5th) 74 (Alta. Q.B.). Leave to appeal refused 2010 CarswellAlta 744, 2010 CarswellAlta 745, 493 A.R. 254 (note), 407 N.R. 386 (note), 502 W.A.C. 254 (note), [2009] C.S.C.R. No. 498, [2009] S.C.C.A. No. 498 (S.C.C.). Although the appeal was allowed in part, the court stated at para 51: "we do not agree with the appellant's argument that the trial judge erred in law by not averting to the *Spousal Support Advisory Guidelines*. The *Guidelines* do not enjoy the force of law and, while they are a useful tool in a judge's determination of spousal maintenance, there remains more than one route available to trial judges in arriving at an appropriate result."

*Where a recipient spouse has not made sufficient efforts to become self-sufficient, income will be imputed to her, but the SSAG will nonetheless apply* — F. (L.) v. F. (B.), 2012 CarswellBC 2137, 2012 BCSC 1073 (B.C.S.C.). The husband proposed that the SSAG not be applied in this case as the wife had not made any effort to become self-sufficient. The judge found that the correct approach was to impute income to the wife rather than departing entirely from the Guidelines.

*Where support is only needs-based and not compensatory, the SSAG will not be of assistance and support will be ordered based on the need of the recipient alone* — Puddicombe v. Vrban, 2012 CarswellAlta 2266, 2012 ABQB 781 (Alta. Q.B.). The parties were married for 25 years and had no children. The judge determined that the wife was not entitled to compensatory support but was entitled to needs-based support. The judge awarded interim support below the low end of the Guidelines, on the basis that the Guidelines are more helpful as a guide when compensatory support is ordered.

*Where support has been "front-end loaded", duration will reflect this fact and a shorter duration will be ordered* — Maber v. Maber, 2012 CarswellNB 706, 2012 CarswellNB 707, 2012 NBQB 337, 397 N.B.R. (2d) 41, 1028 A.P.R. 41 (N.B.Q.B.). This was a review decision for spousal support 12 years after separation. The wife had made reasonable efforts to become self-sufficient, and the children were independent. The judge found that the wife had received support above the top range of the SSAG (with child formula) for a number of years and, as such, duration should reflect the "front-end load". As the children were now independent, support was to be ordered at the low end of the without child range. Support for 2 more years was ordered.

*Utility of SSAG — appellate review — Fisher v. Fisher*, 2008 CarswellOnt 43, 2008 ONCA 11, 47 R.F.L. (6th) 235, 88 O.R. (3d) 241, 288 D.L.R. (4th) 513, 232 O.A.C. 213, [2008] O.J. No. 38 (Ont. C.A.). With regard to appellate review, the court found as follows at para. 103: "when counsel fully address the Guidelines in argument, and a trial judge decides to award a quantum of support outside the suggested range, appellate review will be assisted by the inclusion of reasons explaining why the Guidelines do not provide an appropriate result." The global amount suggested by the SSAG (the quantum per month multiplied by the number of months) can be used as a "litmus test" for the global amount ordered by the trial judge. In this case, the trial judge's spousal support award (which was below the SSAG minimum) was replaced by the Court of Appeal by an amount which was within the SSAG range.

*Trial judge intended to order amount above SSAG range — Court of Appeal gives effect to trial judge's intention — Wang v. Poon*, 2008 CarswellBC 2333, 2008 BCCA 442, 58 R.F.L. (6th) 235, 84 B.C.L.R. (4th) 199, 302 D.L.R. (4th) 679, [2008] B.C.J. No. 2113 (B.C.C.A.), varying 2007 CarswellBC 297, 2007 BCSC 194, 70 B.C.L.R. (4th) 120, [2007] B.C.J. No. 271 (B.C.S.C.). The trial judge made an award whose global amount was at the low end of the SSAG range, but stated incorrectly that the award was above the SSAG range for quantum and duration. The Court of Appeal held at para. 58: "on the result, I conclude that the trial judge erred in making an award of spousal support which did not reflect her stated intention of providing more generous support for Ms. Wang than was reflected in the SSAG." The Court of Appeal substituted a more generous spousal support award.

*Support claimant found no longer entitled — support terminated retroactively — Redpath v. Redpath*, 2008 CarswellBC 72, 2008 BCSC 68, 48 R.F.L. (6th) 373, 79 B.C.L.R. (4th) 137, [2008] 10 W.W.R. 362, [2008] B.C.J. No. 68 (B.C.S.C. [In Chambers]). The support recipient had investment and employment income, and had remarried a man earning $658,000 per year. Although her counsel argued for a continuation of spousal support based on the SSAG range, she was not found to be entitled to spousal support and it was therefore terminated retroactively.

*Appellate review of award outside SSAG range — Garritsen v. Garritsen*, 2009 CarswellBC 868, 2009 BCSC 124, 71 R.F.L. (6th) 106, [2009] B.C.J. No. 691 (B.C.S.C.). In this appeal of a Master's award, Melnick J. quoted the judgement of L'Heureux-Dubé J.in *Hickey* regarding the standard of appellate review for support orders. However, he went on to observe that "now that the SSAG are available to provide what is effectively a range within which the awards in most cases of this kind should fall, it may be that if a particular award is substantially lower or higher than the range and there are no exceptional circumstances to explain the anomaly, appellate intervention should be permitted."

*Arrears reduced because prior order had exceeded SSAG range — Hampton v. Hampton*, 2008 CarswellBC 340, 2008 BCSC 209, [2008] B.C.J. No. 292 (B.C.S.C.). The husband had been ordered to pay interim support in an amount greater than the SSAG range. Arrears had accumulated. At trial, these arrears were reduced because of the difference between the interim quantum ordered and the SSAG range.

Two main formulas — without child formula and with child formula

There are two basic formulas in the proposal: the **without child support formula** and the **with child support formula**. The dividing line between the two is the absence or presence of a dependent child or children of the marriage, and a concurrent child support obligation, at the time spousal support is determined. Both formulas use **income sharing** as the method for determining the amount of spousal support, not budgets. The formulas produce **ranges** for the amount and duration of support, not just a single number. The precise number chosen within

> that range is a matter for negotiation or adjudication, depending upon the facts of a particular case. (SSAG Executive Summary)

*Erroneous application of without child support formula for duration in marriages longer than 25 years — Pettigrew v. Pettigrew*, 2006 CarswellNS 349, 2006 NSCA 98, 30 R.F.L. (6th) 7, 246 N.S.R. (2d) 298, 780 A.P.R. 298, [2006] N.S.J. No. 321 (N.S.C.A.). The trial court stated, and the Court of Appeal repeated, that the amount ordered at trial was less than the bottom of the SSAG range. However, the amount was in fact within the range. This error was caused by a misapplication of the "without child support" formula for quantum in marriages longer than 25 years.

*Length of the marriage — Tran v. Tran*, 2009 CarswellBC 3229, 2009 BCSC 1647 (B.C.S.C.). Where, after the parties' marriage, one party is compelled to stay in another country, the time spent in that other country is still included in the period of the marriage when determining the length of the marriage for spousal support purposes.

*SSAG under Divorce Act; effect of prior agreement on SSAG*

> The Advisory Guidelines have been developed specifically for use under the federal Divorce Act. Provincial/territorial laws differ in some respects and any use of these Guidelines in the provincial/territorial context must take account of these distinctive statutes, especially on matters of entitlement for unmarried couples and agreements. A prior agreement may limit the application of the Guidelines, as the Advisory Guidelines cannot be used to override existing agreements, especially agreements that time limit or waive spousal support. (SSAG Executive Summary)
>
> A final agreement — i.e. one waiving or terminating spousal support or setting a fixed amount with no provision for review or variation — will thus preclude the application of the Advisory Guidelines unless the agreement can be it set aside or overridden under existing law.... If the agreement is not a final agreement, but one which provides for review or for variation upon a material change of circumstances, the Advisory Guidelines may be applicable to the determination of the amount and duration of spousal support on review or variation. (SSAG Chapter 5.2)

*Due to nature of parties' agreement, it did not preclude use of SSAG — trial court judgement overturned and award substantially in compliance with SSAG made — McEachern v. McEachern*, 2006 CarswellBC 2750, 2006 BCCA 508, 33 R.F.L. (6th) 315, 62 B.C.L.R. (4th) 95, [2007] 3 W.W.R. 471, 232 B.C.A.C. 185, 385 W.A.C. 185, [2006] B.C.J. No. 2917 (B.C.C.A.). The parties' separation agreement was not found to preclude the use of the SSAG, because it had not provided for a specific spousal support payment over a specific period of time. The Court of Appeal ordered spousal support in an amount slightly below the SSAG range, reversing a trial court award of substantially less. At para. 64, the court made the following comments regarding the general applicability of the SSAG: "the Advisory Guidelines are simply guidelines; they are not law. The formulas need not be slavishly adhered to by judges, who must always have regard to the particular facts before them. Those facts may disclose valid reasons why the Advisory Guidelines are not of particular assistance in a given case, or why an award may justifiably be greater or less than that set out in the applicable formula. But, it is fair to say that the Advisory Guidelines have been accepted by this Court, and by the trial courts, as a useful tool in determining the appropriate range of awards in most cases."

*Agreement which was of no legal effect nonetheless among reasons to order support quantum below SSAG range* — *K. (S.) v. K. (L.)*, 2009 CarswellBC 125, 2009 BCSC 69, 64 R.F.L. (6th) 441, [2009] B.C.J. No. 105 (B.C.S.C.). The wife had waived her entitlement to support in an agreement which was found to be unfair and not binding. However, an amount below the SSAG range was ordered, a decision which was justified in part by her waiver of support and in part by the fact that 14 years passed between the separation and the support application.

*Challenged agreements — role of SSAG*

> Where the validity or enforceability of an agreement is being challenged under existing law, courts *may* use the ranges under the Advisory Guidelines to assist in identifying unfair agreements, for example in determining whether there is substantial compliance with the *Divorce Act* objectives under either stage 1 or 2 of a *Miglin* analysis. . . . If a spousal support agreement is set aside or overridden on the basis of *Miglin* or other applicable legal doctrines, the Advisory Guidelines may be relied upon in determining the amount and duration of support. (SSAG User's Guide, section 3)

"The Advisory Guidelines, as informal, non-legislated guidelines, confer no power to re-open or override final spousal support agreements [User's Guide, March 31, 2010, section 3.]

> The Advisory Guidelines may be helpful in three ways in cases involving agreement:
>
> 1. To determine spousal support where the agreement provides for a review or variation.
> 2. To provide a standard for assessing the fairness of an agreement.
> 3. To determine the amount or duration of support if a final agreement is set aside or overridden. [See User's Guide, March 31, 2010, section 3.]

*Where a judge awards spousal support pursuant to the SSAG, and the award is similar to the provisions of a Divorce Contract, this award will not be found unreasonable on appeal* — *O'Grady v. O'Grady*, 2010 CarswellAlta 752, 2010 ABCA 109, 82 R.F.L. (6th) 59, 319 D.L.R. (4th) 301, 477 A.R. 216, 483 W.A.C. 216, [2010] A.J. No. 446 (Alta. C.A.). After 25 years of marriage, the parties divorced in 2002 and concluded a Divorce Contract. The pertinent provision of their Divorce Contract for the purposes of this appeal stated that, from 2006 to 2008, the husband would pay the wife 37.5% of his gross income. Another provision, which was not incorporated into the Divorce Contract although the parties conducted themselves as if it had been, required the husband to pay the wife 37.5% of his annual bonus. The wife brought an application for further support in 2008. The chambers judge awarded the wife $12,000 monthly in support. This decision was upheld by a majority judgement of the Court of Appeal. The Court of Appeal found that the award of the chambers judge was a reasonable quantum of support, given that, had the parties continued to abide by the Divorce Contract's amounts, the wife would have received $11,517 (37.5% of the husband's gross income). The Spousal Support Guidelines provide for a range between, $11,137 to $14,730 per month for a long-range marriage, given an income of $367,439. The husband had an income of about $1,000 more than that amount.

*SSAG used to bring support in line with objectives of the Act — Turpin v. Clark*, 2008 CarswellBC 2238, 2008 BCSC 1425, [2008] B.C.J. No. 2013 (B.C.S.C. [In Chambers]), reversed 2009 CarswellBC 3149, 2009 BCCA 530, 80 R.F.L. (6th) 239, 4 B.C.L.R. (5th) 48, 313 D.L.R. (4th) 452, [2010] 6 W.W.R. 613, 278 B.C.A.C. 220, 471 W.A.C. 220, [2009] B.C.J. No. 2328

(B.C.C.A.). Leave to appeal refused 2010 CarswellBC 1055, 2010 CarswellBC 1056, 297 B.C.A.C. 320 (note), 407 N.R. 396 (note), 504 W.A.C. 320 (note), [2010] S.C.C.A. No. 5 (S.C.C.). The parties had agreed upon spousal support which was below the SSAG ranges for both quantum and duration. The Chambers judge held that in light of an unexpected deterioration in the recipient's health and her unforeseen challenges in becoming self-sufficient, the second stage of the *Miglin* test was found to justify an upward variation. The quantum of support was increased to an amount at the bottom of the SSAG range. However, the 8-year time limit in the agreement was maintained, despite the fact that the SSAG called for indefinite support. The Court of Appeal considered whether the degree of intervention imposed by the variation order was appropriate in the circumstances. It observed that in the *Turpin* case, the minutes provided that "under no circumstances" would spousal support be increased and described the support provisions as "fair and adequate under all foreseeable circumstances including any increase in the Plaintiff's income." The parties were utterly clear that there would be no increase in spousal support in the future. The minutes were not as rigid in respect to the duration of support, which did not "terminate absolutely" until the later of September 1, 2012, or the husband's retirement. The minutes also stated that the wife was to become financially self-sufficient insofar as was practicable, within a reasonable period of time. The court observed that the support was specified, but there was a general term "within a reasonable time." What is reasonable at one point in time can change at a later period of time. The appellate court held the chambers judge erred in law by intervening to the extent that he did in varying the spousal support provisions of the divorce order. Applying the deferential standard required by *Miglin*, the court would not interfere with the step-down provisions of the divorce order. However, because of the delay in the wife's achievement of economic self-sufficiency, caused by her unanticipated health complications and inability to earn income, the court extended the duration of the final amount of the award ($4,000) for an additional 3 years until 2015 or when the husband retired, whichever event occurred later.

*Utility of SSAG in assessing pre-2005 agreements — Hartshorne v. Hartshorne*, 2009 CarswellBC 1398, 2009 BCSC 698, 70 R.F.L. (6th) 106, [2009] B.C.J. No. 1050 (B.C.S.C.), reversed 2010 CarswellBC 1618, 2010 BCCA 327, 82 R.F.L. (6th) 1, 6 B.C.L.R. (5th) 58, 320 D.L.R. (4th) 398, 289 B.C.A.C. 244, 489 W.A.C. 244, [2010] B.C.J. No. 1271 (B.C.C.A.). Because the SSAG were designed to reflect existing practice, they can be useful to test the appropriateness of spousal support agreements even if they were reached before the draft SSAG were introduced in 2005.

*SSAG used to test support arrangements in separation agreement reached before SSAG were written — Leaman v. Leaman*, 2008 CarswellNfld 87, 2008 NLTD 54, 50 R.F.L. (6th) 331, 274 Nfld. & P.E.I.R. 336, 837 A.P.R. 336, [2008] N.J. No. 96 (N.L.T.D.). The parties' 2002 separation agreement was set aside for a number of reasons, among which was the fact that the spousal support provided was well below the bottom of the SSAG range. The court stated at para. 40: "Although I recognize that Divorcemate and spousal support guidelines were not in place in 2001, the current day low end calculation from Divorcemate provides a bench mark for comparison purposes."

*Use of SSAG to challenge a separation agreement — unsuccessful — Carberry v. Stringer*, 2008 CarswellNfld 5, 2008 NLUFC 1, 273 Nfld. & P.E.I.R. 142, 833 A.P.R. 142, [2008] N.J. No. 6 (N.L.U.F.C.). Divergence from SSAG was used among other arguments to challenge a separation agreement. The agreement was upheld.

*Use of SSAG to challenge a separation agreement — unsuccessful — Dobie v. Rautenberg*, 2008 CarswellBC 1390, 2008 BCSC 826, [2008] B.C.J. No. 1199 (B.C.S.C.). The recipient challenged a separation agreement because, among other reasons, the monthly support quantum was at least $500 below the bottom of the SSAG range. The application to increase support from the agreed-upon amount on an interim basis was dismissed.

*See also re use of SSAG in applying Miglin test to an agreement* — *Mirza v. Mirza*, 2006 CarswellBC 1899, 2006 BCCA 362, 31 R.F.L. (6th) 301, 269 D.L.R. (4th) 259, 229 B.C.A.C. 186, 379 W.A.C. 186, [2006] B.C.J. No. 1756 (B.C.C.A.), additional reasons at 2007 CarswellBC 313, 2007 BCCA 106, 237 B.C.A.C. 104, 392 W.A.C. 104 (B.C.C.A.); *W.(C.L.) v. R.(S.U.)*, 2007 CarswellBC 809, 2007 BCSC 453 (B.C.S.C.); *Vanderlans v. Vanderlans*, 2007 CarswellNfld 119, 2007 NLUFC 8, 265 Nfld. & P.E.I.R. 142, 805 A.P.R. 142, [2007] N.J. No. 121 (N.L.U.F.C.), affirmed 2008 CarswellNfld 190, 2008 NLCA 37, 53 R.F.L. (6th) 264, 276 Nfld. & P.E.I.R. 329, 846 A.P.R. 329 (N.L.C.A.); *Rapley v. Rapley*, 2006 CarswellBC 3068, 2006 BCSC 1854, 33 R.F.L. (6th) 430, [2006] B.C.J. No. 3213 (B.C.S.C.); *Barter v. Barter*, 2006 CarswellNfld 238, 2006 NLUFC 39, 260 Nfld. & P.E.I.R. 303, 786 A.P.R. 303, [2006] N.J. No. 237 (N.L.U.F.C.); *Chepil v. Chepil*, 2006 CarswellBC 14, 2006 BCSC 15, 2006 C.E.B. & P.G.R. 8183, [2006] B.C.J. No. 15 (B.C.S.C.); *Leaman v. Leaman*, 2008 CarswellNfld 87, 2008 NLTD 54, 50 R.F.L. (6th) 331, 274 Nfld. & P.E.I.R. 336, 837 A.P.R. 336, [2008] N.J. No. 96 (N.L.T.D.).

*Interim orders*

> The Advisory Guidelines are intended to apply to interim orders as well as final orders. (SSAG Chapter 5.3)

Note that interim orders are exceptions: see SSAG section 12.1 and *Canadian Divorce Law and Practice*, Volume 3, Chapter 17, section 17.1.

*Application to interim orders* — *Fisher v. Fisher*, 2008 CarswellOnt 43, 2008 ONCA 11, 47 R.F.L. (6th) 235, 88 O.R. (3d) 241, 288 D.L.R. (4th) 513, 232 O.A.C. 213, [2008] O.J. No. 38 (Ont. C.A.). The SSAG ranges are designed to apply to interim as well as final orders. In making a new spousal support order or agreement, any support already paid on an interim basis must be included in order to evaluate the global amount against the SSAG ranges. See also *Samis (Litigation Guardian of) v. Samis*, 2011 CarswellOnt 5545, 2011 ONCJ 308 (Ont. C.J. [In Chambers]).

*The SSAG are designed to apply to interim spousal support* — *Loesch v. Walji*, 2007 CarswellBC 3007, 2007 BCSC 1807, 48 R.F.L. (6th) 128, [2007] B.C.J. No. 2663 (B.C.S.C.), affirmed 2008 CarswellBC 982, 2008 BCCA 214, 52 R.F.L. (6th) 33, 81 B.C.L.R. (4th) 271, [2008] 10 W.W.R. 625, 255 B.C.A.C. 264, 430 W.A.C. 264, [2008] B.C.J. No. 897 (B.C.C.A.).

*Interim spousal support will be awarded at a level which will allow the recipient to maintain the standard of living enjoyed during the marriage* — *Bot v. Bot*, 2010 CarswellOnt 5548, 2010 ONSC 3805 (Ont. S.C.J.). The parties had a 25-year marriage and two children. The husband conceded entitlement.

*Where a spouse has shown a basis for compensatory and non-compensatory support, interim support will be ordered at the mid-range of the SSAG* — *MacKenzie v. Flynn*, 2010 ONCJ 184, 2010 CarswellOnt 3450, [2010] O.J. No. 2145 (Ont. C.J.). Interim support was ordered based on compensatory and non-compensatory entitlement as the wife had suffered economic disadvantage. Quantum was at the mid-range of the SSAG.

*Where inadequate financial disclosure is provided by the payor, the quantum of interim support will be determined by the needs of the recipient spouse* — *Bourque-Larivière v. Larivière*, 2010 CarswellOnt 5545, 2010 ONSC 4252 (Ont. S.C.J.). The parties had a longterm, traditional marriage, and the wife did not work outside the home. The husband unilaterally terminated support and provided inadequate financial disclosure to the court. The judge determined quantum of support by assessing the reasonable needs of the wife, in part by examining her spending since separation.

*Where the payor has a very high income and the ability to pay, the lifestyle to which both parties had been accustomed during marriage should form the basis of quantum for interim support* — Elgner v. Elgner, 2009 CarswellOnt 7702, 85 R.F.L. (6th) 51, [2009] O.J. No. 5269 (Ont. S.C.J.); leave to appeal refused 2010 CarswellOnt 1640, 2010 ONSC 1578, 85 R.F.L. (6th) 62, 99 O.R. (3d) 687, 267 O.A.C. 1, [2010] O.J. No. 1139 (Ont. Div. Ct.), additional reasons at 2010 CarswellOnt 3918, 2010 ONSC 2399, 85 R.F.L. (6th) 71 (Ont. Div. Ct.), affirmed 2010 CarswellOnt 6860, 2010 ONSC 3512, 92 R.F.L. (6th) 106, 103 O.R. (3d) 588, 324 D.L.R. (4th) 277, 268 O.A.C. 267, [2010] O.J. No. 3828 (Ont. Div. Ct.), affirmed 2011 CarswellOnt 5673, 2011 ONCA 483, 5 R.F.L. (7th) 1, 105 O.R. (3d) 721, 336 D.L.R. (4th) 159, 282 O.A.C. 28, [2011] O.J. No. 3040 (Ont. C.A.); leave to appeal refused 2011 CarswellOnt 12421, 2011 CarswellOnt 12422, 429 N.R. 398 (note), 294 O.A.C. 396 (note) (S.C.C.). This was a very high-income case where the parties had a traditional, 33-year marriage and three children. The judge found "need" was not the only factor to consider in the circumstances of the case. The wife was responsible for supporting her sister, and the parties had done so prior to separation. In addition, the judge found that as means were not in issue, the award should reflect the goal of the parties being able to enjoy a similar lifestyle.

*Where the recipient spouse is entitled to compensatory support, quantum will reflect an equalization of the income of the parties* — Marbach v. Marbach, 2008 CarswellAlta 1996, 2008 ABQB 516, 99 Alta. L.R. (4th) 265, 296 D.L.R. (4th) 533, [2009] 3 W.W.R. 702, 459 A.R. 43 (Alta. Q.B.). The parties had a long-term, traditional marriage where the wife's career was put on the back burner in part because of frequent moves related to the husband's career in the armed forces. The judge found she was entitled to interim support in a quantum which resulted in the equalization of the incomes of the parties.

*Where entitlement is found, interim spousal support will be ordered based on the SSAG* — Lemcke v. Lemcke, 2008 CarswellBC 1634, 2008 BCSC 1051, 57 R.F.L. (6th) 414 (B.C.S.C. [In Chambers]), additional reasons at 2008 CarswellBC 1840, 2008 BCSC 1173, 62 R.F.L. (6th) 166 (B.C.S.C. [In Chambers]). The parties had a 19-year, traditional marriage. The judge found the wife was entitled to interim spousal support as she had a medical condition (osteoarthritis), which prevented her from working full-time, and had been out of the workforce for many years.

*The SSAG may be considered when making an interim order, and the judge's discretion may be used in departing from the SSAG* — M. (D.R.) v. M. (R.B.), 2006 CarswellBC 3177, 2006 BCSC 1921, 63 B.C.L.R. (4th) 331, [2006] B.C.J. No. 3299 (B.C.S.C.). The parties had a 13-year relationship, including 6 years of marriage, and had three children. The wife was a stay-at-home mother. The wife appealed the decision of a Master which ordered support at significantly above SSAG levels. The appeal was dismissed.

*Interim support in cases where payor incomes are above the SSAG ceiling* — awards of support will reflect the needs of the parties and be awarded at a level which reflects means and needs — Maskobi v. Maskobi, 2010 CarswellOnt 2742, 2010 ONSC 2540 (Ont. S.C.J.). The husband conceded entitlement, and his income was considerably above the SSAG ceiling. As such, the judge awarded interim support at an amount that reflected the means and needs of the parties. Support was awarded at a level that was above the wife's monthly expenses in order for her to relocate and aid in the transitional period. However, it was well below SSAG amounts.

*Where spousal support is required in order to complete an educational venture that will lead to self-sufficiency, temporary spousal support may be ordered at the high end of the SSAG* — Jones v. Hugo, 2012 CarswellOnt 4722, 2012 ONCJ 211, [2012] O.J. No. 1735 (Ont. C.J.), additional reasons at 2012 CarswellOnt 7690, 2012 ONCJ 381 (Ont. C.J. [In Chambers]). This case concerned a claim for temporary spousal support by a man who was in a 7½-year same-sex relationship which included a brief marriage. The parties had run a business together and upon the breakdown of the marriage, the applicant was excluded from access to monies from the business. He had also been studying, which he was forced to suspend due to financial reasons when the marriage collapsed. The respondent had not complied with a previous order for support. Temporary spousal support was ordered in the high range of the SSAG, on the basis that the applicant required the money urgently in order to complete his education, which would make him self-sufficient.

Absent other factors, temporary support will be ordered at mid-range of the SSAG — Strauss v. Strauss, 2012 CarswellOnt 3089, 2012 ONSC 1022, [2012] O.J. No. 884 (Ont. S.CJ.), additional reasons at 2012 CarswellOnt 12220, 2012 ONSC 5553 (Ont. S.CJ.). The recipient wife was awarded temporary spousal support after twenty years of cohabitation. The support was at the mid-range of the SSAG.

SSAG especially useful on interim support applications, especially if spouses' financial situation has stabilized — M. (D.R.) v. M. (R.B.), 2006 CarswellBC 3177, 2006 BCSC 1921, 63 B.C.L.R. (4th) 331, [2006] B.C.J. No. 3299 (B.C.S.C.). At para. 19, the Court made the following findings about the utility of the SSAG on interim support applications: "They are a useful tool to have when determining interim spousal support. By focusing on income differences they provide a helpful measure of needs and means. Their use is consistent with the purposes of interim orders: to bridge the gap between the start of the litigation and the time when a resolution is reached at trial or by agreement; to avoid lengthy and costly interim litigation; to move the litigation to a timely resolution; and to reduce conflict." However, the Court went on at para. 21 to distinguish between two types of fact pattern at the interim stage: "The more the financial situation of the spouses has stabilized at the interim stage, the more helpful the quantum found in the SSAG may be; adjustments can be made at trial. The more the situation is one of financial transition, where a spouse may be temporarily paying disproportionately more of or fewer of the ongoing financial obligations, the less helpful the quantum may be."

## 11.3 Income

See also **Chapter 8 Determination of Income**.

*Definition of income under Federal Child Support Guidelines*

> The starting point under both formulas is the definition of income used in the *Federal Child Support Guidelines*, subject to some minor adjustments for spousal support purposes, explained in Chapter 6. (SSAG Executive Summary)

The calculation of income under the *Federal Child Support Guidelines* (*FCSG*) is dealt with comprehensively in MacDonald and Wilton, *Child Support Guidelines Law and Practice*, 2d Ed.

*Calculation of income for the purposes of SSAG differs from calculation of income for the purpose of the FCSG in the following ways:*

In every spousal support case, two incomes are in issue. (SSAG Chapter 6.1)

2. For purposes of the *Advisory Guidelines*, section 4 of Schedule III [of the *FCSG*] does not apply. **No amount of social assistance should be treated as income, for either the recipient or the payor.** (SSAG Chapter 6.2)

3. Under the *with child support* formula, included in each spouse's income are the amounts identified for various child-related government benefits and refundable credits: the Canadian Child Tax Benefit, the National Child Benefit Supplement, the GST credit (including any portion for the children), the refundable medical expense credit, the Child Disability Benefit, and the various provincial benefit and credit schemes. Under the *Federal Child Support Guidelines*, these benefits and credits are not treated as income for table amount purposes: see note 6 to Schedule I. (SSAG Chapter 6.3)

4. If these benefits are "rotated" between parents in a shared custody situation (paid to one parent in certain months and to another parent in other months) then both of their incomes must reflect the amounts received. (SSAG Chapter 8.6.1)

5. Consistent with our treatment of the Child Tax Benefit under the with child support formula, the [Universal Child Care Benefit] for a child who is a child of the marriage will also be included in the income of the custodial parent in determining spousal support. (SSAG Chapter 6.4)

6. Income. . . received on a non-taxable basis . . . has to be 'grossed up' to approximate the equivalent taxable employment income" under "the *without child support formula*, while the net or non-taxable amount can be used for the basic *with child support* formula. (SSAG Chapter 6.6)

The following instructions are also relevant in calculating income for SSAG purposes.

the relevant time for determining the incomes of the spouses is the date of the hearing or the date of the agreement, at both interim and initial stages. (SSAG Chapter 6.7)

The *Spousal Support Advisory Guidelines* are income-based guidelines and thus require much more careful attention to the actual incomes, or the income-earning capacities, of both spouses. By focussing on income, the Guidelines actually encourage a more sophisticated analysis of "self-sufficiency" on the part of the recipient, rather than some rough-and-ready downward adjustment of the monthly amount of support. Consistent with *Moge*, the question is usually: what income could this specific recipient earn, with his or her experience, education and qualifications? (SSAG Chapter 13.2)

There are three important differences between the *without child support* formula and the *with child support* formula. First, the *with child support* formula uses the net incomes of the spouses, not their gross incomes. Second, this formula divides the pool of combined net incomes between the two spouses, not the gross income difference. Third, the upper and lower percentage limits of net income division in the *with child support* formula do not change with the length of the marriage. (SSAG Executive Summary) in the Quebec context, the formulas will start with the definition of annual income (revenu annuel) in section 9 of the Regulation Respecting the Determination of Child Support Payments. (SSAG Chapter 15.1)

*Income – potentially non-recurring bonus only partially included – Beninger v. Beninger*, 2008 CarswellBC 2896, 2008 BCSC 1806, [2008] B.C.J. No. 2612 (B.C.S.C. [In Chambers]), affirmed 2009 CarswellBC 2963, 2009 BCCA 458, 77 R.F.L. (6th) 56, 277 B.C.A.C. 36, 469 W.A.C. 36, [2009] B.C.J. No. 2197 (B.C.C.A.). The payor received a bonus of $50,000, which brought his income to $416,000. The recipient applied for an increase on this basis. The court found it uncertain whether the payor's income would stay at this level in future years. The low end SSAG amount would have been $10,885 had the bonus been included, and $9,261 had it been excluded. An award of $10,000 per month was made.

*Severance pay is considered income for the purposes of determining the SSAG ranges – Ellis v. Ellis*, 2010 CarswellOnt 1814, 2010 ONSC 1880, [2010] O.J. No. 1250 (Ont. S.C.J.). The parties were married for 22 years and separated in 1994. The husband sought to vary the spousal support order of the divorce judgement on the grounds that he had reduced income because of losing his job. The judge found that his severance payments should be seen as income for the purposes of *SSAG* and, although he reduced ongoing support payments, he also found that the husband was in arrears because he did not include the severance in his income for the previous years. See also *Scott v. Scott*, 2009 CarswellOnt 7707, [2009] O.J. No. 5279, 2009 C.E.B. & P.G.R. 8371 (Ont. S.C.J.).

*Tax rates and other government benefits and credits where recipient lives outside Canada – Boju v. Corr*, 2009 CarswellOnt 563 (Ont. S.C.J.). The court stated that the premises upon which the SSAG amounts are based "include assumptions relating to taxation rates and other government benefits and credits that are not entirely applicable in the present situation where the child and recipient spouse live in the United States". The court found that the recipient spouse had addressed these concerns by claiming only $500 which was half the lowest amount payable under the SSAG. The court ordered interim spousal support of $500 per month.

*Application – where payor has large asset base and apparent ability to determine his own income – Waters v. Conrod*, 2008 CarswellBC 1398, 2008 BCSC 869, 294 D.L.R. (4th) 655, [2008] B.C.J. No. 1256 (B.C.S.C. [In Chambers]). The payor had several million dollars in assets, and the court found at para. 88 that the SSAG are not "particularly illuminating where, as here, the paying spouse's ability to pay is so heavily influenced by his asset or capital base, and his apparent ability to structure his personal financial affairs in ways that, while they may be entirely legitimate from a business point of view, do not readily adapt themselves to the Guidelines."

*Income – court makes support award contingent on further submissions regarding SSAG inputs – Moniz v. Moniz*, 2008 CarswellBC 1728, 2008 BCSC 1109, 59 R.F.L. (6th) 148, [2008] B.C.J. No. 1555 (B.C.S.C.), additional reasons at 2009 CarswellBC 754, 2009 BCSC 395, [2009] B.C.J. No. 589 (B.C.S.C.). In an earlier ruling, the court varied the spousal support obligation downward to $1100 per month, "subject to verification by the parties regarding my calculation of the range for spousal support" under the SSAG. The parties made submissions regarding the proper SSAG inputs, and the court concluded that the correct range was actually $1,089 to $1,455, rather than $1,026 to $1,347. Because the $1100 award was still within this range, it was not varied further.

*Erroneous application – failure to gross-up wife's tax free income – Benson v. Benson*, 2008 CarswellOnt 745, [2008] O.J. No. 578 (Ont. S.C.J.), additional reasons at 2008 CarswellOnt 1886 (Ont. S.C.J.). The "without child support" SSAG range as stated in this judgement appears to rely on erroneous inputs. The recipient's tax-free worker's compensation income was not grossed up as required by s. 6.6 of the SSAG.

*Erroneous application — special child care expenses under FCSG s. 7 not considered — Boulton v. Beirne*, 2008 CarswellBC 917, 2008 BCSC 577, [2008] B.C.J. No. 832 (B.C.S.C.). The "with child support" SSAG range as stated in this judgement appears to rely on erroneous inputs, insofar as the spousal support payor's contributions to s. 7 expenses were not considered in calculating his net disposable income as required by s. 8.3.1 of the SSAG.

*Importance of SSAG on interim support application with incomplete financial information — Langdon v. Langdon*, 2008 CarswellOnt 545 (Ont. S.C.J.). The court stated, at para. 7, that the SSAG's "importance increases when the court has only limited financial information." On this interim motion, the judge seemed skeptical about the payor's stated income. However, the interim support award was within the SSAG range based on that stated income, albeit toward the high end.

*Suspicion that recipient may be under-reporting income justifies award towards low end of SSAG range — Hernandez v. Hernandez-Trueba*, 2008 CarswellOnt 1879, 53 R.F.L. (6th) 61, [2008] O.J. No. 1287 (Ont. S.C.J.). On an interim basis, the court awarded spousal support towards the low end of the SSAG range. In so doing, the judge noted that " I am not at all clear on the wife's means. It appears that she has funds to pay for expensive vacations for the children.... This, again, is without prejudice to the wife providing better evidence at trial."

*Judge excludes non-taxable income in process of calculating range — Gagnon v. Petke*, 2008 CarswellBC 964, 2008 BCSC 610, [2008] B.C.J. No. 879 (B.C.S.C.). The payor had both taxable and non-taxable sources of income. The judge identified the SSAG range which would apply if only the taxable income were considered, and then ordered a higher quantum because of the additional non-taxable income. However, the SSAG process for income determination (and the software which is used to apply it) is able to take account of varying tax status of different types of income and produce an appropriate range.

*Section 7 child care contributions apparently left out of SSAG inputs — Wu v. Dipopolo*, 2008 CarswellBC 164, 2008 BCSC 112, 78 B.C.L.R. (4th) 165, [2008] B.C.J. No. 150 (B.C.S.C.). It appears that an incorrect SSAG range was used because the parties' s. 7 contributions to child care were not included in the income inputs.

*Erroneous application — Reavie v. Heaps*, 2008 CarswellBC 1624, 2008 BCSC 1038, 58 R.F.L. (6th) 111, [2008] B.C.J. No. 1461 (B.C.S.C.). According to commentary from Professors Rogerson and Thompson, the quantum ordered (which the judge said was at the high end of the range) was actually at the low end or midpoint due to errors in calculation.

*Where payor has large asset base and apparent ability to determine his own income — Waters v. Conrod*, 2008 CarswellBC 1398, 2008 BCSC 869, 294 D.L.R. (4th) 655, [2008] B.C.J. No. 1256 (B.C.S.C. [In Chambers]). The payor had several million dollars in assets, and the court found at para. 88 that the SSAG are not "particularly illuminating where, as here, the paying spouse's ability to pay is so heavily influenced by his asset or capital base, and his apparent ability to structure his personal financial affairs in ways that, while they may be entirely legitimate from a business point of view, do not readily adapt themselves to the Guidelines."

# CHAPTER 12

## WITHOUT CHILD SUPPORT FORMULA

The without child support formula, set out below, is built around two crucial factors: the gross income difference between the spouses and the length of the marriage. Both the amount and the duration of support increase incrementally with the length of the marriage, as can be seen in the summary box below. The idea that explains this formula is merger over time: as a marriage lengthens, spouses more deeply merge their economic and non-economic lives, with each spouse making countless decisions to mould his or her skills, behaviours and finances around those of the other spouse. The gross income difference measures their differential loss of the marital standard of living at the end of the marriage. The formulas for both amount and duration reflect the idea that the longer the marriage, the more the lower income spouse should be protected against such a differential loss. Merger over time captures both the compensatory and non-compensatory spousal support objectives that have been recognized by our law since *Moge* and *Bracklow*. (SSAG Executive Summary)

While we use the convenient term "length of marriage", the actual measure under the Advisory Guidelines is the period of cohabitation. This includes pre-marital cohabitation and ends with separation. . . (SSAG Chapter 7.3)

In calculating the length of the relationship, be sure to include periods of premarital cohabitation. Also, the period ends with the date of separation (not divorce). User's Guide, March 31, 2010, Chapter 7.

When determining duration, even if the relationship is under 20 years in length, indefinite support may be appropriate under the "rule of 65". Duration under the *without child support* formula will be indefinite (duration not specified) even if the relationship is shorter than 20 years, if the length of the relationship in years plus the recipient's age at the date of separation equals or exceeds 65. "Rule of 65" is not applicable to short marriages (under 5 years) (SSAG, Chapter 7 (c)).

In Quebec divorce cases, some judges . . . ignore any period of pre-marital cohabitation, while other judges treat that period as a relevant consideration in determining spousal support in divorce proceedings. That difference of opinion will have important implications for outcomes under the Advisory Guidelines in the application of the without child support formula. (SSAG Chapter 15.2)

This chapter is divided into the following sections:

12.1 Quantum
12.2 Duration

## 12.1 Quantum

> Amount ranges from 1.5 to 2 percent of the difference between the spouses' gross incomes (the gross income difference) for each year of marriage (or, more precisely, years of cohabitation), up to a maximum of 50 percent. The maximum range remains fixed for marriages 25 years or longer at 37.5 to 50 percent of income difference. (The upper end of this maximum range is capped at the amount that would result in equalization of the spouses' net incomes—the net income cap.) (SSAG Executive Summary)
>
> "In computing 'net income' for purposes of this cap, the permitted deductions would be federal and provincial income taxes, employment insurance premiums, Canada Pension Plan contributions, and any deductions that benefit the recipient spouse
>
> (e.g. medical or dental insurance, group life insurance and other benefit plans). Mandatory pension deductions are not permitted. . . For those without software, or more precise net income calculations, this net income cap can be calculated crudely by hand, at 48 percent of the gross income difference. This '48 percent' method is a second-best, but adequate, alternative. (SSAG Chapter 7.4.)
>
> [T]his formula uses gross income (i.e. before tax) figures rather than net (i.e. after tax)." (SSAG Chapter 7.4)

*Where a recipient is entitled to indefinite support with limited ability to earn an income, spousal support at the mid-range will be ordered* — Buttar v. Buttar, 2013 CarswellOnt 11488, 2013 ONCA 517, 35 R.F.L. (7th) 1, 116 O.R. (3d) 481, 309 O.A.C. 222, [2013] O.J. No. 3725 (Ont. C.A.), additional reasons at 2013 CarswellOnt 14061, 2013 ONCA 616 (Ont. C.A.). The Court of Appeal upheld the spousal support order in a trial decision. The parties were married for 36 years and had three adult children. The wife had no income, poor health and limited ability to earn an income. The trial judge had imputed $40,000 in income to the husband and set spousal support at the mid-range of the SSAG amounts. A lump sum award was made on the basis of indefinite support.

*Where the parties have modest incomes, spousal support will be paid at the lower end of the SSAG range* — Campbell v. Campbell, 2012 CarswellNS 594, 2012 NSCA 86, 320 N.S.R. (2d) 223, 1014 A.P.R. 223 (N.S.C.A.). The parties were married for 28 years and had three adult children. The wife's income consisted of disability payments, and the husband's income was also modest. Upon separation in 2006, the parties concluded a separation agreement based on the husband's then income of $65,000. A consent interim order was made in 2010 as the husband had lost his job. The order provided $400 monthly in spousal support, as well as child support. At trial, child support was terminated and spousal support was ordered to continue indefinitely at $400 monthly, which was towards the lower end of the SSAG range.

*Where prospective spousal support is ordered for a situation in which the recipient did not apply until 11 years after separation, support will be awarded at an amount slightly below the SSAG range for current income* — Molloy v. Molloy, 2012 CarswellNS 395, 2012 NSCA 60 (N.S.C.A.). The parties were married for 27 years and had four adult children. The wife made an application for support 11 years after separation. The judge found entitlement existed both at the time of separation and at the time of the current hearing, and ordered prospective spousal support at $800 monthly, which was slightly below the SSAG range for the parties' current incomes but more than at separation. The trial judge found that the wife had been economically disadvantaged by the marriage and had suffered economic hardship in the years since separation.

*Where a recipient spouse is capable of earning income from assets but is not doing so, spousal support will be awarded at the low end of the SSAG range* — Lane v. Lane, 2012 CarswellAlta 67, 2012 ABCA 2 (Alta. C.A.), additional reasons at 2012 CarswellAlta 1085, 2012 ABCA 194 (Alta. C.A.). The parties had a long-term, traditional marriage. The Alberta Court of Appeal upheld a trial judge's decision to award spousal support at the lower end of the SSAG range under the without child formula, factoring in the fact that the wife was not earning income from her significant assets of $1.1 million although the assets could generate income.

*Where spousal support is non-compensatory, it will be awarded at the mid-range of the SSAG* — Beck v. Beckett, 2011 CarswellOnt 8467, 2011 ONCA 559, 4 R.F.L. (7th) 48, 341 D.L.R. (4th) 69, 283 O.A.C. 109, [2011] O.J. No. 3752 (Ont. C.A.). The parties had a 22-year relationship and had two children, one of whom was a dependent at the time of trial. The trial judge had declined to award spousal support given the parties' respective incomes and the fact that he had awarded child support. The Court of Appeal found that the trial judge had left it open for the wife to seek spousal support after the youngest child was independent. This change had occurred between the trial and the appeal and consequently the Court of Appeal exercised its discretion to award spousal support at a rate at the mid-range of the *Spousal Support Guidelines* under the without child formula. The Court of Appeal found that it was not an error for the trial judge to decline to award compensatory support on the basis that the wife had not been economically disadvantaged by the relationship.

*In a long-term marriage with compensatory and non-compensatory entitlement, spousal support will be ordered indefinitely at the mid-range of the SSAG with no reduction for the payor's new family* — Reid v. Carnduff, 2014 CarswellOnt 1566, 2014 ONSC 605 (Ont. S.C.J.). The parties had a 24-year marriage, in a 27-year relationship, and one adult child. The wife was entitled to compensatory and non-compensatory support.

*Where non-compensatory entitlement is found, support will be ordered for a limited term at the high end of the SSAG range in order to assist with re-training* — Dhillon v. Dhillon, 2014 CarswellBC 1180, 2014 BCSC 740 (B.C.S.C.). The parties were married for approximately 8 years and had no children. The wife was employed full-time, as was the husband. She was found to have non-compensatory entitlement in order to upgrade her qualifications and enhance her ability to be self-sufficient. Spousal support was ordered for 1 year at the high end of the SSAG range.

*Where a party has not demonstrated need beyond the amount paid by an interim order and has made no steps towards self-sufficiency, support will be ordered below the SSAG amounts* — Pothier v. Taillefer, 2014 CarswellOnt 895, 2014 ONSC 812, 42 R.F.L. (7th) 184 (Ont. S.C.J.). The parties cohabited for 26 years and had two adult children. The husband had income over $100,000, but was now receiving WSIB benefits. The wife had not been employed since 1983 and had no income. Indefinite entitlement was found. The judge ordered support of $1,200 monthly, which was below the SSAG range, finding that the SSAG was not appropriate as the wife had little need beyond the amount of $1,000 which was being paid pursuant to an interim order. The judge found that the wife had not taken steps towards self-sufficiency and had alcohol problems.

*Where the recipient has need, spousal support will be ordered indefinitely at the high end of the range when the payor has engaged in blameworthy conduct* — Dufour v. Dufour, 2014 CarswellOnt 415, 2014 ONSC 166 (Ont. S.C.J.). The parties were married for 16 years in an 18-year relationship with no children. The husband was 24 years older than the wife. The wife had health problems and no income. Indefinite support was ordered at the high end of the SSAG amounts. The husband was found to have engaged in blameworthy conduct by not disclosing income earned at an earlier date, but retroactive support was not ordered because of his current modest lifestyle and lack of assets or earning potential.

*Support at the mid-high range will be ordered when the recipient is unable to work due to disability* — *Stannett v. Green*, 2014 CarswellOnt 40, [2014] O.J. No. 47 (Ont. S.C.J.). The parties cohabited for 9 years and had no children. They separated in 2009. The wife had not worked since separation and was receiving CPP disability for depression and anxiety. The judge imputed income of $75,000 to the husband. The wife was found to have need; and, given her disability, support at the mid-high range of the SSAG was ordered in a lump sum in order to facilitate a clean break.

*Where a party has seriously delayed bringing an application, support will be paid well below the low end of the SSAG range* — *Quackenbush v. Quackenbush*, 2013 CarswellOnt 17344, 2013 ONSC 7547 (Ont. S.C.J.). The parties were married for 19 years and had two children, one of whom had died and the other was an adult. The parties separated in 1990. The wife had serious health problems and was receiving disability social assistance. The husband was now retired and had a new partner. The judge held the SSAG did not apply where there was serious delay in applying and ordered support at $300 monthly. The SSAG range would have begun at $1,000.

*Where there is a short-term marriage in which the recipient was pressured to give up a secure job and suffered economic disadvantage from the breakdown of the marriage, the SSAG will not be applied and a lump sum award of support will be ordered* — *Davis v. Tatton*, 2013 CarswellBC 3554, 2013 BCSC 2126 (B.C.S.C.). The parties were married for a year and had no children. The judge found that the wife suffered economic disadvantage from the breakdown of the marriage from resulting anxiety and depression. The husband was found to have pressured the wife to give up a secure job. The Guidelines were not applied, and a lump sum of $125,000 was ordered to help the wife re-establish self-sufficiency.

*Where a recipient is disabled and cannot survive on the amounts within the SSAG range, support above the range will be ordered* — *Este v. Blais*, 2013 CarswellOnt 16474, 2013 ONSC 7389 (Ont. S.C.J.). The wife was receiving CPP disability, and the husband's income was $60,252 annually. Support above the SSAG ranges was ordered as the wife had argued that she could not survive on an award within the ranges. The high end of the range was $737 per month, and an order for $1,000 was made. No discussion of the disability exception occurred, and it is unclear if it was applied.

*Where no evidence of compensatory support is led, a step-down order will issue at the low end of the SSAG range* — *Colley v. Colley*, 2013 CarswellOnt 12531, 2013 ONSC 5666, 40 R.F.L. (7th) 209 (Ont. S.C.J.). The parties were married for 23 years and had two adult children. They separated in 2000, and a 2005 consent order provided for spousal support at the low end of the SSAG. The husband sought to terminate support. There was insufficient evidence to find compensatory support. The judge ordered step-down termination of support at the low end of the range. The wife had repartnered.

*Support below the SSAG range will be ordered when the recipient is not entitled to compensatory support* — *Gray v. Gray*, 2013 CarswellOnt 11867, 2013 ONSC 5478 (Ont. S.C.J.), additional reasons at 2013 CarswellOnt 13812, 2013 ONSC 6231 (Ont. S.C.J.). The parties were married for 16 years and had four adult children. The husband had repartnered and had three young children. The wife had leukemia and was receiving disability benefits. On a variation application, the judge held that the wife was not entitled to compensatory support. Support below the SSAG range was ordered with a review in 3 years.

*Where there is insufficient evidence of income, an interim interim order of support will be made at less than the SSAG range* — *Strutzenberger v. Strutzenberger*, 2013 CarswellOnt 11889, 2013 ONSC 5224 (Ont. S.C.J.). The parties were married for 34 years, and the wife sought interim spousal support. The judge found that there was insufficient evidence to determine the husband's income and made an interim interim order for 4 months at slightly less than the SSAG range.

*Where a recipient has suffered a heart attack which affects his or her ability to work, interim spousal support will be ordered at the higher end of the range* — *Wallace v. Wallace*, 2013 CarswellOnt 11098, 2013 ONSC 4324 (Ont. S.C.J.), additional reasons at 2013 CarswellOnt 18604, 2013 ONSC 8007 (Ont. S.C.J.). The parties were married for 25 years and had two children in university who were not eligible for child support. The husband claimed spousal support.

*Where a recipient seeks support in an amount below the SSAG range, support may be ordered below the SSAG range* — *McConnell v. McConnell*, 2013 CarswellOnt 11129, 2013 ONSC 4528 (Ont. S.C.J.). The parties were married for 34 years and had four children, the youngest of whom was living with the wife and receiving disability social assistance and paying rent. The other children were independent. The wife sought to continue the interim award, which was slightly less than the low end of the SSAG range. Once the husband's pension was split, support would change to the low end of the SSAG range.

*Where support within the SSAG range is insufficient to provide adequate spousal support and the payor's income is not accurate because of tax consequences, support above the SSAG will be ordered* — *Tasman v. Henderson*, 2013 CarswellOnt 9222, 2013 ONSC 4377 (Ont. S.C.J.). The parties were together for 6 years including 5 years of marriage and had no children. The wife sought interim interim support. The judge found that the SSAG were not appropriate as they did not adequately provide for spousal support in this case of a short marriage with no children. The husband's income did not reflect his true income because of tax issues, and he had a pattern of RRSP withdrawals during the relationship. Interim interim support was ordered at three times the mid-point of the SSAG range.

*Where the parties had a mid-length marriage and the wife was entitled to compensatory and non-compensatory support, indefinite support will be awarded at the mid-point of the SSAG range* — *Kovac v. Kovac*, 2013 CarswellOnt 9767, 2013 ONSC 4593 (Ont. S.C.J.). The parties were married for 15 years and had two adult children. Both parties were employed.

*Where a party seeks support lower than the SSAG and for a shorter duration than indicated by the SSAG, it will be ordered absent other factors* — *McKay v. Adams*, 2013 CarswellMan 555, 2013 MBQB 236, 298 Man. R. (2d) 97 (Man. Q.B.). The parties were married for 19 years with no children. Spousal support was set by a final order in 2010. The husband retired at age 59 in 2012 and sought variation. The wife sought ongoing support as set in the original order, which was below the SSAG range. The length of support sought was also lower than the Guidelines indicated. The judge found there was no reason for the retirement, and spousal support was ordered to continue.

*Mid-range support will be ordered when compensatory and non-compensatory entitlement is found in a 16-year marriage* — *J. (R.D.) v. L. (D.)*, 2013 CarswellNB 229, 2013 NBQB 12, 404 N.B.R. (2d) 73, 1048 A.P.R. 73 (N.B.Q.B.). The parties were married for 16 years and separated in 2010. The husband suffered from depression, had no income, and was found to be entitled to compensatory and non-compensatory support. Indefinite support at the mid-range was ordered.

*Where a payor spouse has retired, support will be ordered below the SSAG range* — *O'Neil v. O'Neil*, 2013 CarswellNS 1048, 2013 NSSC 44, 36 R.F.L. (7th) 203, 326 N.S.R. (2d) 290, 1033 A.P.R. 290, [2013] N.S.J. No. 67 (N.S.S.C.), additional reasons at 2013 CarswellNS 144, 2013 NSSC 64, 326 N.S.R. (2d) 308, 1033 A.P.R. 308 (N.S.S.C.). The parties were married for 33 years and had three adult children. The wife had been at home for 20 years and was now teaching part-time. The husband argued support should terminate after his retirement. Pursuant to a 2005 order, the husband had been paying $3,000 monthly. Despite the wife's compensatory claim, the judge ordered support below the SSAG. The husband's counsel had argued spousal support including the husband's RRIF income amounted to double dipping, which the judge held was partially true but justified.

*Where a recipient spouse has the qualifications necessary to earn an income but is not doing so because of ongoing studies, spousal support below the SSAG range will be ordered — A. (N.) v. R. (S.),* 2013 CarswellBC 26, 2013 BCSC 42 (B.C.S.C.). The parties had a 17-year marriage with no children. They were both highly educated, however the judge found that the wife forwent some educational opportunities during the marriage, triggering compensatory support. The wife was still a student and was entitled to needs-based support as well. The judge awarded spousal support below the low end of the SSAG as he found that, with the qualifications held by the wife (M.Sc.), she was capable of earning income, which she was not doing.

*Where the parties have a long-term, traditional marriage, the wife suffered from the economic consequences of the marriage breakdown and she was not covered by the husband's medical insurance, support at the high end of the range will be ordered — MacNeil v. MacNeil,* 2013 CarswellNS 23, 2013 NSSC 23 (N.S.S.C.). The parties cohabited for 28 years in a traditional marriage prior to divorce in 2008. Indefinite support was ordered at the high end of the SSAG range.

*Where child support is no longer being paid, spousal support will be ordered at the midrange of the SSAG — Mills v. Mills,* 2012 CarswellNS 1043, 2012 NSFC 5 (N.S. Fam. Ct.). The parties were together for 18 years, including 14 years of marriage. Support was ordered at the mid-range of the SSAG. The wife was found to be entitled to compensatory and non-compensatory support. The husband had previously paid child support, which had now terminated.

*Where the recipient has no means to retire matrimonial debt, spousal support will be ordered for a limited time at above the SSAG range, including a portion applied to matrimonial debt, and will continue indefinitely at the SSAG range in a long-term marriage — Crowe v. Crowe,* 2012 CarswellNS 307, 2012 NSSC 180, 318 N.S.R. (2d) 219, 1005 A.P.R. 219 (N.S.S.C.). The parties cohabited for 20 years, including 14 years of marriage, and had two adult children. The husband had been disabled since 1991 and had stayed in the household with the children. The husband sought spousal support. Spousal support was ordered for 2 years above the SSAG range, a portion of which was to be applied to the matrimonial debt. After the 2 years, spousal support would continue indefinitely at slightly below the SSAG range.

*Where there are no factors to indicate a high- or low-end award, mid-range support will be ordered — A. v. B.,* 2012 CarswellNS 1042, 2012 NSFC 9 (N.S. Fam. Ct.). The parties were together for 3.5 years, including 2 years of marriage. The husband was 71, had retired and had claimed bankruptcy. The wife was 67 and was a nurse. Upon marriage, the husband had a modest income; and the wife was aware of his limited resources. He was awarded non-compensatory spousal support in a restructured order of $700 monthly for 6 months, which reflected a mid-range award of 2 years, which was also mid-range in duration. A mid-range award was found to be appropriate absent factors that would indicate a high- or low-end award.

*In a very long-term marriage, support will be ordered at the mid-high range of the SSAG based on the husband's pension income to ensure comparable standards of living for the parties — Mullins v. Mullins,* 2012 CarswellNS 251, 2012 NSSC 143 (N.S.S.C.). The parties were married for 36 years and had three adult children. The wife was found to be entitled to compensatory and non-compensatory support. The judge considered the husband's full pension income despite pension division to determine the SSAG amounts. The judge held the parties deserved comparable standards of living and made an order at the mid-high range of the SSAG range.

*Where spousal support is requested below the SSAG range, such an order will be made — Jenkins v. Jenkins,* 2012 CarswellNS 234, 2012 NSSC 117 (N.S.S.C.). The parties were married for 38 years. The wife sought interim support and was found to have compensatory and non-compensatory entitlement. She applied for an order below the SSAG range, and the order was granted. The wife's income was $15,500, and the husband's was $82,500.

*Where the parties have a long-term marriage and there are no grounds for compensatory support, support will be awarded slightly below the middle of the SSAG* — *E. (S.) v. E. (N.)*, 2012 CarswellBC 3745, 2012 BCSC 1803 (B.C.S.C.). The parties were married for 22 years and had no children. The wife was awarded non-compensatory support. Both parties worked throughout the marriage and kept their finances separate. Although the wife had health problems and was not working, the judge found that these problems were not related to the breakdown of the marriage. Spousal support at slightly below the mid-range was ordered.

*Mid-range support at the low end for duration will be awarded after a long-term marriage with no children where the recipient has a university degree and is relatively young* — *Tamaki v. Dahlie*, 2012 CarswellBC 4058, 2012 BCSC 1917 (B.C.S.C.). The parties had a long-term marriage with no children. The judge found compensatory and non-compensatory entitlement despite the fact that the wife had worked throughout most of the marriage. The judge awarded lump sum support based on a mid-range of the SSAG amounts at the low end for duration to take into account the wife's relatively young age at separation and her qualifications, as well as the roles played by the spouses during the marriage and the absence of children.

*When a recipient spouse has both a high needs-based claim and a strong compensatory claim, support will be awarded at the high end of the range* — *Seabrook v. Seabrook*, 2012 CarswellBC 1166, 2012 BCSC 606 (B.C.S.C.). The parties had a lengthy traditional marriage, and the wife had extremely limited work experience. She also suffered from cancer and carpal tunnel syndrome. For these reasons, spousal support was awarded at the top end of the range under the without child formula.

*A lack of children is not a relevant factor in determining which end of the SSAG ranges should be used as the without child formula takes this factor into account* — *Fernandez Rojas v. Kindle*, 2012 CarswellOnt 3956, 2012 ONSC 2011 (Ont. S.C.J.). The parties had no children. The judge found the wife was entitled to compensatory and needs-based support. She had moved from Mexico to marry the husband and had limited English skills as well as needs which were well above the low end of the range. Support was awarded at the mid-range of the SSAG to allow the wife time to obtain a part-time job, and support would be reduced after 3 months.

*Where the payor spouse has significant undisclosed income and the recipient spouse was sponsored by the payor to come to Canada, support above the SSAG amounts will be ordered* — *Kkabbazy v. Esfahani*, 2012 CarswellOnt 11411, 2012 ONSC 4591 (Ont. S.C.J.). The parties had a very brief marriage. They were married in Iran, and the husband sponsored the wife to come to Canada. He claimed he only made $26,000 yearly. However the judge found that the husband had access to significantly more wealth, and the parties lived a lifestyle commensurate with a much higher income. The judge found that even if he imputed an income of $200,000 to the husband, this would not result in giving the wife a reasonable amount of income under the SSAG. Spousal support was ordered at above Guidelines amounts.

*Where limited-term spousal support is ordered after a long-term marriage, support at the high end of the SSAG range will be awarded* — *Friedl v. Friedl*, 2012 CarswellOnt 16530, 2012 ONSC 6337, 24 R.F.L. (7th) 429 (Ont. S.C.J.). The parties had a long-term marriage during which the wife generally worked full-time. The judge found little professional disadvantage to the wife as a result of the marriage. There was no compensatory support as the parties shared domestic duties. There was some non-compensatory support ordered to reflect the difference in the parties' incomes and to soften the transition for the wife. The judge ordered support at the high end of the range of the Guidelines, which reflected the fact that the judge had ordered a termination date for support and no retroactive support to the date of separation.

*Spousal support will be ordered at the low end of the SSAG range where to do so would result in equal net disposable income for both parties* — *MacDonald v. MacDonald*, 2012 CarswellOnt 15337, 2012 ONSC 6657, [2012] O.J. No. 5757 (Ont. S.C.J.), additional reasons at

2013 CarswellOnt 191, 2013 ONSC 287 (Ont. S.CJ.). The parties negotiated an agreement which provided for above SSAG spousal support at the expense of child support in order to mitigate the tax burden for the payor husband. The parties separated in 2006. The husband sought termination of support. The judge found that the wife had ongoing need and ordered support at the low end of the SSAG range, taking into account a balancing of net disposable income between the parties, under the with child formula.

Where the low end of the SSAG range equals the original consent order amount and sufficiently meets the needs of the recipient, low end support will be ordered — Bewza v. Bewza, 2012 CarswellBC 3648, 2012 BCSC 1736 (B.C.S.C.). The wife sought a variation of spousal support on the grounds that the husband's income had increased since the last order. The parties had a long-term marriage and originally had a consent order as to spousal support that provided for $2,000 monthly. Sixteen months prior to this hearing, the amount was varied to $1,000. The judge found a material change in circumstances and ordered a return to $2,000 monthly, which was at the low end of the SSAG range given the circumstances. The low end was sufficient to meet the parties' objectives in the original consent order, provide for the recipient's needs, and account for the husband's fluctuating work income. (He owned a logging company.)

Where neither party is required to pay income tax, support may be awarded at the low end of the SSAG range — Syrette v. Syrette, 2011 CarswellOnt 10640, 2011 ONSC 6108, 8 R.F.L. (7th) 293, 82 C.B.R. (5th) 316, [2011] O.J. No. 4551 (Ont. S.CJ.). The parties were married for 24 years and both parties lived and worked on a reserve, so neither of them was required to pay income tax. Spousal support was awarded at the low end of the SSAG range. [No reference was made to the non-taxable exception found in the SSAG.]

Mere subsistence should not be the basis of a spousal support order — Enemark v. Enemark, 2009 CarswellBC 188, 2009 BCSC 104, 65 R.F.L. (6th) 414 (B.C.S.C. [In Chambers]). After a 27-year marriage, the former wife, from 2005 to 2007, survived onconsiderably less income than what her property and financial statement indicated. She had relinquished the standard of living she had enjoyed while married. She is entitled to make that decision. At a later point in time, she may use her wealth to enjoy the higher standard of living the law recognizes she is entitled to after a 27-year marriage. The court extended permanent spousal support at $1,950.00 per month, without theneed for a further review.

Where the parties' incomes are likely to change, the Spousal Support Guidelines are of limited assistance in determining quantum — Mechefske v. Mechefske, 2009 CarswellOnt 2696, [2009] O.J. No. 2004 (Ont. S.CJ.). The parties were married for 19 years. The wife sought ongoing spousal support. The husband had paid $1,520 in spousal support for 4 years at the time of the new application. The judge found the wife had ongoing need for support caused by economic disadvantage stemming from the marriage. However, he found that she was relatively young and industrious and declined to award indefinite support. The judge found that the Guidelines were of little use in this case because the parties' incomes were not indicative of what they were likely to earn in the future. The wife was awarded $1,200 a month for 5 years.

Where the recipient spouse has not made all possible efforts to increase her income, an award in the middle of the Spousal Support Advisory Guidelines will be indicated — Shorey v. Shorey, 2009 CarswellOnt 7514, [2009] O.J. No. 5136 (Ont. S.CJ.). The parties were married for approximately 15 years. The wife had two children from a previous marriage who lived with the parties. They separated in 2005 and the applicant wife applied for retro-active spousal support back to 2006. The judge found that the wife had the ability to increase her income and that her decision to work only 2 days a week was not justified.The judge imputed income to her based on a 3-day work week.

## 12.2 Duration

Duration ranges from .5 to 1 year for each year of marriage. However, support will be indefinite (duration not specified) if the marriage is 20 years or longer in duration or, if the marriage has lasted 5 years or longer, when the years of marriage and age of the support recipient (at separation) added together total 65 or more (the rule of 65). (SSAG Executive Summary)

Any periods of interim spousal support are to be included within the durational limits fixed by the Advisory Guidelines under either formula. (SSAG Chapter 5.3)

Time limits under this formula can be used . . . to structure the on-going process of review and variation. While the initial order is indefinite (duration not specified), a time limit may be imposed on a subsequent review or variation. (SSAG Chapter 7.5.6)

*Relationship between length of marriage and length of support — Fisher v. Fisher*, 2008 CarswellOnt 43, 2008 ONCA 11, 47 R.F.L. (6th) 235, 88 O.R. (3d) 241, 288 D.L.R. (4th) 513, 232 O.A.C. 213, [2008] O.J. No. 38 (Ont. C.A.). Even if applying the Guidelines, a court may order indefinite support for marriages of less than 20 years, or may order time-limited support, even if the marriage lasted for more than 20 years.

*Where support has been "front-end loaded", duration will reflect this fact and a shorter duration will be ordered — Maber v. Maber*, 2012 CarswellNB 706, 2012 CarswellNB 707, 2012 NBQB 337, 397 N.B.R. (2d) 41, 1028 A.P.R. 41 (N.B.Q.B.). This was a review decision for spousal support, 12 years after separation. The wife had made reasonable efforts to become self-sufficient and the children were independent. The judge found that the wife had received support above the top range of the SSAG (with child formula) for a number of years, and as such, duration should reflect "front-end load". As the children were now independent, support was to be ordered at the low end of the without child range. Support for two more years was ordered.

### Indefinite spousal support

Generally, duration under the without child formula is "indefinite" when the relationship is 20 years or longer or when the "rule of 65" applies.

*Time-limited order inappropriate — self-sufficiency does not outweigh other factors — Tedham v. Tedham*, 2005 CarswellBC 2346, 2005 BCCA 502, 20 R.F.L. (6th) 217, 47 B.C.L.R. (4th) 254, 261 D.L.R. (4th) 332, [2006] 3 W.W.R. 212, [2005] B.C.J. No. 2186 (B.C.C.A.), additional reasons at 2005 CarswellBC 2699, 2005 BCCA 553, 47 B.C.L.R. (4th) 276, 261 D.L.R. (4th) 332 at 359, [2006] 3 W.W.R. 234, 217 B.C.A.C. 250, 358 W.A.C. 250 (B.C.C.A.). The court considered the appropriate order for spousal support where there was a 16-year marriage and the court was utilizing the "without child support formula" which would yield a support order in the range of $6,300 to $8,500 per month with a duration of between 8 and 16 years, assuming the husband's income was in the range of $343,000 per year and the wife's was in the range of $30,000 per year. The court ordered indefinite spousal support of $6,000 per month.

*In a long-term marriage with compensatory and non-compensatory entitlement, spousal support will be ordered indefinitely at the mid-range with no reduction for the payor's new family — Reid v. Carnduff*, 2014 CarswellOnt 1566, 2014 ONSC 605 (Ont. S.C.J.). The parties had a 24-year marriage, in a 27-year relationship, and one adult child. The judge ordered support at mid-SSAG range from 2013 on indefinitely with no reduction for the husband's new family obligations. The wife was entitled to compensatory and non-compensatory support.

*Where the recipient has need, spousal support will be ordered indefinitely at the high end of the range when the payor has engaged in blameworthy conduct* — Dufour v. Dufour, 2014 CarswellOnt 415, 2014 ONSC 166 (Ont. S.C.J.). The parties were married for 16 years in an 18-year relationship with no children. The husband was 24 years older than the wife. The wife had health problems and no income. Indefinite support was ordered at the high end of the SSAG amounts. The husband was found to have engaged in blameworthy conduct by not disclosing income earned at an earlier date, but retroactive support was not ordered because of his current modest lifestyle and lack of assets or earning potential.

*Indefinite support will be ordered when compensatory and non-compensatory entitlement is found in a 16-year marriage* — J. (R.D.) v. L. (D.), 2013 CarswellNB 229, 2013 NBQB 12, 404 N.B.R. (2d) 73, 1048 A.P.R. 73 (N.B.Q.B.). The parties were married for 16 years and separated in 2010. The husband suffered from depression, had no income and was found to be entitled to compensatory and non-compensatory support. Indefinite support at the mid-range was ordered.

*Where the parties had a medium-length marriage and the wife was entitled to compensatory and non-compensatory support, indefinite support will be awarded at the midrange of the SSAG amounts* — Kovac v. Kovac, 2013 CarswellOnt 9767, 2013 ONSC 4593 (Ont. S.C.J.). The parties were married for 15 years and had two adult children. Both parties were employed.

*Indefinite support at the low range support was ordered, to be reviewed upon the wife's retirement* — Aubé v. Aubé, 2013 CarswellNB 170, 2013 NBQB 128, 402 N.B.R. (2d) 342, 1044 A.P.R. 342 (N.B.Q.B.). The parties were married for 33 years and had one adult child. The husband had health problems and was found to have non-compensatory entitlement due to interdependency and disability. The wife argued the debt exception applied. However, the court noted that the debt was considered in the property division. As the assets exceeded the debts, the court held the debt exception did not apply. Retroactive support to separation (2008) was ordered at the low end of the SSAG range.

*Where the recipient is not working full-time, a step-down order to the mid-low SSAG range will be made* — Kopp v. Kopp, 2012 CarswellMan 3, 2012 MBQB 2, 2012 C.E.B. & P.G.R. 8468, 273 Man. R. (2d) 257 (Man. Q.B.), additional reasons at 2012 CarswellMan 46, 2012 MBQB 41, 274 Man. R. (2d) 237 (Man. Q.B.). The parties were married for 29 years and had two adult children. They separated in 2005 and had a series of consent orders for support. The husband, aged 57, sought to terminate support based on his retirement. The judge found he was underemployed, but ordered a stepdown order from $725, the current support amount, to $600, which was mid-low in the SSAG range, in order to reflect the wife's obligation to become self-sufficient.

*Where there has been a long-term marriage, and the recipient has no means to retire matrimonial debt, spousal support will be ordered for a limited time at above the SSAG range, including a portion applied to matrimonial debt, and will continue indefinitely at SSAG range* — Crowe v. Crowe, 2012 CarswellNS 307, 2012 NSSC 180, 318 N.S.R. (2d) 219, 1005 A.P.R. 219 (N.S.S.C.). The parties cohabited for 20 years, including 14 years of marriage, and had two adult children. The husband had been disabled since 1991 and had stayed in the household with the children. The husband sought spousal support. Spousal support was ordered for 2 years above the SSAG range, a portion of which was to be applied to the matrimonial debt. After the 2 years, spousal support would continue indefinitely at slightly below the SSAG range. The husband was to declare the entire amount as taxable income.

*Where child support has been prioritized to the detriment of spousal support, duration of spousal support will be extended under the s. 15.3 exception* — Abernethy v. Peacock, 2012 CarswellOnt 3368, 2012 ONCJ 145, [2012] O.J. No. 1203 (Ont. C.J.). On this application to vary spousal support after the youngest child had left home, the judge found that the recipient spouse was entitled to an extended duration of spousal support and applied the s. 15.3 exception. Child support had been prioritized prior to the application. The termination of child support left the recipient impoverished and she had made adequate, if unsuccessful, efforts to become self-sufficient. Spousal support was awarded indefinitely at the top end of the SSAG range, using the without child calculations.

*Where the parties had a traditional long-term marriage, indefinite spousal support will be ordered at the mid-range under the without child formula* — *DelGuidice v. Menard*, 2012 CarswellOnt 8477, 2012 ONSC 2756 (Ont. S.C.J.). The parties had been married for more than 20 years. The wife suffered from serious mental health issues which required intermittent hospitalization. She had not had any sort of paid employment since 1994.

*Where the wife's need continues, ongoing support will be ordered at the low end of the SSAG range* — *S. (J.R.G.) v. S. (J.A.)*, 2011 CarswellBC 3290, 2011 BCSC 1612 (B.C.S.C. [In Chambers]). The parties had an 18-year relationship which ended in 1994. The husband, who had been paying support under a separation agreement since that time, sought to terminate support on the grounds that his income had decreased because he had retired. The judge found this was a material change; however the wife had mental health issues that prevented her from becoming self-sufficient. As well, she had an ongoing need. The wife's needs were increasing. The judge ordered spousal support at the low end of the SSAG range, which was above the amount set out in the separation agreement.

*Where the payor spouse has a reduced ability to pay and the parties have maintained similar lifestyles since separation, indefinite spousal support may be awarded at the lower end of the SSAG range* — *Guignard v. Guignard*, 2011 CarswellOnt 14411, 2011 ONSC 7078, [2011] O.J. No. 5812 (Ont. S.C.J.). The parties were married for 24 years. The husband had a significant debt load. Spousal support was awarded at the low end of the SSAG range because of the husband's reduced ability to pay and the similar lifestyles the parties had enjoyed since separation. The recipient wife, although she earned significantly less than the husband, was employed in a stable job. Support was awarded indefinitely as the wife was unlikely to advance further in her career.

*Indefinite support does not necessarily mean permanent support or that support will continue indefinitely at the level set by the formula, as such orders are open to review and variation.* See *Banziger v. Banziger*, 2010 CarswellBC 333, 2010 BCSC 179 (B.C.S.C. [In Chambers]), for the meaning of "indefinite" support (SSAG, s. 7(c)).

## Time limited spousal support

*Where a party seeks support lower than amounts set out in the SSAG and for a shorter duration than indicated by the SSAG, support in that amount will be ordered absent other factors* — *McKay v. Adams*, 2013 CarswellMan 555, 2013 MBQB 236, 298 Man. R. (2d) 97 (Man. Q.B.). The parties were married for 19 years with no children. Spousal support was set by a final order in 2010. The husband retired at age 59 in 2012 and sought variation. The wife sought ongoing support as set in the original order, which was below the SSAG range. The length of support sought was also lower than the Guidelines indicated. The judge found there was no reason for the retirement, and spousal support was ordered to continue.

*Where there are no factors to indicate a high or low end award, mid-range support will be ordered at the mid-duration indicated by the SSAG* — *A. v. B.*, 2012 CarswellNS 1042, 2012 NSFC 9 (N.S. Fam. Ct.). The parties were together for 3.5 years, including 2 years of marriage. The husband was 71, had retired and had claimed bankruptcy. The wife was 67 and was a nurse. Upon marriage, the husband had a modest income; and the wife was aware of his limited resources. He was awarded non-compensatory spousal support in a restructured order of $700 monthly for 6 months, which reflected a mid-range award of 2 years, which was also mid-range in duration. A mid-range award was found to be appropriate absent factors that would indicate a high- or low-end award.

*Where limited-term spousal support is ordered after a long-term marriage, support at the high end of the SSAG range will be awarded* — *Friedl v. Friedl*, 2012 CarswellOnt 16530, 2012 ONSC 6337, 24 R.F.L. (7th) 429 (Ont. S.C.J.). The parties had a long-term marriage during which the wife generally worked full-time. The judge found little professional disadvantage to the wife as a result of the marriage. There was no compensatory support as the parties shared domestic duties. There was some non-compensatory support ordered to reflect the difference in the parties' incomes and to soften the transition for the wife. The judge ordered support at the high range of the Guidelines, which reflected the fact that the judge had ordered a termination date for support and no retroactive support to the date of separation.

*Where the wife suffered only minimal financial disadvantage, she was awarded mid-range spousal support after a 12-year marriage.* — *Barraco v. Scott*, 2011 CarswellOnt 8325, 2011 ONSC 4467, 9 R.F.L. (7th) 126 (Ont. S.C.J.). The parties had three children. Although the marriage was one of financial inter-dependence, any advantage the husband received was minimal. The husband was supportive of the wife's return to school and her career changes throughout the marriage. While the wife did not suffer economic hardship because her income was lower than the husband's, she did suffer hardship as a result of the reduction in her standard of living following the separation. The wife was entitled to $2,100 per month in spousal support, which was within the mid-range of the *Spousal Support Advisory Guidelines*. Support was payable for 11 years from the date of separation.

*Five-year step down spousal support order* — *common-law relationship* — Spousal Support Advisory Guidelines *used as a "useful benchmark"* — *Thompson v. Williams*, 2011 CarswellAlta 762, 2011 ABQB 311, 97 R.F.L. (6th) 133 (Alta. Q.B.). The parties were in an 18-year common-law relationship. During the course of the relationship the man purchased four houses that the couple used to start a vacation rental business. The man paid the wife a consulting fee to manage the properties, including arranging advertising, rental and cleaning. When asked, the man refused to make the woman part owner of the properties. The man also purchased a condominium, which was transferred into the woman's name and was to be the woman's home upon separation. The court determined that the man was unjustly enriched at the woman's expense. Although their finances were kept primarily separate, the couple engaged in a joint family venture. The woman's overall contribution to the accumulated assets was 30%. The parties were adult independent partners and the woman was entitled to spousal support. Despite stress-related headaches suffered by the woman, the court determined that she should be able to return to full-time employment, earning approximately $20,000 to $25,000 per year. The woman was awarded spousal support on a declining basis. For the first year following separation, the woman was awarded $2,400, which was at the top end of the *Spousal Support Advisory Guidelines* range. In the second and third years the woman was awarded $2,000 per month. For the fourth and fifth year the woman would receive $1,500 per month, which was lower than the bottom end of the SSAG range. Support ceased after the fifth year.

*Limited-term support where parties provided equal financial contribution and lived financially separate lives* — *Hayes v. Hanrieder*, 2009 CarswellOnt 490, 66 R.F.L. (6th) 112 (Ont. S.C.J.). The real basis for support was transitional needs-based support. The court made a step-down order starting on February 1, 2009 at $750 per month and ending on September 1, 2011.

*Where both parties worked during the marriage, even if it was fairly long, support will not be indefinite; step-down order granted* — *Klimm v. Klimm*, 2010 CarswellOnt 1419, 2010 ONSC 1479, [2010] O.J. No. 968 (Ont. S.C.J.); additional reasons at 2010 CarswellOnt 2267, 2010 ONSC 2156 (Ont. S.C.J.). The parties married in 1985 and were married for 18 or 19 years.

They had no children. Both parties worked during the marriage and both had secure employment thereafter. The husband earned significantly more than the wife and the judge found that that discrepancy was due in part to her performance of most of the household tasks during the marriage. The judge awarded $1,800 (the middle range of the SSAG amounts) for 2 years, followed by 4 years of "stepped down" support at $900 a month, as the wife had a duty to become self-sufficient.

*Time-limited spousal support orders as wife's income had grown steadily and she was employed full-time — Malesh v. Malesh,* 2008 CarswellOnt 3258, [2008] O.J. No. 2207 (Ont. S.C.J.). The parties were together for 18 years. The husband earned approximately $90,790 per year and the wife earned $76,000. The wife sought spousal support. The court ordered the husband to pay spousal support of $1,233 per month for 9 years, or a lesser period, if a material change in circumstances occurs. According to the SSAG, the duration of support fell between 9 and 18 years from the date of separation. The court found that the shorter duration was appropriate given that the wife's income had grown steadily and she had finally achieved full-time employment status. Nine years would be sufficient for the wife to achieve self-sufficiency.

# CHAPTER 13

## WITH CHILD SUPPORT FORMULA

There are several different formulas for spousal support depending on the arrangement for care of the children. There is the basic formula where the recipient has primary care of the children and receives both child and spousal support. There are also other formulas: the shared custody formula, the split custody formula, the step-parent formula, the custodial payor formula and the adult child formula.

> Cases with dependent children and concurrent child support obligations require a different formula, the with child support formula, set out in Chapter 8. These cases raise different considerations: priority must be given to child support; there is usually reduced ability to pay; and particular tax and benefit issues arise. The rationale for spousal support is also different. Where there are dependent children, the primary rationale is compensatory, as both *Moge* and *Bracklow* made clear. What drives support is not the length of the marriage, or marital interdependency, or merger over time, but the presence of dependent children and the need to provide care and support for those children. This parental partnership rationale looks at not just past loss, but also at the continuing economic disadvantage that flows from present and future child care responsibilities, anchored in s. 15.2(6)(b) of the *Divorce Act*. (SSAG Executive Summary)

This chapter is divided into the following sections:

13.1 Basic Formula: Quantum
13.2 Basic Formula: Duration
13.3 Shared Custody
13.4 Split Custody
13.5 Step-Children
13.6 Custodial Payor
13.7 Adult Children

## 13.1  Basic Formula: Quantum

The basic with child support formula [is] used to determine the amount of spousal support to be paid where the payor spouse pays both child and spousal support to the lower income recipient spouse who is also the parent with custody or primary care of the children. (SSAG Executive Summary)

1.   Determine the individual net disposable income (INDI) of each spouse:
   1.1  Payor's INDI = Guidelines Income minus Payor's Child Support minus Taxes and Deductions
   1.2  Recipient's INDI = Guidelines Income minus Recipient's Notional Child Support minus Taxes and Deductions Plus Government Benefits and Credits
2.   Add together the individual net disposable incomes. By iteration, determine the range of spousal support amounts that would be required to leave the lower income recipient spouse with between 40 and 46 percent of the combined INDI." (SSAG Executive Summary)
3.   Explanation of Terms:
   3.1  Guidelines Income = Income calculated per section 1.2 of this volume (SSAG Section 6)
   3.2  Payor's Child Support = "usually the table amount, plus any contributions to special or extraordinary expenses, or any other amount fixed under any other provisions of the Federal Child Support Guidelines" (SSAG Sections 8.3 and 8.3.1)
   3.3  Recipient's Notional Child Support = "notional table amount . . . plus any contributions by the recipient spouse to s. 7 expenses" (SSAG Sections 8.3 and 8.3.1)
   3.4  Deductions = "federal and provincial income taxes, as well as employment insurance premiums and Canada Pension Plan contributions. . . . Deductions should be recognized for certain benefits, e.g. medical or dental insurance, group life insurance, and other benefit plans, especially those that provide immediate or contingent benefits to the former spouse or the children of the marriage" (SSAG Sections 8.3 and 8.3.1)
   NOT including "deductions for mandatory pension contributions" (SSAG Section 8.3 and 8.3.1)
   3.5  To Iterate = "to estimate hypothetical spousal support repeatedly, in order to determine the amount of spousal support that will leave the lower income recipient spouse with between 40 and 46 percent of the combined pool of individual net disposable income ... net income computations like these require computer software. (SSAG Section 8.3.2)

Step-by-step, here is how the with child support formula works with the Quebec child support rules:

First, the Quebec rules use an income-shares formula, where the table sets out the basic annual contribution for the child required jointly from the parents based upon their combined disposable incomes as defined in the Regulation.

Second, to this basic annual contribution are added any child-care expenses, post-secondary education expenses and any other special expenses.

Third, to determine the payor's child support, the Quebec rules calculate the respective parental child support contributions based upon each parent's disposable income. The Quebec rules thus calculate an actual contribution for the recipient spouse, avoiding any need to compute a notional table amount.

Fourth, the Quebec rules adjust parental child support contributions explicitly and mathematically for different custodial arrangements, including sole custody, sole custody with access between 20 and 40 per cent of the time (described as sole custody with visiting and prolonged outing rights), split custody (described as sole custody granted to each parent), shared custody, and any combinations of the foregoing arrangements.

The respective contributions, after any such adjustments, then become the basis for calculating individual net disposable income for each spouse and in turn for determining the ranges of spousal support. Apart from these adjustments, the *Spousal Support Advisory Guidelines* operate in essentially the same fashion in divorce cases in Quebec as in the other provinces and territories. (SSAG Section 15.3)

*Where an award within the SSAG range properly considers Divorce Act criteria, the appellate court will defer to the discretion of the trial judge* — De Winter v. De Winter, 2013 CarswellAlta 1721, 2013 ABCA 311, [2013] A.J. No. 972 (Alta. C.A.). Leave to appeal refused 2014 CarswellAlta 180, 2014 CarswellAlta 181, [2013] S.C.C.A. No. 457 (S.C.C.). The parties were married for 24 years and had a blended family, with the husband bringing one child and the wife two children to the relationship. The wife had been out of the workforce since 1977, and the trial judge declined to impute income to her, finding she was unemployable. The husband argued that the judge had simply chosen a figure in the SSAG range for support. The Court of Appeal found that the trial judge had properly considered *Divorce Act* criteria in making an award at the low end of the SSAG range.

*Where there is a large disparity in incomes, spousal support at the mid-high end of the SSAG will be ordered* — G. (J.S.) v. G. (M.F.), 2013 CarswellMan 354, 2013 MBCA 66, 34 R.F.L. (7th) 15, 363 D.L.R. (4th) 240, [2013] M.J. No. 227 (Man. C.A.). The parties were married for 8 years and cohabited for 1 year. They had three dependent children, two of whom were in shared custody. The trial judge awarded prospective spousal support at the mid-high point of the SSAG range, as well as retroactive spousal support and full table child support. The parties' incomes were separated by more than $100,000.

*Where the parties waived spousal support in a domestic contract, a court awarding interim spousal support pending trial, where the recipient has made out a prima facie case for support, will be limited to providing for basic needs and support will fall within the SSAG range* — Burden v. Burden, 2013 CarswellNS 526, 2013 NSCA 30, 34 R.F.L. (7th) 255, 328 N.S.R. (2d) 104, 1039 A.P.R. 104 (N.S.C.A.). The parties were married for 11 years, within a 14-year relationship, and had one child, who resided with the wife. They had concluded a cohabitation agreement which waived spousal support. The husband's income had increased from $100,000 to $250,000, and the wife's had diminished. She had returned to school and had no income. The husband appealed a motion judge's decision to award interim spousal support to the wife. The amount ordered by the motion judge was $3,000 monthly, which was approximately half of the amount at the low end of the range under the with child formula. The motion judge limited spousal support in order to provide for the wife's basic needs, while recognizing that the parties, with the assistance of counsel, had negotiated a comprehensive agreement that waived support. The motion judge found the wife had made out a reasonable prospect of success in setting aside the agreement. The Court of Appeal upheld this decision.

*Where the recipient is impoverished by the marriage, has a young child and limited ability to support herself, support slightly below the SSAG range will be awarded for a period of 9 years where there was a one-year marriage — Werner v. Werner*, 2013 CarswellNS 20, 2013 NSCA 6, 325 N.S.R. (2d) 175, 1031 A.P.R. 175 (N.S.C.A.). The parties had a 1-year marriage and one young child in the sole custody of the wife with no access. The husband was about 30 years older than the wife and was retired. The judge found the husband was hiding assets and imputed income to him. The judge also found the wife had been impoverished by the marriage and had very little education with which to support herself. The wife sought indefinite support. The trial judge ordered a lump sum award for child and spousal support that reflected a spousal support award of $1,100 monthly, slightly below the lower end of the SSAG range, for 9 years, within the time periods prescribed by the SSAG. The decision was upheld by the Court of Appeal.

*Where a party suffers economic disadvantage from the breakdown of the marriage, spousal support at the mid-range of the SSAG will be ordered regardless of new family obligations — V. (B.) v. V. (P.)*, 2012 CarswellOnt 4738, 2012 ONCA 262, 19 R.F.L. (7th) 292, [2012] O.J. No. 1778 (Ont. C.A.). The parties were married for 12 years and had two children, who resided with the wife. Spousal support was awarded at the mid-range of the SSAG on the basis that the wife had suffered from the breakdown of the marriage and the husband had benefited from the marriage. The Court of Appeal held that the trial judge did not err in declining to reduce support to reflect the fact the husband had a new family.

*Where entitlement is made out, and the recipient has demonstrated need and has made an effort to become self-sufficient, spousal support will be awarded at the middle of the SSAG range — Karges v. Karges*, 2014 CarswellOnt 2404, 2014 ONCA 163 (Ont. C.A.), affirming 2012 CarswellOnt 13169, 2012 ONSC 6033 (Ont. S.C.J.). The parties had two children and were married for 7 years. The Court of Appeal upheld a trial decision ordering spousal support at the mid-range of the SSAG. The trial judge had found need and ability to pay, given that the husband had a significantly higher income.

*A trial decision which follows the "first family first" principle will be upheld when midrange support under the SSAG has been awarded at trial — V. (B.) v. V. (P.)*, *supra*. The Ontario appellate court upheld the trial decision, which found that spousal support should not be reduced on account of the remarriage of the father and his resulting child. The trial judge found that the first wife had suffered economic disadvantage from the breakdown of the marriage and had awarded spousal support in the mid-range of the SSAG.

*Interim support at the low end of the SSAG range may be ordered when there is a large disparity in income between the parties, even in situations where the recipient's expenses are low — Pelley v. Pelley*, 2014 CarswellBC 749, 2014 BCSC 473 (B.C.S.C.). The payor husband's income was significantly higher than that of the wife. The judge found that this indicated an award of interim support despite the fact that the wife and child were living with the wife's parents, which reduced their costs. Spousal support was ordered at the low end of the SSAG range.

*Where compensatory and non-compensatory entitlement are found, spousal support will be awarded at the mid-low point of the SSAG range in a medium-length marriage — Kish v. Kish*, 2014 CarswellAlta 667, 2014 ABQB 241 (Alta. Q.B.). The parties were married for approximately 15 years and had two children. The wife was entitled to compensatory and non-compensatory support. Interim support was awarded at the mid-low point of the SSAG range.

*Where the recipient spouse is a stay-at-home mother, support will be ordered at the midrange of the SSAG — Gibbons v. Gibbons*, 2012 CarswellBC 4034, 2012 BCSC 1967 (B.C.S.C.). The parties had a 14-year relationship (including a one-year marriage-like relationship), and the judge awarded interim spousal support in the mid-range based on the parties' decision in their marriage that the wife would be a stay-at-home mother.

*Mid-range spousal support was awarded to the wife under the with child formula — Ma v. Zhang*, 2012 CarswellOnt 2489, 2012 ONSC 1147 (Ont. S.C.J.).

*Mid-range support will be ordered on an interim decision* — Mistretta v. Cunningham, 2012 CarswellOnt 16544, 2012 ONSC 7283 (Ont. S.C.J.). The parties had a 3-year relationship and one child together. The mother did not work during the relationship and had been diagnosed with lupus following separation. She sought temporary spousal and child support. Support at the mid-range was ordered.

*Where the recipient spouse and children continue to reside in the matrimonial home with its related expenses, spousal support will be ordered between the mid and high end of the SSAG range* — Matson v. Matson, 2012 CarswellOnt 16839, 2012 ONSC 6499 (Ont. S.C.J.). The parties jointly owned a Tim Horton's franchise which the husband ran. Interim spousal support was ordered between the mid and high end of the range to take into account that the wife would be responsible for the expenses related to the matrimonial home, in which she and the children continued to reside.

*Where the parties have a shared parenting arrangement facilitated by the payor spouse obtaining a second residence, spousal support will be ordered at the low end of the SSAG* — B. (A.H.) v. B. (C.L.), 2012 CarswellBC 4076, 2012 BCSC 1930 (B.C.S.C.). The parties were married for slightly less than 4 years and had one child. The low end was chosen to reflect the fact that the wife's costs would be lowered by the shared parenting regime that was also ordered. In order to participate in this shared parenting arrangement, the husband also had to obtain a second residence in the wife's community. This also was factored into the spousal support (with child) award.

*Where the parties have had a long-term, traditional marriage, spousal support will be awarded at slightly above the mid-range of the SSAG even when the recipient spouse has received a substantial property division award* — M. (P.R.) v. M. (B.J.), 2012 CarswellBC 3748, 2012 BCSC 1795 (B.C.S.C.). The parties were married for 23 years in a traditional marriage and had four children. The wife had received more than $4 million in assets as a result of the property division. The judge found she was entitled to compensatory and non-compensatory support as she did not have a realistic chance of achieving the standard of living she was accustomed to prior to the marriage breakdown. The wife was awarded support at slightly above the mid-range of the SSAG.

*Where the recipient spouse is in a new relationship that provides her with economic benefits, spousal support will be ordered below the SSAG range* — Eyking v. Eyking, 2012 CarswellNS 914, 2012 NSSC 409, 30 R.F.L. (7th) 386, 323 N.S.R. (2d) 213, 1025 A.P.R. 213 (N.S.S.C.). The parties had an 18½-year marriage. The judge found the wife was entitled to support on a compensatory and non-compensatory basis. She performed much of the childcare and was out of the workforce for a portion of the marriage. The wife was in a new relationship, however, did not reside with her new partner. She had purchased a cottage with him, however. The judge found the new relationship was not a common-law marriage, but was a factor in determining quantum of support, which was set at slightly below the low end of the SSAG.

*Spousal support below the SSAG range will be awarded when the recipient is largely self-sufficient and has attained a lifestyle commensurate with that enjoyed during the relationship* — Lawlor v. Lawlor, 2012 CarswellAlta 2218, 2012 ABQB 723 (Alta. Q.B.). The parties were married for 16 years and had four children who were independent. The wife had achieved self-sufficiency. However, the judge found she was entitled to compensatory support given the educational upgrading that the husband had acquired during the marriage. Spousal support was awarded for three years prior to the date of the Statement of Claim and in an ongoing manner, at below the SSAG range.

*Where a wife gave up her career to stay home with the children but has the capacity to earn income, support at the mid-range of the SSAG will be ordered* — V. (L.S.C.M.) v. V. (D.W.E.), 2012 CarswellBC 3632, 2012 BCSC 1734 (B.C.S.C.). The parties were married for 12 years and had three children. The wife sought to enforce an interim order of spousal and child support. The judge found she was entitled to compensatory support as she had given up her career to be the primary caregiver to the children. Spousal support was awarded at the midrange of the SSAG. The wife was found to be educated and capable of self-sufficiency.

*Where no persuasive factors are put forward for deviating from an award at the midrange of the SSAG, support at the mid-range of the SSAG will be awarded* — Overell v. Overell, 2012 CarswellOnt 14616, 2012 ONSC 6615 (Ont. S.C.J.). The parties were married for 17 years and had two children in university. The wife was a stay-at-home mother.

*Where a recipient spouse is substantially self-sufficient but there is a disparity in the parties' incomes, mid-range support will be ordered* — Young v. Young, 2012 CarswellBC 3645, 2012 BCSC 1727 (B.C.S.C.). The recipient wife in this case owned a window-treatment business, and the husband was a nurse. The dependent adult daughter resided with the wife. It was a long-term relationship. The judge found that the wife was entitled on needs-based grounds only. The judge found that the disparity in the parties' incomes meant that the wife's standard of living had decreased somewhat post-separation even though she was substantially self-sufficient. Indefinite mid-range support was ordered under the with child formula.

*Where a recipient spouse is making reasonable efforts at self-sufficiency, spousal support will be ordered at the mid-range of the SSAG* — Kelsch v. Chaput, 2012 CarswellBC 362, 2012 BCCA 64, 317 B.C.A.C. 59, 540 W.A.C. 59 (B.C.C.A.). Spousal support was awarded at the mid-range of the SSAG under the with child formula. The wife was making reasonable efforts at self-sufficiency, and the fact that she had well-off parents did not absolve the husband of his obligation to support.

*Where the wife in a 24-year traditional marriage has limited marketable skills and is the sole caregiver to the child, spousal support between the mid and high ranges will be awarded* — Damaschin-Zamfirescu v. Damaschin-Zamfirescu, 2012 CarswellOnt 14841, 2012 ONSC 6689, [2012] O.J. No. 5586 (Ont. S.C.J.). The parties had one child who was an adolescent. The wife had been educated in Romania and had no real marketable skills. The judge here awarded spousal support between the mid to high ranges of the SSAG, based on the recipient spouse's caregiving role for the child, the high caregiving needs of the child, the 24-year traditional marriage, and the wife's limited education and skills.

*Where the wife in a long-term marriage has a limited education and suffers from cancer, support will be awarded at the top of the SSAG range* — T. (E.E.) v. T. (A.N.), 2012 CarswellAlta 858, 2012 ABQB 298 (Alta. Q.B.). The parties had a long-term (26-year), traditional marriage, and the wife had a grade 10 education. The husband was an engineer earning $102,000 annually. The judge awarded spousal support at the high end of the SSAG, based on the wife's limited education and the fact that she was also suffering from cancer and would not realistically be able to attempt to enter the workforce for another year according to her doctor. The parties had an 11-year-old daughter for whom the wife was the primary caregiver.

*A wife in an 18-year, mainly traditional marriage was awarded support between the mid and high range of the SSAG* — Meeser v. Meeser, 2012 CarswellOnt 15902, 2012 ONSC 7085, 30 R.F.L. (7th) 204 (Ont. S.C.J.), additional reasons at 2013 CarswellOnt 1271, 2013 ONSC 898 (Ont. S.C.J.). The wife worked part-time in a factory after separation, and the parties had one child who was still dependent.

*Absent other factors, spousal support will be ordered at the mid-range of the SSAG* — G. (J.P.) v. G. (V.S.), 2012 CarswellBC 1871, 2012 BCSC 946, 35 B.C.L.R. (5th) 367 (B.C.S.C.). The parties cohabited and were married for a total of 16 years. Spousal support at the mid-range was awarded for a period of 8 years on compensatory and needs-based grounds under the with child formula. The wife was employed and on her way to becoming self-sufficient.

When using the with child formula, child support must be factored into the calculations — *Watson v. Watson*, 2012 CarswellBC 1473, 2012 BCSC 730, 2012 C.E.B. & P.G.R. 8488 (B.C.S.C.). The parties had two children. When the two children were young, the parties decided the wife should give up her job to care for the children and she was out of the workforce for 9 years of the parties' approximately 17-year marriage. The judge did not accept the mother's calculations of potential support, which were calculated under the with child formula but without child support received factored in. The wife satisfied the test for compensatory spousal support, but based on the parties' incomes she was only entitled to $50 monthly.

Where the recipient's entitlement to support is needs-based and compensatory in a 6-year relationship, support will be ordered at the mid-range of the SSAG — *Kostin v. Eaket*, 2012 CarswellAlta 2280, 2012 ABQB 756 (Alta. Q.B.). The parties cohabited for 6 years and had one child together. The mother stayed home with the child until the child started kindergarten. The judge found the mother was entitled to compensatory and need-based spousal support for a period of 3 years at the mid-range of the SSAG under the with child formula.

Where a recipient spouse conceals the fact she has remarried and does not offer adequate evidence concerning her new spouse's ability to provide support, spousal support below the SSAG range will be ordered to reflect only the compensatory aspect of her claim — *Qaraan v. Qaraan*, 2012 CarswellOnt 15895, 2012 ONSC 6017 (Ont. S.C.J.). The parties were married for 17 years and had three children. Retroactive spousal support for 2009 was ordered at the low end of the range to reflect the fact that the wife had the benefit of living in the matrimonial home rent-free and mortgage-free. For 2010 and 2011, spousal support below the SSAG ranges was awarded to reflect the fact that the wife had received a substantial equalization payment and her concealment from the court of the fact of her remarriage and new husband's ability to support her. Support ordered was to reflect the compensatory nature of her claim.

Where support is within the SSAG ranges and no material change in circumstances is found, support will continue as previously ordered on consent — *Brooks v. Brooks*, 2012 CarswellNB 713, 2012 NBQB 401, 397 N.B.R. (2d) 361, 1028 A.P.R. 361 (N.B.Q.B.). The parties had a 10-year marriage, and the children resided with the husband. Spousal support was fixed by a consent order in 2008. The wife applied for variation. Her application was dismissed on the grounds that the support found in the consent order was within the SSAG ranges and there was no material change in circumstances since the original order was made.

Where a child has been apprehended by CAS, the with child formula will nonetheless be used to determine spousal support — *G. (D.K.) v. T. (T.L.A.)*, 2012 CarswellBC 1592, 2012 BCPC 162 (B.C. Prov. Ct.). The parties had one child who had significant medical needs. The mother had supervised access to the child, and a child protection trial was to occur some months later to determine where the child would live. The judge found that the with child formula under the SSAG was appropriate as, should the child be found no longer in need of protection, she would be returned to the wife.

Where the recipient has need and the payor spouse has the means to pay, support will be ordered at the mid-range of the SSAG — *Arnott v. Arnott*, 2012 CarswellOnt 3712, 2012 ONSC 1822, [2012] O.J. No. 1357 (Ont. S.C.J.). The parties were married for 9 years and had two children in the wife's custody, with access by the husband. A final order of spousal support was made at the mid-range of the SSAG for a duration of 9 years.

Where the family is living beyond its means, income may be imputed to the recipient spouse once circumstances would reasonably allow her to become employed for the purposes of the determining the SSAG amount — *Alden v. Thomas*, 2011 CarswellOnt 13376, 2011 ONSC 7003, [2011] O.J. No. 5374 (Ont. S.C.J.), additional reasons at 2012 CarswellOnt 584, 2012 ONSC 422 (Ont. S.C.J.). The parties cohabited for 3§ years and had two young children. The parties had joint custody with primary residence with the mother. Spousal support was ordered at the mid-range of the SSAG. Income was imputed to the wife after the younger child was of an age to be in school.

*Where the recipient spouse is young and has earning potential, is not overly oppressed by childcare duties, and has retained the major asset of the family, support will be ordered at the low- to mid-range of the SSAG* — Dickey v. Morrel, 2011 CarswellOnt 14630, 2011 ONCJ 707, [2011] O.J. No. 5631 (Ont. C.J.). The parties were in a common-law relationship and had one child. The child resided with the mother. The judge found that the mother had suffered economic consequences as a result of the relationship and was entitled to compensatory and non-compensatory support. Support was awarded at the low to mid range of the SSAG because the wife retained the major asset of the family, the child was entering his adolescent years and would require less hands-on care in the near future, and the wife was young and had earning potential. Support was reviewable after five years depending on the level of self-sufficiency achieved by the wife.

*A lump-sum payment may be awarded in accordance with the* Spousal Support Advisory Guidelines — M. (A.A.) v. K. (R.P.), 2010 CarswellOnt 1139, 2010 ONSC 930, 81 R.F.L. (6th) 370, [2010] O.J. No. 807 (Ont. S.C.J.). The parties were both veterinarians and had two children together during their 9-year marriage. The wife sought to set aside their separation agreement and claimed spousal support and child support. The judge set aside the Agreement and awarded compensatory and non-compensatory support in a lump-sum payment.

*The judge may award spousal support in the lower end of the SSAG range when the payor spouse's income is largely performance-based* — Chapman v. Chapman, 2009 CarswellOnt 8915, [2009] O.J. No. 5994 (Ont. S.C.J.), additional reasons at 2010 CarswellOnt 2343 (Ont. S.C.J.). The parties were married for 23 years and had two children together. The judge rejected the idea that the wife was not entitled to any of the increase from the husband's income from a new job he started after separation, which was in the same field as his previous job. The wife's support over the years had allowed the husband to progress to his new position. However, the judge included the husband's bonus money in calculations for the SSAG, but set support in the lower range to account for the fact that some of the husband's income was performance-based.

*Factors such as length of the marriage, economic disadvantage stemming from the marriage, and expenses of the parties are considered when determining where in the SSAG range an award should be placed* — Guignard v. Guignard, 2009 CarswellOnt 3127, [2009] O.J. No. 2267 (Ont. S.C.J.). The judge took into account "the incomes which I have found for the parties, the length of the marriage, the economic disadvantages to Ms. Guignard arising out of the marriage and the breakdown of the marriage, the reasonable expenses of the parties on an interim basis, and the *Spousal Support Advisory Guidelines*" when deciding that the wife should be awarded an amount at the lower end of the Guidelines range. The parties were married for 25 years and had two children. The wife had an income of approximately $32,000 which she earned as an educational assistant and lifeguard. The husband had an income of $106, 000. During the marriage, the parties relocated several times for the husband's career, which the court found had a negative economic effect on the wife.

## 13.2  Basic Formula: Duration

Duration under this basic with child support formula also reflects the underlying parental partnership rationale. Initial orders are indefinite (duration not specified), subject to the usual process of review or variation. The formula does, however, provide a durational range which is intended to structure the process of review and variation and to limit the cumulative duration of spousal support. The durational limits under this formula can be thought of as "soft" time limits. There are two tests for duration and whichever produces the longer duration at each end of the range is to be employed (SSAG Executive Summary)

- The first test for duration is the same as the test for duration under the without child support formula. It will typically be the applicable test for longer marriages, marriage of ten years or more. The upper end is one year of support for each year of marriage, subject to the provisions under the without child support formula for indefinite (duration not specified) support after 20 years of marriage. The lower end is one-half year of support for each year of marriage. If the children are already in school at the time of separation, then the lower end of the range will always be determined by this length-of-marriage test. (SSAG Section 8.5.2)
- The second test for duration under the basic with child support formula is driven by the age of the children of the marriage. It usually operates where the period of time until the last or youngest child finishes high school is greater than the length of the marriage. These are mostly short or short-to-medium marriages, typically (but not always) under 10 years in length. . . The upper end of the range for spousal support under this test is the date when the last or youngest child finishes high school. . . The lower end of the range under this test is also tied to the age of the youngest child and schooling, once again reflecting the parental partnership model. In shorter marriages, spousal support should continue at least until the date the youngest child starts attending school full-time. (SSAG Section 8.5.3)

*Appropriate to rely on SSAG to order indefinite duration* — Michaud v. Kuszelewski, 2009 CarswellNS 646, 2009 NSCA 118, 75 R.F.L. (6th) 3, 312 D.L.R. (4th) 598, 284 N.S.R. (2d) 310, 901 A.P.R. 310 (N.S.C.A.), affirming 2008 CarswellNS 498, 2008 NSSC 276, 269 N.S.R. (2d) 35, 860 A.P.R. 35 (N.S.S.C.). Despite the existence of an interim order for child and spousal support, the husband had paid very little during a period of 6 years. The wife thereafter obtained an upward variation of the order for spousal support. The Nova Scotia Court of Appeal found that it was "appropriate in the circumstances of this case for the trial judge to rely on the *Spousal Support Advisory Guidelines*" in ordering an award with indefinite duration. The appeal was dismissed.

*Where there is a stark contrast between lifestyles of the parents and uncertainty of the mother's career, spousal support will continue longer than indicated by the SSAG* — Q. (G.V.) v. Q. (M.L.), 2012 CarswellOnt 9626, 2012 ONSC 4250 (Ont. S.C.J.). The parties had one child. The wife was awarded spousal support at slightly above the mid-range of the SSAG for a duration that was longer than that indicated by the SSAG. The parties were relatively wealthy and they had separated when the child was 2 years of age. Spousal support was to continue to the later of 2018 or until the child was finished high school.

*Where the economic situation of the payor spouse indicates a quantum lower than the SSAG range, the duration may nonetheless be as indicated by the SSAG* — Heath v. Heath, 2012

CarswellSask 732, 2012 SKQB 436, 410 Sask. R. 85 (Sask. Q.B.). The judge awarded indefinite spousal support below the low end of the without child formula on the basis that spousal support must take into account the economic realities of the parties. Indefinite support was indicated by the SSAG. While the wife continued to suffer the economic consequences of the marriage breakdown and had continuing need, the husband had accumulated significant debt since the end of the marriage. The wife had previously been receiving support under the with child formula until the child became independent.

*SSAG among reasons to replace lump sum with indefinite periodic support — trial decision on quantum not interfered with — P. (J.B.) v. S. (L.J.),* 2008 CarswellNS 91, 2008 NSCA 19, 291 D.L.R. (4th) 477, 263 N.S.R. (2d) 192, 843 A.P.R. 192, [2008] N.S.J. No. 77 (N.S.C.A.). In this proceeding under provincial legislation, the SSAG were relied upon to replace the trial court's lump sum spousal support award with an indefinite award. However, the monthly quantum of support deemed appropriate by the court below was not interfered with. The SSAG were not considered with regard to quantum.

*Where the recipient spouse is employed full-time, spousal support may be ordered at the mid-range of the SSAG amounts for a limited period of time — Ma v. Zhang,* 2012 CarswellOnt 2489, 2012 ONSC 1147 (Ont. S.C.J.). The parties were married for seven years and had one child with Asperger's syndrome. The wife was granted sole custody with reasonable access on reasonable notice. Spousal support of eight months was ordered at a midrange of the SSAG, with the judge citing the wife's economic recovery since the breakdown of the marriage. She was employed with a salary of $39,000, in contrast with the husband's salary which was approximately $75,000 per year.

*Where the recipient spouse is unable to work because of illness, which might be terminal, indefinite spousal support may be ordered at the middle of the SSAG range — Purgavie v. Purgavie,* 2012 CarswellOnt 4296, 2012 ONSC 2268, [2012] O.J. No. 1630 (Ont. S.C.J.). The parties had been married for 16 years and had one child. The wife was unable to work because of ongoing treatment for cancer. Her prognosis was unknown. Spousal support was ordered at the mid-range of the SSAG for an indefinite period of time.

*Where relief sought is below the usual duration as set out by the SSAG, spousal support may be ordered for a shorter duration than that found in the SSAG — Rambarran v. Bissessar,* 2012 CarswellOnt 1182, 2012 ONSC 144, [2012] O.J. No. 292 (Ont. S.C.J.). The parties had three children and were married for 16 years. The wife had custody. The judge awarded compensatory spousal support in the mid-range of the SSAG. The applicant agreed to a limit of two and one-half years until the youngest child was in school full-time.

*Midpoint of quantum range used but time limit imposed despite SSAG — Pagnotta v. Malozewski,* 2008 CarswellOnt 1896, 54 R.F.L. (6th) 173, [2008] O.J. No. 1318 (Ont. Div. Ct.), varying 2007 CarswellOnt 9117 (Ont. S.C.J.). This appeal of an interim spousal support order was heard by Ontario's Divisional Court. At para. 13, the court stated that "there appears to be no articulated basis for departing from the Spousal Support Guidelines." The Divisional Court chose the midpoint of the "with child support" quantum range, but limited the support period to only 2 years despite the parties' 20-year marriage and a substantial disparity in their incomes.

*SSAG "with child support" formula followed for both duration and quantum — Dabrowska v. Bragagnolo,* 2008 CarswellOnt 4763, 2008 ONCJ 360, [2008] O.J. No. 3155 (Ont. C.J.). The Court stated, at para. 26: "I find that the SSAG achieve a fair result in this case and that there are no variables (as set out in the SSAG) that would have me deviate from them." Quantum was set at the top of the SSAG range, providing 51.3% of the family's net disposable income to the recipient's household. The Court also said that it was following the SSAG in declining to set a duration in this initial "with child support" order.

## Interim support; indefinite support

> Any periods of interim spousal support are to be included within the durational limits fixed by the Advisory Guidelines under either formula. (SSAG Section 5.3)

> Indefinite support does not necessarily mean permanent support. And it certainly does not mean that support will continue indefinitely at the level set by the formula, as such orders are open to variation as circumstances change over time. . . . such orders or agreements are subject to variation and review and, through that process, even to time limits and termination. . . . When a support award is "indefinite", recipients are under an obligation to make reasonable efforts toward self-sufficiency. (SSAG User's Guide, Section 5(b))

*Where both parties continue to occupy the matrimonial home, the high end of the SSAG range will be appropriate to reflect the benefit of occupancy to the payor spouse* — Menchella v. Menchella, 2012 CarswellOnt 3510, 2012 ONSC 1861, [2012] O.J. No. 1257 (Ont. S.C.J.). The parties were married for 15 years and had one child. The wife was granted custody of the child and received spousal and child support. Interim spousal support was ordered in the high range of the SSAG to reflect the fact that exclusive possession was not granted to the wife and the husband continued to reside in the home, which was 6,000 square feet.

*Where the parties have no equalization of property 10 years after a separation agreement and the parties had disparate net family property, temporary spousal support at the mid-range will be ordered* — Massai v. Massai, 2012 CarswellOnt 14515, 2012 ONSC 6467 (Ont. S.C.J.). The parties had signed an interim separation agreement 10 years prior that waived spousal support. However, the agreement was not signed in unimpeachable circumstances, and thus support could be ordered in face of a waiver. No property equalization had been made post-separation. Temporary mid-range support was granted. The judge noted that the outstanding property equalization and the parties disparate net family property post-separation could have warranted a higher award.

*Where the payor spouse has a low income and child support has been ordered, temporary spousal support will not be ordered* — Pinto v. Pinto, 2011 CarswellOnt 15061, 2011 ONSC 7403, [2011] O.J. No. 5728 (Ont. S.C.J.). The parties were in a relationship for 16 years and had three children. The wife had custody, with access to the husband. It had been a traditional marriage. The judge found that, due to the low income of the husband and the award of child support to the wife, SSAG did not indicate a temporary spousal support award. The husband was required to pay the property taxes.

*Where there is uncertainty as to the recipient spouse's employment and future education plans, an indefinite award may be awarded under the* Spousal Support Advisory Guidelines — Rivard v. Rivard, 2010 CarswellOnt 3361, 2010 ONSC 2711, [2010] O.J. No. 2039 (Ont. S.C.J.). The parties in this case were together for 9 years, married for 7 years, and had two children. There was a wide disparity in their incomes ($22,000 for the wife and almost $100,000 for the husband). The judge found that the wife's career was interrupted by the marriage and that she was entitled to compensatory spousal support. The judge awarded spousal support of an indefinite length with an automatic review after 5 years. The wife had plans to complete a degree during that time. There was uncertainty surrounding her future employment and the judge found that an indefinite award was warranted for these reasons. The judge considered the SSAG as well as the factors set out in s. 15.2(4) of the *Divorce Act*, the objectives of an order for spousal support as set out in s. 15.2(6) of the *Divorce Act*, the financial need of the applicant and the ability to pay of the respondent and all the needs, means and circumstances of the parties in determining the quantum of support ($1,400/month).

*Where the parties have children, support will be indefinite subject to review* — *Berry v. Edge*, 2010 CarswellOnt 25, 2010 ONSC 171, [2010] O.J. No. 25 (Ont. S.C.J.). The parties, who had a 10-year common law relationship, were the parents of two children. The female spouse did not work outside the home during the relationship except for a small amount of babysitting, and at the time of trial was receiving public assistance. The judge awarded indefinite support with an automatic review 2 years later, during which time the judge urged the female spouse to make serious efforts to become self-sufficient. He awarded $800 a month, as well as $18,500 in retroactive spousal support to the date of separation.

## 13.3 Shared Custody

### Straight set-off amount; amount greater than set-off amount

> Assume for the moment that the payor is paying only the straight set-off amount of child support in a shared custody case . . . the full table amount (plus any s. 7 contributions) is . . . deducted from the payor spouse's net disposable income. For the recipient, the notional table amount (plus any contribution to s. 7 expenses) is deducted from his or her income. This would be done in the calculation of INDI . . . Shared custody arrangements do not result in any automatic lowering of spousal support. (SSAG Chapter 8.6)

> in some shared custody cases, the amount of support is increased beyond the straight set-off amount . . . If [the child support payor] pays a higher amount of child support because [the child support recipient] spends more on the children or because of the increased costs of shared custody, no adjustment should be made. . . . If [the child support payor] pays more child support simply to reduce the disparity in household standards of living, an adjustment should probably be made to the ranges for spousal support, as there is less need for the same function to be performed by spousal support. (SSAG Chapter 8.6.2)

> 50/50 split of the couple's family net disposable income or monthly cash flow after the payment of child and spousal support . . . in some cases this 50/50 split falls just outside the upper or lower end of the range. In these cases, the shared custody range has been broadened to include this 50/50 split . . . These adjustments are made automatically by the software programs" (SSAG Chapter 8.6.3)

> [I]t is critical to determine which spouse is receiving which child-related government benefits in shared custody cases before calculating the range for spousal support.). User's Guide, March 31, 2010, section 8(a).

*Modified "without child support" formula used instead of "shared custody" formula* — *Mann v. Mann*, 2009 CarswellBC 1065, 2009 BCCA 181, 68 R.F.L. (6th) 1, 95 B.C.L.R. (4th) 201, 461 W.A.C. 1, 273 B.C.A.C. 1 (B.C.C.A.), additional reasons at 2009 CarswellBC 3513, 2009 BCCA 603, 74 R.F.L. (6th) 18 (B.C.C.A.). The court found at para. 83: "As commentators have noted, the application of the 'with child' formula is problematic in shared custody situations, particularly where a payor spouse is paying the full table amount of child support." Instead of applying the SSAG's shared custody formula, it applied a modified version of the "without child support" formula. The formula was modified by subtracting from each spouse's income the amount of child support paid.

*Where the payor has significant access costs and significant debt, support at the low end of the SSAG ranges will be ordered* — *Matthews v. Taylor*, 2012 CarswellNfld 77, 2012 NLTD(G) 24, 320 Nfld. & P.E.I.R. 5, 993 A.P.R. 5 (N.L.T.D.). The parties had an 11 year relationship and 2 children in a shared parenting arrangement. Support was ordered at the low range of the with child formula to reflect the fact that the payor husband had incurred significant debt meeting his support obligations during a period of unemployment as well as high access costs.

*Where spousal support is compensatory, a quantum in the mid to high range of the SSAG may be ordered* — *Dewan v. Dewan*, 2012 CarswellOnt 1656, 2012 ONSC 503, 19 R.F.L. (7th) 132, [2012] O.J. No. 363 (Ont. S.C.J.). The parties had a 14-year relationship. They had joint custody of their three children. Compensatory spousal support was ordered in the mid- to high range of the SSAG range for a total of 12 years.

*Mid-range spousal support ordered to ensure consistent standard of living in both parents' households* — *Fell v. Fell*, 2007 CarswellOnt 1604 (Ont. S.C.J.), additional reasons at 2007 CarswellOnt 3447 (Ont. S.C.J.). The parties were married for 12 years and had three children. The wife was employed part-time as a nurse and was the primary caregiver. The wife earned approximately $44,000 per year and the husband earned $96,000. The parties shared parenting of their children and the wife sought spousal support. The court granted the wife spousal support in the amount of $450 per month, the mid-range, since the parties' shared parenting of their children and this amount would ensure that the children enjoyed a consistent standard of living in the home of both their parents.

*Shared custody — interim spousal support* — *Guignard v. Guignard*, 2009 CarswellOnt 3127, [2009] O.J. No. 2267 (Ont. S.C.J.). The wife's income was $32,256. The husband's income was $106,211.69. Taking into account the shared custody of the parties' child, and the incomes of the parties, the Spousal Support Advisory Guidelines indicate a range of spousal support of $1,142.00 per month at the lower end, $1,512.00 per month in the middle and $1,874.00 at the upper end. The court took into account the parties' incomes, the length of the marriage, the economic disadvantages to the wife arising out of the marriage and the breakdown of the marriage, the reasonable expenses of the parties on an interim basis, and the *Spousal Support Advisory Guidelines*, viewed in light of *Fisher v. Fisher*, 2008 CarswellOnt 43, 2008 ONCA 11, 47 R.F.L. (6th) 235, 88 O.R. (3d) 241, 232 O.A.C. 213, 288 D.L.R. (4th) 513, [2008] O.J. No. 38 (Ont. C.A.). The court held that the husband should pay interim spousal support in the sum of $1,200 per month.

*Shared custody — SSAG not applied due to parties' high debt load* — *B. (P.S.O.) v. B. (L.M.)*, 2008 CarswellBC 346, 2008 BCSC 213, [2008] B.C.J. No. 299 (B.C.S.C.), original reasons at 2007 CarswellBC 1768, 2007 BCSC 1138, [2007] B.C.J. No. 1695 (B.C.S.C.). In this shared custody situation, the court declined to apply the SSAG because of the parties' high debt load.

*Use of SSAG in shared custody situation where child support equal to set-off table amount plus $250 per month* — *Bekkers v. Bekkers*, 2008 CarswellOnt 173, 49 R.F.L. (6th) 119, [2008] O.J. No. 140 (Ont. S.C.J.). The parties had equal shared custody of their two children. The difference between the child support Table Amounts for the two parties was $683; pursuant to *Contino v. Leonelli-Contino*, 2005 CarswellOnt 6281, 2005 CarswellOnt 6282, 2005 SCC 63, 19 R.F.L. (6th) 272, [2005] 3 S.C.R. 217, 259 D.L.R. (4th) 388, 341 N.R. 1, 204 O.A.C. 311, 80 O.R. (3d) 480 (note), [2005] S.C.J. No. 65 (S.C.C.), $250 per month was added to this amount producing a total child support obligation on the husband of $933 per month. The SSAG range would have been $141-$829 per month if the straight set-off child support amount had been ordered. Interim spousal support of $600 per month was ordered.

*Equal shared custody — midpoint of SSAG range ordered — Pedersen v. Pedersen*, 2008 CarswellBC 564, 2008 BCSC 342, [2008] B.C.J. No. 490 (B.C. Master). On an interim basis, the court applied the SSAG shared custody formula and ordered the midpoint quantum.

## 13.4 Split Custody

> In the split custody situation, a notional table amount must be deducted from each parent, not just the recipient but the payor as well. (SSAG Chapter 8.7)

> In some split custody cases, the higher-income spouse will not claim any child support from the lower-income spouse. In these cases, an adjustment must be made, to avoid stating too high a range for spousal support (which assumes that the recipient of spousal support is in fact paying an amount for child support). (SSAG, Chapter 8.7.)

*Where there is an overpayment of support, support amounts may be ordered at levels below the SSAG — Cherry-Francey v. Francey*, 2012 CarswellOnt 4123, 2012 ONSC 2109, [2012] O.J. No. 1537 (Ont. S.C.J.). The parties in this case were married for 15 years and had two children in a split-custody arrangement. Indefinite compensatory and needs-based support was ordered on a final basis at a level below the SSAG amounts. The judge found that there was an overpayment in support in favour of the recipient post-separation and reduced the amounts payable to one-half the SSAG amount to take into account these overpayments. The judge correctly treated the recipient spouse's ODSP as not part of her income.

## 13.5 Step-Children

> Under section 8 of the Child Support Guidelines, it is possible for a step-parent to pay less than the table amount of child support if appropriate. A reduced amount is only ordered or agreed upon when the biological parent is already paying child support. [citation removed] Where the amount of child support is reduced under s. 8, the with child support formula range should be calculated using the full table amount rather than the reduced amount. (SSAG Chapter 8.8)

*Application of the step-children formula — Collins v. Collins*, 2008 CarswellNfld 272, 2008 NLUFC 31, 281 Nfld. & P.E.I.R. 1, 863 A.P.R. 1, [2008] N.J. No. 296 (N.L.U.F.C.). After ordering that the step-father pay $200 per month for his step-child, in awarding spousal support, the court took into account the actual amount that the step-father would have paid under the "with child support" formula to ensure that the step-father was not overpaying on spousal support.

## 13.6  Custodial Payor

> 1)  Reduce the payor spouse's Guidelines income by the grossed-up notional table amount for child support (plus a gross-up of any contributions to s. 7 expenses).
> 2)  If the recipient spouse is paying child support, reduce the recipient's Guidelines income by the grossed-up amount of child support paid (table amount plus any s. 7 contributions). ["To gross up the child support will require a calculation of the gross value of the non-taxable child support, using the appropriate marginal tax rate for the payor or recipient spouse."]
> 3)  Determine the adjusted gross income difference between the spouses and then quantum ranges from 1.5 percent to 2 percent for each year of marriage, up to a maximum of 50.
> 4)  Duration ranges from .5 to 1 year of support for each year of marriage, with the same rules for indefinite (duration not specified) support as under the without child support formula.(SSAG Chapter 8.9)

[An exception specific to this formula is described in s. 7.9 of this Volume and in s. 12.9 of the SSAG.]

*Where the parties were in a marriage of long duration and fell within the "65 rule", the SSAG presumed an indefinite award of spousal support* — *Cassidy v. McNeil*, 2010 CarswellOnt 1637, 2010 ONCA 218, 99 O.R. (3d) 81, [2010] O.J. No. 1158 (Ont. C.A.). The parties were married for 23 years and had three children who all resided with the husband after separation. The parties both worked during the marriage, the husband as a university professor and the wife as a teacher. This was an appeal from a trial decision which awarded $1,200 in monthly spousal support for a limited term of 5 years to the mother, and also awarded prospective child support to the father. The Court of Appeal reduced the quantum of spousal support to $975, and based the award on mainly compensatory grounds, although need was also found to be a factor. During the parties' marriage, the wife had put her career on the back burner to raise the children. She worked at a private school, where she was able to pay reduced tuition for the children. The Court of Appeal also removed the limited term and made the order of support indefinite based on the presumption found in the SSAG for marriages of longer than 20 years. The situation of the wife also fell within the "rule of 65", in that she was 48 years old at the time of separation and the parties had been married for 23 years. Lang J.A. found that the SSAG presumption reflected case law, which took into account the dependency on lifestyle and the relevancy of the recipient's age in becoming self-supporting. Further grounds for an indefinite award in this case were found to be the uncertainty of the wife's employment and the certainty of the husband's employment, as he was a tenured professor. This is an example of the "custodial payor" formula.

*Where the children are older and do not require childcare, this will lower the amount of spousal support payable according to the SSAG range* — *Domirti v. Domirti*, 2010 CarswellBC 518, 2010 BCCA 112 (B.C.C.A. [In Chambers]). The parties were married from 1979 to 1994 and had three children. The husband appealed an award of $1,250 per month of spousal support made by a judge of the Supreme Court of B.C. The chambers judge found that, despite ongoing attempts to find full-time employment and upgrade her skills, after many years of receiving spousal support Ms. Skinner (formerly Mrs. Domirti) had not yet reached self-sufficiency. The chambers judge awarded her $1,250 per month in spousal support, which was in the middle of the *SSAG* range. The Court of Appeal used the *custodial payor* formula found in the SSAG to determine quantum because the husband had custody of the parties' three children. Factors for quantum in this case were the older age of the remaining custodial children, the lack of childcare responsibilities, and the non-custodial parent's pre-separation contributions to the children's expenses. This led to an award at the lower end of the SSAG range.

*Appellant's failure to apply custodial payor formula correctly not apparently noted by respondent or by court* — Lust v. Lust, 2007 CarswellAlta 808, 2007 ABCA 202, 417 A.R. 106, 410 W.A.C. 106, [2007] A.J. No. 654 (Alta. C.A.), reversing in part 2007 CarswellAlta 864, 2007 ABQB 214, 413 A.R. 1, [2007] A.J. No. 635 (Alta. Q.B.). This was a custodial payor situation in which the recipient appealed from the trial court decision. She claimed that the SSAG suggested an award of $1229 per month, but she had mistakenly relied upon the basic child support forumla rather than the custodial payor formula. According to the case report, neither the respondent nor the court pointed out this erroneous application of the SSAG. The appeal was dismissed.

*The "Custodial Payor" formula takes into account a payor's present child care responsibility.* — L. (R.) v. L. (N.), 2012 CarswellNB 258, 2012 NBQB 123, 22 R.F.L. (7th) 82, 388 N.B.R. (2d) 220, 1006 A.P.R. 220 (N.B.Q.B.).

*Where the father, the payor parent has become the primary parent of the children, because of his high-handedness,, the court may award support above the range given in the custodial parent formula may be awarded to the mother* — Osanlo v. Onghaei, 2012 CarswellOnt 4139, 2012 ONSC 2158 (Ont. S.C.J.). The father had, after a family vacation to Iran, returned to Canada with the children. The wife's passport had disappeared and she had great difficulty returning to Canada. She was then destitute and had no means of support. The children were being cared for by the husband's second wife. The husband's finances were extremely opaque, but the lifestyle enjoyed by the parties was lavish. Interim spousal support above the SSAG range for a custodial parent payor was awarded to the first wife to allow her to re-establish herself in Canada and as a parent. The judge found that because the primary parent was changed through high-handedness by the father, this was not an appropriate situation to limit support to the custodial parent formula.

*Where a recipient spouse has made a decision not to pursue more lucrative employment, this decision will have an effect on spousal support entitlement and support at the mid-range, rather than the high range, of the SSAG may be ordered* — de la Sablonniere v. Castagner, 2012 CarswellOnt 969, 2012 ONSC 176 (Ont. S.C.J.). The parties were in a relationship for 19 years and had three children. The children had decided to reside with the husband. This decision followed the custodial payor formula with support awarded at the midrange for a total of twelve years.

*The ability of a custodial payor to pay spousal support when also owing a large amount of debt is a scenario which will prompt the application of the compelling financial circumstances exception in the SSAG* — Fyfe v. Jouppien, 2011 CarswellOnt 9295, 2011 ONSC 5462, 10 R.F.L. (7th) 336 (Ont. S.C.J.). Here, the exception for compelling financial circumstances in the interim period was applied. The parties were together for 23 years and had two children. At separation, both parties were self-sufficient and the children resided with their mother. After separation, the husband was diagnosed with terminal cancer and began receiving disability payments. The judge determined that the husband was entitled to support, but that the wife had no ability to pay because of significant debt stemming from her role as the sole provider to the children.

*SSAG not used due to access costs and other facts* — D. (D.A.) v. D. (A.N.), 2008 CarswellNS 103, 2008 NSFC 2, 269 N.S.R. (2d) 161, 860 A.P.R. 161, [2008] N.S.J. No. 88 (N.S. Fam. Ct.). In this custodial payor case under the provincial support legislation, the court found the SSAG "not applicable in this case because of a number of variables including the requirement of the Applicant-father/spouse to pay access costs for the children to see their mother."

*Custodial payor case with above-ceiling income: $1500 per month ordered* — Campbell v. Campbell, 2008 CarswellBC 230, 2008 BCSC 154, [2008] B.C.J. No. 202 (B.C.S.C. [In

Chambers]). In this custodial payor case, given the income imputed to the recipient, the SSAG range was $2,552-$3,403. Interim support of $1500 per month was ordered.

## 13.7 Adult Children

> This adult children formula will only apply where the child support for all the remaining children of the marriage is determined under section 3(2)(b) of the Child Support Guidelines and there are no children for whom a table amount of child support is being paid under section 3(1) or section 3(2)(a). . . Once each parent's contribution to the child's budget has been allocated under s. 3(2)(b), those actual child support amounts are grossed up and deducted from each spouse's gross income. Then the without child support formula is applied, using the adjusted gross income difference and the length of marriage factor to determine amount and duration . . . The [formula] for the custodial payor can be used to describe the calculations, with one change: the actual amounts of each parent's contribution to child support will be grossed up, rather than table and section 7 amounts. (SSAG Chapter 8.10)

"When deducting child support in this hybrid formula, the child support amount must be *grossed up*, as this is a gross income formula. If child support is not grossed up, then the spousal support range will be too high" (SSAG, Chapter 8.10). See *Buchanan v. Goldberg*, 2010 CarswellOnt 74, 2010 ONSC 268 (Ont. S.C.J.), where child support was not grossed up.

# CHAPTER 14

## USING THE RANGES

This chapter is divided into the following sections:

14.1 Effect of property awards, exempt or excluded assets, debts, if any

14.2 Compensatory or non-compensatory basis for support; longer marriages under with child formula; recipients limited income; children's age, number and needs; standard of living; payor's need and ability to pay; net income; need to preserve work incentive; self-sufficiency; net disposable income

14.3 Other

### 14.1 Effect of Property Awards, Exempt or Excluded Assets, Debts, If Any

An absence of property to be divided might suggest an award at the higher end of the range. If the recipient receives a large amount of property, the low end of the range might be more appropriate. Similarly, if the recipient holds sizeable exempt or excluded assets after division, that too might militate in favour of the lower end of the range. Where one spouse assumes a disproportionate share of the family debts, it may be necessary to use the debt payment exception described below in Chapter 12. But there will be other cases, not so severe, where the debt payments of one spouse will just be a factor pushing the amount higher or lower within the range, depending upon which spouse is paying the debts. (SSAG Section 9.6)

#### Spousal Support Awards — Low End of Range

*Spousal support was set at the low end of the SSAG range because of the effect of the division of family assets — Yang v. Ren*, 2012 CarswellBC 1085, 2012 BCCA 164, 321 B.C.A.C. 178, 547 W.A.C. 178 (B.C.C.A.). At the Court of Appeal, the father appealed from a judgement regarding custody and guardianship of the parties' child. The parties were married in 2006, had a child and separated in 2008. The father, entirely with his own funds, acquired a condominium in Vancouver after the marriage registration in China. However, equal division of the family assets was ordered, as the wife had a need to become economically independent and the husband had a superior financial capacity in comparision to the wife. The award of spousal support was affirmed on appeal. There was no further discussion of spousal support on appeal.

*Reference to wife's spousal support being lower than SSAG ranges was sufficient to indicate that the wife's occupation of the matrimonial home was taken into account in giving her an unusually low amount of spousal support — Haraphongse v. Haraphongse*, 2011 CarswellAlta 2321, 2011 ABCA 343 (Alta. C.A.). The appellant claimed that the trial judge "never indicated the exact amount by which he reduced the spousal support to take account of the wife's occupation of the home, making it unclear if the proper test was applied." However, the appellate court concluded that the trial judge had noted that the amount for interim spousal support was lower than the amount in the SSAG as the wife had occupied the matrimonial home since day one. Consequently, the appellate court considered that the reduced amount took into account the occupation of the house. While the court did not explicitly take into account the claim for occupation rent, in fact it was considered. The reasons could have been more specific, but there was no reviewable error. The wife had sought $8,000 to $12,000 in monthly spousal support but was awarded $7,500.

*Property distribution justifies lower-end award* — *Holmes v. Matkovich*, 2008 CarswellYukon 55, 2008 YKCA 10, 59 R.F.L. (6th) 60, 258 B.C.A.C. 86, 434 W.A.C. 86, [2008] Y.J. No. 51 (Y.T.C.A.). In a judgement which was affirmed on appeal, the trial court chose an amount at the lower end of the SSAG range because the support recipient was to receive the parties' farm.

*Reapportionment of debts and assets a reason to move within range* — *award at low end* — *McEachern v. McEachern*, 2006 CarswellBC 2750, 2006 BCCA 508, 33 R.F.L. (6th) 315, 62 B.C.L.R. (4th) 95, [2007] 3 W.W.R. 471, 232 B.C.A.C. 185, 385 W.A.C. 185, [2006] B.C.J. No. 2917 (B.C.C.A.). The reapportionment of the parties' property and debt was accounted for by making an award at the low end of the SSAG range.

*Where the effect of the property division is advantageous to the recipient spouse, support will be at the low end of the SSAG range* — *Yang v. Ren*, supra. The father appealed a spousal support order in which he was ordered to pay support at the upper end of the SSAG range because of the nature of the property division. (It was divided equally.) Although the marriage was only 2 years long, the wife was disadvantaged by it as it entailed a move to Canada. She had limited English skills and no education or training and was not able to support herself.

*Where the recipient spouse has a superior asset position after equalization, support at the low end of the range will be awarded* — *Brisson v. Brisson*, 2012 CarswellBC 3051, 2012 BCCA 396, 22 R.F.L. (7th) 1, 39 B.C.L.R. (5th) 1, 355 D.L.R. (4th) 720, 328 B.C.A.C. 163, 558 W.A.C. 163 (B.C.C.A.). The parties had a very long-term marriage (37 years), and at trial the judge determined no spousal support was payable because the current and future financial circumstances of the parties would be roughly equivalent. The Court of Appeal overturned this decision and ordered $500 monthly in support, which was at the low end of the without child SSAG range, in recognition of the wife's superior asset position post-equalization.

*The range of support was largely dependent on the father's ability to pay; support awarded below the low end of the range* — *Caldarola v. Buscemi*, 2012 CarswellMan 403, 2012 MBQB 203, 22 R.F.L. (7th) 406, 281 Man. R. (2d) 159 (Man. Q.B.). The parties were married for almost 14 years and had been separated for two and one-half years. They had three children, the oldest of whom was mildly autistic and the youngest of whom might be autistic. The mother was a registered nurse, but had not worked since the youngest child was born. The father was a mechanical engineering technologist, whose earnings for 2010 were $78,700, and $73,400 in 2011. The spousal support issues before the court were: whether income should be imputed to the mother and the appropriate amount of spousal support, both retroactive and ongoing, to be paid. The mother had primary care of the children. The oldest child refused to see his father. The court considered that the range of support related more to the father's ability to pay than the mother's needs, as even the high end of the range could not meet her present budget requirements. In determining which range high, mid or low to choose, the court considered the following factors: 1. The father's "net disposable income" was not truly all disposable income. The father had a mandatory pension deduction and also paid into a health plan, which payment benefits the mother and the children. 2. He had a significant amount of debt incurred during the marriage and was carrying the entire burden of that debt repayment. 3. He has not had the advantage of his equity in the martial home since separation, and had been living at his parents through this time. The mother would have child support income of $1,440 per month, together with other child-related benefits and credits which would not be taxed. The court imputed a modest amount of income to the mother. The court observed that her refusal to recognize her responsibility to earn income commensurate with her training was concerning. Her refusal to participate with the son's counseling meant she had less time in which to earn an income without requiring child care. In considering the parties' condition, means, needs and other circumstances, the court ordered spousal support in an amount between the low end and the mid-range of the SSAG which was $400 per month.

*Support in lower amount of range where reapportionment had compensated payee to certain extent* — Holland v. Novotony, 2009 CarswellBC 3478, 2009 BCSC 1754 (B.C.S.C.). The husband had an annual income of $102,000. The wife had no income. The wife claimed to have a medical disability. She had applied for CPP disability benefits, but her application had not been processed. The range under the SSAG was $2,040 at the lower end, $2,380 at the middle, and $2,720 at the upper end. As a result of the reapportionment in favour of the wife and on the facts of this case, the court considered that it was appropriate to look to the lower end of the range with respect to quantum. The court ordered spousal support of $2,200 per month.

*Support in lower amount of range where reapportionment had compensated payee to certain extent* — C. (S.) v. D. (A.), 2009 CarswellBC 3475, 2009 BCSC 1749 (B.C.S.C.). The wife was entitled to support on both a compensatory and non-compensatory basis. The court recognized that the reapportionment of the family home compensated the wife to an extent for the economic dislocation flowing from the breakdown of the marriage. Consequently, the spousal support should be somewhat lower than what it would otherwise be. The marriage had lasted 14 years. The parties had three children. The wife had largely been a homemaker and had no real world work experience. She had obtained her university degree 15 years previously. She had a history of medical difficulties. The incomes of the husband and wife were imputed into each party's calculations at $423,000 and $3,000 respectively. The resultant range from the DivorceMate calculation was the following: $8,184, $9,059, and $9,932. The court held that there was no reason to depart from the SSAG range for duration. The appropriate level of spousal support was $8,300 per month for a period of 10 years.

*Potential to earn income from asset justifies choosing lower extremity of range as support quantum* — Chow v. Ng, 2008 CarswellBC 255, 2008 BCSC 172, [2008] B.C.J. No. 217 (B.C.S.C.). The midpoint of the SSAG range was ordered for an initial period. The recipient was to have an additional $30,000 in annual income imputed to her as of February 2010. From this point forward, she was to receive spousal support equal to the bottom of the new SSAG range because she would be the sole owner of a large house and would be in a position to downsize and obtain investment income.

*Reapportionment justifies low end award* — Williams v. Williams, 2008 CarswellBC 2500, 2008 BCSC 1603, [2008] B.C.J. No.2267 (B.C.S.C.). The reapportionment of assets in favour of the support recipient was the court's reason for ordering a quantum equal to the low end of the SSAG range.

*Reapportionment in favour of recipient justifies award close to bottom of SSAG range* — Lucik v. Lucik, 2008 CarswellBC 949, 2008 BCSC 531, [2008] B.C.J. No. 759 (B.C.S.C.). In light of the reapportionment of marital property, a spousal support award toward the bottom of the SSAG range was made.

*Reapportionment relevant in using range* — Rayvals v. Rayvals, 2008 CarswellBC 270, 2008 BCSC 176, 51 R.F.L. (6th) 391, 80 B.C.L.R. (4th) 191, [2008] B.C.J. No. 233 (B.C.S.C.), additional reasons at 2008 CarswellBC 1143, 2008 BCSC 718, 56 R.F.L. (6th) 127 (B.C.S.C.). The family assets had been reapportioned in favour of the wife, who received 80% of them. This was a relevant factor in ordering a monthly quantum less than the SSAG range.

*Reapportionment suggests that lower end of range should be used* — Freeman v. Freeman, 2008 CarswellBC 1366, 2008 BCSC 857, [2008] B.C.J. No. 1247 (B.CS.C.), additional reasons at

2008 CarswellBC 2386, 2008 BCSC 1462, [2008] B.C.J. No. 2065 (B.C.S.C.). After identifying the SSAG quantum range, the court stated at para. 124: "The economic advantages and disadvantages have, to some extent, been taken into account in the reapportionment decision. On the facts of this case it is appropriate, as a result, to look to the lower end of the range with respect to quantum."

### Middle of range

*Where mortgage and other costs have been paid by the payor spouse, support in the midrange of the SSAG may be ordered* — Colosimo v. Colosimo, 2012 CarswellOnt 83, 2012 ONSC 162, [2012] O.J. No. 26 (Ont. S.C.J.). The parties were married for 17 years and had two children in split custody. Interim spousal support was ordered at the mid-range of the SSAG in order to recognize the husband's payment of housing expenses for the wife.

*Spousal support ordered at mid-range of* Spousal Support Advisory Guidelines, *to be reduced to low-end of Guidelines upon payment of monetary award based on unjust enrichment* — Jackson v. McNee, 2011 CarswellOnt 9185, 2011 ONSC 4651, 12 R.F.L. (7th) 190 (Ont. S.C.J.). The parties lived in a common law relationship for 18.5 years and had three children. The parties had a primarily traditional relationship in which the man worked outside the home, and controlled the finances and the couple's rental properties, and the woman raised the children and maintained the house. The woman was awarded $739 per month for spousal support. An income of $75,000 was imputed to the man and the award was in the mid-range of the *Spousal Support Advisory Guidelines*. The evidence indicated that the parties were in a joint-family venture and the contribution of each party was linked to the accumulation of family wealth. By caring for the children and home while the man worked, the woman clearly established her claim of unjust enrichment. In the circumstances, a monetary award was appropriate. Despite being in a new relationship, the woman was entitled to spousal support because her ability to earn income during the parties' relationship was negatively impacted by her role in the relationship. The spousal support award was to be reduced to the low-end of the SSAG range after the woman received the monetary award based on unjust enrichment.

### High end of range

*Where the payor spouse is residing in the matrimonial home, spousal support may be awarded at the high end of the SSAG ranges* — Czegledy-Nagy v. Seirli, 2011 CarswellOnt 12789, 2011 ONSC 6488, 11 R.F.L. (7th) 310 (Ont. S.C.J.), additional reasons at 2012 CarswellOnt 1077, 2012 ONSC 119, 11 R.F.L. (7th) 323 (Ont. S.C.J.). The parties were in a relationship for 7 years and had triplets. They shared custody. Interim spousal support was sought and granted at the high end of the SSAG as the husband was residing in the matrimonial home, which was one of the wife's principal assets.

## 14.2  Compensatory or non-compensatory basis for support; longer marriages under with child formula; recipients limited income; children's age, number and needs; standard of living; payor's need and ability to pay; net income; need to preserve work incentive; self-sufficiency; net disposable income

The delineation of the compensatory and/or non-compensatory basis for entitlement in a particular case is relevant . . . to determine location within the ranges. (SSAG Section 4.2)

A strong compensatory claim will be a factor that favours a support award at the higher end of the ranges both for amount and duration. A spouse who has suffered significant economic disadvantage as a result of the marital roles and whose claims are based on both compensatory and non-compensatory grounds may have a stronger support claim under the *without child support* formula than a spouse whose economic circumstances are not the result of marital roles and who can only claim non-compensatory support based upon loss of the marital standard of living . . . Under the *with child support* formula, compensatory principles would also suggest that the more the recipient spouse gave up in the paid labour market, the higher one would go within the range. (SSAG Section 9.1)

In the longer marriage cases under the *with child support* formula, where the length-of-marriage test defines the durational range, most cases will tend towards the longer end of the durational range and few cases should see support terminate at the lower end, given the strong compensatory claims that are typically present in these cases. (SSAG Section 8.5.2)

In a case where the recipient has limited income and/or earning capacity, because of age or other circumstances, the recipient's needs may push an award to the higher end of the ranges for amount and duration. Conversely, the absence of compelling need may be a factor that pushes an award to the lower end of the range. (SSAG Section 9.2)

The age, number and needs of the children will affect placement within the range under the with child support formula . . . Generally speaking, when ability to pay is in issue, the larger the number of children, the less income is left available to pay spousal support, and the ranges will be lower, consistent with s. 15.3 of the *Divorce Act*. In these cases of squeezed ranges for spousal support, there will be strong reasons to go higher in this "depressed" range, to generate some compensatory support for the primary parent. As income levels rise for the parents of three or more children, the spousal support ranges will adjust upwards and there will be more flexibility for the location of amount within the ranges. (SSAG Section 9.3)

Standard of living concerns may also tend to push spousal support awards towards the higher end of the range. Even when spousal support is at the maximum 46 percent of individual net disposable income, a homemaker recipient and the children will be left with a noticeably lower household standard of living (assuming no new partners or children for either spouse). At lower income levels, the needs of the children's household will create pressure to move to the higher end of the range. (SSAG Section 9.5)

Need and limited ability to pay on the part of the payor spouse may push an award to the lower ends of the ranges. These factors will clearly have special importance at the lower end of the income spectrum, even above the floor of $20,000. (SSAG Section 9.4)

it is always important to look at the net income consequences of any particular amount of spousal support, especially for the payor. In longer marriages under this formula, where the formula percentages are higher, this is critical, especially where the payor has large mandatory deductions, including any pension deductions, compared to the recipient. These deductions may be a factor in going lower in the range for amount. (SSAG Section 9.4)

"A lower income payor should be left with sufficient funds to exercise meaningful access to his or her children." (SSAG Section 9.4)

a separate concern, the need to preserve work incentives for the payor. . . . This concern will be particularly important in two situations: long marriages under the without child support formula and most cases of substantial child support under the with child support formula. The problem will be most acute at low-to-middle income levels. (SSAG Section 9.5)

Self-sufficiency incentives may push in different directions. (SSAG Section 9.7)

Although the formula works with gross income figures, it is always important, in determining a precise amount of support within the range to do a "reality check" by looking at net disposable income positions after payment of a given amount of spousal support, particularly in cases of long marriages. (SSAG User's Guide, Section 5)

### Low End of the Range

*Where restructuring does not result in a lump sum amount that is consistent with the Divorce Act, an exception to the SSAG will be found in determining quantum of the lump sum where the payor has serious health issues — Robinson v. Robinson,* 2011 CarswellBC 3271, 2011 BCSC 1489, 14 R.F.L. (7th) 141 (B.C.S.C.), affirmed 2012 CarswellBC 3789, 2012 BCCA 497, 25 R.F.L. (7th) 47, 40 B.C.L.R. (5th) 108, [2012] B.C.J. No. 2572 (B.C.C.A.). The trail judge awarded lump sum spousal support under the without child formula. The parties were married for 28 years and had two adult, independent children. The trial judge found that the wife had a claim for compensatory support and used the SSAG in order to determine monthly support of $6,000, or a mid-range amount. She then found that lump sum spousal support was indicated given the possible difficulty of collecting payments as the husband had moved to Germany, the husband's poor health, and his income. However, the trial judge found that the lump sum indicated by the computer analysis did not meet the objectives of the *Divorce Act* and the trial judge preferred another method of calculation. Consequently, the trial judge made an order based on "the factors of relative tax situations, an appropriate discount rate for the present value, and a contingency rate where necessary". Given the poor health of the husband, the lump sum award was less than it would have been otherwise. The judge found that this case fell into the exceptions of the SSAG found at s. 3.4.2. The decision was upheld by the Court of Appeal.

*Low end support awarded indefinitely — Cassidy v. McNeil,* 2010 CarswellOnt 1637, 2010 ONCA 218, 99 O.R. (3d) 81, 266 O.A.C. 62, [2010] O.J. No. 1158 (Ont. C.A.). The parties were married for 23 years and had two children, who were living with the husband. The wife's annual income was $85,000 and the husband's was $137,000. The trial judge ordered the husband to pay the wife $1,200 per month in spousal support, limited to 5 years. The parties appealed the support order. On appeal, the spousal support order was reduced to the lower end of the Guidelines range and set at $950 per month, but was made indefinite. The court noted that the trial judge had ordered spousal support on the high end of the range, which was inappropriate given the husband's obligations for the children and the wife's relatively high income.

*After 16 years of support following a 12-year marriage, support will be awarded at the low end of the low range of the SSAG for a definitive duration — Aspe v. Aspe,* 2010 CarswellBC 3077, 2010 BCCA 508, 89 R.F.L. (6th) 245, 11 B.C.L.R. (5th) 309, 327 D.L.R. (4th) 231, 294

B.C.A.C. 290, 498 W.A.C. 290 (B.C.C.A.). The parties had three children, were married for 12 years, and separated in 1993, at which time the wife was awarded indefinite support. The wife applied for a variation and increase of spousal support in 2008 after the children decided to live with their father. The wife claimed she was disabled and could not work, but was unable to present admissible expert evidence on this point. The chambers judge found that the Advisory Guidelines addressed issues that were no longer relevant to the case and that the range of acceptable amounts ("depending upon the assumptions made") was overly broad. The chambers judge awarded ongoing spousal support at the low end of the SSAG for a duration of 2 years, at which point the order was reviewable. The Court of Appeal further lowered the amount. The apellate court did not address the SSAG.

*The Court of Appeal will award the minimum amount of support provided for in the SSAG if it finds a sufficiently demonstrated material change in circumstances such as early retirement and debt load* — Emery v. Emery, 2010 CarswellBC 2137, 2010 BCCA 376, 100 R.F.L. (6th) 154 (B.C.C.A.), additional reasons to 2010 CarswellBC 1170, 2010 BCCA 229, 85 R.F.L. (6th) 251, 287 B.C.A.C. 116, 485 W.A.C. 116 (B.C.C.A.). The parties had a 23-year "traditional" marriage. They had seven children and separated in 2000. By the time of the proceedings in 2006, five of their seven children were living independently while two of them, who were disabled, remained in the wife's care. The wife worked 20 hours a week. In 2006, the Supreme Court ordered the husband to pay $1,750 per month in spousal support, to be reviewed in 2007. When the husband made a review application in 2007, the court applied the SSAG in calculating support at $1,300 per month, payable beginning in 2008, based on the husband's projected income. In 2009, the husband took early retirement from the police force for psychological reasons and sought to terminate support. The chambers judge did not find that the husband's retirement demonstrated a material change of circumstances, but vacated the spousal support order for 4 months to give the husband time to secure other employment. In 2010, the Court of Appeal disagreed, finding that early retirement did constitute a material change of circumstances. The court noted that the Advisory Guidelines provide a range of $1,139 to $1,886 and awarded exactly $1,139 for 2009 due to the husband's retirement and debt load.

*A lower court decision to award support in the low range of the SSAG will be affirmed, given the brief marriage, the wife's prospect of self-sufficiency, and the husband's increased access with the child* — Reis v. Bucholtz, 2010 CarswellBC 509, 2010 BCCA 115, 3 B.C.L.R. (5th) 71, [2010] B.C.J. No. 382 (B.C.C.A.).

*The income prospects of a support recipient (a 40-year-old medical doctor) can justify an award at the low end of the SSAG for a reasonably short period of time* —Gonabady-Namadon v. Mohammadzadeh, 2009 CarswellBC 2767, 2009 BCCA 448, 74 R.F.L. (6th) 1, 98 B.C.L.R. (4th) 23, 277 B.C.A.C. 48, 469 W.A.C. 48 (B.C.C.A), varying 2008 CarswellBC 968, 2008 BCSC 606, 54 R.F.L. (6th) 408 (B.C.S.C.), varying 2008 CarswellBC 1120, 2008 BCSC 706, 58 R.F.L. (6th) 205 (B.C.S.C.). Support was ordered with a quantum at the bottom of the SSAG range and a duration slightly below the bottom. The professional income and future prospects of the wife were given as the reasons for this choice. At trial, the trial judge found that the wife was not entitled to spousal support due to her annual income of $150,000. On appeal, the income imputed to the husband was $350,000; the wife was found to be entitled to spousal support and awarded $2,300 a month for 6 years.

*The SSAG are helpful in establishing a range of appropriate support — a modified version of the "without child" support formula was applied* — Mann v. Mann, 2009 CarswellBC 1065, 2009 BCCA 181, 68 R.F.L. (6th) 1, 95 B.C.L.R. (4th) 201, 273 B.C.A.C. 1, 461 W.A.C. 1 (B.C.C.A.), additional reasons at 2009 CarswellBC 3513, 2009 BCCA 603, 74 R.F.L. (6th) 18 (B.C.C.A.). The parties separated in 1999 after a 15-year marriage. The wife applied for spousal support in 2006 when she instituted divorce proceedings. The trial judge found that the wife had become self-sufficient by the time of trial, as her income permitted the lifestyle that the parties had enjoyed before separation. At trial, the wife was awarded lump sum support of $25,000. The trial court considered the SSAG, but did not find them useful. The husband's income increased significantly post-separation. On appeal, the court questioned whether the trial judge's award of a lump sum of $25,000 was an award that could and should be changed. The Court of Appeal held, at para. 82, that:

> The *Spousal Support Guidelines* cannot be applied in the circumstances of this case, without adjustment for the deferred application for spousal support, consideration of the respondent's significant post-separation income increase, his underpayment for the family assets in 2001, as well as the amounts he actually paid under the parties' shared custody arrangement. But, they are helpful in establishing a range of appropriate support and their consideration in this case provides a better range than the needs-based approach the trial judge took that caused the compensatory factor to be confined to the years when the appellant forewent spousal support after the separation agreement and overlooked the disadvantage to her and the advantage to her husband of the role she played during the marriage.

Instead of applying the SSAG's shared custody formula, it applied a modified version of the "without child support" formula. The formula was modified by subtracting from each spouse's income the amount of child support paid.

*Where the parties have concluded Minutes of Settlement, variation may result in an award that is outside of the range (in this case below the range) found in the* Spousal Support Advisory Guidelines — *Turpin v. Clark*, 2009 CarswellBC 3149, 2009 BCCA 530, 80 R.F.L. (6th) 239, 4 B.C.L.R. (5th) 48, 313 D.L.R. (4th) 452, [2010] 6 W.W.R. 613, 278 B.C.A.C. 220, 471 W.A.C. 220, [2009] B.C.J. No. 2328 (B.C.C.A.), leave to appeal refused 2010 CarswellBC 1055, 2010 CarswellBC 1056, 297 B.C.A.C. 320 (note), 407 N.R. 396 (note), 504 W.A.C. 320 (note), [2010] S.C.C.A. No. 5 (S.C.C.). The parties were married for approximately 20 years and had two children. They divorced in 2005 and signed Minutes of Settlement. The Minutes of Settlement provided for spousal support, but at levels lower than would be indicated by the SSAG. Twenty-seven months after, the wife applied for and received variation of the spousal support agreement to bring support in line with SSAG. The Court of Appeal found that the trial judge had erred in assessing spousal support at Guidelines amounts, as the Guidelines themselves state that agreements between the parties should be seen as reflecting their intentions, which should be respected. Although variation of such agreements is possible under the SSAG, consideration of the parties' intentions may lead to an award outside the SSAG range. The Court of Appeal recognized that Ms. Clark's continued need required variation of the Minutes of Settlement, but upheld the step-down provisions and the quantum originally determined by the parties, and extended the time limit of support by 3 years.

*Income prospects of recipient justify award at low end* — *Gonabady-Namadon v. Mohammadzadeh, supra.* Support was ordered with a quantum at the bottom of the SSAG range, and a duration slightly below the bottom. The "professional income and future prospects" of the wife (a 40-year-old doctor) were given at para. 61 as the reasons for this choice.

*Payor's employment-related expenses cited as reason for ordering amount slightly below SSAG range* — *Yemchuk v. Yemchuk*, 2005 CarswellBC 1881, 2005 BCCA 406, 16 R.F.L. (6th) 430, 44 B.C.L.R. (4th) 77, 257 D.L.R. (4th) 476, [2005] 10 W.W.R. 634, 215 B.C.A.C. 193, 355 W.A.C. 193, [2005] B.C.J. No. 1748 (B.C.C.A.), additional reasons at 2005 CarswellBC 2540, 2005 BCCA 527, 22 R.F.L. (6th) 60, [2005] B.C.J. No. 2319 (B.C.C.A.). The trial court had found no entitlement to spousal support, but the appeal court found that the appellant was entitled. The SSAG range was $1,190 to $1,580 per month; the court endorsed the SSAG but ordered $1,100 per month in light of the payor's employment-related expenses.

Where a spousal support payor has custody of the children and has received no child support, and the recipient has made few efforts towards self-sufficiency, support below the without child SSAG range will be ordered — Chiasson v. Chiasson, 2012 CarswellNB 759, 2013 NBQB 3, 398 N.B.R. (2d) 110, 1032 A.P.R. 110 (N.B.Q.B.). The parties had two independent children. They had a 17-year traditional marriage, and the wife had little education. The judge found entitlement on a non-compensatory basis and found that the wife had need, as she had very little income post-separation. The husband had custody of the children, and the wife was unable to pay child support. The judge found that support should be ordered at less than the Guidelines amounts because the husband had borne the entire financial responsibility for the children on his income of $46,000 and the wife had not made efforts to become self-sufficient since separation. The wife was young at the time of separation (30 years of age).

Spousal support below the SSAG range will be awarded when the recipient is largely self-sufficient and has attained a lifestyle commensurate with that enjoyed during the relationship — Lawlor v. Lawlor, 2012 CarswellAlta 2218, 2012 ABQB 723 (Alta. Q.B.). The parties were married for 16 years and had four children who were independent. The wife had achieved self-sufficiency. However, the judge found she was entitled to compensatory support given the educational upgrading that the husband had acquired during the marriage. Spousal support was awarded for 3 years prior to the date of the Statement of Claim and in an ongoing manner at below the SSAG range.

Where the payor spouse's income is extremely high, support will be ordered at a level below the SSAG range — McCain v. McCain, 2012 CarswellOnt 16853, 2012 ONSC 7344, 34 R.F.L. (7th) 82 (Ont. S.C.J.). The wife in this case was awarded temporary spousal support at below the SSAG range under the ceiling. The husband had an annual income of more than $9 million, and it was a long-term, traditional marriage. The judge, after setting aside the support provision in the parties' marriage contract, found that the wife was entitled to compensatory support and ordered $175,000 monthly.

Where spousal support is ordered on a non-compensatory basis after a long-term, non-traditional marriage, support may be ordered in the lower end of the SSAG range — Cook v. Cook, 2011 CarswellOnt 10276, 2011 ONSC 5920, [2011] OJ No 4399 (Ont. S.C.J.), additional reasons at 2012 CarswellOnt 2022, 2012 ONSC 1141, [2012] O.J. No. 677 (Ont. S.C.J.). The parties were married for 22 years prior to their separation. The respondent husband was awarded means-based, rather than compensatory, spousal support in the lower end of the SSAG range. The judge reasoned that the lower range was appropriate because it was meansbased support and also because, although it was a long-term marriage, it was not traditional. The recipient spouse was employed, although at a lower salary than the payor spouse.

Temporary spousal support set at low end of the range of the Spousal Support Advisory Guidelines — Perry v. Fujimoto, 2011 CarswellOnt 4180, 2011 ONSC 3334 (Ont. S.C.J.), additional reasons at 2011 CarswellOnt 11164, 2011 ONSC 6129 (Ont. S.C.J.). The parents were married for 18 years and had two children. The wife was awarded $4,000 per month for temporary spousal support. The support awarded was at the low end of the SSAG range because the husband's income exceeded the SSAG ceiling. The wife had a much higher net worth than the husband, the wife would benefit indirectly from the child support order and her claim for support on a non-compensatory basis rested on the outcome of a pending motor vehicle action.

On an application for temporary spousal support where the payee's income was only estimated, the court should award support at the low end of the range — Atkins v. Burgess, 2010 CarswellOnt 339, 2010 ONSC 557, [2010] O.J. No. 275 (Ont. S.C.J.). The court held that the wife was entitled to temporary spousal support, given the roles of the parties during their short marriage and the financial consequences for the wife, because of her care of the children. She was attempting to achieve self-sufficiency, but had not yet met with significant success. She was in dire need of support and the husband clearly had the means to pay support. The temporary spousal support was required to relieve the wife from economic hardship arising from the breakdown of the marriage and in order to promote her economic self-sufficiency. The husband had an imputed income of $90,000. The wife estimated her income for the upcoming year to be $15,000. With an income of $15,000, the wife stated that the range of spousal support under SSAG would be $719 to $1,330 per month. The court accepted the wife's estimate of her present income at $15,000. However, the court decided that, as the wife had only estimated her income, the quantum of spousal support should be at the low end of the range. The court ordered temporary spousal support in the amount of $719 per month.

*Low end of range as wife had maintained qualifications and was fully employed* — Ross v. Ross, 2010 CarswellBC 84, 2010 BCSC 52 (B.C.S.C.). The court found that the wife was entitled to support on the basis of compensatory and non-compensatory models. The husband's income, averaged over the past 3 years, was $64,220. Based upon the wife's 2009 income of $24,100 it was argued that the Guidelines supported a range of spousal support of $1,053 at the low end, $1,229 at the mid-range, and $1,404 at the high end for an indefinite period of time. The parties had been married for 21 years. The wife had worked part-time during the marriage and now worked full-time. However, her employment prospects had been negatively affected by her primary care of the children and home during the marriage. The court stated that the Guidelines suggested that "where the claim for compensatory spousal support is strong, it favours an award at the higher end because of the economic disadvantages created by the marriage roles." However, in this case, the wife maintained her qualifications as a ski instructor during the marriage by re-certifying and working part time. She had also been able to obtain full-time work in this field since the parties separated. In addition, she would be able to earn income from her share of the sale proceeds from the matrimonial home without depleting this capital resource. These factors supported an award at the lower end of the range. The court found an award of spousal support in the amount of $1,100 per month was appropriate in all of the circumstances. The court ordered indefinite support, as in the past 3 years, both parties had been able to work full-time all year round.

*Lower range support ordered* — Cecutti v. Cecutti, 2009 CarswellOnt 714 (Ont. S.C.J.), additional reasons at 2009 CarswellOnt 4245 (Ont. S.C.J.). The parties were married for 40 years and the wife was seeking spousal support. In ordering the lower amount of spousal support, the court noted, "considering the length of the marriage, the recipient's age and financial dependency on the respondent, given the husband's present capacity to pay and the standard of living this couple enjoyed, Mr. Cecutti's current higher standard of living and what his wife could have perhaps expected but for the separation, the payor's age, the equalization payment to be received by the wife and its impact on Mrs. Cecutti's future financial needs and the tax implications of payments to each party, I feel the lower end of the range of the above calculations is an appropriate level of spousal support."

*Lower range support ordered because wife's parents testified they would support her* — Novlesky v. Novlesky, 2009 CarswellBC 2638, 2009 BCSC 1328, [2009] B.C.J. No. 195 (B.C.S.C.). In ordering support at the low end of the SSAG range, the court noted that the husband had significant ongoing financial obligations of child support and access costs. The court also considered that the wife's parents had testified that they would help her financially until she was economically self-sufficient (although the court recognized that they were not legally obliged to do so).

*Where the husband lacked the ability to afford spousal support after taking into account his child support obligations and the lower- end of the range under the SSAG was zero, the court did not make an order for spousal support* — MacFarland v. MacFarland, 2009 CarswellOnt 2949, 70

R.F.L. (6th) 196, [2009] O.J. No. 2149 (Ont. S.C.J.). The court stated that when child support was no longer payable, the provisions of the *Divorce Act*, s. 15.3(3) might become applicable.

*Spousal support should be at lower end of the range because of the delay in bringing the matter before the courts* — Courtney v. Courtney, 2009 CarswellOnt 6465 (Ont. S.C.J.).

*Various factors led to lower end of range of spousal support* — Gibson v. Gibson, 2009 CarswellOnt 6082, [2009] O.J. No. 4172 (Ont. S.C.J.). The husband had an income of $90,000 and the wife had an imputed income of $15,000. The spousal support according to the Guidelines ranged from $737 to $1,356, with a mid-range of $1,036. The parties had been married for 12 years. There was a significant discrepancy between the parties' incomes. The wife had suffered both an economic disadvantage and economic hardship resulting from the breakdown of the marriage. In determining the level of support which should be ordered, the court took into account the parties' incomes, both actual and imputed, the length of the marriage and that the wife had the sole care of the children, one of whom, had anorexia nervosa, which required the wife's time and attention. The husband was paying Guideline child support of $1,221. He had to incur significant expense to exercise access to his children who are over 900 kilometres away. He was making payments on the line of credit, $18,654.27 of which was incurred prior to separation. The court granted the wife interim spousal support of $800 per month which was at the lower end of the range.

*Lower end of the range* — Trewern v. Trewern, 2009 CarswellBC 451, 2009 BCSC 236 (B.C.S.C.). The court found that given the difference in income ($36,509 for the husband — $21,333 for the wife = $15,176) and the length of marriage being 21 years, the "without child support" formula under the Guidelines would result in a range of support between $398 per month to $531 per month for an indefinite duration. The court ordered support of $400 per month on non-compensatory grounds as: (1) the husband's income was and would continue to be greater than that of the wife; (2) support would allow the wife to come closer to an equality of lifestyles; and (3) the husband would be able to pay provided he gained control of his debts through management of his capital asset.

*Lower than mid-range as amount meets all of payees needs and preserves work incentives for the husband* — Savoie v. Savoie, 2009 CarswellNB 187, 2009 NBQB 134, 345 N.B.R. (2d) 214, 889 A.P.R. 214, [2009] N.B.J. No. 138 (N.B.Q.B.). Having regard to the application of the Advisory Guidelines, and taking into consideration the court's finding that the wife's income is $10,000 per year and the husband's income is $160,000, the ranges of spousal support for 27 years of cohabitation are $4,688 per month at the low end to $6,153 per month at the upper end with a mid-range quantum of $5,420, based on the figures generated by the Childview Software 2009.1.0. An award of $5,200 per month produces a sufficient amount of spousal support for the wife that will allow her to meet all of her needs. As well it recognizes the need to preserve work incentives for the husband. The court had regard to the means and needs of the parties as well as the factors and objectives of spousal support orders pursuant to s. 15.2 of the *Divorce Act*. Given the wife's age and considering the 27 years of cohabitation, the spousal support was payable until further order of the court.

*Factors leading to low end of range* — Arnold v. Arnold, 2009 CarswellBC 2684, 2009 BCSC 1384 (B.C.S.C.), additional reasons at 2010 CarswellBC 278, 2010 BCSC 166 (B.C.S.C.). The court awarded support at the low end of the range, after considering the wife's need in reapportioning assets, the short duration of the marriage, and the fact there was no compensatory or contractual basis for a claim for spousal support. The court also kept in mind the wife's need and the husband's means. He earned US$156,000 per annum. The low end of the range of support suggested by the Guidelines (assuming incomes of $166,000 — the current equivalent of US$156,000 — for the husband and $10,000 for the wife) is $1,365 per month for 3.5 years. The parties requested that payment be made as a lump sum. The court awarded a lump sum for spousal support of $57,330.

*Where the SSAG suggests a range of $0, there will not necessarily be any reason to depart from this amount even where compensatory entitlement has been found* — *P. (C.E.A.) v. P. (P.E.)*, 2006 CarswellBC 3207, 2006 BCSC 1913, [2006] B.C.J. No. 3295 (B.C.S.C.). The wife was diagnosed with bipolar disorder after separation. The parties began to cohabit in 1983, marrried in 1992 and separated in 2004. They had four children together. The wife had stopped work in 2002. The judge found that both parties had income which was only sufficient to meet their individual budgets, and they were earning roughly the same amount. The wife was found to be capable of caring for the children, however. Although the judge found that the wife had an entitlement to spousal support on a compensatory basis, the SSAG produced a quantum of $0 at both the lower and upper range of the Guidelines.

*Recipient cohabiting therefore not in need* — *amount near bottom of SSAG range ordered* — *M. (K.A.) v. M. (P.K.)*, 2008 CarswellBC 135, 2008 BCSC 93, 50 R.F.L. (6th) 165, [2008] B.C.J. No. 121 (B.C.S.C.). The recipient was cohabiting with a new partner. The court stated at para. 73: "I have chosen an amount near the bottom of the range suggested by the SSAG, in part, because there is no needs basis to her entitlement."

*Lower end of range used for retroactive lump sum spousal support order* — *Lake v. Lake*, 2008 CarswellNfld 147, 2008 NLUFC 12, [2008] N.J. No. 160 (N.L.U.F.C.). The low end of the SSAG range was chosen for this retroactive lump sum support order.

*Helping to support a child of the marriage can justify lower-end spousal support award if this fact not otherwise dealt with* — *Gehla v. Gehla*, 2008 CarswellBC 249, 2008 BCSC 175, [2008] B.C.J. No. 218 (B.C.S.C. [In Chambers]). The parties' 21-year-old daughter resided with and was, to some extent, supported by the spousal support payor; he did not seek child support from the recipient. This fact was cited by the court as a reason to order spousal support at the low end of the SSAG range.

## Middle of the Range

*Setting of spousal support award at mid-range of SSAG where evidence before the court was wanting* — *Stace-Smith v. Lecompte*, 2011 CarswellBC 573, 2011 BCCA 129, 97 R.F.L. (6th) 91, 16 B.C.L.R. (5th) 119, 302 B.C.A.C. 250, 511 W.A.C. 250 (B.C.C.A.). The trial judge erred in finding that the parties were not in a "marriage-like" relationship, the woman was not a "spouse" and she was not entitled to spousal support. The Court of Appeal determined the woman's entitlement to and award of spousal support. The range of support, as set out by the *Spousal Support Advisory Guidelines*, was one factor in the determination of the support award. This was an appropriate case to award a lump sum payment as the man was not reliable in meeting his child support obligations and seemed to view his child and former spouse as less of a priority over time. The award was set at the mid-range under the SSAG and for the duration of 3 years, at which point the child would attend school full-time.

*Where the recipient claims support on compensatory and non-compensatory grounds, the payor is responsible for high access costs, and the parties were married for 9 years, support at the mid-range will be ordered* — *Jardine v. Jardine*, 2013 CarswellNS 64, 2013 NSSC 30 (N.S.S.C.). The parties had two children.

*Where the wife suffered only minimal financial disadvantage, she was awarded mid-range spousal support for a 12-year marriage.* — *Barraco v. Scott*, 2011 CarswellOnt 8325, 2011 ONSC 4467, 9 R.F.L. (7th) 126 (Ont. S.C.J.). The parties were married for 12 years and had three children. Although the marriage was one of financial inter-dependence, any advantage the husband received was minimal. The husband was supportive of the wife's return to school and career changes throughout the marriage. While the wife did not suffer economic hardship because her income was lower than the husband's, she did suffer hardship as a result of the reduction in her standard of living following the separation. The wife was entitled to $2,100 per month in spousal support, which was within the mid-range of the *Spousal Support Advisory Guidelines*. Support was payable for 11 years from the date of separation.

*Slightly lower than middle of range ordered on motion for interim support* — Morey v. Morey, 2009 CarswellOnt 1502, [2009] O.J. No. 1160 (Ont. S.C.J.). The husband earned $212,000 a year and the wife $104,000 a year. They had two children. The Guidelines suggested a range of spousal support, for a couple with two children, of between about $700 and $2,150 per month, with mid-range support being about $1,450 per month. The court, independently of the Guidelines, concluded that the wife was entitled to a relatively modest amount of spousal support pending trial. She had the lower income and was paying many of the expenses for which both parties had been responsible while they were still living together. The husband's expenses may have been reduced, even taking into account his payment of child support. In addition, he was taking a vacation in Costa Rica in the near future. The court made an interim order for spousal support in the amount of $1,200 per month, and that is slightly less than the mid-range set out in the Guidelines.

*Where the recipient claims support on compensatory and non-compensatory grounds, the payor is responsible for high access costs, and the parties were married for nine years, support at the mid-range will be ordered* — Jardine v. Jardine, 2013 CarswellNS 64, 2013 NSSC 30 (N.S.S.C.). The parties had two children.

*Where evidence about the payor's income is conflicting, support will be awarded which would be appropriate for both of the income possibilities* — Muzaffar v. Mohsin, 2009 CarswellOnt 5783, [2009] O.J. No. 4005 (Ont. S.C.J.). The parties were married for 16 years and had no children. There was conflicting evidence of the husband's income, which put it somewhere between $48,000 and $68,000, resulting in an *SSAG* range of $900-$1200 and $1200-$1,675 respectively. The judge awarded interim spousal support within the *SSAG* range close to the overlap point, at $1,300 a month.

*Where the payor's income fluctuates, spousal support will be fixed in the middle of the range provided by the SSAG* — D. (K.) v. D. (N.), 2009 CarswellBC 2021, 2009 BCSC 995 (B.C.S.C.). The parties had a marriage of medium duration (9 years) and had two children together. At the time of trial, the wife had been out of the work force for 5 years to raise the children, and the judge found that she had been economically disadvantaged by the marriage. Although the wife did not wish to go back to work, she had the skills to become self-sufficient and should be expected to do so. The judge gave her a year to find a job and imputed income for her after that time. The judge used this income and the *SSAG* to determine the appropriate range. Because of the husband's fluctuating income, the judge fixed spousal support at a medium range to take this fluctuation into account.

*On an interim support application, where the income of the payor spouse is highly disputed, the judge may use the ranges provided for in the SSAG to arrive at an intermediate figure* — Kozek v. Kozek, 2009 CarswellBC 3452, 2009 BCSC 1745 (B.C. Master); affirmed 2009 CarswellBC 3260, 2009 BCSC 1663 (B.C.S.C.). The parties cohabited for 23 years, including 17 years of marriage. The wife was attempting to complete her high school education and the husband worked in the forestry industry. In this interim motion, there were significant questions about the actual income of the husband, with his estimate being approximately $40,000 and the wife's estimate at approximately $140,000. The judge awarded support at an amount which essentially split the difference and came to an intermediate amount between those suggested by the parties, with a more in-depth evaluation to be conducted at the trial on the merits. On appeal, the court, *inter alia*, stated that the issue was not whether the method used by the master in calculating the husband's income was correct, but rather whether the order that resulted was clearly wrong. The appellate court concluded that it was not.

*Mid-range support ordered — Savoie v. Savoie*, 2009 CarswellNB 187, 2009 NBQB 134, 345 N.B.R. (2d) 214, 889 A.P.R. 214 (N.B.Q.B.). In this case, the parties cohabitated for 27 years. Based on the parties' income the spousal support range was from $4,688 to $6,153 per month. The court ordered the mid-range of spousal support which would allow Ms. Savoie to meet her needs as well as recognize the need to preserve work incentives for Mr. Savoie who was trying to save his company.

*Mid-range support ordered — Willi v. Chapple*, 2009 CarswellOnt 5398, [2009] O.J. No. 3752 (Ont. S.C.J.). The parties cohabitated for 16 years and had one child. The mother was a day-care worker and the father a wealthy businessman. The mother ceased working upon cohabitation. The mother brought an application for spousal support. The range for support pursuant to the SSAG was between $4,250 and $5,667 per month. The court ordered $5,500 based on the father's high income and since the mother was only seeking support for 6 years.

*Mid-range of support awarded where the applicant had not exploited opportunities to increase her income potential — Shorey v. Shorey*, 2009 CarswellOnt 7514 (Ont. S.C.J.).

*Medium amount of support in the range unless there is a reason to depart from this amount — Hall v. Mougan*, 2009 CarswellBC 1287, 2009 BCSC 645 (B.C.S.C.); additional reasons at 2009 CarswellBC 3283, 2009 BCSC 1667 (B.C.S.C. [In Chambers]). The court ordered the payor to pay the payee $3,086 per month.

*Where a support recipient is cohabiting with a new partner, which reduces accommodation expenses, support in the mid-range of the SSAG may be awarded — Boland v. Boland*, 2012 CarswellOnt 2748, 2012 ONCJ 102, [2012] O.J. No. 925 (Ont. C.J.), additional reasons at 2012 CarswellOnt 5050, 2012 ONCJ 239, 22 R.F.L. (7th) 368 (Ont. C.J.). This case was a review under a separation agreement made after a 20-year marriage. The wife established ongoing need and established her entitlement to compensatory support. She was awarded support in the mid-range of the SSAG, rather than high-range, because she was cohabiting with a new partner who benefited her in terms of accommodation expenses.

## High end of range

*Where particular circumstances exist, such as the extreme economic disadvantage and hardship of the recipient spouse since separation, and such circumstances are adequately described by the trial judge, a decision to award support above the SSAG amounts may be upheld — Stergios v. Kim*, 2011 CarswellOnt 14815, 2011 ONCA 836, [2011] O.J. No. 5900 (Ont. C.A.). The Court of Appeal upheld the trial decision, finding that there was significant evidence supporting the decision to award compensatory and non-compensatory support to the wife. The trial judge awarded spousal support above the Guidelines amount, finding that the respondent wife had exceptional circumstances, namely that she had been living on charity and accumulating debt for five years.

*Husband to pay indefinite support at the high end of the range to compensate for the wife's diminished earning capacity as she assumed full-time housekeeping and child-rearing responsibilities in a long-term marriage and in consideration of the husband's failure to disclose his resources fairly — Gagne v. Gagne*, 2011 CarswellOnt 1476, 2011 ONCA 188, 99 R.F.L. (6th) 1, [2011] O.J. No. 1015 (Ont. C.A.). The parties were married for 18 years with three children. The husband was a self-employed real estate broker and the wife was a stay-at-home mother with primary care of the children. Following separation she obtained work as a secretary. The parties signed a separation agreement that provided that the husband pay undifferentiated spousal and child support for 24 months after which support was to be reviewed. At trial, the judge ordered the husband to pay $8,000 per month spousal support and $2,000 per month child support. On appeal by the husband, the Court of Appeal held that the trial judge's reasons for judgement were insufficient in failing to explain the basis for support, and accepting the respondent's compromise, by ordering overvalued spousal support and undervalued child support without explanation. The Court of Appeal imputed an income of $250,000 to the husband and $45,000 to the wife and ordered the husband to pay to the wife $4,597 per month, which was at the high end of the *Spousal Support Advisory Guidelines*, because of his failure to make fair disclosure of his resources. Child support was ordered at $4,072 per month.

*Where the recipient party has financial need and is entitled to compensatory support, support may be ordered slightly above the top end of the SSAG range* — *Hipel v. Hipel*, 2011 CarswellOnt 13042, 2011 ONSC 6411, 14 R.F.L. (7th) 343, [2011] O.J. No. 4769 (Ont. S.C.J.). The relationship between the parties lasted 3 years. The parties had two children and the judge found that the wife was entitled to compensatory support because of the role she had adopted during the marriage. She had made efforts to become self-supporting since the breakdown of the relationship but was still in need of financial support, which the husband had the ability to provide. Spousal support was ordered slightly above the top end of the SSAG range for a period of 24 months.

*Top of range chosen to allow wife to afford medical costs* — *Kerr v. Baranow*, 2007 CarswellBC 3047, 2007 BCSC 1863, 47 R.F.L. (6th) 103, [2007] B.C.J. No. 2737 (B.C.S.C.), reversed 2009 CarswellBC 642, 2009 BCCA 111, 66 R.F.L. (6th) 1, 93 B.C.L.R. (4th) 201, [2009] 9 W.W.R. 285, 266 B.C.A.C. 298, 449 W.A.C. 298, [2009] B.C.J. No. 474 (B.C.C.A.), additional reasons at 2010 CarswellBC 108, 2010 BCCA 32, 78 R.F.L. (6th) 305, 2 B.C.L.R. (5th) 197, [2010] 4 W.W.R. 465, [2010] B.C.J. No. 88 (B.C.C.A.), reversed 2011 CarswellBC 240, 2011 CarswellBC 241, 2011 SCC 10, 93 R.F.L. (6th) 1, [2011] 1 S.C.R. 269, 108 O.R. (3d) 399, 14 B.C.L.R. (5th) 203, 328 D.L.R. (4th) 577, 64 E.T.R. (3d) 1, [2011] 3 W.W.R. 575, 300 B.C.A.C. 1, 411 N.R. 200, 274 O.A.C. 1, 509 W.A.C. 1, 108 O.R. (3d) 399 (note), [2011] S.C.J. No. 10 (S.C.C.). The case was sent back for retrial on the issue of unjust enrichment. See *Kerr v. Baranow*, 2012 CarswellBC 2450, 2012 BCSC 1222, 22 R.F.L. (7th) 335, 37 B.C.L.R. (5th) 398, 353 D.L.R. (4th) 146 (B.C.S.C.). The wife was hospitalized. The trial judge had chosen a quantum at the top of the SSAG range in order to allow her to afford hospital costs. The Court of Appeal found no error in this aspect of the decision. Entitlement, quantum, and the indefinite duration of the order were not appealed at the Supreme Court of Canada.

*Upper range of support ordered as the marriage was traditional* — *M. (S,J.) v. M. (J.L.)*, 2010 CarswellBC 247, 2010 BCSC 154 (B.C.S.C.). The parties were married for 33 years. The husband was an engineer and the wife taught for 10 years. The parties decided to adopt a child and the wife stayed at home to care for him. Since separation, the husband had been voluntarily paying $4,000 per month in spousal support and then unilaterally reduced it to $3,000 per month. The wife could only work part-time due to her health issues. The husband was ordered to pay spousal support of $4,500 per month which was at the upper end of the Guidelines because the marriage was traditional, and the wife would incur extra medical and dental insurance costs after the divorce.

*High end of the range* — *Hartshorne v. Hartshorne*, 2009 CarswellBC 1398, 2009 BCSC 698, 70 R.F.L. (6th) 106, [2009] B.C.J. No. 1050 (B.C.S.C.), reversed 2010 CarswellBC 1618, 2010 BCCA 327, 82 R.F.L. (6th) 1, 6 B.C.L.R. (5th) 58, 320 D.L.R. (4th) 398, 289 B.C.A.C. 244, 489 W.A.C. 244, [2010] B.C.J. No. 1271 (B.C.C.A.), additional reasons at 2011 CarswellBC 107, 2011 BCCA 29, 95 R.F.L. (6th) 14, 14 B.C.L.R. (5th) 33, 330 D.L.R. (4th) 503, 299 B.C.A.C. 6, 508 W.A.C. 6, [2011] B.C.J. No. 107 (B.CC.A.). The parties' marriage agreement did not operate to create an equal division of property. While the SSAG are usually used prospectively, in this case the court applied them after the period in question had elapsed with the knowledge of what had actually happened to the parties. Although the court acknowledged that SSAG does not automatically apply to payor incomes that exceed $350,000, it was not concerned that in 1 year the husband had an income over $350,000. The court found that there was no evidence to suggest that awarding the wife support at the highrange of SSAG for either duration or quantum would cause the husband hardship or interfere with his obligations to any of his children. The award covered the period from January 1, 2000, until December 31, 2009.

*Given the low income estimate and low duration, it is appropriate that spousal support be ordered at the upper end of the range* — Willi v. Chappie, 2009 CarswellOnt 5398, [2009] O.J. No. 3752 (Ont. S.C.J.). On an income of $200,000, the SSAG show a range of monthly support between $4,250 and $5,667. The court had reviewed the payee's financial statement and it was quite reasonable. Her needs were at least $4,700 per month. The court awarded her $5,500 per month.

*Upper amount in range paid on interim support motion, as no reason not to do so* — Morrison v. Morrison, 2009 CarswellBC 474, 2009 BCSC 256 (B.C. Master). The husband currently supports the parties' son with no contribution from the wife. The court took support of this child into account and the fact that the *Spousal Support Advisory Guidelines* suggested a low of $792, a medium of $924, and an upper figure of $1,056 as monthly spousal support. The court could not see any reason why the wife should not be entitled to receive the highest amount. The husband was ordered to pay interim spousal support of $1,056 per month, until further order of the court.

*High end of range where parties had low incomes and wife's disability was directly caused by husband's abuse* — Paheerding v. Palihati, 2009 CarswellBC 1077, 2009 BCSC 557 (B.C.S.C.). The husband had an imputed income of $28,471 and the wife received EI disability income of $12,168. The court took into account: the fact that the husband had two children living with him (his son still being a "child of the marriage" as a post-secondary student), and the wife had one child with her, and that the SSAG provided a range of monthly support between $253 to $479, with a mid-range amount of $365. This range was classified as "indefinite" and "duration unspecified" with a maximum duration of 9 years, the length of the marriage. The court considered all the relevant statutory provisions, the guiding case law, the SSAG, and all the evidence. Spousal support was set at the high end of the range at $479 per month, as provided for under the SSAG calculation. The court was of the opinion that this result was justified because the evidence disclosed entitlement based on both compensatory and non-compensatory grounds as the plaintiff's current disability arose directly from the husband's severe spousal abuse during the marriage. The order was of an indefinite duration, but subject to variation or review.

*Non-disclosure and failure to comply among reasons for ordering retroactive support at high end of the SSAG range* — Kerman v. Kerman, 2008 CarswellBC 793, 2008 BCSC 500, 53 R.F.L. (6th) 156, [2008] B.C.J. No. 710 (B.C.S.C.), additional reasons at 2008 CarswellBC 1358, 2008 BCSC 852, 58 R.F.L. (6th) 157 (B.C.S.C.). The Court stated at para. 78: "Since the spousal support that I am awarding in this section is for past spousal support that ought to have been paid and was not paid due to the non-disclosure and resulting in non-payment by Mr. Kerman, and because the non-receipt of that money caused significant hardship to Ms. Hillier, including her need to cash in RRSP's and carry credit card debt, I conclude that spousal support should be at the high range for the period 2001-2007."

*Where the payor's income had declined from $168,000 at the time of the consent order to an imputed income of $80,000 at the time of the variation hearing, the wife's acute needs militated strongly in favour of an award in the high end of the range for a payor income of $80,000,* *according to the Guidelines — Fraser v. Fraser*, 2012 CarswellBC 2093, 2011 BCSC 1852 (B.C.S.C.).

## 14.3 Other

Where a trial judge has found that the support recipient has a prospect for early self-sufficiency, spousal support will be reviewed rather than terminated prior to the time range indicated by the SSAG — *Lightle v. Kotar*, 2014 CarswellBC 428, 2014 BCCA 69, 43 R.F.L. (7th) 20, 59 B.C.L.R. (5th) 75, 371 D.L.R. (4th) 269, [2014] 5 W.W.R. 615, 352 B.C.A.C. 39, 601 W.A.C. 39, [2014] B.C.J. No. 294 (B.C.C.A.). The parties were married for 9 years and had two children. The Court of Appeal found that the trial judge had incorrectly determined the husband's annual income and, subsequently, the amount of spousal support that should be paid. The Court of Appeal substituted an order for support at the mid-point of the SSAG, finding at para. 62 that "substantial deviation from the range of outcomes established by the SSAG must be justified by special circumstances." The trial judge had used incorrect figures of a range provided by husband's counsel. The Court of Appeal applied mid-range amounts and gave deference to the trial judge's finding that the wife could achieve early self-sufficiency. However, under the with child formula, the suggested time range was an indefinite order with review after 8 to 16 years. The Court of Appeal ordered a review after 5 years, rather than termination, as ordered at trial.

Where prospective spousal support is ordered for a situation in which the recipient did not apply until 11 years after separation, support will be awarded at an amount slightly below the SSAG range for current income — *Molloy v. Molloy*, 2012 CarswellNS 395, 2012 NSCA 60 (N.S.C.A.). The parties were married for 27 years and had four adult children. The wife made an application for support 11 years after separation. The judge found entitlement existed both at the time of separation and now, and ordered prospective spousal support at $800 monthly, which was slightly below the SSAG range for the parties' current incomes but more than at separation. The trial judge found that the wife had been economically disadvantaged by the marriage and had suffered economic hardship in the years since separation.

Where spousal support is awarded above the SSAG range based on incorrect application of the Moge and Leskun principles, the trial judge will be found to have erred — *Armstrong v. Armstrong*, 2012 CarswellBC 1095, 2012 BCCA 166, 33 B.C.L.R. (5th) 86, 350 D.L.R. (4th) 186, 320 B.C.A.C. 94, 543 W.A.C. 94, [2012] B.C.J. No. 770 (B.C.C.A.). The Court of Appeal considered whether or not a trial judge had erred in awarding support above the SSAG range. It found that the trial judge had based his award of support not on the SSAG or applicable principles about the economic consequences of the marriage breakdown, but rather on equalization of net disposable income.

Insufficient evidence to determine income is sufficient reason to deviate from the SSAG — *Flieger v. Adams*, 2012 CarswellNB 219, 2012 CarswellNB 220, 2012 NBCA 39, 18 R.F.L. (7th) 28, 387 N.B.R. (2d) 322, 1001 A.P.R. 322, [2012] N.B.J. No. 137 (N.B.C.A.). The motions judge declined to apply the SSAG, finding that there was insufficient evidence to determine the husband's income, the Guidelines gave no guidance as to how to quantify the benefit derived from expense sharing between the husband and his new partner or how to deal with "double dipping". The Court of Appeal found the latter two factors could be dealt with by movement within the SSAG range, but determined insufficient evidence regarding income was grounds to depart from the Guidelines amounts. The husband's income reporting was missing information about pension, and the motions judge imputed income to him because of his earning capacity. The decision to award above-SSAG support was upheld on appeal.

Where the recipient spouse has transportation costs and the payor spouse is living with his parent, support will be awarded at the high end of the SSAG — McMahon v. Coulis, 2012 CarswellOnt 15211, 2012 ONSC 6552 (Ont. S.C.J.). Spousal support was ordered at the high end of the SSAG, plus the father was ordered to pay a transportation allowance as the mother had no transportation. The judge also took into account tax repercussions. The husband also had fewer expenses as he was living with his mother.

The Court of Appeal will examine the SSAG to determine whether duration of support ordered is in error — McIntire v. McIntire, 2012 CarswellBC 1479, 2012 BCCA 214, 19 R.F.L. (7th) 284, 35 B.C.L.R. (5th) 245, 322 B.C.A.C. 139, 549 W.A.C. 139 (B.C.C.A.). This was an appeal of a judgement in which spousal support was ordered for 2 years after a 5½-year marriage (with an additional year of cohabitation). The Court of Appeal found that this was overly short with reference to duration as set out in the SSAG and ordered an additional year of support.

Where a party has not demonstrated need beyond the amount paid by an interim order and has made no steps towards self-sufficiency, support will be ordered below the SSAG amounts — Pothier v. Taillefer, 2014 CarswellOnt 895, 2014 ONSC 812, 42 R.F.L. (7th) 184 (Ont. S.C.J.). The parties cohabited for 26 years and had two adult children. The husband had income over $100,000, but was now receiving WSIB benefits. The wife had not been employed since 1983 and had no income. Indefinite entitlement was found. The judge ordered support of $1,200 monthly, which was below the SSAG range, finding that the SSAG was not appropriate as the wife had little need beyond the amount of $1,000 which was being paid pursuant to an interim order. The judge found that the wife had not taken steps towards self-sufficiency and had alcohol problems.

The purpose of interim spousal support is to address need, rather than compensatory entitlement, which will result in an award below the SSAG range when other factors are present — Betts v. Betts, 2014 CarswellNB 63, 2014 NBQB 47, 416 N.B.R. (2d) 355, 1079 A.P.R. 355 (N.B.Q.B.). The parties were married for 38 years and had five adult children. There was an unenforceable agreement between the parties, and the wife also claimed there were collateral agreements. The judge found the existence of collateral agreements required findings of credibility and a full hearing. The wife had no high school diploma and had never worked. The judge found she needed support and that interim support was intended to address need, rather than compensatory issues to be determined at trial, which indicated an award at the low end of the SSAG range. The judge considered other factors, such as the wife living rent-free in the marital home, the husband's income of over $350,000, and the property had not yet been equalized, which pointed to an award below the SSAG range.

Where a payor spouse is solely responsible for child-related costs, spousal support will be at the low end of the SSAG range — Wang v. Song, 2013 CarswellOnt 204, 2013 ONSC 42 (Ont. S.C.J.), additional reasons at 2013 CarswellOnt 2059, 2013 ONSC 1265 (Ont. S.C.J.). The parties had a 16-year marriage and one dependent child. The husband was working part-time at McDonald's, and medical evidence was led and accepted by the court that he was unable to return to his professional career due to mental illness. The wife was an engineer and ordered to pay spousal support at the low end of the Guidelines, taking into account that she was solely responsible for the costs associated with the parties' daughter.

Where there is a large disparity in incomes, spousal support at the mid-high end of the SSAG will be ordered — G. (J.S.) v. G. (M.F.), 2013 CarswellMan 354, 2013 MBCA 66, 34 R.F.L. (7th) 15, 363 D.L.R. (4th) 240, [2013] M.J. No. 227 (Man. C.A.). The parties were married for 8 years and cohabited for 1 year. They had three dependent children, two of whom in shared custody. The trial judge awarded prospective spousal support at the mid-high end of the SSAG range, as well as retroactive spousal support and full table child support. The parties' incomes were separated by more than $100,000.

*Where the recipient spouse is deliberately underemployed, increasing income may be imputed to him or her to determine SSAG ranges for support* — E. (P.D.) v. E. (A.J.), 2009 CarswellBC 3388, 2009 BCSC 1712, [2009] B.C.J. No. 2497 (B.C.S.C.). The parties were married for 15 years. The judge found that the wife was earning $20,000 annually, which was less than she should be making given her education and experience. He imputed income to her on the grounds that she was deliberately underemployed. The judge examined the SSAG ranges for a recipient spouse income of $20,000, $30,000 and $40,000. The judge created a "step-down" order for spousal support where the support was gradually decreased based on these ranges.

*Where the bottom of the SSAG range is 0, a court will order no spousal support* — MacFarland v. MacFarland, 2009 CarswellOnt 2949, 70 R.F.L. (6th) 196, [2009] O.J. No. 2149 (Ont. S.C.J.). Where the husband lacked the ability to afford spousal support after taking into account his child support obligations and the lower end of the range under SSAG was zero, the court made no order for spousal support. The court stated that when child support was no longer payable, the provisions of the *Divorce Act*, s. 15.3(3) might become applicable.

*Where a support applicant lives in the United States, the court can take into account the fact that she would not have to pay taxes on spousal support in the United States, balanced against the costs of medical expenses in that country* — Samis (Litigation Guardian of) v. Samis, 2011 CarswellOnt 5545, 2011 ONCJ 308 (Ont. C.J. [In Chambers]). The applicant was an 80-year-old woman who resided in a nursing home in Vermont and suffered from dementia. Her son was her legal guardian. In the United States, a spousal support recipient does not have to pay taxes on spousal support until her income reaches $80,000 per annum. The court made interim orders for two separate periods: the first where the applicant did not receive subsidization of other expenses through Medicaid and the second when because of Medicaid subsidization, the applicant's monthly deficit was reduced to $1,300 per month. The court made a temporary retroactive spousal support order in the mid-range SSAG level of spousal support of $3,992 per month for the first period and $1,300 per month for the second period.

# CHAPTER 15

# RESTRUCTURING

*Trading off amount and duration; calculation of global amounts generated by formulas; types of restructuring; restructured awards*

Restructuring allows the amount and duration under the formulas to be traded off against each other, so long as the overall value of the restructured award remains within the total or global amounts generated by the formula when amount and duration are combined. (SSAG Executive Summary)

Restructuring requires the calculation of the global or total amounts generated by the formula when amount is multiplied by duration. . . it would also be possible to restructure using stepdown awards, as long as the total amount of the award falls within the range set by the formula. (SSAG Section 10.2.1)

There are three types of restructuring:

- front-end loading to increase the amount outside the formula's range by reducing duration. This involves choosing a durational limit at the low end of the formula's range or below it. Front-end loading may be appropriate in shorter marriages under the without child support formula where the monthly formula amounts are relatively modest. (SSAG Section 10.2.1)
- to extend duration by cutting back on amount. Depending on how much of an extension of duration is required, this can be accomplished either by choosing an amount at the lower end of the formula's range for amount or by setting an amount below the formula's range. This use of restructuring might be desirable in medium-length marriages where the recipient spouse will have long-term need and would be better off with modest supplements to income over a longer period of time than with more generous payments over the time period suggested by the formula (SSAG Section 10.2.2)
- to formulate a lump sum by combining amount and duration. (SSAG Executive Summary)

When restructuring is relied upon to resolve issues of inappropriate formula outcomes for amount or duration, awards remain consistent with the overall or global amounts generated by the Advisory Guidelines. (SSAG Section 10.1)

The primary use of restructuring will be under the without child support formula. . . restructuring should be kept in mind in three particular kinds of cases . . . (i) shorter marriages without children; (ii) long-term disability after a medium-length marriage . . . (iii) longer marriages where the formula generates a time limit but current practice dictates indefinite support (SSAG Section 10.3.1)

The most likely circumstances for the use of front-end loading or a lump sum under the basic *with child support* formula will be cases where the recipient wants spousal support above the

> upper end of the range for a shorter period, e.g. to pursue a more expensive educational program. (SSAG Section 10.3.2)
>
> time-value of money or . . . various future contingencies . . . could affect the value of awards over time. In practice, more sophisticated calculations may take such factors into account. [citation omitted] Computer software programs may assist in some of the calculations required by restructuring. [citation omitted] If periodic payments are converted into a lump sum, the different tax consequences must be taken into account in arriving at a comparable lump sum. (SSAG Section 10.2)

This chapter is divided into the following sections:

15.1 Front-end Loading
15.2 Extending Duration
15.3 Lump Sum

## 15.1 Front-end Loading

*The court will vary spousal support where changed circumstances render the original agreement for front-end loaded support unfair* — Turpin v. Clark, 2009 CarswellBC 3149, 2009 BCCA 530, 80 R.F.L. (6th) 239, 4 B.C.L.R. (5th) 48, 313 D.L.R. (4th) 452, [2010] 6 W.W.R. 613, 278 B.C.A.C. 220, 471 W.A.C. 220, [2009] B.C.J. No. 2328 (B.C.C.A.). Leave to appeal refused 2010 CarswellBC 1055, 2010 CarswellBC 1056, 297 B.C.A.C. 320 (note), 407 N.R. 396 (note), 504 W.A.C. 320 (note), [2010] S.C.C.A. No. 5 (S.C.C.). The parties separated after almost 20 years of marriage. The wife earned $2,000, while the husband earned $350,000. At separation the wife was preparing to undergo cancer-related surgery. The parties agreed to a front-end loaded support award so that it would gradually decrease as the wife attained self-sufficiency. The wife found out that she had further health problems and applied to increase support. The chambers judge found that a variation was appropriate because of the wife's additional medical issues and inability to work, and because the parties had not contemplated these possibilities. The Court of Appeal affirmed the decision.

*On appeal, an order providing support to the wife in the amount above the SSAG range for a shorter period overturned* — S. (J.K.) v. S. (H.G.), 2008 CarswellBC 1218, 2008 BCCA 245, 54 R.F.L. (6th) 38, 83 B.C.L.R. (4th) 102, 257 B.C.A.C. 16, 432 W.A.C. 16, [2008] B.C.J. No. 1068 (B.C.C.A.), varying 2006 CarswellBC 2255, 2006 BCSC 1356, [2006] B.C.J. No. 2051 (B.C.S.C.). The parties were married for 10 years and at the time of separation the husband was 55 and the wife was 44 years old. Following separation, they continued to see each other until the husband realized there was no chance of reconciliation. At the time of trial, the husband was 63 years of age and the wife was 51 years of age. The husband was an orthodontist and the wife had retired from her work as a flight attendant in 2005. There was one child of the marriage, who at the time of trial was suffering from chronic psychological difficulties. The parties agreed to joint custody but the child resided primarily with the wife. At trial, it was held the wife was capable of earning $35,000 per year and the husband's income was $477,206 per year. The trial judge ordered that the wife would receive spousal support in the amount of $13,750 per month until June 30, 2009, $11,000 per month until June 30, 2011, and $8,000 per month until June 30, 2013 when support would terminate. The Court of Appeal set aside this spousal support order and held that the wife would receive instead $8,000 per month from July 1, 2006 until June 30, 2011 and then $6,500 per month until otherwise ordered or agreed by the parties. The trial judge considered the SSAG and concluded that, as the husband was 63 years of age and would probably retire at 70 years of age, she would award to the wife more money for a lesser period of time. On appeal, it was held that the trial judge had discretion to depart from the Guidelines but the evidence indicated that it was unlikely the wife would curb her spending or find employment while receiving these generous amounts and it was not sensible for her support to cease when she was 65 when she would be more likely to be unemployable.

*Restructured amount where the quantum was above the range, the duration was below the range* — Fisher v. Fisher, 2008 CarswellOnt 43, 2008 ONCA 11, 47 R.F.L. (6th) 235, 88 O.R. (3d) 241, 288 D.L.R. (4th) 513, 232 O.A.C. 213, [2008] O.J. No. 38 (Ont. C.A.). The parties separated after 19 years of marriage. There were no children. The trial judge awarded the wife a time-limited award of spousal support, citing speculation of future self-sufficiency. Finding that the trial judge made two errors of fact that caused the trial award to be set aside, the Court of Appeal determined the quantum for spousal support. The evidence did not support the finding that the wife would be self-sufficient in a reasonable time. However, indefinite support was not reasonable in the circumstances. Seven years of support, commencing at separation, encouraged self-sufficiency while recognizing the economic disadvantage the wife suffered as a result of the breakdown of the marriage. The SSAG amount on a global or overall basis as generated by the formulas ranged from $147,088 to $392,236, with a duration of 9.5 to 19 years. The Court of Appeal made a spousal support order for $3,000 per month for the first 3.5 years and $1,500 per month for the remaining 3.5 years. The monthly payments of the restructured order were initially higher than the SSAG, but this was balanced by a duration shorter than that set out in the Guidelines. The amount of the global order was $189,000, which was within the SSAG range, as determined on a global basis.

*Front-end loading to fund education* — Vynnyk v. Baisa, 2008 CarswellOnt 5629, 2008 ONCA 657, 55 R.F.L. (6th) 239, [2008] O.J. No. 3747 (Ont. C.A.), affirming 2007 CarswellOnt 403, 38 R.F.L. (6th) 344, [2007] O.J. No. 274 (Ont. S.C.J.). Although restructuring was not explicitly mentioned, an amount substantially higher than the SSAG range was ordered for a period which was substantially shorter. This arrangement was at least partially designed to facilitate the wife's education which would promote her self-sufficiency.

*A court is not required to use incomes as of the date of separation; consequently, the use of incomes as of the time of trial does not necessarily indicate an attempt at restructuring. The fact that the trial judge placed the monthly award at the high end of the range disclosed by the appropriate SSAG formula does not indicate that the award was subject to restructuring either. The trial judge merely exercised his discretion to award support using the high end of the range* — L. (R.) v. L. (N.), 2012 CarswellNB 258, 2012 NBQB 123, 22 R.F.L. (7th) 82, 388 N.B.R. (2d) 220, 1006 A.P.R. 220 (N.B.Q.B.). The court held that the spousal support award was not "front end loaded". The husband's obligations under the *Divorce Act* remained, because the wife had not been able to achieve economic self-sufficiency. After separation, the wife had graduated from university, but had not been able to find a teaching position. Duration was set at the upper end of the range — 16 years, because of: the wife's age, 49, her health issues — rheumatoid arthritis necessitating surgeries, the uncertainty regarding her ability to be self-sufficient, and the fact that she would need to be state supported, if she did not receive spousal support. The court ordered spousal support of $950 per month until August, 2020 or until varied or terminated under the *Divorce Act*. The court acknowledged that the award was earlier set at the high end of the range for amount. The court also took into account that the amount remains based on: the husband's 2007 income level (and his income had increased steadily since then), that the award remained based on an attributed income level to the wife that she had not yet attained, and that the "Custodial Payor" formula used to calculate the amount takes into account his present child care responsibility. The court also considered that the wife remained in dire "need" of support. She had no other real income, nor any other significant means beyond a little but rapidly depleting capital against retirement, which she was not required to deplete before retirement.

*Support award calculation software is not helpful in the case of lump sum awards based on restructured support* — Robinson v. Robinson, 2011 CarswellBC 3271, 2011 BCSC 1489, 14 R.F.L. (7th) 141 (B.C.S.C.), affirmed 2012 CarswellBC 3789, 2012 BCCA 497, 25 R.F.L. (7th) 47, 40 B.C.L.R. (5th) 108, [2012] B.C.J. No. 2572 (B.C.C.A.). The parties separated after over 25 years of marriage. The husband earned a comfortable income, and the wife made much less. The court stated, at para. 128:

> The lump sum calculations provided by the computer application of the Formula do not provide an appropriate result in this case where there is a restructuring of support (s. 3.4.2 of the *SSAG*) to arrive at a lump sum. This is an example of an exception (s. 3.4.3 of the *SSAG*) where the "formula outcomes, even after consideration of restructuring, will not generate results consistent with the support objectives and factors under the *Divorce Act*." As was the case in *Hartshorne*, the computer applications provide a reference point but an award that meets the requirements of the *Divorce Act* and *Family Relations Act* requires another method of calculation.

The court arrived at the lump sum of $330,000, payable within 45 days, by way of the following calculation: "There are 9 and one-half years or 114 months remaining for the payment of spousal support from December 2011, for a total of $684,000. From this gross amount, I would deduct tax which would be payable by the wife at an assumed rate of 35%. The discount rate for present value is 7%. To that amount I apply a contingency discount of 20%" (para. 129).

*Where the parties had been in a mid-length relationship and both parties were autonomous, mid-range support may be ordered and restructured to reflect the disability exception and ease the transition to independence* — Broadbear v. Prothero, 2011 CarswellOnt 6129, 2011 ONSC 3656, 6 R.F.L. (7th) 342, [2011] O.J. No. 3136 (Ont. S.C.J.). The parties cohabited for a total of six and a quarter years. The female spouse suffered from PTSD following an incident that occurred after the end of the relationship. The judge found that during the relationship, the parties operated as autonomous individuals who both contributed financially to joint expenses. The support was ordered on a needs-based basis. The judge made a final order of support in the mid-range of the SSAG, noting the disability exception. Support payments were restructured to reflect a higher amount in the short term and the payments were to continue for 18 months.

*A specific plan must be in place to justify restructuring a support award for the purpose of returning to school* — D. (T.A.) v. D. (M.K.), 2010 CarswellBC 1623, 2010 BCSC 898 (B.C.S.C.). The wife was awarded $2,000 per month in spousal support on an interim basis. The award, which was approximately double the high end of the SSAG range, was restructured to enable the wife to return to school full-time and work part-time. By failing to consider quantum and duration together, the "restructured" award fell outside the SSAG formula. Without a specific plan to return to school, which the wife did not have, there was no justification to depart from the Guidelines. Interim spousal support was reduced to $622 per month.

*Where a shorter duration of spousal support is awarded, an award in the higher range of the SSAG may be indicated* — Willi v. Chappie, 2009 CarswellOnt 5398, [2009] O.J. No. 3752 (Ont. S.C.J.). The parties had an off-and-on cohabitation relationship of 16 years and had one child together. The judge awarded a relatively short term of support based on the application by Ms. Willi, which imputed annual income to Mr. Chappie in the amount of $200,000. The judge stated that he found this to be a conservative estimate, as the husband's annual income could be over $600,000. Ms. Willi also applied for a short duration of support (6 years in total, including retroactive support which was necessary because of the respondent's lack of cooperation). Based on the duration and the low imputed income, the judge awarded support at the upper end of the SSAG range, being $5,500 per month until November 2009, retroactive to October 2003.

The court will use a front-end-loaded payment structure in order to compensate the payee party for loss of employment as well as to encourage self-sufficiency — McCulloch v. Bawtinheimer, 2006 CarswellAlta 397, 2006 ABQB 232, 24 R.F.L. (6th) 312, 423 A.R. 88, [2006] A.J. No. 361 (Alta. Q.B.). The parties separated after 6 years of living together. The wife earned about $27,000 each year, and the husband's annual salary was about $100,000. The wife had moved twice for the husband's employment during the relationship and this negatively affected her ability to find employment. The court granted the wife 9 months' retroactive support in the amount of $1,000 per month and ongoing support of $500 per month for the following 7 months. The court "front-loaded" the support payments in order to compensate the wife for her "current state of unemployment and risk of being on welfare, to compensate her for giving up employment opportunities as a result of the Respondent's multiple job transfers, and to encourage [her] self-sufficiency" (para. 62).

A court's use of the term "restructuring" does not necessarily mean that true support award restructuring has taken place — D. (T.A.) v. D. (M.K.), 2010 CarswellBC 1623, 2010 BCSC 898 (B.C.S.C.). The parties lived together for almost 15 years. The husband's income was $42,000, and the wife earned no income. In awarding $2,000 a month in support, the Master stated that she had "restructured" spousal support omitting to describe what duration was adjusted but noting that a higher amount was needed "for a shorter duration". The award is described in para. 16 as:

> [A]t the rim of the high end of the global range for the full duration (($2,000 6(6.5 6 12) = $156,000) vs. ($1,008 6 (13 6 12) = $157,248)). If applied for a shorter duration as would be expected for an interim order, the amount of $2,000 per month is well outside the global ranges generated by the formula. Use of the higher duration intended for final orders is false in the circumstances of an interim order which is purposefully intended to have short duration, as here.

The court found that the restructured support amount was not within the range contemplated in the SSAG and noted that the "restructuring was not according to the formula in the guidelines, and the term was used loosely. The award was based more upon concern for the plaintiff's needs in the interim if she was to attend school full time." (para. 16) The judge noted that the range of support in this case would be between $466 and $622, and awarded the latter.

## 15.2 Extending Duration

The Court of Appeal upheld a lower court decision that awarded the wife a relatively low amount of support over a long period of time — Caldwell v. Caldwell, 2013 CarswellAlta 1241, 2013 ABCA 268, 33 R.F.L. (7th) 285 (Alta. C.A.). The chambers judge awarded the wife retroactive support in the amount of $790 per month until her 60th birthday, subject to variation in the case of a significant change in circumstances. The husband appealed. The Court of Appeal dismissed his appeal, noting that while long-term spousal support is unusual after a medium-length marriage, it was appropriate in these circumstances. [The court did not refer to restructuring.]

Time-limited award at high end of SSAG range changed to indefinite award at low end of SSAG range — Cassidy v. McNeil, 2010 CarswellOnt 1637, 2010 ONCA 218, 99 O.R. (3d) 81, 266 O.A.C. 62, [2010] O.J. No. 1158 (Ont. C.A.), reversing in part 2008 CarswellOnt 110, [2008] O.J. No. 112 (Ont. S.C.J.), affirming 2009 CarswellOnt 8859 (Ont. S.C.J.). At trial, the wife was awarded prospective child support of $1,200 for a limited time of 5 years. On appeal, the

wife was awarded $950 per month for an indefinite period. The trial judge erred by considering
only need in his award. The wife was able to demonstrate entitlement. If the trial judge's award
was an attempt to restructure, no explanation was given. There was no basis for a time-limited
award and an indefinite award was in line with the SSAG. However, the circumstances did not
support a monthly payment at the high end of the SSAG range.

Where a payor has significant arrears of support, ongoing support would be subject to
restructuring and would begin after the payment of arrears was completed — Hadjioannou v.
Hadjioannou, 2013 CarswellBC 27, 2013 BCSC 43, [2013] B.C.J. No. 49 (B.C.S.C.). The parties
were married for just over 10 years and had three children together. The husband had significant
spousal and child support arrears, and the judge found that this was an appropriate case for
restructuring. Ongoing spousal support was to begin immediately after arrears had been paid off.

Limited financial means precluded restructuring — Tessaro v. Tessaro, 2010 CarswellOnt
7583, 2010 ONSC 5342 (Ont. S.C.J.). The wife was entitled to spousal support within the SSAG
range of 9 to 18 years from the date of separation. The husband's limited finances precluded
restructuring the prospective support payments. Although there was no current requirement for
spousal support, a claim could be advanced in the future.

Low spousal support for indefinite period — Bockhold v. Bockhold, 2010 CarswellBC 369,
2010 BCSC 214, [2010] B.C.J. No. 283 (B.C.S.C. [In Chambers]). The parties were married for
17 years and had two children. Pursuant to a consent order entered into in 2003, the husband
agreed to pay the wife spousal and child support with spousal support subject to review upon
cessation of child support. The court found that the wife was not self-sufficient despite entering
into a new relationship and receiving spousal support for 10 years, because she had been out of
work during most of the marriage and was diagnosed with a disability. The court noted that for a
payor with an annual income of $540,000, the SSAG would suggest a range of support at the low
end of $11,093, mid-range of $12,941 and high range of $14,790 per month. The court awarded
the wife $10,000 per month in spousal support for an indefinite duration due to the wife's
disability.

## 15.3 Lump Sum

Retroactive spousal support awards may be paid in a lump sum and the lump sum reduced
by a percentage to adjust for the lost tax deductibility to the payer — Samoilova v. Mahnic, 2014
CarswellAlta 224, 2014 ABCA 65, 41 R.F.L. (7th) 83, [2014] A.J. No. 154 (Alta. C.A.). The
parties had agreed that the SSAG should form the basis of any award. The trial judge made an
award of lump sum, retroactive support. After the reasons were released, but prior to the entry of
the order, husband's counsel wrote a letter to the judge noting that the judge had not taken into
account the tax ramifications of the order, which was not taxable in the hands of the recipient, nor
deductible by the payor. Husband's counsel asked that the tax ramifications be considered. The
wife's counsel took the position that any change to the order would result in hardship. The judge
subsequently reduced the amount of the lump sum to reflect the fact that the parties had agreed
the SSAG would apply, and the presumption in the SSAG is that support will be taxable in the
hands of the recipient and deductible by the payor. In order to achieve fairness, the lump sum was
reduced by 30%. The appellate court upheld this decision, ruling that it would likely be an error
not to consider tax consequences once raised as an issue.

Where there is animosity, ability to pay, history of non-payment, a retroactive award and
other factors, a lump sum award will be ordered — Racco v. Racco, 2014 CarswellOnt 5377, 2014
ONCA 330, 44 R.F.L. (7th) 348, 373 D.L.R. (4th) 240, 318 O.A.C. 374, [2014] O.J. No. 2000
(Ont. C.A.). The husband appealed, inter alia, the payment of spousal support in a lump sum to

the wife. The Court of Appeal found that the trial judge had appropriately used his discretion in considering the following factors when awarding a lump sum:

> ... a high level of animosity between the parties, a history of non-payment by the appellant, the possibility that the appellant's financial situation would continue to be precarious, the desirability of terminating personal contact, the need to effect a retroactive award of support and the need to provide capital to the respondent ... [para. 31].

The Court of Appeal also held that the quantum was appropriate when measured against the suggested range of the SSAG, although the trial judge did not refer to the SSAG.

*A large spousal support amount awarded to a party may not be a lump sum, but rather a calculation of periodic spousal support payments due to the party in the specified periods of time* — *Edgar v. Edgar*, 2012 CarswellOnt 11952, 2012 ONCA 646 (Ont. C.A.). The trial judge had calculated arrears of periodic payments based on the *Spousal Support Advisory Guidelines* and provided that the credits due to the respondent husband for spousal and child support were to be set off against his obligation to the appellant wife for ongoing child support. The husband was awarded $28,000 in spousal support.

*Where a court awards lump sum spousal support instead of periodic support, it is preferable that the court considers whether the amount awarded is in keeping with the* Spousal Support Advisory Guidelines. *If it is not, some reasons should be provided for why the Guidelines do not provide an appropriate result* — *Davis v. Crawford*, 2011 CarswellOnt 2512, 2011 ONCA 294, 95 R.F.L. (6th) 257, 106 O.R. (3d) 221, 332 D.L.R. (4th) 508, 277 O.A.C. 200, [2011] O.J. No. 1719 (Ont. C.A.), additional reasons at 2011 CarswellOnt 4562, 2011 ONCA 423, [2011] O.J. No. 2637 (Ont. C.A.).

*The Spousal Support Advisory Guidelines will be used to determine the amount of a lump sum award of spousal support* — *Karisik v. Chow*, 2010 CarswellBC 3272, 2010 BCCA 548, 94 R.F.L. (6th) 70, 12 B.C.L.R. (5th) 107, 301 B.C.A.C. 133, 510 W.A.C. 133 (B.C.C.A.). Leave to appeal refused 2011 CarswellBC 1436, 2011 CarswellBC 1437, 425 N.R. 390 (note), 305 B.C.A.C. 320 (note), 515 W.A.C. 320 (note), [2011] S.C.C.A. No. 59 (S.C.C.). The wife appealed a trial decision which awarded her lump sum spousal support based on a monthly periodic amount. The trial judge used the *Spousal Support Advisory Guidelines* in order to determine an appropriate amount and duration of support. The wife objected to the award of lump sum rather than periodic support. The Court of Appeal held that the trial judge reasonably exercised his discretion in awarding lump sum support on the basis that this would assist the wife in retaining the matrimonial home.

*Where the parties had a long, 20-year marriage, a court may still make a time-limited, 10-year award of spousal support at the low end of the range where other financial relief, such as lump sum support, has been granted* — *Reisman v. Reisman*, 2014 CarswellOnt 1496, 2014 ONCA 109, 42 R.F.L. (7th) 1, 118 O.R. (3d) 721, 371 D.L.R. (4th) 164, 315 O.A.C. 333 (Ont. C.A.). The monthly support figure should not be considered alone. There was also a lump sum support order of $119,956.34, an equalization amount that the husband had overpaid in the interim domestic contract and agreed to forgo in return for paying lower monthly support. The lump sum amount of $119,000 was equivalent to monthly payments of $1,500 for 10 years. Consequently for at least 10 years, the mother's effective monthly spousal support was $6,000, which was above the high end of the range established by the Guidelines for a "without child" support scenario and for a couple with the income or imputed income of the parties. The appellate court did not adjust the amount of support.

*Where compensatory entitlement is found, retroactive support may be ordered in a lump sum reflecting the high end of SSAG range* — *Soutar v. Soutar*, 2014 CarswellOnt 704, 2014

ONSC 470 (Ont. S.C.J.). The parties were married for 18 years, in a 20-year relationship, and had three adult children. The parties separated in 2005, and the wife sought retroactive support. The wife was entitled to compensatory support, and a lump sum reflecting support at the high end of the SSAG range was ordered for the period from 2009 to 2012.

A *lump sum award will be made when a clean break would be appropriate, in part because the recipient lives in another jurisdiction* — Stannett v. Green, 2014 CarswellOnt 40, [2014] O.J. No. 47 (Ont. S.C.J.). The parties cohabited for 9 years and had no children. They separated in 2009. The wife had not worked since separation and was receiving CPP disability for depression and anxiety. The judge imputed income to the husband of $75,000. The wife was found to have need; and, given her disability, support at the mid-high range of the SSAG was ordered in a lump sum in order to facilitate a clean break.

*Spousal Support Advisory Guidelines and the parties' separation agreement used to determine a lump sum spousal support award* — Luehr v. Luehr, 2011 CarswellBC 652, 2011 BCSC 359, 1 R.F.L. (7th) 400 (B.C.S.C.). The wife suffered from severe mental illness years after the parties separated. In a separation agreement, incorporated into a consent order, the parties implicitly acknowledged the wife's entitlement to support by permitting her to occupy the mortgage-free matrimonial home and receive any rental income from the home. Since the sale of the house, the wife continued to be entitled to support on a compensatory, non-compensatory and contractual basis. The wife's need for support was greater than it had been when the parties separated. But for her illness, the wife would have likely remained in the home and generated rental income from it until she was 65. There was a significant risk that the husband's employment would be interrupted for significant periods before the wife reached 65. In the circumstances a lump sum payment of $75,000, which considered both the mid-range obligations under the *Spousal Support Advisory Guidelines*, and the parties' intentions in their separation agreement, was reasonable.

*Where the payor is unlikely to be in the workforce for much longer, lump sum support may be ordered* — A. v. B., 2012 CarswellNS 1042, 2012 NSFC 9 (N.S. Fam. Ct.). The parties were together for 3.5 years, including 2 years of marriage. The husband was 71, had retired and had claimed bankruptcy. The wife was 67 and was a nurse. Upon marriage, the husband had a modest income; and the wife was aware of his limited resources. He was awarded non-compensatory spousal support in a restructured order of $700 monthly for 6 months, which reflected a mid-range award of 2 years, which was also mid-range in duration. A mid-range award was found to be appropriate absent factors that would indicate a high- or low-end award.

*Where lump sum spousal support, in accordance with the SSAG, was appropriate to address a multitude of complex support issues* — M. (A.A.) v. K. (R.P.), 2010 CarswellOnt 1139, 2010 ONSC 930, 81 R.F.L. (6th) 370, [2010] O.J. No. 807 (Ont. S.C.J.). The parties, who were both veterinarians, had a 9-year relationship and two children. The husband had an estimated income of $189,900, and the wife had an estimated income of $100,000 in 2009. The parties entered a separation agreement that included a mutual release of spousal support. They did not discuss the spousal support clause, thereby failing to focus on the circumstances in which the agreement was executed and departing significantly from the overall objectives of the *Divorce Act*. The wife was entitled to compensatory and non-compensatory support. A lump sum payment, as a form of restructuring in accordance with the SSAG, was appropriate. The lump sum payment would address the various complex issues of the commencement date, delay, post-separation increases in income and the balance of compensatory and non-compensatory aspects of the order. The wife was awarded a lump sum of $44,000, netted down for tax purposes.

*Order for lump sum spousal support where the husband had a history of non-payment and his unemployment jeopardized future payments* — Vanos v. Vanos, 2009 CarswellOnt 6420, 77 R.F.L. (6th) 123, [2009] O.J. No. 4217 (Ont. S.C.J.), reversed 2010 CarswellOnt 9680, 2010

ONCA 876, 94 R.F.L. (6th) 312, 271 O.A.C. 222, [2010] O.J. No. 5539 (Ont. C.A.). The wife was entitled to spousal support for an indefinite period. The husband was ordered to make monthly payments of $1,489, which was the middle figure of the SSAG range. Given the husband's history of non-payment of support orders and his current unemployment, an order for a lump sum payment and a vesting order were justified. The lump sum support payment for future spousal support was $121,500. The order for lump sum spousal support was upheld on appeal.

Determining the correct lump sum is not a simple mathematical exercise — Hartshorne v. Hartshorne, 2009 CarswellBC 1398, 2009 BCSC 698, 70 R.F.L. (6th) 106, [2009] B.C.J. No. 1050 (B.C.S.C.), reversed in part 2010 CarswellBC 1618, 2010 BCCA 327, 82 R.F.L. (6th) 1, 6 B.C.L.R. (5th) 58, 320 D.L.R. (4th) 398, 289 B.C.A.C. 244, 489 W.A.C. 244, [2010] B.C.J. No. 1271 (B.C.C.A.), additional reasons at 2011 CarswellBC 107, 2011 BCCA 29, 95 R.F.L. (6th) 14, 14 B.C.L.R. (5th) 33, 330 D.L.R. (4th) 503, 299 B.C.A.C. 6, 508 W.A.C. 6, [2011] B.C.J. No. 107 (B.C.C.A.). The court considered the award it would have made without the assistance of SSAG, the quantums generated by the wife's counsel, and the quantum the court calculated using 2 years of SSAG monthly support, plus an 8-year lump sum. It found that the wife was entitled to lump sum retroactive spousal support in the amount of $350,000 payable on February 28, 2001, the date of Beames J.'s second and final judgement. The court decided that the amount was not too high considering the standard of living that the parties had during their marriage.

Non-compensatory claim for spousal support awarded as a lump sum and later reduced to reflect the tax consequences — Arnold v. Arnold, 2009 CarswellBC 2684, 2009 BCSC 1384 (B.C.S.C.), additional reasons at 2010 CarswellBC 278, 2010 BCSC 166 (B.C.S.C.). The wife had a reasonable claim for non-compensatory spousal support at the low end of the SSAG range. She was awarded support of $1,365 per month for a period of 3½ years. In accordance with the parties' preference, a lump sum award of $57,330 was made. In additional reasons, the court reduced the support order by 30% to reflect the tax consequences of a lump sum award.

Lump sum spousal support award for mid-length marriage — Venco v. Lie, 2009 CarswellBC 1639, 2009 BCSC 831 (B.C.S.C.). Following the breakdown of a 9-year marriage, the wife had made efforts to become self-sufficient, but was not yet completely so. She was entitled to time-limited spousal support on a compensatory and non-compensatory basis. The SSAG range was from nil to $98 per month for 4½ to 11 years. The wife was awarded a lump sum payment of $5,000. The lump sum payment was prudent given the husband's hostility towards the wife, his stated intention to prevent her from receiving any monetary compensation following the divorce, and his history of non-payment of spousal support.

Conversion to lump sum by comparison of cost-to-payor or versus value-to-recipient — Roach v. Dutra, 2009 CarswellBC 487, 2009 BCSC 229, [2009] B.C.J. No. 353 (B.C.S.C.), additional reasons at 2009 CarswellBC 1375, 2009 BCSC 693, 70 R.F.L. (6th) 410 (B.C.S.C.), affirmed 2010 CarswellBC 1267, 2010 BCCA 264, 82 R.F.L. (6th) 42, 5 B.C.L.R. (5th) 95, 87 C.P.C. (6th) 239, 288 B.C.A.C. 141, 488 W.A.C. 141 (B.C.C.A.). An appropriate periodic award was determined through reference to the SSAG. The court then found that the cost to the payor of paying the global amount as a lump sum would be between $25,000 and $34,000, while the value of the benefit to the recipient would be between $31,000 and $43,000. The lump sum owing was fixed at $30,000.

Where the parties had a short marriage, lump sum spousal support was ordered after a consideration of SSAG — Drake v. Drake, 2009 CarswellBC 3604, 2009 BCSC 1815 (B.C.S.C.). According to the Spousal Support Advisory Guidelines, the relative incomes of the parties should result in a range of support between $416 to $554 per month, for a duration of 3 to 6 years, with a possible review and variation built in. The wife sought a lump sum of $10,000 which was equivalent of 2 years of support at the lowest end of the range. The court accepted this approach, finding that it recognized that the marriage was of short duration.

*Lump sum ordered to affect a clean break* — Fountain v. Fountain, 2009 CarswellOnt 6342, 77 R.F.L. (6th) 255 (Ont. S.C.J.). The court found that the parties needed a clean break and that the husband was able to pay the wife a lump sum spousal support amount. The court ordered support for 15 years which totalled $90,000. It reduced this amount by 22% for tax, 6% for a discount rate, and then finally 25% for negative contingencies.

*Lump sum and ongoing spousal support ordered* — Card v. Card, 2009 CarswellBC 1696, 2009 BCSC 865 (B.C.S.C.), additional reasons at 2009 CarswellBC 2484, 2009 BCSC 1268 (B.C.S.C.). The parties were married for 18 years and had three children. The wife was a traditional stay-at-home mother for the majority of the marriage. The wife brought an application for spousal support. The court ordered that the husband pay the wife $60,000 in lump sum and $500 per month in spousal support for an indefinite period (the court allowed for a review after 6 years). The wife needed the $60,000 to pay for the husband's share of the matrimonial home. The court noted that the combination of lump sum and ongoing spousal support was warranted based on the 18-year marriage which significantly disadvantaged the wife economically.

*Modest amount of spousal support for short marriage paid as lump sum* — Abuzokkar v. Farag, 2009 CarswellOnt 4046, [2009] O.J. No. 2915 (Ont. S.C.J.). The wife sought spousal support in this case. The husband earned $61,800 per year and the wife earned $30,000. The court found that there was no evidence that the wife stayed at home during the marriage or that she gave up jobs or education. She was not disadvantaged by the marriage and was employed full-time. The court noted that the parties were only married for just over 4 years and accordingly spousal support should be for a limited period and not be substantial. In this case, the Guidelines suggested spousal support of a range of $0 to $444 per month for a period of 2 to 12 years. The court awarded $200 per month for a period of 3 years, to be paid in a lump sum from the net equalization.

*Lump sum reduced by 50% to account for future contingencies* — Raymond v. Raymond, 2008 CarswellOnt 7939, 64 R.F.L. (6th) 160, [2008] O.J. No. 5294 (Ont. S.C.J.). Having chosen the mid-range SSAG figure as appropriate and having decided to order a lump sum, the judge calculated the lump sum at para. 27. The SSAG quantum of $3,246 per month was reduced to a net amount of $2,240. This was multiplied by the number of months in the mid-range SSAG duration, then reduced by 6% to account for the time- value of money. Finally, it was reduced by 50% "to take into account future contingencies".

*Lump sum ordered* — *no adjustment for tax implications* — Reavie v. Heaps, 2008 CarswellBC 1624, 2008 BCSC 1038, 58 R.F.L. (6th) 111, [2008] B.C.J. No. 1461 (B.C.S.C.). The trial judge found that the SSAG quantum range was $2,175 to $2,900 per year, and that the duration range was 0.5 to 1.0 years. A lump sum of $2,900 was ordered, without any adjustment for tax implications.

*Lump sum ordered* — Durakovic v. Durakovic, 2008 CarswellOnt 5329, [2008] O.J. No. 3537 (Ont. S.C.J.). The court summarized when lump sum awards should be awarded and then determined that the wife was entitled to a lump sum award. The court awarded the wife spousal support of $3,500 for 28 months, reduced 30% for income tax, 3% for present value, and 25% for negative contingencies.

*Conversion to lump sum with tax adjustment* — Martin v. Martin, 2007 CarswellOnt 683, [2007] O.J. No. 467 (Ont. S.C.J.), additional reasons at 2007 CarswellOnt 1574 (Ont. S.C.J.). This case offers an example of conversion of a SSAG-based periodic support award being converted to a lump sum. See also Smith v. Smith, 2006 CarswellBC 2761, 2006 BCSC 1655, [2006] B.C.J. No. 2920 (B.C.S.C.).

# CHAPTER 16

## CEILINGS AND FLOORS

*Income boundaries before SSAG applied*

"Ceilings" and "floors" in Chapter 11 define the boundaries of the typical incomes to which the formulas can be applied. The ceiling is the income level for the payor spouse above which any formula gives way to discretion, set here at a gross annual income for the payor of $350,000. The floor is the income level for the payor below which no support is usually paid, here set at $20,000. To avoid a cliff effect, there is an exception for cases where the payor spouse's gross income is more than $20,000 but less than $30,000, where spousal support may not be awarded or may be reduced below the low end of the range. An additional exception is also necessary, to allow an award of spousal support below the income floor in particular cases. (SSAG Executive Summary)

Where a payor parent earns over $350,000, the closer his or her earnings are to $350,000, the more likely the courts seem willing to follow the SSAG in determining spousal support.

This chapter is divided into the following sections:

16.1 Ceilings
16.2 Floors

## 16.1 Ceilings

*Ceilings — approaches using with child support formula*

The ceiling is not a "cap" on spousal support, nor does it bar the continued use of the formulas as one method of arriving at an amount in a particular case. (SSAG Chapter 11.3)

We can suggest two possible approaches for these very high income cases using the with child support formula: (SSAG Chapter 11.3)

1) The first approach uses the formula to determine a minimum amount for spousal support, an approach we can call "minimum plus". A notional calculation would be required to calculate spousal support at the $350,000 ceiling, using the child support payable at the ceiling. This would determine the "minimum" spousal support range. In Example 11.2, that range would be $7,585 to $9,160. There would be discretion to add to that minimum for incomes over $350,000, after taking into account the actual amount of child support being paid by the payor at that higher income level, which would be $6,052 per month at $500,000. This approach might make more sense where the payor's income is closer to the ceiling. (SSAG Chapter 11.3)

> 2)   The second approach would be one of pure discretion. Once the payor's income exceeded the ceiling, then there would be no "minimum" for spousal support, just a dollar figure that would take into account the actual amount of child support paid, an amount which can be very large for high income cases. At some point, the large amounts of child support include a component that compensates the recipient spouse for the indirect costs of child-care responsibilities, leaving less need for spousal support to do so. This approach will become more important where the payor's income is well above the ceiling. (SSAG Chapter 11.3)

Spousal Support Advisory Guidelines *considered but not used* — *Vanasse v. Seguin*, 2008 CarswellOnt 4265, [2008] O.J. No. 2832 (Ont. S.C.J.), additional reasons at 2009 CarswellOnt 606, 77 R.F.L. (6th) 109, [2009] O.J. No. 483 (Ont. S.C.J.), reversed 2009 CarswellOnt 4407, 2009 ONCA 595, 77 R.F.L. (6th) 118, 96 O.R. (3d) 321, 252 O.A.C. 218, [2009] O.J. No. 3211 (Ont. C.A.), reversed [indexed as: *Kerr v. Baranow*] 2011 CarswellBC 240, 2011 CarswellBC 241, 2011 SCC 10, 93 R.F.L. (6th) 1, [2011] 1 S.C.R. 269, 108 O.R. (3d) 399, 14 B.C.L.R. (5th) 203, 328 D.L.R. (4th) 577, 64 E.T.R. (3d) 1, [2011] 3 W.W.R. 575, 300 B.C.A.C. 1, 411 N.R. 200, 274 O.A.C. 1, 509 W.A.C. 1, [2011] S.C.J. No. 10 (S.C.C.). The parties lived together in a common-law relationship for approximately 12 years and had two children, a son 10 years of age and a daughter 8 years of age at the time of trial. The trial judge imputed an annual income to the man of $450,000 and to the woman of $85,000. While the trial judge considered that the *Spousal Support Advisory Guidelines* did not apply where the payor's income exceeded $350,000, it was helpful to consider the comparative net disposable incomes ("NDI") in each household in assessing the appropriate amount of spousal support. The SUPPORTmate calculations indicated that the woman would receive 48% of the parties' NDI, if support were ordered in the amount of $3,800 per month, which the court considered would be a reasonable amount in light of the objectives and factors outlined in s. 33 of the *Family Law Act*. The woman had already received some spousal support for 3 years. That amount would be stepped down as of July 1, 2008, in light of her imputed income. The woman was to receive a further 7 years of spousal support, subject to a variation or earlier termination based on a "material change in circumstances" as outlined in s. 37 of the *Family Law Act*. The woman was also entitled to spousal support from the date that she commenced her application for spousal support in September 2005. The man was ordered to pay the woman $70,000 in retroactive support which took account of the support that he had already paid from September 2005 to June 30, 2008 and tax considerations. In the additional reasons at 2008 CarswellOnt 4265, the woman was granted, *inter alia*, an interest on the lump sum spousal support. Spousal support was not an issue on appeal at the Court of Appeal or at the Supreme Court of Canada. [Retroactive spousal support was considered in the *Kerr v. Baranow* appeal heard at the same time as the *Vanasse* appeal at the Supreme Court of Canada. However, this was not a case where the payor had an income over $350,000.]

*The court is not obliged to consider deviation from the table amount explicitly under s. 11 of the SSAG regarding support awards for income exceeding $350,000* — *H. (J.E.) v. H. (P.L.)*, 2014 CarswellBC 2259, 2014 BCCA 310, 49 R.F.L. (7th) 285, 63 B.C.L.R. (5th) 107, 376 D.L.R. (4th) 670, [2014] 12 W.W.R. 265, 360 B.C.A.C. 15, 617 W.A.C. 15 (B.C.C.A.). At trial, the husband did not raise the issue of deviation from the table amount of support under s. 11 of the SSAG, which establish a ceiling income of $350,000 for table support applicability. The trial judge found the husband's annual income to be $1 million and ordered spousal support in the SSAG mid-range at $24,124 per month without explicitly considering the implications of s. 11. The husband submitted that the judge's decision to follow the SSAG formula rather than exercise his discretion was an error of law. The appellate court found that s. 11 recognizes that the judge's determination of an appropriate quantum of spousal support may be a matter of pure discretion and that, therefore, the issue of whether the SSAG apply to income above the ceiling is not a matter of law. The court dismissed the appeal.

*The SSAG calculations which were considered together with the evidence and the authorities are regarded as unreliable and likely excessive in cases where a payor's income exceeds $350,000 per annum* — Dickson v. Dickson, 2011 CarswellMan 96, 2011 MBCA 26, 93 R.F.L. (6th) 241, 333 D.L.R. (4th) 179, [2011] 5 W.W.R. 219, 262 Man. R. (2d) 247, 507 W.A.C. 247 (Man. C.A.), affirming 2009 CarswellMan 515, 2009 MBQB 274, 247 Man. R. (2d) 56, [2009] M.J. No. 374 (Man. Q.B.). The parties cohabited for 1 year, married in 1982, and separated in 2005, when the husband moved out. There were 4 children, ages 24, 22, 20 and 17 at the time of the proceedings. The wife was a homemaker with minimal income. During the marriage the family was substantially supported by money from the husband's family. The husband and wife had an organic food company, which performed badly. Following the separation, the husband withdrew money from his RRSP and reorganized the business structure excluding the wife. The trial judge held that the average income of the husband between 2005 and 2007 was $520,877 and for the year 2008, $303,320. The husband was in arrears and presented a misleading financial picture. The trial judge ordered the husband to pay child support, plus school payments from the RESP, and spousal support of $4,485 per month from April 2005 to Dec 2007 and thereafter $5,741 per month.

*Wife granted time-limited support at the low end of the range* — Davies v. Quantz, 2010 CarswellOnt 9748, 2010 ONCA 896, 100 R.F.L. (6th) 176, [2010] O.J. No. 5629 (Ont. C.A.), affirming 2010 CarswellOnt 10064, 2010 ONSC 416, 100 R.F.L. (6th) 156 (Ont. S.C.J.). The parties cohabitated for 18 years before they separated. They were both highly educated. For the first 9 years of the relationship the parties were "equals". After the birth of their children, the wife gave up her successful career to become the primary caregiver, at which point the parties transitioned into a traditional marriage. The wife's application for spousal support was granted. The husband's annual income was $428,000. The wife's career was severely disadvantaged by her assuming the role of fulltime mother and by moving from Quebec to Ontario to advance the husband's career. The wife was aware that the husband expected her to resume her career once the children were in school full-time. The wife was entitled to support on a compensatory basis and because of need. She was awarded $9,440 per month based on the lowest end of the *Spousal Support Advisory Guidelines* range for a payor earning $428,000. As the children were both in school full-time, the wife was in a position to seek work. A time-limited support order was made for 8 years, at which point the wife was expected to be self-supporting. The court noted that it was not realistic for her to wait until she was over 50 to even consider re-entering the workforce. The spousal support order was upheld on appeal with the Court of Appeal noting that the wife could seek variation of the order in the future if the circumstances permitted.

*Where the parties' income is over the $350,000 threshold, the parties should enjoy an income that is similar to what they had while married* — Elgner v. Elgner, 2009 CarswellOnt 7702, 85 R.F.L. (6th) 51, [2009] O.J. No. 5269 (Ont. S.C.J.), leave to appeal refused 2010 CarswellOnt 1640, 2010 ONSC 1578, 85 R.F.L. (6th) 62, 99 O.R. (3d) 687, 267 O.A.C. 1, [2010] O.J. No. 1139 (Ont. Div. Ct.), additional reasons at 2010 CarswellOnt 3918, 2010 ONSC 2399, 85 R.F.L. (6th) 71 (Ont. Div. Ct.), affirmed 2010 CarswellOnt 6860, 2010 ONSC 3512, 92 R.F.L. (6th) 106, 103 O.R. (3d) 588, 324 D.L.R. (4th) 277, 268 O.A.C. 267, [2010] O.J. No. 3828 (Ont. Div. Ct.), affirmed 2011 CarswellOnt 5673, 2011 ONCA 483, 5 R.F.L. (7th) 1, 105 O.R. (3d) 721, 336 D.L.R. (4th) 159, 282 O.A.C. 28, [2011] O.J. No. 3040 (Ont. C.A.), leave to appeal refused 2011 CarswellOnt 12421, 2011 CarswellOnt 12422, 429 N.R. 398 (note), 294 O.A.C. 396 (note) (S.C.C.). The parties were married for 33 years and had three adult children. The husband had an income of between $2.8 and $3.9 million annually. The wife had sacrificed her career for that of the husband. The judge ordered interim support at the lower end of the SSAG range. The judge determined the parties' circumstances did not indicate an award based purely on need, but rather considered that the wife had the right to a similar lifestyle that the parties enjoyed while married. He emphasized that the wife was not required to deplete her capital in order to fund\ that lifestyle.

*SSAG are a starting point for determining the quantum of temporary spousal support —* *Elgner v. Elgner, supra.* The SSAG's, under para. 11.1 "The Ceiling", provide: "Our preference is to use the payor's gross income as the basis for the ceiling." The husband's income in the previous 3 years was in the in the range of $2,800,000 to $3,900,000. The court noted that the wife's expenses were particularly high in 2008, as she paid for renovations to her new home. The court awarded the wife retroactive spousal support commencing in January 2008 to the date when the temporary spousal support commenced, without prejudice to the wife to argue at trial that it should go back to the date of separation. The court found that the wife's expenses were known for the 2008 and 2009 years and she was entitled to retroactive spousal support for those years. The court fixed the quantum of such support as follows:

(a) For 2008, the wife's budget was $115,439 per month. This included a monthly payment of $10,652 for income taxes estimated to be $127,824 for the year. The court stated that this amount was not sufficient to cover what the wife's true income taxes would be. The wife had certain non-recurring expenses for the 2 years after separation. Therefore, the wife was entitled to the higher end of the scale and the court set her support at $140,000 per month. An order was made that the husband reimburse the wife in the amount of $1,680,000 for retroactive spousal support.

(b) For the 2009 year, the wife's expenses decreased to $88,790.33 per month. In her budget for 2009, the wife showed an income tax payment of $5,000 per month. The court held that the $140,000 per month retroactive spousal support should continue for the year 2009. The husband was ordered to reimburse the wife in the amount of $1,680,000 for such retroactive spousal support.

(c) The court ordered that the husband pay on-going periodic temporary spousal support in the amount of $110,000 per month until further order of the court or the parties reached an agreement in writing, reduced the on-going support payment by deleting the wife's payments for furnishing the condominium, for her legal fees and her sister's expenses, and took into account some income from her investments.

*SSAG used an award at lower end of the range — the trial judge had failed to consider the relevance and allocation of family assets and debts — Gonabady-Namadon v. Mohammazadeh,* 2009 CarswellBC 2767, 2009 BCCA 448, 74 R.F.L. (6th) 1, 98 B.C.L.R. (4th) 23, 277 B.C.A.C. 48, 469 W.A.C. 48 (B.C.C.A.). The husband and wife and their two young children emigrated from Iran in 2001 and separated in 2006. The husband returned to Iran, where he ran a successful business. His financial disclosure was questionable, but the trial judge imputed an income of $250,000 to him. The wife re-qualified as a medical doctor in Canada, and earned $156,000 per year. She was 49 years old. At trial, the wife's application for support was dismissed. On appeal, the court grossed up the husband's income to $350,000 because he was not taxed, and ordered him to pay the wife $2,300 per month for 6 years, retroactive to the date of trial.

*The judge made use of SSAG to determine spousal support based on evidence of potential income dependent on a discretionary bonus — Beninger v. Beninger,* 2009 CarswellBC 818, 2009 BCCA 145, 78 R.F.L. (6th) 37, 99 B.C.L.R. (4th) 72, 269 B.C.A.C. 56, 453 W.A.C. 56, [2009] B.C.J. No. 638 (B.C.C.A.). The parties were married for 25 years in a traditional marriage and were approaching age 60. They had 4 children, but only one was still a dependant. The husband, a tax lawyer, had an income that was held to be $416,400 and the wife had no income. The wife appealed an order for spousal support of $10,000 per month, which was in the in the mid-range of the SSAG, alleging an error in the determination of the husband's income. The appeal was dismissed.

*No specific reference to SSAG, although amount ordered at lower end of SSAG range — T. (R.) v. D. (D.)*, 2009 CarswellBC 1223, 2009 BCCA 198, 64 R.F.L. (6th) 233, 92 B.C.L.R. (4th) 277, [2009] 7 W.W.R. 246, 270 B.C.A.C. 114, 454 W.A.C. 114, [2009] B.C.J. No. 928 (B.C.C.A.), affirming 2007 CarswellBC 1967, 2007 BCSC 1247, 42 R.F.L. (6th) 230, [2007] B.C.J. No. 1853 (B.C.S.C.), and affirming 2008 CarswellBC 1176, 2008 BCSC 733, 55 R.F.L. (6th) 322 (B.C.S.C.). The husband was a physician and the wife had trained as a lawyer, but had not worked since 2007. There was one child of the marriage. At trial, the husband's income was imputed to be $625,000 per year and he was ordered to pay the wife $10,500 per month which was reviewable in 4 years, subject to a material change in circumstances. The wife's appeal for an increase in child support was granted; retroactivity of spousal support was upheld, as was the amount of child support, but the date of review was changed to the earlier date of May 2010, when the child would start school.

*Multi-year average income used for SSAG calculation includes 1 year above ceiling —* Hartshorne v. Hartshorne, 2009 CarswellBC 1398, 2009 BCSC 698, 70 R.F.L. (6th) 106, [2009] B.C.J. No. 1050 (B.C.S.C.), reversed in part 2010 CarswellBC 1618, 2010 BCCA 327, 82 R.F.L. (6th) 1, 6 B.C.L.R. (5th) 58, 320 D.L.R. (4th) 398, 289 B.C.A.C. 244, 489 W.A.C. 244, [2010] B.C.J. No. 1271 (B.C.C.A.), additional reasons at 2011 CarswellBC 107, 2011 BCCA 29, 95 R.F.L. (6th) 14, 14 B.C.L.R. (5th) 33, 330 D.L.R. (4th) 503, 299 B.C.A.C. 6, 508 W.A.C. 6, [2011] B.C.J. No. 107 (B.C.C.A.). The trial judge observed that the SSAG do not "automatically" apply to incomes in excess of $350,000. In this case, the payor's income had fluctuated dramatically from year to year and a multi-year average was used. The judge stated at para. 125 that in reaching this average he was "untroubled by including one year that [was] over $350,000".

*Where income is over $350,000 some discretion can be exercised in utilizing the SSAG —* James v. James, 2009 CarswellBC 1490, 2009 BCCA 261, 66 R.F.L. (6th) 246, 94 B.C.L.R. (4th) 183, [2009] 10 W.W.R. 11, 273 B.C.A.C. 75, 461 W.A.C. 75, [2009] B.C.J. No. 1151 (B.C.C.A.). In 2004, the parties had entered into a consent order. At the time, the husband's annual income was estimated to be about $500,000. The husband was ordered to pay $5,750 per month in spousal support. Subsequently, the wife obtained financial information from the husband and the court concluded that the husband's income for 2005 and 2006 was in the range of $1 million per year. The wife had a measure of need in order to maintain a lifestyle consonant with what she had during the marriage. On the variation application, the court held that the wife was entitled to a level of support that could maintain a lifestyle not dramatically different from that which she enjoyed during the years when the parties were married. The husband had the ability to pay. The court varied the amount of spousal support to $9,000 per month.

*$650,000 income — SSAG "not useful" — Bell v. Bell*, 2009 CarswellBC 1588, 2009 BCCA 280, 69 R.F.L. (6th) 21, 97 B.C.L.R. (4th) 55, [2010] 1 W.W.R. 98, 272 B.C.A.C. 207, 459 W.A.C. 207, [2009] B.C.J. No. 1201 (B.C.C.A.), additional reasons at 2010 CarswellBC 625, 2010 BCCA 138, 76 R.F.L. (6th) 257, 2 B.C.L.R. (5th) 200, [2010] 7 W.W.R. 453, 284 B.C.A.C. 316 (B.C.C.A.). The husband's annual income was found to be $650,000, and the trial and appellate courts were of the opinion that the SSAG would not be useful in the circumstances.

*On appeal an order providing support to the wife in amount above the SSAG range for a shorter period overturned — S. (J.K.) v. S. (H.G.)*, 2008 CarswellBC 1218, 2008 BCCA 245, 54 R.F.L. (6th) 38, 83 B.C.L.R. (4th) 102, 257 B.C.A.C. 16, 432 W.A.C. 16, [2008] B.C.J. No. 1068 (B.C.C.A.), varying 2006 CarswellBC 2255, 2006 BCSC 1356, [2006] B.C.J. No. 2051 (B.C.S.C.). The parties were married for 10 years and at the time of separation the husband was 55 and the wife was 44 years old. Following separation, they continued to see each other until the husband realized there was no chance of reconciliation. At the time of trial, the husband was 63 years of age and the wife was 51 years of age. The husband was an orthodontist and the wife had retired from her work as a flight attendant in 2005. There was one child of the marriage, who at the time of trial was suffering from chronic psychological difficulties. The parties agreed to joint custody but the child resided primarily with the wife. At trial, it was held that the wife was capable of earning $35,000 per year and the husband's income was $477,206 per year. The trial judge ordered that the wife would receive spousal support in the amount of $13,750 per month until June 30, 2009, $11,000 per month until June 30, 2011, and $8,000 per month until June 30, 2013, when support would terminate. The Court of Appeal set aside this spousal support order and held that the wife would receive instead $8,000 per month from July 1, 2006 until June 30, 2011 and then $6,500 per month until otherwise ordered or agreed by the parties. The trial judge considered the SSAG and concluded that, as the husband was 63 of age and would probably retire at 70 years of age, she would award to the wife more money for a lesser period of time. On appeal, it was held that the trial judge had discretion to depart from the Guidelines, but the evidence indicated that it was unlikely the wife would curb her spending or find employment while receiving these generous amounts and it was not sensible for her support to cease when she was 65 when she would be more likely to be unemployable.

*Judge noted that parties had agreed that the SSAG would be inapplicable in the calculation of the appropriate spousal support in this case as they were never intended to apply to income differentials exceeding $350,000 − P. (T.L.) v. P. (F.J.),* 2008 CarswellAlta 1619, 2008 ABCA 334 (Alta. C.A.), reversing in part 2007 CarswellAlta 1344, 2007 ABQB 600, [2007] A.J. No. 1114 (Alta. Q.B.). The parties were married for 21 years. At the time of the separation, the wife was 46 years old and the husband was 50 years old. There were 3 children of the marriage. One of the children lived with the husband and the other two children lived with the wife. An income of $68,000 was imputed to the wife, although she had not worked outside the home for 20 years. The husband was a Vice President and Director at an investment firm and his income was $670,965 for 2006. He was ordered to pay spousal support in the amount of $5,000 per month with a review in 2.5 years. The Court of Appeal held that although there is deference to a trial judge's findings in matrimonial property and support orders, there is a reviewable issue here in the failure of the trial judge to explain how the evidence related to his finding that the parties were living beyond their means. The appeal was, therefore, allowed in part, and the issue of spousal support referred back for re-consideration.

*Courts can use two approaches when payor's income at ceiling − Loesch v. Walji,* 2008 CarswellBC 982, 2008 BCCA 214, 52 R.F.L. (6th) 33, 81 B.C.L.R. (4th) 271, [2008] 10 W.W.R. 625, 255 B.C.A.C. 264, 430 W.A.C. 264, [2008] B.C.J. No. 897 (B.C.C.A.). In this case, the court addressed the different methods that judges can employ when a payor's income is above $350,000. The parties were married for 17 years and had 4 children. The husband had an estimated annual income of $1,600,000. During the marriage, the parties had lived an expensive and luxurious lifestyle. The wife brought a motion for interim spousal support and the judge awarded her $50,000 per month. The husband appealed. The Court of Appeal found that the trial judge did not err given the substantial wealth of the husband and the high standard of living during the marriage. The Court of Appeal further noted that under the SSAG, with child formula, when the payor's income is in excess of $350,000 the court can take two approaches. First, the court can employ the "minimal plus" approach which uses the formula to determine a minimum amount for spousal support. The second method is "pure discretion" where there is no minimum amount, just a dollar figure that would take into account the actual amount of child support being paid. The court of appeal concluded that the judge was correct in applying the "pure discretion" approach and taking into account the wife's needs and the husband's ability to pay.

*Income of $500,000, SSAG used as a comparative tool to arrive at the appropriate amount of support payable* — *Milton v. Milton,* 2008 CarswellNB 591, 2008 CarswellNB 592, 2008 NBCA 87, 62 R.F.L. (6th) 286, 305 D.L.R. (4th) 94, 338 N.B.R. (2d) 300, 866 A.P.R. 300, [2008] N.B.J. No. 467 (N.B.C.A.). The marriage was traditional and long-term as it had lasted 21 years. The trial judge found that the husband had an annual income of $500,000. He estimated that the wife would have an income of approximately $40,000, taking into account her anticipated investment income. The wife's standard of living decreased after separation while the husband's did not. The trial judge used the *Spousal Support Advisory Guidelines* as a comparative tool to arrive at the correct amount of spousal support to be paid. The range for monthly support found in the guidelines was between $7,952 and $10,603. The trial judge ordered the husband to pay spousal support of $6,500 per month indefinitely. The appellate court held that in so doing the trial judge made no reversible error and consequently the court dismissed this ground of appeal.

*Support above ceiling for several years, then reduced to amount at ceiling* — *S. (J.K.) v. S. (H.G.),* 2006 CarswellBC 2255, 2006 BCSC 1356, [2006] B.C.J. No. 2051 (B.C.S.C.), varied 2008 CarswellBC 1218, 2008 BCCA 245, 54 R.F.L. (6th) 38, 83 B.C.L.R. (4th) 102, 257 B.C.A.C. 16, 432 W.A.C. 16, [2008] B.C.J. No. 1068 (B.C.C.A.). The wife was a 51-year-old retired air stewardess and the husband was a 62-year-old orthodontist who had an income for *Child Support Guidelines* purposes of $477,206. The parties lived together for 10 years. The parties continued to spend time together and vacationed together after separation for another 6 years until the husband realized there was no hope of reconciliation. The wife submitted that she was entitled to indefinite spousal support in the range of $11,000 to $15,000 based on the defendant's Guidelines income of $450,000 to $500,000. The defendant submitted that the court should award her $5,000 per month for 12 months only. The court stated that the SSAG provide a parameter of $6,500 per month for 10 years based on the highest Guidelines income of $350,000. However, the court recognized that the Guidelines are advisory only and may not be applicable. The court stated that due to the unique circumstances of this case, it would award the wife more money for a lesser period of time. The husband was 63 years old and would likely retire by age 70. At that point it would be unlikely he would receive income anywhere near $477,000 per annum. The wife would be 58 and would have another 7 years or more of employability. The child should no longer be dependent and the wife should still have capital from her share of the family assets. The court ordered a step down order. For the 36 months commencing July 1, 2006, the husband would pay the wife $13,750 per month. For the 24 months following July 1, 2009, the husband would pay the wife $11,000 per month. For the 24 months following July 2011, the husband would pay the wife $8,000 per month. After June 2013 all spousal support payments would cease.

*The court has discretion whether to apply the SSAG in a high-income case and has discretion to depart from the SSAG both with respect to the quantum and duration of the spousal support award, citing S. (J.K.) v. S. (H.G.), supra* — *Bozak v. Bozak,* 2008 CarswellBC 2398, 2008 BCSC 1458, [2008] B.C.J. No. 2080 (B.C.S.C.).

*Spousal support payable for high earners discretionary* — *payor worked time and a half* — *T. (R.) v. D. (D.),* 2007 CarswellBC 1967, 2007 BCSC 1247, 42 R.F.L. (6th) 230, [2007] B.C.J. No. 1853 (B.C.S.C.), additional reasons at 2008 CarswellBC 1176, 2008 BCSC 733, 55 R.F.L. (6th) 322 (B.C.S.C.), affirmed 2009 CarswellBC 1223, 2009 BCCA 198, 64 R.F.L. (6th) 233, 92 B.C.L.R. (4th) 277, [2009] 7 W.W.R. 246, 270 B.C.A.C. 114, 454 W.A.C. 114, [2009] B.C.J. No. 928 (B.C.C.A.). The husband was a physician and the mother had trained as a lawyer, but had worked in human resources. The parties had one child. The husband left the wife for the wife's sister-in-law. The husband earned $630,000 (rounded down from $633,030). The husband argued that his income for Guidelines purposes should be set at $350,000 on the basis that he worked time and a half all of the time, and he was entitled to a fair compensation for himself for the time he worked. The wife received $315,000, and there was no evidence that either wife or child did without on the support that has been paid. The court stated, at para. 58, that it was not given any authority "that suggests that a payor who works double the time and earns double the money only needs to pay support based on half of his or her earnings. While the Guidelines allow the court to increase the income of underachievers, the Guidelines do not reduce the income of overachievers." It did note that for income over $350,000, the amount of support was discretionary. The husband conceded that the wife was entitled to compensatory support. The husband stated that he expected his personal income to average about $400,000. Using the 2007 SSAG CHEQUEmate Calculator and 12 years of marriage/cohabitation (the figure used by the wife in her SSAG calculations) produced spousal support ranging from $10,067 to $12,199. Attributing no income to the wife and $425,000 to the husband produced a range of $10,979 to $13,020. The court found that the wife was entitled to child support of $3,447 and spousal support of $10,500 each month. The order for spousal support was reviewable in 4 years, subject to any material change in circumstance in the interim.

In assessing a recipient's need in above-ceiling interim claims, the judge will consider the recipient's living situation — A. (J.L.) v. G. (M.J.G.), 2014 CarswellBC 2177, 2014 BCSC 1391 (B.C.S.C.). The husband's income was $890,532. The court found that the wife's stated "need" of $23,836, which was just slightly below the SSAG mid-range, was excessive. In its assessment of need, the court included the fact that the wife lived rent-free, although she paid taxes and utilities. The husband argued that she should pay rent, but the judge found that this was a matter for trial. The court ordered interim support of $12,000 per month.

The court may exercise its discretion where the payor's income is above the SSAG ceiling amount, using the Divorce Act objectives as a guideline — M. (S.R.) v. M. (N.G.T.), 2014 CarswellBC 697, 2014 BCSC 442 (B.C.S.C.). The court noted that the table amounts greatly exceeded the amount required to support a lifestyle similar to that enjoyed by the parties at separation. The court looked to the objectives set out in s. 15.2(6) of the Divorce Act to guide its decision, which involved an examination of all of the parties' circumstances, including the amount of child support and s. 7 expenses, the parties' pre-separation lifestyle, their means and needs, and their ages and future prospects.

The purpose of interim spousal support is to address need, rather than compensatory entitlement, which will result in an award below the SSAG range when other factors are present — Betts v. Betts, 2014 CarswellNB 63, 2014 NBQB 47, 416 N.B.R. (2d) 355, 1079 A.P.R. 355 (N.B.Q.B.). The parties were married for 38 years and had five adult children. There was an unenforceable agreement between the parties, and the wife also claimed there were collateral agreements. The judge found the existence of collateral agreements required findings of credibility and a full hearing. The wife had no high school diploma and had never worked. The judge found she needed support and that interim support was intended to address need, rather than compensatory issues to be determined at trial, which indicated an award at the low end of the SSAG range. The judge considered other factors, such as the wife living rent-free in the marital home, the husband's income of over $350,000, and the property had not yet been equalized, which pointed to an award below the SSAG range. In these circumstances, an award below the low end of the SSAG range was warranted.

With incomes over $350,000, the amounts set out in the SSAG are one factor in determining spousal support but their application is not automatic — Cork v. Cork, 2014 CarswellOnt 5516, 2014 ONSC 2488, 44 R.F.L. (7th) 276, 97 E.T.R. (3d) 304 (Ont. S.C.J.). The parties were married for 24 years and had three adult children. The wife had been out of the workforce for 17 years and had no income. The husband's income was $536,674. The judge found that a cap at $350,000 was not required, but that he had discretion to cap at that amount and not automatically apply the Guidelines amounts. The parties had separated 2 years previously, interim spousal support at the high end of the SSAG had been paid, and the wife had not taken steps to achieve self-sufficiency. Income of $40,000 per year was imputed to her. The court ordered the husband to pay spousal support to the wife in the amount of $16,000 per month from the date of trial followed by a review.

*Where the payor's income is greater than $350,000, a court can determine spousal support on the basis of the needs of the payee and the fact that the SSAG should not automatically be followed* — M. (K.R.) v. M. (F.B.), 2013 CarswellBC 468, 2013 BCSC 286 (B.C.S.C.). The parties began cohabiting in 2001, were married in 2006, and separated in 2012. They had three children. The husband was a very successful businessman whose income was $895,898 a year. The wife did not work outside the home. The court determined that with an income of $895,898, the SSAG indicated a range of $18,555 at the low end, $20,199 at the mid-range and $21,843 at the high end. However, as the SSAG clearly stated that when the payor's income was greater than the $350,000 ceiling, these formulas should no longer be automatically applied to divide income beyond that threshold. The court noted that where the payor's income is $350,000, the SSAG provided a range of $6,468 at the low end, $7,160 at the mid-range and $7,893 at the high end. The wife estimated her total monthly expenses at $20,861.67. The court considered that the wife's expenses for the categories of household expense, vacation and personal expenses were excessive. The court took into account the wife's needs and the fact that with incomes over $350,000 the SSAG should not be followed automatically in deciding that spousal support should be fixed at $8,000 a month.

*Where spousal support is ordered above the SSAG ceiling, it is not necessary to make a finding on the payor's income* — Colivas v. Colivas, 2013 CarswellOnt 193, 2013 ONSC 168 (Ont. S.C.J.). Here, the wife sought interim spousal and child support. The judge found that the husband's finances were opaque in the extreme and ordered spousal support and child support based on the lifestyle the parties had enjoyed prior to separation. True determination of income was to be done at trial. The judge found that spousal support did not require a particular income to be found, but child support did.

*Where the payor spouse's income is extremely high, support will be ordered at a level below the SSAG range* — McCain v. McCain, 2012 CarswellOnt 16853, 2012 ONSC 7344, 34 R.F.L. (7th) 82 (Ont. S.C.J.). The wife was awarded temporary spousal support at below the SSAG range. The husband had an annual income of more than $9 million, and it was a long-term, traditional marriage. The judge, after setting aside the support provision in the parties' marriage contract, found that the wife was entitled to compensatory support and ordered $175,000 monthly.

*Interim support in cases where payor incomes are above the SSAG ceiling — awards of support will reflect the needs of the parties and be awarded at a level which reflects means and needs* — Maskobi v. Maskobi, 2010 CarswellOnt 2742, 2010 ONSC 2540 (Ont. S.C.J.). The husband conceded entitlement, and his income was considerably above the SSAG ceiling. As such, the judge awarded interim support at an amount that reflected the means and needs of the parties. Support was awarded at a level that was above the wife's monthly expenses in order for her to relocate and to aid her in the transitional period. However, it was well below SSAG amounts.

*The SSAG rejected — high spousal support award* —Martin v. Martin, 2006 CarswellOnt 4876, 40 R.F.L. (6th) 32, 81 O.R. (3d) 503, 81 O.R. (3d) 495, 272 D.L.R. (4th) 666, 214 O.A.C. 140, [2006] O.J. No. 3238 (Ont. C.A.), affirming 2004 CarswellOnt 5438, 12 R.F.L. (6th) 415, [2004] O.T.C. 1139, [2004] O.J. No. 5170 (Ont. S.C.J.). The parties were married for about 26 years. The husband's gross income was $1,382,000. The wife's investment income was $80,000. The husband was a professional hockey coach and the wife primarily looked after the children. The husband was ordered to continue paying the $1,000 child support that he had been paying under the interim separation agreement. The biggest issue was spousal support. The wife argued that the husband should pay to her 35 to 45% of his gross income. The trial judge, Power J., rejected any formulaic approach and the SSAG. He noted that the wife received $1.7 million in equalization, a significant amount of which was income-generating wealth. Further, no case was made out to justify an equitable apportionment of the husband's income as Power J. rejected that the wife had contributed equally to acquiring the husband's income. Power J. instead noted that this would ignore the husband's talents as a hockey coach. He awarded spousal support of $27,000/month. This award was upheld on appeal. Armstrong J.A. concluded that the spousal support award was not a redistribution of capital. Further, the case was unique in that the parties saved large sums of money due to the instability of the husband's job as a hockey coach. The spousal support amount was a high award, but it was justified in that it met the wife's day-to-day needs (which were modest during the marriage and continued to be modest) and it satisfied her need for financial security.

The SSAG should not be applied on a secondary arbitration where the payor's income is over $350,000, the order requested is effectively a variation order, and the parties had an arbitration agreement which did not specify the use of the SSAG — Myers v. Vickar, 2012 CarswellOnt 11113, 2012 ONSC 5004, 26 R.F.L. (7th) 227 (Ont. S.C.J.). The wife argued that the arbitrator erred in not considering the Spousal Support Advisory Guidelines. The court noted that the parties' arbitration agreement did not address the use of the SSAG and that the SSAG are not binding legislation. The particular circumstances of the parties formed exceptions to the SSAG in any case. The judge found the arbitrator had not erred in declining to apply the SSAG.

Where the payor's income is above the SSAG ceiling, the SSAG will be of limited assistance — Bodenstein v. Bodenstein, 2012 CarswellOnt 2938, 2012 ONSC 1493, [2012] O.J. No. 996 (Ont. S.C.J.). This was an interim variation of support. The parties were married for 20 years and had two children whose custody followed a dual nesting arrangement. Ongoing spousal support was ordered on a non-compensatory basis. The SSAG was considered, but was found to be of limited assistance, as the payor spouse's income was above the ceiling of the SSAG at $413,000.

Payor's income $9,740,000 — SSAG not followed — Goriuk v. Turton, 2011 CarswellBC 1216, 2011 BCSC 652, 2 R.F.L. (7th) 180 (B.C.S.C.). The parties were common-law spouses who cohabited for 7 years. There were no children. At the time of the separation in September 2009, the man was 36 and the woman was 40 years old. The man was a musician with an annual income of approximately $9,740,000. The woman was a horse trainer who was receiving $10,000 per month in voluntary payments from the man. Noting that under the SSAG the mid range was $95,760 per month, the judge considered Professors Rogerson and Thompson's "The Advisory Guidelines Three Months Later" which stated "When the payor's income exceeds the ceiling, the formulas no longer operate and you are into the wild blue yonder of individual decisionmaking." Holding that the woman's expenses represent the reasonable elements of the parties' previous lifestyle, the judge ordered the man to pay interim support in the amount of $25,000 per month based on the parties' means and needs. The trial was to take place in 4 months time.

Payor's income over $350,000 — SSAG used — Gibson v. Gibson, 2011 CarswellOnt 6951, 2011 ONSC 4406 (Ont. S.C.J.), additional reasons at 2011 CarswellOnt 10072, 2011 ONSC 5602 (Ont. S.C.J.). The parties were married for 19 years and had two children, one at university and the other 13 years of age. Although the husband, a successful financial expert, had previously earned $1 million per year, his income for 2010 was $696,838. The wife, aged 47, who had not worked throughout the marriage had retrained and was held to have an imputed income of $30,000 per year. The husband paid the younger child's school fees, a proportionate share of the sports and activities and medical expenses, and one half of the older child's expenses. In considering the SSAG calculations, the judge commented that "despite the fact [the husband] is a high income earner I find no reason to depart from the SSAG to determine an appropriate range of spousal support for [him] to pay". The court ordered that the husband pay $19,000 per month, in the mid range, until the husband's income for 2011 was determined. No order as to duration was made.

*Imputed income of payor $628,586, SSAG a starting point and cross check of judicial analysis* — *Berta v. Berta*, 2011 CarswellOnt 3, 2012 ONSC 42 (Ont. S.C.J.). The parties had been married for 27 years and were joint owners of a successful company of which the husband was president and CEO. There were no children. On an application for interim spousal support by the wife, the court imputed to the husband an income of $628,586 and to the wife an income of $227,300. The judge commented that the wife was entitled to the standard of living that she had enjoyed prior to the separation. The court ordered that the husband pay to the wife $13,200 per month for interim spousal support, in light of the long-term marriage and other considerations under the Act. The SSAG, he said, "are instructive, but not wholly applicable in this case as the income levels exceed $350,000. However, I have utilized the Guidelines as a starting point and cross check of my analysis."

*Payor's income deemed to be $660,000* — *ceiling provided by SSAG should not be considered a basis for denying appropriate interim support* — *Trombetta v. Trombetta*, 2011 CarswellOnt 318, 2011 ONSC 394, [2011] O.J. No. 281 (Ont. S.C.J.). The parties had been married for 20 years and were divorced in 1996. There were two children of the marriage who were adults. In an interim motion for interim spousal support in the context of a Motion to Change a Final Order, the husband's income was deemed to be $660,000 per year (although the judge mentioned that his income jumped from $43,000 in 1996 to over $2 million in 2008). The wife, aged 52, was not working as she suffered from breast cancer. The husband was ordered to pay the amount of $15,000 per month interim support, up from $3,500 per month, until trial. The judge indicated that this amount was at the low end of the range for the SSAG based on the deemed income amount of $660,000 per year, and would be higher if the husband's income was deemed to be $1 or $2 million per year.

*Support ordered at low end of SSAG* — *Marzara v. Marzara*, 2011 CarswellBC 742, 2011 BCSC 408 (B.C.S.C.). The parties were married in Iran and, with their two children, emigrated to Canada where their third child was born. When the parties separated, they had been married for 26 years. The wife was 51, and the husband was 59 years of age. They had had a traditional marriage. The husband's income was held to be $374,018. Although the wife had worked very little outside of the home during the marriage, an income of $12,000 plus considerable income from investments resulted in a total income of $92,800 to $104,400 being imputed to her. Given the uncertainties in determining the incomes of both parties, an amount at the low end was chosen and the husband was ordered to pay indefinite spousal support to the wife in the amount of $9,200 per month.

*Payor's income $540,000* — *support lower than the SSAG, but of longer duration due to the wife's learning disability* — *Bockhold v. Bockhold*, 2010 CarswellBC 369, 2010 BCSC 214, [2010] B.C.J. No. 283 (B.C.S.C. [In Chambers]). At the time of separation, the wife was 45 and the husband was 43 years of age. There were two children of the marriage, each under 17, at the time of separation. The husband's income was $540,000 and the wife's income was fixed at $18,000.The judge ordered indefinite spousal support for the wife in the amount of $10,000 per month.

*Where the husband's income was $372,000, the SSAG were applied and the high amount, $14,954, was found to be appropriate to take into account investment income which was available to the husband from a holding company* — *Bot v. Bot*, 2010 CarswellOnt 5548, 2010 ONSC 3805 (Ont. S.C.J.).

*Interim support ordered at the higher end of the SSAG range to take into account the availability of investment income to the husband from his holding company* — *Bot v. Bot, supra*.

The parties were married for 25 years and had two adult children who were no longer dependants. The parties owned an engineering and construction company. The husband's income was held to be $372,000 for support purposes and incidental income of $9,600 was attributed to the wife. The court ordered that the husband pay support for the wife in the amount of $14,954 per month.

Where the payor's income is above the $350,000 ceiling an examination of the recipient's budget, when reasonable, may result in an interim support award below the formula amounts — Maskobi v. Maskobi, 2010 CarswellOnt 2742, 2010 ONSC 2540 (Ont. S.C.J.). The parties began cohabiting in 2000 and married in 2002. They had two children before separating in 2009. The wife was a stay-at-home mother and the husband earned $1.1 million annually. The judge ordered interim support lower than the SSAG formula would indicate, in addition to child support. He emphasized the need to avoid income-sharing prior to the trial on the merits, and carefully examined the wife's proposed budget. He awarded an amount higher than her proposed monthly budget in order to allow for relocation costs.

Where there is unsatisfactory evidence available, a lump-sum payment for interim spousal support will not be ordered and Guideline amounts will be appropriate — Poirier v. Poirier, 2010 CarswellOnt 744, 2010 ONSC 920, 81 R.F.L. (6th) 161, [2010] O.J. No. 536 (Ont. S.C.J.), additional reasons at 2010 CarswellOnt 4889, 2010 ONSC 2291, 89 R.F.L. (6th) 459 (Ont. S.C.J.). The parties were married for 26 years and had six children, three of whom lived with the wife. The husband's income was between $360,000 and $568,000 annually. The wife requested a lump-sum payment of $100,000 interim spousal support. The judge ordered spousal support of $10,000 a month, which was towards the lower end of the SSAG formula range. This was, in part, to allow the parties to gather better evidence to allow the court to make an appropriate determination of support at trial.

Where the payor's income is above the $350,000 ceiling, long-term needs of both parties must be considered in determining an interim amount of spousal support — Denofrio v. Denofrio, 2009 CarswellOnt 4601, 72 R.F.L. (6th) 52, [2009] O.J. No. 3295 (Ont. S.C.J.), additional reasons at 2009 CarswellOnt 7172, 75 R.F.L. (6th) 417 (Ont. S.C.J.). The parties were married for 54 years and had four children. The husband's annual income was $4.1 million (including the receipt of capital assets from the dissolution of his companies). The wife applied for $150,000 monthly in support. The judge awarded interim support of $15,000 monthly, on the ground that payments in the amount requested by the wife would have the effect of distributing marital property, which would be more properly effected by the trial on the merits. The judge found that it would not be just, fair or reasonable to go beyond the $350,000 payor income threshold found in the SSAG, especially because to do so could compromise the long-term needs of both parties. The husband, who was represented by his litigation guardians, suffered from Alzheimer's disease and was in a long-term care facility which was a significant drain on his finances.

Spousal support of $20,000 per month found to be appropriate — Dyck v. Dyck, 2009 CarswellMan 176, 2009 MBQB 112, 239 Man. R. (2d) 137, [2009] M.J. No. 139 (Man. Q.B.). The parties were marred for 8 years and had two children. The husband's income was $3,045,205 per year. The wife brought a motion for interim spousal support of $20,000 per month, which the court awarded. The court found that the wife's request for $20,000 per month was reasonable in the context of her budget, cash flow and lifestyle during the marriage. The husband had enough funds to ensure that the needs of both households were met.

Although the court referred to a presumption that SSAG was used as a cross-check or starting point, SSAG was not used — Korkola v. Korkola, 2009 CarswellOnt 395, [2009] O.J. No. 343 (Ont. S.C.J.). The parties cohabited for 2 years and were married for 7 years. There were 2 children of the marriage, aged 7 and 4. The husband was 36 years old and had an income of

$540,000 (with a projected $19,000 RRSP contribution). The wife was 32 years old and had an imputed income of $50,000. The court ordered the husband to pay spousal support to the wife in the amount of $9,212 per month.

*Income over $750,000 — interim support — SSAG applied — amount at low end of the range — Wilson v. Wilson*, 2009 CarswellBC 3504, 2009 BCSC 1777 (B.C.S.C.). The parties had been married for 7 years. The husband had an income of at least $750,000 per year. The wife had no marketable skills and was a stay-at-home mother. The court was satisfied that the wife had reasonable annual expenses of $270,000 and the husband had the ability to pay. The range of spousal support was $14,204 to $16,737 per month. Given the amount of child support that was $14,265 a month and the family's expenses, the court awarded spousal support of $11,600 per month for 11 years.

*Income over $350,000, SSAG not used — Dobbin v. Dobbin*, 2009 CarswellNfld 50, 2009 NLUFC 11, 284 Nfld. & P.E.I.R. 6, 875 A.P.R. 6[2009] N.J. No. 52 (N.L.U.F.C.). The husband had an income not lower than $1,500,000 and the wife an income of between $75,000 and $100,000. The parties had been married for 39 years. The court used the Divorce-mate Software to consider the ranges of spousal support utilizing the SSAG. However, it did not use the ranges suggested because of the ceiling rationale in the Guidelines. It did use the software to consider the final apportionment of annual income based upon certain spousal support payments. The court ordered spousal support of $20,000 net of taxes per month.

*Although SSAG not referred to, interim spousal support order close to the SSAG amount — Turk v. Turk*, 2008 CarswellOnt 512, 50 R.F.L. (6th) 211, [2008] O.J. No. 397 (Ont. S.C.J.). The parties were married for 22 years and had 2 children who were in university. The 51-year-old husband was a lawyer and a real estate developer who ran 3 companies. The 48-year-old wife was a homemaker and occasionally assisted the husband. The judge attributed income of $1 million a year to the husband. In determining that interim spousal support of $20,000 per month was to be paid to the wife, the court commented that it was a long-term marriage and the lifestyle was very high. There were the resources to continue that lifestyle notwithstanding that there were now two households. It was appropriate in this case that the two households each had approximately 50% of the net disposable income.

*The SSAG used when income just above ceiling — Abelson v. Mitra*, 2008 CarswellBC 1873, 2008 BCSC 1197, 59 R.F.L. (6th) 364, [2008] B.C.J. No. 1672 (B.C.S.C.). When the payor's income is close to the ceiling, the formula ranges will often be used to determine the amount of spousal support. In this case, the husband's income was $355,000 per year. The court used the SSAG to determine spousal support since the husband's income was close to the ceiling.

*Different incomes used for child and spousal support calculation — B. (J.E.) v. B. (G.)*, 2008 CarswellBC 1589, 2008 BCSC 528, 57 R.F.L. (6th) 422, [2008] B.C.J. No. 758 (B.C. Master). In some high-income with child support formula cases, the courts have calculated the Table Amount of child support on the payor's full income and then calculated the formula range for spousal support based on a payor's gross income of $350,000 per annum. In this case, child support for two children was based on the husband's actual income of $1,356,374.62 per year and spousal support was based on $350,000 per year.

*Pure discretion approach appropriate for support above the ceiling — Bozak v. Bozak*, 2008 CarswellBC 2398, 2008 BCSC 1458, [2008] B.C.J. No. 2080 (B.C.S.C.). The wife's income was imputed to be $78,000 annually and the husband's income was $512,000 for spousal support purposes. The parties had two children, aged 9 and 11. Under the SSAG, the suggested range of spousal support was between approximately $6,448 and $11,617, for an indefinite period. The "pure discretion" approach takes into account the actual amount of child support to avoid an absurd result. The wife left the marriage with $1 million dollars in assets. She was young and she had an ability to earn a significant income. Given all the circumstances, in order to meet compensatory and any possible non-compensatory objectives for spousal support, the court awarded $6,000 a month, to terminate June 30, 2016 when the younger child was expected to finish high school.

*Payor income of $672K per year — below-guideline range ordered* — M. (C.L.) v. M. (R.A.), 2008 CarswellBC 695, 2008 BCSC 217, [2008] B.C.J. No. 608 (B.C.S.C.), additional reasons at 2008 CarswellBC 1931, 2008 BCSC 1240 (B.C.S.C.). The parties, who were divorced, had three children. The wife had remarried. Her second husband, Mr. B., was paying support to his former spouse. If the SSAG were applied to the first husband, Mr. M.'s support obligation, it would have resulted in a range from $7,736 to $19,500 per month. The court ordered Mr. M. to continue to pay her spousal support at $6,000 a month until the first day of the month following the month in 2009 in which Mr. B was no longer required to pay spousal support. At that time, the B. family unit would have more financial resources at its disposal. For 1 year afterwards, Mr. M. was to pay spousal support of $4,000 a month, reduced by $2,000 a month in the following year, so that Mr. M.'s obligation to pay spousal support should end in the year 2011. In its additional reasons at 2008 CarswellBC 1931, the court accepted that Mr. B.'s obligation to pay spousal support was "to decrease by $1,000 a month in July, 2009 and that he has an obligation to continue to pay $1,000 a month for two years after July 2009." Ms. B. submitted that the continued obligation of Mr. B. should be reflected in the court's award of spousal support. The court accepted the argument and found that it was appropriate and fair to change the directions for payment of spousal support. Thus, Mr. M.'s obligation to pay spousal support was to continue at $6,000 a month until August 2009 when it would be reduced to $4,500 a month. It was to be further reduced to $2,500 a month in August 2010. His obligation to pay spousal support would end with the July 2011 payment.

*Payor income of $750 per year — below guidance quantum ordered* — Campbell v. Campbell, 2008 CarswellBC 230, 2008 BCSC 154, [2008] B.C.J. No. 202 (B.C.S.C. [In Chambers]). Interim spousal support of $1,500 per month was ordered. The wife, the custodial payor, had an income of $750,000 per year and the recipient husband had an imputed income of $6,000 in 2007. The SSAG range was $2,552 to $3,403 per month. This was an interim application and the evidence had not been tested by cross-examination and full document disclosure. The court stated that while it considered that a court should try to maintain the status quo and apply the SSAG unless there were exceptional circumstances, in the case at bar the court found that there were exceptional circumstances, including the husband's past substance abuse and his failure to work to his ability. Although there was evidence that he had recently abstained from the use of cocaine, the wife's submission that he would use spousal support to finance his habit has some credence.

*Payor income of $850k — SSAG not used* — Lewis v. Lewis, 2008 CarswellOnt 3263, 55 R.F.L. (6th) 454, [2008] O.J. No. 2227 (Ont. S.C.J.). On this interim application, the husband was found to have an average income of $850,000 per year. The SSAG were found to have "little, if any, application" and were not used.

*Payor income $1.09 million — amount below SSAG range ordered* — O. (S.) v. O. (C.S.), 2008 CarswellBC 444, 2008 BCSC 283, [2008] B.C.J. No. 407 (B.C. Master). The range was $29,493-$34,324/month; $25,000 per month was ordered on an interim basis.

*For an income of $823,322, SAGG is an important tool in determination of the quantum and duration of temporary spousal support* — Jackson v. Boyle-Jackson, 2009 CarswellOnt 861 (Ont. S.C.J.), additional reasons at 2009 CarswellOnt 1414 (Ont. S.C.J.). The parties were married for 29 years and there was one child of the marriage. The husband was 55 years old and earned an income of $823,322 per annum. The wife was 53 years old and because she suffered from a brain injury in a car accident in 1988, she had not worked since that time. She received $8,000 per annum from structured settlement payments and from CPP. The judge stated that the family's lifestyle was high and, therefore, it was appropriate for an approximate equal division of net disposable income. Accordingly, the court ordered that the husband pay the wife $18,900 per month, which he stated was approximately in the middle of the SSAG range.

On the payor's application to terminate spousal support in a separation agreement, held support increased to high end of SAGG range as support compensatory — M. (J.W.J.) v. R. (T.E.), 2007 CarswellBC 383, 2007 BCSC 252, [2007] B.C.J. No. 358 (B.C.S.C.). The parties married young, at 21 and 22 years of age and the wife left a nursing programme and worked at a clerical job while the husband completed his undergraduate degree and attended law school. The wife later withdrew from employment to manage their household and to remain home with the couples' three children. The husband worked long hours and had a successful practice. The parties lived on a farm (she owned 25% with her family) and then in a house purchased from the proceeds of her inheritance. When the parties were 40 and 41 years old respectively, 19 years after their marriage, they separated. The children were 15, 14, and 11 years of age and resided with the wife. The husband was earning $400,000, and they entered into a separation agreement by which he was to pay child support, plus spousal support in the amount of $2,841 per month, as well as an annual $10,000 per year. The assets were divided 66% in favour of the wife. The wife retained the 25% interest she had in the farm from her family. Four years later, the husband had remarried with 2 additional children and the wife had also remarried. The husband was earning between $600,000 and $700,000. At the time, the wife's assets were somewhat higher than the husband's, because the farm sold for more than anticipated, but she had cashed in her RRSP and spent the funds. The judge held that the wife had suffered economic disadvantage arising from the marriage and its breakdown and had not been fully compensated for that loss. At separation, she was 40 years old, unemployed, had minimal marketable skills and ongoing child-care responsibilities. The husband had a well-established law practice. Despite the asset distribution, the wife was unlikely to recover from the economic disadvantage. The court imputed to her an income of $30,000 and held that the SSAG were a useful mechanism to calculate the wife's shortfall in income. Since the SSAG do not provide for income over $350,000, $350,000 was used for the calculation and it was ordered that the wife would receive spousal support in the amount of $3,772 per month, reviewable in 2020.

Spousal support above SSAG range for high-income case not clearly wrong — M. (D.R.) v. M. (R.B.), 2006 CarswellBC 3177, 2006 BCSC 1921, 63 B.C.L.R. (4th) 331, [2006] B.C.J. No. 3299 (B.C.S.C.). The court affirmed a Master's order which had found the husband's annual income to be $750,000 and awarded the wife $8,500 per month for interim spousal support. This amount was above the SSAG range. The decision, however, was not clearly wrong and was allowed to stand.

Mid range Guideline amount granted without explanation — E. (Y.J.) v. R. (Y.N.), 2007 CarswellBC 782, 2007 BCSC 509, [2007] B.C.J. No. 771 (B.C.S.C.). Both parties qualified as chartered accountants. The husband developed a very successful career and the wife, while she had done some part-time work over the course of the marriage, was at the time of the hearing, unemployed and had thus far been unsuccessful in reintegrating into the work force. The court found that it was unrealistic to expect the wife to return to work before the end of 2007. The court calculated spousal support based on a Guidelines income of $602,400 and assuming no salary for the wife, and awarded spousal support in the sum of $15,128 per month (being the middle range figure) commencing April 1, 2007 and each month thereafter including December 1, 2007. Commencing January 1, 2008 and based on the husband's Guideline Income of $602,400 and the wife's imputed Guideline Income of $35,000, the court awarded spousal support of $14,148 per month, being the middle range between $12,849 and $15,447. This amount would continue to be paid indefinitely, pending some material change in circumstances which triggers a review which is sought by either spouse.

## 16.2 Floors

*Caution against using the SSAGS where a payor's income is between $20,000 and $30,000 per year is directed to persons whose real income is between $20,000 and $30,000 and not where parts of real income are not included for spousal support purposes – Brisson v. Brisson*, 2012 CarswellBC 3051, 2012 BCCA 396, 22 R.F.L. (7th) 1, 39 B.C.L.R. (5th) 1, 328 B.C.A.C. 163, 558 W.A.C. 163 (B.C.C.A.). The caution is based on the idea that "support should not be paid until the payor's gross income is sufficient to support the payor and leave something over to pay the spouse." In this case, the husband's income was comfortably in excess of the amounts where the caution should be used. The husband had an annual real income of $38,875 comprised of income from a public service pension, Old Age Security, Canada Pension Plan and a Veterans Affairs disability benefit. The wife had an income of $11,550 from part-time employment.

*Where a payor's real income is greater than $20,000, the SSAG floor will not be taken into account – Brisson v. Brisson*, 2012 CarswellBC 3051, 2012 BCCA 396, 22 R.F.L. (7th) 1, 39 B.C.L.R. (5th) 1, 355 D.L.R. (4th) 720, 328 B.C.A.C. 163, 558 W.A.C. 163 (B.C.C.A.). The parties had a very long-term marriage (37 years) and at trial, the judge determined no spousal support was payable because the current and future financial circumstances of the parties would be roughly equivalent. The Court of Appeal rejected the husband's argument that no spousal support should be payable as his income was less than $20,000 when CPP and pension were removed. The Court found that the SSAG floor referred to a payor's real income, rather than pre-tax income, and ordered support.

*Need on the part of a recipient spouse will not be sufficient alone to disregard the floor in the SSAG – D. (I.) v. D. (D.)*, 2013 CarswellBC 28, 2013 BCSC 45 (B.C.S.C.). This was an appeal concerning spousal and child support. The payor husband's income for spousal support purposes was determined to be $19,000. The judge found no spousal support should be payable based on the "floor" of the SSAG. The judge found that need on the part of the recipient spouse was not sufficient to disregard the floor, especially when the marriage was short (as in this case).

*Where a payor has no ability to pay without causing himself or herself hardship, spousal support will not be ordered – Heywood v. Heywood*, 2013 CarswellOnt 189, 2013 ONSC 58 (Ont. S.C.J.). The parties were married for over 35 years and had adult children. They concluded a separation agreement which provided for spousal support. The husband had been laid off subsequent to the agreement and had a job working at minimum wage resulting in not more than $20,000 annually. The judge determined the wife had no ability to earn employment income. The husband sought termination of support on the basis of the SSAG floors. The judge found that to disregard the rationale of the "floors" would cause the husband hardship and reduce his motivation to continue employment. The judge found any spousal support order was destined to fail and would result in both parties being on social assistance. The husband was not obligated to liquidate his RRSPs as to do so would result in "double dipping".

*Where the payor spouse has 'means', although below the floor for support, arrears of support will not be completely rescinded – Oliver v. Flanagan*, 2012 CarswellNB 64, 2012 NBQB 49, 18 R.F.L. (7th) 390, 384 N.B.R. (2d) 181, 995 A.P.R. 181 (N.B.Q.B.). The parties had been separated for fifteen years after a 28 year marriage. An equalization had never been made. The judge found that, for the majority of the time when arrears were accruing, the husband did not have income above the "floor" found in the SSAG. He ordered $200 monthly in support to reflect the fact that the husband had additional means other than his income, because he had received a pay-out of his pension. The wife had an order to the effect that she was entitled to half the pension but there was no realistic prospect she would be able to enforce that judgment. The judge used his discretion in deciding that total rescission of arrears would be unfair, as the wife had some prospect on collecting through garnishment.

*SSAG assume that the "without children" formula should apply to spouses earning over $20,000 — That low threshold may be appropriate in some situations, such as when spouses own their own homes, but not in circumstances where the application of the SSAG would result in the payor spouse no longer being self-sufficient — House v. House*, 2012 CarswellBC 372, 2012 BCSC 197, 19 R.F.L. (7th) 92 (B.C.S.C.).

*Spousal support ordered — Gustafson v. Gustafson*, 2010 CarswellMan 17, 2010 MBQB 10, 248 Man. R. (2d) 255 (Man. Q.B.). In this case, the court addressed whether the husband was financially able to pay spousal support to his wife. The husband earned $20,476 and the wife earned $17,898 per year. The court acknowledged that the husband's income was just over the threshold for support suggested by the SSAG. The SSAG guidelines indicated a range of support from $81 to $100 per month. The court analyzed the husband's budget and concluded that he was able to pay the wife $75 in spousal support per month.

*No spousal support ordered because husband could not pay — Scheiris v. Scheiris*, 2009 CarswellOnt 5405, [2009] O.J. No. 3795 (Ont. S.C.J.). The parties were married for 42 years. The husband earned just over $10,000 per year based on his Canada pension and old age security benefits. The wife received $299.45 per month from her share of the husband's Canada pension plan benefits. The SSAG suggested a range of support of $188 to $250 per month. The court found that the husband did not have an ability to pay spousal support.

*SSAG indicated that neither party entitled to spousal support — Kajorinne v. Kajorinne*, 2008 CarswellOnt 4229 (Ont. S.C.J.). The parties separated after 10 years of marriage and two children. The wife sought spousal support. The husband was laid off from his employment as a construction electrician. His income was determined to be $22,000 based on employment insurance benefits and the wife's income was $26,000; however, she had recently been laid off as well. The SSAG indicated that no spousal support should be paid at their income levels, which the court followed.

*Spousal support ordered despite husband's income less than $20,000 — M. (W.M.) v. M. (H.S.)*, 2007 CarswellBC 2667, 2007 BCSC 1629 (B.C.S.C.). The parties were married for 27 years. The wife was in her late fifties and had no income while the husband was 63 and had an annual income of $17,800. The wife brought an application for spousal support. Although spousal support is generally not paid if the payor's income is less than $20,000, in this case the court made an exception because the marriage was long-term. The SSAG range of support was $550 to $750 per month and the husband was ordered to pay spousal support of $600 per month for an indefinite period of time.

*Court ordered spousal support despite payor's low income — Skirten v. Lengyel*, 2007 CarswellOnt 1020 (Ont. S.C.J.). The parties cohabitated for 5 years and had one child. In addressing the issue of spousal support, the court noted that based on Mr. Lengyel's income at $24,960 and Ms. Skirten's income at $16,682 the SSAG suggested that no spousal support is payable. Notwithstanding the SSAG, the court stated that since Mr. Lengyel owned an unencumbered home and a motorcycle valued at approximately $20,000, some spousal support was appropriate. Accordingly, the court ordered spousal support of $50 per month.

*Where the payor spouse is found to have no ability to pay, support will be terminated — Scheiris v. Scheiris*, 2009 CarswellOnt 5405, [2009] O.J. No. 3795 (Ont. S.C.J.). The parties were married for 42 years and, prior to his retirement, the husband's income was approximately $35,000 in worker's compensation payments. He made a motion to vary support from $900 monthly based on his changed income. The husband's income after retirement was only $10,000 a year of CPP and OAS, lower than the "floor" of the SSAG of $20,000. He had received worker's compensation, but this ended after retirement. The judge terminated support payments.

Although the wife in this case was only receiving $3,600 a year in CPP payments, the judge found the husband had no ability to pay. The wife was being supported by the parties' children.

*Spousal support ordered despite the fact the payor's income was below the floor amount —* Pratt v. Pratt, 2008 CarswellNB 116, 2008 NBQB 94, 334 N.B.R. (2d) 22, 858 A.P.R. 22, [2008] N.B.J. No. 85 (N.B.Q.B.). The court stated that it had "considered" the SSAG, but did not elaborate.

# CHAPTER 17

## EXCEPTIONS

*Where use of ranges and restructuring have not yielded appropriate result; compensatory or non-compensatory support; exceptions triggered by compensatory claims*

> Exceptions are the last step in a support determination in cases covered by formulas. The formulas provide two other opportunities, discussed above, to shape awards that are responsive to the exigencies of individual cases. First, the ranges for amount and duration provide considerable scope to adjust within those ranges to the particular facts of any case (Chapter 9). Second, restructuring provides a further means to push and pull amount and duration above and below the ranges generated by the formula (Chapter 10). Only if neither of these steps can accommodate the unusual facts of a specific case should it become necessary to resort to these exceptions. (SSAG Chapter 12)
>
> The delineation of the compensatory and/or non-compensatory basis for entitlement in a particular case is relevant . . . to determine whether or not the case justifies a departure from the ranges as an exception. (SSAG Chapter 4.2)
>
> two exceptions are triggered by compensatory claims that may not be adequately satisfied by the formula ranges: the compensatory exception for short marriages without children and, in cases with children, the s. 15.3 exception for compensatory claims that must be deferred because of the priority of child support. The application of both of these exceptions therefore requires a delineation of the basis for entitlement. (SSAG Chapter 4.2)

This chapter is divided into the following sections:

17.1 General
17.2 Compelling Financial Circumstances in the Interim Period
17.3 Debt Payment
17.4 Prior Support Obligations
17.5 Illness and Disability
17.6 Compensatory Exception in Short Marriages Without Children
17.7 Property Division, Reapportionment of Property
17.8 Basic Needs/Hardship: Without Child Support, Custodial Payor Formulas
17.9 Non-taxable Payor Income
17.10 Non-primary Parent to Fulfil Parenting Role under the Custodial Payor Formula
17.11 Special Needs of Child
17.12 Small Amounts, Inadequate Compensation under the With Child Support Formula
17.13 Other Grounds for Exceptions

## 17.1 General

The exceptions are departures from the *Spousal Support Advisory Guideline* formula ranges. They are to be used when neither the Guideline ranges nor restructuring provides the appropriate result. The British Columbia Court of Appeal case of *S. (R.M.) v. S. (F.P.C.)*, 2011 CarswellBC 170, 2011 BCCA 53, 90 R.F.L. (6th) 1, 14 B.C.L.R. (5th) 84, 299 B.C.A.C. 186, 508 W.A.C. 186, [2011] B.C.J. No. 174 (B.C.C.A.), gives a clear statement of the proper use of the exceptions. Smith, J.A., writing for the majority at paragraphs 66 and 68, states that Professors Carol Rogerson and Rollie Thompson, the authors of the *Spousal Support Advisory Guidelines*

> ... recognized that there would be exceptions to the *SSAG* formulas where circumstances might require a deviation from the ranges. In that regard, they defined certain exceptions to the formulas that would provide "considerable room for the exercise of discretion under the Advisory Guidelines but [the discretion] will be exercised within a much more defined structure than existed before — one with clearer starting points" (see *SSAG: The Final Version*, July 2008, at p. 2).

The SSAG exceptions come into play after considering the ranges and restructuring: only if neither of these can adequately accommodate the facts in a particular case does one need to turn to the exceptions. See Professors Rogerson and Thompson's *The Spousal Support Advisory Guidelines: A New and Improved User's Guide to the Final Version* at chapter 12.

Thus, where the formula ranges and restructuring under the *Spousal Support Advisory Guidelines* have not yielded an appropriate result in terms of the quantum of spousal support, exceptions to the formula ranges should be considered. When circumstances fall within the Guideline exceptions, there is considerable opportunity for the exercise of discretion. The exceptions are available to either the potential support payor or payee. They can be invoked either to justify higher or lower spousal support than the amounts provided in the formula ranges.

In some of the early cases, the courts departed from the ranges, but not in fact on the basis of the exceptions. Instead, it seems that the courts did not like the current support law or did not apply the current law properly.

So far, courts and counsel have been reluctant to use the exceptions. Further, courts occasionally apply the logic behind the exceptions without explicitly referring to them in cases which seem to warrant a departure from the formula ranges for disability or other reasons, and instead, rely on judicial discretion to depart from formula ranges.

There are eleven exceptions set out in the *Spousal Support Advisory Guidelines* and this chapter is divided accordingly with a final section on other possible grounds for exceptions. Further grounds for exceptions have been and will be found. See 17.12, below. However, as the SSAG are advisory only, it would still be possible for the court to find that the SSAG do not have any application to a particular case. The court could then simply use its discretion in determining quantum.

## Burden of proof

Following conventional legal principles, a spouse who claims to fall within one of these exceptions ought to bear the burden of proof. (SSAG s. 12)

*"A spouse who claims to fall within an exception from the SSAGs bears the burden of proof to establish the exception"* — *Zdrill v. Zdrill*, 2011 CarswellOnt 2886, 2011 ONSC 2188 (Ont. S.C.J.). The parties in this case had two young children who resided with the father. During the

marriage, the mother was essentially a stay-at-home parent. Post-separation, she experienced financial difficulties and was subsisting on social assistance at the time of trial. The court found that no income should be attributed to the wife, who was clearly entitled to compensatory support, because of her role in the marriage. At the time of this interim motion for spousal support, she was suffering from depression and had never worked full-time. The husband argued that he did not have the ability to pay and invoked a number of exceptions found in the SSAG, namely the compelling financial circumstances post-separation and the "custodial payor" exception. He also invoked the basic needs/hardship exception. The court found that the fact that the father was paying the familial debts after separation merely continued the situation that was present before separation. A payor will not meet the onus of showing that the Custodial Payor exception applies where the ranges within the regular formula are sufficient to take account of this fact. The test for basic needs/ hardship is not met where the payor had not shown that there would be a sufficient change in the standard of living of the children that this should be considered an exception. The husband earned $58,407 and the wife received social assistance of $6,089, which resulted in a range from a low of $803 to a high of $1,071. The court, taking into account that the father had custody of the children, ordered interim spousal support in the amount of $803 per month until further order of the court.

*Burden of proving exception* — *Garritsen v. Garritsen*, 2009 CarswellBC 868, 2009 BCSC 124, 71 R.F.L. (6th) 106, [2009] B.C.J. No. 691 (B.C.S.C.). Melnick J. stated at para. 13: "It is noted in the SSAG that the spouse who claims to fall within one of the categorical exceptions ought to bear the burden of proof."


## Judicial comment on the use of the exceptions

*Judges have a discretion to award spousal support above or below the Guideline ranges, even where the circumstances do not fall within the exceptions set out in the Guidelines; the exceptional circumstances set out in s. 12 of the Guidelines are not an exhaustive list* — *Smith v. Smith*, 2011 CarswellNB 377, 2011 NBCA 66, 9 R.F.L. (7th) 286, 336 D.L.R. (4th) 285, 969 A.P.R. 208, 375 N.B.R. (2d) 208 (N.B.C.A.). The parties had been married for 28 years and had two children who were financially independent. At the time of the appeal, the wife was 52 and the husband was 54. The wife had worked throughout the marriage at a variety of jobs and was earning $15,600 a year. However, her employment was uncertain. The husband was earning $62,000 a year. At trial, the wife was awarded $1,000 a month, well below the SSAG range. One of the grounds of appeal was that the trial judge committed an error in law in not applying the SSAG to determine the appropriate quantum of spousal support when the husband had admitted entitlement. The court based its decision on the fact that the trial judge had made a palpable and overriding error in considering the husband's possible debt to be present-day actual debt, a view that was merely speculative. The decision, accordingly, was reviewable and the court could adjust the amount of spousal support. The appeal succeeded on an error of fact. However, in an obiter remark, the court addressed the issue of whether or not a court needs to follow the SSAG. The court stated, at paragraph 37:

> While the Guidelines help to promote consistency in judgments, and therefore a greater measure of certainty in law, they do not constitute law. Therefore, while judges would be wise to follow the Guidelines, and usually do so, they should not be mandated to do so even when their reasons for decision do not bring into play an exception listed in ch.12 of the Guidelines.

The court was of the opinion that there is an obligation upon a judge to explain why he or she departed from the Guideline amounts. The appellate court awarded the wife $1,709.50 in spousal support, an amount at the mid-point of the Guideline range. The Court of Appeal made its calculation using the "Without Children Support Formula" and taking into account the parties' incomes, the length of cohabitation, the wife's age and the fact that she had income at the time of trial.

*Failure to consider the exceptions provided for by the SSAG specifically constitutes an error in principle unless there is another reasonable explanation for the deviance* — D. (T.A.) v. D. (M.K.), 2010 CarswellBC 1623, 2010 BCSC 898 (B.C.S.C.). This case was an appeal from the decision of a Master granting interim compensatory and non-compensatory spousal support to a wife in a long-term, traditional marriage. The Master had awarded an amount that was double the top end of the SSAG range. The judge of the Superior Court found that in a case where the award deviates substantially from the SSAG ranges, and was so much higher that the SSAG, there must be compelling financial circumstances to justify such an extreme departure. There was no such evidence found in this case, where the husband was a custodial payor and the wife did not provide any child support. The court found the award was unreasonable. Spousal support was fixed at the high end of the SSAG range, given the wife's need.

*Where neither the SSAG, nor its exceptions adequately encompass the situation of a given case, the judge may use his discretion to award a different amount of spousal support* — L. (J.A.) v. L. (S.B.J.), 2009 CarswellNS 148, 2009 NSSC 87 (N.S.S.C.), additional reasons at 2009 CarswellNS 223, 2009 NSSC 135 (N.S.S.C.). The judge in this case found that the wife had ongoing need which entitled her to support, and she did not have a stable living situation. However, he found that the husband was simply unable to pay the Guidelines amount suggested by the Custodial Payor exception, because "[t]he custodial parent as payor formula does not provide him with sufficient net disposable income to pay his reasonable living expenses, which include expenses for the children, and to pay the range of spousal support suggested." The wife was awarded $300 in monthly support.

### 17.2 Compelling Financial Circumstances in the Interim Period

When spouses separate, it is not always possible to adjust the household finances quickly. One of the spouses may have to bear large and often unmovable (at least in the short run) expenses, most likely for housing or debts. In most instances, the ranges generated by the formulas will cover these exceptional cases, but there may be some difficulties where marriages are shorter or incomes are lower or property has not yet been divided. Interim spousal support can be adjusted back to the formula amounts once a house has been sold or a spouse has moved or debts have been refinanced. (SSAG Chapter 12.1)

*Where the recipient spouse is paying the expenses for the matrimonial home, this contribution may be considered as a compelling financial circumstance* — Heisler v. Heisler, 2013 CarswellNS 413, 2013 NSFC 3 (N.S. Fam. Ct.). The parties were married for approximately 24 years and had three children. The wife was a homemaker during the marriage and sought, *inter alia*, interim spousal support. Since separation, the husband had been late with mortgage payments, and the wife proposed that interim spousal support should be awarded at the upper end of the table amounts on the basis that she would be responsible for paying the mortgage. The judge found that this was a compelling financial circumstance under the exception to the Guidelines and awarded spousal support at the top end of the range.

*Where a party is not able to support herself post-separation because of issues faced as a newcomer to Canada as a result of the marriage, the compelling financial circumstances in the interim period exception will be used and support above the table amounts will be ordered* — *Singh v. Singh*, 2013 CarswellOnt 14291, 2013 ONSC 6476, 40 R.F.L. (7th) 78, [2013] O.J. No. 4699 (Ont. S.C.J.). The wife applied for interim spousal support. The parties were married for only 7 months. The wife had relocated from India and had left a well-paying job there in order to marry. Her qualifications were not recognized in Canada, and the husband had not paid spousal support since the separation. The judge found the wife was entitled to compensatory, contractual and needs-based spousal support, in part because of the immigration sponsorship undertaken by the husband which was found to constitute an agreement to support. The SSAG were applied using the exception for compelling financial circumstances in the interim period as well as the hardship exception. Spousal support above the table amounts was ordered.

*Where a recipient spouse is paying for all the familial housing expenses, including those of the payor spouse, this will be a compelling financial circumstance in the interim period, and support will be awarded above the high end of the table amounts* — *Kramchynsky v. Kramchynsky*, 2013 CarswellMan 73, 2013 MBQB 56, 289 Man. R. (2d) 85 (Man. Q.B.). The husband sought a review of a consent order for interim spousal support, *inter alia*. The wife had primary care of the two minor children, and they resided in the former matrimonial home. The judge found that the fact that the wife paid all costs associated with the former matrimonial home, as well as the cottage property in which the husband resided, was a factor when considering the compelling financial circumstances in the interim period exception. Spousal support was awarded that was significantly more than the high end of the table amounts.

*Where the recipient spouse has a limited education, high debt load and few assets post-separation, compelling financial circumstances will cause an award above the Guidelines on an interim basis* — *Thiyagarajah v. Paramsothy*, 2011 CarswellOnt 15091, 2011 ONSC 7368 (Ont. S.C.J.). The parties in this case were married for 5 years in a traditional marriage where the wife had left her job at the request of the husband. The parties had no children. She was entitled to compensatory and non-compensatory support on an interim basis. The judge found that the wife had compelling financial circumstances on an interim basis as contemplated by the SSAG exceptions. Spousal support was awarded at above-Guidelines levels.

*The ability of a custodial payor to pay spousal support when also owing a large amount of debt is a scenario which will prompt the application of the compelling financial circumstances exception in the SSAG* — *Fyfe v. Jouppien*, 2011 CarswellOnt 9295, 2011 ONSC 5462, 10 R.F.L. (7th) 336 (Ont. S.C.J.). Here, the exception for compelling financial circumstances in the interim period was applied. The parties were together for 23 years and had two children. At separation, both parties were self-sufficient and the children resided with their mother. After separation, the husband was diagnosed with terminal cancer and began receiving disability payments. The judge determined that the husband was entitled to support, but that the wife had no ability to pay because of significant debt stemming from her role as the sole provider to the children.

*The compelling financial circumstances exception is not available where the father was paying the familial debts after separation which merely continued the situation that was present before separation* — *Zdrill v. Zdrill*, 2011 CarswellOnt 2886, 2011 ONSC 2188 (Ont. S.C.J.). See case discussed in detail at **17 General**, above.

*Former husband in compelling financial circumstances* — *Marche v. Marche*, 2009 CarswellNfld 53, 2009 NLTD 31 (N.L.T.D.) The former husband's assumption of full responsibility for the joint line of credit, together with the requirement that he borrow $36,000 to settle the division of the matrimonial home with his former wife and her receipt of this money, are circumstances which qualify for exceptions to the formulas on the basis of compelling financial circumstances in the interim period. The court ordered that the former husband pay spousal support to his former wife of $416 per month.

*Paying rent insufficient to justify use of this exception* — *Garritsen v. Garritsen*, 2009 CarswellBC 868, 2009 BCSC 124, 71 R.F.L. (6th) 106, [2009] B.C.J. No. 691 (B.C.S.C.). The Master had found that the compelling interim circumstances exception was appropriate because the recipient had to pay rent after leaving the matrimonial home. Given that the marriage was not especially short and given that the payor was required to carry the matrimonial home expenses, the court which heard the appeal found that the Master's invocation of this exception was unwarranted. Support was reduced to $868 per month, an amount equal to the top of the SSAG range.

## 17.3 Debt Payment (SSAG, s. 12.2)

> If the payor is required to pay a disproportionate share of the debts, then there may have to be some reduction in support from the lower end of the range generated by the formulas. The reduction may only be for a specified period, depending upon the balance remaining to be paid. At the end of that period, support could automatically revert to an amount within the range or, in some cases, a review may be ordered at that time. Conversely, if less frequently, the recipient may sometimes need an amount of support above the upper end of the range, in order to make payments on a family debt.
>
> Where assets exceed debts, however, there can be little reason for a debt exception, as the party responsible for the debt will usually also hold the corresponding asset or other assets.
>
> The limits of this exception can be refined, thanks in part to feedback received since the Draft Proposal:
>
> - the total family debts must exceed the total family assets, or the payor's debts must exceed his or her assets;
> - the qualifying debts must be "family debts";
> - the debt payments must be "excessive or unusually high" (SSAG Chapter 12.2)

### Debt exception applied to reduce spousal support or spousal support not ordered

*Where a payor spouse has no capacity to pay spousal support because of high levels of family debt, spousal support will not be ordered* — *Goodine v. Goodine*, 2013 CarswellNS 211, 2013 NSSC 98 (N.S.S.C.). The wife claimed ongoing spousal support. The parties had significant debt. The husband was responsible for paying the matrimonial debts under an interim order. The wife had made no steps to become economically self-sufficient. The judge found the husband could not realistically service the matrimonial debt and pay spousal support. The wife had frustrated attempts to restructure debt. The judge considered the debt exception, and spousal support was terminated.

*Arrears will be calculated at a discount when the payor spouse has assumed the burden of the matrimonial debts during separation* — *Carrier c. Ponn*, 2013 CarswellNB 271, 2013 CarswellNB 272, 2013 NBQB 146, 403 N.B.R. (2d) 31, 1045 A.P.R. 31 (N.B.Q.B.). The parties had a 14-year relationship, and the judge found that the husband was entitled to spousal support on a compensatory and non-compensatory basis for the role that he had played in the wife's medical career as well as his "extreme" poverty. He was 67 years old and suffered from heart problems which prevented him from working and which also meant self-sufficiency in the future was not realistic. The wife had assumed the burden of the parties' debts. Spousal support arrears were calculated at a 25% deduction from the lower end of the SSAG tables to account for the wife's contribution to the debt. Ongoing support was calculated based on the table amounts.

*Where the parties' joint debt exceeds their assets, their situation constitutes an exception under the Guidelines* — Dunn v. Dunn, 2011 CarswellOnt 14551, 2011 ONSC 6899, 16 R.F.L. (7th) 156 (Ont. S.C.J.), additional reasons at 2011 CarswellOnt 15285, 2011 ONSC 6899, 16 R.F.L. (7th) 174 (Ont. S.C.J.). The parties had been in a long-term traditional marriage which had lasted 26 years. They had cohabited for 3 years before they were married. They had three independent adult children. The husband was a financial advisor who had made a significant income during the marriage and the wife had mostly worked in the home, except for some low paying occasional work. The parties separated in June 2009. Their current joint debt was $138,023. The husband had an additional debt of $123,077.33 for a combined total of $261,100.33. In order to calculate support, the court looked at the income available to the husband after financing his share of the joint debt and his own debt total (approximately $192,000), which includes liability for income taxes. The court imputed income of $25,000 to the wife. The court assumed that the husband would continue to earn at the rate of $225,000 per annum. The court, when assessing the range of spousal support, took into consideration the possibility that the husband would have to satisfy the entire joint debt. He would have $148,600 after servicing the debt from which he could pay support. It found that support should be towards the lower end of the range. The court ordered support of $4,000 a month during this 5-year period when the couple must deal with the debt built up during the marriage.

*With the husband's current income and level of child support payments, no spousal support or arrears of support would be ordered until the husband's Revenue Canada debt is satisfied* — Andreychuk v. Andreychuk, 2009 CarswellBC 1063, 2009 BCSC 549 (B.C.S.C.).

*The fact that the payor spouse was maintaining significant family debt was a major factor in awarding support below the range* — TenHoeve v. TenHoeve, 2009 CarswellOnt 1882, [2009] O.J. No. 1423 (Ont. S.C.J.). The decision was made on an interim, interim basis.

*The husband's assumption of debts as a result of the wife's bankruptcy was a factor in awarding the wife well below the SSAG range* — Metlin v. Metlin, 2009 CarswellOnt 3047, [2009] O.J. No. 2211 (Ont. S.C.J.). The parties had lived together for 17 years. They were married for 12 years. In 2008, the husband earned $47,796 and the wife $20,000. The court awarded the wife $500 a month in spousal support. [The debt exception was not mentioned.]

*Husband assumed marital debt* — Marche v. Marche, 2009 CarswellNfld 53, 2009 NLTD 31 (N.L.T.D.). The husband's assumption of full responsibility for the joint line of credit, together with the requirement that he borrow $36,000 to settle the division of the matrimonial home with his former wife, and her receipt of this money, are circumstances which qualify for exceptions to the formulas on the basis of debt payment. The court ordered that the former husband pay spousal support to his former wife of $416 per month.

*Cases in which the SSAG's debt exception was not explicitly mentioned, but debt appeared to be relevant in going beyond the quantum range* — Munro v. Munro, 2006 CarswellBC 2906, 2006 BCSC 1758, [2006] B.C.J. No. 3069 (B.C.S.C.); British Columbia (Director of Maintenance Enforcement) v. G. (C.), 2006 CarswellBC 1247, 2006 BCPC 204, [2006] B.C.J. No. 1157 (B.C. Prov. Ct.); Frouws v. Frouws, 2007 CarswellBC 301, 2007 BCSC 195, [2007] B.C.J. No. 282 (B.C.S.C.); P. (M.) v. F. (S.), 2006 CarswellBC 1570, 2006 BCPC 289, [2006] B.C.J. No. 1434 (B.C. Prov. Ct.).

## Debt exception not applicable

*The wife's debts were not sufficiently high to invoke the SSAG "debt exception"* — *S. (R.M.)* v. *S. (F.P.C.)*, 2011 CarswellBC 170, 2011 BCCA 53, 90 R.F.L. (6th) 1, 14 B.C.L.R. (5th) 84, 299 B.C.A.C. 186, 508 W.A.C. 186, [2011] B.C.J. No. 174 (B.C.C.A.). Under a reapportionment order, the wife would receive an amount that would assist her in meeting her debt obligations. Her monthly support payments would be tax deductible.

*Where efforts to improve the family debt situation have not been made, debts will not be found to be excessive or unusually high and the debt exception will not be applied* — *Robles v. Kuhn*, 2012 CarswellBC 1492, 2012 BCSC 752 (B.C.S.C.). The parties had two children and were married for approximately 10 years. They had approximately $70,000 in family debts for a sailboat and lines of credit. The wife was granted sole custody of the children. The judge found the family debts were not excessive or unusually high as required under the debt exception in the SSAG. He found the father had not made efforts to reduce the debt load by selling the sailboat, which formed the bulk of the debt.

*Where assets exceed debts, the debt exception will not apply* — *Aubé v. Aubé*, 2013 CarswellNB 170, 2013 NBQB 128, 402 N.B.R. (2d) 342, 1044 A.P.R. 342, [2013] N.B.J. No. 103 (N.B.Q.B.). The parties were married for 33 years and had one adult child. The husband had health problems and was found to have non-compensatory entitlement due to interdependency and disability. The wife argued the debt exception applied, but the debt was considered in the property division. As the assets exceeded the debts, the judge held the debt exception did not apply. Retroactive support to separation (2008) was ordered at the low end of the SSAG range. Indefinite support was ordered to be reviewed upon the wife's retirement.

*The husband's servicing of debt after separation while wife worked part time and his delay in dealing with some financial issues led the court to look at the low end of the SSAG ranges* — *no retroactive spousal support granted* — *Calder v. Calder*, 2011 CarswellNS 612, 2011 NSSC 328 (N.S.S.C.). Both parties had the right to apply for spousal support for a period of 2 years should their employment circumstances change.

*The debt payment exception is not applicable where a substantial portion of the respondent's debt is post-separation debt* — *McFadden v. Sprague*, 2009 CarswellOnt 294, [2009] O.J. No. 258 (Ont. S.C.J.). Further there was "no evidence to indicate that the respondent was required to pay a disproportionate share of the debts nor is there any evidence that her existing debt load is significantly out of proportion to her income. The evidence does not support a finding that the respondent assumed a disproportionate share of the family debts."

*Gambling and legal debts arising post-separation are not justification for the use of the debt exception under the SSAG* — *Dingle v. Dingle*, 2010 CarswellOnt 10743, 2010 ONCJ 731, 100 R.F.L. (6th) 459, [2010] O.J. No. 6029 (Ont. C.J.), additional reasons at 2010 CarswellOnt 10756, 2010 ONCJ 734, 100 R.F.L. (6th) 479, [2010] O.J. No. 6034 (Ont. C.J.). The husband argued that his gambling and legal debts of $91,000 should affect the amount of support awarded to his former wife whose situation fell under the disability exception in the SSAG. The judge found that the debt exception does not apply to debts of this nature and that these debts had no relationship to the marriage.

*The debt payment exception not applicable where some of the husband's debts arose because he was living beyond his means* — *Van Wieren v. Van Wieren*, 2008 CarswellBC 23, 2008 BCSC 31 (B.C.S.C.). The husband had a significant amount of debt and was attempting to use the debt payment exception to reduce spousal support. The court found that the husband's debt issues were a result of living beyond his means. Further, the court noted that the wife desired to purchase her husband's half interest in the matrimonial home which would provide him with funds to pay off some of his debt. Accordingly, spousal support was ordered.

*The parties have high debt load, but SSAG not applied* — *B. (P.S.O.) v. B. (L.M.)*, 2008 CarswellBC 346, 2008 BCSC 213, [2008] B.C.J. No. 299 (B.C.S.C.), original reasons at *B. (P.S.O.) v. B. (L.M.)*, 2007 CarswellBC 1768, 2007 BCSC 1138, [2007] B.C.J. No. 1695 (B.C.S.C.). In this shared custody situation, the court declined to apply the SSAG, because of the parties' high debt load.

## 17.4 Prior Support Obligations

> Under the current law, courts determine the amount of any support for the second spouse taking into account the prior support obligations and the payor's budget. We have created an exception for these prior support obligations. Most often, the prior support obligation will involve child support, but spousal support may also be involved after a longer first marriage and then a shorter second marriage. In the vast majority of cases, the prior support obligation will involve a payment to another party. But there can also be cases where a spouse is a custodial parent for a prior child in his or her care who is not a "child of the marriage". A custodial parent in this case has as much of a "prior support obligation" as does a support payor. (SSAG Chapter 12.3)
>
> Under the without child support formula . . . Where there are prior support obligations, the payor's gross income will have to be adjusted to reflect those obligations, before computing the gross income difference and applying the percentage ranges to that difference. Adjusting for a prior spousal support obligation is simple, as spousal support is paid on a gross or before-tax basis: deduct the amount of spousal support paid from the spouse's gross income to establish the spouse's gross income. For a prior child support obligation, as child support is paid on a net or after-tax basis, the calculation is slightly more complicated: first, gross up the child support amount to reflect the payor's marginal tax rate on the amount paid and then deduct the grossed up amount from the spouse's gross income. (SSAG Chapter 12.3.1)
>
> Under the with child support formula ...an obligation to pay support for a prior spouse or prior children requires a slightly different adjustment under this formula, which works with net incomes rather than the gross incomes of the without child support formula. In calculating the payor spouse's individual net disposable income, this exception will require that any amounts of support paid to prior spouses or children be deducted, thereby reducing the size of the pool of individual net disposable income between the current spouses and also reducing the payor's share of that smaller pool. Because we are working with net income under this formula, there is no need to gross up any child support amounts and the software can work out the after-tax value of the gross amount of spousal support. (SSAG Chapter 12.3.2)
>
> Where a payor has a child of a prior relationship in his or her care after separation, a child who is not a 'child of the marriage' . . . the custodial parent's support obligation towards that prior child can be estimated by using an amount of 'notional child support,' based upon the table amount for that child or children for a person with the custodial parent's Guidelines income. In some cases, a further adjustment may have to be made for any section 7 expenses paid by the custodial parent. (SSAG Chapter 12.3.3)

This exception recognizes the financial realities faced by parties who have more than one family to support. Where resources are stretched to their limit, which may be the case where there are multiple spousal or child support obligations, it may not be possible for a payor spouse to provide spousal support to a subsequent spouse at Guidelines amounts.

*No spousal support payable; child support for child from previous relationship and child from parties' relationship had priority* — *Lickfold v. Robichaud*, 2008 CarswellOnt 6138, [2008] O.J. No. 4117 (Ont. S.C.J.). The father's income was $52,243 per year and he was paying child support for his child from another relationship. The parties also had one child together for whom the father was ordered to pay child support pursuant to the Guidelines. The mother sought spousal support, but the court found that although the mother was entitled to support, the father was unable to pay spousal support at that time.

*Support payor had prior support obligation to a former spouse* — *support at middle or lower end of range, depending on scenario used* — *exception not mentioned* — *Robertson v. Williams*, 2009 CarswellOnt 8022, [2009] O.J. No. 5451 (Ont. S.C.J.). The husband's income was $34,611. He was previously married and divorced and a support order required him to pay his former spouse $800 per month. He claimed a tax deduction of $9,600 for this support payment. The wife was injured at work a number of years previously and was in receipt of non-taxable benefits from WSIB. The amount received by her was approximately $10,700 per year which was indexed each year for inflation. The court provided each party with two scenarios based on Chequemate Spousal Guidelines. Considering the parties' 16 years of cohabitation and the gross income difference between the parties, a middle range figure of spousal support would be $334. If income were imputed to her of $1,800 per year for CPP benefits available, but not taken, the middle range support would be $292. In light of the evidence before the court and with some assistance from the SSAG scenarios, the court awarded spousal support of $300 per month for an indefinite period. [There was no specific mention of an exception under the Guidelines.]

*SSAG not applicable where payor has a prior financial obligation to his parents* — *Wang v. Seow*, 2008 CarswellMan 431, 2008 MBQB 218, 232 Man. R. (2d) 151 (Man. Q.B.). The parties were married for 5 years and had one child. The husband was primarily responsible for the child who lived with the husband's parents. The husband worked in the United States and earned $70,548 and the wife earned $19,500 per year. Prior to and during the marriage, the husband was the sole financial support for his parents and sister. The court held that this factor was not accounted for in the Guidelines. The wife brought a motion for interim spousal support. The husband was ordered to pay $600 per month, since the wife was dependent on the husband during the marriage. The quantum of spousal support ordered was influenced by the husband's financial obligations to his extended family since the wife knew about this obligation before and during the marriage.

## 17.5 Illness and Disability (SSAG s. 12.4)

For many cases . . . neither the breadth of the ranges nor the expanded possibilities of restructuring are seen to provide an adequate response to illness or disability. In these cases, there are three distinct approaches to long-term disability, three approaches that became more sharply defined after *Bracklow* in 1999. Because these are "hard" cases, more of them turn up in the reported decisions. Below we have framed these three approaches using the language of the Advisory Guidelines, as courts increasingly have used the Guidelines to consider these issues.

Faced with a recipient with a long-term disability, Canadian courts have responded with one of three approaches, here stated in declining order of frequency.

1)  Lower Amount, Extend Duration: most courts will extend duration, even to be "indefinite", while keeping the amount within the range, at or near the low end;

2)  No Exception: a slightly smaller number of courts will fix an amount in the range, often towards the upper end, and use the maximum duration, even though that means support will end while need continues;

3)  Increase Amount, Extend Duration: a much smaller group of courts will respond to the greater need in disability cases by increasing amount and extending duration. (SSAG Chapter 12.4)

The illness or disability exception will usually arise where there are problems with the maximum duration under the without child support formula, where the marriage is of short-to-medium duration. Under the basic with child support formula, there will be much less need for this exception, given the lengthy maximum duration available to a primary parent under the shorter-marriage test for duration. (SSAG Chapter 12.4)

Cases involving the disability of one or both spouses prompt the most frequent application of the exceptions, perhaps because this seems like an obvious situation where departure from Guideline amounts would be appropriate. The disability exception, and the way judges choose to apply it in determining quantum and duration of support, is often closely linked to the recipient spouse's projected ability to become self-sufficient and to enter or re-enter the workforce. However, use of the disability exception will not necessarily lead to indefinite support, even in situations where the recipient spouse will never re-enter the workforce. A number of cases have been found to depart from the Guideline amounts because of disability, without explicitly making use of the exceptions.

## Illness or disability exception considered

*Where the relationship is of short duration, little medical evidence relating to disability is led and the recipient is able to work to some extent, the disability exception will not be applied —* Shen v. Tong, 2013 CarswellBC 3620, 2013 BCCA 519, 40 R.F.L. (7th) 257, 54 B.C.L.R. (5th) 115, 347 B.C.A.C. 233, 593 W.A.C. 233 (B.C.C.A.). The parties were married for 3.5 years. The wife was disabled after an accident which had occurred 8 years prior to the separation, although there was little medical evidence led at trial. At trial, $50,000 in annual income was imputed to her despite no finding that she was underemployed or a malingerer. The Court of Appeal found this was an error. There was no evidence that she could earn this amount of income or that she was not disabled, and the husband did not allege same. She was now employed. It was held by the Court of Appeal that her disability could be accommodated within the ranges of the table amounts in the SSAG, which the Court of Appeal noted was the approach taken in many cases involving a disabled recipient. Spousal support was ordered for 3 years, which was the approach the SSAG mandated.

*Where a payor is of retirement age and spousal support has been paid for some years, the disability exception will be considered but no change may be made —* L. (R.) v. B. (L.A.), 2013 CarswellPEI 48, 2013 PESC 24, 342 Nfld. & P.E.I.R. 220, 1064 A.P.R. 220 (P.E.I.S.C.). The parties were married for approximately 14 years. They had no children. The wife suffered from anorexia nervosa, and medical evidence that she was unable to work was accepted. The judge found that she was in dire need of non-compensatory spousal support. The wife had not applied for CPP disability, and the judge opined that she would likely be entitled and had an obligation to mitigate her circumstances. The husband had experienced some windfalls due to tax implications stemming from the breakdown of the marriage. The debt exception was considered but not applied because the husband's age precluded a longer term of spousal support than usual. Spousal support had been paid since 2005. Medical evidence showed that the wife should recover in 1 to 2 years. Support was ordered at the midrange of the table amounts until 2016.

*Where the recipient spouse is disabled, the disability exception may be applied and support above the SSAG range may be awarded indefinitely* — Aujla v. Singh, 2012 CarswellOnt 11695, 2012 ONSC 5217, [2012] O.J. No. 4395 (Ont. S.C.J.). The parties were both in their 30s. The wife lived in a nursing home as she had multiple sclerosis, which had been diagnosed shortly after the marriage. The applicant husband was employed. Her sources of income were GST rebate and disability. The parties were married for 5 years. The wife's counsel requested $1,000 monthly for support. Income attributed to the husband based on his income during the marriage put the SSAG range at $154 to $208 monthly. The judge found that this was not a case for compensatory support and that the husband had already paid almost the maximum duration of support under the Guidelines under an interim order. However, he considered the disability exception in awarding $300 monthly for an indefinite period, as the wife's need was extreme and the husband had put forward $400 monthly as an amount he was willing to pay.

*Where the parties had been in a mid-length relationship and both parties were autonomous, mid-range support may be ordered and restructured to reflect the disability exception and ease the transition to independence* — Broadbear v. Prothero, 2011 CarswellOnt 6129, 2011 ONSC 3656, 6 R.F.L. (7th) 342, [2011] O.J. No. 3136 (Ont. S.C.J.). The parties cohabited for a total of six and a quarter years. The female spouse suffered from PTSD following an incident that occurred after the end of the relationship. The judge found that during the relationship, the parties operated as autonomous individuals who both contributed financially to joint expenses. The support was ordered on a needs-based basis. The judge made a final order of support in the mid-range of the SSAG, noting the disability exception. Support payments were restructured to reflect a higher amount in the short term and the payments were to continue for 18 months.

*Where the recipient spouse has a long-term disability which prevents her from working lower support for an extended period of time will be awarded under the disability exception* — Dingle v. Dingle, 2010 CarswellOnt 10743, 2010 ONCJ 731, 100 R.F.L. (6th) 459, [2010] O.J. No. 6029 (Ont. C.J.), additional reasons at 2010 CarswellOnt 10756, 2010 ONCJ 734, 100 R.F.L. (6th) 479, [2010] O.J. No. 6034 (Ont. C.J.). The parties in this case were in their late 40s and had no children. They had been married for approximately 20 years when they separated. The wife suffered from fibromyalgia and Chronic Pain Syndrome, which was diagnosed prior to the marriage. The court found that the wife was entitled to needs-based, non-compensatory support. The court found that a delay of 7 years before the application for support was fatal to a finding of retroactive support, but not to ongoing support. The court also found that the award suggested by the Guidelines was inappropriate in this case and that restructuring would also not result in a fair outcome for the plaintiff. The long delay between separation and the award of support and, more importantly, the disability/illness exception, applied in this case. The wife was incapable of supporting herself and had relied on the kindness of friends and family and frugality to make ends meet in the interim. The judge awarded a lower amount for an extended time-frame than would normally be awarded under the SSAG. He declined to time-limit the award.

*Spousal support within SSAG range despite disability* — McFadden v. Sprague, 2009 CarswellOnt 294, [2009] O.J. No. 258 (Ont. S.C.J.). The parties separated after 20 years of marriage and two children. The husband sought spousal support from the wife. He was found, due to his physical and emotional problems, to be unable to seek and maintain employment and in need of spousal support. In determining the quantum of spousal support, the court acknowledged that the disability exception under the SSAG applied to this case; however, the court concluded that this was not a case where the quantum of spousal support should fall outside of the suggested ranges of support.

*Disability exception considered — SSAG not used as issues were very complex — Lepp v. Lepp,* 2008 CarswellBC 717, 2008 BCSC 448, 52 R.F.L. (6th) 423, [2008] B.C.J. No. 640 (B.C.S.C.). The court held at para. 39: "Many of the complex issues that arise on variation applications are present in this case including the impact of remarriage and a second family, the passage of time and the impact of inflation. In addition, disability, one of the five exceptions to the application of the SSAG, is present here. In my view, the SSAG do not account for the multiple factors to be considered in this case both with regard to quantum and duration of the spousal support." On the variation application, the court increased the amount of spousal support payable.

*Where the nature of the parties' relationship created economic dependence, the plaintiff was severely disabled and destitute, the disability exception to the SSAG will apply to interim support regardless of the short duration of the relationship — Kirk v. Hackl,* 2007 SKQB 82, 2007 CarswellSask 78, 292 Sask. R. 109, [2007] S.J. No. 87 (Sask. Q.B.). This case concerned a motion for interim spousal support by the plaintiff, a common-law wife who had inexplicably lost her sight and became functionally blind during the relationship. The parties cohabited for 44 months. The wife was awarded $1,000 monthly in interim support after a survey of the jurisprudence of the disability exception found in the SSAG. The judge rejected the defendant's request that the support awarded be at the low end of the SSAG which would amount to only $134 per month. The judge found that the plaintiff was destitute and relying on friends and family for support, and that the nature of the parties' relationship had created a dependence on the defendant for support.

*Where the disability exception applies, the award may be in increased amount and extended duration — Pegler v. Avio,* 2008 CarswellBC 169, 2008 BCSC 128, 49 R.F.L. (6th) 145, [2008] B.C.J. No. 159 (B.C.S.C.). The parties were common-law spouses with one child. The female spouse suffered from multiple sclerosis and it was found she should be awarded need-based and compensatory support for her contribution to the parties' life together, which was a traditional relationship. In recognition of the disability, the judge awarded support at the high end of the Guidelines, but departed from the Guidelines in declining to make a time limitation on the support, although the parties' relationship was of a medium-length.

*In a case where the disability exception would normally apply, it will be preferable to consider an alternative award that does not result in loss of third-party benefits — A. (S.) v. A. (E.),* 2010 CarswellNB 86, 2010 NBQB 61, 358 N.B.R. (2d) 34, 924 A.P.R. 34 (N.B.Q.B.). The parties were married for 12 years and had four children together. The wife had multiple sclerosis and was in receipt of CPP disability for herself and the children. In addition, she received a child tax credit. The wife brought a motion for interim spousal support which was dismissed. The wife had significant medical expenses related to her condition and was residing in the marital home with the children. The husband was found to have sufficient means to pay support and the wife was shown to have need. The judge explicitly considered the application of the SSAG exception for disability or illness. However, he found that it would be selfdefeating to award interim support to the point where the wife would lose some of the thirdparty benefits she was receiving. Without support, however, it was found that the wife did not have sufficient means to support herself and the children and maintain the marital home. The judge therefore ordered the husband to contribute one-half of the expenses of the mortgage, property tax and property insurance on the marital home, as a way of providing the wife with more discretionary income, yet maintaining her low taxable income.

*Even in a situation where both parties are facing financial difficulties, where a recipient spouse is disabled, the disability exception may apply — lower amount, extended duration awarded — Campbell v. Campbell*, 2009 CarswellBC 2606, 2009 BCSC 1330, [2009] B.C.J. No. 1944 (B.C.S.C.). The parties were in a situation the judge decried as "tragic". The wife was suffering from a number of medical conditions and was in need of support. She existed on disability payments and lived in subsidized housing. The husband had suffered a very debilitating stroke in 2006, and in 2007 filed for bankruptcy which left him without savings. He had no realistic hope of ever being employable again. The husband made an application to vary the previous spousal support order and cancel arrears of support. The petitioner wife applied to increase spousal support. The judge found that there had been a material change in circumstances sufficient to vary, given the change in financial circumstances of the parties. The disability exception applied and the support was awarded indefinitely at the low end of the Guideline amounts, although arrears were reduced. This case followed the "lower amount, extend duration" approach to the exception.

*Disability exception found not to apply on the facts — Rayvals v. Rayvals*, 2008 CarswellBC 270, 2008 BCSC 176, 51 R.F.L. (6th) 391, 80 B.C.L.R. (4th) 191, [2008] B.C.J. No. 233 (B.C.S.C.), additional reasons at 2008 CarswellBC 1143, 2008 BCSC 718, 56 R.F.L. (6th) 127 (B.C.S.C.). The wife suffered from fibromyalgia. The court found that the parties' circumstances were not so exceptional that the illness or disability exception to the Guidelines applied. One spouse is not the insurer of the other. "[The wife] has been disadvantaged from the breakdown of the marriage because she is no longer advantaged to the extent she was during the marriage by [the husband's] income. However, [the husband] has been disadvantaged by the marriage breakdown because he has had to pay $500 a month for spousal support since 2000. He wants to be able to move on in his new life. [His] income has increased by some $15,000 since separation, but his obligations have also increased because of his remarriage and two infant children."

*Where the income of the payor spouse is modest, support will be awarded at Guideline amounts regardless of the disability of the recipient spouse — Bramhill v. Dick*, 2007 CarswellBC 411, 2007 BCSC 262, [2007] B.C.J. No. 387 (B.C.S.C.). The wife was diagnosed with multiple sclerosis 4 year before the parties began to cohabit. They cohabited for approximately 14 years. The plaintiff wife claimed compensatory and non-compensatory spousal support on the grounds that her disability prevented her from working and she was unable to support herself. The judge also found that the relationship was to the benefit of both parties. He considered applying the disability exception, but found that there was not enough income for both parties, which he distinguished from Wise and Williston, where the payor spouse was making more than $60,000 annually. The judge awarded interim support at the upper level of Guideline amounts, pending receipt of financial information from the sale of the family home.

*Despite the application of the disability exception, the Bracklow principles will not require a support payor to meet the total needs of the recipient spouse after a short- to mid-length relationship, but rather dictate a contribution to the recipient spouse's needs — Wise v. Wise*, 2006 CarswellBC 1540, 2006 BCSC 945, 56 B.C.L.R. (4th) 186, [2006] B.C.J. No. 1413 (B.C.S.C.). The parties cohabited and then married for a total of 7.5 years. The wife, prior to the marriage, developed multiple sclerosis which made her unemployable. The payor husband had already paid 4 years of support and the judge awarded another 4 years of support at an amount slightly above the Guideline ranges to take into consideration the wife's disability.

*Where a recipient parent is caring exclusively for a disabled child, the SSAG will not apply and support above the SSAG range may be ordered — Jans v. Jans*, 2013 CarswellAlta 2192, 2013 ABPC 199, 41 R.F.L. (7th) 500 (Alta. Prov. Ct.). The parties were married for 19 years and cohabited for 21. They had two adult children and a younger child, who had Down syndrome and was in the exclusive care of the wife. The wife had been a homemaker during the marriage and had found two part-time jobs after separation. The judge found that the Guidelines amounts did not adequately reflect the wife's responsibility in having to care for a disabled child. Support above the SSAG amount was ordered, which resulted in the wife having slightly more money than the husband after each party paid support to a child at university. However, the judge noted that the wife was supporting two people on that sum, whereas the husband was only supporting himself.

## Disability or illness cases, exception not mentioned

*The disability exception will not be considered when the payor spouse has retired — Powell v. Levesque,* 2014 CarswellBC 186, 2014 BCCA 33, 38 R.F.L. (7th) 261, 57 B.C.L.R. (5th) 132, 370 D.L.R. (4th) 370, 350 B.C.A.C. 43, 598 W.A.C. 43 (B.C.C.A.). The parties, who were women, cohabited for 8 years between 1990 and 1998. Subsequent to the relationship, the respondent became disabled and unable to work. The judge found she had a need for support. The appellant applied to vary spousal support on the basis of her early retirement. She had retired at 44, and the judge at first instance found the medical reasons for her retirement were not compelling. The Court of Appeal did not consider the disability exception in finding that the motions judge had erred in not finding a material change in circumstances. The appellant had retired from the Armed Forces with a full pension after completing her full term of service in the face of mounting health issues, which the Court of Appeal found was not unreasonable. The Court of Appeal applied the SSAG, which suggested a duration of 4 to 8 years. As the appellant had paid support for 12 years, the court considered her obligation extinguished, and spousal support was terminated.

*The court awarded support until the wife turned 60 because the husband was absent from the children's lives, the wife was ill and the children had medical issues — Caldwell v. Caldwell,* 2013 CarswellAlta 1241, 2013 ABCA 268, 33 R.F.L. (7th) 285 (Alta. C.A.). The parties separated after 12 years of marriage. The chambers judge awarded the wife spousal support in the amount of $790 per month until her 60th birthday, subject to variation in the case of a significant change in circumstances. The husband appealed, citing the relatively short length of the marriage and the 18 years he had been paying support. The Court of Appeal noted that while long-term spousal support is unusual after a medium-length marriage, it was appropriate in these circumstances.

*Where a recipient is entitled to non-compensatory support but the payor is found to have no ability to pay, no spousal support will be ordered and the disability exception will not be considered — Hurley v. Hurley,* 2012 CarswellNS 201, 2012 NSCA 32, 14 R.F.L. (7th) 10, 314 N.S.R. (2d) 346, 994 A.P.R. 346 (N.S.C.A.). The parties were in a relationship for 10 years, including 7 years of marriage, and had no children. The wife was unable to work during the marriage due to mental health issues and was receiving disability payments. The trial judge found she had need, but the husband had no ability to pay because of high motor vehicle expenses. No spousal support was awarded, and this decision was upheld by the Court of Appeal. [No reference to the disability exception was made.]

*Wife's disability could both justify a more generous property division and a support award in excess of the SSAG quantum range — Shellito v. Bensimhon,* 2008 CarswellBC 469, 2008 BCCA 68, 50 R.F.L. (6th) 263, 79 B.C.L.R. (4th) 45, 251 B.C.A.C. 225, 420 W.A.C. 225 (B.C.C.A.). The wife suffered from debilitating headaches which rendered her unable to work. This fact was among the trial court's reasons for ordering a 50/50 division of property despite the facts that the marriage had lasted less than 6 years and the husband had brought much of the property into the marriage. With regard to spousal support, the wife's disability was also found to justify an award in excess of the SSAG range. This decision was upheld on appeal with the court rejecting the contention that the respondent's disability had been "doublecounted" by affecting both property and support. Neither trial nor appellate court acknowledged that the SSAG explicitly recognize a disability exception.

*Spousal support will be awarded between the mid and high range in situations where the recipient spouse has a disability* — H. (M.) v. H. (R.), 2013 CarswellBC 62, 2013 BCSC 57 (B.C.S.C.). In this case, the recipient wife had a neurological condition which prevented her from working and essentially incapacitated her. No mention of the disability exception was made.

*The presence of a disability will not always result in increased spousal support under the Guidelines* — Depatie v. Squires, 2012 CarswellOnt 2701, 2012 ONSC 1399, [2012] O.J. No. 965 (Ont. Div. Ct.). The parties were together for 12.5 years. The wife had a child from a previous relationship and the husband was found to stand in the place of a parent for this child. The husband was ordered to pay a small amount of child support (with the majority paid by the biological father of the child), as well as spousal support. The spousal support was timelimited, despite the wife's disability, as it was found that the disability did not cause her economic problems and compensatory support was not warranted. This decision upheld the lower court decision.

*The wife's severe disability and in particular her significant ongoing and uninsured medical expenses served to increase her need and may have led to a higher level of support* — Haggerty v. Haggerty, 2010 CarswellNS 6, 2010 NSSC 9, 80 R.F.L. (6th) 227, [2010] N.S.J. No. 5 (N.S.S.C.). The husband had an income of $65,000 and the wife an income of $6,000. The parties had lived together for 10 years, including 7 years of marriage. If the relationship were considered to have lasted 7 years, support would be $467 to $688 per month for 3.5 to 7 years. If the relationship were considered to be 10 years long, the range would be $737.50 to $983.33 per month for 5 to 10 years. The court awarded support of $900 per month for 7 years.

*Support at the mid-high range will be ordered when the recipient is unable to work due to disability (exception not considered)* — Stannett v. Green, 2014 CarswellOnt 40, [2014] O.J. No. 47 (Ont. S.C.J.). The parties cohabited for 9 years and had no children. They separated in 2009. The wife had not worked since separation and was receiving CPP disability for depression and anxiety. The judge imputed income to the husband of $75,000. The wife was found to have need; and, given her disability, support at the mid-high range of the SSAG was ordered in a lump sum in order to facilitate a clean break.

*Where a recipient is disabled and cannot survive on the amounts within the SSAG range, support above the range may be ordered* — Este v. Blais, 2013 CarswellOnt 16474, 2013 ONSC 7389 (Ont. S.C.J.). Reasons were very brief. The wife was receiving CPP disability, and the husband's income was $60,252 annually. Support above the SSAG ranges was ordered as the wife had argued that she could not survive on an award within the ranges. The high end of the range was $737 per month, and an order for $1,000 was made. [No discussion of the disability exception occurred and it is unclear if it was applied.]

*Disabled father, support payable in the mid range amount despite waiver of support in agreement* — Barton v. Sauvé, 2010 CarswellOnt 1509, 2010 ONSC 1072, 100 O.R. (3d) 763, [2010] O.J. No. 1008 (Ont. S.C.J.), additional reasons at 2010 CarswellOnt 5973, 2010 ONSC 4538 (Ont. S.C.J.). The parties had an 8-year common-law relationship and had two children. Both parties worked during the relationship. The father sustained a work-related injury and eventually stopped working and received Workers' Compensation Benefits. After the mother received $2 million from an aunt, the parties signed a cohabitation agreement in which the parties waived spousal support. After separation, the man lived in a small onebedroom apartment and his only income was approximately $15,000 per year in Worker's Compensation payments. He was unable to provide for his children when they visited at the same level that they enjoyed at their mother's home. The court set aside the waiver of spousal support provision in the cohabitation agreement pursuant to s. 33(4) of the *Family Law Act* on the basis that it had resulted in unconscionable circumstances and ordered spousal support. The Guidelines indicated a range of

$396 to $527 per month. Support was ordered in the mid-range amount of $462 per month for 6 years or, if the parties preferred, a lump sum of $25,000.

*Increased spousal support due to wife's illnesses* — van Rythoven v. van Rythoven, 2009 CarswellOnt 5187, [2009] O.J. No. 3648 (Ont. S.C.J.), affirmed 2010 CarswellOnt 10590, 2010 ONSC 5923, 99 R.F.L. (6th) 152 (Ont. Div. Ct.), additional reasons at 2011 CarswellOnt 1688, 2011 ONSC 1369 (Ont. Div. Ct.). The parties were married for 13 years and had two children. In determining an appropriate amount of spousal support, the court considered the wife's extensive illnesses and concluded that in this case the SSAG was inapplicable. After analyzing the parties' situation, the court awarded the wife $1,950 in spousal support per month which was at the top of the SSAG range that would normally be applicable.

*Indefinite duration* — Steele v. Steele, 2009 CarswellOnt 2788, [2009] O.J. No. 2062 (Ont. S.C.J.), additional reasons at 2009 CarswellOnt 3985 (Ont. S.C.J.). The parties were married for 12 years and had four children. At the time of separation, the wife was dealing with Crohn's disease, which made it difficult for her to work. The wife argued that a portion of her spousal support would go towards paying for her prescription medication since she had no medical coverage. In determining the appropriate duration of spousal support, the court noted that the SSAG recommends a maximum duration of 13 years; however, given the wife's medical condition this amount would be inappropriate and instead awarded her $650 per month indefinitely.

*Wife awarded support which gave her 40% of family income* — Shaw v. Shaw, 2009 CarswellNS 648, 2009 NSSC 353, 283 N.S.R. (2d) 388, 900 A.P.R. 388 (N.S.S.C.). The parties separated after 15 years of marriage. At the time of separation, the wife was not employed due to her medical disability. The wife sought spousal support from the husband. The court found that the wife was in need due to her medical disability and awarded her $650 per month indefinitely, which left her with 40% of the family income.

*Payee terminally ill* — Robertson v. Williams, 2009 CarswellOnt 8022, [2009] O.J. No. 5451 (Ont. S.C.J.). The husband's income was $34,611. The wife was injured at work a number of years before the hearing and was in receipt of non-taxable benefits from WSIB. The amount she received was approximately $10,700 per year which was indexed each year for inflation. The court provided each party with two scenarios based on *Chequemate Spousal Guidelines*. Considering the parties' 16 years of cohabitation and the gross income difference between them, a middle range figure of spousal support would be $334. If income were imputed to the wife of $1,800 per year for CPP benefits available, but not taken, the middle range of support would be $292. In light of the evidence before the court and with some assistance from the SSAG scenarios, the court awarded spousal support of $300 per month for an indefinite period.

*Reduction in payor's income, but Guidelines not strictly followed where payee suffered from disability* — Rhynold v. Rhynold, 2009 CarswellOnt 6260 (Ont. S.C.J.). The husband's income was in the $59,000 range. The *Chequemate Spousal Guidelines* provided that this income would yield a monthly support payment of $591 for the lower range, $690 for the mid-range and $788 for the upper range. The court ordered spousal support in the sum of $788 for ongoing spousal support.

*The SSAG not applied where parties had disabilities and lump sum agreed to be appropriate* — Mohajeriko v. Gandomi, 2009 CarswellBC 748, 2009 BCSC 393, [2009] B.C.J. No. 576 (B.C.S.C.). The Court stated, at para. 185: "Because this is a case involving some illness or disability of both parties and because they agree that lump sum spousal support is appropriate, I will not address the *SSAG* further."

*Disability among reasons to order quantum above custodial payor range* — Mumford v. Mumford, 2008 CarswellNS 171, 2008 NSSC 82, 266 N.S.R. (2d) 11, 851 A.P.R. 11, [2008] N.S.J. No. 138 (N.S.S.C.). The duration was fixed at 16 years, which was the maximum suggested by the SSAG range. The court ordered a quantum of support in excess of the SSAG custodial payor range, after making the following findings at para. 92: "The court has decided to order an amount greater than the Guidelines given the Petitioner's severe disability and in particular her obvious inability to manage her affairs. This serves to increase her need." However, the SSAG's "disability exception" was not specifically mentioned.

*Quantum well in excess of SSAG range ordered for disabled recipient* — *Smith v. Smith,* 2008 CarswellOnt 1921, [2008] O.J. No. 1330 (Ont. S.C.J.), additional reasons at 2008 CarswellOnt 4644, 56 R.F.L. (6th) 148, [2008] O.J. No. 1674 (Ont. S.C.J.), affirmed 2010 CarswellOnt 9220, 2010 ONSC 6430, 1 R.F.L. (7th) 70 (Ont. Div. Ct.). The support claimant was disabled and any support she received would have been deducted dollar-for-dollar from her Ontario Disability Support Plan entitlement. The SSAG were rejected because the top of the quantum range would "not address her needs." The court added at para. 80: "this is an atypical case, due to the wife's intense need for support, her medical problems and her restricted ability to work. The Guidelines will not produce a reasonable award which will reflect the unique circumstances of this case." The quantum of support ordered was over twice the top of the SSAG range. [The judgement did not mention the SSAG "disability exception".]

*When a recipient spouse suffering from mental health problems may improve after the conclusion of trial, indefinite support subject to review will be ordered* — *Peterson v. Peterson,* 2007 CarswellSask 496, 2007 SKQB 316, 301 Sask. R. 37 (Sask. Q.B.). The parties were married for 4 years and had a child together. The wife suffered from anxiety and depression which the judge found was a pre-existing circumstance exacerbated by problems within the marriage. Because of her health issues, she was not yet able to achieve economic self-sufficiency after the marriage, which the judge underlined was the goal of spousal support. The judge ordered spousal support, while maintaining that "any order of spousal support should not be an excuse or even a subconscious motivation to languish in anxiety/depression or lack of self-esteem triggered or exacerbated by the stress experienced years ago within the marriage." The judge ordered indefinite spousal support of $500 monthly which was subject to review after a year.

*In a spousal relationship of short duration where the recipient spouse is disabled, fixed term spousal support will be ordered regardless of whether the spouse can ever return to work when disabled* — *Wilson v. Marchand,* 2007 CarswellOnt 6230, 2007 ONCJ 408, 43 R.F.L. (6th) 356 (Ont. C.J.), additional reasons at 2007 CarswellOnt 6469, 2007 ONCJ 455, 43 R.F.L. (6th) 369 (Ont. C.J.). The parties had a child together during their common-law relationship. Shortly after the child's birth, the wife was diagnosed with a brain tumour and suffered from seizures. It was unclear whether the wife would ever be able to return to work or what her long-term health prospects would be. The judge found that she was entitled to spousal support, despite the short length of the cohabitation and the absence of legal marriage. The parties comported themselves as if they were in a spousal relationship, purchasing a house together and having a planned child. The judge found that "it is necessary to balance the need for closure to the payor in a short relationship with the moral obligation to support an ill or disabled spouse regardless of the length of the relationship" (para. 18). Under the SSAG, Mr. Wilson would not have to pay support. However, the judge found that the wife's disability dictated otherwise. Spousal support was ordered in the amount of $500 for another 2 years in addition to the support that had already been paid since 2006.

*Where the payor spouse has ample means and the recipient spouse is unable to support herself due to disability, the short duration of a marriage will not be a bar to an award of indefinite support* — *Eng v. Eng,* 2006 CarswellBC 2237, 2006 BCSC 1353, 31 R.F.L. (6th) 407, [2006] B.C.J. No. 2044 (B.C.S.C.). The parties were married for 3-and-a-half years, following a 6-month period of cohabitation. The wife had serious health issues necessitating the use of a wheelchair and the judge found it was unlikely she would ever work again. The health issues arose before the marriage. A few months before the parties began living together, the husband inherited a substantial amount of property and shares on the death of his father. The judge found that the wife had an "obvious and significant" ongoing need of support, given her disability. Although the wife had benefitted in some ways from the marriage, these benefits were offset by the losses of her prior spousal support from her first marriage, her home, and other disadvantages caused by the breakdown of the marriage. Despite the short duration of the relationship, the judge found that the husband had expressly and implicitly agreed that he would provide for the wife for the rest of her life. The judge awarded non-compensatory support. The judge found that the short duration of the marriage prompted an award which allowed the wife to live with comfort and dignity, but not at the same level she enjoyed during the marriage. The husband's ample means and the ongoing support needed by the wife dictated an indefinite duration of spousal support.

## 17.6 Compensatory Exception in Short Marriages Without Children

Some short- or medium-length marriages can involve large compensatory claims, disproportionate to the length of the marriage, even without any children involved. These compensatory claims may relate to an economic loss or may involve a restitutionary claim for an economic advantage conferred. Some examples come to mind:

- One spouse is transferred for employment purposes, on one or more occasions, forcing the other spouse to give up his or her job and to become a secondary earner.
- One spouse moves across the country to marry, giving up his or her job or business to do so. [citation omitted]
- One spouse works to put the other through a post-secondary or professional program but the couple separates shortly after graduation as in *Caratun v. Caratun* [citation omitted] before the supporting spouse has been able to enjoy any of the benefits of the other spouse's enhanced earning capacity.

There could undoubtedly be other examples.

If a claimant spouse can prove such a disproportionate compensatory claim, then this exception allows for an individualized determination of the amount of spousal support, based upon the size and nature of that claim. The formula will not offer much assistance. (SSAG Chapter 12.5)

The majority of cases recently of compensatory support in short marriages without children have been found to be in situations where the recipient spouse has made a dramatic relocation for the sake of the relationship, often giving up a good job to do so.

*Spousal support awarded on a compensatory basis because both the "compensatory" and the "non-primary parent to fulfill parenting role" exceptions to the SSAG applied — S. (R.M.) v. S. (F.P.C.)*, 2011 CarswellBC 170, 2011 BCCA 53, 90 R.F.L. (6th) 1, 14 B.C.L.R. (5th) 84, 299 B.C.A.C. 186, 508 W.A.C. 186, [2011] B.C.J. No. 174 (B.CC.A.). The parties married in 2004 and separated in 2007. They had two children. The wife was ordered to pay the husband spousal support over and above the Spousal Support Advisory Guidelines ranges He was awarded spousal support on a compensatory basis, because he suffered considerable economic disadvantage during the short course of the marriage. He quit his job in Mexico and relocated to British Columbia, where he was unable to find equivalent work. Although the trial judge did not expressly state that the husband was entitled to support over the SSAG ranges, he seemed to apply both the "compensatory exception" and the "non-primary parent to fulfil parenting role exception". Both exceptions were relevant in this case, particularly the latter to ensure that the husband could fulfil his parenting role when the children were in his custody. Based on these exceptions there was no error in awarding spousal support above the SSAG ranges. The review condition was varied in scope to "a review on entitlement and quantum for non-compensatory support related directly to the ability of the [husband] to financially meet his parenting role under the joint custody order".

*Where support determined in reference to the SSAG is insufficient to provide adequate support and the payor's income is not accurate because of tax consequences, support above the SSAG range will be ordered* — Tasman v. Henderson, 2013 CarswellOnt 9222, 2013 ONSC 4377 (Ont. S.C.J.). The parties were together for 6 years including 5 years of marriage and had no children. The wife sought interim interim support. The judge found that the SSAG were not appropriate as they did not adequately provide for spousal support in this case of a short marriage with no children. The husband's income did not reflect his true income because of tax issues, and he had a pattern of RRSP withdrawals during the relationship. Interim interim support was ordered at three times the mid-range of the SSAG range.

*Majority of cases recently of compensatory support in short marriages without children have been found to be in situations where the recipient spouse has made a dramatic relocation for the sake of the relationship, often giving up a good job to do so* — spousal support awarded on a compensatory basis because both the "compensatory" and the "non-primary parent to fulfill parenting role" exceptions to the SSAG applied — S. (R.M.) v. S. (F.P.C.), 2011 CarswellBC 170, 2011 BCCA 53, 90 R.F.L. (6th) 1, 14 B.C.L.R. (5th) 84, 299 B.C.A.C. 186, 508 W.A.C. 186 (B.C.C.A.). The parties married in 2004 and separated in 2007. They had two children. The wife was ordered to pay the husband spousal support over and above the *Spousal Support Advisory Guidelines* ranges He was awarded spousal support on a compensatory basis, because he suffered considerable economic disadvantage during the short course of the marriage. He quit his job in Mexico and relocated to B.C., where he was unable to find equivalent work. Although the trial judge did not expressly state that the husband was entitled to support over the SSAG ranges, he seemed to apply both the "compensatory exception" and the "non-primary parent to fulfil parenting role exception". Both exceptions were relevant in this case, particularly the latter to ensure that the husband could fulfil his parenting role when the children were in his custody. Based on these exceptions there was no error in awarding spousal support above the SSAG ranges. The review condition was varied in scope to "a review on entitlement and quantum for non-compensatory support related directly to the ability of the [husband] to financially meet his parenting role under the joint custody order".[Autors' note: This is an unusual 1 case where the compensatory exception is invoked in a short marriage with children].

*Compensatory exception applied after 4-year marriage* — Beardsall v. Dubois, 2009 CarswellOnt 559, [2009] O.J. No. 416 (Ont. S.C.J.). The wife had moved from Ottawa to London to be with the husband, and had quit her job. The court quoted the SSAG text about the compensatory exception, which appeared to apply on the facts. The spousal support order made was substantially more generous than the SSAG range for this 4-year marriage.

*Where one party has relocated, giving up a well-paying job or career, even when the marriage is of a short duration with no children, the compensatory exception will apply* — Volik v. Lisovska, 2011 CarswellBC 12, 2011 BCSC 22, [2011] B.C.J. No. 28 (B.C.S.C.). The parties were married for less than a year. The wife had been living in Ukraine when the parties decided they would marry and live in Victoria. The claimant left a well-paying job in Ukraine to relocate and the judge found she had been economically disadvantaged by the marriage. This case fell under the compensatory exception because the wife had made a large sacrifice for the marriage. The judge granted compensatory, non-compensatory (need-based) support, and contractual support, in that the husband agreed to sponsor the wife for immigration purposes and then withdrew that support.

*Despite the short length of a marriage, where a spouse relocates and suffers economic disadvantage from a marriage, the marriage may fall within the compensatory exception and the spouse may be entitled to compensatory spousal support* — *Ahn v. Ahn*, 2007 CarswellBC 2227, 2007 BCSC 1148, [2007] B.C.J. No. 1702 (B.C.S.C.). The parties were married for shortly over a year and were both in their fifties. The wife had relocated from the U.S. and had given up a well-paying, stable job to marry the husband. The parties had a traditional marriage with the wife taking care of household duties, while the husband was a successful businessman. The judge found that the wife was entitled to compensatory spousal support stemming from the breakdown of the marriage, which caused her economic disadvantage due to the fact she had given up her employment and relocated in order to marry.

*Where the recipient spouse quits his/her job to relocate to live with the payor spouse, compensatory support above the Guidelines range will be appropriate* — *Fuller v. Matthews*, 2007 CarswellBC 1018, 2007 BCSC 444, [2007] B.C.J. No. 656 (B.C.S.C.), additional reasons at 2007 CarswellBC 1683, 2007 BCSC 1099 (B.C.S.C.). The parties lived together in a short relationship which nonetheless met the requirements for a spousal relationship under the *Family Relations Act*. The common-law wife claimed spousal support on a compensatory basis because she moved to the defendant's house and, in a mutual decision with the defendant, she quit her job and moved cities (within B.C.) to reside with him. The judge awarded an amount above the Guidelines range. The judge found that the Guidelines range did not "adequately address the very specific financial sacrifice the plaintiff made when she quit her teaching job in Courtney to join the defendant in Delta". [There was no specific mention of the compensatory exception.]

## 17.7 Property Division, Reapportionment of Property

Spousal support is only determined after the division of family or matrimonial property. In Canada, there is a different regime for property division in every province and territory. All the property regimes have a few common characteristics: special rules governing the matrimonial home, a defined pool of family or matrimonial property, and a strong presumption of equal division of that pool. In most cases, there will be some net accumulation of property and it will be divided equally. Apart from the debt payment exception already mentioned, there are two other situations where a possible "property" exception has been suggested in determining spousal support: unequal division of property, or high property awards.

The remedies of property division and spousal support perform distinct functions and have different rationales. In the Draft Proposal, we therefore did not propose a general exception for unequal property division. We were less categorical about any exception for high property awards. We do recognize that British Columbia's property law is different and thus justifies an exception, as B.C. law allows unequal division or "reapportionment" on grounds that ordinarily are taken into consideration for the spousal support remedy. (SSAG, Section 12.6)

Unlike any other Canadian matrimonial property statute, the British Columbia *Family Relations Act* empowers a court to reapportion, or divide unequally, property between spouses on grounds that overlap with spousal support considerations:

> s. 65(1) If the provisions for division of property between spouses under section 56, Part 6 or their marriage agreement, as the case may be, would be unfair having regard to. . .

> (e) the needs of each spouse to become or remain economically independent and self-sufficient, or
>
> (f) any other circumstances relating to the acquisition, preservation, maintenance, improvement or use of property or the capacity or liabilities of a spouse, the Supreme Court, on application, may order that the property covered by section 56, Part 6 or the marriage agreement, as the case may be, be divided into shares fixed by the court.
>
> Factors (e) (self-sufficiency) and (f) (capacity or liabilities) are frequently used to adjust for the economic disadvantage of the lower-income spouse at the end of the marriage. . . In the distinctive property regime in British Columbia, and only in British Columbia, there is thus an exception available where a sufficiently large reapportionment order has been made on these 'spousal support' grounds. (SSAG Chapter 12.6.1)

## Reapportionment of property

The B.C. reapportionment exception has not had very much effect on spousal support awards, not even in location within the ranges, chiefly because the amounts are quite small: *see* Carol Rogerson and Rollie Thompson, "Complex Issues Bring us Back to Basics" 28 CFLQ 263 at pages 297-298; 308-309.

*The SSAG exception for reapportionment of property applies to short relationships and/or no children where it can be demonstrated that both compensatory and non-compensatory bases for an award of spousal support can be adequately met by a reapportionment of property — Does not necessarily require a spousal support award outside the SSAG ranges — Where unequal reapportionment of property does not adequately reflect compensatory and non-compensatory needs resulting from a long-term, traditional marriage, support at the low end of the SSAG range will be ordered — Marquez v. Zapiola*, 2013 CarswellBC 3038, 2013 BCCA 433, 36 R.F.L. (7th) 22, 51 B.C.L.R. (5th) 55, 344 B.C.A.C. 133, 587 W.A.C. 133 (B.C.C.A.), additional reasons at 2014 CarswellBC 202, 2014 BCCA 35, 40 R.F.L. (7th) 53, 54 B.C.L.R. (5th) 1, 50 C.P.C. (7th) 95, 349 B.C.A.C. 302, 596 W.A.C. 302 (B.C.C.A.). The parties were married for 19 years and had two children in the mother's custody. The trial judge found the wife was entitled to compensatory and non-compensatory support. The trial judge awarded spousal support within the SSAG range to the wife on the basis that there was an unequal division of property. Income was imputed to the wife. The judge found that, although the SSAG exception relating to reapportionment of property could result in an order where the reapportionment met compensatory and non-compensatory needs, this will not necessarily result in an order of support below the SSAG range. The Court of Appeal awarded support at the low end of the range, finding the amount awarded by the trial judge did not adequately reflect the wife's compensatory and non-compensatory requirements. The wife was not required to deplete her capital in order to achieve the marital standard of living.

*Reapportionment of matrimonial home — Young v. Young*, 2009 CarswellBC 3587, 2009 BCCA 518, 76 R.F.L. (6th) 75, 278 B.C.A.C. 129, 471 W.A.C. 129 (B.C.C.A.). The parties were married for 16 years. The husband earned $65,500 per year. After paying child support for the parties' three children, the husband could not afford to pay spousal support. Accordingly, the court, having regard to all of the circumstances, divided the matrimonial home 64/36 so that the wife got the higher share. The appellate court affirmed the reapportionment of the net proceeds of the sale of the matrimonial home 64/36 in favour of the wife under s. 65 of the *Family Relations Act*. The Court of Appeal held that the trial judge had not overlooked the contributions of the husband to the matrimonial home before and during the marriage and after separation. He had ordered a lower reapportionment in the wife's favour than in the cases to which he referred indicated that he took the husband's contributions into account. He referred explicitly to the husband's pre-marital contribution. An SSAG spousal support comparison does not undermine the reapportionment.

*Reapportionment justifies support quantum slightly below SSAG range — Tedham v. Tedham*, 2005 CarswellBC 2346, 2005 BCCA 502, 20 R.F.L. (6th) 217, 47 B.C.L.R. (4th) 254, [2006] 3 W.W.R. 212, 261 D.L.R. (4th) 332, [2005] B.C.J. No. 2186 (B.C.C.A.); additional reasons at 2005 CarswellBC 2699, 2005 BCCA 553, 47 B.C.L.R. (4th) 276, 261 D.L.R. (4th) 332 at 359, [2006] 3 W.W.R. 234, 217 B.C.A.C. 250, 358 W.A.C. 250 (B.C.C.A.). Marital property had been reapportioned in the wife's favour and this was a reason to fix the support quantum at $6,000, whereas the bottom of the SSAG range was $6,260.

*Where the recipient spouse has obtained the majority of the family assets and other factors are present, exceptions to the SSAG will apply — L. (E.A.) v. G. (H.M.)*, 2010 CarswellBC 1612, 2010 BCSC 892, 83 R.F.L. (6th) 125 (B.C.S.C.). The judge in this case reviewed spousal support after a 3-year initial period had elapsed. He found that there was a material change in circumstances. The judge had previously made orders granting the wife the real property of the family, including the marital home and the family cottage, and granting the husband business assets including shares. The value of the real estate was found to greatly outstrip the value of the business assets. The judge considered this fact, as well as the wife's increased ability to earn income post-relocation, the increased cost of access for the father, the debt repayments he was compelled to make in the context of his bankruptcy, in determining that the situation fell within the exceptions to the SSAG. The judge awarded significantly less than the amount suggested in the SSAG ranges.

*No spousal support awarded — D. (C.J.) v. E. (J.H.)*, 2009 CarswellBC 2248, 2009 BCSC 1168 (B.C.S.C.). The court declined to award the husband spousal support as the reapportionment was in his favour.

*SSAG not appropriate where reapportioning in wife's favour — Mandreck v. Mandreck*, 2009 CarswellBC 2968, 2009 BCSC 1511, 75 R.F.L. (6th) 339 (B.C.S.C.). The wife received her entire teacher's pension as well as other assets.

*Where one party has dissipated family assets, is unlikely to pay support, and the other party has been economically disadvantaged by the marriage, an unequal division of assets under s. 65(1) of the Family Relations Act will be appropriate — N. (M.L.) v. N. (D.)*, 2006 CarswellBC 3043, 2006 BCCA 561, 34 R.F.L. (6th) 272, 62 B.C.L.R. (4th) 116, 233 B.C.A.C. 261, 386 W.A.C. 261, [2006] B.C.J. No. 3178 (B.C.C.A.). The husband appealed from an order reapportioning the matrimonial home 100% in favour of the wife. At the time of trial, the husband had accrued child support arrears of more than $6,000. The trial judge decided that the husband would likely be similarly uncooperative in payment of eventual spousal support payments and therefore the wife agreed to forego spousal support (compensatory and non-compensatory) in return for reapportionment of property. The trial judge found that an unequal division of property was appropriate given the arrears and the irresponsible behaviour of the husband post-separation, including dissipation of assets and gambling. He apportioned the assets 75% to the wife, including the matrimonial home, and 25% to the husband, including the RRSPs. The Court of Appeal found that dissipation of assets and material non-disclosure were "relevant circumstances which the court is entitled to take into account in making compensation orders". The Court of Appeal upheld the trial judge's decision, although it emphasized that property should first be allocated under a s. 65(1) analysis prior to turning to the issue of spousal support, where the trial judge somewhat conflated the issues. However, when the Court of Appeal used the trial judge's findings of fact in determining the "appropriate reapportionment" under s. 65(1), it came to the conclusion that the award made by the trial judge was appropriate.

*Fact of reapportionment (of both assets and debt) is a factor which should be taken into account in applying the Advisory Guidelines* — McEachern v. McEachern, 2006 CarswellBC 2750, 2006 BCCA 508, 33 R.F.L. (6th) 315, [2007] 3 W.W.R. 471, 62 B.C.L.R. (4th) 95, 385 W.A.C. 185, 232 B.C.A.C. 185, [2006] B.C.J. No. 2917 (B.C.C.A.). Where there is a small reapportionment, given the length of the marriage and the roles played by the parties in the marriage, the reapportionment can properly be taken into account by considering an award at the lower end of the range suggested by the Advisory Guidelines.

## Property division — high property awards

The remedies of property division and spousal support perform distinct functions and have different rationales. In the Draft proposal, we therefore did not propose a general exception for unequal property division. We were less categorical about any exception for high property awards. (SSAG S. 12.6)

*Where a party has received a very substantial property award under equalization and the spousal support under the SSAG falls under the over $350,000 exception, support under the SSAG range may be awarded* — H. (W.) v. R. (I.), 2012 CarswellBC 3065, 2012 BCSC 1483 (B.C.S.C.). The husband in this case had a business empire worth $41 million. The parties met in Cuba while the husband was on vacation, where the wife was working as a pharmacist and scuba diving instructor. The parties had a marriage contract which was set aside on the grounds that the execution was substantially unfair. The Court used its discretion under the SSAG for incomes above $350,000, considering the conditions, means, needs and other circumstances of each spouse in finding that spousal support should be below the SSAG ranges. The wife had received a very substantial property award under the equalization process.

*Wife had over $4 million in assets — spousal support below SSAG quantum ordered* — Chutter v. Chutter, 2008 CarswellBC 2661, 2008 BCCA 507, 60 R.F.L. (6th) 263, 301 D.L.R. (4th) 297, [2009] 3 W.W.R. 246, 443 W.A.C. 109, 263 B.C.A.C. 109, 86 B.C.L.R. (4th) 233, [2008] B.C.J. No. 2398 (B.C.C.A.); additional reasons at 2009 CarswellBC 1028, 2009 BCCA 177, 97 B.C.L.R. (4th) 32, 70 R.F.L. (6th) 1, [2009] 12 W.W.R. 100, 269 B.C.A.C. 206, 453 W.A.C. 206, 309 D.L.R. (4th) 670 (B.C.C.A.); reversing 2007 CarswellBC 1296, 2007 BCSC 814, [2007] B.C.J. No. 1247 (B.C.S.C.). The parties' settlement agreement had left the wife with over $4 million in assets, and the trial judge had found her not entitled to spousal support, despite the husband's significantly higher income. The Court of Appeal overturned this finding, and then considered the SSAG with regard to amount and duration after noting at paragraph 107 that "the fact that this is a high asset case does not make the Guidelines irrelevant." However, the court ordered spousal support in an amount below the SSAG range, because of the wife's large asset holdings. [The property division exception was not mentioned].

*Where the recipient spouse has obtained the majority of the family assets and other factors are present, exceptions to the SSAG will apply* — L. (E.A.) v. G. (H.M.), 2010 CarswellBC 1612, 2010 BCSC 892, 83 R.F.L. (6th) 125 (B.C. S.C.), additional reasons to 2010 CarswellBC 896, 2010 BCSC 509, 83 R.F.L. (6th) 72 (B.C.S.C.). The judge in this case reviewed spousal support after a 3-year initial period had elapsed. He found that there was a material change in circumstances. The judge had previously made orders granting the wife the family's real property, including the marital home and the family cottage, and granting the husband business assets including shares. The value of the real estate was found to greatly outstrip the value of the business assets. The judge considered this fact, as well as the wife's increased ability to earn income post-relocation, the increased cost of access for the father, the debt repayments he was compelled to make in the context of his bankruptcy, in determining that the situation fell within the exceptions to the SSAG. The court referred in particular to "both parties' changed financial circumstances, their new geographic circumstances, the debt payments that the defendant is obliged to make in the context of his bankruptcy (which the support payments and arrears survive), the plaintiff's enhanced ability to earn income in Prince Edward Island . . ., and the apportionment of matrimonial property." The judge awarded significantly less than the amount suggested in the SSAG ranges.

*Exceptions — property division — apply SSAG with care when property not divided equally — Hartshorne v. Hartshorne*, 2009 CarswellBC 1398, 2009 BCSC 698, 70 R.F.L. (6th) 106, [2009] B.C.J. 1050 (B.C. S.C.); reversed in part 2010 CarswellBC 1618, 2010 BCCA 327, 82 R.F.L. (6th) 1, 6 B.C.L.R. (5th) 58, 289 B.C.A.C. 244, 489 W.A.C. 244 (B.C. C.A.); additional reasons 2011 CarswellBC 107, 2011 BCCA 29, 95 R.F.L. (6th) 14, B.C.L.R. (5th) 33, 330 D.L.R. (4th) 503, 299 B.C.A.C. 6, 508 W.A.C. 6, [2011] B.C.J. No. 107 (B.C.C.A.). Among the reasons for applying the SSAG only "with care" in this case, the judge observed at paragraph 123 that "the ranges are based on a strong presumption that the parties accumulated property during their marriage which has been divided equally. Here. . . the parties' marriage agreement. . . did not operate to create an equal division of property." [*Authors' Note*: More properly, there is an assumption that property has been divided equally. There may be many different reasons for unequal division that may have little effect on spousal support.]

## Boston v. Boston

> . . . [T]he Advisory Guidelines on amount and duration do not change the law from *Boston v. Boston* governing double-dipping, mostly from pensions. That law remains in place, as a possible constraint upon the amount of support, determining if some portion of income should be excluded from the formula because it has been previously shared under property division. SSAG, s. 12.6.3

An extensive discussion of the complexities of this exception and the cases where an adjustment has been made to prevent "double-dipping" can be found . . . under "The Without Child Support Formula (Retirement cases under the without child support formula." *(New and Improved User's Guide, March 31, 2010)*.

*There is no double recovery contrary to* Boston v. Boston *where 'the proper basis of compensation, the divided public service pension and Canada Pension Plan benefits are excluded in respect to both parties — Brisson v. Brisson*, 2012 CarswellBC 3051, 2012 BCCA 396, 22 R.F.L. (7th) 1, 39 B.C.L.R. (5th) 1, 328 B.C.A.C. 163, 558 W.A.C. 163 (B.C.C.A.). The husband had an annual real income of $38,875 comprised of income from a public service pension, Old Age Security, Canada Pension Plan and a Veterans Affairs disability benefit. The wife had an income of $11,550 from part-time employment.

*There is no error in failing to order spousal support in accordance with the SSAGs where the sole source of income for the parties is income from assets that have been divided under the Family Relations Act — Puiu v. Puiu*, 2011 CarswellBC 3174, 2011 BCCA 480, 10 R.F.L. (7th) 108, 313 B.C.A.C. 76, 533 W.A.C. 76, [2011] B.C.J. No. 2308 (B.C.C.A.). The parties were in their sixties and no longer worked. Neither of them had any income other than from their assets.

Spousal Support Advisory Guidelines *were not applicable where the husband's income could not be determined and the SSAG formulae did not consider the exception to double-dipping from pension income* — Flieger v. Adams, 2011 CarswellNB 444, 2011 NBQB 237, 14 R.F.L. (7th) 125, 379 N.B.R. (2d) 110, 978 A.P.R. 110 (N.B.Q.B.). The parties had a 35-year, primarily traditional, marriage. During the marriage the wife held various low-paying jobs and was financially dependent on the husband. On consent the husband was ordered to pay the wife $1,750 per month in spousal support. The husband's motion to vary support to reflect his early retirement was granted in part. The wife conceded that the quantum of support should be varied. The wife continued to be entitled to support on a compensatory and needs basis. The support that the wife had received prior to the husband's retirement did not meet her financial needs and she was required to encroach on her capital. The wife neither had the skills nor was sufficiently healthy to work outside the home. The husband had not proven that he was medically unable to continue to work. Support was awarded on an indefinite basis, but the *Spousal Support Advisory Guidelines* were not applicable. There was insufficient evidence to determine the husband's potential income and his current pension income. The SSAG did not consider the financial advantage that the husband had by sharing expenses with his current partner. The SSAG also did not consider the exception to double-dipping from pension income, which applied to the wife. The court awarded the wife $405 bi-weekly in spousal support, subject to variation and review.

*A pension asset may be included for Guidelines income purposes when the income generated from it is less for one party than for the other* — Mullins v. Mullins, 2012 CarswellNS 251, 2012 NSSC 143 (N.S.S.C.). The parties had a long-term marriage. The judge found that the wife was entitled to support. The parties' assets had already been divided, and the husband's portion of the pension was found to generate significantly more income than the wife's income. The judge found that, given the length of the marriage, the parties' standards of living should be similar. The husband had the ability to pay support without hardship.

*Court took into account that the parties had agreed that the already equalized portion of the husband's pension should not be considered for spousal support purposes and the court then applied the without child support formula* — Hurst v. Hurst, 2008 CarswellOnt 5707, 58 R.F.L. (6th) 377 (Ont. S.C.J.). See also Gammon v. Gammon, 2008 CarswellOnt 802, [2008] O.J. No. 603 (Ont. S.C.J.); additional reasons at 2008 CarswellOnt 6319, 60 R.F.L. (6th) 208, [2008] O.J. No. 4252 (Ont. S.C.J.) and Ellis v. Ellis, 2010 CarswellOnt 1814, 2010 ONSC 1880, 84 R.F.L. (6th) 263, [2010] O.J. No. 1250 (Ont. S.C.J.).

*Where the parties equalized the value of the husband's pension on separation, his pension income should be considered for purposes of determining support* — Scott v. Scott, 2009 CarswellOnt 7707, 2009 C.E.B. & P.G.R. 8371, [2009] O.J. No. 5279 (Ont. S.C.J.). The wife continued to need financial support and the husband had the ability to pay and consequently double recovery would be permitted in accordance with the Boston decision. The wife continued to experience economic hardship from the marriage breakdown. See also *Jenkins v. Jenkins*, 2009 CarswellMan 365, 2009 MBQB 189, 243 Man. R. (2d) 68 (Man. Q.B.).

*A support recipient is not required to access her portion of the split pension where the payee spouse retires early and add the pension income to her employment income, so her entitlement to spousal support is reduced or terminated* — Szczerbaniwicz v. Szczerbaniwicz, 2010 CarswellBC 759, 2010 BCSC 421, 84 R.F.L. (6th) 166 (B.C.S.C.). This ruling is especially important where there is a compensatory component to the spousal support, as opposed to support based strictly on need. See also *Swales v. Swales*, 2010 CarswellAlta 1946, 2010 ABCA 292, 90 R.F.L. (6th) 314 (Alta. C.A.); reversing 2010 CarswellAlta 507, 2010 ABQB 187, 26 Alta. L.R. (5th) 341, 2010 C.E.B. & P.G.R. 8382 (Alta. Q.B.).

*Pension division justifies spousal support below the SSAG range* — Oyama v. Oyama, 2009 CarswellBC 692, 2009 BCCA 114, 63 R.F.L. (6th) 1 (B.C.C.A.); affirming 2007 CarswellBC 632,

2007 BCSC 428 (B.C.S.C.). Because the support payor's pension had been divided to the benefit of the recipient, spousal support was awarded in an amount less than that called for by the SSAG. [The property division exception was not mentioned].

## 17.8 Basic Needs/Hardship: Without Child Support, Custodial Payor Formulas

The basic needs/hardship exception is non-compensatory. In other cases, in shorter marriages, the compelling financial circumstances at the interim stage can provide for a higher amount of support for a transitional period, such that no further exception need be applied by the time of trial. . . . [the] basic needs/hardship exception should only be considered at the trial or initial determination stage, after a full review of the merits on all the evidence, including any interim exception granted.

The basic needs/hardship exception applies under the without child support formula and the custodial payor formula, only in these circumstances:

- the formula range, even after restructuring, will not provide sufficient income for the recipient to meet her or his basic needs
- the reason will be that the recipient's base or non-support income is zero or too low
- the marriage will typically be short to medium in length, e.g. 1 to 10 years
- the payor spouse will have the ability to pay.

We should be clear that this exception is only intended to ease the transition in these hardship cases. It is not intended to provide the marital standard of living, but only a standard of basic needs. And it is not intended to provide support for a long period of time after a shorter marriage, but only for a short transition period. . . . One situation where the basic needs/hardship exception has been applied is immigration sponsorship cases . . . For the most part, those who pressed for this exception can be found in big cities and it may be that this specific exception is not necessary outside of those big cities. (SSAG Chapter 12.7)

*Fact pattern suggests applicability of this exception* — Simpson v. Grignon, 2007 CarswellOnt 3095, 39 R.F.L. (6th) 329, [2007] O.J. No. 1915 (Ont. S.C.J.). The court found at para. 20 that "[t]he range of support indicated by the Spousal Support Advisory Guidelines is much lower than what would be considered customary in Ontario, even having regard to the short duration of this marriage." The parties had cohabited for roughly 4.5 years. The amount of support ordered was well above the SSAG range, although the duration was within it. The facts of the case seem appropriate for the "basic needs/hardship exception" as it is described in the SSAG.

*Immigration cases with fact patterns to which this exception might be applicable* — Gidey v. Abay, 2007 CarswellOnt 6145, [2007] O.J. No. 3693 (Ont. S.C.J.); M. (T.) v. G. (M.A.), 2006 CarswellBC 3438, 2006 BCPC 604, [2006] B.C.J. No. 3479 (B.C. Prov. Ct.).

## 17.9  Non-taxable Payor Income

> What warrants this non-taxable exception is when the non-deductibility of the spousal support poses a problem for the payor's ability to pay, as the non-taxable payor is unable to pay the gross amount of spousal support that would be required of a payor with the benefits of deductibility.
>
> Under the without child support formula, ability to pay will usually only become an issue in longer marriage cases, marriages of 15 years or more. In these longer marriage cases, the 50/50 net income "cap" will simplify the use of this exception, as the upper limit on spousal support will be equalization of the spouses' net incomes. (SSAG Chapter 12.8)
>
> In every one of these non-taxable exception cases, it is necessary to balance the tax positions of the spouses — the reduced ability to pay of the payor spouse, who can't deduct the support paid, and the needs or loss of the recipient spouse, who still has to pay taxes on spousal support and only receives after-tax support. (SSAG Chapter 12.8)

*Amount below range chosen in part due to payor's inability to deduct payment from income* — *Paul v. Paul*, 2008 CarswellNS 197, 2008 NSSC 124, [2008] N.S.J. No. 157 (N.S.S.C.). The court stated at para. 35: "Any spousal support paid by the husband to the wife is not deductible for income tax purposes by the husband or included in the income of the wife since the parties are First Nation individuals. The Court is unclear whether the 'Without Child Support Formula' in the Spousal Support Advisory Guidelines takes this factor into account." The support quantum ordered was below the SSAG range for this among other reasons. No explicit reference was made in the case report to the "Non-Taxable Payor Income" exception.

Payments where this exception may be used would include: Workers' Compensation, disability payments, income earned by an aboriginal person on reserve and some overseas employment arrangements. "In these cases, the payor is unable to deduct the support paid, contrary to the assumption built into the formulas for amount. In most cases, the recipient of spousal support will still have to include the support as income and pay tax on it." See User's Guide, March 31, 2010, s. 12, Exceptions.

*Lower amount of support where government credits and benefits not entirely applicable as recipient spouse and child live outside Canada* — *Boju v. Corr*, 2009 CarswellOnt 563 (Ont. S.C.J.). The husband payor lived in Ontario and the wife recipient lived in Phoenix, Arizona. According to the SSAG, the range of support was between $1,008 per month (40% of the net family income) and $1,093 per month (46% of the net family income). The payor submitted that the amounts were premised on taxation rates and other government credits and benefits that were not entirely applicable to a child and recipient spouse living in the U.S. However, the court found that the recipient had addressed this concern by "dramatically reducing" the amount she was claiming to $500 per month. This was the amount ordered by the court on an interim basis. There was no calculation provided for the way in which this amount was determined.

*Where neither party is required to pay income tax, support may be awarded at the low end of the SSAG range* — *Syrette v. Syrette*, 2011 CarswellOnt 10640, 2011 ONSC 6108, 8 R.F.L. (7th) 293, 82 C.B.R. (5th) 316 (Ont. S.C.J.). The parties were married for 24 years and both parties lived and worked on a reserve, so neither of them was required to pay income tax. Spousal support was awarded at the low end of the SSAG range. No reference was made to the non-taxable exception found in the SSAG.

*Lower amount of spousal support ordered because husband did not receive tax relief* — *James v. Torrens*, 2007 CarswellSask 356, 2007 SKQB 219 (Sask. Q.B.). The wife was seeking spousal support in this case. The court noted that "the issue of spousal support in this case is complicated by the fact that the husband is not able to deduct the value of the award against his income." The court awarded the wife $350 per month in spousal support.

## 17.10 Non-primary Parent to Fulfil Parenting Role under the Custodial Payor Formula

To come within this exception:

- the recipient spouse and non-custodial parent must play an important role in the child's care and upbringing after separation
- the marriage is shorter and the child is younger
- the ranges for amount and duration are low enough and short enough under the custodial payor formula that the non-custodial parent may not be able to continue to fulfil his or her parental role.

. . . Most often, the exception will be used to extend the duration of spousal support, until the child is old enough and the parenting functions are much reduced. Less frequently, the amount of support might need to be increased, to ensure the recipient spouse has sufficient resources to meet the specific demands of parenting. In practical terms, this parenting exception should be considered first, before reaching the more general illness and disability exception discussed above. (SSAG Chapter 12.9)

This exception may be used where the support recipient does not have the resources to meet the requirements of parenting. A notable situation that has prompted application of this exception is when travel costs for access are significant, where parents may need to travel hundreds or thousands of kilometers in order to both exercise access and maintain gainful employment.

*Spousal support awarded on the basis of the "non-primary parent to fulfil parenting role" exceptions to the SSAG applied* — S. (R.M.) v. S. (F.P.C.), 2011 CarswellBC 170, 2011 BCCA 53, 90 R.F.L. (6th) 1, 14 B.C.L.R. (5th) 84, 299 B.C.A.C. 186, 508 W.A.C. 186 (B.C.C.A.). The parties had married in 2004 and separated in 2007. They had two young children. The wife was an anesthetist and the husband had been a sports director at a Club Med in Mexico when they met. He gave up his job to move to B.C. when they married. When the wife ended the marriage, the husband moved into the basement of the parties' home. The wife was ordered to pay the husband spousal support over and above the *Spousal Support Advisory Guidelines* ranges. Although the trial judge did not expressly state that the husband was entitled to support over the SSAG ranges, he seemed to apply both the "compensatory exception" and the "non-primary parent to fulfil parenting role exception". Both exceptions were relevant in this case, particularly the latter to ensure that the husband could fulfil his parenting role when the children were in his custody. Based on these exceptions there was no error in awarding spousal support above the SSAG ranges. The review condition was varied in scope to "a review on entitlement and quantum for non-compensatory support related directly to the ability of the [husband] to financially meet his parenting role under the joint custody order".

*An award in excess of the SSAG range and duration was upheld because the recipient mother fell within the exception of a non-primary parent fulfilling a parenting role* — Kelly v. Kelly, 2011 CarswellBC 842, 2011 BCCA 173, 18 B.C.L.R. (5th) 99, 303 B.C.A.C. 209, 512 W.A.C. 209 (B.C.C.A.). The trial judge awarded the wife periodic spousal support that exceeded the *Spousal Support Advisory Guidelines* calculations, both in amount and duration. The husband's appeal of the award was dismissed. Although it would have been preferable if the trial judge had allowed the parties to review and make submissions on his SSAG calculations, in this case the result would not have differed. The award of a greater amount and longer duration of support was justified because the wife fell within the exception of a non-primary parent fulfilling a parenting role under the custodial payor formula. The exception can apply if the support recipient does not have the resources to meet the demands of parenting. The trial judge considered the parties' financial circumstances and the best interests of the children in applying the exception.

*A payor will not meet the onus of showing that the "custodial payor exception" applies where the ranges within the regular formula are sufficient to take account that he was the custodial payor* — Zdrill v. Zdrill, 2011 CarswellOnt 2886, 2011 ONSC 2188 (Ont. S.C.J.). The parties had two young children who resided with the father. During the marriage, the mother was essentially a stay-at-home parent. Post-separation, she experienced financial difficulties and was subsisting on social assistance at the time of trial. The court found that no income should be attributed to the wife, who was clearly entitled to compensatory support, because of her role in the marriage. At the time of this interim motion for spousal support, she was suffering from depression and had never worked full-time. The husband argued that he did not have the ability to pay and invoked a number of exceptions found in the SSAG, including the "custodial payor exception". The court held that a payor will not meet the onus of showing that the custodial payor exception applies where the ranges within the regular formula are sufficient to take account of this fact. The husband earned $58,407 and the wife received social assistance of $6,089, which resulted in a range from a low of $803 to a high of $1,071. The court, taking into account that the father had custody of the children, ordered interim spousal support in the amount of $803 per month until further order of the court.

*Exception applied in light of substantial access travel costs for non-custodial spousal support recipient* — Petit v. Petit, 2008 CarswellOnt 8257, [2008] O.J. No. 5437 (Ont. S.C.J.), additional reasons at 2009 CarswellOnt 3841, [2009] O.J. No. 2795 (Ont. S.C.J.). The court specifically acknowledged and applied the "non-primary parenting role" exception in this case. The spousal support recipient lived approximately 1000 km away from the spousal support payor, and would incur substantial travel costs in order to exercise access. An amount in excess of the SSAG ranges was ordered.

*Custodial payor situation — access costs justify quantum above range* — Mumford v. Mumford, 2008 CarswellNS 171, 2008 NSSC 82, 266 N.S.R. (2d) 11, 851 A.P.R. 11, [2008] N.S.J. No. 138 (N.S.S.C.). The duration was fixed at 16 years, which was the maximum suggested by the SSAG range. The court ordered an amount in excess of the SSAG custodial payor range after making the following findings at para. 92: "She is also still required to provide for her son when he is visiting and to incur access expenses." [However, the SSAG's "Non-Primary Parent to Fulfil Parenting Role under the Custodial Payor Formula" exception was not specifically mentioned. The recipient also had substantial medical problems.]

## 17.11 Special Needs of Child

First, duration. A child with special needs can obviously affect the ability of the primary parent to obtain employment, whether part-time or full-time. This may require that the duration of support be extended beyond the length of the marriage or beyond the last child finishing high school, the two possible maximum time limits under the with child support formula.

Second, amount. Again, a special needs child will often mean that the primary parent cannot work as much, perhaps not even part-time, and thus the amount of spousal support will be increased because of the recipient's lower income, an adjustment that can be accommodated by the with child support formula. But even then, there may be a need to go above the upper end of the range, to leave an even larger percentage of the family's net disposable income in the hands of the primary parent. . . (SSAG Chapter 12.10)

The court awarded support until the wife turned 60 because the husband was absent from the children's lives, the wife was ill and the children had medical issues — Caldwell v. Caldwell, 2013 CarswellAlta 1241, 2013 ABCA 268, 33 R.F.L. (7th) 285 (Alta. C.A.). The parties separated after 12 years of marriage. The chambers judge awarded the wife spousal support in the amount of $790 per month until her 60th birthday, subject to variation in the case of a significant change in circumstances. The husband appealed, citing the relatively short length of the marriage and the 18 years he had been paying support. The Court of Appeal noted that while long-term spousal support is unusual after a medium-length marriage, it was appropriate in these circumstances. [The SSAG exception for special needs of a child was not mentioned in this case.]

Where the recipient spouse has no ability to earn income because she is the caregiver for the parties' disabled children, this fact will be taken into account in imputing income for the purposes of the SSAG — Misner v. Misner, 2010 CarswellOnt 2713, 2010 ONSC 2284, 83 R.F.L. (6th) 264 (Ont. S.C.J.), additional reasons at 2011 CarswellOnt 3182, 2011 ONSC 2932, 5 R.F.L. (7th) 196 (Ont. S.C.J.), further additional reasons at 2011 CarswellOnt 8134, 2011 ONSC 4811, 5 R.F.L. (7th) 200 (Ont. S.C.J.). The parties were married for 20 years, and had four children. The judge recognized the inability of the wife to work given the huge effort required to care for the parties two special-needs children, whom the judge found would need assistance all their lives. The judge ordered spousal support at the high end of the Guidelines range.

Wife unable to work due to children's illnesses — Yeates v. Yeates, 2008 CarswellOnt 3842, 2008 ONCA 519 (Ont. C.A.). The parties separated after 15 years of marriage and three children. The eldest child had epilepsy and cerebral palsy, and would never become self-sufficient. The middle child suffered from autism. The husband's income was $108,872 per year. The wife argued that the care of the children made it impossible for her to return to work. The trial judge ordered $2,500 per month in spousal support. The husband appealed and the appeal was dismissed. The Court of Appeal noted that the amount of $2,500 per month was within the parameters of what was available and what the parties' real needs were. [The case did not specifically refer to the "special needs exception".]

Where disability payments to the child, child support can be reduced and interim spousal support can be ordered at the upper end of the SSAG range — Blonski v. Blonski, 2010 CarswellOnt 2768, 2010 ONSC 2552, [2010] O.J. No. 1781 (Ont. S.C.J.). A developmentally delayed child, aged 18, lived with his mother. The child received $796 monthly in government assistance. This assistance caused the judge to reduce child support payments, which in turn prompted the judge to award interim spousal support at the upper end of the SSAG range.

*Where the payor spouse has no ability to pay, even when the parties have a disabled child, nominal spousal support will be ordered* — Dhanesar v. Dhanesar, 2009 CarswellOnt 7173 (Ont. S.C.J.). The parties were married for approximately 16 years and had two minor children, one of whom was autistic. The husband was unemployed and had no ability to pay. The judge ordered nominal spousal support of $1 to be varied when the husband became employed.

## 17.12 Small Amounts, Inadequate Compensation under the With Child Support Formula

> The Advisory Guidelines must be consistent with section 15.3(2) and (3) of the Divorce Act and thus there must be an exception for duration, using the terms of s. 15.3(2):
>
> - as a result of giving priority to child support
> - the court is unable to make a spousal support order or the court makes a spousal support order in an amount less than it otherwise would have been
> - or the parties agree to those terms as part of an agreement.
>
> This section 15.3 exception would recognize that spousal support may have to continue past the time limits in these cases. And, further, in some of these cases, the amount of spousal support may even have to increase upon variation or review as the children cease to be "children of the marriage", but any of these increases in amount should remain within the formula ranges. (SSAG Chapter 12.11)

*Where priority has been given to child support in an order or agreement, and the amount of spousal support is less than it would otherwise have been, this will prompt an exception to the normal duration found in the SSAG and support will not be time-limited in cases where there is a strong compensatory element* — Abernethy v. Peacock, 2012 CarswellOnt 3368, 2012 ONCJ 145, [2012] O.J. No. 1203 (Ont. C.J.). This was a judgment after a retrial on an application to vary the spousal support provisions in a separation agreement. The judge found that the separation agreement had prioritised child support over spousal support. Now that the children were independent, the wife was still in need and had not obtained reasonable self-sufficiency despite efforts to do so. The 12.11 exception applied. The judge found it was uncertain whether self-sufficiency would ever be attained by the wife and ordered indefinite support.

*Spousal support likely to increase after child support terminated* — Hajir v. Farshidfar, 2008 CarswellOnt 7047 (Ont. S.C.J.). The court acknowledged that the wife had a strong compensatory claim and awarded her the upper range of the SSAG. However, the court further noted that once the eldest child finished university and was no longer a dependent, spousal support would likely increase.

*Retroactive and ongoing spousal support will be granted when previous awards did not adequately take into account the economic hardship caused by the marriage because of the priority of child support obligations* — Danby v. Danby, 2008 CarswellOnt 5512, [2008] O.J. No. 3659 (Ont. S.C.J.). The husband sought a variation lowering his support obligations after he retired. At the time of the prior support order, two of the parties' children were considered dependents. The judge found that the husband's spousal support obligations should continue, given the ongoing need and the fact that previous spousal support payments "did not meet the appropriate support objectives but, rather, were slightly more than nominal" in order to allow the payment of child support, which was given precedence when means were limited. Therefore, the obligation to support was ongoing, and as the older child was no longer dependent, money was now available for spousal support. The judge found that the wife was entitled to compensatory and noncompensatory support and that economic hardship had not been adequately addressed in the previous order. He granted retroactive and ongoing support.

*Where the SSAG suggests a range of $0, there will not necessarily be any reason to depart from this amount, even where compensatory entitlement has been found — P. (C.E.A.) v. P. (P.E.)*, 2006 CarswellBC 3207, 2006 BCSC 1913, [2006] B.C.J. No. 3295 (B.C.S.C.). The wife was diagnosed with bipolar disorder after separation. The parties began to cohabit in 1983, married in 1992 and separated in 2004. They had four children together. The wife had stopped work in 2002. The judge found that both parties had income which was only sufficient to meet their individual budgets, and they were earning roughly the same amount. The wife was found to be capable of caring for the children, however. Although the judge found that the wife had an entitlement to spousal support on a compensatory basis, the SSAG produced a quantum of $0 at both the lower and upper range of the Guidelines.

## 17.13 Other Grounds for Exceptions

The SSAG grounds for exceptions are not exhaustive. Others may be added in the future. Cases under this section will largely be cases that did not come neatly under the other exceptions set out in the SSAG. Some of the cases below should in fact be placed under existing exceptions. For example, *V. (S.S.) v. V. (G.J.)*, 2009 CarswellNB 303, 72 R.F.L. (6th) 203 (N.B.Q.B.), below, is really a debt case. Most of these cases where other grounds for exceptions will be found will be one of a kind, rather than a new category of exception.

*A long-term spousal support order is not usually granted for a 12-year marriage, but where the husband played no role, apart from financial, in raising the four children, long-term spousal support is justifiable — Caldwell v. Caldwell*, 2013 CarswellAlta 1241, 2013 ABCA 268, 33 R.F.L. (7th) 285 (Alta. C.A.). The wife had health issues, including depression, post-traumatic stress disorder for some time, gastro esophageal reflux disease and inflammatory arthritis, with systemic lupus erythematosis recently diagnosed. She was on extensive medication. The court ordered spousal support of $790 per month until the wife reached 60.

*Where restructuring does not result in a lump sum amount that is consistent with the Divorce Act, an exception to the SSAG will be found in determining quantum of the lump sum where the payor has serious health issues — Robinson v. Robinson*, 2011 CarswellBC 3271, 2011 BCSC 1489, 14 R.F.L. (7th) 141 (B.C.S.C.), affirmed 2012 CarswellBC 3789, 2012 BCCA 497, 40 B.C.L.R. (5th) 108 (B.C.C.A.). The trail judge awarded lump sum spousal support under the without child formula. The parties were married for 28 years and had two adult, independent children. The trial judge found that the wife had a claim for compensatory support and used the SSAG in order to determine monthly support of $6,000, or a mid-range amount. She then found that lump sum spousal support was indicated given the possible difficulty of collecting payments as the husband had moved to Germany, the husband's poor health and his income. However, the trial judge found that the lump sum indicated by the computer analysis did not meet the objectives of the *Divorce Act*, and the trial judge preferred another method of calculation. Consequently, the' trial judge made an order based on "the factors of relative tax situations, an appropriate discount rate for the present value, and a contingency rate where necessary". Given the poor health of the husband, the lump sum award was less than it would have been otherwise. The judge found that this case fell into the exceptions of the SSAG found at 3.4.2 (Restructuring). The decision was upheld by the Court of Appeal.

*Limited-duration, interim spousal award was set significantly below the range of the* Spousal Support Advisory Guidelines *where the dependant spouse lived with her parents — Gray v.*

*Breeze*, 2011 CarswellSask 345, 2011 SKQB 193 (Sask. Q.B.). The parties were married for three and a half years and had one child. After the marriage and the birth of their daughter, the wife significantly reduced her hours working as a chiropractor. The wife was awarded $3,000 per month in interim spousal support. The SSAG range for the husband's income of $223,900 was $5,634 to $6,747. The interim amount was set well below the SSAG range because the wife, who had moved back in with her parents, had minimal need. The court also determined that, although the wife was not expected to become immediately self-sufficient, she had the ability to increase the number of hours she was working. To encourage the wife to find more gainful employment, the award was set for six months, after which the wife could re-apply.

*When the recipient spouse has lower housing costs, this fact will create an exception to the Guidelines amounts — Schloegl v. McCroary*, 2008 CarswellBC 2706, 2008 BCSC 1722, 64 R.F.L. (6th) 343, [2008] B.C.J. No. 2443 (B.C.S.C.). The wife had a permanent arrangement to live with her mother, thereby lowering her expenses. The parties had a short marriage which resulted in the birth of a child, who, at the time of trial was approximately 2 years of age. In light of the wife's intent to live with her own mother until the child had finished high school, and the attendant lower housing costs, the judge awarded spousal support at slightly below Guidelines amounts. A review was to occur when the child entered kindergarten.

*Unconscionable behaviour regarding a separation agreement may prompt an award of support above the Guidelines — Tailor v. Tailor*, 2008 CarswellOnt 5866, 59 R.F.L. (6th) 316, [2008] O.J. No. 3900 (Ont. S.C.J.). The parties were married in India and the wife moved to Canada in 2005. The parties were married for less than 2 years and lived together for only 10 months. The judge set aside a Separation Agreement which had not been freely negotiated. The judge found that the husband's conduct in regard to the Separation Agreement was unconscionable and that this conduct was a factor in his decision to award spousal support slightly above the Guidelines amounts, for a 20-month period.

*Exception found where, after separation, the parties jointly purchased a home which had significant monthly mortgage payments — V. (S.S.) v. V. (G.J.)*, 2009 CarswellNB 303, 72 R.F.L. (6th) 203 (N.B.Q.B.). In light of the parties' joint purchase of a home after separation, the husband had accepted financial responsibility towards his wife and children which exceeded the Advisory Guideline support amounts. The wife would have a monthly shortfall in her budget if she did not receive help from her husband. The parties had been married for 18 years and had two children. The husband had a career in the military and presently earned $60,480. The wife had worked in various low paying jobs, full or part time, and also had had periods of unemployment when she would stay at home with the children. The husband offered to pay spousal support of $300 monthly. He provided Spousal Support Advisory Guideline calculations which ranged from $0 - $105.00 monthly. The court, taking into account the exception where the parties had jointly purchased a home with a significant mortgage, ordered the husband to pay spousal support of $450 per month for 60 months, at which point support would be reviewed.

# CHAPTER 18

## VARIATION AND REVIEW

The Advisory Guidelines do not — and cannot — affect the basic legal structure of variation and review (SSAG Chapter 14.1)

where there has been no incorporation of the agreement . . . the effect of subsequent changes in the parties' situation will be governed by the terms of the agreement. If the agreement provides for reviews by the parties at specified times or if it includes a material change clause, and if the conditions for these are met, it is possible for the Advisory Guidelines to apply to determine amount and duration. However, the Advisory Guidelines will have no application if the agreement is a final agreement in which spousal support has been waived or time-limited. (SSAG Chapter 14.1)

the Advisory Guidelines . . . confer no power to override agreements (SSAG Chapter 14.1)

where a spousal support agreement has been incorporated into the divorce judgment — as is the practice in many parts of the country — the agreement is treated as a court order. If the agreement provides for review or includes a material change clause, and those conditions are met, the Advisory Guidelines may be applicable to determine amount and duration. If the agreement is a final agreement, waiving or time-limiting support, the threshold requirement of a change in circumstances under s. 17 of the Divorce Act would have to be satisfied before a variation could be granted, as well as the causal connection requirement in s. 17(10) if the spousal support had ended at the time of the application. (SSAG Chapter 14.1)

Apart from the issue of the governing legal framework, a review or variation may involve issues of continuing entitlement that would determine the application of the Advisory Guidelines. (SSAG Chapter 14.1)

The largest category of variations and reviews consists of applications seeking a reduction in spousal support based upon a change in the income of one party or the other. One of three reasons provides the foundation for the application:

1) the payor spouse's income goes down;
2) the recipient spouse's income goes up; or
3) the payor spouse applies to reduce or terminate support on the grounds that the recipient spouse ought to have a higher income.

In each of these three situations the Advisory Guidelines can be used to determine the amount of support. (SSAG Chapter 14.1)

If the basis for the variation application is "the payor's post-separation income increase. . . the upper limit upon any increased spousal support ought to be the numbers generated by the formulas" (SSAG Chapter 14.3)

Suppose the recipient loses employment after the initial order, or suffers an illness or disability, or otherwise suffers a reduction in income. If either of the income-sharing formulas were applied, any reduction in the recipient's income after separation would lead to an increase in the spousal support payable. Once again, as with the payor's post-separation increase, some notion of causation seems to operate under the current law, requiring another complex, fact-based decision. While a formulaic solution is thus not possible, the same upper limit can be applied, i.e. the upper limit upon any increased spousal support ought to be the numbers generated by the formulas. (SSAG Chapter 14.4)

In our view, it should be possible for either spouse to apply to cross over from the with child support formula to the without child support formula, by way of application to vary or review. . . The crossover from the one formula to the other will only affect the amount of spousal support, but not the duration. (SSAG Chapter 14.5)

This chapter is divided into the following sections:

18.1 Variation
18.2 Review

## 18.1 Variation

The SSAG will be applied on variation on a case-by-case basis where significant complicating factors are not present — MacQuarrie v. MacQuarrie, 2012 CarswellPEI 5, 2012 PECA 3, 18 R.F.L. (7th) 1, 319 Nfld. & P.E.I.R. 246, 992 A.P.R. 246, [2012] P.E.I.J. No. 5 (P.E.I.C.A.). The Court of Appeal upheld a motion judge's decision to vary spousal support after the husband retired. The judge found that the husband's pre-retirement income was above that contemplated by the divorce provisions and constituted a material change in circumstances for the purpose of variation, and ordered retroactive support at the top of the SSAG range. The motions judge also ordered ongoing support based on the husband's post-retirement income. The Court of Appeal found no reversible error in the motion judge's decision and found that he had correctly considered the factors of the strength of the compensatory claim, the needs of the recipient, and the needs and the ability of the payor in determining quantum under the without child formula.

Incorrect calculation of the husband's income is grounds for variation of the quantum of support — Jakob v. Jakob, 2010 CarswellBC 599, 2010 BCCA 136, 80 R.F.L. (6th) 264, 6 B.C.L.R. (5th) 212 (B.C.C.A.), additional reasons at 2010 CarswellBC 1530, 2010 BCCA 309, 82 R.F.L. (6th) 95, 289 B.C.A.C. 50, 489 W.A.C. 50 (B.C.C.A.). The parties were quite impoverished and the trial judge incorrectly calculated the husband's income to be lower than it actually was, based on an average of the previous 3 years rather than his current income, which had been increasing.

The court approved judicial comments that the SSAG should be aproached with caution on variation applications — James v. James, 2009 CarswellBC 1490, 2009 BCCA 261, 66 R.F.L. (6th) 246, 94 B.C.L.R. (4th) 183, [2009] 10 W.W.R. 11, 273 B.C.A.C. 75, 461 W.A.C. 75, [2009] B.C.J. No. 1151 (B.C.C.A.).

In situations where the payor has an income of over $350,000, which allows for discretion under the SSAG, an increase in spousal support may be ordered where grounds for such an increase are demonstrated, but with consideration that the sum ordered should allow for ongoing business needs where the payor runs a corporation — James v. James, 2009 CarswellBC 1490, 2009 BCCA 261, 66 R.F.L. (6th) 246, 94 B.C.L.R. (4th) 183, [2009] 10 W.W.R. 11, 273 B.C.A.C. 75, 461 W.A.C. 75, [2009] B.C.J. No. 1151 (B.C.C.A.). In this case, the wife's need for more money to allow for housing that met the standard set during the marriage prompted an increase in support to $9,000 monthly, as the husband was found to have a minimum income of $500,000.

*SSAG utilized on variation application* — *Jens v. Jens*, 2008 CarswellBC 2091, 2008 BCCA 392, 57 R.F.L. (6th) 31, 84 B.C.L.R. (4th) 250, 300 D.L.R. (4th) 136, 260 B.C.A.C. 185, 439 W.A.C. 185, [2008] B.C.J. No. 1886 (B.C.C.A.). The Court stated, at para. 48: "I am satisfied that the factors that enter into the determination of spousal support in this case do not raise the complexities that arise on some variation applications, and that it is appropriate to use the SSAG as a guide to the appropriate level and duration of support."

*Error in law in intervening to the extent of increasing amount of support on variation application* — *SSAG used to bring support in line with objectives of the Act* —*Turpin v. Clark*, 2008 CarswellBC 2238, 2008 BCSC 1425, [2008] B.C.J. No. 2013 (B.C.S.C. [In Chambers]), reversed 2009 CarswellBC 3149, 2009 BCCA 530, 80 R.F.L. (6th) 239, 4 B.C.L.R. (5th) 48, 313 D.L.R. (4th) 452, [2010] 6 W.W.R. 613, 278 B.C.A.C. 220, 471 W.A.C. 220, [2009] B.C.J. No. 2328 (B.C.C.A.). The parties had agreed upon spousal support which was below the SSAG ranges for both quantum and duration. The Chambers judge held that in light of an unexpected deterioration in the recipient's health and her unnforseen challenges in becoming self-sufficient, the second stage of the *Miglin* test was found to justify an upward variation. The quantum of support was increased to an amount at the bottom of the SSAG range. However, the 8-year time limit in the agreement was maintained despite the fact that the SSAG called for indefinite support. The Court of Appeal considered whether the degree of intervention imposed by the variation order was appropriate in the circumstances. It observed that in the *Turpin* case, the minutes provided that "under no circumstances" would spousal support be increased and described the support provisions as "fair and adequate under all foreseeable circumstances including any increase in the Plaintiff's income". The parties were utterly clear that there would be no increase in spousal support in the future. The minutes were not as rigid in respect to the duration of support, which did not "terminate absolutely" until the later of September 1, 2012, or the husband's retirement. The minutes also stated that the wife was to become financially self-sufficient insofar as was practicable within a reasonable period of time. The court observed that the support was specified, but there was a general term "within a reasonable time." What is reasonable at one point in time can change at a later period of time. The court held the chambers judge erred in law by intervening to the extent that he did in varying the spousal support provisions of the divorce order. Applying the deferential standard required by *Miglin*, the court would not interfere with the step-down provisions of the divorce order. However, because of the delay in the wife's achievement of economic self-sufficiency, caused by her unanticipated health complications and inability to earn income, the court extended the duration of the final amount of the award ($4,000) for an additional 3 years until 2015 or when the husband retired, whichever event occurred later.

*Use of SSAG on support variation application* — *Beninger v. Beninger*, 2007 CarswellBC 2984, 2007 BCCA 619, 47 R.F.L. (6th) 11, 75 B.C.L.R. (4th) 228, [2008] 4 W.W.R. 193, 249 B.C.A.C. 193, 414 W.A.C. 193, [2007] B.C.J. No. 2657 (B.C.C.A.). The use of the SSAG may be appropriate on variation applications. However, by contrast to an initial application, they must be utilized cautiously in the variation context. The Court held, at para. 55 that "the decision whether to use the SSAG as a guide on variation applications will have to be made cautiously and on a fact-specific basis." On the facts of this case, the SSAG were applied to increase the support quantum in light of the payor's increasing income.

*Where a spousal support application is fatally flawed because of a change in division of property, a new application will require new examination of the evidence and will be treated as a new application rather than as variation* — *Hartshorne v. Hartshorne*, 2010 CarswellBC 1618, 2010 BCCA 327, 82 R.F.L. (6th) 1, 6 B.C.L.R. (5th) 58, 320 D.L.R. (4th) 398, 289 B.C.A.C.

244, 489 W.A.C. 244, [2010] B.C.J. No. 1271 (B.C.C.A.) . The parties separated in 1998 after 12½ years of cohabitation, including 9 years of marriage. They were involved in extensive litigation, which culminated in a case at the Supreme Court of Canada (*Hartshorne v. Hartshorne*, 2004 CarswellBC 603, 2004 CarswellBC 604, 2004 SCC 22, REJB 2004-55588, 47 R.F.L. (5th) 5, [2004] 1 S.C.R. 550, 25 B.C.L.R. (4th) 1, 236 D.L.R. (4th) 193, [2004] 6 W.W.R. 1, 194 B.C.A.C. 161, 318 N.R. 1, 317 W.A.C. 161, [2004] S.C.J. No. 20 (S.C.C.)), which radically changed the division of property. The SCC decision directed that therefore, the wife's right to spousal support could be determined by a "new application". In the new application, the wife filed for spousal support as well as increased child support for the parties' two children. This decision was an appeal of a trial decision awarding a lump-sum spousal support award of $350,000, retroactive to February 28, 2001, when the initial order for the division of property under Part 5 of the *Family Relations Act* was concluded. The Court of Appeal found that, rather than a variation, the trial judge was correct in approaching the calculation of spousal support under the SSAG as a new application, because "the initial order for spousal support was fundamentally flawed and therefore could not be the starting point for the respondent's new application" (para. 49). The trial judge had the advantage of examining all the evidence that had come to light since the SCC judgements. He was correct in examining anew the evidence of the wife's economic disadvantage, rather than relying on the findings of fact in other applications.

*Variation granted — new duration within SSAG range but quantum above SSAG range —* Kun v. Toth, 2006 CarswellBC 836, 2006 BCCA 173, 25 R.F.L. (6th) 1, [2006] B.C.J. No. 739 (B.C.C.A.). The husband's application for variation was granted. The new spousal support order was within the SSAG range for duration, but above the quantum range.

*The SSAG may be applied on variation even when the SSAG were not yet written at the time of the original order —* Misztal v. Karpynczyk, 2012 CarswellOnt 14730, 2012 ONSC 6474 (Ont. S.C.J.), additional reasons at 2013 CarswellOnt 346, 2013 ONSC 113 (Ont. S.C.J.). The parties were married for 23 years and had one child. They consented to an order including spousal support which could be varied when there was a material change in circumstances. Seven years after the consent order, the wife brought a Motion to Change seeking an increase in spousal support and a retroactive increase in support. The judge considered the SSAG over the objections of husband's counsel, who proposed that the SSAG should not be applied as they were not yet written at the time of the original order. Spousal support was ordered at the low end of the SSAG.

*Where the recipient spouse has not made a prima facie case of hardship or increased expenses on an interim motion for increased support, support will remain at the original level even if it is significantly lower than the quantum indicated by the SSAG —* Kuziora v. Fournier, 2012 CarswellOnt 2890, 2012 ONSC 1569, [2012] O.J. No. 1043 (Ont. S.C.J.). This decision arose from a Motion to Change. The parties were married for 18 years and had two children. The wife had custody. The husband had a debilitating illness and was unable to work. The judge declined to increase the amount of spousal support from $590/month. The low-range amount in this case indicated by the SSAG was $1,149. The judge cited the fact that the wife was supporting the two children, and found that the recipient spouse had not made out a *prima facie* case of hardship.

*Where the SSAG indicate that the result of a variation would be minimal based on the increase in both parties' incomes, an increase in spousal support will not be made —* Kaulback v. Kaulback, 2011 CarswellOnt 7688, 2011 ONSC 4337, [2011] O.J. No. 3587 (Ont. S.C.J.). The recipient spouse brought a Motion to Vary a final order of support. The parties had been married for 12 years and the wife had primary care of the two children. The incomes of both parents had risen since the previous order but the wife was not yet self-sufficient. The wife sought retroactive and ongoing support. Retroactive and ongoing support was not awarded as there was evidence the wife was aware of the husband's increased income significantly prior to the time she brought the

Motion to Vary and, because her income increased as well, the increase in support would have been very minimal when based on the SSAG.

*Where a spousal support decision was made before the advent of the SSAG, it will not be considered when a variation is brought before the courts* — *Racki v. Racki*, 2011 CarswellOnt 13385, 2011 ONSC 6733, [2011] O.J. No. 5063 (Ont. S.C.J.). The parties were married for 12 years and had three children. The husband sought termination of spousal support. The wife was unemployed and the husband had recently filed for bankruptcy. The husband was ordered to pay $500 a month, which was at the high end of the SSAG if the wife earned $10,000 a year, but was at the low end of the SSAG if the wife earned nothing. However, the judge noted the SSAG was not a factor at the time indefinite spousal support was originally ordered and that it would be unfair to use it as a factor at this point. Spousal support was reviewable in three years.

*Duration set at the top range of the SSAG with step-down order over the full duration of the payments* — *Poon v. Chung*, 2011 CarswellBC 118, 2011 BCSC 98, 94 R.F.L. (6th) 493 (B.C.S.C.). The parties separated after a 15-year marriage. The wife, who was unable to work at the time of separation due to mental illness, had recovered significantly and had been gainfully employed for the preceding 4 years. The husband's application to vary spousal support was granted. Given the wife's state of health, spousal support was ordered for the *Spousal Support Advisory Guidelines'* upper limit of 15 years. Although the amount started at $1,800, which was at the high end of the SSAG range, it decreased on a descending basis to $500 per month by the end of the 15-year duration.

*The termination of spousal support following a 9-year marriage* — *Bierman v. Bierman*, 2011 CarswellSask 211, 2011 SKQB 115, 99 R.F.L. (6th) 122, 369 Sask. R. 295, [2011] S.J. No. 192 (Sask. Q.B.). The parties were married for 9 years. The wife received spousal support, primarily on a non-compensatory basis, for 10 years following separation. On the husband's application to vary support, the court terminated spousal support forthwith. Any economic hardship suffered by the wife had likely ceased when she remarried, and had definitely ceased by the date of the application. The court further found that the wife was purposely underemployed and imputed income of $25,000 to her so that she may pay a proportionate amount of s. 7 expenses.

*Variation — silence in minutes of settlement and consent order does not negate support recipient's obligation to contribute to support of herself and children* — *Moon v. Moon*, 2011 CarswellOnt 2086, 2011 ONSC 1834, 3 R.F.L. (7th) 381, [2011] O.J. No. 1315 (Ont. S.C.J.). At the time of the minutes of settlement and consent order in 2007, following a 14-year marriage with three children, the husband was 35 and the wife was 44 years old. At the time of this application, the husband worked as an IT Manager and earned $90,000 per year. The wife was a homemaker and had not worked in 11 years although prior to 2000, she had work as an ESL instructor and had significant education and training. The court ordered support to be varied downward 6 months following the judgement by imputing an income to the wife of $25,000 and based on the husband paying child support in accordance with the *Child Support Guidelines*. The court further ordered that effective 2016 support would terminate. Given the length of this marriage and the ages of the parties at separation, the wife was not entitled to support for life.

*Where self-sufficiency is attained, even where the "Rule of 65" applies, support will be terminated* — *Roberts v. Cantu-Roberts*, 2010 CarswellOnt 2030, 2010 ONSC 1883, [2010] O.J. No. 1392 (Ont. S.C.J.), additional reasons at 2010 CarswellOnt 5018, 2010 ONSC 3969 (Ont. S.C.J.). The parties in this case were a dentist and his former wife who suffered from health problems preventing her from working. They separated in 1997 and concluded a separation agreement providing for $7,000 monthly in spousal support to be paid to the wife. This amount was variable when there was a material change in circumstances, including the husband's retirement. The husband applied for termination of support; the wife claimed support should be ongoing at $2,000 a month. The judge recognized the application of the "Rule of 65" found in the SSAG, but emphasized that although this rule would have indicated an indefinite support award, such an award was not indicative of permanent entitlement to support. The judge found that the support had been sufficient to allow the wife to attain self-sufficiency. Her net worth was approximately twice that of her former husband's. Support was terminated.

Indefinite support is subject to variation and review — Boucher v. Boucher, 2010 CarswellBC 24, 2010 BCSC 21 (B.C.S.C.). The parties cohabited for 23 years. The husband was 57 years of age and the wife 48 years of age at the time of the trial. Entitlement was not an issue. Given the length of the marriage and the age of the wife, the duration of the payment was indefinite. However, as stated in the Guidelines, indefinite does not mean permanent. Such support is subject to variation and review. The husband's Guideline income was $147,655 and the wife's $42,000. As there was no reason to deviate from the midpoint amount of support, the court awarded the wife indefinite spousal support of $2,577 per month.

SSAG can be used as a "guide" in variation but parties did not submit SSAG calculations — Conner v. Conner, 2009 CarswellBC 792, 2009 BCSC 423, [2009] B.C.J. No. 616 (B.C.S.C.). In this variation case, the court held that the SSAG "can be referred to as a guide" but observed that the parties had not submitted SSAG ranges. The new quantum of support awarded was substantially below the bottom of the applicable SSAG range.

SSAG should be used cautiously and in context on review hearings — Al Hosseini v. Kazemi, 2009 CarswellBC 942, 2009 BCSC 502, [2009] B.C.J. No. 743 (B.C.S.C.). The court cited M. (J.) v. M. (L.D.), 2008 CarswellBC 1930, 2008 BCSC 1235 (B.C.S.C. [In Chambers]).

SSAG can be utilized on a variation application, even though not available at the time of the original support order — E. (P.D.) v. E. (A.J.), 2009 CarswellBC 3388, 2009 BCSC 1712, [2009] B.C.J. No. 2497 (B.C.S.C.).

Variation application — SSAG not used — Lepp v. Lepp, 2008 CarswellBC 717, 2008 BCSC 448, 52 R.F.L. (6th) 423, [2008] B.C.J. No. 640 (B.C.S.C.). The SSAG ranges were disregarded in this case for a number of reasons, among them was the fact that it was a variation application and the disability exception applied. The Court held, at para. 39: "Many of the complex issues that arise on variation applications are present in this case including the impact of remarriage and a second family, the passage of time and the impact of inflation. In addition, disability, one of the five exceptions to the application of the SSAG, is present here. In my view, the SSAG do not account for the multiple factors to be considered in this case both with regard to quantum and duration of the spousal support."

Despite many comments to the contrary, the Spousal Support Advisory Guidelines do apply on variation and review applications. How they apply depends on the issues raised on the particular application to vary or to review. The Guidelines have frequently been applied to the most common issues on variation or review, such as a decrease in the payor's income or an increase in the recipient's income. For a review of the conflicting authorities on the application of the Guidelines on variation, see Bockhold v. Bockhold, 2010 CarswellBC 369, 2010 BCSC 214, [2010] B.C.J. No. 283 (B.C.S.C. [In Chambers]).

Where existing payments are within the SSAG ranges, and no hardship has been made out, spousal support will not be varied on an interim basis in the context of a Motion to Change — McKeen v. McKeen, 2011 CarswellOnt 14437, 2011 ONCJ 602, [2011] O.J. No. 5446 (Ont. C.J.). This was a variation of an interim order in which the wife sought increased spousal support in the context of a Motion to Change a final order, as she was no longer receiving child support and the payor husband's income had increased. In addition, the recipient had multiple sclerosis and her health had deteriorated since spousal support was agreed upon in the Separation Agreement. The judge declined to make a temporary order. The threshold in such a case was hardship, which the wife did not demonstrate. In addition, the amount of the husband's income was a triable issue and the issue of whether or not the spousal support was reviewable at this time, given the provisions of the Separation Agreement, was also a triable issue. The judge also found that the wife's behaviour was unreasonable given her financial circumstances and that she was living alone in a five bedroom house.

*Utility of SSAG on retroactive variation application* — *Mann v. Mann*, 2008 CarswellOnt 4474, 2008 ONCJ 331, [2008] O.J. No. 2942 (Ont. C.J.), affirmed 2009 CarswellOnt 2631, [2009] O.J. No. 1960 (Ont. S.C.J.). With regard to variation motions, the Court stated, at para. 9: "the spousal support guidelines . . . have relevance as a starting point, especially when the court is essentially being asked to adjust the spousal support calculation back to the time when the final order was made, as I have been asked to do in this case."

## 18.2 Review

The *Spousal Support Advisory Guidelines* (Ottawa: Department of Justice, 2005, later amended in 2008) (the "SSAG") may be considered on a review, however in doing so the court must be cautious and cognisant that as a general matter, the guidelines are directed to the initial order: see *Kerman v. Kerman*, 2008 CarswellBC 793, 2008 BCSC 500, 53 R.F.L. (6th) 156, [2008] B.C.J. No. 710 (B.C.S.C.); *M. (J.) v. M. (L.D.)*, 2008 CarswellBC 1930, 2008 BCSC 1235 (B.C.S.C. [In Chambers]); *Beninger v. Beninger*, 2007 CarswellBC 2984, 2007 BCCA 619, 47 R.F.L. (6th) 11, 75 B.C.L.R. (4th) 228, [2008] 4 W.W.R. 193, 249 B.C.A.C. 193, 414 W.A.C. 193, [2007] B.C.J. No. 2657 (B.C.C.A.); and the commentary on *Beninger* and *Fisher v. Fisher*, 2008 CarswellOnt 43, 2008 ONCA 11, 47 R.F.L. (6th) 235, 88 O.R. (3d) 241, 288 D.L.R. (4th) 513, 232 O.A.C. 213, [2008] O.J. No. 38 (Ont. C.A.), by the authors of the *Spousal Support Advisory Guidelines* in Carol Rogerson and Rollie Thompson, *The Spousal Support Advisory Guidelines Three Years Later* (8 February 2008). See *Bockhold v. Bockhold*, 2009 CarswellBC 248, 2009 BCSC 130 (B.C.S.C.), per Ross J., at para. 15(c).

As well as their applicability to initial orders, the Guidelines appear equally amenable to review or variation proceedings — *L. (R.) v. L. (N.)*, 2012 CarswellNB 258, 2012 NBQB 123, 22 R.F.L. (7th) 82, 388 N.B.R. (2d) 220, 1006 A.P.R. 220 (N.B.Q.B.). (See: C. Rogerson and R. Thompson, *The Spousal Support Advisory Guidelines: A New and Improved User's Guide to the Final Version*, March 2010 (Department of Justice Canada), Section 13 at p. 49).

*SSAG may be considered on review* — *Beck v. Beck*, 2012 CarswellNfld 419, 2012 NLTD(F) 34, 329 Nfld. & P.E.I.R. 287, 1022 A.P.R. 287 (N.L.T.D.). This was a review hearing for support. The wife had found a job paying $38,000 yearly, and the husband earned $106,000. The parties had two adult children and had a long-term, traditional marriage. The judge found spousal support should continue and used the SSAG in determining quantum. However, he awarded support below the SSAG range under the without child formula, finding that the wife's decision to allow her adult children to live with her rent-free was unreasonable. Spousal support continued at the same levels as before the review.

Where a child of the marriage has special needs, the recipient spouse is the caregiver for the child, and the payor spouse has the means to pay, spousal support will not be reviewable until the child is a pre-adolescent — *Ruffalo v. David*, 2011 CarswellOnt 14459, 2011 ONSC 7234 (Ont. S.C.J.). The parties were married for eight years and had two children, one of whom had significant special needs. The wife was the custodial parent. Spousal support was ordered at the low end of the SSAG range and was not reviewable until the child with special needs was a pre-adolescent (in three and one-half years), as it was not realistic to expect the wife to work until that time, given the demands of the child and the fact that she had not been employed since before the marriage. The payor husband had the means to pay.

   *Applicability of SSAG on support review proceeding* — Cavanaugh v. Cavanaugh, 2008
CarswellNB 590, 2008 NBQB 387, 77 R.F.L. (6th) 355, 341 N.B.R. (2d) 166, 876 A.P.R. 166,
[2008] N.B.J. No. 464 (N.B.Q.B.), reversed in part 2008 CarswellNB 630 (N.B.C.A.). The Court
found, at para. 57: " in the absence of any indication in the order which gives rise to a review as to
the reason for it, the inquiry to be conducted by the reviewing court, or the parameters under
which the review should take place, the argument that the SSAG should be looked to becomes
more compelling. If the parties choose, effectively, to re-litigate their case, they should expect to
do so in the shadow of the Guidelines."

# CHAPTER 19
# JUDICIAL RECEPTION OF THE SSAG

Unlike the *Child Support Guidelines*, the SSAG are not legislated, and there is no plan to enact them. Their relevance to the practitioner therefore depends substantially on the extent to which courts are likely to follow them in adjudicated cases.

This chapter seeks to assess judicial reception of the SSAG. Section 19.1 reproduces comments made by the SSAG's authors about this issue. Section 19.2.3 provides a review of the use of the *Spousal Support Advisory Guidelines* in appellate decisions from mid-2008, the date of the final draft, to mid-2013, a period of 5 years. The appellate case law is extensive with over 100 Court of Appeal decisions. The review of appellate cases contains a chart of Court of Appeal decisions dealing directly with the SSAG during the 5 year period, commentary and annotations of key cases in which the judges have commented on the utility of the Advisory Guidelines. Only Court of Appeal cases that deal explicitly with the Guidelines have been reviewed; the Supreme Court of Canada has not, as yet, considered the SSAG.

Case summaries of the appellate decisions of general application are found at 19.2.3 of this chapter, and other case summaries are found under the appropriate chapters in Part II of of *Canadian Divorce Law and Practice*. All of these sections — the observations of the SSAG authors in 19.1, the 5-year review in 19.2, and the case law with respect to the SSAG — reach the same conclusion: there is broad and general judicial acceptance of the SSAG ranges, despite a few areas in which deviation from them is more likely.

This chapter is divided into the following sections:

19.1 Observations of the SSAG Authors
19.2 Review of Appellate Decisions Dealing with the *Spousal Support Guidelines*
    19.2.1 Chart
    19.2.2 SSAG Commentary: Appellate Decisions mid-2008 to mid-2013
    19.2.3 Cases

## 19.1 Observations of the SSAG Authors

Our monitoring of the use of the Advisory Guidelines since the release of the Draft Proposal has shown that in practice the durational aspect of the *without child support* formula is often ignored. . . . To ignore duration is to misapply the *without child support* formula (SSAG Section 7.5.1)

In practice, restructuring has often been ignored. In many cases, particularly short marriages under the without child support formula, courts have found the amounts generated by the formula too low and have then simply concluded that the Advisory Guidelines do not yield an appropriate outcome and are of no further use [citation removed]. The failure to consider restructuring is unfortunate because it means that an important element of flexibility is not being utilized. The structure and guidance provided by the Guidelines are thus being lost in a number of cases where these benefits would otherwise be available. (SSAG Section 10.1)

Since the release of the Draft Proposal, one surprise has been the failure of lawyers and judges to use the listed "exceptions" to the formulas. (SSAG Section 12)

## 19.2 Review of Appellate Decisions Dealing with the *Spousal Support Guidelines*

### 19.2.1 Chart Appellate Decisions mid-2008 to mid-2013 *

| | |
|---|---|
| **BC** | *Marquez v. Zapiola*, 2013 BCCA 433; *Hepburn v. Hepburn*, 2013 BCCA 383; *Brandl v. Rolston*, 2013 BCCA 235; *Morck v. Morck*, 2013 BCCA 186; *Armstrong v. Armstrong*, 2012 BCCA 166; *Brisson v. Brisson*, 2012 BCCA 396; *Kelsch v. Chaput*, 2012 BCCA 64; *Ouellette v. Ouellette*, 2012 BCCA 145; *Q. (R.E.) v. K. (G.J.)*, 2012 BCCA 146; *Robinson v. Robinson*, 2012 BCCA 497; *Kelly v. Kelly*, 2011 BCCA 173; *Puiu v. Puiu*, 2011 BCCA 480; *S. (R.M.) v. S. (F.P.C.)*, 2011 BCCA 53; *Stace-Smith v. Lecompte*, 2011 BCCA 129; *Pinder v. Pinder*, 2010 BCCA 235; *Aelbers v. Aelbers*, 2010 BCCA 197; *Dima v. Dima*, 2010 BCCA 557; *Domirti v. Domirti*, 2010 BCCA 472; *Emery v. Emery*, 2010 BCCA 376; *Hartshorne v. Hartshorne*, 2010 BCCA 327; *Jakob v. Jakob*, 2010 BCCA 136; *Karisik v. Chow*, 2010 BCCA 548; *Shortridge-Tsuchiya v. Tsuchiya*, 2010 BCCA 61; *Beninger v. Beninger*, 2009 BCCA 458; *James v. James*, 2009 BCCA 261; *Kerr v. Baranow*, 2009 BCCA 111; *Bell v. Bell*, 2009 BCCA 280; *Gonabady-Namadon v. Mohammadzadeh*, 2009 BCCA 448; *Mann v. Mann*, 2009 BCCA 181; *Redpath v. Redpath*, 2009 BCCA 168; *Rozendaal v. Rozendaal*, 2009 BCCA 234; *Young v. Young*, 2009 BCCA 518; *Chutter v. Chutter*, 2008 BCCA 507; *Turpin v. Clark*, 2008 BCSC 1425; *Beese v. Beese*, 2008 BCCA 396; *Jens v. Jens*, 2008 BCCA 392; *Loesch v. Walji*, 2008 BCCA 214; *S. (J.K.) v. S. (H.G.)* , 2008 BCCA 245; *Wang v. Poon*, 2008 BCCA 442 |
| **Alberta** | *Caldwell v. Caldwell*, 2013 ABCA 268; *De Winter v. De Winter*, 2013 ABCA 311; *Elfar v. Elfar*, 2012 ABCA 375; *Haraphongse v. Haraphongse*, 2011 ABCA 343; *O'Grady v. O'Grady*, 2010 ABCA 109; *Rockall v. Rockall*, 2010 ABCA 278; *Taylor v. Taylor*, 2009 ABCA 354; *Sawatzky v. Sawatzky*, 2008 ABCA 355; *Lapp v. Lapp*, 2008 ABCA 15 |
| **Manitoba** | *Kynoch v. Kynoch*, 2013 MBCA 73; *Thomson v. Thomson*, 2011 MBCA 28; *Scott v. Scott*, 2011 MBCA 21 |
| **Ontario** | *Buttar v. Buttar*, 2013 ONCA 517; *Ruffalo v. David*, 2012 ONCA 698; *Edgar v. Edgar*, 2012 ONCA 646; *V. (B.) v. V. (P.)*, 2012 ONCA 262; *Stergios v. Kim*, 2011 ONCA 836; *Davis v. Crawford*, 2011 ONCA 294; *Gagne v. Gagne*, 2011 ONCA 188; *Ward v. Ward*, 2011 ONCA 178; *Greenglass v. Grennglass*, 2010 ONCA 675; *Cassidy v. McNeil*, 2010 ONCA 218; *Carr v. Parlee*, 2010 ONCA 254; *Catsoudas v. Catsoudas*, 2009 ONCA 706; *Rioux v. Rioux*, 2009 ONCA 569; *Jessop v. Wright*, 2008 ONCA 673; *Fisher v. Fisher*, 2008 ONCA 11 |

---

* There have been no decisions at the appellate level in Newfoundland and Labrador, Nunavut, and the Northwest Territories. Two Saskatchewan decisions — *Albers v. Albers*, 2013 SKCA 64; and *MacDonald v. MacDonald*, 2010 SKCA 60 — make reference to the SSAG but do not deal directly with them.

| Quebec | *Droit de la famille - 131531*, 2013 QCCA 1044; *Droit de la famille - 122683*, 2012 QCCA 1742; *Droit de la famille - 112606*, 2011 QCCA 1554 |
|---|---|
| NB | *LeBlanc v. LeBlanc*, 2013 NBCA 22; *Flieger v. Adams*, 2012 NBCA 39; *Grant v. Grant*, 2012 NBCA 101; *B. (P.M.) v. B. (M.L.)*, 2012 NBCA 11; *Smith v. Smith*, 2011 NBCA 66; *M. (J.A.) v. M. (D.L.)*, 2008 NBCA 2; *Milton v. Milton*, 2008 NBCA 87 |
| NS | *Baker v. Baker*, 2012 NSCA 24; *Hurst v. Gill*, 2011 NSCA 100; *Michaud v. Kuzelweski*, 2009 NSCA 118 |
| PEI | *MacQuarrie v. MacQuarrie*, 2012 PECA 3 |
| Yukon | *Holmes v. Matkovich*, 2008 YKCA 10 |

## 19.2.2  SSAG Commentary: Appellate Decisions mid-2008 to mid-2013

The most striking feature of the preceding chart is the sheer number of the judgements from the British Columbia Court of Appeal. The B.C. Court of Appeal was the first appellate court in Canada to provide a general endorsement of the SSAG as "a useful tool to assist judges in assessing the quantum and duration of spousal support" (*Yemchuk v. Yemchuk*, 2005 CarswellBC 1881, 2005 BCCA 406, 16 R.F.L. (6th) 430, 44 B.C.L.R. (4th) 77, 257 D.L.R. (4th) 476, [2005] 10 W.W.R. 634, 215 B.C.A.C. 193, 355 W.A.C. 193, [2005] B.C.J. No. 1748 (B.C.C.A.), at para. 64) and has dealt extensively with them since. During the second stage of the SSAG, mid-2008 to mid-2013, the B.C. Court of Appeal moved to a much wider range of issues, including discussion of some of the listed exceptions to use of the SSAG, factors to consider when determining the appropriate place within the amount and duration ranges, and appropriate use of the SSAG for variation orders, interim orders and reviews.

A steady rise in the use of the SSAG in Ontario has occurred since *Fisher v. Fisher*, 2008 CarswellOnt 43, 2008 ONCA 11, 47 R.F.L. (6th) 235, 88 O.R. (3d) 241, 288 D.L.R. (4th) 513, 232 O.A.C. 213, [2008] O.J. No. 38 (Ont. C.A.), provided a general endorsement of the SSAG as a "useful" tool" that is likely to bring consistency and predictability to the law. In more recent years, the Ontario Court of Appeal has provided guidance on factors determining appropriate amounts and durations within the ranges and substituting its own SSAG numbers when income had been reassessed, an indication of comfort and familiarity with the SSAG. While there are many fewer cases at the appellate level in Ontario than in British Columbia, the absolute number of cases at the superior court level in Ontario making reference to the SSAG has now surpassed the number in British Columbia.

The case of *Droit de la famille - 112606*, 2011 CarswellQue 8981, 2011 CarswellQue 15234, 2011 QCCA 1554, EYB 2011-194830, 8 R.F.L. (7th) 1, [2011] R.J.Q. 1745, [2011] J.Q. No. 11097, [2011] Q.J. No. 11097 (C.A. Que.), provides an extensive discussion of the SSAG and a general endorsement for its use both as a cross-check and a starting point. In doing so, it basically reversed the earlier decision of *G. (C.) c. V. (G.)*, 2006 CarswellQue 4931, 2006 QCCA 763, EYB 2006-106167, [2006] R.J.Q. 1519, [2006] J.Q. No. 5231 (C.A. Que.). A later decision, *Droit de la famille - 131531*, 2013 CarswellQue 5424, 2013 QCCA 1044, EYB 2013-223013 (C.A. Que.), cites this decision, noting the SSAG are advisory only but the amount being appealed from is within the SSAG. However, a decision at the superior court level, *Droit de la famille - 123274*, 2012 CarswellQue 12535, 2012 QCCS 5873, EYB 2012-214451 (C.S. Que.), by Justice J-P Senécal echoes many of the earlier criticisms in the 2006 decision and appears to have blunted much of the impact of the 2011 decision. The SSAG remain least used, on a per population basis, in the province of Quebec.

Until 2013, there were no cases in the Prairie provinces which provided a discussion or opinion of the SSAG beyond their strictly voluntary use. All three provinces have had cases which found that failure to refer to the SSAG in the situation before them was not an appealable error (*Scott v. Scott*, 2011 CarswellMan 52, 2011 MBCA 21, 97 R.F.L. (6th) 119, 262 Man. R. (2d) 237, 507 W.A.C. 237 (Man. C.A.); *Aalbers v. Aalbers*, 2013 CarswellSask 394, 2013 SKCA 64, 417 Sask. R. 69, 580 W.A.C. 69 (Sask. C.A.); and *Rockall v. Rockall*, 2010 CarswellAlta 1859, 2010 ABCA 278, 90 R.F.L. (6th) 317, 35 Alta. L.R. (5th) 1, 490 A.R. 135, 497 W.A.C. 135, [2010] A.J. No. 1064 (Alta. C.A.)). In 2013, both the Alberta and Manitoba Courts of Appeal found the SSAG to be a useful tool when determining spousal support (*De Winter v. De Winter*, 2013 CarswellAlta 1721, 2013 ABCA 311, [2013] A.J. No. 972 (Alta. C.A.); *Kynoch v. Kynoch*, 2013 CarswellMan 441, 2013 MBCA 73, 294 Man. R. (2d) 250, 581 W.A.C. 250 (Man. C.A.)) and, in the latter Manitoba case, a tool which "... can bring some measure of consistency and predictability to a sorely inconsistent area and thereby encourage settlement" (para. 48).

This is in contrast to the Maritimes where New Brunswick provided a general endorsement early in *C. (J.D.E.) v. C. (S.M.)*, 2006 CarswellNB 242, 2006 CarswellNB 243, 2006 NBCA 46, 299 N.B.R. (2d) 334, 27 R.F.L. (6th) 19, 778 A.P.R. 334, [2006] N.B.J. No. 186 (N.B.C.A.), and a positive tone in subsequent decisions, although noting the SSAG are not mandatory. Both the Prince Edward Island and Nova Scotia Courts of Appeal found application of the SSAG appropriate to a variation application on the particular facts, although one had to be particularly cautious in the case of variation applications (*MacQuarrie v. MacQuarrie*, 2012 CarswellPEI 5, 2012 PECA 3, 18 R.F.L. (7th) 1, 319 Nfld. & P.E.I.R. 246, 992 A.P.R. 246, [2012] P.E.I.J. No. 5 (P.E.I.C.A.); and *Michaud v. Kuzelweski*, 2009 CarswellNS 646, 2009 NSCA 118, 75 R.F.L. (6th) 3, 312 D.L.R. (4th) 598, 284 N.S.R. (2d) 310, 901 A.P.R. 310 (N.S.C.A.)). The Nova Scotia Court of Appeal has also used the SSAG to analyze the adequacy of the equalization agreement (*Baker v. Baker*, 2012 CarswellNS 139, 2012 NSCA 24, 9 R.F.L. (7th) 325, 348 D.L.R. (4th) 485, 314 N.S.R. (2d) 189, 994 A.P.R. 189 (N.S.C.A.)).

The Yukon is the only one of the three territories where the Court of Appeal makes reference to the SSAG. In *Holmes v. Matkovich*, 2008 CarswellYukon 55, 2008 YKCA 10, 59 R.F.L. (6th) 60, 258 B.C.A.C. 86, 434 W.A.C. 86, [2008] Y.J. No. 51 (Y.T.C.A.), the Yukon appellate court affirmed on appeal, the trial court choosing an amount at the lower end of the SSAG range because the support recipient was to receive the parties' farm.

### Tests for General Applicability of the SSAG to Initial Orders of Support at the Trial and Appeal Levels

As Madam Justice Larlee of New Brunswick's Court of Appeal noted in the early decision of *C. (J.D.E.) v. C. (S.M.)*, supra, at para. 5, "The guidelines have been referred to in many ways: a check, a cross-check, a litmus test, a useful tool and a starting point." The *Spousal Support Advisory Guidelines* state that they are intended as a starting point for negotiation and adjudication (p. 28). In *Fisher v. Fisher*, supra, it was noted that the bar in London, Ontario, frequently used them in this way as a starting point for assessing the appropriate level of support. Indeed, in *Carr v. Parlee*, 2010 CarswellOnt 2040, 2010 ONCA 254, [2010] O.J. No. 1397 (Ont. C.A.), a lawyer was found negligent for not advising his client of the range of support under the SSAG.

At the appeal level, the SSAG may operate as a litmus test when used to consider the reasonableness of the award. *Fisher* held that at the same time the reasonableness of the award produced by the Guidelines must be balanced in light of the circumstances of the individual case, including the financial history of the parties during the marriage and their likely future circumstances.

Madam Justice Lang in *Fisher v. Fisher, supra*, at para. 102, cites the higher test proposed by Newbury J.A. in *Redpath v. Redpath*, 2006 CarswellBC 1709, 2006 BCCA 338, 33 R.F.L. (6th) 91, 62 B.C.L.R. (4th) 233, 228 B.C.A.C. 272, 376 W.A.C. 272, [2006] B.C.J. No. 1550 (B.C.C.A.), for using the SSAG to inform an appellate standard of review:

> ... [where the] award is substantially lower or higher than the range and there are no exceptional circumstances to explain the anomaly, the standard of review should be reformulated to permit appellate intervention.

This test has been followed in *Kerr v. Baranow*, 2009 CarswellBC 642, 2009 BCCA 111, 93 B.C.L.R. (4th) 201, 66 R.F.L. (6th) 1, [2009] 9 W.W.R. 285, 266 B.C.A.C. 298, 449 W.A.C. 298, [2009] B.C.J. No. 474 (B.C.C.A.), additional reasons at 2010 BCCA 32, 2010 CarswellBC 108, 2 B.C.L.R. (5th) 197, 78 R.F.L. (6th) 305, [2010] 4 W.W.R. 465, [2010] B.C.J. No. 88 (B.C.C.A.), reversed 2011 CarswellBC 240, 2011 CarswellBC 241, 2011 SCC 10, 93 R.F.L. (6th) 1, [2011] 1 S.C.R. 269, 108 O.R. (3d) 399, 14 B.C.L.R. (5th) 203, 328 D.L.R. (4th) 577, 64 E.T.R. (3d) 1, [2011] 3 W.W.R. 575, 300 B.C.A.C. 1, 411 N.R. 200, 274 O.A.C. 1, 509 W.A.C. 1, [2011] S.C.J. No. 10 (S.C.C.) (in calculating amount and duration of spousal support, the jurisprudence requires an application of the SSAG unless reasons are provided as to why the SSAG are not appropriate); *Gagne v. Gagne*, 2011 CarswellOnt 1476, 2011 ONCA 188, 99 R.F.L. (6th) 1, [2011] O.J. No. 1015 (Ont. C.A.) (there is an obligation upon a judge to explain why he or she departed from the SSAG). A less stringent version of the test was used in *Beninger v. Beninger*, 2009 CarswellBC 2963, 2009 BCCA 458, 77 R.F.L. (6th) 56, 277 B.C.A.C. 36, 469 W.A.C. 36, [2009] B.C.J. No. 2197 (B.C.C.A.) (trial courts are not required to explain all deviations from the SSAG, but doing so would be "best practice"). Another early case of strong general endorsements of the SSAG is *Yemchuk v. Yemchuk, supra* (the Advisory Guidelines are viewed "as a useful tool to assist judges in assessing the quantum and duration of spousal support").

This test has also been specifically rejected. See *Smith v. Smith*, 2011 CarswellNB 377, 2011 CarswellNB 378, 2011 NBCA 66, 9 R.F.L. (7th) 286, 336 D.L.R. (4th) 285, 375 N.B.R. (2d) 208, 969 A.P.R. 208, [2011] N.B.J. No. 245 (N.B.C.A.) (where the wife's argument, that whenever there was no exception to the normal ranges as set out in the SSAG exceptions the standard SSAG ranges must be applied, failed; a judge will not be mandated to apply the usual SSAG ranges, even when none of the exceptions applied); *Scott v. Scott, supra* (failure to refer to the SSAG was not an error in law); and *Rockall v. Rockall, supra* (if amount of spousal support exceeds amount recommended under the *Spousal Support Guidelines*, this fact is irrelevant as the SSAG do not have the force of law; not using the SSAG will not in itself constitute a reversible error); *Droit de la famille - 112606, supra*; *Taylor v. Taylor*, 2009 CarswellAlta 1701, 2009 ABCA 354, 72 R.F.L. (6th) 249, 15 Alta. L.R. (5th) 303, 312 D.L.R. (4th) 448, 464 A.R. 245, 467 W.A.C. 245, [2009] A.J. No. 1162 (Alta. C.A.), at para. 51 (a trial judge does not err in law by not averting to the SSAG, as the Guidelines do not enjoy the force of law; while they are a useful tool in a judge's determination of spousal maintenance, there is more than one route available to trial judges in arriving at an appropriate award of spousal support).

Other appellate courts have emphasized that the SSAG are advisory only. *Droit de la famille - 131531, supra* (use of the SSAG is advisory only and does not replace the broad discretion of judges to determine support based on applicable legal principles); *Brisson v. Brisson*, 2012 CarswellBC 3051, 2012 BCCA 396, 22 R.F.L. (7th) 1, 39 B.C.L.R. (5th) 1, 355 D.L.R. (4th) 720, 328 B.C.A.C. 163, 558 W.A.C. 163 (B.C.C.A.) (in considering the appropriate amount of spousal support, the courts should consider the *Spousal Support Advisory Guidelines*; although they do not have legal force, they do provide an indication of a level of support that may be appropriate).

## Proceedings where the SSAG have been applied

While the *Spousal Support Advisory Guidelines* have been utilized on initial applications, there have been appellate decisions about the Guidelines' use in other proceedings.

### Interim Orders

Appellate courts have found that the SSAG apply on interim proceedings: *Shortridge-Tsuchiya v. Tsuchiya*, 2010 CarswellBC 276, 2010 BCCA 61, 79 R.F.L. (6th) 7, 2 B.C.L.R. (5th) 24, 315 D.L.R. (4th) 498, [2010] 8 W.W.R. 629, 283 B.C.A.C. 117, 480 W.A.C. 117, [2010] B.C.J. No. 217 (B.C.C.A.) (an expenses order calculated in accordance with the SSAG may be used as a *de facto* interim support order); *Fisher v. Fisher, supra* (SSAG ranges are designed to apply to interim as well as final orders); and *Loesch v. Walji*, 2007 CarswellBC 3007, 2007 BCSC 1807, 48 R.F.L. (6th) 128, [2007] B.C.J. No. 2663 (B.C.S.C.), affirmed 2008 CarswellBC 982, 2008 BCCA 214, 52 R.F.L. (6th) 33, 81 B.C.L.R. (4th) 271, [2008] 10 W.W.R. 625, 255 B.C.A.C. 264, 430 W.A.C. 264, [2008] B.C.J. No. 897 (B.C.C.A.).

### Variation

The appellate courts have approached variation applications more tentatively. See *James v. James*, 2009 CarswellBC 1490, 2009 BCCA 261, 66 R.F.L. (6th) 246, 94 B.C.L.R. (4th) 183, [2009] 10 W.W.R. 11, 273 B.C.A.C. 75, 461 W.A.C. 75, [2009] B.C.J. No. 1151 (B.C.C.A.) (on a variation application the SSAG are a good starting point, but the SSAG should be approached with caution); *Jens v. Jens*, 2008 CarswellBC 2091, 2008 BCCA 392, 57 R.F.L. (6th) 31, 84 B.C.L.R. (4th) 250, 300 D.L.R. (4th) 136, 260 B.C.A.C. 185, 439 W.A.C. 185, [2008] B.C.J. No. 1886 (B.C.C.A.) (the SSAG utilized on variation application); *MacQuarrie v. MacQuarrie, supra* (when it is appropriate to apply the SSAG to a variation application); and *Aelbers v. Aelbers*, 2010 CarswellBC 1464, 2010 BCCA 197, 86 R.F.L. (6th) 261 (B.C.C.A.) (a court must consider whether it is appropriate to apply the SSAG in an application to vary support).

### Review

The SSAG may be applied on a review; the issues on review are similar to those in an initial application: *Morck v. Morck*, 2013 CarswellBC 1032, 2013 BCCA 186, 28 R.F.L. (7th) 279, 44 B.C.L.R. (5th) 235, 337 B.C.A.C. 125, 576 W.A.C. 125, [2013] B.C.J. No. 803 (B.C.C.A.).

### Restructuring

The appellate courts have ruled on the matter of restructuring. "Restructuring allows the amount and duration under the formulas to be traded off against each other" (SSAG Executive Summary). See: *S. (J.K.) v. S. (H.G.)*, 2008 CarswellBC 1218, 2008 BCCA 245, 54 R.F.L. (6th) 38, 83 B.C.L.R. (4th) 102, 257 B.C.A.C. 16, 432 W.A.C. 16, [2008] B.C.J. No. 1068 (B.C.C.A.), varying 2006 CarswellBC 2255, 2006 BCSC 1356, [2006] B.C.J. No. 2051 (B.C.S.C.); *Fisher v. Fisher, supra* (order providing support to the wife in an amount above the SSAG range for a shorter period overturned; restructured amount where the quantum was above the range, the duration was below the range; time-limited award at high end of the SSAG range changed to indefinite award at low end of the range); *Cassidy v. McNeil*, 2010 CarswellOnt 1637, 2010 ONCA 218, 99 O.R. (3d) 81, 266 O.A.C. 62, [2010] O.J. No. 1158 (Ont. C.A.), reversing in part 2008 CarswellOnt 110, [2008] O.J. No. 112 (Ont. S.C.J.), affirming 2009 CarswellOnt 8859 (Ont. S.C.J.) (time-limited award at high end of the SSAG range changed to indefinite award at low end of the SSAG range); *Vanos v. Vanos*, 2009 CarswellOnt 6420, 77 R.F.L. (6th) 123, [2009] O.J. No. 4217 (Ont. S.C.J.), reversed 2010 CarswellOnt 9680, 2010 ONCA 876, 94 R.F.L. (6th) 312, 271 O.A.C. 222, [2010] O.J. No. 5539 (Ont. C.A.) (order for lump sum spousal support where husband had a history of non-payment and his unemployment jeopardized future payments); and *Hartshorne v. Hartshorne*, 2009 CarswellBC 1398, 2009 BCSC 698, 70 R.F.L. (6th) 106, [2009] B.C.J. No. 1050 (B.C.S.C.), reversed 2010 CarswellBC 1618, 2010 BCCA 327, 82 R.F.L. (6th) 1, 6 B.C.L.R. (5th) 58, 320 D.L.R. (4th) 398, 289 B.C.A.C. 244, 489 W.A.C. 244, [2010] B.C.J. No. 1271 (B.C.C.A.), additional reasons at 2011 BCCA 29, 2011 CarswellBC 107, 95 R.F.L. (6th) 14, 14 B.C.L.R. (5th) 33, 330 D.L.R. (4th) 503, 299 B.C.A.C. 6, 508 W.A.C. 6, [2011] B.C.J. No. 107 (B.C.C.A.) (retroactive calculation of lump sum award); *Robinson v. Robinson*, 2012 CarswellBC 3789, 2012 BCCA 497, 25 R.F.L. (7th) 47, 40 B.C.L.R. (5th) 108, [2012] B.C.J. No. 2572 (B.C.C.A.) (lump sum award upheld; summary trial judge calculated the lump sum award with reference to the principles and formulas; the SSAG cited and various cases of assistance); and *Davis v. Crawford*, 2011 CarswellOnt 2512, 2011 ONCA 294, 95 R.F.L. (6th) 257, 106 O.R. (3d) 221, 332 D.L.R. (4th) 508, 277 O.A.C. 200, [2011] O.J. No. 1719 (Ont. C.A.) (application of SSAG to lump sum orders).

## Exceptions

There are a number of appellate cases dealing with exceptions under the SSAG. These are: *Young v. Young*, 2009 CarswellBC 3587, 2009 BCCA 518, 76 R.F.L. (6th) 75, 278 B.C.A.C. 129, 471 W.A.C. 129 (B.C.C.A.) (reapportionment of matrimonial home in wife's favour when spousal support not available; consideration of the SSAG in determining the amount of reapportionment award); *Kelly v. Kelly*, 2011 CarswellBC 842, 2011 BCCA 173, 18 B.C.L.R. (5th) 99, 303 B.C.A.C. 209, 512 W.A.C. 209 (B.C.C.A.) (discussion of non-primary parent exception); *S. (R.M.) v. S. (F.P.C.)*, 2011 CarswellBC 170, 2011 BCCA 53, 90 R.F.L. (6th) 1, 14 B.C.L.R. (5th) 84, 299 B.C.A.C. 186, 508 W.A.C. 186, [2011] B.C.J. No. 174 (B.C.C.A.) (compensatory exception and non-primary parent to fulfill parenting role exception); *Cassidy v. McNeil*, 2010 CarswellOnt 1637, 2010 ONCA 218, 99 O.R. (3d) 81, 266 O.A.C. 62, [2010] O.J. No. 1158 (Ont. C.A.) (application of custodial payor formula; discussion of where within range is appropriate); and *Puiu v. Puiu*, 2011 CarswellBC 3174, 2011 BCCA 480, 10 R.F.L. (7th) 108, 313 B.C.A.C. 76, 533 W.A.C. 76, [2011] B.C.J. No. 2308 (B.C.C.A.) (exception where parties living on assets alone).

## Specific Rulings

The SSAG may be used in cases where income is imputed: *Brandl v. Rolston*, 2013 CarswellBC 1273, 2013 BCCA 235, 31 R.F.L. (7th) 296, 362 D.L.R. (4th) 439, 338 B.C.A.C. 141, 577 W.A.C. 141 (B.C.C.A.); but see *Aalbers v. Aalbers*, *supra* (where the payor's income must be imputed because of uncertainty caused by attempts to hide his true financial status, the SSAG will not be applicable).

In still other cases there is only one decision on a particular issue, but in some cases these decisions may be widely applied. See *Beese v. Beese*, 2008 CarswellBC 2103, 2008 BCCA 396, 60 R.F.L. (6th) 31, 87 B.C.L.R. (4th) 286, 261 B.C.A.C. 35, 440 W.A.C. 35 (B.C.C.A.), additional reasons at 2008 CarswellBC 2715, 2008 BCCA 525, 60 R.F.L. (6th) 49, 86 B.C.L.R. (4th) 360, 261 B.C.A.C. 35 at 51, 440 W.A.C. 35 at 51 (B.C.C.A.). Leave to appeal refused 2009 CarswellBC 2674, 2009 CarswellBC 2675, 401 N.R. 392 (note), 289 B.C.A.C. 318 (note), 489 W.A.C. 318 (note), [2009] S.C.C.A. No. 73 (S.C.C.) (the SSAG are particularly useful where there is no evidentiary record); *Stace-Smith v. Lecompte*, 2011 CarswellBC 573, 2011 BCCA 129, 97 R.F.L. (6th) 91, 16 B.C.L.R. (5th) 119, 302 B.C.A.C. 250, 511 W.A.C. 250 (B.C.C.A.) (the SSAG-calculated support will be awarded in the case of a marriage-like relationship as though the parties had been married); *Lapp v. Lapp*, 2008 CarswellAlta 267, 2008 ABCA 15, 51 R.F.L. (6th) 11, 93 Alta. L.R. (4th) 1, 425 A.R. 232, 418 W.A.C. 232, [2008] A.J. No. 208 (Alta. C.A.) (application to retroactive support award on appeal); and *Dima v. Dima*, 2010 CarswellBC 3684, 2010 BCCA 557 (B.C.C.A.) (the trial judge must carefully consider whether the SSAG are applicable when the marriage is brief and there is a child).

There have been three Court of Appeal decisions holding that the SSAG are not applicable where the payor's income is above the ceiling set out in the SSAG which is $350,000. These cases are: *Bell v. Bell*, 2009 CarswellBC 1588, 2009 BCCA 280, 69 R.F.L. (6th) 21, 97 B.C.L.R. (4th) 55, [2010] 1 W.W.R. 98, 272 B.C.A.C. 207, 459 W.A.C. 207, [2009] B.C.J. No. 1201 (B.C.C.A.), additional reasons at 2010 CarswellBC 625, 2010 BCCA 138, 76 R.F.L. (6th) 257, 2 B.C.L.R. (5th) 200, [2010] 7 W.W.R. 453, 284 B.C.A.C. 316 (B.C.C.A.) (the SSAG are not useful, particularly as payor's income was well over $300,000; party entitled to spousal support where she had been disadvantaged by the loss of the standard of living husband's income provided and currently there was a considerable difference in the parties' incomes); *Loesch v. Walji, supra* (the SSAG are not useful where the payor's income was well over $350,000, in this case $900,000 per year with admitted non-resident tax-free status grossed up to $1.6 million); and *Domirti v. Domirti*, 2011 CarswellBC 108, 2011 BCCA 30, 13 B.C.L.R. (5th) 208 (B.C.C.A.) (when it is appropriate to consider the SSAG, an award that falls substantially outside the SSAG ranges may permit appellate intervention).

**Practice and Procedure**

***Role of the Trial Court***

It is an error for the trial judge not to consider the SSAG when they are fully addressed by counsel: *Q. (R.E.) v. K. (G.J.)*, 2012 CarswellBC 887, 2012 BCCA 146, 17 R.F.L. (7th) 255, 31 B.C.L.R. (5th) 264, 348 D.L.R. (4th) 622, [2012] 8 W.W.R. 270, 319 B.C.A.C. 98, 542 W.A.C. 98 (B.C.C.A.), additional reasons at 2012 CarswellBC 1774, 2012 BCCA 267, 17 R.F.L. (7th) 291, 31 B.C.L.R. (5th) 300, [2012] 8 W.W.R. 306 (B.C.C.A.) (when at trial, parties prepared submissions regarding spousal support using the SSAG, the British Columbia Court of Appeal held it open to the trial judge to choose a figure for lump sum support which lay approximately midway between the amounts sought by the respective parties). Conversely, if the SSAG are not put forward by counsel, the court need not consider them: *Jessop v. Wright*, 2008 CarswellOnt 5785, 2008 ONCA 673, 56 R.F.L. (6th) 29 (Ont. C.A.).

The appellate courts have emphasized the need to have reasons where there is a departure from the SSAG. See *Kerr v. Baranow, supra* (in calculating amount and duration of spousal support, the jurisprudence requires an application of the SSAG unless reasons are provided as to why the SSAG are not appropriate); *Kelsch v. Chaput*, 2012 CarswellBC 362, 2012 BCCA 64,

317 B.C.A.C. 59, 540 W.A.C. 59 (B.C.C.A.) (where reasons for using the SSAG are brief, they may still meet the "functional" test of the Supreme Court of Canada and reflect the principles the court was obliged to consider); *Gagne v. Gagne, supra* (need to provide reasons for departure from the SSAG; there is an obligation upon a judge to explain why he or she departed from the SSAG). However, see *Beninger v. Beninger, supra* (trial courts are not required to explain all deviations from SSAG, but doing so would be "best practice"); *Scott v. Scott, supra* (failure to refer to the SSAG was not an error in law); and *Smith v. Smith, supra* (a judge will not be mandated to apply the usual SSAG ranges, even when none of the exceptions applied.

## Role of the Appellate Court

In circumstances where the appellate court rules that the SSAG should have been applied at trial, the appeal court can apply the SSAG rather than remitting the matter to trial: *Stace-Smith v. Lecompte, supra; Domirti v. Domirti*, 2010 CarswellBC 2864 , 2010 BCCA 472, 10 B.C.L.R. (5th) 281, 294 B.C.A.C. 127, 498 W.A.C. 127, [2010] B.C.J. No. 2074 (B.C.C.A.); *Domirti v. Domirti*, 2010 CarswellBC 518, 2010 BCCA 112 (B.C.C.A. [In Chambers]) (where a trial judge bases a support award on an incorrect application of the SSAG, the Court of Appeal may vary the order to reflect the correct application). However, see *M. (J.A.) v. M. (D.L.)*, 2008 CarswellNB 24, 2008 CarswellNB 25, 2008 NBCA 2, 289 D.L.R. (4th) 37, 326 N.B.R. (2d) 111, 838 A.P.R. 111, [2008] N.B.J. No. 9 (N.B.C.A.) (the SSAG should be applied if entitlement exists; Court of Appeal remitted this matter to the trial court for reconsideration).

Where use of the SSAG is not disputed at trial, the SSAG may not be disputed on appeal: *Elfar v. Elfar*, 2012 CarswellAlta 2091 , 2012 ABCA 375, 539 A.R. 268, 561 W.A.C. 268 (Alta. C.A.), additional reasons at 2013 CarswellAlta 88, 2013 ABCA 33 (Alta. C.A.).

## Determination of Quantum and Duration within the Ranges

A number of the decisions are fact-based considerations of whether or not the correct amount or duration of spousal support has been awarded. These cases include: *Haraphongse v. Haraphongse*, 2011 CarswellAlta 2321, 2011 ABCA 343 (Alta. C.A.) (reference to wife's spousal support being lower than the SSAG ranges was sufficient to indicate that the wife's occupation of the matrimonial home was taken into account in giving her an unusually low amount of spousal support); *McIntire v. McIntire*, 2012 CarswellBC 1479, 2012 BCCA 214, 19 R.F.L. (7th) 284, 35 B.C.L.R. (5th) 245, 322 B.C.A.C. 139, 549 W.A.C. 139 (B.C.C.A.) (given the SSAG range, the duration for spousal support seemed unduly short but as the husband paid $25,000 to the wife post-separation the duration was less anomalous; nonetheless, the duration of support could not be upheld); *Emery v. Emery*, 2010 CarswellBC 2137, 2010 BCCA 376, 100 R.F.L. (6th) 154 (B.C.C.A.), additional reasons to 2010 BCCA 229, 2010 CarswellBC 1170, 2010 BCCA 229, 2010 CarswellBC 1170, 85 R.F.L. (6th) 251, 287 B.C.A.C. 116, 485 W.A.C. 116 (B.C.C.A.) (the Court of Appeal will award the minimum amount of support provided for in the SSAG if it finds a sufficiently demonstrated material change in circumstances such as early retirement); *Gonabady-Namadon v. Mohammadzadeh*, 2009 CarswellBC 2767, 2009 BCCA 448, 74 R.F.L. (6th) 1, 98 B.C.L.R. (4th) 23, 277 B.C.A.C. 48, 469 W.A.C. 48 (B.C.C.A.), varying 2008 BCSC 606, 2008 CarswellBC 968, 54 R.F.L. (6th) 408 (B.C.S.C.), varying 2008 BCSC 706, 2008 CarswellBC 1120, 58 R.F.L. (6th) 205 (B.C.S.C.) (the income prospects of a support recipient (a 40-year-old medical doctor) can justify an award at the low end of the SSAG for a reasonably short period of time); *S. (J.K.) v. S. (H.G.), supra* (on appeal, an order providing support to the wife in an amount above the SSAG range for a shorter period was overturned; the court awarded an amount above the SSAG range for 5 years and thereafter an amount at the highest end of the Guideline range, as it was unlikely the wife would curb her spending or find employment while receiving these generous amounts and it was not sensible for her support to cease when she was 65 and more likely to be unemployable).

In many cases, the trial courts consider the SSAG in their awards of spousal support and the appellate courts merely affirm the result. See *Ouellette v. Ouellette*, 2012 CarswellBC 904, 2012 BCCA 145, 16 R.F.L. (7th) 39, 32 B.C.L.R. (5th) 67, 319 B.C.A.C. 160, 542 W.A.C. 160 (B.C.C.A.); *V. (B.) v. V. (P.)*, 2012 CarswellOnt 4738, 2012 ONCA 262, 19 R.F.L. (7th) 292, [2012] O.J. No. 1778 (Ont. C.A.); *O'Grady v. O'Grady*, 2010 CarswellAlta 752 , 2010 ABCA 109, 82 R.F.L. (6th) 59, 319 D.L.R. (4th) 301, 477 A.R. 216, 483 W.A.C. 216, [2010] A.J. No. 446 (Alta. C.A.); *Weinkauf v. Weinkauf*, 2010 CarswellAlta 1981, 2010 ABCA 293 (Alta. C.A.); *Michaud v. Kuszelewski*, 2009 CarswellNS 646 , 2009 NSCA 118, 75 R.F.L. (6th) 3, 312 D.L.R. (4th) 598, 284 N.S.R. (2d) 310, 901 A.P.R. 310 (N.S.C.A.); and *Mirza v. Mirza*, 2006 CarswellBC 1899, 2006 BCCA 362, 31 R.F.L. (6th) 301, 269 D.L.R. (4th) 259, 229 B.C.A.C. 186, 379 W.A.C. 186, [2006] B.C.J. No. 1756 (B.C.C.A.), additional reasons at 2007 CarswellBC 313, 2007 BCCA 106, 237 B.C.A.C. 104, 392 W.A.C. 104 (B.C.C.A.).

## 19.2.3 Cases

The case section is divided into the following headings:

- General principles
- Practice and Procedure
- Various Types of Proceedings

## General Principles

*The SSAG amounts are not binding, but can act as a litmus test for the appropriateness of a spousal support order* — Kynoch v. Kynoch, 2013 CarswellMan 441, 2013 MBCA 73, 294 Man. R. (2d) 250, 581 W.A.C. 250 (Man. C.A.). The parties were married for 30 years and had three adult children. Prior to separation, the parties worked the family farm. The wife had been awarded interim spousal support at $1,000 monthly, which was reduced by the trial judge to $250 monthly. The Court of Appeal found that amounts calculated with reference to the SSAG were $878 to $1,134 monthly. The trial judge had not explained how he arrived at the $250 amount, nor discussed the SSAG, although they were pleaded by the wife. The judge found that, although the SSAG amounts are not binding, reference to them can act as a litmus test and, in this case, demonstrated that the quantum awarded by the trial judge was too low. The Court of Appeal awarded $600 monthly to reflect the fact that the wife's father had bought her a home and the husband was living with his mother.

*The SSAG are a useful tool* — Caldwell v. Caldwell, 2013 CarswellAlta 1241, 2013 ABCA 268, 33 R.F.L. (7th) 285 (Alta. C.A.).

*Use of the SSAG is advisory only and does not replace the broad discretion of judges to determine support based on applicable legal principles* — Droit de la famille - 131531, 2013 CarswellQue 5424, 2013 QCCA 1044, EYB 2013-223013 (C.A. Que.). The payor husband appealed an order of spousal support. The parties had been married for 17 years, and the wife had suffered significant economic disadvantage as a result of the marriage and its breakdown. The parties had two children, aged 12 and 18 at the time of trial. Prior to the breakdown of the marriage, the wife was a stay-at-home mother and the husband was a financial advisor whose annual income was in excess of $250,000. The trial judge ordered compensatory and non-compensatory spousal support at levels which the husband claimed exceeded the SSAG amounts. This order was upheld by the Court of Appeal, which noted that the SSAG were advisory only and that in fact the quantum awarded was within the SSAG ranges, although the trial judge did not make reference to the SSAG. The Court of Appeal found that the trial judge had broad discretion to determine support and had not made an error in principle or a misapprehension of the evidence.

*In considering the appropriate amount of spousal support, the courts should consider the* Spousal Support Advisory Guidelines; *although they do not have legal force, they do provide an indication of a level of support that may be appropriate — Brisson v. Brisson,* 2012 CarswellBC 3051, 2012 BCCA 396, 22 R.F.L. (7th) 1, 39 B.C.L.R. (5th) 1, 355 D.L.R. (4th) 720, 328 B.C.A.C. 163, 558 W.A.C. 163 (B.C.C.A.). The court relied on *Yemchuk v. Yemchuk,* 2005 CarswellBC 1881, 2005 BCCA 406, 16 R.F.L. (6th) 430, 44 B.C.L.R. (4th) 77, 257 D.L.R. (4th) 476, [2005] 10 W.W.R. 634, 215 B.C.A.C. 193, 355 W.A.C. 193, [2005] B.C.J. No. 1748 (B.C.C.A.); and *Redpath v. Redpath,* 2006 CarswellBC 1709, 2006 BCCA 338, 33 R.F.L. (6th) 91, 62 B.C.L.R. (4th) 233, 228 B.C.A.C. 272, 376 W.A.C. 272, [2006] B.C.J. No. 1550 (B.C.C.A.). In the Brisson decison, the court was of the opinion that the Guidelines informed, but did not determine, the appropriate level of support. The parties had been married for 37 years. The husband's income, if including his public service pension and Canada Pension Plan benefit, was comfortably above the floor of $20,000 to $30,000 at which point the SSAG raise a caution that spousal support should likely not be awarded. Further, there is no double recovery contrary to *Boston* where, as here, the "proper basis of compensation" excludes the divided public service pension and Canada Pension Plan benefits in respect to both parties. The current income disparity was about $16,000 to $17,000 per annum. Given the Guideline approach, the wife's greater asset position, and the evidence before the court, the amount of spousal support was set at $500 per month, which was the lower value the Guidelines suggested, in recognition of the wife's favourable asset position. The court allowed the appeal, set aside the order terminating spousal support and ordered support in the amount of $500 per month commencing in August 2011.

*A trial judge is not mandated to rely on the* Spousal Support Advisory Guidelines; *but once they are put into play, a party is entitled to know why the trial judge has deviated from them — Grant v. Grant,* 2012 CarswellNB 700, 2012 CarswellNB 701, 2012 NBCA 101, 29 R.F.L. (7th) 244, 397 N.B.R. (2d) 254, 1028 A.P.R. 254, [2012] N.B.J. No. 415 (N.B.C.A.).

*A judge will not be mandated to apply the usual SSAG ranges, even when none of the exceptions apply — Smith v. Smith,* 2011 CarswellNB 377, 2011 CarswellNB 378, 2011 NBCA 66, 9 R.F.L. (7th) 286, 336 D.L.R. (4th) 285, 375 N.B.R. (2d) 208, 969 A.P.R. 208, [2011] N.B.J. No. 245 (N.B.C.A.). The parties were married for 28 years and had two independent adult children. The husband had a large amount of debt, and the parties had lived beyond their means during the marriage. The judge ordered the husband to pay $1,000 monthly, which was less than the wife had requested. The wife appealed on the grounds that the judge had not applied the SSAG. The Court of Appeal found that the judge had misapprehended the wife's circumstances, but that as the husband had conceded entitlement the only issue to determine was whether the trial judge had misapprehended the evidence concerning the husband's ability to pay. The Court of Appeal found that there was palpable and overriding error in the trial judge's findings concerning the husband's debt and, as such, the quantum of spousal support could be adjusted by the Court of Appeal. The Court of Appeal found that there was an error of fact in the case at bar. However, there was no error of law made by the trial judge in not applying the SSAG, as the Guidelines are advisory only. The wife's argument, that whenever there was no exception to the normal ranges, as set out in the SSAG exceptions the standard SSAG ranges must be applied, failed. The Court of Appeal did apply the SSAG when determining quantum, which was set at the middle range of the SSAG amounts.

*Failure to refer to the SSAG was not an error in law* — Scott v. Scott, 2011 CarswellMan 52, 2011 MBCA 21, 97 R.F.L. (6th) 119, 262 Man. R. (2d) 237, 507 W.A.C. 237 (Man. C.A.). The wife's appeal of a variation in child support was dismissed. The motions judge's failure to refer to the *Spousal Support Advisory Guidelines* in his otherwise detailed and cogent reasons was not an error in law that justified appellate intervention. While it is useful for a motions judge to refer to the SSAG, the guidelines are neither legislated nor binding on courts and have not replaced judicial discretion.

*Not using the SSAG will not in itself constitute a reversible error* — Droit de la famille - 112606, 2011 CarswellQue 8981, 2011 CarswellQue 15234, 2011 QCCA 1554, EYB 2011-194830, 8 R.F.L. (7th) 1, [2011] R.J.Q. 1745, [2011] Q.J. No. 11097 (C.A. Que.). The parties had a traditional, 24-year marriage and had two children, one of whom was still a dependant and resided with the wife. The trial judge did not consider whether or not the SSAG were applicable, and the wife appealed partly on the basis that the SSAG should have been used to calculate support and that not doing so was a reversible error. The Quebec Court of Appeal considered the applicability of the SSAG and found that, although a useful tool, they do not replace an analysis under s. 15(2) of the *Divorce Act*. The Court of Appeal found that not using the SSAG could not itself constitute a reversible error when a proper analysis was performed under s. 15(2). Parliament has not seen fit to make the SSAG binding law rather than advisory in nature. Spousal support was increased on other grounds.

*If the amount of spousal support awarded exceeds the amount recommended under the Spousal Support Guidelines, this fact is irrelevant as the SSAG do not have the force of law* — a trial judge cannot rely on the recommendations generated under the SSAG, if his or her own proper analysis requires a different conclusion — Rockall v. Rockall, 2010 CarswellAlta 1859, 2010 ABCA 278, 90 R.F.L. (6th) 317, 35 Alta. L.R. (5th) 1, 490 A.R. 135, 497 W.A.C. 135, [2010] A.J. No. 1064 (Alta. C.A.). The parties cohabited for a year before they married. They were married for 5 years and did not have children. The husband was aware that the wife was HIV positive when they began their relationship. By the time of the trial, the wife had AIDS and the court found that her illness affected her ability to work. She was awarded lump sum arrears of spousal support in the sum of $120,000 in addition to the $58,418.05 in support already received. The trial judge ordered a further lump sum of $28,800 to be paid, representing an entitlement to support in the amount of $800 a month payable over 3 years. In 2009 the husband's income was $140,000 to $150,000. The wife's income was modest or non-existent, although she did receive some assistance as a member of a First Nation. The wife was living in a women's shelter. Her standard of living had dropped markedly since cohabitation. Spousal support was awarded on a non-compensatory basis on account of the wife's health and the parties' disparate financial circumstances. The decision was upheld on appeal as to entitlement but varied from lump sum support to periodic support, as no exceptional circumstances justifying lump sum support were indicated.

*In calculating the amount and duration of spousal support, the jurisprudence requires an application of the SSAG unless reasons are provided as to why the SSAG are not appropriate* — Kerr v. Baranow, 2009 CarswellBC 642, 2009 BCCA 111, 66 R.F.L. (6th) 1, 93 B.C.L.R. (4th) 201, [2009] 9 W.W.R. 285, 266 B.C.A.C. 298, 449 W.A.C. 298, [2009] B.C.J. No. 474 (B.C.C.A.), additional reasons at 2010 CarswellBC 108, 2010 BCCA 32, 78 R.F.L. (6th) 305, 2 B.C.L.R. (5th) 197, [2010] 4 W.W.R. 465, [2010] B.C.J. No. 88 (B.C.C.A.), reversed 2011 CarswellBC 240, 2011 CarswellBC 241, 2011 SCC 10, 93 R.F.L. (6th) 1, [2011] 1 S.C.R. 269, 108 O.R. (3d) 399, 14 B.C.L.R. (5th) 203, 328 D.L.R. (4th) 577, 64 E.T.R. (3d) 1, [2011] 3

W.W.R. 575, 411 N.R. 200, 274 O.A.C. 1, 300 B.C.A.C. 1, 509 W.A.C. 1, [2011] S.C.J. No. 10 (S.C.C.).

A trial judge does not err in law by not averting to the Spousal Support Advisory Guidelines — "The Guidelines do not enjoy the force of law and, while they are a useful tool in a judge's determination of spousal maintenance, there remains more than one route available to trial judges in arriving at an appropriate result" — Taylor v. Taylor, 2009 CarswellAlta 1701, 2009 ABCA 354, 72 R.F.L. (6th) 249, 15 Alta. L.R. (5th) 303, 312 D.L.R. (4th) 448, 464 A.R. 245, 467 W.A.C. 245, [2009] A.J. No. 1162 (Alta. C.A.), at para. 51.

The SSAG reflect existing law — Hartshorne v. Hartshorne, 2009 CarswellBC 1398, 2009 BCSC 698, 70 R.F.L. (6th) 106, [2009] B.C.J. No. 1050 (B.C.S.C.), reversed 2010 CarswellBC 1618, 2010 BCCA 327, 82 R.F.L. (6th) 1, 6 B.C.L.R. (5th) 58, 320 D.L.R. (4th) 398, 289 B.C.A.C. 244, 489 W.A.C. 244, [2010] B.C.J. No. 1271 (B.C.C.A.). The objectives and factors listed in ss. 15.2(4) and (6) of the Divorce Act remain the relevant guiding principles in determining quantum and duration of spousal support. The SSAG are merely intended to reflect the existing law, rather than to modify it.

The SSAG are helpful in establishing a range of appropriate support — a modified version of the "without child support" formula applied — Mann v. Mann, 2009 CarswellBC 1065, 2009 BCCA 181, 68 R.F.L. (6th) 1, 95 B.C.L.R. (4th) 201, 273 B.C.A.C. 1, 461 W.A.C. 1 (B.C.C.A.), additional reasons at 2009 CarswellBC 3513, 2009 BCCA 603, 74 R.F.L. (6th) 18 (B.C.C.A.). The parties separated in 1999 after a 15-year marriage. The wife applied for spousal support in 2006 when she instituted divorce proceedings. The trial judge found that the wife had become self-sufficient by the time of trial, as her income permitted the lifestyle that the parties had enjoyed before separation. At trial, the wife was awarded lump sum support of $25,000. The trial court considered the SSAG, but did not find them useful. The husband's income increased significantly post-separation. On appeal, the court questioned whether the trial judge's award of a lump sum of $25,000 was an award that could and should be changed. The Court of Appeal held, at para. 82:

> The Spousal Support Guidelines cannot be applied in the circumstances of this case, without adjustment for the deferred application for spousal support, consideration of the respondent's significant post-separation income increase, his underpayment for the family assets in 2001, as well as the amounts he actually paid under the parties' shared custody arrangement. But, they are helpful in establishing a range of appropriate support and their consideration in this case provides a better range than the needs-based approach the trial judge took that caused the compensatory factor to be confined to the years when the appellant forewent spousal support after the separation agreement and overlooked the disadvantage to her and the advantage to her husband of the role she played during the marriage.

Instead of applying the SSAG's shared custody formula, it applied a modified version of the "without child support" formula. The formula was modified by subtracting from each spouse's income the amount of child support paid.

While it was not apparent whether or not the trial court had relied on the SSAG, the Court of Appeal noted the discrepancy between the amounts under the SSAG and the amount actually awarded, a discrepancy which the trial judge did not explain — support varied to amount at high end of the SSAG and made indefinite — Rozendaal v. Rozendaal, 2009 CarswellBC 3814, 2009 BCCA 234, 90 R.F.L. (6th) 347 (B.C.C.A.). The trial judge ordered the husband to pay the wife spousal support of $3,000 per month from June 2008 for 12 months, and $2,500 per month for an additional 12 months, after which time support terminated. On the basis of the income of $50,000 imputed to the wife, the range of support suggested by the Spousal Support Guidelines was $691 to $1,478 per month. On appeal, the court upheld the imputation of income of $50,000 even though the wife was 54 years of age and the 6 years before the trial her average income was $23,000. The appellate court considered the trial judge's finding of an income of $50,000 a matter of fact which, absent palpable and overriding error, it could not disturb. However, support was varied and instead awarded on an indefinite basis. The court varied the order in light of the length of the marriage, the wife's age, the age of the youngest child and her anticipated completion of education, and the authorities referred to the court. Support would continue indefinitely from June 1, 2010 in the amount of $1,478 (the high end of the SSAG), subject to the husband's application to vary.

*Use of the SSAG to assess reasonableness of amount requested — duration under the SSAG ignored — Rioux v. Rioux*, 2009 CarswellOnt 4077, 2009 ONCA 569, 66 R.F.L. (6th) 256, 97 O.R. (3d) 102, 252 O.A.C. 126, [2009] O.J. No. 2949 (Ont. C.A.). The parties were married for 21 years when they separated in 2001, and they had one daughter who was enrolled in university. The husband had an income of approximately $100,000 a year and the wife earned $16,000. The trial judge ordered interim child support of $916 per month and a lump sum payment for equalization and spousal support. This decision was overturned by the Court of Appeal, which ordered the $1,500 sought by the wife for 5 years, at which point a review could be sought. The SSAG were explicitly referenced by the Court of Appeal. The court handed down a limited-term award, which it based on the wife's relative youth, the fact that she had remained in the workforce to some extent during the marriage, and because the support was found to be non-compensatory in nature. [It is unclear what SSAG formula would result in an award of only $1,500. Furthermore, the SSAG would dictate an indefinite award because of the parties' traditional, long-term marriage.]

*The court is not obligated to apply the SSAG — Beninger v. Beninger*, 2009 CarswellBC 2963, 2009 BCCA 458, 77 R.F.L. (6th) 56, 277 B.C.A.C. 36, 469 W.A.C. 36, [2009] B.C.J. No. 2197 (B.C.C.A.). The wife argued that the chambers judge was required to apply the SSAG "with child" formula or justify the decision not to apply it. The Court of Appeal stated at para. 28 that, "while it is preferable for a court to organize its analysis by reference to the Guidelines", compliance is not required: "[a]s their name indicates, they are advisory and without statutory effect. That said, they provide helpful advice and this Court has been clear that their advice must be taken seriously and that best practice would include an explanation of any deviation from them." The Court of Appeal upheld the chambers judge's decision, making an award within the SSAG range.

*Utility of the SSAG — Fisher v. Fisher*, 2008 CarswellOnt 43, 2008 ONCA 11, 47 R.F.L. (6th) 235, 88 O.R. (3d) 241, 288 D.L.R. (4th) 513, 232 O.A.C. 213, [2008] O.J. No. 38 (Ont. C.A.). The Ontario Court of Appeal endorsed the B.C. Appellate court's description of the SSAG as a "useful tool", and suggested that they are likely to bring consistency and predictability to the law. However, they do not obviate the need for an individualized analysis, and they must be applied in their entirety (including the sections pertaining to exceptions and restructuring). Part of the usefulness of the SSAG is due to the fact that they are based on case law. However, if they suggest a range which is contrary to the applicable authorities, the authorities prevail. It was an error for the trial judge to not consider the SSAG when fully addressed by counsel. There was extensive discussion of the SSAG and the court applied restructuring.

*The SSAG used to bring quantum of support in line with objectives of the Act; duration set out in agreement maintained — Turpin v. Clark*, 2008 CarswellBC 2238, 2008 BCSC 1425, [2008] B.C.J. No. 2013 (B.C.S.C. [In Chambers]), reversed 2009 CarswellBC 3149, 2009 BCCA 530, 80 R.F.L. (6th) 239, 4 B.C.L.R. (5th) 48, 313 D.L.R. (4th) 452, [2010] 6 W.W.R. 613, 278 B.C.A.C. 220, 471 W.A.C. 220, [2009] B.C.J. No. 2328 (B.C.C.A.). The parties had agreed upon spousal support which was below the SSAG ranges for both quantum and duration. The chambers judge held that in light of an unexpected deterioration in the recipient's health and her unforeseen challenges in becoming self-sufficient, the second stage of the *Miglin* test was found to justify an upward variation. The quantum of support was increased to an amount at the bottom of the SSAG range. The appellate court held the chambers judge erred in law by intervening to the extent that he did in varying the spousal support provisions of the divorce order. Applying the deferential standard required by *Miglin*, the court would not interfere with the step-down provisions of the divorce order. However, because of the delay in the wife's achievement of economic self-sufficiency, caused by her unanticipated health complications and inability to earn income, the court extended the duration of the final amount of the award ($4,000) for an additional 3 years until 2015 or when the husband retired, whichever event occurred later.

*It is only after entitlement to spousal support has been established that the SSAG become relevant — consideration must be given to the SSAG in arriving at the spousal support to be paid; while the SSAG are advisory only, B.C. courts have endorsed them as a "useful tool" in determining issues of quantum and duration of spousal support and B.C. courts have deemed them to be consistent with the law in British Columbia — the SSAG do not necessarily apply in all cases as indicated in the list of exceptions set out in the SSAG; however, the fact that a case is a high asset case does not make the SSAG irrelevant —* Chutter v. Chutter, 2008 CarswellBC 2661, 2008 BCCA 507, 60 R.F.L. (6th) 263, 86 B.C.L.R. (4th) 233, 301 D.L.R. (4th) 297, [2009] 3 W.W.R. 246, 263 B.C.A.C. 109, 443 W.A.C. 109, [2008] B.C.J. No. 2398 (B.C.C.A.).

*The SSAG should be applied if entitlement exists —* M. (J.A.) v. M. (D.L.), 2008 CarswellNB 24, 2008 CarswellNB 25, 2008 NBCA 2, 289 D.L.R. (4th) 37, 326 N.B.R. (2d) 111, 838 A.P.R. 111, [2008] N.B.J. No. 9 (N.B.C.A.). The Court of Appeal remitted this matter to the trial court for reconsideration. In so doing, it included the following instruction regarding the use of SSAG at para. 45: "A judge must first determine entitlement, and then, if entitlement exists, should apply the *Federal Spousal Support Advisory Guidelines*."

*The SSAG not to be substituted for consideration of* Divorce Act *—* Sawatzky v. Sawatzky, 2008 CarswellAlta 1626, 2008 ABCA 355, 59 R.F.L. (6th) 88, 97 Alta. L.R. (4th) 225, 302 D.L.R. (4th) 516, 440 A.R. 267, 438 W.A.C. 267 (Alta. C.A.), varying 2007 CarswellAlta 216, 2007 ABQB 103, [2007] A.J. No. 102 (Alta. Q.B.). The trial judge's award of spousal support was overturned because he appeared to have used the SSAG as a formula and not to have considered the *Divorce Act* factors and objectives. The Alberta Court of Appeal made the following statements about the SSAG, at paras. 15-16: "while it is tempting to resort to a recipe for a mathematical formula instead of going to the difficult analysis in the *Divorce Act*, this approach should not be adopted since, as stated in *Moge v. Moge*, [1992] 3 S.C.R. 813, (S.C.C.) there is no 'magic recipe' or a grid for determining spousal support... [T]he Advisory Spousal Support Guidelines are not mandatory and do not have the force of law. They are a useful tool. While they are instructive as to one route to proper exercise of discretion in arriving at an award, they do not and should not fully fetter a trial judge's discretion."

*The SSAG instructive but do not fetter discretion —* Lust v. Lust, 2007 CarswellAlta 808, 2007 ABCA 202, 417 A.R. 106, 410 W.A.C. 106, [2007] A.J. No. 654 (Alta. C.A.), reversing in part 2007 CarswellAlta 864, 2007 ABQB 214, 413 A.R. 1, [2007] A.J. No. 635 (Alta. Q.B.). The Alberta Court of Appeal stated, at para. 10, that the SSAG are "instructive as to one route to proper exercise of discretion in arriving at an award" but "they do not fully fetter a trial judge's discretion."

*"Might have been preferable" for trial court to use the SSAG —* Carrier c. Carrier, 2007 CarswellNB 155, 2007 CarswellNB 156, 2007 NBC A 23, 281 D.L.R. (4th) 740, 312 N.B.R. (2d) 285, 806 A.P.R. 285, [2007] N.B.J. No. 115 (N.B.C.A.). The trial judge ordered spousal support in an amount below the SSAG range. On appeal, the parties did not challenge the quantum and so it was not varied on appeal. However, the Court noted, at para. 28 that "[i]t might have been

preferable for the trial judge to rely upon the spousal support advisory guidelines to determine an amount."

*The SSAG provides "guide to a range" and not a "set figure"* — Dunnigan v. Park, 2007 CarswellBC 1441, 2007 BCCA 329, 38 R.F.L. (6th) 241 (B.C.C.A.). The trial judge's use of the SSAG was upheld. The Court of Appeal found at para. 16 that he had "properly used the Spousal Support Advisory Guidelines as just that, a guide to a range of awards, rather than as a set figure which must be applied or awarded."

*Failure to use the SSAG not in of itself a reversible error, but comparison of trial decision to the SSAG may permit appellate intervention in some cases* — Redpath v. Redpath, 2006 CarswellBC 1709, 2006 BCCA 338, 33 R.F.L. (6th) 91, 62 B.C.L.R. (4th) 233, 228 B.C.A.C. 272, 376 W.A.C. 272, [2006] B.C.J. No. 1550 (B.C.C.A.). The trial court had ordered spousal support in an amount substantially less than the SSAG minimum and did so without referring to the SSAG. The recipient alleged on appeal that not having done so constituted a reversible error. The Court of Appeal rejected this contention, but stated the following regarding the effect of the SSAG on the standard of appellate review:

> [42] Cases such as *Hickey*, however, were decided prior to the introduction of the Advisory Guidelines. Now that they are available to provide what is effectively a "range" within which the awards in most cases of this kind should fall, it may be that if a particular award is substantially lower or higher than the range and there are no exceptional circumstances to explain the anomaly, the standard of review should be reformulated to permit appellate intervention. In the case at bar, I find that although the trial judge obviously considered the appropriate factors and did not misapprehend the evidence, the figure of $3,500 per month reached by him is simply too low in light of the Guidelines range of $4,542 and $5,510 per month.

Spousal support was increased from $3,500 per month to $5,000 per month, near the midpoint of the applicable SSAG range. See also *Lightle v. Kotar*, 2014 CarswellBC 428, 2014 BCCA 69, 43 R.F.L. (7th) 20, 59 B.C.L.R. (5th) 75, 371 D.L.R. (4th) 269, [2014] 5 W.W.R. 615, 352 B.C.A.C. 39, 601 W.A.C. 39, [2014] B.C.J. No. 294 (B.C.C.A.).

*Award within SSAG range replaced with one below it, criticisms of the SSAG identified* — G. (C.) c. V. (G.), 2006 CarswellQue 4931, 2006 QCCA 763, EYB 2006-106167, [2006] R.J.Q. 1519, [2006] J.Q. No. 5231 (C.A. Que.). The trial judge's award of spousal support amount within the SSAG range was overturned on appeal and replaced with an amount which was less than half of the SSAG minimum quantum. No ruling was made about the general applicability of the SSAG in Quebec, with the court stating that the dossier as it is and the brief pleadings of counsel on this aspect do not permit us, in my opinion, to pronounce a judgment of principle upon the utilization of the Advisory Guidelines. However, previous criticisms of the SSAG made in Quebec courts were identified, and the concern that formulas not replace individualized justice was described as important.

*The SSAG approved as encouraging consistency and predictability but deference paid to trial court's deviation from duration formula* — C. (J.D.E.) v. C. (S.M.), 2006 CarswellNB 242, 2006 CarswellNB 243, 2006 NBCA 46, 27 R.F.L. (6th) 19, 299 N.B.R. (2d) 334, 778 A.P.R. 334, [2006] N.B.J. No. 186 (N.B.C.A.), leave to appeal refused 2006 CarswellNB 579, 2006 CarswellNB 580, 309 N.B.R. (2d) 400 (note), 799 A.P.R. 400 (note), 361 N.R. 392 (note), [2006] S.C.C.A. No. 246 (S.C.C.). The trial court's spousal support award used the SSAG minimum value as a quantum, but imposed a time limit of 5 years, whereas the SSAG call for indefinite support. The wife's appeal was dismissed, and the Court of Appeal stated the following, at para. 5, about the place of the SSAG in the law:

The guidelines have been referred to in many ways: a check, a cross-check, a litmus test, a useful tool and a starting point. But it is my view that whichever term one likes to employ, their use, through the available software, will help in the long run to bring consistency and predictability to spousal support awards. Not only will they foster settlement, they will also allow spouses to anticipate their support responsibilities at the time of separation.

However, on the particular facts of this case deference was paid to the trial judge's decision to impose a 5-year limit.

*Use of the SSAG after a traditional spousal support analysis not an error on the part of the trial judge* — *Pettigrew v. Pettigrew*, 2006 CarswellNS 349, 2006 NSCA 98, 30 R.F.L. (6th) 7, 246 N.S.R. (2d) 298, 780 A.P.R. 298, [2006] N.S.J. No. 321 (N.S.C.A.). The parties separated in 2003 after a 29-year marriage. The trial judge determined that the husband earned $110,000 and the wife earned $20,000. The trial judge ordered the husband to pay $2,900 per month in spousal support as well as a lump sum $30,000 in retroactive support. The Court of Appeal found that the lower court had correctly applied the SSAG in awarding support and dismissed the appeal. The SSAG were relied upon by the trial judge as a "cross-check" after conducting a traditional spousal support analysis. The husband argued on appeal that using the SSAG was an error justifying appellate intervention, but the Court of Appeal upheld the judgement. [There was no additional discussion of the SSAG at the appellate level.]

*The SSAG used to replace support amount specified by agreement not in compliance with Miglin* — *Mirza v. Mirza*, 2006 CarswellBC 1899, 2006 BCCA 362, 31 R.F.L. (6th) 301, 269 D.L.R. (4th) 259, 229 B.C.A.C. 186, 379 W.A.C. 186, [2006] B.C.J. No. 1756 (B.C.C.A.), additional reasons at 2007 CarswellBC 313, 2007 BCCA 106, 237 B.C.A.C. 104, 392 W.A.C. 104 (B.C.C.A.). The parties' separation agreement failed the *Miglin* tests and spousal support was increased from the agreed-upon level. The new support quantum was fixed at trial after considering the SSAG range and was within that range. This result was upheld on appeal.

*Trial court's 3-year time limit and step-down quantum replaced with indefinite award after considering the SSAG* — *certain SSAG details ignored* — *Tedham v. Tedham*, 2005 CarswellBC 2346, 2005 BCCA 502, 20 R.F.L. (6th) 217, 47 B.C.L.R. (4th) 254, 261 D.L.R. (4th) 332, [2006] 3 W.W.R. 212, [2005] B.C.J. No. 2186 (B.C.C.A.), additional reasons at 2005 CarswellBC 2699, 2005 BCCA 553, 47 B.C.L.R. (4th) 276, 261 D.L.R. (4th) 332 at 359, [2006] 3 W.W.R. 234, 217 B.C.A.C. 250, 358 W.A.C. 250 (B.C.C.A.). The parties had been married for 16 years. The time limit imposed at trial was removed after consideration of the "without child support" formula. However, the SSAG's rule of 65 and custodial payor formulas, which may have been relevant on the facts, were not considered.

*Utility of the SSAG* — *Yemchuk v. Yemchuk*, 2005 CarswellBC 1881, 2005 BCCA 406, 16 R.F.L. (6th) 430, 44 B.C.L.R. (4th) 77, 257 D.L.R. (4th) 476, [2005] 10 W.W.R. 634, 215 B.C.A.C. 193, 355 W.A.C. 193, [2005] B.C.J. No. 1748 (B.C.C.A.), additional reasons at 2005 CarswellBC 2540, 2005 BCCA 527, 22 R.F.L. (6th) 60, [2005] B.C.J. No. 2319 (B.C.C.A.). The British Columbia made the following comments regarding the utility of the SSAG and their function in judicial decision-making, at para. 64:

> I have no hesitation in viewing the Advisory Guidelines as a useful tool to assist judges in assessing the quantum and duration of spousal support. They do not operate to displace the courts' reliance on decided authorities (to the extent that relevant authorities are forthcoming) but to supplement them. In that regard, they do not constitute evidence, but are properly considered as part of counsels' submissions.

The *SSAG are guidelines, not rules, and consequently it is open to a court to set the term of spousal support for the period of dependency, not the number of years of the relationship* — *Kilbreath v. Morgan*, 2012 CarswellOnt 5256, 2012 ONSC 2494, 20 R.F.L. (7th) 317 (Ont. S.C.J.). The period of the parties' relationship was 15 or 16 years. The period of dependency was three years, from sometime in 2003 to November 2006. The court ordered the woman's obligation to end in December, 2012, a period of roughly 6 years. When the parties met, the man was a skilled photographer and had a good business dealing with acoustic tiles and office interiors. He had not worked since 2003, claiming that he had health issues (depression, ADD and dyslexia). The court found that the man suffered from chronic low grade depression, but he was not disabled and was employable. The court considered the factors set out in s. 33(9) of the *Family Law Act*, R.S.O. 1990, c. F.3, that were relevant: the period of cohabitation; the period of dependency; the circumstances under which the dependency occurred; the parties' respective assets and means; the assets and means that each was likely to have in the future; the man's capacity to contribute to his own support; the woman's capacity to provide support; their ages and physical and mental health; the man's needs relative to the standard of living while the parties resided together; and the measures available for the man to become able to provide for his own support and the length of time and cost involved to enable him to take those measures. (See para. 202.)

The *threshold for determining increased spousal support is not connected to the threshold for increased child support* — *Sarophim v. Sarophim*, 2010 CarswellBC 370, 2010 BCSC 216, 82 R.F.L. (6th) 318 (B.C.S.C. [In Chambers]). The parties were married for 19 years and had two children. At the time of their divorce, they signed a consent order which provided for spousal support reviewable after 2008. The wife applied for a variation or review of spousal support. The judge declined to order retroactive increased spousal support despite an adjustment of child support based on the payor's increased income after separation. There was no automatic increase of spousal support linked to increase in income, as there were many other factors at play including entitlement and need by the recipient spouse, as well as capacity for self-support.

The *SSAG "of little use" where 16 years had passed since separation, but award equal to top of SSAG range made* — *van Rythoven v. van Rythoven*, 2009 CarswellOnt 5187, [2009] O.J. No. 3648 (Ont. S.C.J.). The parties had separated in 1993, and spousal support had been paid in 1996 and 1997 pursuant to an agreement between the parties. In the wife's 2009 application for further spousal support, the judge held, at para. 75, that the SSAG "are of little use in this situation . . . the circumstances of most awards on which the *Guidelines* are based would not be analogous to the circumstances of this case. Most awards for spousal support are arrived at within a reasonable period of time after the parties separate. At the very least, they contemplate support that is based on the circumstances arising at the time of separation, or shortly thereafter." However, the quantum ordered was equal to the top of the SSAG range.

*Where the parties' incomes are likely to change, the* Spousal Support Guidelines *are of limited assistance* — *Mechefske v. Mechefske*, 2009 CarswellOnt 2696, [2009] O.J. No. 2004 (Ont. S.C.J.). The parties were married for 19 years. The wife sought ongoing spousal support. The husband had paid $1,520 in spousal support for 4 years at the time of the new application. The judge found the wife had ongoing need for support caused by economic disadvantage stemming from the marriage. However, he found that she was relatively young and industrious and declined to award indefinite support. The judge found that the SSAG were of little use in this case because the parties' incomes were not indicative of what they were likely to earn in the future. The wife was awarded $1,200 a month for 5 years.

*"The* Spousal Support Guidelines *are of course simply advisory, that is, a guide in an attempt to provide some element of predictability, certainty and uniformity as between like merited cases"* — *Maier v. Maier*, 2009 CarswellSask 613, 2009 SKQB 359, 75 R.F.L. (6th) 152

(Sask. Q.B.), per C.L. Dawson J. The wife was 54 years of age. The parties were married for 34 years. The wife did not work outside the home for a number of years. She was employed, but her future earning prospects were limited. There was nothing in the law or evidence to justify a time-limited order. If the court applied the SSAG without child formula, using the 1.5% formula, it would suggest the husband pay the wife spousal support of $1,450 per month indefinitely. If the 1.99% formula were used, it would suggest the husband pay the wife $1,925 per month indefinitely. Having regard to all the circumstances, the court ordered the husband to pay to the wife spousal support of $1,500 per month indefinitely.

*The disadvantage of the Guidelines is their lack of flexibility* — *Terry-Lancaster v. Terry*, 2009 CarswellOnt 6141 (Ont. S.C.J.). When the court, in *Moge v. Moge*, 1992 CarswellMan 143, 1992 CarswellMan 222, EYB 1992-67141, 43 R.F.L. (3d) 345, [1992] 3 S.C.R. 813, 99 D.L.R. (4th) 456, [1993] 1 W.W.R. 481, 81 Man. R. (2d) 161, 145 N.R. 1, [1993] R.D.F. 168, 30 W.A.C. 161, [1992] S.C.J. No. 107 (S.C.C.), at para. 90, was considering the advantages of some sort of spousal guideline, it stated, "one possible disadvantage of such a solution lies in the risk that it may impose a straight jacket which precludes the accommodation of the many economic variables susceptible to be encountered in spousal support litigation." This statement was quoted with approval in *Terry-Lancaster v. Terry*. The father acknowledged his estimated income to be $100,099. The parties had a long-term marriage of 22 years. The mother was 48 when the parties separated and the youngest children of the marriage were twins who at that time were 4 years old. At the time of the motion, two of the children of the marriage were residing with the father and four of the children of the marriage were residing with the mother. The previous order which was in place for some time and then stayed required the father to pay spousal support of $1,000 per month. The court ordered spousal support of $438 per month on a temporary basis. The final determination of spousal support would be made at trial. The mother's income could also be determined at that point.

*The SSAG useful as a "check" on support analysis but on facts of case SSAG duration range too long* — *Ellis v. Ellis*, 2008 CarswellNS 126, 2008 NSSC 78, [2008] N.S.J. No. 102 (N.S.S.C.), additional reasons at 2008 CarswellNS 486, 2008 NSSC 262, 269 N.S.R. (2d) 25, 860 A.P.R. 25 (N.S.S.C.). The court stated that the SSAG were "some help, as a check" on a conclusion already reached about spousal support. The court chose a duration of support which was below the SSAG range for the following stated reasons: "The parties are only thirty-nine years of age. They have both achieved professional designations in the course of their marriage/cohabitation. Today, they also enjoy comparable incomes" (para. 35).

*Legitimacy of the SSAG* — *A. (J.H.) v. A. (C.G.)*, 2008 CarswellMan 126, 2008 MBQB 62, 58 R.F.L. (6th) 327, [2008] M.J. No. 94 (Man. Q.B.). The Court made the following comments about the place of the SSAG in litigation at paras. 162-163:

> Given the broad and growing use of and reference to the SSAG by appellate courts in other jurisdictions, and as a matter of comity within this court, I think it would take an appellate decision in this Province to direct me not to use or consider the SSAG, should I regard them as applicable or helpful in this or another case...
>
> That said, I do not think the SSAG create a regime where evidence, its reliability or completeness, no longer matters. I do not think that the SSAG have created a regime (at least not yet) where one can stand up, file three tax returns, a financial statement dealing with assets, debts and expenses and a computer generated calculation offered by the SSAG, close the evidence and proceed to argument.

**Practice and Procedure**

Where reasons for using the SSAG are brief, they may still meet the "functional" test of the Supreme Court of Canada in cases such as R. v. Sheppard, 2002 SCC 26; and C. (R.) v. McDougall, 2008 SCC 53; and reflect the principles the court was obliged to consider — Kelsch v. Chaput, 2012 CarswellBC 362, 2012 BCCA 64, 317 B.C.A.C. 59, 540 W.A.C. 59 (B.C.C.A.). The husband had appealed on various grounds including, inter alia, that the judge below should not have set spousal support at the mid-range indicated by the Spousal Support Guidelines and failed to give reasons for doing so. The reasons were brief, but did make reference to the wife's economic position, which was significantly less favourable than the husband's, and to the fact that in this case support was awarded on a compensatory and non-compensatory basis. The appellate court found that the mid-range was entirely appropriate. The court noted that if the wife remained in the matrimonial home, it would provide significant security for her in later life as she would not have a pension from her tutoring business. While her family was described as affluent, there was no authority that required her to turn to her parents in substitution for the husband's support under the Divorce Act.

Where the use of the SSAG is not disputed at trial, it may not be disputed on appeal — Elfar v. Elfar, 2012 CarswellAlta 2091, 2012 ABCA 375, 539 A.R. 268, 561 W.A.C. 268 (Alta. C.A.), additional reasons at 2013 CarswellAlta 88, 2013 ABCA 33 (Alta. C.A.). The husband argued, among other grounds of appeal, that the trial judge gave undue weight to the SSAG and that the spousal support award was punitive. The Alberta Court of Appeal noted that the husband had not objected to the use of the Guidelines at trial and it was too late to do so at the appeal stage. The appeal was dismissed.

When at trial, the parties prepared submissions regarding spousal support using the SSAG, the appellate court held that it was open to the trial judge to choose the sum ($150,000) for lump sum support, an amount which lay approximately mid-way between the amounts sought by the respective parties — Q. (R.E.) v. K. (G.J.), 2012 CarswellBC 887, 2012 BCCA 146, 17 R.F.L. (7th) 255, 31 B.C.L.R. (5th) 264, 348 D.L.R. (4th) 622, [2012] 8 W.W.R. 270, 319 B.C.A.C. 98, 542 W.A.C. 98 (B.C.C.A.), additional reasons at 2012 BCCA 267, 2012 CarswellBC 1774, 17 R.F.L. (7th) 291, 31 B.C.L.R. (5th) 300, [2012] 8 W.W.R. 306 (B.C.C.A.). The parties were both practising lawyers, although the wife did not work to her full capacity but instead spent considerable time with the parties' children.

Husband to pay indefinite support at the high end of the range to compensate for the wife's diminished earning capacity as she assumed full-time housekeeping and child-rearing responsibilities in a long-term marriage and in consideration of the husband's failure to disclose his resources fairly — need to provide reasons for departure from SSAG — Gagne v. Gagne, 2011 CarswellOnt 1476, 2011 ONCA 188, 99 R.F.L. (6th) 1, [2011] O.J. No. 1015 (Ont. C.A.). The parties were married for 18 years with three children. The husband was a self-employed real estate broker, and the wife was a stay-at-home mother with primary care of the children. Following separation she obtained work as a secretary. The parties signed a separation agreement which provided that the husband would pay undifferentiated spousal and child support for 24 months after which support was to be reviewed. At trial, the judge ordered the husband to pay $8,000 per month spousal support and $2,000 per month child support. The Court of Appeal held that the trial judge's reasons for judgement insufficiently explained the basis for support, accepted the respondent's compromise, ordered overvalued spousal support and undervalued child support without explanation. The Court of Appeal imputed an income of $250,000 to the husband and $45,000 to the wife, and ordered the husband to pay to the wife $4,597 per month, which was at the high end of the Spousal Support Advisory Guidelines, because of the husband's failure to make fair disclosure of his resources. Child support was ordered at $4,072 per month.

*Where an error in assessing income is made by a trial judge, the Court of Appeal may award support based on the Guidelines — Pinder v. Pinder,* 2010 CarswellBC 1207, 2010 BCCA 235, 83 R.F.L. (6th) 3, 5 B.C.L.R. (5th) 86 (B.C.C.A.). The parties had a 10-year marriage which ended in 2002. The wife received spousal support beginning in 2007. Later in 2007, the husband's employment was terminated and he successfully applied to cease support payments and have the support arrears, which had accrued, cancelled. The judge found that the parties had "virtually the same" incomes and that the husband no longer had the means to pay support. The wife appealed to the British Columbia Court of Appeal. The husband had demonstrated a material change in circumstances (his retirement), but the Court of Appeal found that the trial judge erred in finding the incomes of the parties to be virtually the same. They found on the evidence that the husband had an income in 2007 of $62,000 and used the *Spousal Support Advisory Guidelines* to award the wife monthly support in the amount of $1,000, which fell in the middle of the Guideline range.

*Where a trial judge bases a support award on an incorrect application of the SSAG, the Court of Appeal may vary the order to reflect the correct application — Domirti v. Domirti,* 2010 CarswellBC 2864, 2010 BCCA 472, 10 B.C.L.R. (5th) 281, 294 B.C.A.C. 127, 498 W.A.C. 127, [2010] B.C.J. No. 2074 (B.C.C.A.), additional reasons at 2011 CarswellBC 108, 2011 BCCA 30, 13 B.C.L.R. (5th) 208 (B.C.C.A.); and see *Domirti v. Domirti,* 2010 CarswellBC 518, 2010 BCCA 112 (B.C.C.A. [In Chambers]). The parties were in a relationship for 14 years and separated in 1994. In 1996 the court made an order on consent that the husband pay a low amount of spousal support. In 2004 the wife applied for a variation of the order, and the court increased the amount to $1,000. In 2005 the wife sought another increase, and the court, finding that despite her efforts to become self-sufficient the wife's circumstances had deteriorated, increased the amount to $1,250 per month subject to review. In 2008 the husband made a review application, and the judge found that the husband had failed to demonstrate a material change in circumstances and ordered him to continue to pay support indefinitely. The husband appealed to the Court of Appeal in 2010. The Court of Appeal found that the trial judge's decision to apply the SSAG to a pre-SSAG order regarding the amount and duration of support (but not entitlement) was appropriate. The appellate court also found, however, that the judge had misinterpreted the Advisory Guidelines when basing the award of indefinite support on the wife's age at the time of the review rather than her age at the date of separation, as required by Rule 65. The court found that a correct application of the SSAG would result in an amount of support ranging from $1,021 to $1,362 and lasting from 8 to 16 years. After correctly applying the SSAG, the appellate court determined that the husband's support obligation had been fulfilled and that the wife's circumstances did not "fall within any of the exceptions for extending spousal support beyond the ranges of the *SSAG.*" The court terminated support as of the date of the husband's retirement earlier in 2010.

*The court must have sufficient evidence of the payor's income in order to apply the* Spousal Support Advisory Guidelines *on an interim order for support — MacDonald v. MacDonald,* 2010 CarswellSask 250, 2010 SKCA 60, 350 Sask. R. 245, 487 W.A.C. 245 (Sask. C.A.). This is an appeal from a decision of the Court of Queen's Bench to grant interim spousal support of $5,045 per month to the respondent wife. The parties were married from 1977 to 2006 and had two children who were adults at the time of the appeal. During the marriage they ran a family business together, and after their separation the wife had a full-time job as a librarian, while the husband continued to manage the business. The Court of Appeal overturned the trial judgement on the grounds that the trial judge had insufficient evidence to make such an award, as it had very limited evidence concerning the husband's income, since the majority of his 2008 income was dividends from the company. The trial judge appears to have used the husband's income from the dividends as well in determining support under the SSAG (which at that point were in draft form). Division of the dividends was found by the Court of Appeal to be a decision better left for trial.

Trial courts are not required to explain all deviations from the SSAG, but doing so would be "best practice" — Beninger v. Beninger, 2009 CarswellBC 2963, 2009 BCCA 458, 77 R.F.L. (6th) 56, 277 B.C.A.C. 36, 469 W.A.C. 36, [2009] B.C.J. No. 2197 (B.C.C.A.), affirming 2008 CarswellBC 2896, 2008 BCSC 1806, [2008] B.C.J. No. 2612 (B.C.S.C. [In Chambers]). Huddart J.A., speaking for the Court, stated at para. 28:

> While it is preferable for a court to organize its analysis by reference to the Guidelines as well as the statutory requirements and authorities applying them, neither the Divorce Act nor the authorities require justification for deviation from them... As their name indicates, they are advisory and without statutory effect. That said, they provide helpful advice and this Court has been clear that their advice must be taken seriously and that best practice would include an explanation of any deviation from them.

See also Lightle v. Kotar, 2014 CarswellBC 428, 2014 BCCA 69, 43 R.F.L. (7th) 20, 59 B.C.L.R. (5th) 75, 371 D.L.R. (4th) 269, [2014] 5 W.W.R. 615, 352 B.C.A.C. 39, 601 W.A.C. 39, [2014] B.C.J. No. 294 (B.C.C.A.).

In calculating the amount and duration of spousal support, the jurisprudence requires an application of the SSAG unless reasons are provided as to why the SSAG are not appropriate — Kerr v. Baranow, 2009 CarswellBC 642, 2009 BCCA 111, 66 R.F.L. (6th) 1,93 B.C.L.R. (4th) 201, [2009] 9 W.W.R. 285, 266 B.C.A.C. 298, 449 W.A.C. 298, [2009] B.C.J. No. 474 (B.C.C.A.), additional reasons at 2010 CarswellBC 108, 2010 BCCA 32, 78 R.F.L. (6th) 305, 2 B.C.L.R. (5th) 197, [2010] 4 W.W.R. 465, [2010] B.C.J. No. 88 (B.C.C.A.), reversed 2011 CarswellBC 240, 2011 CarswellBC 241, 2011 SCC 10, 93 R.F.L. (6th) 1, [2011] 1 S.C.R. 269, 108 O.R. (3d) 399, 14 B.C.L.R. (5th) 203, 328 D.L.R. (4th) 577, 64 E.T.R. (3d) 1, [2011] 3 W.W.R. 575, 300 B.C.A.C. 1, 411 N.R. 200, 274 O.A.C. 1, 509 W.A.C. 1, [2011] S.C.J. No. 10 (S.C.C.).

Utility of the SSAG — trial judge erred by not considering the SSAG when fully addressed by counsel — Fisher v. Fisher, 2008 CarswellOnt 43, 2008 ONCA 11, 47 R.F.L. (6th) 235, 88 O.R. (3d) 241, 288 D.L.R. (4th) 513, 232 O.A.C. 213, [2008] O.J. No. 38 (Ont. C.A.). The Ontario Court of Appeal endorsed the B.C. Appellate court's description of the SSAG as a "useful tool", and suggested that they are likely to bring consistency and predictability to the law. However, they do not obviate the need for an individualized analysis, and they must be applied in their entirety (including the sections pertaining to exceptions and restructuring). Part of the usefulness of the SSAG is due to the fact that they are based on case law. However, if they suggest a range which is contrary to the applicable authorities, the authorities prevail. There was extensive discussion of the SSAG, and the court applied restructuring.

Trial court award not within SSAG range set aside and replaced with mid-range award — the SSAG particularly useful where there is no evidentiary record — Beese v. Beese, 2008 CarswellBC 2103, 2008 BCCA 396, 60 R.F.L. (6th) 31, 87 B.C.L.R. (4th) 286, 261 B.C.A.C. 35, 440 W.A.C. 35 (B.C.C.A.), additional reasons at 2008 CarswellBC 2715, 2008 BCCA 525, 60 R.F.L. (6th) 49, 86 B.C.L.R. (4th) 360, 261 B.C.A.C. 35 at 51, 440 W.A.C. 35 at 51 (B.C.C.A.). Leave to appeal refused (2009), 2009 CarswellBC 2674, 2009 CarswellBC 2675, 401 N.R. 392 (note), 289 B.C.A.C. 318 (note), 489 W.A.C. 318 (note), [2009] S.C.C.A. No. 73 (S.C.C.). The parties began living together in 1993, married in 1997, separated in 2000 and were divorced in 2003. During the marriage, the wife had been in a serious accident, had received $264,000 which the parties spent partially on the husband's unsuccessful business ventures. The trial judge had made an order in proceedings under the Family Relations Act ("FRA") whereby the husband received all of the family assets and was ordered to pay compensation to the wife of $175,000 or lump sum spousal support in the same amount. The husband was made responsible for all family debts which were greater than the family assets by $77,900. The court was satisfied that the trial judge erred in making an award of spousal support without considering the factors under ss. 89 and 93 of the FRA and in an amount which could not be justified having regard to those factors or the SSAG. The appellate court found that the wife was entitled to spousal support based on a compensatory, rather than a needs-based, model and granted her lump sum support in the amount of $12,000. The Court of Appeal found, at para. 65:

> In determining the appropriate award, particularly in circumstances where there is no evidentiary record before the court, I find recourse to the *SSAG* to be helpful. As earlier stated, the trial judge referred to the *SSAG*, but he did not apply them, apparently because he was of the view that support should be based on compensation for Ms. Cramer's "loss" of her settlement funds. Based on the factors to which I have referred, and bearing in mind that Mr. Beese has already assumed a disproportionate share of the family debt, I would make an award in the mid-range of the figures set forth by the trial judge as applying under the *SSAG* then in effect.

*If SSAG ranges not provided to the court, it cannot commit an error by failing to apply the SSAG* — *Jessop v. Wright*, 2008 CarswellOnt 5785, 2008 ONCA 673, 56 R.F.L. (6th) 29 (Ont. C.A.). The Ontario Court of Appeal held, at para. 9: "In arriving at the appropriate amount of support, the motion judge did not apply the *Spousal Support Advisory Guidelines* to these incomes. However, ranges under the *Guidelines* were not provided to the motions judge. In these circumstances, there can be no error in failing to apply the *Guidelines*". However, the court found it to have been an error to order the same amount of support in various years despite differences in the recipient's income between those years. The quantum was reduced during certain years to an amount within the SSAG range.

*Where spousal support decisions depart from the* Spousal Support Advisory Guidelines, *courts should provide reasons for doing so* — *Hong v. Silva*, 2009 CarswellOnt 8103, [2009] O.J. No. 5543 (Ont. S.C.J.). The parties had a 9-year common law relationship that resulted in a child. They separated in 2006 and the wife applied for spousal support. The judge awarded her the mid-range figure in the "with child" category based on the parties respective incomes, for an award of $319 per month. The judge noted the direction in Fisher that decisions which depart from the SSAG should provide reasons for which the Guidelines were found to be inapplicable. The judge also ordered that review may be requested after 3 years (6 years after separation, which fell within the SSAG time frame).

*Support extended where the trial judge had intended to make a spousal support award greater than the SSAG but had failed to do so* — *the appellate court noted the payee's precarious financial circumstances caused by the marriage breakdown* — *Wang v. Poon*, 2008 CarswellBC 2333, 2008 BCCA 442, 58 R.F.L. (6th) 235, 84 B.C.L.R. (4th) 199, 302 D.L.R. (4th) 679, [2008] B.C.J. No. 2113 (B.C.C.A.), varying 2007 CarswellBC 297, 2007 BCSC 194, 70 B.C.L.R. (4th) 120, [2007] B.C.J. No. 271 (B.C.S.C.). The court on appeal extended the period of time during which the wife was to receive spousal support. The wife was 47 years old, spoke little English, and the trial award did not properly take into account her precarious financial circumstances arising from the breakdown of the marriage. While she had obtained employment as a hairdresser, the trial award, when combined with her income, would barely meet her modest projected expenses. The trial judge had awarded support believing it to be above the SSAG ranges but it was not. The Court of Appeal made an order extending spousal support for a further 2 years, thus increasing spousal support by $14,400.

## Various Types of Proceedings

### Interim Orders

An expenses order calculated in accordance with the SSAG may be used as a de facto interim support order — Shortridge-Tsuchiya v. Tsuchiya, 2010 CarswellBC 276, 2010 BCCA 61, 79 R.F.L. (6th) 7, 2 B.C.L.R. (5th) 24, 315 D.L.R. (4th) 498, [2010] 8 W.W.R. 629, 283 B.C.A.C. 117, 480 W.A.C. 117, [2010] B.C.J. No. 217 (B.C.C.A.). Leave to appeal refused 2010 CarswellBC 1797, 2010 CarswellBC 1798, 409 N.R. 397 (note), 300 B.C.A.C. 319 (note), 509 W.A.C. 319 (note) (S.C.C.). The mother was Canadian, and the father was Japanese. The parties lived in Japan. They had one child, whom the mother brought to Canada in 2008 after the separation. The father did not pay any child or spousal support. The chambers judge made an expenses order which was the equivalent of a spousal support order calculated in accordance with the SSAG. The father claimed it went beyond the scope of an expenses order. The Court of Appeal judge found the order to be appropriate given that the father had not paid any support.

The court must have sufficient evidence of the payor's income in order to apply the Spousal Support Advisory Guidelines on an interim order for support — MacDonald v. MacDonald, 2010 CarswellSask 250, 2010 SKCA 60, 350 Sask. R. 245, 487 W.A.C. 245 (Sask. C.A.). This is an appeal from a decision of the Court of Queen's Bench to grant interim spousal support of $5,045 per month to the respondent wife. The parties were married from 1977 to 2006 and had two children who were adults at the time of the appeal. During the marriage they ran a family business together, and after their separation the wife had a full-time job as a librarian, while the husband continued to manage the business. The Court of Appeal overturned the trial judgement on the grounds that the trial judge had insufficient evidence to make such an award, as it had very limited evidence concerning the husband's income, since the majority of his 2008 income was dividends from the company. The trial judge appears to have used the husband's income from the dividends as well in determining support under the SSAG (which at that point were in draft form). Division of the dividends was found by the Court of Appeal to be a decision better left to the trial.

The SSAG rejected on interim basis as the quantum ranges were so intertwined with issues of duration of support — Martin v. Orris, 2009 CarswellMan 522, 2009 MBQB 290, 246 Man. R. (2d) 262 (Man. Q.B.), affirmed 2010 CarswellMan 246, 2010 MBCA 59, 255 Man. R. (2d) 126, 486 W.A.C. 126, [2010] M.J. No. 180 (Man. C.A.).

It is usually appropriate to give consideration to the SSAG when determining interim spousal support — van de Wint v. McArthur, 2009 CarswellBC 2528, 2009 BCSC 1283 (B.C.S.C.).

### Variation

The SSAG will be applied on variation cautiously on a case-by-case basis where significant complicating factors are not present — MacQuarrie v. MacQuarrie, 2012 CarswellPEI 5, 2012 PECA 3, 18 R.F.L. (7th) 1, 319 Nfld. & P.E.I.R. 246, 992 A.P.R. 246, [2012] P.E.I.J. No. 5 (P.E.I.C.A.). The Court of Appeal upheld a motion judge's decision to vary spousal support after the husband retired. The judge found that the husband's preretirement income was above that contemplated by the divorce provisions and constituted a material change in circumstances for the purpose of variation, and ordered retroactive support at the top of the SSAG range. The motions judge also ordered ongoing support based on the husband's post-retirement income. The Court of Appeal found no reversible error in the motions judge's decision and found that he had correctly considered the factors of the strength of the compensatory claim, the needs of the recipient, and the needs and the ability of the payor in determining quantum under the without child formula.

*The court must consider whether it is appropriate to apply the SSAG in an application to vary support* — *Aelbers v. Aelbers*, 2010 CarswellBC 1464, 2010 BCCA 197, 86 R.F.L. (6th) 261 (B.C.C.A.). The husband earned a substantial income, and the wife was unable to work due to a documented illness. In 2005 the chambers judge ordered the husband to pay $2,100 per month in spousal support. In 2008 the Supreme Court found that the husband had failed to disclose a portion of his earnings and varied the order, increasing the amount prospectively as well as retroactively to the date of the original order. The husband appealed to the Court of Appeal. The Court of Appeal noted that the 2008 decision did not address whether the application of the SSAG to a variation application was appropriate. The appeal was allowed.

*On a variation application, the SSAG is a good starting point however should be approached with caution* — *James v. James*, 2009 CarswellBC 1490, 2009 BCCA 261, 66 R.F.L. (6th) 246, 94 B.C.L.R. (4th) 183, [2009] 10 W.W.R. 11, 273 B.C.A.C. 75, 461 W.A.C. 75, [2009] B.C.J. No. 1151 (B.C.C.A.). After 19 years of marriage, the parties entered into a consent order in 2004 which provided for spousal support of $5,750 per month. The wife had been a flight attendant for 22 years, but was encouraged by the husband to accept a $100,000 severance package in 2001 and retire from the airline. The husband's yearly income for 2004 to 2006 ranged from $986,000 to $1.3 million per year. The husband applied to vary or terminate spousal support, and the chambers judge granted the variation. On appeal, the court noted that the wife was entitled to retroactive spousal support because of the husband's increased income and because he encouraged the wife to leave her employment. The court found that the wife was in need of increased spousal support. Retroactive spousal support was awarded because of the husband's increased income.

*Where income is imputed by a judge because of intentional underemployment, spousal support may be based on the SSAG as applied to that income* — *LeBlanc v. LeBlanc*, 2013 CarswellNB 122, 2013 CarswellNB 123, 2013 NBCA 22, 401 N.B.R. (2d) 334, 1041 A.P.R. 334, [2013] N.B.J. No. 79 (N.B.C.A.). The husband appealed an order allowing variation of spousal support in favour of his wife. The parties were married for 17 years and had an adult son. The wife was unable to work because of a disability. The order in question reduced spousal support from $1,700 to $1,000 monthly in light of the husband's retirement. The trial judge imputed income to the husband after finding he was intentionally underemployed. She then applied the *Spousal Support Advisory Guidelines* to that imputed income. The husband was 54 years old and in good health. The Court of Appeal found that it was open to the lower court judge to exercise her discretion as she had and the decision was upheld. [There was no further discussion of the SSAG on appeal.]

*The SSAG utilized on variation application* — *Jens v. Jens*, 2008 CarswellBC 2091, 2008 BCCA 392, 57 R.F.L. (6th) 31, 84 B.C.L.R. (4th) 250, 300 D.L.R. (4th) 136, 260 B.C.A.C. 185, 439 W.A.C. 185, [2008] B.C.J. No. 1886 (B.C.C.A.). The Court stated, at para. 48: "I am satisfied that the factors that enter into the determination of spousal support in this case do not raise the complexities that arise on some variation applications, and that it is appropriate to use the SSAG as a guide to the appropriate level and duration of support."

## Review

*Where a spousal support order is being reviewed, the SSAG may be applied because the issues on review are similar to those in an initial application.* — *Morck v. Morck*, 2013 CarswellBC 1032, 2013 BCCA 186, 28 R.F.L. (7th) 279, 44 B.C.L.R. (5th) 235, 337 B.C.A.C. 125, 576 W.A.C. 125, [2013] B.C.J. No. 803 (B.C.C.A.). The husband appealed an order which dismissed his application to review, reduce or terminate spousal support to his wife. They had a 24-year marriage and two adult sons when they separated in 2005. Spousal support was set out in a 2006 separation agreement, which provided for $3,000 monthly reviewable after 2 years or in the event of a change of circumstances. The application judge determined that the husband was capable of earning the same income he did at the time the separation agreement was signed and that he was deliberately underemployed. He also found there was no change in circumstances. The wife had mental health issues that were known to the parties when the agreement was signed that currently prevented her from working. The Court of Appeal found that the application judge had erred in treating the application as a variation rather than as a review. No change in circumstances need be made out in a review application, so the judge erred in considering this. The Court of Appeal also found that the *Spousal Support Advisory Guidelines* may provide guidance as to quantum on a review because the issues on review are similar to an initial application.

*Where there are dependent children, indefinite orders subject to review are appropriate* — *P. (J.B.) v. S. (L.J.)*, 2008 CarswellNS 91, 2008 NSCA 19, 291 D.L.R. (4th) 477, 263 N.S.R. (2d) 192, 843 A.P.R. 192, [2008] N.S.J. No. 77 (N.S.C.A.). The wife was not working, and the husband earned $40,000 as a long-distance truck driver. The issue in this case was whether the trial judge should have made an award of two lump sums of $2,200 and $2,500 in full satisfaction of obligation for spousal support. The Court of Appeal found that this was an error. However, in determining quantum, the appellate court used the same amount as the trial judge, $214 per month, but made the award indefinite.

## Specific Situations

### Imputed Income

 *The SSAG may be used in cases where income is imputed* — *Brandl v. Rolston*, 2013 CarswellBC 1273, 2013 BCCA 235, 31 R.F.L. (7th) 296, 362 D.L.R. (4th) 439, 338 B.C.A.C. 141, 577 W.A.C. 141 (B.C.C.A.). The trial judge applied the SSAG in determining support. She based the amount awarded on imputed income to the husband as well as to the wife and then applied the SSAG. The husband appealed the order. The Court of Appeal found that the appeal should be dismissed as the trial judge had made findings of fact based on the evidence of the husband's income, which should be granted deference. The Court of Appeal also noted that the SSAG, along with the *Child Support Guidelines*, give broad discretion to the judge to impute income.

 *Where the payor's income must be imputed because of uncertainty caused by attempts to hide his true financial status, the SSAG will not be applicable* — *Aalbers v. Aalbers*, 2013 CarswellSask 394, 2013 SKCA 64, 417 Sask. R. 69, 580 W.A.C. 69 (Sask. C.A.). The parties were married for 19 years and had five children ranging in age from 9 years to 19 years at the time of trial. The husband owned an agricultural business. The judge found that the husband was attempting to hide his assets and diminish the value of the company by moving assets to his father and presenting his farm business as faltering. The judge rejected the husband's financial statement. The trial judge found that the SSAG were only of use when the income of the parties is known or closely approximated. Because of the husband's financial obfuscation, the trial judge had imputed income to him and thus did not find the SSAG of use. The judge ordered the husband to pay $1,500 monthly in ongoing, non-compensatory spousal support. The Court of Appeal upheld this award, but did not specifically address the issue of the use of the SSAG.

## Common-law union

*SSAG-calculated support will be awarded in the case of a marriage-like relationship as though the parties had been married* — *Stace-Smith v. Lecompte*, 2011 CarswellBC 573, 2011 BCCA 129, 97 R.F.L. (6th) 91, 16 B.C.L.R. (5th) 119, 302 B.C.A.C. 250, 511 W.A.C. 250 (B.C.C.A.). The parties lived together for 4 years and had one child, who remained with the wife after the separation. They separated in 2009. The trial judge dismissed the wife's claim for spousal support on the basis that she had not established that she was a "spouse" within the definition of the British Columbia *Family Relations Act*. The wife appealed, and the Court of Appeal found that trial judge had erred in finding that wife had neither pleaded nor led evidence that she was in a "marriage-like" relationship and found that she was entitled to support based on both compensation and need. The Court of Appeal judge awarded the wife a lump sum payment of $18,000, which reflected 3 years of $500 per month payments, a mid-range amount under the SSAG.

*Application of the SSAG when awarding a lump sum; where a spousal support lump sum award is not outside what would be generated by the SSAG, it will be upheld on appeal* — *Davis v. Crawford*, 2011 CarswellOnt 2512, 2011 ONCA 294, 95 R.F.L. (6th) 257, 106 O.R. (3d) 221, 332 D.L.R. (4th) 508, 277 O.A.C. 200, [2011] O.J. No. 1719 (Ont. C.A.); additional reasons at 2011 CarswellOnt 4562, 2011 ONCA 423, [2011] O.J. No. 2637 (Ont. C.A.). The trial judge had awarded lump sum spousal support of $135,000. It was a 23-year common-law relationship with no children. The lump sum amount was upheld on appeal. The wife was 64, and the husband 66.

## Brief marriage and a child

*The trial judge must carefully consider whether the SSAG are applicable when the marriage is brief and there is one child* — *Dima v. Dima*, 2010 CarswellBC 3684, 2010 BCCA 557 (B.C.C.A.). The parties had a one-year marriage. The wife gave birth to their son in 2009 after the separation and applied to the Provincial Court for a spousal and child support order. The judge relied on the *Spousal Support Advisory Guidelines* when awarding $523 per month in spousal support as well as a retroactive lump sum for the period during which the husband was not paying support. The husband appealed to the Supreme Court, which found that the chambers judge should have imputed net income rather than gross income and remitted the matter to the Provincial Court to reconsider the quantum of support as well as the applicability of the Guidelines in the circumstances. The husband appealed to the Court of Appeal, which remitted the matter to the Provincial Court regarding the issue of the retroactive lump sum award.

## Indication that trial judge will rely on the SSAG

*Trial judge entitled to indicate intention to rely on SSAG* — *Barter v. Barter*, 2006 CarswellNfid 59, 2006 NLCA 13, [2006] N.J. No. 52 (N.L.C.A.). The trial judge suggested to the parties that he would be generally guided by the SSAG in determining the amount and duration of a spousal support order. The parties subsequently negotiated a resolution which was issued as a consent order. The judge's reference to the SSAG did not constitute a reversible error.

## Income over $350,000

*The SSAG are not useful, particularly as the payor's income was well over $300,000* — a *party is entitled to spousal support where she had been disadvantaged by the loss of the standard of living the husband's income provided and currently there was a considerable difference in the* *parties' incomes* — *Bell v. Bell*, 2009 CarswellBC 1588, 2009 BCCA 280, 69 R.F.L. (6th) 21, 97 B.C.L.R. (4th) 55, [2010] 1 W.W.R. 98, 272 B.C.A.C. 207, 459 W.A.C. 207, [2009] B.C.J. No. 1201 (B.C.C.A.), additional reasons at 2010 CarswellBC 625, 2010 BCCA 138, 76 R.F.L. (6th) 257, 2 B.C.L.R. (5th) 200, [2010] 7 W.W.R. 453, 284 B.C.A.C. 316 (B.C.C.A.). The husband's income was $649,959 and the wife's income was $140,000. The parties divorced in 2006 after reaching an agreement on an equal division of their property, valued at $12 million. The court recognized that the wife had sufficient capital and income to meet her needs and was economically self-sufficient. However, without spousal support, she would not be compensated in terms of her lower standard of living caused by the breakdown of the marriage. Neither party should be required to encroach on capital to deal with the difference in his or her standard of living compared to that of a spouse. The husband's current income was half the amount of his income at the time of the parties' agreement, predicated largely on his 2005 income. Consequently, the court reduced spousal support from $10,000 a month to $5,000 a month. The SSAG are not useful in this case, particularly as the husband's income is well in excess of $300,000.

See also **Chapter 16 — Ceilings and Floors.**

### *Re-partnering*

*Where the recipient spouse has "re-partnered", support lower than the* Spousal Support Advisory Guidelines *may be ordered* — *Fountain v. Fountain*, 2009 CarswellOnt 6342, 77 R.F.L. (6th) 255 (Ont. S.C.J.). The parties were married for 24 years and had two adult children. The judge found that both parties had "re partnered" and therefore awarded spousal support lower than that found in the SSAG.

*Assistance from the SSAG somewhat limited where each of the parties cohabits with a new partner* — *Balazsy v. Balazsy*, 2009 CarswellOnt 5982, 75 R.F.L. (6th) 315, [2009] O.J. No. 4113 (Ont. S.C.J.).

### *Government assistance*

*There is no obligation for the payor to consider support according to the SSAG when the husband is responsible for the wife for government assistance payments* — *Moro v. El Mantari*, 2009 CarswellBC 2700, 2009 BCSC 1399 (B.C.S.C. [In Chambers]), additional reasons at 2010 CarswellBC 1098, 2010 BCSC 631, [2010] B.C.J. No. 811 (B.C.S.C.). The husband had an obligation to support the wife on an interim basis because of his sponsorship agreement. He also had an obligation to support her on non-compensatory or needs-based principles. The parties married in Morocco in 2005, when the husband was 50 and the wife 20. The wife came to Canada in August 2006. They had a child and decided to separate in November 2008.

# CHAPTER 20

# RETROACTIVE SUPPORT AND THE SSAG

This chapter is divided into the following sections:

20.1 General
20.2 Retroactive Spousal Support for the Interim Period
20.3 Variation Applications
20.4 Separation Agreement Set Aside
20.5 Tax Issues and Lump Sum Retroactive Awards

## 20.1 General

> The Spousal Support Advisory Guidelines are being used to determine quantum of support for retroactive spousal support.
>
> There are two settings where "retroactive" spousal support is raised most frequently. At trial where the court is asked to revisit the amount and duration of interim spousal support or on an application to vary spousal support, with a claim for retroactive support accompanying the claim for varied prospective support. [User's Guide, March 31, 2010, section 14.]

See also Chapter 7, section **7.1.1 Retroactive Spousal Support** and Chapter 10, section **10.7 Retroactive Variation of Support Orders**.

The Supreme Court of Canada case *D.B.S. v. S.R.G.; T.A.R. v. L.J.W.; Henry v. Henry; — S. (D.B.) v. G. (S.R.)*, 2006 CarswellAlta 976, 2006 CarswellAlta 977, 2006 SCC 37, 31 R.F.L. (6th) 1, [2006] 2 S.C.R. 231, 61 Alta. L.R. (4th) 1, 270 D.L.R. (4th) 297, [2006] 10 W.W.R. 379, 351 N.R. 201, 391 A.R. 297, 377 W.A.C. 297, [2006] S.C.J. No. 37 (S.C.C.) although a case dealing with retroactive child support, has had a significant effect upon retroactive spousal support. See summary below. For a detailed discussion of this case, see Chapter 7, section **7.1.1**, and *Canadian Divorce Law and Practice*, Volume 1, section **15§85**.

*Situations where awarding retroactive support may be appropriate* — *D.B.S. v. S.R.G.; T.A.R. v. L.J.W.; Henry v. Henry* — *S. (D.B.) v. G. (S.R.)*, *supra*. In this case, the court noted that there are three situations in which it may be appropriate for a court to order a retroactive award. The first is where there is an existing order for support because the order is presumptively valid. The second is where support has been previously set out in an agreement between the parents. The third is where the status quo does not involve payment of child support. The court further noted that, "in exercising their discretion to order retroactive support, courts must balance the payor's interest in certainty with the need for fairness and flexibility. In doing so, a court should consider the reasonableness of the delay in seeking support, the conduct of the payor, the circumstances of the child, and the hardship occasioned by a retroactive award." The award should generally be retroactive to the date when effective notice was given to the payor. Although this is a child support case, the principles are applicable to spousal support cases as well.

*No error in awarding retroactive spousal support based on post-separation income and in applying the high range of the SSAG to the 10-year period commencing January 1, 2000 — no error in principle in trial judge's quantification of the lump sum award — Hartshorne v. Hartshorne*, 2010 CarswellBC 1618, 2010 BCCA 327, 82 R.F.L. (6th) 1, 6 B.C.L.R. (5th) 58, 320 D.L.R. (4th) 398, 289 B.C.A.C. 244, 489 W.A.C. 244, [2010] B.C.J. No. 1271 (B.C.C.A.). The parties separated in 1998 after 12½ years of cohabitation, including 9 years of marriage. They were the parties in extensive litigation, which culminated in a case at the Supreme Court of Canada (*Hartshorne v. Hartshorne*, 2004 CarswellBC 603, 2004 CarswellBC 604, 2004 SCC 22, REJB 2004-55588, 47 R.F.L. (5th) 5, [2004] 1 S.C.R. 550, 25 B.C.L.R. (4th) 1, 236 D.L.R. (4th) 193, [2004] 6 W.W.R. 1, 318 N.R. 1, 194 B.C.A.C. 161, 317 W.A.C. 161, [2004] S.C.J. No. 20 (S.C.C.)), which radically changed the division of property. The SCC decision directed that the wife's right to spousal support could be determined by a "new application". In the new application, the wife filed for spousal support as well as increased child support for the parties' two children. This decision is the appeal of a trial decision awarding a lump-sum spousal support award of $350,000, retroactive to February 28, 2001, when the initial order for the division of property under Part 5 of the *FRA* was concluded. The appellate court held that there was no error in trial judge's order of increased retroactive support, but the award of ongoing prospective support amounted to palpable and overriding error.

*Trial judge should discuss reasons for retroactive orders — Reis v. Bucholtz*, 2010 CarswellBC 509, 2010 BCCA 115, 3 B.C.L.R. (5th) 71, [2010] B.C.J. No. 382 (B.C.C.A.). The trial judge awarded the mother $26,567 in retroactive child support and $68,429 in spousal support. The husband appealed. In dismissing the appeal, the Court of Appeal held that while it was not mandatory for a court making a retroactive order to explicitly refer to the *D.B.S. v. S.R.G.; T.A.R. v. L.J.W.; Henry v. Henry; S. (D.B.) v. G. (S.R.)*, 2006 CarswellAlta 976, 2006 CarswellAlta 977, 2006 SCC 37, 31 R.F.L. (6th) 1, [2006] 2 S.C.R. 231, 61 Alta. L.R. (4th) 1, 270 D.L.R. (4th) 297, [2006] 10 W.W.R. 379, 351 N.R. 201, 391 A.R. 297, 377 W.A.C. 297, [2006] S.C.J. No. 37 (S.C.C.) decision, some discussion of the reasons for retroactive orders was to be expected. The Court of Appeal applied the factors set out in *S. (D.B.) v. G. (S.R.)* and concluded that the trial judge's retroactive order was correct.

*SSAG used in retroactive case — Milton v. Milton*, 2008 CarswellNB 591, 2008 CarswellNB 592, 2008 NBCA 87, 62 R.F.L. (6th) 286, 305 D.L.R. (4th) 94, 338 N.B.R. (2d) 300, 866 A.P.R. 300, [2008] N.B.J. No. 467 (N.B.C.A.). The parties were married for 21 years. In February 2006, the wife was awarded interim spousal support of $4,000 per month retroactive to October 2005. At trial, the wife sought an increased amount of spousal support pursuant to the SSAG. The trial judge used the *Guidelines* amount which ranged from $7,952 to $10,603 monthly and found that spousal support of $6,500 per month indefinitely was appropriate. The husband appealed. The appellate court found that the trial judge made no error and utilized the SSAG appropriately.

*Spousal support retroactive to date wife began looking for employment — Paleczny v. Paleczny*, 2010 CarswellBC 36, 2010 BCSC 36 (B.C.S.C.). In this case, the court awarded the wife spousal support retroactive to September 2008, which was the date the wife began retraining and looking for employment. The court used the SSAG to determine that the mid-range of spousal support was appropriate and calculated retroactive spousal support based on this amount.

*Retroactive spousal support awarded in accordance with the SSAG — Elgner v. Elgner*, 2009 CarswellOnt 7702, 85 R.F.L. (6th) 51, [2009] O.J. No. 5269 (Ont. S.C.J.). Leave to appeal refused 2010 CarswellOnt 1640, 2010 ONSC 1578, 85 R.F.L. (6th) 62, 99 O.R. (3d) 687, 267 O.A.C. 1, [2010] O.J. No. 1139 (Ont. Div. Ct.), additional reasons at 2010 CarswellOnt 3918,

2010 ONSC 2399, 85 R.F.L. (6th) 71 (Ont. Div. Ct.), affirmed 2010 CarswellOnt 6860, 2010 ONSC 3512, 92 R.F.L. (6th) 106, 103 O.R. (3d) 588, 324 D.L.R. (4th) 277, 268 O.A.C. 267, [2010] O.J. No. 3828 (Ont. Div. Ct.). The parties separated in 2007 after 33 years of marriage. The husband's income for 2007, 2008, and 2009 ranged between $2,800,000 and $3,900,000 annually. The wife brought a motion for retroactive and interim ongoing spousal support. The husband was ordered to pay $140,000 per month in spousal support retroactive to January 2008 and ongoing interim support of $110,000 per month effective January 2010. In determining the retroactive and ongoing spousal support amounts, the court used the SSAG as a guideline and noted that it is applicable despite the husband's income being in excess of the $350,000 ceiling.

*Retroactive support will be determined based on SSAG ranges using an average of the parties' incomes during the relevant years* — Bastarache v. Bastarache, 2012 CarswellNB 102, 2012 NBQB 75, 387 N.B.R. (2d) 152, 1001 A.P.R. 152, [2012] N.B.J. No. 77 (N.B.Q.B.). Retroactive support was ordered for five years based on an average of the husband's income. Support was awarded between the mid to top range of the SSAG under the without child formula. The wife had suffered poverty post-separation and the husband was making on average $56,000, with the wife making on average $13,000 a year.

## 20.2 Retroactive Spousal Support for the Interim Period

*An order of spousal support is effective as of the date that proceedings are commenced where the recipient spouse is in need prior to trial and she has not delayed in bringing her application — Kerr v. Baranow*, 2011 CarswellBC 240, 2011 CarswellBC 241, 2011 SCC 10, 93 R.F.L. (6th) 1, [2011] 1 S.C.R. 269, 108 O.R. (3d) 399, 14 B.C.L.R. (5th) 203, 328 D.L.R. (4th) 577, 64 E.T.R. (3d) 1, [2011] 3 W.W.R. 575, 411 N.R. 200, 274 O.A.C. 1, 300 B.C.A.C. 1, 509 W.A.C. 1, [2011] S.C.J. No. 10 (S.C.C.).

*Retroactive support ordered because wife was not working — T. (R.) v. D. (D.)*, 2009 CarswellBC 1223, 2009 BCCA 198, 64 R.F.L. (6th) 233, 92 B.C.L.R. (4th) 277, [2009] 7 W.W.R. 246, 270 B.C.A.C. 114, 454 W.A.C. 114, [2009] B.C.J. No. 928 (B.C.C.A.). The parties separated in November 2005. At trial, the court used the SSAG to calculate the appropriate amount of spousal support and determined that the mid-range was appropriate. The court ordered spousal support retroactive to May 2006 which was the date when the regular interim payments had commenced. The husband appealed. On appeal, the court found that the wife had to encroach on her capital and was not working during this time. Accordingly, the retroactive date and mid-range amount were appropriate and the appeal was dismissed.

*SSAG considered in retroactive case — Dickson v. Dickson*, 2009 CarswellMan 515, 2009 MBQB 274, 247 Man. R. (2d) 56 (Man. Q.B.), additional reasons at, 2010 MBQB 164, 2010 CarswellMan 388 (Man. Q.B.). An interim order was made in this case where the husband's income was found to be $687,534 per year. At trial, in analyzing ongoing and retroactive spousal support, the court considered the SSAG and noted that, "these advisory guidelines are not law but rather a useful guide and crosscheck on one's own calculations after considering the evidence and in particular, the evidence of income and expense of the parties and the children and after considering the authorities. The SSAG had been widely accepted as useful in this way throughout the country and are referred to and accepted in most of the modern spousal support cases." The court analyzed the husband's income from the date of separation and accordingly used the SSAG to determine the quantum of spousal support and the retroactive amount.

*Final support order retroactive to the date of the interim order — Fisher v. Fisher*, 2008 CarswellOnt 43, 2008 ONCA 11, 47 R.F.L. (6th) 235, 88 O.R. (3d) 241, 288 D.L.R. (4th) 513, 232 O.A.C. 213, [2008] O.J. No. 38 (Ont. C.A.). This is a significant decision which addresses both retroactive spousal support and the SSAG. In this case, the parties were married for 19 years. At an interim motion, the husband was ordered to pay temporary spousal support, which commenced in October 2004, in the amount of $2,000 monthly. At trial, the trial judge refused to order that the support order be retroactive to October 2004. The wife appealed. The appellate court found that the trial judge erred in refusing the wife's request that the final support order be retroactive to October 2004. The court noted that, "retroactive support should be available when the recipient establishes at trial that he or she was entitled to a greater amount of interim support, the respondent had the ability to pay, and the imposition of retroactive support would not create undue hardship for the payor." The court concluded that the final support order should be retroactive to October 2004. In determining whether the quantum and duration of spousal support was appropriate, the court did an excellent job of analyzing the SSAG, and the case law and stated that, "when counsel fully addresses the *Guidelines* in argument, and a trial judge decides to award a quantum of support outside the suggested range, appellate review will be assisted by the inclusion of reasons explaining why the *Guidelines* do not provide an appropriate result. This is no different than a trial court distinguishing a significant authority relied upon by a party".

*Retroactive support awarded* — *Purdue v. Purdue*, 2009 CarswellNB 538, 2009 NBQB 303, 351 N.B.R. (2d) 215, 904 A.P.R. 215 (N.B.Q.B.). The parties separated after being married for 17 years and had 2 children. An interim order was made awarding the wife child and spousal support. The father did not pay any child or spousal support since the interim order. The court awarded the mother retroactive child support from March 2006 in the amount of $7,847 and found that the expenses that the father paid for from March to November 2006 — he paid the household bills — were more reasonably characterized as in lieu of spousal support than child support. The court further noted that the divorce petition was filed in May 2006; thus, the father was clearly put on notice at that time of the mother's request for retroactive support. There was also blameworthy conduct on the part of the father, who knew, or should have known, the nature of the claim and his duty to disclose all of his income. The retroactive order would not impose hardship on the father, as he made more than five times the income of the mother. The court also awarded the wife spousal support retroactive to the date of the interim order. The court used the SSAG to determine the quantum of spousal support and found that the mid-range was appropriate.

*Court orders spousal support retroactive to the date of trial* — *Kerr v. Baranow*, 2009 CarswellBC 642, 2009 BCCA 111, 66 R.F.L. (6th) 1, 93 B.C.L.R. (4th) 201, [2009] 9 W.W.R. 285, 266 B.C.A.C. 298, 449 W.A.C. 298, [2009] B.C.J. No. 474 (B.C.C.A.), additional reasons at, 2010 BCCA 32, 2010 CarswellBC 108, 78 R.F.L. (6th) 305, 2 B.C.L.R. (5th) 197, [2010] 4 W.W.R. 465, [2010] B.C.J. No. 88 (B.C.C.A.). In this case, the trial judge awarded the wife $1,739 per month in retroactive spousal support from the date of the application pursuant to the SSAG. The husband appealed. On appeal, the court reversed the decision and ordered spousal support retroactive to the date of trial. The court noted that the wife's financial need did not exceed her means, she did not demand interim support and she established no blameworthy conduct on the husband's part.

*Retroactive spousal support awarded to the date of the interim order* — *Willi v. Chapple*, 2009 CarswellOnt 5398, [2009] O.J. No. 3752 (Ont. S.C.J.). The parties cohabitated for 16 years and had one child. An interim interim order was made in 2004 where the father was ordered to make a combined payment of $3,500 in child and spousal support. The mother brought a motion for retroactive spousal support based on the father's increased income. In awarding retroactive spousal support of $5,500 per month retroactive to October 2003, the date of the interim interim order, the court noted that the SSAG suggested a range from $4,250 to $5,667 per month and concluded that the upper range was appropriate.

## 20.3 Variation Applications

*Retroactive support awarded because of husband's increased income* — *James v. James*, 2009 CarswellBC 1490, 2009 BCCA 261, 66 R.F.L. (6th) 246, 94 B.C.L.R. (4th) 183, [2009] 10 W.W.R. 11, 273 B.C.A.C. 75, 461 W.A.C. 75, [2009] B.C.J. No. 1151 (B.C.C.A.). After 19 years of marriage, the parties entered into a consent order in 2004 which provided for spousal support of $5,750 per month. The wife was a flight attendant for 22 years, but was encouraged by the husband to accept $100,000 in a severance package in 2001 and retire from the airline. The husband's yearly income for 2004 to 2006 ranged from $986,000 to $1.3 million per year. The husband applied to vary or terminate spousal support and the chambers judge granted the variation. On appeal, the court noted that the wife was entitled to retroactive spousal support due to the husband's increased income and because he encouraged the wife to leave her employment. The court also noted that on a variation application the SSAG is a good starting point; however, the SSAG should be approached with caution. The court found that the wife was in need of increased spousal support.

*Child and spousal support arrears treated the same* — *Brown v. Brown*, 2010 CarswellNB 30, 2010 CarswellNB 31, 2010 NBCA 5, 76 R.F.L. (6th) 33, 315 D.L.R. (4th) 293, 353 N.B.R. (2d) 323, 910 A.P.R. 323, [2010] N.B.J. No. 18 (N.B.C.A.). The court held that while *D.B.S. v. S.R.G.; T.A.R. v. L.J.W.; Henry v. Henry; S. (D.B.) v. G. (S.R.)*, 2006 CarswellAlta 976, 2006 CarswellAlta 977, 2006 SCC 37, 31 R.F.L. (6th) 1, [2006] 2 S.C.R. 231, 61 Alta. L.R. (4th) 1, 270 D.L.R. (4th) 297, [2006] 10 W.W.R. 379, 351 N.R. 201, 391 A.R. 297, 377 W.A.C. 297, [2005] S.C.C.A. No. 100, [2006] S.C.J. No. 37 (S.C.C.), speaks only of variation orders involving child support, it does not consider spousal support. The court stated that there is, as a general proposition, "no valid policy reason for distinguishing between child and spousal support when it comes to the retroactive variation of support arrears."

*Retroactive support ordered because of husband's severance package* — *Ellis v. Ellis*, 2010 CarswellOnt 1814, 2010 ONSC 1880,, 84 R.F.L. (6th) 263 [2010] O.J. No. 1250 (Ont. S.C.J.). The parties separated in 1999 after 22 years of marriage. A final consent order fixed spousal support at $2,233 per month and provided for variation in the event of a material change in circumstances. Subsequently, the husband received a severance package of 95 weeks when his employment was terminated. The husband brought a motion to retroactively decrease spousal support and the wife brought a cross-motion to retroactively increase spousal support. The husband's motion was dismissed and the wife's was granted in part. The court analyzed the ranges suggested by the SSAG, the wife's need and the husband's ability to pay. The court ordered that the husband pay retroactive spousal support of $4,000 per month for the years 2006 through 2008, which was between the mid to upper range of the SSAG and ongoing spousal support of $2,000 per month for 2009. The court noted that the retroactive support reflected the husband's temporarily increased ability to pay resulting from his severance package.

*SSAG considered in variation application* — *Mann v. Mann*, 2008 CarswellOnt 4474, 2008 ONCJ 331, [2008] O.J. No. 2942 (Ont. C.J.), affirmed 2009 CarswellOnt 2631, [2009] O.J. No. 1960 (Ont. S.C.J.). In this case, an order was made fixing the husband's income at $58.500 per year, the wife's income at $28,700 per year, child support at $879, and spousal support at $150 per month. The husband lost his job the day after the hearing and went on employment insurance until he found full-time employment. He now earned $42,900 per year and brought a motion to vary or eliminate spousal support and rescind all or part of the support arrears under the order. The court noted that had spousal support been paid while the husband was unemployed, the wife would have received 57.5% of the parties' combined net disposable income which was appropriate given the length of marriage and that the parties had 2 children. The court noted that although the SSAG were only advisory and not designed for variation motions, spousal support guidelines still had relevance as a starting point and must be balanced in light of the circumstances of each individual case.

*Retroactive support ordered due to husband's lack of disclosure* — *Krane v. Krane*, 2010 CarswellOnt 1471, 2010 ONSC 1488, [2010] O.J. No. 1009 (Ont. S.C.J.). The parties were married for 19 years and had 3 children. The husband was ordered to pay spousal support of $995 per month, which was subsequently varied a few times and was to be terminated if the wife earned in excess of $35,500. The wife brought a motion for retroactive and ongoing variation of spousal support based on the husband's annual income being more than he claimed. The court analyzed the husband's income from 2003 and used the SSAG after 2005 to determine the appropriate amount of spousal support. The court awarded retroactive and ongoing spousal support and noted that the retroactive variation was warranted as the husband had engaged in blameworthy conduct by failing to make full financial disclosure.

*Retroactive reduction in spousal support awarded* — *Pandya v. Pandya*, 2010 CarswellOnt 2475, 2010 ONSC 2026 (Ont. S.C.J.). In this case, the husband was paying $9,000 per month in spousal support pursuant to a court order. Subsequently, the husband, who was a doctor, was involved in litigation with his partners resulting in reduced income. The husband brought a motion to vary spousal support and was seeking a retroactive reduction of spousal support to $5,000 per month from March 1, 2009. The court noted that based on the husband's income, the SSAG suggested a range from $5,761 to $6,903. In considering the means and needs of the parties, the court awarded an amount at the lower range retroactive to March 1, 2009.

*No retroactive spousal support ordered* — *Sarophim v. Sarophim*, 2010 CarswellBC 370, 2010 BCSC 216, 82 R.F.L. (6th) 318 (B.C.S.C. [In Chambers]). The parties separated after 29 years of marriage and entered into a separation agreement. Pursuant to the agreement, the husband paid the wife $1,250 per month in spousal support and either party could apply for a review after September 2008. The wife brought a motion to retroactively vary spousal support because the husband's income was higher. The court concluded that there was no case for a retroactive award because the husband had disclosed his income. The court awarded the wife an amount at the lower end of the SSAG range.

## 20.4 Separation Agreement Set Aside

*Retroactive support ordered after separation agreement set aside* — *Leaman v. Leaman*, 2009 CarswellNfld 328, 2009 NLTD 199, 293 Nfld. & P.E.I.R. 108, 906 A.P.R. 108 (N.L.T.D.). The parties separated in 2001 after 19 years of marriage. The husband retired in 2008 and ceased paying spousal support, but maintained contract work with his former employer. The wife was seeking retroactive and ongoing spousal support. A separation agreement that the husband was relying upon was set aside by a court order. The court stated that "although [it] recognized that Divorcemate and spousal support guidelines were not in place in 2001, the current day low end calculation from Divorcemate provides a bench mark to assist in determination of the appropriate quantum and duration." Accordingly, the court ordered that the husband pay retroactive spousal support of $50,000. The court did not award any future spousal support.

## 20.5 Tax Issues and Lump Sum Retroactive Awards

Tax issues can complicate any retroactive spousal support order. If the retroactive support is calculated using the Advisory Guidelines and converted into a lump sum payment, then the lump sum should be discounted for income tax, as the lump sum will usually not be deductible. On the other hand, if it is the intention to make the retroactive support deductible and to reassess and adjust prior years' taxes, then that should be made clear and the proper forms filed with the Canada Revenue Agency. . [User's Guide, March 31, 2010, section 14.]

Orders should be structured to take tax implications into account. For an example of a court acknowledging and providing for this uncertainty in its order, see *Chapman v. Chapman*, 2010 CarswellOnt 2343 (Ont. S.C.J.).

# APPENDIX 1

## DIVORCE ACT

R.S.C. 1985, c. 3 (2nd Supp.), as am. R.S.C. 1985, c. 27 (2nd Supp.), s. 10;
S.C. 1990, c. 18, ss. 1, 2; 1992, c. 51, s. 46; 1993, c. 8, ss. 1-5;
1993, c. 28, s. 78 (Sched. III, items 41-43) [Amended 1998, c. 15, ss. 22, 23;
1999, c. 3, s. 12 (Sched., item 11).]; 1997, c. 1, ss. 1-15; 1998, c. 30, ss. 13(f) (Fr.), 15(f);
1999, c. 3, s. 61; 1999, c. 31, s. 74 (Fr.); 2002, c. 7, ss. 158-160; 2002, c. 8, s. 183(1)(i);
2005, c. 33, s. 8(1), (2) (Fr.); 2007, c. 14; 2014, c. 2, s. 33; 2015, c. 3, s. 76.

. . . . .

## INTERPRETATION

**2. (1) Definitions** — In this Act,

**"age of majority"**, in respect of a child, means the age of majority as determined by the laws of the province where the child ordinarily resides, or, if the child ordinarily resides outside of Canada, eighteen years of age;

**"appellate court"**, in respect of an appeal from a court, means the court exercising appellate jurisdiction with respect to that appeal;

**"applicable guidelines"**, means

(a) where both spouses or former spouses are ordinarily resident in the same province at the time an application for a child support order or a variation order in respect of a child support order is made, or the amount of a child support order is to be recalculated pursuant to section 25.1, and that province has been designated by an order made under subsection (5), the laws of the province specified in the order, and

(b) in any other case, the Federal Child Support Guidelines;

**"child of the marriage"** means a child of two spouses or former spouses who, at the material time,

(a) is under the age of majority and who has not withdrawn from their charge, or

(b) is the age of majority or over and under their charge but unable, by reason of illness, disability or other cause, to withdraw from their charge or to obtain the necessaries of life;

**"child support order"**, means an order made under subsection 15.1(1);

**"corollary relief proceeding"** means a proceeding in a court in which either or both former spouses seek a child support order, a spousal support order or a custody order;

**"court"**, in respect of a province, means

(a) for the Province of Ontario, the Superior Court of Justice,

(a.1) for the Province of Newfoundland and Labrador, the Trial Division of the Supreme Court of the Province,

(b) for the Province of Quebec, the Superior Court,

(c) for the Provinces of Nova Scotia, British Columbia and Prince Edward Island, the Supreme Court of the Province,

(d) for the Province of New Brunswick, Manitoba, Saskatchewan or Alberta, the Court of Queen's Bench for the Province, and

(e) for Yukon or the Northwest Territories, the Supreme Court, and in Nunavut, the Nunavut Court of Justice,

and includes such other court in the province the judges of which are appointed by the Governor General as is designated by the Lieutenant Governor in Council of the province as a court for the purposes of this Act;

**"custody"** includes care, upbringing and any other incident of custody;

**"custody order"** means an order made under subsection 16(1);

**"divorce proceeding"** means a proceeding in a court in which either or both spouses seek a divorce alone or together with a child support order, a spousal support order or a custody order;

**"Federal Child Support Guidelines"** means the guidelines made under section 26.1;

**"provincial child support service"** means any service, agency or body designated in an agreement with a province under subsection 25.1(1);

**"spousal support order"** means an order made under subsection 15.2(1);

**"spouse"** means either of two persons who are married to each other;

**"support order"** means a child support order or a spousal support order;

**"variation order"** means an order made under subsection 17(1);

**"variation proceeding"** means a proceeding in a court in which either or both former spouses seek a variation order.

. . . . .

(3) **Term not restrictive** — The use of the term "application" to describe a proceeding under this Act in a court shall not be construed as limiting the name under which and the form and manner in which that proceeding may be taken in that court, and the name, manner and form of the proceeding in that court shall be such as is provided for by the rules regulating the practice and procedure in that court.

(4) **Idem** — The use in section 21.1 of the terms "affidavit" and "pleadings" to describe documents shall not be construed as limiting the name that may be used to refer to those documents in a court and the form of those documents, and the name and form of the documents shall be such as is provided for by the rules regulating the practice and procedure in that court.

. . . . .

R.S.C. 1985, c. 27 (2nd Supp.), s. 10 (Sched., item 7(1), (2)); 1990, c. 18, s. 1; 1992, c. 51, s. 46; 1993, c. 28, s. 78 (Sched. III, item 41) [Repealed 1999, c. 3, s. 12 (Sched., item 11).]; 1997, c. 1, s. 1; 1998, c. 30, s. 15(f); 1999, c. 3, s. 61; 2002, c. 7, s. 158; 2005, c. 33, s. 8(1); 2015, c. 3, s. 76.

# JURISDICTION

. . . . .

**4. (1) Jurisdiction in corollary relief proceedings** – A court in a province has jurisdiction to hear and determine a corollary relief proceeding if

(a)  either former spouse is ordinarily resident in the province at the commencement of the proceeding; or

(b)  both former spouses accept the jurisdiction of the court.

**(2) Jurisdiction where two proceedings commenced on different days** – Where corollary relief proceedings between the same former spouses and in respect of the same matter are pending in two courts that would otherwise have jurisdiction under subsection (1) and were commenced on different days and the proceeding that was commenced first is not discontinued within thirty days after it was commenced, the court in which a corollary relief proceeding was commenced first has exclusive jurisdiction to hear and determine any corollary relief proceeding then pending between the former spouses in respect of that matter and the second corollary relief proceeding shall be deemed to be discontinued.

**(3) Jurisdiction where two proceedings commenced on same day** – Where proceedings between the same former spouses and in respect of the same matter are pending in two courts that would otherwise have jurisdiction under subsection (1) and were commenced on the same day and neither proceeding is discontinued within thirty days after it was commenced, the Federal Court has exclusive jurisdiction to hear and determine any corollary relief proceeding then pending between the former spouses in respect of that matter and the corollary relief proceedings in those courts shall be transferred to the Federal Court on the direction of that Court.

1993, c. 8, s. 1; 2002, c. 8, s. 183(1)(i)

. . . . .

# COROLLARY RELIEF

## *Interpretation*

**15. Definition of "spouse"** – In section 15.1 to 16, **"spouse"** has the meaning assigned by subsection 2(1), and includes a former spouse.

1997, c. 1, s. 2

. . . . .

## *Spousal Support Orders*

**15.2 (1) Spousal support order** – A court of competent jurisdiction may, on application by either or both spouses, make an order requiring a spouse to secure or pay, or to secure and pay, such lump sum or periodic sums, or such lump sum and periodic sums, as the court thinks reasonable for the support of the other spouse.

**(2) Interim order** – Where an application is made under subsection (1), the court may, on application by either or both spouses, make an interim order requiring a spouse to secure or pay, or to secure and pay, such lump sum or periodic sums, or such lump sum and periodic sums, as the court thinks reasonable for the support of the other spouse, pending the determination of the application under subsection (1).

**(3) Terms and conditions** — The court may make an order under subsection (1) or an interim order under subsection (2) for a definite or indefinite period or until a specified event occurs, and may impose terms, conditions or restrictions in connection with the order as it thinks fit and just.

**(4) Factors** — In making an order under subsection (1) or an interim order under subsection (2), the court shall take into consideration the condition, means, needs and other circumstances of each spouse, including

(a)   the length of time the spouses cohabited;

(b)   the functions performed by each spouse during cohabitation; and

(c)   any order, agreement or arrangement relating to support of either spouse.

**(5) Spousal misconduct** — In making an order under subsection (1) or an interim order under subsection (2), the court shall not take into consideration any misconduct of a spouse in relation to the marriage.

**(6) Objectives of spousal support order** — An order made under subsection (1) or an interim order under subsection (2) that provides for the support of a spouse should

(a)   recognize any economic advantages or disadvantages to the spouses arising from the marriage or its breakdown;

(b)   apportion between the spouses any financial consequences arising from the care of any child of the marriage over and above any obligation for the support of any child of the marriage;

(c)   relieve any economic hardship of the spouses arising from the breakdown of the marriage; and

(d)   in so far as practicable, promote the economic self-sufficiency of each spouse within a reasonable period of time.

1997, c. 1, s. 2

## *Priority*

**15.3 (1) Priority to child support** — Where a court is considering an application for a child support order and an application for a spousal support order, the court shall give priority to child support in determining the applications.

**(2) Reasons** — Where, as a result of giving priority to child support, the court is unable to make a spousal support order or the court makes a spousal support order in an amount that is less than it otherwise would have been, the court shall record its reasons for having done so.

**(3) Consequences of reduction or termination of child support order** — Where, as a result of giving priority to child support, a spousal support order was not made, or the amount of a spousal support order is less than it otherwise would have been, any subsequent reduction or termination of that child support constitutes a change of circumstances for the purposes of applying for a spousal support order, or a variation order in respect of the spousal support order, as the case may be.

1997, c. 1, s. 2

. . . . .

## Variation, Rescission or Suspension of Orders

**17. (1) Order for variation, rescission or suspension** — A court of competent jurisdiction may make an order varying, rescinding or suspending, prospectively or retroactively,

    (a) a support order or any provision thereof on application by either or both former spouses; or

    (b) a custody order or any provision thereof on application by either or both former spouses or by any other person.

**(2) Application by other person** — A person, other than a former spouse, may not make an application under paragraph (1)(b) without leave of the court.

**(3) Terms and conditions** — The court may include in a variation order any provision that under this Act could have been included in the order in respect of which the variation order is sought.

**(4) Factors for child support order** — Before the court makes a variation order in respect of a child support order, the court shall satisfy itself that a change of circumstances as provided for in the applicable guidelines has occurred since the making of the child support order or the last variation order made in respect of that order.

**(4.1) Factors for spousal support order** — Before the court makes a variation order in respect of a spousal support order, the court shall satisfy itself that a change in the condition, means, needs or other circumstances of either former spouse has occurred since the making of the spousal support order or the last variation order made in respect of that order, and, in making the variation order, the court shall take that change into consideration.

**(5) Factors for custody order** — Before the court makes a variation order in respect of a custody order, the court shall satisfy itself that there has been a change in the condition, means, needs or other circumstances of the child of the marriage occurring since the making of the custody order or the last variation order made in respect of that order, as the case may be, and, in making the variation order, the court shall take into consideration only the best interests of the child as determined by reference to that change.

**(5.1) Variation order** — For the purposes of subsection (5), a former spouse's terminal illness or critical condition shall be considered a change of circumstances of the child of the marriage, and the court shall make a variation order in respect of access that is in the best interests of the child.

**(6) Conduct** — In making a variation order, the court shall not take into consideration any conduct that under this Act could not have been considered in making the order in respect of which the variation order is sought.

**(6.1) Guidelines apply** — A court making a variation order in respect of a child support order shall do so in accordance with the applicable guidelines.

**(6.2) Court may take agreement, etc., into account** — Notwithstanding subsection (6.1), in making a variation order in respect of a child support order, a court may award an amount that is different from the amount that would be determined in accordance with the applicable guidelines if the court is satisfied

    (a) that special provisions in an order, a judgment or a written agreement respecting the financial obligations of the spouses, or the division or transfer of their property, directly or indirectly benefit a child, or that special provisions have otherwise been made for the benefit of a child; and

(b) that the application of the applicable guidelines would result in an amount of child support that is inequitable given those special provisions.

**(6.3) Reasons** – Where the court awards, pursuant to subsection (6.2), an amount that is different from the amount that would be determined in accordance with the applicable guidelines, the court shall record its reasons for having done so.

**(6.4) Consent orders** – Notwithstanding subsection (6.1), a court may award an amount that is different from the amount that would be determined in accordance with the applicable guidelines on the consent of both spouses if it is satisfied that reasonable arrangements have been made for the support of the child to whom the order relates.

**(6.5) Reasonable arrangements** – For the purposes of subsection (6.4), in determining whether reasonable arrangements have been made for the support of a child, the court shall have regard to the applicable guidelines. However, the court shall not consider the arrangements to be unreasonable solely because the amount of support agreed to is not the same as the amount that would otherwise have been determined in accordance with the applicable guidelines.

**(7) Objectives of variation order varying spousal support order** – A variation order varying a spousal support order should

(a) recognize any economic advantages or disadvantages to the former spouse arising from the marriage or its breakdown;

(b) apportion between the former spouses any financial consequences arising from the care of any child of the marriage over and above any obligation for the support of any child of the marriage;

(c) relieve any economic hardship of the former spouses arising from the breakdown of the marriage; and

(d) in so far as practicable, promote the economic self-sufficiency of each former spouse within a reasonable period of time.

**(8)** [Repealed 1997, c. 1, s. 5(5).]

**(9) Maximum contact** – In making a variation order varying a custody order, the court shall give effect to the principle that a child of the marriage should have as much contact with each former spouse as is consistent with the best interests of the child and, for that purpose, where the variation order would grant custody of the child to a person who does not currently have custody, the court shall take into consideration the willingness of that person to facilitate such contact.

**(10) Limitation** – Notwithstanding subsection (1), where a spousal support order provides for support for a definite period or until a specified event occurs, a court may not, on an application instituted after the expiration of that period or the occurrence of the event, make a variation order for the purpose of resuming that support unless the court is satisfied that

(a) a variation order is necessary to relieve economic hardship arising from a change described in subsection (4.1) that is related to the marriage; and

(b) the changed circumstances, had they existed at the time of the making of the spousal support order or the last variation order made in respect of that order, as the case may be, would likely have resulted in a different order.

**(11) Copy of order** – Where a court makes a variation order in respect of a support order or a custody order made by another court, it shall send a copy of the variation order, certified by a judge or officer of the court, to that other court.

1997, c. 1, ss. 4, 5; 2007, c. 14, s. 1

**17.1 Variation order by affidavit, etc.** — Where both former spouses are ordinarily resident in different provinces, a court of competent jurisdiction may, in accordance with any applicable rules of the court, make a variation order pursuant to subsection 17(1) on the basis of the submissions of the former spouses, whether presented orally before the court or by means of affidavits or any means of telecommunication, if both former spouses consent thereto.

1993, c. 8, s. 2

## *Provisional Orders*

**18. (1) Definitions** — In this section and section 19,

**"Attorney General"**, in respect of a province, means

(a) for Yukon, the member of the Executive Council of Yukon designated by the Commissioner of Yukon,

(b) for the Northwest Territories, the member of the Executive Council of the Northwest Territories designated by the Commissioner of the Northwest Territories,

(b.1) for Nunavut, the member of the Executive Council of Nunavut designated by the Commissioner of Nunavut, and

(c) for the other provinces, the Attorney General of the province,

and includes any person authorized in writing by the member or Attorney General to act for the member or Attorney General in the performance of a function under this section or section 19;

**"provisional order"** means an order made pursuant to subsection (2).

**(2) Provisional order** — Notwithstanding paragraph 5(1)(a) and subsection 17(1), where an application is made to a court in a province for a variation order in respect of a support order and

(a) the respondent in the application is ordinarily resident in another province, and has not accepted the jurisdiction of the court, or both former spouses have not consented to the application of section 17.1 in respect of the matter, and

(b) in the circumstances of the case, the court is satisfied that the issues can be adequately determined by proceeding under this section and section 19,

the court shall make a variation order with or without notice to and in the absence of the respondent, but such order is provisional only and has no legal effect until it is confirmed in a proceeding under section 19 and, where so confirmed, it has legal effect in accordance with the terms of the order confirming it.

**(3) Transmission** — Where a court in a province makes a provisional order, it shall send to the Attorney General for the province

(a) three copies of the provisional order certified by a judge or officer of the court;

(b) a certified or sworn document setting out or summarizing the evidence given to the court; and

(c) a statement giving any available information respecting the identification, location, income and assets of the respondent.

**(4) Idem** — On receipt of the documents referred to in subsection (3), the Attorney General shall send the documents to the Attorney General for the province in which the respondent is ordinarily resident.

**(5) Further evidence** — Where, during a proceeding under section 19, a court in a province remits the matter back for further evidence to the court that made the provisional order, the court that made the order shall, after giving notice to the applicant, receive further evidence.

**(6) Transmission** — Where evidence is received under subsection (5), the court that received the evidence shall forward to the court that remitted the matter back a certified or sworn document setting out or summarizing the evidence, together with such recommendations as the court that received the evidence considers appropriate.

1993, c. 8, s. 2; 1993, c. 28, s. 78 (Sched. III, item 43); 1997, c. 1, s. 6; 2002, c. 7, s. 159; 2014, c. 2, s. 33

**19. (1) Transmission** — On receipt of any documents sent pursuant to subsection 18(4), the Attorney General for the province in which the respondent is ordinarily resident shall send the documents to a court in the province.

**(2) Procedure** — Subject to subsection (3), where documents have been sent to a court pursuant to subsection (1), the court shall serve on the respondent a copy of the documents and a notice of a hearing respecting confirmation of the provisional order and shall proceed with the hearing, in the absence of the applicant, taking into consideration the certified or sworn document setting out or summarizing the evidence given to the court that made the provisional order.

**(3) Return to Attorney General** — Where documents have been sent to a court pursuant to subsection (1) and the respondent apparently is outside the province and is not likely to return, the court shall send the documents to the Attorney General for that province, together with any available information respecting the location and circumstances of the respondent.

**(4) Idem** — On receipt of any documents and information sent pursuant to subsection (3), the Attorney General shall send the documents and information to the Attorney General for the province of the court that made the provisional order.

**(5) Right of respondent** — In a proceeding under this section, the respondent may raise any matter that might have been raised before the court that made the provisional order.

**(6) Further evidence** — Where, in a proceeding under this section, the respondent satisfies the court that for the purpose of taking further evidence or for any other purpose it is necessary to remit the matter back to the court that made the provisional order, the court may so remit the matter and adjourn the proceeding for that purpose.

**(7) Order of confirmation or refusal** — Subject to subsection (7.1), at the conclusion of a proceeding under this section, the court shall make an order

(a)   confirming the provisional order without variation;
(b)   the provisional order with variation; or
(c)   refusing confirmation of the provisional order.

**(7.1) Guidelines apply** — A court making an order under subsection (7) in respect of a child support order shall do so in accordance with the applicable guidelines.

**(8) Further evidence** — The court, before making an order confirming the provisional order with variation or an order refusing confirmation of the provisional order, shall decide whether to remit the matter back for further evidence to the court that made the provisional order.

**(9) Interim order for support of children** — Where a court remits a matter pursuant to this section in relation to a child support order, the court may, pending the making of an order under subsection (7), make an interim order in accordance with the applicable guidelines requiring a spouse to pay for the support of any or all children of the marriage.

**(9.1) Interim order for support of spouse** — Where a court remits a matter pursuant to this section in relation to a spousal support order, the court may make an interim order requiring a spouse to secure or pay, or to secure and pay, such lump sum or periodic sums, or such lump sum and periodic sums, as the court thinks reasonable for the support of the other spouse, pending the making of an order under subsection (7).

**(10) Terms and conditions** — The court may make an order under subsection (9) or (9.1) for a definite or indefinite period or until a specified event occurs, and may impose terms, conditions or restrictions in connection with the order as it thinks fit and just.

**(11) Provisions applicable** — Subsection 17(4), (4.1) and (6) to (7) apply, with such modifications as the circumstances require, in respect of an order made under subsection (9) or (9.1) as if it were a variation order referred to in those subsections.

**(12) Report and filing** — On making an order under subsection (7), the court in a province shall

(a) send a copy of the order, certified by a judge or officer of the court, to the Attorney General for that province, to the court that made the provisional order and, where that court is not the court that made the support order in respect of which the provisional order was made, to the court that made the support order;

(b) where an order is made confirming the provisional order with or without variation, file the order in the court; and

(c) where an order is made confirming the provisional order with variation or refusing confirmation of the provisional order, give written reasons to the Attorney General for that province and to the court that made the provisional order.

1993, c. 8, s. 4; 1997, c. 1, s. 7

**20. (1) Definition of court** — In this section, **"court"**, in respect of a province, has the meaning assigned by subsection 2(1) and includes such other court having jurisdiction in the province as is designated by the Lieutenant Governor in Council of the province as a court for the purposes of this section.

**(2) Legal effect throughout Canada** — Subject to subsection 18(2), an order made under any of sections 15.1 to 17 or subsection 19(7), (9) or (9.1) has legal effect throughout Canada.

**(3) Enforcement** — An order that has legal effect throughout Canada pursuant to subsection (2) may be

(a) registered in any court in a province and enforced in like manner as an order of that court; or

(b) enforced in a province in any other manner provided for by the laws of that province, including its laws respecting reciprocal enforcement between the province and a jurisdiction outside Canada.

**(4) Variation of orders** — Notwithstanding subsection (3), a court may only vary an order that has legal effect throughout Canada pursuant to subsection (2) in accordance with this Act.

1997, c. 1, s. 8

**20.1 (1) Assignment of order** — A support order may be assigned to

(a) any minister of the Crown for Canada designated by the Governor in Council;

(b) any minister of the Crown for a province, or any agency in a province, designated by the Lieutenant Governor in Council of the province;

(c) any member of the Legislative Assembly of Yukon, or any agency in Yukon, designated by the Commissioner of Yukon;

(d) any member of the Legislative Assembly of the Northwest Territories, or any agency in the Northwest Territories, designated by the Commissioner of the Northwest Territories; or

(e) any member of the Legislative Assembly of Nunavut, or any agency in Nunavut, designated by the Commissioner of Nunavut.

**(2) Rights** — A minister, member or agency referred to in subsection (1) to whom an order is assigned is entitled to the payments due under the order, and has the same right to be notified of, and to participate in, proceedings under this Act to vary, rescind, suspend or enforce the order as the person who would otherwise be entitled to the payments.

1993, c. 28, s. 78 (Sched. III, item 43.1) [As enacted by 1998, c. 15, s. 23.]; 1997, c. 1, s. 9; 2002, c. 7, s. 160; 2014, c. 2, s. 34

## *Appeals*

**21. (1) Appeal to appellate court** — Subject to subsections (2) and (3), an appeal lies to the appellate court from any judgment or order, whether final or interim, rendered or made by a court under this Act.

**(2) Restriction on divorce appeals** — No appeal lies from a judgment granting a divorce on or after the day on which the divorce takes effect.

**(3) Restriction on order appeals** — No appeal lies from an order made under this Act more than thirty days after the day on which the order was made.

**(4) Extension** — An appellate court or a judge thereof may, on special grounds, either before or after the expiration of the time fixed by subsection (3) for instituting an appeal, by order extend that time.

**(5) Powers of appellate court** — The appellate court may

(a) dismiss the appeal; or

(b) allow the appeal and

(i) render the judgment or make the order that ought to have been rendered or made, including such order or such further or other order as it deems just, or

(ii) order a new hearing where it deems it necessary to do so to correct a substantial wrong or miscarriage of justice.

**(6) Procedure on appeals** — Except as otherwise provided by this Act or the rules or regulations, an appeal under this section shall be asserted, heard and decided according to the ordinary procedure governing appeals to the appellate court from the court rendering the judgment or making the order being appealed.

## *Divorce Act, R.S.C. 1970, c. D-8*

. . . . .

**34. (1) Variation and enforcement of orders previously made** — Subject to subsection (1.1), any order made under subsection 11(1) of the *Divorce Act*, chapter D-8 of the Revised Statutes of Canada, 1970, including any order made pursuant to section 33 of this Act, and any order to the like effect made corollary to a decree of divorce granted in Canada before July 2, 1968 or granted on or after that day pursuant to subsection 22(2) of that Act may be varied, rescinded, suspended or enforced in accordance with sections 17 to 20, other than subsection 17(10), of this Act as if

(a) the order were a support order or custody order, as the case may be; and

(b) in subsections 17(4), (4.1) and (5), the words **"or the last order made under subsection 11(2) of the *Divorce Act*, chapter D-8 of the Revised Statutes of Canada, 1970, varying that order"** were added immediately before the words **"or the last variation order made in respect of that order"**.

**(1.1) Combined orders** — Where an application is made under subsection 17(1) to vary an order referred to in subsection (1) that provides a single amount of money for the combined support of one or more children and a former spouse, the court shall rescind the order and treat the application as an application for a child support order and an application for a spousal support order.

**(2) Enforcement of interim orders** — Any order made under section 10 of the *Divorce Act*, chapter D-8 of the Revised Statutes of Canada, 1970, including any order made pursuant to section 33 of this Act, may be enforced in accordance with section 20 of this Act as if it were an order made under subsection 15.1(1) or 15.2(1) or section 16 of this Act, as the case may be.

**(3) Assignment of orders previously made** — Any order for the maintenance of a spouse or child of the marriage made under section 10 or 11 of the *Divorce Act*, chapter D-8 of the Revised Statutes of Canada, 1970, including any order made pursuant to section 33 of this Act, and any order to the like effect made corollary to a decree of divorce granted in Canada before July 2, 1968 or granted on or after that day pursuant to subsection 22(2) of that Act may be assigned to any minister, member or agency designated pursuant to section 20.1

1997, c. 1, s. 14

**35. Procedural laws continued** — The rules and regulations made under the *Divorce Act*, chapter D-8 of the Revised Statutes of Canada, 1970, and the provisions of any other law or of any rule, regulation or other instrument made thereunder respecting any matter in relation to which rules may be made under subsection 25(2) that were in force in Canada or any province immediately before the day on which this Act comes into force and that are not inconsistent with this Act continue in force as though made or enacted by or under this Act until they are repealed or altered by rules or regulations made under this Act or are, by virtue of the making of rules or regulations under this Act, rendered inconsistent with those rules or regulations.

## Divorce Act, R.S.C. 1985, c. 3 (2nd Supp.)

**35.1 (1) Variation and enforcement of support orders previously made** — Subject to subsection (2), any support order made under this Act before the coming into force of this section may be varied, rescinded, suspended or enforced in accordance with sections 17 to 20 as if the support order were a child support order or a spousal support order, as the case may be.

**(2) Combined orders** — Where an application is made under subsection 17(1) to vary a support order made under this Act before the coming into force of this section that provides for the combined support of one or more children and a former spouse, the court shall rescind the order and treat the application as an application for a child support order and an application for a spousal support order.

**(3) Assignment of orders previously made** — Any support order made under this Act before the coming into force of this section may be assigned to any minister, member or agency designated pursuant to section 20.1.

1997, c. 1, s. 15

# APPENDIX 2
# Spousal Support Advisory Guidelines July 2008

Prepared by:

**Professor Carol Rogerson**

Faculty of Law
University of Toronto

and

**Professor Rollie Thompson**

Dalhousie Law School

*This final version of the Spousal Support Advisory Guidelines was prepared by the authors with the support of the Department of Justice Canada. The Spousal Support Advisory Guidelines do not necessarily reflect the views of the Department of Justice Canada.*
*[Reproduced with permission as an unofficial version of the original publication.]*

# TABLE OF CONTENTS

# EXECUTIVE SUMMARY

The **Spousal Support Advisory Guidelines** were developed to bring more certainty and predictability to the determination of spousal support under the federal *Divorce Act*. The Advisory Guidelines project has been supported by the federal Department of Justice. The Advisory Guidelines were released three years ago, in January 2005, in the form of a Draft Proposal and have been used across Canada since then. Comments and feedback were provided and some revisions made. This document is the final version.

The *Spousal Support Advisory Guidelines* are very different from the *Federal Child Support Guidelines*. They **have not been legislated** by the federal government. They are informal guidelines that will operate on **an advisory basis only**. The Advisory Guidelines will be used to determine the amount and duration of spousal support within the existing legal framework of the *Divorce Act* and the judicial decisions interpreting its provisions. The Guidelines are not legally binding and their adoption and use will be voluntary. They are intended as a practical tool to assist spouses, lawyers, mediators and judges in determining the amount and duration of spousal support in typical cases. The various components of the Guidelines — the basic formulas, restructuring, and exceptions — are intended to build upon current practice, reflecting best practices and emerging trends across the country. The process of developing the Advisory Guidelines is described in Chapter 2.

An overview of the structure of the Guidelines is found in Chapter 3.

The Advisory Guidelines do **not** deal with **entitlement**, just amount and duration once entitlement has been found. A mere disparity of income that would generate an amount under the Guidelines does not automatically lead to entitlement. As is set out in Chapter 4, there must be a finding (or an agreement) on entitlement, on a compensatory or non-compensatory or contractual basis, *before* the formulas and the rest of the Guidelines are applied. The basis of entitlement is important, not only as a threshold issue, but also to determine location within the formula ranges or to justify departure from the ranges as an exception. Entitlement issues also arise frequently on review and variation, especially applications to terminate support.

Some limitations on the application of the Guidelines are dealt with in Chapter 5. The Advisory Guidelines have been developed specifically for use under the federal *Divorce Act*. **Provincial/territorial laws** differ in some respects and any use of these Guidelines in the provincial/territorial context must take account of these distinctive statutes, especially on matters of entitlement for unmarried couples and agreements. A **prior agreement** may limit the application of the Guidelines, as the Advisory Guidelines cannot be used to override existing agreements, especially agreements that time limit or waive spousal support.

There are two basic formulas in the proposal: the *without child support* **formula** and the *with child support* **formula**. The dividing line between the two is the absence or presence of a dependent child or children of the marriage, and a concurrent child support obligation, at the time spousal support is determined. Both formulas use **income sharing** as the method for determining the amount of spousal support, not budgets. The formulas produce **ranges** for the amount and duration of support, not just a single number. The precise number chosen within that range is a matter for negotiation or adjudication, depending upon the facts of a particular case.

The starting point under both formulas is the definition of **income** used in the *Federal Child Support Guidelines*, subject to some minor adjustments for spousal support purposes, explained in Chapter 6.

The *without child support* **formula**, set out below, is built around two crucial factors: the **gross income difference** between the spouses and the **length of the marriage**. Both the amount and the duration of support increase incrementally with the length of the marriage, as can be seen in the summary box below. The idea that explains this formula is **merger over time**: as a marriage lengthens, spouses more deeply merge their economic and non-economic lives, with each spouse making countless decisions to mould his or her skills, behaviours and finances around those of the other spouse. The gross income difference measures their differential loss of the marital standard of living at the end of the marriage. The formulas for both amount and duration reflect the idea that the longer the marriage, the more the lower income spouse should be protected against such a differential loss. Merger over time captures both the compensatory and non-compensatory spousal support objectives that have been recognized by our law since *Moge* and *Bracklow*.

---

### The *Without Child Support* Formula

**Amount** ranges from 1.5 to 2 percent of the difference between the spouses' gross incomes (the **gross income difference**) for each year of marriage (or, more precisely, years of cohabitation), up to a maximum of 50 percent. The maximum range remains fixed for marriages 25 years or longer at 37.5 to 50 percent of income difference. (The upper end of this maximum range is capped at the amount that would result in equalization of the spouses' net incomes — the **net income cap**.)

**Duration** ranges from .5 to 1 year for each year of marriage. However, support will be **indefinite (duration not specified)** if the marriage is **20 years or longer** in duration *or*, if the marriage has lasted 5 years or longer, when the years of marriage and age of the support recipient (at separation) added together total 65 or more (the **rule of 65**).

---

Chapter 7 contains examples of the application of the *without child support* formula and the ranges it produces for marriages of different lengths and incomes.

Cases with dependent children and concurrent child support obligations require a different formula, the **with child support formula**, set out in Chapter 8. These cases raise different considerations: priority must be given to child support; there is usually reduced ability to pay; and particular tax and benefit issues arise. The rationale for spousal support is also different. Where there are dependent children, the primary rationale is compensatory, as both *Moge* and *Bracklow* made clear. What drives support is not the length of the marriage, or marital interdependency, or merger over time, but the presence of dependent children and the need to provide care and support for those children. This **parental partnership** rationale looks at not just past loss, but also at the continuing economic disadvantage that flows from present and future child care responsibilities, anchored in s. 15.2(6)(b) of the *Divorce Act*.

There are three important differences between the *without child support* formula and the *with child support* formula. First, the *with child support* formula uses the **net incomes** of the spouses, not their gross incomes. Second, this formula divides the **pool** of combined net incomes between the two spouses, not the gross income difference. Third, the upper and lower percentage limits of net income division in the *with child support* formula **do not change with the length of the marriage**.

Set out below is a summary version of the **basic *with child support* formula**, used to determine the amount of spousal support to be paid where the payor spouse pays both child and spousal support to the lower income recipient spouse who is also the parent with custody or primary care of the children.

## The Basic *With Child Support* Formula for Amount

(1) Determine the **individual net disposable income (INDI)** of each spouse:

- Guidelines Income *minus* Child Support *minus* Taxes and Deductions = Payor's INDI
- Guidelines Income *minus* Notional Child Support minus Taxes and Deductions *Plus* Government Benefits and Credits = Recipient's INDI

(2) Add together the individual net disposable incomes. By iteration, determine the range of spousal support amounts that would be required to leave the lower income recipient spouse with between 40 and 46 percent of the combined INDI.

Net income computations like these require computer software. Basic to this formula is the concept of **individual net disposable income**, an attempt to isolate a **pool** of net disposable income available after adjustment for each spouse's child support obligations. This is done by deducting or backing out their respective **contributions to child support**. The details of these calculations are set out in Chapter 8, along with several examples.

**Duration** under this basic *with child support* formula also reflects the underlying parental partnership rationale. Initial orders are **indefinite (duration not specified)**, subject to the usual process of review or variation. The formula does, however, provide a **durational range** which is intended to structure the process of review and variation and to limit the cumulative duration of spousal support. The durational limits under this formula can be thought of as "soft" time limits. There are two tests for duration and whichever produces the longer duration at each end of the range is to be employed:

- First is the **length-of-marriage** test, which is modelled on the duration under the *without child support* formula, i.e. one-half to one year of support for every year of marriage, and which will likely govern for most marriages of ten years or more.
- Second is the **age-of-children** test. The lower end of the durational range is until the youngest child starts full-time school. The upper end of the durational range is until the last or youngest child finishes high school. This test will typically apply to marriages of less than ten years.

**Shared and split custody** situations require slight variations in the computation of individual net disposable income, as the backing out of child support obligations is a bit more complicated. There is also a different, hybrid formula for cases where **spousal support is paid by the custodial parent**. Under this formula, the spouses' Guidelines incomes are reduced by the grossed-up amount of child support (actual or notional) and then the *without child support* formula is applied to determine amount and duration. Finally, there is one more hybrid formula for those spousal support cases where the child support for **adult children** is determined under section 3(2)(b) of the *Child Support Guidelines*.

The formulas provide ranges for the amount and duration of spousal support. The location of a precise amount or duration within those ranges — what we refer to as **using the ranges** — will be driven by the **factors** detailed in Chapter 9: the strength of any compensatory claim; the recipient's needs; the age, number, need and standard of living of any children; the needs and ability to pay or the payor; work incentives for the payor; property division and debts; and self-sufficiency incentives.

**Restructuring** allows the amount and duration under the formulas to be traded off against each other, so long as the overall value of the restructured award remains within the total or global amounts generated by the formula when amount and duration are combined. Chapter 10 shows how restructuring can be used in three different ways:

- to **front-end load** awards by increasing the amount beyond the formula's range and shortening duration;
- to **extend duration** beyond the formula's range by lowering the monthly amount; or
- to formulate a **lump sum** by combining amount and duration.

**"Ceilings" and "floors"** in Chapter 11 define the boundaries of the typical incomes to which the formulas can be applied. The **ceiling** is the income level for the payor spouse above which any formula gives way to discretion, set here at **a gross annual income for the payor of $350,000**. The **floor** is the income level for the payor below which no support is usually paid, here set at **$20,000**. To avoid a cliff effect, there is an **exception** for cases where the payor spouse's gross income is **more than $20,000 but less than $30,000**, where spousal support may not be awarded or may be reduced below the low end of the range. An additional **exception** is also necessary, to allow an award of spousal support **below the income floor** in particular cases.

Any formula, even with restructuring, will have its limits and there will always be exceptional cases. Because the Guidelines are only advisory, departures are always possible on a case-by-case basis where the formula outcomes are inappropriate. The Guidelines do contain a short list of **exceptions** in Chapter 12, intended to identify common categories of departures:

- compelling financial circumstances in the interim period;
- debt payment;
- prior support obligations;
- illness and disability;
- the compensatory exception in short marriages without children;
- reapportionment of property (British Columbia);
- basic needs/hardship under the *without child support* and *custodial payor* formulas;
- non-taxable payor income;
- non-primary parent to fulfil parenting role under the *custodial payor* formula;
- special needs of a child; and
- section 15.3 for small amounts and inadequate compensation under the *with child support* formula.

Self-sufficiency is a central concept in the law of spousal support and Chapter 13 draws together in one place all the aspects of the Advisory Guidelines that promote self-sufficiency, one of the objectives of the *Divorce Act*.

The formulas are intended to apply to initial orders and to the negotiation of initial agreements, including interim arrangements. Given the uncertain state of the current law, it is not possible to make the Advisory Guidelines apply to the full range of issues that can arise on **variation and review**, issues that are considered in Chapter 14. The Advisory Guidelines can be applied on applications to reduce spousal support because of changes in income, for example, when the payor spouse's income goes down or the recipient spouse's income goes up (or ought to have gone up). In some cases, one spouse may wish to apply to vary to **cross over** between the two formulas, mostly in longer marriages once the children are no longer dependent, where *without child support* formula produces higher ranges.

More difficult issues arise where the payor's income increases or the recipient's income is reduced after separation. The most the formula can do is to establish an upper limit upon any increase in spousal support in such cases. At the present time, no formula can be constructed to resolve issues around the recipient spouse's remarriage or re-partnering, or subsequent children.

Quebec has different guidelines for determining child support, which have an impact on spousal support determinations. The application of the Advisory Guidelines to *Divorce Act* cases in Quebec raises special issues that are dealt with in Chapter 15.

## INTRODUCTION

In 2001 the federal Department of Justice identified the need for a project to explore the possibility of developing some form of advisory spousal support guidelines. The aim of the project was to bring more certainty and predictability to the determination of spousal support under the *Divorce Act*.[1] The project was a response to growing concerns expressed by lawyers, judges, mediators and the public about the lack of certainty and predictability in the current law of spousal support, creating daily dilemmas in advising clients, and negotiating, litigating or – in the case of judges – deciding spousal support issues. We were retained to direct that project.

In January 2005, the Draft Proposal was released, setting out a comprehensive set of Spousal Support Advisory Guidelines. These Advisory Guidelines have been used by spouses, lawyers, mediators and judges across Canada over the past three years. We received detailed comments and feedback on the Draft Proposal. What you hold in your hands is the final version of the Spousal Support Advisory Guidelines. It is the revised version of the earlier Draft Proposal and is now the authoritative document on the Spousal Support Advisory Guidelines. The Draft Proposal is now only of historical interest.

The term "guidelines" inevitably brings to mind the *Federal Child Support Guidelines*, enacted in 1997.[2] We need to emphasize at the beginning that this comparison must be resisted. This project **does not involve formal, legislative reform.** Unlike the federal, provincial and territorial child support guidelines, these Advisory Guidelines are not legislated. They are instead intended to be **informal guidelines** that operate on an **advisory** basis only, **within the existing legislative framework. They do not have the binding force of law** and are applied only to the extent that lawyers and judges find them useful. They are guidelines in the true sense of the word. We have called them *Advisory* Guidelines to differentiate them from the child support guidelines.

### Nature and status of the Advisory Guidelines

The Advisory Guidelines are intended as a practical tool to assist in determinations of spousal support **within the current legal framework** – to operate primarily as a starting point in negotiations and settlements. The project was not directed at a theoretical re-ordering of the law of spousal support or at creating a new model of spousal support. The formulas we have developed are intended as proxies for the spousal support objectives found in the *Divorce Act* as elaborated upon by the Supreme Court of Canada. Our goal was to develop guidelines that would achieve appropriate results over a wide range of typical cases.

Given the informal nature of these advisory guidelines, they have been developed with the recognition that they must be broadly consistent with current support outcomes while also providing some much needed structure and consistency to this area of law – a not insignificant challenge. As informal guidelines, they **do not address entitlement**, but deal only with the amount and duration of support **once entitlement has been established.** In the same vein they confer **no power to re-open existing spousal support agreements** beyond what exists under current law.

---

[1] *Divorce Act*, R.S.C. 1995, c. 3 (2nd Supp).

[2] The *Federal Child Support Guidelines*, SOR/ 97-175, which were enacted as regulations pursuant to the *Divorce Act, ibid*, came into force in May, 1997. All provinces and territories save Quebec (where a different guidelines model applies) have adopted child support guidelines that are either identical or similar to the *Federal Child Support Guidelines*. The Guidelines are based on a percentage-of-income formula.

## Content of the Advisory Guidelines

The Advisory Guidelines are based on what is called "income sharing". Contrary to popular conception, income sharing does not necessarily mean equal sharing. It simply means that spousal support is determined as a percentage of spousal incomes. The percentages can vary according to a number of factors. The Advisory Guidelines offer two basic formulas that base spousal support on spousal incomes and other relevant factors such as the presence or absence of dependent children, and the length of the marriage. The formulas deal with the amount (sometimes referred to as quantum) and duration of spousal support once entitlement to support has been established. The formulas generate ranges of outcomes, rather than precise figures for amount and duration, which may be restructured by trading off amount against duration.

The Guidelines are advisory only and thus always allow for departures from the outcomes generated by the formulas on a case-by-case basis where they are not appropriate. While we have tried to specify exceptions to assist the parties and the courts in framing and assessing any departures from the formulas' ranges, they are not exhaustive of the grounds for departure. There is still considerable room for the exercise of discretion under the Advisory Guidelines but it will be exercised within a much more defined structure than existed before – one with clearer starting points. Budgets, which are currently the primary tool in spousal support determinations, increasingly play a reduced and less central role.

## Documents accompanying this final version

There are two documents being released together:

1.  this completely-revised final version of the reference document, entitled "The Spousal Support Advisory Guidelines"; and
2.  a brief "Report on Revisions" which notes the changes made from the Draft Proposal to this final version.

Still to come, in the near future, is an "Operating Manual", which will provide a summary step-by-step guide to the Advisory Guidelines, cross-referenced to the final version.

## Structure of this final version

While much of the content of this final version has not changed from the Draft Proposal, we have moved it around, by changing the structure and presentation. Some issues that seemed important at the time of the Draft Proposal are no longer issues, and thus some parts of the Draft Proposal have been removed or shortened. Now that the Advisory Guidelines are better known and widely used, we have highlighted some topics that are often forgotten, topics like entitlement, using the ranges, restructuring, exceptions and self-sufficiency. We have also drawn on the experience with the Advisory Guidelines in the three years since the release of the Draft Proposal in explaining the operation of the scheme.

Before we reach the actual content of the Spousal Support Advisory Guidelines, there are many preliminary matters that must be addressed so that the Advisory Guidelines can be properly understood. In Chapter 1 we provide some necessary background to the project. We review the current legal framework for spousal support – the framework within which the Advisory Guidelines operate – and also discuss the problems within the current law that led to this guidelines initiative.

In Chapter 2 we discuss in more detail the nature of this project, the challenges it raised, and the process by which the Advisory Guidelines were developed

With Chapter 3, we move into the actual substance of the Advisory Guidelines, providing an overview of their basic structure.

Chapters 4 and 5 deal with two critical threshold questions to be considered before reaching the Advisory Guidelines: is there entitlement to spousal support? and do the Advisory Guidelines apply in this case? The issues of entitlement and the basis for entitlement arise, not only at this threshold point, but also throughout the application of the Guidelines.

Chapter 6 highlights another critical step in the Guidelines analysis, the determination of the incomes of the spouses.

Chapter 7 deals with the first of the two basic formulas around which the Advisory Guidelines are structured — the *without child support* formula, which applies in cases where there are no dependent children and hence no concurrent child support obligation.

Chapter 8 details the other basic formula — the *with child support* formula, which applies in cases where there are dependent children.

Chapter 9 focuses upon how these formula ranges can be used, and the factors that can affect the location of the precise amount and duration within the ranges. Chapter 10 then takes the next step, how the formula ranges can be restructured, by trading off amount against duration, to produce larger amounts or longer durations or lump sum amounts.

Chapter 11 explains how to apply the ceilings and floors, the upper and lower boundaries of the range of incomes for which the formulas operate. Further, this chapter offers guidance on the determination of spousal support in cases above the ceiling or around the floor.

Chapter 12 sets out the exceptions to the use of the formula ranges. The exceptions have been ignored too often in practice and we have therefore given them greater emphasis in this final version. Some of the older exceptions have been clarified, while new ones have been added.

In Chapter 13, we have gathered together all the aspects of the Advisory Guidelines that serve to promote self-sufficiency. Self-sufficiency is an important and difficult issue in the law of spousal support and we thought it deserved a separate chapter in the final version.

Chapter 14 looks at the subsequent uses of the Advisory Guidelines in the process of variation and review. The Advisory Guidelines may have more limited application at these later stages, as issues of continuing entitlement often arise.

Chapter 15 discusses the application of the Advisory Guidelines to divorce cases in Quebec, and some of the adjustments that had to be made for Quebec cases

At the end of the document, after the conclusion, there can be found a glossary of terms that offers a handy reference point for many of the terms used in this document. Some of these terms will be familiar to family lawyers and judges but not to other readers; others are new terms specific to these Spousal Support Advisory Guidelines.

# 1 BACKGROUND — THE CURRENT LAW OF SPOUSAL SUPPORT

## 1.1 The Legislative Framework

Spousal support, when sought in the context of a divorce, is governed by the federal *Divorce Act*. There are also provincial and territorial laws that govern spousal support outside the divorce context, applying to unmarried couples and to married couples who have separated but are not applying for a divorce. The statutory provisions are an important starting point in understanding the law around spousal support; they provide the framework within which the proposed advisory guidelines will operate. The Advisory Guidelines do nothing to alter that legislative framework.

Federal and provincial/territorial spousal support legislation in Canada tends to take the form of relatively open-ended provisions incorporating a variety of factors and objectives. Much room is left for judicial discretion in the interpretation and application of the legislation. Judicial interpretations in turn guide lawyers and mediators advising clients negotiating spousal support settlements.

The specific focus of this project has been on developing informal guidelines to assist in the determination of the amount and duration of spousal support under the *Divorce Act*. The current *Divorce Act*, enacted in 1985, attempts to provide guidance for spousal support determinations by setting out, in s. 15.2 (6), four objectives for spousal support:

> **15.2 (6)** An order ... that provides for the support of a spouse should
>
> 1. recognize any economic advantages or disadvantages to the spouses arising from the marriage or its breakdown;
>
> 2. apportion between the spouses any financial consequences arising from the care of any child of the marriage over and above the obligation apportioned between the spouses pursuant to subsection (8) [i.e. through child support];
>
> 3. relieve any economic hardship of the spouses arising from the breakdown of the marriage; and
>
> 4. in so far as practicable, promote the economic self-sufficiency of each spouse within a reasonable period of time.

In addition, s. 15.2 (4) lists certain factors to be taken into account in making support orders for a spouse:

> **15.2 (4)** In making an order . . . the court shall take into consideration the condition, means, needs and other circumstances of each spouse including
>
> 1. the length of time the spouses cohabited;
>
> 2. the functions performed by the spouse during cohabitation; and
>
> 3. any order, agreement or arrangement relating to support of the spouse or child.

Finally, s. 15.2 (5) is more specific, indicating one factor that may *not* be taken into account — spousal misconduct:

> **15.2 (5)** In making an order [for spousal support or an interim order] the court shall not take into consideration any misconduct of a spouse in relation to the marriage.

Provincial/territorial support law is governed by distinctive statutory regimes. However, in practice there is much overlap between federal and provincial/territorial support laws. The leading Supreme Court of Canada decisions on spousal support, *Moge* and *Bracklow*, which will be discussed in more detail below, articulated a broad conceptual framework for spousal support that has been relied upon in decisions under both provincial/territorial and federal legislation. Indeed *Bracklow*, which combined claims under both the *Divorce Act* and provincial legislation, made no real distinction between the two.

**The Advisory Guidelines were specifically developed for use under the federal** *Divorce Act*. However, given the overlap between the spousal support regimes in practice, it is not surprising that lawyers and judges have used the Advisory Guidelines under provincial/

territorial support legislation. It is important that such use take account of the distinctive features of these statutes. In Chapter 5 on application, below, we discuss in more detail some of the specific issues that arise in the application of the Advisory Guidelines to support determinations under provincial/territorial spousal support laws.

## 1.2 Judicial Interpretation[3]

In two important decisions, *Moge v. Moge*[4] in 1992 and *Bracklow v. Bracklow*,[5] in 1999, the Supreme Court of Canada has attempted to clarify the general principles that structure our law of spousal support. These decisions, together with the legislation, constitute the current legal framework for spousal support. Our proposed advisory guidelines do nothing to displace these decisions, but are rather an attempt to develop formulas to better implement the principles these decisions recognize.

The combined effect of these two decisions is a very broad basis for spousal support under the *Divorce Act*. Both *Moge* and *Bracklow* can be seen as responses to, and rejections of, the very limited view of spousal support that had emerged from the Supreme Court of Canada's 1987 *Pelech* trilogy[6] which had emphasized the importance of finality and promoting a clean break between divorced spouses. In the wake of *Pelech*, spousal support came to be viewed as a transitional or rehabilitative remedy. Time-limited spousal support orders came to be the norm, even in cases of long, traditional marriages.

In the ground-breaking *Moge* decision in 1992, the Supreme Court of Canada clearly rejected the *Pelech* trilogy and the clean-break model of spousal support. The Court emphasized that all four support objectives in the 1985 *Divorce Act* had to be given weight and that the clean-break model of spousal support unduly emphasized only one of those objectives — the promotion of spousal self-sufficiency after divorce — at the expense of all the others. Former spouses were obligated to make reasonable efforts to maximize their earning capacity and contribute to their own support but the Court recognized that some spouses, despite their best efforts, would not be able to become self-sufficient. In the Court's view, the clean-break model went too far in deeming spouses to be self-sufficient when they were not. In *Moge* the Court endorsed an expansive compensatory basis for spousal support, portraying its purpose as the equitable distribution between the spouses of the *economic* consequences of the marriage — both its economic advantages and disadvantages. While the Court recognized that many different circumstances could give rise to compensatory claims, the decision focused on the most common situation — where a spouse has sacrificed labour force participation to care for children, both during the marriage and after marriage breakdown. Under the compensatory approach of *Moge*, spousal

---

[3] For a more detailed review of the judicial interpretation of the *Divorce Act*'s spousal support provisions see Carol Rogerson, "The Canadian Law of Spousal Support" (2004), 38 *Family Law Quarterly* 69; Carol Rogerson, "Spousal Support Post-*Bracklow*: The Pendulum Swings Again?" (2001), 19 *Canadian Family Law Quarterly* 185; Rollie Thompson "Everything is Broken: No More Spousal Support Principles?" unpublished paper prepared for the Continuing Legal Education Society of British Columbia Family Law Conference, July 12-13, 2001 available online at www. cle.bc.ca. The Background Paper, discussed at note 11 below and accompanying text, also reviews the current law of spousal support.

[4] *Moge v. Moge*, [1992] 3 S.C.R. 813.

[5] *Bracklow v. Bracklow*, [1999] 1 S.C.R. 420.

[6] The three cases were *Pelech v. Pelech*, [1987] 1 S.C.R. 801, *Richardson v. Richardson*, [1987] 1 S.C.R. 857 and *Caron v. Caron*, [1987] 1 S.C.R. 892. All three cases were decided under the earlier, 1968 *Divorce Act* and all three also involved separation agreements in which the former wives had waived their rights to ongoing spousal support. In each case the Court refused to override the agreement and the application for spousal support was dismissed.

support came to be understood primarily as a form of compensation for the loss of economic opportunity — or in the language of the *Divorce Act*, the economic disadvantage — resulting from the roles adopted during the marriage.

The compensatory principle from *Moge* continues to play a significant role in structuring our law of spousal support. However, when lower courts attempted to implement the compensatory principle, which the Supreme Court of Canada had presented at a high level of generality, they ran into some difficulties on both the practical and theoretical fronts.

On the practical front, the compensatory principle is difficult to implement. Establishing a support claim requires, in principle, individualized evidence of earning capacity loss. As the Supreme Court of Canada itself acknowledged in *Moge*, providing this form of expert evidence can be costly. Evidence of earning capacity loss can also be difficult to obtain and somewhat hypothetical, particularly in cases of long marriages where the spouse claiming spousal support had no established career before assuming the role of homemaker. Difficult questions of causation can also arise as to why a spouse remained out of the labour force or chose lowly paid employment. On a practical level, effective implementation of the compensatory principle requires the development of proxy measures of economic loss that will inevitably involve some sacrifice of accuracy and theoretical purity.

After *Moge*, Canadian courts showed no enthusiasm for reliance upon expert economic evidence documenting loss of earning capacity.[7] Instead, "need" — the traditional conceptual anchor of spousal support — became a convenient proxy measure of economic disadvantage. A spouse in economic need was presumed to be suffering economic disadvantage as a result of the marriage; conversely, a spouse not in need was presumed not to have suffered any economic disadvantage as a result of the marriage. The use of need and standard of living as proxy measures for loss of opportunity was expressly endorsed by Bastarache J. A. (as he then was) in *Ross v. Ross*, a New Brunswick case involving a long traditional marriage:

> It is in cases where it is not possible to determine the extent of the economic loss of the disadvantaged spouse that the Court will consider need and standard of living as the primary criteria, together with the ability to pay of the other spouse.[8]

At least in longer marriages, need came to be measured against the marital standard of living, a measure suggested by the Supreme Court of Canada itself in *Moge*:

> As marriage should be regarded as a joint endeavour, the longer the relationship endures, the closer the economic union, the greater will be the presumptive claim to equal standards of living upon its dissolution.[9]

The rule that emerged in many lower court decisions was that the goal of spousal support, *after a long marriage*, was to provide the support claimant with a reasonable standard of living judged in light of the marital standard of living. In some cases, as in *Ross*, the principle for long marriages has been expressed as providing similar lifestyles or roughly equivalent standards of living for each of the spouses.

---

[7] After the Ontario Court of Appeal's refusal to base an award on such evidence in *Elliot v. Elliot* (1993), 48 R.F.L. (3d) 237 (Ont. C.A.) it virtually disappeared from spousal support cases.
[8] *Ross v. Ross* (1995), 16 R.F.L. (4th) 1 (N.B.C.A.) at 7.
[9] See *Moge, supra* note 4 at 870.

On the theoretical front, the post-*Moge* case law also revealed concerns with the limitations of a pure compensatory analysis that would confine the basis for spousal support to economic loss caused by the roles adopted during the marriage. Some judges shifted the compensatory focus to the economic *advantages* of the marriage in the form of the earning capacity the payor spouse was able to maintain and enhance. Other judges found the compensatory framework itself too restrictive. Compensatory theories narrowed the basis for entitlement. This was something many judges resisted. Some judges read the *Divorce Act* spousal support objectives more broadly, focussing on the section referring to the relief of economic hardship caused by the marriage breakdown. Others read *Moge* as a general directive to ameliorate the post-divorce impoverishment of former spouses. The most serious limitations of a compensatory analysis arose in cases involving ill or disabled spouses whose economic needs were not related to marital roles and who could not claim spousal support based on losses or gains in earning capacity during the marriage.

The Supreme Court of Canada directly addressed these limitations of the compensatory principle in its 1999 decision in *Bracklow*. In that case the Court ruled that there is also a non-compensatory basis for spousal support under the *Divorce Act* based on "need alone." Thus a former spouse has an obligation to pay spousal support if the other spouse is experiencing economic need at the point of marriage breakdown, even when that need does not arise from the roles adopted during the marriage. The Court based this obligation on a view of marriage as a relationship involving mutual obligations and complex interdependencies that may be difficult to unravel when the marriage breaks down. The Court also spoke of marriage as involving the assumption of basic social obligations, reflecting the view that primary responsibility for support of a needy partner rests upon the family rather than the state. The Court went on to say that the extent of a former spouse's obligation to meet his or her former partner's post-divorce needs would be dependent upon many factors, including the length of the relationship, the way the parties had structured their relationship, ability to pay, and the re-partnering or remarriage of the former spouses.

*Bracklow* clearly expanded the basis of the spousal support obligation under the *Divorce Act* to include need as well as compensation. However, in the course of doing so the decision increased the level of uncertainty about the nature and extent of the spousal support obligation, well beyond what had existed after *Moge*. The Supreme Court of Canada failed to provide a definition of "need," leaving open the question of whether it meant an inability to provide a basic standard of living or whether it should be assessed in the context of the marital standard of living. After *Bracklow*, many argued that any spouse who experienced a significant decline in standard of living after marriage breakdown was entitled to spousal support.

Even more significantly, *Bracklow* emphasized the highly discretionary, individualized nature of spousal support decisions. The Court was clear that the *Divorce Act* endorses no single theory of spousal support and must retain flexibility to allow judges to respond appropriately to the diverse forms that marital relationships can take. The Court presented spousal support determinations as first and foremost exercises of discretion by trial judges who were required to "balance" the multiple support objectives and factors under the *Divorce Act* and apply them in the context of the facts of particular cases. One of the main messages of *Bracklow* was that there were no rules in spousal support.

## 1.3 The Problem of Spousal Support and the Need for Guidelines

The culture of spousal support after *Bracklow* was one that emphasized individualized decision making and an absence of rules. Multiple theories of spousal support competed with each other while, on the ground, spousal support cases were negotiated and argued under an amorphous needs-and-means framework dominated by budgets. "Need" means many different things to different people and many different theories of spousal support can be couched in the language of need. The guidelines project sprang from the growing concern expressed by lawyers and judges that the highly discretionary nature of the current law of spousal support had created an unacceptable degree of uncertainty and unpredictability.[10]

Similar fact situations could generate a wide variation in results. Individual judges were provided with little concrete guidance in determining spousal support outcomes and their subjective perceptions of fair outcomes played a large role in determining the spousal support ultimately ordered. Appeals were often be of little help because appeal courts frequently dispose of appeals with little explanation, deferring to trial judges on issues of quantum and duration. Lawyers in turn had difficulty predicting outcomes, thus impeding their ability to advise clients and to engage in cost-effective settlement negotiations.

And for those without legal representation or in weak bargaining positions, support claims were simply not pursued. Despite a very broad basis for entitlement under the existing law, many spouses did not claim spousal support, being unwilling to engage in the difficult and costly process required.

More generally, the uncertainty and unpredictability that pervaded the law of spousal support was undermining the legitimacy of the spousal support obligation. The widely differing understandings of the nature of the spousal support obligation generated concerns about unfair outcomes at both ends of the spectrum. In some cases awards were perceived as too low, in others as unjustifiably high.

The Advisory Guidelines were a response to these concerns. They were developed for the purpose of bringing more certainty and predictability to spousal support determinations. They incorporate the basic principles of compensation and need that the Supreme Court of Canada has identified as the bases for spousal support under the *Divorce Act* but provide a more structured way of implementing those principles through formulas based on income sharing, i.e. formulas based on sharing specified percentages of spousal incomes.

## 1.4 Why Guidelines Now?

Spousal support guidelines rely upon mathematical formulas that determine spousal support as a percentage of spousal incomes. When spousal support guidelines were considered in the past, the idea was rejected as both impossible and undesirable. The conclusion was that it would be impossible to draft guidelines with sufficient flexibility to respond to the diversity of marriages and the multiple objectives of spousal support. The disadvantages of guidelines, in terms of a loss of flexibility, were seen to outweigh any advantages in terms of efficient dispute resolution. In our view, when the Advisory Guidelines project commenced in 2001, the time was ripe for reconsideration. What had changed?

First and foremost, the law of spousal support had become more unstructured, more discretionary and more uncertain over time, particularly since 1999 in the wake of *Bracklow*. After *Moge* and prior to *Bracklow*, there had been some hope that a principled approach to spousal support was developing through the case law. It subsequently became clear that the

---

[10] The past tense is used to describe the problems in the law of spousal support that the Advisory Guidelines were intended to address. Since their release in draft form in January of 2005, the Advisory Guidelines have already had an impact in reducing the degree of uncertainty and unpredictability in the current law of spousal support. The use of the past tense should not be taken as suggesting, however, that these problems have been eliminated.

normal process of judicial development had effectively come to a halt. In that situation, spouses, lawyers and judges began to find attractive the greater certainty and predictability that guidelines would bring, even guidelines that were not perfect.

Second, since 1997 experience with child support guidelines, both at the federal and provincial/territorial levels, had changed the legal culture. Their formulaic approach had accustomed lawyers and judges to the systemic advantages of *average* justice rather than individualized justice, to determining support without budgets and to the concept of income sharing after divorce.

Third, spousal support advisory guidelines were not simply an abstract concept any more. Some American jurisdictions had successfully experimented with such guidelines for more than a decade, as explained in the Background Paper that was prepared for this project.[11] Most recently, the influential American Law Institute (ALI) had recommended a formulaic approach to spousal support as part of its comprehensive rethinking of the law of family dissolution, a process begun in the 1990s and culminating in the Institute's final report in 2002.[12] Some American jurisdictions had begun to implement the ALI guidelines. Greater experience with guidelines was yielding more sophisticated models.

Finally, we could see the beginnings of formulaic approaches to the determination of spousal support in the current law. With the greater prevalence of computer software, especially since the *Federal Child Support Guidelines* came into effect in 1997, lawyers and judges could have readily available information on net disposable incomes or monthly cash flow, tax calculations and household standards of living. Armed with this information, some courts began looking to income sharing and standards of living, rather than budgets, to resolve spousal support issues.

All of these changes made spouses, lawyers, mediators and judges more interested in spousal support guidelines. In weighing the advantages and disadvantages of such guidelines, more saw the balance tipping in favour of some type of spousal support advisory guidelines.

As we embarked upon this project we identified four advantages of a scheme of spousal support advisory guidelines. These became the objectives of the project:

1. *To reduce conflict and to encourage settlement.* All other financial matters on family dissolution are now governed by rules — property division, pensions, child support. Spousal support is the last remaining pool of unfettered discretion. It is also typically the last financial issue to be resolved. Spousal support thus becomes the flashpoint for unhappiness with all the other financial rules, as well as for any remaining bitterness between spouses. Advisory guidelines can limit the range of results and constrain the issues and information required, thereby encouraging settlement and damping down some of the conflict between the parties.

2. *To create consistency and fairness.* When spousal support is determined in an excessively discretionary context, similar fact situations can generate wide variations in results. Moreover, the widely differing understandings of the nature of the spousal support obligation generate concerns about unfairness at both ends of the spectrum — in some cases awards may be too high, and in others too low. Advisory guidelines should create more consistent treatment of spouses who are in similar circumstances

---

[11] Carol Rogerson, *Developing Spousal Support Guidelines in Canada: Beginning the Discussion* (December, 2002), available on the Department of Justice website at: http://canada.justice.gc.ca/en/dept/pub/spousal/index.html. The Background Paper is discussed in Chapter 2.

[12] American Law Institute, *Principles of the Law of Family Dissolution: Analysis and Recommendations* (LexisNexis, 2002). The recommendations with respect to spousal support are found in Chapter 5, "Compensatory Spousal Payments."

as well as more open explanations of how those outcomes were reached. This can enhance the legitimacy and perceived fairness of spousal support awards, as has been the case with the child support amounts.

3. *To reduce the costs and improve the efficiency of the process.* In financial matters, it is ultimately dollars weighed against dollars, i.e. the cost of legal fees and disbursements weighed against the money gained or lost in support or property. Advisory guidelines can provide a starting point from which the parties can each decide whether further negotiation or litigation is warranted. Moreover, some spouses who previously would have given up on seeking spousal support because of the costs and unpredictable results of the highly discretionary regime will be more likely to obtain support if advisory guidelines are in place. Guidelines are even more important where one or both parties are unrepresented.

4. *To provide a basic structure for further judicial elaboration.* Advisory guidelines can act to encourage or more accurately, kick start, the normal process of legal development in an area of judicial discretion. Under the current discretionary law, that process had nearly ground to a halt. Advisory guidelines can give basic structure and shape to the law, with room left for lawyers and courts to adjust, modify, and identify possible new exceptions, etc. By their very existence, advisory guidelines will create pressure to give reasons for any departures in negotiations or decisions.

**The goal of the project was not to raise the current levels of support over the broad run of cases.** Greater consistency under a scheme of advisory guidelines would mean that some spouses would see higher support awards and others would see lower awards. We did recognize that a scheme of advisory guidelines would likely lead to more frequent spousal support awards as spouses who previously would have given up on seeking spousal support because of the costs and unpredictable results of the highly discretionary regime would find it easier to claim spousal support.

We move next, in Chapter 2, to a more detailed description of the Advisory Guidelines project, including a discussion of the nature of the guidelines developed and the process that was used to develop them.

## 2 THE GUIDELINES PROJECT

### 2.1 The Nature of the Guidelines: Informal and Advisory

There are many preconceptions about what spousal support guidelines are and how they work. Any talk of spousal support guidelines immediately brings to mind the *Federal Child Support Guidelines*. As we emphasized in the introduction, this comparison should be resisted. These Advisory Guidelines are very different.

Unlike the *Federal Child Support Guidelines*, the Spousal Support **Advisory Guidelines** do not involve formal legislative reform. They have not been legislated by the federal government. They are intended to be **informal** guidelines that operate on an **advisory** basis only, within the existing legislative framework.

We know that this concept of informal guidelines is one that many have difficulty understanding initially. Yet think of the early days of the *Federal Child Support Guidelines* before they were formally enacted. Many judges and lawyers used the draft proposed tables informally to assist in the determination of child support. Think also of the normal process of legal development and the ways that various presumptions can develop over time to structure judicial discretion. Such presumptions were starting to develop in the post-*Moge* law of spousal support, but since *Bracklow,* that process has broken down. The Advisory Guidelines project can be thought of as an attempt to facilitate the normal process of legal development by providing a broad structure that can then be adjusted over time as it is tested by individual cases.

The inspiration for the process chosen for the development of these Advisory Guidelines came from the experience of many of the American jurisdictions that have adopted spousal support guidelines. In the American context, spousal support guidelines have generally been the product of bench and bar committees of local bar associations. They were created with the intention of reflecting local practice and providing a more certain framework to guide settlement negotiations. While some of the American guidelines subsequently evolved into legislation, at the initial stages they were informal.

A similar process was adopted for the development of these Advisory Guidelines. They have been created through a process that involves working with judges, lawyers and mediators who have expertise in family law. The goal of the process was to articulate informal guidelines based on emerging patterns embedded in current practice. As for their application, the Advisory Guidelines do not have the force of law. They are advisory in nature, and they acquire their force through their usefulness.

The federal Department of Justice has supported the development of the Advisory Guidelines by providing financial support, communicating information on the project, participating in the discussions with the working group of family law experts, and keeping provincial and territorial governments informed.

We have called this process for developing the Advisory Guidelines one of working "from the ground up", in contrast to the "from the top down" process of formal legislative reform. The process, described in more detail below, was a long one involving many different stages. But before we get to that, we would like to say a bit more about the general nature of this project and some of the challenges it has raised.


## 2.2 The Challenges of the Project

### 2.2.1 Theory and practice

As stated in the introduction, this project was not directed at a theoretical re-ordering of the law of spousal support. Its aims were practical rather than theoretical — to provide a practical tool to assist family lawyers, mediators and judges who are confronted daily with the dilemma of determining appropriate levels of spousal support, as well as divorcing and separating spouses. As *Bracklow* has made clear, the *Divorce Act* does not mandate any one model of spousal support. We kept this in mind in constructing these guidelines. Reflecting current practice meant reflecting a wide range of competing views of spousal support. No one theory or model or ideology or formula could be used. The formulas, described in more detail below, incorporate elements of different theories. In addition, the exceptions recognize alternate or subsidiary models of spousal support. There is no theoretical purity in the guidelines we have constructed — they are the product of much compromise, compromises already found in the law of spousal support.

But increased consistency and predictability — the goals of the project — do require structure, even if it does not come from theoretical purity. The project was premised on the view that patterns and structure were beginning to emerge in the law, at least in a range of typical cases — the beginnings of guidelines.[13] But in the current culture of spousal support, these were often

---

[13] See for example V. Jennifer Mackinnon and E. Jane Murray, "Magical Mystery Tour: Seeking Greater Consistency in Spousal Support Awards" (2004), 22 *Canadian Family Law Quarterly* 215.

not discussed or articulated or openly acknowledged within the family law system. This project has attempted to build upon and facilitate those developments.

### 2.2.2 Reflecting current practice, changing current practice

Admittedly, there has been a central tension in the project between reflecting practice and changing practice. As informal rules of practice without the force of law, the Guidelines had to reflect current practice and could not stray too far from existing results over all. That said, there was also much in current practice that was inconsistent, arbitrary and hard to explain. The Advisory Guidelines were developed because of their potential to constrain some of those current practices. In building upon current practice the project has drawn on best practices or emerging trends. The Advisory Guidelines incorporate and reflect much of the current practice of spousal support while at the same time seeking greater consistency and logic in the results.

### 2.2.3 National guidelines and local spousal support cultures

Early on we faced the problem of squaring national guidelines with local and regional patterns of support. To the extent that local variations reflect higher or lower incomes, income-based guidelines such as these can adjust for that. The ranges provided by the Advisory Guidelines also leave some scope for adjustment towards local patterns and local conditions. It was also our hope that the Advisory Guidelines might lead to some cross-fertilisation of ideas amongst regions, forcing reconsideration of some local practices. The *Divorce Act* is a national statute and it can be argued that the spousal support received in one part of the country should not differ significantly from that received in another. We did worry, however, about whether regional and local variations were so great that any national advisory guidelines based on current practice would be of limited usefulness and that the only solution might lie in "regional" or "provincial" guidelines.

In the three years since the release of the Draft Proposal we have found that by and large the ranges generated by the Advisory Guidelines are able to accommodate the variations in local and regional practices. Some parts of the country inhabit the high end of the ranges, and some the low end, but lawyers and judges have generally found that some part of the "national" ranges is "about right" for their area. In the course of gathering feedback, we did receive comments about particular fact situations and specific subsets of cases, where the ranges seemed "high" or "low" in particular localities or regions. Some of the modest revisions that we have made introduce adjustments to accommodate these fact situations.

### 2.3 The Development of the Guidelines and the Release of the Draft Proposal

The first stage of the Advisory Guidelines project, which commenced in September 2001, involved the preparation of a lengthy background paper by Professor Rogerson: *Developing Spousal Support Guidelines in Canada: Beginning the Discussion* (December, 2002) (the "Background Paper"). The paper and the project were first discussed at the National Family Law Program in Kelowna, B.C. in July 2002, with the paper being completed in December 2002.

The paper laid the groundwork for exploring the possibility of developing spousal support guidelines. It reviewed in detail the basic building blocks that could be drawn upon in creating guidelines: emerging patterns in the current law, the various theories of spousal support, as well as various models of guidelines that are in effect or proposed in the United States and elsewhere.

The Background Paper also laid out a possible process for the development of guidelines – one of building informal guidelines that would reflect current practice and that would operate on an advisory basis only within the existing legislative framework.

For those who want more detail about the multiple sources that have influenced the crafting of the Advisory Guidelines, we encourage you to read the Background Paper.[14]

The second stage of the project involved working with a small group of family law experts to discuss developing spousal support guidelines. Those discussions were supplemented by some additional small-scale consultations with other groups of lawyers and judges. The federal Department of Justice constituted what was initially a twelve (now thirteen) person Advisory Working Group on Family Law composed of lawyers, judges, and mediators from across the country. Its purpose was to advise the Department on family law matters generally, one of which was the Guidelines project. (A list of the members of the Advisory Working Group can be found in Appendix A.)

We brought to the project a knowledge of the law of spousal support based upon our own research and our comprehensive reading of reported spousal support decisions. Given that the guidelines were to build on current practice and that litigated cases represent only a very small percentage of the spousal support cases that make their way through the family law system, we knew we needed to draw on practice outside the realm of reported cases. We needed the on-the-ground experience of judges, lawyers and mediators who deal with spousal support issues every day and in many different contexts – advice to clients, negotiations with other lawyers, separation agreements, settlement conferences, mediations and collaborative law. The Advisory Working Group essentially played a consultative role. As directors of the project, we had had the responsibility for making the final judgement calls on the contents of the Advisory Guidelines.

We had five meetings with the Advisory Working Group during this stage of the project: the first in Ottawa (February 2003), the second in Montreal (May 2003), the third in Toronto (November 2003), the fourth in Ottawa (April 2004), and the fifth in Toronto (October 2004).

The discussions within the Advisory Working Group were directed first at determining the desirability and feasibility of developing advisory guidelines. Initially, not every member of the Group was supportive of spousal support advisory guidelines, but all were receptive to the general idea. There was also agreement that there were certain patterns in spousal support, at least at the level of outcomes and at least in certain kinds of cases. We then began the process of trying to craft advisory guidelines.

At this stage of the project we had already immersed ourselves in reported spousal support decisions to identify dominant patterns and to begin thinking about framing formulas that might capture those patterns. We had also read decisions on a province-by-province, territory-by-territory basis, looking for local patterns. We had identified certain categories of marriages and certain typical fact situations within them. To enhance our understanding of patterns in practice, we started, within the Advisory Working Group, with concrete fact situations to draw out group members' views of likely outcomes. In reviewing the group's responses we identified where the answers clustered. We used the responses, in addition to our knowledge of reported decisions, to develop mathematical formulas which would generate amounts of spousal support as a percentage of spousal incomes. From these responses we also developed formulas for duration, the concept of restructuring (trading off amount against duration to increase amount or to extend duration) and exceptions to the formulas.

---

[14]  The Background Paper has been translated and is available on the Department of Justice web site at http://canada.justice.gc.ca/en/dept/pub/spousal/index.html and on the Advisory Guidelines web site of the Faculty of Law, University of Toronto, see note 16, below.

We then tested out our formulas, restructuring and exceptions on more fact situations. Finally, to ensure that they were acceptable when compared to current practice, we took the revised formulas, restructuring and exceptions and demonstrated the range of outcomes they would generate. Throughout this process of finalizing the formulas, we continued to read decisions, this time to test whether reported decisions fell within the formula ranges and, if not, whether restructuring or exceptions might account for the outcomes.

Given the practical nature of the project, the primary focus of the process was on support outcomes rather than on appropriate theories of spousal support. While people might often disagree at the level of theory, there can be a fair amount of consistency in actual award levels. We also began with the easiest categories of marriages where patterns in the current law are the clearest and where we expected the greatest consistency in outcomes. We began with long marriages, then moved to short marriages without dependent children, and then to marriages with dependent children. Lastly, we tackled the most difficult category, medium duration marriages without dependent children, where there is the most diversity of outcomes and the least consistency in the current law.

We then began the process of crystallizing the guidelines that were emerging in our discussions within the Advisory Working Group into a comprehensive draft proposal for spousal support advisory guidelines. A "Sneak Preview" of the draft proposal was presented at the National Family Law Program in La Malbaie, Quebec in July 2004. The feedback we received there, combined with further discussions within the Advisory Working Group, resulted in some fine-tuning of the proposal. The final version of the document entitled "Spousal Support Advisory Guidelines: A Draft Proposal" was released in January, 2005.[15] At the time we realized that we could work longer on the Draft Proposal and continue to perfect it, but we were of the view that it was important to begin to broaden the discussion, by a public release of the proposed Advisory Guidelines.

## 2.4 The Second Stage of the Process: Information, Feedback and Revision

With the issuance of the Draft Proposal, the next stage of the process in the guidelines project began — one of discussion, experimentation, feedback and revision. The Draft Proposal was widely circulated amongst family lawyers, mediators and judges and posted on the Department of Justice website. There was also national media coverage of the release of the Draft Proposal.

Although the Advisory Guidelines were presented as a draft, subject to ongoing discussion and revision, it was a comprehensive and detailed draft. We fully expected that lawyers, judges and mediators would begin to use the Advisory Guidelines, despite their draft status, and in fact encouraged them to do so as the best way to test the Guidelines — to find out if they were useful, if they generated generally acceptable results within the current legal framework and to discover their flaws and limitations. We suggested that lawyers, for example, could begin to use the draft Advisory Guidelines to assist in structuring and guiding negotiations about spousal support, either explicitly as a principled basis for negotiation or, more modestly, as a litmus test of the reasonableness of offers or counter-offers derived by budgets or other methods. Judges were informed that they might use the guidelines in a similar fashion. The ranges could provide a check

---

[15] Carol Rogerson and Rollie Thompson, *Spousal Support Advisory Guidelines: A Draft Proposal* (January, 2005), available on-line at: http://www.justice.gc.ca/en/dept/pub/spousal/project/index.html and also on the Advisory Guidelines web site, see note 16, below. The paper was also issued in French under the title *Lignes directrices facultatives en matière de pensions alimentaires pour époux — Ébauche d'une proposition.*

or litmus test to assess the positions of the parties in settlement conferences or in argument in hearings and trials. The Advisory Guidelines could also assist in adjudication, in providing one more way of approaching the discretionary decision to be made in spousal support cases.

The use of the draft Guidelines by lawyers and judges was facilitated by the speedy development and release of software programs to perform the calculations under the Advisory Guidelines' formulas. These software programs found their genesis in the introduction of the *Federal Child Support Guidelines* in 1997 and were already being used by many lawyers and judges prior to the release of the Draft Proposal in 2005. Each of the software suppliers — DIVORCEmate, ChildView and AliForm — incorporated the Spousal Support Advisory Guidelines into their software. We have worked closely with the software suppliers throughout the project and they have been a regular and helpful source of feedback.

After the release of the Draft Proposal we traveled across the country talking to groups of lawyers and judges, groups both large and small. For the most part the sessions were focused on education and information: we explained how the Advisory Guidelines were constructed and how they could be used to improve the consistency and predictability of spousal support awards. We picked up comments and reactions from those who attended these sessions, but many of the early comments reflected lack of knowledge of the Guidelines, or misconceptions or lack of use.

We continued to read reported decisions: to track the courts' use of the Advisory Guidelines, to look at cases where the Guidelines were considered but rejected, to note judicial criticisms and comments, and to refine the exceptions. Even after the release of the Draft Proposal, we continued to read reported spousal support decisions in every province and territory that made no mention of the Advisory Guidelines to determine whether the outcomes were nonetheless consistent with the formulas' ranges.

Monthly updates were prepared, reporting on on-going developments, including judicial decisions considering the Guidelines, feedback that we received in our travels, and any problems or issues that were emerging. These updates were widely disseminated, posted not only on a web site created for the project[16] but also on a number of other websites used by lawyers and judges.[17]

Another meeting of the Advisory Working Group was held in March of 2006 to review on-going developments and discuss emerging issues. By the summer of 2006, a year and half after the release of the Draft Proposal, there was sufficient familiarity and experience with the Advisory Guidelines that it was possible to move into the next phase of the project — one of seeking informed feedback in a structured way with a view to making revisions to the *Draft Proposal*. A new document was prepared to structure that feedback process, the "Issues Paper," a draft of which was released at the National Family Law Program in Kananaskis, Alberta, in July 2006, and the final version in August 2006.[18] The paper identified issues for revision and, on some issues, possible options for revision.

In September of 2006 we began another cross-Canada tour, this time seeking out feedback from lawyers, mediators and judges, in small groups where the discussion could be very focused. We also invited written responses to the Draft Proposal. We received written comments from members of the public, from individual lawyers and from bar associations.[19]

---

[16] This web site is located at the Faculty of Law, University of Toronto: English: http://www.law.utoronto.ca/faculty/rogerson/ssag.html; French: http://www.law.utoronto.ca/faculty/rogerson/ssag_fr.html

[17] These include QuickLaw, WestlaweCARSWELL, the Canadian Bar Association National Family Law Section website, and for judges, the judicial library on Judicom.

[18] Carol Rogerson and Rollie Thompson, "Issues for Discussion: Revising the Spousal Support Advisory Guidelines" (August 2006), posted on the Advisory Guidelines web site, *supra* note 16.

[19] Comments were received from the Canadian Bar Association, National Family Law Section and from the Family Law Committee of the Barreau du Québec.

As a result of the feedback we obtained from these sources, supplemented by our continued reading of a steady stream of reported spousal support decisions, we developed a detailed and practical sense of how the Advisory Guidelines were being used on the ground, and a more finely-tuned understanding of what revisions were necessary. With the assistance of the Advisory Working Group at two further meetings (Toronto, November 2006 and Montreal, June 2007) we began to reflect upon the feedback and work on issues for revision. This document, the final version of the Advisory Guidelines, reflects those revisions.

In the next section we discuss in more detail the responses to the Draft Proposal which have shaped the revision process. As will be shown, in general the Advisory Guidelines have had a very warm reception from lawyers, mediators and judges, and the revisions have involved fine-tuning rather than radical revision.

## 2.5 The Response to the Advisory Guidelines

### 2.5.1 Widespread use of the Advisory Guidelines

The Draft Proposal very quickly achieved one of its goals: the rekindling of serious debate in Canada about the law of spousal support as lawyers, judges and members of the public reacted to its contents. Discussions of developments and issues in spousal support law now invariably focus on the Advisory Guidelines.

Awareness has increased over time, not only within the professional community of family law judges, lawyers, and mediators, but also within the larger population of divorcing spouses trying to navigate their way through the family law system. Over 50,000 copies of the Draft Proposal were downloaded from the Justice web site in the first year after its release. Family law clients now often walk into their lawyers' offices knowing about the Advisory Guidelines. As of February, 2008 there were over 400 judicial decisions from across the country in which the Advisory Guidelines have been considered, including strong endorsements from appellate courts in three provinces: British Columbia, New Brunswick and Ontario. The judicial response to the Guidelines will be discussed in more detail below.

But decided cases are only the tip of the iceberg, as few spousal support cases go to trial. Even more significantly, we learned in our travels across the country that the Advisory Guidelines are being widely used in discussions with clients, in negotiations with other lawyers, and in settlement conferences with judges. In general, the Advisory Guidelines have had a very warm reception from lawyers, mediators and judges, as people appreciate the benefit of greater consistency and predictability. Again and again, we heard that it is helpful to have a range to know that one's claim, offer, settlement or decision is "in the ballpark".

### 2.5.2 Criticisms of the Guidelines

There have certainly been criticisms of the Advisory Guidelines. Some criticisms were easily dealt with: they were based on misunderstandings about the Draft Proposal and quickly disappeared with a more accurate understanding of the scheme. Other criticisms flagged problems and concerns with specific parts of the Draft Proposal and were very helpful in the process of revising and improving the scheme.

However, there were also more fundamental criticisms leading some to reject the Advisory Guidelines outright. Some critics were fundamentally opposed to the concept of any "guidelines" for spousal support, viewing the nature of the decision-making in spousal support cases as necessarily discretionary and individualized. They criticized the Guidelines for their rigidity — for offering "cookie cutter" answers that fail to deliver individual justice in each case. It was suggested that some judges would simply apply the Guidelines rather than engaging in the hard analytic work demanded by the *Divorce Act*. Other critics were troubled by the informal, advisory status of the guidelines, seeing them as an illegitimate attempt to change the law outside of the legislative process. These criticisms found judicial expression.[20]

These criticisms do not represent the dominant view of the Advisory Guidelines that has emerged as the Guidelines have become better understood. We believe it is important, nonetheless, to address the criticisms briefly here.

Criticisms of the Advisory Guidelines as "too rigid" have often assumed a more rigid scheme than the one we actually developed. Some of the concerns about undue rigidity also embodied a fear that the Guidelines would be applied in a rigid and inflexible fashion, whatever our intentions. Our consultations since the release of the Draft Proposal have revealed that unsophisticated use of the Advisory Guidelines by both judges and lawyers is a concern. However, the appropriate remedy, in the minds of most lawyers and judges, is further education rather than rejection of the Advisory Guidelines and the benefits of increased certainty and predictability that they have brought. We have also seen many cases where use of the Advisory Guidelines has enhanced the quality of judicial reasons as judges respond to the benchmarks provided by the Guidelines and decide whether or not the formula outcomes are appropriate.

Those who oppose any form of guidelines for spousal support and who stress the unique nature of every case ignore the fact that there are many typical cases with very similar facts. They also undervalue the importance of consistency. Consistency is related to a fundamental principle of law: equal treatment, the similar treatment of similar cases. The formulas found in the Advisory Guidelines generate outcomes across a wide range of cases in a consistent, principled fashion, serving as a healthy check upon one's "gut feeling" or budget-based result.

As for the criticism that the Advisory Guidelines are an illegitimate attempt to change the law, it is true that the formulas at the core of the Advisory Guidelines can easily be taken, at first glance, as an entirely new scheme of income-sharing that has been superimposed on the *Divorce Act*. But an understanding of the intentions informing the project and the way in which the Advisory Guidelines were developed counters this first impression. The Advisory Guidelines are intended to reflect current law, not to change it. The formulas were developed to embody, or act as "proxy measures" of, the principles and factors which structure the current law of spousal support. The formula ranges are intended to capture the dominant ranges of support outcomes under the current law and practice.

It must be recognized that some criticisms of the Advisory Guidelines are really criticisms of the current law, reflecting a preference for a stricter compensatory approach, as if *Bracklow* never happened, or a pre-*Moge* approach that placed heavy emphasis on achieving a clean break. The open-ended discretion under the current law allows lawyers and judges to insert their personal theories of spousal support into their determinations of the amount and duration of spousal support. Guidelines, even Advisory Guidelines, serve to reveal and hence constrain outcomes at odds with the principles and dominant patterns of the current law.

---

[20] See, for example, the decisions of Justice Trussler in *V.S. v. A.K.*, [2005] A.J. No. 1357, 2005 ABQB 754 (Alta.Q.B), Justice Julien in *D.S. c. M.S.*, [2006] J.Q. no. 506, 2006 QCCS 334 (C.S), and Justice Campbell in *Vanderlinden v. Vanderlinden*, [2007] N.S.J. No. 107, 2007 NSSC 80. The criticisms voiced by Justice Julien were echoed at the appellate level by Quebec Court of Appeal *G.V. v. C.G.*, [2006] J.Q. no. 5231.

## 2.5.3 The Advisory Guidelines in the Courts

The case law under the Advisory Guidelines has been burgeoning since the release of the Draft Proposal. As of November 2008 there were over 400 judicial decisions in which the Advisory Guidelines have been considered. There are trial level decisions from every province and territory.[21] In addition, in their brief lifetime since the release of the Draft Proposal, the Advisory Guidelines have been considered by five provincial courts of appeal. There are 19 appellate level decisions: 12 from the British Columbia Court of Appeal, three from the New Brunswick Court of Appeal, and one each from the Nova Scotia, Alberta, Quebec and Ontario Courts of Appeal.[22]

The Advisory Guidelines have received strong endorsement from the British Columbia, New Brunswick and Ontario Courts of Appeal and have been referred to with approval by the Alberta and Nova Scotia Courts of Appeal. They have, however, received what can at best be described as a lukewarm reception from the Quebec Court of Appeal.[23] They have not yet been considered by the Supreme Court of Canada.[24]

The single most important judicial decision on the Advisory Guidelines to date remains that of the British Columbia Court of Appeal in *Yemchuk v. Yemchuk*,[25] released in late August of 2005. In this ground-breaking decision, which was the first appeal court consideration of the Guidelines, the B.C. Court of Appeal approved of the Advisory Guidelines "as a useful tool to assist judges in assessing the quantum and duration of spousal support." The Court of Appeal stated that the Advisory Guidelines "are intended to reflect the current law rather than to change it", "to build upon the law as it exists". The Court described "the move away from a budget-laden analysis" as "appealing".

In *Yemchuk*, the Court also clarified the legal status of the Guidelines in the courtroom, an issue that had been troubling lawyers and judges. The Advisory Guidelines were not "law" and would not be legislated. Were they then "evidence" or "expert evidence" and was there a need to "prove" the document? Justice Prowse, writing for the Court, described the Advisory Guidelines in terms similar to a compilation of precedent:

> It should also be stressed that the Advisory Guidelines are intended to reflect the current law, rather than to change it. They were drafted by the authors after extensive analyses of the authorities regarding spousal support across the country, particularly

---

[21] As of February 8, 2008 the Advisory Guidelines had been considered in 425 reported cases. British Columbia generated the highest number of decisions (167), far surpassing the other provinces. Ontario came in second (107). A significant number of cases were from Alberta (42) and Nova Scotia (29). After this came Newfoundland and Labrador (23), Saskatchewan (19) and New Brunswick (18).

[22] See Carol Rogerson and Rollie Thompson, "The Advisory Guidelines 31 Months Later" (September 12, 2007) and "The Spousal Support Advisory Guidelines Three Years Later" (February 8, 2008), both posted on the Advisory Guidelines web site, *supra* note 16.

[23] *G.V. v. C.G.*, *supra* note 20. At worst the decision can be read as an adoption by the Court of the rigidity and illegitimacy criticisms discussed above, and hence as a rejection of the Advisory Guidelines. At best the decision can be read as a ruling on the facts in which the trial judge was found to have used the Guidelines inappropriately by failing to engage in any of the necessary analysis apart from the Guidelines formula. The use of the Advisory Guidelines in Quebec is discussed more fully in Chapter 15.

[24] Leave to appeal was sought but denied in *S.C. v. J.C.*, [2006] N.B.J. No. 186, a decision of the New Brunswick Court of Appeal which endorsed the use of the Advisory Guidelines by the trial judge; see note 26, below.

[25] [2005] B.C.J. No. 1748, 2005 BCCA 406.

> the *Moge* and *Bracklow* decisions and those following thereafter. ... While decisions can undoubtedly be found in which the result would not accord with the Advisory Guidelines, I am satisfied that their intention and general effect is to build upon the law as it exists, rather than to present an entirely new approach to the issue of spousal support... They do not operate to displace the courts' reliance on decided authorities (to the extent that relevant authorities are forthcoming) but to supplement them.

The *Draft Proposal* was thus not evidence, but part of legal argument and reasoning, and could be cited like any other article, text or government document. For the judge, the Advisory Guidelines could be used as one more piece of useful information in the determination of the amount and duration of spousal support.

In April of 2006, the New Brunswick Court of Appeal became the second appellate court to approve of the Advisory Guidelines with its decision in *S.C. v. J.C.*[26] Following the reasoning in *Yemchuk* on the issue of the Guidelines' consistency with current law, Justice Larlee, writing for the Court of Appeal, approved of the Advisory Guidelines in the following terms:

> The guidelines have been referred to in many ways: a check, a cross-check, a litmus test, a useful tool and a starting point. But it is my view that whichever term one likes to employ, their use, through the available software, will help in the long run to bring consistency and predictability to spousal support awards. Not only will they foster settlement, they will also allow spouses to anticipate their support responsibilities at the time of separation.

Since *Yemchuk*, the B.C. Court of Appeal has considered the Advisory Guidelines in 10 other decisions. The most important of these, in terms of the evolving legal status of the Guidelines, is the July 2006 decision in *Redpath v. Redpath*.[27] In *Redpath*, the Court incorporated the Guidelines ranges into the standard of appellate review:

> Cases such as *Hickey*, however, were decided prior to the introduction of the Advisory Guidelines. Now that they are available to provide what is effectively a "range" within which the awards in most cases of this kind should fall, it may be that if a particular award is substantially lower or higher than the range and there are no exceptional circumstances to explain the anomaly, the standard of review should be reformulated to permit appellate intervention.

The Court of Appeal thus recognized that the Advisory Guidelines now offer some bench marks for the range of acceptable trial results, making it possible to justify appellate intervention when trial decisions fall substantially outside those benchmarks.

In January of 2008, as we were putting the finishing touches to the final version of the Advisory Guidelines, the Ontario Court of Appeal released its decision in *Fisher v. Fisher*.[28] In *Fisher* the Ontario Court of Appeal followed *Yemchuk* in endorsing the Advisory Guidelines as a useful tool and a "litmus test" for the reasonableness of spousal support awards, while adding the

---

[26] [2006] N.B.J. No. 186, leave to appeal to the SCC denied, [2006] S.C.C.A. No. 246 (Oct. 19, 2006))
[27] [2006] B.C.J. No. 1550, 2006 BCCA 338.
[28] *Fisher v. Fisher*, [2008] O.J. No. 38, 2008 ONCA 11.

important caveat that the Advisory Guidelines do not replace an individualized analysis and must be applied in their entirety.

As a result of the appellate endorsement of the Advisory Guidelines in British Columbia and New Brunswick, trial courts in those provinces now refer to the Guidelines in virtually every spousal support decision. But even in provinces where there has not been such strong appellate endorsement or any appellate endorsement at all — Ontario (prior to the release of *Fisher*), Nova Scotia, Saskatchewan, Alberta, and Newfoundland and Labrador — we have also seen wide-spread and growing use of the Guidelines by trial judges, in settlement conferences, on applications for interim support and in trials.

### 2.5.4 Results of the feedback: "the ranges are about right"

The feedback we have gathered since the release of the Draft Proposal, has confirmed the basic structure of the Guideline formulas.[29] Some parts of the country inhabit the high end of ranges and some the low ends, but current practice across the country is by and large accommodated by the formula ranges. We did hear about problems with the application of the formulas to particular fact situations and specific subsets of cases, and we took these into account in the revision process, as will be discussed in the chapters that follow. As a result of the feedback we received, the revisions we have made to the Draft Proposal in this final version of the Advisory Guidelines have involved fine-tuning rather than radical revision: some modest tweaking of the formulas and the addition of some new exceptions.[30]

### 2.5.5 Unsophisticated use

The main problem that emerged both from the feedback process[31] and our reading of Guidelines cases is that the Advisory Guidelines are often used in an unsophisticated fashion by both lawyers and judges. Some lawyers and judges seem to focus only on the formulas and to ignore other parts of the Guidelines scheme, such as entitlement, exceptions and restructuring. The choice of a particular amount or duration within the range is often left unexplained. There has been a tendency to convert the Guidelines into default rules, even when such was not intended.

We have tried to be conscious of unsophisticated use in revising the Draft Proposal. While much of the actual content has not changed, we have changed the structure and presentation. We have tried to write more clearly, to respond to some of the misinterpretations and misunderstandings of the Draft Proposal. And we have highlighted topics that are often forgotten, topics like entitlement, using the ranges, restructuring, exceptions and self-sufficiency.[32]

---

[29] A more detailed discussion of our findings can be found in Carol Rogerson and Rollie Thompson, "The Advisory Guidelines 31 Months Later" (September 12, 2007), posted on the Advisory Guidelines web site, *supra* note 16.

[30] The revisions are detailed in the accompanying "Report on Revisions".

[31] This concern was emphasized in the submission of the Canadian Bar Association, National Family Law Section, "Spousal Support Advisory Guidelines," May 2007, referred to *supra*, note 19.

[32] As part of the revision process we also plan to produce an "operating manual" which will present in a concise format the various steps and considerations involved the use of the Advisory Guidelines. To the extent that the use of computer software has contributed to the problem of unsophisticated use by presenting the formula outcomes without analysis or reasons, we will be working with the software suppliers to encourage the use of more prompts and reminders, to ensure that lawyers and judges remain alert to the full operation of the Advisory Guidelines, before and beyond the formulaic ranges.

To some extent, unsophisticated use was to be expected in the first year or two of the Advisory Guidelines. Over time, as lawyers and judges become more experienced, we would expect to see a more sophisticated use of all the various parts of the Guidelines — and indeed we have already started to see this happen in places such as British Columbia where the Guidelines are used extensively on a province-wide basis.

## 3 AN OVERVIEW OF THE ADVISORY GUIDELINES

Spousal support guidelines can be structured in many different ways. For those who are interested, the Background Paper reviews in detail other models of spousal support guidelines. This chapter presents a structural overview of this scheme of Advisory Guidelines. Some of what you will find here has already been touched on, in a less systematic way, in Chapter 2. As well, many of the individual components of the Advisory Guidelines will be discussed more extensively in subsequent chapters. However, we thought it would be helpful for readers to have a sense of the big picture at the beginning.

We begin with a discussion of the basic concept of income sharing on which the Advisory Guidelines are constructed and then move into an organized, step-by-step review of the specific components of the Advisory Guidelines. We have divided this review into three main sections. First, we deal with the preliminary issues that arise *before* any consideration of the formulas — what might be called issues of application. Then we deal with the basic structure of the income-sharing formulas for determination of amount and duration of support that are at the heart of the proposed approach. The outcomes generated by the formulas are not necessarily determinative, however. The final section deals with the steps that can be taken *after* the formula calculations: locating a specific amount or duration within the ranges, restructuring the formula outcomes (by trading off amount against duration), and departing from the amounts and durations generated by the formulas, through exceptions.

### 3.1 Income Sharing

The core concept on which the Spousal Support Advisory Guidelines are built is **income sharing**. Under the Advisory Guidelines, budgets play a diminished role in determining spousal support outcomes. Instead the Advisory Guidelines look primarily to the incomes of the parties and rely on a mathematical formula to determine the portion of spousal incomes to be shared. Contrary to common perception, **income sharing does not mean equal sharing**. There are many ways of sharing income; it all depends on the formula that is adopted.

You will see below that other factors are also relevant in determining support outcomes under the Advisory Guidelines, such as the presence of dependent children or the length of the marriage. But the income levels of the parties and, and more specifically the income disparity between them, become the primary determinants of support outcomes. Under the Spousal Support Advisory Guidelines, as under the *Child Support Guidelines*, the precise determination of income, including the imputing of income, becomes a much more significant issue than it has been in the past.

**Income sharing here is a method, and not a new theory of spousal support.** As we have noted earlier, the Advisory Guidelines project has not been driven by a desire to theoretically reorder the law of spousal support. Rather it has been driven by the practical needs of family law practitioners and judges who deal with the daily dilemmas of advising, negotiating, litigating and deciding spousal support.

It is therefore important to emphasize that **the use of income sharing as a method** for determining the amount of spousal support does not necessarily imply adoption of the income-sharing theories of spousal support identified in the Background Paper. Some of these theories, which are admittedly contentious, rest upon a view of marriage as a relationship of trust and community, which justifies treating marital incomes as joint incomes.

The method of income sharing can be used, however, as a practical and efficient way of implementing many support objectives such as compensation for the economic advantages and disadvantages of the marriage or the recognition of need and economic dependency. Such use of proxy measures already exists in spousal support law – think of the prevalent use of standard of living and a "needs and means" analysis to quantify compensatory support.

The Guidelines do not commit to any particular theory of spousal support. As will become clear in the discussion of the different formulas under these Advisory Guidelines, they aim to accommodate the multiple theories that now inform our law and, to generate results that are in broad conformity with existing patterns in the law.

We now move on to an overview of the basic framework of the specific scheme of income sharing found in the Advisory Guidelines.

## 3.2 Preliminary Issues — The Applicability of the Advisory Guidelines

### 3.2.1 Form and force

Unlike the *Federal Child Support Guidelines*, the Spousal Support Advisory Guidelines **have not been legislated**. Following the practice in some American jurisdictions, these are **informal guidelines. They are not legally binding. Their use is completely voluntary**. They have been and will be adopted by lawyers and judges to the extent they find them useful, and will operate as a practical tool within **the existing legal framework**. As non-legislated, informal guidelines, these Guidelines are **advisory only**. They are intended as a **starting point** for negotiation and adjudication.

### 3.2.2 Entitlement

The Advisory Guidelines do **not** deal with entitlement. The informal status of the Guidelines means that they must remain subject to the entitlement provisions of the *Divorce Act*, notably ss. 15.2(4) and (6) as interpreted by the courts. Entitlement therefore remains a threshold issue to be determined before the guidelines will be applicable.

**On its own, a mere disparity of income that would generate an amount under the Advisory Guidelines formulas, does not automatically lead to entitlement**. There must be a finding (or an agreement) on entitlement, on a compensatory or non-compensatory or contractual basis, *before* the formulas and the rest of the Guidelines are applied.

The Advisory Guidelines were drafted on the assumption that the current law of spousal support, post-*Bracklow*, continues to offer a very expansive basis for entitlement to spousal support. Effectively any significant income disparity generates an entitlement to some support, leaving amount and duration as the main issues to be determined in spousal support cases. However, the Guidelines leave the issue of when an income disparity is significant, in the sense of signaling entitlement, to the courts. It is open to a court to find no entitlement on a particular set of facts, despite income disparity, and the Advisory Guidelines do not speak to that issue.

The basis of entitlement is important, not only as a threshold issue, but also to determine location within the formula ranges or to justify departure from the ranges as an exception.

Entitlement issues also arise frequently on review and variation, especially applications to terminate support.

Entitlement is dealt with in Chapter 4.

### 3.2.3 Application to provincial/territorial law

The Advisory Guidelines have specifically been developed under the federal *Divorce Act* and are intended for use under that legislation. Provincial/territorial support law is governed by distinct statutory regimes. However, in practice there is much overlap between federal and provincial/territorial support laws.

The broad conceptual framework for spousal support articulated by the Supreme Court of Canada in *Moge* and *Bracklow* has been relied upon under both provincial and federal legislation. Indeed *Bracklow*, which combined claims under the *Divorce Act* and provincial legislation, made no real distinction between the two. Given this overlap, the Advisory Guidelines have been used under provincial/territorial support legislation.

There are some distinctive features of provincial/territorial spousal support laws that need to be taken into account when using the Advisory Guidelines. Many provincial/territorial laws have specific provisions governing entitlement, for example provisions determining which non-marital relationships give rise to a spousal support obligation. Like other issues of entitlement discussed above, this must be a threshold determination before the Advisory Guidelines are applied to determine amount and duration of support. We also note that the list of specific factors to be considered in determining spousal support does vary from statute to statute, with some provincial/territorial legislation making explicit reference, for example, to factors such as property and conduct, although the impact of these differences in wording on spousal support outcomes is unclear.

Provincial laws differ from the *Divorce Act* in their application to unmarried couples but this should not cause any difficulties with respect to the operation of the Advisory Guidelines. Although we conveniently refer to "length of marriage" as a relevant factor in the operation of the formulas, the formulas actually rely upon the period of spousal cohabitation (including any periods of pre-marital cohabitation), thus easily meshing with provincial/territorial legislation.

The application of the Advisory Guidelines under provincial/territorial legislation is dealt with in Chapter 5.

### 3.2.4 Application to agreements

The Advisory Guidelines **do not confer any power to re-open or override final agreements on spousal support**. This issue, like entitlement, is outside the scope of the Advisory Guidelines and will continue to be dealt with under the common law doctrine of unconscionability, provincial/territorial statutes and the evolving interpretation of the Supreme Court of Canada's recent decision in *Miglin*.[33] Agreements limiting or waiving spousal support may therefore preclude the application of the Guidelines.

If a final agreement is set aside or overridden under existing law, the Advisory Guidelines *may* be of assistance in determining the amount and duration of support, although the intentions of the parties as reflected in the agreement may also continue to influence the outcome.

As well, the Advisory Guidelines *may* be applicable if a spousal support agreement provides for review or variation.

---

[33] *Miglin v. Miglin*, [2003] 1 S.C.R. 303.

Further discussion of the application of the Advisory Guidelines in the cases where there are spousal support agreements can be found in Chapters 5 and 14.

## 3.2.5 Interim orders

The Advisory Guidelines are intended to apply to interim orders as well as final orders. We anticipate, in fact, that they will be particularly valuable at the interim stage, which is now dominated by a needs-and-means analysis — budgets, expenses and deficits that require individualized decision-making.

**Any periods of interim support clearly have to be included within the durational limits set by the Advisory Guidelines.** Otherwise, if duration were only to be fixed in final orders, there would be incentives in both directions — for some to drag out proceedings and for others to speed them up — and general inequity. Interim support is discussed in Chapter 5.

The Advisory Guidelines do recognize that the amount may need to be set differently during the interim period while parties are sorting out their financial situation immediately after separation. To accommodate these short-term concerns, the Guidelines recognize an exception for compelling financial circumstances in the interim period, considered in Chapter 12.

## 3.2.6 Review and variation

The primary application of the Advisory Guidelines is to **initial determinations** of spousal support at the point of separation or divorce, whether through negotiated agreements or court orders. Ideally a truly comprehensive set of guidelines would apply not only to the initial determination of support but also to subsequent reviews and variations over time. However, these issues have proven the most difficult to reduce to a formula given the uncertainty in the current law concerning the effect of post-separation income changes, remarriage and repartnering, and subsequent children.

In the end, we chose a more modest course, identifying certain situations where the Advisory Guidelines can apply on reviews and variations, including increases in the recipient's income and decreases in the payor's income. We have left others, such as post-separation increases in the payor's income, re-partnering, remarriage and second families, to more discretionary determinations under the evolving framework of current law.

The application of the Advisory Guidelines in the context of review and variation is dealt with more extensively in Chapter 14.

## 3.3 The Formulas

## 3.3.1 Two basic formulas

The Advisory Guidelines are constructed around **two basic formulas**, rather than just one formula: the *without child support* **formula** and the *with child support* **formula**. The dividing line between the two is the absence or presence of a dependent child or children of the marriage, and a concurrent child support obligation, at the time spousal support is determined.

### 3.3.2  Determining income

Both formulas use **income sharing** as the method for determining the amount of spousal support, not budgets. Income-sharing formulas work directly from income, as income levels essentially determine the amount of support to be paid. Under the Advisory Guidelines, the accurate determination of income becomes a much more significant issue in spousal support cases than it has in the past, and there may be more incentives to dispute income. However, because the Advisory Guidelines generate ranges and not specific amounts, absolute precision in the determination of income may not be as crucial as under the *Federal Child Support Guidelines*. Many cases will involve combined claims for child and spousal support, where a precise determination of income is already required for child support purposes.

**The starting point for the determination of income under both formulas is the definition of income under the *Federal Child Support Guidelines*, including the Schedule III adjustments**. More details on the determination of income are found in Chapter 6.

The Advisory Guidelines do not solve the complex issues of income determination that arise in cases involving self-employment income and other forms of non-employment income. In determining income it may be necessary, as under the *Federal Child Support Guidelines*, to **impute income** in situations where a spouse's actual income does not appropriately reflect his or her earning capacity. In some cases the issue will be imputing income to the payor spouse. On variation and review the issue may be imputing income to the recipient spouse if it is established that the he or she has failed to make appropriate efforts towards self-sufficiency.

### 3.3.3  The *without child support* formula

In cases where there are no dependent children, the ***without child support* formula** applies. This formula relies heavily upon length of marriage — or more precisely, the length of relationship, including periods of pre-marital cohabitation — to determine both the amount and duration of support. Both amount and duration increase with the length of the relationship. This formula is constructed around the concept of **merger over time** which offers a useful tool for implementing both compensatory and non-compensatory support objectives in cases where there are no dependent children in a way that reflects general patterns in the current law.

#### Under the basic without child support formula:

- The *amount* of spousal support is 1.5 to 2 percent of the difference between the spouses' gross incomes for each year of marriage, to a maximum range of 37.5 to 50 per cent of the gross income difference for marriages of 25 years or more (The upper end of this maximum range is capped at the amount that would result in equalization of the spouses' net incomes — the net income cap.)
- *Duration* is .5 to 1 year of support for each year of marriage, with duration becoming indefinite (duration not specified) after 20 years *or*, if the marriage has lasted 5 years or longer, when the years of marriage and age of the support recipient (at separation) added together total 65 or more (the "rule of 65").

The *without child support* formula is discussed in detail in Chapter 7.

## 3.3.4 The *with child support* formula

In cases where there are dependent children, the ***with child support* formula** applies. The distinctive treatment of marriages with dependent children and concurrent child support obligations is justified by both theoretical and practical considerations and is reflected in current case law.

On the theoretical front, marriages with dependent children raise strong compensatory claims based on the economic disadvantages flowing from assumption of primary responsibility for child care, not only during the marriage, *but also after separation.* We have identified this aspect of the compensatory principle as it operates in cases involving dependent children as the **parental partnership principle**, and have drawn on this concept in structuring the *with child support* formula. For marriages with dependent children, length of marriage is not the most important determinant of support outcomes as compared to post-separation child-care responsibilities.

On the practical front, child support must be calculated first and given priority over spousal support. As well, the differential tax treatment of child and spousal support must be taken into account, complicating the calculations. The *with child support* formula thus works with computer software calculations of net disposable incomes

### Under the basic *with child support* formula:

- Spousal support is an *amount* that will leave the recipient spouse with between 40 and 46 percent of the spouses' net incomes *after child support has been taken out.* (We refer to the spouses' net income after child support has been taken out as Individual Net Disposable Income or INDI).
- The approach to *duration* under this formula is more complex and flexible than under the *without child support* formula; orders are initially indefinite in form (duration not specified) but the formula also establishes durational ranges which are intended to structure the process of review and variation and which limit the cumulative duration of awards under this formula. These durational limits rely upon both length of marriage and the ages of the children.

The *with child support* formula is really a cluster of formulas dealing with different custodial arrangements. **Shared and split custody** situations require slight variations in the computation of individual net disposable income, as the backing out of child support obligations is a bit more complicated. There is also a different, hybrid formula for cases where **spousal support is paid by the custodial parent**. Under this formula, the spouses' Guidelines incomes are reduced by the grossed-up amount of child support (actual or notional) and then the *without child support* formula is applied to determine amount and duration. Finally, there is one more hybrid formula for those spousal support cases where the child support for **adult children** is determined under section 3(2)(b) of the *Child Support Guidelines.*

The *with child support* formula is discussed in detail in Chapter 8.

## 3.3.5 Length of marriage

Under the Advisory Guidelines length of marriage is a primary determinant of support outcomes in cases *without* dependent children. Under the *without child support* formula the percentage of income sharing increases with length of the marriage; the same is true for duration of support.

Length of marriage is much less relevant under the *with child support* formula, although it still plays a significant role in determining duration under that formula.

Given the relevance of length of marriage under the Advisory Guidelines, it is important to clarify its meaning. **While we use the convenient term length of marriage, the more accurate description is the length of the cohabitation, which includes periods of pre-marital cohabitation, and ends with separation.**

### 3.3.6 Ranges

The Advisory Guidelines do not generate a fixed figure for either amount or duration, but instead produce **a range of outcomes** that provide a starting point for negotiation or adjudication.

Ranges create scope for more individualized decision-making, allowing for argument about where a particular case should fall within the range in light of the *Divorce Act*'s multiple support objectives and factors. Ranges can also accommodate some of the variations in current practice, including local variations in spousal support cultures.

### 3.3.7 Ceilings and floors

As with the *Federal Child Support Guidelines*, the Spousal Support Advisory Guidelines establish ceilings and floors in terms of the income levels to which they are applicable. Both the ceiling and the floor have been set by reference to the annual gross income of the payor. The ceiling has been set at a gross annual income for the payor of $350,000 and the floor at a gross annual income of $20,000. Ceiling and floors are dealt with more extensively in Chapter 11.

### 3.4 After the Formulas Have Been Applied

Under the Advisory Guidelines there is still much room for flexibility to respond to the facts of particular cases. First, there is considerable room for discretion in the fixing of precise amounts and durations within the ranges generated by the formulas. Second, there is the ability to restructure the formula outcomes by trading off amount against duration. Third the other is the possibility of departing from the formula outcomes by relying upon exceptions.

### 3.4.1 Using the ranges

The location of a precise amount or duration within those ranges will be driven by the factors detailed in Chapter 9: the strength of any compensatory claim, the recipient's needs, the age, number, needs and standard of living of any children, the needs and ability to pay of the payor, work incentives for the payor, property division and debts, and self-sufficiency incentives.

### 3.4.2 Restructuring

Although the formulas generate separate figures for amount and duration, the Advisory Guidelines explicitly recognize that these awards can be restructured by trading off amount against duration.

In *Bracklow* the Supreme Court of Canada explicitly recognized that the amount and duration of awards can be configured in different ways to yield awards of similar value (what the

719

Court called quantum). Thus the Court noted that an order for a smaller amount paid out over a long period of time can be equivalent to an order for a higher amount paid out over a shorter period of time.

Restructuring can be used in three ways:

- to **front-end load** awards by increasing the amount beyond the formulas' ranges and shortening duration;
- to **extend duration** beyond the formulas' ranges by lowering the monthly amount; and
- to formulate a **lump sum** payment by combining amount and duration.

When restructuring is relied upon to resolve issues of inappropriate formula outcomes, awards remain consistent with the overall or global amounts generated by the Advisory Guidelines. **Restructuring thus does not involve an exception or departure from the formulas.**

Restructuring works best when duration is clearly defined, and will thus have its primary application under the *without child support* formula.

Restructuring is dealt with in more detail in Chapter 10.

### 3.4.3 Exceptions

The formulas are intended to generate appropriate outcomes in the majority of cases. We recognize, however, that there will be cases where the formula outcomes, even after consideration of restructuring, will not generate results consistent with the support objectives and factors under the *Divorce Act*. The informal, advisory nature of the Guidelines means that the formula outcomes are never binding and departures are always possible on a case-by-case basis where the formula outcomes are found to be inappropriate. The Advisory Guidelines do, however, itemize a series of exceptions which, although clearly not exhaustive, are intended to assist lawyers and judges in framing and assessing departures from the formulas. The exceptions create room both for the operation of competing theories of spousal support and for consideration of the particular factual circumstances in individual cases where these may not be sufficiently accommodated by restructuring.

The exceptions are listed and explained in Chapter 12:

- compelling financial circumstances in the interim period;
- debt payments;
- prior support obligations;
- illness or disability of a recipient spouse;
- a compensatory exception for shorter marriages under the *with child support* formula;
- reapportionment of property (British Columbia);
- basic needs/hardship under the *without child support* and *custodial payor* formulas;
- non-taxable payor income;
- non-primary parent to fulfil a parenting role under the *custodial payor* formula;
- special needs of a child; and
- section 15.3 for small amounts and inadequate compensation under the *with child support* formula.

## 4 ENTITLEMENT

The Advisory Guidelines do **not** deal with entitlement. They deal with the amount and duration of support after a finding of entitlement. The informal status of the Guidelines means that they must remain subject to the entitlement provisions of the *Divorce Act*, notably ss. 15.2(4) and (6), as interpreted by the courts. Entitlement therefore remains a threshold issue to be determined before the Guidelines will be applicable. **On its own, a mere disparity of income that would generate an amount under the Advisory Guidelines formulas does not automatically lead to entitlement.**

The Advisory Guidelines were drafted on the assumption that the current law of spousal support, post-*Bracklow*, offers a very expansive basis for entitlement to spousal support. As a general matter, if there is a significant income disparity at the end of the marriage, there will be an entitlement to some support, leaving amount and duration as the main issues to be determined in spousal support cases. The Advisory Guidelines do not, however, pre-determine when an income disparity will be large enough to create entitlement, leaving that issue to the courts. Nor do the Guidelines preclude the possibility that courts may find no entitlement on particular facts despite a fairly significant income disparity.

We recognize that the Advisory Guidelines may, over time, shape understandings of entitlement.[34] But this will be part of the normal evolution of the law in this area. It is also possible that the law of entitlement may change over time, if the Supreme Court of Canada or an appellate court were to decide to narrow or refine *Bracklow*.

Concerns have been raised that the Advisory Guidelines will generate more litigation, or more potential for litigation, on the issue of entitlement as payors will view this as a way of avoiding the application of the Guidelines. In our view, an increased focus on the issue of entitlement would not necessarily be a bad thing given the absence of analysis that tends to prevail in this area of law. And realistically, serious entitlement issues arise only in a relatively narrow range of cases.[35] At this point, we have seen no evidence of increased litigation on entitlement.

Since the release of the Draft Proposal we have found that the threshold issue of entitlement is often ignored in practice, with entitlement simply being assumed because there is a difference in spousal incomes that generates an amount of support under the formulas as displayed by the software. We emphasize once again that this is incorrect. **There must be a finding (or agreement) on entitlement *before* the formulas and the rest of the Guidelines are applied.**

**Furthermore, entitlement is not just a threshold issue; entitlement matters throughout the Guidelines.** Even where entitlement is found, as it often will be where there is a substantial income disparity, the basis for entitlement in a particular case, e.g. compensatory or non-compensatory, informs the whole subsequent Guidelines analysis, including the discretionary judgments that need to be made on location within the ranges, restructuring and exceptions. As well, issues of continuing entitlement arise on variation and review, most obviously in the context of applications to terminate spousal support. **A crucial step in a Guidelines case is identifying the basis for entitlement with reference to the *Divorce Act* objectives and the leading decisions, such as *Moge* and *Bracklow*.**[36]

---

[34] For an example of a case in which the Advisory Guidelines were considered in the entitlement analysis see *R.S.R. v. S.M.R.*, [2006] B.C.J. No. 2109, 2006 BCSC 1404.

[35] As will be shown in the discussion below, findings of "no entitlement" are most likely in shorter marriages, which are "small stakes" cases. At the other end of the spectrum, entitlement issues are usually fairly clear in ""large stakes" cases like long marriages. This means that entitlement is most likely to arise as a contested issue in medium-length cases under the *without child support* formula.

[36] A good example is the leading B.C.C.A. decision in *Yemchuk v. Yemchuk*, [2005] B.C.J. No. 1748,

## 4.1 Entitlement as a Threshold Issue: The "No Entitlement" Cases

In some cases the threshold entitlement analysis will determine that there is no entitlement to spousal support and hence that the Advisory Guidelines are not applicable. As noted above, current spousal support law, post-*Bracklow*, does provide a broad basis for entitlement. *Moge* created a broad basis for compensatory claims for spousal support based on economic disadvantage from the marriage or the conferral of an economic advantage upon the other spouse. But even if it is not possible for a lower-income spouse to make a compensatory claim, *Bracklow* has provided the possibility of a non-compensatory claim based on need or hardship created by the loss of the marital standard of living. Typically a significant disparity in income at the point of marriage breakdown will create an entitlement to some support – at the very least to some time-limited, transitional support.

However, the case law does show that there may be a finding of "no entitlement" despite income disparity. Under the current law it is possible to argue that an income disparity reflects neither economic disadvantage flowing from the marriage nor economic need and hence that there is no entitlement to support. Lawyers using the Advisory Guidelines need to remain aware of these possibilities.

We do not offer here a comprehensive review of the case law on entitlement, as this issue is outside the scope of the Guidelines, but merely flag some of the kinds of cases in which courts have found no entitlement to spousal support. Some "no entitlement" cases involve findings that the parties, because of differences in their asset positions or their costs of living, have similar standards of living despite an income disparity.[37] In others, the income disparity is the result of post-separation events or choices, such as a job loss on the recipient's part[38] or a post-separation increase in the payor's income.[39] Finally, in some cases courts have found that any compensatory or needs-based claims have been met through property division,[40] including in B.C a reapportionment of assets to meet self-sufficiency concerns, thus eliminating entitlement to spousal support.[41]

There are relatively few reported cases where entitlement has not been found. This could be read as confirming the broad basis for entitlement under the current law; alternatively, it could suggest that entitlement issues, even if raised on the facts of particular cases, are often not worth litigating and are settled. Significantly, many of the no entitlement cases involve somewhat atypical fact situations: short marriages, second marriages, claims by men, or claims by non-custodial parents.

## 4.2 Entitlement at Other Stages of the Guidelines Analysis

Cases where no entitlement is found despite a significant income disparity are infrequent. However, an analysis of entitlement is not only relevant at the threshold stage of determining whether any spousal support at all is to be paid. Even in cases where entitlement is found and

---

2005 B.C.C.A. The support claim was brought by the husband who had retired early to facilitate the wife's relocation because of her employment. The trial judge had found no entitlement on the husband's part. The Court of Appeal overturned that decision, engaging in an extensive analysis of the husband's entitlement on compensatory grounds, before turning to the Advisory Guidelines as a useful tool in determining the appropriate amount of support.

[37] A good example is *Eastwood v. Eastwood*, 2006 CarswellNB 655, 2006 NBQB 413.
[38] See *Rezel v. Rezel*, [2007] O.J. No. 1460 (S.C.J.).
[39] See *Eastwood*, *supra* note 37.
[40] See *Chutter v. Chutter*, [2007] B.C.J. No. 1247, 2007 BCSC 814.
[41] See *W.J. M. v. L.A.M.*, [2007] B.C.J. No. 1283, 2007 BCSC 842.

spousal support is awarded, **an analysis of *the basis of entitlement* is a necessary underpinning to the determination of the amount and duration of support.**

The compensatory and non-compensatory bases for spousal support need to be delineated as they generate different support outcomes. The Advisory Guidelines reflect these different bases. For example, as will be shown in Chapters 7 and 8, the *without child support* formula reflects non-compensatory support considerations in its application to cases of short and medium length marriages with no children while the *with child support formula* is largely compensatory. In cases of longer marriages under the *without child support* formula the awards reflect a mix of compensatory and non-compensatory claims.

The delineation of the compensatory and/or non-compensatory basis for entitlement in a particular case is relevant at two particular points in the application of the Guidelines

- to determine location within the ranges; and
- to determine whether or not the case justifies a departure from the ranges as an exception

With respect to determining location within the range, in longer marriages under the *without child support* formula, a strong compensatory claim may, for example, suggest an award at the high end of the range whereas a non-compensatory claim based only upon loss of the marital standard of living may suggest an award at the lower end of the range. As well, compensatory claims can be more or less extensive, depending upon the degree of economic disadvantage experienced because of labour force withdrawal. A fuller discussion of using the ranges is found in Chapter 9.

The use of the exceptions is dealt with in more detail in Chapter 12. We simply note here that two exceptions are triggered by compensatory claims that may not be adequately satisfied by the formula ranges: the compensatory exception for short marriages without children and, in cases with children, the s. 15.3 exception for compensatory claims that must be deferred because of the priority of child support. The application of both of these exceptions therefore requires a delineation of the basis for entitlement.

## 4.3 Entitlement Issues on Review and Variation

Entitlement issues can also arise on review and variation, most obviously in the context of applications to terminate spousal support. Such applications may be triggered by the recipient's remarriage or by the recipient's employment or simply by the passage of time. In many cases duration under the Advisory Guidelines is indefinite (duration not specified), thus requiring a discretionary determination of whether termination is appropriate. Even in cases where the Advisory Guidelines generate a range for duration, courts may sometimes prefer to make the initial order indefinite and later deal with the issue of termination on a subsequent review or variation, particularly where the suggested time limits are fairly lengthy.

Determining whether termination is appropriate will often require an analysis of whether the initial basis for entitlement continues to exist. Although the issue on termination is often framed in terms of whether the recipient has become "self-sufficient", the issue can also be seen as one of whether there is a continuing entitlement to support. The determination of when a spouse has become self-sufficient is one of those "hard" issues in the law of spousal support that was there before the Advisory Guidelines. While the Guidelines, as discussed in Chapter 13, take into account the obligation to make reasonable efforts towards self-sufficiency, they do not determine the hard issue of when self-sufficiency has been achieved and the law on this continues to evolve.

The result on a termination application may differ depending on whether the initial award was compensatory or non-compensatory in nature, reinforcing once again the need for a delineation of the basis for entitlement.[42] For example, remarriage may not mean an end to entitlement if the original basis for the support order was compensatory,[43] but it may if the basis was non-compensatory.[44]

Thus far we have talked about how entitlement issues arise in the context of applications to reduce or terminate spousal support. Reviews or variations may also give rise to entitlement issues of a somewhat different sort when the recipient applies for an increase in spousal support, either because of a decrease in the recipient's income or a post-separation increase in the payor's income.

As we emphasize in Chapter 14 which deals with the application of the Guidelines in the context of review and variation, one cannot determine the spousal support outcome in these cases simply by applying the formulas to the new incomes. The current law requires in each of these cases that there be a threshold determination of whether the change in income is relevant to the support obligation and if so, to what extent. The issue can be seen as one of "entitlement," although it is not always framed in that language, and the analysis requires going back to the compensatory and non-compensatory bases for spousal support. Cases involving a post-separation increase in the payor's income, for example, can be thought of as raising the issue of the recipient's entitlement to share in that increase.[45]


# 5 APPLICATION

In Chapter 4 we dealt with the threshold issue of entitlement that must be addressed before the Advisory Guidelines, and more specifically the formulas, are applied. In this chapter we deal with several other preliminary issues of application that, like entitlement, must be addressed before the formulas are applied.


## 5.1 Application to provincial/territorial law

The Advisory Guidelines were specifically developed under the federal *Divorce Act* and intended for use under that legislation. Provincial/territorial support law is governed by specific statutory regimes.

However, in practice there is much overlap between federal and provincial/territorial support laws. The broad conceptual framework for spousal support articulated by the Supreme Court of Canada in *Moge* and *Bracklow* has been applied under both provincial and federal legislation. Indeed *Bracklow*, which combined claims under the *Divorce Act* and provincial legislation, made no real distinction between the two.

In the Draft Proposal we recognized that it was possible, given this overlap, that the Advisory Guidelines would be used under provincial/territorial support legislation. In our view there was sufficient flexibility in the Advisory Guidelines, given their informal and non-binding nature and their use of ranges for both amount and duration, to deal with any distinctive patterns in

---

[42] See *Rezansoff v. Rezansoff*, [2007] S.J. No. 37, 2007 SKQB 32 for an excellent discussion of this in the context of a case involving non-compensatory support.

[43] See *J.W.J.McC. v. T.E.R.*, [2007] B.C.J. No. 358, 2007 BCSC 252.

[44] See *Kelly v. Kelly*, [2007] B.C.J. No. 324, 2007 BCSC 227.

[45] See for example *D.B.C. v. R.M.W.*, [2006] A.J. No. 1629, 2006 ABQB 905 where the wife was found not entitled to a share of the husband's increased income after separation both because she had not contributed to that increase and because it was unrelated to the marital lifestyle. In fact the husband had decreased his income during the marriage because of a joint marital decision to alter their lifestyle.

provincial/territorial law. The three years of experience with the Advisory Guidelines since the release of the Draft Proposal have borne out this prediction. The Advisory Guidelines have frequently been used in spousal support determinations under provincial legislation, in cases involving both married couples who have separated but not yet commenced divorce proceedings[46] and unmarried couples.[47]

We recognize that there are some differences between provincial/territorial support laws and the *Divorce Act*. Many provincial/territorial laws have specific provisions governing entitlement, for example provisions determining which non-marital relationships give rise to a spousal support obligation. However, as discussed in Chapter 4, the Advisory Guidelines only deal with the amount and duration, and not entitlement.

Once an unmarried couple satisfies this additional provincial requirement, e.g. cohabitation for two or three years and proves entitlement, the Advisory Guidelines can then be applied. Under the *without child support* formula, the period of cohabitation for an unmarried couple is the same as the "length of the marriage" for a married couple. Similarly, under the *with child support* formula, there is no distinction drawn, as this formula is driven by net incomes, custodial arrangements and child support obligations.

Provincial/territorial statutes often include specific provisions governing the effect of agreements. However, as will be discussed immediately below, because the Advisory Guidelines do not deal with the effect of agreements there will be no conflict.

Finally, it is important to note that the list of specific factors to be considered in determining spousal support does vary from statute to statute, with some provincial/territorial legislation making explicit reference, for example, to factors such as property[48] and conduct,[49] although the impact of these differences in wording on spousal support outcomes is unclear.[50]

## 5.2 Application to agreements

The Advisory Guidelines **confer no power to re-open or override** *final* **spousal support agreements**. This issue like entitlement, is outside the scope of the Advisory Guidelines and continues to be dealt with under existing law – the common law doctrine of unconscionability, the evolving law applying the Supreme Court of Canada's recent decision in *Miglin*,[51] and provincial statutory provisions which deal with the effect of a prior agreement on spousal support. When the *Federal Child Support Guidelines* were brought into force, changes

---

[46] See for example, *Brown v. Brown*, [2007] N.B.J. No. 330, 2007 NBQB 227 (application to married couple under *Family Services Act*) and *Barter v. Barter*, [2006] N.J. No. 237, 2006 NLUFC 39 (used under *Family Law Act* to determine that agreement satisfies provincial support objectives).

[47] See for example *McCulloch v. Bawtinheimer*, [2006] A.J. No. 361 (Q.B.) using the Advisory Guidelines in a case involving a six year relationship between "adult interdependent partners" as defined under Alberta legislation,. The result in *Bawtinheimer* was consistent with the ranges generated by the *without child support* formula after an explicit use of restructuring. See also *Foley v. Girard*, [2006] O.J. No. 2496, which involved a 20-year same-sex relationship and a result consistent with the *without child support* formula.

[48] See for example s. 7(1) of Manitoba's *Family Maintenance Act*, C.C.S.M. cF20, s. 4(k) of Nova Scotia's *Family Maintenance and Custody Act*, R.S.N.S. 1989, c. 160 and ss. 8(d) and 9(a) and (b) of Ontario's *Family Law Act*, R.S.O. 1990, c. F.3.

[49] See for example s. 33(10) of Ontario 's *Family Law Act, ibid.*

[50] For example the concept of "needs and means" of the spouses under both the *Divorce Act* and provincial/territorial legislation that does not specifically refer to property as a factor arguably encompasses consideration of the spouses' assets and it is universal practice to determine property division before dealing with spousal support.

[51] *Miglin v. Miglin*, [2003] 1 S.C.R. 303.

were made to the *Divorce Act* providing, in essence, that the *Guidelines* would prevail over inconsistent child support agreements. The Spousal Support Advisory Guidelines, given their informal nature, do not have such an effect. They do not confer any power to override existing agreements. **A final agreement – i.e. one waiving or terminating spousal support or setting a fixed amount with no provision for review or variation – will thus preclude the application of the Advisory Guidelines unless the agreement can be it set aside or overridden under existing law.**[52]

The Advisory Guidelines do have an important role to play in the *negotiation* of agreements by providing a more structured framework for negotiation and some benchmarks of fairness. One possible effect of the Advisory Guidelines may thus be a reduction over time in the number of agreements that are subsequently perceived to be unfair by one of the parties. Furthermore, when an agreement is challenged, courts may use the outcome under the Advisory Guidelines to assist in identifying unfair agreements. The case law offers several examples of the Advisory Guidelines being used in this way, in the context of either a *Miglin* analysis or an application to override an agreement under provincial legislation.[53]

If a final spousal support agreement is set aside or over-ridden on the basis of *Miglin* or other applicable legal doctrines, the Advisory Guidelines may be relied upon in determining the amount and duration of support.[54] However, as is recognized in *Miglin*, in some cases the parties' intentions, as reflected in their agreement, may still continue to influence the spousal support outcome and lead the courts to an outcome different from that suggested by the Advisory Guidelines.[55]

It should not be assumed that the mere presence of a spousal support agreement precludes the application of the Advisory Guidelines. **If the agreement is not a final agreement, but one which provides for review or for variation upon a material change of circumstances, the Advisory Guidelines may be applicable to the determination of the amount and duration of spousal support on review or variation.** This application of the Advisory Guidelines is discussed further in Chapter 14 which deals with variation and review.

## 5.3 Interim orders

The Advisory Guidelines are intended to apply to interim orders as well as final orders. The interim support setting is an ideal situation for the use of guidelines. There is a need for a quick, easily calculated amount, knowing that more precise adjustments can be made at trial.[56] Once an income can be established for each party it is possible under the formulas to generate ranges of monthly amounts with relative ease.

---

[52] For a cases where the Advisory Guidelines were found inapplicable because of an agreement see *Woodall v. Woodall*, [2005] O.J. No. 3826, 2005 ONCJ 253 (Ont. C.J.).

[53] See *R.S.M. v. M.S.M.*, [2006] B.C.J. No. 1756, 2006 BCCA 362, *W.(C.L.) v. R.(S.U.)*, 2007 CarswellBC 666, 2007 BCSC 453, *Vanderlans v. Vanderlans*, 2007 CarswellNfld 119, 2007 NLUFC 8; *Rapley v. Rapley*, [2006] B.C.J. No. 3213, 2006 BCSC 18541 *Barter v. Barter*, [2006] N.J. No. 237, 2006 NLUFC 39 and *Chepil v. Chepil*, [2006] B.C.J. No. 15, 2006 BCSC 15.

[54] See *R.S.M. v. M.S.M* ., *ibid.*

[55] See *Santoro v. Santoro*, [2006] B.C.J. No. 453, 2006 BCSC 331 (*Miglin* used to override agreement; however guidelines of "limited use" because of prior agreement; spousal support set well below the range under the *without child support* formula).

[56] Not surprisingly, two of the early American guidelines found their origins in the assessment of interim spousal support, those in California counties and Pennsylvania .

Traditionally, interim spousal support has been based upon a needs-and-means analysis, assessed through budgets, current and proposed expenses, etc. All of that can be avoided with guidelines formulas, apart from exceptional cases. Further, conflict between spouses at this interim stage can be significantly reduced and settlements encouraged, another benefit for the spouses and any children of the marriage.[57]

The Advisory Guidelines do recognize that the amount may need to be different during the interim period while parties are sorting out their financial situation immediately after separation. To accommodate these short-term concerns, the Advisory Guidelines recognize an exception for compelling financial circumstances in the interim period which is discussed in Chapter 12, dealing with exceptions.

There is another critical way that the Advisory Guidelines apply to interim orders. Any periods of interim spousal support are to be included within the durational limits fixed by the Advisory Guidelines under either formula. If the computation of duration did not include the period of interim orders, there would be incentives for some parties to drag out proceedings and for others to speed them up. Further, differing periods of interim support would result in inequities amongst spouses, with some receiving support longer and others shorter, a concern especially in cases of shorter marriages.

## 5.4 Review and Variation

The primary application of the Advisory Guidelines is to **interim and initial determinations** of spousal support at the point of separation or divorce, whether through negotiated agreements or court orders. The Advisory Guidelines also have a role to play in the determination of spousal support in the context of variation and review, but it is a somewhat more limited role. We set out three aspects of this limited role below.

First, the Advisory Guidelines do nothing to change the current structure of the law governing variation and review, including the threshold determinations of whether the conditions for a variation or review have been met.

Second, given that the Advisory Guidelines are based on income sharing, they are well-suited to adjusting spousal support amounts to changing incomes over time. The Guidelines can thus be applied in a very straightforward way to increases in the recipient's income and decreases in the payor's income. However, in some cases, such as post-separation increases in the payor's income or reductions in the recipient's income, there are threshold issues of the relevance of the changed income to the spousal claim — issues essentially of "entitlement." These threshold issues must be dealt with first, to determine to what extent, if any, the income change is to be taken into account, before the Guidelines can be applied.

Third, the impact of re-partnering, re-marriage and second families on spousal support have proven the most difficult to reduce to a formula given the uncertainty in the current law. We have left these issues to discretionary determinations under the evolving framework of the current law.

The application of the Advisory Guidelines in the context of review and variation is dealt with more extensively in Chapter 14.

---

[57] In *D.R.M. v. R.B.M.*, [2006] B.C.J. No. 3299, 2006 Carswell BC 3177 (S.C.), Justice Martinson set out in detail the rationale for the application of the Advisory Guidelines to interim spousal support orders.

## 6 INCOME

The accurate determination of spousal incomes is critical to the proper application of the Advisory Guidelines. The Advisory Guidelines do not, and cannot, solve the complex issues of income determination that can arise in cases involving self-employment income and various forms of non-employment income. In the majority of cases, income issues are relatively straightforward and any disputes are limited in scope. Because the Advisory Guidelines generate ranges, and not specific amounts, absolute precision in the determination of income may not be as crucial as under the *Federal Child Support Guidelines*.

### 6.1 The Starting Point for Income Determination

**The starting point for the determination of income under the Spousal Support Advisory Guidelines is the definition of income under the *Federal Child Support Guidelines*.**

The *Federal Child Support Guidelines* provide an expansive definition of "income" for child support purposes, one that reflects and clarifies much of the pre-Guidelines law on income determination. Sections 15 to 20 of the *Child Support Guidelines*, along with Schedule III, create a framework for income determination. Prior to the release of the Spousal Support Advisory Guidelines, most courts used the same definition of income for both child support and spousal support purposes and that practise has continued since January 2005.

The Child Support Guidelines use a "gross" income measure, income before taxes and other deductions. This same gross income provides the basis for the calculations under all the formulas found in the Spousal Support Advisory Guidelines.

Some of the technicalities of Schedule III are sometimes forgotten in spousal cases. The income imputing provisions of section 19 are, if anything, even more important than in child support cases. In every spousal support case, two incomes are in issue. Income may need to be imputed to a payor spouse, but in addition a spousal support case may also require that an income be imputed to the recipient spouse, because of self-sufficiency issues. In these cases, income is imputed to the recipient under s. 19(1)(a), for under/unemployment. These imputing issues are considered at greater length in Chapter 13 on Self-sufficiency.

There are a few distinctive income issues that do arise in the spousal support context, addressed below.

### 6.2 Social Assistance Is Not "Income"

Under s. 4 of Schedule III to the *Federal Child Support Guidelines*, social assistance is treated as income, but only "the amount attributable to the spouse". This adjustment is required as social assistance is included in line 150 income. For spousal support purposes, any social assistance received by the recipient spouse has traditionally not been viewed as income, so that a recipient relying entirely on social assistance would be treated as person with zero income.[58] Turning to the payor spouse, a payor who receives social assistance is by definition unable to support himself or herself and thus has no ability to pay.[59]

---

[58] *Lawrence v. Lawrence*, [2006] B.C.J. No. 210, 2006 BCSC 167 at para. 84.
[59] *Kortlever v. Kortlever*, [2007] B.C.J. No. 758, 2007 BCSC 487 at para. 39 (both spouses on social assistance, no spousal support).

For purposes of the Advisory Guidelines, section 4 of Schedule III does not apply. **No amount of social assistance should be treated as income, for either the recipient or the payor.**

## 6.3  The Child Tax Benefit and Other Child Benefits

Under the *with child support* formula, included in each spouse's income are the amounts identified for various child-related government benefits and refundable credits: the Canadian Child Tax Benefit, the National Child Benefit Supplement, the GST credit (including any portion for the children), the refundable medical expense credit, the Child Disability Benefit, and the various provincial benefit and credit schemes.

Under the *Federal Child Support Guidelines*, these benefits and credits are not treated as income for table amount purposes: see note 6 to Schedule I. There is some controversy about their consideration for section 7 purposes, or for the determination of undue hardship under section 10, with a number of judges now including them.[60]

For lower-income custodial parents, typically the support recipients, these amounts are significant. As for payors, only low-income spouses obtain any of these, basically the GST Credit, and most of these low-income spouses will not be paying spousal support. In some circumstances, the custodial parent and recipient of these benefits and credits will also be the payor of spousal support.

We did consider backing out the child portion of these benefits, since the bulk of the benefits and credits are tied to the children of the marriage in the recipient spouse's care, e.g. the Child Tax Benefit, the child portion of the GST Credit, and the various provincial programs. The logic of doing so would be similar to that applied in respect of the spouses' child support obligations, i.e. to get at the remaining net disposable income available to the spouses as individuals.

In the end, **we decided to include these child-related benefits in income under the *with child support* formula**, for three reasons.

First, these benefits and credits reduce, sometimes dramatically, with increasing amounts of spousal support transferred to the recipient spouse, especially through the lower and middle income brackets. Including these benefits and credits in the recipient's income gives a much clearer picture of the impact of spousal support upon the recipient's actual net disposable income. Second, some fine lines would have to be drawn between child- and non-child related portions of these benefits and credits. A precise disentanglement would be complicated and for little practical gain. Third, for lower income recipient spouses, these amounts are sizeable, more than $7,000-$8,000 annually for two children. Their removal would produce significantly higher amounts of spousal support, which would cause significant hardship for payor spouses, especially those with lower incomes, unless the formula percentages were adjusted.

## 6.4  The Universal Child Care Benefit (UCCB)

The Universal Child Care Benefit (UCCB) came into effect in July 2006, after the release of the Spousal Support Advisory Guidelines. Under the UCCB, parents receive a taxable benefit of $100 per month for each child under the age of 6. For a custodial parent, the UCCB provides an additional source of taxable income, included in line 150 income.

---

[60] Rollie Thompson, "The Chemistry of Support: The Interaction of Spousal and Child Support" (2006), 25 C.F.L.Q. 251 at 284-288.

The UCCB required amendments to the *Federal Child Support Guidelines*, effective March 22, 2007 (SOR/2007-59). The UCCB is not included in income for table amount purposes, under s. 3 of Schedule III. By reason of a new s. 3.1, the UCCB is included in parental incomes for purposes of section 7 expense sharing, but only for those children for whom section 7 expenses are requested. Any UCCB for another child is not to be included in a parent's income. The UCCB is also considered as income for section 10 undue hardship calculations.

Consistent with our treatment of the Child Tax Benefit under the *with child support* formula, **the UCCB for a child who is a child of the marriage will also be included in the income of the custodial parent in determining spousal support.**

## 6.5 Benefits for Children Other Than Children of the Marriage

Spouses may be receiving child-related benefits for children other than "children of the marriage", children of prior or subsequent relationships. Under the *Federal Child Support Guidelines*, these benefits are generally not treated as part of income for child support purposes at all, thus avoiding the issue. With the 2007 UCCB amendments, section 3.1(b) specifically does exclude any UCCB for a child for whom a section 7 expense is not requested.

Under the *with child support* formulas in the Advisory Guidelines, these benefits are included for "children of the marriage", for the reasons explained above.

**Child-related benefits received by a spouse for children other than "children of the marriage" should not be included in income for spousal support purposes, under either formula.**

This is consistent with our general approach to child support obligations towards other children, discussed at greater length below in Chapter 12 on Exceptions. As the exclusion of these benefits for other children is consistent with the definition of income under the *Federal Child Support Guidelines*, no further adjustments need to be made to income under the Spousal Support Advisory Guidelines.

## 6.6 Non-Taxable Incomes

There are a number of sources of income that are received on a non-taxable basis, most commonly some disability payments, workers' compensation, and income of aboriginal persons earned on reserve. For child support purposes, this income has to be "grossed up" to approximate the equivalent taxable employment income, under s. 19(1)(b). For spousal support purposes, the same grossing-up is required by the *without child support* formula, while the net or non-taxable amount can be used for the basic *with child support* formula.

A complication does arise in the spousal support setting, as spousal support is deductible for the payor and taxable for the recipient. The Advisory Guidelines formulas generate "gross" amounts of spousal support on the assumption that the payor will be able to deduct the support and the recipient will pay tax upon it. What if the payor spouse has only non-taxable income, so that he or she cannot get the benefit of the tax deductibility?

If the payor receives a mix of taxable and non-taxable income, then the payor can get the full benefit of the deduction so long as the spousal support paid is less than the taxable portion of his or her income. The problem only arises where that is not the case, where the payor's income is entirely from non-taxable sources. To be clear, we are speaking here only of income sources that are *legitimately* non-taxable, as opposed to income illegally earned "under the table" and hence not taxed.

In our view, **where a payor spouse has an income entirely or mostly from legitimately non-taxable sources, then an exception must be created**, under both formulas, to take into account the reduced ability to pay of the payor spouse, who can't deduct the support paid, and the needs or loss of the recipient spouse, who still has to pay taxes on spousal support and only receives after-tax support. This exception is discussed in more detail in Chapter 12.

### 6.7 Time for Determining Income

The proper time for determining income under the Advisory Guidelines is both a theoretical and a practical issue. Spousal incomes will inevitably change between the date of separation and the date when interim matters are resolved, and then again by the date of the trial or trial settlement. In Chapter 14, we consider the difficulties that can arise when the payor's income increases, or the recipient's income decreases, at the stage of variation and review. Here we focus upon income determination at the interim and initial stages.

The *without child support* formula gives theoretical emphasis to the marital standard of living, as measured by the spouses' incomes at or near the date of separation. The marital standard of living during cohabitation ought not be affected by a substantial post-separation increase in the payor's income. The *with child support* formula is not tied so tightly to living standards and incomes at separation, as ability to pay issues loom larger where both child and spousal support have to be paid. Under both formulas post-separation increases in the recipient's income are relevant given the obligation to pursue self-sufficiency.

The "timing" issue often proves to be a minor one, as not much time passes between separation and interim arrangements, and not much more to the initial divorce order. More importantly, payor incomes do not usually increase that much in the intervening period. Further, where income must be determined for both child support and spousal support, there are practical pressures to use the same income for both purposes, in the interests of simplicity and consistency. The formulas provide ranges for amount, and adjustments can be made through selecting a particular amount within the ranges. Finally, we do not wish to create an unduly technical approach that might encourage litigation over income issues.

**The Advisory Guidelines start from the practical position that the relevant time for determining the incomes of the spouses is the date of the hearing or the date of the agreement, at both interim and initial stages.**

There will be two situations where there may need to be some adjustment to this general approach:

- where there has been a lengthy period of time between the separation and the initial order or agreement, it is more likely that the payor will have experienced a substantial increase in income after separation or that the recipient will have had an income reduction.
- in a small number of cases, even with a shorter separation, the payor can experience a substantial increase in income between separation and the date of initial determination of spousal support.

In these situations, it may be necessary to look more closely at the post-separation income changes, applying the principles set out in Chapter 14.

## 7 THE *WITHOUT CHILD SUPPORT* FORMULA

Here we examine the first of the two basic formulas that lie at the core of the Advisory Guidelines — the ***without child support* formula**. This formula applies in cases where there are no dependent children and hence no concurrent child support obligations. Assuming entitlement, the formula generates ranges for amount and duration of spousal support.

The *without child support* formula covers a diverse range of fact situations, the only unifying factor being the absence of a concurrent child support obligation for a child or children of the marriage.[61] It covers marriages of all lengths where the spouses never had children. It also applies to long marriages where there were children, but they are no longer dependent.[62] The support claims in these cases involve a mix of compensatory and non-compensatory rationales.

It might seem impossible to develop one formula that could yield appropriate support outcomes over such a wide array of marital situations. In developing the formula we turned to the concept of **merger over time**, which incorporates both compensatory and non-compensatory rationales for spousal support. Put simply, the idea is that as a marriage lengthens, spouses more deeply merge their economic and non-economic lives, resulting in greater claims to the marital standard of living.[63] Using that concept, which relates support outcomes to the length of the marriage, we developed a formula that surprisingly generates results consistent with much of current practice, while bringing some much-needed structure.

In what follows we first introduce the basic structure of the *without child support* formula and provide an example of its operation. We then discuss the concept of merger over time that underlies the formula and its relation to existing rationales for spousal support. This is followed by a more detailed examination of the different parts of the formula and a series of further examples illustrating the formula's application in a variety of factual contexts.

### 7.1 The Basic Structure of the *without child support* formula

The *without child support* formula is set out in the box below in its most basic form. The formula is in fact two formulas — one for amount and one for duration. The formula generates **ranges** for amount and duration, rather than fixed numbers.

There are two crucial factors under the formula:

- the gross income difference between the spouses, and
- the length of the marriage, or more precisely, as will be explained below, the length of the period of cohabitation.

Both amount and duration increase incrementally with the length of marriage.

---

[61] Support obligations to children or spouses from prior relationships are dealt with as exceptions under both formulas; see Chapter 11.
[62] Some medium length marriages with dependent children in which support is initially determined under the *with child support* formula may cross-over to the without child support formula for a re-determination of amount after child support ceases. Crossover is discussed in Chapter 14, Variation and Review, below.
[63] In developing this formula we drew in part on the American Law Institute (ALI) proposals referred to in Chapter 1, including the concept of merger over time. As we discuss further below, this concept-although not the terminology-is strongly anchored in our current law of spousal support.

## The *Without Child Support* Formula

**Amount** ranges from 1.5 to 2 percent of the difference between the spouses' gross incomes (the **gross income difference**) for each year of marriage (or more precisely, year of cohabitation), up to a maximum of 50 percent. The range remains fixed for marriages 25 years or longer, at 37.5 to 50 percent of income difference. (The upper end of this maximum range is capped at the amount that would result in equalization of the spouses' net incomes – the **net income cap**).

**Duration** ranges from .5 to 1 year for each year of marriage. However support will be **indefinite (duration not specified)** if the marriage is **20 years or longer** in duration *or*, if the marriage has lasted five years or longer, when years of marriage and age of the support recipient (at separation) added together total 65 or more (the **rule of 65**).

A simple example illustrating the basic operation of the *without child support* formula will be helpful at this point before we venture further into its more complex details. The primary purpose of this example is to show the basic calculations required under the formula and to give a sense of the outcomes the formula generates.

### Example 7.1

Arthur and Ellen have separated after a 20-year marriage and one child. During the marriage Arthur, who had just finished his commerce degree when the two met, worked for a bank, rising through the ranks and eventually becoming a branch manager. He was transferred several times during the course of the marriage. His gross annual income is now $90,000. Ellen worked for a few years early in the marriage as a bank teller, then stayed home until their son was in school full time. She worked part time as a store clerk until he finished high school. Their son is now independent. Ellen now works full time as a receptionist earning $30,000 gross per year. Both Arthur and Ellen are in their mid forties.

Assuming entitlement has been established in this case, here is how support would be determined under the *without child support* formula.

To determine the **amount** of support:

- Determine the gross income difference between the parties:
  $90,000 -$30,000 = $60,000
- Determine the applicable percentage by multiplying the length of the marriage by 1.5-2 percent per year:
  1.5 X 20 years = 30 percent
  to
  2 X 20 years = 40 percent
- Apply the applicable percentage to the income difference:
  30 percent X $60,000 = $18,000/year ($1,500/month)
  to
  40 percent X $60,000 = $24,000/year ($2,000/month)

**Duration** would be indefinite (duration not specified) in this case because the length of the marriage was 20 years.

**Thus, assuming entitlement, spousal support under the formula would be in the range of $1,500 to $2,000 per month for an indefinite (not specified) duration. This formula amount assumes the usual tax consequences, i.e. deductible to the payor and taxable to the recipient. It would also be open to the normal process of variation and review.**

An award of $1,500 per month, at the low end of the range, would leave Ellen with a gross annual income of $48,000 and Arthur with one of $72,000. An award of $2,000 per month, at the high end of the range, would leave Ellen with a gross annual income of $54,000 and Arthur with one of $66,000. In Chapter 9 we deal with the factors that determine the setting of a precise amount within that range.

On first glance, this formula no doubt looks like an entirely new approach to spousal support, far removed both from the *Divorce Act* and its spousal support objectives and factors and from the principles of compensatory and non-compensatory support that the Supreme Court of Canada articulated in *Moge* and *Bracklow*. Before we examine the operation and application of this formula in more detail, we explain the concept of "merger over time" that underlies this formula and how it relates to existing theories of spousal support and the current law. We will show that the formula is a "proxy measure" for factors such as economic disadvantage, need, and standard of living that are currently used to determine spousal support outcomes.

## 7.2 Merger over Time and Existing Theories of Spousal Support

The idea that underlies the *without child support* formula and explains sharing income in proportion to the length of the marriage is **merger over time**. We use this term[64] to capture the idea that as a marriage lengthens, spouses merge their economic and non-economic lives more deeply, with each spouse making countless decisions to mould his or her skills, behaviour and finances around those of the other spouse. Under the *without child support* formula, the income difference between the spouses represents their differential loss of the marital standard of living. The formulas for both amount and duration reflect the idea that the longer the marriage, the more the lower-income spouse should be protected against such a differential loss.

Under this formula, short marriages without children will generate very modest awards, both in terms of amount and duration. In cases where there are adequate resources, the support could be paid out in a single lump sum. Medium length marriages will generate transitional awards of varying lengths and in varying amounts, increasing with the length of the relationship. Long marriages will generate generous spousal support awards on an indefinite basis that will provide the spouses with something approaching equivalent standards of living after marriage breakdown. The formula generates the same ranges for long marriages in which the couple have never had children as for long marriages in which there have been children who are now grown.

While the label may be unfamiliar, the concept of merger over time, which relates the extent of the spousal support claim to the length of the marriage, underlies much of our current law. Its clearest endorsement can be found in Justice L'Heureux-Dubé's much-quoted passage from *Moge*:

> Although the doctrine of spousal support which focuses on equitable sharing does not guarantee to either party the marital standard of living enjoyed during the marriage, this standard is far from irrelevant to support entitlement. . . As marriage should be regarded as a joint endeavour, the longer the relationship endures, the closer the economic union, the greater will be the presumptive claim to equal standards of living upon its dissolution.[65]

---

[64] We have taken this term from the American Law Institute (ALI) proposals which are referred to in Chapter 1 above and discussed in more detail in the Background Paper.

[65] *Moge v. Moge*, [1992] 3 S.C.R. 813 at 870.

Merger over time offers an effective way of capturing both the compensatory and non-compensatory spousal support objectives that have been recognized by our law since *Moge* and *Bracklow*. Under our current law, both kinds of support claims have come to be analyzed in terms of loss of the marital standard of living. Budgets, and more specifically budgetary deficits, now play a central role in quantifying this drop in standard of living. Under the *without child support* formula, the spousal income difference serves as a convenient and efficient **proxy measure** for loss of the marital standard of living, replacing the uncertainty and imprecision of budgets. The length of marriage then determines the extent of the claim to be protected against this loss of the marital standard of living.

Merger over time can have a significant compensatory component. One of the common ways in which spouses merge their economic lives is by dividing marital roles to accommodate the responsibilities of child-rearing. Compensatory claims will loom large in one significant segment of marriages covered by the *without child support* formula — long marriages in which there were children of the marriage who are now independent.

Compensatory claims, in theory, focus on the lower income spouse's loss of earning capacity, career development, pension benefits etc. as a result of having assumed primary responsibility for child care. However in practice, after *Moge*, courts began to respond to the difficulties of quantifying such losses with any accuracy, particularly in longer marriages, by developing proxy measures of economic loss that focussed on the marital standard of living. When awarding spousal support in cases involving long traditional marriages, courts began to articulate their goal as providing the lower income spouse with a reasonable standard of living as assessed against the marital standard of living. And increasingly the standard for determining spousal support in long marriages has become a rough equivalency of standards of living.

Merger over time also has a significant non-compensatory component. In cases of long traditional marriages where the children are grown, it is now common to see spousal support justified on a dual basis. Non-compensatory support claims based on dependency over a long period of time are commonly relied upon to supplement compensatory claims based on earning-capacity loss. In marriages where the spouses have never had children — the other segment of marriages covered by the *without child support* formula — spousal support claims are usually non-compensatory in nature, based on need, dependency, and loss of the marital standard of living. Merger over time addresses these non-compensatory claims.

Giving precise content to the concept of non-compensatory or needs-based support has been one of the main challenges in spousal support law since *Bracklow*. One reading of *Bracklow* suggests that non-compensatory support is grounded in the economic dependency or, in Justice McLachlin's words, the "interdependency" of the spouses. It recognizes the difficulties of disentangling lives that have been intertwined in complex ways over lengthy periods of time. On this broad reading of *Bracklow*, which many courts have accepted, need is not confined to situations of absolute economic necessity, but is a relative concept related to the previous marital standard of living.[66] On this view entitlement to non-compensatory support arises whenever a lower income spouse experiences a significant drop in standard of living after marriage breakdown as a result of loss of access to the other spouse's income, with amount and duration resolved by an individual judge's sense of fairness.

---

[66] Some read *Bracklow* as grounding non-compensatory support in a "basic social obligation" theory of spousal support. This somewhat questionable theory, which is discussed in more detail in the Background Paper, understands need in the absolute sense of an inability to meet basic needs and grounds the obligation to meet that need in the status of marriage itself.

Merger over time incorporates this broad view of non-compensatory support and provides some structure for quantifying awards made on this basis.[67] It takes account not just of obvious economic losses occasioned by the marriage, but also of the elements of reliance and expectation that develop in spousal relationships and increase with the length of the relationship.

The *without child support* formula generates the same ranges for long marriages in which the couple have never had children as for long marriages in which there have been children who are now grown. This result, which flows from the merger over time principle, mirrors what we find in the current law — lengthy marriages involving economic dependency give rise to significant spousal support obligations without regard to the source of the dependency.

We recognize that in some specific situations the *without child support* formula, based as it is on the concept of merger over time which gives significant weight to the length of the marriage, may not adequately satisfy either compensatory or non-compensatory (needs-based) support objectives. Rather than modifying the formula, which in general works well across a wide-range of fact situations and incomes, we have dealt with these problems through exceptions — the exception for disproportionate compensatory claims in shorter marriages; the illness and disability exception, and the basic needs/undue hardship exception in short marriages. These exceptions are discussed in Chapter 12, below.

We now turn to a more detailed examination of the operation and application of the formula.

## 7.3 Determining the Length of the Relationship

The *without child support* formula relies upon length of marriage for determining both amount and duration of support. While we use the convenient term "length of marriage", the actual measure under the Advisory Guidelines is the **period of cohabitation**. This includes pre-marital cohabitation and ends with separation. Inclusion of pre-marital cohabitation in determining length of marriage is consistent with what most judges do now in determining spousal support. This way of defining length of marriage also makes the Advisory Guidelines more easily used under provincial spousal support laws, which apply to non-marital relationships.

We have not set precise rules for determining the length of marriage. The simplest approach would be to round up or down to the nearest full year, and this is what we have done in our examples. Another, slightly more complicated, approach would be to allow for half years and round up or down to that. Because the formula generates ranges and not a fixed number, absolute precision in the calculation of the length of the marriage is not required. Addition or subtraction of half a year will likely make little or no difference to the outcome.

## 7.4 The Formula for Amount

Several aspects of the formula for amount should be noted. First, this formula uses **gross income** (i.e. before tax) figures rather than net (i.e. after tax). (The determination of income is

---

[67] Building as it does on the concept of merger over time, the *without child support* formula does not directly incorporate the "basic social obligation" theory of non-compensatory support that some read *Bracklow* as supporting, see footnote immediately above. The *without child support* formula produces awards that will go some way toward meeting basic needs where they exist, but limits the extent of any basic social obligation by the length of the marriage. However, some of the exceptions identified in Chapter 12, such as the illness/disability exception and the basic needs/hardship exception in short marriages do provide some accommodation for elements of basic social obligation.

dealt with more fully in Chapter 6.) While net income figures may be marginally more accurate, familiarity and ease of calculation tipped the scales in favour of using gross income figures.[68] As you will see in Chapter 8, net income figures are used under the *with child support* formula because of the need to deal with the differential tax treatment of spousal and child support.

Second, this formula applies a specified percentage to the **income difference** between the spouses rather than allocating specified percentages of the pool of combined spousal incomes. In applying income sharing to the spousal income difference this formula once again differs from the *with child support* formula where the use of net income figures requires a model of income sharing that applies to a combined pool of spousal incomes.

Third, the formula for amount does not use a fixed or flat percentage for sharing the income differential. Instead, drawing on the underlying concept of merger of time, the formula incorporates a **durational factor** to increase the percentage of income shared as the marriage increases in length.[69] The durational factor is 1.5 to 2 percent of the gross income difference for each year of marriage.

The **ranges for amount** were developed by first determining the point when maximum sharing would be reached, which we set at 25 years. We also started with the assumption that maximum sharing would involve something close to equalization of incomes, or sharing 50 percent of the gross income difference. We then essentially worked backwards to determine what level of income sharing per year would be required to reach maximum sharing at year 25. The answer was 2 percent per year. In the course of developing the formula, we experimented with different percentage ranges, but the range of 1.5 to 2 percent provided the best fit with outcomes under current practice.

We chose income equalization (50 per cent of the gross income difference) as the **maximum level of income sharing**, potentially reached after 25 years of marriage and representing the full merger of the spouses" lives. Much time was spent considering the arguments for a somewhat lower maximum to take into account incentive effects and the costs of going out to work in situations where only the payor is employed. However, we also recognized that there would be cases where equalization of income would be appropriate. For example where only pension income is being shared after a very long marriage, where both spouses are low income, or perhaps where both spouses are employed after a long marriage, but with a significant income disparity. We drafted the formula to allow for that possibility.

After the release of the Draft Proposal we sought feedback on the issue of whether the maximum level of sharing should be set lower than 50 percent of the gross income difference. We concluded that income equalization should be retained as the maximum level of sharing, but that it should be expressed as equalization of net incomes rather than of gross incomes. The formula has therefore been adjusted by capping the upper end of the maximum range at equalization of the spouses' net incomes — the **net income cap**.

## 7.4.1 The equalization of net income cap

In long marriages where the formula generates the maximum range of 37.5 to 50 percent of the gross income difference the recipient can end up with more than 50 per cent of the spouses' net income, notably where the payor spouse is still employed and subject to tax and employment deductions, and the recipient has little or no income. This result should never occur.

---

[68] In the revision process we introduced one small element of a net income calculation-an "equalization of net income" cap on the formula, which is discussed below.

[69] The concept of the durational factor is drawn from the ALI and Maricopa County guidelines; see Chapter 1.

To avoid this result, shortly after the release of the Draft Proposal we began advising lawyers and judges to look closely at the net incomes of the spouses in these longer marriages when determining an appropriate amount within the range. We have now decided to modify the *without child support* formula itself by introducing a **net income cap. The recipient of spousal support should never receive an amount of spousal support that will leave him or her with more than 50 percent of the couple's net disposable income or monthly cash flow.**

Effectively, the introduction of the net income cap retains income equalization as the maximum level of sharing under the *without child support* formula. It simply provides for a more accurate calculation of income equalization. As for lowering the high end of the maximum range below equalization of net income, we concluded that the arguments that supported the initial choice of income equalization as the maximum level of sharing continued to be persuasive. As well, there was no obvious consensus around a lower percentage cap.

The software programs can calculate the "50 percent of net income" limit with precision and the formula range presented on the screen will reflect this limit at the upper end of the range. In computing "net income" for purposes of this cap, the permitted deductions would be federal and provincial income taxes, employment insurance premiums, Canada Pension Plan contributions, and any deductions that benefit the recipient spouse (e.g. medical or dental insurance, group life insurance and other benefit plans). Mandatory pension deductions are not permitted, for the same reasons as under the basic *with child support* formula, explained below in Chapter 8. Union dues and professional fees are already deducted from the spouses' gross incomes, consistent with the *Federal Child Support Guidelines* (see Chapter 6).

One of the advantages of the *without child support* formula is that the calculations can be done without a computer. For those without software, or more precise net income calculations, this net income cap can be calculated crudely by hand, at 48 percent of the gross income difference. This "48 percent" method is a second-best, but adequate, alternative.[70]

In thinking about the maximum level of sharing under this formula it is important to keep in mind that the formula does not **require** an award that would equalize spousal incomes after 25 years, but rather **permits** awards in the range of between 37.5 to 50 per cent of the gross income difference (capped at net income equalization). Consistent with current law, the formula does not generate a general rule of income equalization; it simply provides for the possibility of equalization.

## 7.4.2 The problem of amount in short marriages

The feedback we received after the release of the Draft Proposal, combined with our continued reading of Guidelines cases, has confirmed that the ranges for amount generated by the *without child support* formula are "about right" and require no major adjustment beyond the net income cap.

We have generally found that the *without child support* formula works well, generating a reasonable range of outcomes across a wide range of cases from short to long marriages with varying incomes. The formula works extremely well for long marriages, which constitute the majority of the cases in which this formula is applied.[71] For medium length marriages, in some

---

[70] The "48 percent" cap will work well in cases where the payor is working and the recipient is not. It will not necessarily be a good proxy for the equalization of net income cap where both parties are working; that will depend upon the spouses' respective tax rates and deductions.

[71] This is true not only for long marriages/relationships in which there were children who are now adults, but also long marriages/relationships in which the parties had no children. See *Foley v.*

cases the monthly amounts need to be adjusted (i.e. increased) through restructuring (see Chapter 10), but we were well aware of this when we developed the formula. We placed heavy emphasis on restructuring to render the results of the formula consistent with current practice. These are also the cases — medium-length marriages without children — that frequently give rise to exceptions.

During the feedback process we did hear criticisms in some parts of the country that the amounts produced by the formula in shorter marriage cases were "too low".

In some of these cases, there was a failure to consider the **compensatory exception** — the exception for disproportionate compensatory claims in shorter marriages. In these cases, one spouse may have experienced a significant economic loss as a result of the marriage, by moving or by giving up employment, for example. Or, one spouse may have conferred an economic benefit on the other spouse by funding his or her pursuit of a professional degree or other education and training. This exception is considered in more detail in Chapter 12.

In other, non-compensatory cases, the formula was criticized as not providing enough support for the transition from the marital standard of living back to a lower standard of living based upon the recipient's earning ability. In these cases, involving marriages of less than 6 or 7 years, there is also little scope for much restructuring. This raised the issue of whether the structure of the formula needed to be fundamentally changed by increasing the percentage level of income-sharing in shorter marriages.

In the end, we concluded against any change to the basic structure of the formula. In the majority of cases across the country the formula works well for short marriages without children, which under current law typically give rise to very limited support obligations, if entitlement is found at all. The modest amounts generated by the formula are typically restructured into a lump sum or into a very short transitional award. In most of these cases, the recipient has a base income, which is supplemented by spousal support. In some parts of the country one does find more generous transitional awards providing the marital standard of living even after short marriages. This is a limited, regional pattern that is difficult to justify under the current principles that govern spousal support.

We do recognize, however, that there is a specific problem for shorter marriages where the recipient has little or no income. In these shorter marriage cases, the formula may generate too little support for the low income recipient even to meet her or his basic needs for a transitional period. The amount required to meet those basic needs will vary from big city to small city to town to rural area. Whether restructuring provides a satisfactory outcome, i.e. more support for a shorter time, will depend upon where the recipient lives. Thus the problem for these short-to-medium-marriage-low-income cases is most acute in big cities.

We did not wish to change the structure of the formula itself for this one sub-set of cases. The best approach to these cases was to create a carefully-tailored exception — the **basic needs/ undue hardship exception for short marriages** — discussed further in Chapter 12 on Exceptions below.

---

*Girard*, [2006] O.J. No. 2496 (S.C.J.) which involved a 20 year same-sex relationship and *Long-Beck v. Beck*, [2006] N.B.J. No. 398, 2006 NBQB 317 which involved a 22 year marriage without children in which the wife quit work with the husband's consent.

## 7.5 The Formula for Duration

As with amount, duration under the *without child support* formula increases with the length of marriage. Subject to the provisions for indefinite support (duration not specified), the formula generates ranges for duration with the ends of the ranges determined as follows:

- **a minimum duration of half the length of the marriage and**
- **a maximum duration of the length of the marriage**

**It is important to remember, as discussed in Chapter 5 on application, that any periods of interim support are to be included in the durational ranges.**

The ranges for duration under the *without child support* formula are admittedly very broad, allowing for an award at the top end of the range that is effectively double in value that at the bottom end. This will be particularly significant in medium-length marriages. Given the uncertainties in the current law on duration, it was not possible to come up with tighter ranges.

The formula also provides for indefinite support (duration not specified) in two circumstances:

- when the marriage has been 20 years or longer in length; or
- when the marriage has lasted five years or longer, **if the years of marriage plus the** *age* **of the support recipient** *at the time of separation* **equals or exceeds 65 and (the rule of 65).**

The "rule of 65" recognizes that length of marriage cannot be the only factor in determining the duration of spousal support in marriages without dependent children. **Age** is also a significant factor as it affects the ability to become self-supporting.

### 7.5.1 The tendency to ignore duration

Our monitoring of the use of the Advisory Guidelines since the release of the Draft Proposal has shown that **in practice the durational aspect of the *without child support* formula is often ignored.** The formula is used to determine the amount of spousal support, but not duration. In some cases awards are for shorter periods of time than the formula suggests. In other cases the durational limits are ignored in favour of indefinite orders.

To ignore duration is to misapply the *without child support* formula. Amount and duration are interrelated parts of the formula — they are a package deal. Using one part of the formula without the other undermines its integrity and coherence. If the durational limits were to be systematically increased, for example, by lowering the threshold for indefinite support, the formula would have to be redesigned and the amounts decreased. Within the scheme of the Advisory Guidelines itself, adjustment of duration beyond the formula requires restructuring and will involve a corresponding adjustment of amount.

In what follows we discuss in more detail four aspects of the formula for duration under the *without child support* formula: indefinite support, the "rule of 65", time limits in short marriages, and time limits in medium-length marriages. The real problem of duration under this formula has proven to be this last aspect, the use of time limits in marriages that are neither long nor short.

### 7.5.2 The meaning of "indefinite" support

In using the term "indefinite" we simply adopted a word that had been used for years in spousal support law to mean "an order for support without a time limit at the time it is made". Under the Advisory Guidelines an order for indefinite support does not necessarily mean permanent support, and it certainly does not mean that support will continue indefinitely at the level set by the formula.

Under the current law, orders for indefinite support are open to variation as the parties' circumstances change over time and may also have review conditions attached to them. The Advisory Guidelines do nothing to change this: **"indefinite" support means support that is subject to the normal process of variation and review.**

Through the process of review and variation the amount of spousal support may be reduced, for example if the recipient's income increases or if the recipient fails to make reasonable efforts to earn income and income is imputed. Support may even be terminated if the basis for entitlement disappears. It is true that current law supports the idea that after long marriages spousal support will often be permanent, even if the amount is subject to reduction to reflect the recipient's obligation to pursue self-sufficiency.

In practice, however, most orders for indefinite support after long marriages will be significantly modified, if not eliminated, after the retirement of the payor and the receipt of pension income by the payor and the recipient. "Indefinite" often means "until the payor reaches 65". Variation and review in the context of the Advisory Guidelines are discussed in more detail in Chapter 14.

After the release of the Draft Proposal we were very surprised to learn from our feedback sessions that the term "indefinite" in the Advisory Guidelines was being misinterpreted by many as meaning "infinite" or "permanent."

We realized that we would have to develop a new term to express the concept that indefinite orders are not necessarily permanent, that they are subject to review and variation and, through that process, even to time limits and termination. Our solution has been to add "duration not specified" as a parenthetical explanation whenever the term "indefinite" is used in the formulas, i.e. **indefinite (duration not specified).**

## 7.5.3 The "rule of 65": the age factor and indefinite support

The *without child support* formula provides that indefinite (duration not specified) support will be available even in cases where the marriage is shorter than 20 years **if the years of marriage plus the *age* of the support recipient *at the time of separation* equals or exceeds 65.** In a shorthand expression, we described this as the **"rule of 65".**

Thus, if a 10 year marriage ends when the recipient is 55, indefinite (duration not specified) support will be available because years of marriage (10) plus age (55) equals 65. Note that this is only a "rule" about duration, as the amount of support would be limited by the length of the marriage, i.e. 1.5 to 2 per cent per year or 15 to 20 per cent of the gross income difference in a 10-year marriage.

In reality, given the ages of the parties in the cases covered by the rule of 65, there will likely be significant changes in the amount of support ordered upon the retirement of one or both of the spouses. This refinement to the formula for duration is intended to respond to the situation of older spouses who were economically dependent during a medium length marriage and who may have difficulty becoming self-sufficient given their age.

**The "rule of 65" for indefinite (duration not specified) support is not available in short marriages (under 5 years in length).** The assumption in the current law is that short marriages generate only limited support obligations.

In the Draft Proposal, we struggled with the issue of whether an age component should always be required for indefinite (duration not specified) support — i.e. whether the "rule of 65" should apply even in long marriages. Under a 20 year rule with no age requirement, for example, a 38 year-old spouse leaving a 20 year marriage would be entitled to indefinite (duration not specified) support. Some would argue that indefinite (duration not specified) support is not appropriate for a spouse who is still relatively young and capable of becoming self-sufficient. If the "rule of 65" were generally applicable, support would not become indefinite (duration not specified) even after a 20 year marriage unless the recipient were 45 years of age or older.

Several considerations led us to the conclusion that a 20-year rule without any age requirement was the more appropriate choice. First, a spouse who married young and spent the next 20 years caring for children could be more disadvantaged than someone who married when they were older and had been able to acquire some job skills before withdrawing from the labour force. As well, under the current law it would be very difficult to impose a time-limit on support after a 20 year marriage, even if self-sufficiency and an eventual termination of support were contemplated at some point in the future. The typical order would be an indefinite order subject to review and/or variation. An order for indefinite support (duration not specified) under the Advisory Guidelines is no different.

Despite the frequent misinterpretation of the meaning of "indefinite", there was no pressure to change either of the conditions for indefinite support. Most of the feedback about the "rule of 65" focussed on technical issues of its application, as there was general agreement on the "rule".

## 7.5.4 Time limits in short marriages

The current law of spousal support has no difficulty with time limits in short marriages without children. Time limits, or lump sum orders, are common in these cases. Even in those jurisdictions where appeal courts have discouraged the use of time-limited support, discussed below, short marriages without children are identified as permissible exceptions. In practice, we were told in the feedback phase, these cases are not a problem.

## 7.5.5 Lowering the threshold for indefinite support?

In some parts of the country, it is very difficult to time limit spousal support, by reason of appellate decisions or local practices. For marriages of less than 20 years, the Draft Proposal incorporated time limits, although these were generous time limits. During the feedback phase, we did canvass the possibility of lowering the threshold for indefinite support, below 20 years.

We found little support for such a change. Even those who wanted to lower the threshold could not agree on what that new threshold should be. Many lawyers, mediators and judges expressed their frustration with the current law on duration, especially their perceived inability to use time limits in a sensible way. The durational limits in the Advisory Guidelines were seen as providing some structure for negotiations, initial decisions and variation or review. Lowering the threshold for indefinite support would not solve the problem and would in practice undermine the usefulness of the Guidelines.

## 7.5.6 The problem of time limits in medium length marriages

The real "problems" for time limits under the *without child support* formula are concentrated in marriages that are neither "long" (20 years or more) or "short" (under 5 years). For marriages that last 6 to 19 years, in every jurisdiction we were told, it becomes increasingly difficult to impose time limits on initial support orders as the marriage lengthens. At some point, in each jurisdiction, the time limits were seen as inconsistent with the current law on duration. At the same time, as we explained above, many lawyers, mediators and judges wanted to see more use of time limits.

It is certainly true that after *Moge* time limits fell into disfavour because of the associated problems of "crystal ball gazing" and arbitrary terminations of spousal support where self-sufficiency was "deemed" rather than actually achieved. Time-limited orders became less common. However, since *Bracklow*, some judges have brought back time limits, at least for non-compensatory support orders. While time limits are frequently negotiated by parties in agreements and consent orders, the law on time limits remains uncertain. In some parts of the country trial courts feel bound by appellate court rulings confining time-limited orders to a narrow range of exceptional cases, primarily short marriages without children.

It is in marriages of medium length that duration remains uncertain. Here practice varies and depends upon many factors — regional support cultures and the governing provincial appellate court jurisprudence; whether the context is negotiation or court-ordered support; and whether the support claim is compensatory or non-compensatory in nature. The most that can be said is that current law is inconsistent on the issue of time limits in medium-length marriages.

In practice the issue of duration in medium-length marriages is often put off to the future, to be dealt with through ongoing reviews and variations. In some cases this process of review and variation may eventually generate a time-limited order leading to termination. Under current practice uncertainty about duration can generate low monthly awards, as judges or lawyers fear that any monthly amount of support could continue for a long time, even permanently.

In developing the Draft Proposal, it was our view that reasonable time limits for medium length marriages would be an essential element of the scheme, under both the without child support and *with child support* formulas, especially if the Guidelines were to generate reasonable monthly amounts. *Bracklow* emphasized this interrelationship between amount and duration, recognizing that a low award paid out over a lengthy period of time is equivalent to an award for a higher amount paid out over a shorter period of time. As well, we were aware of the importance of providing structure in this area to facilitate negotiation and settlement. Recognizing that this was an area of law in flux, we saw a role for the Advisory Guidelines in helping to shape the developing law.

In assessing the compatibility of the time limits generated by the *without child support* formula with current law it is important to keep in mind that they are potentially very generous; in medium length marriages they can extend for up to 19 years. These time limits are thus very different from the short and arbitrary time limits, typically of between three to five years, that became standard under the clean-break model of spousal support for medium-to-long marriages and which *Moge* rejected. The time limits generated by the formula should be assessed in context — they are potentially for lengthy periods of time and, once marriages are of any significant length, operate in conjunction with generous monthly amounts.

As well, it is important to keep in mind that in the context of the *without child support* formula, support claims in medium-length marriages will typically be non-compensatory. In non-compensatory support cases, one strand of the post-*Bracklow* case law recognizes the appropriateness of time limited orders when the purpose of the support order is to provide a period of transition to a lower standard of living rather than compensation for lost career opportunities. Such use of time limits does not involve "crystal-ball gazing" and the making of arbitrary assumptions about future developments, but rather reflects the basis of entitlement.

In Chapter 8 you will see that we dealt with the issue of time limits in short and medium-length marriages with children somewhat differently, because of the strong compensatory claims in such cases and the need for individualized assessment of recipients' challenges in over-coming disadvantage resulting from the assumption of the child-rearing role.

We recognize that some provincial appellate court jurisprudence may at this point create barriers to the use of the formula's time-limits by trial judges. We also recognize that the lengthy time limits potentially generated under the *without child support* formula – up to 19 years in duration – are very different from the typical kinds of time limits with which our law of spousal support is familiar and raise some distinct problems of foreseeability. In our view, the law around time limits will continue to develop and to respond to the durational ranges under the formula. We already see signs of this in the Guidelines case law since the release of the Draft Proposal which offers several examples of judges making somewhat novel time-limited orders for the lengthy durations generated by the *without child support* formula.[72] In assessing the feasibility of these orders, it is important to remember that time-limited orders are subject to variation. It is thus possible to avoid some of the problems of arbitrary "crystal ball gazing" while reinforcing expectations with respect to the eventual termination of the support order.[73]

As well, in cases where it is not feasible for courts to impose the time limits generated by the formula in initial orders, the time limits can still be used in a "softer", more indirect way to structure the on-going process of review and variation and to reinforce expectations of the eventual termination of the order. This is not dissimilar to the use of the time limits under the *with child support* formula where they establish the outside limit for indefinite (duration not specified) orders. The fact that courts are reluctant to make time limited orders on initial applications does not preclude the eventual use of time limits on subsequent reviews or variations. The Guidelines case law already offers several examples of this "softer" use of time limits in subsequent variations or reviews to bring an eventual termination to what was initially an indefinite order.[74]

Finally, if the durational limits under this formula, even in their "softer" form, are found to be inappropriate in cases close to the 20 year threshold for indefinite support, restructuring can be used to extend duration. As is explained in Chapter 10, duration can be extended by restructuring so long as an appropriate downward adjustment is made to amount so as to keep the total value of the award within the global ranges generated by the formula.

## 7.6 Making the Formula Concrete — Some Examples

### 7.6.1 A short-marriage example

In cases of short marriages, marriages of less than 5 years, the *without child support* formula generates very small amounts for a very short duration. The formula will always generate time-limits in these cases.[75]

---

[72] See for example, *Hance v. Carbone*, 2006 CarswellOnt 7063 (Ont.S.C.J.) (17 1/2 yr. marriage; spousal support ordered for 15 years in addition to 6 years time-limited provided under separation agreement) and *Bishop v. Bishop*, [2005] N.S.J. No. 324, 2005 NSSC 220 (N.S.S.C.) (13 year marriage; final order spousal support for 10 years in addition to 1 year interim). For an example under the *with child support* formula, discussed in Chapter 8, see *Fewer v. Fewer*, [2005] N.J. No. 303, 2005 NLTD 163 (N.L.S.C.) (16 1/2 yr. marriage; 1 child 15 with wife; spousal support ordered for 16 1/2 yrs from separation, subject to variation).

[73] The variation of time-limited orders is explicitly discussed in *Fewer, ibid.*

[74] One of the best examples is *Kelly v. Kelly*, [2007] B.C.J. No. 324, 2007 BCSC 227 (17 year relationship, no children, support paid for 9 years; wife remarried; on variation application support recognized as non-compensatory; time-limited to further 19 months, 10 years total.) Another good example under the *custodial payor* formula is *Puddifant v. Puddifant*, [2005] N.S.J. No. 558, 2005 NSSC 340 (S.C.F.D.) (12 year marriage, 1 child with husband, wife mental illness, support paid for 9 years; on husband's application to terminate support ordered for further 3 years, total 12 years.)

[75] The "rule of 65", which allows for indefinite support to older spouses in marriages of less than 20 years in length, does not apply to short marriages (under 5 years).

*Example 7.2*

Karl and Beth were married for only four years. They had no children. Beth was 25 when they met and Karl was 30. When they married, Beth was a struggling artist. Karl is a music teacher with a gross annual income of $60,000. Beth now earns $20,000 per year, selling her work and giving art lessons to children. Entitlement is a threshold issue before the Advisory Guidelines apply. On these facts, given the disparity in income and Beth's limited income at the point of marriage breakdown, entitlement is likely to be found.

The conditions for indefinite (duration not specified) support do not apply and duration would be calculated on the basis of .5 to 1 year of support for each year of marriage.

To determine the amount of support under the formula:

- Determine the gross income difference between the parties:
  $60,000 − $20,000 = $40,000
- Determine the applicable percentage by multiplying the length of the marriage by 1.5-2 percent per year:
  1.5 X 4 years = 6 percent
  to
  2 X 4 years = 8 percent
- Apply the applicable percentage to the income difference:
  6 percent X $40,000 = $2,400/year ($200/month)
  to
  8 percent X $40,000 = $3,200/year ($267/month)

**Duration** of spousal support = (.5-1) X 4 years of marriage = 2 to 4 years

**The result under the formula is support in the range of $200 to $267 per month for a duration of 2 to 4 years.**

In practice, this modest award would likely be converted into a lump sum using restructuring, discussed in Chapter 10.

## 7.6.2 Some medium-length marriage examples

In medium-length marriages (5 to 19 years), the formula generates increasing amounts of support as the marriage increases in length, moving from relatively small percentages at the shorter end of the spectrum to relatively generous amounts after 15 years, when awards of 30 percent of the gross income difference become possible. Except where the rule of 65 is applicable, the formula generates time limits of varying lengths depending on the length of the marriage. The ranges for duration are, however, very wide, leaving much opportunity to respond to the facts of particular cases.

This category covers a diverse array of cases raising a variety of support objectives. Current law is at its most inconsistent in its handling of these cases. This area posed the greatest challenges to developing a single formula that would yield appropriate results. We concluded that our formula based on merger over time provided the best starting point. But not surprisingly, it is in these cases that there will be the most frequent need to rely upon restructuring to massage the formula outcomes and where there will likely be the greatest resort to exceptions.

### Example 7.3

Bob and Susan have been married 10 years. They married in their late twenties and Sue is now 38. Bob is employed as a computer salesman and Sue is a hairdresser. Both worked throughout the marriage. There were no children. Bob's gross annual income is $65,000; Sue's is $25,000.

Entitlement is a threshold issue before the Advisory Guidelines are applicable. An argument might be made that there is no entitlement to support: Sue is employed full time and could support herself, and there is no compensatory basis for support. However, Sue will suffer a significant drop in standard of living as result of the marriage breakdown and, at an income of $25,000, will likely experience some economic hardship. Current law would suggest an entitlement to at least transitional support on a non-compensatory basis to allow Sue to adjust to a lower standard of living.

The case does not satisfy the conditions for indefinite (duration not specified) support. The marriage is under 20 years and the case does not fall within the "rule of 65" for indefinite support because Sue's age at separation plus years of marriage is below 65 (38+10=48).

To determine the **amount** of support under the formula:

- Determine the **gross income difference** between the parties:
  $65,000 − $25,000 = $40,000
- Determine the **applicable percentage** by multiplying the length of the marriage by 1.5-2 percent per year:
  1.5 X 10 years = **15 percent**
  to
  2 X 10 years = **20 percent**
- Apply the applicable percentage to the income difference:
  15 percent X $40,000 = $6,000/year (**$500/month**)
  to
  20 percent X $40,000 = $8,000/year (**$667/month**)

**Duration** of spousal support = (.5-1) X 10 years of marriage = 5 to 10 years

**The result under the formula is support in the range of $500 to $667 per month for a duration of 5 to 10 years.**

Consistent with current law, the formula essentially generates modest top-up support for a transitional period to assist Sue in adjusting from the marital standard of living.

An award of $500 per month, at the low end of the range, would leave Sue with a gross annual income of $31,000 and Bob with one of $59,000. An award of $667 per month, at the high end of the range, would leave Sue with a gross annual income of $33,000 and Bob with one of $57,000. In a marriage of this length the formula does not equalize incomes.

Some might find the amounts generated by the formula too low, even at the high end of the range. An argument could be made that, consistent with current law, any transitional order should put Sue somewhat closer to the marital standard of living for the period of gearing down. As will be discussed in Chapter 10, a **restructuring** of the formula outcome is possible to produce larger amounts for a shorter duration.

### Example 7.4

David and Jennifer were married for 12 years. It was a second marriage for both. David was 50 when they met. He is a businessman whose gross annual income is now $100,000 per year. Now 62, he is in good health, loves his work, and has no immediate plans to retire.

Jennifer was 45 when they met, while Jennifer was working in his office. She had been a homemaker for 20 years during her first marriage and had received time-limited support. When they met she was working in a low-level clerical position earning $20,000 gross per year. Jennifer, now 57, did not work outside the home during the marriage.

Entitlement is a threshold issue before the Advisory Guidelines are applicable. Given the length of the marriage and Jennifer's lack of income, entitlement to support on non-compensatory grounds would be relatively uncontentious.

The **amount** of support on an income difference of $18,000 and a 12 year marriage would be calculated as follows:

- 18 percent X $100,000 = $18,000/year **($1,500/month)**
  to
  24 percent X $100,000 = $24,000/year **($2,000/month)**

This is a case where the "rule of 65" would govern duration. Because Jennifer's age at separation plus years of marriage is 65 or over (57+12= 69), the formula provides for indefinite (duration not specified) support, rather than the durational range of 6 to 12 years based on length of marriage alone. A variation in amount would, however, be likely when David retires.

**The result under the formula is support in the range of $1,500 to $2,000 a month on an indefinite (duration not specified) basis, subject to variation and possibly review.**

Support at the low end of the range would leave Jennifer with a gross annual income of $18,000 and David with one of $72,000. Support at the high end of the range would leave Jennifer with a gross annual income of $24,000 and David with one of $66,000. Again, because of the length of the marriage (12 years), the formula does not generate results that approach income equalization.

### 7.6.3 Some long-marriage examples

In cases of long marriages (20 years or longer) the formula generates generous levels of spousal support for indefinite periods, reflecting the fairly full merger of the spouses' lives. The long marriages covered by the *without child support* formula fall into two categories: those where there have been children who are no longer dependent and those where the couple did not have children.

*Example 7.1* provides an example of the formula's application to a long marriage with children where the wife was a secondary earner. *Example 7.5*, presented below, involves the familiar scenario of a very long traditional marriage.

### Example 7.5

John and Mary were married for 28 years. Theirs was a traditional marriage in which John worked his way up the career ladder and now earns $100,000 gross per year, while Mary stayed home and raised their two children, both of whom are now grown up and on their own. Mary is 50 years of age and has no income. John is 55.

Entitlement to spousal support is clear on these facts and thus the Advisory Guidelines are applicable. Because the length of the marriage is over 25 years, the maximum range for amount applies — 37.5 to 50 percent of the gross income difference (capped at equalization of net incomes).

The range for amount on an income difference of $100,000 after a 28 year marriage would be:

- 37.5 percent X $100,000 = $37,500/year **($3,125/month)**
  to
  50 percent X $100,000 = $50,000/year **($4,167/month, capped at $4048[76])**

**Duration** is indefinite (duration not specified) because the marriage is 20 years or over in length.

**The formula results in a range for support of $3,125 to $4,048 per month for an indefinite (unspecified) duration, subject to variation and possibly review.**

An award of $3,125 per month, at the low end of the range, would leave Mary with a gross income of $37,500 per year and John with one of $62,500. An award of $4,048 per month, at the high end of the range, would equalize the net incomes of the parties.

As will be discussed further in Chapter 14, the order is open to variation over time in response to changes in the parties' circumstances, including increases in Mary's income or the imputation of income to her if she fails to make reasonable efforts to contribute to her own support. John's retirement would also likely be grounds for variation.

**Example 7.6 involves a long marriage without children.**

### Example 7.6

Richard is a teacher with a gross annual income of $75,000. He is in his late forties. His wife, Judy, is the same age. She trained as a music teacher but has worked as a freelance violinist for most of the marriage, with a present gross income of $15,000 a year. Judy has also been responsible for organizing their active social life and extensive vacations. They were married 20 years. They had no children.

Entitlement will easily be established in this case given the significant income disparity, Judy's limited employment income, and the length of the marriage.

The range for amount under the formula, based on income difference of $60,000 and a 20 year marriage is:

- 30 percent X $60,000 = $18,000/year **($1,500/month)**
  to
  40 percent X $60,000 = $24,000/year **($2,000/month)**

**Duration** would be indefinite (duration not specified) because the marriage was 20 years in length.

**The result under the formula is support in the range from of $1,500 to $2,000 per month for an indefinite (unspecified) duration, subject to variation and possibly review.**

An award at the lower end of the range would leave Judy with a gross annual income of $33,000 and Richard with one of $57,000. An award at the high end of the range would leave Judy with a gross annual income of $39,000 and Richard with one of $51,000.

Judy will certainly be expected to increase her income and contribute to her own support. The issue in applying the formula will be whether a gross income of $30,000 a year, for example,

---

[76] This is based on an assumption of Ontario residence and the applicable tax rates and mandatory deductions in November 2007.

should be attributed to Judy for the purposes of an initial determination of support. If so, support under the formula would be lowered to a range of $1,125 to $1,500 per month (or $13,500 to $18,000 per year).

More likely, Judy would be given some period of time (for example one or two years) before she would be expected to earn at that level, with support to be adjusted at that point, after a review.

## 7.7 After the Formula

As the examples in this chapter indicate, many issues remain after the application of the *without child support* formula — issues of choosing an amount and duration within the ranges, restructuring, and exceptions, all addressed in separate chapters below. It is important to keep these other parts of the Advisory Guidelines in mind, particularly in cases involving the *without child support* formula where restructuring and exceptions will frequently need to be used.

## 8 THE *WITH CHILD SUPPORT* FORMULA

The dividing line between the two proposed formulas under the Advisory Guidelines is the presence of a child support obligation.[77] Where the spouses have not had children or the children have grown up and are on their own, the *without child support* formula will apply. Where a spouse is paying child support, the *with child support* formula will apply.

From a technical perspective, there must be a different formula for spousal support in these cases, a formula that takes into account the payment of child support and its priority over spousal support as set out in s. 15.3 of the *Divorce Act*. Further, because of tax and benefit issues, we have to use net rather than gross incomes. Practically, the payment of child support usually means reduced ability to pay spousal support. And, theoretically, there are different rationales for the amount and duration of spousal support where there are still dependent children to be cared for and supported.

This category of cases dominates in practice, in support statistics and in jurisprudence. Any guidelines must generate a workable formula for amount and duration for this category, a formula that can adjust across a wide range of incomes and family circumstances. For the most part, marriages with dependent children will involve spousal support paid by a parent who is also paying child support to the recipient spouse. The basic formula in this chapter is constructed around this typical situation. Variations on the basic formula are required to accommodate cases of shared and split custody. There are also a sizeable number of cases where the spouse paying spousal support has primary parental responsibility for the children. In these custodial payor situations, an alternative formula must be constructed. Finally, we have added one more hybrid formula, applicable in cases where the only remaining children are away at university or otherwise have their child support determined under section 3(2)(b) of the Child Support Guidelines.

The *with child support* formula is thus really a family of formulas, adjusted for different parenting arrangements.

---

[77] The child support obligation must be for a child of the marriage. A child support obligation to a child from a prior marriage or relationship is dealt with as an exception under both formulas, explained in more detail in Chapter 12 on Exceptions below.

## 8.1 The Compensatory Rationale for Spousal Support

Where there are dependent children, the primary rationale for spousal support is compensatory. After *Moge*, spouses must, as Chief Justice McLachlin put it in *Bracklow*, "compensate each other for foregone careers and missed opportunities during the marriage upon the breakdown of their union."[78] The main reason for those foregone careers and missed opportunities is the assumption of primary responsibility by one spouse for the care of children during the marriage. Where one spouse, in a marriage with children, has become a full-time homemaker or has worked outside the home part time or has worked as a secondary earner, there will be disadvantage and loss at the end of the marriage, usually warranting compensatory support. This compensatory rationale is encompassed by the first of the four objectives of spousal support, in s. 15.2(6)(a) of the *Divorce Act*.

Under compensatory theory, it is usually necessary to estimate the spouse's disadvantage or loss by determining what the recipient's career or employment path might have been, had the recipient not adopted his or her role during the marriage — not an easy task. The ideal evidence would be individualized economic evidence of earning capacity loss, but few litigants can afford such evidence and often it would be highly speculative. Some spouses never establish a career or employment history. For others, their pre-marital and marital choices were shaped by their future expected role during marriage. And there are short marriages, where past losses are relatively small and most of the spouse's child-rearing and any associated losses are still to come in the future.

As was explained in Chapter 1, after *Moge*, courts had to develop proxies to measure that loss where there was no clear and specific career or employment path. Need became the most common proxy, calculated through the conventional budget analysis. Sometimes standard of living was used, with the post-separation position of the recipient spouse measured against the marital standard or some reasonable standard of living. In practice, crude compromises were made in applying the compensatory approach.

More recently, what we have called the **parental partnership** rationale has emerged in the literature and in the case law. On this approach, the obligation for spousal support flows from parenthood rather than the marital relationship itself. It is not the length of the marriage, or marital interdependency, or merger over time, that drives this theory of spousal support, but the presence of dependent children and the need to provide care and support for those children. Unlike the conventional compensatory approach, parental partnership looks at not just past loss, but also the continuing economic disadvantage that flows from present and future child-care responsibilities. For shorter marriages with younger children, these present and future responsibilities are more telling. Further, the parental partnership rationale better reflects the reality that many women never acquire a career before marriage, or mould their pre-marital employment in expectation of their primary parental role after marriage.

The parental partnership rationale is firmly anchored in one of the four statutory objectives in s. 15.2(6) of the *Divorce Act*, where clause (b) states a spousal support order should:

> apportion between the spouses any financial consequences arising from the care of any child of the marriage over and above any obligation for the support of any child of the marriage.

---

[78] *Bracklow v. Bracklow*, [1999] 1 S.C.R. 420 at para. 1.

The 1997 implementation of the *Federal Child Support Guidelines* has reinforced this rationale. Under the Guidelines, only the direct costs of child-rearing — and not even all of them — are included in child support. The indirect costs of child-rearing were left to be compensated through spousal support, as was recognized by the 1995 Family Law Committee's *Report and Recommendations on Child Support*. Principal amongst these indirect costs is the custodial parent's reduced ability to maximize his or her income because of child-care responsibilities. Now that child support is fixed under the *Child Support Guidelines* and determined by a different method than before 1997, spousal support has to be adjusted to reflect the concerns identified by the parental partnership model.

With the implementation of the *Federal Child Support Guidelines* came the increased use of computer software. The software regularly and graphically displays information like net disposable income, monthly cash flow and household standards of living. This information has made spouses, lawyers, mediators and courts more conscious of the financial implications of child and spousal support, in turn reflected in the use of these concepts in determining the amount of spousal support. Before the *Federal Child Support Guidelines*, and even afterwards for a while, most courts were not prepared to award more than 50 percent of the family's net disposable income to the recipient spouse and children, leaving the single payor spouse with the other 50 percent. With the new software, many courts began consciously to allocate more than 50 percent of a family's net disposable income to the recipient spouse and children, and even as much as 60 percent, as in the Ontario Court of Appeal decision in *Andrews v. Andrews*[79] and in numerous trial decisions across the country.[80]

These cases also reveal a non-compensatory element found in some decisions where both child and spousal support are paid to the same parent. There is a household standard of living element within the parental partnership rationale that should be openly acknowledged. Both child and spousal support go into the same household, to support the standard of living of both parent and child. In some cases, spousal support is used as a residual financial remedy to shore up the standard of living that the children experience in the recipient's household.

## 8.2 Background to the Basic Formula

There is no simple way to construct a formula for spousal support where the support payor is also paying child support. First, child support must be determined, as it takes priority over spousal support in assessing the payor's ability to pay. Second, child support is not taxable or deductible, but spousal support is taxable to the recipient and deductible for the payor. Third, child and spousal support must be determined separately, but it is very difficult in any formula to isolate spousal finances cleanly from support of children.

This formula for cases with child support — the *with child support* formula — differs from the *without child support* formula set out in Chapter 7. First, the *with child support* formula uses **the net incomes** of the spouses, not their gross incomes. Second, the *with child support* formula divides the **pool** of combined net incomes between the two spouses, not just the difference between the spouses' gross incomes. Third, in the *with child support* formula, the upper and lower percentage limits for net income division **do not change with the length of the marriage.**

---

[79] *Andrews v. Andrews*, (1999), 50 R.F.L. (4 th) 1 (Ont. C.A.).
[80] See for example *Gale v. Gale* (2000), 6 R.F.L. (5 th) 157 (Man.Q.B.), *Bastedo v. Bastedo*, [2000] P.E.I.J. No. 49 (S.C.T.D.), *Lyttle v. Bourget*, [1999] N.S.J. No. 298 (S.C.), *Tedham v. Tedham*, [2002] B.C.J. No. 1635 (S.C.), *Clark v. Cooper-Clark*, [2002] N.B.J. No. 41 (Q.B.).

Unlike the *without child support* formula, this formula must use **net income**. While gross income would be simpler to understand, calculate and implement, nothing remains simple once child support has to be considered. Different tax treatment demands more detailed after-tax calculations, and ability to pay must be more accurately assessed. Net income computations will usually require computer software, another unavoidable complication.

Thanks to that same computer software, many lawyers had become familiar with net disposable income or monthly cash flow calculations before the release of the Draft Proposal. Judges were using such calculations to underpin their spousal support decisions. In the software programs, these numbers included child and spousal support to produce what can be called **family net disposable income** or monthly cash flow. This larger pool of net income is then divided between the spouses. Often, more than 50 percent of this family net disposable income is allocated to the recipient spouse and children by way of combined child and spousal support, or sometimes as much as 60 percent and occasionally even more. Under the formula proposed here for spousal support, we divide a different and smaller pool of net income, after removing the spouses' respective child support obligations — what we call **individual net disposable income** or **INDI**.

We considered using the more familiar family net disposable income as the basis for the *with child support* formula, rather than this newer variation of individual net disposable income. In the end we opted for individual net disposable income. First, the family net disposable income of the recipient spouse includes both child and spousal support, bulking up the recipient's income in a somewhat misleading fashion and masking the impact of spousal support upon the recipient parent's individual income. Second, allocating family NDI between spouses blurs the distinction between child and spousal support, between child and adult claims upon income. Individual NDI attempts to back out the child support contributions of each spouse, to obtain a better estimate of the income pool that remains to be divided between the adults. Third, after separation, the spouses see themselves, not as one family, but more as individuals with distinct relationships with their children and their former spouses. Fourth, separating out each spouse's individual net disposable income, after removal of child support obligations, produced a more robust and sophisticated formula, one that adjusted better across income levels and numbers of children.

## 8.3 The Basic Formula

Set out in the box below is a summary of how this basic *with child support* formula works. Remember that this formula applies where the higher income spouse is paying both child and spousal support to the lower income spouse who is also the primary parent. By primary parent, we mean the spouse with sole custody or the spouse with primary care of the children in a joint custody arrangement.

---

### The Basic With Child Support Formula for Amount

1. Determine the **individual net disposable income (INDI)** of each spouse:
   - o   Guidelines Income *minus* Child Support *minus* Taxes and Deductions = Payor's INDI
   - o   Guidelines Income *minus* Notional Child Support *minus* Taxes and Deductions *plus* Government Benefits and Credits = Recipient's INDI
2. Add together the individual net disposable incomes. By iteration, determine the range of spousal support amounts that would be required to leave the lower income recipient spouse with between 40 and 46 per cent of the combined INDI.

---

## 8.3.1 Calculating individual net disposable income

Basic to this formula is the concept of **individual net disposable income**, an attempt to isolate a **pool** of net disposable income available after adjustment for child support obligations. The starting point is the Guidelines income of each spouse as is explained in Chapter 6 above. In the interests of uniformity and efficiency, we basically use the same definition of income as that found in the *Federal Child Support Guidelines*. Next, we deduct or back out from each spouse's income their respective **contributions to child support.**

For the child support **payor**, that is usually the table amount, plus any contributions to special or extraordinary expenses, or any other amount fixed under any other provisions of the *Federal Child Support Guidelines*. For the child support **recipient**, a **notional table amount** is deducted, plus any contributions by the recipient spouse to s. 7 expenses. In reality, the recipient will likely spend more than these amounts through direct spending for the children in her or his care. But by this means we make an adjustment, however imperfect, for the recipient's child support obligation. A formula could be constructed without this notional child support number, but such a formula would have adjusted to the number of children and income levels with less precision and with less transparency about the role of the recipient parent.

Second, **income taxes and other deductions** must be subtracted from the incomes of both the payor and the recipient to obtain net incomes. As spousal support is transferred from one spouse to another, because of tax effects, the size of the total pool of individual net disposable income actually changes slightly, which complicates these calculations. The current software does these calculations automatically, as differing hypothetical amounts of spousal support are transferred, a process called "iteration".

Clearly permissible **deductions** are federal and provincial income taxes, as well as employment insurance premiums and Canada Pension Plan contributions. Union dues and professional fees are already deducted from Guidelines income under the adjustments of Schedule III to the *Federal Child Support Guidelines*. Deductions should be recognized for certain benefits, e.g. medical or dental insurance, group life insurance, and other benefit plans, especially those that provide immediate or contingent benefits to the former spouse or the children of the marriage.

More contentious are **deductions for mandatory pension contributions**. We concluded that there should not be an automatic deduction for such pension contributions, but the size of these mandatory deductions may sometimes be used as a factor to justify fixing an amount towards the lower end of the spousal support range.

We reached this conclusion after considerable discussion. Like EI, CPP and other deductions, pension contributions are mandatory deductions, in that the employee has no control over, and no access to, that money. But, unlike other deductions, pension contributions are a form of forced saving that permit the pension member to accumulate an asset. Further, after separation, the spouse receiving support does not usually share in the further pension value being accumulated by post-separation contributions. Finally, there are serious problems of horizontal equity in allowing a deduction for mandatory pension contributions by employees. What about payors with non-contributory pension plans or RRSPs or those without any pension scheme at all? And what about the recipient spouse — would we have to allow a notional or actual deduction for the recipient too, to reflect her or his saving for retirement? In the end, we decided it was fairer and simpler not to allow an automatic deduction for pension contributions.

Third, we **do include** in each spouse's income the amounts identified for **government benefits and refundable credits**. Included are the Child Tax Benefit, the National Child

Benefit Supplement, the GST credit, the refundable medical credit, the Child Disability Benefit, the various provincial benefit and credit schemes, and the new Universal Child Care Benefit. Under the *Federal Child Support Guidelines* these benefits and credits are generally **not** treated as income. For the reasons set out in Chapter 6 on Income above, a different approach is warranted for spousal support purposes.

### 8.3.2　The basic formula: dividing individual net disposable income

Once the individual net disposable income (INDI) of each spouse has been determined, the next step is to add together these individual net disposable incomes. Then we have to iterate, i.e. to estimate hypothetical spousal support repeatedly, in order to determine the amount of spousal support that will leave the lower income recipient spouse with between 40 and 46 percent of the combined pool of individual net disposable income.

How did we arrive at the percentages for the range, from 40 to 46 percent of the individual net disposable income? This was a critical issue in the construction of this formula. In our earlier Sneak Preview in the summer of 2004, we had suggested a higher range, from 44 to 50 percent of INDI. We ultimately opted for a lower range, after much discussion with the Advisory Working Group, some limited feedback from the Sneak Preview, further reviews of the case law in various provinces, and some more hard thought about the upper and lower bounds for these ranges. Since the release of the Draft Proposal and after our meetings across Canada, we can confirm that this percentage range is appropriate.

We found that a range of 40 to 46 percent of individual net disposable income typically covered spousal support outcomes in the **middle** of the very wide range of outcomes now observed in most Canadian provinces. To capture the middle of the range on a national basis means that some areas will find the upper bound (46 percent) a bit low and other areas will consider even the lower bound (40 percent) at the higher end of their local range.

Prior to the Sneak Preview, we had experimented with a range of 40 to 50 percent of INDI. But that produced far too broad a range in absolute dollar terms. One of the objectives of the Advisory Guidelines is to develop more predictability and consistency in spousal support outcomes and a ten-percentage point range simply failed to do that. A narrower five or six percentage point range is about right.

The lower boundary of this range — 40 percent of INDI — does ensure that the recipient spouse will receive not less than 50 percent of the family net disposable income in all cases involving two or more children, and slightly below that in one-child cases.

The upper end of this range — 46 percent of INDI — falls short of an equal split, which would leave both spouses in the same individual position. Despite the intellectual attraction of a 50/50 split, there are a number of practical problems that convinced us that it was not appropriate to set the upper limit of the range there. First, very few courts are currently prepared to push spousal support amounts that high. Second, there is a live concern for the access-related expenses of the payor spouse, expenses that are not otherwise reflected in the formula. Most payors are exercising access and most are spending directly upon their children during the time they spend with their children. Third, there are concerns for the payor in the situation where the payor has employment-related expenses and the recipient spouse is at home full time and receiving large spousal support.

We should repeat here a central difference between this formula and the *without child support* formula: **the length of the marriage does not affect the upper and lower percentages in this *with child support* formula.**

We also wish to stress the inter-relationship between the percentage limits and the precise elements of our version of individual net disposable income. If a notional table amount were not removed from the recipient spouse's income, or if government benefits and refundable credits were excluded, then the formula percentages would have to change. Our objective throughout has been to develop formulas that can capture the bulk of current outcomes, while at the same time demonstrating robustness in adjusting across incomes and child support amounts and custodial situations.

As a result of computer software, lawyers and courts became accustomed to calculating net disposable income or monthly cash flow on a *family* basis: the payor's net disposable income after deduction of child and spousal support and taxes, and the recipient's after addition of child and spousal support (and deduction of taxes). How do these more familiar family net disposable income percentages compare to our range of individual net disposable income divisions? Typically, the 46 percent of INDI at the upper end of our proposed formula generates a family net disposable income for the primary parent spouse of 56 to 58 percent where there are two children. At the lower end of the range, a spousal support amount that leaves the recipient spouse with 40 percent of INDI will typically leave that spouse and the two children with 52 or 53 percent of the family net disposable income. For comparison purposes, we have provided family net disposable income proportions in the examples below.

We recognize that Quebec has a different scheme of determining child support, which in turn has implications for fixing spousal support. The application of the Advisory Guidelines in divorce cases in Quebec is dealt with in more detail in Chapter 15.

## 8.4 Amounts of Spousal Support: Examples of the Basic Formula

At this point it helps to give a few examples of the ranges of monthly spousal support generated by this basic formula. Then we will move to the issue of duration. For illustration purposes, we assume that these parents and children all live in Ontario, as the use of one jurisdiction simplifies the exposition of the formula's operation.

In the earlier Draft Proposal, the formula calculations were done partially with software and partially by hand. With the release of the Draft Proposal, Canada's three major family law software suppliers incorporated the Spousal Support Advisory Guidelines into their programs, so that the calculations can be done easily and with greater precision. In addition, the ranges for amount have changed since the January 2005 release of the Draft Proposal, due to changes in child support table amounts in May 2006, various changes to federal and provincial taxes and changes in child benefits. The result is that the numbers in these examples are different from those set out in the Draft Proposal.

### Example 8.1

Ted and Alice have separated after 11 years together. Ted works at a local manufacturing plant, earning $80,000 gross per year. Alice has been home with the two children, now aged 8 and 10, who continue to reside with her after separation. After the separation, Alice found work, less than full time, earning $20,000 gross per year. Alice's mother provides lunch and after-school care for the children, for nothing, when Alice has to work. Ted will pay the table amount for child support, $1,159 per month. Alice's notional table amount would be $308. There are no s. 7 expenses (if there were, the spousal amounts would be lower).

**Under the formula, Ted would pay spousal support in the range of $474 to $1,025 per month.**

Using the *family* net disposable income figures (or the similar monthly cash flow figures) more familiar to current software users, spousal support of $1,025 monthly along with the child support would leave Alice and the children with $4,003 per month and Ted with $2,976 per month, or 57.4 per cent of the family's net disposable income in favour of Alice and the children. At the lower end of the range, with spousal support of $474 per month, the net disposable income of the family would be split 52.6/47.4 in favour of Alice and the children, leaving Ted with $3,326 monthly and Alice and the children with $3,684. The amount of spousal support is obviously affected by the **number of children**. If Ted and Alice had only one child, the spousal support range would be higher, from $888 to $1,463 per month. If the couple had three children, Ted's ability to pay would be reduced, bringing the range down to $79 to $626 monthly. Four children would lower that range even further, down to a range from zero to $222 per month.

The spousal support range will also be lowered by any payment of section 7 expenses. In our *Example 8.1*, if Alice were paying child care expenses of $8,000 per year for the two children and Ted paid his proportionate share of the net cost, the formula range would reduce to $319 to $925 per month for spousal support.

### Example 8.2

Bob and Carol have separated after eight years of marriage and two children, now aged 4 and 6, who are both living with Carol. Bob earns $40,000 gross annually at a local building supply company, while Carol has found part-time work, earning $10,000 per year. Carol's mother lives with Carol and provides care for the children when needed. Bob pays the table amount of $601 per month for the children. Carol's notional table amount of child support would be $61 per month. There are no s. 7 expenses.

**Under the formula, Bob would pay spousal support in the range of zero to $34 per month.**

Again, by way of comparison to the more familiar numbers, if Bob were to pay child support of $601 and spousal support of $34 monthly, at the upper end of the range, he would be left with $1,951 per month, while Carol and the two children would have *family* net disposable income of $2,325 monthly, or 54.4 percent of the family's net disposable income.

### Example 8.3

Drew and Kate have been married for four years. Drew earns $70,000 gross per year working for a department store. Kate used to work as a clerk in the same store, but she has been home since their first child was born. The children are now 1 and 3, living with Kate. Kate has no Guidelines income (and hence there is no notional table amount for her). Drew will pay the table amount of $1,043 per month for the two children.

**Under the formula, Drew would pay spousal support to Kate in the range of $908 to $1,213 per month.**

If Drew were to pay spousal support of $1,213 monthly, he would have $2,394 per month, while Kate and the children would have family net disposable income of $3,084 monthly, or 56.3 percent of the total family NDI. At the lower end of the range, spousal support of $908 per month would leave Drew with $2,604 in family NDI, while Kate and the children would have $2,780 monthly, or 51.6 percent of the family's NDI.

The formula generates ranges for the amount of spousal support. Chapter 9 below discusses the factors to be considered in fixing a particular amount within the ranges.

## 8.5  Duration under the Basic Formula

In most cases where there are dependent children, the courts order "indefinite" spousal support, usually subject to review or sometimes just left to variation. Even when the recipient spouse is expected to become self-sufficient in the foreseeable future, courts typically have not often imposed time limits in initial support orders. Where the recipient spouse is not employed outside the home, or is employed part-time, the timing of any review is tied to the age of the children, or to some period of adjustment after separation, or to the completion of a program of education or training. As the recipient spouse becomes employed or more fully employed, spousal support will eventually be reduced, to top up the recipient's employment earnings, or support may even be terminated. In other cases, support is reduced or terminated if the recipient spouse remarries or re-partners.

In practice, where there are dependent children, few "indefinite" orders are permanent. Many intervening events will lead to changes or even termination. Some of these issues are canvassed in Chapter 14, which deals with variation, review, remarriage, second families, etc. By making initial orders indefinite, the current law simply postpones many of the difficult issues relating to duration and recognizes the fact-specific nature of these determinations.

Under the *without child support* formula, discussed in Chapter 7, there are time limits keyed to the length of the marriage, i.e. .5 to 1 year of spousal support for each year the spouses have cohabited, subject to the exceptions for indefinite (duration not specified) support.

Under the *with child support* formula, one option was simply to leave duration indefinite in all cases, with no durational limits of any kind, thereby avoiding all of the difficult issues of duration where there are dependent children. Such an approach would, however, be inconsistent with our durational approach under the *without child support* formula. It would also be inconsistent with the underlying parental partnership rationale for spousal support. This rationale emphasizes the ongoing responsibilities for child-care after separation and the resulting limitations on the custodial or residential parent's earning abilities. When those responsibilities cease, there must be some other reason for support to continue, such as the length of the marriage.

Our approach to duration for marriages with dependent children maintains current practices, while introducing the general idea of a range for duration. Initial orders continue to be indefinite (duration not specified) in form, subject to the usual processes of review or variation. That does not change. What our approach adds is the acceptance of generally understood outside limits on the cumulative duration of spousal support that will inform the process of review and variation.[81]

The durational limits under this formula combine the factors of length of marriage and length of the remaining child-rearing period, under two different tests for duration. For longer marriages, it makes sense that a recipient spouse should get the benefit of the time limits based upon length of marriage that might be obtained under the *without child support* formula, as these will typically run well beyond the end of any child-rearing period. More difficult are shorter marriages where the recipient parent has the care of young children. To deal with these cases we have, under this formula, developed additional durational limits based on the responsibilities of child-rearing and the age of the children.

In what follows we explain in more detail the different elements of the admittedly complex approach to duration under this formula, and then draw these elements together in a concise summation in s. 8.5.4.

---

[81] The approach to duration under this formula involves fairly extensive reliance upon review orders. We discuss review orders and the leading Supreme Court of Canada decision, *Leskun v. Leskun*, [2006] 1 S.C.R. 920 in more detail in Chapters 13 and 14. In our view, the role contemplated for review orders under this formula is not inconsistent with *Leskun*.

## 8.5.1 The creation of a range for duration in the basic formula

In this final version we have made some changes to the language used to describe and present the two tests for duration under this formula. More importantly, we have also added a lower end for the range under the basic *with child support* formula.

In the Draft Proposal, we did not propose any minimum duration or lower end of the range for duration under the *with child support* formula, only a maximum outside duration. Through the feedback process, we became convinced that some range for duration was required, for three reasons. First, absent a lower end of the range, the maximum duration was not treated as an outside time limit, but instead as a default time limit, i.e. a recipient was seen as possessing an entitlement to receive spousal support for the length of the marriage or until the youngest child finished high school, no matter what. That was never our intention. Second, absent a lower end and following upon the default approach just described, there was no room created for negotiation around duration between the spouses, unlike under the *without child support* formula. Third, after further feedback across Canada and further research, we did get a strong sense of what the lower end of the range could be under the current law.

The real crux of any range is for shorter marriages with pre-school children, where we feared that these recipients might be seriously disadvantaged by creating a lower end of the range. This remains a concern, especially since it appears that the duration of support in these cases is lengthening, as the courts continue to develop an appreciation of the serious continuing disadvantage flowing from a spouse's on-going child care obligations.

We emphasise that the durational limits under this formula must be seen as "softer", more flexible than under the *without child support* formula given the prominence of the compensatory rationale under this formula. First, the durational limits are not intended to be implemented as time limits on initial orders, but rather to give structure to an on-going process of review and variation. Second, determinations of duration in cases with dependent children are very fact-specific and vary enormously based upon the education, skills and work-experience of the dependent spouse, the ages of the children and the available arrangements for child-care. Our suggested durational range is at best a typical range that will not be appropriate in all cases. And third, this is an area of law in flux. We see the law over time giving increased emphasis to what we have termed the "parental partnership" concept, which recognizes the ongoing responsibilities for child-care after separation and the resulting limitations on the custodial or residential parent's earning abilities.

As we explain in more detail below, there are two tests that establish the range for duration under the basic *with child support* formula. We have renamed these tests to clarify their rationale and operation: the *length-of-marriage* test and the age-of-children test. Under these two tests the upper and lower end of the range in each case will be the **longer duration** produced by either test.

Before we explain the two tests for duration, it is import to remember that **the durational limits under the *with child support* formula include any period of spousal support paid at the interim stage**, the same treatment as under the *without child support* formula.

## 8.5.2 The *length-of-marriage* test for duration

The first test for duration is the same as the test for duration under the *without child support* formula. It will typically be the applicable test for longer marriages, marriage of ten years or more. The **upper end** is one year of support for each year of marriage, subject to the provisions under the *without child support* formula for indefinite (duration not specified) support after 20 years of marriage. The **lower end** is one-half year of support for each year of marriage. If the children are already in school at the time of separation, then the lower end of the range will always be determined by this *length-of-marriage* test.

Once again, we emphasize that these "softer" time limits are intended to structure the process of review and variation of initial orders that are indefinite in form; they are not intended to give rise to time-limited orders, at least not initially.

We can use *Example 8.1* above to explain this test. Ted and Alice cohabited for 11 years during their marriage and are now in their late thirties or early forties, with two children, aged 8 and 10 at separation. The initial support order would be indefinite (duration not specified), but it would be expected that the ultimate, cumulative duration of the award would fall somewhere within the range of 5.5 years (lower end) to 11 years (upper end). The maximum outside time limit would be 11 years. Reviews and variations in the meantime may bring support to an end before 11 years, and certainly the amount may have been reduced significantly during this period. But if support is still in pay after 11 years, there would be an expectation, barring exceptional circumstances, that support would be terminated at that point on an application for review or variation.

In the longer marriage cases under the *with child support* formula, where the *length-of-marriage* test defines the durational range, most cases will tend towards the longer end of the durational range and few cases should see support terminate at the lower end, given the strong compensatory claims that are typically present in these cases. The age of the children will be a critical factor in location with the range. Consider *Example 8.1* again: if support terminated for Alice at lower end of 5.5 years, the children would be only 13 and 15, an age at which the demands of child care can still have considerable impact upon Alice's income-earning abilities. By contrast, if Ted and Alice had been married for 14 years, and the children were 10 and 12 at separation, the lower end of the durational range would see support last until the children were 17 and 19. The choice of a particular duration within this range would be affected by these and other factors set out in Chapter 9.

### 8.5.3 The *age-of-children* test for duration

The second test for duration under the basic *with child support* formula is driven by the age of the children of the marriage. It usually operates where the period of time until the last or youngest child finishes high school is greater than the length of the marriage. These are mostly short or short-to-medium marriages, typically (but not always) under 10 years in length. The current case law is inconsistent and erratic on duration for these marriages, ranging from indefinite orders without conditions, to indefinite orders with short review periods and sometimes stringent review conditions, and even occasionally to time limits. Despite the language of indefinite support, the reality in most cases is that support does not continue for long, as re-employment, retraining, remarriage and other changes often intervene to bring spousal support to an end.

We too have struggled with duration for this category of cases. On the one hand, many of these custodial parents face some of the most serious disadvantages of all spouses, especially mothers with little employment history who have very young children in their care, all of which militates in favour of no time limits or very long time limits. On the other hand, many recipient spouses do have good education and employment backgrounds, are younger, and are emerging from shorter marriages and briefer periods out of the paid labour market, all indicators of quicker recovery of earning capacity. Inevitably, as under the current law, this means that reviews are a critical means of sorting out the individual circumstances of the recipient spouses.

The **upper end of the range** for spousal support under this test is the **date when the last or youngest child finishes high school**. Relatively few cases will reach this outside time limit and those that do will likely involve reduced amounts of top-up support by that date. Hence, extensions beyond that date would involve cases that fall within any of the exceptions described in Chapter 12, like the exception for the special needs of a child or the exception under s. 15.3 of the *Divorce Act*.

The **lower end of the range** under this test is also tied to the age of the youngest child and schooling, once again reflecting the parental partnership model. In shorter marriages, spousal support should continue at least until the **date the youngest child starts attending school full-time**. The school date will vary from province to province and from school district to school district, based upon the availability of junior kindergarten, the age rules governing school registration and the program the child takes.

Keep in mind that these tests for duration say nothing about the proper *amount* of spousal support during this period. That will be a function of the recipient's income-earning ability, her or his ability to undertake part-time or full-time employment. The amount of support may be significantly reduced over the course of any order, or even reduced to zero.

As with longer marriages with dependent children, the **initial support order in these shorter marriage cases will still be indefinite (duration not specified)**, as the determination of self-sufficiency remains an individualized decision. Any time limit will typically only appear after a review or variation hearing, especially in these cases involving young children. This appears to be the pattern in the current Canadian practice, as best as we can discern from the few reported decisions, the feedback we received since the Draft Proposal and the Advisory Working Group.

Take our *Example 8.3* where Drew and Kate have only been married four years, with two pre-school children aged 1 and 3 and Kate at home with them. The upper end of the range for duration would be 17 years, while the lower end would be 5 years, the latter assuming that children in their area start full-time school at age 6. In this typical case, any initial order would likely include a review provision, the review to occur at some point before the youngest child starts school.

### 8.5.4 The use of the two tests for duration: whichever is longer

In most cases, only one of the two tests, either the *length-of-marriage* test or the *age-of-children* test, will apply to determine both the upper and lower ends of the range. In general, the *length-of-marriage* test applies for longer marriages, marriages of ten years or more, while the *age-of-children* test applies for shorter marriages, those under ten years. But the two tests must be used together, **as it is the longer of the two tests that applies for each end of the range**. Remember that this is a range for duration, and that the actual outcome in any particular case will be worked out within that range over a series of orders or agreements, by way or review or variation of an initial order or agreement.

**The Basic *With Child Support* Formula for Duration**
**Initial orders indefinite (duration not specified)**

subject to cumulative durational limits implemented by review or variation:

### Upper End of the Range: the longer of

- o    the length of marriage, or
- o    the date the last or youngest child finishes high school

### Lower End of the Range: the longer of

o   one-half the length of marriage, or

o   the date the youngest child starts full-time school

Take our *Example 8.2* where Bob and Carol have been married for 8 years, with two children aged 4 and 6. The *length-of-marriage* test suggests a durational range of 4 to 8 years, while the *age-of-children* test would suggest a range of 2 to 14 years. The result for Bob and Carol would be a durational range where the lower end of the range is 4 years (from the *length-of-marriage* test) and of the upper end of the range is 14 years (from the *age-of-children* test). As can be seen, much turns upon the interaction of the length of the marriage and the age of the children.

## 8.5.5 The problem of short marriages with young children

Applying the two tests for duration under the *with child support* formula, the range for duration will be determined by whichever test produces the longer duration at both the lower and upper ends of the range. Where those bounds are determined by the *length-of-marriage* test, there seems to be little difficulty. The range is the same as that under the *without child support* formula. A durational range of half the length of the marriage to the length of the marriage is intuitively understandable.

The *age-of-children* test is not as simple. It is tied to the presence of children in the marriage, and the economic disadvantages that come with the obligation to care for children. Length of marriage alone no longer provides a measure of the duration of the spousal support obligation, as the case law increasingly demonstrates, even if some spouses think it should. The *age-of-children* test will usually apply in shorter marriages. For shorter marriages with young children, this test will generate a long potential duration at the upper end of the range, one that can run as long as the date that the last or youngest child finishes high school, an outcome that raised some concerns during the feedback process. For very short marriages with very young children, the lower end of the range under the *age-of-children* test, added in the revision process, has also raised some concerns.

Critical to understanding these durational issues is the compensatory rationale for spousal support in these shorter marriage cases. Most of the economic disadvantage in these cases is not in the past, but in the future; it is the continuing disadvantage that flows from the obligations of child care and their impact upon the ability of the recipient parent to obtain and maintain employment. Hence the importance of the age of the children in fashioning durational limits. Our understanding of the current law, based both upon reported cases and discussions with lawyers and judges in our cross-country consultations, is that the law applicable to these cases is in flux, showing increasing recognition over time of the on-going economic disadvantage flowing from post-separation child-care responsibilities.

The upper end of the range for duration under the *age-of-children* test — up until the last or youngest child finishes high school — may appear long in a shorter marriage case. Consider Bob and Carol again in *Example 8.2*, where spousal support could potentially last as long as 14 years after an 8-year marriage, if the children are 4 and 6 in Carol's primary care at the date of separation. If duration were tied to the length of the marriage alone, spousal support would otherwise terminate when the children were 12 and 14 years old. But at this point, Carol's employment position may still reflect continuing economic disadvantage and limitations placed on her ability to achieve full-self-sufficiency by her post-separation custodial responsibilities. It may only be as the children reach their teenage years that she can focus more on improving her employment position. Termination at this point might also fail, depending on the facts, to recognize Carol's continuing child care obligations. A good way to test this outside durational limit is to think about the labour market position of the primary parent if one of those children had special needs or developed problems in their teenage years.

Slightly different problems are raised by the lower end of the durational range under the *age-of-children* test — until the youngest child starts attending school full-time. In the majority of cases, as our consultations revealed, this lower end of the durational range will not be contentious. In marriages of even four or five years, the age of children test will begin to yield results similar to the lower end of the durational range under the *length-of-marriage* test. Indeed, the major concern raised by the introduction of the lower end of the durational range in cases of shorter marriages with children, whether defined by length of marriage or age of youngest child starting full-time school, has been that it will create a "ceiling" and stunt the progressive development of the law in this area.

However, in some cases, of very short marriages, the *age-of-children* test has raised concerns that it sets the lower end of the durational range too high — i.e., that it establishes a "minimum duration" that is too long because it exceeds the length of the marriage. The kind of case that raises this concern is a fairly extreme set of facts: a marriage as brief as one or two years, with an infant less than a year old. In this hypothetical case, assuming the child would start full-time school at age 6, the lower end of the range for duration under the *age-of-children* test would be five years, which some would suggest is too long for such a short marriage.

In responding to this concern, we note that there are a number of other important dimensions to spousal support in these cases, in addition to duration, that soften the impact of this lower end of the range for duration. First, the lower end of the range for duration does not guarantee any particular *amount* of support. The formula range is driven by the number and age of the children, the spousal incomes, the child custody arrangements, child support amounts, section 7 contributions and tax positions. Much will turn upon the employment status of the recipient, and the recipient's ability to return to the paid labour market. A recipient is always under an obligation to make reasonable efforts towards self-sufficiency, and, on particular facts, those efforts may be subject to scrutiny in a review scheduled well before the youngest child starts full-time school. Second, in some situations, income will have to be imputed to the recipient, either part-time or full-time, on an individualized basis, often through the process of review. Third, entitlement is always an issue, before reaching the questions of amount and duration under the Advisory Guidelines. In some cases of strong facts — i.e. a recipient with a strong connection to the work-force — there may even be a finding of no entitlement so that the lower end of the range for duration is not engaged. The lower end of the durational range does not create a "minimum entitlement." Finally, we have said all along that the durational limits under the *with child support* formula are "softer", less formulaic, than those under the *without child support* formula. In *Moge*, the Supreme Court of Canada emphasized the need for individualized decision-making on self-sufficiency in compensatory support cases and duration under the *with child support* formula must therefore not be too rigidly applied.

## 8.6 Shared Custody

The basic formula is constructed around the typical fact situation, where the higher income spouse pays child and spousal support to the lower income spouse who has the primary care of the children. Here we address custodial variations, the first being shared custody.

Where the spouses have **shared custody**, the starting point for the calculation of child support under s. 9(a) of the *Federal Child Support Guidelines* is the straight set-off of table amounts for the number of children subject to shared custody, as set out in the Supreme Court decision in *Contino v. Leonelli-Contino.*[82] That amount is then adjusted, usually upwards, but occasionally downwards, based upon s. 9(b) (increased costs of shared custody and actual spending on children by the spouses) and s. 9(c) (other circumstances, including relative incomes, income levels, assets and debts, household standards of living, any reliance upon previous levels of child support paid). The *Contino* decision was handed down after the release of the Draft Proposal, but the shared custody formula anticipated that outcome. The majority in *Contino* emphasised that there is no presumption in favour of the full table amount for the payor, nor is there any presumption in favour of the straight set-off, under section 9.

Under the basic *with child support* formula, child support is deducted from the payor's income and then that child support amount plus a notional amount for child support is deducted from the recipient's income, to obtain individual net disposable income. Shared custody requires some changes to this basic formula.

Assume for the moment that the payor is paying *only* the straight set-off amount of child support in a shared custody case. If we were only to deduct the smaller set-off amount of child support for the payor spouse in a shared custody situation, that would misrepresent and understate the payor parent's contribution to child support. Shared custody assumes that both parents spend directly upon the child in their shared care. The full table amount (plus any s. 7 contributions) is thus deducted from the payor spouse's net disposable income. For the recipient, the notional table amount (plus any contribution to s. 7 expenses) is deducted from his or her income. This would be done in the calculation of INDI, even though the child support paid by the payor and received by the recipient would be the straight set-off amount.

If the straight set-off of child support is calculated as above, it turns out that the spousal support ranges are basically the same in these shared custody situations as in sole custody situations. Shared custody arrangements do not result in any automatic lowering of spousal support. It was important that the shared custody formula not provide any false financial incentives to encourage shared custody litigation, while at the same time providing ample room within the range to adjust for the realities of shared parenting.

### Example 8.4

Peter and Cynthia have separated after nine years together. Peter works as a reporter at the local television station, earning $65,000 gross per year, while his wife Cynthia works for a local arts organization, earning $39,000 gross per year.

Peter and Cynthia share custody of their two children, aged 8 and 7 on a week about, 50/50 basis. In these circumstances, there could be entitlement issues, but we will assume entitlement here for exposition purposes.

First, assume Peter only pays the straight set-off amount of child support, i.e. $972 - $584 = $388. We would deduct from Peter's income the full table amount of $972, of which $584 is spent by him directly for the children in his care and $388 is paid as child support to Cynthia. Cynthia's income would still be reduced by her notional table amount of $584. If Cynthia receives the full amount of the child benefits, and assuming entitlement, then the range for spousal support would be zero to $142 per month.

---

[82] [2005] 3 S.C.R. 217, 19 R.F.L. (6 th) 272.

## 8.6.1 Adjusting for rotating child benefits

Since the release of the Draft Proposal, there has been a change in policy governing the receipt of the Child Tax Benefit and the child portion of the GST/HST Credit. The Canada Revenue Agency (CRA) decided that parents in shared custody cases "will have their benefits rotated between them only on a six-month on, six-month off basis". According to the CRA policy, it is possible for only one shared custody parent to receive the full child benefits provided that the parents do not self-identify or otherwise come to CRA's attention. The same approach has now been extended to the Universal Child Care Benefit (UCCB) in shared custody situations. As with all tax matters, the CRA policy cannot be altered by the parents' agreement or by a court order.

Under the *with child support* formula, these child benefits are treated as income and thus the allocation of the Child Tax Benefit, GST Credit and UCCB can affect the spousal support range for amount. It is therefore critical to be clear on this income issue.

In our *Example 8.4*, if the child benefits are rotated, thereby reducing Cynthia's income, the formula range would be higher, **from zero to $289 per month**.

## 8.6.2 Adjusting the ranges for child support that departs from the set-off

To make matters more difficult, in some shared custody cases, the amount of support is increased beyond the straight set-off amount, for various reasons: to reflect the increased costs of shared custody (or the respective abilities of the parents to incur those increased costs); to adjust for the recipient parent's larger share of actual child care costs; to reflect a parent's reliance upon a previous higher amount of child support, as in *Contino*; or to reduce disparities in the standards of living between the parental households. A central concern expressed in *Contino* was that the children not experience any dramatic change in standards of living as they move between the two parental households.

To return to *Example 8.4*, what if Peter pays more than the straight set-off amount of $388 per month? Much depends upon why Peter pays more. If Peter pays a higher amount of child support because Cynthia spends more on the children or because of the increased costs of shared custody, no adjustment should be made.

On the other hand, if Peter pays more child support simply to reduce the disparity in household standards of living, an adjustment should probably be made to the ranges for spousal support, as there is less need for the same function to be performed by spousal support. For example, if Peter were to pay child support of $569 per month on this standard-of-living rationale, rather than $388, then the range for spousal support would be **zero to zero** after adjustment (assuming the full child benefits are paid to Cynthia). At child support of $569 per month, Cynthia would have noticeably more of the family's net disposable income than Peter, leaving no room for spousal support under the *with child support* formula.

*Contino* emphasized the discretionary nature of child support in shared custody cases. Departures from the set-off can even sometimes go below the set-off amount. There can be a number of reasons for departing from the set-off amount, either above or below. A careful analysis of those reasons is thus necessary, to determine whether any adjustment should be made in calculating the formula ranges and, eventually, in choosing the appropriate amount within the ranges.

## 8.6.3 Adjusting the limits of the range

We received much feedback from mediators and lawyers working with shared custody parents, stating that these parents often opt for a 50/50 split of the couple's family net disposable income or monthly cash flow after the payment of child and spousal support (remember that this is a broader and different measure from INDI or individual net disposable income). This option leaves the children with roughly the same resources and standard of living in each household. We agree that this equal split of net income should be available as one of the normal range of outcomes — not mandated, just available — in every shared custody case.

The shared custody formula for spousal support usually includes this 50/50 split within the range, but in some cases this 50/50 split falls just outside the upper or lower end of the range. In these cases, the shared custody range has been broadened to include this 50/50 split. Take *Example 8.4* which shows a range of zero to $142 per month where Peter pays the set-off amount of $388 as child support (and assuming that Cynthia receives the full child benefits). At the upper end of the range, Cynthia would be left with 49.7 per cent of the family net disposable income. To increase her share to 50 per cent, the upper end of the spousal support range would have to be $179. Under our revised shared custody formula, the range here would become zero to $179 per month, to ensure that the 50/50 split falls within the range.

In what cases has the formula range been adjusted? In cases where parental incomes are lower or not that far apart (like Peter and Cynthia), the upper end of the range has been adjusted upwards a bit. In cases where the recipient parent has little or no income and there are two or more children subject to shared custody, then the lower end of the range has been adjusted downwards, to ensure that the 50/50 split falls within the range. These adjustments are made automatically by the software programs.

In these latter cases, where there are two or more children subject to shared custody and the recipient has little or no income, the formula will produce a range with a lower end that leaves the lower-income recipient with 50 per cent of the family's net disposable income and the rest of the range will obviously go higher. During the feedback process, some criticized this range of outcomes, suggesting that a shared custody recipient should never receive spousal support that would give her or him more than 50 per cent of the family's net disposable income. After all, they suggested, under this arrangement, both parents face the same ongoing obligations of child care going into the future, with neither parent experiencing more disadvantage.

The answer to these criticisms is that the past is relevant in these cases, as there is a reason the recipient has little or no income, usually explained by that parent's past shouldering of the bulk of child care responsibilities. In most shared custody cases, both parents have shared parenting during the relationship, so that there is less disadvantage and less disparity in their incomes at the end of the marriage. Where the recipient has little or no income, she or he will have a greater need for increased support in the short run. But the shared custody arrangement will reduce the impact of ongoing child care upon the recipient's employment prospects, such that progress towards self-sufficiency should occur more quickly. In these cases, spousal support will likely be reduced in the near future on review or variation, and the duration of support may be shorter.

## 8.7 Split custody

In a split custody situation, more significant changes to the basic formula are required. If each parent has one or more children in their primary care or custody, then s. 8 of the *Federal Child Support Guidelines* requires a set-off of table amounts, with each spouse paying the table amount for the number of children in the other spouse's custody. But this means that each parent will also be considered to support the child or children in their care directly, out of their remaining income. Thus, in the split custody situation, a notional table amount must be deducted from *each* parent, not just the recipient but the payor as well.

Since there is one child in each household, there are no economies of scale and accordingly larger proportions of their incomes are devoted to child support, leaving a smaller pool of INDI to be divided by way of spousal support. Again, as with shared custody, this would be done in the calculation of INDI, even though the child support paid by the payor and received by the recipient would be the set-off amount directed by the s. 8 formula.

### Example 8.5

Take the case of Peter and Cynthia again, and assume that each parent has custody of one child, same incomes, same facts. Peter's one child table amount would be $601 per month, Cynthia's $358 per month. Under s. 8 of the *Federal Child Support Guidelines*, these table amounts would be offset, with Peter paying Cynthia $243 per month. In calculating Peter's individual net disposable income, for spousal support purposes, the full one child amount is deducted, twice, once for the table amount effectively paid to Cynthia and once for the notional amount spent directly on the child in his care. Similarly, in calculating Cynthia's INDI, a double deduction of her one-child table amount is made, once for the amount effectively paid to Peter for the child in his care, plus a notional table amount for the child in Cynthia's own care.

The actual child support paid by Peter to Cynthia would be $243, the one-child set-off amount under s. 8. Using the split custody formula for spousal support, Peter would pay spousal support to Cynthia in the range of **zero to $445 per month**.

## 8.8 Step-Children

Under the *Divorce Act* and provincial family law statutes, a spouse can be found to stand in the place of a parent towards a child who is not his or her biological or adoptive child.[83] With that finding, a step-parent becomes liable to pay child support, in an amount that is "appropriate" under section 5 of the *Child Support Guidelines*, "having regard to these *Guidelines* and any other parent's legal duty to support the child". For the most part, the threshold for finding step-parent status is fairly high, not easily satisfied in short marriages except for very young children.[84] After the Supreme Court decision in *Chartier*,[85] some courts have lowered that threshold, making it more likely that a spouse will be found to stand in the place of a parent after a shorter marriage. In British Columbia, the Family Relations Act imposes a step-parent child support obligation if "the step-parent contributed to the support and maintenance of the child for at least one year".[86]

During the feedback phase, especially in British Columbia, there were questions about which formula is appropriate to apply in short-marriage step-parent situations or whether there

---

[83] *Divorce Act*, s. 2(2).
[84] Carol Rogerson, "The Child Support Obligations of Step-Parents" (2001), 18 Can.J.Fam.L. 9; Nick Bala, "Who is a 'Parent'? 'Standing in the Place of a Parent' and Section 5 of the Child Support Guidelines" in Law Society of Upper Canada, *Special Lectures 2006: Family Law* (Toronto: Irwin Law, 2007) at 71.
[85] *Chartier v. Chartier*, [1999] 1 S.C.R. 242.
[86] *Family Relations Act*, R.S.B.C. 1996, c. 128, s. 1 "parent". Section 1(2) requires that the step-parent be married to the parent or that they lived together in a marriage-like relationship for at least two years.

should be an exception under the *with child support* formula for step-parent cases. There were concerns that this formula generated spousal support obligations that were too substantial in such cases.

In the vast majority of step-parent cases, the *with child support* formula will apply with no difficulty. In many cases, the step-parent will treat the children as his or her own after the breakdown of the marriage. In some of these cases, there will be both step-children and biological children, with all of them treated alike. In other cases, the threshold for the finding of step-parent status will be high enough that the marriage will be a medium-to-long one, with substantial spousal support obligations.

In our view, the short marriage concerns are now resolved by the creation of a range for duration under this formula. Upon closer analysis, the difficulty in these stepparent cases was not the range for amount, but the potentially long duration under the *age-of-children* test for the upper end of the range and its use as a "default rule". An example can demonstrate how the addition of a lower end for the durational range allows for a reasonable range of outcomes in step-parent cases.

### Example 8.6

Art and Kathie have been married for 5 years. Art earns $80,000 per year and Kathie earns $20,000. Kathie had two children from a previous relationship at the time she and Art got married, two girls who are now 10 and 12. Assume that Kathie does not receive any child support from the girls' father and that she has sole custody of the girls.

Under the *Federal Child Support Guidelines*, Art could be required to pay as much as the table amount of child support, $1,159 per month. If Art pays the full table amount, **the basic *with child support* formula would produce an amount for spousal support in the range of $474 to $1,025 per month.**

As for the duration of spousal support, the order would be **indefinite (duration not specified), with a cumulative durational range of 2.5 years at the lower end to 8 years at the upper end.** The upper end of the durational range here is determined by the *age-of-children* test, i.e. when the youngest daughter (now 10) finishes high school at age 18, or 8 years. The lower end, however, is fixed by the *length-of-marriage* test, as both children are older and in full-time school, i.e. one-half the length of the marriage, or 2 = years. Upon a future review or a variation application, a court could put a relatively short time limit on spousal support, depending upon the facts.

The facts of this simple example can be modified to strengthen or weaken the spousal support claim. If the girls are younger during their relationship with Art, so that they are only 6 and 8 at separation, then the durational range would be 2 = to 12 years and there would be strong factors pushing towards the upper end of the range. Contrast the effect of the low British Columbia threshold under the *Family Relations Act*. The girls are 6 and 8 at separation, but assume that Art was only married to Kathie for two years. The upper end of the durational range would still be 12 years, but the lower end would be reduced to one year, i.e. one-half year for each year of marriage.

Under section 8 of the *Child Support Guidelines*, it is possible for a step-parent to pay less than the table amount of child support if appropriate. A reduced amount is only ordered or agreed upon when the biological parent is already paying child support.[87] Where the amount of

---

[87] Sometimes a court will order the step-parent to pay less than the full table amount, leaving the custodial parent to take steps to obtain or increase child support from the biological parent.

child support is reduced under s. 8, the *with child support* formula range should be calculated using the full table amount rather than the reduced amount.[88]

## 8.9 A Hybrid Formula for Spousal Support Paid by the Custodial Parent (The *Custodial Payor* Formula)

The basic formula for marriages with dependent children assumes that the higher income spouse pays both child and spousal support to the recipient parent, who also has sole custody or primary care of the children. The spousal support to be paid must then adjust for the payor's child support payments. The shared and split custody situations may change the math, but both still involve the higher income spouse paying both child and spousal support to the recipient.

A different formula is required where the higher income spouse paying spousal support is also the parent with sole custody or primary care of the children. Now spousal support and child support flow in opposite directions. the *without child support* formula does not apply, however, as it assumes no dependent children. While we could have left this situation as an exception, with no formulaic solution, it is common enough that we constructed a formula to guide outcomes in this situation.

Either of the two formulas could be used as a starting point and then modified to accommodate custodial payors. We chose to start from the *without child support* formula for custodial payors. In this situation the recipient parent does not have the primary care of children and thus more closely resembles the single recipient in the *without child support* formula. The primary rationale for the payment of spousal support in these cases will be merger over time, rather than parental partnership. That said, a number of lower income recipient spouses in this situation will continue to play an important role in their children's lives and any formula must be able to adjust in such cases. The other advantage of the *without child support* formula is ease of calculation, but the formula will have to be modified to back out child support and to take into account tax implications.

Most of these cases will involve older children and longer marriages, where the husband is the higher-income payor and the parent with primary care. In many of these cases, the non-custodial wife may have a sizeable compensatory claim from her past role in child-rearing, which will be reflected in the range for spousal support, and the location of any amount within that range. In these cases involving older children and longer marriages, the children will cease to be children of the marriage within a few years and the wife will cross-over into the *without child support* formula, as is explained below in Chapter 14 on variation and review. In a subset of custodial payor cases, there will be illness or disability issues for the non-custodial spouses, many of which can be accommodated within the ranges or restructuring, but exceptions will be made in some cases, as discussed below in Chapter 12 below. There is a small minority of custodial payor cases that involve young children, shorter marriages and husbands claiming spousal support from their wives.

---

[88] Given the way the formula works, any reduction in the step-parent's child support would otherwise lead to an increase in the range for spousal support, an inappropriate result.

**Formula for Spousal Support Paid by Custodial Parent (The *Custodial Payor* Formula)**

1. Reduce the payor spouse's Guidelines income by the **grossed-up notional table amount** for child support (plus a gross-up of any contributions to s. 7 expenses).

2. If the recipient spouse is paying child support, reduce the recipient's Guidelines income by the **grossed-up amount of child support paid** (table amount plus any s. 7 contributions).

3. Determine the **adjusted gross income difference** between the spouses and then quantum ranges from 1.5 percent to 2 percent for each year of marriage, up to a maximum of 50.

4. **Duration** ranges from .5 to 1 year of support for each year of marriage, with the same rules for indefinite (duration not specified) support as under the without child support formula.

In reducing gross incomes by grossed-up amounts for child support, this formula does the same thing conceptually as the basic *with child support* formula — it establishes the spouses' available incomes after their child support obligations are fulfilled. To gross up the child support will require a calculation of the gross value of the non-taxable child support, using the appropriate marginal tax rate for the payor or recipient spouse.

### Example 8.6

Matt earns $100,000 gross per year and has custody of two teenage children. Anna earns $30,000 gross per year. The spouses separated after 16 years together. There are no s. 7 expenses.

Assume entitlement to spousal support has been established.

First, Matt's income is reduced by the table amount for two children, $1,404, grossed-up to $2,525 per month or $30,300 annually. Matt's reduced income would thus be $69,700. Anna is required to pay child support at the table amount of $444 per month, grossed-up to $625 monthly or $7,500 annually. Anna's reduced income would be $22,500. After a 16-year marriage, Anna would receive a range of 24 to 32 percent of the adjusted gross income difference of $47,200.

**Under the *custodial payor* formula, Matt would pay spousal support in a range from $944 to $1,259 per month, for a duration of 8 to 16 years.**

There is one **exception** distinctive to this *custodial payor* formula, discussed in more detail below in Chapter 12. Where the recipient spouse and non-primary parent plays an important role in the child's care and upbringing after separation, yet the marriage is shorter and the child is younger, the ranges for amount and duration applied under this *custodial payor* formula may not allow that spouse to continue to fulfil that parental role. In our view, in such cases, under this **parenting exception**, it should be possible to exceed the upper limits on both amount and duration for that purpose.

### 8.10 A Hybrid Formula for Adult Children and Section 3(2)(b)

After the release of the Draft Proposal, we added another formula to this family of formulas, another hybrid formula, this time for adult children whose child support is determined under section 3(2)(b) of the *Federal Child Support Guidelines*. In these cases of children who are the age of majority or over, the table-amount-plus-section-7-expenses approach is considered "inappropriate". Under the case law, these are usually cases where:

1. the adult child attends a post-secondary institution away from home;
2. the adult child makes a sizeable contribution to his or her own education expenses; or
3. there are other non-parental resources to defray education expenses, like scholarships or RESP's or grandparent monies.

Under section 3(2)(b), an individual budget is usually prepared for the adult child and, after the child and other contributions are deducted, the remaining deficit is then apportioned between the parents, based upon their incomes or some other arrangement. These child support amounts will differ significantly from any amounts using the table and section 7 expenses, almost invariably lower.

This *adult children* formula will *only* apply where the child support for *all* the remaining children of the marriage is determined under section 3(2)(b) of the Child Support Guidelines and there are *no* children for whom a table amount of child support is being paid under section 3(1) or section 3(2)(a). It should not be used, for example, where there is one older child away at university and another still at home in high school. In that case, the basic *with child support* formula would be used, with any necessary adjustment to the amounts of child support contributed by each parent for the child away at school.

Under this *adult children* formula, like the *custodial payor* formula, the framework of the *without child support* formula is used, but adjusted for the child support amounts paid, another hybrid formula. Once each parent's contribution to the child's budget has been allocated under s. 3(2)(b), those actual child support amounts are grossed up and deducted from each spouse's gross income. Then the *without child support* formula is applied, using the adjusted gross income difference and the length of marriage factor to determine amount and duration. The box above for the *custodial payor* can be used to describe the calculations, with one change: the actual amounts of each parent's contribution to child support will be grossed up, rather than table and section 7 amounts.

### Example 8.7

Take Matt and Anna from the previous *Example 8.6* and assume that there is only one child of the marriage, now 20 years old and attending university away from home. Matt earns $100,000 and Anna earns $30,000. Their son's tuition, books and living expenses total $20,000 and, through a mix of summer employment and scholarships, he can contribute $5,000. The parents have agreed to divide the remaining $15,000 between them, $12,000 by Matt ($1,000 per month) and $3,000 by Anna ($250 per month).

Under this formula, Matt's gross income would be reduced by the grossed up amount of the child support, or $21,300, while Anna's grossed up contribution would be $4,100. The adjusted gross income difference would be $78,700 less $25,900, leaving $52,800.

**After a 16-year marriage, under this formula, the range for spousal support for Anna is 24 to 32 per cent of $52,800, or $1,056 to $1,408 per month, for whatever duration would remain of the original 8 to 16 years.**

Another practical advantage of this formula is that it eases the transition between formulas. Most of these cases are longer marriages and, once the last child ceases to be a "child of the marriage" and child support stops, the spouses will "cross over" to the unadjusted without child support formula, described briefly below. In *Example 8.7*, when the son ceases to a "child of the marriage" in a few years, Anna's spousal support would be determined by crossing over to the *without child support* formula, with no adjustment any longer for child support. The range for amount would be 24 to 32 per cent of the gross income difference of $70,000, or $1,400 to $1,867 per month, again for whatever duration would remain of the original 8 to 16 years.

## 8.11 Crossover to the *with child support* formula

There is one last issue to be flagged here, that of crossover between the two formulas. The most frequent crossover situation will be in cases where child support ceases after a medium-to-long marriage, where the children were older or even university-age at the time of the initial order, as in *Example 8.7* above. At this point, either spouse can apply to vary, to bring spousal support under the *without child support* formula. In most cases, it will be the recipient making the application, to obtain an increase in support under the *without child support* formula, once child support is no longer payable and the payor's ability to pay is improved as a result. Specific examples of crossover are considered in Chapter 14 on variation and review.

## 9 USING THE RANGES

The formulas generate **ranges** for amount and for duration as well unless the conditions for indefinite (duration not specified) support are met. The ranges allow the parties and their counsel, or a court, to adjust amount and duration to accommodate the specifics of the individual case in light of the support factors and objectives found in the *Divorce Act*.

In this section we can only highlight in the most general way the sorts of factors that could be taken into account in fixing precise amounts and time periods and that might push a determination up or down within the ranges. Most of the relevant factors will be the same as those that now operate within the present discretionary case law, the difference being that here they will operate within the boundaries created by the formulas. Also, as under current law, no single factor will be determinative and several factors may be at play in any given case, sometimes pushing in different directions.

## 9.1 Strength of Any Compensatory Claim

A strong compensatory claim will be a factor that favours a support award at the higher end of the ranges both for amount and duration. A spouse who has suffered significant economic disadvantage as a result of the marital roles and whose claims are based on both compensatory and non-compensatory grounds may have a stronger support claim under the *without child support* formula than a spouse whose economic circumstances are not the result of marital roles and who can only claim non-compensatory support based upon loss of the marital standard of living. In *Examples 7.1* and *7.5*, both of which involved long marriages where one spouse sacrificed employment opportunities as a result of child care responsibilities, this factor of a strong compensatory claim could weigh in favour of an award at the higher end of the range in as compared to some of our other examples where there were no children.

Under the *with child support* formula, compensatory principles would also suggest that the more the recipient spouse gave up in the paid labour market, the higher one would go within the range. To give a simple example, two tax lawyers marry fresh out of law school, but one stays home with the children and the other pursues a career within a large law firm. Compensatory logic would dictate that something close to the maximum 46 percent of INDI would make sense here, as the payor spouse's income is a very good proxy measure of where the recipient spouse would have been. Given the presence of dependent children under this formula, almost every case will have a compensatory element and the lower and higher ends of the range reflect that. What moves a case up or down the range is the relative strength or weakness of the compensatory claim.

## 9.2  Recipient's Needs

In a case where the recipient has limited income and/or earning capacity, because of age or other circumstances, the recipient's needs may push an award to the higher end of the ranges for amount and duration.

Conversely, the absence of compelling need may be a factor that pushes an award to the lower end of the range, for example, where the recipient already has a solid base of employment or other income. Or the recipient spouse may have reduced living expenses, living in a mortgage-free matrimonial home or subsidized housing or family-provided housing. Or the recipient may be cohabiting with a new partner, thereby reducing her or his expenses.

In *Example 7.4*, where Jennifer is unemployed at the age of 57, this need factor might weigh in favour of an award at the higher end of the range. *Example 7.2*, in contrast, where Sue is only 38 and earning $25,000 per year, the need factor may not be as compelling, suggesting an award at the lower end of the range. In *Example 7.1* the absence of compelling need on Ellen's part, given her income of $30,000 per year, might suggest an award at the lower end of the range, but this would be counter-balanced by Ellen's strong compensatory claim.

## 9.3  Age, Number, Needs and Standard of Living of Children

The age, number and needs of the children will affect placement within the range under the *with child support* formula. A child with special needs will usually demand more time and resources from the care-giving parent, thus reducing that parent's ability to earn in the paid labour market and pushing spousal support towards the upper end. The same will generally be true for the parent with primary care of an infant or toddler, as contrasted to care of an older child or adolescent. That lower base of income will generate a higher range for amount, of course, but here we speak of location within the range as well.

Generally speaking, when ability to pay is in issue, the larger the number of children, the less income is left available to pay spousal support, and the ranges will be lower, consistent with s. 15.3 of the *Divorce Act*. In these cases of squeezed ranges for spousal support, there will be strong reasons to go higher in this "depressed" range, to generate some compensatory support for the primary parent. As income levels rise for the parents of three or more children, the spousal support ranges will adjust upwards and there will be more flexibility for the location of amount within the ranges.

Standard of living concerns may also tend to push spousal support awards towards the higher end of the range. Even when spousal support is at the maximum 46 percent of individual net disposable income, a homemaker recipient and the children will be left with a noticeably lower household standard of living (assuming no new partners or children for either spouse). At lower income levels, the needs of the children's household will create pressure to move to the higher end of the range.

## 9.4 Needs and Ability to Pay of Payor

Need and limited ability to pay on the part of the payor spouse may push an award to the lower ends of the ranges. These factors will clearly have special importance at the lower end of the income spectrum, even above the floor of $20,000. (The floor is discussed further in Chapter 11 below.) In some cases where the need of the lower-income recipient spouse is pressing, the lower-income payor spouse may also be struggling to maintain some modest standard of living.

Even though the *without child support* formula uses gross incomes to work out the amounts, it is always important to look at the net income consequences of any particular amount of spousal support, especially for the payor. In longer marriages under this formula, where the formula percentages are higher, this is critical, especially where the payor has large mandatory deductions, including any pension deductions, compared to the recipient. These deductions may be a factor in going lower in the range for amount.[89]

The *with child support* formula uses net incomes for its calculations, adjusting for tax and certain standardized deductions. But this formula does not deduct mandatory pension contributions, for the reasons explained in Chapter 8 above. Mandatory pension deductions may become an important factor to select a lower amount within the ranges at lower income levels, to ensure that the payor spouse has enough net income for his or her own needs.[90]

Also a concern for lower income payors under the *with child support* formula will be their direct spending on expenses for the children during their time with the children. A lower income payor should be left with sufficient funds to exercise meaningful access to his or her children.

## 9.5 Work Incentives for Payor

The previous factor focussed upon the needs and ability to pay of the payor. Here we want to isolate a separate concern, the need to preserve work incentives for the payor. This concern will be particularly important in two situations: long marriages under the *without child support* formula and most cases of substantial child support under the *with child support* formula. The problem will be most acute at low-to-middle income levels.

Here we are not speaking about employment deductions from the payor's pay, discussed immediately above. One obvious concern here is the additional out-of-pocket costs of going to work every day, not covered by any employer and not reflected in income or deductions from pay, e.g. clothing, commuting to work, parking, tools, etc. For example, where a payor has substantial commuting expenses in an urban area, this may be a factor for going lower in the range.

A less precise, but perhaps more important, concern under this heading is the payor's net income after payment of taxes, deductions, child support (if any) and spousal support, and the marginal gain in this remaining income from any additional gross income earned. This more nebulous work incentive concern will come to the fore where the payor is working in the paid labour market and the recipient is not, especially under the *without child support* formula. In longer marriage cases under this formula, the percentages of gross income will be high enough to raise this issue, making it a factor to go lower in the range for amount.

---

[89] It is not correct, as some have done, to reduce the payor's gross income by the amount of the deductions. The formula range must first be calculated properly, using the gross incomes, and then judgment exercised about location within that range, with the amount of the deductions used as one factor amongst others.

[90] Again, it is not correct to deduct the mandatory pension contribution from a spouse's INDI and lower the whole range. These contributions are just one factor in locating an amount within the range.

Under the *with child support* formula, the recipient may be home full time with the care of children, so that this argument of "work incentive" is less compelling. And, under either formula, if the recipient of spousal support is also working, whether full-time or part-time, this version of "work incentive" for the payor virtually disappears.

## 9.6 Property Division and Debts

Underpinning the Advisory Guidelines is a basic assumption that the parties have accumulated the typical family or matrimonial property for couples of their age, incomes and obligations, and that their property is divided equally under the matrimonial property laws. Significant departures from those assumptions may affect where support is fixed within the ranges for amount and duration.

An absence of property to be divided might suggest an award at the higher end of the range. If the recipient receives a large amount of property, the low end of the range might be more appropriate. Similarly, if the recipient holds sizeable exempt or excluded assets after division, that too might militate in favour of the lower end of the range.

Where one spouse assumes a disproportionate share of the family debts, it may be necessary to use the debt payment exception described below in Chapter 12. But there will be other cases, not so severe, where the debt payments of one spouse will just be a factor pushing the amount higher or lower within the range, depending upon which spouse is paying the debts.

## 9.7 Self-Sufficiency Incentives

Self-sufficiency incentives may push in different directions. As often happens under the current case law, support might be fixed at the lower end of the ranges to encourage the recipient to make greater efforts to self-sufficiency, although imputing income also goes a long way towards responding to this concern. On the other hand, the need to promote self-sufficiency might lead to an award at the higher end of the range where this could mean that a recipient spouse obtains re-training or education leading to more remunerative employment and less support in the long term. Self-sufficiency issues are discussed at greater length in the separate Chapter 13 below.

This is not an exhaustive list, but rather an attempt to identify some of the more obvious factors that might affect how and where amount and duration are fixed within the ranges. The ranges also allow room for local and regional differences in support outcomes, recognizing that awards in some parts of the country are higher than in others.

## 10 RESTRUCTURING

## 10.1 The General Concept: Trading Off Amount Against Duration

Under the Advisory Guidelines there are several mechanisms that allow outcomes to be adjusted in response to the facts of particular cases. As discussed in Chapter 9, above, there is considerable flexibility in the fixing of precise amounts and durations within the ranges generated by the formulas. Here we discuss a second mechanism for flexibility – the ability to "restructure" the formula outcomes by trading off amount against duration. In Chapter 12, which follows, we discuss the third method – that of departing from the formula outcomes by relying upon exceptions.

Although the formulas generate separate figures for amount and duration, the Advisory Guidelines explicitly recognize that these awards can be "restructured" by trading off amount against duration. The only limit is that the overall value of the restructured award should remain within the global — or total — amounts generated by the formula when amount is multiplied by duration.

While the terminology of restructuring is new, the concept of trading off amount against duration is an established feature of current spousal support practice. Such tradeoffs are commonly made in separation agreements and consent orders. In *Bracklow* the Supreme Court of Canada acknowledged that such an adjustment can also be made by judges, explicitly recognizing that the amount and duration of awards can be configured in different ways to yield awards of similar value (or quantum). Thus the Court noted that an order for a smaller amount paid out over a long period of time can be equivalent to an order for a higher amount paid out over a shorter period of time.

Under the Advisory Guidelines a certain degree of adjustment of amount against duration will occur when precise amounts and duration are being fixed within the ranges (see Chapter 9). However, in particular cases an appropriate award will require an adjustment beyond the limits of the formula's ranges. Restructuring allows the formula to continue to act as a tool to guide such deviations from the ranges because the overall value of the award remains within the global amounts set by the formula. In this way restructuring differs from exceptions, discussed below in Chapter 12, which involve an actual departure from the global range of outcomes suggested by the formula.

**When restructuring is relied upon to resolve issues of inappropriate formula outcomes for amount or duration, awards remain consistent with the overall or global amounts generated by the Advisory Guidelines.**

Restructuring can be used in three ways:

- first, to **front-end load** awards by increasing the amount beyond the formulas' ranges and shortening duration[91]
- second, to **extend duration** beyond the formulas' ranges by lowering the monthly amount; and
- third, to formulate a **lump sum** payment by combining amount and duration[92]

Restructuring was a crucial component in the development of the Advisory Guidelines, particularly the development of the *without child support* formula. It was the only way in which some of the results generated by the formula could be rendered consistent with current practice. **Restructuring is thus an important aspect of a SSAG analysis after the formulas have been applied to generate ranges for amount and duration.**[93]

**In practice, restructuring has often been ignored.** In many cases, particularly short marriages under the *without child support* formula, courts have found the amounts generated by the formula too low and have then simply concluded that the Advisory Guidelines do not yield an appropriate outcome and are of no further use.[94] The failure to consider restructuring is unfortunate because it means that an important element of flexibility is not being utilized. The

---

[91] See for example *McCulloch v. Bawtinheimer*, [2006] A.J. No. 361 (Q.B.).

[92] See *Smith v. Smith*, [2006] B.C.J. No. 2920, 2006 BCSC 1655 and *Martin v. Martin*, [2007] O.J. No. 467.

[93] A good discussion of restructuring and its place within the overall scheme of the Advisory Guidelines is found in *McCulloch v. Bawtinheimer, supra* note 91.

[94] For an appellate example see the B.C. Court of Appeal decision in *Toth v. Kuhn*, [2007] B.C.J. No. 244, BCCA 83; for a trial level example see *Wang v. Poon*, [2007] B.C.J. No. 271, 2007 BCSC 194.

structure and guidance provided by the Guidelines are thus being lost in a number of cases where these benefits would otherwise be available.

## 10.2  How Does Restructuring Work? Some Examples

We now provide some examples of the different ways restructuring might be used and set out the basic calculation of the "global ranges" generated by the formulas. **Note that the calculations provided in these examples are very simplified** and do *not* take into account the time-value of money or the various future contingencies that could affect the value of awards over time. In practice, more sophisticated calculations may take such factors into account.[95] Computer software programs may assist in some of the calculations required by restructuring.[96] If periodic payments are converted into a lump sum, the different tax consequences must be taken into account in arriving at a comparable lump sum.

Despite such software programs, however, there will also be a certain amount of guess-work involved in restructuring. But this is already familiar to family law lawyers who frequently make trade-offs between amount and duration in settlement negotiations and spousal support agreements. Restructuring by means of a lump sum payment or an increase in amount above the formula amounts will also require a finding of ability to pay on the payor's part.

Our examples focus on the first and second uses of restructuring. We have assumed that the third use of restructuring — converting a periodic order to a lump sum in a short marriage — is familiar and straightforward, and so we have not provided a specific example.

As will be discussed further below, the primary use of restructuring will be under the *without child support* formula which generates fixed time limits. Our examples reflect this. Following these examples we will discuss in more detail the use of restructuring under each of the Guideline formulas.

### 10.2.1  Example 1: restructuring by front-end loading

Our first example involves front-end loading to increase the amount outside the formula's range by reducing duration. This involves choosing a durational limit at the low end of the formula's range or below it. Front-end loading may be appropriate in shorter marriages under the *without child support* formula where the monthly formula amounts are relatively modest. Restructuring will provide a generous but relatively short transitional award. Under current practice, spousal support awards in such cases will be shaped by the goal of cutting the ties between the parties fairly quickly and allowing them to go their separate ways. Front-end loading may also be desirable in cases where the recipient spouse needs significant support for a short period to undertake a program of retraining or education, or where the recipient spouse has a low base income.

---

[95] Two cases offer careful examples of restructuring to fix a lump sum. From B.C. see *Smith v. Smith, supra* note 92 (present value of monthly support if paid until payor 65, discounted for tax and adjusted for reapportionment, resulting in lump sum of $25,0000). From Ontario see *Martin v. Martin, supra* note 92, (9 year marriage with 2 children, husband the support claimant, lump sum support at the low end of the global range awarded under the custodial payor formula adjusted for tax).

[96] See for example DIVORCEmate's new SUMmate Quantum v. Duration Analyzer.

### Example 10.1

Here we return to the case of Bob and Susan in *Example 7.3*, who were married 10 years and had no children. They are both in their late thirties and employed full time. Bob's gross annual income as a computer salesman is $65,000; Sue's as a hairdresser is $25,000.

Under the *without child support* formula a 10 year marriage such as this gives rise to a range for amount of 1.5 to 20 percent of the gross income difference. Under the formula, spousal support would be in the range of $500 to $667 per month (or $6,000 to $8,000 per year) for a period of 5 to 10 years.

Given the parties' ages and employment situations and the length of the marriage, the appropriate award in this case would likely be one that cut the ties between the parties fairly quickly. The monthly amounts generated by the formula might also appear low when assessed against current practice. Both of these concerns could be met by providing transitional support at a higher level than the formula allows, for example $1,300 per month (which represents roughly 39 percent of the income difference) for only 3 years, rather than the 5 year minimum duration under the formula.

Restructuring requires the calculation of the global or total amounts generated by the formula when amount is multiplied by duration. On the facts of this example, the simplified calculation of the minimum and maximum global awards under the *without child support* formula would be as follows:

- low end of global range (low end of range for monthly amount x low end of range for duration in months)

**$500 per month for 5 years ($500 x 60 months) = $30,000**

- high end of global range (high end of range for monthly amount x high end of range for duration in months)

**$667 per month for 10 years ($667 x 120 months) = $80,040**

The global range in this example would therefore be between $30,000 and $80,040.

The proposed award of $1,300 per month for three years, which has a total value of $46,800 ($1,300 x 36 months), would be permissible under restructuring as it falls within the global ranges generated by the formula, even though it falls outside the formula's specific ranges for amount and duration.

Although this example uses a fixed monthly amount for the duration of the restructured award, it would also be possible to restructure using step-down awards, as long as the total amount of the award falls within the range set by the formula. In the example above, restructuring would allow an award of $1,500 per month for the first year, 1,000 per month for the second year, and $750 per month for the third year. The total value of the award — $39,000 — falls within the global amounts generated by the formula.

## 10.2.2 Example 2: restructuring by extending duration and reducing amount

Our second example shows the use of restructuring to extend duration by cutting back on amount. Depending on how much of an extension of duration is required, this can be accomplished either by choosing an amount at the lower end of the formula's range for amount or by setting an amount below the formula's range. This use of restructuring might be desirable in medium-length marriages where the recipient spouse will have long-term need and would be better off with modest supplements to income over a longer period of time than with more generous payments over the time period suggested by the formula.

### Example 10.2

Brian and Gail were married for 15 years and had no children. Both are 45. Gail is a phys ed teacher earning $70,000 gross per year. Brian worked as a trainer in the early years of the marriage but was forced to stop working because of a debilitating illness. He now receives CPP disability of $10,000 per year.

For a 15-year marriage, the *without child support* formula generates an amount ranging from 22.5 to 30 percent of the gross income difference. Here the formula results in a range for spousal support of $1,125 to $1,500 per month (or $13,500 to $18,000 per year), for a duration of from 7.5 to 15 years.

An award of 15 years' duration would take Brian to the age of 60. The desirable result in this case might be to provide support until Brian reaches age 65 when he will start to receive pension benefits. Restructuring would permit this.

On the facts of this example, the simplified calculation of the minimum and maximum global awards under the *without child support* formula would be as follows:

- low end of global range (low end of range for monthly amount x low end of range for duration in months)

**$1,125 per month for 7.5 years ($1,125 X 90 months) = $101,250**

- high end of global range (high end of range for monthly amount x high end of range for duration in months)

**$1,500 per month for 15 years ($1,500 X 180 months) = $270,000**

The global range in this example would therefore be between $101,250 and $270,000.

Because of Brian's need and the length of the marriage, absent restructuring, this would likely be a case where the award would tend towards the upper end of the ranges for both amount and duration. Using restructuring, the award could be extended to 20 years to take Brian to age 65 if the amount were set at the lowest end of the formula's range: $1,125 per month. In this case, the total amount of the award ($1,125 x 240 months) would equal the maximum global amount set by the formula, $270,000.

Although this example extends duration for a defined period, it might also be possible to use restructuring to extend duration indefinitely, recognizing, however, that the total value of an indefinite (duration not specified) award cannot be calculated with precision. A certain amount of guesswork would inevitably be involved in determining how low the amount of the indefinite award should be set to achieve some rough equivalence with the formula amounts.

## 10.3 When Should You Think About Restructuring?

In practice, restructuring has often been ignored. Here we try to flag the different kinds of fact situations, under each formula, where restructuring should be considered as an option.

## 10.3.1 Restructuring under the *without child support* formula

The primary use of restructuring will be under the *without child support* formula. To trade off amount against duration ideally requires a fixed duration for the award. As a result, restructuring will generally only be advisable in cases where the formula generates time limits rather than indefinite (duration not specified) support. It will thus have limited application under the *with child support* formula where duration is often uncertain.

More specifically, restructuring should be kept in mind in three particular kinds of cases under the *without child support* formula where it may often be appropriate:

- **shorter marriages without children**

    In some very short marriages cases where the support entitlement is limited and there is available property, a lump sum award that allows for a clean break may be appropriate. Restructuring allows for this.

    In other short marriage cases without children the purpose of the award is to provide a period of transition to allow the recipient an opportunity to adjust to a lower standard of living. Such awards, under current practice, often provide fairly generous levels of support during this transitional period. The amounts generated under the formula in the case of shorter marriages are often lower than current practice. Restructuring should be considered as a way to increase the amount of the award beyond the high end of the formula's range by reducing duration.

    The possibility of this use of restructuring to generate amounts consistent with current practice was a crucial factor in the development of the *without child support* formula. We knew that the amounts generated by the formula in some medium-length marriages, assessed on their own, would often be lower than current practice. But we also recognized that current awards were consistent with the total value of the awards generated by the formula when amount and duration were combined to yield global ranges.

    *Example 10.1 illustrates this use.*[97]

- **long-term disability after a medium-length marriage**

    The use of restructuring to extend duration should be considered in medium-length marriages where the recipient spouse will have long-term need because of illness or disability. The recipient may prefer more modest supplements to income over a longer period of time than more generous payments over the maximum time period permitted by the formula.

    *Example 10.2 illustrates this use.*

    We do recognize, as discussed in Chapter 12 on exceptions, that current law is uncertain in its treatment of illness and disability cases. In some cases, therefore, courts may find restructuring inadequate and then treat these cases as exceptions warranting a departure from the global ranges generated by the formula.

- **longer marriages where the formula generates a time limit but current practice dictates indefinite support**

---

[97] For an example in the Guidelines case law see *McCulloch v. Bawtinheimer*, *supra* note 91.

Under the *without child support* formula, support becomes indefinite (duration not specified) after 20 years of marriage. For marriages under that length, the formula generates time limits. Current practice, however, may preclude time limits in marriages shorter than 20 years, for example after 15 or 18 years.

What often happens in practice is that these longer durational limits of the Advisory Guidelines are simply ignored and only the ranges for amount are considered. In Chapter 7 we recognize that some courts may not be willing to implement the longer time limits under the *without child support* formula in initial orders and we suggest a "softer" use of the time limits to structure the on-going process of variation and review. But if it is contemplated that the support will likely not terminate at the end of maximum duration, even on this "softer" use of time-limits, restructuring should be applied. The extension of duration beyond the maximum end of the formula's range will require some trade-off of amount, at least a reduction to the low end of the range, if not below.

By way of example, this use of restructuring may arise in cases where there were dependent children at the time of separation who have since become independent and there has been a cross-over from the *with child support* formula. The age of the recipient may be such that the maximum duration based on length of marriage will not run to age 60 or 65 for the recipient, whenever pension income kicks in. Restructuring may be used to extend duration to that age by adjusting amount downward.

## 10.3.2 Restructuring under the *with child support* formula

For the most part, restructuring has less relevance for marriages with dependent children, for a number of reasons. After explaining these limitations, we will identify the circumstances in which restructuring is a practical option under this formula.

First, under the basic *with child support* formula, all orders are indefinite in form, within the framework of the two tests for determining the durational range that will structure the process of review and variation. The "softer" nature of the time limits under this formula make restructuring a more uncertain enterprise.

Second, restructuring to extend duration is unlikely to turn up under this formula. By the time the spouses reach the end of this formula's maximum duration, they will most likely have "crossed over" to the *without child support* formula, as explained above.

The third important limit on restructuring under this formula is the payor's ability to pay, applicable to the options of front-end loading or a lump sum. Where there are three children or more (or sometimes two children plus large section 7 expenses), there is little or no room to increase spousal support above the ranges, except for very high payor incomes.

The most likely circumstances for the use of front-end loading or a lump sum under the basic *with child support* formula will be cases where the recipient wants spousal support above the upper end of the range for a shorter period, e.g. to pursue a more expensive educational program. Many of these will be shorter marriage cases. To convert periodic payments to a lump sum, obviously there will have to be assets or resources available to the payor to make the lump sum payment. For front-end loading to occur, the following cases would be prime candidates, as there will be some additional ability to pay available:

- only one child;
- shared custody

- two children, no s. 7 expenses and higher incomes
- higher incomes generally.

The addition of a lower end to the durational range under this formula in this final version does create more room for negotiation over duration, which creates the conditions amenable to restructuring in these cases and perhaps some others.

### 10.3.3 Restructuring under the *custodial payor* formula

The *custodial payor* formula, applicable in cases where there are dependent children but the recipient spouse is not the custodial parent, is a modified version of the without child formula. Its adoption of the *without child support* formula's durational ranges means that restructuring may be used the same way under this formula as under the *without child support* formula, discussed above.[98]

## 11 CEILINGS AND FLOORS

Any guidelines must address the question of "ceilings" and "floors". The **ceiling** is the income level for the paying spouse above which any income-sharing formula gives way to discretion. The **floor** is the income level for the payor below which no support would generally be payable.

In the case of the *Federal Child Support Guidelines*, to take a familiar example, once the payor's income is over $150,000, section 4 provides that the amount of child support is the table amount for the first $150,000 plus any additional discretionary amount on the balance of the payor's income above $150,000. In practice courts have been prepared to follow the table formula for child support up to much higher income levels. At the other end, the floor for child support under the table formula is an income of about $8,000, based upon the personal tax exemption for a single person. This is a true floor in that the paying parent is deemed unable to pay any child support below that income level.

Ceilings and floors are trickier to establish for any spousal support formula. In practical terms, ceilings and floors attempt to define the upper and lower bounds of the typical case, for which guideline formulas can generate acceptable results. The benefits of consistency and predictability should be extended as far upwards and downwards as possible, while we recognise the important practical issues at each end of the income spectrum.

First we will explain the reasons for the ceiling and the floor: **the ceiling of $350,000 of gross payor income, and the floor of $20,000 of gross payor income.**

Above the ceiling and below the floor, the formulas do not operate, leaving these very high and very low income cases to be dealt with like "exceptions", which we discuss next in this Chapter. But these situations are not really "exceptions", as they lie outside the typical income levels for which the formulas were constructed.

---

[98] The Ontario case of *Martin, supra* note 92, is a good example of restructuring under the *custodial payor* formula, used to create a lump sum award at the low end of the global range for the husband after a nine year marriage.

## 11.1 The Ceiling

The shorthand term "ceiling" may be misleading. Under the *Federal Child Support Guidelines*, there is no absolute ceiling, just an income level above which the standard fixed-percentage-of-income formula can be varied, to generate a lesser percentage of income above that level. We propose a similar approach here.

Under the Spousal Support Advisory Guidelines, a ceiling could be based on the payor's income, or the monthly amount of support paid, or the recipient's income, or some form of standard of living test. Our preference is to use the payor's gross income as the basis for the ceiling.

**The ceiling is a gross annual payor income of $350,000.** After the payor's gross income reaches the ceiling of $350,000, the formulas should no longer be automatically applied to divide income beyond that threshold. But the $350,000 is not a "cap" either, as spousal support can and often will increase for income above that ceiling, on a case-by-case basis. Below, we discuss possible approaches for cases above the ceiling.

In the feedback on the Draft Proposal, we heard very few suggestions for a lower or higher income level for the ceiling. In large urban areas, an income of $350,000 was seen as a reasonable upper boundary for the use of formulas. By contrast, in rural areas and in other lower-income areas, some judges and lawyers began to feel uneasy with the higher-income ranges under the formulas somewhere between $150,000 and $250,000, leading to the development of informal "ceilings" at lower levels in these first few years under the Advisory Guidelines. Based on this experience, we have not revised the ceiling, leaving the law to develop further in this small number of high income cases.

## 11.2 The Floor

A floor for the Advisory Guidelines is more significant, if it sets the amount of support at zero below that floor. In our view, that should generally be the effect of the floor. The *Federal Child Support Guidelines* use a very low floor, about $8,000 gross per year. The floor for spousal support has to be higher than that.

**There should generally not be any amount of spousal support payable until the payor's gross income exceeds $20,000 per year.** A minimum wage or poverty line income would be too low for a floor, providing too little incentive for the payor to continue working, given prevailing tax rates. A review of the case law suggests that judges almost never order spousal support where payors make less than $20,000, or even slightly more. According to child support database information, where dependent children are involved, if the payor's income is below $20,000 gross annually, spousal support is only ordered or agreed upon in less than 2 percent of cases and the percentages for incomes of $20,000 to $29,000 are only about 2.5 percent.

Below this floor, there will be occasional cases where there will be entitlement to spousal support. There is also a need for flexibility for incomes just above the floor, to avoid any "cliff effect" and to accommodate ability to pay concerns. These are discussed below.

## 11.3 Payor Income Above the $350,000 Ceiling

To repeat, the ceiling is not a "cap" on spousal support, nor does it bar the continued use of the formulas as one method of arriving at an amount in a particular case. The examples below illustrate the operation of the ceiling and some of the issues that arise in cases above the ceiling.

**Example 11.1**

In a long-marriage case, assume one spouse earns $350,000 gross per year and the other has no income, after 25 years of marriage. Under the *without child support* formula, a 25-year marriage would call for sharing between 37.5 to 50 percent of the gross income difference, i.e., annual spousal support in the range of $131,250 to $175,000 (capped at $173,232), or $10,937 to $14,583 (capped at $14,436) monthly.

If the payor earned more, say $500,000, a court could leave spousal support in that same range or, in its discretion, a court might go higher, but no formula would push the court or the parties to do so and it would be an individualized decision. If the formula were to be applied for an income of $500,000, the support would rise to $15,625 to $20,833 (capped at $20,688) monthly. Or the court or the parties might settle upon an amount somewhere in between these two ranges. These are large numbers for support in this case, but keep in mind that this is the very top end of the formula, with a long marriage, a high payor income and no income for the recipient.[99]

**Example 11.2**

Take the same facts as *Example 11.1* above, with the payor earning $350,000 gross per year and the recipient having no income, but add two teenage children living with the recipient. Assume that child support would follow the table formula, with child support of $4,312 per month (using the Ontario tables).

Spousal support under the *with child support* formula, would produce a range from $7,585 to $9,160 per month.

If the payor earns more than $350,000, e.g. $500,000, a court can decide to go higher or not. Under the *with child support* formula the operation of the ceiling is complicated by the fact that child support increases as incomes rise above the ceiling. We can suggest two possible approaches for these very high income cases using the *with child support* formula.

The first approach uses the formula to determine a minimum amount for spousal support, an approach we can call "minimum plus". A notional calculation would be required to calculate spousal support at the $350,000 ceiling, using *the child support payable at the ceiling*. This would determine the "minimum" spousal support range. In Example *11.2*, that range would be $7,585 to $9,160. There would be discretion to add to that minimum for incomes over $350,000, after taking into account the actual amount of child support being paid by the payor at that higher income level, which would be $6,052 per month at $500,000. This approach might make more sense where the payor's income is closer to the ceiling.[100]

The second approach would be one of pure discretion. Once the payor's income exceeded the ceiling, then there would be no "minimum" for spousal support, just a dollar figure that would take into account the actual amount of child support paid, an amount which can be very large for

---

[99] For an early case under this formula, well above the ceiling at a payor income of $1.26 million, see *Modry v. Modry*, [2005] A.J. No. 442 (Alta.Q.B.). For a custodial payor case, where the amount was below the low end of the range on an income of $500,000, see *Milton v. Milton*, [2007] N.B.J. No. 414, 2007 NBQB 363 (N.B.Q.B.).

[100] For a case that took this approach, see *J.W.McC. v. T.E.R.*, [2007] B.C.J. No. 358, 2007 BCSC 252 (B.C.S.C.), where the range was calculated for $350,000 and then the high end of that range used, as the payor earned $400,000. Other B.C. judges have used the formula above the ceiling in *with child support* formula cases: *Teja v. Dhanda*, [2007] B.C.J. No. 1853, 2007 BCSC 1247 (B.C.S.C.)(just below low end of range, $425,000); and *E.(Y.J.) v. R.(Y.N.)*, 2007 CarswellBC 782, 2007 BCSC 509 (B.C.S.C.)(mid-point of range, $602,400).

high income cases. At some point, the large amounts of child support include a component that compensates the recipient spouse for the indirect costs of child-care responsibilities, leaving less need for spousal support to do so. This approach will become more important where the payor's income is well above the ceiling.[101]

What is clear is that the larger stakes at these income levels and the complexities of the individual cases mean that the Advisory Guidelines will have less significance to the outcomes above the ceiling, whether negotiated or litigated.

## 11.4  Payor Income Below $20,000/$30,000

The "floor" for the use of the formulas is a gross payor income of $20,000 per year. Below that floor, spousal support orders are rare and thus exceptional. For payor incomes between $20,000 and $30,000, there is no presumption against support, but it may be necessary to depart from the lower end of the formula ranges, in light of ability to pay considerations.

First is the situation involving payor incomes **below the floor of $20,000**. In general, the formulas for amount and duration will not operate where the payor spouse's gross income is less than $20,000 per year, as it will be rare that there will be sufficient ability to pay.[102] There may, however, be exceptional cases where spousal support might be paid, e.g. where the payor spouse is living with parents or otherwise has significantly reduced living expenses, or where both spouses are retired and on low incomes after a long marriage.[103] Formulas may be less helpful in determining amounts in such cases.

There is another good reason for allowing for spousal support in exceptional situations below the income floor. The Advisory Guidelines address amount and duration, not entitlement. An absolute income floor for amount would effectively create an entitlement rule, something that these guidelines should not do, in light of their informal and advisory nature. The issue of entitlement must always remain open, as a threshold issue, to be defined by the legislation and judicial interpretation of that legislation.

The examples below illustrate the operation of this $20,000 floor.

### Example 11.3

To take an example at the lower extreme, assume the higher income spouse earns $18,000 gross per year as employment income, after a 25-year marriage, but the other spouse has no income at all.

With a floor of $20,000, there would usually be zero spousal support payable at $18,000, despite the income difference. The range for spousal support generated by the *without child support* formula would have been $562 to $750 (capped at $706) per month. At the top end of this range, using Ontario figures, each spouse would have 50 per cent of the net income, but only $737 per month each, below social assistance rates in most jurisdictions. Even at the low end of this range, the payor would only have monthly net income of $880 compared to the recipient's $596 monthly.

---

[101]  In one Alberta case, where the payor earned $670,965, the full table amount of child support was ordered, but spousal support was much lower than a formulaic result (but in the middle of the range for an income of $350,000): *T.L.P. v. F.J.P.*, [2007] A.J. No. 1114, 2007 ABQB 600 (Alta.Q.B.).

[102]  For example, *A.M.R. v. B.E.R.*, [2005] P.E.I.J. No. 83, 2005 PESCTD 62 (P.E.I.S.C.)(wife earned $18,557, husband received workers compensation grossed up to $13,525).

[103]  For example, *M.(W.M.) v. M.(H.S.)*, 2007 CarswellBC 2667, 2007 BCSC 1629 (B.C.S.C.)(older couple, husband on disability income $17,800, wife no income, $600/mo. ordered, middle of range).

*Example 11.4*

Assume the payor earns $20,000 gross per year, the other spouse has no income and they have one child, which would mean a table amount of child support of $172 per month in Ontario.

If we applied the *with child support* formula here, spousal support would range from $319 to $436 per month. At these levels, the custodial parent and one child would be left at around 80 per cent of the already-too-low low-income measure used in Schedule II of the *Federal Child Support Guidelines* to compare household standards of living, while leaving the paying spouse a net monthly income of about $925 per month.

These numbers only improve slightly, even in the one-child case, for those earning $25,000 per year. The table amount of child support would be $211 per month. After payment of spousal support in the range of $436 to $569 per month the payor's net disposable income inches up just below $1,100 per month.

For spouses with low incomes, we must be particularly concerned about work incentives, welfare rates and net disposable incomes. There may be compelling arguments for low-income payors to pay child support at very low income levels, but the same arguments cannot be made for support for adult spouses.

There is a second related concern for those payors whose incomes are **more than $20,000 but less than $30,000**. For these payors, assuming entitlement, consideration should be given to the percentages sought under the applicable formula, the net disposable income left to the payor spouse, and the impact of a spousal support payment upon the work incentives and marginal gains of the payor.[104] For example, under the *without child support* formula, a shorter marriage would mean a smaller percentage and hence a smaller bite of the payor's income, in contrast to our 25-year marriage examples above. Or, to take another example, for a payor with an income in this $20,000 to $30,000 region and whose shifts, overtime hours or seasonal work are changeable, there are realistic concerns about disincentives to work. This flexibility will also avoid a "cliff effect" for payors just above the $20,000 floor, where a payor would suddenly go from zero spousal support to a formula amount simply because of making a few dollars more per year.

As these cases are just above the income floor, these are situations that could be treated as "exceptions" to the operation of the formulas, unlike those cases where the payor's income is below the floor. But the concerns in these two situations both arise from the operation of the floor, so we have dealt with them here together.

## 12 EXCEPTIONS

The formulas are intended to generate appropriate outcomes in the majority of cases. The formulas set out in Chapters 7 and 8 have been designed to cover a wide range of *typical* cases. There will be unusual or atypical cases, however, where the formulas generate results inconsistent with the support factors and objectives found in the *Divorce Act* and an appropriate result can only be achieved by departing from the formula.

The term **exceptions** refers, under the Advisory Guidelines, to recognized **categories of departures** from the ranges of amounts and durations for spousal support under the formulas. Exceptions are the last step in a support determination in cases covered by formulas. The formulas provide two other opportunities, discussed above, to shape awards that are responsive to

---

[104] For a careful analysis of this exception, see *Maitland v. Maitland*, [2005] O.J. No. 2252 (Ont.S.C.J.) (husband truck driver earned $28,439, wife no income, amount below range ordered).

the exigencies of individual cases. First, the ranges for amount and duration provide considerable scope to adjust **within those ranges** to the particular facts of any case (Chapter 9). Second, **restructuring** provides a further means to push and pull amount and duration above and below the ranges generated by the formula (Chapter 10). Only if *neither* of these steps can accommodate the unusual facts of a specific case should it become necessary to resort to these exceptions.

As we emphasize throughout this document, the Advisory Guidelines are informal rules and are not legally binding. In principle, the formula outcomes can be ignored whenever they are viewed as inappropriate. Departures from the formula outcomes could thus have been left entirely to case-by-case determination, without any need for categorical exceptions. In our view, however, it is important to the integrity of the Advisory Guidelines that exceptions be listed and defined. It is only the systemic benefits of consistency, predictability, coherence and fairness that encourage all concerned to work within the formula ranges. We took the view that exceptions should be stated, to structure and constrain departures from the formula in the interests of consistency and predictability.

We recognize that any list of itemized exceptions will not be exhaustive. There will always be unusual and even one-of-a-kind fact situations in spousal support cases, as in family law generally. But there are certain familiar categories of "hard" cases that come up with sufficient regularity that an exception can both recognize their existence and offer some guidance to their resolution. Following conventional legal principles, a spouse who claims to fall within one of these exceptions ought to bear the burden of proof.

Since the release of the Draft Proposal, one surprise has been the failure of lawyers and judges to use the listed "exceptions" to the formulas. In this final version, we have therefore assembled all the exceptions in one chapter, with more refinements and specifics about their potential use. We have also added some new exceptions, reflecting the feedback received since the Draft Proposal. For ease of reference, we will first list all the exceptions, before discussing each in turn:

1. Compelling financial circumstances in the interim period
2. Debt payment
3. Prior support obligations
4. Illness and disability
5. Compensatory exception in shorter marriages without children
6. Property division: reapportionment of property (B.C.), high property awards?
7. Basic needs/hardship: without child support, custodial payor formulas
8. Non-taxable payor income
9. Non-primary parent to fulfil parenting role under the custodial payor formula
10. Special needs of child
11. Section 15.3: small amounts, inadequate compensation under the *with child support* formula

## 12.1 Compelling Financial Circumstances in the Interim Period

We have listed this exception first, as it is the first exception that most will encounter. There are some situations in the interim period where there may have to be an exception for compelling financial circumstances. When spouses separate, it is not always possible to adjust the household finances quickly. One of the spouses may have to bear large and often unmovable (at least in the short run) expenses, most likely for housing or debts. In most instances, the ranges generated by the formulas will cover these exceptional cases, but there may be some difficulties where marriages are shorter or incomes are lower or property has not yet been divided. Interim spousal support can be adjusted back to the formula amounts once a house has been sold or a spouse has moved or debts have been refinanced.

Below we offer some examples of how this exception might operate.

### Example 12.1

In *Example 8.1*, Ted earns $80,000 gross per year and Alice makes $20,000. Alice and the two children remain in the family home after the separation. Assume that Alice has to make a large monthly mortgage payment, in the amount of $2,100 per month, as the couple had recently purchased a new home. Under the *with child support* formula, the range for spousal support would be $471 to $1,021 per month, on top of child support of $1,159 monthly.

At the interim stage, spousal support might have to be increased above the upper end of the range if Alice continues to make the mortgage payments. If Ted were to make the mortgage payments, then spousal support might have to be reduced below the lower end of the range at this interim stage.

The "compelling financial circumstances" in the interim period will usually involve such mortgage or debt expenses, especially under the *with child support* formula where the spouses are more often at the limit of their abilities to pay after separation. But there can also be other kinds of "compelling financial circumstances" at this interim stage, as in the next example.

### Example 12.2

In a modification of *Example 7.2*, Karl and Beth have been married for only two years. They have no children. Beth was 25 when they met and Karl was 30. When they married, Beth was a struggling artist who earned a meagre gross income of $12,000 a year giving art lessons to children. Karl is a music teacher with a gross annual income of $60,000. With Karl's encouragement, Beth stopped working during the marriage to devote herself to her painting. They lived in a house Karl owned before the marriage, which Beth will get some share of when the property is eventually divided. Beth has gone to live with a friend, but wants to rent her own apartment.

Using the *without child support* formula, a two-year marriage would generate a range for amount of 3 to 4 percent of the gross income difference of $60,000 (assessing Beth's income as zero, which it would be at the point when interim support is claimed). The result would be support in the range of $150 to $200 per month for between one and two years.

Until Beth finds work and gets her share of the property, she is going to require a minimum of $1000 per month. Even restructuring the award to provide $400 per month for a year would not meet these needs. The **interim exception** could be relied upon to make an interim award in a higher amount.[105]

While we have added another exception below for "basic needs/hardship" under the *without child support* formula more generally, it is preferable to use this interim exception for shorter term or purely transitional needs. The "basic needs/hardship" exception should only be considered at the trial or initial determination stage, after a full review of the merits on all the evidence, including any interim exception granted.

---

[105] In *Kirk v. Hackl*, [2007] S.J. No. 87, 2007 SKQB 82 (Sask.Q.B.), two exceptions were at work, both disability and interim circumstances.

## 12.2 Debt Payment

The existence of marital debts does not necessarily affect spousal support. In many cases debts are adequately taken into account in property division, reducing the amount of shareable property. However, where a couple has a negative net worth, i.e., debts greater than assets, then the allocation of the debt payments can have a dramatic impact upon ability to pay.

If the payor is required to pay a disproportionate share of the debts, then there may have to be some reduction in support from the lower end of the range generated by the formulas. The reduction may only be for a specified period, depending upon the balance remaining to be paid. At the end of that period, support could automatically revert to an amount within the range or, in some cases, a review may be ordered at that time. Conversely, if less frequently, the recipient may sometimes need an amount of support above the upper end of the range, in order to make payments on a family debt.

Where assets exceed debts, however, there can be little reason for a debt exception, as the party responsible for the debt will usually also hold the corresponding asset or other assets.

The limits of this exception can be refined, thanks in part to feedback received since the Draft Proposal:

- the total family debts must exceed the total family assets, or the payor's debts must exceed his or her assets;
- the qualifying debts must be "family debts";
- the debt payments must be "excessive or unusually high".

Each of these three refinements deserves comment.

In all property regimes, this spousal support exception can apply where total family debts exceed total family assets. In some Canadian property regimes, however, courts are empowered to allocate specific assets to a particular spouse, so that it is possible to leave one spouse with net assets and the other spouse is left with the family debts. In these regimes, the debt payment exception should be extended to this situation where one spouse has a "net debt" position.

The debts must be "family debts", i.e. debts taken into account in the division of the family or marital property or debts incurred to support the family during cohabitation.

Further, most debt payments can be accommodated within the formula ranges and it is only "excessive or unusually high" debt payments that compel going outside the ranges to make an exception. Implicit in this latter condition is that the debtor has made all reasonable efforts to refinance and reduce the debt payments first.

## 12.3 Prior Support Obligations

An obligation to pay support for a prior spouse or for prior children will affect the support to be paid to a subsequent spouse. Generally speaking, the courts have adopted a first-family-first approach for payors in such cases, subject to a very limited exception for low-income payors. Under the current law, courts determine the amount of any support for the second spouse taking into account the prior support obligations and the payor's budget.

We have created an exception for these prior support obligations. Most often, the prior support obligation will involve child support, but spousal support may also be involved after a longer first marriage and then a shorter second marriage.

In the vast majority of cases, the prior support obligation will involve a payment to another party. But there can also be cases where a spouse is a custodial parent for a prior child in his or her care who is not a "child of the marriage". A custodial parent in this case has as much of a "prior support obligation" as does a support payor. We have modified this exception since the Draft Proposal to recognize this reality.

### 12.3.1 Prior support under the *without child support* formula

Where there are prior support obligations, the payor's gross income will have to be adjusted to reflect those obligations, *before* computing the gross income difference and applying the percentage ranges to that difference. Adjusting for a **prior spousal support obligation** is simple, as spousal support is paid on a gross or before-tax basis: deduct the amount of spousal support paid from the spouse's gross income to establish the spouse's gross income. For a prior **child support obligation,** as child support is paid on a net or after-tax basis, the calculation is slightly more complicated: first, gross up the child support amount to reflect the payor's marginal tax rate on the amount paid and then deduct the grossed up amount from the spouse's gross income.

The effect of this prior support deduction is to leave the payor spouse with a lower gross income. The payor would thus have a lower income, the size of the gross income difference would be reduced and hence the formula amount of support for the second spouse would be lower.

### 12.3.2 Prior support under the *with child support* formula

An obligation to pay support for a prior spouse or prior children requires a slightly different adjustment under this formula, which works with net incomes rather than the gross incomes of the *without child support* formula. . In calculating the payor spouse's individual net disposable income, this exception will require that any amounts of support paid to prior spouses or children be deducted, thereby reducing the size of the pool of individual net disposable income between the current spouses and also reducing the payor's share of that smaller pool. Because we are working with net income under this formula, there is no need to gross up any child support amounts and the software can work out the after-tax value of the gross amount of spousal support.

### 12.3.3 Prior children in the spouse's care

Where a payor has a child of a prior relationship in his or her care after separation, a child who is not a "child of the marriage", the spouse has a different sort of "prior support obligation" towards that child, one not fixed in a support agreement or order, but an obligation nonetheless. Consistent with our approach for custodial parents under the *with child support* formula, the custodial parent's support obligation towards that prior child can be estimated by using an amount of "notional child support", based upon the table amount for that child or children for a person with the custodial parent's Guidelines income. In some cases, a further adjustment may have to be made for any section 7 expenses paid by the custodial parent.

#### *Example 12.3*

Assume the same facts for Ted and Alice in *Example 8.1*, but this time assume that Ted's 16-year-old son of an earlier marriage comes to live with Ted after separation. In calculating the range under the *with child support* formula, Ted's income would have to be reduced by the one-child table amount ($719, using Ontario figures), which would reduce the range for spousal support to Alice, down from $471 to $1,021 **to $15 to $471 monthly**.

## 12.4 Illness and disability

Many cases of illness or disability can be accommodated within the formulas. The central concern in many of these cases will be the recipient's need for long-term or indefinite support. Indefinite (duration not specified) support would be available under the formulas after 20 years of marriage or based upon the "rule of 65". And, in most medium-to-long marriages, with or without children, the ranges for duration and amount offer considerable scope to accommodate the needs of an ill or disabled spouse. Disability will be an important factor in locating the amount and duration within the ranges in these cases, a point already noted above in Chapter 9.

In some medium-length marriages, where the formulas generate time limits, **restructuring** may have to be employed (Chapter 10). Under restructuring, the monthly amount can be reduced and the duration extended beyond the maximum, especially where spousal support is effectively bridging until retirement, when the recipient's pension and old age benefits become payable. For this to be effective, the support amounts generated by the formula would have to be large enough to allow for a reasonable lower amount of monthly support. *Example 7.8*, the case of Gail and Brian, where Brian is suffering from a chronic illness at the end of their 15 year marriage, illustrates the use of restructuring to deal with the needs of an ill or disabled spouse.

For many cases, however, neither the breadth of the ranges nor the expanded possibilities of restructuring are seen to provide an adequate response to illness or disability. In these cases, there are three distinct approaches to long-term disability, three approaches that became more sharply defined after *Bracklow* in 1999. Because these are "hard" cases, more of them turn up in the reported decisions. Below we have framed these three approaches using the language of the Advisory Guidelines, as courts increasingly have used the Guidelines to consider these issues.

Faced with a recipient with a long-term disability, Canadian courts have responded with one of three approaches, here stated in declining order of frequency:

1.  *Lower Amount, Extend Duration*: most courts will extend duration, even to be "indefinite", while keeping the amount within the range, at or near the low end;
2.  *No Exception*: a slightly smaller number of courts will fix an amount in the range, often towards the upper end, and use the maximum duration, even though that means support will end while need continues;
3.  *Increase Amount, Extend Duration*: a much smaller group of courts will respond to the greater need in disability cases by increasing amount and extending duration.

After *Bracklow*, the law in this area remains uncertain. In our view, the third approach is the least consistent with *Bracklow*. The case law is dominated by the first two approaches, each of which can find support in the *Bracklow* decision. Our preference would be the second, "no exception" approach, which seems more consistent with the modern limits of spousal support as a remedy. But a slight majority of the reported cases see these cases as exceptions, mostly preferring the first, "lower amount, extended duration" approach. For now, as there is no dominant pattern or trend in the case law, we must recognize the possibility of an exception for these cases and leave the law to develop.

In order to explain the use of the ranges, restructuring and these three alternative approaches, it is best to use an example. We will change the facts slightly in Example 7.3, the case of Bob and Sue.

### Example 12.4

Bob and Sue have been married for 10 years. Sue is now 38, and Bob earns $65,000 per year. There are no children. Assume that Sue worked as a hairdresser, earning $25,000 a year, but then became ill and unable to work towards the end of the marriage, with no prospect of future improvement. She now receives $10,000 per year thanks to CPP disability.

Under the *without child support* formula, the applicable percentages for amount after a 10 year marriage would still be, as on the original facts, 15 to 20 percent, but now applied to a gross income difference of $55,000. **Spousal support under the formula would be in the range of $687 to $917 per month (or $8,250 to $11,000 annually) for a duration ranging from 5 to 10 years.**

At the maximum duration, Sue would only obtain spousal support until age 48. Suppose Sue wants to receive support until age 60, another 12 years or 22 years in total.

Restructuring could be attempted. The maximum global amount under the formula would be $110,000 ($917 per month for 10 years). If this global amount were stretched over 22 years (and ignoring any discounting for time), that could generate an annual amount of $5,000 per year or $417 per month.

Under the "no exception" approach, Sue's support would be limited by the maximum amount and duration generated by the formula, subject to an extension of the maximum duration by means of restructuring. Current law offers support for this "no exception" approach, specifically the *Bracklow* case itself. *Bracklow* involved a support claim by a disabled spouse on facts quite similar to those in our example of Bob and Sue. The final result in *Bracklow* is consistent with the *without child support* formula, without resort to an exception.[106]

*Bracklow* involved a seven-year relationship. At the time of the original trial, Mr. *Bracklow* was earning $44,000 gross per year and Mrs. *Bracklow*'s income from CPP was $787 per month, or roughly $9,500 per year. The final result in the case, taking into account the interim support paid, was a time-limited order of $400 per month for slightly more than seven years. The *with child support* formula yields a similar result. Under the formula, after a 7 year marriage the range for support is 10.5 to 14 percent of the gross income difference, which in *Bracklow* was $34,500. The range for support would therefore be $301 to $402 per month (or $3623 to $4830 per year) for a duration of 3.5 to 7 years duration. Thus the results generated by the formula might also be seen as appropriate for the case of Bob and Sue.[107]

**If Sue's claim for support is seen as warranting an exception**, our preferred solution would be to extend the duration of support to age 60 as Sue requests, but for an amount at the low end of the range, i.e. $687 monthly or $8,250 per year. Typically these will be cases where the recipient is younger or the marriage is shorter or the payor's income is not high. Under this exception, we suggest that it is best to **lengthen the maximum durational limit, while keeping the amount within the range, more specifically at or near the lower end of the range.**

Under the third approach above, a court might order the upper end of the range, or $917 per month in Sue's case, but without any time limit of 5 to 10 years. Duration would be thus be "indefinite (duration not specified)", which for practical purposes might be "permanent" in such a case.[108] As stated earlier, this third approach is used much less often and is least consistent with *Bracklow*.

---

[106] The result of the Supreme Court of Canada decision was to return the case for a rehearing of Mrs. Bracklow's claim for spousal support. The rehearing decision is reported at (1999), 3 R.F.L. (5 th) 179 (B.C.S.C.).

[107] For examples of cases where no exception was made, see *Puddifant v. Puddifant*, [2005] N.S.J. No. 558, 2005 NSSC 340 (N.S.S.C.F.D.); *Williston v. Williston*, [2006] B.C.J. No. 3248, 2006 BCSC 1869 (B.C.S.C.); and *Wise v. Wise*, [2006] B.C.J. No. 1143, 2006 BCSC 945 (B.C.S.C.).

[108] For example, *Bramhill v. Dick*, [2007] B.C.J. No. 387, 2007 BCSC 262 (B.C.S.C.).

At most, what we propose here is a limited exception for illness and disability cases, as these are the cases that the courts often treat as exceptional. Some might propose that there be a similar and additional exception based upon age for older recipient spouses. In our view, there are sufficient accommodations for age in the *without child support* formula. The recipient's age will be a factor in fixing amount and duration within the ranges and there is also the rule of 65 for indefinite support.

Some would even broaden this exception beyond illness and disability, into something more like a "basic social obligation" exception, where the recipient has basic needs beyond any formula support for one of any number of reasons. We believe that the sheer breadth of a basic social obligation exception would undermine the integrity and consistency of any formula or guidelines.

The illness or disability exception will usually arise where there are problems with the maximum duration under the *without child support* formula, where the marriage is of short-to-medium duration. Under the basic *with child support* formula, there will be much less need for this exception, given the lengthy maximum duration available to a primary parent under the shorter-marriage test for duration.

Disability does come up regularly under the *custodial payor* formula, as it often explains why the mother is the non-custodial parent. Under the *custodial payor* formula, there is another exception described below, an exception for a non-custodial parent to fulfil her or his parenting role, a parenting exception that may provide more spousal support for an ill or disabled non-custodial parent. However, if the non-custodial parent is not actively involved in parenting, perhaps because of the illness or disability, then the illness or disability exception might be applied.

Three years after the release of the Draft Proposal, the language of the Advisory Guidelines is now being used to address these difficult issues of illness and disability, but the law remains in a state of flux. Some courts make an exception, others don't, and we have to await further developments.

## 12.5 The Compensatory Exception in Short Marriages Without Children

The merger over time concept incorporates both compensatory and non-compensatory elements. In longer marriages the *without child support* formula thus generates high percentage ranges for sharing the gross income difference. In these longer marriages, by recognizing strong non-compensatory claims to the marital standard of living, the formula amounts also fully recognize any compensatory claims based on loss of earning capacity or career damage.

For short-or medium-length marriages, however, the *without child support* formula produces smaller amounts of support, reflecting the reduced importance of compensatory considerations, especially as most of these will be marriages without children. More important in these short-to-medium marriages is the transitional function of non-compensatory support, with the transition being longer or shorter depending upon the expectation and reliance interests flowing from the length of the marriage.

But some short-or medium-length marriages can involve large *compensatory* claims, disproportionate to the length of the marriage, even without any children involved. These compensatory claims may relate to an economic loss or may involve a restitutionary claim for an economic advantage conferred. Some examples come to mind:

- One spouse is transferred for employment purposes, on one or more occasions, forcing the other spouse to give up his or her job and to become a secondary earner.

- One spouse moves across the country to marry, giving up his or her job or business to do so.[109]
- One spouse works to put the other through a post-secondary or professional program but the couple separates shortly after graduation as in *Caratun v. Caratun*[110] before the supporting spouse has been able to enjoy any of the benefits of the other spouse's enhanced earning capacity.

There could undoubtedly be other examples.

If a claimant spouse can prove such a disproportionate compensatory claim, then this exception allows for an individualized determination of the amount of spousal support, based upon the size and nature of that claim. The formula will not offer much assistance. The compensatory principles set out in *Moge*, and reaffirmed in *Bracklow*, continue to develop in the case law. Thus, the precise scope of this exception will reflect the evolution of those principles.

A compensatory exception is unnecessary under the *with child support* formula, given the weight given to compensatory considerations in the construction of this formula and the generous maximum durations available under the two tests for duration.

## 12.6 Property Division, Reapportionment of Property

Spousal support is only determined after the division of family or matrimonial property. In Canada, there is a different regime for property division in every province and territory. All the property regimes have a few common characteristics: special rules governing the matrimonial home, a defined pool of family or matrimonial property, and a strong presumption of equal division of that pool. In most cases, there will be some net accumulation of property and it will be divided equally. Apart from the debt payment exception already mentioned, there are two other situations where a possible "property" exception has been suggested in determining spousal support: unequal division of property, or high property awards.

The remedies of property division and spousal support perform distinct functions and have different rationales. In the Draft Proposal, we therefore did not propose a general exception for unequal property division. We were less categorical about any exception for high property awards. We do recognize that British Columbia's property law is different and thus justifies an exception, as B.C. law allows unequal division or "reapportionment" on grounds that ordinarily are taken into consideration for the spousal support remedy.

Before considering these exceptions, we realise that, in many settlements, the division of property is used to fund a lump sum payment of spousal support. The Advisory Guidelines can actually assist in negotiating that outcome, as the ranges for amount and duration can offer guidance in converting all or a portion of periodic spousal support into a lump sum amount through restructuring. But this is not an "exception", just restructuring and paying the lump sum spousal support through property division. Any "property exception" would work the other way,

---

[109] For example, *Ahn v. Ahn*, [2007] B.C.J. No. 1702, 2007 BCSC 1148 (B.C.S.C.); *Fuller v. Matthews*, [2007] B.C.J. No. 656, 2007 BCSC 444 (B.C.S.C.).

[110] *Caratun v. Caratun* (1993), 42 R.F.L. (3d) 113 (Ont. C.A.). The ALI proposals also contain an exception for disproportionate compensatory losses in short marriages. With respect to *Caratun*-type cases, the ALI's proposals frame these as reimbursement support cases which involve compensation for a *loss*, i.e., the loss either spouse incurs when the marriage is dissolved before that spouse realizes a fair return from his or her investment in the other spouse's earning capacity. Spousal support in these cases, the ALI suggests, ought to be the reimbursement of living and other expenses contributed by the claimant spouse.

i.e. the unequal division or high property award is made first and then spousal support is reduced below the ranges because of the property division.

## 12.6.1  Reapportionment of property (British Columbia)

Unlike any other Canadian matrimonial property statute, the British Columbia *Family Relations Act* empowers a court to reapportion, or divide unequally, property between spouses on grounds that overlap with spousal support considerations. Among the grounds in section 65(1), entitled "Judicial reapportionment based on fairness", can be found factor (e):

---

1.   If the provisions for division of property between spouses under section 56, Part 6 or their marriage agreement, as the case may be, would be unfair having regard to
   a.   the duration of the marriage,
   b.   the duration of the period during which the spouses have lived separate and apart,
   c.   the date when property was acquired or disposed of,
   d.   the extent to which property was acquired by the spouse through inheritance or gift,
   e.   the needs of each spouse to become or remain economically independent and self-sufficient, or
   f.   any other circumstances relating to the acquisition, preservation, maintenance, improvement or use of property or the capacity or liabilities of a spouse, the Supreme Court, on application, may order that the property covered by section 56, Part 6 or the marriage agreement, as the case may be, be divided into shares fixed by the court.

---

Factors (e) (self-sufficiency) and (f) (capacity or liabilities) are frequently used to adjust for the economic disadvantage of the lower-income spouse at the end of the marriage. There is a substantial case law on reapportionment on these grounds, which we do not need to repeat here.[111] One of the concerns of the case law has been to avoid double recovery.

In its spousal support decisions since the release of the Draft Proposal, the British Columbia Court of Appeal has applied reapportionment law in the context of the Spousal Support Advisory Guidelines. In many instances, any adjustment for reapportionment can be made by reducing support within the ranges. But sometimes an exception has to be recognized: spousal support may have to be reduced below the formula ranges where a sufficiently large reapportionment order has been made under section 65 on the grounds stated in clauses (1)(e) and (f).[112]

In the distinctive property regime in British Columbia, **and only in British Columbia**, there is thus an exception available where a sufficiently large reapportionment order has been made on these "spousal support" grounds.

---

[111] The leading decision would be *Toth v. Toth* (1995), 13 B.C.L.R. (3d) 1, 17 R.F.L. (4 th) 55 (B.C.C.A.).
[112] *Tedham v. Tedham*, [2005] B.C.J. No. 2186, 2005 BCCA 502, 261 D.L.R. (4 th) 332, 47 B.C.L.R. (4 th) 254, 20 R.F.L. (6 th) 217; *Narayan v. Narayan*, [2006] B.C.J. No. 3178, 2006 BCCA 561, 62 B.C.L.R. (4 th) 116, 34 R.F.L. (6 th) 272; *MacEachern v. MacEachern*, [2006] B.C.J. No. 2917, 2006 BCCA 508, 62 B.C.L.R. (4 th) 95, 33 R.F.L. (6 th) 315, [2007] 3 W.W.R. 471; *Foster v. Foster*, [2007] B.C.J. No. 244, 2007 BCCA 83, 64 B.C.L.R. (4 th) 259, 37 R.F.L. (6 th) 139.

## 12.6.2 An exception for high property awards?

Some have suggested that a high property award should constitute an exception for spousal support purposes. On this view, property and support are alternative financial remedies that can be substituted, one for the other, so that a high property award always justifies lower spousal support. While this view does find some acceptance in the case law, so too does the more compelling view that property and support are governed by distinctive laws and serve different purposes and that a high property award should not in and of itself dictate a significant reduction of spousal support. Recognizing high property awards as an explicit exception would, in our view, inappropriately entrench a contested view. Again, we have to leave the law to develop further in this area.

If there were an exception of this kind, it would result in an amount of spousal support set below the low end of the range or for a shorter duration, where there is a high property award.

It should be kept in mind that the Advisory Guidelines can already accommodate some of these "high property" concerns, without any exception. First, each spouse is expected to generate reasonable income from his or her assets and income can be imputed where a spouse fails to do so. The income imputed will affect the operation of the formula (Chapter 6). Second, as discussed above, property-related concerns may, in some cases, determine whether support is fixed at the upper or lower ends of the ranges for amount or duration, e.g. an absence of property to be divided or a large amount of property or continuing equalization payments (Chapter 9). Third, many high property cases are also high-income cases, bringing into play the ceiling above which the formula will not necessarily apply (Chapter 11).

Finally, there will be some cases where a high property award means no entitlement to spousal support, as the recipient of the property will thereby become economically self-sufficient, overcoming any disadvantage or need at the end of the marriage (Chapter 4). This is not an "exception" to the Advisory Guidelines, however, but an instance where the threshold requirement of entitlement is not met, so that the Advisory Guidelines are not engaged.

## 12.6.3 Boston v. Boston

One last property point: the Advisory Guidelines on amount and duration do not change the law from *Boston v. Boston*[113] governing double-dipping, mostly from pensions. That law remains in place, as a possible constraint upon the amount of support, determining if some portion of income should be excluded from the formula because it has been previously shared under property division.[114]

## 12.7 Basic Needs/Hardship: Without Child Support, Custodial Payor Formulas

The *without child support* formula works well across a wide range of cases from short to long marriages with varying incomes. In some parts of the country and in some cases, there is a specific problem for shorter marriages where the recipient has little or no income. In these shorter-marriage cases, the formula is seen as generating too little support for the low income

---

[113] *Boston v. Boston*, [2001] 2 S.C.R. 413.
[114] For examples of Guidelines cases applying *Boston*, see *Pettigrew v. Pettigrew*, [2006] N.S.J. No. 321, 2006 NSCA 98 (N.S.C.A.), affirming [2005] N.S.J. No. 616, 2005 NSSC 219 (N.S.S.C.); *Puddifant v. Puddifant*, [2005] N.S.J. No. 558, 2005 NSSC 340 (N.S.S.C.F.D.); *Vanderlans v. Vanderlans*, [2007] N.J. No. 121, 2007 NLUFC 8 (N.L.U.F.C.).

recipient to meet her or his basic needs for a transitional period that goes beyond any interim exception.

Restructuring in these cases will sometimes still not generate an amount or a duration that is sufficient, in the eyes of some, to "relieve any economic hardship of the spouses arising from the breakdown of the marriage", as stated in section 15.2(6)(c) of the *Divorce Act*. To complicate matters further, the amount required to meet basic needs will vary from big city to small city to town to rural area. Whether restructuring provides a satisfactory outcome, i.e. more support for a shorter time, will depend upon where the recipient lives. Thus the problem for these short-to-medium-marriage-low-income cases seems to be most acute in big cities.[115]

We did not wish to change the structure of the formula itself for this one sub-set of cases. The best approach to these cases was to create a carefully-tailored exception, the **basic needs/hardship exception**, leaving the basic formula intact for the vast majority of cases where the formula produces a reasonable range of outcomes.

**Other exceptions** may avoid the need to resort to this basic needs/hardship exception. In some short marriages without children, the **compensatory exception** may apply, with more generous outcomes than under this exception. The basic needs/hardship exception is non-compensatory. In other cases, in shorter marriages, the **compelling financial circumstances at the interim stage** can provide for a higher amount of support for a transitional period, such that no further exception need be applied by the time of trial. Earlier, we made clear that basic needs/hardship exception should only be considered at the trial or initial determination stage, after a full review of the merits on all the evidence, including any interim exception granted.

The basic needs/hardship exception applies under the *without child support* formula and the *custodial payor* formula, *only* in these circumstances:

- the formula range, even after restructuring, will not provide sufficient income for the recipient to meet her or his basic needs
- the reason will be that the recipient's base or non-support income is zero or too low
- the marriage will typically be short to medium in length, e.g. 1 to 10 years
- the payor spouse will have the ability to pay.

We should be clear that this exception is only intended to ease the transition in these hardship cases. It is not intended to provide the marital standard of living, but only a standard of basic needs. And it is not intended to provide support for a long period of time after a shorter marriage, but only for a short transition period.

One situation where the **basic needs/hardship exception** has been applied is immigration sponsorship cases, where a marriage breaks down while a sponsorship agreement is in place. Most spousal sponsorship agreements now run for a period of three years from the date the immigrating spouse becomes a permanent resident.[116] In some cases of very short marriages, the three-year agreement has been used as a measure of the appropriate duration for the period that the payor spouse covers basic needs through spousal support.[117]

A simple example will illustrate the application of this exception:

---

[115] For example, *Simpson v. Grignon*, [2007] O.J. No. 1915, 2007 CarswellOnt 3095 (Ont.S.C.J.).

[116] The duration of such sponsorship agreements was once as long as 10 years, reduced now to 3 years: *Immigration and Refugee Protection Regulations*, SOR/2002-227, as am. SOR/2004-167 and SOR/2005-61, s. 132.

[117] For example, *Gidey v. Abay*, [2007] O.J. No. 3693 (Ont.S.C.J.); *T.M. v. M.A.G.*, [2006] B.C.J. No. 3479, 2006 BCPC 604 (B.C.P.C.).

## Example 12.5

Rob and Donna have been married for 5 years, a second marriage with no children. Rob earns $60,000 per year. Donna is 53 years old and has no income. Much turns upon why Donna has no income.

If Donna has no income because she moved twice in the past 5 years to accommodate Rob's employment transfers, then the compensatory exception would apply, with spousal support based upon Donna's loss.

But if Donna has no income because she has few skills and is unemployed at the end of the marriage, then her entitlement will be non-compensatory. Under the *without child support* formula, the range would be $4,500 to $6000 per year ($375 to $500 per month) for 2 = to 5 years. This range would not meet Donna's basic needs in any part of Canada.

By means of restructuring, using the maxima for amount and duration, the formula could generate as much as $15,000 per year for 2 years. In some parts of Canada, that might be enough to meet Donna's basic needs. In a city, however, Donna might need $20,000 a year for those two years to meet her basic needs, as part of the transition from married life.

In the end, we remain uneasy about recognizing this exception. Many would suggest that the restructured outcome for Donna of $15,000 per year for two years is perfectly reasonable, even in a big city, so that no exception is warranted at all. Others would see the restructured amount as too low, or the duration as too short, thus warranting an exception, and cases to that effect can be found in the post-Guidelines case law. For the most part, those who pressed for this exception can be found in big cities and it may be that this specific exception is not necessary outside of those big cities.

## 12.8 Non-Taxable Payor Income

Both formulas produce a "gross" amount of spousal support, i.e. an amount that is deductible from taxable income for the payor and included in taxable income for the recipient. As we noted in Chapter 6 on Income, some payors have incomes based entirely on legitimately non-taxable sources, usually workers' compensation or disability payments or income earned by an aboriginal person on reserve.[118] In these cases, the payor is unable to deduct the support paid, contrary to the assumption built into the formulas for determining amount.

Some of the recipients may pay little or no tax on the support income received, due to their low incomes, but that is not our concern here. Nor are we concerned with payors who earn income tax-free by working "under the table" or by understating their income for tax purposes. Here we are concerned with payors who legitimately receive their income on a non-taxable basis.

What warrants this **non-taxable exception** is when the non-deductibility of the spousal support poses a problem for the payor's ability to pay, as the non-taxable payor is unable to pay the gross amount of spousal support that would be required of a payor with the benefits of deductibility.

Under the *without child support* formula, ability to pay will usually only become an issue in longer marriage cases, marriages of 15 years or more. In these longer marriage cases, the 50/50 net income "cap" will simplify the use of this exception, as the upper limit on spousal support will be equalization of the spouses' net incomes. A simple example helps to explain why.

---

[118] For a case of an aboriginal person earning income on reserve, see *James v. Torrens*, [2007] S.J. No. 334, 2007 SKQB 219 (Sask.Q.B.).

## Example 12.6

Donna and Jeff have been married for many years, with two adult children. Later in his career, Jeff experienced became unable to work and Jeff now receives a disability pension of $37,500 per year, non-taxable. Grossed up, his disability pension would be worth $50,000 per year. Donna works part-time on account of health issues and earns $10,000 gross per year.

Under the *without child support* formula, if Donna and Jeff have been married for 25 years and using the gross income difference, spousal support would be **$1,250 to $1,667 per month, indefinite (duration not specified)**. But Jeff cannot deduct any amount for the spousal support paid, even though Donna will have to include it as taxable income.

In this final version, we have added a net income "cap" under this formula, so that the upper end of the range for support would leave both Jeff and Donna with 50 per cent of the net income. This net income calculation takes into account Jeff's inability to deduct his support and Donna's payment of tax on that support. The "cap" would kick in at **$1,318 per month** (using Ontario tax rates), well below the formula's upper limit of $1,667 monthly (if Jeff's income were taxable, the "cap" would still take effect, but much higher, at $1,575 per month).

That would only leave a narrow range of **$1,250 to $1,318 per month** if we applied the "cap" literally. Practically, the **non-taxable exception** would mean that a court or the parties will likely have to go lower than $1,250 per month in most cases, in consideration of Jeff's ability to pay.

What if Donna and Jeff were married for 20 years? Using the gross income difference, the range would be $1,000 to $1,333 per month, indefinite (duration not specified). The net income "cap" would only have a small impact here, as it would limit the upper end of the range to $1,318. Ability to pay concerns for Jeff's position would be much diminished and this non-taxable exception may not be required.

The problems are actually more serious at higher income levels, especially where the support recipient has to pay a higher rate of tax. If the payor receives $68,388 non-taxable, the equivalent of a grossed-up income of $100,000 and the recipient earned $30,000 per year, the net income "cap" has an even greater impact than it does for Donna and Jeff. Most cases of non-taxable income involve low-to-middle incomes rather than such higher incomes.

Because the *with child support* formula already uses net incomes for its calculations, the basic formula automatically adjusts for the non-deductibility of support. The result is that the whole range under this formula is reduced downward, but it is important to be aware of the reduction and the amounts involved. Another example can help, if we go back to the familiar example of Ted and Alice.

## Example 12.7

Ted and Alice have been married for 11 years and have two children aged 8 and 10, as in *Example 8.1*. Alice still earns $20,000, but Ted now receives a non-taxable disability pension totalling $56,900 per year (grossed-up, this would be equivalent to $80,000 of employment income). This means that Ted still pays $1,159 per month in child support and there are no section 7 expenses. When Ted earned $80,000 per year in employment income, the spousal support range was **$474 to $1,025 per month**, using Ontario rates. Now that Ted receives a non-taxable disability pension, the range is **reduced to $380 to**

**$797 per month**. The difference in the two ranges reflects the effect of Ted being unable to deduct the spousal support for tax purposes.

It might be possible to make an exception here, to increase spousal support above the upper end of the automatically-reduced non-taxable range, pushing up towards $1,025 per month, in order to improve the financial situation of the recipient and the children. At $1,025 per month, however, almost 61 per cent of the family's net disposable income or monthly cash flow would be left in Alice's household.

The important point is to appreciate how much the basic *with child support* formula has reduced the range for amount when the payor's income is non-taxable, in order to make the necessary judgment about whether an exception should be made, to increase spousal support above the calculated range.

In every one of these **non-taxable exception** cases, it is necessary to balance the tax positions of the spouses — the reduced ability to pay of the payor spouse, who can't deduct the support paid, and the needs or loss of the recipient spouse, who still has to pay taxes on spousal support and only receives after-tax support.

## 12.9 Non-Primary Parent to Fulfil Parenting Role under the *Custodial Payor* Formula

In many cases, the *custodial payor* formula will apply because a father has become the custodial or primary parent of older children, after a medium to long marriage. In these cases, this hybrid formula will provide reasonable amounts of spousal support for durations that will extend beyond the children reaching the age of majority. But in some cases the *custodial payor* formula will be applied after a shorter marriage, with younger children.

There is an exception distinctive to the custodial payor formula, flagged earlier in Chapter 8 and reflected in the Nova Scotia case of *Davey v. Davey*.[119] It is quite a narrow exception, unlikely to be raised very often, but worth noting. To come within this exception:

- the recipient spouse and non-custodial parent must play an important role in the child's care and upbringing after separation
- the marriage is shorter and the child is younger
- the ranges for amount and duration are low enough and short enough under the custodial payor formula that the non-custodial parent may not be able to continue to fulfil his or her parental role.

Some of these cases may involve an element of illness or disability, as in *Davey*. Under this exception, however, the focus is upon the recipient's parenting role, rather than the disability. Most often, the exception will be used to extend the **duration** of spousal support, until the child is old enough and the parenting functions are much reduced. Less frequently, the **amount** of support might need to be increased, to ensure the recipient spouse has sufficient resources to meet the specific demands of parenting.

In practical terms, this parenting exception should be considered first, before reaching the more general illness and disability exception discussed above. If the non-custodial parent does not play an important parenting role, perhaps because of the illness or disability, then the more general exception can be properly used.

---

[119] *Davey v. Davey* (2003), 36 R.F.L. (5th) 297 (N.S.C.A.), affirming (2002), 205 N.S.R. (2d) 367 (N.S.S.C.).

## Special Needs of Child

A child with special needs can raise issues of both amount and duration in spousal support law, issues that may require an exception.[120]

First, **duration**. A child with special needs can obviously affect the ability of the primary parent to obtain employment, whether part-time or full-time. This may require that the duration of support be extended beyond the length of the marriage or beyond the last child finishing high school, the two possible maximum time limits under the *with child support* formula.

Second, **amount**. Again, a special needs child will often mean that the primary parent cannot work as much, perhaps not even part-time, and thus the amount of spousal support will be increased because of the recipient's lower income, an adjustment that can be accommodated by the *with child support* formula. But even then, there may be a need to go above the upper end of the range, to leave an even larger percentage of the family's net disposable income in the hands of the primary parent, above the typical maxima of 54 per cent (1 child) or 58 per cent (2 children) or even 61 per cent (3 children). In these cases, spousal support awards go beyond the usual compensatory rationale under the *with child support* formula, to reflect a larger component of supplementing the children's household standard of living. The table amount of child support and section 7 expenses for the special needs child may not fully reflect all the costs imposed upon the recipient spouse's household by that child.

## 12.11 Section 15.3: Small Amounts, Inadequate Compensation under the *With Child Support* Formula

The *with child support* formula gives priority to child support, as required by s. 15.3(1) of the *Divorce Act* and by similar provisions found in provincial statutes. In cases where the spouses have three or four children, or where there are large section 7 expenses, there may be little or no room left for spousal support, despite the substantial economic disadvantage to the custodial parent.[121] The maximum time limits may end spousal support after the last child finishes high school or after the length of the marriage, despite the potential inadequacy of the compensation in such cases. The Advisory Guidelines must be consistent with section 15.3(2) and (3) of the *Divorce Act* and thus there must be an exception for **duration**, using the terms of s. 15.3(2):

- as a result of giving priority to child support
- the court is unable to make a spousal support order or the court makes a spousal support order in an amount less than it otherwise would have been
- or the parties agree to those terms as part of an agreement.

This **section 15.3** exception would recognize that spousal support may have to continue past the time limits in these cases. And, further, in some of these cases, the amount of spousal support may even have to increase upon variation or review as the children cease to be "children of the marriage", but any of these increases in amount should remain within the formula ranges. These outcomes are entirely consistent with compensatory theory and section 15.3 of the *Divorce Act*.

---

[120] *Yeates v. Yeates*, 2007 CarswellOnt 2107 (Ont.S.C.J.); *Frouws v. Frouws*, [2007] B.C.J. No. 282, 2007 BCSC 195 (B.C.S.C.).
[121] For an example, see *C.E.A.P. v. P.E.P.*, [2006] B.C.J. No. 3295, 2006 BCSC 1913 (B.C.S.C.).

## 13 SELF-SUFFICIENCY

A central topic of every conference and meeting about the Advisory Guidelines has been self-sufficiency. It is not surprising that any attempt to bring greater consistency and predictability to spousal support awards should bring this topic to the forefront. Some have criticized the Advisory Guidelines for generating "entitlements" to support, "entitlements" seen as too generous in amount and duration, eliminating any incentives for recipients to pursue self-sufficiency. Others have criticized the Advisory Guidelines for not producing "answers" or "rules" on the hard issues of self-sufficiency.

The language of the fourth objective in section 15.2(6)(d) of the *Divorce Act* has been parsed and argued in case after case: "in so far as practicable, promote the economic self-sufficiency of each spouse within a reasonable period of time." We were frequently asked, "How do the Spousal Support Advisory Guidelines promote self-sufficiency?"

To understand what the Advisory Guidelines can and can't do under the rubric of self-sufficiency, it is important to start with the legal framework within which the Guidelines operate.

After *Pelech* in 1987 and before *Moge* in 1992, the Canadian law of spousal support gave priority to self-sufficiency as part of a "clean break" approach, as spousal support was only intended to facilitate the transition to independence for the recipient.[122] A recipient could be "deemed" to be self-sufficient, based upon optimistic projections of training or likely employment, even after lengthy traditional marriages. Once the recipient found full-time employment of any kind, spousal support would often be terminated or entitlement would be denied. The *Moge* decision rejected this approach, emphasizing that self-sufficiency is only one of the four objectives set out in s. 15.2(6) and all four objectives must be considered in determining spousal support. Self-sufficiency is no longer to be "deemed" where a spouse continues to experience economic disadvantage after the end of a marriage. *Moge* directed Canadian courts to take a more realistic view of self-sufficiency, not to underestimate the effects of post-marital disadvantage nor to overestimate the labour market prospects of separated and divorced spouses. Self-sufficiency requires an individualized decision, based upon evidence specific to this recipient and *this* payor.

The 1999 *Bracklow* decision said little new about self-sufficiency, as its focus was upon the non-compensatory basis for support, this in a case where the wife was ill and unable to work.

Self-sufficiency was very much an issue in *Leskun*, where the husband argued that the wife had breached her legal duty to become self-sufficient, eliciting this response from the Court: "Failure to achieve self-sufficiency is not breach of 'a duty' and is simply one factor amongst others to be taken into account."[123] *Leskun* also affirmed the use of review orders, which have proved useful in encouraging and monitoring self-sufficiency in cases of indefinite spousal support orders.

After *Moge*, self-sufficiency has not been treated as an absolute standard, requiring the recipient to take any job at the end of a marriage. As the Ontario Court of Appeal said in *Allaire v. Allaire*, "self-sufficiency is not a free-standing concept. It must be seen in the context of the standard of living previously enjoyed by the parties."[124]

These are very general directions on the subject of self-sufficiency, leaving lawyers, mediators and trial judges to work out specifics in each case. After *Moge*, the determination of self-sufficiency requires a highly individualized analysis, not amenable to "guidelines". What the Advisory Guidelines can do is to encourage self-sufficiency through various aspects of their design, aspects described below.

---

[122] Carol Rogerson, "The Canadian Law of Spousal Support" (2004), 38 F.L.Q. 69.
[123] *Leskun v. Leskun*, [2006] 1 S.C.R. 920, 34 R.F.L. (6 th) 1 at para. 27.
[124] (2003), 35 R.F.L. (5 th) 256 (Ont.C.A.) at para. 21.

Strictly speaking, "self-sufficiency" is a concept primarily of importance in compensatory cases, which can arise under either formula: always under the *with child support* formula, and in many longer marriages and a few shorter ones under the *without child support* formula. In these longer marriages under the latter formula, there will be grown up children or one spouse will have subordinated his or her career and employment, leaving one spouse disadvantaged at the end of the marriage. The compensatory exception, described above in Chapter 12, will also raise self-sufficiency issues.

The term "self-sufficiency" has often taken on a broader meaning in practice, with some application to non-compensatory cases too. It can refer to the recipient's obligation to earn income to his or her present capacity. Or, used even more loosely, it sometimes just means that the payor's obligation to pay spousal support should be ended and the recipient should be required to live within her or his means.

## 13.1 Entitlement

Entitlement is the first step in the spousal support analysis, before reaching the Advisory Guidelines as to amount and duration. Self-sufficiency is one of the major arguments against entitlement, i.e. the recipient cannot show any "economic disadvantage" or "need" at the end of the marriage. Entitlement issues are discussed at greater length in Chapter 4 above.

"Self-sufficiency" as a threshold entitlement issue comes up more often in cases of shorter, childless marriages or in cases where the recipient already has a significant income, whether from employment or investments. Occasionally, as mentioned in Chapter 12 on Exceptions, there will be a very large property award that raises an issue of threshold entitlement.

## 13.2 Imputing Income

The Spousal Support Advisory Guidelines are income-based guidelines and thus require much more careful attention to the actual incomes, or the income-earning capacities, of both spouses. By focussing on income, the Guidelines actually encourage a more sophisticated analysis of "self-sufficiency" on the part of the recipient, rather than some rough-and-ready downward adjustment of the monthly amount of support. Consistent with *Moge*, the question is usually: what income could this specific recipient earn, with his or her experience, education and qualifications? As the B.C. Court of Appeal explained in MacEachern, imputing income provides a ready means of assessing and encouraging self-sufficiency. In that case, the Court imputed a low-wage full-time retail sales income to the wife who was working only part-time and who had not made "wholehearted" efforts, and then fixed the amount of spousal support at the low end of the range under the *with child support* formula.[125]

Imputing income imposes a discipline on our thinking about self-sufficiency. What sort of employment might the recipient find? Is the employment available full-time or part-time? How much can the recipient realistically contribute to her or his own support? What are the prospects of any improvement in that income? If there is training or education required, how will that change the employment prospects of the support recipient?

The answers to these questions will often generate different estimates of potential income. These estimated incomes can in turn be used to generate ranges under the formulas. Where the recipient's income, actual or imputed, is lower and the payor has a much higher income, as in many long traditional marriages, then the different estimates of income will often produce little

---

[125] *MacEachern v. MacEachern*, [2006] B.C.J. No. 2917, 2006 BCCA 508 (B.C.C.A.).

change in the ranges, making the imputation of income less telling to the final outcome. In other cases, however, the spouses' competing views on how much income to impute to a recipient will be the crux of the spousal support dispute, usually where the recipient might have considerable earning power.

## 13.3 Using the Ranges

We have already discussed self-sufficiency as a factor affecting location with the ranges in Chapter 9 above.

In some cases, as in *MacEachern*, a court may opt for the lower end of the formula range for amount, in order to provide the recipient an incentive to earn more. A court may do this even after imputing income to the recipient, especially if the court has been kind in the income imputed.

In other cases, a court may push the amount to the upper end of the range, to provide a recipient with the necessary funds to undertake education or training, all with a view eventually to reduce or even eliminate the support once the recipient obtains higher paying employment. For this option, the court will need a specific plan brought forward by the recipient.

## 13.4 Restructuring

As is explained in Chapter 10 on Restructuring, a court or the parties can "frontend load" spousal support by restructuring, in order to generate a large enough amount of support for a period of education or training by the recipient. Restructuring may be necessary to accomplish this self-sufficiency purpose when even the upper end of the ranges on amount and duration do not generate enough support. Most likely examples would be shorter marriages or lower incomes under the *without child support* formula or cases of higher child support or lower incomes under the *with child support* formula.

Another form of restructuring that can promote self-sufficiency is the "step-down order", with the amount of spousal support reducing over time at fixed intervals.

Finally, the lump sum support order is often justified as encouraging self-sufficiency, both by its implicit time limit and by its assurance that the lump sum will not be reduced by any future new employment or income.

## 13.5 Time Limits: the *without child support* formula

For marriages under 20 years in length, apart from the "rule of 65", the *without child support* formula produces time limits on the payment of spousal support. After a ten-year marriage, for example, the duration of support will be 5 to 10 years. In these cases without children, spousal support will usually be non-compensatory, providing a period of transition from the higher shared standard of living during the marriage back to whatever standard the recipient can sustain by herself or himself. The time limit defines the end of that period.

Time limits provide clear direction to the recipient that support will end and that the recipient will have to obtain income from another source or live at the lower standard of living from that time forward. In this sense, time limits in the non-compensatory setting further the more limited notion of self-sufficiency that operates in such cases.

Many Canadian courts are uneasy about time limits in some longer marriages under 20 years in length and currently prefer to make indefinite (duration not specified) orders. Even in these cases, the Advisory Guidelines still seek to implement time limits, albeit in a "softer" way, by using the process of review and variation to signal the eventual termination of support.

## 13.6 Time Limits: The *with child support* formula

Implicit in *Moge* is that the Court's concerns about "deemed self-sufficiency" were largely focussed upon the compensatory setting. Time limits will operate differently in compensatory cases, especially in those cases that fall under the *with child support* formula. Individual orders will be indefinite in duration, unlike the time-limited orders found in most cases under the *without child support* formula. The upper and lower ends of the durational range under the *with child support* formula provide the outer limits of the process of review and variation.

At some point, the recipient's disadvantage may be fully compensated and complete "self-sufficiency" attained, such that spousal support can terminate in a compensatory case. Under the *with child support* formula, any termination of support will usually happen through the process of variation or review, as there must be evidence on these issues before a court can terminate or time limit support. In this sense, time limits under the *with child support* formula are "softer", more flexible than in most cases under the *without child support* formula.

Even in this "softer" form, however, the time limits under this formula encourage self-sufficiency, in a more structured way than a succession of indefinite orders with no defined end-point.

## 13.7 Review Orders

Along with imputing income, the most frequent mechanism used in our law to promote self-sufficiency has become the review order, a form of order that was developed after *Moge* and once described as "the halfway house between indefinite orders and time-limited orders".[126] The review order is grounded in s. 15.2(3) of the *Divorce Act*, the court's power to "impose terms, conditions or restrictions in connection with the [spousal support] order as it thinks fit and just". In its 2006 Leskun decision, the Supreme Court of Canada affirmed the use of review orders and identified as three examples justifying their use, "the need to. . . start a program of education, train or upgrade skills, or obtain employment".[127] As part of the infrastructure of support law, review orders are a critical element of the Advisory Guidelines.

Review orders can permit a court to monitor a recipient's progress towards self-sufficiency, without any need to prove a change in circumstances.[128] Review hearings can be scheduled at critical times, like the completion of a training or education program or after a child starts full-time school or after a period of job-seeking. After *Leskun*, the terms of review should be more clearly set out in the terms of the order, "to tightly circumscribe the issue" for the review hearing and thus to avoid relitigation. The court can set out in the court order, or the parties in an agreement, the recipient's plan, which will form the basis for the review.

Where there are serious questions about the self-sufficiency efforts of a recipient, a court can even make a "terminating review order", i.e. spousal support is time limited, but the time limit is made subject to review and possible extension. This offers an example of a "softer" use of time limits in compensatory cases.

---

126  Rogerson, "Spousal Support Post *Bracklow:* The Pendulum Swings Again?", *supra* note 3 at 255.
127  *Leskun v. Leskun,* [2006] 1 S.C.R. 920 at para. 36.
128  For a recent discussion of review orders, see David Aston, "Review Orders: Let's Have Another Look" (2007), 26 C.F.L.Q. 253.

## 13.8 Indefinite Support Is Not Permanent Support

Under the Advisory Guidelines duration of spousal support will be indefinite, under both formulas, where the parties have been married for 20 years or more, or where the "rule of 65" applies. But indefinite support, under the Guidelines as under the current law, does not necessarily mean that support is "permanent" or "infinite", only that the duration has not been specified. We have purposely changed the language in this final version to convey that notion; our new terminology is "indefinite (duration not specified)". Duration may be specified at some point in the future and support terminated, if entitlement ceases.

Even in long traditional marriages, self-sufficiency remains a consideration, "in so far as practicable", to use the language of s. 15.2(6)(d). For the most part, these self-sufficiency issues will come up on a variation where there is a change of circumstances or on a review as described above. Entitlement may then be revisited for any number of reasons — the recipient finding employment, the recipient's remarriage or repartnering, the payor's retirement or loss of employment, etc. — and support may be terminated if entitlement has ceased.

Where the recipient does remain entitled to spousal support under an indefinite (duration not specified) order or agreement, the amount of support will inevitably change over time through the process of variation or review. As described above, in some circumstances, income may be imputed to a recipient, to assess or encourage the recipient's contribution to his or her own support.

## 13.9 Real Incentives for Self-Sufficiency

All of the above reflect various ways that the Spousal Support Advisory Guidelines can "promote self-sufficiency" as required by s. 15.2(6)(d) of the *Divorce Act*. In the end, however, the real encouragement for self-sufficiency is not found in spousal support law, or in the Advisory Guidelines, but in the harsh economic reality facing most separated or divorced spouses. In all but the highest income cases, a recipient must find more income in order to avoid a drop in her or his standard of living, as spousal support is limited by the payor's ability to pay. The limits of that ability to pay spousal support will be reached more quickly under the *with child support* formula, given the priority to child support.

## 14 VARIATION, REVIEW, REMARRIAGE, SECOND FAMILIES

The formulas proposed in Chapters 7 and 8 are intended to apply to initial orders and to the negotiation of initial agreements. Where there is an entitlement to support, the formulas generate ranges for both amount and duration of spousal support at the time of divorce. The formulas will also determine a range of amounts for interim orders under the *Divorce Act*. What role do the Advisory Guidelines play thereafter, upon variation or review? What about remarriage or re-partnering or second families? These issues proved to be some of the most difficult of all in constructing spousal support guidelines. In the earlier parts we have touched upon some of these issues.

Ideally a truly comprehensive set of advisory guidelines would apply to the full range of issues that can arise on variation and review. The current state of the law renders that impossible at the present time. We opted for a more modest approach at this stage — to apply the Guideline formulas as far as consensus and the current case law allow, and no more. We identified certain situations where the Advisory Guidelines would apply on reviews and variations, including increases in the recipient's income and decreases in the payor's income. We have left others, such as post-separation increases in the payor's income, re-partnering, remarriage and second families, to discretionary, case-by-case determinations under the evolving framework of current law. We hope that, at some later stage, after a period of experience with the Advisory Guidelines, it will be possible to develop formulaic ranges to guide resolution of these remaining issues.

### 14.1 Material Changes, Reviews and Issues of Continuing Entitlement

**We should make clear at the outset that the Advisory Guidelines do not – and cannot – affect the basic legal structure of variation and review.** Under section 17(4.1) of the *Divorce Act*, a material change of circumstances is a threshold requirement for the variation of court-ordered spousal support. Section 17(7) sets out the objectives of an order varying spousal support and section 17(10) addresses variations after spousal support has ended, imposing a further condition that the changed circumstances be related to the marriage.

The process of review allows for reassessments of support without the requirement of a material change in circumstances, a process elaborated by appeal and trial courts in case law. The Supreme Court of Canada approved the use of review orders in *Leskun* in 2006.[129] Review orders are justified where there is "genuine and material uncertainty at the time of the original trial" as to the spouses' finances in the near future. "Common examples are the need to establish a new residence, start a program of education, train or upgrade skills, or obtain employment", stated the Court. If a review term is included in an order, the issues to be reviewed should be precisely identified in the order, to avoid mere relitigation of the whole case.

None of this is affected by the Advisory Guidelines, which deal with the amount and duration of spousal support. The spouse seeking to vary court-ordered support will still have to prove a material change before the advisory guidelines can operate to determine amount and duration. In a similar vein, a review is possible only if a provision for review was included in the initial order and only if any preconditions for review are met, e.g. the passage of a period of time or the completion of a training program. Only then will it be possible for the Advisory Guidelines to be applied to determine amount and duration.

If spousal support has been negotiated, the result will be a separation agreement that deals with spousal support. The possibilities for reviewing or modifying spousal support that the spouses have agreed upon will depend on many factors, including the drafting of the agreement and whether or not the agreement has subsequently been incorporated into the divorce judgement.

We will deal first with the situation where there has been no incorporation of the agreement. The effect of subsequent changes in the parties' situation will be governed by the terms of the agreement. If the agreement provides for reviews by the parties at specified times or if it includes a material change clause, and if the conditions for these are met, it is possible for the Advisory Guidelines to apply to determine amount and duration. However, the Advisory Guidelines will have no application if the agreement is a final agreement in which spousal support has been waived or time-limited.

As has been emphasized at many points in this document, the Advisory Guidelines do not deal with the effect of a prior agreement on spousal support. As informal guidelines, they confer no power to override agreements. The *Miglin*[130] case continues to govern the issue of the effect of a prior agreement on a court's ability to award spousal support. The Advisory Guidelines will

---

[129] *Leskun v. Leskun*, [2006] 1 S.C.R. 920.
[130] *Miglin v. Miglin*, [2003] 1 S.C.R. 303.

only be helpful *after* the *Miglin* analysis, if a finding has been made that a final agreement is not determinative and spousal support is to be determined afresh by the court.

In cases where a spousal support agreement has been incorporated into the divorce judgment — as is the practice in many parts of the country — the agreement is treated as a court order. If the agreement provides for review or includes a material change clause, and those conditions are met, the Advisory Guidelines may be applicable to determine amount and duration. If the agreement is a final agreement, waiving or time-limiting support, the threshold requirement of a change in circumstances under s. 17 of the *Divorce Act* would have to be satisfied before a variation could be granted, as well as the causal connection requirement in s. 17(10) if the spousal support had ended at the time of the application. Given that the court order in these cases rests upon an agreement, the *Miglin* analysis would also be relevant in determining whether the requirement of material change had been met and whether a variation was appropriate.

Apart from the issue of the governing legal framework, **a review or variation may involve issues of continuing entitlement that would determine the application of the Advisory Guidelines.** Entitlement is always a live issue, a precondition to determining amount and duration under the Guidelines, as is discussed in Chapter 2 above. As circumstances change, with changes in employment and income, retirement, remarriage, re-partnering and second families, entitlement may come to the forefront as a threshold issue.

Variations and reviews raise many different issues for resolution.[131] In Chapters 7 and 8, we canvassed some of these issues, especially in our discussions of duration. In what follows we will organize our discussion of this material around the different kinds of issues that are raised on variations and reviews.

### 14.2 Applications to Reduce Spousal Support Because of Changes in Income

The largest category of variations and reviews consists of applications seeking a reduction in spousal support based upon a change in the income of one party or the other. One of three reasons provides the foundation for the application:

1. the payor spouse's income goes down;
2. the recipient spouse's income goes up; or
3. the payor spouse applies to reduce or terminate support on the grounds that the recipient spouse ought to have a higher income.

In each of these three situations the Advisory Guidelines can be used to determine the amount of support. In some situations, the Advisory Guidelines can even result in the termination of spousal support, if the amount of support falls to zero with little or no prospect of future change.

In situations (i) and (iii), difficult questions of imputing income can arise. In situation (i), there can be questions about the good faith and reasonableness of the payor spouse who alleges an income reduction, which in turn may call for imputing income to the payor. In situation (iii), income may have to be imputed to a recipient spouse who has failed to maximize earning capacity, as has been discussed above in Chapter 13 on self-sufficiency.

---

[131] For an excellent discussion of the use of the Advisory Guidelines in variation applications which touches on many of the issues we deal with below see the British Columbia Court of Appeal's December 2007 decision in *Beninger v. Beninger*, [2007] B.C.J. No. 2657, 2007 BCCA. Justice Prowse, writing for the Court, dispels the common misunderstanding that Advisory Guidelines have no application in variation applications, finding instead that they may be applied, but with careful attention to the limits of their applicability.

Under the *without child support* formula, as the gross income difference between the spouses narrows, spousal support will be reduced. Similarly, under the *with child support* formula, as the disparity between the spouses' net incomes is reduced, so too is the amount of spousal support required to bring the income of the lower income recipient spouse up to the desired percentage. In some cases with children, this may mean the end of entitlement, but in others it may just reflect a current inability to pay and the postponement of payment of spousal support, consistent with section 15.3 of the *Divorce Act*. At some point, as the disparity in spousal incomes narrows under either formula, entitlement may disappear.

We provide below some examples of how the Advisory Guidelines would apply to variation or review applications in this category.

### Example 14.1

In *Example 7.2* John and Mary had been married for 25 years in a traditional marriage, with two grown-up children. Mary had no income, but John was earning $100,000 gross per year. Now assume that John has lost his previous job and changed employers, with a reduction in his annual gross income down to $80,000, while Mary still has no income.

On a variation application by John, the range for spousal support would be reduced, under the *without child support* formula, from the initial $3,125 to $4,167 (capped at $4,046) per month, down to $2,500 to $3,333 (capped at $3,216) per month.

### Example 14.2

In *Example 8.1* Ted was earning $80,000 gross per year at the end of an 11-year marriage, with two children aged 8 and 10, while Alice was working part time, earning $20,000 gross per year. Now assume that Alice has found a full-time job, increasing her gross annual income to $35,000, while Ted still earns $80,000.

On a variation or review under the *with child support* formula, Alice's increase in income would reduce the range for spousal support, from the original $474 to $1,025, down to $52 to $741 per month.

### Example 14.3

Again using *Example 6.1* above, now assume that the children are 13 and 14 and Alice is still working part-time, but Ted alleges that Alice was offered a full-time job by her employer and she turned it down.

Upon review or variation, a court might decide to impute the full-time income of $35,000 per year to Alice and to reduce support to the same range as above, of $52 to $741 per month. Or a court might not be prepared to go to that full amount, instead imputing a slightly lower income, such as $30,000, which would produce a range of $163 to $846 per month.

## 14.3 The Payor's Post-Separation Income Increase

There are two possible formulaic extremes here. At one extreme, one could decide that any post-separation income increase of the payor spouse should not affect the amount of spousal support. After all, some would suggest, the recipient is entitled to a sharing of the marital standard of living, but no more. Certainly, this bright-line method would be predictable and administratively simple. At the other extreme, one could argue that the formulas should just continue to be applied to any income increase for the payor. This again would offer a predictable result, but one which the basic principles of spousal support would not justify in all cases. This approach is most compelling after a long traditional marriage.

Under the current law, it is impossible to maintain either of these approaches to the exclusion of the other. Some rough notion of causation is applied to post-separation income increases for the payor, in determining both whether the income increase should be reflected in increased spousal support and, if it should, by how much. It all depends on the length of the marriage, the roles adopted during the marriage, the time elapsed between the date of separation and the subsequent income increase, and the reason for the income increase (e.g. new job vs. promotion within same employer, or career continuation vs. new venture). The extent of sharing of these post-separation increases involves a complex, fact-based decision.[132]

We can propose one formulaic limit in these cases: the upper limit upon any increased spousal support ought to be the numbers generated by the formulas. As the following examples show, that upper limit offers some help in defining a range of possible results after a post-separation income increase.

### Example 14.4

In *Example 7.1*, Arthur and Ellen were married for 20 years and had one grown-up child. At the time of the initial order, Arthur earned $90,000 gross per year and Ellen earned $30,000, both working full time. Under the *without child support* formula, spousal support was indefinite (duration not specified), in the range of $1,500 to $2,000 per month. Arthur's income increases to $110,000 gross per year, while Ellen's remains unchanged.

A court, on an application for variation, might order that none, some or all of Arthur's post-separation income increase be taken into account. If all the increase were taken into account, the formula would define the upper limits of any varied spousal support within a range of $2,000 to $2,666 per month.

### Example 14.5

The arithmetic becomes more complicated under the *with child support* formula. When the payor spouse's income increases, then child support will usually increase too, if requested. Let's go back once again to Ted and Alice in *Example 6.1*. At the time of the initial order, Ted earned $80,000 gross per year and Alice earned $20,000, after 11 years together. Their two children were aged 8 and 10 at that time. Spousal support under the formula was in a range from $474 to $1,025 monthly. Assume Ted's income subsequently increases, to $100,000 gross per year. His child support for two children will rise from $1,159 to $1,404 per month.

If none of Ted's increase were taken into account for spousal support purposes, then Ted would pay child support of $1,404 and the range for spousal support would remain unchanged at $474 to $1,025 per month. The result would be that Alice's percentage of family net disposable income would drop, as would her percentage of INDI, calculated

---

[132] Most of the major cases on this issue are reviewed in *D.B.C. v. R.M.W.*, [2006] A.J. No. 1629, 2006 ABQB 905 (Alta.Q.B.) at paras. 22-32. See also *Kelly v. Kelly*, [2007] B.C.J. No. 324, 2007 BCSC 227 (B.C.S.C.), where both spouses had also remarried. In *Beninger, supra* note 131, the B.C.C.A. found on the facts that the wife was entitled to share in the increased income and used the Advisory Guidelines ranges based on the husband's current income to determine the amount of support.

using Ted's new income. At the other extreme, the full amount of the increase might be taken into account under the spousal support formula, generating a new and higher range of $961 to $1,715 per month.

## 14.4 The Recipient's Reduced Income After Separation

Suppose the recipient loses employment after the initial order, or suffers an illness or disability, or otherwise suffers a reduction in income. If either of the income-sharing formulas were applied, any reduction in the recipient's income after separation would lead to an increase in the spousal support payable. Once again, as with the payor's post-separation increase, some notion of causation seems to operate under the current law, requiring another complex, fact-based decision. While a formulaic solution is thus not possible, the same upper limit can be applied, i.e. the upper limit upon any increased spousal support ought to be the numbers generated by the formulas.

### Example 14.6

In *Example 7.1*, Ellen was working full time and earning $30,000 gross per year at the time of the initial determination. Assume Ellen has been reduced to part-time hours and now earns $20,000 gross per year, while Arthur's income is unchanged at $90,000.

The initial range of spousal support was $1,500 to $2,000 monthly, where it would remain if none of Ellen's income reduction were taken into account. The range could rise as high as $1,750 to $2,333 monthly if the full amount of Ellen's reduction were considered.

## 14.5 Crossover Between the Two Formulas

As children get older, finish their education or otherwise cease to be children of the marriage, then the child support obligation ends. What happens at that point? In our view, it should be possible for either spouse to apply to cross over from the *with child support* formula to the *without child support* formula, by way of application to vary or review. This crossover would be entirely consistent with the approach and language of s. 15.3 of the *Divorce Act*, especially s. 15.3(3). Section 15.3(3) provides that in cases where spousal support was reduced or not ordered because of the priority given to child support, any subsequent reduction or termination of child support constitutes a change of circumstances for the purposes of bringing an application to vary spousal support.

The crossover from the one formula to the other will only affect the **amount** of spousal support, but not the duration. Under the first, longer-marriage test for duration under the *with child support* formula, which applies to medium-to-long marriages with dependent children, the outcome will tend towards the upper end of the range for duration in most cases.

Crossover situations will mostly arise in medium-to-long marriages, where the children are older at the time of the initial order. These are the cases where duration is driven by the length of the marriage, so that after child support ceases, spousal support will usually remain payable for a further period. In short-to-medium length marriages with dependent children, the outside limit of duration is the end of the child-rearing period, so no spousal support would ordinarily be payable after child support has ended, subject to section 15.3(3). Thus there is little potential for crossover between the formulas.

Often the application to vary, to cross over to the *without child support* formula, will come from the recipient spouse in a longer marriage. Consider the following example.

**Example 14.7**

Take once again the example of Ted and Alice in *Example 8.1*. At the time of the divorce Ted made $80,000 gross per year and Alice earned $20,000. They had been married 11 years with children aged 8 and 10 at separation.

Under the *with child support* formula, spousal support was initially in the range of $474 to $1,025 per month. Under the longer-marriage test for duration, the range for duration was 5 = to 11 years. Recall that the 11-year maximum was derived from the first test for duration, based upon the length of their marriage, as that was longer than the time remaining to the end of high school for the youngest child (which was 10 years). If their two children pursued any post-secondary studies, then child support would still be payable and the *with child support* formula would continue to apply right to the end of the 11-year maximum for spousal support, although the amount of support would likely have changed based on improvements in Alice's employment situation.

If we change those facts slightly, however, then the potential for crossover emerges. If Ted and Alice had been married for 20 years at separation and thereafter their children finished school and child support terminated, Alice might wish to apply to vary, to cross over.

Under the *with child support* formula, the initial range of spousal support was $474 to $1,025 per month with two children in the primary care of Alice. Before reaching the crossover stage, the *with child support* formula could adjust to just one child being left at home, as the table amount of child support would reduce to $719 and the spousal support range would rise to $1,217 to $1,703 if Ted still earns $80,000 and Alice $20,000. At the crossover stage, assuming the spouses' incomes remained the same, the range would be higher under the *without child support* formula: $1,500 to $2,000 per month for a 20 year marriage with that gross income difference.

If Ted and Alice had been together for 25 years, the new range after crossover would be even higher. The new range would be between $1,875 and $2,500 (capped at $2,428) per month. These higher numbers flow from two factors: the impact of length of marriage upon the without child support ranges, and the additional ability to pay freed up by the absence of a child support obligation.

In drawing out these possibilities, we have assumed that both spouses' incomes and circumstances have remained unchanged over time, which is very unlikely. It would be much more likely that Alice's income would be higher, as she was working part time at the time of the initial order. Her higher income would likely have reduced her spousal support. But Ted's income might have gone up too, which may have affected his spousal support, depending upon the treatment of his post-separation income increase as discussed above.

Situations where the payor spouse would be the one applying to vary and cross over to the *without child support* formula would be fewer. Given the way the two formulas operate, for the most part, these would be cases where the marriage lasted 15 years or less. In these cases, the payor spouse would argue that the *without child support* formula, where the percentages are driven by the length of the marriage, would produce a lower range for spousal support compared to the *with child support* formula. We provide an example below.

**Example 14.8**

Let's start again with Ted and Alice, assuming they have the same incomes they did at the point of separation as in *Example 14.7*. Assume that their children pursue no post-secondary employment and that child support ends after 10 years. Spousal support will likely still be paid for another year based upon their 11-year marriage.

Ted might apply to vary, arguing that spousal support should be fixed in the without child support range of $825 to $1100 if the initial support had been determined by the range for one child of $1,217 to $1,703 monthly. Again, however, it must be remembered that incomes *will* change over time, which in turn will alter the stakes and the incentives involved in crossover questions.

## 14.6 The Payor's Remarriage or Re-partnering

The payor's remarriage or re-partnering usually is **not** grounds for a reduction in spousal support under the current law, apart from some exceptional cases. Where there were ability to pay limitations upon the support previously ordered, the payor's remarriage or re-partnering may even improve the payor's ability to pay, as a result of the sharing of expenses with the new spouse or partner. There is no need for any formulaic adjustment here.

## 14.7 The Recipient's Remarriage or Re-partnering

The remarriage or re-partnering of the support recipient does have an effect on spousal support under the current law, but how much and when and why are less certain. There is little consensus in the decided cases. Remarriage does not mean automatic termination of spousal support, but support is often reduced or suspended or sometimes even terminated. Compensatory support is often treated differently from non-compensatory support. Much depends upon the standard of living in the recipient's new household. The length of the first marriage seems to make a difference, consistent with concepts of merger over time. The age of the recipient spouse also influences outcomes.

In particular fact situations, usually at the extremes of these sorts of factors, we can predict outcomes. For example, after a short-to-medium first marriage, where the recipient spouse is younger and the support is non-compensatory and for transitional purposes, remarriage by the recipient is likely to result in termination of support. At the other extreme, where spousal support is being paid to an older spouse after a long traditional marriage, remarriage is unlikely to terminate spousal support, although the amount may be reduced.

An ability to predict in some cases, however, is not sufficient to underpin a formula for adjustment to the new spouse's or partner's income. Ideally, a formula would provide a means of incorporating some amount of gross income from the new spouse or partner, to reduce the income disparity under either formula. Any such incorporation could increase with each year of the new marriage or relationship. Where the recipient remarries or re-partners with someone who has a similar or higher income than the previous spouse, eventually — faster or slower, depending upon the formula adopted — spousal support would be extinguished. Where the recipient remarries or re-partners with a lower income spouse, support might continue under such a formula until the maximum durational limit, unless terminated earlier.

We have been unable to construct a formula with sufficient consensus or flexibility to adjust to these situations, despite considerable feedback that a formula would be desirable. In this final version, we still have to leave the issues surrounding the recipient's remarriage or re-partnering to individual case-by-case negotiation and decision making.

## 14.8 Second Families

Second families — or, more accurately, subsequent children — raise some of the most difficult issues in support law. We have already addressed prior support obligations for prior spouses and prior children as an exception under both formulas in Chapter 12. We have also addressed remarriage and re-partnering in this Chapter. Under this heading, we consider a different issue, that of support for subsequent children.

By "subsequent children", we mean children who are born or adopted after the separation of the spouses. For the most part, subsequent children will be an issue upon variation or review, but it is possible that these issues can arise at the point of the initial determination of spousal support.

Since the coming into force of the *Federal Child Support Guidelines*, courts have struggled with these issues in the child support setting, left largely to discretionary decision making, mostly under the undue hardship provisions in the *Child Support Guidelines*.[133] The issues do not get any easier when the potential conflict between child support and spousal support is added to the mix.

The first-family-first philosophy is the most common approach. On this view, the payor's obligations to the children and spouse of the first marriage take priority over any subsequent obligations. Most who adopt the first-family-first principle will acknowledge a narrow exception: where payment of first-family support would drive the second family onto social assistance or otherwise into poverty, relief may be granted, but only in extreme cases. Other than this narrow exception, first-family-first provides a simple rule for child and spousal support: no change for subsequent children.

If child support is the only issue, there is a strong second philosophy that runs through the cases: to determine child support in a way that treats all the payor's children equally. This is usually done through the use of household standard of living calculations. This equal-treatment-of-children approach gives greater weight to the interests of subsequent children, but gives no guidance to balancing the demands of spousal support to a first spouse vs. support for subsequent children. There is a tendency on this approach to give reduced weight to spousal support, given the concern for equal treatment of the payor's *children*. Reduced spousal support is often used as a means of adjustment between the households.

In the absence of any clear policy in the *Federal Child Support Guidelines* on this issue, it is difficult, if not impossible, to articulate any related policy on spousal support vs. subsequent children. For now, again with some regret, we must leave the issues of quantum and duration to discretion or case-by-case decision making. Any changes in child support policy on second families would have important implications for spousal support issues.

## 15 THE ADVISORY GUIDELINES IN QUEBEC

Inevitably, the application of the Spousal Support Advisory Guidelines to divorce cases in Quebec requires some modifications. The most obvious modifications flow from Quebec's guidelines for the determination of child support, which differ in important ways from the *Federal Child Support Guidelines*. A few other modifications are also noted below.

---

[133] See Rollie Thompson, "The Second Family Conundrum in Child Support" (2001), 18 *Canadian Journal of Family Law* 227.

The bulk of Quebec's guidelines are found in the *Regulation Respecting the Determination of Child Support Payments*, to which are attached as schedules the child support determination form and the table.[134] The *Regulation* is made under authority of the *Code of Civil Procedure* and the *Civil Code*, both of which also contain provisions governing the determination of child support.[135] These provisions will be referred to here as the child support rules. These rules apply to determine child support under the *Civil Code* and under the federal *Divorce Act*.

For these Quebec rules to become the "applicable guidelines" for child support in Quebec divorce proceedings, Quebec was designated by the federal government under the *Divorce Act*.[136] The Quebec rules thus apply to determine child support in divorce proceedings when both spouses are ordinarily resident in Quebec. Where one of the parents resides outside Quebec, then the *Federal Child Support Guidelines* apply. The Quebec child support rules therefore apply to most divorces in Quebec.

In Quebec, the computer software used to make income, support and tax calculations is AliForm. AliForm has added the Advisory Guidelines to its collection of family law programs.

## 15.1 The Definition of Income

In the formulas, the starting point for the determination of income is Guidelines income, a measure of gross income defined in considerable detail under the *Federal Child Support Guidelines*. The major reason for this choice was to simplify the determination of income by using the same definition for both child and spousal support.

For the same reason, in the Quebec context, the formulas will start with the definition of annual income (revenu annuel) in section 9 of the *Regulation Respecting the Determination of Child Support Payments*. It too is a gross income measure, with a broad scope very similar to Guidelines income.

## 15.2 Length of Marriage Under the *without child support* formula

Under the *without* child support formula set out in Chapter 7, length of marriage is critical in determining both the amount and the duration of spousal support. Length of marriage is defined as the period of spousal cohabitation, including any period of pre-marital cohabitation, and ending with the date of separation. The inclusion of premarital cohabitation in part reflects provincial/territorial family laws accepting cohabitation for a specified period as a basis for spousal support in non-marital relationships.

Under the *Civil Code*, by contrast, there is no entitlement to spousal support for unmarried cohabitants. In Quebec divorce cases, some judges therefore ignore any period of pre-marital cohabitation, while other judges treat that period as a relevant consideration in determining spousal support in divorce proceedings. That difference of opinion will have important implications for outcomes under the Advisory Guidelines in the application of the *without child support* formula.

---

[134] Decret 484-97, 1997 G.O. II, 2117 and 2605, modified by Decret 777-97, 1997 G.O. II, 3648 and Decret 1312-2003, 2003 G.O. II, 5396. The form is Schedule I and the table is Schedule II.

[135] L.Q. 1996, c. 68 and L.Q. 2004, c. 5. Sections 585 to 596 of the *Civil Code* govern the support of children, with sections 587.1 to 587.3 implementing the child support rules. Sections 825.8 to 825.14 of the *Code of Civil Procedure* regulate the procedure for deter mining child support

[136] *Divorce Act*, R.S.C. 1985, c. 3 (2nd Supp), ss. 2(1) applicable guidelines, (5) and (6). The designation is S.O.R./97-237.

## 15.3 Child Support and the *with child support* formula

In the few circumstances where one party lives outside the province and the federal guidelines apply in a Quebec divorce, no adjustments to the *with child support* formula are necessary. The Quebec child support rules apply in most divorce cases, however, and when these rules apply, some modifications *are* required.

It should be noted that section 825.13 of the Quebec *Code of Civil Procedure* clearly gives priority to child support over spousal support, in language similar to s. 15.3(1) of the *Divorce Act*.[137]

While there are some broad similarities between the two schemes, the Quebec child support rules differ from the federal guidelines in significant respects:

- both parents' incomes are taken into account;
- the floor is higher, as there is a $10,000 basic deduction for self-support;
- the ceiling for the combined disposable incomes of the parents is $200,000 annually;
- access to the child of between 20 and 40 per cent of the time by the non-custodial parent affects the amount of child support;
- additional expenses are defined somewhat differently, especially for extracurricular activities (which need not be extraordinary);
- the value of the assets of a parent may affect the amount of child support, as may the resources available to the child;
- an adjustment can be made if child support is more than 50 per cent of a parent's disposable income;
- undue hardship does not include a standard-of-living test; and
- only simple hardship is now required for any adjustment for a parent's support obligations respecting other children.[138]

The *with child support* formula set out in Chapter 8 works easily and effectively with the Quebec child support rules. The Quebec rules first generate the respective contributions to child support – the amounts to be backed out in determining each spouse's individual net disposable income. The percentage ranges under the basic formula are then applied to the remaining pool of INDI to generate the amount of spousal support.

Government benefits and refundable credits also have to be added back to the recipient spouse's INDI in cases under the Quebec child support rules. As with Guidelines income, these sources of income are not included under the definition of annual income in the Quebec rules.

Step-by-step, here is how the *with child support* formula works with the Quebec child support rules:

- First, the Quebec rules use an income-shares formula, where the table sets out the basic annual contribution for the child required jointly from the parents based upon their combined disposable incomes as defined in the Regulation.
- Second, to this basic annual contribution are added any child-care expenses, post-secondary education expenses and any other special expenses.

---

[137] Section 825.13 states: "The support to be provided to a child is determined without regard to support claimed by a parent of the child for himself."

[138] See Jean-Marie Fortin and Jocelyn Verdon, *AliForm annoté Barème québécois: Aspects civils et fiscaux,* 2nd ed. (Brossard: Publications CCH, 2004) and also Dominique Goubau, "Comparison of Federal and Quebec Regulations for Determining Child Support," and Jean-Marie Fortin, "Quebec Guidelines for the Determination of Child Support," in *Federal Child Support Guidelines Reference Manual* (Ottawa, 1998) at J-7 to J-25 and J-29 to J-41. The Quebec rules are also explained in Department of Justice, *Children Come First: A Report to Parliament Reviewing the Provisions and Operation of the Federal Child Support Guidelines* (Ottawa, 2002), Volume 2 at 23-28.

- Third, to determine the payor's child support, the Quebec rules calculate the respective parental child support contributions based upon each parent's disposable income. The Quebec rules thus calculate an actual contribution for the recipient spouse, avoiding any need to compute a notional table amount.
- Fourth, the Quebec rules adjust parental child support contributions explicitly and mathematically for different custodial arrangements, including sole custody, sole custody with access between 20 and 40 per cent of the time (described as sole custody with visiting and prolonged outing rights), split custody (described as sole custody granted to each parent), shared custody, and any combinations of the foregoing arrangements.

The respective contributions, after any such adjustments, then become the basis for calculating individual net disposable income for each spouse and in turn for determining the ranges of spousal support.

Apart from these adjustments, the Spousal Support Advisory Guidelines operate in essentially the same fashion in divorce cases in Quebec as in the other provinces and territories.

## 15.4 The Current State of the Advisory Guidelines in Quebec

Until the Quebec Court of Appeal decision in *G.V. v. C.G.* in June of 2006,[139] there had been a great deal of interest in the Advisory Guidelines amongst lawyers and mediators.[140] There were a number of reported trial decisions, some using the Guidelines, others criticising them. After the Court of Appeal decision, the use of the Advisory Guidelines was dramatically reduced. As a result, three years after the Draft Proposal, unlike in the rest of Canada, there has been little practical experience with the Advisory Guidelines in Quebec and thus little feedback to be provided for the final version.

The appeal in *G.V. v. C.G.* involved a 32-year marriage with three children, two of whom were independent and the youngest resided with the husband. The wife was 55, earning $50,000 per year, while the husband earned $227,000 per year. The wife paid child support to the husband of $15,948 per year. The trial judge had applied the Advisory Guidelines, which produced a range of $4,500 to $6,000 per month under the custodial payor formula, to order spousal support of $4,500 per month, on an indefinite basis.

The Court of Appeal allowed the husband's appeal and reduced spousal support to $2,705 per month, after engaging in a detailed analysis of the wife's expense budget. The trial judge was found to have erred in relying heavily upon the Advisory Guidelines rather than engaging in a detailed individual analysis.

The decision did not reject in principle the use of the Advisory Guidelines. For the Court, Forget J.A. stated: "the dossier as it is and the brief pleadings of counsel on this aspect do not permit us, in my opinion, to pronounce a judgment of principle upon the utilization of the Advisory Guidelines." The Court of Appeal did refer to earlier criticisms of the Guidelines contained in trial judgments by Justices Julien and Gendreau. The Court did not disagree with the decision in *Yemchuk*, but emphasised that the B.C. Court of Appeal had not endorsed an "automatic" application of the Advisory Guidelines without an individual analysis.

Since the Quebec Court of Appeal decision, there have been virtually no trial decisions even referring to the Guidelines. In turn, lawyers and mediators rarely use the Advisory

---

[139] [2006] J.Q. no. 5231 (Que.C.A.).

[140] In particular, the Family Law Committee of the Barreau du Québec has supported the principles and objectives of the Advisory Guidelines and their use as a tool for reference, orientation, consultation and validation of spousal support.

Guidelines now in negotiations and mediations, apart from the occasional reference in preparing a case. Lawyers and mediators now await some sign from the Courts that the Advisory Guidelines can be a useful tool in spousal support cases. Only after a period of prolonged use will it be possible to obtain the necessary practical feedback to make further changes to the Advisory Guidelines in Quebec.

## 16 CONCLUSION

For those of you who have read this document from beginning to end, we know that it has been a long and winding road to get here The Advisory Guidelines are admittedly complex. But spousal support raises many difficult issues. There are no simple solutions and there is no "one big formula". That is why the Advisory Guidelines contain two formulas, not one: the *without child support* formula and the *with child support* formula. The formulas generate not precise numbers but ranges for both the amount and the duration of spousal support. The *with child support* formula is actually a family of formulas, each one adjusting for different custodial arrangements. The formulas become even more flexible with the use of restructuring. Finally, there are a series of exceptions to both formulas.

In the three years since the release of the Draft Proposal, the Advisory Guidelines have been used by spouses, lawyers, mediators and judges to assist in the resolution of thousands of cases across Canada. The Advisory Guidelines have already served to refocus and revitalize discussions about the law and practice of spousal support in Canada. Over that three-year period, revisions and adjustments have been made to the Advisory Guidelines in response to comments, criticisms and suggestions from those same spouses, lawyers, mediators and judges. This final version of the Spousal Support Advisory Guidelines brings to an end the most intensive part of the process.

The Department of Justice continues to monitor developments in the law of spousal support and will now be monitoring the Advisory Guidelines. If there is a major appellate decision, that may spark a need for review as well. It must not be forgotten that the Advisory Guidelines are intended to be a reflection of the current law.

The software suppliers make regular adjustments to their programs for changes in tax rates and structures, changes in government benefits and the like. This means that the formulas will be updated regularly on these technical matters.

Finally, it now appears that the Spousal Support Advisory Guidelines have become entrenched as a useful tool in the law of spousal support. As such, they have now become part of the everyday analysis employed by spouses, lawyers, mediators and judges. Undoubtedly legal publishers will step in, to provide analysis and updates on the case law. The Advisory Guidelines will continue to be a topic on family law programs for lawyers, mediators and judges. In only a few short years, the Spousal Support Advisory Guidelines have gone from concept to Draft Proposal to final version, and now belong to all those who operate in the field of family law.

# INDEX

[References are to page number]